THE PEARSON SERIES IN ECONOMICS

*denotes  Visit www.

MyEconLab® Provides the Power of Practice

Optimize your study time with **MyEconLab**, the online assessment and tutorial system. When you take a sample test online, **MyEconLab** gives you targeted feedback and a personalized Study Plan to identify the topics you need to review.

Study Plan

The Study Plan shows you the sections you should study next, gives easy access to practice problems, and provides you with an automatically generated quiz to prove mastery of the course material.

Unlimited Practice

As you work each exercise, instant feedback helps you understand and apply the concepts. Many Study Plan exercises contain algorithmically generated values to ensure that you get as much practice as you need.

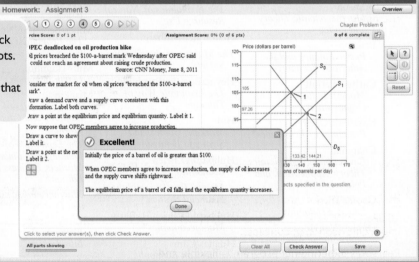

Learning Resources

Study Plan problems link to learning resources that further reinforce concepts you need to master.

- **Help Me Solve This** learning aids help you break down a problem much the same way as an instructor would do during office hours. Help Me Solve This is available for select problems.

- **eText links** are specific to the problem at hand so that related concepts are easy to review just when they are needed.

- A **graphing tool** enables you to build and manipulate graphs to better understand how concepts, numbers, and graphs connect.

Find out more at www.myeconlab.com

Real-Time Data Analysis Exercises

Up-to-date macro data is a great way to engage in and understand the usefulness of macro variables and their impact on the economy. Real-Time Data Analysis exercises communicate directly with the Federal Reserve Bank of St. Louis's FRED® site, so every time FRED posts new data, students see new data.

End-of-chapter exercises accompanied by the Real-Time Data Analysis icon 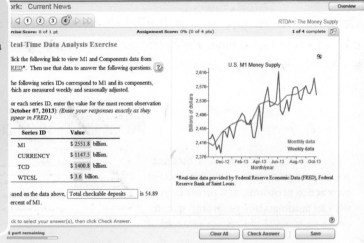 include Real-Time Data versions in **MyEconLab**.

Select in-text figures labeled **MyEconLab** Real-Time Data update in the electronic version of the text using FRED data.

Current News Exercises

Posted weekly, we find the latest microeconomic and macroeconomic news stories, post them, and write auto-graded multi-part exercises that illustrate the economic way of thinking about the news.

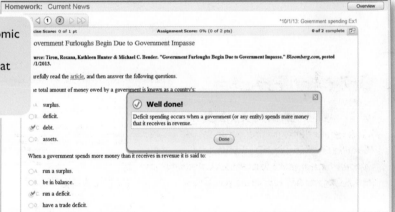

Interactive Homework Exercises

Participate in a fun and engaging activity that helps promote active learning and mastery of important economic concepts.

Pearson's experiments program is flexible and easy for instructors and students to use. For a complete list of available experiments, visit *www.myeconlab.com*.

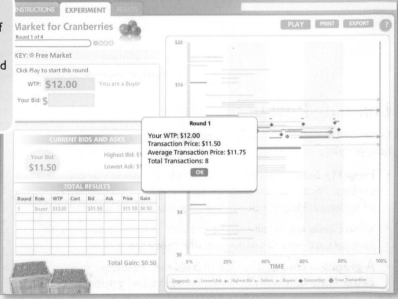

International Economics

| THEORY AND POLICY |

TENTH EDITION

GLOBAL EDITION

Paul R. Krugman
Princeton University

Maurice Obstfeld
University of California, Berkeley

Marc J. Melitz
Harvard University

PEARSON

Boston   Columbus   Indianapolis   New York   San Francisco   Upper Saddle River
Amsterdam   Cape Town   Dubai   London   Madrid   Milan   Munich   Paris   Montréal   Toronto
Delhi   Mexico City   São Paulo   Sydney   Hong Kong   Seoul   Singapore   Taipei   Tokyo

For Robin—P.K.
For my family—M.O.
For Clair, Benjamin, and Max—M.M.

Editor in Chief: Donna Battista
Managing Editor: Jeff Holcomb
Head of Learning Asset Acquisition, Global Editions:
    Laura Dent
Associate Editor, Global Editions: Toril Cooper
Program Manager: Carolyn Philips
International Marketing Manager: Kristin Schneider
Production Project Manager: Carla Thompson
Assistant Project Editor, Global Editions: Paromita Banerjee
Procurement Specialist: Carol Melville
Senior Operations Supervisor: Arnold Vila
Operations Specialist: Michelle Klein
Senior Art Director: Jonathan Boylan
Text Permissions Associate Project Manager:
    Samantha Graham

Interior Design: Integra-Chicago
Image Manager: Rachel Youdelman
Photo Research: Aptara, Inc.
Director of Media: Susan Schoenberg
Content Leads, MyEconLab: Courtney Kamauf and
    Noel Lotz
Senior Media Producer: Melissa Honig
Senior Production Manufacturing Controller, Global Editions:
    Trudy Kimber
Full-Service Project Management and Composition:
    Integra Software Services, Inc.
Media Producer, Global Editions: Vikram Kumar
Cover Image Credit: © Denis Vrublevski/ Shutterstock
Cover Designer: PreMedia Global USA, Inc.

Pearson Education Limited
Edinburgh Gate
Harlow
Essex CM20 2JE
England

and Associated Companies throughout the world

Visit us on the World Wide Web at:
www.pearsonglobaleditions.com

© Pearson Education Limited 2015

Authorized adaptation from the United States edition, entitled International Economics: Theory and Policy, 10th Edition
ISBN 978-0-13-342364-8 by Paul R. Krugman, Maurice Obstfeld, and Marc J. Melitz, published by Pearson Education © 2015.

ISBN 10: 1-292-01955-7
ISBN 13: 978-1-292-01955-0

British Library Cataloguing-in-Publication Data
A catalogue record for this book is available from the British Library

10 9 8 7 6 5 4
19 18 17 16

Typeset in 10/12 Times New Roman, Integra Software Services, Inc.

Printed in Malaysia (CTP-VVP)

Brief Contents

Contents

PART 4   International Macroeconomic Policy   **570**

19   INTERNATIONAL MONETARY SYSTEMS: AN HISTORICAL OVERVIEW   570

Preface

Years after the global financial crisis that broke out in 2007–2008, the industrial world's economies are still growing too slowly to restore full employment. Emerging markets, despite impressive income gains in many cases, remain vulnerable to the ebb and flow of global capital. And finally, an acute economic crisis in the euro area has lasted since 2009, bringing the future of Europe's common currency into question. This tenth edition therefore comes out at a time when we are more aware than ever before of how events in the global economy influence each country's economic fortunes, policies, and political debates. The world that emerged from World War II was one in which trade, financial, and even communication links between countries were limited. More than a decade into the 21st century, however, the picture is very different. Globalization has arrived, big time. International trade in goods and services has expanded steadily over the past six decades thanks to declines in shipping and communication costs, globally negotiated reductions in government trade barriers, the widespread outsourcing of production activities, and a greater awareness of foreign cultures and products. New and better communications technologies, notably the Internet, have revolutionized the way people in all countries obtain and exchange information. International trade in financial assets such as currencies, stocks, and bonds has expanded at a much faster pace even than international product trade. This process brings benefits for owners of wealth but also creates risks of contagious financial instability. Those risks were realized during the recent global financial crisis, which spread quickly across national borders and has played out at huge cost to the world economy. Of all the changes on the international scene in recent decades, however, perhaps the biggest one remains the emergence of China—a development that is already redefining the international balance of economic and political power in the coming century.

Imagine the astonishment of the generation that lived through the depressed 1930s as adults, had its members been able to foresee the shape of today's world economy! Nonetheless, the economic concerns that continue to cause international debate have not changed that much from those that dominated the 1930s, nor indeed since they were first analyzed by economists more than two centuries ago. What are the merits of free trade among nations compared with protectionism? What causes countries to run trade surpluses or deficits with their trading partners, and how are such imbalances resolved over time? What causes banking and currency crises in open economies, what causes financial contagion between economies, and how should governments handle international financial instability? How can governments avoid unemployment and inflation, what role do exchange rates play in their efforts, and how can countries best cooperate to achieve their economic goals? As always in international economics, the interplay of events and ideas has led to new modes of analysis. In turn, these analytical advances, however abstruse they may seem at first, ultimately do end up playing a major role in governmental policies, in international negotiations, and in people's everyday lives. Globalization has made citizens of all countries much more aware than ever before of the worldwide economic forces that influence their fortunes, and globalization is here to stay.

New to the Tenth Edition

For this edition, we are offering an Economics volume as well as Trade and Finance splits. The goal with these distinct volumes is to allow professors to use the book that best suits their needs based on the topics they cover in their International Economics course. In the Economics volume for a two-semester course, we follow the standard practice of dividing the book into two halves, devoted to trade and to monetary questions. Although the trade and monetary portions of international economics are often treated as unrelated subjects, even within one textbook, similar themes and methods recur in both subfields. We have made it a point to illuminate connections between the trade and monetary areas when they arise. At the same time, we have made sure that the book's two halves are completely self-contained. Thus, a one-semester course on trade theory can be based on Chapters 2 through 12, and a one-semester course on international monetary economics can be based on Chapters 13 through 22. For professors' and students' convenience, however, they can now opt to use either the Trade or the Finance volume, depending on the length and scope of their course.

We have thoroughly updated the content and extensively revised several chapters. These revisions respond both to users' suggestions and to some important developments on the theoretical and practical sides of international economics. The most far-reaching changes are the following:

- **Chapter 5, Resources and Trade: The Heckscher-Ohlin Model** This edition offers expanded coverage of the effects on wage inequality of North-South trade, technological change, and outsourcing. The section describing the empirical evidence on the Heckscher-Ohlin model has been rewritten, emphasizing new research. That section also incorporates some new data showing how China's pattern of exports has changed over time in a way that is consistent with the predictions of the Heckscher-Olhin model.

- **Chapter 6, The Standard Trade Model** This chapter has been updated with some new data documenting how the terms of trade for the U.S. and Chinese economies have evolved over time.

- **Chapter 8, Firms in the Global Economy: Export Decisions, Outsourcing, and Multinational Enterprises** The coverage emphasizing the role of firms in international trade has been revised. There is also a new Case Study analyzing the impact of offshoring in the United States on U.S. unemployment.

- **Chapter 9, The Instruments of Trade Policy** This chapter features an updated treatment of the effects of trade restrictions on United States firms. This chapter now describes the recent trade policy dispute between the European Union and China regarding solar panels and the effects of the "Buy American" restrictions that were written into the American Recovery and Re-Investment Act of 2009.

- **Chapter 12, Controversies in Trade Policy** A new case study discusses the recent garment factory collapse in Bangladesh (in April 2013) and the tension between the costs and benefits of Bangladesh's rapid growth as a clothing exporter.

- **Chapter 17, Output and the Exchange Rate in the Short Run** In response to the global economic crisis of 2007–2009, countries throughout the world adopted countercyclical fiscal responses. Renewed academic research on the size of the fiscal multiplier soon followed, although most of it was set in the closed economy and so ignored the exchange rate effects stressed in this chapter's model. For this edition, we have added a new Case Study on the size of the fiscal multiplier in the open economy.

In line with recent academic literature, which focuses on fiscal policy at the zero lower interest-rate bound, we integrate the discussion with our model of the liquidity trap.

- **Chapter 18, Fixed Exchange Rates and Foreign Exchange Intervention** The chapter now includes additional discussion of "inflow attacks" on exchange rates being held at appreciated levels through foreign exchange intervention and other measures, a phenomenon seen in China and other countries. A new Case Study focuses on the Swiss National Bank's policy of capping the Swiss franc's level against the euro.
- **Chapter 19, International Monetary Systems: An Historical Overview** A detailed derivation of an open economy's multi-period intertemporal budget constraint now complements the discussion of external balance. (Instructors who do not want to cover this relatively more technical material can skip it without loss of continuity.) The intertemporal analysis is applied to analyze the sustainability of New Zealand's persistent foreign borrowing. In addition, the chapter's discussion of recent events in the global economy has been updated.
- **Chapter 20, Financial Globalization: Opportunity and Crisis** For this new edition, we have switched the earlier order of Chapters 20 and 21 so that the book now covers the international capital market before covering optimum currency areas and the euro crisis. Our reasoning is that the euro crisis is in large part a crisis of the banks, which students cannot understand without a good prior grasp of international banking and its problems. Consistent with this approach, the new Chapter 20 covers bank balance sheets and bank fragility in detail, with emphasis on bank capital and capital regulation. Ever since this book's first edition, we have stressed the global context of banking regulation. In this edition, we explain the "financial trilemma," which forces national policymakers to choose at most two from among the potential objectives of financial openness, financial stability, and national control over financial policy.
- **Chapter 21, Optimum Currency Areas and the Euro** The crisis in the euro area escalated dramatically after the last edition of this book went to press. For this new edition, we have brought our coverage of the euro crisis up to date with new material on initiatives for closer policy coordination in the euro countries, such as banking union. Our theoretical discussion of optimum currency areas also reflects lessons of the euro crisis.
- **Chapter 22, Developing Countries: Growth, Crisis, and Reform** Our coverage of capital flows to developing countries now includes recent research on the small size of those flows, as well as their paradoxical tendency to favor low-growth over high-growth developing economies. We point out the close link between theories of capital allocation to developing countries and theories of the cross-country distribution of income.

In addition to these structural changes, we have updated the book in other ways to maintain current relevance. Thus, we examine the educational profile of foreign born workers in the United States and how it differs from the overall population (Chapter 4); we review recent anti-dumping disputes involving China (Chapter 8); we discuss the causes of the large measured global current account surplus (Chapter 13); we describe the outbreak and resolution of Zimbabwe's hyperinflation (Chapter 15); and we describe the evolving infrastructure of international bank regulation, including Basel III and the Financial Stability Board (Chapter 20).

About the Book

The idea of writing this book came out of our experience in teaching international economics to undergraduates and business students since the late 1970s. We perceived two main challenges in teaching. The first was to communicate to students the exciting intellectual advances in this dynamic field. The second was to show how the development of international economic theory has traditionally been shaped by the need to understand the changing world economy and analyze actual problems in international economic policy.

We found that published textbooks did not adequately meet these challenges. Too often, international economics textbooks confront students with a bewildering array of special models and assumptions from which basic lessons are difficult to extract. Because many of these special models are outmoded, students are left puzzled about the real-world relevance of the analysis. As a result, many textbooks often leave a gap between the somewhat antiquated material to be covered in class and the exciting issues that dominate current research and policy debates. That gap has widened dramatically as the importance of international economic problems—and enrollments in international economics courses—have grown.

This book is our attempt to provide an up-to-date and understandable analytical framework for illuminating current events and bringing the excitement of international economics into the classroom. In analyzing both the real and monetary sides of the subject, our approach has been to build up, step by step, a simple, unified framework for communicating the grand traditional insights as well as the newest findings and approaches. To help the student grasp and retain the underlying logic of international economics, we motivate the theoretical development at each stage by pertinent data and policy questions.

The Place of This Book in the Economics Curriculum

Students assimilate international economics most readily when it is presented as a method of analysis vitally linked to events in the world economy, rather than as a body of abstract theorems about abstract models. Our goal has therefore been to stress concepts and their application rather than theoretical formalism. Accordingly, the book does not presuppose an extensive background in economics. Students who have had a course in economic principles will find the book accessible, but students who have taken further courses in microeconomics or macroeconomics will find an abundant supply of new material. Specialized appendices and mathematical postscripts have been included to challenge the most advanced students.

Some Distinctive Features

This book covers the most important recent developments in international economics without shortchanging the enduring theoretical and historical insights that have traditionally formed the core of the subject. We have achieved this comprehensiveness by stressing how recent theories have evolved from earlier findings in response to an evolving world economy. Both the real trade portion of the book (Chapters 2 through 12) and the monetary portion (Chapters 13 through 22) are divided into a core of chapters focused on theory, followed by chapters applying the theory to major policy questions, past and current.

In Chapter 1, we describe in some detail how this book addresses the major themes of international economics. Here we emphasize several of the topics that previous authors failed to treat in a systematic way.

Increasing Returns and Market Structure

Even before discussing the role of comparative advantage in promoting international exchange and the associated welfare gains, we visit the forefront of theoretical and empirical research by setting out the gravity model of trade (Chapter 2). We return to the research frontier (in Chapters 7 and 8) by explaining how increasing returns and product differentiation affect trade and welfare. The models explored in this discussion capture significant aspects of reality, such as intraindustry trade and shifts in trade patterns due to dynamic scale economies. The models show, too, that mutually beneficial trade need not be based on comparative advantage.

Firms in International Trade

Chapter 8 also summarizes exciting new research focused on the role of firms in international trade. The chapter emphasizes that different firms may fare differently in the face of globalization. The expansion of some and the contraction of others shift overall production toward more efficient producers within industrial sectors, raising overall productivity and thereby generating gains from trade. Those firms that expand in an environment of freer trade may have incentives to outsource some of their production activities abroad or take up multinational production, as we describe in the chapter.

Politics and Theory of Trade Policy

Starting in Chapter 4, we stress the effect of trade on income distribution as the key political factor behind restrictions on free trade. This emphasis makes it clear to students why the prescriptions of the standard welfare analysis of trade policy seldom prevail in practice. Chapter 12 explores the popular notion that governments should adopt activist trade policies aimed at encouraging sectors of the economy seen as crucial. The chapter includes a theoretical discussion of such trade policy based on simple ideas from game theory.

Asset Market Approach to Exchange Rate Determination

The modern foreign exchange market and the determination of exchange rates by national interest rates and expectations are at the center of our account of open-economy macroeconomics. The main ingredient of the macroeconomic model we develop is the interest parity relation, augmented later by risk premiums (Chapter 14). Among the topics we address using the model are exchange rate "overshooting"; inflation targeting; behavior of real exchange rates; balance-of-payments crises under fixed exchange rates; and the causes and effects of central bank intervention in the foreign exchange market (Chapters 15 through 18).

International Macroeconomic Policy Coordination

Our discussion of international monetary experience (Chapters 19 through 22) stresses the theme that different exchange rate systems have led to different policy coordination problems for their members. Just as the competitive gold scramble of the interwar years showed how beggar-thy-neighbor policies can be self-defeating, the current float challenges national policymakers to recognize their interdependence and formulate policies cooperatively.

The World Capital Market and Developing Countries

A broad discussion of the world capital market is given in Chapter 20 which takes up the welfare implications of international portfolio diversification as well as problems of prudential supervision of internationally active banks and other financial institutions. Chapter 22 is devoted to the long-term growth prospects and to the specific macroeconomic stabilization and liberalization problems of industrializing and newly industrialized countries. The chapter reviews emerging market crises and places in historical perspective the interactions among developing country borrowers, developed country lenders, and official financial institutions such as the International Monetary Fund. Chapter 22 also reviews China's exchange-rate policies and recent research on the persistence of poverty in the developing world.

Learning Features

This book incorporates a number of special learning features that will maintain students' interest in the presentation and help them master its lessons.

Case Studies

Case studies that perform the threefold role of reinforcing material covered earlier, illustrating its applicability in the real world, and providing important historical information often accompany theoretical discussions.

Special Boxes

Less central topics that nonetheless offer particularly vivid illustrations of points made in the text are treated in boxes. Among these are U.S. President Thomas Jefferson's trade embargo of 1807–1809 (Chapter 3); the astonishing ability of disputes over banana trade to generate acrimony among countries far too cold to grow any of their own bananas (Chapter 10); markets for nondeliverable forward exchange (Chapter 14); and the rapid accumulation of foreign exchange reserves by developing countries (Chapter 22).

Captioned Diagrams

More than 200 diagrams are accompanied by descriptive captions that reinforce the discussion in the text and help the student in reviewing the material.

Learning Goals

A list of essential concepts sets the stage for each chapter in the book. These learning goals help students assess their mastery of the material.

Summary and Key Terms

Each chapter closes with a summary recapitulating the major points. Key terms and phrases appear in boldface type when they are introduced in the chapter and are listed at the end of each chapter. To further aid student review of the material, key terms are italicized when they appear in the chapter summary.

Problems

Each chapter is followed by problems intended to test and solidify students' comprehension. The problems range from routine computational drills to "big picture" questions suitable for classroom discussion. In many problems we ask students to apply what they have learned to real-world data or policy questions.

Further Readings

For instructors who prefer to supplement the textbook with outside readings, and for students who wish to probe more deeply on their own, each chapter has an annotated bibliography that includes established classics as well as up-to-date examinations of recent issues.

MyEconLab

MyEconLab

MyEconLab is the premier online assessment and tutorial system, pairing rich online content with innovative learning tools. MyEconLab includes comprehensive homework, quiz, test, and tutorial options, allowing instructors to manage all assessment needs in one program. Key innovations in the MyEconLab course for the tenth edition of *International Economics: Theory & Policy* include the following:

- *Real-Time Data Analysis Exercises,* marked with 🌐, allow students and instructors to use the latest data from FRED, the online macroeconomic data bank from the Federal Reserve Bank of St. Louis. By completing the exercises, students become familiar with a key data source, learn how to locate data, and develop skills to interpret data.
- In the *enhanced eText* available in MyEconLab, figures labeled MyEconLab Real-Time Data allow students to display a pop-up graph updated with real-time data from FRED.
- *Current News Exercises,* new to this edition of the MyEconLab course, provide a turnkey way to assign gradable news-based exercises in MyEconLab. Every week, Pearson scours the news, finds a current article appropriate for an economics course, creates an exercise around the news article, and then automatically adds it to MyEconLab. Assigning and grading current news-based exercises that deal with the latest economic events has never been more convenient.

Students and MyEconLab

This online homework and tutorial system puts students in control of their own learning through a suite of study and practice tools correlated with the online, interactive version of the textbook and learning aids such as animated figures. Within MyEconLab's structured environment, students practice what they learn, test their understanding, and then pursue a study plan that MyEconLab generates for them based on their performance.

Instructors and MyEconLab

MyEconLab provides flexible tools that allow instructors easily and effectively to customize online course materials to suit their needs. Instructors can create and assign tests, quizzes, or homework assignments. MyEconLab saves time by automatically grading all questions and tracking results in an online gradebook. MyEconLab can even grade assignments that require students to draw a graph.

After registering for MyEconLab instructors have access to downloadable supplements such as an instructor's manual, PowerPoint lecture notes, and a test bank. The test bank can also be used within MyEconLab, giving instructors ample material from which they can create assignments—or the Custom Exercise Builder makes it easy for instructors to create their own questions.

Weekly news articles, video, and RSS feeds help keep students updated on current events and make it easy for instructors to incorporate relevant news in lectures and homework.

For more information about MyEconLab or to request an instructor access code, visit www.myeconlab.com.

Additional Supplementary Resources

A full range of additional supplementary materials to support teaching and learning accompanies this book.

- The Online Instructor's Manual—updated by Hisham Foad of San Diego State University—includes chapter overviews and answers to the end-of-chapter problems.
- The Online Test Bank offers a rich array of multiple-choice and essay questions, including some mathematical and graphing problems, for each textbook chapter. It is available in Word, PDF, and TestGen formats. This Test Bank was carefully revised and updated by Robert F. Brooker of Gannon University.
- The Computerized Test Bank reproduces the Test Bank material in the TestGen software that is available for Windows and Macintosh. With TestGen, instructors can easily edit existing questions, add questions, generate tests, and print the tests in variety of formats.
- The Online PowerPoint Presentation with Tables, Figures, & Lecture Notes was revised by Amy Glass of Texas A&M University. This resource contains all text figures and tables and can be used for in-class presentations.
- The Companion Web Site at www.pearsonglobaleditions.com/Krugman contains additional appendices. (See page 21 of the Contents for a detailed list of the Online Appendices.)

Instructors can download supplements from our secure Instructor's Resource Center. Please visit www.pearsonglobaleditions.com/Krugman.

Acknowledgments

Our primary debt is to Christina Masturzo, the Acquisitions Editor in charge of the project. We also are grateful to the Program Manager, Carolyn Philips, and the Project Manager, Carla Thompson. Heather Johnson's efforts as Project Manager with Integra-Chicago were essential and efficient. We would also like to thank the media team at Pearson—Denise Clinton, Noel Lotz, Courtney Kamauf, and Melissa Honig—for all their hard work on the MyEconLab course for the tenth edition. Last, we thank the other editors who helped make the first nine editions of this book as good as they were.

We also wish to acknowledge the sterling research assistance of Tatjana Kleineberg and Sandile Hlatshwayo. Camille Fernandez provided superb logistical support, as usual. For helpful suggestions and moral support, we thank Jennifer Cobb, Gita Gopinath, Vladimir Hlasny, and Phillip Swagel.

We thank the following reviewers, past and present, for their recommendations and insights:

Jaleel Ahmad, *Concordia University*

Lian An, *University of North Florida*

Anthony Paul Andrews, *Governors State University*

Myrvin Anthony, *University of Strathclyde, U.K.*

Michael Arghyrou, *Cardiff University*

Richard Ault, *Auburn University*

Amitrajeet Batabyal, *Rochester Institute of Technology*

Tibor Besedes, *Georgia Tech*

George H. Borts, *Brown University*

Robert F. Brooker, *Gannon University*

Francisco Carrada-Bravo, *W.P. Carey School of Business, ASU*

Debajyoti Chakrabarty, *University of Sydney*

Adhip Chaudhuri, *Georgetown University*

Jay Pil Choi, *Michigan State University*

Jaiho Chung, *National University of Singapore*

Jonathan Conning, *Hunter College and The Graduate Center, The City University of New York*

Brian Copeland, *University of British Columbia*

Kevin Cotter, *Wayne State University*

Barbara Craig, *Oberlin College*

Susan Dadres, *University of North Texas*

Ronald B. Davies, *University College Dublin*

Ann Davis, *Marist College*

Gopal C. Dorai, *William Paterson University*

Robert Driskill, *Vanderbilt University*

Gerald Epstein, *University of Massachusetts at Amherst*

JoAnne Feeney, *State University of New York at Albany*

Robert Foster, *American Graduate School of International Management*

Patrice Franko, *Colby College*

Diana Fuguitt, *Eckerd College*

Byron Gangnes, *University of Hawaii at Manoa*

Ranjeeta Ghiara, *California State University, San Marcos*

Neil Gilfedder, *Stanford University*

Amy Glass, *Texas A&M University*

Patrick Gormely, *Kansas State University*

Thomas Grennes, *North Carolina State* University

Bodil Olai Hansen, *Copenhagen Business School*

Michael Hoffman, *U.S. Government Accountability Office*

Henk Jager, *University of Amsterdam*

Arvind Jaggi, *Franklin & Marshall College*

Mark Jelavich, *Northwest Missouri State University*

Philip R. Jones, *University of Bath and University of Bristol, U.K.*

Tsvetanka Karagyozova, *Lawrence University*

Hugh Kelley, *Indiana University*

Michael Kevane, *Santa Clara University*

Maureen Kilkenny, *University of Nevada*

Hyeongwoo Kim, *Auburn University*

Stephen A. King, *San Diego State University, Imperial Valley*

Faik Koray, *Louisiana State University*

Corinne Krupp, *Duke University*

Bun Song Lee, *University of Nebraska, Omaha*

Daniel Lee, *Shippensburg University*

Francis A. Lees, *St. Johns University*

Jamus Jerome Lim, *World Bank Group*

Rodney Ludema, *Georgetown University*

Stephen V. Marks, *Pomona College*

Michael L. McPherson, *University of North Texas*

Marcel Mérette, *University of Ottawa*

Shannon Mitchell, *Virginia Commonwealth University*

Kaz Miyagiwa, *Emory University*

Shannon Mudd, *Ursinus College*

Marc-Andreas Muendler, *University of California, San Diego*

Ton M. Mulder, *Erasmus University, Rotterdam*

Robert G. Murphy, *Boston College*

E. Wayne Nafziger, *Kansas State University*

Steen Nielsen, *University of Aarhus*

Dmitri Nizovtsev, *Washburn University*

Terutomo Ozawa, *Colorado State University*

Arvind Panagariya, *Columbia University*

Nina Pavcnik, *Dartmouth College*

Iordanis Petsas, *University of Scranton*

Thitima Puttitanun, *San Diego State University*

Peter Rangazas, *Indiana University-Purdue University Indianapolis*

James E. Rauch, *University of California, San Diego*

Michael Ryan, *Western Michigan University*

Donald Schilling, *University of Missouri, Columbia*

Patricia Higino Schneider, *Mount Holyoke College*

Ronald M. Schramm, *Columbia University*

Craig Schulman, *Texas A&M University*

Yochanan Shachmurove, *University of Pennsylvania*

Margaret Simpson, *The College of William and Mary*

Enrico Spolaore, *Tufts University*

Robert Staiger, *University of Wisconsin-Madison*

Jeffrey Steagall, *University of North Florida*

Robert M. Stern, *University of Michigan*

Abdulhamid Sukar, *Cameron University*

Rebecca Taylor, *University of Portsmouth, U.K.*

Scott Taylor, *University of British Columbia*

Aileen Thompson, *Carleton University*

Sarah Tinkler, *Portland State University*

Arja H. Turunen-Red, *University of New Orleans*

Dick vander Wal, *Free University of Amsterdam*

Gerald Willmann, *University of Kiel*

Rossitza Wooster, *California State University, Sacramento*

Bruce Wydick, *University of San Francisco*

Jiawen Yang, *The George Washington University*

Kevin H. Zhang, *Illinois State University*

Although we have not been able to make each and every suggested change, we found reviewers' observations invaluable in revising the book. Obviously, we bear sole responsibility for its remaining shortcomings.

Paul R. Krugman
Maurice Obstfeld
Marc J. Melitz
October 2013

Pearson would like to thank and acknowledge the following people for their work on the Global Edition:

Contributors:

Stefania Paladini, *Coventry University*

Pritish Kumar Sahu, *Multimedia University*

Reviewers:

Lap-kei Chow, *CUHK Business School*

Timo Korkeamäki, *Hanken School of Economics*

Joyce Chai Hui Ming, *Temasek Polytechnic*

Erkan Ilgün, *International Burch University*

Yue (Lucy) Liu, *University of Edinburgh*

Özlem Olgu, *Koç University*

CHAPTER 1

INTRODUCTION

You could say that the study of international trade and finance is where the discipline of economics as we know it began. Historians of economic thought often describe the essay "Of the Balance of Trade" by the Scottish philosopher David Hume as the first real exposition of an economic model. Hume published his essay in 1758, almost 20 years before his friend Adam Smith published *The Wealth of Nations*. And the debates over British trade policy in the early 19th century did much to convert economics from a discursive, informal field to the model-oriented subject it has been ever since.

Yet the study of international economics has never been as important as it is now. In the early 21st century, nations are more closely linked than ever before through trade in goods and services, flows of money, and investment in each other's economies. And the global economy created by these linkages is a turbulent place: Both policy makers and business leaders in every country, including the United States, must now pay attention to what are sometimes rapidly changing economic fortunes halfway around the world.

A look at some basic trade statistics gives us a sense of the unprecedented importance of international economic relations. Figure 1-1 shows the levels of U.S. exports and imports as shares of gross domestic product from 1960 to 2012. The most obvious feature of the figure is the long-term upward trend in both shares: International trade has roughly tripled in importance compared with the economy as a whole.

Almost as obvious is that, while both imports and exports have increased, imports have grown more, leading to a large excess of imports over exports. How is the United States able to pay for all those imported goods? The answer is that the money is supplied by large inflows of capital—money invested by foreigners willing to take a stake in the U.S. economy. Inflows of capital on that scale would once have been inconceivable; now they are taken for granted. And so the gap between imports and exports is an indicator of another aspect of growing international linkages—in this case the growing linkages between national capital markets.

Finally, notice that both imports and exports took a plunge in 2009. This decline reflected the global economic crisis that began in 2008 and is a reminder of the close links between world trade and the overall state of the world economy.

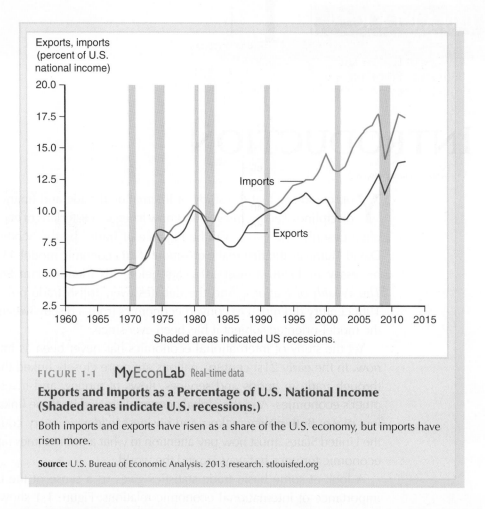

FIGURE 1-1   MyEconLab Real-time data

**Exports and Imports as a Percentage of U.S. National Income
(Shaded areas indicate U.S. recessions.)**

Both imports and exports have risen as a share of the U.S. economy, but imports have
risen more.

Source: U.S. Bureau of Economic Analysis. 2013 research. stlouisfed.org

If international economic relations have become crucial to the United States,
they are even more crucial to other nations. Figure 1-2 shows the average of
imports and exports as a share of GDP for a sample of countries. The United
States, by virtue of its size and the diversity of its resources, relies less on international trade than almost any other country.

This text introduces the main concepts and methods of international
economics and illustrates them with applications drawn from the real world. Much
of the text is devoted to old ideas that are still as valid as ever: The 19th-century trade
theory of David Ricardo and even the 18th-century monetary analysis of David
Hume remain highly relevant to the 21st-century world economy. At the same time,
we have made a special effort to bring the analysis up to date. In particular, the
economic crisis that began in 2007 threw up major new challenges for the global
economy. Economists were able to apply existing analyses to some of these challenges, but they were also forced to rethink some important concepts. Furthermore,
new approaches have emerged to old questions, such as the impacts of changes in
monetary and fiscal policy. We have attempted to convey the key ideas that have
emerged in recent research while stressing the continuing usefulness of old ideas.

FIGURE 1-2

Average of Exports and Imports as Percentages of National Income in 2011

International trade is even more important to most other countries than it is to the United States.

Source: Organization for Economic Cooperation and Development.

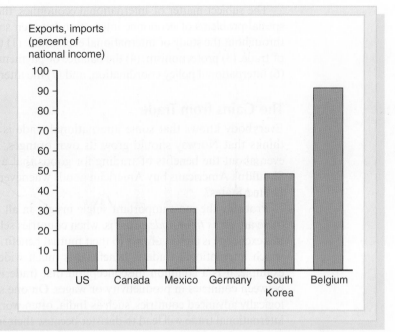

Exports, imports (percent of national income)

LEARNING GOALS

After reading this chapter, you will be able to:

- Distinguish between international and domestic economic issues.
- Explain why seven themes recur in international economics, and discuss their significance.
- Distinguish between the trade and monetary aspects of international economics.

What Is International Economics About?

International economics uses the same fundamental methods of analysis as other branches of economics because the motives and behavior of individuals are the same in international trade as they are in domestic transactions. Gourmet food shops in Florida sell coffee beans from both Mexico and Hawaii; the sequence of events that brought those beans to the shop is not very different, and the imported beans traveled a much shorter distance than the beans shipped within the United States! Yet international economics involves new and different concerns because international trade and investment occur between independent nations. The United States and Mexico are sovereign states; Florida and Hawaii are not. Mexico's coffee shipments to Florida could be disrupted if the U.S. government imposed a quota that limits imports; Mexican coffee could suddenly become cheaper to U.S. buyers if the peso were to fall in value against the dollar. By contrast, neither of those events can happen in commerce within the United States because the Constitution forbids restraints on interstate trade and all U.S. states use the same currency.

The subject matter of international economics, then, consists of issues raised by the special problems of economic interaction between sovereign states. Seven themes recur throughout the study of international economics: (1) the gains from trade, (2) the pattern of trade, (3) protectionism, (4) the balance of payments, (5) exchange rate determination, (6) international policy coordination, and (7) the international capital market.

The Gains from Trade

Everybody knows that some international trade is beneficial—for example, nobody thinks that Norway should grow its own oranges. Many people are skeptical, however, about the benefits of trading for goods that a country could produce for itself. Shouldn't Americans buy American goods whenever possible to help create jobs in the United States?

Probably the most important single insight in all of international economics is that there are *gains from trade*—that is, when countries sell goods and services to each other, this exchange is almost always to their mutual benefit. The range of circumstances under which international trade is beneficial is much wider than most people imagine. For example, it is a common misconception that trade is harmful if large disparities exist between countries in productivity or wages. On one side, businesspeople in less technologically advanced countries, such as India, often worry that opening their economies to international trade will lead to disaster because their industries won't be able to compete. On the other side, people in technologically advanced nations where workers earn high wages often fear that trading with less advanced, lower-wage countries will drag their standard of living down—one presidential candidate memorably warned of a "giant sucking sound" if the United States were to conclude a free trade agreement with Mexico.

Yet the first model this text presents of the causes of trade (Chapter 3) demonstrates that two countries can trade to their mutual benefit even when one of them is more efficient than the other at producing everything and when producers in the less efficient country can compete only by paying lower wages. We'll also see that trade provides benefits by allowing countries to export goods whose production makes relatively heavy use of resources that are locally abundant while importing goods whose production makes heavy use of resources that are locally scarce (Chapter 5). International trade also allows countries to specialize in producing narrower ranges of goods, giving them greater efficiencies of large-scale production.

Nor are the benefits of international trade limited to trade in tangible goods. International migration and international borrowing and lending are also forms of mutually beneficial trade—the first a trade of labor for goods and services (Chapter 4), the second a trade of current goods for the promise of future goods (Chapter 6). Finally, international exchanges of risky assets such as stocks and bonds can benefit all countries by allowing each country to diversify its wealth and reduce the variability of its income (Chapter 20). These invisible forms of trade yield gains as real as the trade that puts fresh fruit from Latin America in Toronto markets in February.

Although nations generally gain from international trade, it is quite possible that international trade may hurt particular groups *within* nations—in other words, that international trade will have strong effects on the distribution of income. The effects of trade on income distribution have long been a concern of international trade theorists who have pointed out that:

International trade can adversely affect the owners of resources that are "specific" to industries that compete with imports, that is, cannot find alternative employment in other industries. Examples would include specialized machinery, such as power looms made less valuable by textile imports, and workers with specialized skills, like fishermen who find the value of their catch reduced by imported seafood.

Trade can also alter the distribution of income between broad groups, such as workers and the owners of capital.

These concerns have moved from the classroom into the center of real-world policy debate as it has become increasingly clear that the real wages of less-skilled workers in the United States have been declining—even though the country as a whole is continuing to grow richer. Many commentators attribute this development to growing international trade, especially the rapidly growing exports of manufactured goods from low-wage countries. Assessing this claim has become an important task for international economists and is a major theme of Chapters 4 through 6.

The Pattern of Trade

Economists cannot discuss the effects of international trade or recommend changes in government policies toward trade with any confidence unless they know their theory is good enough to explain the international trade that is actually observed. As a result, attempts to explain the pattern of international trade—who sells what to whom—have been a major preoccupation of international economists.

Some aspects of the pattern of trade are easy to understand. Climate and resources clearly explain why Brazil exports coffee and Saudi Arabia exports oil. Much of the pattern of trade is more subtle, however. Why does Japan export automobiles, while the United States exports aircraft? In the early 19th century, English economist David Ricardo offered an explanation of trade in terms of international differences in labor productivity, an explanation that remains a powerful insight (Chapter 3). In the 20th century, however, alternative explanations also were proposed. One of the most influential, explanations links trade patterns to an interaction between the relative supplies of national resources such as capital, labor, and land on one side and the relative use of these factors in the production of different goods on the other. We present this theory in Chapter 5. We then discuss how this basic model must be extended in order to generate accurate empirical predictions for the volume and pattern of trade. Also, some international economists have proposed theories that suggest a substantial random component, along with economies of scale, in the pattern of international trade, theories that are developed in Chapters 7 and 8.

How Much Trade?

If the idea of gains from trade is the most important theoretical concept in international economics, the seemingly eternal debate over how much trade to allow is its most important policy theme. Since the emergence of modern nation-states in the 16th century, governments have worried about the effect of international competition on the prosperity of domestic industries and have tried either to shield industries from foreign competition by placing limits on imports or to help them in world competition by subsidizing exports. The single most consistent mission of international economics has been to analyze the effects of these so-called protectionist policies—and usually, though not always, to criticize protectionism and show the advantages of freer international trade.

The debate over how much trade to allow took a new direction in the 1990s. After World War II the advanced democracies, led by the United States, pursued a broad policy of removing barriers to international trade; this policy reflected the view that free trade was a force not only for prosperity but also for promoting world peace.

In the first half of the 1990s, several major free trade agreements were negotiated. The most notable were the North American Free Trade Agreement (NAFTA) between the United States, Canada, and Mexico, approved in 1993, and the so-called Uruguay Round agreement, which established the World Trade Organization in 1994.

Since that time, however, an international political movement opposing "globalization" has gained many adherents. The movement achieved notoriety in 1999, when demonstrators representing a mix of traditional protectionists and new ideologies disrupted a major international trade meeting in Seattle. If nothing else, the anti-globalization movement has forced advocates of free trade to seek new ways to explain their views.

As befits both the historical importance and the current relevance of the protectionist issue, roughly a quarter of this text is devoted to this subject. Over the years, international economists have developed a simple yet powerful analytical framework for determining the effects of government policies that affect international trade. This framework helps predict the effects of trade policies, while also allowing for cost-benefit analysis and defining criteria for determining when government intervention is good for the economy. We present this framework in Chapters 9 and 10 and use it to discuss a number of policy issues in those chapters and in the two that follow.

In the real world, however, governments do not necessarily do what the cost-benefit analysis of economists tells them they should. This does not mean that analysis is useless. Economic analysis can help make sense of the politics of international trade policy by showing who benefits and who loses from such government actions as quotas on imports and subsidies to exports. The key insight of this analysis is that conflicts of interest *within* nations are usually more important in determining trade policy than conflicts of interest *between* nations. Chapters 4 and 5 show that trade usually has very strong effects on income distribution within countries, while Chapters 10 through 12 reveal that the relative power of different interest groups within countries, rather than some measure of overall national interest, is often the main determining factor in government policies toward international trade.

Balance of Payments

In 1998, both China and South Korea ran large trade surpluses of about $40 billion each. In China's case, the trade surplus was not out of the ordinary—the country had been running large surpluses for several years, prompting complaints from other countries, including the United States, that China was not playing by the rules. So is it good to run a trade surplus and bad to run a trade deficit? Not according to the South Koreans: Their trade surplus was forced on them by an economic and financial crisis, and they bitterly resented the necessity of running that surplus.

This comparison highlights the fact that a country's *balance of payments* must be placed in the context of an economic analysis to understand what it means. It emerges in a variety of specific contexts: in discussing foreign direct investment by multinational corporations (Chapter 8), in relating international transactions to national income accounting (Chapter 13), and in discussing virtually every aspect of international monetary policy (Chapters 17 through 22). Like the problem of protectionism, the balance of payments has become a central issue for the United States because the nation has run huge trade deficits every year since 1982.

Exchange Rate Determination

In September 2010, Brazil's finance minister, Guido Mantegna, made headlines by declaring that the world was "in the midst of an international currency war." The occasion for his remarks was a sharp rise in the value of Brazil's currency, the *real*, which was worth less than 45 cents at the beginning of 2009 but had risen to almost 60 cents when he spoke (and would rise to 65 cents over the next few months). Mantegna accused wealthy countries—the United States in particular—of engineering this rise, which was devastating to Brazilian exporters. However, the surge in the *real* proved short-lived; the currency began dropping in mid-2011, and by the summer of 2013 it was back down to only 45 cents.

A key difference between international economics and other areas of economics is that countries usually have their own currencies—the euro, which is shared by a number of European countries, being the exception that proves the rule. And as the example of the *real* illustrates, the relative values of currencies can change over time, sometimes drastically.

For historical reasons, the study of exchange rate determination is a relatively new part of international economics. For much of modern economic history, exchange rates were fixed by government action rather than determined in the marketplace. Before World War I, the values of the world's major currencies were fixed in terms of gold; for a generation after World War II, the values of most currencies were fixed in terms of the U.S. dollar. The analysis of international monetary systems that fix exchange rates remains an important subject. Chapter 18 is devoted to the working of fixed-rate systems, Chapter 19 to the historical performance of alternative exchange-rate systems, and Chapter 21 to the economics of currency areas such as the European monetary union. For the time being, however, some of the world's most important exchange rates fluctuate minute by minute and the role of changing exchange rates remains at the center of the international economics story. Chapters 14 through 17 focus on the modern theory of floating exchange rates.

International Policy Coordination

The international economy comprises sovereign nations, each free to choose its own economic policies. Unfortunately, in an integrated world economy, one country's economic policies usually affect other countries as well. For example, when Germany's Bundesbank raised interest rates in 1990—a step it took to control the possible inflationary impact of the reunification of West and East Germany—it helped precipitate a recession in the rest of Western Europe. Differences in goals among countries often lead to conflicts of interest. Even when countries have similar goals, they may suffer losses if they fail to coordinate their policies. A fundamental problem in international economics is determining how to produce an acceptable degree of harmony among the international trade and monetary policies of different countries in the absence of a world government that tells countries what to do.

For almost 70 years, international trade policies have been governed by an international agreement known as the General Agreement on Tariffs and Trade (GATT). Since 1994, trade rules have been enforced by an international organization, the World Trade Organization, that can tell countries, including the United States, that their policies violate prior agreements. We discuss the rationale for this system in Chapter 9 and look at whether the current rules of the game for international trade in the world economy can or should survive.

While cooperation on international trade policies is a well-established tradition, coordination of international macroeconomic policies is a newer and more uncertain topic. Attempts to formulate principles for international macroeconomic coordination date to the 1980s and 1990s and remain controversial to this day. Nonetheless, attempts at international macroeconomic coordination are occurring with growing frequency in the real world. Both the theory of international macroeconomic coordination and the developing experience are reviewed in Chapter 19.

The International Capital Market

In 2007, investors who had bought U.S. mortgage-backed securities—claims on the income from large pools of home mortgages—received a rude shock: as home prices began to fall, mortgage defaults soared, and investments they had been assured were safe turned out to be highly risky. Since many of these claims were owned by financial institutions, the housing bust soon turned into a banking crisis. And here's the thing: it wasn't just a U.S. banking crisis, because banks in other countries, especially in Europe, had also bought many of these securities.

The story didn't end there: Europe soon had its own housing bust. And while the bust mainly took place in southern Europe, it soon became apparent that many northern European banks—such as German banks that had lent money to their Spanish counterparts—were also very exposed to the financial consequences.

In any sophisticated economy, there is an extensive capital market: a set of arrangements by which individuals and firms exchange money now for promises to pay in the future. The growing importance of international trade since the 1960s has been accompanied by a growth in the *international* capital market, which links the capital markets of individual countries. Thus in the 1970s, oil-rich Middle Eastern nations placed their oil revenues in banks in London or New York, and these banks in turn lent money to governments and corporations in Asia and Latin America. During the 1980s, Japan converted much of the money it earned from its booming exports into investments in the United States, including the establishment of a growing number of U.S. subsidiaries of Japanese corporations. Nowadays, China is funneling its own export earnings into a range of foreign assets, including dollars that its government holds as international reserves.

International capital markets differ in important ways from domestic capital markets. They must cope with special regulations that many countries impose on foreign investment; they also sometimes offer opportunities to evade regulations placed on domestic markets. Since the 1960s, huge international capital markets have arisen, most notably the remarkable London Eurodollar market, in which billions of dollars are exchanged each day without ever touching the United States.

Some special risks are associated with international capital markets. One risk is currency fluctuations: If the euro falls against the dollar, U.S. investors who bought euro bonds suffer a capital loss. Another risk is national default: A nation may simply refuse to pay its debts (perhaps because it cannot), and there may be no effective way for its creditors to bring it to court. Fears of default by highly indebted European nations have been a major concern in recent years.

The growing importance of international capital markets and their new problems demand greater attention than ever before. This text devotes two chapters to issues arising from international capital markets: one on the functioning of global asset markets (Chapter 20) and one on foreign borrowing by developing countries (Chapter 22).

International Economics: Trade and Money

The economics of the international economy can be divided into two broad subfields: the study of *international trade* and the study of *international money*. International trade analysis focuses primarily on the *real* transactions in the international economy, that is, transactions involving a physical movement of goods or a tangible commitment of economic resources. International monetary analysis focuses on the *monetary* side of the international economy, that is, on financial transactions such as foreign purchases of U.S. dollars. An example of an international trade issue is the conflict between the United States and Europe over Europe's subsidized exports of agricultural products; an example of an international monetary issue is the dispute over whether the foreign exchange value of the dollar should be allowed to float freely or be stabilized by government action.

In the real world, there is no simple dividing line between trade and monetary issues. Most international trade involves monetary transactions, while, as the examples in this chapter already suggest, many monetary events have important consequences for trade. Nonetheless, the distinction between international trade and international money is useful. The first half of this text covers international trade issues. Part One (Chapters 2 through 8) develops the analytical theory of international trade, and Part Two (Chapters 9 through 12) applies trade theory to the analysis of government policies toward trade. The second half of the text is devoted to international monetary issues. Part Three (Chapters 13 through 18) develops international monetary theory, and Part Four (Chapters 19 through 22) applies this analysis to international monetary policy.

MyEconLab Can Help You Get a Better Grade

MyEconLab   If your exam were tomorrow, would you be ready? For each chapter, MyEconLab Practice Tests and Study Plans pinpoint sections you have mastered and those you need to study. That way, you are more efficient with your study time, and you are better prepared for your exams.

Here's how it works:

1. Make sure you have a Course ID from your instructor. Register and log in at www.myeconlab.com
2. Click on "Study Plan" and select the "Practice" button for the first section in this chapter.
3. Work the Practice questions. MyEconLab will grade your work automatically.
4. The Study Plan will serve up additional Practice Problems and tutorials to help you master the specific areas where you need to focus. By practicing online, you can track your progress in the Study Plan.
5. If you do well on the practice questions, the "Quiz Me" button will become highlighted. Work the Quiz questions.
6. Once you have mastered a section via the "Quiz Me" test, you will receive a Mastery Point and be directed to work on the next section.

CHAPTER 2

WORLD TRADE: AN OVERVIEW

I n 2013, the world as a whole produced goods and services worth about $74 trillion at current prices. Of this total, more than 30 percent was sold across national borders: World trade in goods and services exceeded $23 trillion. That's a whole lot of exporting and importing.

In later chapters, we'll analyze why <u>countries</u> sell much of what they produce to other countries and why they purchase much of what they consume from other countries. We'll also examine the benefits and costs of international trade and the motivations for and effects of government policies that restrict or encourage trade.

Before we get to all that, however, let's begin by describing who trades with whom. An empirical relationship known as the *gravity model* helps to make sense of the value of trade between any pair of countries and sheds light on the impediments that continue to limit international trade even in today's global economy.

We'll then turn to the changing structure of world trade. As we'll see, recent decades have been marked by a large increase in the share of world output sold internationally by a shift in the world's economic center of gravity toward Asia and by major changes in the types of goods that make up that trade.

LEARNING GOALS

After reading this chapter, you will be able to:

- Describe how the value of trade between any two countries depends on the size of these countries' economies and explain the reasons for that relationship.
- Discuss how distance and borders reduce trade.
- Describe how the share of international production that is traded has fluctuated over time and why there have been two ages of globalization.
- Explain how the mix of goods and services that are traded internationally has changed over time.

Who Trades with Whom?

Figure 2-1 shows the total value of trade in goods—exports plus imports—between the United States and its top 15 trading partners in 2012. (Data on trade in services are less well broken down by trading partner; we'll talk about the rising importance of trade in

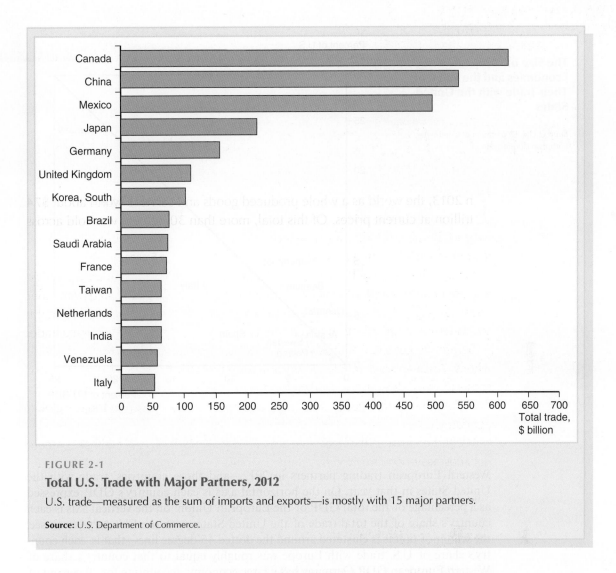

FIGURE 2-1

Total U.S. Trade with Major Partners, 2012

U.S. trade—measured as the sum of imports and exports—is mostly with 15 major partners.

Source: U.S. Department of Commerce.

services, and the issues raised by that trade, later in this chapter.) Taken together, these 15 countries accounted for 69 percent of the value of U.S. trade in that year.

Why did the United States trade so much with these countries? Let's look at the factors that, in practice, determine who trades with whom.

Size Matters: The Gravity Model

Three of the top 15 U.S. trading partners are European nations: Germany, the United Kingdom, and France. Why does the United States trade more heavily with these three European countries than with others? The answer is that these are the three largest European economies. That is, they have the highest values of **gross domestic product (GDP),** which measures the total value of all goods and services produced in an economy. There is a strong empirical relationship between the size of a country's economy and the volume of both its imports and its exports.

Figure 2-2 illustrates this relationship by showing the correspondence between the size of different European economies—specifically, America's 15 most important

FIGURE 2-2

The Size of European Economies and the Value of Their Trade with the United States

Source: U.S. Department of Commerce, European Commission.

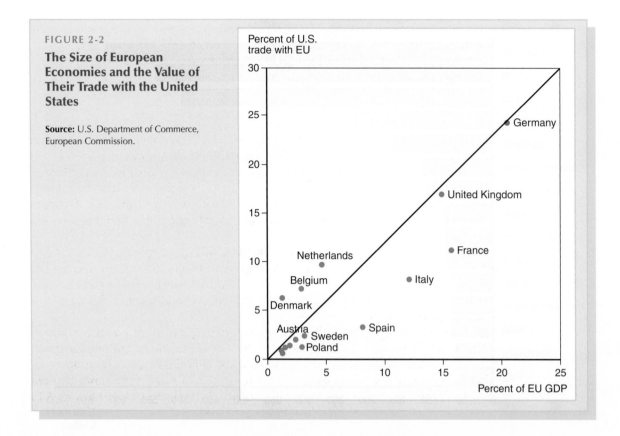

Western European trading partners in 2012—and those countries' trade with the United States in that year. On the horizontal axis is each country's GDP, expressed as a percentage of the total GDP of the European Union; on the vertical axis is each country's share of the total trade of the United States with the EU. As you can see, the scatter of points is clustered around the dotted 45-degree line—that is, each country's share of U.S. trade with Europe was roughly equal to that country's share of Western European GDP. Germany has a large economy, accounting for 20 percent of Western European GDP; it also accounts for 24 percent of U.S. trade with the region. Sweden has a much smaller economy, accounting for only 3.2 percent of European GDP; correspondingly, it accounts for only 2.3 percent of U.S.–Europe trade.

Looking at world trade as a whole, economists have found that an equation of the following form predicts the volume of trade between any two countries fairly accurately,

$$T_{ij} = A \times Y_i \times Y_j/D_{ij}, \tag{2-1}$$

where A is a constant term, T_{ij} is the value of trade between country i and country j, Y_i is country i's GDP, Y_j is country j's GDP, and D_{ij} is the distance between the two countries. That is, the value of trade between any two countries is proportional, other things equal, to the *product* of the two countries' GDPs and diminishes with the distance between the two countries.

An equation such as (2-1) is known as a **gravity model** of world trade. The reason for the name is the analogy to Newton's law of gravity: Just as the gravitational attraction between any two objects is proportional to the product of their masses and diminishes with distance, the trade between any two countries is, other things equal, proportional to the product of their GDPs and diminishes with distance.

Economists often estimate a somewhat more general gravity model of the following form:

$$T_{ij} = A \times Y_i^a \times Y_j^b / D_{ij}^c. \tag{2-2}$$

This equation says that the three things that determine the volume of trade between two countries are the size of the two countries' GDPs and the distance between the countries, without specifically assuming that trade is proportional to the product of the two GDPs and inversely proportional to distance. Instead, a, b, and c are chosen to fit the actual data as closely as possible. If a, b, and c were all equal to 1, Equation (2-2) would be the same as Equation (2-1). In fact, estimates often find that (2-1) is a pretty good approximation.

Why does the gravity model work? Broadly speaking, large economies tend to spend large amounts on imports because they have large incomes. They also tend to attract large shares of other countries' spending because they produce a wide range of products. So, other things equal, the trade between any two economies is larger—the larger is *either* economy.

What other things *aren't* equal? As we have already noted, in practice countries spend much or most of their income at home. The United States and the European Union each account for about 25 percent of the world's GDP, but each attracts only about 2 percent of the other's spending. To make sense of actual trade flows, we need to consider the factors limiting international trade. Before we get there, however, let's look at an important reason why the gravity model is useful.

Using the Gravity Model: Looking for Anomalies

It's clear from Figure 2-2 that a gravity model fits the data on U.S. trade with European countries pretty well—but not perfectly. In fact, one of the principal uses of gravity models is that they help us to identify anomalies in trade. Indeed, when trade between two countries is either much more or much less than a gravity model predicts, economists search for the explanation.

Looking again at Figure 2-2, we see that the Netherlands, Belgium, and Ireland trade considerably more with the United States than a gravity model would have predicted. Why might this be the case?

For Ireland, the answer lies partly in cultural affinity: Not only does Ireland share a language with the United States, but tens of millions of Americans are descended from Irish immigrants. Beyond this consideration, Ireland plays a special role as host to many U.S.-based corporations; we'll discuss the role of such *multinational corporations* in Chapter 8.

In the case of both the Netherlands and Belgium, geography and transport costs probably explain their large trade with the United States. Both countries are located near the mouth of the Rhine, Western Europe's longest river, which runs past the Ruhr, Germany's industrial heartland. So the Netherlands and Belgium have traditionally been the point of entry to much of northwestern Europe; Rotterdam in the Netherlands is the most important port in Europe, as measured by the tonnage handled, and Antwerp in Belgium ranks second. The large trade of Belgium and the Netherlands suggests, in other words, an important role of transport costs and geography in determining the volume of trade. The importance of these factors is clear when we turn to a broader example of trade data.

Impediments to Trade: Distance, Barriers, and Borders

Figure 2-3 shows the same data as Figure 2-2—U.S. trade as a percentage of total trade with Western Europe in 2012 versus GDP as a percentage of the region's total GDP—but adds two more countries: Canada and Mexico. As you can see, the two neighbors of the United States do a lot more trade with the United States than European economies of equal size. In fact, Canada, whose economy is roughly the same size as Spain's, trades as much with the United States as all of Europe does.

Why does the United States do so much more trade with its North American neighbors than with its European partners? One main reason is the simple fact that Canada and Mexico are much closer.

All estimated gravity models show a strong negative effect of distance on international trade; typical estimates say that a 1 percent increase in the distance between two countries is associated with a fall of 0.7 to 1 percent in the trade between those countries. This drop partly reflects increased costs of transporting goods and services. Economists also believe that less tangible factors play a crucial role: Trade tends to be intense when countries have close personal contact, and this contact tends to diminish when distances are large. For example, it's easy for a U.S. sales representative to pay a quick visit to Toronto, but it's a much bigger project for that representative to go to Paris. Unless the company is based on the West Coast, it's an even bigger project to visit Tokyo.

In addition to being U.S. neighbors, Canada and Mexico are part of a **trade agreement** with the United States, the North American Free Trade Agreement, or NAFTA, which ensures that most goods shipped among the three countries are not subject to tariffs or

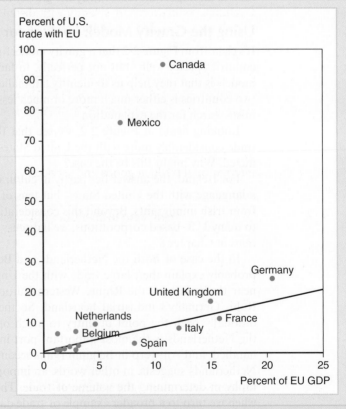

other barriers to international trade. We'll analyze the effects of barriers to international trade in Chapters 8–9, and the role of trade agreements such as NAFTA in Chapter 10. For now, let's notice that economists use gravity models as a way of assessing the impact of trade agreements on actual international trade: If a trade agreement is effective, it should lead to significantly more trade among its partners than one would otherwise predict given their GDPs and distances from one another.

It's important to note, however, that although trade agreements often end all formal barriers to trade between countries, they rarely make national borders irrelevant. Even when most goods and services shipped across a national border pay no tariffs and face few legal restrictions, there is much more trade between regions of the same country than between equivalently situated regions in different countries. The Canadian–U.S. border is a case in point. The two countries are part of a free trade agreement (indeed, there was a Canadian–U.S. free trade agreement even before NAFTA); most Canadians speak English; and the citizens of either country are free to cross the border with a minimum of formalities. Yet data on the trade of individual Canadian provinces both with each other and with U.S. states show that, other things equal, there is much more trade between provinces than between provinces and U.S. states.

Table 2-1 illustrates the extent of the difference. It shows the total trade (exports plus imports) of the Canadian province of British Columbia, just north of the state of Washington, with other Canadian provinces and with U.S. states, measured as a percentage of each province or state's GDP. Figure 2-4 shows the location of these provinces and states. Each Canadian province is paired with a U.S. state that is roughly the same distance from British Columbia: Washington State and Alberta both border British Columbia; Ontario and Ohio are both in the Midwest; and so on. With the exception of trade with the far eastern Canadian province of New Brunswick, intra-Canadian trade drops off steadily with distance. But in each case, the trade between British Columbia and a Canadian province is much larger than trade with an equally distant U.S. state.

Economists have used data like those shown in Table 2-1, together with estimates of the effect of distance in gravity models, to calculate that the Canadian–U.S. border, although it is one of the most open borders in the world, has as much effect in deterring trade as if the countries were between 1,500 and 2,500 miles apart.

Why do borders have such a large negative effect on trade? That is a topic of ongoing research. Chapter 21 describes one recent focus of that research: an effort to determine how much effect the existence of separate national currencies has on international trade in goods and services.

TABLE 2-1	Trade with British Columbia, as Percent of GDP, 2009		
Canadian Province	Trade as Percent of GDP	Trade as Percent of GDP	U.S. State at Similar Distance from British Columbia
Alberta	6.9	2.6	Washington
Saskatchewan	2.4	1.0	Montana
Manitoba	2.0	0.3	California
Ontario	1.9	0.2	Ohio
Quebec	1.4	0.1	New York
New Brunswick	2.3	0.2	Maine

Source: Statistics Canada, US Department of Commerce

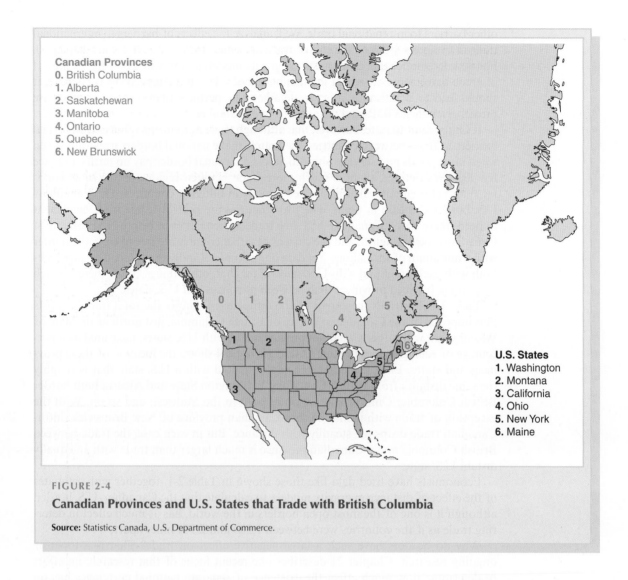

Canadian Provinces
0. British Columbia
1. Alberta
2. Saskatchewan
3. Manitoba
4. Ontario
5. Quebec
6. New Brunswick

U.S. States
1. Washington
2. Montana
3. California
4. Ohio
5. New York
6. Maine

FIGURE 2-4

Canadian Provinces and U.S. States that Trade with British Columbia

Source: Statistics Canada, U.S. Department of Commerce.

The Changing Pattern of World Trade

World trade is a moving target. The direction and composition of world trade is quite different today from what it was a generation ago and even more different from what it was a century ago. Let's look at some of the main trends.

Has the World Gotten Smaller?

In popular discussions of the world economy, one often encounters statements that modern transportation and communications have abolished distance, so that the world has become a small place. There's clearly some truth to these statements: The Internet makes instant and almost free communication possible between people thousands of miles apart, while jet transport allows quick physical access to all parts of the globe. On the other hand, gravity models continue to show a strong negative relationship between distance and international trade. But have such effects grown weaker over time? Has the progress of transportation and communication made the world smaller?

The answer is yes—but history also shows that political forces can outweigh the effects of technology. The world got smaller between 1840 and 1914, but it got bigger again for much of the 20th century.

Economic historians tell us that a global economy, with strong economic linkages between even distant nations, is not new. In fact, there have been two great waves of globalization with the first wave relying not on jets and the Internet but on railroads, steamships, and the telegraph. In 1919, the great economist John Maynard Keynes described the results of that surge of globalization:

> What an extraordinary episode in the economic progress of man that age was which came to an end in August 1914!...The inhabitant of London could order by telephone, sipping his morning tea in bed, the various products of the whole earth, in such quantity as he might see fit, and reasonably expect their early delivery upon his doorstep.

Notice, however, Keynes's statement that the age "came to an end" in 1914. In fact, two subsequent world wars, the Great Depression of the 1930s and widespread protectionism, did a great deal to depress world trade. Figure 2-5 shows one measure of international trade: the ratio of an index of world exports of manufactured goods

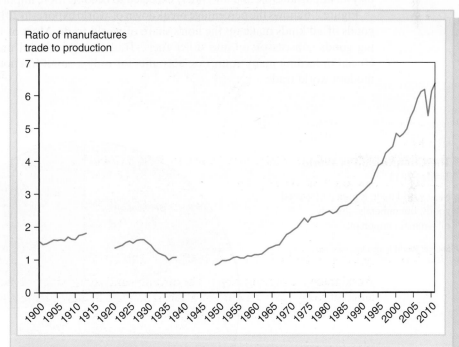

FIGURE 2-5

The Fall and Rise of World Trade

The ratio of world exports of manufactured goods to world industrial production—shown here as an index with 1953=1—rose in the decades before World War I but fell sharply in the face of wars and protectionism. It didn't return to 1913 levels until the 1970s but has since reached new heights.

Source: UN Monthly Bulletin of Statistics, World Trade Organization

to an index of world industrial production. World trade grew rapidly in the decades leading up to World War I but then fell significantly. As you can see, by this measure globalization didn't return to pre-World-War-I levels until the early 1970s.

Since then, however, world trade as a share of world production has risen to unprecedented heights. Much of this rise in the value of world trade reflects the so-called "vertical disintegration" of production: Before a product reaches the hands of consumers, it often goes through many production stages in different countries. For example, consumer electronic products—cell phones, iPods, and so on—are often assembled in low-wage nations such as China from components produced in higher-wage nations like Japan. Because of the extensive cross-shipping of components, a $100 product can give rise to $200 or $300 worth of international trade flows.

What Do We Trade?

When countries trade, what do they trade? For the world as a whole, the main answer is that they ship manufactured goods such as automobiles, computers, and clothing to each other. However, trade in mineral products—a category that includes everything from copper ore to coal, but whose main component in the modern world is oil—remains an important part of world trade. Agricultural products such as wheat, soybeans, and cotton are another key piece of the picture, and services of various kinds play an important role and are widely expected to become more important in the future.

Figure 2-6 shows the percentage breakdown of world exports in 2011. Manufactured goods of all kinds make up the lion's share of world trade. Most of the value of mining goods consists of oil and other fuels. Trade in agricultural products, although crucial in feeding many countries, accounts for only a small fraction of the value of modern world trade.

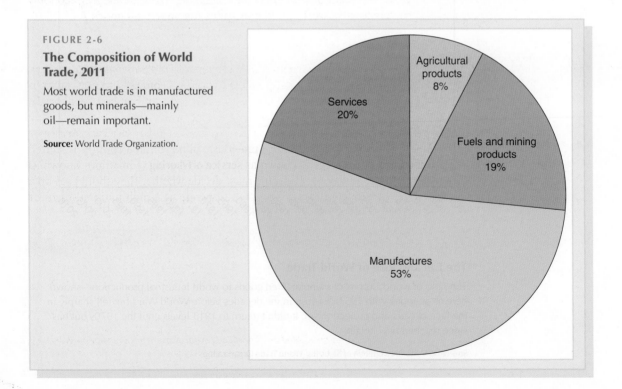

FIGURE 2-6

The Composition of World Trade, 2011

Most world trade is in manufactured goods, but minerals—mainly oil—remain important.

Source: World Trade Organization.

Meanwhile, service exports include traditional transportation fees charged by airlines and shipping companies, insurance fees received from foreigners, and spending by foreign tourists. In recent years, new types of service trade, made possible by modern telecommunications, have drawn a great deal of media attention. The most famous example is the rise of overseas call and help centers: If you call an 800 number for information or technical help, the person on the other end of the line may well be in a remote country (the Indian city of Bangalore is a particularly popular location). So far, these exotic new forms of trade are still a relatively small part of the overall trade picture, but as explained below, that may change in the years ahead.

The current picture, in which manufactured goods dominate world trade, is relatively new. In the past, primary products—agricultural and mining goods—played a much more important role in world trade. Table 2-2 shows the share of manufactured goods in the exports and imports of the United Kingdom and the United States in 1910 and 2011. In the early 20th century Britain, while it overwhelmingly exported manufactured goods (manufactures), mainly imported primary products. Today, manufactured goods dominate both sides of its trade. Meanwhile, the United States has gone from a trade pattern in which primary products were more important than manufactured goods on both sides to one in which manufactured goods dominate.

A more recent transformation has been the rise of third world exports of manufactured goods. The terms **third world** and **developing countries** are applied to the world's poorer nations, many of which were European colonies before World War II. As recently as the 1970s, these countries mainly exported primary products. Since then, however, they have moved rapidly into exports of manufactured goods. Figure 2-7 shows the shares of agricultural products and manufactured goods in developing-country exports since 1960. There has been an almost complete reversal of relative importance. For example, more than 90 percent of the exports of China, the largest developing economy and a rapidly growing force in world trade, consists of manufactured goods.

Service Offshoring

One of the hottest disputes in international economics right now is whether modern information technology, which makes it possible to perform some economic functions at long range, will lead to a dramatic increase in new forms of international trade. We've already mentioned the example of call centers, where the person answering your request for information may be 8,000 miles away. Many other services can also be done in a remote location. When a service previously done within a country is shifted to a foreign location, the change is known as **service offshoring** (sometimes known as **service outsourcing**). In addition, producers must decide whether they should set up a foreign subsidiary to provide those services (and operate as a multinational firm) or

TABLE 2-2	Manufactured Goods as Percent of Merchandise Trade			
	United Kingdom		**United States**	
	Exports	Imports	Exports	Imports
1910	75.4	24.5	47.5	40.7
2011	72.1	69.1	65.3	67.2

Source: 1910 data from Simon Kuznets, *Modern Economic Growth: Rate, Structure and Speed.* New Haven: Yale Univ. Press, 1966. 2011 data from World Trade Organization.

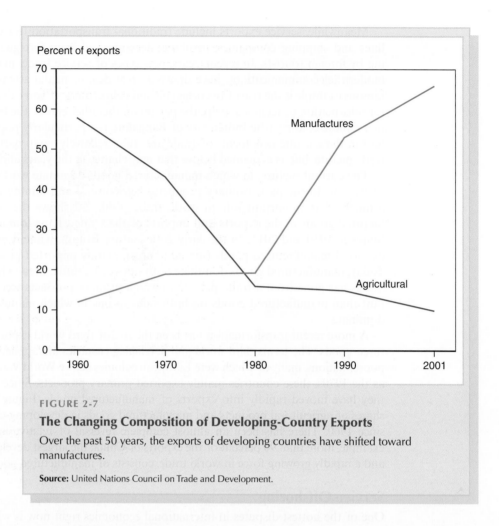

FIGURE 2-7

The Changing Composition of Developing-Country Exports

Over the past 50 years, the exports of developing countries have shifted toward manufactures.

Source: United Nations Council on Trade and Development.

outsource those services to another firm. In Chapter 8, we describe in more detail how firms make these important decisions.

In a famous *Foreign Affairs* article published in 2006, Alan Blinder, an economist at Princeton University, argued that "in the future, and to a great extent already in the present, the key distinction for international trade will no longer be between things that can be put in a box and things that cannot. It will, instead, be between services that can be delivered electronically over long distances with little or no degradation of quality, and those that cannot." For example, the worker who restocks the shelves at your local grocery has to be on site, but the accountant who keeps the grocery's books could be in another country, keeping in touch over the Internet. The nurse who takes your pulse has to be nearby, but the radiologist who reads your X-ray could receive the images electronically anywhere that has a high-speed connection.

At this point, service outsourcing gets a great deal of attention precisely because it's still fairly rare. The question is how big it might become, and how many workers who currently face no international competition might see that change in the future. One way economists have tried to answer this question is by looking at which services are traded at long distances *within* the United States. For example, many financial services are provided to the nation from New York, the country's financial capital; much of the country's software publishing takes place in Seattle, home of Microsoft; much

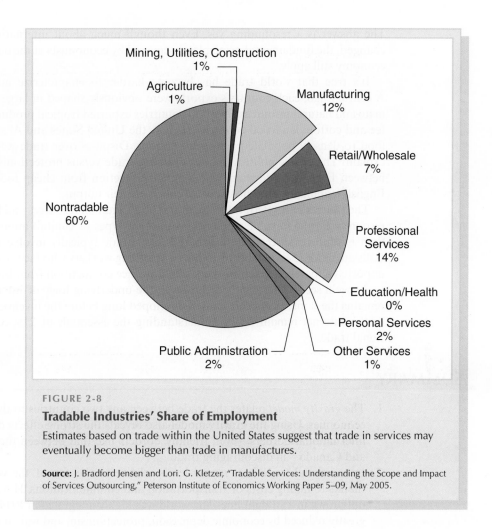

FIGURE 2-8

Tradable Industries' Share of Employment

Estimates based on trade within the United States suggest that trade in services may eventually become bigger than trade in manufactures.

Source: J. Bradford Jensen and Lori. G. Kletzer, "Tradable Services: Understanding the Scope and Impact of Services Outsourcing," Peterson Institute of Economics Working Paper 5–09, May 2005.

of America's (and the world's) Internet search services are provided from the Googleplex in Mountain View, California, and so on.

Figure 2-8 shows the results of one study that systematically used data on the location of industries within the United States to determine which services are and are not tradable at long distances. As the figure shows, the study concluded that about 60 percent of total U.S. employment consists of jobs that must be done close to the customer, making them nontradable. But the 40 percent of employment that is in tradable activities includes more service than manufacturing jobs. This suggests that the current dominance of world trade by manufactures, shown in Figure 2-6, may be only temporary. In the long run, trade in services, delivered electronically, may become the most important component of world trade. We discuss the implication of these trends for U.S. employment in Chapter 8.

Do Old Rules Still Apply?

We begin our discussion of the causes of world trade in Chapter 3 with an analysis of a model originally put forth by the British economist David Ricardo in 1819. Given all the changes in world trade since Ricardo's time, can old ideas still be relevant?

The answer is a resounding yes. Even though much about international trade has changed, the fundamental principles discovered by economists at the dawn of a global economy still apply.

It's true that world trade has become harder to characterize in simple terms. A century ago, each country's exports were obviously shaped in large part by its climate and natural resources. Tropical countries exported tropical products such as coffee and cotton; land-rich countries such as the United States and Australia exported food to densely populated European nations. Disputes over trade were also easy to explain: The classic political battles over free trade versus protectionism were waged between English landowners who wanted protection from cheap food imports and English manufacturers who exported much of their output.

The sources of modern trade are more subtle. Human resources and human-created resources (in the form of machinery and other types of capital) are more important than natural resources. Political battles over trade typically involve workers whose skills are made less valuable by imports—clothing workers who face competition from imported apparel and tech workers who now face competition from Bangalore.

As we'll see in later chapters, however, the underlying logic of international trade remains the same. Economic models developed long before the invention of jet planes or the Internet remain key to understanding the essentials of 21st-century international trade.

SUMMARY

1. The *gravity model* relates the trade between any two countries to the sizes of their economies. Using the gravity model also reveals the strong effects of distance and international borders—even friendly borders like that between the United States and Canada—in discouraging trade.

2. International trade is at record levels relative to the size of the world economy, thanks to falling costs of transportation and communications. However, trade has not grown in a straight line: The world was highly integrated in 1914, but trade was greatly reduced by economic depression, protectionism, and war, and took decades to recover.

3. Manufactured goods dominate modern trade today. In the past, however, primary products were much more important than they are now; recently, trade in services has become increasingly important.

4. *Developing countries*, in particular, have shifted from being mainly exporters of primary products to being mainly exporters of manufactured goods.

KEY TERMS

developing countries, p. 51	service offshoring (service	third world, p. 51
gravity model, p. 44	outsourcing), p. 51	trade agreement, p. 46
gross domestic product		
(GDP), p. 43		

PROBLEMS   MyEconLab

1. Explain why Canada and South Korea are similar in terms of population and GDP but differ in trade—the US arguably Canada's largest trading partner, whilst Korea divides 60 percent of its exports among China, ASEAN, the US and the EU.

2. The gravity model is often used to not only explain trade between two countries, but also to investigate the reasons why they don't. Illustrate this anomaly with suitable examples and reasons.

3. Equation (2.1) says that trade between any two countries is proportional to the product of their GDPs. Does this mean that if the GDP of every country in the world doubled, world trade would quadruple?

4. Over the past few decades, East Asian economies have increased their share of world GDP. Similarly, intra–East Asian trade—that is, trade among East Asian nations—has grown as a share of world trade. More than that, East Asian countries do an increasing share of their trade with each other. Explain why, using the gravity model.

5. A century ago, most British imports came from relatively distant locations: North America, Latin America, and Asia. Today, most British imports come from other European countries. How does this fit in with the changing types of goods that make up world trade?

FURTHER READINGS

Paul Bairoch. *Economics and World History*. London: Harvester, 1993. A grand survey of the world economy over time.

Alan S. Blinder. "Offshoring: The Next Industrial Revolution?" *Foreign Affairs*, March/April 2006. An influential article by a well-known economist warning that the growth of trade in services may expose tens of millions of previously "safe" jobs to international competition. The article created a huge stir when it was published.

Frances Cairncross. *The Death of Distance*. London: Orion, 1997. A look at how technology has made the world smaller.

Keith Head. "Gravity for Beginners." A useful guide to the gravity model, available at http:// pacific. commerce.ubc.ca/keith/gravity.pdf

Harold James. *The End of Globalization: Lessons from the Great Depression*. Cambridge: Harvard University Press, 2001. A survey of how the first great wave of globalization ended.

J. Bradford Jensen and Lori G. Kletzer. "Tradable Services: Understanding the Scope and Impact of Services Outsourcing." Peterson Institute Working Paper 5–09, May 2005. A systematic look at which services are traded within the United States, with implications about the future of international trade in services.

World Bank. *World Development Report 1995*. Each year the World Bank spotlights an important global issue; the 1995 report focused on the effects of growing world trade.

World Trade Organization. *World Trade Report*. An annual report on the state of world trade. Each year's report has a theme; for example, the 2004 report focused on the effects on world trade of domestic policies such as spending on infrastructure.

MyEconLab Can Help You Get a Better Grade

MyEconLab If your exam were tomorrow, would you be ready? For each chapter, MyEconLab Practice Tests and Study Plans pinpoint sections you have mastered and those you need to study. That way, you are more efficient with your study time, and you are better prepared for your exams.

To see how it works, turn to page 41 and then go to

www.myeconlab.com

CHAPTER 3

LABOR PRODUCTIVITY AND COMPARATIVE ADVANTAGE: THE RICARDIAN MODEL

Countries engage in international trade for two basic reasons, each of which contributes to their gains from trade. First, countries trade because they are different from each other. Nations, like individuals, can benefit from their differences by reaching an arrangement in which each does the things it does relatively well. Second, countries trade to achieve economies of scale in production. That is, if each country produces only a limited range of goods, it can produce each of these goods at a larger scale and hence more efficiently than if it tried to produce everything. In the real world, patterns of international trade reflect the interaction of both these motives. As a first step toward understanding the causes and effects of trade, however, it is useful to look at simplified models in which only one of these motives is present.

The next four chapters develop tools to help us to understand how differences between countries give rise to trade between them and why this trade is mutually beneficial. The essential concept in this analysis is that of comparative advantage.

Although comparative advantage is a simple concept, experience shows that it is a surprisingly hard concept for many people to understand (or accept). Indeed, the late Paul Samuelson—the Nobel laureate economist who did much to develop the models of international trade discussed in Chapters 4 and 5— once described comparative advantage as the best example he knows of an economic principle that is undeniably true yet not obvious to intelligent people.

In this chapter, we begin with a general introduction to the concept of comparative advantage, then proceed to develop a specific model of how comparative advantage determines the pattern of international trade.

LEARNING GOALS

After reading this chapter, you will be able to:

- Explain how the *Ricardian model*, the most basic model of international trade, works and how it illustrates the principle of *comparative advantage*.

■ Demonstrate *gains from trade* and refute common fallacies about international trade.

■ Describe the empirical evidence that wages reflect productivity and that trade patterns reflect relative productivity.

The Concept of Comparative Advantage

On Valentine's Day, 1996, which happened to fall less than a week before the crucial February 20 primary in New Hampshire, Republican presidential candidate Patrick Buchanan stopped at a nursery to buy a dozen roses for his wife. He took the occasion to make a speech denouncing the growing imports of flowers into the United States, which he claimed were putting American flower growers out of business. And it is indeed true that a growing share of the market for winter roses in the United States is supplied by imports flown in from South American countries, Colombia in particular. But is that a bad thing?

The case of winter roses offers an excellent example of the reasons why international trade can be beneficial. Consider first how hard it is to supply American sweethearts with fresh roses in February. The flowers must be grown in heated greenhouses, at great expense in terms of energy, capital investment, and other scarce resources. Those resources could be used to produce other goods. Inevitably, there is a trade-off. In order to produce winter roses, the U.S. economy must produce fewer of other things, such as computers. Economists use the term **opportunity cost** to describe such trade-offs: The opportunity cost of roses in terms of computers is the number of computers that could have been produced with the resources used to produce a given number of roses.

Suppose, for example, that the United States currently grows 10 million roses for sale on Valentine's Day and that the resources used to grow those roses could have produced 100,000 computers instead. Then the opportunity cost of those 10 million roses is 100,000 computers. (Conversely, if the computers were produced instead, the opportunity cost of those 100,000 computers would be 10 million roses.)

Those 10 million Valentine's Day roses could instead have been grown in Colombia. It seems extremely likely that the opportunity cost of those roses in terms of computers would be less than it would be in the United States. For one thing, it is a lot easier to grow February roses in the Southern Hemisphere, where it is summer in February rather than winter. Furthermore, Colombian workers are less efficient than their U.S. counterparts at making sophisticated goods such as computers, which means that a given amount of resources used in computer production yields fewer computers in Colombia than in the United States. So the trade-off in Colombia might be something like 10 million winter roses for only 30,000 computers.

This difference in opportunity costs offers the possibility of a mutually beneficial rearrangement of world production. Let the United States stop growing winter roses and devote the resources this frees up to producing computers; meanwhile, let Colombia grow those roses instead, shifting the necessary resources out of its computer industry. The resulting changes in production would look like Table 3-1.

Look what has happened: The world is producing just as many roses as before, but it is now producing more computers. So this rearrangement of production, with the United States concentrating on computers and Colombia concentrating on roses, increases the size of the world's economic pie. Because the world as a whole is producing more, it is possible in principle to raise everyone's standard of living.

TABLE 3-1	Hypothetical Changes in Production	
	Million Roses	**Thousand Computers**
United States	−10	+100
Colombia	+10	−30
Total	0	+70

The reason that international trade produces this increase in world output is that it allows each country to specialize in producing the good in which it has a comparative advantage. A country has a **comparative advantage** in producing a good if the opportunity cost of producing that good in terms of other goods is lower in that country than it is in other countries.

In this example, Colombia has a comparative advantage in winter roses and the United States has a comparative advantage in computers. The standard of living can be increased in both places if Colombia produces roses for the U.S. market, while the United States produces computers for the Colombian market. We therefore have an essential insight about comparative advantage and international trade: *Trade between two countries can benefit both countries if each country exports the goods in which it has a comparative advantage.*

This is a statement about possibilities—not about what will actually happen. In the real world, there is no central authority deciding which country should produce roses and which should produce computers. Nor is there anyone handing out roses and computers to consumers in both places. Instead, international production and trade are determined in the marketplace, where supply and demand rule. Is there any reason to suppose that the potential for mutual gains from trade will be realized? Will the United States and Colombia actually end up producing the goods in which each has a comparative advantage? Will the trade between them actually make both countries better off?

To answer these questions, we must be much more explicit in our analysis. In this chapter, we will develop a model of international trade originally proposed by British economist David Ricardo, who introduced the concept of comparative advantage in the early 19th century.[1] This approach, in which international trade is solely due to international differences in the productivity of labor, is known as the **Ricardian model**.

A One-Factor Economy

To introduce the role of comparative advantage in determining the pattern of international trade, we begin by imagining that we are dealing with an economy—which we call Home—that has only one factor of production. (In Chapter 4 we extend the analysis to models in which there are several factors.) We imagine that only two goods, wine and cheese, are produced. The technology of Home's economy can be summarized by labor productivity in each industry, expressed in terms of the **unit labor requirement,** the number of hours of labor required to produce a pound of cheese or a gallon of wine. For example, it might require one hour of labor to produce a pound of cheese and two hours to produce a gallon of wine. Notice, by the way, that we're defining unit

[1]The classic reference is David Ricardo, *The Principles of Political Economy and Taxation*, first published in 1817.

labor requirements as the *inverse* of productivity—the more cheese or wine a worker can produce in an hour, the *lower* the unit labor requirement. For future reference, we define a_{LW} and a_{LC} as the unit labor requirements in wine and cheese production, respectively. The economy's total resources are defined as L, the total labor supply.

Production Possibilities Because any economy has limited resources, there are limits on what it can produce, and there are always trade-offs; to produce more of one good, the economy must sacrifice some production of another good. These trade-offs are illustrated graphically by a **production possibility frontier** (line *PF* in Figure 3-1), which shows the maximum amount of wine that can be produced once the decision has been made to produce any given amount of cheese, and vice versa.

When there is only one factor of production, the production possibility frontier of an economy is simply a straight line. We can derive this line as follows: If Q_W is the economy's production of wine and Q_C its production of cheese, then the labor used in producing wine will be $a_{LW}Q_W$, and the labor used in producing cheese will be $a_{LC}Q_C$. The production possibility frontier is determined by the limits on the economy's resources—in this case, labor. Because the economy's total labor supply is L, the limits on production are defined by the inequality

$$a_{LC}Q_C + a_{LW}Q_W \leq L. \tag{3-1}$$

Suppose, for example, that the economy's total labor supply is 1,000 hours, and that it takes 1 hour of labor to produce a pound of cheese and 2 hours of labor to produce a gallon of wine. Then the total labor used in production is (1 × pounds of cheese produced) + (2 × gallons of wine produced), and this total must be no more than the 1,000 hours of labor available. If the economy devoted all its labor to cheese production, it could, as shown in Figure 3-1, produce L/a_{LC} pounds of cheese (1,000 pounds). If it devoted all its labor to wine production instead, it could produce L/a_{LW} gallons—1000/2 = 500 gallons—of wine. And it can produce any mix of wine and cheese that lies on the straight line connecting those two extremes.

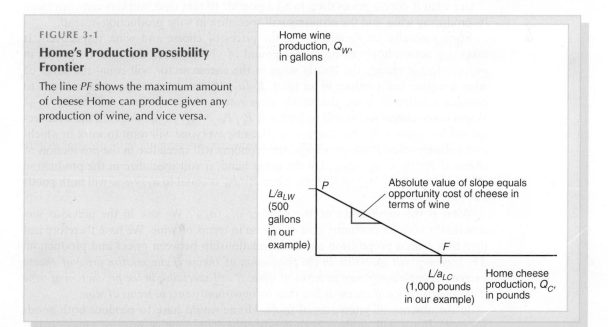

FIGURE 3-1

Home's Production Possibility Frontier

The line *PF* shows the maximum amount of cheese Home can produce given any production of wine, and vice versa.

Home wine production, Q_W, in gallons

L/a_{LW} (500 gallons in our example)

P

Absolute value of slope equals opportunity cost of cheese in terms of wine

F

L/a_{LC} (1,000 pounds in our example)

Home cheese production, Q_C, in pounds

When the production possibility frontier is a straight line, the *opportunity cost* of a pound of cheese in terms of wine is constant. As we saw in the previous section, this opportunity cost is defined as the number of gallons of wine the economy would have to give up in order to produce an extra pound of cheese. In this case, to produce another pound would require a_{LC} person-hours. Each of these person-hours could in turn have been used to produce $1/a_{LW}$ gallons of wine. Thus, the opportunity cost of cheese in terms of wine is a_{LC}/a_{LW}. For example, if it takes one person-hour to make a pound of cheese and two hours to produce a gallon of wine, the opportunity cost of each pound of cheese is half a gallon of wine. As Figure 3-1 shows, this opportunity cost is equal to the absolute value of the slope of the production possibility frontier.

Relative Prices and Supply

The production possibility frontier illustrates the different mixes of goods the economy *can* produce. To determine what the economy will actually produce, however, we need to look at prices. Specifically, we need to know the relative price of the economy's two goods, that is, the price of one good in terms of the other.

In a competitive economy, supply decisions are determined by the attempts of individuals to maximize their earnings. In our simplified economy, since labor is the only factor of production, the supply of cheese and wine will be determined by the movement of labor to whichever sector pays the higher wage.

Suppose, once again, that it takes one hour of labor to produce a pound of cheese and two hours to produce a gallon of wine. Now suppose further that cheese sells for $4 a pound, while wine sells for $7 a gallon. What will workers produce? Well, if they produce cheese, they can earn $4 an hour. (Bear in mind that since labor is the only input into production here, there are no profits, so workers receive the full value of their output.) On the other hand, if workers produce wine, they will earn only $3.50 an hour, because a $7 gallon of wine takes two hours to produce. So if cheese sells for $4 a pound while wine sells for $7 a gallon, workers will do better by producing cheese—and the economy as a whole will specialize in cheese production.

But what if cheese prices drop to $3 a pound? In that case, workers can earn more by producing wine, and the economy will specialize in wine production instead.

More generally, let P_C and P_W be the prices of cheese and wine, respectively. It takes a_{LC} person-hours to produce a pound of cheese; since there are no profits in our one-factor model, the hourly wage in the cheese sector will equal the value of what a worker can produce in an hour, P_C/a_{LC}. Since it takes a_{LW} person-hours to produce a gallon of wine, the hourly wage rate in the wine sector will be P_W/a_{LW}. Wages in the cheese sector will be higher if $P_C/P_W > a_{LC}/a_{LW}$; wages in the wine sector will be higher if $P_C/P_W < a_{LC}/a_{LW}$. Because everyone will want to work in whichever industry offers the higher wage, the economy will specialize in the production of cheese if $P_C/P_W > a_{LC}/a_{LW}$. On the other hand, it will specialize in the production of wine if $P_C/P_W < a_{LC}/a_{LW}$. Only when P_C/P_W is equal to a_{LC}/a_{LW} will both goods be produced.

What is the significance of the number a_{LC}/a_{LW}? We saw in the previous section that it is the opportunity cost of cheese in terms of wine. We have therefore just derived a crucial proposition about the relationship between prices and production: *The economy will specialize in the production of cheese if the relative price of cheese exceeds its opportunity cost in terms of wine; it will specialize in the production of wine if the relative price of cheese is less than its opportunity cost in terms of wine.*

In the absence of international trade, Home would have to produce both goods for itself. But it will produce both goods only if the relative price of cheese is just equal to its opportunity cost. Since opportunity cost equals the ratio of unit labor requirements in cheese and wine, we can summarize the determination of prices in the absence of international trade with a simple labor theory of value: *In the absence of international trade, the relative prices of goods are equal to their relative unit labor requirements.*

Trade in a One-Factor World

To describe the pattern and effects of trade between two countries when each country has only one factor of production is simple. Yet the implications of this analysis can be surprising. Indeed, to those who have not thought about international trade, many of these implications seem to conflict with common sense. Even this simplest of trade models can offer some important guidance on real-world issues, such as what constitutes fair international competition and fair international exchange.

Before we get to these issues, however, let us get the model stated. Suppose there are two countries. One of them we again call Home and the other we call Foreign. Each of these countries has one factor of production (labor) and can produce two goods, wine and cheese. As before, we denote Home's labor force by L and Home's unit labor requirements in wine and cheese production by a_{LW} and a_{LC}, respectively. For Foreign, we will use a convenient notation throughout this text: When we refer to some aspect of Foreign, we will use the same symbol that we use for Home, but with an asterisk. Thus Foreign's labor force will be denoted by L^*, Foreign's unit labor requirements in wine and cheese will be denoted by a_{LW}^* and a_{LC}^*, respectively, and so on.

In general, the unit labor requirements can follow any pattern. For example, Home could be less productive than Foreign in wine but more productive in cheese, or vice versa. For the moment, we make only one arbitrary assumption: that

$$a_{LC}/a_{LW} < a_{LC}^*/a_{LW}^* \qquad (3\text{-}2)$$

or, equivalently, that

$$a_{LC}/a_{LC}^* < a_{LW}/a_{LW}^*. \qquad (3\text{-}3)$$

In words, we are assuming that the ratio of the labor required to produce a pound of cheese to that required to produce a gallon of wine is lower in Home than it is in Foreign. More briefly still, we are saying that Home's relative productivity in cheese is higher than it is in wine.

But remember that the ratio of unit labor requirements is equal to the opportunity cost of cheese in terms of wine; and remember also that we defined comparative advantage precisely in terms of such opportunity costs. So the assumption about relative productivities embodied in equations (3-2) and (3-3) amounts to saying that *Home has a comparative advantage in cheese.*

One point should be noted immediately: The condition under which Home has this comparative advantage involves all four unit labor requirements, not just two. You might think that to determine who will produce cheese, all you need to do is compare the two countries' unit labor requirements in cheese production, a_{LC} and a_{LC}^*. If $a_{LC} < a_{LC}^*$, Home labor is more efficient than Foreign in producing cheese. When one country can produce a unit of a good with less labor than another country, we say that the first country has an **absolute advantage** in producing that good. In our example, Home has an absolute advantage in producing cheese.

What we will see in a moment, however, is that we cannot determine the pattern of trade from absolute advantage alone. One of the most important sources of error

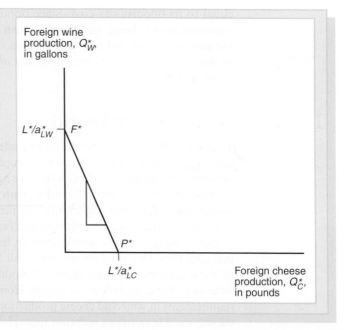

FIGURE 3-2

Foreign's Production Possibility Frontier

Because Foreign's relative unit labor requirement in cheese is higher than Home's (it needs to give up many more units of wine to produce one more unit of cheese), its production possibility frontier is steeper.

in discussing international trade is to confuse comparative advantage with absolute advantage.

Given the labor forces and the unit labor requirements in the two countries, we can draw the production possibility frontier for each country. We have already done this for Home, by drawing PF in Figure 3-1. The production possibility frontier for Foreign is shown as P^*F^* in Figure 3-2. Since the slope of the production possibility frontier equals the opportunity cost of cheese in terms of wine, Foreign's frontier is steeper than Home's.

In the absence of trade, the relative prices of cheese and wine in each country would be determined by the relative unit labor requirements. Thus, in Home the relative price of cheese would be a_{LC}/a_{LW}; in Foreign it would be a_{LC}^*/a_{LW}^*.

Once we allow for the possibility of international trade, however, prices will no longer be determined purely by domestic considerations. If the relative price of cheese is higher in Foreign than in Home, it will be profitable to ship cheese from Home to Foreign and to ship wine from Foreign to Home. This cannot go on indefinitely, however. Eventually, Home will export enough cheese and Foreign enough wine to equalize the relative price. But what determines the level at which that price settles?

Determining the Relative Price after Trade

Prices of internationally traded goods, like other prices, are determined by supply and demand. In discussing comparative advantage, however, we must apply supply-and-demand analysis carefully. In some contexts, such as some of the trade policy analysis in Chapters 9 through 12, it is acceptable to focus only on supply and demand in a single market. In assessing the effects of U.S. import quotas on sugar, for example, it is reasonable to use **partial equilibrium analysis,** that is, to study a single market, the sugar market. When we study comparative advantage, however, it is crucial to keep track of the relationships between markets (in our example, the markets for wine and cheese). Since Home exports cheese only in return for imports of wine, and Foreign

FIGURE 3-3

World Relative Supply and Demand

The *RD* and *RD'* curves show that the demand for cheese relative to wine is a decreasing function of the price of cheese relative to that of wine, while the *RS* curve shows that the supply of cheese relative to wine is an increasing function of the same relative price.

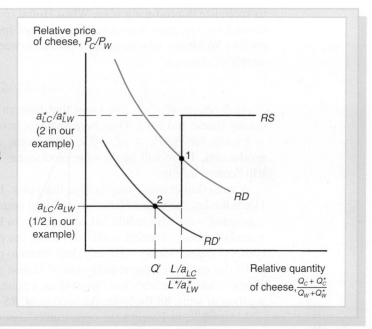

exports wine in return for cheese, it can be misleading to look at the cheese and wine markets in isolation. What is needed is **general equilibrium analysis,** which takes account of the linkages between the two markets.

One useful way to keep track of two markets at once is to focus not just on the quantities of cheese and wine supplied and demanded but also on the *relative* supply and demand, that is, on the number of pounds of cheese supplied or demanded divided by the number of gallons of wine supplied or demanded.

Figure 3-3 shows world supply and demand for cheese relative to wine as functions of the price of cheese relative to that of wine. The **relative demand curve** is indicated by *RD*; the **relative supply curve** is indicated by *RS*. World general equilibrium requires that relative supply equal relative demand, and thus the world relative price is determined by the intersection of *RD* and *RS*.

The striking feature of Figure 3-3 is the funny shape of the relative supply curve *RS*: It's a "step" with flat sections linked by a vertical section. Once we understand the derivation of the *RS* curve, we will be almost home-free in understanding the whole model.

First, as drawn, the *RS* curve shows that there would be *no* supply of cheese if the world price dropped below a_{LC}/a_{LW}. To see why, recall that we showed that Home will specialize in the production of wine whenever $P_C/P_W < a_{LC}/a_{LW}$. Similarly, Foreign will specialize in wine production whenever $P_C/P_W < a_{LC}^*/a_{LW}^*$. At the start of our discussion of equation (3-2), we made the assumption that $a_{LC}/a_{LW} < a_{LC}^*/a_{LW}^*$. So at relative prices of cheese below a_{LC}/a_{LW}, there would be no world cheese production.

Next, when the relative price of cheese P_C/P_W is exactly a_{LC}/a_{LW}, we know that workers in Home can earn exactly the same amount making either cheese or wine. So Home will be willing to supply any relative amount of the two goods, producing a flat section to the supply curve.

We have already seen that if P_C/P_W is above a_{LC}/a_{LW}, Home will specialize in the production of cheese. As long as $P_C/P_W < a_{LC}^*/a_{LW}^*$, however, Foreign will continue to specialize in producing wine. When Home specializes in cheese production, it produces L/a_{LC} pounds. Similarly, when Foreign specializes in wine, it produces L^*/a_{LW}^* gallons. So for any relative price of cheese between a_{LC}/a_{LW} and a_{LC}^*/a_{LW}^*, the relative supply of cheese is

$$(L/a_{LC})/(L^*/a_{LW}^*). \tag{3-4}$$

At $P_C/P_W = a_{LC}^*/a_{LW}^*$, we know that Foreign workers are indifferent between producing cheese and wine. Thus, here we again have a flat section of the supply curve.

Finally, for $P_C/P_W > a_{LC}^*/a_{LW}^*$, both Home and Foreign will specialize in cheese production. There will be no wine production, so that the relative supply of cheese will become infinite.

A numerical example may help at this point. Let's assume, as we did before, that in Home it takes one hour of labor to produce a pound of cheese and two hours to produce a gallon of wine. Meanwhile, let's assume that in Foreign it takes six hours to produce a pound of cheese—Foreign workers are much less productive than Home workers when it comes to cheesemaking—but only three hours to produce a gallon of wine.

In this case, the opportunity cost of cheese production in terms of wine is $1/2$ in Home—that is, the labor used to produce a pound of cheese could have produced half a gallon of wine. So the lower flat section of RS corresponds to a relative price of $1/2$.

Meanwhile, in Foreign the opportunity cost of cheese in terms of wine is 2: The six hours of labor required to produce a pound of cheese could have produced two gallons of wine. So the upper flat section of RS corresponds to a relative price of 2.

The relative demand curve RD does not require such exhaustive analysis. The downward slope of RD reflects substitution effects. As the relative price of cheese rises, consumers will tend to purchase less cheese and more wine, so the relative demand for cheese falls.

The equilibrium relative price of cheese is determined by the intersection of the relative supply and relative demand curves. Figure 3-3 shows a relative demand curve RD that intersects the RS curve at point 1, where the relative price of cheese is between the two countries' pretrade prices—say, at a relative price of 1, in between the pretrade prices of $1/2$ and 2. In this case, each country specializes in the production of the good in which it has a comparative advantage: Home produces only cheese, while Foreign produces only wine.

This is not, however, the only possible outcome. If the relevant RD curve were RD', for example, relative supply and relative demand would intersect on one of the horizontal sections of RS. At point 2, the world relative price of cheese after trade is a_{LC}/a_{LW}, the same as the opportunity cost of cheese in terms of wine in Home.

What is the significance of this outcome? If the relative price of cheese is equal to its opportunity cost in Home, the Home economy need not specialize in producing either cheese or wine. In fact, at point 2 Home must be producing both some wine and some cheese; we can infer this from the fact that the relative supply of cheese (point Q' on the horizontal axis) is less than it would be if Home were in fact completely specialized. Since P_C/P_W is below the opportunity cost of cheese in terms of wine in Foreign, however, Foreign does specialize completely in producing wine. It therefore remains true that if a country does specialize, it will do so in the good in which it has a comparative advantage.

For the moment, let's leave aside the possibility that one of the two countries does not completely specialize. Except in this case, the normal result of trade is that the price of a traded good (e.g., cheese) relative to that of another good (wine) ends up somewhere in between its pretrade levels in the two countries.

COMPARATIVE ADVANTAGE IN PRACTICE: THE CASE OF BABE RUTH

Everyone knows that Babe Ruth was the greatest slugger in the history of baseball. Only true fans of the sport know, however, that Ruth also was one of the greatest *pitchers* of all time. Because Ruth stopped pitching after 1918 and played outfield during all the time he set his famous batting records, most people don't realize that he even could pitch. What explains Ruth's lopsided reputation as a batter? The answer is provided by the principle of comparative advantage.

As a player with the Boston Red Sox early in his career, Ruth certainly had an *absolute* advantage in pitching. According to historian Geoffrey C. Ward and filmmaker Ken Burns:

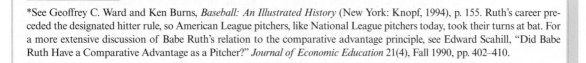

> In the Red Sox's greatest years, he was their greatest player, the best left-handed pitcher in the American League, winning 89 games in six seasons. In 1916 he got his first chance to pitch in the World Series and made the most of it. After giving up a run in the first, he drove in the tying run himself, after which he held the Brooklyn Dodgers scoreless for eleven innings until his teammates could score the winning run.... In the 1918 series, he would show that he could still handle them, stretching his series record to

$29^2/_3$ scoreless innings, a mark that stood for forty-three years.*

The Babe's World Series pitching record was broken by New York Yankee Whitey Ford in the same year, 1961, that his teammate Roger Maris shattered Ruth's 1927 record of 60 home runs in a single season.

Although Ruth had an absolute advantage in pitching, his skill as a batter relative to his teammates' abilities was even greater: His *comparative* advantage was at the plate. As a pitcher, however, Ruth had to rest his arm between appearances and therefore could not bat in every game. To exploit Ruth's *comparative* advantage, the Red Sox moved him to center field in 1919 so that he could bat more frequently.

The payoff to having Ruth specialize in batting was huge. In 1919, he hit 29 home runs, "more than any player had ever hit in a single season," according to Ward and Burns. The Yankees kept Ruth in the outfield (and at the plate) after they acquired him in 1920. They knew a good thing when they saw it. That year, Ruth hit 54 home runs, set a slugging record (bases divided by at bats) that remains untouched to this day, and turned the Yankees into baseball's most renowned franchise.

*See Geoffrey C. Ward and Ken Burns, *Baseball: An Illustrated History* (New York: Knopf, 1994), p. 155. Ruth's career preceded the designated hitter rule, so American League pitchers, like National League pitchers today, took their turns at bat. For a more extensive discussion of Babe Ruth's relation to the comparative advantage principle, see Edward Scahill, "Did Babe Ruth Have a Comparative Advantage as a Pitcher?" *Journal of Economic Education* 21(4), Fall 1990, pp. 402–410.

The effect of this convergence in relative prices is that each country specializes in the production of that good in which it has the relatively lower unit labor requirement. The rise in the relative price of cheese in Home will lead Home to specialize in the production of cheese, producing at point *F* in Figure 3-4a. The fall in the relative price of cheese in Foreign will lead Foreign to specialize in the production of wine, producing at point F^* in Figure 3-4b.

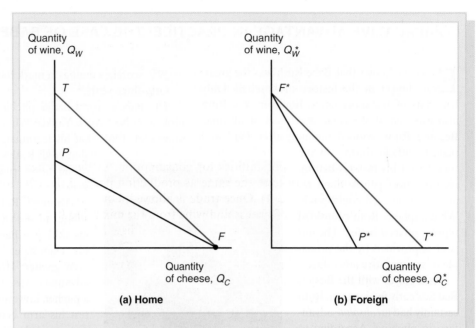

FIGURE 3-4

Trade Expands Consumption Possibilities

International trade allows Home and Foreign to consume anywhere within the colored lines, which lie outside the countries' production frontiers.

The Gains from Trade

We have now seen that countries whose relative labor productivities differ across industries will specialize in the production of different goods. We next show that both countries derive **gains from trade** from this specialization. This mutual gain can be demonstrated in two alternative ways.

The first way to show that specialization and trade are beneficial is to think of trade as an indirect method of production. Home could produce wine directly, but trade with Foreign allows it to "produce" wine by producing cheese and then trading the cheese for wine. This indirect method of "producing" a gallon of wine is a more efficient method than direct production.

Consider our numerical example yet again: In Home, we assume that it takes one hour to produce a pound of cheese and two hours to produce a gallon of wine. This means that the opportunity cost of cheese in terms of wine is $1/2$. But we know that the relative price of cheese after trade will be higher than this, say 1. So here's one way to see the gains from trade for Home: Instead of using two hours of labor to produce a gallon of wine, it can use that labor to produce two pounds of cheese, and trade that cheese for *two* gallons of wine.

More generally, consider two alternative ways of using an hour of labor. On one side, Home could use the hour directly to produce $1/a_{LW}$ gallons of wine. Alternatively, Home could use the hour to produce $1/a_{LC}$ pounds of cheese. This cheese could then be traded for wine, with each pound trading for P_C/P_W gallons, so our original hour of labor yields $(1/a_{LC})(P_C/P_W)$ gallons of wine. This will be more wine than the hour could have produced directly as long as

$$(1/a_{LC})(P_C/P_W) > 1/a_{LW},$$ (3-5)

or

$$P_C/P_W > a_{LC}/a_{LW}.$$

But we just saw that in international equilibrium, if neither country produces both goods, we must have $P_C/P_W > a_{LC}/a_{LW}$. This shows that Home can "produce" wine more efficiently by making cheese and trading it than by producing wine directly for itself. Similarly, Foreign can "produce" cheese more efficiently by making wine and trading it. This is one way of seeing that both countries gain.

Another way to see the mutual gains from trade is to examine how trade affects each country's possibilities for consumption. In the absence of trade, consumption possibilities are the same as production possibilities (the solid lines PF and P*F* in Figure 3-4). Once trade is allowed, however, each economy can consume a different mix of cheese and wine from the mix it produces. Home's consumption possibilities are indicated by the colored line TF in Figure 3-4a, while Foreign's consumption possibilities are indicated by T*F* in Figure 3-4b. In each case, trade has enlarged the range of choice, and therefore it must make residents of each country better off.

A Note on Relative Wages

Political discussions of international trade often focus on comparisons of wage rates in different countries. For example, opponents of trade between the United States and Mexico often emphasize the point that workers in Mexico are paid only about $6.50 per hour, compared with more than $35 per hour for the typical worker in the United States. Our discussion of international trade up to this point has not explicitly compared wages in the two countries, but it is possible in the context of our numerical example to determine how the wage rates in the two countries compare.

In our example, once the countries have specialized, all Home workers are employed producing cheese. Since it takes one hour of labor to produce one pound of cheese, workers in Home earn the value of one pound of cheese per hour of their labor. Similarly, Foreign workers produce only wine; since it takes three hours for them to produce each gallon, they earn the value of $1/3$ of a gallon of wine per hour.

To convert these numbers into dollar figures, we need to know the prices of cheese and wine. Suppose that a pound of cheese and a gallon of wine both sell for $12; then Home workers will earn $12 per hour, while Foreign workers will earn $4 per hour. The **relative wage** of a country's workers is the amount they are paid per hour, compared with the amount workers in another country are paid per hour. The relative wage of Home workers will therefore be 3.

Clearly, this relative wage does not depend on whether the price of a pound of cheese is $12 or $20, as long as a gallon of wine sells for the same price. As long as the relative price of cheese—the price of a pound of cheese divided by the price of a gallon of wine—is 1, the wage of Home workers will be three times that of Foreign workers.

Notice that this wage rate lies between the ratios of the two countries' productivities in the two industries. Home is six times as productive as Foreign in cheese, but only one-and-a-half times as productive in wine, and it ends up with a wage rate three times as high as Foreign's. It is precisely because the relative wage is between the relative productivities that each country ends up with a *cost* advantage in one good. Because of its lower wage rate, Foreign has a cost advantage in wine even though it

THE LOSSES FROM NONTRADE

Our discussion of the gains from trade took the form of a "thought experiment" in which we compared two situations: one in which countries do not trade at all and another in which they have free trade. It's a hypothetical case that helps us to understand the principles of international economics, but it does not have much to do with actual events. After all, countries don't suddenly go from no trade to free trade or vice versa. Or do they?

As economic historian Douglas Irwin* has pointed out, in the early history of the United States the country actually did carry out something very close to the thought experiment of moving from free trade to no trade. The historical context was as follows: In the early 19th century Britain and France were engaged in a

massive military struggle, the Napoleonic Wars. Both countries endeavored to bring economic pressures to bear: France tried to keep European countries from trading with Britain, while Britain imposed a blockade on France. The young United States was neutral in the conflict but suffered considerably. In particular, the British navy often seized U.S. merchant ships and, on occasion, forcibly recruited their crews into its service.

In an effort to pressure Britain into ceasing these practices, President Thomas Jefferson declared a complete ban on overseas shipping. This embargo would deprive both the United States and Britain of the gains from trade, but Jefferson hoped that Britain would be hurt more and would agree to stop its depredations.

Irwin presents evidence suggesting that the embargo was quite effective: Although some smuggling took place, trade between the United States and the rest of the world was drastically reduced. In effect, the United States gave up international trade for a while.

The costs were substantial. Although quite a lot of guesswork is involved, Irwin suggests that real income in the United States may have fallen by about 8 percent as a result of the embargo. When you bear in mind that in the early 19th century only a fraction of output could be traded—transport costs were still too high, for example, to allow large-scale shipments of commodities like wheat across the Atlantic—that's a pretty substantial sum.

Unfortunately for Jefferson's plan, Britain did not seem to feel equal pain and showed no inclination to give in to U.S. demands. Fourteen months after the embargo was imposed, it was repealed. Britain continued its practices of seizing American cargoes and sailors; three years later the two countries went to war.

*Douglas Irwin, "The Welfare Cost of Autarky: Evidence from the Jeffersonian Trade Embargo, 1807–1809," *Review of International Economics* 13 (September 2005), pp. 631–645.

has lower productivity. Home has a cost advantage in cheese, despite its higher wage rate, because the higher wage is more than offset by its higher productivity.

We have now developed the simplest of all models of international trade. Even though the Ricardian one-factor model is far too simple to be a complete analysis of either the causes or the effects of international trade, a focus on relative labor productivities can be a very useful tool for thinking about trade issues. In particular, the simple one-factor model is a good way to deal with several common misconceptions about the meaning of comparative advantage and the nature of the gains from free trade. These misconceptions appear so frequently in public debate about international economic policy, and even in statements by those who regard themselves as experts, that in the next section we take time out to discuss some of the most common misunderstandings about comparative advantage in light of our model.

Misconceptions about Comparative Advantage

There is no shortage of muddled ideas in economics. Politicians, business leaders, and even economists frequently make statements that do not stand up to careful economic analysis. For some reason this seems to be especially true in international economics. Open the business section of any Sunday newspaper or weekly news magazine and you will probably find at least one article that makes foolish statements about international trade. Three misconceptions in particular have proved highly persistent. In this section we will use our simple model of comparative advantage to see why they are incorrect.

Productivity and Competitiveness

Myth 1: Free trade is beneficial only if your country is strong enough to stand up to foreign competition. This argument seems extremely plausible to many people. For example, a well-known historian once criticized the case for free trade by asserting that it may fail to hold in reality: "What if there is nothing you can produce more cheaply or efficiently than anywhere else, except by constantly cutting labor costs?" he worried.[2]

The problem with this commentator's view is that he failed to understand the essential point of Ricardo's model—that gains from trade depend on *comparative* rather than *absolute* advantage. He is concerned that your country may turn out not to have anything it produces more efficiently than anyone else—that is, that you may not have an absolute advantage in anything. Yet why is that such a terrible thing? In our simple numerical example of trade, Home has lower unit labor requirements and hence higher productivity in both the cheese and wine sectors. Yet, as we saw, both countries gain from trade.

It is always tempting to suppose that the ability to export a good depends on your country having an absolute advantage in productivity. But an absolute productivity advantage over other countries in producing a good is neither a necessary nor a sufficient condition for having a *comparative* advantage in that good. In our one-factor model, the reason that an absolute productivity advantage in an industry is neither necessary nor sufficient to yield competitive advantage is clear: *The competitive advantage of an industry depends not only on its productivity relative to the foreign industry, but also on the domestic wage rate relative to the foreign wage rate.* A country's wage rate, in turn, depends on relative productivity in its other industries. In our numerical example, Foreign is less efficient than Home in the manufacture of wine, but it is at an even greater relative productivity disadvantage in cheese. Because of its overall lower productivity, Foreign must pay lower wages than Home, sufficiently lower that it ends up with lower costs in wine production. Similarly, in the real world, Portugal has low productivity in producing, say, clothing as compared with the United States, but because Portugal's productivity disadvantage is even greater in other industries, it pays low enough wages to have a comparative advantage in clothing over the United States all the same.

But isn't a competitive advantage based on low wages somehow unfair? Many people think so; their beliefs are summarized by our second misconception.

---

[2]Paul Kennedy, "The Threat of Modernization," *New Perspectives Quarterly* (Winter 1995), pp. 31–33. Used by permission of John Wiley & Sons, Ltd.

DO WAGES REFLECT PRODUCTIVITY?

In the numerical example that we use to puncture common misconceptions about comparative advantage, we assume the relative wage of the two countries reflects their relative productivity—specifically, that the ratio of Home to Foreign wages is in a range that gives each country a cost advantage in one of the two goods. This is a necessary implication of our theoretical model. But many people are unconvinced by that model. In particular, rapid increases in productivity in "emerging" economies like China have worried some Western observers, who argue that these countries will continue to pay low wages even as their productivity increases—putting high-wage countries at a cost disadvantage—and dismiss the contrary predictions of orthodox economists as unrealistic theoretical speculation. Leaving aside the logic of this position, what is the evidence?

The answer is that in the real world, national wage rates do, in fact, reflect differences in productivity. The accompanying figure compares estimates of productivity with estimates of wage rates for a selection of countries in 2011 (except for China, where the data are for 2009). Both measures are expressed as percentages of U.S. levels. Our estimate of productivity is GDP per worker measured in U.S. dollars. As we'll see in the second half of this text, that basis should indicate productivity in the production of traded goods. Wage rates are measured by wages in manufacturing.

If wages were exactly proportional to productivity, all the points in this chart would lie along the indicated 45-degree line. In reality, the fit isn't bad. In particular, low wage rates in China and India reflect low productivity.

The low estimate of overall Chinese productivity may seem surprising, given all the stories one hears about Americans who find themselves competing with Chinese exports. The Chinese workers producing those exports don't seem to have extremely low productivity. But remember what the theory of comparative advantage says: Countries export the goods in which they have relatively high productivity. So it's only to be expected that China's overall relative productivity is far below the level of its export industries.

The figure that follows tells us that the orthodox economists' view that national wage rates reflect national productivity is, in fact, verified by the data at a point in time. It's also true that in the past, rising relative productivity led to rising wages. Consider, for example, the case of South Korea. In 2011, South Korea's labor productivity was a bit less than half of the U.S. level, and its

The Pauper Labor Argument

Myth 2: Foreign competition is unfair and hurts other countries when it is based on low wages. This argument, sometimes referred to as the **pauper labor argument,** is a particular favorite of labor unions seeking protection from foreign competition. People who adhere to this belief argue that industries should not have to cope with foreign industries that are less efficient but pay lower wages. This view is widespread and has acquired considerable political influence. In 1993, Ross Perot, a self-made billionaire and former presidential candidate, warned that free trade between the United States and Mexico, with the latter's much lower wages, would lead to a "giant sucking sound" as U.S. industry moved south. In the same year, another self-made billionaire, Sir James Goldsmith, who was an influential member of the European Parliament, offered similar if less picturesquely expressed views in his book *The Trap*, which became a best seller in France.

Again, our simple example reveals the fallacy of this argument. In the example, Home is more productive than Foreign in both industries, and Foreign's lower cost of wine production is entirely due to its much lower wage rate. Foreign's lower wage rate, however, is irrelevant to the question of whether Home gains from trade. Whether the lower cost

wage rate was actually slightly higher than that. But it wasn't always that way: In the not too distant past, South Korea was a low-productivity, low-wage economy. As recently as 1975, South Korean wages were only 5 percent those of the United States. But when South Korea's productivity rose, so did its wage rate.

In short, the evidence strongly supports the view, based on economic models, that productivity increases are reflected in wage increases.

Productivity and Wages

A country's wage rate is roughly proportional to the country's productivity

Source: International Monetary Fund, Bureau of Labor Statistics, and The Conference Board.

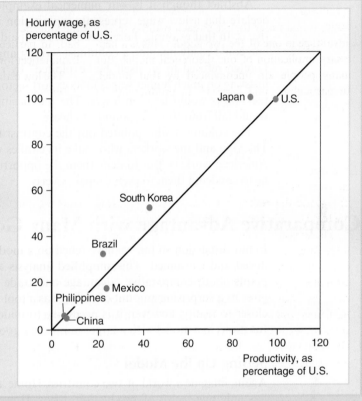

of wine produced in Foreign is due to high productivity or low wages does not matter. All that matters to Home is that it is cheaper *in terms of its own labor* for Home to produce cheese and trade it for wine than to produce wine for itself.

This is fine for Home, but what about Foreign? Isn't there something wrong with basing one's exports on low wages? Certainly it is not an attractive position to be in, but the idea that trade is good only if you receive high wages is our final fallacy.

Exploitation

Myth 3: Trade exploits a country and makes it worse off if its workers receive much lower wages than workers in other nations. This argument is often expressed in emotional terms. For example, one columnist contrasted the multimillion-dollar income of the chief executive officer of the clothing chain The Gap with the low wages—often less than $1 an hour—paid to the Central American workers who produce some of its merchandise.[3]

---

[3]Bob Herbert, "Sweatshop Beneficiaries: How to Get Rich on 56 Cents an Hour," *New York Times* (July 24, 1995), p. A13.

It can seem hard-hearted to try to justify the terrifyingly low wages paid to many of the world's workers.

If one is asking about the desirability of free trade, however, the point is not to ask whether low-wage workers deserve to be paid more but to ask whether they and their country are worse off exporting goods based on low wages than they would be if they refused to enter into such demeaning trade. And in asking this question, one must also ask, *What is the alternative?*

Abstract though it is, our numerical example makes the point that one cannot declare that a low wage represents exploitation unless one knows what the alternative is. In that example, Foreign workers are paid much less than Home workers, and one could easily imagine a columnist writing angrily about their exploitation. Yet if Foreign refused to let itself be "exploited" by refusing to trade with Home (or by insisting on much higher wages in its export sector, which would have the same effect), real wages would be even lower: The purchasing power of a worker's hourly wage would fall from $1/3$ to $1/6$ pound of cheese.

The columnist who pointed out the contrast in incomes between the executive at The Gap and the workers who make its clothes was angry at the poverty of Central American workers. But to deny them the opportunity to export and trade might well be to condemn them to even deeper poverty.

Comparative Advantage with Many Goods

In our discussion so far, we have relied on a model in which only two goods are produced and consumed. This simplified analysis allows us to capture many essential points about comparative advantage and trade and, as we saw in the last section, gives us a surprising amount of mileage as a tool for discussing policy issues. To move closer to reality, however, it is necessary to understand how comparative advantage functions in a model with a larger number of goods.

Setting Up the Model

Again, imagine a world of two countries, Home and Foreign. As before, each country has only one factor of production, labor. However, let's assume that each of these countries consumes and is able to produce a large number of goods—say, N different goods altogether. We assign each of the goods a number from 1 to N.

The technology of each country can be described by its unit labor requirement for each good, that is, the number of hours of labor it takes to produce one unit of each good. We label Home's unit labor requirement for a particular good as a_{Li}, where i is the number we have assigned to that good. If cheese is assigned the number 7, a_{L7} will mean the unit labor requirement in cheese production. Following our usual rule, we label the corresponding Foreign unit labor requirement a_{Li}^*.

To analyze trade, we next pull one more trick. For any good, we can calculate a_{Li}/a_{Li}^*, the ratio of Home's unit labor requirement to Foreign's. The trick is to relabel the goods so that the lower the number, the lower this ratio. That is, we reshuffle the order in which we number goods in such a way that

$$a_{L1}/a_{L1}^* < a_{L2}/a_{L2}^* < a_{L3}/a_{L13}^* < \ldots < a_{LN}/a_{LN}^*. \tag{3-6}$$

Relative Wages and Specialization

We are now prepared to look at the pattern of trade. This pattern depends on only one thing: the ratio of Home to Foreign wages. Once we know this ratio, we can determine who produces what.

Let w be the wage rate per hour in Home and w^* be the wage rate in Foreign. The ratio of wage rates is then w/w^*. The rule for allocating world production, then, is simply this: Goods will always be produced where it is cheapest to make them. The cost of making some good, say good i, is the unit labor requirement times the wage rate. To produce good i in Home will cost wa_{Li}. To produce the same good in Foreign will cost $w^* a_{Li}^*$. It will be cheaper to produce the good in Home if

$$wa_{Li} < w^* a_{Li}^*,$$

which can be rearranged to yield

$$a_{Li}^* / a_{Li} > w/w^*.$$

On the other hand, it will be cheaper to produce the good in Foreign if

$$wa_{Li} > w^* a_{Li}^*,$$

which can be rearranged to yield

$$a_{Li}^* / a_{Li} < w/w^*.$$

Thus, we can restate the allocation rule: Any good for which $a_{Li}^* / a_{Li} > w/w^*$ will be produced in Home, while any good for which $a_{Li}^* / a_{Li} < w/w^*$ will be produced in Foreign.

We have already lined up the goods in increasing order of a_{Li}/a_{Li}^* (equation (3-6)). This criterion for specialization tells us that there is a "cut" in the lineup determined by the ratio of the two countries' wage rates, w/w^*. All the goods to the left of that point end up being produced in Home; all the goods to the right end up being produced in Foreign. (It is possible, as we will see in a moment, that the ratio of wage rates is exactly equal to the ratio of unit labor requirements for one good. In that case, this borderline good may be produced in both countries.)

Table 3-2 offers a numerical example in which Home and Foreign both consume and are able to produce *five* goods: apples, bananas, caviar, dates, and enchiladas.

The first two columns of this table are self-explanatory. The third column is the ratio of the Foreign unit labor requirement to the Home unit labor requirement for each good—or, stated differently, the relative Home productivity advantage in each good. We have labeled the goods in order of Home productivity advantage, with the Home advantage greatest for apples and least for enchiladas.

Which country produces which goods depends on the ratio of Home and Foreign wage rates. Home will have a cost advantage in any good for which its relative productivity is

TABLE 3-2	**Home and Foreign Unit Labor Requirements**		
Good	**Home Unit Labor Requirement a_{Li}**	**Foreign Unit Labor Requirement (a_{Li}^*)**	**Relative Home Productivity Advantage (a_{Li}^*/a_{Li})**
Apples	1	10	10
Bananas	5	40	8
Caviar	3	12	4
Dates	6	12	2
Enchiladas	12	9	0.75

higher than its relative wage, and Foreign will have the advantage in the others. If, for example, the Home wage rate is five times that of Foreign (a ratio of Home wage to Foreign wage of five to one), apples and bananas will be produced in Home and caviar, dates, and enchiladas in Foreign. If the Home wage rate is only three times that of Foreign, Home will produce apples, bananas, and caviar, while Foreign will produce only dates and enchiladas.

Is such a pattern of specialization beneficial to both countries? We can see that it is by using the same method we used earlier: comparing the labor cost of producing a good directly in a country with that of indirectly "producing" it by producing another good and trading for the desired good. If the Home wage rate is three times the Foreign wage (put another way, Foreign's wage rate is one-third that of Home), Home will import dates and enchiladas. A unit of dates requires 12 units of Foreign labor to produce, but its cost in terms of Home labor, given the three-to-one wage ratio, is only 4 person-hours ($12/4 = 3$). This cost of 4 person-hours is less than the 6 person-hours it would take to produce the unit of dates in Home. For enchiladas, Foreign actually has higher productivity along with lower wages; it will cost Home only 3 person-hours to acquire a unit of enchiladas through trade, compared with the 12 person-hours it would take to produce it domestically. A similar calculation will show that Foreign also gains; for each of the goods Foreign imports, it turns out to be cheaper in terms of domestic labor to trade for the good rather than produce the good domestically. For example, it would take 10 hours of Foreign labor to produce a unit of apples; even with a wage rate only one-third that of Home workers, it will require only 3 hours of labor to earn enough to buy that unit of apples from Home.

In making these calculations, however, we have simply assumed that the relative wage rate is 3. How does this relative wage rate actually get determined?

Determining the Relative Wage in the Multigood Model

In the two-good model, we determined relative wages by first calculating Home wages in terms of cheese and Foreign wages in terms of wine. We then used the price of cheese relative to that of wine to deduce the ratio of the two countries' wage rates. We could do this because we knew that Home would produce cheese and Foreign wine. In the many-good case, who produces what can be determined only after we know the relative wage rate, so we need a new procedure. To determine relative wages in a multigood economy, we must look behind the relative demand for goods to the implied relative demand for labor. This is not a direct demand on the part of consumers; rather, it is a **derived demand** that results from the demand for goods produced with each country's labor.

The relative derived demand for Home labor will fall when the ratio of Home to Foreign wages rises, for two reasons. First, as Home labor becomes more expensive relative to Foreign labor, goods produced in Home also become relatively more expensive, and world demand for these goods falls. Second, as Home wages rise, fewer goods will be produced in Home and more in Foreign, further reducing the demand for Home labor.

We can illustrate these two effects using our numerical example as illustrated in Table 3-2. Suppose we start with the following situation: The Home wage is initially 3.5 times the Foreign wage. At that level, Home would produce apples, bananas, and caviar while Foreign would produce dates and enchiladas. If the relative Home wage were to increase from 3.5 to 3.99, the pattern of specialization would not change. However, as the goods produced in Home became relatively more expensive, the relative demand for these goods would decline and the relative demand for Home labor would decline with it.

Suppose now that the relative wage increased slightly from 3.99 to 4.01. This small further growth in the relative Home wage would bring about a shift in the pattern of specialization. Because it is now cheaper to produce caviar in Foreign than in Home, the production of caviar shifts from Home to Foreign. What does this imply for the relative demand for Home labor? Clearly it implies that as the relative wage rises from a little less than 4 to a little more than 4, there is an abrupt drop-off in the relative demand, as Home production of caviar falls to zero and Foreign acquires a new industry. If the relative wage continues to rise, relative demand for Home labor will gradually decline, then drop off abruptly at a relative wage of 8, at which point production of bananas shifts to Foreign.

We can illustrate the determination of relative wages with a diagram like Figure 3-5. Unlike Figure 3-3, this diagram does not have relative quantities of goods or relative prices of goods on its axes. Instead it shows the relative quantity of labor and the relative wage rate. The world demand for Home labor relative to its demand for Foreign labor is shown by the curve *RD*. The world supply of Home labor relative to Foreign labor is shown by the line *RS*.

The relative supply of labor is determined by the relative sizes of Home's and Foreign's labor forces. Assuming the number of person-hours available does not vary with the wage, the relative wage has no effect on relative labor supply and *RS* is a vertical line.

Our discussion of the relative demand for labor explains the "stepped" shape of *RD*. Whenever we increase the wage rate of Home workers relative to that of Foreign workers, the relative demand for goods produced in Home will decline and the demand for Home labor will decline with it. In addition, the relative demand for Home labor will drop off abruptly whenever an increase in the relative Home wage makes a good cheaper to produce in Foreign. So the curve alternates between smoothly

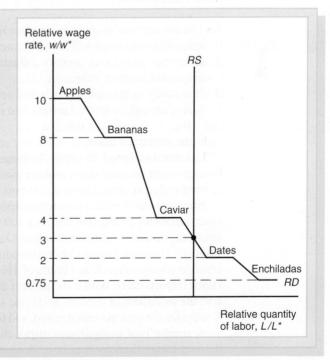

FIGURE 3-5

Determination of Relative Wages

In a many-good Ricardian model, relative wages are determined by the intersection of the derived relative demand curve for labor, *RD*, with the relative supply, *RS*.

downward-sloping sections where the pattern of specialization does not change and "flats" where the relative demand shifts abruptly because of shifts in the pattern of specialization. As shown in the figure, these "flats" correspond to relative wages that equal the ratio of Home to Foreign productivity for each of the five goods.

The equilibrium relative wage is determined by the intersection of *RD* and *RS*. As drawn, the equilibrium relative wage is 3. At this wage, Home produces apples, bananas, and caviar while Foreign produces dates and enchiladas. The outcome depends on the relative size of the countries (which determines the position of *RS*) and the relative demand for the goods (which determines the shape and position of *RD*).

If the intersection of *RD* and *RS* happens to lie on one of the flats, both countries produce the good to which the flat applies.

Adding Transport Costs and Nontraded Goods

We now extend our model another step closer to reality by considering the effects of transport costs. Transportation costs do not change the fundamental principles of comparative advantage or the gains from trade. Because transport costs pose obstacles to the movement of goods and services, however, they have important implications for the way a trading world economy is affected by a variety of factors such as foreign aid, international investment, and balance of payments problems. While we will not deal with the effects of these factors yet, the multigood one-factor model is a good place to introduce the effects of transport costs.

First, notice that the world economy described by the model of the last section is marked by very extreme international specialization. At most, there is one good that both countries produce; all other goods are produced either in Home or in Foreign, but not in both.

There are three main reasons why specialization in the real international economy is not this extreme:

1. The existence of more than one factor of production reduces the tendency toward specialization (as we will see in the next two chapters).
2. Countries sometimes protect industries from foreign competition (discussed at length in Chapters 9 through 12).
3. It is costly to transport goods and services; in some cases the cost of transportation is enough to lead countries into self-sufficiency in certain sectors.

In the multigood example of the last section, we found that at a relative Home wage of 3, Home could produce apples, bananas, and caviar more cheaply than Foreign, while Foreign could produce dates and enchiladas more cheaply than Home. *In the absence of transport costs*, then, Home will export the first three goods and import the last two.

Now suppose there is a cost to transport goods, and that this transport cost is a uniform fraction of production cost, say 100 percent. This transportation cost will discourage trade. Consider dates, for example. One unit of this good requires 6 hours of Home labor or 12 hours of Foreign labor to produce. At a relative wage of 3, 12 hours of Foreign labor costs only as much as 4 hours of Home labor; so in the absence of transport costs, Home imports dates. With a 100 percent transport cost, however, importing dates would cost the equivalent of 8 hours of Home labor (4 hours of labor plus the equivalent of 4 hours for the transportation costs), so Home will produce the good for itself instead.

A similar cost comparison shows that Foreign will find it cheaper to produce its own caviar than to import it. A unit of caviar requires 3 hours of Home labor to produce. Even at a relative Home wage of 3, which makes this the equivalent of 9 hours of Foreign labor, this is cheaper than the 12 hours Foreign would need to produce caviar for itself. In the absence of transport costs, then, Foreign would find it cheaper to import caviar than to make it domestically. With a 100 percent cost of transportation, however, imported caviar would cost the equivalent of 18 hours of Foreign labor and would therefore be produced locally instead.

The result of introducing transport costs in this example, then, is that Home will still export apples and bananas and import enchiladas, but caviar and dates will become **nontraded goods,** which each country will produce for itself.

In this example, we have assumed that transport costs are the same fraction of production cost in all sectors. In practice there is a wide range of transportation costs. In some cases transportation is virtually impossible: Services such as haircuts and auto repair cannot be traded internationally (except where there is a metropolitan area that straddles a border, like Detroit, Michigan–Windsor, Ontario). There is also little international trade in goods with high weight-to-value ratios, like cement. (It is simply not worth the transport cost of importing cement, even if it can be produced much more cheaply abroad.) Many goods end up being nontraded either because of the absence of strong national cost advantages or because of high transportation costs.

The important point is that nations spend a large share of their income on nontraded goods. This observation is of surprising importance in our later discussion of international monetary economics.

Empirical Evidence on the Ricardian Model

The Ricardian model of international trade is an extremely useful tool for thinking about the reasons why trade may happen and about the effects of international trade on national welfare. But is the model a good fit to the real world? Does the Ricardian model make accurate predictions about actual international trade flows?

The answer is a heavily qualified yes. Clearly there are a number of ways in which the Ricardian model makes misleading predictions. First, as mentioned in our discussion of nontraded goods, the simple Ricardian model predicts an extreme degree of specialization that we do not observe in the real world. Second, the Ricardian model assumes away effects of international trade on the distribution of income *within* countries, and thus predicts that countries as a whole will always gain from trade; in practice, international trade has strong effects on income distribution. Third, the Ricardian model allows no role for differences in resources among countries as a cause of trade, thus missing an important aspect of the trading system (the focus of Chapters 4 and 5). Finally, the Ricardian model neglects the possible role of economies of scale as a cause of trade, which leaves it unable to explain the large trade flows between apparently similar nations—an issue discussed in Chapters 7 and 8.

In spite of these failings, however, the basic prediction of the Ricardian model— that countries should tend to export those goods in which their productivity is relatively high—has been strongly confirmed by a number of studies over the years.

Several classic tests of the Ricardian model, performed using data from the early post-World War II period, compared British with American productivity and trade.[4]

---

[4]The pioneering study by G. D. A. MacDougall is listed in Further Readings at the end of the chapter. A well-known follow-up study, on which we draw here, was Bela Balassa, "An Empirical Demonstration of Classical Comparative Cost Theory," *Review of Economics and Statistics* 45 (August 1963), pp. 231–238; we use Balassa's numbers as an illustration.

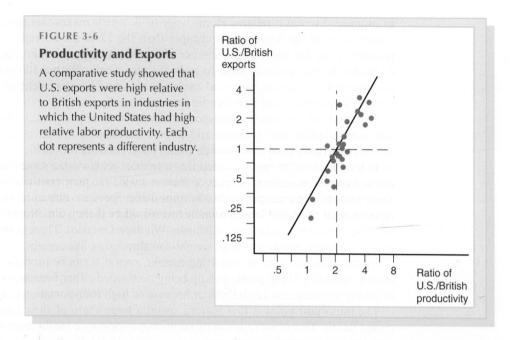

FIGURE 3-6

Productivity and Exports

A comparative study showed that U.S. exports were high relative to British exports in industries in which the United States had high relative labor productivity. Each dot represents a different industry.

This was an unusually illuminating comparison, because it revealed that British labor productivity was lower than American productivity in almost every sector. As a result, the United States had an absolute advantage in everything. Nonetheless, the amount of overall British exports was about as large as the amount of American exports at the time. Despite its lower absolute productivity, there must have been some sectors in which Britain had a comparative advantage. The Ricardian model would predict that these would be the sectors in which the United States' productivity advantage was smaller.

Figure 3-6 illustrates the evidence in favor of the Ricardian model, using data presented in a paper by the Hungarian economist Bela Balassa in 1963. The figure compares the ratio of U.S. to British exports in 1951 with the ratio of U.S. to British labor productivity for 26 manufacturing industries. The productivity ratio is measured on the horizontal axis, the export ratio on the vertical axis. Both axes are given a logarithmic scale, which turns out to produce a clearer picture.

Ricardian theory would lead us broadly to expect that the higher the relative productivity in the U.S. industry, the more likely U.S. rather than U.K. firms would export in that industry. And that is what Figure 3-6 shows. In fact, the scatterplot lies quite close to an upward-sloping line, also shown in the figure. Bearing in mind that the data used for this comparison are, like all economic data, subject to substantial measurement errors, the fit is remarkably close.

As expected, the evidence in Figure 3-6 confirms the basic insight that trade depends on *comparative*, not *absolute* advantage. At the time to which the data refer, U.S. industry had much higher labor productivity than British industry—on average about twice as high. The commonly held misconception that a country can be competitive only if it can match other countries' productivity, which we discussed earlier in this chapter, would have led one to predict a U.S. export advantage across the board. The Ricardian model tells us, however, that having high productivity in an industry compared with that of foreigners is not enough to ensure that a country will export that industry's products; the relative productivity must be high compared with relative productivity in other sectors. As it happened, U.S. productivity exceeded British productivity in all 26 sectors (indicated by dots) shown in Figure 3-6, by margins ranging from 11 to 366 percent. In 12 of the sectors, however, Britain actually had larger exports than the United States. A glance at the figure shows that, in general, U.S. exports were larger than U.K. exports only in industries where the U.S. productivity advantage was somewhat more than two to one.

More recent evidence on the Ricardian model has been less clear-cut. In part, this is because the growth of world trade and the resulting specialization of national economies means that we do not get a chance to see what countries do badly! In the world economy of the 21st century, countries often do not produce goods for which they are at a comparative disadvantage, so there is no way to measure their productivity in those sectors. For example, most countries do not produce airplanes, so there are no data on what their unit labor requirements would be if they did. Nonetheless, several pieces of evidence suggest that differences in labor productivity continue to play an important role in determining world trade patterns.

Perhaps the most striking demonstration of the continuing usefulness of the Ricardian theory of comparative advantage is the way it explains the emergence of countries with very low overall productivity as export powerhouses in some industries. Consider, for example, the case of clothing exports from Bangladesh. The Bangladeshi clothing industry received the worst kind of publicity in April 2013, when a building housing five garment factories collapsed, killing more than a thousand people. The backstory to this tragedy, however, was the growth of Bangladesh's clothing exports, which were rapidly gaining on those of China, previously the dominant supplier. This rapid growth took place even though Bangladesh is a very, very poor country, with extremely low overall productivity even compared with China, which as we have already seen is still low-productivity compared with the U.S.

What was the secret of Bangladesh's success? It has fairly low productivity even in the production of clothing – but its productivity disadvantage there is much smaller than in other industries, so that the nation has a comparative advantage in clothing. Table 3-3 illustrates this point with some estimates based on 2011 data.

Compared with China, Bangladesh still has an *absolute* disadvantage in clothing production, with significantly lower productivity. But because its relative productivity in apparel is so much higher than in other industries, Bangladesh has a strong comparative advantage in apparel—and its apparel industry is giving China a run for the money.

In sum, while few economists believe that the Ricardian model is a fully adequate description of the causes and consequences of world trade, its two principal implications—that productivity differences play an important role in international trade and that it is comparative rather than absolute advantage that matters—do seem to be supported by the evidence.

TABLE 3-3	**Bangladesh versus China, 2011**	
	Bangladeshi Output per Worker as % of China	**Bangladeshi exports as % of China**
All industries	28.5	1.0
Apparel	77	15.5

Source: McKinsey and Company, "Bangladesh's ready-made garments industry: The challenge of growth," 2012; UN Monthly Bulletin of Statistics.

SUMMARY

1. We examined the Ricardian model, the simplest model that shows how differences between countries give rise to trade and gains from trade. In this model, labor is the only factor of production, and countries differ only in the productivity of labor in different industries.

2. In the Ricardian model, countries will export goods that their labor produces relatively efficiently and will import goods that their labor produces relatively inefficiently. In other words, a country's production pattern is determined by comparative advantage.

3. We can show that trade benefits a country in either of two ways. First, we can think of trade as an indirect method of production. Instead of producing a good for itself, a country can produce another good and trade it for the desired good. The simple model shows that whenever a good is imported, it must be true that this indirect "production" requires less labor than direct production. Second, we can show that trade enlarges a country's consumption possibilities, which implies gains from trade.

4. The distribution of the gains from trade depends on the relative prices of the goods countries produce. To determine these relative prices, it is necessary to look at the relative world supply and demand for goods. The relative price implies a relative wage rate as well.

5. The proposition that trade is beneficial is unqualified. That is, there is no requirement that a country be "competitive" or that the trade be "fair." In particular, we can show that three commonly held beliefs about trade are wrong. First, a country gains from trade even if it has lower productivity than its trading partner in all industries. Second, trade is beneficial even if foreign industries are competitive only because of low wages. Third, trade is beneficial even if a country's exports embody more labor than its imports.

6. Extending the one-factor, two-good model to a world of many commodities does not alter these conclusions. The only difference is that it becomes necessary to focus directly on the relative demand for labor to determine relative wages rather than to work via relative demand for goods. Also, a many-commodity model can be used to illustrate the important point that transportation costs can give rise to a situation in which some goods are nontraded.

7. While some of the predictions of the Ricardian model are clearly unrealistic, its basic prediction—that countries will tend to export goods in which they have relatively high productivity—has been confirmed by a number of studies.

KEY TERMS

absolute advantage, p. 61
comparative advantage, p. 58
derived demand, p. 74
gains from trade, p. 66
general equilibrium analysis, p. 63
nontraded goods, p. 77

opportunity cost, p. 57
partial equilibrium analysis, p. 62
pauper labor argument, p. 70
production possibility frontier, p. 59
relative demand curve, p. 63

relative supply curve, p. 63
relative wage, p. 67
Ricardian model, p. 58
unit labor requirement, p. 58

PROBLEMS

MyEconLab

1. Home has 1,200 units of labor available. It can produce two goods, apples and bananas. The unit labor requirement in apple production is 3, while in banana production it is 2.
   a. Graph Home's production possibility frontier.
   b. What is the opportunity cost of apples in terms of bananas?
   c. In the absence of trade, what would be the price of apples in terms of bananas? Why?
2. Home is as described in problem 1. There is now also another country, Foreign, with a labor force of 800. Foreign's unit labor requirement in apple production is 5, while in banana production it is 1.
   a. Graph Foreign's production possibility frontier.
   b. Construct the world relative supply curve.
3. Now suppose world relative demand takes the following form: Demand for apples/demand for bananas = price of bananas/price of apples.
   a. Graph the relative demand curve along with the relative supply curve.
   b. What is the equilibrium relative price of apples?
   c. Describe the pattern of trade.
   d. Show that both Home and Foreign gain from trade.
4. Suppose an hour's labor produces 10 kg of rice and 5 meter of cloth in India, and 5 kg and 2 meter in Thailand. Using opportunity costs, explain which country will export cloth and which will export paddy in trade.
5. Suppose Mike and Johnson produce two products—hamburgers and T-shirts. Mike produces 10 hamburgers or 3 T-shirts a day and Johnson produces 7 hamburgers or 4 T-shirts. Assuming they can devote time in making either hamburgers or T-shirts.
   a. Draw the production possibility curve.
   b. Who enjoys the absolute advantage of producing both?
   c. Who has a higher opportunity cost of making T-shirts?
   d. Who has a comparative advantage in producing hamburgers?
6. "Chinese workers earn only $.75 an hour; if we allow China to export as much as it likes, our workers will be forced down to the same level. You can't import a $10 shirt without importing the $.75 wage that goes with it." Discuss.
7. Japanese labor productivity is roughly the same as that of the United States in the manufacturing sector (higher in some industries, lower in others), while the United States is still considerably more productive in the service sector. But most services are nontraded. Some analysts have argued that this poses a problem for the United States, because our comparative advantage lies in things we cannot sell on world markets. What is wrong with this argument?
8. Anyone who has visited Japan knows it is an incredibly expensive place; although Japanese workers earn about the same as their U.S. counterparts, the purchasing power of their incomes is about one-third less. Extend your discussion from question 7 to explain this observation. (Hint: Think about wages and the implied prices of nontraded goods.)
9. International immobility of resources is compensated by the international flow of goods—justify.
10. We have focused on the case of trade involving only two countries. Suppose that there are many countries capable of producing two goods, and that each country has only one factor of production, labor. What could we say about the pattern of production and trade in this case? (Hint: Try constructing the world relative supply curve.)

FURTHER READINGS

Donald Davis. "Intraindustry Trade: A Heckscher-Ohlin-Ricardo Approach." *Journal of International Economics* 39 (November 1995), pp. 201–226. A recent revival of the Ricardian approach to explain trade between countries with similar resources.

Rudiger Dornbusch, Stanley Fischer, and Paul Samuelson. "Comparative Advantage, Trade and Payments in a Ricardian Model with a Continuum of Goods." *American Economic Review* 67 (December 1977), pp. 823–839. More recent theoretical modeling in the Ricardian mode, developing the idea of simplifying the many-good Ricardian model by assuming that the number of goods is so large as to form a smooth continuum.

Giovanni Dosi, Keith Pavitt, and Luc Soete. *The Economics of Technical Change and International Trade.* Brighton: Wheatsheaf, 1988. An empirical examination that suggests that international trade in manufactured goods is largely driven by differences in national technological competencies.

Stephen Golub and Chang-Tai Hsieh. "Classical Ricardian Theory of Comparative Advantage Revisited." *Review of International Economics* 8(2), 2000, pp. 221–234. A modern statistical analysis of the relationship between relative productivity and trade patterns, which finds reasonably strong correlations.

G. D. A. MacDougall. "British and American Exports: A Study Suggested by the Theory of Comparative Costs." *Economic Journal* 61 (December 1951), pp. 697–724; 62 (September 1952), pp. 487–521. In this famous study, MacDougall used comparative data on U.S. and U.K. productivity to test the predictions of the Ricardian model.

John Stuart Mill. *Principles of Political Economy.* London: Longmans, Green, 1917. Mill's 1848 treatise extended Ricardo's work into a full-fledged model of international trade.

David Ricardo. *The Principles of Political Economy and Taxation.* Homewood, IL: Irwin, 1963. The basic source for the Ricardian model is Ricardo himself in this book, first published in 1817.

MyEconLab Can Help You Get a Better Grade

MyEconLab If your exam were tomorrow, would you be ready? For each chapter, MyEconLab Practice Tests and Study Plans pinpoint sections you have mastered and those you need to study. That way, you are more efficient with your study time, and you are better prepared for your exams.

To see how it works, turn to page 41 and then go to

www.myeconlab.com

CHAPTER 4

Specific Factors and Income Distribution

A s we saw in Chapter 3, international trade can be mutually beneficial to the nations engaged in it. Yet throughout history, governments have protected sectors of the economy from import competition. For example, despite its commitment in principle to free trade, the United States limits imports of apparel, textiles, sugar, ethanol, and dairy products, among many other commodities. During presidential re-election cycles, punitive tariffs are often imposed on import of goods produced in key political swing states.[1] If trade is such a good thing for the economy, why is there opposition to its effects? To understand the politics of trade, it is necessary to look at the effects of trade not just on a country as a whole, but on the distribution of income within that country.

The Ricardian model of international trade developed in Chapter 3 illustrates the potential benefits from trade. In that model, trade leads to international specialization, with each country shifting its labor force from industries in which that labor is relatively inefficient to industries in which it is relatively more efficient. Because labor is the only factor of production in that model, and it is assumed that labor can move freely from one industry to another, there is no possibility that individuals will be hurt by trade. The Ricardian model thus suggests not only that all *countries* gain from trade, but also that every *individual* is made better off as a result of international trade, because trade does not affect the distribution of income. In the real world, however, trade has substantial effects on the income distribution within each trading nation, so that in practice the benefits of trade are often distributed very unevenly.

There are two main reasons why international trade has strong effects on the distribution of income. First, resources cannot move immediately or without cost from one industry to another—a short-run consequence of trade. Second, industries differ in the factors of production they demand. A shift in the mix of goods a country produces will ordinarily reduce the demand for some factors of production, while raising the demand for others—a long-run consequence of trade. For

---

[1]The latest examples are the 35 percent tariff imposed on tires (imported from China) during Barack Obama's first term and a 30 percent tariff on steel imports during Georges W. Bush's first term. Production of both steel and tires is concentrated in Ohio, a key swing state in the past several U.S. presidential elections.

both of these reasons, international trade is not as unambiguously beneficial as it appeared to be in Chapter 3. While trade may benefit a nation as a whole, it often hurts significant groups within the country in the short run, and potentially, but to a lesser extent, in the long run.

Consider the effects of Japan's rice policy. Japan allows very little rice to be imported, even though the scarcity of land means that rice is much more expensive to produce in Japan than in other countries (including the United States). There is little question that Japan as a whole would have a higher standard of living if free imports of rice were allowed. Japanese rice farmers, however, would be hurt by free trade. While the farmers displaced by imports could probably find jobs in manufacturing or services, they would find changing employment costly and inconvenient: The special skills they developed for rice farming would be useless in those other jobs. Furthermore, the value of the land that the farmers own would fall along with the price of rice. Not surprisingly, Japanese rice farmers are vehemently opposed to free trade in rice, and their organized political opposition has counted for more than the potential gains from trade for the nation as a whole.

A realistic analysis of trade must go beyond the Ricardian model to models in which trade can affect income distribution. In this chapter, we focus on the short-run consequences of trade on the income distribution when factors of production cannot move without cost between sectors. To keep our model simple, we assume that the sector-switching cost for some factors is high enough that such a switch is impossible in the short run. Those factors are *specific* to a particular sector.

LEARNING GOALS

After reading this chapter, you will be able to:

- Understand how a mobile factor will respond to price changes by moving across sectors.
- Explain why trade will generate both winners and losers in the short run.
- Understand the meaning of gains from trade when there are losers.
- Discuss the reasons why trade is a politically contentious issue.
- Explain the arguments in favor of free trade despite the existence of losers.

The Specific Factors Model

The **specific factors model** was developed by Paul Samuelson and Ronald Jones.[2] Like the simple Ricardian model, it assumes an economy that produces two goods and that can allocate its labor supply between the two sectors. Unlike the Ricardian model, however, the specific factors model allows for the existence of factors of production

---

[2]Paul Samuelson, "Ohlin Was Right," *Swedish Journal of Economics* 73 (1971), pp. 365–384; and Ronald W. Jones, "A Three-Factor Model in Theory, Trade, and History," in Jagdish Bhagwati et al., eds., *Trade, Balance of Payments, and Growth* (Amsterdam: North-Holland, 1971), pp. 3–21.

WHAT IS A SPECIFIC FACTOR?

In the model developed in this chapter, we assume two factors of production—land and capital—are permanently tied to particular sectors of the economy. In advanced economies, however, agricultural land receives only a small part of national income. When economists apply the specific factors model to economies like those of the United States or France, they typically think of factor specificity not as a permanent condition but as a matter of time. For example, the vats used to brew beer and the stamping presses used to build auto bodies cannot be substituted for each other, and so these different kinds of equipment are industry-specific. Given time, however, it would be possible to redirect investment from auto factories to breweries or vice versa. As a result, in a long-term sense both vats and stamping presses can be considered two manifestations of a single, mobile factor called capital.

In practice, then, the distinction between specific and mobile factors is not a sharp line. Rather, it is a question of the speed of adjustment, with factors being more specific the longer it takes to redeploy them between industries. So how specific are the factors of production in the real economy?

Worker mobility varies greatly with the characteristics of the worker (such as age) and the job occupation (whether it requires general or job-specific skills). Nevertheless, one can measure an average rate of mobility by looking at the duration of unemployment following a worker's displacement. After four years, a displaced worker in the United States has the same probability of being employed as a similar worker who was not displaced.* This four-year time-span compares with a lifetime of 15 or 20 years for a typical specialized machine, and 30 to 50 years for structures (a shopping mall, office building, or production plant). So labor is certainly a less specific factor than most kinds of capital. However, even though most workers can find new employment in other sectors within a four-year time-span, switching occupations entails additional costs: A displaced worker who is re-employed in a different occupation suffers an 18 percent permanent drop in wages (on average). This compares with a 6 percent drop if the worker does not switch occupations.† Thus, labor is truly flexible only before a worker has invested in any occupation-specific skills.

*See Bruce Fallick, "The Industrial Mobility of Displaced Workers," *Journal of Labor Economics* 11 (April 1993), pp. 302–323.
†See Gueorgui Kambourov and Iourii Manovskii, "Occupational Specificity of Human Capital," *International Economic Review* 50 (February 2009), pp. 63–115.

besides labor. Whereas labor is a **mobile factor** that can move between sectors, these other factors are assumed to be **specific.** That is, they can be used only in the production of particular goods.

Assumptions of the Model

Imagine an economy that can produce two goods, cloth and food. Instead of one factor of production, however, the country has *three*: labor (L), capital (K), and land (T for *terrain*). Cloth is produced using capital and labor (but not land), while food is produced using land and labor (but not capital). Labor is therefore a *mobile* factor that can be used in either sector, while land and capital are both *specific* factors that can be used only in the production of one good. Land can also be thought of as a different type of capital, one that is specific to the food sector (see box above).

How much of each good does the economy produce? The economy's output of cloth depends on how much capital and labor are used in that sector. This relationship is summarized by a **production function** that tells us the quantity of cloth that can be produced given any input of capital and labor. The production function for cloth can be summarized algebraically as

$$Q_C = Q_C(K, L_C), \tag{4-1}$$

where Q_C is the economy's output of cloth, K is the economy's capital stock, and L_C is the labor force employed in cloth. Similarly, for food we can write the production function

$$Q_F = Q_F(T, L_F), \tag{4-2}$$

where Q_F is the economy's output of food, T is the economy's supply of land, and L_F is the labor force devoted to food production. For the economy as a whole, the labor employed must equal the total labor supply L:

$$L_C + L_F = L. \tag{4-3}$$

Production Possibilities

The specific factors model assumes that each of the specific factors, capital and land, can be used in only one sector, cloth and food, respectively. Only labor can be used in either sector. Thus, to analyze the economy's production possibilities, we need only to ask how the economy's mix of output changes as labor is shifted from one sector to the other. This can be done graphically, first by representing the production functions (4-1) and (4-2), and then by putting them together to derive the **production possibility frontier**.

Figure 4-1 illustrates the relationship between labor input and output of cloth. The larger the input of labor for a given capital supply, the larger the output. In Figure 4-1, the slope of $Q_C(K, L_C)$ represents the **marginal product of labor**, that is, the addition to output generated by adding one more person-hour. However, if labor input is increased without increasing capital, there will normally be **diminishing returns**: Because adding a worker means that each worker has less capital to work with, each successive increment of labor will add less to production than the last. Diminishing returns are reflected in the shape of the production function: $Q_C(K, L_C)$ gets flatter as we move to

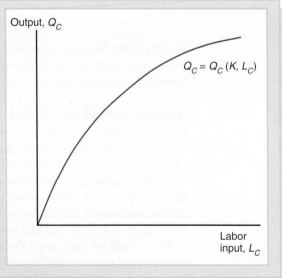

FIGURE 4-1

The Production Function for Cloth

The more labor employed in the production of cloth, the larger the output. As a result of diminishing returns, however, each successive person-hour increases output by less than the previous one; this is shown by the fact that the curve relating labor input to output gets flatter at higher levels of employment.

Output, Q_C

$Q_C = Q_C(K, L_C)$

Labor input, L_C

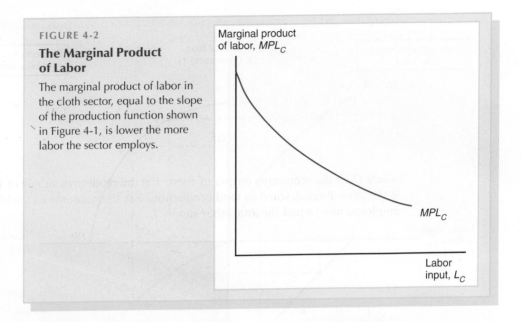

FIGURE 4-2

The Marginal Product of Labor

The marginal product of labor in the cloth sector, equal to the slope of the production function shown in Figure 4-1, is lower the more labor the sector employs.

the right, indicating that the marginal product of labor declines as more labor is used.[3] Figure 4-2 shows the same information a different way. In this figure, we directly plot the marginal product of labor as a function of the labor employed. (In the appendix to this chapter, we show that the area under the marginal product curve represents the total output of cloth.)

A similar pair of diagrams can represent the production function for food. These diagrams can then be combined to derive the production possibility frontier for the economy, as illustrated in Figure 4-3. As we saw in Chapter 3, the production possibility frontier shows what the economy is capable of producing; in this case, it shows how much food it can produce for any given output of cloth and vice versa.

Figure 4-3 is a four-quadrant diagram. In the lower-right quadrant, we show the production function for cloth illustrated in Figure 4-1. This time, however, we turn the figure on its side: A movement downward along the vertical axis represents an increase in the labor input to the cloth sector, while a movement to the right along the horizontal axis represents an increase in the output of cloth. In the upper-left quadrant, we show the corresponding production function for food; this part of the figure is also flipped around, so that a movement to the left along the horizontal axis indicates an increase in labor input to the food sector, while an upward movement along the vertical axis indicates an increase in food output.

The lower-left quadrant represents the economy's allocation of labor. Both quantities are measured in the reverse of the usual direction. A downward movement along the vertical axis indicates an increase in the labor employed in cloth; a leftward movement along the horizontal axis indicates an increase in labor employed in food. Since an increase in employment in one sector must mean that less labor is available for the other, the possible allocations are indicated by a downward-sloping line. This line, labeled AA, slopes downward at a 45-degree angle, that is, it has a slope of -1.

---

[3]Diminishing returns to a single factor does not imply diminishing returns to scale when all factors of production are adjusted. Thus, diminishing returns to labor is entirely consistent with constant returns to scale in both labor and capital.

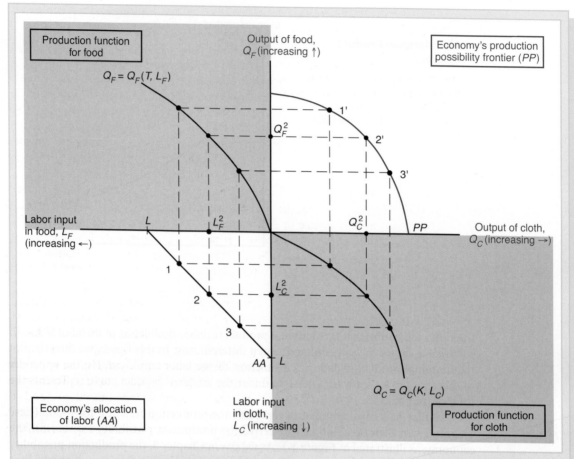

FIGURE 4-3

The Production Possibility Frontier in the Specific Factors Model

Production of cloth and food is determined by the allocation of labor. In the lower-left quadrant, the allocation of labor between sectors can be illustrated by a point on line *AA*, which represents all combinations of labor input to cloth and food that sum up to the total labor supply *L*. Corresponding to any particular point on *AA*, such as point 2, is a labor input to cloth (L_C^2) and a labor input to food (L_F^2). The curves in the lower-right and upper-left quadrants represent the production functions for cloth and food, respectively; these allow determination of output (Q_C^2, Q_F^2) given labor input. Then in the upper-right quadrant, the curve *PP* shows how the output of the two goods varies as the allocation of labor is shifted from food to cloth, with the output points 1′, 2′, 3′ corresponding to the labor allocations 1, 2, 3. Because of diminishing returns, *PP* is a bowed-out curve instead of a straight line.

To see why this line represents the possible labor allocations, notice that if all labor were employed in food production, L_F would equal *L*, while L_C would equal 0. If one were then to move labor gradually into the cloth sector, each person-hour moved would increase L_C by one unit while reducing L_F by one unit, tracing a line with a slope of −1, until the entire labor supply *L* is employed in the cloth sector. Any particular allocation of labor between the two sectors can then be represented by a point on *AA*, such as point 2.

We can now see how to determine production given any particular allocation of labor between the two sectors. Suppose the allocation of labor were represented by point 2 in the lower-left quadrant, that is, with L_C^2 hours in cloth and L_F^2 hours in food. Then we can use the production function for each sector to determine output: Q_C^2 units of cloth, Q_F^2 units of food. Using coordinates Q_C^2, Q_F^2, point $2'$ in the upper-right quadrant of Figure 4-3 shows the resulting outputs of cloth and food.

To trace the whole production possibility frontier, we simply imagine repeating this exercise for many alternative allocations of labor. We might start with most of the labor allocated to food production, as at point 1 in the lower-left quadrant, then gradually increase the amount of labor used in cloth until very few workers are employed in food, as at point 3; the corresponding points in the upper-right quadrant will trace out the curve running from $1'$ to $3'$. Thus, *PP* in the upper-right quadrant shows the economy's production possibilities for given supplies of land, labor, and capital.

In the Ricardian model, where labor is the only factor of production, the production possibility frontier is a straight line because the opportunity cost of cloth in terms of food is constant. In the specific factors model, however, the addition of other factors of production changes the shape of the production possibility frontier *PP* to a curve. The curvature of *PP* reflects diminishing returns to labor in each sector; these diminishing returns are the crucial difference between the specific factors and the Ricardian models.

Notice that when tracing *PP*, we shift labor from the food to the cloth sector. If we shift one person-hour of labor from food to cloth, however, this extra input will increase output in that sector by the marginal product of labor in cloth, MPL_C. To increase cloth output by one unit, then, we must increase labor input by $1/MPL_C$ hours. Meanwhile, each unit of labor input shifted out of food production will lower output in that sector by the marginal product of labor in food, MPL_F. To increase output of cloth by one unit, then, the economy must reduce output of food by MPL_F/MPL_C units. The slope of *PP*, which measures the opportunity cost of cloth in terms of food—that is, the number of units of food output that must be sacrificed to increase cloth output by one unit—is therefore

$$\text{Slope of production possibilities curve} = -MPL_F/MPL_C.$$

We can now see why *PP* has the bowed shape it does. As we move from $1'$ to $3'$, L_C rises and L_F falls. We saw in Figure 4-2, however, that as L_C rises, the marginal product of labor in cloth falls; correspondingly, as L_F falls, the marginal product of labor in food rises. As more and more labor is moved to the cloth sector, each additional unit of labor becomes less valuable in the cloth sector and more valuable in the food sector: The opportunity cost (foregone food production) of each additional cloth unit rises, and *PP* thus gets steeper as we move down it to the right.

We have shown how output is determined, given the allocation of labor. The next step is to ask how a market economy determines what the allocation of labor should be.

Prices, Wages, and Labor Allocation

How much labor will be employed in each sector? To answer this, we need to look at supply and demand in the labor market. The demand for labor in each sector depends on the price of output and the wage rate. In turn, the wage rate depends on the combined demand for labor by food and cloth producers. Given the prices of cloth and food together with the wage rate, we can determine each sector's employment and output.

First, let's focus on the demand for labor. In each sector, profit-maximizing employers will demand labor up to the point where the value produced by an additional person-hour equals the cost of employing that hour. In the cloth sector, for example, the value of an additional person-hour is the marginal product of labor in cloth multiplied by the price of one unit of cloth: $MPL_C \times P_C$. If w is the wage rate of labor, employers will therefore hire workers up to the point where

$$MPL_C \times P_C = w. \tag{4-4}$$

But the marginal product of labor in cloth, already illustrated in Figure 4-2, slopes downward because of diminishing returns. So for any given price of cloth P_C, the value of that marginal product, $MPL_C \times P_C$, will also slope down. We can therefore think of equation (4-4) as defining the demand curve for labor in the cloth sector: If the wage rate falls, other things equal, employers in the cloth sector will want to hire more workers.

Similarly, the value of an additional person-hour in food is $MPL_F \times P_F$. The demand curve for labor in the food sector may therefore be written

$$MPL_F \times P_F = w. \tag{4-5}$$

The wage rate w must be the same in both sectors because of the assumption that labor is freely mobile between sectors. That is, because labor is a mobile factor, it will move from the low-wage sector to the high-wage sector until wages are equalized. The wage rate, in turn, is determined by the requirement that total labor demand (total employment) equals total labor supply. This equilibrium condition for labor is represented in equation (4-3).

By representing these two labor demand curves in a diagram (Figure 4-4), we can see how the wage rate and employment in each sector are determined given the prices of food and cloth. Along the horizontal axis of Figure 4-4, we show the total labor supply L. Measuring from the left of the diagram, we show the value of the marginal

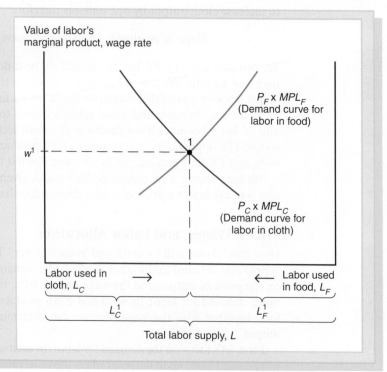

FIGURE 4-4

The Allocation of Labor

Labor is allocated so that the value of its marginal product ($P \times MPL$) is the same in the cloth and food sectors. In equilibrium, the wage rate is equal to the value of labor's marginal product.

product of labor in cloth, which is simply the MPL_C curve from Figure 4-2 multiplied by P_C. This is the demand curve for labor in the cloth sector. Measuring from the right, we show the value of the marginal product of labor in food, which is the demand for labor in food. The equilibrium wage rate and allocation of labor between the two sectors is represented by point 1. At the wage rate w^1, the sum of labor demanded in the cloth (L_C^1) and food (L_F^1) sectors just equals the total labor supply L.

A useful relationship between relative prices and output emerges clearly from this analysis of labor allocation; this relationship applies to more general situations than that described by the specific factors model. Equations (4-4) and (4-5) imply that

$$MPL_C \times P_C = MPL_F \times P_F = w$$

or, rearranging, that

$$-MPL_F / MPL_C = -P_C / P_F. \tag{4-6}$$

The left side of equation (4-6) is the slope of the production possibility frontier at the actual production point; the right side is minus the relative price of cloth. This result tells us that *at the production point, the production possibility frontier must be tangent to a line whose slope is minus the price of cloth divided by that of food.* As we will see in the following chapters, this is a very general result that characterizes production responses to changes in relative prices along a production possibility frontier. It is illustrated in Figure 4-5: If the relative price of cloth is $(P_C/P_F)^1$, the economy produces at point 1.

What happens to the allocation of labor and the distribution of income when the prices of food and cloth change? Notice that any price change can be broken into two parts: an equal-proportional change in both P_C and P_F and a change in only one price. For example, suppose the price of cloth rises 17 percent and the price of food rises 10 percent. We can analyze the effects of this by first asking what happens if cloth and food prices both rise by 10 percent and then by finding out what happens if only cloth prices rise by 7 percent. This allows us to separate the effect of changes in the overall price level from the effect of changes in relative prices.

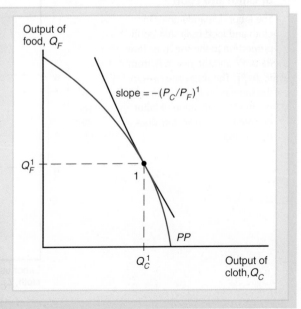

FIGURE 4-5

Production in the Specific Factors Model

The economy produces at the point on its production possibility frontier (*PP*) where the slope of that frontier equals minus the relative price of cloth.

Output of food, Q_F

slope $= -(P_C/P_F)^1$

Q_F^1

1

PP

Q_C^1

Output of cloth, Q_C

An Equal-Proportional Change in Prices Figure 4-6 shows the effect of an equal-proportional increase in P_C and P_F. P_C rises from P_C^1 to P_C^2; P_F rises from P_F^1 to P_F^2. If the prices of both goods increase by 10 percent, the labor demand curves will also shift up by 10 percent. As you can see from the diagram, these shifts lead to a 10 percent increase in the wage rate from w^1 (point 1) to w^2 (point 2). However, the allocation of labor between the sectors and the outputs of the two goods does not change.

In fact, when P_C and P_F change in the same proportion, no real changes occur. The wage rate rises in the same proportion as the prices, so *real* wage rates, the ratios of the wage rate to the prices of goods, are unaffected. *With the same amount of labor employed in each sector, receiving the same real wage rate, the real incomes of capital owners and landowners also remain the same. So everyone is in exactly the same position as before.* This illustrates a general principle: Changes in the overall price level have no real effects, that is, do not change any physical quantities in the economy. Only changes in relative prices—which in this case means the price of cloth relative to the price of food, P_C/P_F—affect welfare or the allocation of resources.

A Change in Relative Prices Consider the effect of a price change that *does* affect relative prices. Figure 4-7 shows the effect of a change in the price of only one good, in this case a 7 percent rise in P_C from P_C^1 to P_C^2. The increase in P_C shifts the cloth labor demand curve in the same proportion as the price increase and shifts the equilibrium from point 1 to point 2. Notice two important facts about the results of this shift. First, although the wage rate rises, it rises by *less* than the increase in the price of cloth. If wages had risen in the same proportion as the price of cloth (7 percent increase), then wages would have risen from w^1 to $w^{2'}$. Instead, wages rise by a smaller proportion, from w^1 to w^2.

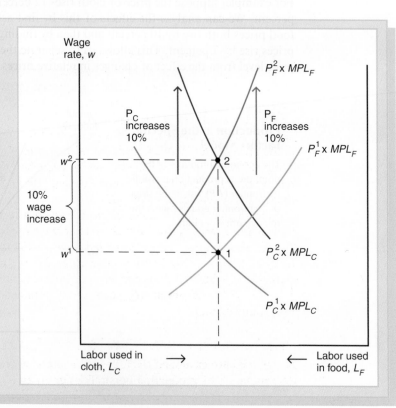

FIGURE 4-6

An Equal-Proportional Increase in the Prices of Cloth and Food

The labor demand curves in cloth and food both shift up in proportion to the rise in P_C from P_C^1 to P_C^2 and the rise in P_F from P_F^1 to P_F^2. The wage rate rises in the same proportion, from w^1 to w^2, but the allocation of labor between the two sectors does not change.

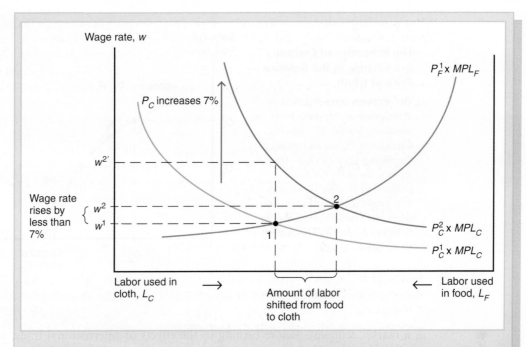

FIGURE 4-7

A Rise in the Price of Cloth

The cloth labor demand curve rises in proportion to the 7 percent increase in P_C, but the wage rate rises less than proportionately. Labor moves from the food sector to the cloth sector. Output of cloth rises; output of food falls.

Second, when only P_C rises, in contrast to a simultaneous rise in P_C and P_F, labor shifts from the food sector to the cloth sector and the output of cloth rises while that of food falls. (This is why w does not rise as much as P_C: Because cloth employment rises, the marginal product of labor in that sector falls.)

The effect of a rise in the relative price of cloth can also be seen directly by looking at the production possibility curve. In Figure 4-8, we show the effects of the same rise in the price of cloth, which raises the *relative* price of cloth from $(P_C/P_F)^1$ to $(P_C/P_F)^2$. The production point, which is always located where the slope of PP equals minus the relative price, shifts from 1 to 2. Food output falls and cloth output rises as a result of the rise in the relative price of cloth.

Since higher relative prices of cloth lead to a higher output of cloth relative to that of food, we can draw a relative supply curve showing Q_C/Q_F as a function of P_C/P_F. This relative supply curve is shown as RS in Figure 4-9. As we showed in Chapter 3, we can also draw a relative demand curve, which is illustrated by the downward-sloping line RD. In the absence of international trade, the equilibrium relative price $(P_C/P_F)^1$ and output $(Q_C/Q_F)^1$ are determined by the intersection of relative supply and demand.

Relative Prices and the Distribution of Income

So far, we have examined the following aspects of the specific factors model: (1) the determination of production possibilities given an economy's resources and technology and (2) the determination of resource allocation, production, and relative prices

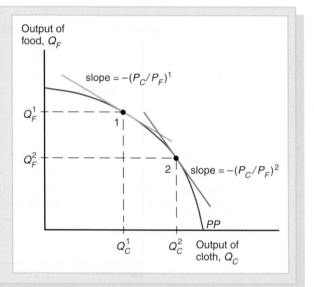

FIGURE 4-8

The Response of Output to a Change in the Relative Price of Cloth

The economy always produces at the point on its production possibility frontier (*PP*) where the slope of *PP* equals minus the relative price of cloth. Thus, an increase in P_C/P_F causes production to move down and to the right along the production possibility frontier corresponding to higher output of cloth and lower output of food.

in a market economy. Before turning to the effects of international trade, we must consider the effect of changes in relative prices on the distribution of income.

Look again at Figure 4-7, which shows the effect of a rise in the price of cloth. We have already noted that the demand curve for labor in the cloth sector will shift upward in proportion to the rise in P_C, so that if P_C rises by 7 percent, the curve defined by $P_C \times MPL_C$ also rises by 7 percent. We have also seen that unless the price of food also rises by at least 7 percent, w will rise by *less* than P_C. Thus, if only cloth prices rise by 7 percent, we would expect the wage rate to rise by only, say, 3 percent.

Let's look at what this outcome implies for the incomes of three groups: workers, owners of capital, and owners of land. Workers find that their wage rate has risen, but less than in proportion to the rise in P_C. Thus, their real wage in terms of cloth (the

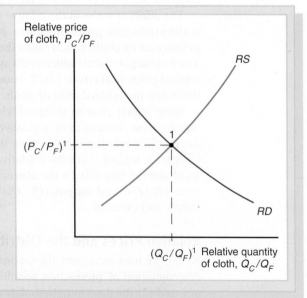

FIGURE 4-9

Determination of Relative Prices

In the specific factors model, a higher relative price of cloth will lead to an increase in the output of cloth relative to that of food. Thus, the relative supply curve *RS* is upward sloping. Equilibrium relative quantities and prices are determined by the intersection of *RS* with the relative demand curve *RD*.

amount of cloth they can buy with their wage income), w/P_C, falls, while their real wage in terms of food, w/P_F, rises. Given this information, we cannot say whether workers are better or worse off; this depends on the relative importance of cloth and food in workers' consumption (determined by the workers' preferences), a question we will not pursue further.

Owners of capital, however, are definitely better off. The real wage rate in terms of cloth has fallen, so the profits of capital owners in terms of what they produce (cloth) rises. That is, the income of capital owners will rise more than proportionately with the rise in P_C. Since P_C in turn rises relative to P_F, the income of capitalists clearly goes up in terms of both goods. Conversely, landowners are definitely worse off. They lose for two reasons: The real wage in terms of food (the good they produce) rises, squeezing their income, and the rise in cloth price reduces the purchasing power of any given income. (The chapter appendix describes the welfare changes of capitalists and landowners in further detail.)

If the relative price had moved in the opposite direction and the relative price of cloth had *decreased*, then the predictions would be reversed: Capital owners would be worse off, and landowners would be better off. The change in the welfare of workers would again be ambiguous because their real wage in terms of cloth would rise, but their real wage in terms of food would fall. The effect of a relative price change on the distribution of income can be summarized as follows:

- The factor specific to the sector whose relative price increases is definitely better off.
- The factor specific to the sector whose relative price decreases is definitely worse off.
- The change in welfare for the mobile factor is ambiguous.

International Trade in the Specific Factors Model

We just saw how changes in relative prices have strong repercussions for the distribution of income, creating both winners and losers. We now want to link this relative price change with international trade and match up the predictions for winners and losers with the trade orientation of a sector.

For trade to take place, a country must face a world relative price that differs from the relative price that would prevail in the absence of trade. Figure 4-9 shows how this relative price was determined for our specific factors economy. In Figure 4-10, we also add a relative supply curve for the world.

Why might the relative supply curve for the world be different from that for our specific factors economy? The other countries in the world could have different technologies, as in the Ricardian model. Now that our model has more than one factor of production, however, the other countries could also differ in their resources: the total amounts of land, capital, and labor available. What is important here is that the economy faces a different relative price when it is open to international trade.

The change in relative price is shown in Figure 4-10. When the economy is open to trade, the relative price of cloth is determined by the relative supply and demand for the world; this corresponds to the relative price $(P_C/P_F)^2$. If the economy could not trade, then the relative price would be lower, at $(P_C/P_F)^1$.[4] The increase in the relative price from $(P_C/P_F)^1$ to $(P_C/P_F)^2$ induces the economy to produce relatively more cloth. (This is also shown as the move from point 1 to point 2 along the economy's

---

[4]In the figure, we assumed there were no differences in preferences across countries, so we have a single relative demand curve for each country and the world as a whole.

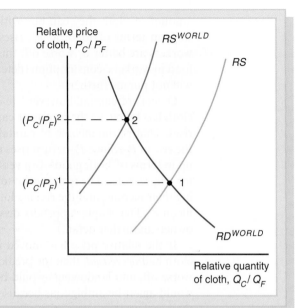

FIGURE 4-10

Trade and Relative Prices

The figure shows the relative supply curve for the specific factors economy along with the world relative supply curve. The differences between the two relative supply curves can be due to either technology or resource differences across countries. There are no differences in relative demand across countries. Opening up to trade induces an increase in the relative price from $(P_C/P_F)^1$ to $(P_C/P_F)^2$.

production possibility frontier in Figure 4-8.) At the same time, consumers respond to the higher relative price of cloth by demanding relatively more food. At the higher relative price $(P_C/P_F)^2$, the economy thus exports cloth and imports food.

If opening up to trade had been associated with a decrease in the relative price of cloth, then the changes in relative supply and demand would be reversed, and the economy would become a food exporter and a cloth importer. We can summarize both cases with the intuitive prediction that—when opening up to trade—an economy exports the good whose relative price has increased and imports the good whose relative price has decreased.[5]

Income Distribution and the Gains from Trade

We have seen how production possibilities are determined by resources and technology; how the choice of what to produce is determined by the relative price of cloth; how changes in the relative price of cloth affect the real incomes of different factors of production; and how trade affects both relative prices and the economy's response to those price changes. Now we can ask the crucial question: Who gains and who loses from international trade? We begin by asking how the welfare of particular groups is affected, and then how trade affects the welfare of the country as a whole.

To assess the effects of trade on particular groups, the key point is that international trade shifts the relative price of the goods traded. We just saw in the previous section that opening to trade will increase the relative price of the good in the new export sector. We can link this prediction with our results regarding how relative price changes translate into changes in the distribution of income. More specifically, we saw that the specific factor in the sector whose relative price increases will gain and that the specific factor in the other sector (whose relative price decreases) will lose. We also saw that the welfare changes for the mobile factor are ambiguous.

---

[5]We describe how changes in relative prices affect a country's pattern of trade in more detail in Chapter 6.

The general outcome, then, is simple: *Trade benefits the factor specific to the export sector of each country but hurts the factor specific to the import-competing sectors, with ambiguous effects on mobile factors.*

Do the gains from trade outweigh the losses? One way to try to answer this question would be to sum up the gains of the winners and the losses of the losers and compare them. The problem with this procedure is that we are comparing welfare, which is inherently subjective. A better way to assess the overall gains from trade is to ask a different question: Could those who gain from trade compensate those who lose and still be better off themselves? If so, then trade is *potentially* a source of gain to everyone.

In order to show aggregate gains from trade, we need to state some basic relationships among prices, production, and consumption. In a country that cannot trade, the output of a good must equal its consumption. If D_C is consumption of cloth and D_F consumption of food, then in a closed economy, $D_C = Q_C$ and $D_F = Q_F$. International trade makes it possible for the mix of cloth and food consumed to differ from the mix produced. While the amounts of each good that a country consumes and produces may differ, however, a country cannot spend more than it earns: The *value* of consumption must be equal to the value of production. That is,

$$P_C \times D_C + P_F \times D_F = P_C \times Q_C + P_F \times Q_F. \qquad (4\text{-}7)$$

Equation (4-7) can be rearranged to yield the following:

$$D_F - Q_F = (P_C/P_F) \times (Q_C - D_C). \qquad (4\text{-}8)$$

$D_F - Q_F$ is the economy's food *imports*, the amount by which its consumption of food exceeds its production. The right-hand side of the equation is the product of the relative price of cloth and the amount by which production of cloth exceeds consumption, that is, the economy's *exports* of cloth. The equation, then, states that imports of food equal exports of cloth times the relative price of cloth. While it does not tell us how much the economy will import or export, the equation does show that the amount the economy can afford to import is limited, or constrained, by the amount it exports. Equation (4-8) is therefore known as a **budget constraint**.[6]

Figure 4-11 illustrates two important features of the budget constraint for a trading economy. First, the slope of the budget constraint is minus P_C/P_F, the relative price of cloth . The reason is that consuming one less unit of cloth saves the economy P_C; this is enough to purchase P_C/P_F extra units of food. In other words, one unit of cloth can be exchanged on world markets for P_C/P_F units of food. Second, the budget constraint is tangent to the production possibility frontier at the chosen production point (shown as point 1 here and in Figure 4-5). Thus, the economy can always afford to consume what it produces.

To illustrate that trade is a source of potential gain for everyone, we proceed in three steps:

1. First, we notice that in the absence of trade, the economy would have to produce what it consumed, and vice versa. Thus, the *consumption* of the economy in the absence of trade would have to be a point on the *production* possibility frontier. In Figure 4-11, a typical pretrade consumption point is shown as point 2.

---

[6]The constraint that the value of consumption equals that of production (or, equivalently, that imports equal exports in value) may not hold when countries can borrow from other countries or lend to them. For now, we assume that these possibilities are not available and that the budget constraint (equation (4-8)) therefore holds. International borrowing and lending are examined in Chapter 6, which shows that an economy's consumption *over time* is still constrained by the necessity of paying its debts to foreign lenders.

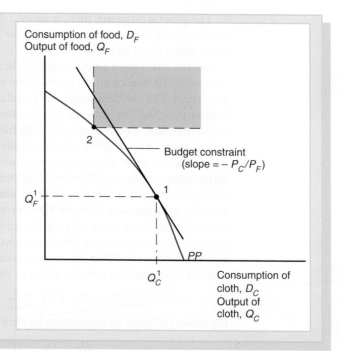

FIGURE 4-11

Budget Constraint for a Trading Economy and Gains from Trade

Point 1 represents the economy's production. The economy can choose its consumption point along its budget constraint (a line that passes through point 1 and has a slope equal to minus the relative price of cloth). Before trade, the economy must consume what it produces, such as point 2 on the production possibility frontier (*PP*). The portion of the budget constraint in the colored region consists of feasible post-trade consumption choices, with consumption of both goods higher than at pretrade point 2.

2. Next, we notice that it is possible for a trading economy to consume more of *both* goods than it would have in the absence of trade. The budget constraint in Figure 4-11 represents all the possible combinations of food and cloth that the country could consume given the world relative price of cloth. Part of that budget constraint—the part in the colored region—represents situations in which the economy consumes more of both cloth and food than it could in the absence of trade. Notice that this result does not depend on the assumption that pretrade production and consumption is at point 2; unless pretrade production is at point 1, so that trade has no effect on production at all, there is always a part of the budget constraint that allows the consumption of more of both goods.

3. Finally, observe that if the economy as a whole consumes more of both goods, then it is possible in principle to give each *individual* more of both goods. This would make everyone better off. This shows, then, that it is possible to ensure that everyone is better off as a result of trade. Of course, everyone might be even better off if they had less of one good and more of the other, but this only reinforces the conclusion that everyone has the potential to gain from trade.

The fundamental reason why trade potentially benefits a country is that it *expands the economy's choices*. This expansion of choice means that it is always possible to redistribute income in such a way that everyone gains from trade.[7]

That everyone *could* gain from trade unfortunately does not mean that everyone actually does. In the real world, the presence of losers as well as winners from trade is one of the most important reasons why trade is not free.

---

[7]The argument that trade is beneficial because it enlarges an economy's choices is much more general than this specific example. For a thorough discussion, see Paul Samuelson, "The Gains from International Trade Once Again," *Economic Journal* 72 (1962), pp. 820–829.

The Political Economy of Trade: A Preliminary View

Trade often produces losers as well as winners. This insight is crucial to understanding the considerations that actually determine trade policy in the modern world economy. Our specific factors model informs us that those who stand to lose most from trade (at least in the short run) are the immobile factors in the import-competing sector. In the real world, this includes not only the owners of capital but also a portion of the labor force in those importing-competing sectors. Some of those workers (especially lower-skilled workers) have a hard time transitioning from the import-competing sectors (where trade induces reductions in employment) to export sectors (where trade induces increases in employment). Some suffer unemployment spells as a result. In the United States, workers in the import-competing sectors earn wages substantially below the average wage, and those workers earning the lowest wage face the highest risk of separation from their current employer due to import competition. (For example, the average wage of production workers in the apparel sector in 2012 was 35 percent below the average wage for all production workers.) One result of this disparity in wages is widespread sympathy for the plight of those workers and, consequently, for restrictions on apparel imports. The gains that more affluent consumers would realize if more imports were allowed and the associated increases in employment in the export sectors (which hire, on average, relatively higher-skilled workers) do not matter as much.

Does this mean that trade should be allowed only if it doesn't hurt lower-income people? Few international economists would agree. In spite of the real importance of income distribution, most economists remain strongly in favor of more or less free trade. There are three main reasons why economists do *not* generally stress the income distribution effects of trade:

1. Income distribution effects are not specific to international trade. Every change in a nation's economy—including technological progress, shifting consumer preferences, exhaustion of old resources and discovery of new ones, and so on—affects income distribution. Why should an apparel worker, who suffers an unemployment spell due to increased import competition, be treated differently from an unemployed printing machine operator (whose newspaper employer shuts down due to competition from Internet news providers) or an unemployed construction worker laid off due to a housing slump?

2. It is always better to allow trade and compensate those who are hurt by it than to prohibit the trade. All modern industrial countries provide some sort of "safety net" of income support programs (such as unemployment benefits and subsidized retraining and relocation programs) that can cushion the losses of groups hurt by trade. Economists would argue that if this cushion is felt to be inadequate, more support rather than less trade is the answer. (This support can also be extended to all those in need, instead of indirectly assisting only those workers affected by trade.)[8]

3. Those who stand to lose from increased trade are typically better organized than those who stand to gain (because the former are more concentrated within regions and industries). This imbalance creates a bias in the political process that requires a counterweight, especially given the aggregate gains from trade. Many trade restrictions tend to favor the most organized groups, which are often not the most in need of income support (in many cases, quite the contrary).

---

[8]An op-ed by Robert Z. Lawrence and Matthew J. Slaughter in the *New York Times*, "More Trade and More Aid," argues this point (June 8, 2011).

the average price of sugar in the U.S. market has been about twice the average price on the world market. A 2000 study by the U.S. General Accounting Office estimated that those import restrictions and the associated higher sugar prices generated annual losses of $2 billion for U.S. consumers. This study was recently updated in 2013, and this cost has now risen above $3 billon, representing $10 a year for every man, woman, and child. The gains to sugar producers are substantially smaller because the import restrictions also generate distortions in the sugar market and foreign producers assigned the rights to sell sugar to the United States keep the differential between the higher U.S. price and the lower world price.

If producers and consumers were equally able to get their interests represented, this policy would never have been enacted. In absolute terms, however, each consumer suffers very little. Ten dollars a year is not much; furthermore, most of the cost is hidden, because most sugar is consumed as an ingredient in other foods rather than purchased directly. As a result, most consumers are unaware that the import quota even exists, let alone that it reduces their standard of living. Even if they were aware, $10 is not a large enough sum to provoke people into organizing protests and writing letters to their congressional representatives.

The situation of the sugar producers (those who would lose from increased trade) is quite different. The higher profits from the import quota are highly concentrated in a small number of producers. (Seventeen sugar cane farms generate more than half of the profits for the whole sugar cane industry.) Those producers are organized in trade associations that actively lobby on their members' behalf, and make large campaign contributions. (The American Sugar Alliance spent nearly $3 million in lobbying expenses in a single 12-month period leading up to the 2013 congressional vote on the U.S. Farm Bill, which reauthorizes the restrictions on U.S. imports of sugar.)

As one would expect, most of the gains from the sugar import restrictions go to that small group of sugar cane farm owners and not to their employees. Of course, the trade restrictions do prevent job losses for those workers, but the consumer cost per job saved is astronomically high: over $3 million per job saved. In addition, the sugar import restrictions also reduce employment in other sectors that rely on large quantities of sugar in their production processes. In response to the high sugar prices in the United States, for example, candy-making firms have shifted their production sites to Canada, where sugar prices are substantially lower. (There are no sugar farmers in Canada, and hence no political pressure for restrictions on sugar imports.) On net, the sugar restrictions thus generate employment *losses* for U.S. workers.

As we will see in Chapters 9 through 12, the politics of import restriction in the sugar industry is an extreme example of a kind of political process that is common in international trade. That world trade in general became steadily freer from 1945 to 1980 depended, as we will see in Chapter 10, on a special set of circumstances that controlled what is probably an inherent political bias against international trade.

International Labor Mobility

In this section, we will show how the specific factors model can be adapted to analyze the effects of labor mobility. In the modern world, restrictions on the flow of labor are legion—just about every country imposes restrictions on immigration. Thus, labor mobility is less prevalent in practice than capital mobility. However, the analysis of physical capital movements is more complex, as it is embedded along with other factors in a multinational's decision to invest abroad (see Chapter 8). Still, it is important to understand the international economic forces that drive *desired* migration of workers across borders and the short-run consequences of those migration flows whenever they are realized. We will also explore the long-run consequences of changes in a country's labor and capital endowments in the next chapter.

In the previous sections, we saw how workers move between the cloth and food sectors within one country until the wages in the two sectors are equalized. Whenever international migration is possible, workers will also want to move from the low-wage to the high-wage country.[10] To keep things simple and to focus on international migration, let's assume that two countries produce a single good with labor and an immobile factor, land. Since there is only a single good, there is no reason to trade it; however, there will be "trade" in labor services when workers move in search of higher wages. In the absence of migration, wage differences across countries can be driven by technology differences, or alternatively, by differences in the availability of land relative to labor.

Figure 4-13 illustrates the causes and effects of international labor mobility. It is very similar to Figure 4-4, except that the horizontal axis now represents the total world labor force (instead of the labor force in a given country). The two marginal product curves now represent production of the same good in different countries (instead of the production of two different goods in the same country). We do not multiply those curves by the prices of the good; instead, we assume the wages measured on the vertical axis represent real wages (the wage divided by the price of the unique good in each country). Initially, we assume there are OL^1 workers in Home and L^1O^* workers in Foreign. Given those employment levels, technology and land endowment differences are such that real wages are higher in Foreign (point B) than in Home (point C).

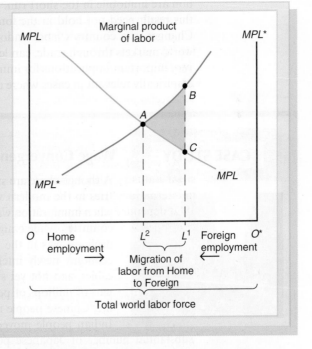

FIGURE 4-13

Causes and Effects of International Labor Mobility

Initially, OL^1 workers are employed in Home, while L^1O^* workers are employed in Foreign. Labor migrates from Home to Foreign until OL^2 workers are employed in Home, L^2O^* in Foreign, and wages are equalized.

[10]We assume workers' tastes are similar so location decisions are based on wage differentials. Actual wage differentials across countries are very large—large enough that, for many workers, they outweigh personal tastes for particular countries.

Now suppose that workers are able to move between these two countries. Workers will move from Home to Foreign. This movement will reduce the Home labor force and thus raise the real wage in Home, while increasing the labor force and reducing the real wage in Foreign. If there are no obstacles to labor movement, this process will continue until the real wage rates are equalized. The eventual distribution of the world's labor force will be one with OL^2 workers in Home and L^2O^* workers in Foreign (point A).

Three points should be noted about this redistribution of the world's labor force.

1. It leads to a convergence of real wage rates. Real wages rise in Home and fall in Foreign.
2. It increases the world's output as a whole. Foreign's output rises by the area under its marginal product curve from L^1 to L^2, while Home's falls by the corresponding area under its marginal product curve. (See appendix for details.) We see from the figure that Foreign's gain is larger than Home's loss, by an amount equal to the colored area ABC in the figure.
3. Despite this gain, some people are hurt by the change. Those who would originally have worked in Home receive higher real wages, but those who would originally have worked in Foreign receive lower real wages. Landowners in Foreign benefit from the larger labor supply, but landowners in Home are made worse off.

As in the case of the gains from international trade, then, international labor mobility, while allowing everyone to be made better off in principle, leaves some groups worse off in practice. This main result would not change in a more complex model where countries produce and trade different goods, so long as some factors of production are immobile in the short run. However, we will see in the following chapter that this result need not hold in the long run when all factors are mobile across sectors. Changes in a country's labor endowment, so long as the country is integrated into world markets through trade, can leave the welfare of all factors unchanged. This has very important implications for immigration in the long run and has been shown to be empirically relevant in cases where countries experience large immigration increases.

CASE STUDY

Wage Convergence in the Age of Mass Migration

Although there are substantial movements of people between countries in the modern world, the truly heroic age of labor mobility—when immigration was a major source of population growth in some countries, while emigration caused population in other countries to decline—was in the late 19th and early 20th centuries. In a global economy newly integrated by railroads, steamships, and telegraph cables, and not yet subject to many legal restrictions on migration, tens of millions of people moved long distances in search of a better life. Chinese people moved to Southeast Asia and California, while Indian people moved to Africa and the Caribbean; in addition, a substantial number of Japanese people moved to Brazil. However, the greatest migration involved people from the periphery of Europe—from Scandinavia, Ireland, Italy, and Eastern Europe—who moved to places where land was abundant and wages were high: the United States, Canada, Argentina, and Australia.

TABLE 4-1	Real Wage, 1870 (U.S. = 100)	Percentage Increase in Real Wage, 1870–1913
Destination Countries		
Argentina	53	51
Australia	110	1
Canada	86	121
United States	100	47
Origin Countries		
Ireland	43	84
Italy	23	112
Norway	24	193
Sweden	24	250

Source: Jeffrey G. Williamson, "The Evolution of Global Labor Markets Since 1830: Background Evidence and Hypotheses," *Explorations in Economic History* 32 (1995), pp. 141–196.

Did this process cause the kind of real wage convergence that our model predicts? Indeed, it did. Table 4-1 shows real wages in 1870, and the change in these wages up to the eve of World War I, for four major "destination" countries and for four important "origin" countries. As the table shows, at the beginning of the period, real wages were much higher in the destination than in the origin countries. Over the next four decades real wages rose in all countries, but (except for a surprisingly large increase in Canada) they increased much more rapidly in the origin than in the destination countries, suggesting that migration actually did move the world toward (although not by any means all the way to) wage equalization.

As documented in the case study on the U.S. economy, legal restrictions put an end to the age of mass migration after World War I. For that and other reasons (notably a decline in world trade and the direct effects of two world wars), convergence in real wages came to a halt and even reversed itself for several decades, only to resume in the postwar years.

CASE STUDY   Foreign Workers: The Story of the GCC

Following the discovery of large oil and natural gas reserves in the mid-1900s, the Gulf Cooperation Council (GCC) countries' economies have relied heavily on foreign workers.[11] As Figure 4-14 shows, the mean share of foreign workers in the GCC countries has steadily increased, and made up

[11]See GCC countries: Bahrain, Kuwait, Oman, Qatar, Saudi Arabia, and United Arab Emirates.

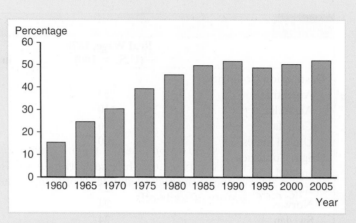

FIGURE 4-14

Mean Migrant Stock as a Percentage of the GCC Population

Source: World Development Indicators Online database.

50 percent of the population in 2005. While the influx of workers to the Gulf has been mainly from Arab and Indian subcontinent countries, recently there has been a significant inflow of people from Europe and North America.[12] The Gulf has become home to the regional headquarters of many multinational corporations (for instance, Oracle, Microsoft, and IBM) generating demand for highly skilled foreign workers mainly from the West with professional and technical skills needed to run these companies in sync with their home country operations. With such a large presence, one has to wonder about the implications for the GCC economies of large numbers of expatriates. First of all, the standards of living reflected in Gross Domestic Product (GDP) per capita have increased tremendously in the last three decades. Kuwait, Qatar and the United Arab Emirates (UAE) consistently rank in the top 15 countries in terms of standards of living.

The large number of foreigners puts serious pressures on the GCC economies. The proportion of foreign workers to the total population is even higher when one looks only at the labor force.[13] This fact results in severe competition for local workers, which prompted all GCC governments to issue labor protective policies that have their own share of consequences.[14] Furthermore, foreigners are separated into two types of accommodations based on their skill level.[15] While no foreign

---

[12]See G. Naufal and C. Vargas-Silva. "Migrant Transfers in the MENA Region: A Two Way Street in Which Traffic Is Changing." *Migration Letters* 7(2), 2010, pp. 168–178.

[13]See N. Ann Colton. "The International Political Economy of Gulf Migration." *Viewpoints* Special Edition Migration and the Gulf. *Middle East Institute Viewpoints* (February 2010), pp. 34–36.

[14]For example, in the United Arab Emirates, the government has introduced Emiratization as a policy aimed at securing jobs for the local labor force.

[15]Low-skilled workers are housed in labor camps (similar to army barracks), and high-skilled workers are housed in regular accommodations.

worker can become a citizen or own property, low-skilled workers cannot even sponsor their families to join them. These restrictions have turned migration to the Gulf into a temporary guest worker program. The nature of the foreign labor market in the Gulf has installed a sense of unease among foreign workers, which is explicitly expressed in the size of remittances. The official remittances from the GCC economies in 2007 surpassed US$37 billion, making the Gulf one of the most active remitting regions in the world.

Thus, the GCC countries present a unique and interesting case of migration. While the large share of foreigners in the population has subjected the local economies to certain complications, foreign workers have also helped the local population achieve one of the highest standards of living in the world. This is the story of the GCC; a story of trade-offs.

SUMMARY

1. International trade often has strong effects on the distribution of income within countries, so that it often produces losers as well as winners. Income distribution effects arise for two reasons: Factors of production cannot move instantaneously and costlessly from one industry to another, and changes in an economy's output mix have differential effects on the demand for different factors of production.

2. A useful model of income distribution effects of international trade is the *specific factors* model, which allows for a distinction between general-purpose factors that can move between sectors and factors specific to particular uses. In this model, differences in resources can cause countries to have different relative supply curves and thus cause international trade.

3. In the specific factors model, factors specific to export sectors in each country gain from trade, while factors specific to import-competing sectors lose. Mobile factors that can work in either sector may either gain or lose.

4. Trade nonetheless produces overall gains in the limited sense that those who gain could in principle compensate those who lose while still remaining better off than before.

5. Most economists do not regard the effects of international trade on income distribution a good reason to limit this trade. In its distributional effects, trade is no different from many other forms of economic change, which are not normally regulated. Furthermore, economists would prefer to address the problem of income distribution directly, rather than by interfering with trade flows.

6. Nonetheless, in the actual politics of trade policy, income distribution is of crucial importance. This is true in particular because those who lose from trade are usually a much more informed, cohesive, and organized group than those who gain.

7. International factor movements can sometimes substitute for trade, so it is not surprising that international migration of labor is similar in its causes and effects to international trade. Labor moves from countries where it is abundant to countries where it is scarce. This movement raises total world output, but it also generates strong income distribution effects, so that some groups are hurt as a result.

KEY TERMS

budget constraint, p. 97
diminishing returns, p. 86
marginal product of labor,
    p. 86

mobile factor, p. 85
production function, p. 86
production possibility frontier,
    p. 86

specific factor, p. 85
specific factors model, p. 84
U.S. Trade Adjustment
    Assistance program, p. 101

| PROBLEMS | MyEconLab |

1. A country opts for free trade while some workers remain unemployed in the import-competing sector. Why? Given real wage rate in Thailand is higher than Bangladesh, how would international trade affect real wages between them under perfectly mobile labor movement?

2. An economy can produce good 1 using labor and capital and good 2 using labor and land. The total supply of labor is 100 units. Given the supply of capital, the outputs of the two goods depend on labor input as follows:

Labor Input to Good 1	Output of Good 1	Labor Input to Good 2	Output of Good 2
0	0.0	0	0.0
10	25.1	10	39.8
20	38.1	20	52.5
30	48.6	30	61.8
40	57.7	40	69.3
50	66.0	50	75.8
60	73.6	60	81.5
70	80.7	70	86.7
80	87.4	80	91.4
90	93.9	90	95.9
100	100	100	100

a. Graph the production functions for good 1 and good 2.
b. Graph the production possibility frontier. Why is it curved?

3. The marginal product of labor curves corresponding to the production functions in problem 2 are as follows:

Workers Employed	MPL in Sector 1	MPL in Sector 2
10	1.51	1.59
20	1.14	1.05
30	1.00	.82
40	.87	.69
50	.78	.60
60	.74	.54
70	.69	.50
80	.66	.46
90	.63	.43
100	.60	.40

a. Suppose the price of good 2 relative to that of good 1 is 2. Determine graphically the wage rate and the allocation of labor between the two sectors.
b. Using the graph drawn for problem 2, determine the output of each sector. Then confirm graphically that the slope of the production possibility frontier at that point equals the relative price.
c. Suppose the relative price of good 2 falls to 1.3. Repeat (a) and (b).
d. Calculate the effects of the price change from 2 to 1.3 on the income of the specific factors in sectors 1 and 2.

4. Consider two countries (Home and Foreign) that produce goods 1 (with labor and capital) and 2 (with labor and land) according to the production functions described in problems 2 and 3. Initially, both countries have the same supply of labor (100 units each), capital, and land. The capital stock in Home then grows. This change shifts out both the production curve for good 1 as a function of labor employed (described in problem 2) and the associated marginal product of labor curve (described in problem 3). Nothing happens to the production and marginal product curves for good 2.
   a. Show how the increase in the supply of capital for Home affects its production possibility frontier.
   b. On the same graph, draw the relative supply curve for both the Home and the Foreign economy.
   c. If those two economies open up to trade, what will be the pattern of trade (i.e., which country exports which good)?
   d. Describe how opening up to trade affects all three factors (labor, capital, land) in both countries.

5. In Home and Foreign, there are two factors each of production, land, and labor used to produce only one good. The land supply in each country and the technology of production are exactly the same. The marginal product of labor in each country depends on employment as follows:

Number of Workers Employed	Marginal Product of Last Worker
1	20
2	19
3	18
4	17
5	16
6	15
7	14
8	13
9	12
10	11
11	10

Initially, there are 11 workers employed in Home, but only 3 workers in Foreign. Find the effect of free movement of labor from Home to Foreign on employment, production, real wages, and the income of landowners in each country.

6. Using the numerical example in problem 5, assume now that Foreign limits immigration so that only 2 workers can move there from Home. Calculate how the movement of these two workers affects the income of five different groups:
   a. Workers who were originally in Foreign
   b. Foreign landowners
   c. Workers who stay in Home
   d. Home landowners
   e. The workers who do move

7. A country produces two crops—paddy and wheat. Given the price of paddy (Pp) and wheat (Pw), the relationship of labor allocation is shown as $MPLp \times Pp = MPLw \times Pw = w$, where $MPLp$ and $MPLw$ are marginal products of labor for the two. If wheat's price increases by 10 percent with no changes in paddy prices, what will happen to labor demand for wheat production, and the market wage rate?

FURTHER READINGS

Avinash Dixit and Victor Norman. *Theory of International Trade.* Cambridge: Cambridge University Press, 1980. The problem of establishing gains from trade when some people may be made worse off has been the subject of a long debate. Dixit and Norman show it is always possible in principle for a country's government to use taxes and subsidies to redistribute income in such a way that everyone is better off with free trade than with no trade.

Lawrence Edwards and Robert Z. Lawrence. 2013. *Rising Tide: Is Growth in Emerging Economies Good for the United States?* Peterson Institute for International Economics. An accessible book that examines how increased trade with emerging economies (such as China and India) has affected the United States and its workers.

Hanson, Gordon H. 2009. "The Economic Consequences of the International Migration of Labor." *Annual Review of Economics* 1 (1): 179–208. A survey paper reviewing how increased migration has affected both sending and recipient countries.

Douglas A. Irwin, *Free Trade under Fire,* 3rd edition. Princeton, NJ: Princeton University Press, 2009. An accessible book that provides numerous details and supporting data for the argument that freer trade generates overall welfare gains. Chapter 4 discusses the connection between trade and unemployment in detail (an issue that was briefly discussed in this chapter).

Charles P. Kindleberger. *Europe's Postwar Growth: The Role of Labor Supply.* Cambridge: Harvard University Press, 1967. A good account of the role of labor migration during its height in Europe.

Robert A. Mundell. "International Trade and Factor Mobility." *American Economic Review* 47 (1957), pp. 321–335. The paper that first laid out the argument that trade and factor movement can substitute for each other.

Michael Mussa. "Tariffs and the Distribution of Income: The Importance of Factor Specificity, Substitutability, and Intensity in the Short and Long Run." *Journal of Political Economy* 82 (1974), pp. 1191–1204. An extension of the specific factors model that relates it to the factor proportions model of Chapter 5.

J. Peter Neary. "Short-Run Capital Specificity and the Pure Theory of International Trade." *Economic Journal* 88 (1978), pp. 488–510. A further treatment of the specific factors model that stresses how differing assumptions about mobility of factors between sectors affect the model's conclusions.

Mancur Olson. *The Logic of Collective Action.* Cambridge: Harvard University Press, 1965. A highly influential book that argues the proposition that in practice, government policies favor small, concentrated groups over large ones.

David Ricardo. *The Principles of Political Economy and Taxation.* Homewood, IL: Irwin, 1963. While Ricardo's *Principles* emphasizes the national gains from trade at one point, elsewhere in his book the conflict of interest between landowners and capitalists is a central issue.

MyEconLab Can Help You Get a Better Grade

MyEconLab   If your exam were tomorrow, would you be ready? For each chapter, MyEconLab Practice Tests and Study Plans pinpoint sections you have mastered and those you need to study. That way, you are more efficient with your study time, and you are better prepared for your exams.

To see how it works, turn to page 41 and then go to

www.myeconlab.com

Further Details on Specific Factors

The specific factors model developed in this chapter is such a convenient tool of analysis that we take the time here to spell out some of its details more fully. We give a fuller treatment of two related issues: (1) the relationship between marginal and total product within each sector and (2) the income distribution effects of relative price changes.

Marginal and Total Product

In the text, we illustrated the production function of cloth in two different ways. In Figure 4-1, we showed total output as a function of labor input, holding capital constant. We then observed that the slope of that curve is the marginal product of labor and illustrated that marginal product in Figure 4-2. We now want to demonstrate that the total output is measured by the area under the marginal product curve. (Students familiar with calculus will find this obvious: Marginal product is the derivative of total, so total is the integral of marginal. Even for these students, however, an intuitive approach can be helpful.)

In Figure 4A-1, we show once again the marginal product curve in cloth production. Suppose we employ L_C person-hours. How can we show the total output of cloth? Let's approximate this using the marginal product curve. First, let's ask what would happen if we used slightly fewer person-hours, say dL_C fewer. Then output would be less. The fall in output would be approximately

$$dL_C \times MPL_C,$$

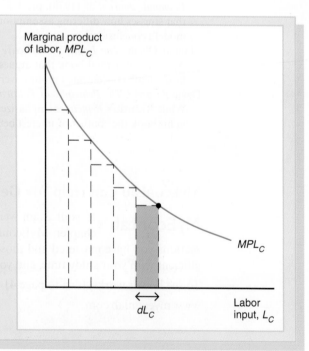

FIGURE 4A-1

Showing that Output Is Equal to the Area under the Marginal Product Curve

By approximating the marginal product curve with a series of thin rectangles, one can show that the total output of cloth is equal to the area under the curve.

that is, the reduction in the work force times the marginal product of labor at the initial level of employment. This reduction in output is represented by the area of the colored rectangle in Figure 4A-1. Now subtract another few person-hours; the output loss will be another rectangle. This time the rectangle will be taller because the marginal product of labor rises as the quantity of labor falls. If we continue this process until all the labor is gone, our approximation of the total output loss will be the sum of all the rectangles shown in the figure. When no labor is employed, however, output will fall to zero. So we can approximate the total output of the cloth sector by the sum of the areas of all the rectangles under the marginal product curve.

This is, however, only an approximation because we used the marginal product of only the first person-hour in each batch of labor removed. We can get a better approximation if we take smaller groups—the smaller the better. As the groups of labor removed get infinitesimally small, however, the rectangles get thinner and thinner, and we approximate ever more closely the total area under the marginal product curve. In the end, then, we find the total output of cloth produced with labor L_C, Q_C is equal to the area under the marginal product of labor curve MPL_C up to L_C.

Relative Prices and the Distribution of Income

Figure 4A-2 uses the result we just found to show the distribution of income within the cloth sector. We saw that cloth employers hire labor L_C until the value of the workers' marginal product, $P_C \times MPL_C$, is equal to the wage w. We can rewrite this in terms of the real wage of cloth as $MPL_C = w/P_C$. Thus, at a given real wage, say $(w/P_C)^1$, the marginal product curve in Figure 4A-2 tells us that L_C^1 worker-hours will be employed. The total output produced with those workers is given by the area under the marginal product curve up to L_C^1. This output is divided into the real income (in terms of cloth) of workers and capital owners. The portion paid to workers is the real wage $(w/P_C)^1$ times the employment level L_C^1, which is the area of the rectangle shown. The remainder is the real income of the capital owners. We can determine the

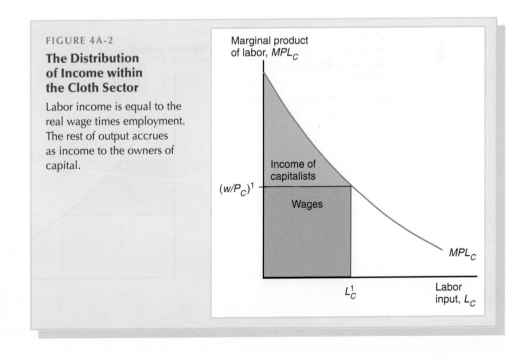

FIGURE 4A-2

The Distribution of Income within the Cloth Sector

Labor income is equal to the real wage times employment. The rest of output accrues as income to the owners of capital.

distribution of food production between labor and landowners in the same way, as a function of the real wage in terms of food, w/P_F.

Suppose the relative price of cloth now rises. We saw in Figure 4-7 that a rise in P_C/P_F lowers the real wage in terms of cloth (because the wage rises by less than P_C) while raising it in terms of food. The effects of this on the income of capitalists and landowners can be seen in Figures 4A-3 and 4A-4. In the cloth sector, the real wage falls from $(w/P_C)^1$ to $(w/P_C)^2$; as a result, capitalists receive increased real income in

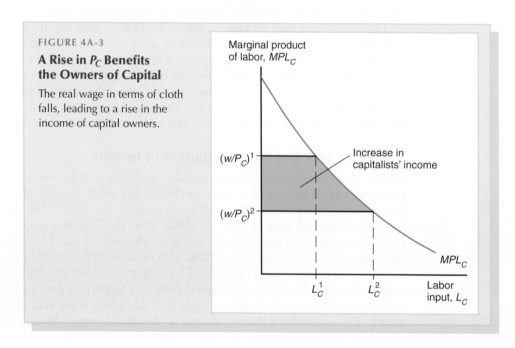

FIGURE 4A-3

A Rise in P_C Benefits the Owners of Capital

The real wage in terms of cloth falls, leading to a rise in the income of capital owners.

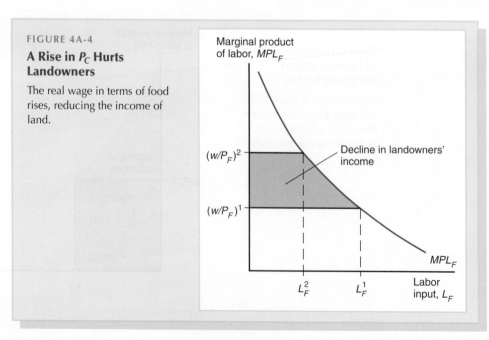

FIGURE 4A-4

A Rise in P_C Hurts Landowners

The real wage in terms of food rises, reducing the income of land.

terms of cloth. In the food sector, the real wage rises from $(w/P_F)^1$ to $(w/P_F)^2$, and landowners receive less real income in terms of food.

This effect on real income is reinforced by the change in P_C/P_F itself. The real income of capital owners in terms of food rises by more than their real income in terms of cloth—because food is now relatively cheaper than cloth. Conversely, the real income of landowners in terms of cloth drops by more than their real income in terms of food—because cloth is now relatively more expensive.

CHAPTER 5

RESOURCES AND TRADE: THE HECKSCHER-OHLIN MODEL

I f labor were the only factor of production, as the Ricardian model assumes, comparative advantage could arise only because of international differences in labor productivity. In the real world, however, while trade is partly explained by differences in labor productivity, it also reflects differences in countries' *resources*. Canada exports forest products to the United States not because its lumberjacks are more productive relative to their U.S. counterparts but because sparsely populated Canada has more forested land per capita than the United States. Thus, a realistic view of trade must allow for the importance not just of labor but also of other factors of production such as land, capital, and mineral resources.

To explain the role of resource differences in trade, this chapter examines a model in which resource differences are the *only* source of trade. This model shows that comparative advantage is influenced by the interaction between nations' resources (the relative **abundance of factors** of production) and the technology of production (which influences the relative **intensity** with which different **factors** of production are used in the production of different goods). Some of these ideas were presented in the specific factors model of Chapter 4, but the model we study in this chapter puts the interaction between abundance and intensity in sharper relief by looking at long-run outcomes when all factors of production are mobile across sectors.

That international trade is largely driven by differences in countries' resources is one of the most influential theories in international economics. Developed by two Swedish economists, Eli Heckscher and Bertil Ohlin (Ohlin received the Nobel Prize in economics in 1977), the theory is often referred to as the **Heckscher-Ohlin theory**. Because the theory emphasizes the interplay between the proportions in which different factors of production are available in different countries and the proportions in which they are used in producing different goods, it is also referred to as the **factor-proportions theory**.

To develop the factor-proportions theory, we begin by describing an economy that does not trade and then ask what happens when two such economies trade with each other. We will see that as opposed to the Ricardian model with a single factor of production, trade can affect the distribution of income across factors, even in the long run. We discuss the extent to which trade may be contributing to increases in wage inequality in developed countries. We then conclude with a further review of the empirical evidence for (and against) the predictions of the factor-proportions theory of trade.

LEARNING GOALS

After reading this chapter, you will be able to:

- Explain how differences in resources generate a specific pattern of trade.
- Discuss why the gains from trade will not be equally spread even in the long run and identify the likely winners and losers.
- Understand the possible links between increased trade and rising wage inequality in the developed world.
- See how empirical patterns of trade and factor prices support some (but not all) of the predictions of the factor-proportions theory.

Model of a Two-Factor Economy

In this chapter, we'll focus on the simplest version of the factor-proportions model, sometimes referred to as "2 by 2 by 2": two countries, two goods, two factors of production. In our example, we'll call the two countries Home and Foreign. We will stick with the same two goods, cloth (measured in yards) and food (measured in calories), that we used in the specific factors model of Chapter 4. The key difference is that in this chapter, we assume that the immobile factors that were specific to each sector (capital in cloth, land in food) are now mobile in the long run. Thus, land used for farming can be used to build a textile plant; conversely, the capital used to pay for a power loom can be used to pay for a tractor. To keep things simple, we model a single additional factor that we call capital, which is used in conjunction with labor to produce either cloth or food. In the long run, both capital and labor can move across sectors, thus equalizing their returns (rental rate and wage) in both sectors.

Prices and Production

Both cloth and food are produced using capital and labor. The amount of each good produced, given how much capital and labor are employed in each sector, is determined by a production function for each good:

$$Q_C = Q_C(K_C, L_C),$$
$$Q_F = Q_F(K_F, L_F),$$

where Q_C and Q_F are the output levels of cloth and food, K_C and L_C are the amounts of capital and labor employed in cloth production, and K_F and L_F are the amounts of capital and labor employed in food production. Overall, the economy has a fixed supply of capital K and labor L that is divided between employment in the two sectors.

We define the following expressions that are related to the two production technologies:

$$a_{KC} = \text{capital used to produce one yard of cloth}$$
$$a_{LC} = \text{labor used to produce one yard of cloth}$$
$$a_{KF} = \text{capital used to produce one calorie of food}$$
$$a_{LF} = \text{labor used to produce one calorie of food}$$

These unit input requirements are very similar to the ones defined in the Ricardian model (for labor only). However, there is one crucial difference: In these definitions, we speak of the quantity of capital or labor *used* to produce a given amount of cloth or food, rather than the quantity *required* to produce that amount. The reason for this change from the Ricardian model is that when there are two factors of production, there may be some room for choice in the use of inputs.

In general, those choices will depend on the factor prices for labor and capital. However, let's first look at a special case in which there is only one way to produce each good. Consider the following numerical example: Production of one yard of cloth requires a combination of two work-hours and two machine-hours. The production of food is more automated; as a result, production of one calorie of food requires only one work-hour along with three machine-hours. Thus, all the unit input requirements are fixed at $a_{KC} = 2$; $a_{LC} = 2$; $a_{KF} = 3$; $a_{LF} = 1$; and there is no possibility of substituting labor for capital or vice versa. Assume that an economy is endowed with 3,000 units of machine-hours along with 2,000 units of work-hours. In this special case of no factor substitution in production, the economy's production possibility frontier can be derived using those two resource constraints for capital and labor. Production of Q_C yards of cloth requires $2Q_C = a_{KC} \times Q_C$ machine-hours and $2Q_C = a_{LC} \times Q_C$ work-hours. Similarly, production of Q_F calories of food requires $3Q_F = a_{KF} \times Q_F$ machine-hours and $1Q_F = a_{LF} \times Q_F$ work-hours. The total machine-hours used for both cloth and food production cannot exceed the total supply of capital:

$$a_{KC} \times Q_C + a_{KF} \times Q_F \le K, \text{ or } 2Q_C + 3Q_F \le 3,000 \qquad (5\text{-}1)$$

This is the resource constraint for capital. Similarly, the resource constraint for labor states that the total work-hours used in production cannot exceed the total supply of labor:

$$a_{LC} \times Q_C + a_{LF} \times Q_F \le L, \text{ or } 2Q_C + Q_F \le 2,000 \qquad (5\text{-}2)$$

Figure 5-1 shows the implications of (5-1) and (5-2) for the production possibilities in our numerical example. Each resource constraint is drawn in the same way we drew the production possibility line for the Ricardian case in Figure 3-1. In this case, however, the economy must produce subject to *both* constraints, so the production possibility frontier is the kinked line shown in red. If the economy specializes in food production (point 1), then it can produce 1,000 calories of food. At that production point, there is spare labor capacity: Only 1,000 work-hours out of 2,000 are employed. Conversely, if the economy specializes in cloth production (point 2), then it can produce 1,000 yards of cloth. At that production point, there is spare capital capacity: Only 2,000 machine-hours out of 3,000 are employed. At production point 3, the economy is employing all of its labor and capital resources (1,500 machine-hours and

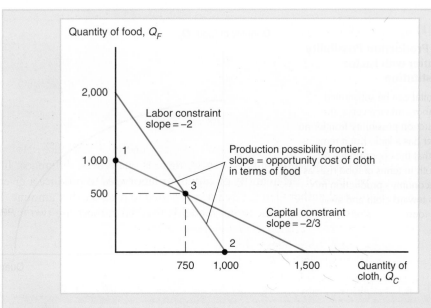

FIGURE 5-1

The Production Possibility Frontier Without Factor Substitution: Numerical Example

If capital cannot be substituted for labor or vice versa, the production possibility frontier in the factor-proportions model would be defined by two resource constraints: The economy can't use more than the available supply of labor (2,000 work-hours) or capital (3,000 machine-hours). So the production possibility frontier is defined by the red line in this figure. At point 1, the economy specializes in food production, and not all available work-hours are employed. At point 2, the economy specializes in cloth, and not all available machine-hours are employed. At production point 3, the economy employs all of its labor and capital resources. The important feature of the production possibility frontier is that the opportunity cost of cloth in terms of food isn't constant: It rises from $^2/_3$ to 2 when the economy's mix of production shifts toward cloth.

1,500 work-hours in cloth production, and 1,500 machine-hours along with 500 work-hours in food production).[1]

The important feature of this production possibility frontier is that the opportunity cost of producing an extra yard of cloth in terms of food is not constant. When the economy is producing mostly food (to the left of point 3), then there is spare labor capacity. Producing two fewer units of food releases six machine-hours that can be used to produce three yards of cloth: The opportunity cost of cloth is $^2/_3$. When the economy is producing mostly cloth (to the right of point 3), then there is spare capital capacity. Producing two fewer units of food releases two work-hours that can be used to produce one yard of cloth: The opportunity cost of cloth is 2. Thus, the opportunity cost of cloth is higher when more units of cloth are being produced.

---

[1]The case of no factor substitution is a special one in which there is only a single production point that fully employs both factors; some factors are left unemployed at all the other production points on the production possibilities frontier. In the more general case below with factor substitution, this peculiarity disappears, and both factors are fully employed along the entire production possibility frontier.

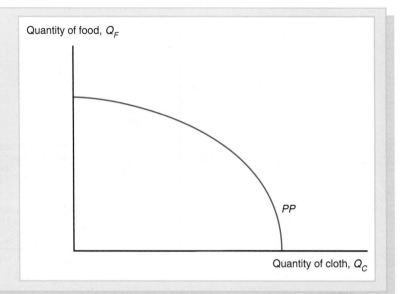

FIGURE 5-2

FIGURE 5-2

The Production Possibility Frontier with Factor Substitution

If capital can be substituted for labor and vice versa, the production possibility frontier no longer has a kink. But it remains true that the opportunity cost of cloth in terms of food rises as the economy's production mix shifts toward cloth and away from food.

Now let's make the model more realistic and allow the possibility of substituting capital for labor and vice versa in production. This substitution removes the kink in the production possibility frontier; instead, the frontier PP has the bowed shape shown in Figure 5-2. The bowed shape tells us that the opportunity cost in terms of food of producing one more unit of cloth rises as the economy produces more cloth and less food. That is, our basic insight about how opportunity costs change with the mix of production remains valid.

Where on the production possibility frontier does the economy produce? It depends on prices. Specifically, the economy produces at the point that maximizes the value of production. Figure 5-3 shows what this implies. The value of the economy's production is

$$V = P_C \times Q_C + P_F \times Q_F,$$

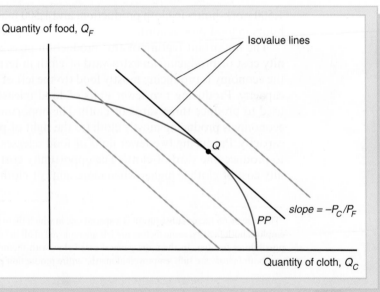

FIGURE 5-3

Prices and Production

The economy produces at the point that maximizes the value of production given the prices it faces; this is the point on the highest possible isovalue line. At that point, the opportunity cost of cloth in terms of food is equal to the relative price of cloth, P_C/P_F.

where P_C and P_F are the prices of cloth and food, respectively. An isovalue line—a line along which the value of output is constant—has a slope of $-P_C/P_F$. The economy produces at the point Q, the point on the production possibility frontier that touches the highest possible isovalue line. At that point, the slope of the production possibility frontier is equal to $-P_C/P_F$. So the opportunity cost in terms of food of producing another unit of cloth is equal to the relative price of cloth.

Choosing the Mix of Inputs

As we have noted, in a two-factor model producers may have room for choice in the use of inputs. A farmer, for example, can choose between using relatively more mechanized equipment (capital) and fewer workers, or vice versa. Thus, the farmer can choose how much labor and capital to use per unit of output produced. In each sector, then, producers will face not fixed input requirements (as in the Ricardian model) but trade-offs like the one illustrated by curve *II* in Figure 5-4, which shows alternative input combinations that can be used to produce one calorie of food.

What input choice will producers actually make? It depends on the relative costs of capital and labor. If capital rental rates are high and wages low, farmers will choose to produce using relatively little capital and a lot of labor; on the other hand, if the rental rates are low and wages high, they will save on labor and use a lot more capital. If w is the wage rate and r the rental cost of capital, then the input choice will depend on the ratio of these two **factor prices**, w/r.[2] The relationship between factor prices and the ratio of labor to capital use in production of food is shown in Figure 5-5 as the curve *FF*.

There is a corresponding relationship between w/r and the labor-capital ratio in cloth production. This relationship is shown in Figure 5-5 as the curve *CC*. As drawn, *CC* is shifted out relative to *FF*, indicating that at any given factor prices, production of cloth will always use more labor relative to capital than will production of food. When this is true, we say that production of cloth is *labor-intensive*, while production of food is *capital-intensive*. Notice that the definition of intensity depends on the ratio of labor to capital used in production, not the ratio of labor or capital to output. Thus a good cannot be both capital- and labor-intensive.

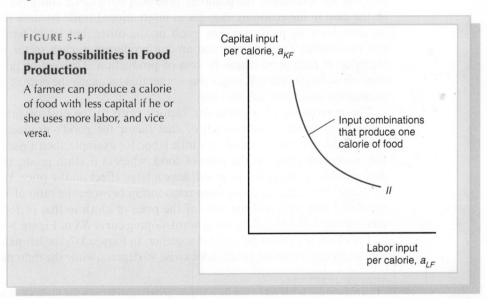

FIGURE 5-4

Input Possibilities in Food Production

A farmer can produce a calorie of food with less capital if he or she uses more labor, and vice versa.

Capital input per calorie, a_{KF}

Input combinations that produce one calorie of food

II

Labor input per calorie, a_{LF}

---

[2] The optimal choice of the labor-capital ratio is explored at greater length in the appendix to this chapter.

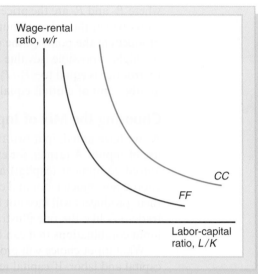

FIGURE 5-5

Factor Prices and Input Choices

In each sector, the ratio of labor to capital used in production depends on the cost of labor relative to the cost of capital, w/r. The curve *FF* shows the labor-capital ratio choices in food production, while the curve *CC* shows the corresponding choices in cloth production. At any given wage-rental ratio, cloth production uses a higher labor-capital ratio; when this is the case, we say that cloth production is *labor-intensive* and that food production is *capital-intensive*.

The *CC* and *FF* curves in Figure 5-5 are called relative factor demand curves; they are very similar to the relative demand curve for goods. Their downward slope characterizes the substitution effect in the producers' factor demand. As the wage w rises relative to the rental rate r, producers substitute capital for labor in their production decisions. The previous case we considered with no factor substitution is a limiting case, where the relative demand curve is a vertical line: The ratio of labor to capital demanded is fixed and does not vary with changes in the wage-rental ratio w/r. In the remainder of this chapter, we consider the more general case with factor substitution, where the relative factor demand curves are downward sloping.

Factor Prices and Goods Prices

Suppose for a moment the economy produces both cloth and food. (This need not be the case if the economy engages in international trade because it might specialize completely in producing one good or the other; but let us temporarily ignore this possibility.) Then competition among producers in each sector will ensure that the price of each good equals its cost of production. The cost of producing a good depends on factor prices: If wages rise—other things equal—the price of any good whose production uses labor will also rise.

The importance of a particular factor's price to the cost of producing a good depends, however, on how much of that factor the good's production involves. If food production makes use of very little labor, for example, then a rise in the wage will not have much effect on the price of food, whereas if cloth production uses a great deal of labor, a rise in the wage *will* have a large effect on the price. We can therefore conclude that there is a one-to-one relationship between the ratio of the wage rate to the rental rate, w/r, and the ratio of the price of cloth to that of food, P_C/P_F. This relationship is illustrated by the upward-sloping curve *SS* in Figure 5-6.[3]

Let's look at Figures 5-5 and 5-6 together. In Figure 5-7, the left panel is Figure 5-6 (of the *SS* curve) turned counterclockwise 90 degrees, while the right panel reproduces

---

[3] This relationship holds only when the economy produces both cloth and food, which is associated with a given range for the relative price of cloth. If the relative price rises beyond a given upper-bound level, then the economy specializes in cloth production; conversely, if the relative price drops below a lower-bound level, then the economy specializes in food production.

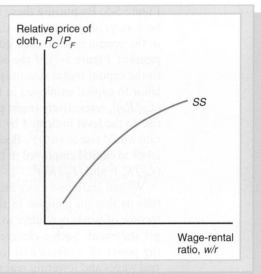

FIGURE 5-6

Factor Prices and Goods Prices

Because cloth production is labor-intensive while food production is capital-intensive, there is a one-to-one relationship between the factor price ratio w/r and the relative price of cloth P_C/P_F; the higher the relative cost of labor, the higher must be the relative price of the labor-intensive good. The relationship is illustrated by the curve SS.

Relative price of cloth, P_C/P_F

SS

Wage-rental ratio, w/r

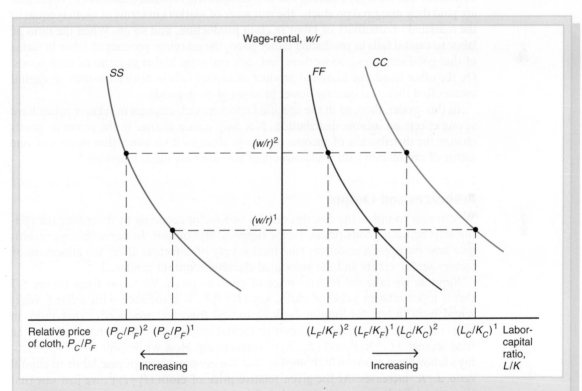

Wage-rental, w/r

SS FF CC

$(w/r)^2$

$(w/r)^1$

Relative price of cloth, P_C/P_F $(P_C/P_F)^2$ $(P_C/P_F)^1$ $(L_F/K_F)^2$ $(L_F/K_F)^1$ $(L_C/K_C)^2$ $(L_C/K_C)^1$ Labor-capital ratio, L/K

← Increasing   Increasing →

FIGURE 5-7

From Goods Prices to Input Choices

Given the relative price of cloth $(P_C/P_F)^1$, the ratio of the wage rate to the capital rental rate must equal $(w/r)^1$. This wage-rental ratio then implies that the ratios of labor to capital employed in the production of cloth and food must be $(L_C/K_C)^1$ and $(L_F/K_F)^1$. If the relative price of cloth rises to $(P_C/P_F)^2$, the wage-rental ratio must rise to $(w/r)^2$. This will cause the labor-capital ratio used in the production of both goods to drop.

Figure 5-5. By putting these two diagrams together, we see what may seem at first to be a surprising linkage of the prices of goods to the ratio of labor to capital used in the production of each good. Suppose the relative price of cloth is $(P_C/P_F)^1$ (left panel of Figure 5-7); if the economy produces both goods, the ratio of the wage rate to the capital rental rate must equal $(w/r)^1$. This ratio then implies that the ratios of labor to capital employed in the production of cloth and food must be $(L_C/K_C)^1$ and $(L_F/K_F)^1$, respectively (right panel of Figure 5-7). If the relative price of cloth were to rise to the level indicated by $(P_C/P_F)^2$, the ratio of the wage rate to the capital rental rate would rise to $(w/r)^2$. Because labor is now relatively more expensive, the ratios of labor to capital employed in the production of cloth and food would therefore drop to $(L_C/K_C)^2$ and $(L_F/K_F)^2$.

We can learn one more important lesson from this diagram. The left panel already tells us that an increase in the price of cloth relative to that of food will raise the income of workers relative to that of capital owners. But it is possible to make a stronger statement: Such a change in relative prices will unambiguously raise the purchasing power of workers and lower the purchasing power of capital owners by raising real wages and lowering real rents in terms of *both* goods.

How do we know this? When P_C/P_F increases, the ratio of labor to capital falls in both cloth and food production. But in a competitive economy, factors of production are paid their marginal product—the real wage of workers in terms of cloth is equal to the marginal productivity of labor in cloth production, and so on. When the ratio of labor to capital falls in producing either good, the marginal product of labor in terms of that good increases—so workers find their real wage higher in terms of both goods. On the other hand, the marginal product of capital falls in both industries, so capital owners find their real incomes lower in terms of both goods.

In this model, then, as in the specific factors model, changes in relative prices have strong effects on income distribution. Not only does a change in the prices of goods change the distribution of income; it always changes it so much that owners of one factor of production gain while owners of the other are made worse off.[4]

Resources and Output

We can now complete the description of a two-factor economy by describing the relationship between goods prices, factor supplies, and output. In particular, we investigate how changes in resources (the total supply of a factor) affect the allocation of factors across sectors and the associated changes in output produced.

Suppose we take the relative price of cloth as given. We know from Figure 5-7 that a given relative price of cloth, say $(P_C/P_F)^1$, is associated with a fixed wage-rental ratio $(w/r)^1$ (so long as both cloth and food are produced). That ratio, in turn, determines the ratios of labor to capital employed in both the cloth and the food sectors: $(L_C/K_C)^1$ and $(L_F/K_F)^1$, respectively. Now we assume that the economy's labor force grows, which implies that the economy's aggregate labor to capital ratio, L/K, increases. At the given relative price of cloth $(P_C/P_F)^1$, we just saw that the ratios of labor to capital employed in both sectors remain constant. How can the economy accommodate the increase in the aggregate relative supply of labor

---

[4] This relationship between goods prices and factor prices (and the associated welfare effects) was clarified in a classic paper by Wolfgang Stolper and Paul Samuelson, "Protection and Real Wages," *Review of Economic Studies* 9 (November 1941), pp. 58–73, and is therefore known as the *Stolper-Samuelson effect*.

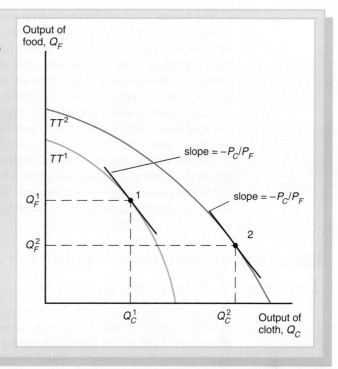

FIGURE 5-8

Resources and Production Possibilities

An increase in the supply of labor shifts the economy's production possibility frontier outward from TT^1 to TT^2, but does so disproportionately in the direction of cloth production. The result is that at an unchanged relative price of cloth (indicated by the slope $-P_C/P_F$), food production actually declines from Q_F^1 to Q_F^2.

L/K if the relative labor demanded in each sector remains constant at $(L_C/K_C)^1$ and $(L_F/K_F)^1$? In other words, how does the economy employ the additional labor hours? The answer lies in the allocation of labor and capital across sectors: The labor-capital ratio in the cloth sector is higher than that in the food sector, so the economy can increase the employment of labor to capital (holding the labor-capital ratio fixed in each sector) by allocating more labor and capital to the production of cloth (which is labor-intensive).[5] As labor and capital move from the food sector to the cloth sector, the economy produces more cloth and less food.

The best way to think about this result is in terms of how resources affect the economy's production possibilities. In Figure 5-8, the curve TT^1 represents the economy's production possibilities before the increase in labor supply. Output is at point 1, where the slope of the production possibility frontier equals minus the relative price of cloth, $-P_C/P_F$, and the economy produces Q_C^1 and Q_F^1 of cloth and food. The curve TT^2 shows the production possibility frontier after an increase in the labor supply. The production possibility frontier shifts out to TT^2. After this increase, the economy can produce more of both cloth and food than before. The outward shift of the frontier is, however, much larger in the direction of cloth than of food—that is, there is a **biased expansion of production possibilities,** which occurs when the production possibility frontier shifts out much more in one direction than in the other. In this case, the expansion is so strongly biased toward cloth production that at unchanged relative prices, production moves from point 1 to point 2, which involves an actual fall in food output from Q_F^1 to Q_F^2 and a large increase in cloth output from Q_C^1 to Q_C^2.

---

[5]See the appendix for a more formal derivation of this result and additional details.

The biased effect of increases in resources on production possibilities is the key to understanding how differences in resources give rise to international trade.[6] An increase in the supply of labor expands production possibilities disproportionately in the direction of cloth production, while an increase in the supply of capital expands them disproportionately in the direction of food production. Thus, an economy with a high relative supply of labor to capital will be relatively better at producing cloth than an economy with a low relative supply of labor to capital. *Generally, an economy will tend to be relatively effective at producing goods that are intensive in the factors with which the country is relatively well endowed.*

We will further see below some empirical evidence confirming that changes in a country's resources lead to growth that is biased toward the sectors that intensively use the factor whose supply has increased. We document this for the Chinese economy, which has recently experienced substantial growth in its supply of skilled labor.

Effects of International Trade between Two-Factor Economies

Having outlined the production structure of a two-factor economy, we can now look at what happens when two such economies, Home and Foreign, trade. As always, Home and Foreign are similar along many dimensions. They have the same tastes and therefore have identical relative demands for food and cloth when faced with the same relative prices of the two goods. They also have the same technology: A given amount of labor and capital yields the same output of either cloth or food in the two countries. The only difference between the countries is in their resources: Home has a higher ratio of labor to capital than Foreign does.

Relative Prices and the Pattern of Trade

Since Home has a higher ratio of labor to capital than Foreign, Home is *labor-abundant* and Foreign is *capital-abundant.* Note that abundance is defined in terms of a ratio and not in absolute quantities. For example, the total number of workers in the United States is roughly three times higher than that in Mexico, but Mexico would still be considered labor-abundant relative to the United States since the U.S. capital stock is more than three times higher than the capital stock in Mexico. "Abundance" is always defined in relative terms, by comparing the ratio of labor to capital in the two countries; thus no country is abundant in everything.

Since cloth is the labor-intensive good, Home's production possibility frontier relative to Foreign's is shifted out more in the direction of cloth than in the direction of food. Thus, other things equal, Home tends to produce a higher ratio of cloth to food.

Because trade leads to a convergence of relative prices, one of the other things that will be equal is the price of cloth relative to that of food. Because the countries differ in their factor abundances, however, for any given ratio of the price of cloth to that of food, Home will produce a higher ratio of cloth to food than Foreign will: Home will have a larger *relative supply* of cloth. Home's relative supply curve, then, lies to the right of Foreign's.

[6] The biased effect of resource changes on production was pointed out in a paper by the Polish economist T. M. Rybczynski, "Factor Endowments and Relative Commodity Prices," *Economica* 22 (November 1955), pp. 336–341. It is therefore known as the *Rybczynski effect.*

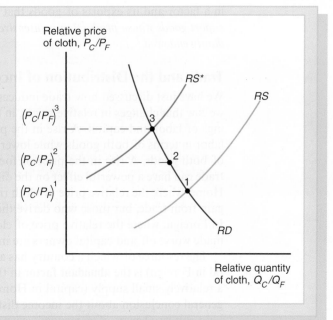

FIGURE 5-9

Trade Leads to a Convergence of Relative Prices

In the absence of trade, Home's equilibrium would be at point 1, where domestic relative supply *RS* intersects the relative demand curve *RD*. Similarly, Foreign's equilibrium would be at point 3. Trade leads to a world relative price that lies between the pretrade prices $(P_C/P_F)^1$ and $(P_C/P_F)^3$, such as $(P_C/P_F)^2$ at point 2.

The relative supply schedules of Home (*RS*) and Foreign (*RS**) are illustrated in Figure 5-9. The relative demand curve, which we have assumed to be the same for both countries, is shown as *RD*. If there were no international trade, the equilibrium for Home would be at point 1, and the relative price of cloth would be $(P_C/P_F)^1$. The equilibrium for Foreign would be at point 3, with a relative price of cloth given by $(P_C/P_F)^3$. Thus, in the absence of trade, the relative price of cloth would be lower in Home than in Foreign.

When Home and Foreign trade with each other, their relative prices converge. The relative price of cloth rises in Home and declines in Foreign, and a new world relative price of cloth is established at a point somewhere between the pretrade relative prices, say at $(P_C/P_F)^2$. In Chapter 4, we discussed how an economy responds to trade based on the direction of the change in the relative price of the goods: The economy exports the good whose relative price increases. Thus, Home will export cloth (the relative price of cloth rises in Home), while Foreign will export food. (The relative price of cloth declines in Foreign, which means that the relative price of food rises there).

Home becomes an exporter of cloth because it is labor-abundant (relative to Foreign) and because the production of cloth is labor-intensive (relative to food production). Similarly, Foreign becomes an exporter of food because it is capital-abundant and because the production of food is capital-intensive. These predictions for the pattern of trade (in the two-good, two-factor, two-country version that we have studied) can be generalized as the following theorem, named after the original developers of this model of trade:

Heckscher-Ohlin Theorem: *The country that is abundant in a factor exports the good whose production is intensive in that factor.*

In the more realistic case with multiple countries, factors of production, and numbers of goods, we can generalize this result as a correlation between a country's abundance in a factor and its exports of goods that use that factor intensively: *Countries tend to export goods whose production is intensive in factors with which the countries are abundantly endowed.*[7]

Trade and the Distribution of Income

We have just discussed how trade induces a convergence of relative prices. Previously, we saw that changes in relative prices, in turn, have strong effects on the relative earnings of labor and capital. A rise in the price of cloth raises the purchasing power of labor in terms of both goods while lowering the purchasing power of capital in terms of both goods. A rise in the price of food has the reverse effect. Thus, international trade can have a powerful effect on the distribution of income, even in the long run. In Home, where the relative price of cloth rises, people who get their incomes from labor gain from trade, but those who derive their incomes from capital are made worse off. In Foreign, where the relative price of cloth falls, the opposite happens: Laborers are made worse off and capital owners are made better off.

The resource of which a country has a relatively large supply (labor in Home, capital in Foreign) is the **abundant factor** in that country, and the resource of which it has a relatively small supply (capital in Home, labor in Foreign) is the **scarce factor.** The general conclusion about the income distribution effects of international trade in the long run is: *Owners of a country's abundant factors gain from trade, but owners of a country's scarce factors lose.*

In our analysis of the specific factors case, we found that factors of production that are "stuck" in an import-competing industry lose from the opening of trade. Here, we find that factors of production that are used intensively by the import-competing industry are hurt by the opening of trade—regardless of the industry in which they are employed. Still, the theoretical argument regarding the aggregate gains from trade is identical to the specific factors case: Opening to trade expands an economy's consumption possibilities (see Figure 4-11), so there is a way to make everybody better off. However, one crucial difference exists regarding the income distribution effects in these two models. The specificity of factors to particular industries is often only a temporary problem: Garment makers cannot become computer manufacturers overnight, but given time the U.S. economy can shift its manufacturing employment from declining sectors to expanding ones. Thus, income distribution effects that arise because labor and other factors of production are immobile represent a temporary, transitional problem (which is not to say that such effects are not painful to those who lose). In contrast, effects of trade on the distribution of income among land, labor, and capital are more or less permanent.

Compared with the rest of the world, the United States is abundantly endowed with highly skilled labor while low-skilled labor is correspondingly scarce. This means that international trade has the potential to make low-skilled workers in the United States worse off—not just temporarily, but on a sustained basis. The negative effect of trade on low-skilled workers poses a persistent political problem, one that cannot be remedied by policies that provide temporary relief (such as unemployment insurance). Consequently, the potential effect of increased trade on income inequality in advanced economies such as the United States has been the subject of a large amount of empirical research. We review some of that evidence in the case study that follows, and conclude that trade has been, at most, a contributing factor to the measured increases in income inequality in the United States.

---

[7]See Alan Deardorff, "The General Validity of the Heckscher-Ohlin Theorem," *American Economic Review* 72 (September 1982), pp. 683–694, for a formal derivation of this extension to multiple goods, factors, and countries.

CASE STUDY

North-South Trade and Income Inequality

The distribution of wages in the United States has become considerably more unequal since the 1970s. In 1970, a male worker with a wage at the 90th percentile of the wage distribution (earning more than the bottom 90 percent but less than the top 10 percent of wage earners) earned 3.2 times the wage of a male worker at the bottom 10th percentile of the distribution. By 2010, that worker at the 90th percentile earned more than 5.2 times the wage of the worker at the bottom 10th percentile. Wage inequality for female workers has increased at a similar rate over that same timespan. Much of this increase in wage inequality was associated with a rise in the premium attached to education, especially since the 1980s. In 1980, a worker with a college degree earned 40 percent more than a worker with just a high school education. This education premium rose steadily through the 1980s and 1990s to 80 percent. Since then, it has been roughly flat (though wage disparities among college graduates continued rising).

Why has wage inequality increased? Many observers attribute the change to the growth of world trade and in particular to the growing exports of manufactured goods from newly industrializing economies (NIEs) such as South Korea and China. Until the 1970s, trade between advanced industrial nations and less-developed economies—often referred to as "North-South" trade because most advanced nations are still in the temperate zone of the Northern Hemisphere—consisted overwhelmingly of an exchange of Northern manufactures for Southern raw materials and agricultural goods, such as oil and coffee. From 1970 onward, however, former raw material exporters increasingly began to sell manufactured goods to high-wage countries like the United States. As we learned in Chapter 2, developing countries have dramatically changed the kinds of goods they export, moving away from their traditional reliance on agricultural and mineral products to a focus on manufactured goods. While NIEs also provided a rapidly growing market for exports from the high-wage nations, the exports of the newly industrializing economies obviously differed greatly in factor intensity from their imports. Overwhelmingly, NIE exports to advanced nations consisted of clothing, shoes, and other relatively unsophisticated products ("low-tech goods") whose production is intensive in unskilled labor, while advanced-country exports to the NIEs consisted of capital- or skill-intensive goods such as chemicals and aircraft ("high-tech goods").

To many observers, the conclusion seemed straightforward: What was happening was a move toward factor-price equalization. Trade between advanced countries that are abundant in capital and skill and NIEs with their abundant supply of unskilled labor was raising the wages of highly skilled workers and lowering the wages of less-skilled workers in the skill- and capital-abundant countries, just as the factor-proportions model predicts.

This is an argument with much more than purely academic significance. If one regards the growing inequality of income in advanced nations as a serious problem, as many people do, and if one also believes that growing world trade is the main cause of that problem, it becomes difficult to maintain economists' traditional support for free trade. (As we have previously argued, in principle, taxes and government payments can offset the effect of trade on income distribution, but one may argue that this is unlikely to happen in practice.) Some influential commentators have argued that advanced nations will have to restrict their trade with low-wage countries if they want to remain basically middle-class societies.

While some economists believe that growing trade with low-wage countries has been the main cause of rising income inequality in the United States, most empirical researchers believed at the time of this writing that international trade has been at most a contributing factor to that growth, and that the main causes lie elsewhere.[8] This skepticism rests on three main observations.

First, the factor-proportions model says that international trade affects income distribution via a change in relative prices of goods. So if international trade was the main driving force behind growing income inequality, there ought to be clear evidence of a rise in the prices of skill-intensive products compared with those of unskilled-labor-intensive goods. Studies of international price data, however, have failed to find clear evidence of such a change in relative prices.

Second, the model predicts that relative factor prices should converge: If wages of skilled workers are rising and those of unskilled workers are falling in the skill-abundant country, the reverse should be happening in the labor-abundant country. Studies of income distribution in developing countries that have opened themselves to trade have shown that at least in some cases, the reverse is true. In Mexico, in particular, careful studies have shown that the transformation of the country's trade in the late 1980s—when Mexico opened itself to imports and became a major exporter of manufactured goods—was accompanied by rising wages for skilled workers and growing overall wage inequality, closely paralleling developments in the United States.

Third, although trade between advanced countries and NIEs has grown rapidly, it still constitutes only a small percentage of total spending in the advanced nations. As a result, estimates of the "factor content" of this trade—the skilled labor exported, in effect, by advanced countries embodied in skill-intensive exports and the unskilled labor, in effect, imported in labor-intensive imports—are still only a small fraction of the total supplies of skilled and unskilled labor. This suggests that these trade flows couldn't have had a very large impact on income distribution.

What, then, *is* responsible for the growing gap between skilled and unskilled workers in the United States? The view of the majority is that the villain is not trade but rather new production technologies that put a greater emphasis on worker skills (such as the widespread introduction of computers and other advanced technologies in the workplace). This is often referred to as a technology-skill complementarity or **skill-biased technological change**.[9]

We discuss the links between this type of technological change and rising wage inequality in the following case study.

---

[8]Among the important entries in the discussion of the impact of trade on income distribution have been Robert Lawrence and Matthew Slaughter, "Trade and U.S. Wages: Giant Sucking Sound or Small Hiccup?" *Brookings Papers on Economic Activity: Microeconomic* 2 (1993), pp. 161–226; Jeffrey D. Sachs and Howard Shatz, "Trade and Jobs in U.S. Manufacturing," *Brookings Papers on Economic Activity* 1 (1994), pp. 1–84; and Adrian Wood, *North-South Trade, Employment, and Income Inequality* (Oxford: Oxford University Press, 1994). For a survey of this debate and related issues, see Chapter 9 in Lawrence Edwards and Robert Z. Lawrence, *Rising Tide: Is Growth in Emerging Economies Good for the United States?* (Peterson Institute for International Economics, 2013).

[9]See Claudia Goldin and Lawrence F. Katz, "The Origins of Technology-Skill Complementarity," *The Quarterly Journal of Economics* (1998), pp. 693–732.

CASE STUDY

Skill-Biased Technological Change and Income Inequality

In this case study, we extend our two-factor production model to incorporate technological change that is skill-biased. We discuss how this provides a much better fit for the empirical patterns associated with rising wage inequality in the United States. We also describe some new research that links back portions of this technological change to trade and outsourcing.

Consider the variant of our two good, two factor model where skilled and unskilled labor are used to produce "high-tech" and "low-tech" goods. Figure 5-10 shows the relative factor demands for producers in both sectors: the ratio of skilled-unskilled workers employed as a function of the skilled-unskilled wage ratio (LL curve for low-tech and HH for high-tech).

We have assumed that production of high-tech goods is skilled-labor intensive, so the HH curve is shifted out relative to the LL curve. In the background, an SS curve

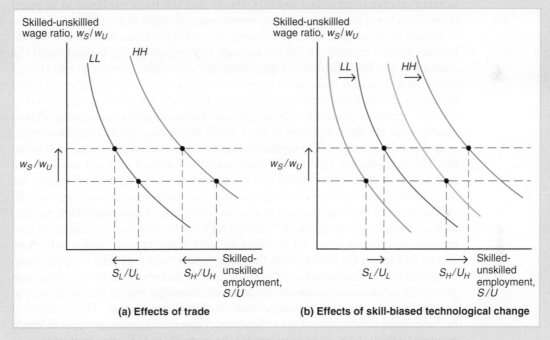

FIGURE 5-10

Increased Wage Inequality: Trade- or Skill-Biased Technological Change?

The LL and HH curves show the skilled-unskilled employment ratio, S/U, as a function of the skilled-unskilled wage ratio, w_S/w_U, in the low-tech and high-tech sectors. The high-tech sector is more skill-intensive than the low-tech sector, so the HH curve is shifted out relative to the LL curve. Panel (a) shows the case where increased trade with developing countries leads to a higher skilled-unskilled wage ratio. Producers in both sectors respond by *decreasing* their relative employment of skilled workers: S_L/U_L and S_H/U_H both decrease. Panel (b) shows the case where skill-biased technological change leads to a higher skilled-unskilled wage ratio. The LL and HH curves shift out (increased relative demand for skilled workers in both sectors). However, in this case producers in both sectors respond by *increasing* their relative employment of skilled workers: S_L/U_L and S_H/U_H both increase.

(see Figures 5-6 and 5-7) determines the skilled-unskilled wage ratio as an increasing function of the relative price of high-tech goods (with respect to low-tech goods).

In panel (a), we show the case where increased trade with developing countries generates an increase in wage inequality (the skilled-unskilled wage ratio) in those countries (via an increase in the relative price of high-tech goods). The increase in the relative cost of skilled workers induces producers in both sectors to *reduce* their employment of skilled workers relative to unskilled workers.

In panel (b), we show the case where technological change in both sectors generates an increase in wage inequality. This technology change is classified as "skill-biased" because it shifts out the relative demand for skilled workers in both sectors (both the LL and the HH curves shift out). It also induces larger productivity gains in the high-tech sector due to its complementarity with skilled workers. Thus, for any given relative price of high-tech goods, the technology change is associated with a higher skilled-unskilled wage ratio (the SS curve shifts). Even though skilled labor is relatively more expensive, producers in both sectors respond to the technological change by *increasing* their employment of skilled workers relative to unskilled workers. (Note that the trade explanation in panel (a) predicts an opposite response for employment in both sectors.)

We can now examine the relative merits of the trade versus skill-biased technological change explanations for the increase in wage inequality by looking at the changes in the skilled-unskilled employment ratio within sectors in the United States. A widespread increase in these employment ratios for all different kinds of sectors (both skilled-labor-intensive and unskilled-labor-intensive sectors) in the U.S. economy points to the skill-biased technological explanation. This is exactly what has been observed in the United States over the last half-century.

In Figure 5-11, sectors are separated into four groups based on their skill intensity. U.S. firms do not report their employment in terms of skill but use a related categorization of production and non-production workers. With a few exceptions, non-production positions require higher levels of education—and so we measure the skilled-unskilled employment ratio in a sector as the ratio of non-production employment to production employment.[10] Sectors with the highest non-production to production employment ratios are classified as most skill-intensive. Each quadrant of Figure 5-11 shows the evolution of this employment ratio over time for each group of sectors (the average employment ratio across all sectors in the group). Although there are big differences in average skill intensity across the groups, we clearly see that the employment ratios are increasing over time for all four groups. This widespread increase across most sectors of the U.S. economy is one of the main pieces of evidence pointing to the technology explanation for the increases in U.S. wage inequality.

Yet, even though most economists agree that skill-biased technological change has occurred, recent research has uncovered some new ways in which trade has been an indirect contributor to the associated increases in wage inequality, by accelerating this process of technological change. These explanations are based on the principle that firms have a choice of production methods that is influenced by openness to trade and foreign investment. For example, some studies show that firms that begin to export also upgrade to more skill-intensive production

---

[10]On average, the wage of a non-production worker is 60 percent higher than that of a production worker.

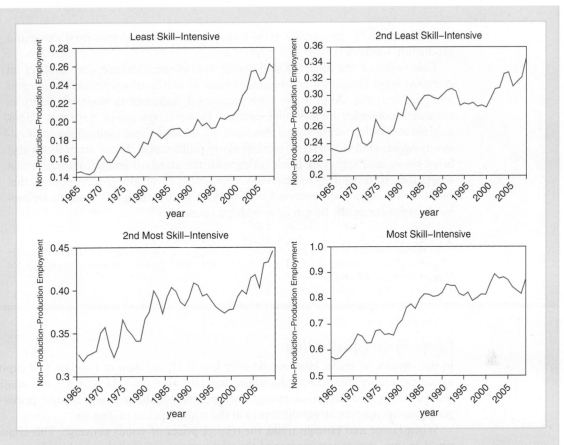

FIGURE 5-11

Evolution of U.S. Non-Production–Production Employment Ratios in Four Groups of Sectors

Sectors are grouped based on their skill intensity. The non-production–production employment ratio has increased over time in all four sector groups.

Source: NBER-CES Manufacturing Productivity Database

technologies. Trade liberalization can then generate widespread technological change by inducing a large proportion of firms to make such technology-upgrade choices.

Another example is related to foreign outsourcing and the liberalization of trade and foreign investment. In particular, the NAFTA treaty (see Chapter 2) between the United States, Canada, and Mexico has made it substantially easier for firms to move different parts of their production processes (research and development, component production, assembly, marketing) across different locations in North America. Because production worker wages are substantially lower in Mexico, U.S. firms have an incentive to move the processes that use production workers more intensively to Mexico (such as component production and assembly). The processes that rely more intensively on higher-skilled, non-production workers (such as research and development and marketing) tend to stay in the United States (or Canada). From the U.S. perspective, this break-up of the production process increases the relative demand for skilled workers and is very similar to skill-biased technological change. One study finds that this outsourcing process from the United States to Mexico can explain

21 to 27 percent of the increase in the wage premium between non-production and production workers.[11]

Thus, some of the observed skill-biased technological change, and its effect on increased wage inequality, can be traced back to increased openness to trade and foreign investment. And, as we have mentioned, increases in wage inequality in advanced economies are a genuine concern. However, the use of trade restrictions targeted at limiting technological innovations—because those innovations favor relatively higher-skilled workers—is particularly problematic: Those innovations also bring substantial aggregate gains (along with the standard gains from trade) that would then be foregone. Consequently, economists favor longer-term policies that ease the skill-acquisition process for all workers so that the gains from the technological innovations can be spread as widely as possible.

---

[11]See Robert Feenstra and Gordon Hanson, "The Impact of Outsourcing and High-Technology Capital on Wages: Estimates for the United States, 1979–1990," *Quarterly Journal of Economics* 144 (August 1999), pp. 907–940.

Factor-Price Equalization

In the absence of trade, labor would earn less in Home than in Foreign, and capital would earn more. Without trade, labor-abundant Home would have a lower relative price of cloth than capital-abundant Foreign, and the difference in relative prices of *goods* implies an even larger difference in the relative prices of *factors*.

When Home and Foreign trade, the relative prices of goods converge. This convergence, in turn, causes convergence of the relative prices of capital and labor. Thus, there is clearly a tendency toward **equalization of factor prices.** How far does this tendency go?

The surprising answer is that in the model, the tendency goes all the way. International trade leads to complete equalization of factor prices. Although Home has a higher ratio of labor to capital than Foreign, once they trade with each other, the wage rate and the capital rent rate are the same in both countries. To see this, refer back to Figure 5-6, which shows that given the prices of cloth and food, we can determine the wage rate and the rental rate without reference to the supplies of capital and labor. If Home and Foreign face the same relative prices of cloth and food, they will also have the same factor prices.

To understand how this equalization occurs, we have to realize that when Home and Foreign trade with each other, more is happening than a simple exchange of goods. In an indirect way, the two countries are in effect trading factors of production. Home lets Foreign use some of its abundant labor, not by selling the labor directly but by trading goods produced with a high ratio of labor to capital for goods produced with a low labor-capital ratio. The goods that Home sells require more labor to produce than the goods it receives in return; that is, more labor is *embodied* in Home's exports than in its imports. Thus Home exports its labor, embodied in its labor-intensive exports. Conversely, since Foreign's exports embody more capital than its imports, Foreign is indirectly exporting its capital. When viewed this way, it is not surprising that trade leads to equalization of the two countries' factor prices.

Although this view of trade is simple and appealing, there is a major problem with it: In the real world, factor prices are *not* equalized. For example, there is an extremely wide range of wage rates across countries (Table 5-1). While some of these differences

TABLE 5-1	Comparative International Wage Rates (United States = 100)
Country	Hourly Compensation of Production Workers, 2011
United States	100
Germany	133
Japan	101
Spain	80
South Korea	53
Brazil	33
Mexico	18
China*	4

*2008

Source: Bureau of Labor Statistics, *Foreign Labor Statistics Home Page.*

may reflect differences in the quality of labor, they are too wide to be explained away on this basis alone.

To understand why the model doesn't give us an accurate prediction, we need to look at its assumptions. Three assumptions crucial to the prediction of factor-price equalization are in reality certainly untrue. These are the assumptions that (1) technologies are the same; (2) costless trade equalizes the prices of goods in the two countries; and (3) both countries produce both goods.

1. The proposition that trade equalizes factor prices will not hold if countries have different technologies of production. For example, a country with superior technology might have both a higher wage rate and a higher rental rate than a country with an inferior technology.
2. Complete factor-price equalization also depends on complete convergence of the prices of goods. In the real world, prices of goods are not fully equalized by international trade. This lack of convergence is due to both natural barriers (such as transportation costs) and barriers to trade such as tariffs, import quotas, and other restrictions.
3. Even if all countries use the same technologies and face the same goods prices, factor price equalization still depends on the assumption that countries produce the same set of goods. We assumed this when we derived the wage and rental rates from the prices of cloth and food in Figure 5-6. However, countries may be induced to specialize in the production of different goods. A country with a very high ratio of labor to capital might produce only cloth, while a country with a very high ratio of capital to labor might produce only food. This implies that factor-price equalization occurs only if the countries involved are sufficiently similar in their relative factor endowments. (A more thorough discussion of this point is given in the appendix to this chapter.) Thus, factor prices need not be equalized between countries with radically different ratios of capital to labor or of skilled to unskilled labor.

Empirical Evidence on the Heckscher-Ohlin Model

The essence of the Heckscher-Ohlin model is that trade is driven by differences in factor abundance across countries. We just saw how this leads to the natural prediction that goods trade is substituting for factor trade, and hence that goods trade across countries should *embody* those factor differences. This prediction, based on the **factor content of trade,** is very powerful and can be tested empirically. However, we will see that the empirical success of this strict test is very limited—mainly due to the same reasons that undermine the prediction for factor-price equalization. Does this mean that differences in factor abundance do *not* help explain the observed patterns of trade across countries? Not at all. First, we will show that relaxing the assumptions generating factor price equalization vastly improves the predictive success for the factor content of trade. Second, we will look directly at the pattern of goods traded between developed and developing countries—and we will see how well they fit with the predictions of the Heckscher-Ohlin model.

Trade in Goods as a Substitute for Trade in Factors: Factor Content of Trade

Tests on U.S. Data Until recently, and to some extent even now, the United States has been a special case among countries. Until a few years ago, the United States was much wealthier than other countries, and U.S. workers visibly worked with more capital per person than their counterparts in other countries. Even now, although some Western European countries and Japan have caught up, the United States continues to be high on the scale of countries as ranked by capital-labor ratios.

One would then expect the United States to be an exporter of capital-intensive goods and an importer of labor-intensive goods. Surprisingly, however, this was not the case in the 25 years after World War II. In a famous study published in 1953, economist Wassily Leontief (winner of the Nobel Prize in 1973) found that U.S. exports were less capital-intensive than U.S. imports.[12] This result is known as the **Leontief paradox.**

Table 5-2 illustrates the Leontief paradox as well as other information about U.S. trade patterns. We compare the factors of production used to produce $1 million worth of 1962 U.S. exports with those used to produce the same value of 1962 U.S. imports. As the first two lines in the table show, Leontief's paradox was still present in that year: U.S. exports were produced with a lower ratio of capital to labor than U.S. imports. As the rest of the table shows, however, other comparisons of imports and exports are more in line with what one might expect. The United States exported products that were more *skilled*-labor-intensive than its imports, as measured by average years of education. We also tended to export products that were

TABLE 5-2	Factor Content of U.S. Exports and Imports for 1962		
		Imports	**Exports**
Capital per million dollars		$2,132,000	$1,876,000
Labor (person-years) per million dollars		119	131
Capital-labor ratio (dollars per worker)		$17,916	$14,321
Average years of education per worker		9.9	10.1
Proportion of engineers and scientists in work force		0.0189	0.0255

Source: Robert Baldwin, "Determinants of the Commodity Structure of U.S. Trade," *American Economic Review* 61 (March 1971), pp. 126–145.

---

[12]See Wassily Leontief, "Domestic Production and Foreign Trade: The American Capital Position Re-Examined," *Proceedings of the American Philosophical Society*7 (September 1953), pp. 331–349.

"technology-intensive," requiring more scientists and engineers per unit of sales. These observations are consistent with the position of the United States as a high-skill country, with a comparative advantage in sophisticated products. Why then do we observe the Leontief paradox? Is it limited to the United States and/or the types of factors considered? The short answer is no.

Tests on Global Data   A study by Harry P. Bowen, Edward E. Leamer, and Leo Sveikauskas[13] extended Leontief's predictions for the factor content of trade to 27 countries and 12 factors of production. Based on the factor content of a country's exports and imports, they checked whether a country was a net exporter of a factor of production whenever it was relatively abundantly endowed with that factor (and conversely, whether the country was a net importer for the other factors). They assessed factor abundance by comparing a country's endowment of a factor (as a share of the world's supply of that factor) with the country's share of world GDP. For example, the United States has about 25 percent of world income in 2011 but only about 5 percent of the world's workers. This yields Leontief's original prediction that the factor content of U.S. trade should show net imports of labor. Bowen et al., tallied the success/failure of this sign test across the 27 countries and 12 factors in their study. They ended up with a success rate of only 61 percent—not much better than what one would obtain from a random coin toss! In other words, the factor content of trade ran in the opposite direction to the prediction of the factor proportions theory in 39 percent of the cases.

These results confirmed that the Leontief paradox was not an isolated case. However, this negative empirical performance is perhaps not surprising—given that it represents a demanding test of a theory that also predicts factor price equalization (which is clearly at odds with the empirical evidence on cross-country wage differences). As we discussed, the assumption of common technology across countries plays a crucial role in delivering this prediction.

The Case of the Missing Trade   Another indication of large technology differences across countries comes from discrepancies between the observed volumes of trade and those predicted by the Heckscher-Ohlin model. In an influential paper, Daniel Trefler[14] at the University of Toronto pointed out that the Heckscher-Ohlin model can also be used to derive predictions for a country's volume of trade based on differences in that country's factor abundance with that of the rest of the world (since, in this model, trade in goods is substituting for trade in factors). In fact, factor trade turns out to be substantially smaller than the Heckscher-Ohlin model predicts.

A large part of the reason for this disparity comes from a false prediction of large-scale trade in labor between rich and poor nations. Consider our example for the United States in 2011, with 25 percent of world income but only 5 percent of the world's workers. Our simple factor-proportions theory should not only predict that U.S. trade should embody net imports of labor—but that the *volume* of those imported labor services should be huge because they need to account for the United States' very low abundance of labor relative to the rest of the world. In fact, the volume of factor content of trade between labor and capital abundant countries is several orders of magnitude smaller than the volume predicted by the factor proportions theory (based on the observed differences in factor abundance across countries).

---

[13]See Harry P. Bowen, Edward E. Leamer, and Leo Sveikauskas, "Multicountry, Multifactor Tests of the Factor Abundance Theory," *American Economic Review* 77 (December 1987), pp. 791–809.
[14]Daniel Trefler, "The Case of the Missing Trade and Other Mysteries," *American Economic Review* 85 (December 1995), pp. 1029–1046.

TABLE 5-3	Estimated Technological Efficiency, 1983 (United States = 1)
Country	
Bangladesh	0.03
Thailand	0.17
Hong Kong	0.40
Japan	0.70
West Germany	0.78

Source: Daniel Trefler, "The Case of the Missing Trade and Other Mysteries," *American Economic Review* 85 (December 1995), pp. 1029–1046.

Trefler showed that allowing for technology differences across countries helped to resolve the predictive success of both the sign test for the direction of the factor content of trade as well as the missing trade (although there was still plenty of trade left missing). The way this resolution works is roughly as follows: If workers in the United States are much more efficient than the world average, then the "effective" labor supply in the United States is correspondingly larger—and hence the expected volume of imported labor services into the United States is correspondingly lower.

If one makes the working assumption that technological differences between countries take a simple multiplicative form—that is, a given set of inputs in any country produces a multiple or fraction of the output produced in the United States—it is possible to use data on factor trade to estimate the relative efficiency of production in different countries. Table 5-3 shows Trefler's estimates for a sample of countries (the multiplicative constant relative to the United States); they suggest that technological differences are in fact very large.

A Better Empirical Fit for the Factor Content of Trade Subsequently, an important study by Donald Davis and David Weinstein at Columbia University showed that if one relaxes this assumption on common technologies along with the remaining two assumptions underlying factor price equalization (countries produce the same set of goods and costless trade equalizes goods prices), then the predictions for the direction and volume of the factor content of trade line-up substantially better with the empirical evidence—ultimately generating a good fit. Table 5-4 shows the improvement in the empirical fit, measured both by the predictive success for the sign test (the

TABLE 5-4	A Better Empirical Fit for the Factor Content of Trade			
	Assumptions Dropped*			
	None	**Drop (1)**	**Drop (1)–(2)**	**Drop (1)–(3)**
Predictive Success (sign test)	0.32	0.50	0.86	0.91
Missing Trade (observed/ predicted)	0.0005	0.008	0.19	0.69

*Assumptions: (1) common technologies across countries; (2) countries produce the same set of goods; and (3) costless trade equalizes goods prices.

Source: Don R. Davis and David Weinstein, "An Account of Global Factor Trade," *American Economic Review* (2001), pp. 1423–1453.

direction of the factor content of trade) and the missing trade ratio: the ratio of the actual volume of factor content trade to the predicted volume (if one, then there is no missing trade; as the ratio decreases below one, an increasing proportion of predicted trade is missing). For this study, the required data (which included detailed information on the technologies used by each country) was only available for two factors (labor and capital) and 10 countries.

In the first column of Table 5-4, all three assumptions behind factor price equalization are imposed (same technologies across countries, countries produce the same set of goods, and costless trade equalizes goods prices). This test is very similar to the one performed by Bowen et al., though the predictive success for the sign test is substantially worse (32 percent success versus 61 percent reported by Bowen et al.). This is due to the different sample of countries and factors considered, and data cleaning procedures based on the newly available information on production techniques. We also see the extent of the missing trade: virtually all of the predicted volume of factor trade is missing. These results confirm once more that this strict test for the Heckscher-Ohlin model performs very poorly.

The results in the second column were obtained once the assumption of common technologies was dropped, as in the study by Trefler. There is a substantial improvement in both empirical tests, although their overall predictive success is still quite weak. In the third column, the assumption that countries produce the same set of goods is also dropped. We see how this induces a massive improvement for the predictive success of the sign test for the direction of the factor content of trade (up to 86 percent success). The extent of missing trade is also vastly reduced, though the observed trade volume still represents only 19 percent of predicted trade. In the fourth and last column, the assumption of goods price equalization via costless trade is also dropped. The predictive success for the direction of trade increases further to 91 percent. At this point, we can say that the Leontief paradox is relegated to a statistical anomaly. Column four also shows a huge improvement in the extent of missing trade: the observed trade now represents 69 percent of predicted trade.

Overall, Table 5-4 highlights vast differences in the predictive success of the factor-proportions theory for the direction and volume of the factor content of trade. At one end (column one), we find virtually no support for the prediction of the Heckscher-Ohlin model; however, we also see how this failure is driven by particular assumptions built-into our "pure" Heckscher-Ohlin model. When those assumptions are dropped, we can reformulate a model of trade based on differences in factor proportions that fits the observed pattern of factor content of trade quite well (column four).

Patterns of Exports between Developed and Developing Countries

Another way to see how differences in factor proportions shape empirical trade patterns is to contrast the exports of labor-abundant, skill-scarce nations in the developing world with the exports of skill-abundant, labor-scarce nations. In our "2 by 2 by 2" theoretical model (2 goods, 2 countries, 2 factors), we obtained the Heckscher-Ohlin theorem stating that the country abundant in a factor exports the good whose production is intensive in that factor. A paper by John Romalis at the University of Sydney[15] showed how this prediction for the pattern of exports can be extended to multiple countries producing multiple goods: As a country's skill abundance increases, its exports are increasingly concentrated in sectors with higher skill intensity. We now

---

[15]John Romalis, "Factor Proportions and the Structure of Commodity Trade," *American Economic Review* 94 (March 2004), pp. 67–97.

see how this prediction holds when comparing the exports of countries at opposite ends of the skill-abundance spectrum as well as when we compare how exports change when a country such as China grows and becomes relatively more skill-abundant.

Figure 5-12 contrasts the exports of three developing countries (Bangladesh, Cambodia, and Haiti) at the lower-end of the skill-abundance spectrum with the three largest European economics (Germany, France, and United Kingdom) at the upper end of the skill-abundance spectrum. The countries' exports to the United States by sector are partitioned into four groups in increasing order of skill intensity. These are the same four sector groups used in Figure 5-11.[16] Figure 5-12 clearly shows how the exports of the three developing countries to the United States are overwhelmingly concentrated in sectors with the lowest skill-intensity. Their exports in high skill-intensity sectors are virtually nil. The contrast with the export pattern for the three European countries is apparent: The exports to the United States for those skill abundant countries are concentrated in sectors with higher skill intensity.

Changes over time also follow the predictions of the Heckscher-Ohlin model. Consider the experience of China over the last three decades, where high growth (especially in the last decade in a half) has been associated with substantial increases in skill

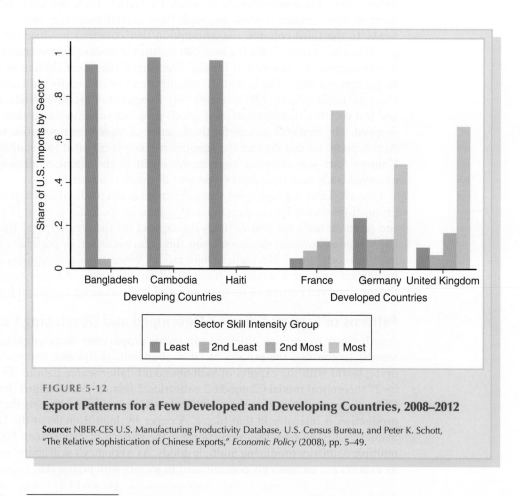

FIGURE 5-12

Export Patterns for a Few Developed and Developing Countries, 2008–2012

Source: NBER-CES U.S. Manufacturing Productivity Database, U.S. Census Bureau, and Peter K. Schott, "The Relative Sophistication of Chinese Exports," *Economic Policy* (2008), pp. 5–49.

---

[16]As previously discussed, a sector's skill intensity is measured by the ratio of non-production to production workers in that sector.

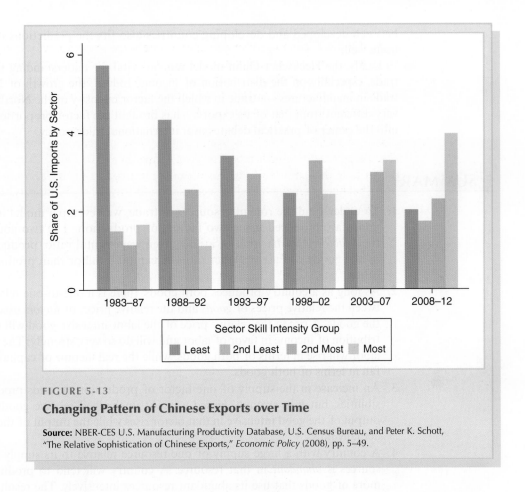

FIGURE 5-13

Changing Pattern of Chinese Exports over Time

Source: NBER-CES U.S. Manufacturing Productivity Database, U.S. Census Bureau, and Peter K. Schott, "The Relative Sophistication of Chinese Exports," *Economic Policy* (2008), pp. 5–49.

abundance. Figure 5-13 shows how the pattern of Chinese exports to the United States by sector has changed over time. Exports are partitioned into the same four groups as Figure 5-12, ordered by the sectors' skill intensity. We clearly see how the pattern of Chinese exports has fundamentally shifted: As predicted by the Chinese change in factor proportions, the concentration of exports in high-skill sectors steadily increases over time. In the most recent years, we see how the greatest share of exports is transacted in the highest skill-intensity sectors—whereas exports were concentrated in the lowest skill-intensity sectors in the earlier years.[17]

Implications of the Tests

We do not observe factor price equalization across countries. When we test the "pure" version of the Heckscher-Ohlin model that maintains all the assumptions behind factor price equalization, we find that a country's factor content of trade bears little resemblance to the theoretical predictions based on that country's factor abundance. However, a less restrictive version of the factor proportions model fits the predicted patterns for the factor content of trade. The pattern of goods trade

---

[17]Comparing Figures 5-12 and 5-13 (latest years), we see that the pattern of Chinese exports to the U.S. is not (yet) as concentrated in high skill-intensity sectors as it is for the three European economies. However, Chinese exports are still remarkably concentrated in high-skill sectors considering China's current GDP per capita. See Peter K. Schott, "The Relative Sophistication of Chinese Exports," *Economic Policy* (2008), pp. 5–49.

between developed and developing countries also fits the predictions of the model quite well.

Lastly, the Heckscher-Ohlin model remains vital for understanding the *effects* of trade, especially on the distribution of income. Indeed, the growth of North-South trade in manufactures—a trade in which the factor intensity of the North's imports is very different from that of its exports—has brought the factor-proportions approach into the center of practical debates over international trade policy.

SUMMARY

1. To understand the role of resources in trade, we develop a model in which two goods are produced using two factors of production. The two goods differ in their *factor intensity*, that is, at any given wage-rental ratio, production of one of the goods will use a higher ratio of capital to labor than production of the other.

2. As long as a country produces both goods, there is a one-to-one relationship between the relative prices of *goods* and the relative prices of *factors* used to produce the goods. A rise in the relative price of the labor-intensive good will shift the distribution of income in favor of labor and will do so very strongly: The real wage of labor will rise in terms of both goods, while the real income of capital owners will fall in terms of both goods.

3. An increase in the supply of one factor of production expands production possibilities, but in a strongly *biased* way: At unchanged relative goods prices, the output of the good intensive in that factor rises while the output of the other good actually falls.

4. A country with a large supply of one resource relative to its supply of other resources is *abundant* in that resource. A country will tend to produce relatively more of goods that use its abundant resources intensively. The result is the basic Heckscher-Ohlin theory of trade: Countries tend to export goods that are intensive in the factors with which they are abundantly supplied.

5. Because changes in relative prices of goods have very strong effects on the relative earnings of resources, and because trade changes relative prices, international trade has strong income distribution effects. The owners of a country's abundant factors gain from trade, but the owners of scarce factors lose. In theory, however, there are still gains from trade, in the limited sense that the winners *could* compensate the losers and everyone would be better off.

6. Increasing trade integration between developed and developing countries could *potentially* explain rising wage inequality in developed countries. However, little empirical evidence supports this direct link. Rather, the empirical evidence suggests that technological change rewarding worker skill has played a much greater role in driving wage inequality.

7. In an idealized model, international trade would actually lead to equalization of the prices of factors such as labor and capital between countries. In reality, complete *factor-price equalization* is not observed because of wide differences in resources, barriers to trade, and international differences in technology.

8. Empirical evidence is mixed on the Heckscher-Ohlin model. Yet, a less restrictive version of the model fits the predicted patterns for the factor content of trade quite well. Also, the Heckscher-Ohlin model does a good job of predicting the pattern of trade between developed and developing countries.

KEY TERMS

abundant factor, p. 128
biased expansion of production
    possibilities, p. 125
equalization of factor prices,
    p. 134
factor abundance, p. 116

factor content of trade, p. 136
factor intensity, p. 116
factor prices, p. 121
factor-proportions theory,
    p. 116
Heckscher-Ohlin theory, p. 116

Leontief paradox, p. 136
scarce factor, p. 128
skill-biased technological
    change, p. 130

PROBLEMS

MyEconLab

1. Go back to the numerical example with no factor substitution that leads to the production possibility frontier in Figure 5-1.
   a. What is the range for the relative price of cloth such that the economy produces both cloth and food? Which good is produced if the relative price is outside of this range?

   For parts (b) through (f), assume the price range is such that both goods are produced.

   b. Write down the unit cost of producing one yard of cloth and one calorie of food as a function of the price of one machine-hour, r, and one work-hour, w. In a competitive market, those costs will be equal to the prices of cloth and food. Solve for the factor prices r and w.
   c. What happens to those factor prices when the price of cloth rises? Who gains and who loses from this change in the price of cloth? Why? Do those changes conform to the changes described for the case with factor substitution?
   d. Now assume the economy's supply of machine-hours increases from 3,000 to 4,000. Derive the new production possibility frontier.
   e. How much cloth and food will the economy produce after this increase in its capital supply?
   f. Describe how the allocation of machine-hours and work-hours between the cloth and food sectors changes. Do those changes conform with the changes described for the case with factor substitution?

2. Suppose in the year 2013, Australia had a population of 45 million and its capital stock is US $90,000 million, and the corresponding figure for Malaysia is 30 million and US $75,000 million. Answer the following, on the basis of this information
   a. Which country is capital abundant and why?
   b. If production of cloth is labor intensive relative to the production of computers, which country would export cloth, if engaged in trade?

3. "The world's poorest countries cannot find anything to export. There is no resource that is abundant—certainly not capital or land, and in small poor nations not even labor is abundant." Discuss.

4. The U.S. labor movement—which mostly represents blue-collar workers rather than professionals and highly educated workers—has traditionally favored limits on imports from less-affluent countries. Is this a shortsighted policy or a rational one in view of the interests of union members? How does the answer depend on the model of trade?

5. Recently, computer programmers in developing countries such as India have begun doing work formerly done in the United States. This shift has undoubtedly led to substantial pay cuts for some programmers in the United States. Answer the following two questions: How is this possible, when the wages of skilled labor

are rising in the United States as a whole? What argument would trade economists make against seeing these wage cuts as a reason to block outsourcing of computer programming?

6. Explain why the Leontief paradox and the more recent Bowen, Leamer, and Sveikauskas results reported in the text contradict the factor-proportions theory.

7. Will free trade and perfect competition lead to an equalization of wage rate internationally? Explain. Why would the wage rate greatly vary between developed and developing countries, in the same sector in a real world situation, even after the adoption of free trade?

FURTHER READINGS

Donald R. Davis and David E. Weinstein. "An Account of Global Factor Trade." *American Economic Review* 91 (December 2001), pp. 1423–1453. This paper confirms the results from earlier studies that the empirical performance of a "pure" Heckscher-Ohlin model is very poor. It then shows how the empirical success of a modified version of the model is vastly improved.

Alan Deardorff. "Testing Trade Theories and Predicting Trade Flows," in Ronald W. Jones and Peter B. Kenen, eds. *Handbook of International Economics.* Vol. 1. Amsterdam: North-Holland, 1984. A survey of empirical evidence on trade theories, especially the factor-proportions theory.

Lawrence Edwards and Robert Z. Lawrence, *Rising Tide: Is Growth in Emerging Economies Good for the United States?* (Peterson Institute for International Economics, 2013). A new book discussing the impact for the United States of increased integration with rapidly growing countries in the develop world.

Gordon Hanson and Ann Harrison. "Trade and Wage Inequality in Mexico." *Industrial and Labor Relations Review* 52 (1999), pp. 271–288. A careful study of the effects of trade on income inequality in our nearest neighbor, showing that factor prices have moved in the opposite direction from what one might have expected from a simple factor-proportions model. The authors also put forward hypotheses about why this may have happened.

Ronald W. Jones. "Factor Proportions and the Heckscher-Ohlin Theorem." *Review of Economic Studies* 24 (1956), pp. 1–10. Extends Samuelson's 1948–1949 analysis (cited on the next page), which focuses primarily on the relationship between trade and income distribution, into an overall model of international trade.

Ronald W. Jones. "The Structure of Simple General Equilibrium Models." *Journal of Political Economy* 73 (December 1965), pp. 557–572. A restatement of the Heckscher-Ohlin-Samuelson model in terms of elegant algebra.

Ronald W. Jones and J. Peter Neary. "The Positive Theory of International Trade," in Ronald W. Jones and Peter B. Kenen, eds. *Handbook of International Economics.* Vol. 1. Amsterdam: North-Holland, 1984. An up-to-date survey of many trade theories, including the factor-proportions theory.

Bertil Ohlin. *Interregional and International Trade.* Cambridge: Harvard University Press, 1933. The original Ohlin book presenting the factor-proportions view of trade remains interesting— its complex and rich view of trade contrasts with the more rigorous and simplified mathematical models that followed.

John Van Reenen. "Wage Inequality, Technology and Trade: 21st Century Evidence." Labour Economics (December 2011), pp. 30–741. A recent survey discussing how trade and new technologies are linked to increases in wage inequality for the United States and the United Kingdom.

John Romalis. "Factor Proportions and the Structure of Commodity Trade." *The American Economic Review* 94 (March 2004), pp. 67–97. A paper showing that a modified version of the Heckscher-Ohlin model has a lot of explanatory power.

Paul Samuelson. "International Trade and the Equalisation of Factor Prices." *Economic Journal* 58 (1948), pp. 163–184; and "International Factor Price Equalisation Once Again." *Economic Journal* 59 (1949), pp. 181–196. The most influential formalizer of Ohlin's ideas is Paul Samuelson (again!), whose two *Economic Journal* papers on the subject are classics.

MyEconLab Can Help You Get a Better Grade

MyEconLab   If your exam were tomorrow, would you be ready? For each chapter, MyEconLab Practice Tests and Study Plans pinpoint sections you have mastered and those you need to study. That way, you are more efficient with your study time, and you are better prepared for your exams.

To see how it works, turn to page 41 and then go to

www.myeconlab.com

Factor Prices, Goods Prices, and Production Decisions

In the main body of this chapter, we made three assertions that are true but not carefully derived. First was the assertion, embodied in Figure 5-5, that the ratio of labor to capital employed in each industry depends on the wage-rental ratio w/r. Second was the assertion, embodied in Figure 5-6, that there is a one-to-one relationship between relative goods prices P_C/P_F and the wage-rental ratio. Third was the assertion that an increase in a country's labor supply (at a given relative goods price P_C/P_F) will lead to movements of both labor and capital from the food sector to the cloth sector (the labor-intensive sector). This appendix briefly demonstrates those three propositions.

Choice of Technique

Figure 5A-1 illustrates again the trade-off between labor and capital input in producing one unit of food—the *unit isoquant* for food production shown in curve *II*. It also, however, illustrates a number of *isocost lines*: combinations of capital and labor input that cost the same amount.

An isocost line may be constructed as follows: The cost of purchasing a given amount of labor L is wL; the cost of renting a given amount of capital K is rK. So if one is able to produce a unit of food using units of labor and units of capital, the total cost of producing that unit, c, is

$$c = wa_{LF} + ra_{KF}.$$

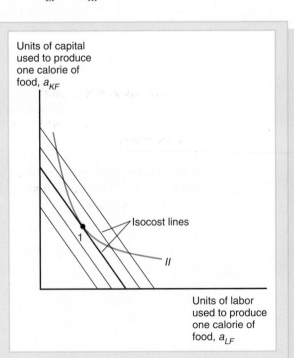

FIGURE 5A-1

Choosing the Optimal Labor-Capital Ratio

To minimize costs, a producer must get to the lowest possible isocost line; this means choosing the point on the unit isoquant (curve *II*) where the slope is equal to minus the wage-rental ratio w/r.

Units of capital used to produce one calorie of food, a_{KF}

Isocost lines

II

1

Units of labor used to produce one calorie of food, a_{LF}

FIGURE 5A-2

Changing the Wage-Rental Ratio

A rise in w/r shifts the lowest-cost input choice from point 1 to point 2; that is, it leads to the choice of a lower labor-capital ratio.

Units of capital used to produce one calorie of food, a_{KF}

slope = $-(w/r)^2$

slope = $-(w/r)^1$

2

1

II

Units of labor used to produce one calorie of food, a_{LF}

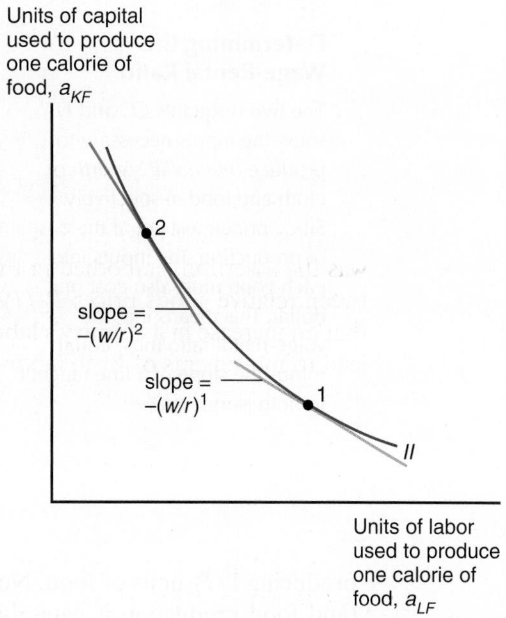

A line showing all combinations of a_{LF} and a_{KF} with the same cost has the equation

$$a_{KF} = (c/r) - (w/r)a_{LF}.$$

That is, it is a straight line with a slope of $-w/r$.

The figure shows a family of such lines, each corresponding to a different level of costs; lines farther from the origin indicate higher total costs. A producer will choose the lowest possible cost given the technological trade-off outlined by curve *II*. Here, this occurs at point 1, where *II* is *tangent* to the isocost line and the slope of *II* equals $-w/r$. (If these results seem reminiscent of the proposition in Figure 4-5 that the economy produces at a point on the production possibility frontier whose slope equals minus P_C/P_F, you are right: The same principle is involved.)

Now compare the choice of labor-capital ratio for two different factor-price ratios. In Figure 5A-2, we show input choices given a low relative price of labor, $(w/r)^1$ and a high relative price of labor $(w/r)^2$. In the former case, the input choice is at 1; in the latter case at 2. That is, the higher relative price of labor leads to the choice of a lower labor-capital ratio, as assumed in Figure 5-5.

Goods Prices and Factor Prices

We now turn to the relationship between goods prices and factor prices. There are several equivalent ways of approaching this problem; here, we follow the analysis introduced by Abba Lerner in the 1930s.

Figure 5A-3 shows capital and labor inputs into both cloth and food production. In previous figures, we have shown the inputs required to produce one unit of a good. In this figure, however, we show the inputs required to produce *one dollar's worth* of each good. (Actually, any dollar amount will do as long as it is the same for both goods.) Thus, the isoquant for cloth, *CC*, shows the possible input combinations for producing $1/P_C$ units of cloth; the isoquant for food, *FF*, shows the possible combinations for

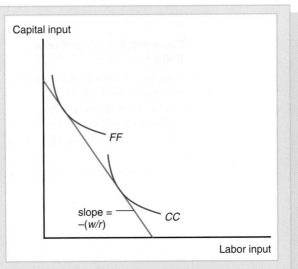

FIGURE 5A-3

Determining the Wage-Rental Ratio

The two isoquants *CC* and *FF* show the inputs necessary to produce *one dollar's worth* of cloth and food, respectively. Since price must equal the cost of production, the inputs into each good must also cost one dollar. This means that the wage-rental ratio must equal minus the slope of a line tangent to both isoquants.

producing $1/P_F$ units of food. Notice that as drawn, cloth production is labor-intensive (and food production is capital-intensive): For any given w/r, cloth production will always use a higher labor-capital ratio than food production.

If the economy produces both goods, then it must be the case that the cost of producing one dollar's worth of each good is, in fact, one dollar. Those two production costs will be equal to one another only if the minimum-cost points of production for both goods lie on the *same* isocost line. Thus, the slope of the line shown, which is just tangent to both isoquants, must equal (minus) the wage-rental ratio w/r.

Finally, now, consider the effects of a rise in the price of cloth on the wage-rental ratio. If the price of cloth rises, it is necessary to produce fewer yards of cloth in order to have one dollar's worth. Thus, the isoquant corresponding to a dollar's worth of cloth shifts inward. In Figure 5A-4, the original isoquant is shown as CC^1, the new isoquant as CC^2.

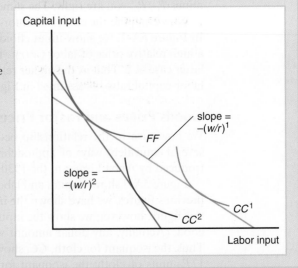

FIGURE 5A-4

A Rise in the Price of Cloth

If the price of cloth rises, a smaller output is now worth one dollar; so CC^1 is replaced by CC^2. The implied wage-rental ratio must therefore rise from $(w/r)^1$ to $(w/r)^2$.

Once again, we must draw a line just tangent to both isoquants; the slope of that line is minus the wage-rental ratio. It is immediately apparent from the increased steepness of the isocost line (slope $= -(w/r)^2$) that the new w/r is higher than the previous one: A higher relative price of cloth implies a higher wage-rental ratio.

More on Resources and Output

We now examine more rigorously how a change in resources—holding the prices of cloth and food constant—affects the allocation of those factors of production across sectors and how it thus affects production responses. The aggregate employment of labor to capital L/K can be written as a weighted average of the labor-capital employed in the cloth sector (L_C/K_C) and in the food sector (L_F/K_F):

$$\frac{L}{K} = \frac{K_C}{K}\frac{L_C}{K_C} + \frac{K_F}{K}\frac{L_F}{K_F} \tag{5A-1}$$

Note that the weights in this average, K_C/K and K_F/K, add up to 1 and are the proportions of capital employed in the cloth and food sectors. We have seen that a given relative price of cloth is associated with a given wage-rental ratio (so long as the economy produces both cloth and food), which in turn is associated with given labor-capital employment levels in both sectors (L_C/K_C and L_F/K_F). Now consider the effects of an increase in the economy's labor supply L at a given relative price of cloth: L/K increases while L_C/K_C and L_F/K_F both remain constant. For equation (5A-1) to hold, the weight on the higher labor-capital ratio, L_C/K_C, must increase. This implies an increase in the weight K_C/K and a corresponding decrease in the weight K_F/K. Thus, capital moves from the food sector to the cloth sector (since the total capital supply K remains constant in this example). Furthermore, since L_F/K_F remains constant, the decrease in K_F must also be associated with a decrease in labor employment L_F in the food sector. This shows that the increase in the labor supply, at a given relative price of cloth, must be associated with movements of *both* labor and capital from the food sector to the cloth sector. The expansion of the economy's production possibility frontier is so biased toward cloth that—at a constant relative price of cloth—the economy produces *less* food.

As the economy's labor supply increases, the economy concentrates more and more of both factors in the labor-intensive cloth sector. If enough labor is added, then the economy specializes in cloth production and no longer produces any food. At that point, the one-to-one relationship between the relative goods price P_C/P_F and the wage-rental ratio w/r is broken; further increases in the labor supply L are then associated with decreases in the wage-rental ratio along the CC curve in Figure 5-7.

A similar process would occur if the economy's capital supply were to increase—again holding the relative goods price P_C/P_F fixed. So long as the economy produces both cloth and food, the economy responds to the increased capital supply by concentrating production in the food sector (which is capital-intensive): Both labor and capital move to the food sector. The economy experiences growth that is strongly biased toward food. At a certain point, the economy completely specializes in the food sector, and the one-to-one relationship between the relative goods price P_C/P_F and the wage-rental ratio w/r is broken once again. Further increases in the capital supply K are then associated with increases in the wage-rental ratio along the FF curve in Figure 5-7.

CHAPTER 6

THE STANDARD TRADE MODEL

Previous chapters developed several different models of international trade, each of which makes different assumptions about the determinants of production possibilities. To bring out important points, each of these models leaves out aspects of reality that the others stress. These models are:

- *The Ricardian model.* Production possibilities are determined by the allocation of a single resource, labor, between sectors. This model conveys the essential idea of comparative advantage but does not allow us to talk about the distribution of income.
- *The specific factors model.* This model includes multiple factors of production, but some are specific to the sectors in which they are employed. It also captures the short-run consequences of trade on the distribution of income.
- *The Heckscher-Ohlin model.* The multiple factors of production in this model can move across sectors. Differences in resources (the availability of those factors at the country level) drive trade patterns. This model also captures the long-run consequences of trade on the distribution of income.

When we analyze real problems, we want to base our insights on a mixture of these models. For example, in the last two decades one of the central changes in world trade was the rapid growth in exports from newly industrializing economies. These countries experienced rapid productivity growth; to discuss the implications of this productivity growth, we may want to apply the Ricardian model of Chapter 3. The changing pattern of trade has differential effects on different groups in the United States; to understand the effects of increased trade on the U.S. income distribution, we may want to apply the specific factors (for the short-run effects) or the Heckscher-Ohlin models (for the long-run effects) of Chapters 4 and 5.

In spite of the differences in their details, our models share a number of features:

1. The productive capacity of an economy can be summarized by its production possibility frontier, and differences in these frontiers give rise to trade.
2. Production possibilities determine a country's relative supply schedule.
3. World equilibrium is determined by world relative demand and a *world* relative supply schedule that lies between the national relative supply schedules.

Because of these common features, the models we have studied may be viewed as special cases of a more general model of a trading world economy. There are many important issues in international economics whose analysis can be conducted in terms of this general model, with only the details depending on which special model you choose. These issues include the effects of shifts in world supply resulting from economic growth and simultaneous shifts in supply and demand resulting from tariffs and export subsidies.

This chapter stresses those insights from international trade theory that are not strongly dependent on the details of the economy's supply side. We develop a standard model of a trading world economy, of which the models of Chapters 3 through 5 can be regarded as special cases, and use this model to ask how a variety of changes in underlying parameters affect the world economy.

LEARNING GOALS

After reading this chapter, you will be able to:

- Understand how the components of the standard trade model, production possibilities frontiers, isovalue lines, and indifference curves fit together to illustrate how trade patterns are established by a combination of supply-side and demand-side factors.
- Recognize how changes in the terms of trade and economic growth affect the welfare of nations engaged in international trade.
- Understand the effects of tariffs and subsidies on trade patterns and the welfare of trading nations and on the distribution of income within countries.
- Relate international borrowing and lending to the standard trade model, where goods are exchanged over time.

A Standard Model of a Trading Economy

The **standard trade model** is built on four key relationships: (1) the relationship between the production possibility frontier and the relative supply curve; (2) the relationship between relative prices and relative demand; (3) the determination of world equilibrium by world relative supply and world relative demand; and (4) the effect of the **terms of trade**—the price of a country's exports divided by the price of its imports—on a nation's welfare.

Production Possibilities and Relative Supply

For the purposes of our standard model, we assume that each country produces two goods, food (F) and cloth (C), and that each country's production possibility frontier is a smooth curve like that illustrated by TT in Figure 6-1.[1] The point on its production possibility frontier at which an economy actually produces depends on the price of cloth relative to food, P_C/P_F. At given market prices, a market economy will choose production levels that maximize the value of its output $P_C Q_C + P_F Q_F$, where Q_C is the quantity of cloth produced and Q_F is the quantity of food produced.

---

[1]We have seen that when there is only one factor of production, as in Chapter 3, the production possibility frontier is a straight line. For most models, however, it will be a smooth curve, and the Ricardian result can be viewed as an extreme case.

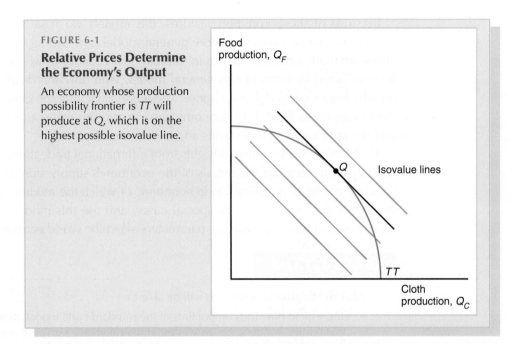

FIGURE 6-1

Relative Prices Determine the Economy's Output

An economy whose production possibility frontier is *TT* will produce at *Q*, which is on the highest possible isovalue line.

We can indicate the market value of output by drawing a number of **isovalue lines**—that is, lines along which the value of output is constant. Each of these lines is defined by an equation of the form $P_C Q_C + P_F Q_F = V$, or, by rearranging, $Q_F = V/P_F - (P_C/P_F)Q_C$, where V is the value of output. The higher V is, the farther out an isovalue line lies; thus isovalue lines farther from the origin correspond to higher values of output. The slope of an isovalue line is $-P_C/P_F$. In Figure 6-1, the highest value of output is achieved by producing at point Q, where TT is just tangent to an isovalue line.

Now suppose that P_C/P_F were to rise (cloth becomes more valuable relative to food). Then the isovalue lines would be steeper than before. In Figure 6-2, the highest isovalue line the economy could reach before the change in P_C/P_F is shown as VV^1; the highest line after the price change is VV^2, the point at which the economy produces shifts from Q^1 to Q^2. Thus, as we might expect, a rise in the relative price of cloth leads the economy to produce more cloth and less food. The relative supply of cloth will therefore rise when the relative price of cloth rises. This relationship between relative prices and relative production is reflected in the economy's relative supply curve shown in Figure 6-2b.

Relative Prices and Demand

Figure 6-3 shows the relationship among production, consumption, and trade in the standard model. As we pointed out in Chapter 5, the value of an economy's consumption equals the value of its production:

$$P_C Q_C + P_F Q_F = P_C D_C + P_F D_F = V,$$

where D_C and D_F are the consumption of cloth and food, respectively. The equation above says that production and consumption must lie on the same isovalue line.

The economy's choice of a point on the isovalue line depends on the tastes of its consumers. For our standard model, we assume the economy's consumption decisions

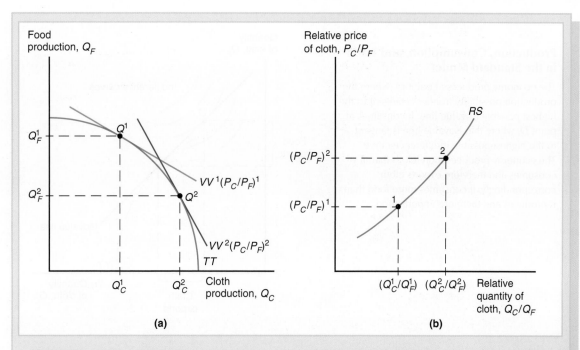

FIGURE 6-2

How an Increase in the Relative Price of Cloth Affects Relative Supply

In panel (a), the isovalue lines become steeper when the relative price of cloth rises from $(P_C/P_F)^1$ to $(P_C/P_F)^2$ (shown by the rotation from VV^1 to VV^2). As a result, the economy produces more cloth and less food and the equilibrium output shifts from Q^1 to Q^2. Panel (b) shows the relative supply curve associated with the production possibilities frontier TT. The rise from $(P_C/P_F)^1$ to $(P_C/P_F)^2$ leads to an increase in the relative production of cloth from Q_C^1/Q_F^1 to Q_C^2/Q_F^2.

may be represented as if they were based on the tastes of a single representative individual.[2]

The tastes of an individual can be represented graphically by a series of **indifference curves.** An indifference curve traces a set of combinations of cloth (C) and food (F) consumption that leave the individual equally well off. As illustrated in Figure 6-3, indifference curves have three properties:

1. They are downward sloping: If an individual is offered less food (F), then to be made equally well off, she must be given more cloth (C).
2. The farther up and to the right an indifference curve lies, the higher the level of welfare to which it corresponds: An individual will prefer having more of both goods to less.
3. Each indifference curve gets flatter as we move to the right (they are bowed-out to the origin): The more C and the less F an individual consumes, the more valuable a unit of F is at the margin compared with a unit of C, so more C will have to be provided to compensate for any further reduction in F.

[2]Several sets of circumstances can justify this assumption. One is that all individuals have the same tastes and the same share of all resources. Another is that the government redistributes income so as to maximize its view of overall social welfare. Essentially, the assumption requires that effects of changing income distribution on demand not be too important.

FIGURE 6-3

Production, Consumption, and Trade in the Standard Model

The economy produces at point Q, where the production possibility frontier is tangent to the highest possible isovalue line. It consumes at point D, where that isovalue line is tangent to the highest possible indifference curve. The economy produces more cloth than it consumes and therefore exports cloth; correspondingly, it consumes more food than it produces and therefore imports food.

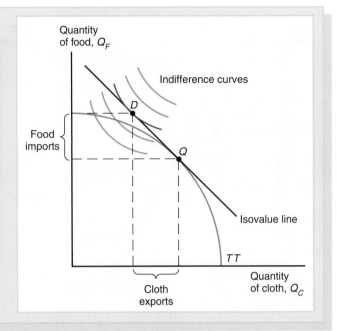

As you can see in Figure 6-3, the economy will choose to consume at the point on the isovalue line that yields the highest possible welfare. This point is where the isovalue line is tangent to the highest reachable indifference curve, shown here as point D. Notice that at this point, the economy exports cloth (the quantity of cloth produced exceeds the quantity of cloth consumed) and imports food.

Now consider what happens when P_C/P_F increases. Panel (a) in Figure 6-4 shows the effects. First, the economy produces more C and less F, shifting production from Q^1 to Q^2. This shifts, from VV^1 to VV^2, the isovalue line on which consumption must lie. The economy's consumption choice therefore also shifts, from D^1 to D^2.

The move from D^1 to D^2 reflects two effects of the rise in P_C/P_F. First, the economy has moved to a higher indifference curve, meaning that it is better off. The reason is that this economy is an exporter of cloth. When the relative price of cloth rises, the economy can trade a given amount of cloth for a larger amount of food imports. Thus, the higher relative price of its export good represents an advantage. Second, the change in relative prices leads to a shift along the indifference curve, toward food and away from cloth (since cloth is now relatively more expensive).

These two effects are familiar from basic economic theory. The rise in welfare is an *income effect*; the shift in consumption at any given level of welfare is a *substitution effect*. The income effect tends to increase consumption of both goods, while the substitution effect acts to make the economy consume less C and more F.

Panel (b) in Figure 6-4 shows the relative supply and demand curves associated with the production possibilities frontier and the indifference curves.[3] The graph shows how the increase in the relative price of cloth induces an increase in the relative production of cloth (move from point 1 to 2) as well as a decrease in the relative

---

[3]For general preferences, the relative demand curve will depend on the country's total income. We assume throughout this chapter that the relative demand curve is independent of income. This is the case for a widely used type of preferences called homothetic preferences.

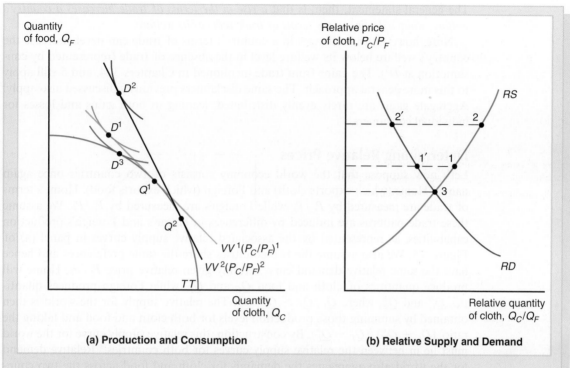

FIGURE 6-4

Effects of a Rise in the Relative Price of Cloth and Gains from Trade

In panel (a), the slope of the isovalue lines is equal to minus the relative price of cloth, P_C/P_F. As a result, when that relative price rises, all isovalue lines become steeper. In particular, the maximum-value line rotates from VV^1 to VV^2. Production shifts from Q^1 to Q^2 and consumption shifts from D^1 to D^2. If the economy cannot trade, then it produces and consumes at point D^3. Panel (b) shows the effects of the rise in the relative price of cloth on relative production (move from 1 to 2) and relative demand (move from 1' to 2'. If the economy cannot trade, then it consumes and produces at point 3.

consumption of cloth (move from point 1' to 2'). This change in relative consumption captures the substitution effect of the price change. If the income effect of the price change were large enough, then consumption levels of both goods could rise (D_C and D_F both increase); but the substitution effect of demand dictates that the *relative* consumption of cloth, D_C/D_F, decrease. If the economy cannot trade, then it consumes and produces at point 3 (associated with the relative price $(P_C/P_F)^3$.

The Welfare Effect of Changes in the Terms of Trade

When P_C/P_F increases, a country that initially exports cloth is made better off, as illustrated by the movement from D^1 to D^2 in panel (a) of Figure 6-4. Conversely, if P_C/P_F were to decline, the country would be made worse off; for example, consumption might move back from D^2 to D^1.

If the country were initially an exporter of food instead of cloth, the direction of this effect would be reversed. An increase in P_C/P_F would mean a fall in P_F/P_C and the country would be worse off: The relative price of the good it exports (food) would drop. We cover all these cases by defining the terms of trade as the price of the good a country initially exports divided by the price of the good it initially imports.

The general statement, then, is that *a rise in the terms of trade increases a country's welfare, while a decline in the terms of trade reduces its welfare.*

Note, however, that changes in a country's terms of trade can never decrease the country's welfare below its welfare level in the absence of trade (represented by consumption at D^3). The gains from trade mentioned in Chapters 3, 4, and 5 still apply to this more general approach. The same disclaimers previously discussed also apply: Aggregate gains are rarely evenly distributed, leading to both gains and losses for individual consumers.

Determining Relative Prices

Let's now suppose that the world economy consists of two countries once again named Home (which exports cloth) and Foreign (which exports food). Home's terms of trade are measured by P_C/P_F while Foreign's are measured by P_C/P_F. We assume these trade patterns are induced by differences in Home's and Foreign's production capabilities, as represented by the associated relative supply curves in panel (a) of Figure 6.5. We also assume the two countries share the same preferences and hence have the same relative demand curve. At any given relative price P_C/P_F, Home will produce quantities of cloth and food Q_C and Q_F, while Foreign produces quantities Q_C^* and Q_F^*, where $Q_C/Q_F > Q_C^*/Q_F^*$. The relative supply for the world is then obtained by summing those production levels for both cloth and food and taking the ratio: $(Q_C + Q_C^*)/(Q_F + Q_F^*)$. By construction, this relative supply curve for the world must lie in between the relative supply curves for both countries.[4] Relative demand for the world also aggregates the demands for cloth and food across the two countries: $(D_C + D_C^*)/(D_F + D_F^*)$. Since there are no differences in preferences across the two countries, the relative demand curve for the world overlaps with the same relative demand curve for each country.

The equilibrium relative price for the world (when Home and Foreign trade) is then given by the intersection of world relative supply and demand at point 1. This relative price determines how many units of Home's cloth exports are exchanged for Foreign's food exports. At the equilibrium relative price, Home's desired exports of cloth, $Q_C - D_C$, match up with Foreign's desired imports of cloth, $D_C^* - Q_C^*$. The food market is also in equilibrium so that Home's desired imports of food, $D_F - Q_F$, match up with Foreign's desired food exports, $Q_F^* - D_F^*$. The production possibility frontiers for Home and Foreign, along with the budget constraints and associated production and consumption choices at the equilibrium relative price $(P_C/P_F)^1$, are illustrated in panel (b).

Now that we know how relative supply, relative demand, the terms of trade, and welfare are determined in the standard model, we can use it to understand a number of important issues in international economics.

Economic Growth: A Shift of the *RS* Curve

The effects of economic growth in a trading world economy are a perennial source of concern and controversy. The debate revolves around two questions. First, is economic growth in other countries good or bad for our nation? Second, is growth in a country more or less valuable when that nation is part of a closely integrated world economy?

In assessing the effects of growth in other countries, commonsense arguments can be made on either side. On one side, economic growth in the rest of the world

---

[4]For any positive numbers X_1, X_2, Y_1, Y_2, if $X_1/Y_1 < X_2/Y_2$, then $X_1/Y_1 < (X_1 + X_2)/(Y_1 + Y_2) < X_2/Y_2$.

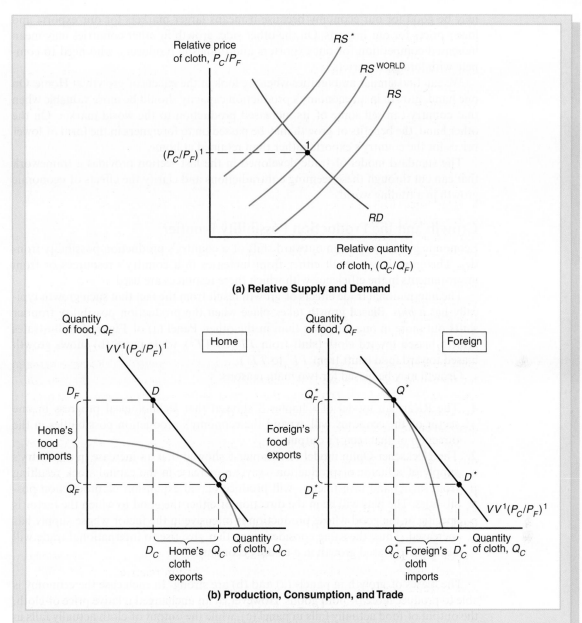

FIGURE 6-5

Equilibrium Relative Price with Trade and Associated Trade Flows

Panel (a) shows the relative supply of cloth in Home (RS), in Foreign (RS*), and for the world. Home and Foreign have the same relative demand, which is also the relative demand for the world. The equilibrium relative price $P_C/P_F)^1$ is determined by the intersection of the world relative supply and demand curves. Panel (b) shows the associated equilibrium trade flows between Home and Foreign. At the equilibrium relative price $(P_C/P_F)^1$, Home's exports of cloth equals Foreign's imports of cloth; and Home's imports of food equals Foreign's exports of food.

may be good for our economy because it means larger markets for our exports and lower prices for our imports. On the other side, growth in other countries may mean increased competition for our exporters and domestic producers, who need to compete with foreign exporters.

We can find similar ambiguities when we look at the effects of growth at Home. On one hand, growth in an economy's production capacity should be more valuable when that country can sell some of its increased production to the world market. On the other hand, the benefits of growth may be passed on to foreigners in the form of lower prices for the country's exports rather than retained at home.

The standard model of trade developed in the last section provides a framework that can cut through these seeming contradictions and clarify the effects of economic growth in a trading world.

Growth and the Production Possibility Frontier

Economic growth means an outward shift of a country's production possibility frontier. This growth can result either from increases in a country's resources or from improvements in the efficiency with which these resources are used.

The international trade effects of growth result from the fact that such growth typically has a *bias*. **Biased growth** takes place when the production possibility frontier shifts out more in one direction than in the other. Panel (a) of Figure 6-6 illustrates growth biased toward cloth (shift from TT^1 to TT^2), while panel (b) shows growth biased toward food (shift from TT^1 to TT^3).

Growth may be biased for two main reasons:

1. The Ricardian model of Chapter 3 showed that technological progress in one sector of the economy will expand the economy's production possibilities in the direction of that sector's output.
2. The Heckscher-Ohlin model of Chapter 5 showed that an increase in a country's supply of a factor of production—say, an increase in the capital stock resulting from saving and investment—will produce biased expansion of production possibilities. The bias will be in the direction of either the good to which the factor is specific or the good whose production is intensive in the factor whose supply has increased. Thus, the same considerations that give rise to international trade will also lead to biased growth in a trading economy.

The biases of growth in panels (a) and (b) are strong. In each case the economy is able to produce more of both goods. However, at an unchanged relative price of cloth, the output of food actually falls in panel (a), while the output of cloth actually falls in panel (b). Although growth is not always as strongly biased as it is in these examples, even growth that is more mildly biased toward cloth will lead, *for any given relative price of cloth*, to a rise in the output of cloth *relative* to that of food. In other words, the country's relative supply curve shifts to the right. This change is represented in panel (c) as the transition from RS^1 to RS^2. When growth is biased toward food, the relative supply curve shifts to the left, as shown by the transition from RS^1 to RS^3.

World Relative Supply and the Terms of Trade

Suppose now that Home experiences growth strongly biased toward cloth, so that its output of cloth rises at any given relative price of cloth, while its output of food declines (as shown in panel (a) of Figure 6-6). Then the output of cloth relative to food will rise at any given price for the world as a whole, and the world relative

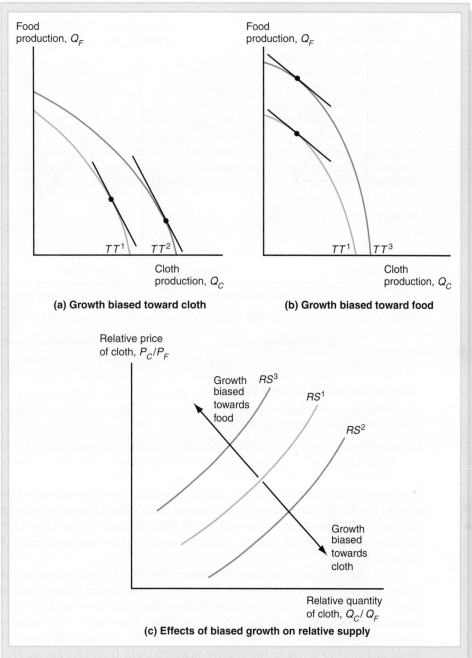

FIGURE 6-6

Biased Growth

Growth is biased when it shifts production possibilities out more toward one good than toward another. In case (a), growth is biased toward cloth (shift from TT^1 to TT^2), while in case (b), growth is biased toward food (shift from TT^1 to TT^3). The associated shifts in the relative supply curve are shown in panel (c): shift to the right (from RS^1 to RS^2) when growth is biased toward cloth, and shift to the left (from RS^1 to RS^3) when growth is biased toward food.

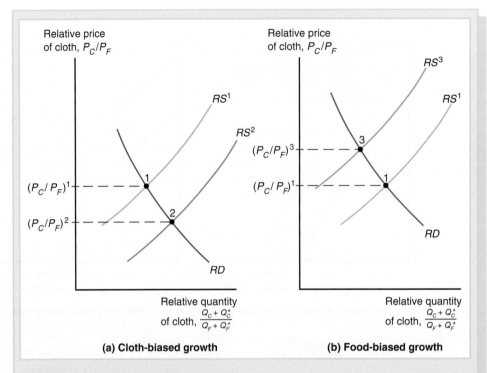

FIGURE 6-7

Growth and World Relative Supply

Growth biased toward cloth shifts the *RS* curve for the world to the right (a), while growth biased toward food shifts it to the left (b).

supply curve will shift to the right, just like the relative supply curve for Home. This shift in the world relative supply is shown in panel (a) of Figure 6-7 as a shift from RS^1 to RS^2. It results in a decrease in the relative price of cloth from $(P_C/P_F)^1$ to $(P_C/P_F)^2$, a worsening of Home's terms of trade and an improvement in Foreign's terms of trade.

Notice that the important consideration here is not *which* economy grows but rather the bias of that growth. If Foreign had experienced growth strongly biased toward cloth, the effect on the world relative supply curve and thus on the terms of trade would have been similar. On the other hand, either Home or Foreign growth strongly biased toward food will lead to a *leftward* shift of the *RS* curve (RS^1 to RS^3) for the *world* and thus to a rise in the relative price of cloth from $(P_C/P_F)^1$ to $(P_C/P_F)^3$ (as shown in panel (b)). This relative price increase is an improvement in Home's terms of trade, but a worsening of Foreign's.

Growth that disproportionately expands a country's production possibilities in the direction of the good it exports (cloth in Home, food in Foreign) is **export-biased growth**. Similarly, growth biased toward the good a country imports is **import-biased growth**. Our analysis leads to the following general principle: *Export-biased growth tends to worsen a growing country's terms of trade, to the benefit of the rest of the world; import-biased growth tends to improve a growing country's terms of trade at the rest of the world's expense.*

International Effects of Growth

Using this principle, we are now in a position to resolve our questions about the international effects of growth. Is growth in the rest of the world good or bad for our country? Does the fact that our country is part of a trading world economy increase or decrease the benefits of growth? In each case the answer depends on the *bias* of the growth. Export-biased growth in the rest of the world is good for us, improving our terms of trade, while import-biased growth abroad worsens our terms of trade. Export-biased growth in our own country worsens our terms of trade, reducing the direct benefits of growth, while import-biased growth leads to an improvement of our terms of trade, a secondary benefit.

During the 1950s, many economists from poorer countries believed that their nations, which primarily exported raw materials, were likely to experience steadily declining terms of trade over time. They believed that growth in the industrial world would be marked by an increasing development of synthetic substitutes for raw materials, while growth in the poorer nations would take the form of a further extension of their capacity to produce what they were already exporting rather than a move toward industrialization. That is, the growth in the industrial world would be import-biased, while that in the less-developed world would be export-biased.

Some analysts even suggested that growth in the poorer nations would actually be self-defeating. They argued that export-biased growth by poor nations would worsen their terms of trade so much that they would be worse off than if they had not grown at all. This situation is known to economists as the case of **immiserizing growth**.

In a famous paper published in 1958, economist Jagdish Bhagwati of Columbia University showed that such perverse effects of growth can in fact arise within a rigorously specified economic model.[5] However, the conditions under which immiserizing growth can occur are extreme: Strongly export-biased growth must be combined with very steep RS and RD curves, so that the change in the terms of trade is large enough to offset the direct favorable effects of an increase in a country's productive capacity. Most economists now regard the concept of immiserizing growth as more a theoretical point than a real-world issue.

While growth at home normally raises our own welfare even in a trading world, this is by no means true of growth abroad. Import-biased growth is not an unlikely possibility, and whenever the rest of the world experiences such growth, it worsens our terms of trade. Indeed, as we point out below, it is possible that the United States has suffered some loss of real income because of foreign growth over the postwar period.

 **CASE STUDY**   **Has the Growth of Newly Industrializing Countries Hurt Advanced Nations?**

In the early 1990s, many observers began warning that the growth of newly industrializing economies would pose a threat to the prosperity of advanced nations. In the Case Study in Chapter 5 on North-South trade, we addressed one way in which that growth might prove to be a problem: It might aggravate the growing gap in incomes between high-skilled and low-skilled workers in advanced nations. Some alarmists, however,

---

[5]"Immiserizing Growth: A Geometrical Note," *Review of Economic Studies* 25 (June 1958), pp. 201–205.

believed that the threat was still broader—that the overall real income of advanced nations, as opposed to its distribution, had been or would be reduced by the appearance of new competitors. This view was also held by a majority of respondents to a 2008 CBS poll: When asked "Do you think the recent economic expansion in countries like China and India has been generally good for the U.S. economy, or bad for the U.S. economy, or had no effect on the U.S. economy?" 62 percent said bad.

These concerns appeared to gain some intellectual support from a 2004 paper by Paul Samuelson, who created much of the modern theory of international trade. In that paper, Samuelson, using a Ricardian model, offered an example of how technological progress in developing countries can hurt advanced countries.[6] His analysis was simply a special case of the analysis we have just described: Growth in the rest of the world can hurt you if it takes place in sectors that compete with your exports. Samuelson took this to its logical conclusion: If China becomes sufficiently good at producing goods it currently imports, comparative advantage disappears—and the United States loses the gains from trade.

The popular press seized on this result, treating it as if it were somehow revolutionary. "The central question Samuelson and others raise is whether unfettered trade is always still as good for the U.S. as they have long believed," wrote *BusinessWeek*, which went on to suggest that such results might "completely derail comparative advantage theory."[7] Politicians also weighed-in, using Samuelson's paper and his towering stature within the economics profession to buttress arguments in favor of more protectionist policies.[8]

But the proposition that growth abroad can hurt your economy isn't a new idea, and it says nothing about whether free trade is better than protection. Also, it's an empirical question whether the growth of newly industrializing countries such as China has actually hurt advanced countries. And the facts don't support the claim.

Bear in mind that the channel through which growth abroad can hurt a country is via the terms of trade. So if the claim that competition from newly industrializing countries hurts advanced economies were true, we should see large negative numbers for the terms of trade of advanced countries and large positive numbers for the terms of trade of the new competitors. In the Mathematical Postscript to this chapter, we show that the percentage real income effect of a change in the terms of trade is approximately equal to the percent change in the terms of trade, multiplied by the share of imports in income. Since advanced countries on average spend about 25 percent of their income on imports (the United States' import share of GDP is lower than this average), a 1 percent decline in the terms of trade would reduce real income by only about 0.25 percent. So the terms of trade would have to decline by several percent a year to be a noticeable drag on economic growth.

Figure 6-8 shows the evolution of the terms of trade for both the United States and China over the last 30 years (normalized at 100 in 2000). We see that the magnitude of the yearly fluctuations in the terms of trade for the United States is small, with no clear trend over time. The U.S. terms of trade in 2011 is essentially at the same level as it was in 1980. Thus, there is no evidence that the United States has

---

[6]Paul Samuelson, "Where Ricardo and Mill Rebut and Confirm Arguments of Mainstream Economists Supporting Globalization," *Journal of Economic Perspectives* 18 (Summer 2004), pp. 135–146.
[7]"Shaking up Trade Theory," *BusinessWeek*, December 6, 2004.
[8]See, for example, "Clinton Doubts Benefits of Doha", *Financial Times*, December 3, 2007.

suffered any kind of sustained loss from a long-term deterioration in its terms of trade. Additionally, there is no evidence that China's terms of trade have steadily appreciated as it has become increasingly integrated into the world economy. If anything, its terms of trade have deteriorated over the last decade. This effect was confirmed in a recent paper using much more detail on Chinese industrial production.[9] The authors isolated the effects of Chinese manufacturing productivity growth (from 1995 to 2007) on its trading partners' terms of trade and found that this effect was positive, though small at .7 percent.

FIGURE 6-8

Evolution of the Terms of Trade for the United States and China (1980–2011, 2000 = 100)

One final point: In Samuelson's example, Chinese technological progress makes the United States worse off by eliminating trade between the two countries! Since what we actually see is rapidly growing China–U.S. trade, it's hard to find much of a relationship between the model and today's reality.

Source: World Development Indicators, World Bank.

Most developed countries tend to experience mild swings in their terms of trade, around 1 percent or less a year (on average), as illustrated for the United States in Figure 6-8. However, some developing countries' exports are heavily concentrated in mineral and agricultural sectors. The prices of those goods on world markets are very

---

[9]See Chang-Tai Hsieh and Ralph Ossa, "A Global View of Productivity Growth in China," National Bureau of Economic Research Working Paper 16778 (2011).

volatile, leading to large swings in the terms of trade. These swings in turn translate into substantial changes in welfare (because trade is concentrated in a small number of sectors and represents a substantial percentage of GDP). In fact, some studies show that most of the fluctuations in GDP in several developing countries (where GDP fluctuations are quite large relative to the GDP fluctuations in developed countries) can be attributed to fluctuations in their terms of trade.[10] For example, Argentina suffered a 6 percent deterioration in its terms of trade in 1999 (due to declining agricultural prices), which induced a 1.4 percent drop in GDP. (The actual GDP loss was higher, but other factors contributed to this deterioration.) On the other hand, Ecuador enjoyed an 18 percent increase in its terms of trade in 2000 (due to increases in oil prices), which added 1.6 percent to the GDP growth rate for that year.[11]

Tariffs and Export Subsidies: Simultaneous Shifts in *RS* and *RD*

Import tariffs (taxes levied on imports) and **export subsidies** (payments given to domestic producers who sell a good abroad) are not usually put in place to affect a country's terms of trade. These government interventions in trade usually take place for income distribution, for the promotion of industries thought to be crucial to the economy, or for balance of payments. (Note: We will examine these motivations in Chapters 10, 11, and 12.) Whatever the motive for tariffs and subsidies, however, they *do* have effects on terms of trade that can be understood by using the standard trade model.

The distinctive feature of tariffs and export subsidies is that they create a difference between prices at which goods are traded on the world market and prices at which those goods can be purchased within a country. The direct effect of a tariff is to make imported goods more expensive inside a country than they are outside the country. An export subsidy gives producers an incentive to export. It will therefore be more profitable to sell abroad than at home unless the price at home is higher, so such a subsidy raises the prices of exported goods inside a country. Note that this is very different from the effects of a production subsidy, which also lowers domestic prices for the affected goods (since the production subsidy does not discriminate based on the sales destination of the goods).

When countries are big exporters or importers of a good (relative to the size of the world market), the price changes caused by tariffs and subsidies change both relative supply and relative demand on world markets. The result is a shift in the terms of trade, both of the country imposing the policy change and of the rest of the world.

Relative Demand and Supply Effects of a Tariff

Tariffs and subsidies drive a wedge between the prices at which goods are traded internationally (**external prices**) and the prices at which they are traded within a country (**internal prices**). This means that we have to be careful in defining the terms of trade, which are intended to measure the ratio at which countries exchange goods; for example, how many units of food can Home import for each unit of cloth that it exports? This means that the terms of trade correspond to external, rather than internal, prices.

---

[10]See M. Ayhan Kose, "Explaining Business Cycles in Small Open Economies: 'How Much Do World Prices Matter?'" *Journal of International Economics* 56 (March 2002), pp. 299–327.
[11]See Christian Broda and Cédric Tille, "Coping with Terms-of-Trade Shocks in Developing Countries," *Current Issues in Economics and Finance* 9 (November 2003), pp 1–7.

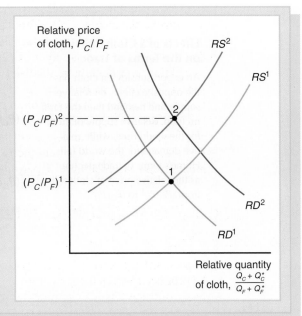

FIGURE 6-9

Effects of a Food Tariff on the Terms of Trade

An import tariff on food imposed by Home both reduces the relative supply of cloth (from RS^1 to RS^2) and increases the relative demand (from RD^1 to RD^2) for the world as a whole. As a result, the relative price of cloth must rise from $(P_C/P_F)^1$ to $(P_C/P_F)^2$.

When analyzing the effects of a tariff or export subsidy, therefore, we want to know how that tariff or subsidy affects relative supply and demand *as a function of external prices.*

If Home imposes a 20 percent tariff on the value of food imports, for example, the internal price of food relative to cloth faced by Home producers and consumers will be 20 percent higher than the external relative price of food on the world market. Equivalently, the internal relative price of cloth on which Home residents base their decisions will be lower than the relative price on the external market.

At any given world relative price of cloth, then, Home producers will face a lower relative cloth price and therefore will produce less cloth and more food. At the same time, Home consumers will shift their consumption toward cloth and away from food. From the point of view of the world as a whole, the relative supply of cloth will fall (from RS^1 to RS^2 in Figure 6-9) while the relative demand for cloth will rise (from RD^1 to RD^2). Clearly, the world relative price of cloth rises from $(P_C/P_F)^1$ to $(P_C/P_F)^2$, and thus Home's terms of trade improve at Foreign's expense.

The extent of this terms of trade effect depends on how large the country imposing the tariff is relative to the rest of the world: If the country is only a small part of the world, it cannot have much effect on world relative supply and demand and therefore cannot have much effect on relative prices. If the United States, a very large country, were to impose a 20 percent tariff, some estimates suggest that the U.S. terms of trade might rise by 15 percent. That is, the price of U.S. imports relative to exports might fall by 15 percent on the world market, while the relative price of imports would rise only 5 percent inside the United States. On the other hand, if Luxembourg or Paraguay were to impose a 20 percent tariff, the terms of trade effect would probably be too small to measure.

Effects of an Export Subsidy

Tariffs and export subsidies are often treated as similar policies, since they both seem to support domestic producers, but they have opposite effects on the terms of trade. Suppose that Home offers a 20 percent subsidy on the value of any cloth

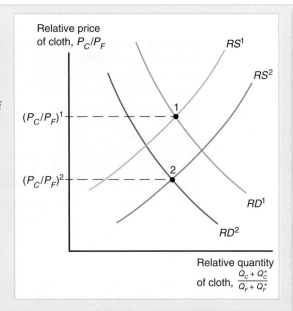

FIGURE 6-10

Effects of a Cloth Subsidy on the Terms of Trade

An export subsidy on cloth has the opposite effects on relative supply and demand than the tariff on food. Relative supply of cloth for the world rises, while relative demand for the world falls. Home's terms of trade decline as the relative price of cloth falls from $(P_C/P_F)^1$ to $(P_C/P_F)^2$.

exported. For any given world prices, this subsidy will raise Home's internal price of cloth relative to that of food by 20 percent. The rise in the relative price of cloth will lead Home producers to produce more cloth and less food, while leading Home consumers to substitute food for cloth. As illustrated in Figure 6-10, the subsidy will increase the world relative supply of cloth (from RS^1 to RS^2) and decrease the world relative demand for cloth (from RD^1 to RD^2), shifting equilibrium from point 1 to point 2. A Home export subsidy worsens Home's terms of trade and improves Foreign's.

Implications of Terms of Trade Effects: Who Gains and Who Loses?

If Home imposes a tariff, it improves its terms of trade at Foreign's expense. Thus, tariffs hurt the rest of the world. The effect on Home's welfare is not quite as clear-cut. The terms of trade improvement benefits Home; however, a tariff also imposes costs by distorting production and consumption incentives within Home's economy (see Chapter 9). The terms of trade gains will outweigh the losses from distortion only as long as the tariff is not too large. We will see later how to define an optimum tariff that maximizes net benefit. (For small countries that cannot have much impact on their terms of trade, the optimum tariff is near zero.)

The effects of an export subsidy are quite clear. Foreign's terms of trade improve at Home's expense, leaving it clearly better off. At the same time, Home loses from terms of trade deterioration *and* from the distorting effects of its policy.

This analysis seems to show that export subsidies never make sense. In fact, it is difficult to come up with situations where export subsidies would serve the national interest. The use of export subsidies as a policy tool usually has more to do with the peculiarities of trade politics than with economic logic.

Are foreign tariffs always bad for a country and foreign export subsidies always beneficial? Not necessarily. Our model is of a two-country world, where the other country exports the good we import and vice versa. In the real, multination world, a foreign government may subsidize the export of a good that competes with U.S. exports; this foreign subsidy will obviously hurt the U.S. terms of trade. A good example of this effect is European subsidies to agricultural exports (see Chapter 9). Alternatively, a country may impose a tariff on something the United States also imports, lowering its price and benefiting the United States. We thus need to qualify our conclusions from a two-country analysis: Subsidies to exports of things *the United States imports* help us, while tariffs *against U.S. exports* hurt us.

The view that subsidized foreign sales to the United States are good for us is not a popular one. When foreign governments are charged with subsidizing sales in the United States, the popular and political reaction is that this is unfair competition. Thus when the Commerce Department determined in 2012 that the Chinese government was subsidizing exports of solar panels to the United States, it responded by imposing a tariff on solar panel imports from China.[12] The standard model tells us that lower prices for solar panels are a good thing for the U.S. economy (which is a net importer of solar panels). On the other hand, some models based on imperfect competition and increasing returns to scale in production point to some potential welfare losses from the Chinese subsidy. Nevertheless, the subsidy's biggest impact falls on the distribution of income within the United States. If China subsidizes exports of solar panels to the United States, most U.S. residents gain from cheaper solar power. However, workers and investors in the U.S. solar panel industry are hurt by the lower import prices.

International Borrowing and Lending

Up to this point, all of the trading relationships we have described were not referenced by a time dimension: One good, say cloth, is exchanged for a different good, say food. In this section, we show how the standard model of trade we have developed can also be used to analyze another very important kind of trade between countries that occurs over time: international borrowing and lending. Any international transaction that occurs over time has a financial aspect, and this aspect is one of the main topics we address in the second half of this book. However, we can also abstract from those financial aspects and think of borrowing and lending as just another kind of trade: Instead of trading one good for another at a point in time, we exchange goods today in return for some goods in the future. This kind of trade is known as **intertemporal trade**; we will have much more to say about it later in this text, but for now we will analyze it using a variant of our standard trade model with a time dimension.[13]

Intertemporal Production Possibilities and Trade

Even in the absence of international capital movements, any economy faces a trade-off between consumption now and consumption in the future. Economies usually do not consume all of their current output; some of their output takes the form of investment in machines, buildings, and other forms of productive capital. The more investment an economy undertakes now, the more it will be able to produce and consume in the future. To invest more, however, an economy must release resources by consuming less (unless there are unemployed resources, a possibility we temporarily disregard). Thus, there is a trade-off between current and future consumption.

---

[12]See "U.S. Will Place Tariffs on Chinese Solar Panels," *New York Times*, October 10, 2012.

[13]See the appendix for additional details and derivations.

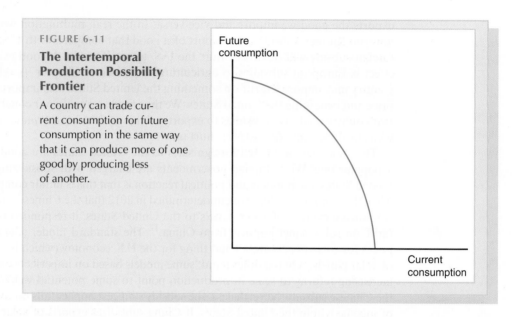

FIGURE 6-11

The Intertemporal Production Possibility Frontier

A country can trade current consumption for future consumption in the same way that it can produce more of one good by producing less of another.

Let's imagine an economy that consumes only one good and will exist for only two periods, which we will call current and future. Then there will be a trade-off between current and future production of the consumption good, which we can summarize by drawing an **intertemporal production possibility frontier**. Such a frontier is illustrated in Figure 6-11. It looks just like the production possibility frontiers between two goods at a point in time that we have been drawing.

The shape of the intertemporal production possibility frontier will differ among countries. Some countries will have production possibilities that are biased toward current output, while others are biased toward future output. We will ask in a moment what real differences these biases correspond to, but first let's simply suppose that there are two countries, Home and Foreign, with different intertemporal production possibilities. Home's possibilities are biased toward current consumption, while Foreign's are biased toward future consumption.

Reasoning by analogy, we already know what to expect. In the absence of international borrowing and lending, we would expect the relative price of future consumption to be higher in Home than in Foreign, and thus if we open the possibility of trade over time, we would expect Home to export current consumption and import future consumption.

This may, however, seem a little puzzling. What is the relative price of future consumption, and how does one trade over time?

The Real Interest Rate

How does a country trade over time? Like an individual, a country can trade over time by borrowing or lending. Consider what happens when an individual borrows: She is initially able to spend more than her income or, in other words, to consume more than her production. Later, however, she must repay the loan with interest, and therefore in the future she consumes *less* than she produces. By borrowing, then, she has in effect traded future consumption for current consumption. The same is true of a borrowing country.

Clearly the price of future consumption in terms of current consumption has something to do with the interest rate. As we will see in the second half of this book, in the real world the interpretation of interest rates is complicated by the possibility of changes in the overall price level. For now, we bypass that problem by supposing that loan contracts are specified in "real" terms: When a country borrows, it gets the right to purchase some quantity of consumption now in return for repayment of some larger quantity in the future. Specifically, the quantity of repayment in the future will be $(1 + r)$ times the quantity borrowed in the present, where r is the **real interest rate** on borrowing. Since the trade-off is one unit of current consumption for $(1 + r)$ units in the future, the relative price of future consumption is $1/(1 + r)$.

When this relative price of future consumption rises (that is, the real interest rate r falls), a country responds by investing more; this increases the supply of future consumption relative to current consumption (a leftward movement along the intertemporal production possibility frontier in Figure 6-11) and implies an upward-sloping relative supply curve for future consumption. We previously saw how a consumer's preferences for cloth and food could be represented by a relative demand curve relating relative consumption to the relative prices of those goods. Similarly, a consumer will also have preferences over time that capture the extent to which she is willing to substitute between current and future consumption. Those substitution effects are also captured by an intertemporal relative demand curve that relates the relative demand for future consumption (the ratio of future consumption to current consumption) to its relative price $1/(1 + r)$.

The parallel with our standard trade model is now complete. If borrowing and lending are allowed, the relative price of future consumption, and thus the world real interest rate, will be determined by the world relative supply and demand for future consumption. The determination of the equilibrium relative price $1/(1 + r^1)$ is shown in Figure 6-12 (notice the parallel with trade in goods and panel (a) of Figure 6-5). The intertemporal relative supply curves for Home and Foreign reflect how Home's production possibilities are biased toward current consumption whereas Foreign's production possibilities are biased toward future consumption. In other words, Foreign's

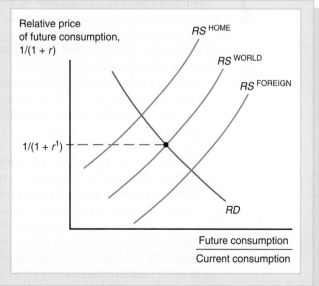

FIGURE 6-12

Equilibrium Interest Rate with Borrowing and Lending

Home, Foreign, and world supply of future consumption relative to current consumption. Home and Foreign have the same relative demand for future consumption, which is also the relative demand for the world. The equilibrium interest rate $1/(1 + r^1)$ is determined by the intersection of world relative supply and demand.

relative supply for future consumption is shifted out relative to Home's relative supply. At the equilibrium real interest rate, Home will export current consumption in return for imports of future consumption. That is, Home will lend to Foreign in the present and receive repayment in the future.

Intertemporal Comparative Advantage

We have assumed that Home's intertemporal production possibilities are biased toward current production. But what does this mean? The sources of intertemporal comparative advantage are somewhat different from those that give rise to ordinary trade.

A country that has a comparative advantage in future production of consumption goods is one that in the absence of international borrowing and lending would have a low relative price of future consumption, that is, a high real interest rate. This high real interest rate corresponds to a high return on investment, that is, a high return to diverting resources from current production of consumption goods to production of capital goods, construction, and other activities that enhance the economy's future ability to produce. So countries that borrow in the international market will be those where highly productive investment opportunities are available relative to current productive capacity, while countries that lend will be those where such opportunities are not available domestically.

SUMMARY

1. The standard trade model derives a world relative supply curve from production possibilities and a world relative demand curve from preferences. The price of exports relative to imports, a country's terms of trade, is determined by the intersection of the world relative supply and demand curves. Other things equal, a rise in a country's terms of trade increases its welfare. Conversely, a decline in a country's terms of trade will leave the country worse off.

2. Economic growth means an outward shift in a country's production possibility frontier. Such growth is usually biased; that is, the production possibility frontier shifts out more in the direction of some goods than in the direction of others. The immediate effect of biased growth is to lead, other things equal, to an increase in the world relative supply of the goods toward which the growth is biased. This shift in the world relative supply curve in turn leads to a change in the growing country's terms of trade, which can go in either direction. If the growing country's terms of trade improve, this improvement reinforces the initial growth at home but hurts the growth in the rest of the world. If the growing country's terms of trade worsen, this decline offsets some of the favorable effects of growth at home but benefits the rest of the world.

3. The direction of the terms of trade effects depends on the nature of the growth. Growth that is export-biased (growth that expands the ability of an economy to produce the goods it was initially exporting more than it expands the economy's ability to produce goods that compete with imports) worsens the terms of trade. Conversely, growth that is import-biased, disproportionately increasing the ability to produce import-competing goods, improves a country's terms of trade. It is possible for import-biased growth abroad to hurt a country.

4. Import tariffs and export subsidies affect both relative supply and relative demand. A tariff raises relative supply of a country's import good while lowering relative demand. A tariff unambiguously improves the country's terms of trade at the rest

of the world's expense. An export subsidy has the reverse effect, increasing the relative supply and reducing the relative demand for the country's export good, and thus worsening the terms of trade. The terms of trade effects of an export subsidy hurt the subsidizing country and benefit the rest of the world, while those of a tariff do the reverse. This suggests that export subsidies do not make sense from a national point of view and that foreign export subsidies should be welcomed rather than countered. Both tariffs and subsidies, however, have strong effects on the distribution of income within countries, and these effects often weigh more heavily on policy than the terms of trade concerns.

5. International borrowing and lending can be viewed as a kind of international trade, but one that involves trade of current consumption for future consumption rather than trade of one good for another. The relative price at which this intertemporal trade takes place is 1 plus the real rate of interest.

KEY TERMS

biased growth, p. 158
export-biased growth, p. 160
export subsidy, p. 164
external price, p. 164
immiserizing growth, p. 161
import-biased growth, p. 160

import tariff, p. 164
indifference curves, p. 153
internal price, p. 164
intertemporal production
   possibility frontier, p. 168
intertemporal trade, p. 167

isovalue lines, p. 152
real interest rate, p. 169
standard trade model, p. 151
terms of trade, p. 151

PROBLEMS

MyEconLab

1. Suppose Indonesia and China are trading partners. Indonesia initially exports palm oil to and imports lubricants from China. Using the standard trade model, explain how an increase in the relative price of palm oil—in relation to lubricant prices—would affect production and consumption of palm oil for Indonesia (assuming that the taste for both goods is the same in both countries). If the income effect of price change of palm oil is greater than the substitution effect, what would happen to palm oil consumption in Indonesia?

2. In the trade scenario in problem 1, due to overfishing, Norway becomes unable to catch the quantity of fish that it could in previous years. This change causes both a reduction in the potential quantity of fish that can be produced in Norway and an increase in the relative world price for fish, P_f/P_a.
   a. Show how the overfishing problem can result in a decline in welfare for Norway.
   b. Also show how it is possible that the overfishing problem could result in an *increase* in welfare for Norway.

3. Imagine the world having two countries producing wheat and cloth, with no difference in preferences across the two countries. If the home country—exporting cloth—experiences a growth strongly biased towards it, what would happen to the home country's terms of trade? How would the terms of trade be affected if the home country's production grows in favor of wheat?

4. The counterpart to immobile factors on the supply side would be lack of substitution on the demand side. Imagine an economy where consumers always buy goods in rigid proportions—for example, one yard of cloth for every pound of

food—regardless of the prices of the two goods. Show that an improvement in the terms of trade benefits this economy as well.

5. Japan primarily exports manufactured goods, while importing raw materials such as food and oil. Analyze the impact on Japan's terms of trade of the following events:
   a. A war in the Middle East disrupts oil supply.
   b. Korea develops the ability to produce automobiles that it can sell in Canada and the United States.
   c. U.S. engineers develop a fusion reactor that replaces fossil fuel electricity plants.
   d. A harvest failure in Russia.
   e. A reduction in Japan's tariffs on imported beef and citrus fruit.

6. The Internet has allowed for increased trade in services such as programming and technical support, a development that has lowered the prices of such services relative to those of manufactured goods. India in particular has been recently viewed as an "exporter" of technology-based services, an area in which the United States had been a major exporter. Using manufacturing and services as tradable goods, create a standard trade model for the U.S. and Indian economies that shows how relative price declines in exportable services that lead to the "outsourcing" of services can reduce welfare in the United States and increase welfare in India.

7. Countries A and B have two factors of production, capital and labor, with which they produce two goods, X and Y. Technology is the same in the two countries. X is capital-intensive; A is capital-abundant.

   Analyze the effects on the terms of trade and on the two countries' welfare of the following:
   a. An increase in A's capital stock.
   b. An increase in A's labor supply.
   c. An increase in B's capital stock.
   d. An increase in B's labor supply.

8. Economic growth is just as likely to worsen a country's terms of trade as it is to improve them. Why, then, do most economists regard immiserizing growth, where growth actually hurts the growing country, as unlikely in practice?

9. From an economic point of view, India and China are somewhat similar: Both are huge, low-wage countries, probably with similar patterns of comparative advantage, which until recently were relatively closed to international trade. China was the first to open up. Now that India is also opening up to world trade, how would you expect this to affect the welfare of China? Of the United States? (Hint: Think of adding a new economy identical to that of China to the world economy.)

10. "In a two country and a two commodity world, an imposition of home country's import tariff increases its terms of trade and export subsidy reduces its terms of trade"—explain. If an import tariff increases the home country's terms of trade, then, at present, why do countries agree to reduce the tariffs under bilateral and multilateral free trade agreements?

11. In a trade-off between current and future consumption, discuss how real interest rates affect the relative price of future consumption.

12. Which of the following countries would you expect to have intertemporal production possibilities biased toward current consumption goods, and which biased toward future consumption goods?
    a. A country like Argentina or Canada in the last century that has only recently been opened for large-scale settlement and is receiving large inflows of immigrants.

   b. A country like the United Kingdom in the late 19th century or the United States today that leads the world technologically but is seeing that lead eroded as other countries catch up.

   c. A country like Saudi Arabia that has discovered large oil reserves that can be exploited with little new investment.

   d. A country that has discovered large oil reserves that can be exploited only with massive investment, such as Norway, whose oil lies under the North Sea.

   e. A country like South Korea that has discovered the knack of producing industrial goods and is rapidly gaining on advanced countries.

FURTHER READINGS

Rudiger Dornbusch, Stanley Fischer, and Paul Samuelson. "Comparative Advantage, Trade, and Payments in a Ricardian Model with a Continuum of Goods." *American Economic Review* 67 (1977). This paper, cited in Chapter 3, also gives a clear exposition of the role of nontraded goods in establishing the presumption that a transfer improves the recipient's terms of trade.

Lawrence Edwards and Robert Z. Lawrence, *Rising Tide: Is Growth in Emerging Economies Good for the United States?* (Peterson Institute for International Economics, 2013), Chapter 5. This chapter provides a detailed analysis of the question raised in the case study on the effects of developing country growth on overall U.S. welfare.

Irving Fisher. *The Theory of Interest.* New York: Macmillan, 1930. The "intertemporal" approach described in this chapter owes its origin to Fisher.

J. R. Hicks. "The Long Run Dollar Problem." *Oxford Economic Papers* 2 (1953), pp. 117–135. The modern analysis of growth and trade has its origins in the fears of Europeans, in the early years after World War II, that the United States had an economic lead that could not be overtaken. (This sounds dated today, but many of the same arguments have now resurfaced about Japan.) The paper by Hicks is the most famous exposition.

Harry G. Johnson. "Economic Expansion and International Trade." *Manchester School of Social and Economic Studies* 23 (1955), pp. 95–112. The paper that laid out the crucial distinction between export- and import-biased growth.

Paul Krugman. "Does Third World Growth Hurt First World Prosperity?" *Harvard Business Review* 72 (July–August 1994), pp. 113–121. An analysis that attempts to explain why growth in developing countries need not hurt advanced countries in principle and probably does not do so in practice.

Jeffrey Sachs. "The Current Account and Macroeconomic Adjustment in the 1970s." *Brookings Papers on Economic Activity*, 1981. A study of international capital flows that views such flows as intertemporal trade.

MyEconLab Can Help You Get a Better Grade

MyEconLab   If your exam were tomorrow, would you be ready? For each chapter, MyEconLab Practice Tests and Study Plans pinpoint sections you have mastered and those you need to study. That way, you are more efficient with your study time, and you are better prepared for your exams.

To see how it works, turn to page 41 and then go to

www.myeconlab.com

More on Intertemporal Trade

This appendix contains a more detailed examination of the two-period intertemporal trade model described in the chapter. First consider Home, whose intertemporal production possibility frontier is shown in Figure 6A-1. Recall that the quantities of current and future consumption goods produced at Home depend on the amount of current consumption goods invested to produce future goods. As currently available resources are diverted from current consumption to investment, production of current consumption, Q_P, falls and production of future consumption, Q_F, rises. Increased investment therefore shifts the economy up and to the left along the intertemporal production possibility frontier.

The chapter showed that the price of future consumption in terms of current consumption is $1/(1 + r)$, where r is the real interest rate. Measured in terms of current consumption, the value of the economy's total production over the two periods of its existence is therefore

$$V = Q_C + Q_F/(1 + r).$$

Figure 6A-1 shows the isovalue lines corresponding to the relative price $1/(1 + r)$ for different values of V. These are straight lines with slope $-(1 + r)$ (because future consumption is on the vertical axis). As in the standard trade model, firms' decisions lead to a production pattern that maximizes the value of production at market prices $Q_C + Q_F/(1 + r)$. Production therefore occurs at point Q. The economy invests the amount shown, leaving Q_C available for current consumption and producing an amount Q_F of future consumption when the first-period investment pays off. (Notice the parallel with Figure 6-1 where production levels of cloth and food are chosen for a single period in order to maximize the value of production.)

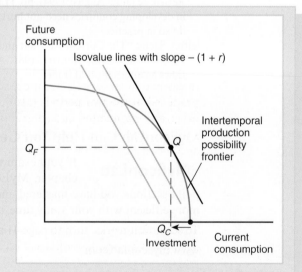

FIGURE 6A-1

Determining Home's Intertemporal Production Pattern

At a world real interest rate of r, Home's investment level maximizes the value of production over the two periods that the economy exists.

FIGURE 6A-2

Determining Home's Intertemporal Consumption Pattern

Home's consumption places it on the highest indifference curve touching its intertemporal budget constraint. The economy exports $Q_C - D_C$ units of current consumption and imports $D_F - Q_F = (1 + r) \times (Q_C - D_C)$ units of future consumption.

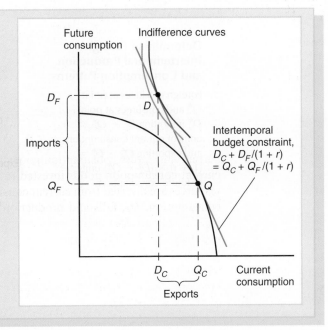

At the chosen production point Q, the extra future consumption that would result from investing an additional unit of current consumption just equals $(1 + r)$. It would be inefficient to push investment beyond point Q because the economy could do better by lending additional current consumption to foreigners instead. Figure 6A-1 implies that a rise in the world real interest rate r, which steepens the isovalue lines, causes investment to fall.

Figure 6A-2 shows how Home's consumption pattern is determined for a given world interest rate. Let D_C and D_F represent the demands for current and future consumption goods, respectively. Since production is at point Q, the economy's consumption possibilities over the two periods are limited by the *intertemporal budget constraint*:

$$D_C + D_F/(1 + r) = Q_C + Q_F/(1 + r).$$

This constraint states that the value of Home's consumption over the two periods (measured in terms of current consumption) equals the value of consumption goods produced in the two periods (also measured in current consumption units). Put another way, production and consumption must lie on the same isovalue line.

Point D, where Home's budget constraint touches the highest attainable indifference curve, shows the current and future consumption levels chosen by the economy. Home's demand for current consumption, D_C, is smaller than its production of current consumption, Q_C, so it exports (that is, lends) $Q_C - D_C$ units of current consumption to Foreigners. Correspondingly, Home imports $D_F - Q_F$ units of future consumption from abroad when its first-period loans are repaid to it with interest. The intertemporal budget constraint implies that $D_F - Q_F = (1 + r) \times (Q_C - D_C)$, so trade is *intertemporally* balanced. (Once again, note the parallel with Figure 6-3, where the economy exports cloth in return for imports of food.)

Figure 6A-3 shows how investment and consumption are determined in Foreign. Foreign is assumed to have a comparative advantage in producing *future* consumption

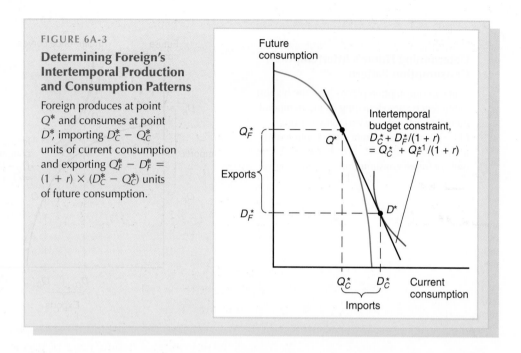

FIGURE 6A-3

Determining Foreign's Intertemporal Production and Consumption Patterns

Foreign produces at point Q^* and consumes at point D^*, importing $D_C^* - Q_C^*$ units of current consumption and exporting $Q_F^* - D_F^* = (1 + r) \times (D_C^* - Q_C^*)$ units of future consumption.

goods. The diagram shows that at a real interest rate of r, Foreign borrows consumption goods in the first period and repays this loan using consumption goods produced in the second period. Because of its relatively rich domestic investment opportunities and its relative preference for current consumption, Foreign is an importer of current consumption and an exporter of future consumption.

The differences between Home and Foreign's production possibility frontiers lead to the differences in the relative supply curves depicted in Figure 6-11. At the equilibrium interest rate $1/(1 + r^1)$, Home's desired export of current consumption equals Foreign's desired import of current consumption. Put another way, at that interest rate, Home's desired first-period lending equals Foreign's desired first-period borrowing. Supply and demand are therefore equal in both periods.

CHAPTER 7

EXTERNAL ECONOMIES OF SCALE AND THE INTERNATIONAL LOCATION OF PRODUCTION

In Chapter 3, we pointed out that there are two reasons why countries specialize and trade. First, countries differ either in their resources or in their technology and specialize in the things they do relatively well; second, economies of scale (or increasing returns) make it advantageous for each country to specialize in the production of only a limited range of goods and services. The past four chapters considered models in which all trade is based on comparative advantage; that is, differences between countries are the only reason for trade. This chapter introduces the role of economies of scale.

The analysis of trade based on economies of scale presents certain problems that we have avoided so far. Until now, we have assumed markets are perfectly competitive, so that all monopoly profits are always competed away. When there are increasing returns, however, large firms may have an advantage over small ones, so that markets tend to be dominated by one firm (monopoly) or, more often, by a few firms (oligopoly). If this happens, our analysis of trade has to take into account the effects of imperfect competition.

However, economies of scale need not lead to imperfect competition if they take the form of *external* economies, which apply at the level of the industry rather than at the level of the individual firm. In this chapter, we will focus on the role of such external economies of scale in trade, reserving the discussion of internal economies for the next chapter.

LEARNING GOALS

After reading this chapter, you will be able to:

- Recognize why international trade often occurs from increasing returns to scale.
- Understand the differences between internal and external economies of scale.
- Discuss the sources of external economies.
- Discuss the roles of external economies and knowledge spillovers in shaping comparative advantage and international trade patterns.

Economies of Scale and International Trade: An Overview

The models of comparative advantage already presented were based on the assumption of constant returns to scale. That is, we assumed that if inputs to an industry were doubled, industry output would double as well. In practice, however, many industries are characterized by **economies of scale** (also referred to as increasing returns), so that production is more efficient the larger the scale at which it takes place. Where there are economies of scale, doubling the inputs to an industry will more than double the industry's production.

A simple example can help convey the significance of economies of scale for international trade. Table 7-1 shows the relationship between input and output of a hypothetical industry. Widgets are produced using only one input, labor; the table shows how the amount of labor required depends on the number of widgets produced. To produce 10 widgets, for example, requires 15 hours of labor, while to produce 25 widgets requires 30 hours. The presence of economies of scale may be seen from the fact that doubling the input of labor from 15 to 30 more than doubles the industry's output—in fact, output increases by a factor of 2.5. Equivalently, the existence of economies of scale may be seen by looking at the average amount of labor used to produce each unit of output: If output is only 5 widgets, the average labor input per widget is 2 hours, while if output is 25 units, the average labor input falls to 1.2 hours.

We can use this example to see why economies of scale provide an incentive for international trade. Imagine a world consisting of two countries, the United States and Britain, both of which have the same technology for producing widgets. Suppose each country initially produces 10 widgets. According to the table, this requires 15 hours of labor in each country, so in the world as a whole, 30 hours of labor produce 20 widgets. But now suppose we concentrate world production of widgets in one country, say the United States, and let the United States employ 30 hours of labor in the widget industry. In a single country, these 30 hours of labor can produce 25 widgets. So by concentrating production of widgets in the United States, the world economy can use the same amount of labor to produce 25 percent more widgets.

But where does the United States find the extra labor to produce widgets, and what happens to the labor that was employed in the British widget industry? To get the labor to expand its production of some goods, the United States must decrease or abandon the production of others; these goods will then be produced in Britain instead, using the labor formerly employed in the industries whose production has expanded in the United States. Imagine there are many goods subject to economies of scale in production, and give them numbers 1, 2, 3,.... To take advantage of economies of scale, each

TABLE 7-1	Relationship of Input to Output for a Hypothetical Industry	
Output	**Total Labor Input**	**Average Labor Input**
5	10	2
10	15	1.5
15	20	1.333333
20	25	1.25
25	30	1.2
30	35	1.166667

of the countries must concentrate on producing only a limited number of goods. Thus, for example, the United States might produce goods 1, 3, 5, and so on, while Britain produces 2, 4, 6, and so on. If each country produces only some of the goods, then each good can be produced at a larger scale than would be the case if each country tried to produce everything. As a result, the world economy can produce more of each good.

How does international trade enter the story? Consumers in each country will still want to consume a variety of goods. Suppose industry 1 ends up in the United States and industry 2 ends up in Britain; then American consumers of good 2 will have to buy goods imported from Britain, while British consumers of good 1 will have to import it from the United States. International trade plays a crucial role: It makes it possible for each country to produce a restricted range of goods and to take advantage of economies of scale without sacrificing variety in consumption. Indeed, as we will see in Chapter 8, international trade typically leads to an increase in the variety of goods available.

Our example, then, suggests how mutually beneficial trade can arise as a result of economies of scale. Each country specializes in producing a limited range of products, which enables it to produce these goods more efficiently than if it tried to produce everything for itself; these specialized economies then trade with each other to be able to consume the full range of goods.

Unfortunately, to go from this suggestive story to an explicit model of trade based on economies of scale is not that simple. The reason is that economies of scale may lead to a market structure other than that of perfect competition, and we need to be careful about analyzing this market structure.

Economies of Scale and Market Structure

In the example in Table 7-1, we represented economies of scale by assuming the labor input per unit of production is smaller the more units produced; this implies that at a given wage rate per hour, the average cost of production falls as output rises. We did not say how this production increase was achieved—whether existing firms simply produced more, or whether there was instead an increase in the number of firms. To analyze the effects of economies of scale on market structure, however, one must be clear about what kind of production increase is necessary to reduce average cost. **External economies of scale** occur when the cost per unit depends on the size of the industry but not necessarily on the size of any one firm. **Internal economies of scale** occur when the cost per unit depends on the size of an individual firm but not necessarily on that of the industry.

The distinction between external and internal economies can be illustrated with a hypothetical example. Imagine an industry that initially consists of 10 firms, each producing 100 widgets, for a total industry production of 1,000 widgets. Now consider two cases. First, suppose the industry were to double in size, so that it now consists of 20 firms, each one still producing 100 widgets. It is possible that the costs of each firm will fall as a result of the increased size of the industry; for example, a bigger industry may allow more efficient provision of specialized services or machinery. If this is the case, the industry exhibits external economies of scale. That is, the efficiency of firms is increased by having a larger industry, even though each firm is the same size as before.

Second, suppose the industry's output is held constant at 1,000 widgets, but that the number of firms is cut in half so that each of the remaining five firms produces 200 widgets. If the costs of production fall in this case, then there are internal economies of scale: A firm is more efficient if its output is larger.

External and internal economies of scale have different implications for the structure of industries. An industry where economies of scale are purely external (that is, where there are no advantages to large firms) will typically consist of many small firms and be perfectly competitive. Internal economies of scale, by contrast, give large firms a cost advantage over small firms and lead to an imperfectly competitive market structure.

Both external and internal economies of scale are important causes of international trade. Because they have different implications for market structure, however, it is difficult to discuss both types of scale economy–based trade in the same model. We will therefore deal with them one at a time. In this chapter, we focus on external economies; in the next, on internal economies.

The Theory of External Economies

As we have already pointed out, not all scale economies apply at the level of the individual firm. For a variety of reasons, it is often the case that concentrating production of an industry in one or a few locations reduces the industry's costs even if the individual firms in the industry remain small. When economies of scale apply at the level of the industry rather than at the level of the individual firm, they are called *external economies*. The analysis of external economies goes back more than a century to the British economist Alfred Marshall, who was struck by the phenomenon of "industrial districts"—geographical concentrations of industry that could not be easily explained by natural resources. In Marshall's time, the most famous examples included such concentrations of industry as the cluster of cutlery manufacturers in Sheffield and the cluster of hosiery firms in Northampton.

There are many modern examples of industries where there seem to be powerful external economies. In the United States, these examples include the semiconductor industry, concentrated in California's famous Silicon Valley; the investment banking industry, concentrated in New York; and the entertainment industry, concentrated in Hollywood. In the rising manufacturing industries of developing countries such as China, external economies are pervasive—for example, one town in China accounts for a large share of the world's underwear production; another produces nearly all of the world's cigarette lighters; yet another produces a third of the world's magnetic tape heads; and so on. External economies have also played a key role in India's emergence as a major exporter of information services, with a large part of this industry still clustered in and around the city of Bangalore.

Marshall argued that there are three main reasons why a cluster of firms may be more efficient than an individual firm in isolation: the ability of a cluster to support **specialized suppliers;** the way that a geographically concentrated industry allows **labor market pooling;** and the way that a geographically concentrated industry helps foster **knowledge spillovers.** These same factors continue to be valid today.

Specialized Suppliers

In many industries, the production of goods and services—and to an even greater extent, the development of new products—requires the use of specialized equipment or support services; yet an individual company does not provide a large enough market for these services to keep the suppliers in business. A localized industrial cluster can solve this problem by bringing together many firms that collectively provide a large enough market to support a wide range of specialized suppliers. This phenomenon has been extensively documented in Silicon Valley: A 1994 study recounts how, as the local industry grew, "engineers left established semiconductor companies to start firms that manufactured capital goods such as diffusion ovens, step-and-repeat cameras, and testers, and materials and components such as photomasks, testing jigs, and specialized chemicals. . . . This independent equipment sector promoted the continuing formation of semiconductor firms by freeing individual producers from the expense of developing capital equipment internally and by spreading the costs of development. It also reinforced the tendency toward industrial localization, as most of these specialized inputs were not available elsewhere in the country."

As the quote suggests, the availability of this dense network of specialized suppliers has given high-technology firms in Silicon Valley some considerable advantages over firms elsewhere. Key inputs are cheaper and more easily available because there are many firms competing to provide them, and firms can concentrate on what they do best, contracting out other aspects of their business. For example, some Silicon Valley firms that specialize in providing highly sophisticated computer chips for particular customers have chosen to become "fabless," that is, they do not have any factories in which chips can be fabricated. Instead, they concentrate on designing the chips, and then hire another firm to actually fabricate them.

A company that tried to enter the industry in another location—for example, in a country that did not have a comparable industrial cluster—would be at an immediate disadvantage because it would lack easy access to Silicon Valley's suppliers and would either have to provide them for itself or be faced with the task of trying to deal with Silicon Valley–based suppliers at long distance.

Labor Market Pooling

A second source of external economies is the way that a cluster of firms can create a pooled market for workers with highly specialized skills. Such a pooled market is to the advantage of both the producers and the workers, as the producers are less likely to suffer from labor shortages and the workers are less likely to become unemployed.

The point can best be made with a simplified example. Imagine there are two companies that both use the same kind of specialized labor, say, two film studios that make use of experts in computer animation. Both employers are, however, uncertain about how many workers they will want to hire: If demand for their product is high, both companies will want to hire 150 workers, but if it is low, they will want to hire only 50. Suppose also that there are 200 workers with this special skill. Now compare two situations: one with both firms and all 200 workers in the same city, the other with the firms, each with 100 workers, in two different cities. It is straightforward to show that both the workers and their employers are better off if everyone is in the same place.

First, consider the situation from the point of view of the companies. If they are in different locations, whenever one of the companies is doing well, it will be confronted with a labor shortage: It will want to hire 150 workers, but only 100 will be available. If the firms are near each other, however, it is at least possible that one will be doing well when the other is doing badly, so both firms may be able to hire as many workers as they want. By locating near each other, the companies increase the likelihood that they will be able to take advantage of business opportunities.

From the workers' point of view, having the industry concentrated in one location is also an advantage. If the industry is divided between two cities, then whenever one of the firms has a low demand for workers, the result will be unemployment: The firm will be willing to hire only 50 of the 100 workers who live nearby. But if the industry is concentrated in a single city, low labor demand from one firm will at least sometimes be offset by high demand from the other. As a result, workers will have a lower risk of unemployment.

Again, these advantages have been documented for Silicon Valley, where it is common both for companies to expand rapidly and for workers to change employers. The same study of Silicon Valley that was quoted previously notes that the concentration of firms in a single location makes it easy to switch employers. One engineer is quoted as saying that "it wasn't that big a catastrophe to quit your job on Friday and have another job on Monday.... You didn't even necessarily have to tell your wife. You just drove off in another direction on Monday morning."[1] This flexibility makes Silicon Valley an attractive location both for highly skilled workers and for the companies that employ them.

Knowledge Spillovers

It is by now a cliché that in the modern economy, knowledge is at least as important an input as are factors of production like labor, capital, and raw materials. This is especially true in highly innovative industries, where being even a few months behind the cutting edge in production techniques or product design can put a company at a major disadvantage.

But where does the specialized knowledge that is crucial to success in innovative industries come from? Companies can acquire technology through their own research and development efforts. They can also try to learn from competitors by studying their products and, in some cases, by taking them apart to "reverse engineer" their design and manufacture. An important source of technical know-how, however, is the informal exchange of information and ideas that takes place at a personal level. And this kind of informal diffusion of knowledge often seems to take place most effectively when an industry is concentrated in a fairly small area, so that employees of different companies mix socially and talk freely about technical issues.

Marshall described this process memorably when he wrote that in a district with many firms in the same industry, "The mysteries of the trade become no mystery, but are as it were in the air.... Good work is rightly appreciated, inventions and improvements in machinery, in processes and the general organization of the business have their merits promptly discussed: If one man starts a new idea, it is taken up by others and combined with suggestions of their own; and thus it becomes the source of further new ideas."

A journalist described how these knowledge spillovers worked during the rise of Silicon Valley (and also gave an excellent sense of the amount of specialized knowledge involved in the industry) as follows: "Every year there was some place, the Wagon Wheel, Chez Yvonne, Rickey's, the Roundhouse, where members of this esoteric fraternity, the young men and women of the semiconductor industry, would head after work to have a drink and gossip and trade war stories about phase jitters, phantom circuits, bubble memories, pulse trains, bounceless contacts, burst modes, leapfrog tests, p-n junctions, sleeping sickness modes, slow-death episodes, RAMs, NAKs, MOSes, PCMs, PROMs, PROM blowers, PROM blasters, and teramagnitudes...."[2] This kind of informal information flow means it is easier for

---

[1]Saxenian, p. 35.

[2]Tom Wolfe, quoted in Saxenian, p. 33.

companies in the Silicon Valley area to stay near the technological frontier than it is for companies elsewhere; indeed, many multinational firms have established research centers and even factories in Silicon Valley simply in order to keep up with the latest technology.

External Economies and Market Equilibrium

As we've just seen, a geographically concentrated industry is able to support specialized suppliers, provide a pooled labor market, and facilitate knowledge spillovers in a way that a geographically dispersed industry cannot. But the strength of these economies presumably depends on the industry's size: Other things equal, a bigger industry will generate stronger external economies. What does this say about the determination of output and prices?

While the details of external economies in practice are often quite subtle and complex (as the example of Silicon Valley shows), it can be useful to abstract from the details and represent external economies simply by assuming that the larger the industry, the lower the industry's costs. If we ignore international trade for the moment, then market equilibrium can be represented with a supply-and-demand diagram like Figure 7-1, which illustrates the market for widgets. In an ordinary picture of market equilibrium, the demand curve is downward sloping, while the supply curve is upward sloping. In the presence of external economies of scale, however, there is a **forward-falling supply curve:** the larger the industry's output, the lower the price at which firms are willing to sell, because their **average cost of production** falls as industry output rises.

In the absence of international trade, the unusual slope of the supply curve in Figure 7-1 doesn't seem to matter much. As in a conventional supply-and-demand analysis, the equilibrium price, P_1, and output, Q_1, are determined by the intersection of the demand curve and the supply curve. As we'll see next, however, external economies of scale make a huge difference to our view of the causes and effects of international trade.

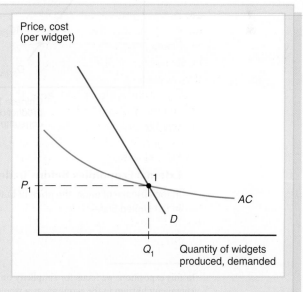

FIGURE 7-1

External Economies and Market Equilibrium

When there are external economies of scale, the average cost of producing a good falls as the quantity produced rises. Given competition among many producers, the downward-sloping average cost curve *AC* can be interpreted as a *forward-falling supply curve.* As in ordinary supply-and-demand analysis, market equilibrium is at point 1, where the supply curve intersects the demand curve, *D*. The equilibrium level of output is Q_1, the equilibrium price P_1.

External Economies and International Trade

External economies drive a lot of trade both within and between countries. For example, New York exports financial services to the rest of the United States, largely because external economies in the investment industry have led to a concentration of financial firms in Manhattan. Similarly, Britain exports financial services to the rest of Europe, largely because those same external economies have led to a concentration of financial firms in London. But what are the implications of this kind of trade? We'll look first at the effects of trade on output and prices; then at the determinants of the pattern of trade; and finally at the effects of trade on welfare.

External Economies, Output, and Prices

Imagine, for a moment, we live in a world in which it is impossible to trade buttons across national borders. Assume, also, there are just two countries in this world: China and the United States. Finally, assume button production is subject to external economies of scale, which lead to a forward-falling supply curve for buttons in each country. (As the box on page 187 shows, this is actually true of the button industry.)

In that case, equilibrium in the world button industry would look like the situation shown in Figure 7-2.[3] In both China and the United States, equilibrium prices and output would be at the point where the domestic supply curve intersects the domestic

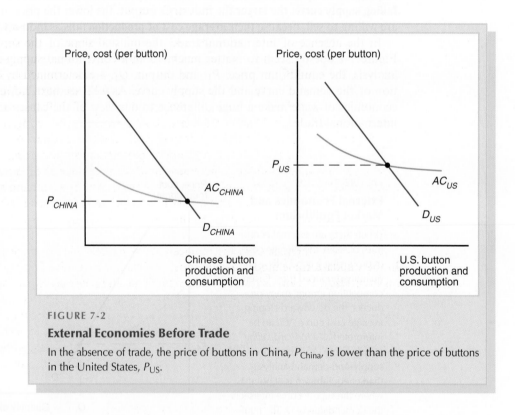

FIGURE 7-2

External Economies Before Trade

In the absence of trade, the price of buttons in China, P_{China}, is lower than the price of buttons in the United States, P_{US}.

---

[3]In this exposition, we focus for simplicity on *partial equilibrium* in the market for buttons, rather than on general equilibrium in the economy as a whole. It is possible, but much more complicated, to carry out the same analysis in terms of general equilibrium.

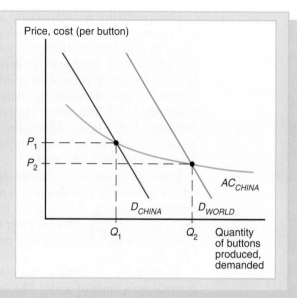

FIGURE 7-3

Trade and Prices

When trade is opened, China ends up producing buttons for the world market, which consists both of its own domestic market and of the U.S. market. Output rises from Q_1 to Q_2, leading to a fall in the price of buttons from P_1 to P_2, which is lower than the price of buttons in either country before trade.

demand curve. In the case shown in Figure 7-2, Chinese button prices in the absence of trade would be lower than U.S. button prices.

Now suppose we open up the potential for trade in buttons. What will happen?

It seems clear that the Chinese button industry will expand, while the U.S. button industry will contract. And this process will feed on itself: As the Chinese industry's output rises, its costs will fall further; as the U.S. industry's output falls, its costs will rise. In the end, we can expect all button production to be concentrated in China.

The effects of this concentration are illustrated in Figure 7-3. Before the opening of trade, China supplied only its own domestic button market. After trade, it supplies the world market, producing buttons for both Chinese and U.S. consumers.

Notice the effects of this concentration of production on prices. Because China's supply curve is forward-falling, increased production as a result of trade leads to a button price that is lower than the price before trade. And bear in mind that Chinese button prices were lower than American button prices before trade. What this tells us is that trade leads to button prices that are lower than the prices in *either* country before trade.

This is very different from the implications of models without increasing returns. In the standard trade model, as developed in Chapter 6, relative prices converge as a result of trade. If cloth is relatively cheap in Home and relatively expensive in Foreign before trade opens, the effect of trade will be to raise cloth prices in Home and reduce them in Foreign. In our button example, by contrast, the effect of trade is to reduce prices everywhere. The reason for this difference is that when there are external economies of scale, international trade makes it possible to concentrate world production in a single location, and therefore to reduce costs by reaping the benefits of even stronger external economies.

External Economies and the Pattern of Trade

In our example of world trade in buttons, we simply assumed the Chinese industry started out with lower production costs than the American industry. What might lead to such an initial advantage?

One possibility is comparative advantage—underlying differences in technology and resources. For example, there's a good reason why Silicon Valley is in California, rather than in Mexico. High-technology industries require a highly skilled work force, and such a work force is much easier to find in the United States, where 40 percent of the working-age population is college-educated, than in Mexico, where the number is below 16 percent. Similarly, there's a good reason why world button production is concentrated in China, rather than in Germany. Button production is a labor-intensive industry, which is best conducted in a country where the average manufacturing worker earns less than a dollar an hour rather than in a country where hourly compensation is among the highest in the world.

However, in industries characterized by external economies of scale, comparative advantage usually provides only a partial explanation of the pattern of trade. It was probably inevitable that most of the world's buttons would be made in a relatively low-wage country, but it's not clear that this country necessarily had to be China, and it certainly wasn't necessary that production be concentrated in any particular location within China.

So what does determine the pattern of specialization and trade in industries with external economies of scale? The answer, often, is historical contingency: Something gives a particular location an initial advantage in a particular industry, and this advantage gets "locked in" by external economies of scale even after the circumstances that created the initial advantage are no longer relevant. The financial centers in London and New York are clear examples. London became Europe's dominant financial center in the 19th century, when Britain was the world's leading economy and the center of a world-spanning empire. It has retained that role even though the empire is long gone and modern Britain is only a middle-sized economic power. New York became America's financial center thanks to the Erie Canal, which made it the nation's leading port. It has retained that role even though the canal currently is used mainly by recreational boats.

Often sheer accident plays a key role in creating an industrial concentration. Geographers like to tell the tale of how a tufted bedspread, crafted as a wedding gift by a 19th-century teenager, gave rise to the cluster of carpet manufacturers around Dalton, Georgia. Silicon Valley's existence may owe a lot to the fact that a couple of Stanford graduates named Hewlett and Packard decided to start a business in a garage in that area. Bangalore might not be what it is today if vagaries of local politics had not led Texas Instruments to choose, back in 1984, to locate an investment project there rather than in another Indian city.

One consequence of the role of history in determining industrial location is that industries aren't always located in the "right" place: Once a country has established an advantage in an industry, it may retain that advantage even if some other country could potentially produce the goods more cheaply.

Figure 7-4, which shows the cost of producing buttons as a function of the number of buttons produced annually, illustrates this point. Two countries are shown: China and Vietnam. The Chinese cost of producing a button is shown as AC_{China}, the Vietnamese cost as $AC_{Vietnam}$. D_{world} represents the world demand for buttons, which we assume can be satisfied either by China or by Vietnam.

Suppose the economies of scale in button production are entirely external to firms. Since there are no economies of scale at the level of the firm, the button industry in each country consists of many small, perfectly competitive firms. Competition therefore drives the price of buttons down to its average cost.

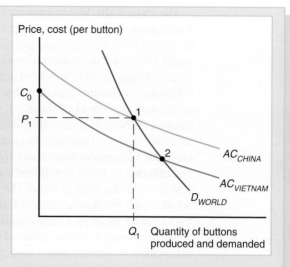

FIGURE 7-4

The Importance of Established Advantage

The average cost curve for Vietnam, $AC_{Vietnam}$, lies below the average cost curve for China, AC_{China}. Thus Vietnam could potentially supply the world market more cheaply than China. If the Chinese industry gets established first, however, it may be able to sell buttons at the price P_1, which is below the cost C_0 that an individual Vietnamese firm would face if it began production on its own. So a pattern of specialization established by historical accident may persist even when new producers could potentially have lower costs.

HOLDING THE WORLD TOGETHER

If you are reading this while fully clothed, the odds are that crucial parts of your outfit—specifically, the parts that protect you from a wardrobe malfunction—came from the Chinese town of Qiaotou, which produces 60 percent of the world's buttons and a large proportion of its zippers.

The Qiaotou fastener industry fits the classic pattern of geographical concentration driven by external economies of scale. The industry's origins lie in historical accident: In 1980, three brothers spotted some discarded buttons in the street, retrieved and sold them, then realized there was money to be made in the button business. There clearly aren't strong internal economies of scale: The town's button and zipper production is carried out by hundreds of small, family-owned firms. Yet there are clearly advantages to each of these small producers in operating in close proximity to the others.

Qiaotou isn't unique. As a fascinating article on the town's industry* put it, in China, "many small towns, not even worthy of a speck on most maps, have also become world-beaters by focusing on labour-intensive niches.... Start at the toothbrush town of Hang Ji, pass the tie mecca of Sheng Zhou, head east to the home of cheap cigarette lighters in Zhang Qi, slip down the coast to the giant shoe factories of Wen Ling, then move back inland to Yiwu, which not only makes more socks than anywhere else on earth, but also sells almost everything under the sun."

At a broad level, China's role as a huge exporter of labor-intensive products reflects comparative advantage: China is clearly labor-abundant compared with advanced economies. Many of those labor-intensive goods, however, are produced by highly localized industries, which benefit strongly from external economies of scale.

*"The Tiger's Teeth," *The Guardian*, May 25, 2005.

We assume the Vietnamese cost curve lies below the Chinese curve because, say, Vietnamese wages are lower than Chinese wages. This means that at any given level of production, Vietnam could manufacture buttons more cheaply than China. One might hope that this would always imply that Vietnam will in fact supply the world market. Unfortunately, this need not be the case. Suppose China, for historical reasons, establishes its button industry first. Then, initially, world button equilibrium will be established at point 1 in Figure 7-4, with Chinese production of Q_1 units per year and a price of P_1. Now introduce the possibility of Vietnamese production. If Vietnam could take over the world market, the equilibrium would move to point 2. However, if there is no initial Vietnamese production ($Q = 0$), any individual Vietnamese firm considering manufacture of buttons will face a cost of production of C_0. As we have drawn it, this cost is above the price at which the established Chinese industry can produce buttons. So although the Vietnamese industry could potentially make buttons more cheaply than China's industry, China's head start enables it to hold on to the industry.

As this example shows, external economies potentially give a strong role to historical accident in determining who produces what, and may allow established patterns of specialization to persist even when they run counter to comparative advantage.

Trade and Welfare with External Economies

In general, we can presume that external economies of scale lead to gains from trade over and above those from comparative advantage. The world is more efficient and thus richer because international trade allows nations to specialize in different industries and thus reap the gains from external economies as well as from comparative advantage.

However, there are a few possible qualifications to this presumption. As we saw in Figure 7-4, the importance of established advantage means that there is no guarantee that the right country will produce a good subject to external economies. In fact, it is possible that trade based on external economies may actually leave a country worse off than it would have been in the absence of trade.

An example of how a country can actually be worse off with trade than without is shown in Figure 7-5. In this example, we imagine that Thailand and Switzerland

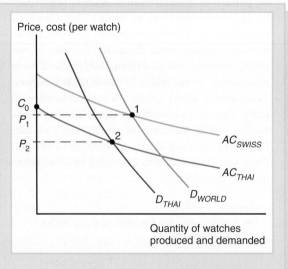

FIGURE 7-5

External Economies and Losses from Trade

When there are external economies, trade can potentially leave a country worse off than it would be in the absence of trade. In this example, Thailand imports watches from Switzerland, which is able to supply the world market (D_{WORLD}) at a price (P_1) low enough to block entry by Thai producers, who must initially produce the watches at cost C_0. Yet if Thailand were to block all trade in watches, it would be able to supply its domestic market (D_{THAI}) at the lower price, P_2.

could both manufacture watches, that Thailand could make them more cheaply, but that Switzerland has gotten there first. D_{WORLD} is the world demand for watches, and, given that Switzerland produces the watches, the equilibrium is at point 1. However, we now add to the figure the Thai demand for watches, D_{THAI}. If no trade in watches were allowed and Thailand were forced to be self-sufficient, then the Thai equilibrium would be at point 2. Because of its lower average cost curve, the price of Thai-made watches at point 2, P_2, is actually lower than the price of Swiss-made watches at point 1, P_1.

We have presented a situation in which the price of a good that Thailand imports would actually be lower if there were no trade and the country were forced to produce the good for itself. Clearly in this situation, trade leaves the country worse off than it would be in the absence of trade.

There is an incentive in this case for Thailand to protect its potential watch industry from foreign competition. Before concluding that this justifies protectionism, however, we should note that in practice, identifying cases like that shown in Figure 7-5 is far from easy. Indeed, as we will emphasize in Chapters 10 and 11, the difficulty of identifying external economies in practice is one of the main arguments against activist government policies toward trade.

It is also worth pointing out that while external economies can sometimes lead to disadvantageous patterns of specialization and trade, it's virtually certain that it is still to the benefit of the *world* economy to take advantage of the gains from concentrating industries. Canada might be better off if Silicon Valley were near Toronto instead of San Francisco; Germany might be better off if the City (London's financial district, which, along with Wall Street, dominates world financial markets) could be moved to Frankfurt. But overall, it's better for the world that each of these industries be concentrated *somewhere*.

Dynamic Increasing Returns

Some of the most important external economies probably arise from the accumulation of knowledge. When an individual firm improves its products or production techniques through experience, other firms are likely to imitate the firm and benefit from its knowledge. This spillover of knowledge gives rise to a situation in which the production costs of individual firms fall as the industry as a whole accumulates experience.

Notice that external economies arising from the accumulation of knowledge differ somewhat from the external economies considered so far, in which industry costs depend on current output. In this alternative situation, industry costs depend on experience, usually measured by the cumulative output of the industry to date. For example, the cost of producing a ton of steel might depend negatively on the total number of tons of steel produced by a country since the industry began. This kind of relationship is often summarized by a **learning curve** that relates unit cost to cumulative output. Such learning curves are illustrated in Figure 7-6. They are downward sloping because of the effect on costs of the experience gained through production. When costs fall with cumulative production over time rather than with the current rate of production, this is referred to as a case of **dynamic increasing returns.**

Like ordinary external economies, dynamic external economies can lock in an initial advantage or head start in an industry. In Figure 7-6, the learning curve L is that of a country that pioneered an industry, while L^* is that of a country that has lower input costs—say, lower wages—but less production experience. Provided the first country has a sufficiently large head start, the potentially lower costs of the second country may not allow the second country to enter the market. For example, suppose

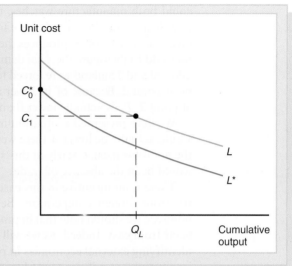

FIGURE 7-6

The Learning Curve

The learning curve shows that unit cost is lower the greater the cumulative output of a country's industry to date. A country that has extensive experience in an industry (L) may have a lower unit cost than a country with little or no experience, even if that second country's learning curve (L^*) is lower—for example, because of lower wages.

the first country has a cumulative output of Q_L units, giving it a unit cost of C_1, while the second country has never produced the good. Then the second country will have an initial start-up cost, C_0^*, that is higher than the current unit cost, C_1, of the established industry.

Dynamic scale economies, like external economies at a point in time, potentially justify protectionism. Suppose a country could have low enough costs to produce a good for export if it had more production experience, but given the current lack of experience, the good cannot be produced competitively. Such a country might increase its long-term welfare either by encouraging the production of the good by a subsidy or by protecting it from foreign competition until the industry can stand on its own feet. The argument for temporary protection of industries to enable them to gain experience is known as the **infant industry argument;** this argument has played an important role in debates over the role of trade policy in economic development. We will discuss the infant industry argument at greater length in Chapter 10, but for now, we simply note that situations like that illustrated in Figure 7-6 are just as hard to identify in practice as those involving nondynamic increasing returns.

Interregional Trade and Economic Geography

External economies play an important role in shaping the pattern of international trade, but they are even more decisive in shaping the pattern of **interregional trade**—trade that takes place between regions *within* countries.

To understand the role of external economies in interregional trade, we first need to discuss the nature of regional economics—that is, how the economies of regions within a nation fit into the national economy. Studies of the location of U.S. industries suggest that more than 60 percent of U.S. workers are employed by industries whose output is nontradable even within the United States—that is, it must be supplied locally. Table 7-2 shows some examples of tradable and nontradable industries. Thus, motion pictures made in Hollywood are shown across the country, and indeed around the world, but newspapers are mainly read in their home cities. Wall Street trades stocks and makes deals for clients across the United States, but savings banks mainly serve local depositors. Scientists at the National Institutes of Health develop

TABLE 7-2	Some Examples of Tradable and Nontradable Industries
Tradable Industries	**Nontradable Industries**
Motion pictures	Newspaper publishers
Securities, commodities, etc.	Savings institutions
Scientific research	Veterinary services

Source: J. Bradford Jensen and Lori. G. Kletzer, "Tradable Services: Understanding the Scope and Impact of Services Outsourcing," in Lael Brainard and Susan M. Collins, eds., *Brookings Trade Forum 2005: Offshoring White Collar Work* (Washington, D.C.: Brookings Institution, 2005), pp. 75–116.

medical knowledge that is applied across the whole country, but the veterinarian who figures out why your pet is sick has to be near your home.

As you might expect, the share of nontradable industries in employment is pretty much the same across the United States. For example, restaurants employ about 5 percent of the work force in every major U.S. city. On the other hand, tradable industries vary greatly in importance across regions. Manhattan accounts for only about 2 percent of America's total employment, but it accounts for a quarter of those employed in trading stocks and bonds and about one-seventh of employment in the advertising industry.

But what determines the location of tradable industries? In some cases, natural resources play a key role—for example, Houston is a center for the oil industry because east Texas is where the oil is. However, factors of production such as labor and capital play a less decisive role in interregional trade than in international trade, for the simple reason that such factors are highly mobile within countries. As a result, factors tend to move to where the industries are rather than the other way around. For example, California's Silicon Valley, near San Francisco, has a very highly educated labor force, with a high concentration of engineers and computer experts. That's not because California trains lots of engineers; it's because engineers move to Silicon Valley to take jobs in the region's high-tech industry.

Resources, then, play a secondary role in interregional trade. What largely drives specialization and trade, instead, is external economies. Why, for example, are so many advertising agencies located in New York? The answer is because so many *other* advertising agencies are located in New York. As one study put it, "Information sharing and information diffusion are critical to a team and an agency's success.... In cities like New York, agencies group in neighborhood clusters. Clusters promote localized networking, to enhance creativity; agencies share information and ideas and in doing this face-to-face contact is critical."[4] In fact, the evidence suggests the external economies that support the advertising business are *very* localized: To reap the benefits of information spillovers, ad agencies need to be located within about 300 yards of each other!

But if external economies are the main reason for regional specialization and interregional trade, what explains how a particular region develops the external economies that support an industry? The answer, in general, is that accidents of history play a crucial role. As noted earlier, a century and a half ago, New York was America's most important port city because it had access to the Great Lakes via the Erie Canal.

---

[4]J. Vernon Henderson, "What Makes Big Cities Tick? A Look at New York," mimeo, Brown University, 2004.

TINSELTOWN ECONOMICS

What is the United States' most important export sector? The answer depends to some extent on definitions; some people will tell you that it is agriculture, others that it is aircraft. By any measure, however, one of the biggest exporters in the United States is the entertainment sector, movies in particular. In 2011, rental fees generated by exports of films and tape were $14.3 billion, compared with only $10.2 billion in domestic box office receipts. American films dominated ticket sales in much of the world; for example, they accounted for about two-thirds of box office receipts in Europe.

Why is the United States the world's dominant exporter of entertainment? There are important advantages arising from the sheer size of the American market. A film aimed primarily at the French or Italian markets, which are far smaller than that of the United States, cannot justify the huge budgets of many American films. Thus, films from these countries are typically dramas or comedies whose appeal fails to survive dubbing or subtitles. Meanwhile, American films can transcend the language barrier with lavish productions and spectacular special effects.

But an important part of the American dominance in the industry also comes from the external economies created by the immense concentration of entertainment firms in Hollywood. Hollywood clearly generates two of Marshall's types of external economies: specialized suppliers and labor market pooling. While the final product is provided by movie studios and television networks, these in turn draw on a complex web of independent producers, casting and talent agencies, legal firms, special effects experts, and so on. And the need for labor market pooling is obvious to anyone who has ever watched the credits at the end of a movie: Each production requires a huge but temporary army that includes not just cameramen and makeup artists but musicians, stuntmen and women, and mysterious occupations like gaffers and grips (and—oh yes—actors and actresses). Whether it also generates the third kind of external economies—knowledge spillovers—is less certain. After all, as the author Nathaniel West once remarked, the key to understanding the movie business is to realize that "nobody knows anything." Still, if there is any knowledge to spill over, surely it does so better in the intense social environment of Hollywood than it could anywhere else.

An indication of the force of Hollywood's external economies has been its persistent ability to draw talent from outside the United States. From Garbo and von Sternberg to Russell Crowe and Guillermo del Toro, "American" films have often been made by ambitious foreigners who moved to Hollywood—and in the end, reached a larger audience even in their original nations than they could have if they had remained at home.

Is Hollywood unique? No, similar forces have led to the emergence of several other entertainment complexes. In India, whose film market has been protected from American domination partly by government policy and partly by cultural differences, a moviemaking cluster known as "Bollywood" has emerged in Bombay. In recent years, Bollywood films have developed a wide following outside India, and film is rapidly becoming a significant Indian export industry. A substantial film industry catering to Chinese speakers has emerged in Hong Kong; in addition, many U.S.-made action films are strongly influenced by Hong Kong style. A specialty industry producing Spanish-language television programs for all of Latin America, focusing on so-called *telenovelas*, long-running soap operas, has emerged in Caracas, Venezuela. And in recent years a Nigerian film complex—"Nollywood"—has emerged, using digital techniques to produce relatively low-budget films that are exported as direct-to-video entertainment, largely but not entirely to other African nations.

That led to New York's becoming America's financial center; it remains America's financial center today thanks to the external economies the financial industry creates for itself. Los Angeles became the center of the early film industry when films were shot outdoors and needed good weather; it remains the center of the film industry today, even though many films are shot indoors or on location, because of the externalities described in the box on page 192.

A question you might ask is whether the forces driving interregional trade are really all that different from those driving international trade. The answer is that they are not, especially when one looks at trade between closely integrated national economies, such as those of Western Europe. Indeed, London plays a role as Europe's financial capital similar to the role played by New York as America's financial capital. In recent years, there has been a growing movement among economists to model interregional and international trade, as well as such phenomena as the rise of cities, as different aspects of the same phenomenon—economic interaction across space. Such an approach is often referred to as **economic geography**.

SUMMARY

1. Trade need not be the result of comparative advantage. Instead, it can result from increasing returns or economies of scale, that is, from a tendency of unit costs to be lower with larger output. Economies of scale give countries an incentive to specialize and trade even in the absence of differences in resources or technology between countries. Economies of scale can be internal (depending on the size of the firm) or external (depending on the size of the industry).

2. Economies of scale can lead to a breakdown of perfect competition, unless they take the form of external economies, which occur at the level of the industry instead of the firm.

3. External economies give an important role to history and accident in determining the pattern of international trade. When external economies are important, a country starting with a large advantage may retain that advantage even if another country could potentially produce the same goods more cheaply. When external economies are important, countries can conceivably lose from trade.

KEY TERMS

average cost of production, p. 183

dynamic increasing returns, p. 189

economic geography, p. 193

economies of scale, p. 178

external economies of scale, p. 179

forward-falling supply curve, p. 183

infant industry argument, p. 190

internal economies of scale, p. 179

interregional trade, p. 190

knowledge spillovers, p. 180

labor market pooling, p. 180

learning curve, p. 189

specialized suppliers, p. 180

PROBLEMS

MyEconLab

1. For each of the following examples, explain whether it is a case of external or internal economies of scale:
   a. A number of firms doing contract research for the drug industry are concentrated in southeastern South Carolina.
   b. All Hondas produced in the United States come from plants in Ohio, Indiana, or Alabama.

    c. All airframes for Airbus, Europe's only producer of large aircraft, are assembled in Toulouse, France.

    d. Cranbury, New Jersey, is the artificial flavor capital of the United States.

2. It is often argued that local knowledge spillover is more feasible for firms existing in clusters. The difficulty in transferring the knowledge lies in the distance. Explain with reference to the situation addressed in the knowledge spillovers section. Give one example of an industry cluster in a developing country.

3. Give two examples of products that are traded on international markets for which there are dynamic increasing returns. In each of your examples, show how innovation and learning-by-doing are important to the dynamic increasing returns in the industry.

4. Evaluate the relative importance of economies of scale and comparative advantage in causing the following:

    a. Most of the world's aluminum is smelted in Norway or Canada.

    b. Half of the world's large jet aircraft are assembled in Seattle.

    c. Most semiconductors are manufactured in either the United States or Japan.

    d. Most Scotch whiskey comes from Scotland.

    e. Much of the world's best wine comes from France.

5. Consider two countries—India and Japan—facing a forward falling supply curve. Both produce two commodities—cloth and radios. India, a labor surplus country, produces cloth using cheap labor. This reduces its domestic price in comparison to Japan. Similarly, Japan being technologically advanced produces radios at a lower cost than India. If both are open to trade, ceteris paribus.

    a. What will happen to the world market price for cloth and radio?

    b. What would you expect of the international trade and who would produce what, if neither India nor Japan has an initial advantage of lower price?

6. It is fairly common for an industrial cluster to break up and for production to move to locations with lower wages when the technology of the industry is no longer rapidly improving—when it is no longer essential to have the absolutely most modern machinery, when the need for highly skilled workers has declined, and when being at the cutting edge of innovation conveys only a small advantage. Explain this tendency of industrial clusters to break up in terms of the theory of external economies.

7. Is it always true that trade increases the welfare of a nation? Under what circumstances would the concentration of industries in one country leave another country worse off when trade resumes between them? Explain with an example.

8. In our discussion of labor market pooling, we stressed the advantages of having two firms in the same location: If one firm is expanding while the other is contracting, it's to the advantage of both workers and firms that they be able to draw on a single labor pool. But it might happen that both firms want to expand or contract at the same time. Does this constitute an argument against geographical concentration? (Think through the numerical example carefully.)

9. Which of the following goods or services would be most likely to be subject to (1) external economies of scale and (2) dynamic increasing returns? Explain your answers.

    a. Software tech-support services

    b. Production of asphalt or concrete

    c. Motion pictures

    d. Cancer research

    e. Timber harvesting

FURTHER READINGS

Frank Graham. "Some Aspects of Protection Further Considered." *Quarterly Journal of Economics* 37 (1923), pp. 199–227. An early warning that international trade may be harmful in the presence of external economies of scale.

Li & Fung Research Centre. *Industrial Cluster Series*, 2006–2010. Li and Fung, a Hong Kong–based trading group, has published a series of reports on rising industrial concentrations in Chinese manufacturing.

Staffan Burenstam Linder. *An Essay on Trade and Transformation.* New York: John Wiley and Sons, 1961. An early and influential statement of the view that trade in manufactures among advanced countries mainly reflects forces other than comparative advantage.

Michael Porter. *The Competitive Advantage of Nations.* New York: Free Press, 1990. A best-selling book that explains national export success as the result of self-reinforcing industrial clusters, that is, external economies.

Annalee Saxenian. *Regional Advantage.* Cambridge: Harvard University Press, 1994. A fascinating comparison of two high-technology industrial districts, California's Silicon Valley and Boston's Route 128.

World Bank. *World Development Report 2009.* A huge survey of the evidence on economic geography, with extensive discussion of industrial clusters in China and other emerging economies.

MyEconLab Can Help You Get a Better Grade

MyEconLab If your exam were tomorrow, would you be ready? For each chapter, MyEconLab Practice Tests and Study Plans pinpoint sections you have mastered and those you need to study. That way, you are more efficient with your study time, and you are better prepared for your exams.

To see how it works, turn to page 41 and then go to
www.myeconlab.com

FIRMS IN THE GLOBAL ECONOMY: EXPORT DECISIONS, OUTSOURCING, AND MULTINATIONAL ENTERPRISES

In this chapter, we continue to explore how economies of scale generate incentives for international specialization and trade. We now focus on economies of scale that are internal to the firm. As mentioned in the previous chapter, this form of increasing returns leads to a market structure that features imperfect competition. **Internal economies of scale** imply that a firm's average cost of production decreases the more output it produces. Perfect competition that drives the price of a good down to marginal cost would imply losses for those firms because they would not be able to recover the higher costs incurred from producing the initial units of output.[1] As a result, perfect competition would force those firms out of the market, and this process would continue until an equilibrium featuring imperfect competition is attained.

Modeling imperfect competition means that we will explicitly consider the behavior of individual firms. This will allow us to introduce two additional characteristics of firms that are prevalent in the real world: (1) In most sectors, firms produce goods that are differentiated from one another. In the case of certain goods (such as bottled water, staples, etc.), those differences across products may be small, while in others (such as cars, cell phones, etc.), the differences are much more significant. (2) Performance measures (such as size and profits) vary widely across firms. We will incorporate this first characteristic (product differentiation) into our analysis throughout this chapter. To ease exposition and build intuition, we will initially consider the case when there are no performance differences between firms. We will thus see how internal economies of scale and product differentiation combine to generate some new sources of gains of trade via economic integration.

---

[1]Whenever average cost is decreasing, the cost of producing one extra unit of output (marginal cost) is lower than the average cost of production (since that average includes the cost of those initial units that were produced at higher unit costs).

We will then introduce differences across firms so that we can analyze how firms respond differently to international forces. We will see how economic integration generates both winners and losers among different types of firms. The better-performing firms thrive and expand, while the worse-performing firms contract. This generates one additional source of gain from trade: As production is concentrated toward better-performing firms, the overall efficiency of the industry improves. Lastly, we will study why those better-performing firms have a greater incentive to engage in the global economy, either by exporting, by outsourcing some of their intermediate production processes abroad, or by becoming multinationals and operating in multiple countries.

LEARNING GOALS

After reading this chapter, you will be able to:

- Understand how internal economies of scale and product differentiation lead to international trade and intra-industry trade.
- Recognize the new types of welfare gains from intra-industry trade.
- Describe how economic integration can lead to both winners and losers among firms in the same industry.
- Explain why economists believe that "dumping" should not be singled out as an unfair trade practice, and why the enforcement of antidumping laws leads to protectionism.
- Explain why firms that engage in the global economy (exporters, outsourcers, multinationals) are substantially larger and perform better than firms that do not interact with foreign markets.
- Understand theories that explain the existence of multinationals and the motivation for foreign direct investment across economies.

The Theory of Imperfect Competition

In a perfectly competitive market—a market in which there are many buyers and sellers, none of whom represents a large part of the market—firms are *price takers.* That is, they are sellers of products who believe they can sell as much as they like at the current price but cannot influence the price they receive for their product. For example, a wheat farmer can sell as much wheat as she likes without worrying that if she tries to sell more wheat, she will depress the market price. The reason she need not worry about the effect of her sales on prices is that any individual wheat grower represents only a tiny fraction of the world market.

When only a few firms produce a good, however, the situation is different. To take perhaps the most dramatic example, the aircraft manufacturing giant Boeing shares the market for large jet aircraft with only one major rival, the European firm Airbus. As a result, Boeing knows that if it produces more aircraft, it will have a significant effect on the total supply of planes in the world and will therefore significantly drive down the price of airplanes. Or to put it another way, Boeing knows that if it wants to sell more airplanes, it can do so only by significantly reducing its price. In **imperfect competition**, then, firms are aware that they can influence the prices of their products and that they can sell more only by reducing their price. This situation occurs in one of two ways: when there are only a few major producers of a particular good, or when each firm produces a good that is differentiated (in the eyes of the consumer) from that of rival firms. As we mentioned in the introduction, this type of competition is an inevitable outcome when there are economies of scale at the level of the firm: The number of surviving firms is forced down to a small number and/or firms must develop products that are clearly differentiated from those produced by their rivals. Under these circumstances, each firm views itself as a *price setter*, choosing the price of its product, rather than a price taker.

When firms are not price takers, it is necessary to develop additional tools to describe how prices and outputs are determined. The simplest imperfectly competitive market structure to examine is that of a **pure monopoly**, a market in which a firm faces no competition; the tools we develop for this structure can then be used to examine more complex market structures.

Monopoly: A Brief Review

Figure 8-1 shows the position of a single monopolistic firm. The firm faces a downward-sloping demand curve, shown in the figure as *D*. The downward slope of *D* indicates that the firm can sell more units of output only if the price of the output falls. As you may recall from basic microeconomics, a **marginal revenue** curve corresponds to the demand curve. Marginal revenue is the extra or marginal revenue the firm gains from selling an additional unit. Marginal revenue for a monopolist is always less than the price because to sell an additional unit, the firm must lower the price of *all* units (not just the marginal one). Thus, for a monopolist, the marginal revenue curve, *MR*, always lies below the demand curve.

Marginal Revenue and Price   For our analysis of the monopolistic competition model later in this section, it is important for us to determine the relationship between the price the monopolist receives per unit and marginal revenue. Marginal revenue is always less than the price—but how much less? The relationship between marginal revenue and price depends on two things. First, it depends on how much output the

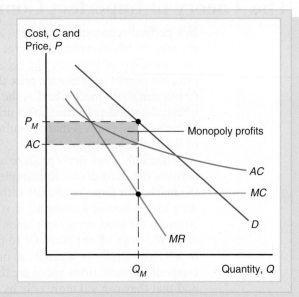

FIGURE 8-1

Monopolistic Pricing and Production Decisions

A monopolistic firm chooses an output at which marginal revenue, the increase in revenue from selling an additional unit, equals marginal cost, the cost of producing an additional unit. This profit-maximizing output is shown as Q_M; the price at which this output is demanded is P_M. The marginal revenue curve *MR* lies below the demand curve *D* because, for a monopoly, marginal revenue is always less than the price. The monopoly's profits are equal to the area of the shaded rectangle, the difference between price and average cost times the amount of output sold.

firm is already selling: A firm not selling very many units will not lose much by cutting the price it receives on those units. Second, the gap between price and marginal revenue depends on the slope of the demand curve, which tells us how much the monopolist has to cut his price to sell one more unit of output. If the curve is very flat, then the monopolist can sell an additional unit with only a small price cut. As a result, he will not have to lower the price by very much on the units he would otherwise have sold, so marginal revenue will be close to the price per unit. On the other hand, if the demand curve is very steep, selling an additional unit will require a large price cut, implying that marginal revenue will be much less than the price.

We can be more specific about the relationship between price and marginal revenue if we assume that the demand curve the firm faces is a straight line. When this is the case, the dependence of the monopolist's total sales on the price it charges can be represented by an equation of the form

$$Q = A - B \times P, \tag{8-1}$$

where Q is the number of units the firm sells, P the price it charges per unit, and A and B are constants. We show in the appendix to this chapter that in this case, marginal revenue is

$$\text{Marginal revenue} = MR = P - Q/B, \tag{8-2}$$

implying that

$$P - MR = Q/B.$$

Equation (8-2) reveals that the gap between price and marginal revenue depends on the initial sales, Q, of the firm and the slope parameter, B, of its demand curve. If sales quantity, Q, is higher, marginal revenue is lower, because the decrease in price required to sell a greater quantity costs the firm more. In other words, the greater is B, the more sales fall for any given increase in price and the closer the marginal revenue is to the price of the good. Equation (8-2) is crucial for our analysis of the monopolistic competition model of trade in the upcoming section.

Average and Marginal Costs   Returning to Figure 8-1, AC represents the firm's **average cost** of production, that is, its total cost divided by its output. The downward slope reflects our assumption that there are economies of scale, so the larger the firm's output, the lower its costs per unit. MC represents the firm's **marginal cost** (the amount it costs the firm to produce one extra unit). In the figure, we assumed the firm's marginal cost is constant (the marginal cost curve is flat). The economies of scale must then come from a fixed cost (unrelated to the scale of production). This fixed cost pushes the average cost above the constant marginal cost of production, though the difference between the two becomes smaller and smaller as the fixed cost is spread over an increasing number of output units.

If we denote c as the firm's marginal cost and F as the fixed cost, then we can write the firm's total cost (C) as

$$C = F + c \times Q, \tag{8-3}$$

where Q is once again the firm's output. Given this linear cost function, the firm's average cost is

$$AC = C/Q = (F/Q) + c. \tag{8-4}$$

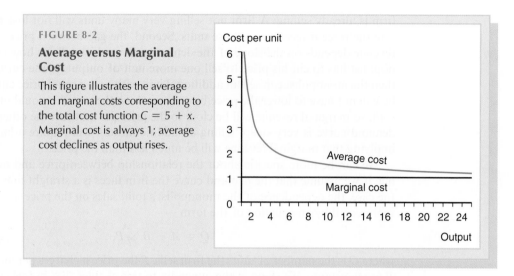

FIGURE 8-2

Average versus Marginal Cost

This figure illustrates the average and marginal costs corresponding to the total cost function $C = 5 + x$. Marginal cost is always 1; average cost declines as output rises.

As we have discussed, this average cost is always greater than the marginal cost c, and declines with output produced Q.

If, for example, $F = 5$ and $c = 1$, the average cost of producing 10 units is $(5/10) + 1 = 1.5$, and the average cost of producing 25 units is $(5/25) + 1 = 1.2$. These numbers may look familiar, because they were used to construct Table 7-1 in the previous chapter. (However, in this case, we assume a unit wage cost for the labor input, and that the technology now applies to a firm instead of an industry.) The marginal and average cost curves for this specific numeric example are plotted in Figure 8-2. Average cost approaches infinity at zero output and approaches marginal cost at very large output.

The profit-maximizing output of a monopolist is that at which marginal revenue (the revenue gained from selling an extra unit) equals marginal cost (the cost of producing an extra unit), that is, at the intersection of the MC and MR curves. In Figure 8-1, we can see that the price at which the profit-maximizing output Q_M is demanded is P_M, which is greater than average cost. When $P > AC$, the monopolist is earning some monopoly profits, as indicated by the shaded box.[2]

Monopolistic Competition

Monopoly profits rarely go uncontested. A firm making high profits normally attracts competitors. Thus, situations of pure monopoly are rare in practice. In most cases, competitors do not sell the same products—either because they cannot (for legal or technological reasons) or because they would rather carve out their own product niche. This leads to a market where competitors sell **differentiated products**. Thus, even when there are many competitors, product differentiation allows firms to remain price setters for their own individual product "variety" or brand. However, more competition implies lower sales for any given firm at any chosen price: Each firm's demand curve shifts in when there are more competitors (we will model this more explicitly in the following sections). Lower demand, in turn, translates into lower profits.

---

[2]The economic definition of *profits* is not the same as that used in conventional accounting, where any revenue over and above labor and material costs is called a profit. A firm that earns a rate of return on its capital less than what that capital could have earned in other industries is not making profits; from an economic point of view, the normal rate of return on capital represents part of the firm's costs, and only returns over and above that normal rate of return represent profits.

The incentive for additional new competitors persists so long as such entry is profitable. Once competition reaches a certain level, additional entry would no longer be profitable and a long-run equilibrium is attained. In some cases, this occurs when there are only a small number of competing firms in the market (such as the market for large jet aircraft). This leads to a market structure called **oligopoly**. In this situation, a single firm has enough market share to influence market aggregates such as total industry output and average industry price.[3] This in turn affects the demand conditions for the other firms. They will therefore have an incentive to adjust their prices in response to the pricing decision of the large firm and vice versa when the other firms are large, too. Thus, pricing decisions of firms are *interdependent* in an oligopoly market structure: Each firm in an oligopoly will consider the expected responses of competitors when setting their price. These responses, however, depend in turn on the competitors' expectations about the firm's behavior—and we are therefore in a complex game in which firms are trying to second-guess each other's strategies. We will briefly discuss an example of an oligopoly model with two firms in Chapter 12.

Let's focus on a much simpler case of imperfect competition known as **monopolistic competition**. This market structure arises when the equilibrium number of competing firms is large and no firm attains a substantial market share. Then, the pricing decision of any given firm will not affect market aggregates and the demand conditions for the other firms, so the pricing decisions of the firms are no longer interrelated. Each firm sets its price given those market aggregates, knowing that the response of any other individual firm would be inconsequential. We next develop such a model of monopolistic competition. We then introduce trade under this market structure in the following section.

Assumptions of the Model   We begin by describing the demand facing a typical monopolistically competitive firm. In general, we would expect a firm to sell more, the larger the total demand for its industry's product and the higher the prices charged by its rivals. On the other hand, we would expect the firm to sell less the greater the number of firms in the industry and the higher its own price. A particular equation for the demand facing a firm that has these properties is[4]

$$Q = S \times [1/n - b \times (P - \overline{P})], \tag{8-5}$$

where Q is the quantity of output demanded, S is the total output of the industry, n is the number of firms in the industry, b is a positive constant term representing the responsiveness of a firm's sales to its price, P is the price charged by the firm itself, and $\overline{P}$ is the average price charged by its competitors. Equation (8-5) may be given the following intuitive justification: If all firms charge the same price, each will have a market share $1/n$. A firm charging more than the average of other firms will have a smaller market share, whereas a firm charging less will have a larger share.[5]

It is helpful to assume that total industry output S is unaffected by the average price $\overline{P}$ charged by firms in the industry. That is, we assume that firms can gain customers only at each other's expense. This is an unrealistic assumption, but it

---

[3]This typically occurs when the fixed cost F is high relative to demand conditions: Each firm must operate at a large scale in order to bring average cost down and be profitable, and the market is not big enough to support many such large firms.

[4]Equation (8-5) can be derived from a model in which consumers have different preferences and firms produce varieties tailored to particular segments of the market. See Stephen Salop, "Monopolistic Competition with Outside Goods," *Bell Journal of Economics* 10 (1979), pp. 141–156, for a development of this approach.

[5]Equation (8-5) may be rewritten as $Q = (S/n) - S \times b \times (P - \overline{P})$. If $P = \overline{P}$, this equation reduces to $Q = S/n$. If $P > \overline{P}$, $Q < S/n$, while if $P < \overline{P}$, $Q > S/n$.

simplifies the analysis and helps us focus on the competition among firms. In particular, it means that S is a measure of the size of the market and that if all firms charge the same price, each sells S/n units.[6]

Next, we turn to the costs of a typical firm. Here we simply assume that total and average costs of a typical firm are described by equations (8-3) and (8-4). Note that in this initial model, we assume all firms are *symmetric* even though they produce differentiated products: They all face the same demand curve (8-5) and have the same cost function (8-3). We will relax this assumption in the next section.

Market Equilibrium   When the individual firms are symmetric, the state of the industry can be described without describing any of the features of individual firms: All we really need to know to describe the industry is how many firms there are and what price the typical firm charges. To analyze the industry—for example, to assess the effects of international trade—we need to determine the number of firms n and the average price they charge $\overline{P}$. Once we have a method for determining n and $\overline{P}$, we can ask how they are affected by international trade.

Our method for determining n and $\overline{P}$ involves three steps. (1) First, we derive a relationship between the number of firms and the *average cost* of a typical firm. We show that this relationship is upward sloping; that is, the more firms there are, the lower the output of each firm—and thus the higher each firm's cost per unit of output. (2) We next show the relationship between the number of firms and the price each firm charges, which must equal $\overline{P}$ in equilibrium. We show that this relationship is downward sloping: The more firms there are, the more intense is the competition among firms, and as a result the lower the prices they charge. (3) Finally, we introduce firm entry and exit decisions based on the profits that each firm earns. When price exceeds average cost, firms earn positive profits and additional firms will enter the industry; conversely, when the price is less than average cost, profits are negative and those losses induce some firms to exit. In the long run, this entry and exit process drives profits to zero. So the price $\overline{P}$ set by each firm must equal the average cost from step (1).

1. *The number of firms and average cost.* As a first step toward determining n and $\overline{P}$, we ask how the average cost of a typical firm depends on the number of firms in the industry. Since all firms are symmetric in this model, in equilibrium they all will charge the same price. But when all firms charge the same price, so that $P = \overline{P}$, equation (8-5) tells us that $Q = S/n$; that is, each firm's output Q is a $1/n$ share of the total industry sales S. But we saw in equation (8-4) that average cost depends inversely on a firm's output. We therefore conclude that average cost depends on the size of the market and the number of firms in the industry:

$$AC = F/Q + c = (n \times F/S) + c. \qquad (8\text{-}6)$$

Equation (8-6) tells us that other things equal, *the more firms there are in the industry, the higher is average cost.* The reason is that the more firms there are, the less each firm produces. For example, imagine an industry with total sales of 1 million widgets annually. If there are five firms in the industry, each will sell 200,000 annually. If there are ten firms, each will sell only 100,000, and therefore each firm will have higher average cost. The upward-sloping relationship between n and average cost is shown as CC in Figure 8-3.

---

[6]Even if firms set different prices, the demand equation (8-5) ensures that the sum of Q over firms is always equal to total output S (because the sum of $P - \overline{P}$ over firms must be zero).

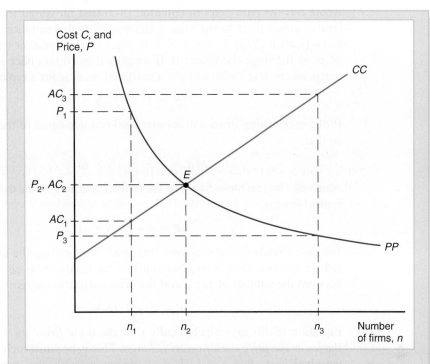

FIGURE 8-3

Equilibrium in a Monopolistically Competitive Market

The number of firms in a monopolistically competitive market, and the prices they charge, are determined by two relationships. On one side, the more firms there are, the more intensely they compete, and hence the lower is the industry price. This relationship is represented by *PP*. On the other side, the more firms there are, the less each firm sells and therefore the higher is the industry's average cost. This relationship is represented by *CC*. If price exceeds average cost (that is, if the *PP* curve is above the *CC* curve), the industry will be making profits and additional firms will enter the industry; if price is less than average cost, the industry will be incurring losses and firms will leave the industry. The equilibrium price and number of firms occurs when price equals average cost, at the intersection of *PP* and *CC*.

2. *The number of firms and the price.* Meanwhile, the price the typical firm charges also depends on the number of firms in the industry. In general, we would expect that the more firms there are, the more intense will be the competition among them, and hence the lower the price. This turns out to be true in this model, but proving it takes a moment. The basic trick is to show that each firm faces a straight-line demand curve of the form we showed in equation (8-1), and then to use equation (8-2) to determine prices.

First recall that in the monopolistic competition model, firms are assumed to take each other's prices as given; that is, each firm ignores the possibility that if it changes its price, other firms will also change theirs. If each firm treats $\overline{P}$ as given, we can rewrite the demand curve (8-5) in the form

$$Q = [\,(S/n) + S \times b \times \overline{P}\,] - S \times b \times P, \qquad (8\text{-}7)$$

where b is the parameter in equation (8-5) that measured the sensitivity of each firm's market share to the price it charges. Now this equation is in the same form as (8-1), with $(S/n) + S \times b \times \overline{P}$ in place of the constant term A and $S \times b$ in place of the slope coefficient B. If we plug these values back into the formula for marginal revenue, (8-2), we have a marginal revenue for a typical firm of

$$MR = P - Q/(S \times b). \tag{8-8}$$

Profit-maximizing firms will set marginal revenue equal to their marginal cost, c, so that

$$MR = P - Q/(S \times b) = c,$$

which can be rearranged to give the following equation for the price charged by a typical firm:

$$P = c + Q/(S \times b). \tag{8-9}$$

We have already noted, however, that if all firms charge the same price, each will sell an amount $Q = S/n$. Plugging this back into (8-9) gives us a relationship between the number of firms and the price each firm charges:

$$P = c + 1/(b \times n). \tag{8-10}$$

Equation (8-10) says algebraically that *the more firms there are in an industry, the lower the price each firm will charge.* This is because each firm's **markup over marginal cost**, $P - c = 1/(b \times n)$, decreases with the number of competing firms. Equation (8-10) is shown in Figure 8-3 as the downward-sloping curve PP.

3. *The equilibrium number of firms.* Let us now ask what Figure 8-3 means. We have summarized an industry by two curves. The downward-sloping curve PP shows that the more firms there are in the industry, the lower the price each firm will charge: The more firms there are, the more competition each firm faces. The upward-sloping curve CC tells us that the more firms there are in the industry, the higher the average cost of each firm: If the number of firms increases, each firm will sell less, so firms will not be able to move as far down their average cost curve.

The two schedules intersect at point E, corresponding to the number of firms n_2. The significance of n_2 is that it is the *zero-profit* number of firms in the industry. When there are n_2 firms in the industry, their profit-maximizing price is P_2, which is exactly equal to their average cost AC_2. This is the long-run monopolistic competition equilibrium that we previously described.

To see why, suppose that n were less than n_2, say n_1. Then the price charged by firms would be P_1, while their average cost would be only AC_1. Thus, firms would be earning positive profits.[7] Conversely, suppose that n were greater than n_2, say n_3. Then firms would charge only the price P_3, while their average cost would be AC_3. Firms would be suffering losses (profit is negative). Over time, firms will enter an industry that is profitable and exit one in which they lose money. The number of firms will rise over time if it is less than n_2, fall if it is greater, leading to the equilibrium price P_2 with n_2 firms.[8]

---

[7]Recall that this represents *economic* profit, which nets out all fixed and capital costs—as opposed to *accounting* profit (which does not).

[8]This analysis slips past a slight problem: The number of firms in an industry must, of course, be a whole number like 5 or 8. What if n_2 turns out to equal 6.37? The answer is that there will be six firms in the industry, all earning a small positive profit. That profit is not challenged by new entrants because everyone knows that a seven-firm industry would lose money. In most examples of monopolistic competition, this whole-number or "integer constraint" problem turns out not to be very important, and we ignore it here.

We have just developed a model of a monopolistically competitive industry in which we can determine the equilibrium number of firms and the average price that firms charge. We now use this model to derive some important conclusions about the role of economies of scale in international trade.

Monopolistic Competition and Trade

Underlying the application of the monopolistic competition model to trade is the idea that trade increases market size. In industries where there are economies of scale, both the variety of goods that a country can produce and the scale of its production are constrained by the size of the market. By trading with each other, and therefore forming an integrated world market that is bigger than any individual national market, nations are able to loosen these constraints. Each country can thus specialize in producing a narrower range of products than it would in the absence of trade; yet by buying from other countries the goods that it does not make, each nation can simultaneously increase the variety of goods available to its consumers. As a result, trade offers an opportunity for mutual gain even when countries do not differ in their resources or technology.

Suppose, for example, there are two countries, each with an annual market for 1 million automobiles. By trading with each other, these countries can create a combined market of 2 million autos. In this combined market, more varieties of automobiles can be produced, at lower average costs, than in either market alone.

The monopolistic competition model can be used to show how trade improves the trade-off between scale and variety that individual nations face. We will begin by showing how a larger market leads to both a lower average price and the availability of a greater variety of goods in the monopolistic competition model. Applying this result to international trade, we observe that trade creates a world market larger than any of the national markets that comprise it. Integrating markets through international trade therefore has the same effects as growth of a market within a single country.

The Effects of Increased Market Size

The number of firms in a monopolistically competitive industry and the prices they charge are affected by the size of the market. In larger markets there usually will be both more firms and more sales per firm; consumers in a large market will be offered both lower prices and a greater variety of products than consumers in small markets.

To see this in the context of our model, look again at the CC curve in Figure 8-3, which showed that average costs per firm are higher the more firms there are in the industry. The definition of the CC curve is given by equation (8-6):

$$AC = F/Q + c = n \times F/S + c.$$

Examining this equation, we see that an increase in total industry output S will reduce average costs for any given number of firms n. The reason is that if the market grows while the number of firms is held constant, output per firm will increase and the average cost of each firm will therefore decline. Thus, if we compare two markets, one with higher S than the other, the CC curve in the larger market will be below that in the smaller one.

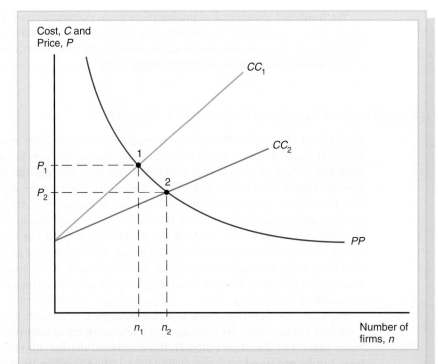

FIGURE 8-4

Effects of a Larger Market

An increase in the size of the market allows each firm, other things equal, to produce more and thus have lower average cost. This is represented by a downward shift from CC_1 to CC_2. The result is a simultaneous increase in the number of firms (and hence in the variety of goods available) and a fall in the price of each.

Meanwhile, the PP curve in Figure 8-3, which relates the price charged by firms to the number of firms, does not shift. The definition of that curve was given in equation (8-10):

$$P = c + 1/(b \times n).$$

The size of the market does not enter into this equation, so an increase in S does not shift the PP curve.

Figure 8-4 uses this information to show the effect of an increase in the size of the market on long-run equilibrium. Initially, equilibrium is at point 1, with a price P_1 and a number of firms n_1. An increase in the size of the market, measured by industry sales S, shifts the CC curve down from CC_1 to CC_2, while it has no effect on the PP curve. The new equilibrium is at point 2: The number of firms increases from n_1 to n_2, while the price falls from P_1 to P_2.

Clearly, consumers would prefer to be part of a large market rather than a small one. At point 2, a greater variety of products is available at a lower price than at point 1.

Gains from an Integrated Market: A Numerical Example

International trade can create a larger market. We can illustrate the effects of trade on prices, scale, and the variety of goods available with a specific numerical example.

Suppose automobiles are produced by a monopolistically competitive industry. The demand curve facing any given producer of automobiles is described by equation (8-5), with $b = 1/30,000$ (this value has no particular significance; it was chosen to make the example come out neatly). Thus, the demand facing any one producer is given by

$$Q = S \times [(1/n) - (1/30,000) \times (P - \overline{P})],$$

where Q is the number of automobiles sold per firm, S is the total number sold for the industry, n is the number of firms, P is the price that a firm charges, and $\overline{P}$ is the average price of other firms. We also assume that the cost function for producing automobiles is described by equation (8-3), with a fixed cost $F = \$750,000,000$ and a marginal cost $c = \$5,000$ per automobile (again, these values were chosen to give nice results). The total cost is

$$C = 750,000,000 + (5,000 \times Q).$$

The average cost curve is therefore

$$AC = (750,000,000/Q) + 5,000.$$

Now suppose there are two countries, Home and Foreign. Home has annual sales of 900,000 automobiles; Foreign has annual sales of 1.6 million. The two countries are assumed, for the moment, to have the same costs of production.

Figure 8-5a shows the PP and CC curves for the Home auto industry. We find that in the absence of trade, Home would have six automobile firms, selling autos at a price of $10,000 each. (It is also possible to solve for n and P algebraically, as shown in the Mathematical Postscript to this chapter.) To confirm that this is the long-run equilibrium, we need to show that the pricing equation (8-10) is satisfied and that the price equals average cost.

Substituting the actual values of the marginal cost c, the demand parameter b, and the number of Home firms n into equation (8-10), we find

$$P = \$10,000 = c + 1/(b \times n) = \$5,000 + 1/[(1/30,000) \times 6$$
$$= \$5,000 + \$5,000,$$

so the condition for profit maximization—marginal revenue equaling marginal cost—is satisfied. Each firm sells 900,000 units/6 firms = 150,000 units/firm. Its average cost is therefore

$$AC = (\$750,000,000/150,000) + \$5,000 = \$10,000.$$

Since the average cost of $10,000 per unit is the same as the price, all monopoly profits have been competed away. Thus six firms, selling each unit at a price of $10,000, with each firm producing 150,000 cars, is the long-run equilibrium in the Home market.

What about Foreign? By drawing the PP and CC curves (panel (b) in Figure 8-5), we find that when the market is for 1.6 million automobiles, the curves intersect at $n = 8$, $P = 8,750$. That is, in the absence of trade, Foreign's market would support eight firms, each producing 200,000 automobiles, and selling them at a price of $8,750. We can again confirm that this solution satisfies the equilibrium conditions:

$$P = \$8,750 = c + 1/(b \times n) = \$5,000 + 1/[(1/30,000) \times 8] = \$5,000 + \$3,750,$$

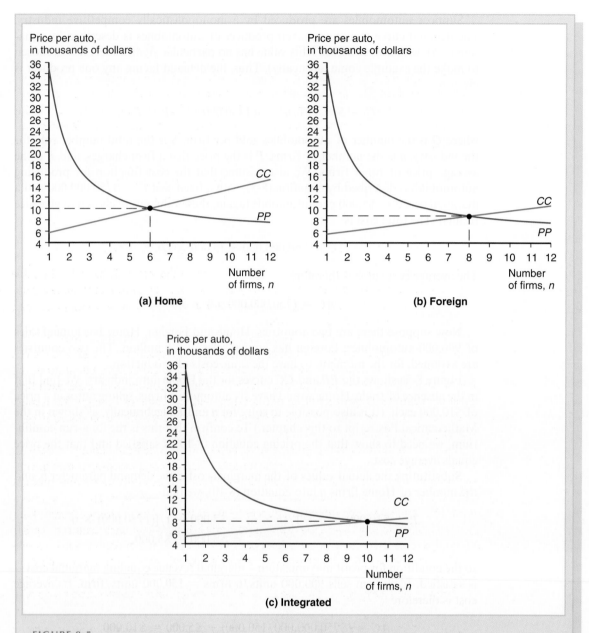

FIGURE 8-5

Equilibrium in the Automobile Market

(a) The Home market: With a market size of 900,000 automobiles, Home's equilibrium, determined by the intersection of the *PP* and *CC* curves, occurs with six firms and an industry price of $10,000 per auto. (b) The Foreign market: With a market size of 1.6 million automobiles, Foreign's equilibrium occurs with eight firms and an industry price of $8,750 per auto. (c) The combined market: Integrating the two markets creates a market for 2.5 million autos. This market supports ten firms, and the price of an auto is only $8,000.

and

$$AC = (\$750{,}000{,}000/200{,}000) + \$5{,}000 = \$8{,}750.$$

Now suppose it is possible for Home and Foreign to trade automobiles costlessly with one another. This creates a new, integrated market (panel (c) in Figure 8-5) with total sales of 2.5 million. By drawing the *PP* and *CC* curves one more time, we find that this integrated market will support ten firms, each producing 250,000 cars and selling them at a price of $8,000. The conditions for profit maximization and zero profits are again satisfied:

$$P = 8{,}000 = c + 1/(b \times n) = 5{,}000 + 1/[(1/30{,}000) \times 10]$$
$$= \$5{,}000 + \$3{,}000,$$

and

$$AC = (\$750{,}000{,}000/250{,}000) + \$5{,}000 = \$8{,}000.$$

We summarize the results of creating an integrated market in Table 8-1. The table compares each market alone with the integrated market. The integrated market supports more firms, each producing at a larger scale and selling at a lower price than either national market does on its own.

Clearly everyone is better off as a result of integration. In the larger market, consumers have a wider range of choices, yet each firm produces more and is therefore able to offer its product at a lower price. To realize these gains from integration, the countries must engage in international trade. To achieve economies of scale, each firm must concentrate its production in one country—either Home or Foreign. Yet it must sell its output to customers in both markets. So each product will be produced in only one country and exported to the other.

This numerical example highlights two important new features about trade with monopolistic competition relative to the models of trade based on comparative advantage that we covered in Chapters 3 through 6: (1) First, the example shows how product differentiation and internal economies of scale lead to trade between similar countries with no comparative advantage differences between them. This is a very different kind of trade than the one based on comparative advantage, where each country exports its comparative advantage good. Here, both Home and Foreign export autos to one another. Home pays for the imports of some automobile models (those produced by firms in Foreign) with exports of different types of models (those produced by firms in Home)—and vice versa. This leads to what is called **intra-industry trade:** two-way

TABLE 8-1	Hypothetical Example of Gains from Market Integration		
	Home Market, Before Trade	**Foreign Market, Before Trade**	**Integrated Market, After Trade**
Industry output (# of autos)	900,000	1,600,000	2,500,000
Number of firms	6	8	10
Output per firm (# of autos)	150,000	200,000	250,000
Average cost	$10,000	$8,750	$8,000
Price	$10,000	$8,750	$8,000

exchanges of similar goods. (2) Second, the example highlights two new channels for welfare benefits from trade. In the integrated market after trade, both Home and Foreign consumers benefit from a greater variety of automobile models (ten versus six or eight) at a lower price ($8,000 versus $8,750 or $10,000) as firms are able to consolidate their production destined for both locations and take advantage of economies of scale.[9]

Empirically, is intra-industry trade relevant, and do we observe gains from trade in the form of greater product variety and consolidated production at lower average cost? The answer is yes.

The Significance of Intra-Industry Trade

The proportion of intra-industry trade in world trade has steadily grown over the last half-century. The measurement of intra-industry trade relies on an industrial classification system that categorizes goods into different industries. Depending on the coarseness of the industrial classification used (hundreds of different industry classifications versus thousands), intra-industry trade accounts for one-quarter to nearly one-half of all world trade flows. Intra-industry trade plays an even more prominent role in the trade of manufactured goods among advanced industrial nations, which accounts for the majority of world trade.

Table 8-2 shows measures of the importance of intra-industry trade for a number of U.S. manufacturing industries in 2009. The measure shown is intra-industry trade as a proportion of overall trade.[10] The measure ranges from 0.97 for metalworking machinery and inorganic chemicals—industries where U.S. exports and imports are nearly equal—to 0.10 for footwear, an industry in which the United States has large imports but virtually no exports. The measure would be 0 for an industry in which the United States is only an exporter or only an importer, but not both; it would be 1 for an industry in which U.S. exports exactly equal U.S. imports.

Table 8-2 shows that intra-industry trade is a very important component of trade for the United States in many different industries. Those industries tend to be ones that produce sophisticated manufactured goods, such as chemicals, pharmaceuticals, and specialized machinery. These goods are exported principally by advanced nations and are probably subject to important economies of scale in production. At the other end of the scale are the industries with very little intra-industry trade, which typically produce labor-intensive products such as footwear and apparel. These are goods that the United States imports primarily from less-developed countries, where comparative advantage is the primary determinant of U.S. trade with these countries.

---

[9]Also note that Home consumers gain more than Foreign consumers from trade integration. This is a standard feature of trade models with increasing returns and product differentiation: A smaller country stands to gain more from integration than a larger country. This is because the gains from integration are driven by the associated increase in market size; the country that is initially smaller benefits from a bigger increase in market size upon integration.

[10]To be more precise, the standard formula for calculating the importance of intra-industry trade within a given industry is

$$I = \frac{min\{\text{exports, imports}\}}{(\text{exports} + \text{imports})/2},$$

where $min\{\text{exports, imports}\}$ refers to the smallest value between exports and imports. This is the amount of two-way exchanges of goods reflected in *both* exports and imports. This number is measured as a proportion of the average trade flow (average of exports and imports). If trade in an industry flows in only one direction, then $I = 0$ since the smallest trade flow is zero: There is no intra-industry trade. On the other hand, if a country's exports and imports within an industry are equal, we get the opposite extreme of $I = 1$.

TABLE 8-2	Indexes of Intra-Industry Trade for U.S. Industries, 2009
Metalworking Machinery	0.97
Inorganic Chemicals	0.97
Power-Generating Machines	0.86
Medical and Pharmaceutical Products	0.85
Scientific Equipment	0.84
Organic Chemicals	0.79
Iron and Steel	0.76
Road Vehicles	0.70
Office Machines	0.58
Telecommunications Equipment	0.46
Furniture	0.30
Clothing and Apparel	0.11
Footwear	0.10

What about the new types of welfare gains via increased product variety and economies of scale? A recent paper by Christian Broda at Duquesne Capital Management and David Weinstein at Columbia University estimates that the number of available products in U.S. imports tripled in the 30-year time-span from 1972 to 2001. They further estimate that this increased product variety for U.S. consumers represented a welfare gain equal to 2.6 percent of U.S. GDP![11]

Table 8-1 from our numerical example showed that the gains from integration generated by economies of scale were most pronounced for the smaller economy: Prior to integration, production there was particularly inefficient, as the economy could not take advantage of economies of scale in production due to the country's small size. This is exactly what happened when the United States and Canada followed a path of increasing economic integration starting with the North American Auto Pact in 1964 (which did not include Mexico) and culminating in the North American Free Trade Agreement (NAFTA, which does include Mexico). The Case Study that follows describes how this integration led to consolidation and efficiency gains in the automobile sector—particularly on the Canadian side (whose economy is one-tenth the size of the U.S. economy).

Similar gains from trade have also been measured for other real-world examples of closer economic integration. One of the most prominent examples has taken place in Europe over the last half-century. In 1957, the major countries of Western Europe established a free trade area in manufactured goods called the Common Market, or European Economic Community (EEC). (The United Kingdom entered the EEC later, in 1973.) The result was a rapid growth of trade that was dominated by intra-industry trade. Trade within the EEC grew twice as fast as world trade as a whole during the 1960s. This integration slowly expanded into what has become the European Union. When a subset of these countries (mostly, those countries that had formed the EEC) adopted the common euro currency in 1999, intra-industry trade among those countries further increased (even relative to that of the other countries in the European Union). Recent studies have also found that the adoption of the euro has led to a substantial increase in the number of different products that are traded within the Eurozone.

---

[11]See Christian Broda and David E. Weinstein, "Globalization and the Gains from Variety," *Quarterly Journal of Economics* 121 (April 2006), pp. 541–585.

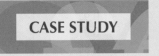

CASE STUDY

The Emergence of the Turkish Automotive Industry

The automotive and automotive spare parts industry is known to be one of the most "open" sectors of a market economy. Mostly dominated by a few large enterprises and transnationals, the sector is often characterized by fierce competition in design and manufacturing, vigorous two-way trade, and significant economies of scale.

The Turkish automotive industry has been one of the fastest expanding export sectors over the 2000s. Currently Turkey is regarded as one of the main automotive producer countries in the world, thanks to its 825,000-vehicle production capacity. As of 2007 (just before the outbreak of the global crisis), the Turkish automotive industry was comprised of 28 firms employing 42,493 people. In addition to the manufacturing of vehicles—which includes the spare parts, accessories, and coach-work segments—motor vehicles trade and repair and maintenance were also a major source of employment. In 2007, motor vehicle-related services (sales, repair and maintenance, gas stations, etc.,) together with land transportation, employed 1,180,000 additional people. The share of the aggregate motor vehicle industry in total manufacturing employment was 4.8 percent, whereas its output and value added shares were almost double, at 9.0 percent. Thus, the industry is about two times more productive than the manufacturing industry as a whole, and pays 60 percent higher wages than the manufacturing average.

Automotive exports increased rapidly in the early 2000s, mainly in response to liberalization of the trade regime starting in 1983. However, the main impetus came in 1996, when Turkey signed a *customs union* agreement with the European Union.

The customs union enabled Turkish manufacturers to import strategic components for the final good duty free, and also to export components of higher value added based on its labor cost advantage. Increased specialization followed, with intensive inter-industry, two-way trading within the sector.

Turkish exports of automotives were only worth US$1,011 million back in 1997. Imports of automotives totalled US$5,596 million. This gave rise to an export-import ratio of barely 0.18. However, by 2007, exports of Turkish automotives reached US$18,059 million, whereas sectoral imports were US$14,043 million. Thus, within a decade the automotive industry turned into a net exporting sector, with an export-import ratio of 1.28.

Trade expansion fed itself in a self-supporting, synergistic expansion of employment and productivity over the early 2000s. As technology had been improved from imports with high value added content, it became the source of a dynamic advantage in exporting.

The automotive industry in Turkey is expected to grow at a rapid pace in the next decade due to the high income elasticity of domestic as well as international demand and the tendency toward regionalization of motor vehicle production chains in the global economy, especially within the European Union. In other words, the automotive industry is expected to play a crucial role in the development of the Turkish economy in the medium term.

Source: E. Taymaz and K. Yilmaz. "Integration with the Global Economy: The Case of Turkish Automobile and Consumer Electronic Industries." *Commission on Growth and Development Working Papers* No. 37, 2008.

Firm Responses to Trade: Winners, Losers, and Industry Performance

In our numerical example of the auto industry with two countries, we saw how economic integration led to an increase in competition between firms. Of the 14 firms producing autos before trade (6 in Home and 8 in Foreign), only 10 firms "survive" after economic integration; however, each of those firms now produces at a bigger scale (250,000 autos produced per firm versus either 150,000 for Home firms or 200,000 for Foreign firms before trade). In that example, the firms were assumed to be symmetric, so exactly which firms exited and which survived and expanded was inconsequential. In the real world, however, performance varies widely across firms, so the effects of increased competition from trade are far from inconsequential. As one would expect, increased competition tends to hurt the worst-performing firms the hardest because they are the ones who are forced to exit. If the increased competition comes from trade (or economic integration), then it is also associated with sales opportunities in new markets for the surviving firms. Again, as one would expect, it is the best-performing firms that take greatest advantage of those new sales opportunities and expand the most.

These composition changes have a crucial consequence at the level of the industry: When the better-performing firms expand and the worse-performing ones contract or exit, then overall industry performance improves. This means that trade and economic integration can have a direct impact on industry performance: It is as if there was technological growth at the level of the industry. Empirically, these composition changes generate substantial improvements in industry productivity.

Take the example of Canada's closer economic integration with the United States (see the preceding Case Study and the discussion in Chapter 2). We discussed how this integration led the automobile producers to consolidate production in a smaller number of Canadian plants, whose production levels rose dramatically. The Canada–U.S. Free Trade Agreement, which went into effect in 1989, extended the auto pact to most manufacturing sectors. A similar process of consolidation occurred throughout the affected Canadian manufacturing sectors. However, this was also associated with a selection process: The worst-performing producers shut down while the better-performing ones expanded via large increases in exports to the U.S. market. Daniel Trefler at the University of Toronto has studied the effects of this trade agreement in great detail, examining the varied responses of Canadian firms.[12] He found that productivity in the most affected Canadian industries rose by a dramatic 14 to 15 percent (replicated economy-wide, a 1 percent increase in productivity translates into a 1 percent increase in GDP, holding employment constant). On its own, the contraction and exit of the worst-performing firms in response to increased competition from U.S. firms accounted for half of the 15 percent increase in those sectors.

Performance Differences across Producers

We now relax the symmetry assumption we imposed in our previous development of the monopolistic competition model so that we can examine how competition from increased market size affects firms differently.[13] The symmetry assumption meant that all firms had the same cost curve (8-3) and the same demand curve (8-5). Suppose now that firms have different cost curves because they produce with different marginal cost levels c_i. We assume all firms still face the same demand curve. Product-quality differences between firms would lead to very similar predictions for firm performance as the ones we now derive for cost differences.

Figure 8-6 illustrates the performance differences between firms 1 and 2 when $c_1 < c_2$. In panel (a), we have drawn the common demand curve (8-5) as well as its associated marginal revenue curve (8-8). Note that both curves have the same intercept on the vertical axis (plug $Q = 0$ into (8-8) to obtain $MR = P$); this intercept is given by the price P from (8-5) when $Q = 0$, which is the slope of the demand curve is $1/(S \times b)$. As we previously discussed, the marginal revenue curve is steeper than the demand curve. Firms 1 and 2 choose output levels Q_1 and Q_2, respectively, to maximize their profits. This occurs where their respective marginal cost curves intersect the common marginal revenue curve. They set prices P_1 and P_2 that correspond to those output levels on the common demand curve. We immediately see that firm 1 will set a lower price and produce a higher output level than firm 2. Since the marginal revenue curve is steeper than the demand curve, we also see that firm 1 will set a higher markup over marginal cost than firm 2: $P_1 - c_1 > P_2 - c_2$.

The shaded areas represent operating profits for both firms, equal to revenue $P_i \times Q_i$ minus operating costs $c_i \times Q_i$ (for both firms, $i = 1$ and $i = 2$). Here, we have assumed the fixed cost F (assumed to be the same for all firms) cannot be recovered and does not enter into operating profits (that is, it is a sunk cost). Since operating profits can be rewritten as the product of the markup times the number of output units sold, $(P_i - c_i) \times Q_i$, we can determine that firm 1 will earn higher profits than firm 2 (recall that firm 1 sets a higher markup and produces more output than firm 2). We can thus summarize all the relevant performance differences based on marginal cost differences across firms. Compared to a firm with a higher marginal cost, a firm with a lower marginal cost will (1) set a lower price but at a higher markup over marginal cost; (2) produce more output; and (3) earn higher profits.[14]

---

[12]See Daniel Trefler, "The Long and Short of the Canada-U.S. Free Trade Agreement," *American Economic Review* 94 (September 2004), pp. 870–895, and the summary of this work in the *New York Times:* "What Happened When Two Countries Liberalized Trade? Pain, Then Gain" by Virginia Postel (January 27, 2005); and Marc J. Melitz and Daniel Trefler, "Gains from Trade When Firms Matter," *Journal of Economic Perspectives* 26 (2012), pp. 91–118.

[13]A more detailed exposition of this model is presented in Marc J. Melitz and Daniel Trefler, "Gains from Trade When Firms Matter," *Journal of Economic Perspectives* 26 (2012), pp. 91–118.

[14]Recall that we have assumed that all firms face the same nonrecoverable fixed cost F. If a firm earns higher operating profits, then it also earns higher overall profits (that deduct the fixed cost F).

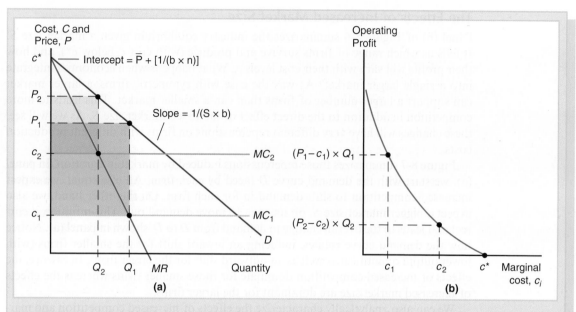

FIGURE 8-6

Performance Differences across Firms

(a) Demand and cost curves for firms 1 and 2. Firm 1 has a lower marginal cost than firm 2: $c_1 < c_2$. Both firms face the same demand curve and marginal revenue curve. Relative to firm 2, firm 1 sets a lower price and produces more output. The shaded areas represent operating profits for both firms (before the fixed cost is deducted). Firm 1 earns higher operating profits than firm 2. (b) Operating profits as a function of a firm's marginal cost c_i. Operating profits decrease as the marginal cost increases. Any firm with marginal cost above c^* cannot operate profitably and shuts down.

Panel (b) in Figure 8-6 shows how a firm's operating profits vary with its marginal cost c_i. As we just mentioned, this will be a decreasing function of marginal cost. Going back to panel (a), we see that a firm can earn a positive operating profit so long as its marginal cost is below the intercept of the demand curve on the vertical axis at $\overline{P} + [1/(b \times n)]$. Let c^* denote this cost cutoff. A firm with a marginal cost c_i above this cutoff is effectively "priced out" of the market and would earn negative operating profits if it were to produce any output. Such a firm would choose to shut down and not produce (incurring an overall profit loss equal to the fixed cost F). Why would such a firm enter in the first place? Clearly, it wouldn't if it knew about its high cost c_i prior to entering and paying the fixed cost F.

We assume that entrants face some randomness about their future production cost c_i. This randomness disappears only *after* F is paid and is sunk. Thus, some firms will regret their entry decision if their overall profit (operating profit minus the fixed cost F) is negative. On the other hand, some firms will discover that their production cost c_i is very low and that they earn high positive overall profit levels. Entry is driven by a similar process as the one we described for the case of symmetric firms. In that previous case, firms entered until profits for all firms were driven to zero. Here, there are profit differences between firms, and entry occurs until *expected* profits across all potential cost levels c_i are driven to zero.

The Effects of Increased Market Size

Panel (b) of Figure 8-6 summarizes the industry equilibrium given a market size S. It tells us which range of firms survive and produce (with cost c_i below c^*), and how their profits will vary with their cost levels c_i. What happens when economies integrate into a single larger market? As was the case with symmetric firms, a larger market can support a larger number of firms than can a smaller market. This leads to more competition in addition to the direct effect of increased market size S. As we will see, these changes will have very different repercussions on firms with different production costs.

Figure 8-7 summarizes those repercussions induced by market integration. In panel (a), we start with the demand curve D faced by each firm. All else equal, we expect increased competition to shift demand in for each firm. On the other hand, we also expect a bigger market size S, on its own, to move demand out. This intuition is correct and leads to the overall change in demand from D to D' shown in panel (a). Notice how the demand curve rotates, inducing an inward shift for the smaller firms (with lower output quantities) as well as an outward shift for the larger firms. In essence, the effects of increased competition dominate for those smaller firms whereas the effects of increased market size are dominant for the larger firms.

We can also analytically characterize the effects of increased competition and market size on the demand curve D. Recall that the vertical intercept of this demand curve is $\overline{P} + [1/(b \times n)]$, while its slope is $1/(S \times b)$. Increased competition (a higher number of firms n) holding market size S constant lowers the vertical intercept for

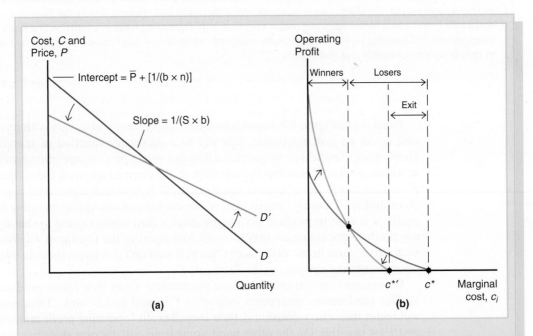

(a)   (b)

FIGURE 8-7

Winners and Losers from Economic Integration

(a) The demand curve for all firms changes from D to D'. It is flatter, and has a lower vertical intercept.
(b) Effects of the shift in demand on the operating profits of firms with different marginal cost c_i. Firms with marginal cost between the old cutoff, c^*, and the new one, $c^{*'}$, are forced to exit. Some firms with the lowest marginal cost levels gain from integration and their profits increase.

demand, leaving its slope unchanged: This is the induced inward shift from more competition.[15] The direct effect of increased market size S flattens the demand curve (lower slope), leaving the intercept unchanged: This generates an outward rotation of demand. Combining these two effects, we obtain the new demand curve D', which has a lower vertical intercept and is flatter than the original demand curve D

Panel (b) of Figure 8-7 shows the consequences of this demand change for the operating profits of firms with different cost levels c_i. The decrease in demand for the smaller firms translates into a new, lower-cost cutoff, $c^{*'}$: Some firms with the high cost levels above $c^{*'}$ cannot survive the decrease in demand and are forced to exit. On the other hand, the flatter demand curve is advantageous to some firms with low cost levels: They can adapt to the increased competition by lowering their markup (and hence their price) and gain some additional market share.[16] This translates into increased profits for some of the best-performing firms with the lowest cost levels c_i.[17]

Figure 8-7 illustrates how increased market size generates both winners and losers among firms in an industry. The low-cost firms thrive and increase their profits and market shares, while the high-cost firms contract and the highest-cost firms exit. These composition changes imply that overall productivity in the industry is increasing as production is concentrated among the more productive (low-cost) firms. This replicates the findings for Canadian manufacturing following closer integration with U.S. manufacturing, as we previously described. These effects tend to be most pronounced for smaller countries that integrate with larger ones, but it is not limited to those small countries. Even for a big economy such as the United States, increased integration via lower trade costs leads to important composition effects and productivity gains.[18]

Trade Costs and Export Decisions

Up to now, we have modeled economic integration as an increase in market size. This implicitly assumes that this integration occurs to such an extent that a single combined market is formed. In reality, integration rarely goes that far: Trade costs among countries are reduced, but they do not disappear. In Chapter 2, we discussed how these trade costs are manifested even for the case of the two very closely integrated economies of the United States and Canada. We saw how the U.S.–Canada border substantially decreases trade volumes between Canadian provinces and U.S. states.

Trade costs associated with this border crossing are also a salient feature of firm-level trade patterns: Very few firms in the United States reach Canadian customers. In fact, most U.S. firms do not report *any* exporting activity at all (because they sell only to U.S. customers). In 2002, only 18 percent of U.S. manufacturing firms reported undertaking some export sales. Table 8-3 shows the proportion of firms that report some export sales across several different U.S. manufacturing sectors. Even

---

[15]In equilibrium, increased competition also leads to a lower average price $\bar{P}$, which will further decrease the intercept.

[16]Recall that the lower the firm's marginal cost c_i, the higher its markup over marginal cost $P_i - c_i$. High-cost firms are already setting low markups and cannot lower their prices to induce positive demand, as this would mean pricing below their marginal cost of production.

[17]Another way to deduce that profit increases for some firms is to use the entry condition that drives average profits to zero: If profit decreases for some of the high-cost firms, then it must increase for some of the low-cost firms, since the average across all firms must remain equal to zero.

[18]See A. B. Bernard, J. B. Jensen, and P. K. Schott, "Trade Costs, Firms and Productivity," *Journal of Monetary Economics* 53 (July 2006), pp. 917–937.

TABLE 8-3	Proportion of U.S. Firms Reporting Export Sales by Industry, 2002
Printing	5%
Furniture	7%
Apparel	8%
Wood Products	8%
Fabricated Metals	14%
Petroleum and Coal	18%
Transportation Equipment	28%
Machinery	33%
Chemicals	36%
Computer and Electronics	38%
Electrical Equipment and Appliances	38%

Source: A. B. Bernard, J. B. Jensen, S. J. Redding, and P. K. Schott, "Firms in International Trade." *Journal of Economic Perspectives* 21 (Summer 2007), pp. 105–130.

in industries where exports represent a substantial proportion of total production, such as chemicals, machinery, electronics, and transportation, fewer than 40 percent of firms export. In fact, one major reason why trade costs associated with national borders reduce trade so much is that they drastically cut down the number of firms willing or able to reach customers across the border. (The other reason is that the trade costs also reduce the export sales of firms that do reach those customers across the border.)

In our integrated economy without any trade costs, firms were indifferent as to the location of their customers. We now introduce trade costs to explain why firms actually do care about the location of their customers and why so many firms choose not to reach customers in another country. As we will see shortly, this will also allow us to explain important differences between those firms that choose to incur the trade costs and export, and those that do not. Why would some firms choose not to export? Simply put, the trade costs reduce the profitability of exporting for all firms. For some, that reduction in profitability makes exporting unprofitable. We now formalize this argument.

To keep things simple, we will consider the response of firms in a world with two identical countries (Home and Foreign). Let the market size parameter S now reflect the size of each market, so that $2 \times S$ now reflects the size of the world market. We cannot analyze this world market as a single market of size $2 \times S$ because this market is no longer perfectly integrated due to trade costs.

Specifically, assume that a firm must incur an additional cost t for each unit of output that it sells to customers across the border. We now have to keep track of the firms' behavior in each market separately. Due to the trade cost t, firms will set different prices in their export market relative to their domestic market. This will lead to different quantities sold in each market and ultimately to different profit levels earned in each market. As each firm's marginal cost is constant (does not vary with production levels), those decisions regarding pricing and quantity sold in each market can be separated: A decision regarding the domestic market will have no impact on the profitability of different decisions for the export market.

Consider the case of firms located in Home. Their situation regarding their domestic (Home) market is exactly as was illustrated in Figure 8-6, except that all

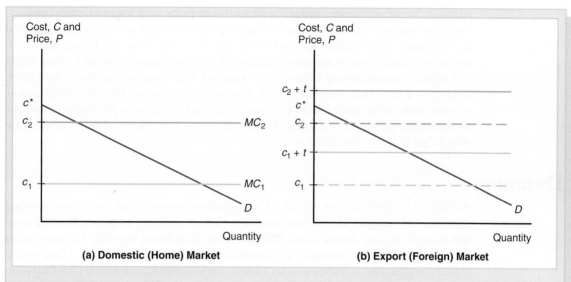

FIGURE 8-8

Export Decisions with Trade Costs

(a) Firms 1 and 2 both operate in their domestic (Home) market. (b) Only firm 1 chooses to export to the Foreign market. It is not profitable for firm 2 to export given the trade cost t.

the outcomes, such as price, output, and profit, relate to the domestic market only.[19] Now consider the decisions of firms 1 and 2 (with marginal costs c_1 and c_2) regarding the export (Foreign) market. They face the same demand curve in Foreign as they do in Home (recall that we assumed the two countries are identical). The only difference is that the firms' marginal cost in the export market is shifted up by the trade cost t. Figure 8-8 shows the situation for the two firms in both markets.

What are the effects of the trade cost on the firms' decisions regarding the export market? We know from our previous analysis that a higher marginal cost induces a firm to raise its price, which leads to a lower output quantity sold and lower profits. We also know that if marginal cost is raised above the threshold level c^*, then a firm cannot profitably operate in that market. This is what happens to firm 2 in Figure 8-8. Firm 2 can profitably operate in its domestic market because its cost there is below the threshold: $c_2 \leq c^*$. However, it cannot profitably operate in the export market because its cost there is above the threshold: $c_2 + t > c^*$. Firm 1, on the other hand, has a low enough cost that it can profitably operate in both the domestic and the export markets: $c_1 + t \leq c^*$. We can extend this prediction to all firms based on their marginal cost c_i. The lowest-cost firms with $c_i \leq c^* - t$ export; the higher-cost firms with $c^* - t < c_i \leq c^*$ still produce for their domestic market but do not export; the highest-cost firms with $c_i > c^*$ cannot profitably operate in either market and thus exit.

We just saw how the modeling of trade costs added two important predictions to our model of monopolistic competition and trade: Those costs explain why only a subset of firms export, and they also explain why this subset of firms will consist of

---

[19] The number of firms n is the total number of firms selling in the Home market. (This includes both firms located in Home as well as the firms located in Foreign that export to Home). $\bar{P}$ is the average price across all those firms selling in Home.

relatively larger and more productive firms (those firms with lower marginal cost c_i). Empirical analyses of firms' export decisions from numerous countries have provided overwhelming support for this prediction that exporting firms are bigger and more productive than firms in the same industry that do not export. In the United States in a typical manufacturing industry, an exporting firm is on average more than twice as large as a firm that does not export. The average exporting firm also produces 11 percent more value added (output minus intermediate inputs) per worker than the average nonexporting firm. These differences across exporters and nonexporters are even larger in many European countries.[20]

Dumping

Adding trade costs to our model of monopolistic competition also added another dimension of realism: Because markets are no longer perfectly integrated through cost-less trade, firms can choose to set different prices in different markets. The trade costs also affect how a firm responds to competition in a market. Recall that a firm with a higher marginal cost will choose to set a lower markup over marginal cost (this firm faces more intense competition due to its lower market share). This means that an exporting firm will respond to the trade cost by lowering its markup for the export market.

Consider the case of firm 1 in Figure 8-8. It faces a higher marginal cost $c_1 + t$ in the Foreign export market. Let P_1^D and P_1^X denote the prices that firm 1 sets on its domestic (Home) market and export (Foreign) market, respectively. Firm 1 sets a lower markup $P_1^X - (c_1 + t)$ on the export market relative to its markup $P_1^X - c_1$ on the domestic market. This in turn implies that $P_1^X - t < P_1^D$ and that firm 1 sets an export price (net of trade costs) lower than its domestic price.

That is considered **dumping** by firm 1 and is regarded by most countries as an "unfair" trade practice. Any firm from Foreign can appeal to its local authorities (in the United States, the Commerce Department and the International Trade Commission are the relevant authorities) and seek punitive damages against firm 1. This usually takes the form of an **antidumping duty** imposed on firm 1 and would usually be scaled to the price difference between P_1^D and $P_1^X - t$.[21]

Dumping is a controversial issue in trade policy; we discuss policy disputes sur-rounding dumping in Chapter 10. For now, we just note that firm 1 is not behaving any differently than the foreign firms it is competing against in the Foreign market. In that market, firm 1 sets exactly the same markup over marginal cost as Foreign firm 2 with marginal cost $c_2 = c_1 + t$. Firm 2's pricing behavior is perfectly legal, so why is firm 1's export pricing decision considered to represent an "unfair" trade practice? This is one major reason why economists believe that the enforcement of dumping claims is misguided (see the Case Study for a further discussion) and that there is no good economic justification for dumping to be considered particularly harmful.

Our model of monopolistic competition highlighted how trade costs have a natural tendency to induce firms to lower their markups in export markets, where they face

---

[20]See A. B. Bernard, J. B. Jensen, S. J. Redding, and P. K. Schott, "Firms in International Trade," *Journal of Economic Perspectives* 21 (Summer 2007), pp. 105–130; and Thierry Mayer and Gianmarco I. P. Ottaviano, "The Happy Few: The Internationalisation of European Firms: New Facts Based on Firm-Level Evidence," *Intereconomics* 43 (May/June 2008), pp. 135–148.

[21]$P_1^X - t$ is called firm 1's *ex* factory price for the export market (the price at the "factory gate" before the trade costs are incurred). If firm 1 incurred some transport or delivery cost in its domestic market, then those costs would be deducted from its domestic price P_1^D to obtain an *ex factory* price for the domestic market. Antidumping duties are based on differences between a firm's ex factory prices in the domestic and export markets.

more intense competition due to their reduced market share. This makes it relatively easy for domestic firms to file a dumping complaint against exporters in their markets. In practice, those antidumping laws can then be used to erect barriers to trade by discriminating against exporters in a market.

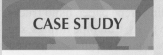

CASE STUDY — Antidumping as Protectionism

In the United States and a number of other countries, dumping is regarded as an unfair competitive practice. U.S. firms that claim to have been injured by foreign firms that dump their products in the domestic market at low prices can appeal, through a quasi-judicial procedure, to the Commerce Department for relief. If their complaint is ruled valid, an "antidumping duty" is imposed, equal to the calculated difference between the actual and the "fair" price of imports. In practice, the Commerce Department accepts the great majority of complaints by U.S. firms about unfair foreign pricing. The determination that this unfair pricing has actually caused injury, however, is in the hands of a different agency, the International Trade Commission, which rejects about half of its cases.

Economists have never been very happy with the idea of singling out dumping as a prohibited practice. For one thing, setting different prices for different customers is a perfectly legitimate business strategy—like the discounts that airlines offer to students, senior citizens, and travelers who are willing to stay over a weekend. Also, the legal definition of dumping deviates substantially from the economic definition. Since it is often difficult to prove that foreign firms charge higher prices to domestic than to export customers, the United States and other nations instead often try to calculate a supposedly fair price based on estimates of foreign production costs. This "fair price" rule can interfere with perfectly normal business practices: A firm may well be willing to sell a product for a loss while it is lowering its costs through experience or breaking into a new market. Even absent such dynamic considerations, our model highlighted how monopolistically competitive firms have an incentive to lower their markups in export markets due to competition effects associated with trade costs.

In spite of almost universally negative assessments from economists, however, formal complaints about dumping have been filed with growing frequency since about 1970. In the early 1990s, the bulk of anti-dumping complaints were directed at developed countries. But since 1995, developing countries have accounted for the majority of anti-dumping complaints. And among those countries, China has attracted a particularly large number of complaints.

There are two main reasons behind this trend. First and foremost has been China's massive export growth. No firm enjoys facing stiff increases in competition, and anti-dumping laws allow firms to insulate themselves from this competition by raising their competitors' costs. Second, proving unfair pricing by a Chinese firm is relatively easier than for exporters from other countries. Most developed countries (including the United States) facing this surge in Chinese exports have labeled China a "non-market" economy. A *BusinessWeek* story describes the difference that this description makes when a U.S. firm files an anti-dumping complaint against a Chinese exporter: "That means the U.S. can simply ignore Chinese data on costs on the assumption they are distorted by subsidized loans, rigged markets, and the controlled yuan. Instead, the government uses data from other developing nations regarded as market economies. In the TV and furniture cases, the U.S. used India—even though it is not a big exporter of these goods. Since India's production costs were higher, China was ruled guilty of dumping."[22]

As the quote suggests, China has been subject to antidumping duties on TVs and furniture, along with a number of other products including crepe paper, hand trucks, shrimp, ironing tables, plastic shopping bags, steel fence posts, iron pipe fittings, saccharin, and most recently solar panels. These duties are high: as high as 78 percent on color TVs and 330 percent on saccharin.

Multinationals and Outsourcing

When is a corporation multinational? In U.S. statistics, a U.S. company is considered foreign-controlled, and therefore a subsidiary of a foreign-based multinational, if 10 percent or more of its stock is held by a foreign company; the idea is that 10 percent is enough to convey effective control. Similarly, a U.S.-based company is considered multinational if it owns more than 10 percent of a foreign firm. The controlling (owning) firm is called the multinational parent, while the "controlled" firms are called the multinational affiliates.

When a U.S. firm buys more than 10 percent of a foreign firm, or when a U.S. firm builds a new production facility abroad, that investment is considered a U.S. outflow of **foreign direct investment (FDI)**. The latter is called *greenfield* FDI, while the former is called *brownfield* FDI (or cross-border mergers and acquisitions). Conversely, investments by foreign firms in production facilities in the United States are considered U.S. FDI inflows. We describe the worldwide patterns of FDI flows in the Case Study that follows. For now, we focus on the decision of a firm to become a multinational parent. Why would a firm choose to operate an affiliate in a foreign location?

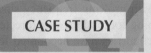

CASE STUDY   **Patterns of Foreign Direct Investment Flows Around the World**

Figure 8-9 shows how the magnitude of worldwide FDI flows has evolved over the last 40 years. We first examine patterns for the world, where FDI flows must be balanced: Hence world inflows are equal to world outflows. We see that there was a massive increase in multinational activity in the mid- to late-1990s, when worldwide FDI flows more than quintupled and then again in the early 2000s. We also see that the growth rate of FDI is very uneven, with huge peaks and troughs. Those peaks and troughs correlate with the gyrations of stock markets worldwide

---

[22]"Wielding a Heavy Weapon Against China," *BusinessWeek*, June 21, 2004.

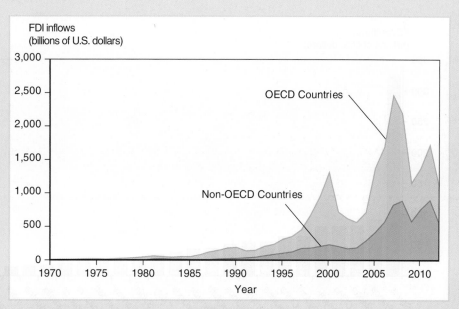

FIGURE 8-9

Inflows of Foreign Direct Investment, 1970–2012 (billions of dollars)

Worldwide flows of FDI have significantly increased since the mid-1990s, though the rates of increase have been very uneven. Historically, most of the inflows of FDI have gone to the developed countries in the OECD. However, the proportion of FDI inflows going to developing and transition economies has steadily increased over time and accounted for over half of worldwide FDI flows since 2009.

Source: World Bank, *World Development Indicators.*

(strongly dominated by fluctuations in the U.S. stock market). The financial collapse in 2000 (the bursting of the dot-com bubble) and the most recent financial crisis in 2007–2009 also induced huge crashes in worldwide FDI flows. Most recently, global FDI flows sharply declined in 2012, even though world GDP grew and the largest stock markets all posted significant gains. (Uncertainty related to the fragility of the economic recovery and political stability played a significant role—as well as the repatriation of profits by multinationals.) Most of those FDI flows related to cross-border mergers and acquisitions, whereas greenfield FDI remained relatively stable.

Looking at the distribution of FDI inflows across groups of countries, we see that historically, the richest OECD countries have been the biggest recipients of inward FDI. However, we also see that those inflows are much more volatile (this is where the FDI related to mergers and acquisitions is concentrated) than the FDI going to the remaining countries with lower incomes. Finally, we also see that there has been a steady expansion in the share of FDI that flows to those countries outside the OECD. This accounted for over half of worldwide FDI flows since 2009. The BRICS countries (Brazil, the Russian Federation, China, India, and South Africa) have accounted for a substantial portion of this increase: FDI flows to those countries increased 20-fold in the past decade.

Figure 8-10 shows the list of the top 25 countries whose firms engage in FDI outflows. Because those flows are very volatile, especially with the recent crisis, they have

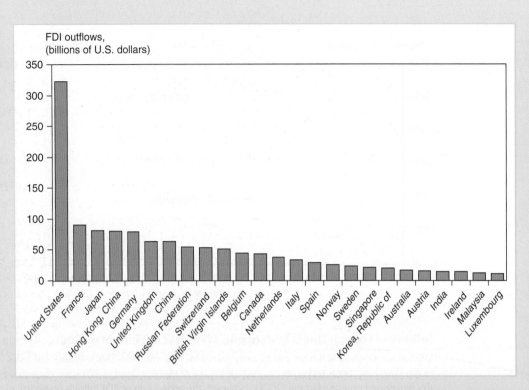

FIGURE 8-10

Outward Foreign Direct Investment for Top 25 Countries, Yearly Average for 2009–2011 (billions of dollars)

Developed countries dominate the list of the top countries whose firms engage in outward FDI. More recently, firms from some big developing countries such as China and India have performed significantly more FDI.

Source: UNCTAD, World Investment Report, 2012.

been averaged over the past three years. We see that FDI outflows are still dominated by the developed economies; but we also see that big developing countries, most notably China (including Hong Kong), are playing an increasingly important role. In fact, one of the fastest-growing FDI segments is flows *from* developing countries *into* other developing countries. Multinationals in both China and India play a prominent role in this relatively new type of FDI. We also see that international tax policies can shape the location of FDI. For example, the British Virgin Islands would not figure in that top-25 list were it not for its status as an international tax haven.[23] Firms from that location that engage in FDI are mainly offshore companies: They are incorporated in the British Virgin Islands, but their productive activities are located elsewhere in the world.

---

[23]The British Virgin Islands is an even bigger recipient of inward FDI: In 2012, it was the fifth largest recipient in the world.

FDI flows are not the only way to measure the presence of multinationals in the world economy. Other measures are based on economic activities such as sales, value added (sales minus purchased intermediate goods), and employment. Sales of FDI affiliates are often used as the benchmark of multinational activity. This provides the relevant benchmark when comparing the activities of multinationals to export volumes. However, the sales of multinationals are also often compared to country GDPs showing, for example, that the big multinationals have higher sales volumes than the GDPs of many countries in the world. For the world as a whole in 2000, the total sales of the largest multinationals (top 200) amounted to more than 27 percent of world GDP.

However striking, this comparison is misleading and overstates the influence of multinationals because country GDP is measured in terms of value added: Intermediate goods used in final production are not double-counted in this GDP measure. On the other hand, the intermediate goods that one multinational sells to another are double-counted in the multinationals' sales totals (once in the sales of the producer of the intermediate goods and another time as part of the final value of the goods sold by the user of the intermediate goods). As a result, the appropriate comparison between multinationals and GDPs should be based on value added. By this metric, the value added produced by the biggest multinationals accounted for 4.3 percent of world GDP in 2000. This is still a big percentage, but not as eye-catching as the 27 percent measure.

The answer depends, in part, on the production activities that the affiliate carries out. These activities fall into two main categories: (1) The affiliate replicates the production process (that the parent firm undertakes in its domestic facilities) elsewhere in the world; and (2) the production chain is broken up, and parts of the production processes are transferred to the affiliate location. Investing in affiliates that do the first type of activities is categorized as **horizontal FDI**. Investing in affiliates that do the second type of activities is categorized as **vertical FDI**.[24]

Vertical FDI is mainly driven by production cost differences between countries (for those parts of the production process that can be performed in another location). What drives those cost differences between countries? This is just the outcome of the theory of comparative advantage that we developed in Chapters 3 through 7. For example, Intel (the world's largest computer chip manufacturer) has broken up the production of chips into wafer fabrication, assembly, and testing. Wafer fabrication and the associated research and development are very skill-intensive, so Intel still performs most of those activities in the United States as well as in Ireland and Israel (where skilled labor is still relatively abundant).[25] On the other hand, chip assembly and testing are labor-intensive, and Intel has moved those production processes to countries where labor is relatively abundant, such as Malaysia, the Philippines, Costa Rica, and China. This type of vertical FDI is one of the fastest-growing types of FDI and is behind the large increase in FDI inflows to developing countries (see Figure 8-9).

---

[24]In reality, the distinctions between horizontal and vertical FDI can be blurred. Some large multinational parents operate large networks of affiliates that replicate parts of the production process, but are also vertically connected to other affiliates in the parent's network. This is referred to as "complex" FDI.

[25]In 2010, Intel opened a new wafer fabrication plant in Dalian, China, where older chip models are produced.

In contrast to vertical FDI, horizontal FDI is dominated by flows between developed countries; that is, both the multinational parent and the affiliates are located in developed countries. The main reason for this type of FDI is to locate production near a firm's large customer bases. Hence, trade and transport costs play a much more important role than production cost differences for these FDI decisions. Consider the example of Toyota, which is the world's largest motor vehicle producer (at least, at the time of writing, though Volkswagen is a closed second). At the start of the 1980s, Toyota produced almost all of its cars and trucks in Japan and exported them throughout the world, but mostly to North America and Europe. High trade costs to those markets (in large part due to trade restrictions; see Chapter 9) and rising demand levels there induced Toyota to slowly expand its production overseas. By 2009, Toyota produced over half of its vehicles in assembly plants abroad. Toyota has replicated the production process for its most popular car model, the Corolla, in assembly plants in Brazil, Canada, China, India, Japan, Pakistan, South Africa, Taiwan, Thailand, Turkey, the United States, the United Kingdom, Vietnam, and Venezuela: This is horizontal FDI in action.

The Firm's Decision Regarding Foreign Direct Investment

We now examine in more detail the firm's decision regarding horizontal FDI. We mentioned that one main driver was high trade costs associated with exporting, which leads to an incentive to locate production near customers. On the other hand, there are also increasing returns to scale in production. As a result, it is not cost effective to replicate the production process too many times and operate facilities that produce too little output to take advantage of those increasing returns. This is called the *proximity-concentration* trade-off for FDI. Empirical evidence on the extent of FDI across sectors strongly confirms the relevance of this trade-off: FDI activity is concentrated in sectors where trade costs are high (such as the automobile industry); however, when increasing returns to scale are important and average plant sizes are large, one observes higher export volumes relative to FDI.

Empirical evidence also shows that there is an even stronger sorting pattern for FDI at the firm level *within* industries: Multinationals tend to be substantially larger and more productive than nonmultinationals in the same country. Even when one compares multinationals to the subset of exporting firms in a country, one still finds a large size and productivity differential in favor of the multinationals. We return to our monopolistic competition model of trade to analyze how firms respond differently to the proximity-concentration trade-off involved with the FDI decision.

The Horizontal FDI Decision   How does the proximity trade-off fit into our model of firms' export decisions captured in Figure 8-8? There, if a firm wants to reach customers in Foreign, it has only one possibility: export and incur the trade cost t per unit exported. Let's now introduce the choice of becoming a multinational via horizontal FDI: A firm could avoid the trade cost t by building a production facility in Foreign. Of course, building this production facility is costly and implies incurring the fixed cost F again for the foreign affiliate. (Note, however, that this additional fixed cost need not equal the fixed cost of building the firm's original production facility in Home; characteristics specific to the individual country will affect this cost.) For simplicity, continue to assume that Home and Foreign are similar countries so that this firm could build a unit of a good at the same marginal cost in this foreign facility. (Recall that horizontal FDI mostly involves developed countries with similar factor prices.)

The firm's export versus FDI choice will then involve a trade-off between the per-unit export cost t and the fixed cost F of setting up an additional production facility. Any such trade-off between a per-unit and a fixed cost boils down to scale. If the firm sells Q units in the foreign market, then it incurs a total trade-related cost $Q \times t$ to export; this is weighed against the alternative of the fixed cost F. If $Q > F/t$, then exporting is more expensive, and FDI is the profit-maximizing choice.

This leads to a scale cutoff for FDI. This cutoff summarizes the proximity-concentration trade-off: Higher trade costs on one hand, and lower fixed production costs on the other hand, both lower the FDI cutoff. The firm's scale, however, depends on its performance measure. A firm with low enough cost c_i will want to sell more than Q units to foreign customers. The most cost-effective way to do this is to build an affiliate in Foreign and become a multinational. Some firms with intermediate cost levels will still want to serve customers in Foreign, but their intended sales Q are low enough that exports, rather than FDI, will be the most cost-effective way to reach those customers.

The Vertical FDI Decision   A firm's decision to break up its production chain and move parts of that chain to a foreign affiliate will also involve a trade-off between per-unit and fixed costs—so the scale of the firm's activity will again be a crucial element determining this outcome. When it comes to vertical FDI, the key cost saving is not related to the shipment of goods across borders; rather, it involves production cost differences for the parts of the production chain that are being moved. As we previously discussed, those cost differences stem mostly from comparative advantage forces.

We will not discuss those cost differences further here, but rather ask why—given those cost differences—all firms do not choose to operate affiliates in low-wage countries to perform the activities that are most labor-intensive and can be performed in a different location. The reason is that, as with the case of horizontal FDI, vertical FDI requires a substantial fixed cost investment in a foreign affiliate in a country with the appropriate characteristics.[26] Again, as with the case of horizontal FDI, there will be a scale cutoff for vertical FDI that depends on the production cost differentials on one hand, and the fixed cost of operating a foreign affiliate on the other hand. Only those firms operating at a scale above that cutoff will choose to perform vertical FDI.

Outsourcing

Our discussion of multinationals up to this point has neglected an important motive. We discussed the **location motive** for production facilities that leads to multinational formation. However, we did not discuss why the parent firm chooses to *own* the affiliate in that location and operate as a single multinational firm. This is known as the **internalization motive**.

As a substitute for horizontal FDI, a parent could license an independent firm to produce and sell its products in a foreign location; as a substitute for vertical FDI, a parent could contract with an independent firm to perform specific parts of the production process in the foreign location with the best cost advantage. This substitute for vertical FDI is known as **foreign outsourcing** (sometimes just referred to as outsourcing, where the foreign location is implied).

---

[26]Clearly, factor prices such as wages are a crucial component, but other country characteristics, such as its transportation/public infrastructure, the quality of its legal institutions, and its tax/regulation policies toward multinationals, can be critical as well.

Offshoring represents the relocation of parts of the production chain abroad and groups together both foreign outsourcing and vertical FDI. Offshoring has increased dramatically in the last decade and is one of the major drivers of the increased worldwide trade in services (such as business and telecommunications services); in manufacturing, trade in intermediate goods accounted for 40 percent of worldwide trade in 2008. When the intermediate goods are produced within a multinational's affiliate network, the shipments of those intermediate goods are classified as intra-firm trade. Intra-firm trade represents roughly one-third of worldwide trade and over 40 percent of U.S. trade.

What are the key elements that determine this internalization choice? Control over a firm's proprietary technology offers one clear advantage for internalization. Licensing another firm to perform the entire production process in another location (as a substitute for horizontal FDI) often involves a substantial risk of losing some proprietary technology. On the other hand, there are no clear reasons why an independent firm should be able to replicate that production process at a lower cost than the parent firm. This gives internalization a strong advantage, so horizontal FDI is widely favored over the alternative of technology licensing to replicate the production process.

The trade-off between outsourcing and vertical FDI is much less clear-cut. There are many reasons why an independent firm could produce some parts of the production process at lower cost than the parent firm (in the same location). First and foremost, an independent firm can specialize in exactly that narrow part of the production process. As a result, it can also benefit from economies of scale if it performs those processes for many different parent firms.[27] Other reasons stress the advantages of local ownership in the alignment and monitoring of managerial incentives at the production facility.

But internalization also provides its own benefits when it comes to vertical integration between a firm and its supplier of a critical input to production: This avoids (or at least lessens) the potential for a costly renegotiation conflict after an initial agreement has been reached. Such conflicts can arise regarding many specific attributes of the input that cannot be specified in (or enforced by) a legal contract written at the time of the initial agreement. This can lead to a holdup of production by either party. For example, the buying firm can claim that the quality of the part is not exactly as specified and demand a lower price. The supplying firm can claim that some changes demanded by the buyer led to increased costs and demand a higher price at delivery time.

Much progress has been made in recent research formalizing those trade-offs. This research explains how this important internalization choice is made, by describing when a firm chooses to integrate with its suppliers via vertical FDI and when it chooses an independent contractual relationship with those suppliers abroad. Developing those theories is beyond the scope of this text; ultimately, many of those theories boil down to different trade-offs between production cost savings and the fixed cost of moving parts of the production process abroad.

Describing which types of firms pick one offshoring option versus the other is sensitive to the details of the modeling assumptions. Nonetheless, there is one prediction that emerges from almost all of those models with respect to the offshoring option. Relative to no offshoring (not breaking up the production chain and moving parts

---

[27]Companies that provide outsourced goods and services have expanded their list of clients to such an extent that they have now become large multinationals themselves. They specialize in providing a narrow set of services (or parts of the production process), but replicate this many times over for client companies across the globe.

of it abroad), both vertical FDI and foreign outsourcing involve lower production costs combined with a higher fixed cost. As we saw, this implies a scale cutoff for a firm to choose either offshoring option. Thus, only the larger firms will choose either offshoring option and import some of their intermediate inputs.

This sorting scheme for firms to import intermediate goods is similar to the one we described for the firm's export choice: Only a subset of relatively more productive (lower-cost) firms will choose to offshore (import intermediate goods) and export (reach foreign customers)—because those are the firms that operate at sufficiently large scale to favor the trade-off involving higher fixed costs and lower per-unit costs (production- or trade-related).

Empirically, are the firms that offshore and import intermediate goods the same set of firms that also export? The answer is a resounding yes. For the United States in 2000, 92 percent of firms (weighed by employment) that imported intermediate goods also exported. Those importers thus also shared the same characteristics as U.S. exporters: They were substantially larger and more productive than the U.S. firms that did not engage in international trade.

CASE STUDY

"We design them here, but the labor is cheaper in Hell."

©2004 Drew Demavich/The New Yorker Collection/www.cartoonbank.com

Shipping Jobs Overseas? Offshoring and Unemployment in the United States

When a company offshores part of its production chain abroad, it is then importing an intermediate good or service. For example, a company may import a part, component, or even an entire assembled product; or it may import business services by using accountants and/or call centers located abroad. As we discuss in the next section, the overall effects of trade in such intermediates are very similar to the trade in final goods that we have focused on up to now. Yet, when it comes to the effects of offshoring on employment, there is one additional dimension: the lower price of the imported intermediates not only benefits a firm's owners and their consumers, it also benefits the firm's remaining workers—because the lower price induces firms to increase their purchases of intermediates, which improves the productivity of the remaining workers.[28]

This productivity effect also induces the offshoring firm to hire additional workers dedicated to the remaining parts of the production process. In many cases, the overall employment effect for the offshoring firm is positive: Several studies of U.S. multinationals have found that when they expand their overseas employment, they concurrently also expand their U.S. employment.[29]

What about foreign outsourcers who no longer maintain ownership of their foreign suppliers? A recent study covering the entire U.S. manufacturing sector found that overall, increases in offshoring from 2001–2007 did have a negative impact on

---

[28]This additional dimension of offshoring, and its effects for low-skilled workers, is emphasized in an influential new paper. See Gene M. Grossman and Esteban Rossi-Hansberg. "The Rise of Offshoring: It's Not Wine for Cloth Anymore." *The New Economic Geography: Effects and Policy Implications*, 2006, pp. 59–102.
[29]See Mihir Desai, C. Fritz Foley, and James R Hines. "Domestic Effects of the Foreign Activities of US Multinationals." *American Economic Journal: Economic Policy*, (January 2009).

U.S. manufacturing employment.[30] However, those losses connected to offshoring accounted for only a tiny fraction (2.3%) of the total employment losses during that period. Those total employment losses were indeed substantial: The decrease in U.S. manufacturing employment totaled 2 million (manufacturing employment has been steadily decreasing over the past 30 years); but offshoring played a very minor role in this trend.

This study also found that the productivity effect for the remaining workers played a very important role: The cost benefits from offshoring lead firms to substantially expand their U.S. operations and hire additional workers. Non-production workers benefited most from this increased employment because they were much less likely to directly suffer from the displacement effect of offshoring in the first place. However, production workers also benefited from this expansion effect tied to offshoring: The initial displacement unemployment for those production workers was cut in half by this increased employment response.

Another channel mitigating the worker displacement effects of offshoring is that—just as with trade in final goods—intermediate goods and services are traded in both directions. In the United States, the popular press and many politicians single-out the employment losses associated with offshoring.[31] Of particular concern are the losses of service jobs to offshoring, given the recent technological trends that have vastly expanded the scope of "offshorable" business services (see the discussion in Chapter 2). This has lead to headlines such as "More U.S. service jobs go overseas; Offshoring is expected to grow" in the *USA Today*.[32] Yet, offshoring in one country is *inshoring* in another country: That is, for every import transaction of an intermediate good or service, there is a corresponding export transaction for the country hosting the offshored part of the production process. And it turns out that for the United States, this inshoring of service jobs (exports of intermediate services) is growing even faster than the offshoring of service jobs out of the United States (imports of intermediate services), leading to a surplus; and one that has been growing over time. Figure 8-11 plots all U.S. cross-border trade over time in service categories related to offshoring (financial, insurance, telecommunications, and business services; that is, all traded services other than tourism, transportation, and royalties).[33] Clearly, there is nothing ominous in the time trend of trade in business services for overall U.S. employment.

Given all these facts on the impact of offshoring for U.S. employment, the view that offshoring simply amounts to "shipping jobs overseas" is misleading. True, when a firm based in the United States moves a call center to India, or moves the assembly of its product to China, then some specific jobs that used to be performed in the United States are now performed in India or China. However, the evidence shows that in terms of overall employment, those jobs are replaced

---

[30]See Greg C. Wright, "Revisiting the Employment Impact of Offshoring." *University of Essex*, mimeo, 2013.

[31]Public Citizen reported a sharp increase in political ads condemning offshoring in the 2012 congressional elections (it tracked 90 ads condemning offshoring in campaigns spanning 30 states).

[32]*USA Today*, December 7, 2012.

[33]Those trade flows also include transactions by multinationals with their affiliates abroad. The net balance of exports over imports is positive for the United States, both among multinational transactions, as well as for transactions between unaffiliated parties.

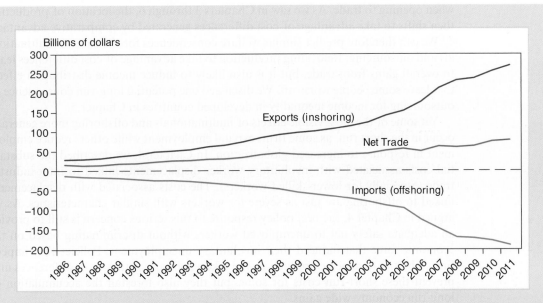

FIGURE 8-11

U.S. International Trade in Business Services (all traded services excluding tourism, transportation, and royalties and license fees), 1986–2011

U.S. service offshoring is captured by U.S. imports of business services. Although service offshoring has dramatically increased over the past decade, U.S. inshoring (exports of business services) has grown even faster. The net balance is positive and has also substantially increased over the past decade.

Source: U.S. Bureau of Economic Analysis.

by other ones in the United States: some related to the expansion effect at the off-shoring firms and others by firms providing intermediate goods and services to firms located abroad (inshoring).

Yet, just as with other forms of trade, trade in intermediates has substantial consequences for the distribution of income. Those call center or manufacturing workers displaced by offshoring are often not the ones who are hired by the expanding firms. Their plight is not made any easier by the gains that accrue to other workers. We discuss these overall welfare consequences in the next section.

Consequences of Multinationals and Foreign Outsourcing

Earlier in this chapter, we mentioned that internal economies of scale, product differentiation, and performance differences across firms combined to deliver some new channels for the gains from trade: increased product variety and higher industry performance as firms move down their average cost curve and production is concentrated in the larger, more productive firms. What are the consequences for welfare of the expansion in multinational production and outsourcing?

We just saw how multinationals and firms that outsource take advantage of cost differentials that favor moving production (or parts thereof) to particular locations. In essence, this is very similar to the relocation of production that occurred *across* sectors when opening to trade. As we saw in Chapters 3 through 6, the location of production then shifts to take advantage of cost differences generated by comparative advantage.

We can therefore predict similar welfare consequences for the case of multinationals and outsourcing: Relocating production to take advantage of cost differences leads to overall gains from trade, but it is also likely to induce income distribution effects that leave some people worse off. We discussed one potential long-run consequence of outsourcing for income inequality in developed countries in Chapter 5.

Yet some of the most visible effects of multinationals and offshoring more generally occur in the short run, as some firms expand employment while others reduce employment in response to increased globalization. In Chapter 4, we described the substantial costs associated with involuntary worker displacements linked to inter-industry trade (especially for lower-skilled workers). The costs associated with displacements linked to offshoring are just as severe for workers with similar characteristics. As we argued in Chapter 4, the best policy response to this serious concern is still to provide an adequate safety net to unemployed workers without discriminating based on the economic force that induced their involuntary unemployment. Policies that impede firms' abilities to relocate production and take advantage of these cost differences may prevent these short-run costs for some, but they also forestall the accumulation of long-run economy-wide gains.

SUMMARY

1. Trade need not be the result of comparative advantage. Instead, it can result from increasing returns or economies of scale, that is, from a tendency of unit costs to be lower with larger output. Economies of scale give countries an incentive to specialize and trade even in the absence of differences between countries in their resources or technology. Economies of scale can be internal (depending on the size of the firm) or external (depending on the size of the industry).

2. Economies of scale internal to firms lead to a breakdown of perfect competition; models of imperfect competition must be used instead to analyze the consequences of increasing returns at the level of the firm. An important model of this kind is the monopolistic competition model, which is widely used to analyze models of firms and trade.

3. In monopolistic competition, an industry contains a number of firms producing differentiated products. These firms act as individual monopolists, but additional firms enter a profitable industry until monopoly profits are competed away. Equilibrium is affected by the size of the market: A large market will support a larger number of firms, each producing at a larger scale and thus a lower average cost, than a small market.

4. International trade allows for the creation of an integrated market that is larger than any one country's market. As a result, it is possible to simultaneously offer consumers a greater variety of products and lower prices. The type of trade generated by this model is intra-industry trade.

5. When firms differ in terms of their performance, economic integration generates winners and losers. The more productive (lower-cost) firms thrive and expand, while the less productive (higher-cost) firms contract. The least-productive firms are forced to exit.

6. In the presence of trade costs, markets are no longer perfectly integrated through trade. Firms can set different prices across markets. These prices reflect trade costs as well as the level of competition perceived by the firm. When there are trade costs, only a subset of more productive firms choose to export; the remaining firms serve only their domestic market.

7. Dumping occurs when a firm sets a lower price (net of trade costs) on exports than it charges domestically. A consequence of trade costs is that firms will feel competition more intensely on export markets because the firms have smaller market shares in those export markets. This leads firms to reduce markups for their export sales relative to their domestic sales; this behavior is characterized as dumping. Dumping is viewed as an unfair trade practice, but it arises naturally in a model of monopolistic competition and trade costs where firms from both countries behave in the same way. Policies against dumping are often used to discriminate against foreign firms in a market and erect barriers to trade.

8. Some multinationals replicate their production processes in foreign facilities located near large customer bases. This is categorized as horizontal foreign direct investment (FDI). An alternative is to export to a market instead of operating a foreign affiliate in that market. The trade-off between exports and FDI involves a lower per-unit cost for FDI (no trade cost) but an additional fixed cost associated with the foreign facility. Only firms that operate at a big enough scale will choose the FDI option over exports.

9. Some multinationals break up their production chain and perform some parts of that chain in their foreign facilities. This is categorized as vertical foreign direct investment (FDI). One alternative is to outsource those parts of the production chain to an independent foreign firm. Both of those modes of operation are categorized as offshoring. Relative to the option of no offshoring, offshoring involves lower production costs but an additional fixed cost. Only firms that operate at a big enough scale will choose to offshore.

10. Multinational firms and firms that outsource parts of production to foreign countries take advantage of cost differences across production locations. This is similar to models of comparative advantage where production at the level of the industry is determined by differences in relative costs across countries. The welfare consequences are similar as well: There are aggregate gains from increased multinational production and outsourcing, but also changes in the income distribution that leaves some people worse off.

KEY TERMS

antidumping duty, p. 220
average cost, p. 199
dumping, p. 220
foreign direct investment
 (FDI), p. 222
foreign outsourcing, p. 227
horizontal FDI, p. 225
imperfect competition,
 p. 197

internal economies of scale,
 p. 196
internalization motive, p. 227
intra-industry trade, p. 209
location motive, p. 227
marginal cost, p. 199
marginal revenue, p. 198
markup over marginal cost,
 p. 204

monopolistic competition,
 p. 201
offshoring, p. 228
oligopoly, p. 201
product differentiation, 200
pure monopoly, p. 198
vertical FDI, p. 225

PROBLEMS

1. Why do firms prefer being price setters over price takers, even in the absence of monopoly? Explain with an example.

2. Suppose the two countries we considered in the numerical example on pages 206–210 were to integrate their automobile market with a third country, which has an annual market for 3.75 million automobiles. Find the number of firms, the output per firm, and the price per automobile in the new integrated market after trade.

3. Suppose that fixed costs for a firm in the automobile industry (start-up costs of factories, capital equipment, and so on) are $5 billion and that variable costs are equal to $17,000 per finished automobile. Because more firms increase competition in the market, the market price falls as more firms enter an automobile market, or specifically, $P = 17,000 + (150/n)$, where n represents the number of firms in a market. Assume that the initial size of the U.S. and the European automobile markets are 300 million and 533 million people, respectively.

   a. Calculate the equilibrium number of firms in the U.S. and European automobile markets *without* trade.

   b. What is the equilibrium price of automobiles in the United States and Europe if the automobile industry is closed to foreign trade?

   c. Now suppose the United States decides on free trade in automobiles with Europe. The trade agreement with the Europeans adds 533 million consumers to the automobile market, in addition to the 300 million in the United States. How many automobile firms will there be in the United States and Europe combined? What will be the new equilibrium price of automobiles?

   d. Why are prices in the United States different in (c) and (b)? Are consumers better off with free trade? In what ways?

4. Go back to the model with firm performance differences in a single integrated market (pages 214–215). Now assume a new technology becomes available. Any firm can adopt the new technology, but its use requires an additional fixed-cost investment. The benefit of the new technology is that it reduces a firm's marginal cost of production by a given amount.

   a. Could it be profit maximizing for some firms to adopt the new technology but not profit maximizing for other firms to adopt that same technology? Which firms would choose to adopt the new technology? How would they be different from the firms that choose not to adopt it?

   b. Now assume there are also trade costs. In the new equilibrium with both trade costs and technology adoption, firms decide whether to export and also whether to adopt the new technology. Would exporting firms be more or less likely to adopt the new technology relative to nonexporters? Why?

5. In the chapter, we described a situation where dumping occurs between two symmetric countries. Briefly describe how things would change if the two countries had different sizes.

   a. How would the number of firms competing in a particular market affect the likelihood that an exporter to that market would be accused of dumping? (Assume the likelihood of a dumping accusation is related to the firm's price difference between its domestic price and its export price: the higher the price difference, the more likely the dumping accusation.)

   b. Would a firm from a small country be more or less likely to be accused of dumping when it exports to a large country (relative to a firm from the large country exporting to the small country)?

6. Which of the following are direct foreign investments?
   a. A Saudi businessman buys $10 million of IBM stock.
   b. The same businessman buys a New York apartment building.
   c. A French company merges with an American company; stockholders in the U.S. company exchange their stock for shares in the French firm.
   d. An Italian firm builds a plant in Russia and manages the plant as a contractor to the Russian government.

7. FDI's, according to their typology, can be divided into (1) horizontal and vertical; (2) inward and outward; (3) portfolio investments and Greenfield. Classify the following cases according to the above parameters:
   a. Huawei (a Chinese corporation) opens up a factory in Indonesia.
   b. Samsung (a Korean chaebol) acquires a minority stake in Japanese stylus maker Wacom.
   c. Geely (a Chinese multinational auto manufacturer) opens some new dealerships in the UK, after having acquired the Swedish Volvo.
   d. Unilever (an Anglo-Dutch corporation and one of the world's main producers of health-care and food products) builds a new production factory in Thailand to produce for regional markets in ASEAN.

8. Sometimes a company, instead of investing directly in a country, chooses alternatives. Provide an example of substitutes for horizontal and vertical FDI and motivations for such choices.

9. Most firms in the apparel and footwear industries choose to outsource production to countries where labor is abundant (primarily, Southeast Asia and the Caribbean)—but those firms do not integrate with their suppliers there. On the other hand, firms in many capital-intensive industries choose to integrate with their suppliers. What could be some differences between the labor-intensive apparel and footwear industries on the one hand and capital-intensive industries on the other hand that would explain these choices?

10. Consider the example of industries in the previous problem. What would those choices imply for the extent of *intra-firm* trade across industries? That is, in what industries would a greater proportion of trade occur within firms?

FURTHER READINGS

Andrew B. Bernard, J. Bradford Jensen, Stephen J. Redding, and Peter K. Schott. "Firms in International Trade." *Journal of Economic Perspectives* 21 (Summer 2007), pp. 105–130. A nontechnical description of empirical patterns of trade at the firm level that focuses on U.S. firms.

Andrew B. Bernard, J. Bradford Jensen, and Peter K. Schott. "Importers, Exporters, and Multinationals: A Portrait of Firms in the US that Trade Goods," in T. Dunne, J. B. Jensen, and M. J. Roberts, eds. *Producer Dynamics: New Evidence from Micro Data*. Chicago: University of Chicago Press, 2009. A nontechnical description of empirical patterns of trade at the firm level that focuses on U.S. firms and multinationals operating in the United States.

Robert Feenstra. "Integration of Trade and Disintegration of Production in the Global Economy." *Journal of Economic Perspectives* 12 (Fall 1998), pp. 32–50. A description of how the supply chain has been broken up into many processes that are then performed in different locations.

Gordon Hanson, Raymond Mataloni, and Matthew Slaughter. "Vertical Production Networks in Multinational Firms." *Review of Economics and Statistics* 87 (March 2005), pp. 664–678. An empirical description of vertical FDI patterns based on multinationals operating in the United States.

Keith Head. *Elements of Multinational Strategy*. New York: Springer, 2007. A recent textbook focused on multinationals.

Elhanan Helpman. "Trade, FDI, and the Organization of Firms." *Journal of Economic Literature* 44 (September 2006), pp. 589–630. A technical survey of recent research on models that incorporate firm performance differences, and on multinationals and outsourcing.

Elhanan Helpman. *Understanding Global Trade*. Cambridge, MA: Harvard University Press, forthcoming. A nontechnical book that covers both comparative advantage theories of trade and more recent theories of trade based on the firm.

Elhanan Helpman and Paul R. Krugman. *Market Structure and Foreign Trade*. Cambridge: MIT Press, 1985. A technical presentation of monopolistic competition and other models of trade with economies of scale.

J. Bradford Jensen. *Global Trade in Services: Fear, Facts, and Offshoring*. Washington, DC: Peterson Institute for International Economics, 2011. A non-technical book focusing on the effects of increased trade in services for the U.S. economy.

James Markusen. "The Boundaries of Multinational Enterprises and the Theory of International Trade." *Journal of Economic Perspectives* 9 (Spring 1995), pp. 169–189. A non-technical survey of models of trade and multinationals.

Thierry Mayer and Gianmarco I. P. Ottaviano. "The Happy Few: The Internationalisation of European Firms: New Facts Based on Firm-Level Evidence." *Intereconomics* 43 (May/June 2008), pp. 135–148.

Marc J. Melitz and Daniel Trefler, "Gains from Trade When Firms Matter," *Journal of Economic Perspectives* 26 (2012), pp. 91–118. A non-technical survey that develops the monopolistic competition model with performance differences across firms in greater detail than in this chapter. The paper also contains a detailed description of the associated evidence for Canadian firms following implementation of the Canada-U.S. Free Trade Agreement.

APPENDIX TO CHAPTER

8

Determining Marginal Revenue

In our exposition of monopoly and monopolistic competition, we found it useful to have an algebraic statement of the marginal revenue faced by a firm given the demand curve it faced. Specifically, we asserted that if a firm faces the demand curve

$$Q = A - B \times P, \tag{8A-1}$$

its marginal revenue is

$$MR = P - (1/B) \times Q. \tag{8A-2}$$

In this appendix, we demonstrate why this is true.

Notice first that the demand curve can be rearranged to state the price as a function of the firm's sales rather than the other way around. By rearranging (8A-1), we get

$$P = (A/B) - (1/B) \times Q. \tag{8A-3}$$

The revenue of a firm is simply the price it receives per unit multiplied by the number of units it sells. Letting R denote the firm's revenue, we have

$$R = P \times Q = [(A/B) - (1/B) \times Q] \times Q. \tag{8A-4}$$

Let us next ask how the revenue of a firm changes if it changes its sales. Suppose the firm decides to increase its sales by a small amount, dX, so that the new level of sales is $Q = Q + dQ$. Then the firm's revenue after the increase in sales, R', will be

$$R' = P' \times Q' = [(A/B) - (1/B) \times (Q + dQ)] \times (Q + dQ) \tag{8A-5}$$
$$= [(A/B) - (1/B) \times Q] \times Q + [(A/B) - (1/B) \times Q] \times dQ$$
$$- (1/B) \times Q \times dQ - (1/B) \times (dQ)^2.$$

Equation (8A-5) can be simplified by substituting in from (8A-1) and (8A-4) to get

$$R' = R + P \times dQ - (1/B) \times Q \times dQ - (1/B) \times (dQ)^2. \tag{8A-6}$$

When the change in sales dQ is small, however, its square $(dQ)^2$ is very small (e.g., the square of 1 is 1, but the square of $1/10$ is $1/100$). So for a small change in Q, the last term in (8A-6) can be ignored. This gives us the result that the *change* in revenue from a small change in sales is

$$R' - R = [(P - (1/B) \times Q)] \times dQ. \tag{8A-7}$$

So the increase in revenue *per unit of additional sales*—which is the definition of marginal revenue—is

$$MR = (R' - R)/dQ = P - (1/B) \times Q,$$

which is just what we asserted in equation (8A-2).

237

CHAPTER 9

THE INSTRUMENTS OF TRADE POLICY

P revious chapters have answered the question, "Why do nations trade?" by *describing* the causes and effects of international trade and the functioning of a trading world economy. While this question is interesting in itself, its answer is even more interesting if it also helps answer the question, "What should a nation's trade policy be?" For example, should the United States use a tariff or an import quota to protect its automobile industry against competition from Japan and South Korea? Who will benefit and who will lose from an import quota? Will the benefits outweigh the costs?

This chapter examines the policies that governments adopt toward international trade, policies that involve a number of different actions. These actions include taxes on some international transactions, subsidies for other transactions, legal limits on the value or volume of particular imports, and many other measures. The chapter thus provides a framework for understanding the effects of the most important instruments of trade policy.

LEARNING GOALS

After reading this chapter, you will be able to:

- Evaluate the costs and benefits of tariffs, their welfare effects, and winners and losers of tariff policies.
- Discuss what export subsidies and agricultural subsidies are, and explain how they affect trade in agriculture in the United States and the European Union.
- Recognize the effect of voluntary export restraints (VERs) on both importing and exporting countries, and describe how the welfare effects of these VERs compare with tariff and quota policies.

Basic Tariff Analysis

A tariff, the simplest of trade policies, is a tax levied when a good is imported. **Specific tariffs** are levied as a fixed charge for each unit of goods imported (for example, $3 per barrel of oil). **Ad valorem tariffs** are taxes that are levied as a fraction of the value of the imported goods (for example, a 25 percent U.S. tariff on imported trucks—see the following box). In either case, the effect of the tariff is to raise the cost of shipping goods to a country.

Tariffs are the oldest form of trade policy and have traditionally been used as a source of government income. Until the introduction of the income tax, for instance, the U.S. government raised most of its revenue from tariffs. Their true purpose, however, has usually been twofold: to provide revenue and to protect particular domestic sectors. In the early 19th century, for example, the United Kingdom used tariffs (the famous Corn Laws) to protect its agriculture from import competition. In the late 19th century, both Germany and the United States protected their new industrial sectors by imposing tariffs on imports of manufactured goods. The importance of tariffs has declined in modern times because modern governments usually prefer to protect domestic industries through a variety of **nontariff barriers,** such as **import quotas** (limitations on the quantity of imports) and **export restraints** (limitations on the quantity of exports—usually imposed by the exporting country at the importing country's request). Nonetheless, an understanding of the effects of a tariff remains vital for understanding other trade policies.

In developing the theory of trade in Chapters 3 through 8, we adopted a *general equilibrium* perspective. That is, we were keenly aware that events in one part of the economy have repercussions elsewhere. However, in many (though not all) cases, trade policies toward one sector can be reasonably well understood without going into detail about those policies' repercussions on the rest of the economy. For the most part, then, trade policy can be examined in a *partial equilibrium* framework. When the effects on the economy as a whole become crucial, we will refer back to general equilibrium analysis.

Supply, Demand, and Trade in a Single Industry

Let's suppose there are two countries, Home and Foreign, both of which consume and produce wheat, which can be costlessly transported between the countries. In each country, wheat is a simple competitive industry in which the supply and demand curves are functions of the market price. Normally, Home supply and demand will depend on the price in terms of Home currency, and Foreign supply and demand will depend on the price in terms of Foreign currency. However, we assume the exchange rate between the currencies is not affected by whatever trade policy is undertaken in this market. Thus, we quote prices in both markets in terms of Home currency.

Trade will arise in such a market if prices are different in the absence of trade. Suppose that in the absence of trade, the price of wheat is higher in Home than it is in Foreign. Now let's allow foreign trade. Since the price of wheat in Home exceeds the price in Foreign, shippers begin to move wheat from Foreign to Home. The export of wheat raises its price in Foreign and lowers its price in Home until the difference in prices has been eliminated.

To determine the world price and the quantity traded, it is helpful to define two new curves: the Home **import demand curve** and the Foreign **export supply curve,** which are derived from the underlying domestic supply and demand curves. Home import demand is the excess of what Home consumers demand over what Home producers supply; Foreign export supply is the excess of what Foreign producers supply over what Foreign consumers demand.

Figure 9-1 shows how the Home import demand curve is derived. At the price P^1, Home consumers demand D^1, while Home producers supply only S^1. As a result, Home import demand is $D^1 - S^1$. If we raise the price to P^2, Home consumers demand only D^2, while Home producers raise the amount they supply to S^2, so import

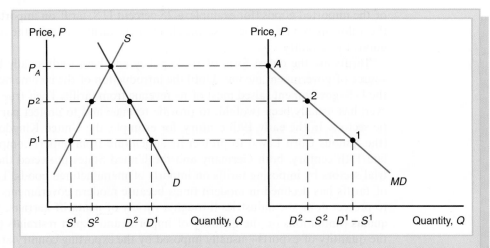

FIGURE 9-1

Deriving Home's Import Demand Curve

As the price of the good increases, Home consumers demand less, while Home producers supply more, so that the demand for imports declines.

demand falls to $D^2 - S^2$. These price-quantity combinations are plotted as points 1 and 2 in the right-hand panel of Figure 9-1. The import demand curve MD is downward sloping because as price increases, the quantity of imports demanded declines. At P_A, Home supply and demand are equal in the absence of trade, so the Home import demand curve intercepts the price axis at P_A (import demand = zero at P_A).

Figure 9-2 shows how the Foreign export supply curve XS is derived. At P^1 Foreign producers supply S^{*1}, while Foreign consumers demand only D^{*1}, so the amount of

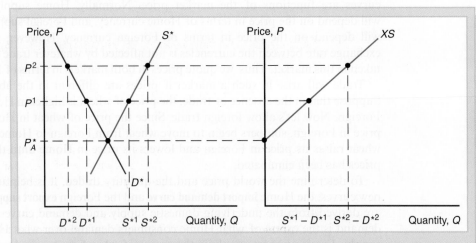

FIGURE 9-2

Deriving Foreign's Export Supply Curve

As the price of the good rises, Foreign producers supply more while Foreign consumers demand less, so that the supply available for export rises.

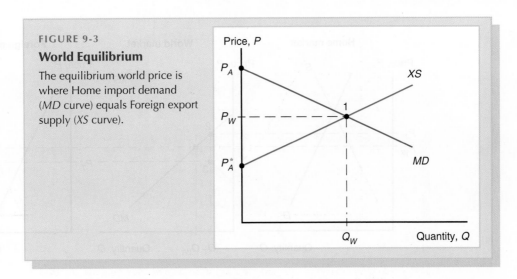

FIGURE 9-3

World Equilibrium

The equilibrium world price is where Home import demand (*MD* curve) equals Foreign export supply (*XS* curve).

the total supply available for export is $S^{*1} - D^{*1}$. At P^2 Foreign producers raise the quantity they supply to S^{*2} and Foreign consumers lower the amount they demand to D^{*2}, so the quantity of the total supply available to export rises to $S^{*2} - D^{*2}$. Because the supply of goods available for export rises as the price rises, the Foreign export supply curve is upward sloping. At P_A^*, supply and demand would be equal in the absence of trade, so the Foreign export supply curve intersects the price axis at P_A^* (export supply = zero at P_A^*).

World equilibrium occurs when Home import demand equals Foreign export supply (Figure 9-3). At the price P_W where the two curves cross, world supply equals world demand. At the equilibrium point 1 in Figure 9-3,

Home demand − Home supply = Foreign supply − Foreign demand.

By adding and subtracting from both sides, this equation can be rearranged to say that

Home demand + Foreign demand = Home supply + Foreign supply

or, in other words,

World demand = World supply.

Effects of a Tariff

From the point of view of someone shipping goods, a tariff is just like a cost of transportation. If Home imposes a tax of $2 on every bushel of wheat imported, shippers will be unwilling to move the wheat unless the price difference between the two markets is at least $2.

Figure 9-4 illustrates the effects of a specific tariff of t per unit of wheat (shown as t in the figure). In the absence of a tariff, the price of wheat would be equalized at P_W in both Home and Foreign, as seen at point 1 in the middle panel, which illustrates the world market. With the tariff in place, however, shippers are not willing to move wheat from Foreign to Home unless the Home price exceeds the Foreign price by at least t. If no wheat is being shipped, however, there will be an excess demand for wheat in Home and an excess supply in Foreign. Thus, the price in Home will rise and that in Foreign will fall until the price difference is t.

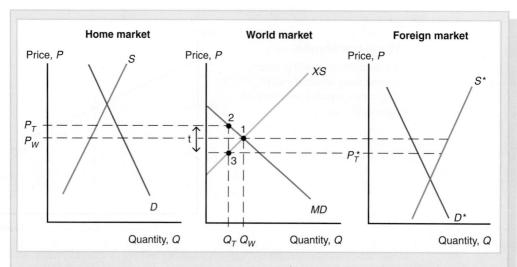

FIGURE 9-4

Effects of a Tariff

A tariff raises the price in Home while lowering the price in Foreign. The volume traded thus declines.

Introducing a tariff, then, drives a wedge between the prices in the two markets. The tariff raises the price in Home to P_T and lowers the price in Foreign to $P_T^* = P_T - t$. In Home, producers supply more at the higher price, while consumers demand less, so that fewer imports are demanded (as you can see in the move from point 1 to point 2 on the MD curve). In Foreign, the lower price leads to reduced supply and increased demand, and thus a smaller export supply (as seen in the move from point 1 to point 3 on the XS curve). Thus, the volume of wheat traded declines from Q_W, the free trade volume, to Q_T, the volume with a tariff. At the trade volume Q_T, Home import demand equals Foreign export supply when $P_T - P_T^* = t$.

The increase in the price in Home, from P_W to P_T, is less than the amount of the tariff because part of the tariff is reflected in a decline in Foreign's export price and thus is not passed on to Home consumers. This is the normal result of a tariff and of any trade policy that limits imports. The size of this effect on the exporters' price, however, is often very small in practice. When a small country imposes a tariff, its share of the world market for the goods it imports is usually minor to begin with, so that its import reduction has very little effect on the world (foreign export) price.

The effects of a tariff in the "small country" case where a country cannot affect foreign export prices are illustrated in Figure 9-5. In this case, a tariff raises the price of the imported good in the country imposing the tariff by the full amount of the tariff, from P_W to $P_W + t$. Production of the imported good rises from S^1 to S^2, while consumption of the good falls from D^1 to D^2. As a result of the tariff, then, imports fall in the country imposing the tariff.

Measuring the Amount of Protection

A tariff on an imported good raises the price received by domestic producers of that good. This effect is often the tariff's principal objective—to *protect* domestic producers from the low prices that would result from import competition. In analyzing trade policy in practice, it is important to ask how much protection a tariff or other trade

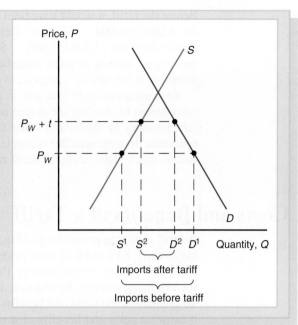

FIGURE 9-5

A Tariff in a Small Country

When a country is small, a tariff it imposes cannot lower the foreign price of the good it imports. As a result, the price of the import rises from P_W to $P_W + t$ and the quantity of imports demanded falls from $D^1 - S^1$ to $D^2 - S^2$.

policy actually provides. The answer is usually expressed as a percentage of the price that would prevail under free trade. An import quota on sugar could, for example, raise the price received by U.S. sugar producers by 35 percent.

Measuring protection would seem to be straightforward in the case of a tariff: If the tariff is an ad valorem tax proportional to the value of the imports, the tariff rate itself should measure the amount of protection; if the tariff is specific, dividing the tariff by the price net of the tariff gives us the ad valorem equivalent.

However, there are two problems with trying to calculate the rate of protection this simply. First, if the small country assumption is not a good approximation, part of the effect of a tariff will be to lower foreign export prices rather than to raise domestic prices. This effect of trade policies on foreign export prices is sometimes significant.

The second problem is that tariffs may have very different effects on different stages of production of a good. A simple example illustrates this point.

Suppose an automobile sells on the world market for $8,000, and the parts out of which that automobile is made sell for $6,000. Let's compare two countries: one that wants to develop an auto assembly industry and one that already has an assembly industry and wants to develop a parts industry.

To encourage a domestic auto industry, the first country places a 25 percent tariff on imported autos, allowing domestic assemblers to charge $10,000 instead of $8,000. In this case, it would be wrong to say that the assemblers receive only 25 percent protection. Before the tariff, domestic assembly would take place only if it could be done for $2,000 (the difference between the $8,000 price of a completed automobile and the $6,000 cost of parts) or less; now it will take place even if it costs as much as $4,000 (the difference between the $10,000 price and the cost of parts). That is, the 25 percent tariff rate provides assemblers with an **effective rate of protection** of 100 percent.

Now suppose the second country, to encourage domestic production of parts, imposes a 10 percent tariff on imported parts, raising the cost of parts of domestic assemblers from $6,000 to $6,600. Even though there is no change in the tariff on assembled automobiles, this policy makes it less advantageous to assemble domestically.

Before the tariff, it would have been worth assembling a car locally if it could be done for $2,000 ($8,000 − $6,000); after the tariff, local assembly takes place only if it can be done for $1,400 ($8,000 − $6,600). The tariff on parts, then, while providing positive protection to parts manufacturers, provides negative effective protection to assembly at the rate of −30 percent (−600/2,000).

Reasoning similar to that seen in this example has led economists to make elaborate calculations to measure the degree of effective protection actually provided to particular industries by tariffs and other trade policies. Trade policies aimed at promoting economic development, for example (Chapter 11), often lead to rates of effective protection much higher than the tariff rates themselves.[1]

Costs and Benefits of a Tariff

A tariff raises the price of a good in the importing country and lowers it in the exporting country. As a result of these price changes, consumers lose in the importing country and gain in the exporting country. Producers gain in the importing country and lose in the exporting country. In addition, the government imposing the tariff gains revenue. To compare these costs and benefits, it is necessary to quantify them. The method for measuring costs and benefits of a tariff depends on two concepts common to much microeconomic analysis: consumer and producer surplus.

Consumer and Producer Surplus

Consumer surplus measures the amount a consumer gains from a purchase by computing the difference between the price he actually pays and the price he would have been willing to pay. If, for example, a consumer would have been willing to pay $8 for a bushel of wheat but the price is only $3, the consumer surplus gained by the purchase is $5.

Consumer surplus can be derived from the market demand curve (Figure 9-6). For example, suppose the maximum price at which consumers will buy 10 units of a good is $10. Then, the 10th unit of the good purchased must be worth $10 to consumers. If it were worth less, they would not purchase it; if it were worth more, they would have been willing to purchase it even if the price were higher. Now suppose that in order to get consumers to buy 11 units, the price must be cut to $9. Then, the 11th unit must be worth only $9 to consumers.

Suppose the price is $9. Then, consumers are willing to purchase only the 11th unit of the good and thus receive no consumer surplus from their purchase of that unit. They would have been willing to pay $10 for the 10th unit, however, and thus receive $1 in consumer surplus from that unit. They would also have been willing to pay $12 for the 9th unit; in that case, they would have received $3 of consumer surplus on that unit, and so on.

---

[1]The effective rate of protection for a sector is formally defined as $(V_T − V_W)/V_W$, where V_W is value added in the sector at world prices, and V_T is value added in the presence of trade policies. In terms of our example, let P_A be the world price of an assembled automobile, P_C the world price of its components, t_A the ad valorem tariff rate on imported autos, and t_C the ad valorem tariff rate on components. You can check that if the tariffs don't affect world prices, they provide assemblers with an effective protection rate of

$$\frac{V_T − V_W}{V_W} = t_A + P_C\left(\frac{t_A − t_C}{P_A − P_C}\right).$$

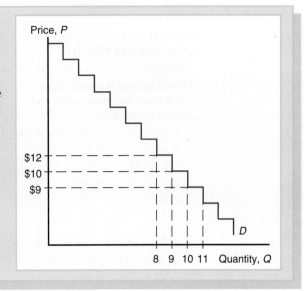

FIGURE 9-6

Deriving Consumer Surplus from the Demand Curve

Consumer surplus on each unit sold is the difference between the actual price and what consumers would have been willing to pay.

Generalizing from this example, if P is the price of a good and Q the quantity demanded at that price, then consumer surplus is calculated by subtracting P times Q from the area under the demand curve up to Q (Figure 9-7). If the price is P^1, the quantity demanded is D^1 and the consumer surplus is measured by the areas labeled a plus b. If the price rises to P^2, the quantity demanded falls to D^2 and consumer surplus falls by b to equal just a.

Producer surplus is an analogous concept. A producer willing to sell a good for $2 but receiving a price of $5 gains a producer surplus of $3. The same procedure used to derive consumer surplus from the demand curve can be used to derive producer surplus from the supply curve. If P is the price and Q the quantity supplied at that price, then producer surplus is P times Q minus the area under the supply curve up to Q

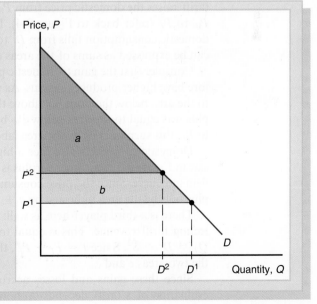

FIGURE 9-7

Geometry of Consumer Surplus

Consumer surplus is equal to the area under the demand curve and above the price.

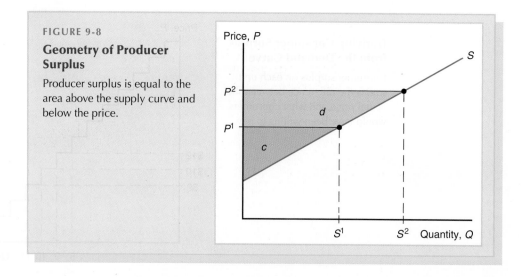

FIGURE 9-8

Geometry of Producer Surplus

Producer surplus is equal to the area above the supply curve and below the price.

(Figure 9-8). If the price is P^1, the quantity supplied will be S^1, and producer surplus is measured by area c. If the price rises to P^2, the quantity supplied rises to S^2, and producer surplus rises to equal c plus the additional area d.

Some of the difficulties related to the concepts of consumer and producer surplus are technical issues of calculation that we can safely disregard. More important is the question of whether the direct gains to producers and consumers in a given market accurately measure the *social* gains. Additional benefits and costs not captured by consumer and producer surplus are at the core of the case for trade policy activism discussed in Chapter 10. For now, however, we will focus on costs and benefits as measured by consumer and producer surplus.

Measuring the Costs and Benefits

Figure 9-9 illustrates the costs and benefits of a tariff for the importing country. The tariff raises the domestic price from P_W to P_T but lowers the foreign export price from P_W to P_T^* (refer back to Figure 9-4). Domestic production rises from S^1 to S^2 while domestic consumption falls from D^1 to D^2. The costs and benefits to different groups can be expressed as sums of the areas of five regions, labeled a, b, c, d, e.

Consider first the gain to domestic producers. They receive a higher price and therefore have higher producer surplus. As we saw in Figure 9-8, producer surplus is equal to the area below the price but above the supply curve. Before the tariff, producer surplus was equal to the area below P_W but above the supply curve; with the price rising to P_T, this surplus rises by the area labeled a. That is, producers gain from the tariff.

Domestic consumers also face a higher price, which makes them worse off. As we saw in Figure 9-7, consumer surplus is equal to the area above the price but below the demand curve. Since the price consumers face rises from P_W to P_T, the consumer surplus falls by the area indicated by $a + b + c + d$. So consumers are hurt by the tariff.

There is a third player here as well: the government. The government gains by collecting tariff revenue. This is equal to the tariff rate t times the volume of imports $Q_T = D^2 - S^2$. Since $t = P_T - P_T^*$, the government's revenue is equal to the sum of the two areas c and e.

Since these gains and losses accrue to different people, the overall cost-benefit evaluation of a tariff depends on how much we value a dollar's worth of benefit to

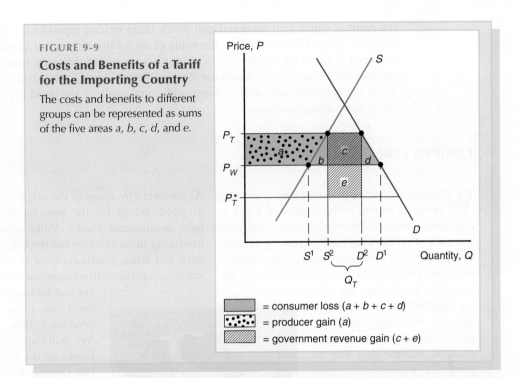

FIGURE 9-9

Costs and Benefits of a Tariff for the Importing Country

The costs and benefits to different groups can be represented as sums of the five areas *a, b, c, d,* and *e.*

▨ = consumer loss ($a + b + c + d$)

▨ = producer gain (a)

▨ = government revenue gain ($c + e$)

each group. If, for example, the producer gain accrues mostly to wealthy owners of resources, while consumers are poorer than average, the tariff will be viewed differently than if the good is a luxury bought by the affluent but produced by low-wage workers. Further ambiguity is introduced by the role of the government: Will it use its revenue to finance vitally needed public services or waste that revenue on $1,000 toilet seats? Despite these problems, it is common for analysts of trade policy to attempt to compute the net effect of a tariff on national welfare by assuming that at the margin, a dollar's worth of gain or loss to each group is of the same social worth.

Let's look, then, at the net effect of a tariff on welfare. The net cost of a tariff is

$$\text{Consumer loss} - \text{producer gain} - \text{government revenue,} \qquad (9\text{-}1)$$

or, replacing these concepts by the areas in Figure 9-9,

$$(a + b + c + d) - a - (c + e) = b + d - e. \qquad (9\text{-}2)$$

That is, there are two "triangles" whose area measures loss to the nation as a whole and a "rectangle" whose area measures an offsetting gain. A useful way to interpret these gains and losses is the following: The triangles represent the **efficiency loss** that arises because a tariff distorts incentives to consume and produce while the rectangle represents the **terms of trade gain** that arise because a tariff lowers foreign export prices.

The gain depends on the ability of the tariff-imposing country to drive down foreign export prices. If the country cannot affect world prices (the "small country" case illustrated in Figure 9-5), region *e*, which represents the terms of trade gain, disappears, and it is clear that the tariff reduces welfare. A tariff distorts the incentives of both producers and consumers by inducing them to act as if imports were more expensive than they actually are. The cost of an additional unit of consumption to the economy is the price of an additional unit of imports, yet because the tariff raises the domestic price above the world price, consumers reduce their consumption to the point at which that marginal unit yields them welfare equal to the tariff-inclusive domestic price. This means that the value of an additional unit of production to the economy is the price of the unit of imports it saves, yet domestic producers expand production to the point at which the marginal cost is equal to the tariff-inclusive price. Thus, the economy produces at home additional units of the good that it could purchase more cheaply abroad.

TARIFFS FOR THE LONG HAUL

We just saw how a tariff can be used to increase producer surplus at the expense of a loss in consumer surplus. There are also many other indirect costs of tariffs: They can lead trading partners to retaliate with their own tariffs (thus hurting exporting producers in the country that first imposed the tariff); they can also be fiendishly hard to remove later on even after economic conditions have completely changed, because they help to politically organize the small group of producers that is protected from foreign competition. (We will discuss this further in Chapter 10.) Finally, large tariffs can induce producers to behave in creative—though ultimately wasteful—ways in order to avoid them.

In the case of the tariff known as the "Chicken Tax," the tariff lasted for so long (47 years and counting) that it ended up hurting the same producers that had intensively lobbied to maintain the tariff in the first place!* This tariff got its name because it was a retaliation by U.S. President Lyndon Johnson's administration against a tariff on U.S. chicken exports imposed by Western Europe in the early 1960s. The U.S. retaliation, focusing on Germany (one of the main political forces behind the original chicken tariff), imposed a 25 percent tariff on imports of light commercial truck vehicles. At the time, Volkswagen was a big producer of such vehicles and exported many of them to the United States.

Before opening production facilities in the United States, Subaru got around the tariff on light commercial trucks by bolting two plastic seats to the open bed of its pickup truck (Subaru BRAT) exported to the United States. Thus, the BRAT was classified as a passenger vehicle thereby avoiding the tariff.

As time went by, many of the original tariffs were dropped, except for the ones on chickens and light commercial trucks. Volkswagen stopped producing those vehicles, but the U.S. "big three" auto and truck producers were then concerned about competition from Japanese truck producers and lobbied to keep the tariff in place. Japanese producers then responded by building those light trucks in the United States (see Chapter 8).

As a result, the latest company to be hit by the consequences of the tariff is Ford, one of those "big three" U.S. producers! Ford produces a small commercial van in Europe, the "Transit Connect," which is designed (with its smaller capacity and ability to navigate old, narrow streets) for European cities. The recent spike in fuel prices sharply increased demand in some U.S. cities for this truck. In 2009, Ford started selling these vehicles in the United States. To get around the 25 percent tariff, Ford installs rear windows, rear seats, and seat belts prior to shipping the vehicles to the United States. These vehicles are no longer classified as commercial trucks but as passenger vehicles, which are subject to the much lower 2.5 percent tariff. Upon arrival in Baltimore, Maryland, the rear seats are promptly removed and the rear windows replaced with metal panels—before delivery to the Ford dealers.

---

*See Matthew Dolan, "To Outfox the Chicken Tax, Ford Strips Its Own Vans," *Wall Street Journal*, September 23, 2009.

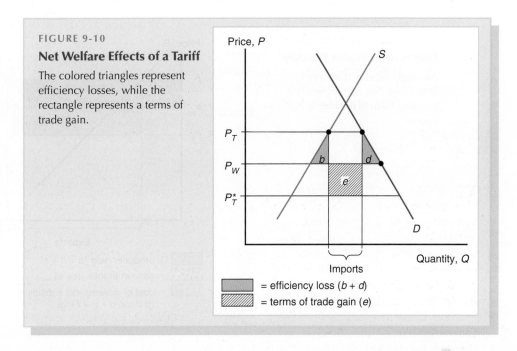

FIGURE 9-10

Net Welfare Effects of a Tariff

The colored triangles represent efficiency losses, while the rectangle represents a terms of trade gain.

The net welfare effects of a tariff are summarized in Figure 9-10. The negative effects consist of the two triangles b and d. The first triangle is the **production distortion loss** resulting from the fact that the tariff leads domestic producers to produce too much of this good. The second triangle is the domestic **consumption distortion loss** resulting from the fact that a tariff leads consumers to consume too little of the good. Against these losses must be set the terms of trade gain measured by the rectangle e, which results from the decline in the foreign export price caused by a tariff. In the important case of a small country that cannot significantly affect foreign prices, this last effect drops out; thus, the costs of a tariff unambiguously exceed its benefits.

Other Instruments of Trade Policy

Tariffs are the simplest trade policies, but in the modern world, most government intervention in international trade takes other forms, such as export subsidies, import quotas, voluntary export restraints, and local content requirements. Fortunately, once we have understood tariffs, it is not too difficult to understand these other trade instruments.

Export Subsidies: Theory

An **export subsidy** is a payment to a firm or individual that ships a good abroad. Like a tariff, an export subsidy can be either specific (a fixed sum per unit) or ad valorem (a proportion of the value exported). When the government offers an export subsidy, shippers will export the good up to the point at which the domestic price exceeds the foreign price by the amount of the subsidy.

The effects of an export subsidy on prices are exactly the reverse of those of a tariff (Figure 9-11). The price in the exporting country rises from P_W to P_S, but because the price in the importing country falls from P_W to P_S^*, the price increase is less than

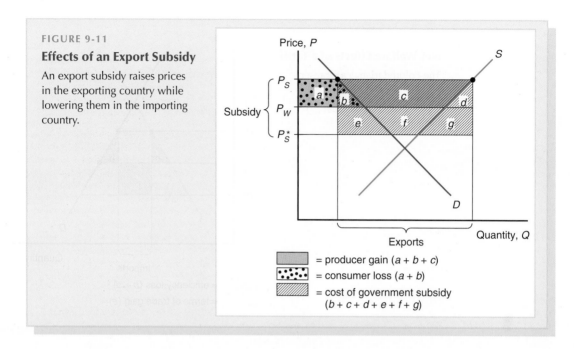

FIGURE 9-11

Effects of an Export Subsidy

An export subsidy raises prices in the exporting country while lowering them in the importing country.

the subsidy. In the exporting country, consumers are hurt, producers gain, and the government loses because it must expend money on the subsidy. The consumer loss is the area $a + b$; the producer gain is the area $a + b + c$; the government subsidy (the amount of exports times the amount of the subsidy) is the area $b + c + d + e + f + g$. The net welfare loss is therefore the sum of the areas $b + d + e + f + g$. Of these, b and d represent consumption and production distortion losses of the same kind that a tariff produces. In addition, and in contrast to a tariff, the export subsidy *worsens* the terms of trade because it lowers the price of the export in the foreign market from P_W to P_S^*. This leads to the additional terms of trade loss $e + f + g$, which is equal to $P_W - P_S^*$ times the quantity exported with the subsidy. So an export subsidy unambiguously leads to costs that exceed its benefits.

CASE STUDY   **Europe's Common Agricultural Policy**

In 1957, six Western European nations—Germany, France, Italy, Belgium, the Netherlands, and Luxembourg—formed the European Economic Community, which has since grown to include most of Europe. Now called the European Union (EU), its two biggest effects are on trade policy. First, the members of the European Union have removed all tariffs with respect to each other, thus creating a customs union (discussed in the next chapter). Second, the agricultural policy of the European Union has developed into a massive export subsidy program.

The European Union's Common Agricultural Policy (CAP) began not as an export subsidy but as an effort to guarantee high prices to European farmers by having the European Union buy agricultural products whenever the prices fell below

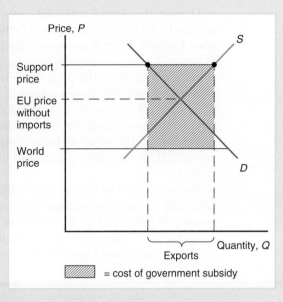

FIGURE 9-12

Europe's Common Agricultural Policy

Agricultural prices are fixed not only above world market levels but also above the price that would clear the European market. An export subsidy is used to dispose of the resulting surplus.

specified support levels. To prevent this policy from drawing in large quantities of imports, it was initially backed by tariffs that offset the difference between European and world agricultural prices.

Since the 1970s, however, the support prices set by the European Union have turned out to be so high that Europe—which, under free trade, would be an importer of most agricultural products—was producing more than consumers were willing to buy. As a result, the European Union found itself obliged to buy and store huge quantities of food. At the end of 1985, for example, European nations had stored 780,000 tons of beef, 1.2 million tons of butter, and 12 million tons of wheat. To avoid unlimited growth in these stockpiles, the European Union turned to a policy of subsidizing exports to dispose of surplus production.

Figure 9-12 shows how the CAP works. It is, of course, exactly like the export subsidy shown in Figure 9-11, except that Europe would actually be an importer under free trade. The support price is set not only above the world price that would prevail in its absence but also above the price that would equate demand and supply even without imports. To export the resulting surplus, an export subsidy is paid that offsets the difference between European and world prices. The subsidized exports themselves tend to depress the world price, increasing the required subsidy. A recent study estimated that the welfare cost to European consumers exceeded the benefits to farm producers by nearly $30 billion (21.5 billion euros) in 2007.[2]

---

[2]See Pierre Boulanger and Patrick Jomini, *Of the Benefits to the EU of Removing the Common Agricultural Policy*, Sciences Politique Policy Brief, 2010.

Despite the considerable net costs of the CAP to European consumers and taxpayers, the political strength of farmers in the EU has been so strong that the program has been difficult to rein in. One source of pressure has come from the United States and other food-exporting nations, which complain that Europe's export subsidies drive down the price of their own exports. The budgetary consequences of the CAP have also posed concerns: In 2013, the CAP cost European taxpayers $78 billion (58 billion euros)—and that figure doesn't include the indirect costs to food consumers. Government subsidies to European farmers are equal to about 22 percent of the value of farm output, more than twice the U.S. figure of 8.6 percent. (U.S. agriculture subsidies are more narrowly targeted on a subset of crops.)

Recent reforms in Europe's agricultural policy represent an effort to reduce the distortion of incentives caused by price support while continuing to provide aid to farmers. If politicians go through with their plans, farmers will increasingly receive direct payments that aren't tied to how much they produce; this should lower agricultural prices and reduce production.

Import Quotas: Theory

An import quota is a direct restriction on the quantity of some good that may be imported. The restriction is usually enforced by issuing licenses to some group of individuals or firms. For example, the United States has a quota on imports of foreign cheese. The only firms allowed to import cheese are certain trading companies, each of which is allocated the right to import a maximum number of pounds of cheese each year; the size of each firm's quota is based on the amount of cheese it imported in the past. In some important cases, notably sugar and apparel, the right to sell in the United States is given directly to the governments of exporting countries.

It is important to avoid having the misconception that import quotas somehow limit imports without raising domestic prices. The truth is that *an import quota always raises the domestic price of the imported good.* When imports are limited, the immediate result is that at the initial price, the demand for the good exceeds domestic supply plus imports. This causes the price to be bid up until the market clears. In the end, an import quota will raise domestic prices by the same amount as a tariff that limits imports to the same level (except in the case of domestic monopoly, in which the quota raises prices more than this; see the appendix to this chapter).

The difference between a quota and a tariff is that with a quota, the government receives no revenue. When a quota instead of a tariff is used to restrict imports, the sum of money that would have appeared with a tariff as government revenue is collected by whoever receives the import licenses. License holders are thus able to buy imports and resell them at a higher price in the domestic market. The profits received by the holders of import licenses are known as **quota rents**. In assessing the costs and benefits of an import quota, it is crucial to determine who gets the rents. When the rights to sell in the domestic market are assigned to governments of exporting countries, as is often the case, the transfer of rents abroad makes the costs of a quota substantially higher than the equivalent tariff.

CASE STUDY

An Import Quota in Practice: U.S. Sugar

The U.S. sugar problem is similar in its origins to the European agricultural problem: A domestic price guarantee by the federal government has led to U.S. prices above world market levels. Unlike the European Union, however, the domestic supply in the United States does not exceed domestic demand. Thus, the United States has been able to keep domestic prices at the target level with an import quota on sugar.

A special feature of the import quota is that the rights to sell sugar in the United States are allocated to foreign governments, which then allocate these rights to their own residents. As a result, rents generated by the sugar quota accrue to foreigners. The quotas restrict the imports of both raw sugar (almost exclusively, sugar cane) as well as refined sugar. Figure 9-13 shows the effect of the U.S. import restrictions on the price of raw sugar in the United States relative to the world price. As we can see, these import restrictions have been quite successful in raising the U.S. domestic price above the world price. When the world sugar price sharply increased in 2010–2011, the import restrictions were eased but not enough to limit sharp increases in the U.S. price—which still remained well above the world price.

We now describe the most recent forecast for the effects of these import restrictions and the associated higher sugar prices.[3] Figure 9-14 shows the raw sugar market equilibrium with and without the quota restriction. Currently, the quota limits imports of raw sugar to $3.4 million tons, while U.S. production totals 8.4 million tons. This leads to a U.S. sugar price that is 34% above the world price. Absent import restrictions, the U.S. price would drop down to the world price level. The figure is drawn assuming the United States is "small" in the world market for raw sugar; that is, removing the quota would not have a significant effect on the world price. According

FIGURE 9-13

U.S. and World Raw Sugar Prices in $ per ton (short ton, raw value), 1989–2011

Source: U.S. Department of Agriculture.

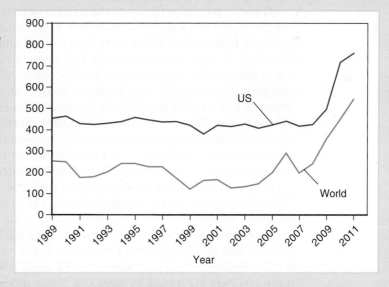

---

[3]These estimates are for 2014, assuming the import restrictions are eliminated in 2013. For further details, see Beghin, John Christopher and Amani Elobeid, "The Impact of the U.S. Sugar Program Redux." *Food and Agricultural Policy Research Institute (FAPRI) Publications*, 2013.

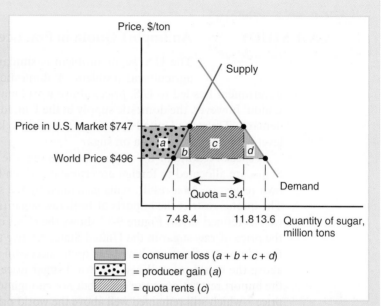

FIGURE 9-14

Effects of the U.S. Import Quota on Sugar

The quota limits imports of raw sugar to 3.4 million tons. Without the quota, imports of sugar would be 84 percent higher, or 6.2 million tons. The result of the quota is that the price of sugar is $747 per ton, versus the $496 price on world markets. This produces a gain for U.S. sugar producers, but a much larger loss for U.S. consumers. There is no offsetting gain in revenue because the quota rents are collected by foreign governments.

to this estimate, free trade would increase sugar imports by 84 percent and an associated 11 percent contraction in domestic production.

The welfare effects of the import quota are indicated by the areas *a, b, c,* and *d.* Consumers lose the surplus *a + b + c + d* associated with the higher price. Part of this consumer loss represents a transfer to U.S. sugar producers, who gain the producer surplus *a.* Part of the loss represents the production distortion *b* and the consumption distortion *d.* The rents to the foreign governments that receive import rights are summarized by area *c.*

In order to put dollar figures on these welfare effects, one must take into account how the higher raw sugar price leads to a higher refined sugar price, which then feeds into higher prices for all food products containing sugar. Even though the ultimate food price increases paid by U.S. consumers are modest—on the order of 0–2 percent—the total consumer surplus losses are massive because those price increases apply to such a large basket of widely consumed goods. The estimated consumer loss for 2014 (relative to a hypothetical outcome where the sugar quota is phased out in 2013) is $3.5 billion! In addition, the higher prices for refined sugar also generate producer surplus losses for the food industry (all food producers who use refined sugar as an ingredient). This adds another $909 million to the consumer losses, for a total cost estimate of $4.4 billion associated with the U.S. sugar quota.

Of course, U.S. sugar producers gain from the higher sugar prices. Their estimated gain for 2014 totals $3.9 billion. (Most of those gains go to sugar processors/refiners, with "only" $486 million going to sugar farmers.) Lastly, foreign sugar exporters who have been allocated the rights to sell sugar into the United States also benefit from those quota rights—as they pocket the difference between the higher U.S. price relative to the world price. (Several of those foreign sugar exporters are owned by large U.S. sugar processors.) This gain makes up most of the differential between the $4.4 billion loss to sugar users (consumers and food producers) and the $3.9 billion gain to sugar producers, as the deadweight losses are relatively minor.

The sugar quota illustrates in an extreme way the tendency of protection to provide benefits to a small group of producers, each of whom receives a large benefit, at the expense of a large number of consumers, each of whom bears only a small cost. In this case, the yearly consumer loss amounts to "only" $11 per capita, or a little under $30 for a typical household. Not surprisingly, the average American voter is unaware that the sugar quota exists, and so there is little effective opposition.

From the point of view of the raw sugar producers (farmers and processors), however, the quota is a life-or-death issue. These producers employ only about 20,000 workers, so the producer gains from the quota represent an implicit subsidy of about $200,000 per worker. It should be no surprise that these sugar producers are very effectively mobilized in defense of their protection. They donated more than $4.5 million in the 2012 congressional races, and the American Sugar Alliance spent an additional $3 million on lobbying expenses in the 12 months period leading up to the 2013 congressional vote on the U.S. farm bill (which reauthorizes the restrictions on U.S. imports of sugar).[4]

Sugar-using food producers, along with consumers, are hurt by the sugar quota, which artificially raises the price of sugar in the United States. It is estimated that employment in chocolate and confectionary manufacturing would rise by 34 percent if the sugar quota were lifted. Dum Dums are still produced in Ohio, though its producer, Spangler Inc., has moved production of its candy canes to Mexico. A substantial portion of the North American confectionary industry has moved to Canada and Mexico, where sugar prices are substantially lower. Spangler CEO Kirk Vashaw estimates that he could save $15,000 *per day* by moving his production facility from Ohio to Canada.[5]

Opponents of protection often try to frame their criticism not in terms of consumer and producer surplus but in terms of the cost to consumers of every job "saved" by an import restriction. Clearly, the loss of the $200,000 subsidy per employee indirectly provided by the quota would force sugar producers to contract and reduce their employment. Estimates for this employment contraction vary between 500 and 2000 workers. Even taking this larger employment loss, the sugar quota would still cost the U.S. consumer $1.75 million per job saved. And this cost does not factor in all the job losses that high sugar prices impose on the food industry.

If the sugar restrictions were lifted, the drop in the refined sugar price would induce a substantial expansion in the sugar-using food industry. We already mentioned the associated $909 million increase in producer surplus for those sectors; but this expansion would also generate 17,000–20,000 new jobs. In fact, the expansion would be big enough to turn the United States from a net importer to a net exporter of sugar-containing foods. Comparing the figures for jobs saved by sugar producers (500–2,000) with the figures for jobs lost in the food sector (17,000–20,000), we see that the employment dimension of protection is no longer that the consumer cost per job saved is astronomically high; rather, it is plainly that jobs are being *lost*, and not saved, by the sugar quota.

---

[4]An amendment to phase out the sugar import restrictions was introduced to the 2013 Farm Bill (Sugar Reform Act of 2013). It was narrowly defeated by votes of 45–54 in the Senate and 206–221 in the House.
[5]See "Farm Bill's Subsidy for Sugar under Pressure" in *Columbia Dispatch*, June 20, 2013.

Voluntary Export Restraints

A variant on the import quota is the **voluntary export restraint (VER)**, also known as a voluntary restraint agreement (VRA). (Welcome to the bureaucratic world of trade policy, where everything has a three-letter symbol!) A VER is a quota on trade imposed from the exporting country's side instead of the importer's. The most famous example is the limitation on auto exports to the United States enforced by Japan after 1981.

Voluntary export restraints are generally imposed at the request of the importer and are agreed to by the exporter to forestall other trade restrictions. As we will see in Chapter 10, certain political and legal advantages have made VERs preferred instruments of trade policy in some cases. From an economic point of view, however, a voluntary export restraint is exactly like an import quota where the licenses are assigned to foreign governments and is therefore very costly to the importing country.

A VER is always more costly to the importing country than a tariff that limits imports by the same amount. The difference is that what would have been revenue under a tariff becomes rents earned by foreigners under the VER, so that the VER clearly produces a loss for the importing country.

A study of the effects of the three major U.S. voluntary export restraints of the 1980s—in textiles and apparel, steel, and automobiles—found that about two-thirds of the cost to consumers of these restraints was accounted for by the rents earned by foreigners.[6] In other words, the bulk of the cost represents a transfer of income rather than a loss of efficiency. This calculation also emphasizes that, from a national point of view, VERs are much more costly than tariffs. Given this fact, the widespread preference of governments for VERs over other trade policy measures requires some careful analysis.

Some voluntary export agreements cover more than one country. The most famous multilateral agreement is the Multi-Fiber Arrangement, which limited textile exports from 22 countries until the beginning of 2005. Such multilateral voluntary restraint agreements are known by yet another three-letter abbreviation: OMA, for "orderly marketing agreement."

CASE STUDY   A Voluntary Export Restraint in Practice

JAPANESE AUTOS

For much of the 1960s and 1970s, the U.S. auto industry was largely insulated from import competition by the difference in the kinds of cars bought by U.S. and foreign consumers. U.S. buyers, living in a large country with low gasoline taxes, preferred much larger cars than Europeans and Japanese, and, by and large, foreign firms had chosen not to challenge the United States in the large-car market.

In 1979, however, sharp oil price increases and temporary gasoline shortages caused the U.S. market to shift abruptly toward smaller cars. Japanese producers, whose costs had been falling relative to those of their U.S. competitors in any case, moved in to fill the new demand. As the Japanese market share soared and U.S. output fell, strong political forces in the United States demanded protection for the U.S.

---

[6]See David G. Tarr, *A General Equilibrium Analysis of the Welfare and Employment Effects of U.S. Quotas in Textiles, Autos, and Steel* (Washington, D.C.: Federal Trade Commission, 1989).

industry. Rather than act unilaterally and risk creating a trade war, the U.S. government asked the Japanese government to limit its exports. The Japanese, fearing unilateral U.S. protectionist measures if they did not do so, agreed to limit their sales. The first agreement, in 1981, limited Japanese exports to the United States to 1.68 million automobiles. A revision raised that total to 1.85 million in 1984. In 1985, the agreement was allowed to lapse.

The effects of this voluntary export restraint were complicated by several factors. First, Japanese and U.S. cars were clearly not perfect substitutes. Second, the Japanese industry to some extent responded to the quota by upgrading its quality and selling larger autos with more features. Third, the auto industry is clearly not perfectly competitive. Nonetheless, the basic results were what the discussion of voluntary export restraints earlier would have predicted: The price of Japanese cars in the United States rose, with the rent captured by Japanese firms. The U.S. government estimates the total costs to the United States to be $3.2 billion in 1984, primarily in transfers to Japan rather than efficiency losses.

CHINESE SOLAR PANELS

Although voluntary export restraints are no longer allowed under WTO rules, this only applies to an agreement negotiated by governments and imposed onto exporters. Recently, a European Union–China trade dispute over a surge in Chinese exports of solar panels was resolved by the Chinese producers "agreeing" to limit their exports to EU countries below 7 gigawatts-worth of solar panels per year—along with a minimum price floor for those units. EU solar panel makers were disappointed, as this agreement forestalled the imposition of 47 percent anti-dumping duties on all Chinese solar panel imports (the threat that generated those concessions by Chinese solar panel producers). However, the imposition of the anti-dumping duties would have triggered a significant retaliation from China, whose officials had already drawn up a list of European products—including luxury fashion goods and wines—that would be subjected to stiff import duties into China. Chinese producers were persuaded to agree to the export limit and price floor instead, since this would allow them to keep the higher prices charged in the European Union. The main losers are European consumers, who will pay substantially more for solar power (and the environment).

Local Content Requirements

A **local content requirement** is a regulation that requires some specified fraction of a final good to be produced domestically. In some cases, this fraction is specified in physical units, like the U.S. oil import quota in the 1960s. In other cases, the requirement is stated in value terms by requiring that some minimum share of the price of a good represent domestic value added. Local content laws have been widely used by developing countries trying to shift their manufacturing base from assembly back into intermediate goods. In the United States, a local content bill for automobiles was proposed in 1982 but was never acted on.

From the point of view of the domestic producers of parts, a local content regulation provides protection in the same way an import quota does. From the point of view of the firms that must buy locally, however, the effects are somewhat different. Local content does not place a strict limit on imports. Instead, it allows firms

BRIDGING THE GAP

In Chapter 8, we discussed how trade in intermediate goods—just like trade in final goods—generates aggregate welfare gains (though gains that are far from evenly distributed). In addition, access to cheaper imported intermediate goods generates private gains for firms as they expand their scale of production. It may therefore seem surprising that U.S. government agencies (at the local, state, and federal level) are expressly forbidden to take advantage of such opportunities. The U.S. Buy American Act, originally passed in 1933, requires those government agencies to purchase many specific inputs from U.S. firms—unless the foreign bid for that input is more than 25 percent below the lowest bid from a U.S. firm. This provision was written into the American Recovery and Re-Investment Act of 2009 (ARRA), the $831 billion stimulus package that was passed in the wake of the severe economic recession. Any public work project funded by the ARRA must use iron, steel, and manufactured goods made in the United States (subject to that same 25 percent differential).

The new Bay Bridge connecting San Francisco and Oakland.

Typically, the percentage difference between the U.S. and foreign bids is substantially below 25 percent, so the Buy American provision results in a cost increase well below the 25 percent maximum. However, China is developing unique capabilities in the production of some highly specialized steel products dedicated to very large-scale infrastructure projects (due in large part to the experience generated from the high demand for such projects in China). For those specialized steel products, the cost difference between Chinese producers and the tiny handful of U.S. firms with the required production capacity is approaching that 25 percent maximum—a very large differential, especially given the massive scale of several infrastructure projects.

For the construction of the new Bay Bridge linking San Francisco and Oakland, the 23 percent difference between the Chinese bid and the lone U.S. bid for some key steel components amounted to a $400 million cost difference, which was so large that the state of California was pushed to forego federal funds under the ARRA and rely instead on bonds financed by future tolls. This financing option is not available for many other infrastructure projects, which must then incur the substantially higher costs associated with the Buy American provisions.

Those provisions not only raise the cost to U.S. taxpayers, they also induce substantial delays in some essential projects as managers navigate the administrative paperwork required to show that some key components are entirely unavailable in the United States. This happened to the Department of Homeland Security, which was unable to operate its electronic baggage screening systems until its contractor was allowed to buy some key foreign components needed for integration with the airports' security systems. Lastly, the Buy American provisions have also triggered similar protectionist clauses from other foreign governments, shutting out U.S. firms from those business opportunities.

to import more, provided that they also buy more domestically. This means that the effective price of inputs to the firm is an average of the price of imported and domestically produced inputs.

Consider, for instance, the earlier automobile example in which the cost of imported parts is $6,000. Suppose purchasing the same parts domestically would cost $10,000, but assembly firms are required to use 50 percent domestic parts. Then, they will face an average cost of parts of $8,000 (0.5 × $6,000 + 0.5 × $10,000), which will be reflected in the final price of the car.

The important point is that a local content requirement does not produce either government revenue or quota rents. Instead, the difference between the prices of imports and domestic goods in effect gets averaged in the final price and is passed on to consumers.

An interesting innovation in local content regulations has been to allow firms to satisfy their local content requirement by exporting instead of using parts domestically. This is sometimes important. For example, U.S. auto firms operating in Mexico have chosen to export some components from Mexico to the United States, even though those components could be produced in the United States more cheaply because doing so allows them to use less Mexican content in producing cars in Mexico for Mexico's market.

Other Trade Policy Instruments

Governments influence trade in many other ways. We list some of them briefly.

   1. *Export credit subsidies.* This is like an export subsidy except that it takes the form of a subsidized loan to the buyer. The United States, like most other countries, has a government institution, the Export-Import Bank, devoted to providing at least slightly subsidized loans to aid exports.

   2. *National procurement.* Purchases by the government or strongly regulated firms can be directed toward domestically produced goods even when these goods are more expensive than imports. The classic example is the European telecommunications industry. The nations of the European Union in principle have free trade with each other. The main purchasers of telecommunications equipment, however, are phone companies—and in Europe, these companies have until recently all been government-owned. These government-owned telephone companies buy from domestic suppliers even when the suppliers charge higher prices than suppliers in other countries. The result is that there is very little trade in telecommunications equipment within Europe.

   3. *Red-tape barriers.* Sometimes a government wants to restrict imports without doing so formally. Fortunately or unfortunately, it is easy to twist normal health, safety, and customs procedures in order to place substantial obstacles in the way of trade. The classic example is the French decree in 1982 that all Japanese videocassette recorders had to pass through the tiny customs house at Poitiers (an inland city nowhere near a major port)—effectively limiting the actual imports to a handful.

The Effects of Trade Policy: A Summary

The effects of the major instruments of trade policy are usefully summarized by Table 9-1, which compares the effect of four major kinds of trade policy on the welfare of consumers.

This table certainly does not look like an advertisement for interventionist trade policy. All four trade policies benefit producers and hurt consumers. The effects of the policies on economic welfare are at best ambiguous; two of the policies definitely hurt the nation as a whole, while tariffs and import quotas are potentially beneficial only for large countries that can drive down world prices.

TABLE 9-1	Effects of Alternative Trade Policies			
Policy	Tariff	Export Subsidy	Import Quota	Voluntary Export Restraint
Producer surplus	Increases	Increases	Increases	Increases
Consumer surplus	Falls	Falls	Falls	Falls
Government revenue	Increases	Falls (government spending rises)	No change (rents to license holders)	No change (rents to foreigners)
Overall national welfare	Ambiguous (falls for small country)	Falls	Ambiguous (falls for small country)	Falls

Why, then, do governments so often act to limit imports or promote exports? We turn to this question in Chapter 10.

SUMMARY

1. In contrast to our earlier analysis, which stressed the general equilibrium interaction of markets, for analysis of trade policy it is usually sufficient to use a partial equilibrium approach.

2. A tariff drives a wedge between foreign and domestic prices, raising the domestic price but by less than the tariff rate. An important and relevant special case, however, is that of a "small" country that cannot have any substantial influence on foreign prices. In the small country case, a tariff is fully reflected in domestic prices.

3. The costs and benefits of a tariff or other trade policy may be measured using the concepts of consumer surplus and producer surplus. Using these concepts, we can show that the domestic producers of a good gain because a tariff raises the price they receive; the domestic consumers lose, for the same reason. There is also a gain in government revenue.

4. If we add together the gains and losses from a tariff, we find that the net effect on national welfare can be separated into two parts: On one hand is an efficiency loss, which results from the distortion in the incentives facing domestic producers and consumers. On the other hand is a terms of trade gain, reflecting the tendency of a tariff to drive down foreign export prices. In the case of a small country that cannot affect foreign prices, the second effect is zero, so that there is an unambiguous loss.

5. The analysis of a tariff can be readily adapted to analyze other trade policy measures, such as export subsidies, import quotas, and voluntary export restraints. An export subsidy causes efficiency losses similar to those of a tariff but compounds these losses by causing a deterioration of the terms of trade. Import quotas and voluntary export restraints differ from tariffs in that the government gets no revenue. Instead, what would have been government revenue accrues as rents to the recipients of import licenses (in the case of a quota) and to foreigners (in the case of a voluntary export restraint).

KEY TERMS

ad valorem tariff, p. 238
consumer surplus, p. 244
consumption distortion loss,
  p. 249
effective rate of protection,
  p. 243
efficiency loss, p. 247
export restraint, p. 239

export subsidy, p. 249
export supply curve, p. 239
import demand curve, p. 239
import quota, p. 239
local content requirement,
  p. 257
nontariff barriers, p. 239
producer surplus, p. 245

production distortion
  loss, p. 249
quota rent, p. 252
specific tariff, p. 238
terms of trade gain, p. 247
voluntary export restraint
  (VER), p. 256

PROBLEMS

MyEconLab

1. Home's demand curve for wheat is

$$D = 100 - 20P.$$

Its supply curve is

$$S = 20 + 20P.$$

Derive and graph Home's *import* demand schedule. What would the price of wheat be in the absence of trade?

2. Now add Foreign, which has a demand curve

$$D^* = 80 - 20P$$

and a supply curve

$$S^* = 40 + 20P.$$

  a. Derive and graph Foreign's export supply curve and find the price of wheat that would prevail in Foreign in the absence of trade.
  b. Now allow Foreign and Home to trade with each other, at zero transportation cost. Find and graph the equilibrium under free trade. What is the world price? What is the volume of trade?

3. Home imposes a specific tariff of 0.5 on wheat imports.
  a. Determine and graph the effects of the tariff on the following: (1) the price of wheat in each country; (2) the quantity of wheat supplied and demanded in each country; (3) the volume of trade.
  b. Determine the effect of the tariff on the welfare of each of the following groups: (1) Home import-competing producers; (2) Home consumers; (3) the Home government.
  c. Show graphically and calculate the terms of trade gain, the efficiency loss, and the total effect on welfare of the tariff.

4. Suppose Foreign had been a much larger country, with domestic demand

$$D^* = 800 - 200P, S^* = 400 + 200P.$$

(Notice that this implies the Foreign price of wheat in the absence of trade would have been the same as in problem 2.)

Recalculate the free trade equilibrium and the effects of a 0.5 specific tariff by Home. Relate the difference in results to the discussion of the small country case in the text.

5. The recent growth in Chinese industries has enabled them to follow the dumping and anti-dumping activities in the international market. Elucidate how dumping and anti-dumping would affect the bargaining power and market price in the dumped country.

6. In a world having two nations, the imposition of tariff adversely affects the import and export of the country that imposes tariff—evaluate. How would the imposition of protective tariff by the home country affect employment? Do you believe that this may also lead to an increase in unemployment in some other industries of the country, which levies tariff?

7. Return to the example of problem 2. Starting from free trade, assume that Foreign offers exporters a subsidy of 0.5 per unit. Calculate the effects on the price in each country and on welfare, both of individual groups and of the economy as a whole, in both countries.

8. Use your knowledge about trade policy to evaluate each of the following statements:
   a. "An excellent way to reduce unemployment is to enact tariffs on imported goods."
   b. "Tariffs have a more negative effect on welfare in large countries than in small countries."
   c. "Automobile manufacturing jobs are heading to Mexico because wages are so much lower there than they are in the United States. As a result, we should implement tariffs on automobiles equal to the difference between U.S. and Mexican wage rates."

9. The nation of Acirema is "small" and unable to affect world prices. It imports peanuts at the price of $10 per bag. The demand curve is

$$D = 400 - 10P.$$

The supply curve is

$$S = 50 + 5P.$$

Determine the free trade equilibrium. Then calculate and graph the following effects of an import quota that limits imports to 50 bags.
   a. The increase in the domestic price.
   b. The quota rents.
   c. The consumption distortion loss.
   d. The production distortion loss.

10. Suppose Brazil—the largest producer of sugar—provides 20 percent export subsidy to sugar companies. By what extent would the domestic prices and the terms of trade be affected in Brazil? If the export subsidy of Brazil hampers the sugar manufacturers of importing countries, what countervailing action would you suggest to protect the domestic industries and prices of the latter?

11. Suppose workers involved in manufacturing are paid less than all other workers in the economy. What would be the effect on the real income *distribution* within the economy if there were a substantial tariff levied on manufactured goods?

FURTHER READINGS

Jagdish Bhagwati. "On the Equivalence of Tariffs and Quotas," in Robert E. Baldwin et al., eds. *Trade, Growth, and the Balance of Payments.* Chicago: Rand McNally, 1965. The classic comparison of tariffs and quotas under monopoly.

W. M. Corden. *The Theory of Protection.* Oxford: Clarendon Press, 1971. A general survey of the effects of tariffs, quotas, and other trade policies.

Robert W. Crandall. *Regulating the Automobile.* Washington, D.C.: Brookings Institution, 1986. Contains an analysis of the most famous of all voluntary export restraints.

Robert C. Feenstra. "How Costly Is Protectionism?" *Journal of Economic Perspectives* 6 (1992), pp. 159–178. A survey article summarizing the empirical work measuring the costs associated with protectionist policies.

Gary Clyde Hufbauer and Kimberly Ann Elliot. *Measuring the Costs of Protection in the United States.* Washington, D.C.: Institute for International Economics, 1994. An assessment of U.S. trade policies in 21 different sectors.

Kala Krishna. "Trade Restrictions as Facilitating Practices." *Journal of International Economics* 26 (May 1989), pp. 251–270. A pioneering analysis of the effects of import quotas when both foreign and domestic producers have monopoly power, showing that the usual result is an increase in the profits of both groups—at consumers' expense.

Patrick Messerlin. *Measuring the Costs of Protection in Europe: European Commercial Policy in the 2000s.* Washington, D.C.: Institute for International Economics, 2001. A survey of European trade policies and their effects, similar to Hufbauer and Elliot's work for the United States.

D. Rousslang and A. Suomela. "Calculating the Consumer and Net Welfare Costs of Import Relief." U.S. International Trade Commission Staff Research Study 15. Washington, D.C.: International Trade Commission, 1985. An exposition of the framework used in this chapter, with a description of how the framework is applied in practice to real industries.

U.S. International Trade Commission. *The Economic Effects of Significant U.S. Import Restraints.* Washington, D.C., 2009. A regularly updated economic analysis of the effects of protection on the U.S. economy.

MyEconLab Can Help You Get a Better Grade

MyEconLab   If your exam were tomorrow, would you be ready? For each chapter, MyEconLab Practice Tests and Study Plans pinpoint sections you have mastered and those you need to study. That way, you are more efficient with your study time, and you are better prepared for your exams.

To see how it works, turn to page 41 and then go to www.myeconlab.com

Tariffs and Import Quotas in the Presence of Monopoly

The trade policy analysis in this chapter assumed that markets are perfectly competitive, so that all firms take prices as given. As we argued in Chapter 8, however, many markets for internationally traded goods are imperfectly competitive. The effects of international trade policies can be affected by the nature of the competition in a market.

When we analyze the effects of trade policy in imperfectly competitive markets, a new consideration appears: International trade limits monopoly power, and policies that limit trade may therefore increase monopoly power. Even if a firm is the only producer of a good in a country, it will have little ability to raise prices if there are many foreign suppliers and free trade. If imports are limited by a quota, however, the same firm will be free to raise prices without fear of competition.

The link between trade policy and monopoly power may be understood by examining a model in which a country imports a good and its import-competing production is controlled by only one firm. The country is small on world markets, so the price of the import is unaffected by its trade policy. For this model, we examine and compare the effects of free trade, a tariff, and an import quota.

The Model with Free Trade

Figure 9A-1 shows free trade in a market where a domestic monopolist faces competition from imports. D is the domestic demand curve: demand for the product by domestic residents. P_W is the world price of the good; imports are available in unlimited quantities at that price. The domestic industry is assumed to consist of only a single firm, whose marginal cost curve is MC.

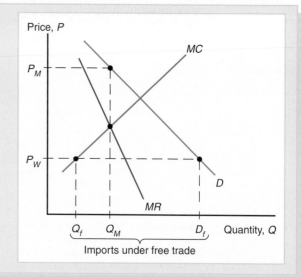

FIGURE 9A-1

A Monopolist under Free Trade

The threat of import competition forces the monopolist to behave like a perfectly competitive industry.

If there were no trade in this market, the domestic firm would behave as an ordinary profit-maximizing monopolist. Corresponding to D is a marginal revenue curve MR, and the firm would choose the monopoly profit-maximizing level of output Q_M and price P_M.

With free trade, however, this monopoly behavior is not possible. If the firm tried to charge P_M, or indeed any price above P_W, nobody would buy its product, because cheaper imports would be available. Thus international trade puts a lid on the monopolist's price at P_W.

Given this limit on its price, the best the monopolist can do is produce up to the point where marginal cost is equal to the world price, at Q_f. At the price P_W, domestic consumers will demand D_f units of the good, so imports will be $D_f - Q_f$. This outcome, however, is exactly what would have happened if the domestic industry had been perfectly competitive. With free trade, then, the fact that the domestic industry is a monopoly does not make any difference in the outcome.

The Model with a Tariff

The effect of a tariff is to raise the maximum price the domestic industry can charge. If a specific tariff t is charged on imports, the domestic industry can now charge $P_W + t$ (Figure 9A-2). The industry still is not free to raise its price all the way to the monopoly price, however, because consumers will still turn to imports if the price rises above the world price plus the tariff. Thus the best the monopolist can do is to set price equal to marginal cost, at Q_t. The tariff raises the domestic price as well as the output of the domestic industry, while demand falls to D_t and thus imports fall. However, the domestic industry still produces the same quantity as if it were perfectly competitive.[7]

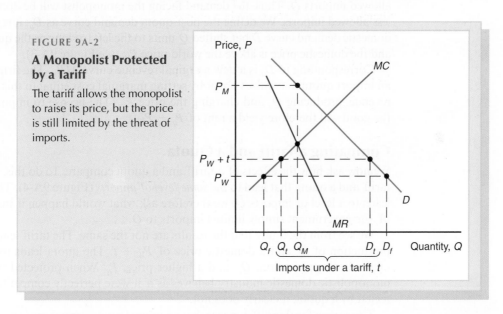

FIGURE 9A-2

A Monopolist Protected by a Tariff

The tariff allows the monopolist to raise its price, but the price is still limited by the threat of imports.

[7]There is one case in which a tariff will have different effects on a monopolistic industry than on a perfectly competitive one. This is the case where a tariff is so high that imports are completely eliminated (a prohibitive tariff). For a competitive industry, once imports have been eliminated, any further increase in the tariff has no effect. A monopolist, however, will be forced to limit its price by the *threat* of imports even if actual imports are zero. Thus, an increase in a prohibitive tariff will allow a monopolist to raise its price closer to the profit-maximizing price P_M.

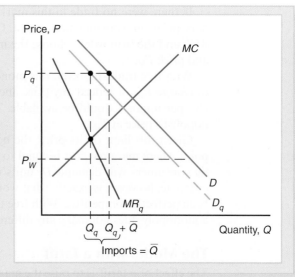

FIGURE 9A-3

A Monopolist Protected by an Import Quota

The monopolist is now free to raise prices, knowing that the domestic price of imports will rise too.

The Model with an Import Quota

Suppose the government imposes a limit on imports, restricting their quantity to a fixed level $\overline{Q}$. Then the monopolist knows that when it charges a price above P_W, it will not lose all its sales. Instead, it will sell whatever domestic demand is at that price, minus the allowed imports $\overline{Q}$. Thus, the demand facing the monopolist will be domestic demand less allowed imports. We define the post-quota demand curve as D_q; it is parallel to the domestic demand curve D but shifted $\overline{Q}$ units to the left (so long as the quota is binding and the domestic price is above the world price P_W, see Figure 9A-3).

Corresponding to D_q is a new marginal revenue curve MR_q. The firm protected by an import quota maximizes profit by setting marginal cost equal to this new marginal revenue, producing Q_q and charging the price P_q. (The license to import one unit of the good will therefore yield a rent of $P_q - P_W$.)

Comparing a Tariff and a Quota

We now ask how the effects of a tariff and a quota compare. To do this, we compare a tariff and a quota that lead to *the same level of imports* (Figure 9A-4). The tariff level t leads to a level of imports $\overline{Q}$; we therefore ask what would happen if instead of a tariff, the government simply limited imports to $\overline{Q}$.

We see from the figure that the results are not the same. The tariff leads to domestic production of Q_t and a domestic price of $P_W + t$. The quota leads to a lower level of domestic production, Q_q, and a higher price, P_q. When protected by a tariff, the monopolistic domestic industry behaves as if it were perfectly competitive; when protected by a quota, it clearly does not.

The reason for this difference is that an import quota creates more monopoly power than a tariff. When monopolistic industries are protected by tariffs, domestic firms know that if they raise their prices too high, they will still be undercut by imports. An import quota, on the other hand, provides absolute protection: No matter how high the domestic price, imports cannot exceed the quota level.

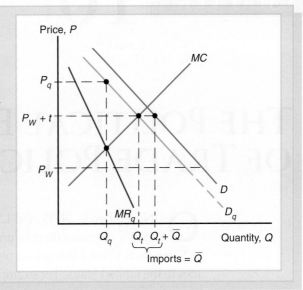

FIGURE 9A-4

Comparing a Tariff and a Quota

A quota leads to lower domestic output and a higher price than a tariff that yields the same level of imports.

This comparison seems to say that if governments are concerned about domestic monopoly power, they should prefer tariffs to quotas as instruments of trade policy. In fact, however, protection has increasingly drifted away from tariffs toward nontariff barriers, including import quotas. To explain this, we need to look at considerations other than economic efficiency that motivate governments.

10

THE POLITICAL ECONOMY OF TRADE POLICY

On November 8, 2005, the U.S. government and the government of China signed a memorandum of understanding under which China agreed, under U.S. pressure, to establish quotas on its exports of various types of clothing and textiles to the United States. For example, China agreed that in 2006 it would not ship more than 772.8 million pairs of socks to America. This agreement significantly raised the price of socks and other goods to American consumers. While China was willing to accommodate the United States on this point, however, it balked at U.S. demands that it reduce its own tariffs on manufactured and agricultural goods.

Both the Chinese and the U.S. governments, then, were determined to pursue policies that, according to the cost-benefit analysis developed in Chapter 9, produced more costs than benefits. Clearly, government policies reflect objectives that go beyond simple measures of cost and benefit.

In this chapter, we examine some of the reasons governments either should not or, at any rate, do not base their trade policy on economists' cost-benefit calculations. The examination of the forces motivating trade policy in practice continues in Chapters 11 and 12, which discuss the characteristic trade policy issues facing developing and advanced countries, respectively. The first step toward understanding actual trade policies is to ask what reasons there are for governments *not* to interfere with trade—that is, what is the case for free trade? With this question answered, arguments for intervention can be examined as challenges to the assumptions underlying the case for free trade.

LEARNING GOALS

After reading this chapter, you will be able to:

- Articulate arguments for free trade that go beyond the conventional gains from trade.
- Evaluate national welfare arguments against free trade.
- Relate the theory and evidence behind "political economy" views of trade policy.
- Explain how international negotiations and agreements have promoted world trade.
- Discuss the special issues raised by preferential trade agreements.

The Case for Free Trade

Few countries have anything approaching completely free trade. The city of Hong Kong, which is legally part of China but maintains a separate economic policy, may be the only modern economy with no tariffs or import quotas. Nonetheless, since the time of Adam Smith, economists have advocated free trade as an ideal toward which trade policy should strive. The reasons for this advocacy are not quite as simple as the idea itself. At one level, theoretical models suggest that free trade will avoid the efficiency losses associated with protection. Many economists believe free trade produces additional gains beyond the elimination of production and consumption distortions. Finally, even among economists who believe free trade is a less-than-perfect policy, many believe free trade is usually better than any other policy a government is likely to follow.

Free Trade and Efficiency

The **efficiency case for free trade** is simply the reverse of the cost-benefit analysis of a tariff. Figure 10-1 shows the basic point once again for the case of a small country that cannot influence foreign export prices. A tariff causes a net loss to the economy measured by the area of the two triangles; it does so by distorting the economic incentives of both producers and consumers. Conversely, a move to free trade eliminates these distortions and increases national welfare.

In the modern world, for reasons we will explain later in this chapter, tariff rates are generally low and import quotas relatively rare. As a result, estimates of the total costs of distortions due to tariffs and import quotas tend to be modest in size. Table 10-1 shows one fairly recent estimate of the gains from a move to worldwide free trade, measured as a percentage of GDP. For the world as a whole, according to these estimates, protection costs less than 1 percent of GDP. The gains from free trade are somewhat smaller for advanced economies such as the United States and Europe and somewhat larger for poorer "developing countries."

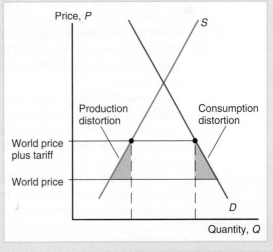

FIGURE 10-1

The Efficiency Case for Free Trade

A trade restriction, such as a tariff, leads to production and consumption distortions.

TABLE 10-1	Benefits of a Move to Worldwide Free Trade (percent of GDP)
United States	0.57
European Union	0.61
Japan	0.85
Developing countries	1.4
World	0.93

Source: William Cline, *Trade Policy and Global Poverty* (Washington, D.C.: Institute for International Economics, 2004), p. 180.

Additional Gains from Free Trade[1]

There is a widespread belief among economists that such calculations, even though they report substantial gains from free trade in some cases, do not represent the whole story. In the case of small countries in general and developing countries in particular, many economists would argue that there are important gains from free trade not accounted for in conventional cost-benefit analysis.

One kind of additional gain involves economies of scale, which were the theme of Chapters 7 and 8. Protected markets limit gains from external economies of scale by inhibiting the concentration of industries; when the economies of scale are internal, they not only fragment production internationally, but by reducing competition and raising profits, they also lead too many firms to enter the protected industry. With a proliferation of firms in narrow domestic markets, the scale of production of each firm becomes inefficient. A good example of how protection leads to inefficient scale is the case of the Argentine automobile industry, which emerged because of import restrictions. An efficient scale assembly plant should make from 80,000 to 200,000 automobiles per year, yet in 1964 the Argentine industry, which produced only 166,000 cars, had no fewer than 13 firms! Some economists argue that the need to deter excessive entry and the resulting inefficient scale of production is a reason for free trade that goes beyond the standard cost-benefit calculations.

Another argument for free trade is that by providing entrepreneurs with an incentive to seek new ways to export or compete with imports, free trade offers more opportunities for learning and innovation than are provided by a system of "managed" trade, where the government largely dictates the pattern of imports and exports. Chapter 11 discusses the experiences of less-developed countries that discovered unexpected export opportunities when they shifted from systems of import quotas and tariffs to more open trade policies.

A related form of gains from free trade involves the tendency, documented in Chapter 8, for more productive firms to engage in exports while less productive firms stay with the domestic market. This suggests that a move to free trade makes the economy as a whole more efficient by shifting the industrial mix toward firms with higher productivity.

These additional arguments for free trade are difficult to quantify, although some economists have tried to do so. In general, models that try to take economies of scale and imperfect competition into account yield bigger numbers than those reported

---

[1]The additional gains from free trade discussed here are sometimes referred to as "dynamic" gains because increased competition and innovation may need more time to take effect than the elimination of production and consumption distortions.

in Table 10-1. However, there is no consensus about just how much bigger the gains from free trade really are. If the additional gains from free trade are as large as some economists believe, the costs of distorting trade with tariffs, quotas, export subsidies, and so on are correspondingly larger than the conventional cost-benefit analysis measures.

Rent Seeking

When imports are restricted with a quota rather than a tariff, the cost is sometimes magnified by a process known as **rent seeking.** Recall from Chapter 9 that to enforce an import quota, a government has to issue import licenses and economic rents accrue to whoever receives these licenses. In some cases, individuals and companies incur substantial costs—in effect, wasting some of the economy's productive resources—in an effort to get import licenses.

A famous example involved India in the 1950s and 1960s. At that time, Indian companies were allocated the right to buy imported inputs in proportion to their installed capacity. This created an incentive to overinvest—for example, a steel company might build more blast furnaces than it expected to need simply because this would give it a larger number of import licenses. The resources used to build this idle capacity represented a cost of protection over and above the costs shown in Figure 10-1.

A more modern and unusual example of rent seeking involves U.S. imports of canned tuna. Tuna is protected by a "tariff-rate quota": A small quantity of tuna (4.8 percent of U.S. consumption) can be imported at a low tariff rate, 6 percent, but any imports beyond that level face a 12.5 percent tariff. For some reason, there are no import licenses; each year, the right to import tuna at the low tariff rate is assigned on a first come, first served basis. The result is a costly race to get tuna into the United States as quickly as possible. Here's how the U.S. International Trade Commission describes the process of rent-seeking:

> Importers attempt to qualify for the largest share of the TRQ [tariff-rate quota] as possible by stockpiling large quantities of canned tuna in Customs-bonded warehouses in late December and releasing the warehoused product as soon as the calendar year begins.

The money importers spend on warehousing lots of tuna in December represents a loss to the U.S. economy over and above the standard costs of protection.

Political Argument for Free Trade

A **political argument for free trade** reflects the fact that a political commitment to free trade may be a good idea in practice even though there may be better policies in principle. Economists often argue that trade policies in practice are dominated by special-interest politics rather than by consideration of national costs and benefits. Economists can sometimes show that in theory, a selective set of tariffs and export subsidies could increase national welfare, but that in reality, any government agency attempting to pursue a sophisticated program of intervention in trade would probably be captured by interest groups and converted into a device for redistributing income to politically influential sectors. If this argument is correct, it may be better to advocate free trade without exceptions even though on purely economic grounds, free trade may not always be the best conceivable policy.

The three arguments outlined in the previous section probably represent the standard view of most international economists, at least those in the United States:

1. The conventionally measured costs of deviating from free trade are large.
2. There are other benefits from free trade that add to the costs of protectionist policies.
3. Any attempt to pursue sophisticated deviations from free trade will be subverted by the political process.

Nonetheless, there are intellectually respectable arguments for deviating from free trade, and these arguments deserve a fair hearing.

CASE STUDY   The Gains from 1992

In 1987, the nations of the European Community (now known as the European Union) agreed on what formally was called the Single European Act, with the intention to create a truly unified European market. Because the act was supposed to go into effect within five years, the measures it embodied came to be known generally as "1992."

The unusual thing about 1992 was that the European Community was already a customs union, that is, there were no tariffs or import quotas on intra-European trade. So, what was left to liberalize? The advocates of 1992 argued that there were still substantial barriers to international trade within Europe. Some of these barriers involved the costs of crossing borders; for example, the mere fact that trucks carrying goods between France and Germany had to stop for legal formalities often resulted in long waits that were costly in time and fuel. Similar costs were imposed on business travelers, who might fly from London to Paris in an hour, then spend another hour waiting to clear immigration and customs. Differences in regulations also had the effect of limiting the integration of markets. For example, because health regulations on food differed among the European nations, one could not simply fill a truck with British goods and take them to France, or vice versa.

Eliminating these subtle obstacles to trade was a very difficult political process. Suppose France decided to allow goods from Germany to enter the country without any checks. What would prevent the French people from being supplied with manufactured goods that did not meet French safety standards, foods that did not meet French health standards, or medicines that had not been approved by French doctors? Thus, the only way that countries can have truly open borders is if they are able to agree on common standards so that a good that meets French requirements is acceptable in Germany and vice versa. The main task of the 1992 negotiations was therefore one of harmonizing regulations in hundreds of areas, negotiations that were often acrimonious because of differences in national cultures.

The most emotional examples involved food. All advanced countries regulate things such as artificial coloring to ensure that consumers are not unknowingly fed chemicals that are carcinogens or otherwise harmful. The initially proposed regulations on artificial coloring would, however, have destroyed the appearance of several traditional British foods: Pink bangers (breakfast sausages) would have become white, golden kippers gray, and mushy peas a drab rather than a brilliant green. Continental consumers did not mind; indeed, they could not understand how the British could eat such things in the first place. But in Britain, the issue became tied up with fear over the loss of national identity, and loosening the proposed regulations became a top priority for the British government, which succeeded in getting the necessary exemptions. On the other hand, Germany was forced to accept imports of beer that do not meet its centuries-old purity laws and Italy to accept pasta made from—horrors!—the wrong kind of wheat.

But why engage in all this difficult negotiating? What were the potential gains from 1992? Attempts to estimate the direct gains have always suggested that they are fairly modest. Costs associated with crossing borders amount to no more than a few percent of the value of the goods shipped; removing these costs adds at best a fraction of a percent to the real income of Europe as a whole. Yet economists at the European Commission (the administrative arm of the European Union) argued that the true gains would be much larger.

Their reasoning relied to a large extent on the view that the unification of the European market would lead to greater competition among firms and to a more efficient scale of production. Much was made of the comparison with the United States, a country whose purchasing power and population are similar to those of the European Union, but that is a borderless, fully integrated market. Commission economists pointed out that in a number of industries, Europe seemed to have markets that were segmented: Instead of treating the whole continent as a single market, firms seemed to have carved it into local zones served by relatively small-scale national producers. The economists argued that with all barriers to trade removed, there would be a consolidation of these producers, with substantial gains in productivity. These putative gains raised the overall estimated benefits from 1992 to several percent of the initial income of European nations. The Commission economists argued further that there would be indirect benefits because the improved efficiency of the European economy would improve the trade-off between inflation unemployment. At the end of a series of calculations, the Commission estimated a gain from 1992 of 7 percent of European income.[2]

While nobody involved in this discussion regarded 7 percent as a particularly reliable number, many economists shared the conviction of the Commission that the gains would be large. There were, however, skeptics who suggested that the segmentation of markets had more to do with culture than with trade policy. For example, Italian consumers wanted washing machines that were quite different from those preferred in Germany. Italians tend to buy relatively few clothes, but those they buy are stylish and expensive, so they prefer slow, gentle washing machines that conserve their clothing investment.

Now that a number of years have passed since 1992, it is clear that both the supporters and the skeptics had valid points. In some cases, there have been notable consolidations of industry; for example, Hoover closed its vacuum cleaner plant in France and concentrated all its production in a more efficient plant in Britain. In other cases, old market segmentations have clearly broken down, and sometimes in surprising ways, like the emergence of British sliced bread as a popular item in France. But in still other cases, markets have shown little sign of merging: Germans have shown little taste for imported beer and Italians none for pasta made with soft wheat.

How large were the economic gains from 1992? By 2003, when the European Commission decided to review the effects of the Single European Act, it came up with more modest estimates than it had before 1992: It put the gains at about 1.8 percent of GDP. If this number is correct, it represents a mild disappointment but hardly a failure.

---

[2]See Michael Emerson, Michel Aujean, Michel Catinat, Philippe Goubet, and Alexis Jacquemin, "The Economics of 1992," *European Economy* 35 (March 1988).

National Welfare Arguments against Free Trade

Most tariffs, import quotas, and other trade policy measures are undertaken primarily to protect the income of particular interest groups. Politicians often claim, however, that the policies are being undertaken in the interest of the nation as a whole, and sometimes they are even telling the truth. Although economists frequently argue that deviations from free trade reduce national welfare, there are some theoretical grounds for believing that activist trade policies can sometimes increase the welfare of the nation as a whole.

The Terms of Trade Argument for a Tariff

One argument for deviating from free trade comes directly out of cost-benefit analysis: For a large country that is able to affect the prices of foreign exporters, a tariff lowers the price of imports and thus generates a terms of trade benefit. This benefit must be set against the costs of the tariff, which arise because the tariff distorts production and consumption incentives. It is possible, however, that in some cases the terms of trade benefits of a tariff outweigh its costs, so there is a **terms of trade argument for a tariff**.

The appendix to this chapter shows that for a sufficiently small tariff, the terms of trade benefits must outweigh the costs. Thus, at small tariff rates, a large country's welfare is higher than with free trade (Figure 10-2). As the tariff rate is increased, however, the costs eventually begin to grow more rapidly than the benefits and the curve relating national welfare to the tariff rate turns down. A tariff rate that completely prohibits trade (t_p in Figure 10-2) leaves the country worse off than with free trade; further increases in the tariff rate beyond t_p have no effect, so the curve flattens out.

At point 1 on the curve in Figure 10-2, corresponding to the tariff rate t_o, national welfare is maximized. The tariff rate t_o that maximizes national welfare is the **optimum tariff.** (By convention, the phrase *optimum tariff* is usually used to refer to the tariff justified by a terms of trade argument rather than to the best tariff given all possible

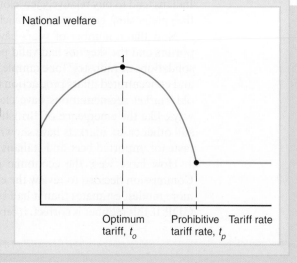

FIGURE 10-2

The Optimum Tariff

For a large country, there is an optimum tariff t_o at which the marginal gain from improved terms of trade just equals the marginal efficiency loss from production and consumption distortion.

considerations.) The optimum tariff rate is always positive but less than the prohibitive rate (t_p) that would eliminate all imports.

What policy would the terms of trade argument dictate for *export* sectors? Since an export subsidy *worsens* the terms of trade, and therefore unambiguously reduces national welfare, the optimal policy in export sectors must be a negative subsidy, that is, a *tax* on exports that raises the price of exports to foreigners. Like the optimum tariff, the optimum export tax is always positive but less than the prohibitive tax that would eliminate exports completely.

The policy of Saudi Arabia and other oil exporters has been to tax their exports of oil, raising the price to the rest of the world. Although oil prices have fluctuated up and down over the years, it is hard to argue that Saudi Arabia would have been better off under free trade.

The terms of trade argument against free trade has some important limitations, however. Most small countries have very little ability to affect the world prices of either their imports or their exports, and thus the terms of trade argument is of little practical importance to them. For big countries like the United States, the problem is that the terms of trade argument amounts to an argument for using national monopoly power to extract gains at other countries' expense. The United States could surely do this to some extent, but such a predatory policy would probably bring retaliation from other large countries. A cycle of retaliatory trade moves would, in turn, undermine the attempts at international trade policy coordination described later in this chapter.

The terms of trade argument against free trade, then, is intellectually impeccable but of doubtful usefulness. In practice, it is more often emphasized by economists as a theoretical proposition than actually used by governments as a justification for trade policy.

The Domestic Market Failure Argument against Free Trade

Leaving aside the issue of the terms of trade, the basic theoretical case for free trade rested on cost-benefit analysis using the concepts of consumer and producer surplus. Many economists have made a case against free trade based on the counterargument that these concepts, producer surplus in particular, do not properly measure costs and benefits.

Why might producer surplus not properly measure the benefits of producing a good? We consider a variety of reasons in the next two chapters: These include the possibility that the labor used in a sector would otherwise be unemployed or underemployed, the existence of defects in the capital or labor markets that prevent resources from being transferred as rapidly as they should be to sectors that yield high returns, and the possibility of technological spillovers from industries that are new or particularly innovative. These can all be classified under the general heading of **domestic market failures**. That is, in each of these examples, some market in the country is not doing its job right—the labor market is not clearing, the capital market is not allocating resources efficiently, and so on.

Suppose, for example, that the production of some good yields experience that will improve the technology of the economy as a whole but that the firms in the sector cannot appropriate this benefit and therefore do not take it into account in deciding how much to produce. Then there is a **marginal social benefit** to additional production that is not captured by the producer surplus measure. This marginal social benefit can serve as a justification for tariffs or other trade policies.

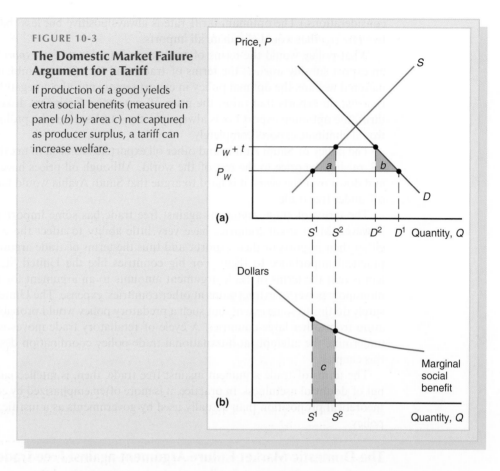

FIGURE 10-3

The Domestic Market Failure Argument for a Tariff

If production of a good yields extra social benefits (measured in panel (b) by area c) not captured as producer surplus, a tariff can increase welfare.

Figure 10-3 illustrates the domestic market failure argument against free trade. Figure 10-3a shows the conventional cost-benefit analysis of a tariff for a small country (which rules out terms of trade effects). Figure 10-3b shows the marginal benefit from production that is not taken account of by the producer surplus measure. The figure shows the effects of a tariff that raises the domestic price from P_W to $P_W + t$. Production rises from S^1 to S^2, with a resulting production distortion indicated by the area labeled a. Consumption falls from D^1 to D^2, with a resulting consumption distortion indicated by the area b. If we considered only consumer and producer surplus, we would find that the costs of the tariff exceed its benefits. Figure 10-3b shows, however, that this calculation overlooks an additional benefit that may make the tariff preferable to free trade. The increase in production yields a social benefit that may be measured by the area under the marginal social benefit curve from S^1 to S^2, indicated by c. In fact, by an argument similar to that in the terms of trade case, we can show that if the tariff is small enough, the area c must always exceed the area $a + b$ and that there is some welfare-maximizing tariff that yields a level of social welfare higher than that of free trade.

The domestic market failure argument against free trade is a particular case of a more general concept known in economics as the **theory of the second best**. This theory states that a hands-off policy is desirable in any one market only if all other markets are working properly. If they are not, a government intervention that appears to distort incentives in one market may actually increase welfare by offsetting the consequences of market failures elsewhere. For example, if the labor market is malfunctioning and fails to deliver full employment, a policy of subsidizing labor-intensive industries, which would be undesirable in a full-employment economy, might turn out to be a good idea. It would be better to fix the labor market by, for example, making wages more flexible, but if for some reason this cannot be done, intervening in other markets may be a "second-best" way of alleviating the problem.

When economists apply the theory of the second best to trade policy, they argue that imperfections in the *internal* functioning of an economy may justify interfering in its external economic relations. This argument accepts that international trade is not the source of the problem but suggests nonetheless that trade policy can provide at least a partial solution.

How Convincing Is the Market Failure Argument?

When they were first proposed, market failure arguments for protection seemed to undermine much of the case for free trade. After all, who would want to argue that the real economies we live in are free from market failures? In poorer nations, in particular, market imperfections seem to be legion. For example, unemployment and massive differences between rural and urban wage rates are present in many less-developed countries (Chapter 11). The evidence that markets work badly is less glaring in advanced countries, but it is easy to develop hypotheses suggesting major market failures there as well—for example, the inability of innovative firms to reap the full rewards of their innovations. How can we defend free trade given the likelihood of interventions that could raise national welfare?

There are two lines of defense for free trade: The first argues that domestic market failures should be corrected by domestic policies aimed directly at the problems' sources; the second argues that economists cannot diagnose market failure well enough to prescribe policy.

The point that domestic market failure calls for domestic policy changes, not international trade policies, can be made by cost-benefit analysis modified to account for any unmeasured marginal social benefits. Figure 10-3 showed that a tariff might raise welfare, despite the production and consumption distortions it causes, because it leads to additional production that yields social benefits. If the same production increase were achieved via a production subsidy rather than a tariff, however, the price to consumers would not increase and the consumption loss *b* would be avoided. In other words, by targeting directly the particular activity we want to encourage, a production subsidy would avoid some of the side costs associated with a tariff.

This example illustrates a general principle when dealing with market failures: It is always preferable to deal with market failures as directly as possible because indirect policy responses lead to unintended distortions of incentives elsewhere in the economy. Thus, trade policies justified by domestic market failure are never the most efficient response; they are always "second-best" rather than "first-best" policies.

This insight has important implications for trade policy makers: Any proposed trade policy should always be compared with a purely domestic policy aimed at correcting the same problem. If the domestic policy appears too costly or has undesirable side effects, the trade policy is almost surely even less desirable—even though the costs are less apparent.

In the United States, for example, an import quota on automobiles has been supported on the grounds that it is necessary to save the jobs of autoworkers. The advocates of an import quota argue that U.S. labor markets are too inflexible for autoworkers to remain employed either by cutting their wages or by finding jobs in other sectors. Now consider a purely domestic policy aimed at the same problem: a subsidy to firms that employ autoworkers. Such a policy would encounter massive political opposition. For one thing, to preserve current levels of employment without protection would require large subsidy payments, which would either increase the federal government's budget deficit or require a tax increase. Furthermore, autoworkers are among the highest-paid workers in the manufacturing sector; the general public would surely object to subsidizing them. It is hard to believe an employment subsidy for autoworkers could pass Congress. Yet an import quota *would be even more expensive* because while it would bring about the same increase in employment, it would also distort consumer choice. The only difference is that the costs would be less visible, taking the form of higher automobile prices rather than direct government outlays.

Critics of the domestic market failure justification for protection argue that this case is typical: Most deviations from free trade are adopted not because their benefits exceed their costs but because the public fails to understand their true costs. Comparing the costs of trade policy with alternative domestic policies is thus a useful way to focus attention on just how large these costs are.

The second defense of free trade is that because market failures are typically hard to identify precisely, it is difficult to be sure what the appropriate policy response should be. For example, suppose there is urban unemployment in a less-developed country; what is the appropriate policy? One hypothesis (examined more closely in Chapter 11) says that a tariff to protect urban industrial sectors will draw the unemployed into productive work and thus generate social benefits that would more than compensate for the tariff's costs. However, another hypothesis says that this policy will encourage so much migration to urban areas that unemployment will, in fact, increase. It is difficult to say which of these hypotheses is right. While economic theory says much about the working of markets that function properly, it provides much less guidance on those that don't; there are many ways in which markets can malfunction, and the choice of a second-best policy depends on the details of the market failure.

The difficulty of ascertaining the correct second-best trade policy to follow reinforces the political argument for free trade mentioned earlier. If trade policy experts are highly uncertain about how policy should deviate from free trade and disagree among themselves, it is all too easy for trade policy to ignore national welfare altogether and become dominated by special-interest politics. If the market failures are not too bad to start with, a commitment to free trade might in the end be a better policy than opening a Pandora's box of a more flexible approach.

This is, however, a judgment about politics rather than about economics. We need to realize that economic theory does *not* provide a dogmatic defense of free trade, even though it is often accused of doing so.

Income Distribution and Trade Policy

The discussion so far has focused on national welfare arguments for and against tariff policy. It is appropriate to start there, both because a distinction between national welfare and the welfare of particular groups helps to clarify the issues and because the advocates of trade policies usually claim that the policies will benefit the nation as a whole. When looking at the actual politics of trade policy, however, it becomes necessary to deal with the reality that there is no such thing as national welfare; there are only the desires of individuals, which get more or less imperfectly reflected in the objectives of government.

How do the preferences of individuals get added up to produce the trade policy we actually see? There is no single, generally accepted answer, but there has been a growing body of economic analysis that explores models in which governments are assumed to be trying to maximize political success rather than an abstract measure of national welfare.

Electoral Competition

Political scientists have long used a simple model of competition among political parties to show how the preferences of voters might be reflected in actual policies.[3] The model runs as follows: Suppose two competing parties are willing to promise whatever will enable each to win the next election, and suppose policy can be described along a single dimension, say, the level of the tariff rate. And finally, suppose voters differ in the policies they prefer. For example, imagine a country exports skill-intensive goods and imports labor-intensive goods. Then voters with high skill levels will favor low tariff rates, but voters with low skills will be better off if the country imposes a high tariff (because of the Stolper-Samuelson effect discussed in Chapter 5). We can therefore think of lining up all the voters in the order of the tariff rate they prefer, with the voters who favor the lowest rate on the left and those who favor the highest rate on the right.

What policies will the two parties then promise to follow? The answer is that they will try to find the middle ground—specifically, both will tend to converge on the tariff rate preferred by the **median voter,** the voter who is exactly halfway up the lineup. To see why, consider Figure 10-4. In the figure, voters are lined up by their preferred tariff rate, which is shown by the hypothetical upward-sloping curve; t_M is the median voter's preferred rate. Now suppose one of the parties has proposed the tariff rate t_A, which is considerably above that preferred by the median voter. Then the other party could propose the slightly lower rate, t_B, and its program would be preferred by almost all voters who want a lower tariff, that is, by a majority. In other words, it would always be in the political interest of a party to undercut any tariff proposal that is higher than what the median voter wants.

FIGURE 10-4

Political Competition

Voters are lined up in order of the tariff rate they prefer. If one party proposes a high tariff of t_A, the other party can win over most of the voters by offering a somewhat lower tariff, t_B. This political competition drives both parties to propose tariffs close to t_M, the tariff preferred by the median voter.

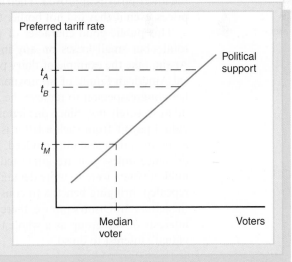

[3]See Anthony Downs, *An Economic Theory of Democracy* (Washington, D.C.: Brookings Institution, 1957).

Similar reasoning shows that self-interested politicians will always want to promise a higher tariff if their opponents propose one that is lower than the tariff the median voter prefers. So both parties end up proposing a tariff close to the one the median voter wants.

Political scientists have modified this simple model in a number of ways. For example, some analysts stress the importance of party activists in getting out the vote; since these activists are often ideologically motivated, the need for their support may prevent parties from being quite as cynical, or adopting platforms quite as indistinguishable, as this model suggests. Nonetheless, the median voter model of electoral competition has been very helpful as a way of thinking about how political decisions get made in the real world, where the effects of policy on income distribution may be more important than their effects on efficiency.

One area in which the median voter model does not seem to work very well, however, is trade policy! In fact, it makes an almost precisely wrong prediction. According to this model, a policy should be chosen on the basis of how many voters it pleases: A policy that inflicts large losses on a few people but benefits a large number of people should be a political winner; a policy that inflicts widespread losses but helps a small group should be a loser. In fact, however, protectionist policies are more likely to fit the latter than the former description. For example, the U.S. dairy industry is protected from foreign competition by an elaborate system of tariffs and quotas. These restrictions impose losses on just about every family in America while providing much smaller benefits to a dairy industry that employs only about 0.1 percent of the nation's work force. How can such a thing happen politically?

Collective Action

In a now famous book, economist Mancur Olson pointed out that political activity on behalf of a group is a public good; that is, the benefits of such activity accrue to all members of the group, not just the individual who performs the activity.[4] Suppose a consumer writes a letter to his congressperson demanding a lower tariff rate on his favorite imported good, and this letter helps change the congressperson's vote so that the lower tariff is approved. Then all consumers who buy the good benefit from lower prices, even if they did not bother to write letters.

This public good character of politics means policies that impose large losses in total—but small losses on any individual—may not face any effective opposition. Again, take the example of dairy protectionism. This policy imposes a cost on a typical American family of approximately $3 per year. Should a consumer lobby his or her congressperson to remove the policy? From the point of view of individual self-interest, surely not. Since one letter has only a marginal effect on the policy, the individual payoff from such a letter is probably not worth the paper it is written on, let alone the postage stamp. (Indeed, it is surely not worth even learning of the policy's existence unless you are interested in such things for their own sake.) And yet, if a million voters were to write demanding an end to dairy protection, it would surely be repealed, bringing benefits to consumers significantly exceeding the costs of sending the letters. In Olson's phrase, there is a problem of **collective action**: While it is in the interests of the group as a whole to press for favorable policies, it is not in any individual's interest to do so.

---

[4]Mancur Olson, *The Logic of Collective Action* (Cambridge: Harvard University Press, 1965).

POLITICIANS FOR SALE: EVIDENCE FROM THE 1990s

As we explain in the text, it's hard to make sense of actual trade policy if you assume governments are genuinely trying to maximize national welfare. On the other hand, actual trade policy does make sense if you assume special-interest groups can buy influence. But is there any direct evidence that politicians really are for sale?

Votes by the U.S. Congress on some crucial trade issues in the 1990s offer useful test cases. The reason is that U.S. campaign finance laws require politicians to reveal the amounts and sources of campaign contributions; this disclosure allows economists and political scientists to look for any relationship between those contributions and actual votes.

A 1998 study by Robert Baldwin and Christopher Magee* focuses on two crucial votes: the 1993 vote on the North American Free Trade Agreement (generally known as NAFTA, and described at greater length below), and the 1994 vote ratifying the latest agreement under the General Agreement on Tariffs and Trade (generally known as the GATT, also described below). Both votes were bitterly fought, largely along business-versus-labor lines—that is, business groups were strongly in favor; labor unions were strongly against. In both cases, the free trade position backed by business won; in the NAFTA vote, the outcome was in doubt until the last minute, and the margin of victory—34 votes in the House of Representatives—was not very large.

Baldwin and Magee estimate an econometric model of congressional votes that controls for such factors as the economic characteristics of members' districts as well as business and labor contributions to the congressional representative. They find a strong impact of money on the voting pattern. One way to assess this impact is to run a series of "counterfactuals": How different would the overall vote had been if there had been no business contributions, no labor contributions, or no contributions of any type at all?

The following table summarizes the results. The first row shows how many representatives

voted in favor of each bill; bear in mind that passage required at least 214 votes. The second row shows the number of votes predicted by Baldwin and Magee's equations: Their model gets it right in the case of NAFTA but overpredicts by a few votes in the case of the GATT. The third row shows how many votes each bill would have received, according to the model, in the absence of labor contributions; the next row shows how many representatives would have voted in favor in the absence of business contributions. The last row shows how many would have voted in favor if both business and labor contributions had been absent.

	Vote for NAFTA	Vote for GATT
Actual	229	283
Predicted by model	229	290
Without labor contributions	291	346
Without business contributions	195	257
Without any contributions	256	323

If these estimates are correct, contributions had big impacts on the vote totals. In the case of NAFTA, labor contributions induced 62 representatives who would otherwise have supported the bill to vote against; business contributions moved 34 representatives the other way. If there had been no business contributions, according to this estimate, NAFTA would have received only 195 votes—not enough for passage.

On the other hand, given that both sides were making contributions, their effects tended to cancel out. Baldwin and Magee's estimates suggest that in the absence of contributions from either labor or business, both NAFTA and the GATT would have passed anyway.

It's probably wrong to emphasize the fact that in these particular cases, contributions from the two sides did not change the final outcome. The really important result is that politicians are, indeed, for sale—which means that theories of trade policy that emphasize special interests are on the right track.

*Robert E. Baldwin and Christopher S. Magee, "Is Trade Policy for Sale? Congressional Voting on Recent Trade Bills," Working Paper 6376, National Bureau of Economic Research, January 1998.

The problem of collective action can best be overcome when a group is small (so that each individual reaps a significant share of the benefits of favorable policies) and/or well organized (so that members of the group can be mobilized to act in their collective interest). The reason that a policy like dairy protection can happen is that dairy producers form a relatively small, well-organized group that is well aware of the size of the implicit subsidy members receive, while dairy consumers are a huge population that does not even perceive itself as an interest group. The problem of collective action, then, can explain why policies that not only seem to produce more costs than benefits but that also seem to hurt far more voters than they help can nonetheless be adopted.

Modeling the Political Process

While the logic of collective action has long been invoked by economists to explain seemingly irrational trade policies, the theory is somewhat vague on the ways in which organized interest groups actually go about influencing policy. A growing body of analysis tries to fill this gap with simplified models of the political process.[5]

The starting point of this analysis is obvious: While politicians may win elections partly because they advocate popular policies, a successful campaign also requires money for advertising, polling, and so on. It may therefore be in the interest of a politician to adopt positions against the interest of the typical voter if the politician is offered a sufficiently large financial contribution to do so; the extra money may be worth more votes than those lost by taking the unpopular position.

Modern models of the political economy of trade policy therefore envision a sort of auction in which interest groups "buy" policies by offering contributions contingent on the policies followed by the government. Politicians will not ignore overall welfare, but they will be willing to trade off some reduction in the welfare of voters in return for a larger campaign fund. As a result, well-organized groups—that is, groups that are able to overcome the problem of collective action—will be able to get policies that favor their interests at the expense of the public as a whole.

Who Gets Protected?

As a practical matter, which industries actually get protected from import competition? Many developing countries traditionally have protected a wide range of manufacturing, in a policy known as import-substituting industrialization. We discuss this policy and the reasons why it has become considerably less popular in recent years in Chapter 11. The range of protectionism in advanced countries is much narrower; indeed, much protectionism is concentrated in just two sectors: agriculture and clothing.

Agriculture   There are not many farmers in modern economies—in the United States, agriculture employs only about 2 million workers out of a labor force of more than 130 million. Farmers are, however, usually a well-organized and politically powerful group that has been able in many cases to achieve very high rates of effective protection. We discussed Europe's Common Agricultural Policy in Chapter 9; the export subsidies in that program mean that a number of agricultural products sell at two or three

[5]See, in particular, Gene Grossman and Elhanan Helpman, "Protection for Sale," *American Economic Review* 89 (September 1994), pp. 833–850.

times world prices. In Japan, the government has traditionally banned imports of rice, thus driving up internal prices of the country's staple food to more than five times as high as the world price. This ban was slightly relaxed in the face of bad harvests in the mid-1990s, but in late 1998—over the protests of other nations, including the United States—Japan imposed a 1,000 percent tariff on rice imports.

The United States is generally a food exporter, which means that tariffs or import quotas cannot raise prices. (Sugar and dairy products are exceptions.) While farmers have received considerable subsidies from the federal government, the government's reluctance to pay money out directly (as opposed to imposing more or less hidden costs on consumers) has limited the size of these subsidies. As a result of the government's reluctance, much of the protection in the United States is concentrated on the other major protected sector: the clothing industry.

Clothing   The clothing industry consists of two parts: textiles (spinning and weaving of cloth) and apparel (assembly of cloth into clothing). Both industries, but especially the apparel industry, historically have been protected heavily through both tariffs and import quotas. Until 2005, they were subject to the Multi-Fiber Arrangement (MFA), which set both export and import quotas for a large number of countries.

Apparel production has two key features. It is labor-intensive: A worker needs relatively little capital, in some cases no more than a sewing machine, and can do the job without extensive formal education. And the technology is relatively simple: There is no great difficulty in transferring the technology even to very poor countries. As a result, the apparel industry is one in which low-wage nations have a strong comparative advantage and high-wage countries have a strong comparative disadvantage. It is also traditionally a well-organized sector in advanced countries; for example, many American apparel workers have long been represented by the International Ladies' Garment Worker's Union.

Later in this chapter, we'll describe how trade negotiations work; one of the most important provisions of the Uruguay Round trade agreements, signed in 1994, was the phaseout of the MFA, which took place at the end of 2004. Although import quotas were reimposed on China in 2005, those quotas have since phased out. At this point, trade in clothing no longer faces many restrictions.

Table 10-2 shows just how important clothing used to be in U.S. protectionism, and how much difference the end of the restrictions on clothing makes. In 2002, with the MFA still in effect, clothing restrictions were responsible for more than 80 percent of the overall welfare costs of U.S. protectionism. Because the MFA assigned import licenses to exporting countries, most of the welfare cost to the United States came not from distortion of production and consumption but from the transfer of quota rents to foreigners.

With the expiration of the MFA, the costs of clothing protection and hence the overall costs of U.S. protection fell sharply.

TABLE 10-2	**Welfare Costs of U.S. Protection ($ billion)**	
	2002 Estimate	**2015 Projected**
Total	14.1	2.6
Textiles and apparel	11.8	0.5
Source: U.S. International Trade Commission.		

International Negotiations and Trade Policy

Our discussion of the politics of trade policy has not been very encouraging. We have argued that it is difficult to devise trade policies that raise national welfare and that trade policy is often dominated by interest group politics. "Horror stories" of trade policies that produce costs that greatly exceed any conceivable benefits abound; it is thus easy to be highly cynical about the practical side of trade theory.

Yet, in fact, from the mid-1930s until about 1980, the United States and other advanced countries gradually removed tariffs and some other barriers to trade, and by so doing aided a rapid increase in international integration. Figure 10-5 shows the average U.S. tariff rate on dutiable imports from 1891 to 2010; after rising sharply in the early 1930s, the rate has steadily declined.[6] Most economists believe this progressive trade liberalization was highly beneficial. Given what we have said about the politics of trade policy, however, how was this removal of tariffs politically possible?

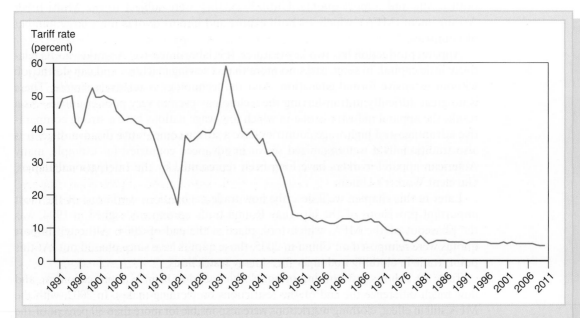

FIGURE 10-5

The U.S. Tariff Rate

After rising sharply at the beginning of the 1930s, the average tariff rate of the United States has steadily declined.

---

[6]Measures of changes in the average rate of protection can be problematic because the composition of imports changes—partly because of tariff rates themselves. Imagine, for example, a country that imposes a tariff on some goods that is so high that it shuts off all imports of these goods. Then the average tariff rate on goods actually imported will be zero! To try to correct for this, the measure we use in Figure 10-5 shows the rate only on "dutiable" imports; that is, it excludes imports that for some reason were exempt from tariffs. At their peak, U.S. tariff rates were so high that goods subject to tariffs accounted for only one-third of imports; by 1975 that share had risen to two-thirds. As a result, the average tariff rate on all goods fell much less than the rate on dutiable goods. The numbers shown in Figure 10-5, however, give a more accurate picture of the major liberalization of trade actually experienced by the United States.

At least part of the answer is that the great postwar liberalization of trade was achieved through **international negotiation**. That is, governments agreed to engage in mutual tariff reduction. These agreements linked reduced protection for each country's import-competing industries to reduced protection by other countries against that country's export industries. Such a linkage, as we will now argue, helps to offset some of the political difficulties that would otherwise prevent countries from adopting good trade policies.

The Advantages of Negotiation

There are at least two reasons why it is easier to lower tariffs as part of a mutual agreement than to do so as a unilateral policy. First, a mutual agreement helps mobilize support for freer trade. Second, negotiated agreements on trade can help governments avoid getting caught in destructive trade wars.

The effect of international negotiations on support for freer trade is straightforward. We have noted that import-competing producers are usually better informed and organized than consumers. International negotiations can bring in domestic exporters as a counterweight. The United States and Japan, for example, could reach an agreement in which the United States refrains from imposing import quotas to protect some of its manufacturers from Japanese competition in return for removal of Japanese barriers against U.S. exports of agricultural or high-technology products to Japan. U.S. consumers might not be effective politically in opposing such import quotas on foreign goods, even though these quotas may be costly to them, but exporters who want access to foreign markets may, through their lobbying for mutual elimination of import quotas, protect consumer interests.

International negotiation can also help to avoid a **trade war**. The concept of a trade war can best be illustrated with a stylized example.

Imagine there are only two countries in the world, the United States and Japan, and these countries have only two policy choices: free trade or protection. Suppose these are unusually clear-headed governments that can assign definite numerical values to their satisfaction with any particular policy outcome (Table 10-3).

The particular values of the payoffs given in the table represent two assumptions. First, we assume that each country's government would choose protection if it could take the other country's policy as given. That is, whichever policy Japan chooses, the U.S. government is better off with protection. This assumption is by no means necessarily true; many economists would argue that free trade is the best policy for the nation, regardless of what other governments do. Governments, however, must act not only in the public interest but also in their own political interest. For the reasons discussed

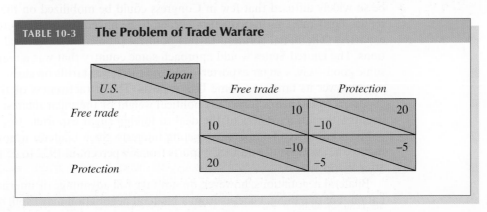

TABLE 10-3   The Problem of Trade Warfare

U.S. \ Japan	Free trade	Protection
Free trade	10 / 10	–10 / 20
Protection	20 / –10	–5 / –5

in the previous section, governments often find it politically difficult to avoid giving protection to some industries.

The second assumption built into Table 10-3 is that even though each government acting individually would be better off with protection, they would both be better off if both chose free trade. That is, the U.S. government has more to gain from an opening of Japanese markets than it has to lose from opening its own markets, and the same is true for Japan. We can justify this assumption simply by appealing to the gains from trade.

To those who have studied game theory, this situation is known as a **Prisoner's dilemma**. Each government, making the best decision for itself, will choose to protect. These choices lead to the outcome in the lower right box of the table. Yet both governments are better off if neither protects: The upper left box of the table yields a payoff that is higher for both countries. By acting unilaterally in what appear to be their best interests, the governments fail to achieve the best outcome possible. If the countries act unilaterally to protect, there is a trade war that leaves both worse off. Trade wars are not as serious as shooting wars, but avoiding them is similar to the problem of avoiding armed conflict or arms races.

Obviously, Japan and the United States need to establish an agreement (such as a treaty) to refrain from protection. Each government will be better off if it limits its own freedom of action, provided the other country limits its freedom of action as well. A treaty can make everyone better off.

This is a highly simplified example. In the real world there are both many countries and many gradations of trade policy between free trade and complete protection against imports. Nonetheless, the example suggests both that there is a need to coordinate trade policies through international agreements and that such agreements can actually make a difference. Indeed, the current system of international trade is built around a series of international agreements.

International Trade Agreements: A Brief History

Internationally coordinated tariff reduction as a trade policy dates back to the 1930s. In 1930, the United States passed a remarkably irresponsible tariff law, the Smoot-Hawley Act. Under this act, tariff rates rose steeply and U.S. trade fell sharply; some economists argue that the Smoot-Hawley Act helped deepen the Great Depression. Within a few years after the act's passage, the U.S. administration concluded that tariffs needed to be reduced, but this posed serious problems of political coalition building. Any tariff reduction would be opposed by those members of Congress whose districts contained firms producing competing goods, while the benefits would be so widely diffused that few in Congress could be mobilized on the other side. To reduce tariff rates, tariff reduction needed to be linked to some concrete benefits for exporters. The initial solution to this political problem was bilateral tariff negotiations. The United States would approach some country that was a major exporter of some good—say, a sugar exporter—and offer to lower tariffs on sugar if that country would lower its tariffs on some U.S. exports. The attractiveness of the deal to U.S. exporters would help counter the political weight of the sugar interest. In the foreign country, the attractiveness of the deal to foreign sugar exporters would balance the political influence of import-competing interests. Such bilateral negotiations helped reduce the average duty on U.S. imports from 59 percent in 1932 to 25 percent shortly after World War II.

Bilateral negotiations, however, do not take full advantage of international coordination. For one thing, benefits from a bilateral negotiation may "spill over" to parties that have not made any concessions. For example, if the United States reduces tariffs on coffee as a result of a deal with Brazil, Colombia will also gain from a higher world coffee price. Furthermore, some advantageous deals may inherently involve more than two partners: The United States sells more to Europe, Europe sells more to Saudi Arabia, Saudi Arabia sells more to Japan, and Japan sells more to the United States. Thus, the next step in international trade liberalization was to proceed to multilateral negotiations involving a number of countries.

Multilateral negotiations began soon after the end of World War II. Originally, diplomats from the victorious Allies imagined such negotiations would take place under the auspices of a proposed body called the International Trade Organization, paralleling the International Monetary Fund and the World Bank (described in the second half of this book). In 1947, unwilling to wait until the ITO was in place, a group of 23 countries began trade negotiations under a provisional set of rules that became known as the **General Agreement on Tariffs and Trade**, or **GATT**. As it turned out, the ITO was never established because it ran into severe political opposition, especially in the United States. So the provisional agreement ended up governing world trade for the next 48 years.

Officially, the GATT was an agreement, not an organization—the countries participating in the agreement were officially designated as "contracting parties," not members. In practice, the GATT did maintain a permanent "secretariat" in Geneva, which everyone referred to as "the GATT." In 1995, the **World Trade Organization**, or **WTO**, was established, finally creating the formal organization envisaged 50 years earlier. However, the GATT rules remain in force, and the basic logic of the system remains the same.

One way to think about the GATT-WTO approach to trade is to use a mechanical analogy: It's like a device designed to push a heavy object, the world economy, gradually up a slope—the path to free trade. To get there requires both "levers" to push the object in the right direction and "ratchets" to prevent backsliding.

The principal ratchet in the system is the process of **binding**. When a tariff rate is "bound," the country imposing the tariff agrees not to raise the rate in the future. At present, almost all tariff rates in developed countries are bound, as are about three-quarters of the rates in developing countries. There is, however, some wiggle room in bound tariffs: A country can raise a tariff if it gets the agreement of other countries, which usually means providing compensation by reducing other tariffs. In practice, binding has been highly effective, with very little backsliding in tariffs over the past half-century.

In addition to binding tariffs, the GATT-WTO system generally tries to prevent non-tariff interventions in trade. Export subsidies are not allowed, with one big exception: Back at the GATT's inception, the United States insisted on a loophole for agricultural exports, which has since been exploited on a large scale by the European Union.

As we pointed out earlier in this chapter, most of the actual cost of protection in the United States comes from import quotas. The GATT-WTO system in effect "grandfathers" existing import quotas, though there has been an ongoing and often successful effort to remove such quotas or convert them to tariffs. New import quotas are generally forbidden except as temporary measures to deal with "market disruption," an undefined phrase usually interpreted to mean surges of imports that threaten to put a domestic sector suddenly out of business.

The lever used to make forward progress is the somewhat stylized process known as a **trade round**, in which a large group of countries get together to negotiate a set of tariff reductions and other measures to liberalize trade. Eight trade rounds have been completed since 1947, the last of which—the Uruguay Round, completed in 1994—established the WTO. In 2001, a meeting in the Persian Gulf city of Doha inaugurated a ninth round, which by 2014 appeared to have failed to achieve an agreement. We'll discuss the reasons for the Doha Round's apparent failure later in this chapter.

The first five trade rounds under the GATT took the form of "parallel" bilateral negotiations, where each country negotiates pairwise with a number of countries at once. For example, if Germany were to offer a tariff reduction that would benefit both France and Italy, it could ask both of them for reciprocal concessions. The ability to make more extensive deals, together with the worldwide economic recovery from the war, helped to permit substantial tariff reductions.

The sixth multilateral trade agreement, known as the Kennedy Round, was completed in 1967. This agreement involved an across-the-board 50 percent reduction in tariffs by the major industrial countries, except for specified industries whose tariffs were left unchanged. The negotiations concerned which industries to exempt rather than the size of the cut for industries not given special treatment. Overall, the Kennedy Round reduced average tariffs by about 35 percent.

The so-called Tokyo Round of trade negotiations (completed in 1979) reduced tariffs by a formula more complex than that of the Kennedy Round. In addition, new codes were established in an effort to control the proliferation of nontariff barriers, such as voluntary export restraints and orderly marketing agreements. Finally, in 1994, an eighth round of negotiations, the so-called Uruguay Round, was completed. The provisions of that round were approved by the U.S. Congress after acrimonious debate; we describe the results of these negotiations below.

The Uruguay Round

Major international trade negotiations invariably open with a ceremony in one exotic locale and conclude with a ceremonial signing in another. The eighth round of global trade negotiations carried out under the GATT began in 1986, with a meeting at the coastal resort of Punta del Este, Uruguay (hence the name Uruguay Round). The participants then repaired to Geneva, where they engaged in years of offers and counteroffers, threats and counterthreats, and, above all, tens of thousands of hours of meetings so boring that even the most experienced diplomat had difficulty staying awake. The round had been scheduled for completion by 1990 but ran into serious political difficulties. In late 1993, the negotiators finally produced a basic document consisting of 400 pages of agreements, together with supplementary documents detailing the specific commitments of member nations with regard to particular markets and products—about 22,000 pages in all. The agreement was signed in Marrakesh, Morocco, in April 1994, and ratified by the major nations—after bitter political controversy in some cases, including in the United States—by the end of that year.

As the length of the document suggests, the end results of the Uruguay Round are not easy to summarize. The most important results, however, may be grouped under two headings, trade liberalization and administrative reforms.

Trade Liberalization

The Uruguay Round, like previous GATT negotiations, cut tariff rates around the world. The numbers can sound impressive: The average tariff imposed by advanced countries fell almost 40 percent as a result of the round. However, tariff rates were already quite low. In fact, the average tariff rate fell only from 6.3 to 3.9 percent, enough to produce only a small increase in world trade.

More important than this overall tariff reduction were the moves to liberalize trade in two important sectors: agriculture and clothing.

World trade in agricultural products has been highly distorted. Japan is notorious for import restrictions that lead to internal prices of rice, beef, and other foods that are several times as high as world market prices; Europe's massive export subsidies under the Common Agricultural Policy were described in Chapter 9. At the beginning of the Uruguay Round, the United States had an ambitious goal: free trade in agricultural products by the year 2000. The actual achievement was far more modest but still significant. The agreement required agricultural exporters to reduce the value of subsidies by 36 percent, and the volume of subsidized exports by 21 percent, over a six-year period. Countries like Japan that protect their farmers with import quotas were required to replace quotas with tariffs, which may not be increased in the future.

World trade in textiles and clothing was also highly distorted by the Multi-Fiber Arrangement, also described in Chapter 9. The Uruguay Round phased out the MFA over a ten-year period, eliminating all quantitative restrictions on trade in textiles and clothing. (Some high tariffs remain in place.) This was a fairly dramatic liberalization—remember, most estimates suggested that protection of clothing imposed a larger cost on U.S. consumers than all other protectionist measures combined. It is worth noting, however, that the formula used in phasing out the MFA was heavily "backloaded": Much of the liberalization was postponed until 2003 and 2004, with the final end of the quotas not taking place until January 1, 2005.

Sure enough, the end of the MFA brought a surge in clothing exports from China. For example, in January 2005, China shipped 27 million pairs of cotton trousers to the United States, up from 1.9 million a year earlier. And there was a fierce political reaction from clothing producers in the United States and Europe. While new restrictions were imposed on Chinese clothing exports, these restrictions were phased out over time; world trade in clothing has, in fact, been largely liberalized. A final important trade action under the Uruguay Round was a new set of rules concerning government procurement, purchases made not by private firms or consumers but by government agencies. Such procurement has long provided protected markets for many kinds of goods, from construction equipment to vehicles. (Recall the box on Hungarian buses in Chapter 9.) The Uruguay Round set new rules that should open up a wide range of government contracts for imported products.

Administrative Reforms: From the GATT to the WTO

Much of the publicity that surrounded the Uruguay Round, and much of the controversy swirling around the world trading system since then, has focused on the round's creation of a new institution, the World Trade Organization. In 1995, this organization replaced the ad hoc secretariat that had administered the GATT. As we'll see in Chapter 12, the WTO has become the organization that opponents of globalization love to hate; it has been accused by both the left and the right of acting as a sort of world government, undermining national sovereignty.

How different is the WTO from the GATT? From a legal point of view, the GATT was a provisional agreement, whereas the WTO is a full-fledged international organization; however, the actual bureaucracy remains small (a staff of 500). An updated version of the original GATT text has been incorporated into the WTO rules. The GATT, however, applied only to trade in goods; world trade in services—that is, intangible things like insurance, consulting, and banking—was not subject to any agreed-upon set of rules. As a result, many countries applied regulations that openly or de facto discriminated against foreign suppliers. The GATT's neglect of trade in services became an increasingly glaring omission, because modern economies have increasingly focused on the production of services rather than physical goods. So the WTO agreement includes rules on trade in services (the General Agreement on Trade in Services, or GATS). In practice, these rules have not yet had much impact on trade in services; their main purpose is to serve as the basis for negotiating future trade rounds.

In addition to a broad shift from producing goods to producing services, advanced countries have also experienced a shift from depending on physical capital to depending on "intellectual property," which is protected by patents and copyrights. (Thirty years ago, General Motors was the quintessential modern corporation; now it's Apple or Google.) Thus, defining the international application of international property rights has also become a major preoccupation. The WTO tries to take on this issue with its Agreement on Trade-Related Aspects of Intellectual Property (TRIPS). The application of TRIPS in the pharmaceutical industry has become a subject of heated debate.

The most important new aspect of the WTO, however, is generally acknowledged to be its "dispute settlement" procedure. A basic problem arises when one country accuses another of violating the rules of the trading system. Suppose, for example, that Canada accuses the United States of unfairly limiting timber imports—and the United States denies the charge. What happens next?

Before the WTO, there were international tribunals in which Canada could press its case, but such proceedings tended to drag on for years, even decades. And even when a ruling had been issued, there was no way to enforce it. This did not mean that the GATT's rules had no force: Neither the United States nor other countries wanted to acquire a reputation as scofflaws, so they made considerable efforts to keep their actions "GATT-legal." But gray-area cases tended to go unresolved.

The WTO contains a much more formal and effective procedure. Panels of experts are selected to hear cases, usually reaching a final conclusion in less than a year; even with appeals, the procedure is not supposed to take more than 15 months.

Suppose the WTO concludes that a nation has, in fact, been violating the rules—and the country nonetheless refuses to change its policy. Then what? The WTO itself has no enforcement powers. What it can do is grant the country that filed the complaint the right to retaliate. To use our Canada–U.S. example, the government of Canada might be given the right to impose restrictions on U.S. exports without being considered in violation of WTO rules. In the case of the banana dispute described in the box on page 298, a WTO ruling found the European Union in violation; when Europe remained recalcitrant, the United States temporarily imposed tariffs on such items as designer handbags.

The hope and expectation is that few disputes will get this far. In many cases, the threat to bring a dispute before the WTO should lead to a settlement; in the great majority of other cases, countries accept the WTO ruling and change their policies.

The following box describes an example of the WTO dispute settlement procedure at work: the U.S.–Venezuela dispute over imported gasoline. As the box explains, this case has also become a prime example for those who accuse the WTO of undermining national sovereignty.

Benefits and Costs

The economic impact of the Uruguay Round is difficult to estimate. If nothing else, think about the logistics: To do an estimate, one must translate an immense document from one impenetrable jargon (legalese) into another (economese), assign numbers to the translation, then feed the whole thing into a computer model of the world economy.

SETTLING A DISPUTE—AND CREATING ONE

The very first application of the WTO's new dispute settlement procedure has also been one of the most controversial. To WTO supporters, it illustrates the new system's effectiveness. To opponents, it shows that the organization stands in the way of important social goals such as protecting the environment.

The case arose out of new U.S. air pollution standards. These standards set rules for the chemical composition of gasoline sold in the United States. A uniform standard would clearly have been legal under WTO rules. However, the new standards included some loopholes: Refineries in the United States, or those selling 75 percent or more of their output in the United States, were given "baselines" that depended on their 1990 pollutant levels. This provision generally set a less strict standard than was set for imported gasoline, and thus in effect introduced a preference for gasoline from domestic refineries.

Venezuela, which ships considerable quantities of gasoline to the United States, brought a complaint against the new pollution rules early in 1995. Venezuela argued that the rules violated the principle of "national treatment," which says that imported goods should be subject to the same regulations as domestic goods (so that regulations are not used as an indirect form of protectionism). A year later, the panel appointed by the WTO ruled in Venezuela's favor; the United States appealed, but the appeal was rejected. The United States and Venezuela then negotiated a revised set of rules.

At one level, this outcome was a demonstration of the WTO doing exactly what it was supposed to do. The United States had introduced measures that pretty clearly violated the letter of its trade agreements; when a smaller, less influential country appealed against those measures, it got fairly quick results.

On the other hand, environmentalists were understandably upset: The WTO ruling, in effect, blocked a measure that would have made the air cleaner. Furthermore, there was little question that the clean-air rules were promulgated in good faith—that is, they were really intended to reduce air pollution, not to exclude exports.

Defenders of the WTO point out that the United States clearly could have written a rule that did not discriminate against imports; the fact that it had not done so was a political concession to the refining industry, which *did* in effect constitute a sort of protectionism. The most you can say is that the WTO's rules made it more difficult for U.S. environmentalists to strike a political deal with the industry.

In the mythology of the anti-globalization movement, which we discuss in Chapter 12, the WTO's intervention against clean-air standards has taken on iconic status: The case is seen as a prime example of how the organization deprives nations of their sovereignty, preventing them from following socially and environmentally responsible policies. The reality of the case, however, is nowhere near that clearcut: If the United States had imposed a "clean" clean-air rule that had not discriminated among sources, the WTO would have had no complaints.

The most widely cited estimates are those of the GATT itself and of the Organization for Economic Cooperation and Development, another international organization (this one consisting only of rich countries and based in Paris). Both estimates suggest a gain to the world economy as a whole of more than $200 billion annually, raising world income by about 1 percent. As always, there are dissenting estimates on both sides. Some economists claim that the estimated gains are exaggerated, particularly because the estimates assume that exports and imports responded strongly to the new liberalizing moves. A probably larger minority of critics argues that these estimates are considerably too low, for the "dynamic" reasons discussed earlier in this chapter.

In any case, it is clear that the usual logic of trade liberalization applies: The costs of the Uruguay Round were felt by concentrated, often well-organized groups, while the benefit accrued to broad, diffuse populations. The progress on agriculture hurt the small but influential populations of farmers in Europe, Japan, and other countries where agricultural prices are far above world levels. These losses were much more than offset by gains to consumers and taxpayers in those countries, but because these benefits were very widely spread, they were little noticed. Similarly, the liberalization of trade in textiles and clothing produced some concentrated pain for workers and companies in those industries, offset by considerably larger but far less visible consumer gains.

Given these strong distributional impacts of the Uruguay Round, it is actually remarkable that an agreement was reached at all. Indeed, after the failure to achieve anything close to agreement by the 1990 target, many commentators began to pronounce the whole trade negotiation process to be dead. That in the end, agreement was achieved, if on a more modest scale than originally hoped, may be attributed to an interlocking set of political calculations. In the United States, the gains to agricultural exporters and the prospective gains to service exporters if the GATT opened the door to substantial liberalization helped offset the complaints of the clothing industry. Many developing countries supported the round because of the new opportunities it would offer to their own textile and clothing exports. Also, some of the "concessions" negotiated under the agreement were an excuse to make policy changes that would eventually have happened anyway. For example, the sheer expense of Europe's Common Agricultural Policy in a time of budget deficits made it ripe for cutting in any case.

An important factor in the final success of the round, however, was fear of what would happen if it failed. By 1993, protectionist currents were evidently running strong in the United States and elsewhere. Trade negotiators in countries that might otherwise have refused to go along with the agreement—such as France, Japan, or South Korea, in all of which powerful farm lobbies angrily opposed trade liberalization—therefore feared that failure to agree would be dangerous. That is, they feared a failed round would not merely mean lack of progress but substantial backsliding on the progress made toward free trade over the previous four decades.

CASE STUDY   The Salmon War

In July 2010, the 20-year-long Salmon War between Norway and Scotland finally came to an end. The dispute dates back to 1989, when the first restrictions on salmon imports from Norway were put into place. Scottish and Irish salmon farmers claimed that Norwegian fish were being exported to the EU at a lower price than the cost of production. At that time the average production cost was 3.7 euros per kilogram in Norway while it was 4.7 euros in Scotland. Later it was shown that the main reason for this difference was a higher rate of wastage in Scottish fish farms.

In response to the claim, the EU Commission proposed a tariff of 11.3 percent on Norwegian salmon. The proposal was repealed after Norway started to freeze and put into storage a large part of its production. In addition, 12 million smolts (young salmons) were destroyed. Both measures were intended to reduce the quantity sent to the market. However, Scottish and Irish fish farmers maintained their complaint, and in 1991 the EU fixed a minimum price on Norwegian salmon; later, a 9.88 percent tariff and an additional 3.8 percent subsidize tax were imposed.

Negotiations in 1997 between Norway and the EU resulted in the "Salmon Agreement." This agreement implied an export tax, a minimum price of 2.9 euros per kilogram, and a cap on the export quantity. Due to economics of scale the most efficient Norwegian salmon producers were able to sell for a price as low as 2.5 euros per kilogram and still make a profit. After an evaluation of Norwegian salmon producers in 2002, the EU scrapped the Salmon Agreement because it found no reason to punish Norway anymore. However, the conflict was not over.

In the spring of 2004, the European Union Salmon Producers Group, a minority group of Irish and Scottish salmon producers, with 20 percent of the EU production, asked for protection from import of salmon to the EU. As a result, a safeguard measurement was imposed in which Norway got an export quota combined with a tariff. The rate of the tariff varied from 6.8 to 24.5 percent. A minimum import price was also fixed. This led to protests from the Danish and French fish-processing industries, which use Norwegian salmon.

In 2006, Norway brought the antidumping measures before the WTO's settlement body. A year later, the WTO stated that the measures were inconsistent with international trade. The European Commission initiated a review of the measures and concluded that there were no grounds for continuing with the measures, as no evidence of dumping had been found. In 2010, the EU Council decided to repeal the antidumping measures on imports of farmed salmon from Norway.

The Doha Disappointment

The ninth major round of world trade negotiations began in 2001 with a ceremony in the Persian Gulf city of Doha. Like previous rounds, this one was marked by difficult negotiation. But as of the summer of 2010, it appeared that something new had happened: For the first time since the creation of the GATT, a round of trade negotiations appeared to have broken down with no agreement in sight.

It's important to understand that the apparent failure of the Doha Round does not undo the progress achieved in previous trade negotiations. Remember that the world trading system is a combination of "levers"—international trade negotiations that push trade liberalization forward—and "ratchets," mainly the practice of binding tariffs, which prevent backsliding. The levers seem to have failed in the latest trade round, but the ratchets are still in place: The reductions in tariff rates that took place in the previous eight rounds remain in effect. As a result, world trade remains much freer than at any previous point in modern history.

In fact, Doha's apparent failure owes a lot to the success of previous trade negotiations. Because previous negotiations had been so successful at reducing trade barriers, the remaining barriers to trade are fairly low, so that the potential gains from further trade liberalization are modest. Indeed, barriers to trade in most manufactured goods other than apparel and textiles are now more or less trivial. Most of the potential gains from a move to freer trade would come from reducing tariffs and export subsidies in agriculture—which has been the last sector to be liberalized because it's the most sensitive sector politically.

Table 10-4 illustrates this point. It shows a World Bank estimate of where the welfare gains from "full liberalization"—that is, the elimination of all remaining barriers to trade and export subsidies—would come from, and how they would be distributed across countries. In the modern world, agricultural goods account for less than 10 percent of total international trade. Nonetheless, according to the World Bank's

TABLE 10-4	Percentage Distribution of Potential Gains from Free Trade			
	Full Liberalization of:			
Economy	Agriculture and Food	Textiles and Clothing	Other Merchandise	All Goods
Developed	46	6	3	55
Developing	17	8	20	45
All	63	14	23	100

Source: Kym Anderson and Will Martin, "Agricultural Trade Reform and the Doha Agenda," *The World Economy* 28 (September 2005), pp. 1301–1327.

estimate, liberalizing agricultural trade would produce 63 percent of the total world gains from free trade for the world as a whole. And these gains are very hard to get at. As already described, farmers in rich countries are highly effective at getting favors from the political process.

The proposals that came closest to actually getting accepted in the Doha Round in fact fell far short of full liberalization. As a result, the likely gains even from a successful round would have been fairly small. Table 10-5 shows World Bank estimates of the welfare gains, as a percentage of income, under two scenarios of how Doha might have played out: an "ambitious" scenario that would have been very difficult to achieve, and a "less ambitious" scenario in which "sensitive" sectors would have been spared major liberalization. The gains for the world as a whole even in the ambitious scenario would have been only 0.18 percent of GDP; in the more plausible scenario, the gains would have been less than a third as large. For middle- and lower-income countries, the gains would have been even smaller. (Why would China have actually lost? Because, as

DO AGRICULTURAL SUBSIDIES HURT THE THIRD WORLD?

One of the major complaints of developing countries during the Doha negotiations was the continuing existence of large agricultural export and production subsidies in rich countries. The U.S. cotton subsidy, which depresses world cotton prices and therefore hurts cotton growers in West Africa, is the most commonly cited example.

But we learned in Chapter 9 that an export subsidy normally raises the welfare of the importing country, which gets to buy goods more cheaply. So shouldn't export subsidies by rich countries actually help poorer countries?

The answer is that in many cases they do. The estimates shown in Table 10-5 indicate that a successful Doha Round would actually have hurt China. Why? Because China, which exports manufactured goods and imports food and other

agricultural products, would be hurt by the removal of agricultural subsidies.

And it's not just China that may actually benefit from rich-country export subsidies. Some third world farmers are hurt by low prices of subsidized food exports from Europe and the United States—but urban residents in the third world benefit, and so do those farmers producing goods, such as coffee, that don't compete with the subsidized products.

Africa is a case in point. A survey of estimates of the likely effects of the Doha Round on low-income African nations found that, in most cases, African countries would actually be made worse off, because the negative effects of higher food prices would more than offset the gains from higher prices for crops such as cotton.

TABLE 10-5	Percentage Gains in Income under Two Doha Scenarios	
	Ambitious	**Less Ambitious**
High-income	0.20	0.05
Middle-income	0.10	0.00
China	−0.02	−0.05
Low-income	0.05	0.01
World	0.18	0.04

Source: See Table 10-4.

explained in the box above, it would have ended up paying higher prices for imported agricultural goods.)

The smallness of the numbers in Table 10-5 helps explain why the round failed. Poor countries saw little in the proposals for them; they pressed for much bigger concessions from rich countries. The governments of rich countries, in turn, refused to take the political risk of crossing powerful interest groups, especially farmers, without something in return—and poor countries were unwilling to offer the deep cuts in their remaining tariffs that might have been sufficient.

There was a more or less desperate attempt to revive the Doha Round in June 2007 because of the U.S. political calendar. Normally, Congress gives U.S. presidents a special privilege called trade promotion authority, also known informally as fast-track. When trade promotion authority is in effect, the president can send Congress a trade agreement and demand an up-or-down vote—members of Congress can't introduce amendments that, say, give special protection to industries in their home districts. Without this authority, trade agreements tend to get warped beyond recognition.

But President Bush's trade promotion authority was scheduled to expire at the end of July 2007, and a Democratic Congress wasn't going to give new authority to a lame-duck Republican president. Everyone realized, then, that a failure to reach a deal in the summer of 2007 would ensure no deal before well into the next president's administration. So a meeting was held in the German city of Potsdam between the four key players: the United States, the European Union, Brazil, and India (China sat on the sidelines). The result was an impasse. The United States and the European Union blamed Brazil and India for being unwilling to open their markets to manufactured goods, while Brazil and India accused the United States and the European Union of doing too little on agriculture.

There was one more attempt to revive the round, in July 2008. But talks collapsed after only eight days, over disagreements on agricultural trade among the United States, India, and China. At the time of writing, the whole round appeared to be in a state of suspension, with nobody admitting failure but no active negotiations underway.

Preferential Trading Agreements

The international trade agreements that we have described so far all involved a "nondiscriminatory" reduction in tariff rates. For example, when the United States agrees with Germany to lower its tariff on imported machinery, the new tariff rate applies to machinery from any nation rather than just imports from Germany. Such nondiscrimination is normal in most tariffs. Indeed, the United States grants many countries a status known formally as that of "most favored nation" (MFN), a guarantee that their exporters will pay tariffs no higher than that of the nation that pays the lowest. All countries granted MFN status thus pay the same rates. Tariff reductions under the GATT always—with one important exception—are made on an MFN basis.

There are some important cases, however, in which nations establish **preferential trading agreements** under which the tariffs they apply to each other's products are lower than the rates on the same goods coming from other countries. The GATT in general prohibits such agreements but makes a rather strange exception: It is against the rules for country A to have lower tariffs on imports from country B than on those from country C, but it is acceptable if countries B and C agree to have zero tariffs on each other's products. That is, the GATT forbids preferential trading agreements in general, as a violation of the MFN principle, but allows them if they lead to free trade between the agreeing countries.[7]

In general, two or more countries agreeing to establish free trade can do so in one of two ways. They can establish a **free trade area** in which each country's goods can be shipped to the other without tariffs, but in which the countries set tariffs against the outside world independently. Or they can establish a **customs union** in which the countries must agree on tariff rates. The North American Free Trade Agreement—which establishes free trade among Canada, the United States, and Mexico—creates a free trade area: There is no requirement in the agreement that, for example, Canada and Mexico have the same tariff rate on textiles from China. The European Union, on the other hand, is a full customs union. All of the countries must agree to charge the same tariff rate on each imported good. Each system has both advantages and disadvantages; these are discussed in the accompanying box.

Subject to the qualifications mentioned earlier in this chapter, tariff reduction is a good thing that raises economic efficiency. At first, it might seem that preferential tariff reductions are also good, if not as good as reducing tariffs all around. After all, isn't half a loaf better than none?

Perhaps surprisingly, this conclusion is too optimistic. It is possible for a country to make itself worse off by joining a customs union. The reason may be illustrated by a hypothetical example using Britain, France, and the United States. The United States is a low-cost producer of wheat ($4 per bushel), France a medium-cost producer ($6 per bushel), and Britain a high-cost producer ($8 per bushel). Both Britain and France maintain tariffs against all wheat imports. If Britain forms a customs union with France, the tariff against French, but not U.S., wheat will be abolished. Is this good or bad for Britain? To answer this, consider two cases.

First, suppose Britain's initial tariff was high enough to exclude wheat imports from either France or the United States. For example, with a tariff of $5 per bushel, it would cost $9 to import U.S. wheat and $11 to import French wheat, so British consumers would buy $8 British wheat instead. When the tariff on French wheat is eliminated, imports from France will replace British production. From Britain's point of view, this is a gain, because it costs $8 to produce a bushel of wheat domestically, while Britain needs to produce only $6 worth of export goods to pay for a bushel of French wheat.

---

[7]The logic here seems to be legal rather than economic. Nations are allowed to have free trade within their boundaries: Nobody insists that California wine pay the same tariff as French wine when it is shipped to New York. That is, the MFN principle does not apply within political units. But what is a political unit? The GATT sidesteps that potentially thorny question by allowing any group of economies to do what countries do, and establish free trade within some defined boundary.

FREE TRADE AREA VERSUS CUSTOMS UNION

The difference between a free trade area and a customs union is, in brief, that the first is politically straightforward but an administrative headache, while the second is just the opposite.

Consider first the case of a customs union. Once such a union is established, tariff administration is relatively easy: Goods must pay tariffs when they cross the border of the union, but from then on can be shipped freely between countries. A cargo that is unloaded at Marseilles or Rotterdam must pay duties there, but will not face any additional charges if it then goes by truck to Munich. To make this simple system work, however, the countries must agree on tariff rates: The duty must be the same whether the cargo is unloaded at Marseilles, Rotterdam, or, for that matter, Hamburg, because otherwise, importers would choose the point of entry that minimizes their fees. So a customs union requires that Germany, France, the Netherlands, and all the other countries agree to charge the same tariffs. This is not easily done: Countries are, in effect, ceding part of their sovereignty to a supranational entity, the European Union.

This has been possible in Europe for a variety of reasons, including the belief that economic unity would help cement the postwar political alliance between European democracies. (One of the founders of the European Union once joked that it should erect a statue of Joseph Stalin, without whose menace the Union might never have been created.) But elsewhere these conditions are lacking. The three nations that formed NAFTA would find it very difficult to cede control over tariffs to any supranational body; if nothing else, it would be hard to devise any arrangement that would give due weight to U.S. interests without effectively allowing the United States to dictate trade policy to Canada and Mexico. NAFTA, therefore, while it permits Mexican goods to enter the United States without tariffs and vice versa, does not require that Mexico and the United States adopt a common external tariff on goods they import from other countries.

This, however, raises a different problem. Under NAFTA, a shirt made by Mexican workers can be brought into the United States freely. But suppose the United States wants to maintain high tariffs on shirts imported from other countries, while Mexico does not impose similar tariffs. What is to prevent someone from shipping a shirt from, say, Bangladesh to Mexico, then putting it on a truck bound for Chicago?

The answer is that even though the United States and Mexico may have free trade, goods shipped from Mexico to the United States must still pass through a customs inspection. And they can enter the United States without duty only if they have documents proving that they are in fact Mexican goods, not transshipped imports from third countries.

But what is a Mexican shirt? If a shirt comes from Bangladesh, but Mexicans sew on the buttons, does that make it Mexican? Probably not. But if everything except the buttons were made in Mexico, it probably should be considered Mexican. The point is that administering a free trade area that is not a customs union requires not only that the countries continue to check goods at the border, but that they specify an elaborate set of "rules of origin" that determine whether a good is eligible to cross the border without paying a tariff.

As a result, free trade agreements like NAFTA impose a large burden of paperwork, which may be a significant obstacle to trade even when such trade is in principle free.

On the other hand, suppose the tariff was lower, for example, $3 per bushel, so that before joining the customs union, Britain bought its wheat from the United States (at a cost to consumers of $7 per bushel) rather than producing its own wheat. When the customs union is formed, consumers will buy French wheat at $6 rather than U.S. wheat at $7. So imports of wheat from the United States will cease. However,

U.S. wheat is really cheaper than French wheat; the $3 tax that British consumers must pay on U.S. wheat returns to Britain in the form of government revenue and is therefore not a net cost to the British economy. Britain will have to devote more resources to exports to pay for its wheat imports and will be worse off rather than better off.

DO TRADE PREFERENCES HAVE APPEAL?

The European Union has slipped repeatedly into bunches of trouble over the question of trade preferences for bananas.

Most of the world's banana exports come from several small Central American nations—the original "banana republics." Several European nations, however, have traditionally bought their bananas instead from their past or present West Indian colonies in the Caribbean. To protect the island producers, France and the United Kingdom have historically imposed import quotas against the "dollar bananas" of Central America, which are typically about 40 percent cheaper than the West Indian product. Germany, however, which has never had West Indian colonies, allowed free entry to dollar bananas.

With the integration of European markets after 1992, the existing banana regime became impossible to maintain because it was easy to import the cheaper dollar bananas into Germany and then ship them elsewhere in Europe. To prevent this outcome, the European Commission announced plans in 1993 to impose a new common European import quota against dollar bananas. Germany angrily protested the move and even denied its legality: The Germans pointed out that the Treaty of Rome, which established the European Community, contains an explicit guarantee (the "banana protocol") that Germany would be able to import bananas freely.

Why did the Germans go ape about bananas? During the years of communist rule in East Germany, bananas were a rare luxury. The sudden availability of inexpensive bananas after the fall of the Berlin Wall made them a symbol of freedom. So the German government was very unwilling to introduce a policy that would sharply increase banana prices.

In the end, the Germans grudgingly went along with a new, unified system of European trade preferences on bananas. But that did not end the controversy: In 1995, the United States entered the fray, claiming that by monkeying around with the existing system of preferences, the Europeans were hurting the interests not only of Central American nations but also those of a powerful U.S. corporation, the Chiquita Banana Company, whose CEO had donated large sums to both Democratic and Republican politicians.

In 1997, the World Trade Organization found that Europe's banana import regime violated international trade rules. Europe then imposed a somewhat revised regime, but this halfhearted attempt to resolve the banana split proved fruitless. The dispute with the United States escalated, with the United States eventually retaliating by imposing high tariffs on a variety of European goods, including designer handbags and pecorino cheese.

In 2001, Europe and the United States agreed on a plan to phase out the banana import quotas over time. The plan created much distress and alarm in Caribbean nations, which feared dire consequences from their loss of privileged access to the European market. But even then the story wasn't over. In January 2005, the European Union announced it would eliminate import quotas on bananas, but that it would *triple* the tariff on bananas that did not come from the so-called ACP countries (African, Caribbean, and Pacific— essentially, former European colonies). Latin American countries immediately moved to challenge the new tariff, and in December 2007 the WTO ruled that Europe's latest banana regime, like its predecessor, was illegal. (Chiquita's stock price jumped with the news.)

Finally, in December 2009, the European Union reached an agreement with Latin American banana producers. It wouldn't completely eliminate trade preferences, but it would cut tariffs on bananas by a third over a seven-year period.

This possibility of a loss is another example of the theory of the second best. Think of Britain as initially having two policies that distort incentives: a tariff against U.S. wheat and a tariff against French wheat. Although the tariff against French wheat may seem to distort incentives, it may actually help to offset the distortion of incentives resulting from the tariff against the United States by encouraging consumption of the cheaper U.S. wheat. Thus, removing the tariff on French wheat can actually reduce welfare.

Returning to our two cases, notice that Britain gains if the formation of a customs union leads to new trade—French wheat replacing domestic production—while it loses if the trade within the customs union simply replaces trade with countries outside the union. In the analysis of preferential trading arrangements, the first case is referred to as **trade creation**, while the second is **trade diversion**. Whether a customs union is desirable or undesirable depends on whether it mainly leads to trade creation or trade diversion.

CASE STUDY   Trade Diversion in South America

In 1991, four South American nations, Argentina, Brazil, Paraguay, and Uruguay, formed a free trade area known as Mercosur. The pact had an immediate and dramatic effect on trade: Within four years, the value of trade among the nations tripled. Leaders in the region proudly claimed Mercosur as a major success, part of a broader package of economic reform.

But while Mercosur clearly was successful in increasing intraregional trade, the theory of preferential trading areas tells us that this need not be a good thing: If the new trade came at the expense of trade that would otherwise have taken place with the rest of the world—that is, if the pact diverted trade instead of created it—it might actually have reduced welfare. And sure enough, in 1996 a study prepared by the World Bank's chief trade economist concluded that despite Mercosur's success in increasing regional trade—or rather, because that success came at the expense of other trade—the net effects on the economies involved were probably negative.

In essence, the report argued that as a result of Mercosur, consumers in the member countries were being induced to buy expensively produced manufactured goods from their neighbors rather than cheaper but heavily tariffed goods from other countries. In particular, because of Mercosur, Brazil's highly protected and somewhat inefficient auto industry had in effect acquired a captive market in Argentina, thus displacing imports from elsewhere, just like our text example in which French wheat displaces American wheat in the British market. "These findings," concluded the initial draft of the report, "appear to constitute the most convincing, and disturbing, evidence produced thus far concerning the potential adverse effects of regional trade arrangements."

But that is not what the final, published report said. The initial draft was leaked to the press and generated a firestorm of protest from Mercosur governments, Brazil in particular. Under pressure, the World Bank first delayed publication, then eventually released a version that included a number of caveats. Still, even in its published version, the report made a fairly strong case that Mercosur, if not entirely counterproductive, nonetheless has produced a considerable amount of trade diversion.

SUMMARY

1. Although few countries practice free trade, most economists continue to hold up free trade as a desirable policy. This advocacy rests on three lines of argument. First is a formal case for the efficiency gains from free trade that is simply the cost-benefit analysis of trade policy read in reverse. Second, many economists believe that free trade produces additional gains that go beyond this formal analysis. Finally, given the difficulty of translating complex economic analysis into real policies, even those who do not see free trade as the best imaginable policy see it as a useful rule of thumb.

2. There is an intellectually respectable case for deviating from free trade. One argument that is clearly valid in principle is that countries can improve their terms of trade through optimal tariffs and export taxes. This argument is not too important in practice, however. Small countries cannot have much influence on their import or export prices, so they cannot use tariffs or other policies to raise their terms of trade. Large countries, on the other hand, can influence their terms of trade, but in imposing tariffs, they run the risk of disrupting trade agreements and provoking retaliation.

3. The other argument for deviating from free trade rests on domestic market failures. If some domestic market, such as the labor market, fails to function properly, deviating from free trade can sometimes help reduce the consequences of this malfunctioning. The theory of the second best states that if one market fails to work properly, it is no longer optimal for the government to abstain from intervention in other markets. A tariff may raise welfare if there is a marginal social benefit to production of a good that is not captured by producer surplus measures.

4. Although market failures are probably common, the domestic market failure argument should not be applied too freely. First, it is an argument for domestic policies rather than trade policies; tariffs are always an inferior, "second-best" way to offset domestic market failure, which is always best treated at its source. Furthermore, market failure is difficult to analyze well enough to be sure of the appropriate policy recommendation.

5. In practice, trade policy is dominated by considerations of income distribution. No single way of modeling the politics of trade policy exists, but several useful ideas have been proposed. Political scientists often argue that policies are determined by competition among political parties that try to attract as many votes as possible. In the simplest case, this leads to the adoption of policies that serve the interests of the median voter. While useful for thinking about many issues, however, this approach seems to yield unrealistic predictions for trade policies, which typically favor the interest of small, concentrated groups over that of the general public. Economists and political scientists generally explain this by appealing to the problem of collective action. Because individuals may have little incentive to act politically on behalf of groups to which they belong, those groups that are well organized—typically small groups with a lot at stake—are often able to get policies that serve their interests at the expense of the majority.

6. If trade policy were made on a purely domestic basis, progress toward freer trade would be very difficult to achieve. In fact, however, industrial countries have achieved substantial reductions in tariffs through a process of international negotiation. International negotiation helps the cause of tariff reduction in two ways: It helps broaden the constituency for freer trade by giving exporters a direct stake, and it helps governments avoid the mutually disadvantageous trade wars that internationally uncoordinated policies could bring.

7. Although some progress was made in the 1930s toward trade liberalization via bilateral agreements, since World War II international coordination has taken place primarily via multilateral agreements under the auspices of the General Agreement on Tariffs and Trade. The GATT, which comprises both a bureaucracy and a set of rules of conduct, is the central institution of the international trading system. The most recent worldwide GATT agreement also set up a new organization, the World Trade Organization (WTO), to monitor and enforce the agreement.

8. In addition to the overall reductions in tariffs that have taken place through multilateral negotiation, some groups of countries have negotiated preferential trading agreements under which they lower tariffs with respect to each other but not the rest of the world. Two kinds of preferential trading agreements are allowed under the GATT: customs unions, in which the members of the agreement set up common external tariffs, and free trade areas, in which members do not charge tariffs on each other's products but set their own tariff rates against the outside world. Either kind of agreement has ambiguous effects on economic welfare. If joining such an agreement leads to replacement of high-cost domestic production by imports from other members of the agreement—the case of trade creation—a country gains. But if joining leads to the replacement of low-cost imports from outside the zone with higher-cost goods from member nations—the case of trade diversion—a country loses.

KEY TERMS

binding, p. 287

collective action, p. 280

customs union, p. 296

domestic market failures, p. 275

efficiency case for free trade, p. 269

free trade area, p. 296

General Agreement on Tariffs and Trade (GATT), p. 287

international negotiation, p. 285

marginal social benefit, p. 275

median voter, p. 279

optimum tariff, p. 274

political argument for free trade, p. 271

preferential trading agreement, p. 296

Prisoner's dilemma, p. 286

rent seeking, p. 271

terms of trade argument for a tariff, p. 274

theory of the second best, p. 276

trade creation, p. 299

trade diversion, p. 299

trade round, p. 287

trade war, p. 285

World Trade Organization (WTO), p. 287

PROBLEMS   MyEconLab

1. According to the WTO and its MFN principle, all preferential tariffs granted to a member have to be extended to all others. However, there are exceptions to this rule; and this is where all preferential trade agreements originate. The EU, for example, is an exception, even if it is of the most complete kind. List the typologies existing in this area and how would a country select which to belong to? Explain with an example.

2. Which of the following are potentially valid arguments for tariffs or export subsidies, and which are not? Explain your answers.

   a. "The more oil the United States imports, the higher the price of oil will go in the next world shortage."

   b. "The growing exports of off-season fruit from Chile, which now accounts for 80 percent of the U.S. supply of such produce as winter grapes, are contributing to sharply falling prices of these former luxury goods."

    c. "U.S. farm exports don't just mean higher incomes for farmers—they mean higher income for everyone who sells goods and services to the U.S. farm sector."

    d. "Semiconductors are the crude oil of technology; if we don't produce our own chips, the flow of information that is crucial to every industry that uses micro-electronics will be impaired."

    e. "The real price of timber has fallen 40 percent, and thousands of timber workers have been forced to look for other jobs."

3. A small country can import a good at a world price of 10 per unit. The domestic supply curve of the good is

$$S = 20 + 10P$$

The demand curve is

$$D = 400 - 5P$$

In addition, each unit of production yields a marginal social benefit of 10.

    a. Calculate the total effect on welfare of a tariff of 5 per unit levied on imports.

    b. Calculate the total effect of a production subsidy of 5 per unit.

    c. Why does the production subsidy produce a greater gain in welfare than the tariff?

    d. What would the optimal production subsidy be?

4. Suppose demand and supply are exactly as described in problem 3, but there is no marginal social benefit to production. However, for political reasons the government counts a dollar's worth of gain to producers as being worth $3 of either consumer gain or government revenue. Calculate the effects *on the government's objective* of a tariff of 5 per unit.

5. Upon Poland's entering the European Union, suppose it is discovered that the cost of automobile production in Poland is €20,000 while it is €30,000 in Germany. Suppose the EU, which has a customs union, has an X percent tariff on automobiles and the costs of production are equal to Y (valued in euros) in Japan. Comment on whether the addition of Poland to the European Union would result in trade *creation* or trade *diversion* under the following scenarios:

    a. $X = 50\%$ and $Y = €18,000$

    b. $X = 100\%$ and $Y = €18,000$

    c. $X = 100\%$ and $Y = €12,000$

6. "There is no point in the United States complaining about trade policies in Japan and Europe. Each country has a right to do whatever is in its own best interest. Instead of complaining about foreign trade policies, the United States should let other countries go their own way, and give up our own prejudices about free trade and follow suit." Discuss both the economics and the political economy of this viewpoint.

7. What is a rent-seeking decision and how is it applied in practice?

8. Free trade is a precise political choice, with arguments for and against it. One of them includes providing incentives to companies to internationalize themselves and export to new countries, thus fostering learning and innovation, which eventually benefits the whole economy and helps competitiveness. Discuss this approach with examples.

9. One argument against free trade is the terms of trade—since an export subsidy worsens the terms, it has to be conceived as a negative one, a tax paid by foreigners. However, the optimum export tax is one that maximizes national gain without harming export. How would it work in the case of a commodity exporting country like Indonesia?

FURTHER READINGS

W. Max Corden. *Trade Policy and Economic Welfare*. Oxford: Clarendon Press, 1974. The classic survey of economic arguments for and against protection.

I. M. Destler. *American Trade Politics*, 4th edition. Washington, D.C.: Peterson Institute for International Economics, 2005. A comprehensive portrait of the real-world process of trade policy making, and its evolution over time.

Gene M. Grossman and Elhanan Helpman. *Interest Groups and Trade Policy*. Princeton: Princeton University Press, 2002. A collection of papers and case studies on modern political economy models of trade policy.

Jeffrey Schott. *The Uruguay Round: An Assessment*. Washington, D.C.: Institute for International Economics, 1994. A mercifully brief and readable survey of the issues and accomplishments of the most recent GATT round, together with a survey of much of the relevant research.

Peter Van den Bossche. *The Law and Policy of the World Trade Organization*. Cambridge: Cambridge University Press, 2008. A comprehensive survey, with texts and other materials, of the legal framework of international trade.

World Trade Organization, *Understanding the WTO*. Geneva: World Trade Organization, 2007. A useful self-survey of the institution's role and history.

MyEconLab Can Help You Get a Better Grade

MyEconLab   If your exam were tomorrow, would you be ready? For each chapter, MyEconLab Practice Tests and Study Plans pinpoint sections you have mastered and those you need to study. That way, you are more efficient with your study time, and you are better prepared for your exams.

To see how it works, turn to page 41 and then go to

www.myeconlab.com

Proving that the Optimum Tariff Is Positive

A tariff always improves the terms of trade of a large country but at the same time distorts production and consumption. This appendix shows that for a sufficiently small tariff, the terms of trade gain is always larger than the distortion loss. Thus, there is always an optimal tariff that is positive.

To make the point, we focus on the case where all demand and supply curves are *linear*, that is, are straight lines.

Demand and Supply

We assume that Home, the importing country, has a demand curve whose equation is

$$D = a - b\widetilde{P}, \tag{10A-1}$$

where $\widetilde{P}$ is the internal price of the good, and a supply curve whose equation is

$$Q = e + f\widetilde{P}. \tag{10A-2}$$

Home's import demand is equal to the difference between domestic demand and supply,

$$D - Q = (a - e) - (b + f)\widetilde{P}. \tag{10A-3}$$

Foreign's export supply is also a straight line,

$$(Q^* - D^*) = g + hP_W, \tag{10A-4}$$

where P_W is the world price. The internal price in Home will exceed the world price by the tariff

$$\widetilde{P} = P_W + t. \tag{10A-5}$$

The Tariff and Prices

A tariff drives a wedge between internal and world prices, driving the internal Home price up and the world price down (Figure 10A-1).

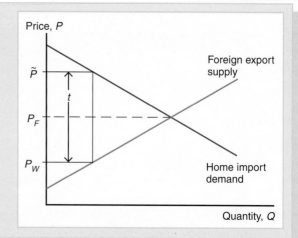

FIGURE 10A-1

Effects of a Tariff on Prices

In a linear model, we can calculate the exact effect of a tariff on prices.

In world equilibrium, Home import demand equals Foreign export supply:

$$(a - e) - (b + f) \times (P_W + t) = g + hP_W. \tag{10A-6}$$

Let P_F be the world price that would prevail if there were no tariff. Then a tariff, t, will raise the internal price to

$$\widetilde{P} = P_F + th/(b + f + h), \tag{10A-7}$$

while lowering the world price to

$$P_W = P_F - t(b + f)/(b + f + h). \tag{10A-8}$$

(For a small country, foreign supply is highly elastic; that is, h is very large. So for a small country, a tariff will have little effect on the world price while raising the domestic price almost one-for-one.)

The Tariff and Domestic Welfare

We now use what we have learned to derive the effects of a tariff on Home's welfare (Figure 10A-2). Q^1 and D^1 represent the free trade levels of consumption and production. With a tariff, the internal price rises, with the result that Q rises to Q^2 and D falls to D^2, where

$$Q^2 = Q^1 + tfh/(b + f + h) \tag{10A-9}$$

and

$$D^2 = D^1 - tbh/(b + f + h). \tag{10A-10}$$

The gain from a lower world price is the area of the rectangle in Figure 10A-2, the fall in the price multiplied by the level of imports after the tariff:

$$\text{Gain} = (D^2 - Q^2) \times t(b + f)/(b + f + h) \tag{10A-11}$$

$$= t \times (D^1 - Q^1) \times (b + f)/(b + f + h) - (t)^2 \times h(b + f)^2/(b + f + h)^2.$$

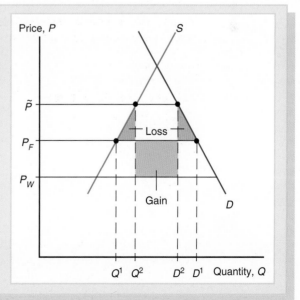

FIGURE 10A-2

Welfare Effects of a Tariff

The net benefit of a tariff is equal to the area of the colored rectangle minus the area of the two shaded triangles.

The loss from distorted consumption is the sum of the areas of the two triangles in Figure 10A-2:

$$\text{Loss} = (1/2) \times (Q^2 - Q^1) \times (\tilde{P} - P_F) + (1/2) \times (D^1 - D^2) \times (\tilde{P} - P_F)$$

$$= (t)^2 \times (b + f) \times (h)^2 / 2(b + f + h)^2. \tag{10A-12}$$

The net effect on welfare, therefore, is

$$\text{Gain} - \text{loss} = t \times U - (t)^2 \times V, \tag{10A-13}$$

where U and V are complicated expressions that are, however, independent of the level of the tariff and positive. That is, the net effect is the sum of a positive number times the tariff rate and a negative number times the *square* of the tariff rate.

We can now see that when the tariff is small enough, the net effect must be positive. The reason is that when we make a number smaller, the square of that number gets smaller faster than the number itself. Suppose a tariff of 20 percent turns out to produce a net loss. Then try a tariff of 10 percent. The positive term in that tariff's effect will be only half as large as with a 20 percent tariff, but the negative part will be only one-quarter as large. If the net effect is still negative, try a 5 percent tariff; this will again reduce the negative effect twice as much as the positive effect. At some sufficiently low tariff, the negative effect will have to be outweighed by the positive effect.

CHAPTER 11

TRADE POLICY IN DEVELOPING COUNTRIES

So far, we have analyzed the instruments of trade policy and its objectives without specifying the context—that is, without saying much about the country undertaking these policies. Each country has its own distinctive history and issues, but in discussing economic policy, one difference between countries becomes obvious: their income levels. As Table 11-1 suggests, nations differ greatly in their per-capita incomes. At one end of the spectrum are the developed or advanced nations, a club whose members include Western Europe, several countries largely settled by Europeans (including the United States), and Japan; these countries have per-capita incomes that in some cases exceed $40,000 per year. Most of the world's population, however, live in nations that are substantially poorer. The income range among these **developing countries**[1] is very wide. Some of these countries, such as South Korea, are now considered members of a group of "newly industrialized" nations with de facto developed-country status, both in terms of official statistics and in the way they think about themselves. Others, such as Bangladesh, remain desperately poor. Nonetheless, for virtually all developing countries, the attempt to close the income gap with more advanced nations has been a central concern of economic policy.

Why are some countries so much poorer than others? Why have some countries that were poor a generation ago succeeded in making dramatic progress, while others have not? These are deeply disputed questions, and to try to answer them—or even to describe at length the answers that economists have proposed over the years—would take us outside the scope of this book. What we can say, however, is that changing views about economic development have had a major role in determining trade policy.

For about 30 years after World War II, trade policies in many developing countries were strongly influenced by the beliefs that the key to economic development was the creation of a strong manufacturing sector, and that the best way to create that manufacturing sector was to protect domestic manufacturers from

---

[1]*Developing country* is a term used by international organizations that has now become standard, even though some "developing" countries have gone through extended periods of declining living standards. A more descriptive but less polite term is *less-developed countries* (LDCs).

MyEconLab Real-time data

TABLE 11-1	Gross Domestic Product Per Capita, 2009 (dollars, adjusted for differences in price levels)
United States	49,428
Germany	40,511
Japan	37,449
South Korea	32,954
Mexico	14,943
China	10,371
Bangladesh	1,929

Source: Conference Board Total Economy Database.

international competition. The first part of this chapter describes the rationale for this strategy of import-substituting industrialization, as well as the critiques of that strategy that became increasingly common after about 1970 and the emergence in the late 1980s of a new conventional wisdom that stressed the virtues of free trade. The second part of the chapter describes the remarkable shift in developing-country trade policy that has taken place since the 1980s.

Finally, while economists have debated the reasons for persistent large income gaps between nations, since the mid-1960s a widening group of Asian nations has astonished the world by achieving spectacular rates of economic growth. The third part of this chapter is devoted to the interpretation of this "Asian miracle" and its (much disputed) implications for international trade policy.

LEARNING GOALS

After reading this chapter, you will be able to:

- Recapitulate the case for protectionism as it has been historically practiced in developing countries and discuss import-substitution-led industrialization and the "infant industry" argument.
- Summarize the basic ideas behind "economic dualism" and its relationship to international trade.
- Discuss the recent economic history of the Asian countries, such as China and India, and detail the relationship between their rapid economic growth and their participation in international trade.

Import-Substituting Industrialization

From World War II until the 1970s, many developing countries attempted to accelerate their development by limiting imports of manufactured goods, in order to foster a manufacturing sector serving the domestic market. This strategy became popular for a number of reasons, but theoretical economic arguments for import substitution played an important role in its rise. Probably the most important of these arguments was the *infant industry argument*, which we mentioned in Chapter 7.

The Infant Industry Argument

According to the infant industry argument, developing countries have a *potential* comparative advantage in manufacturing, but new manufacturing industries in developing countries cannot initially compete with well-established manufacturing in developed countries. To allow manufacturing to get a toehold, then, governments should temporarily support new industries until they have grown strong enough to meet international competition. Thus, it makes sense, according to this argument, to use tariffs or import quotas as temporary measures to get industrialization started. It is a historical fact that some of the world's largest market economies began their industrialization behind trade barriers: The United States had high tariff rates on manufacturing in the 19th century, while Japan had extensive import controls until the 1970s.

Problems with the Infant Industry Argument   The infant industry argument seems highly plausible, and in fact it has been persuasive to many governments. Yet economists have pointed out many pitfalls in the argument, suggesting that it must be used cautiously.

First, it is not always a good idea to try to move today into the industries that will have a comparative advantage in the future. Suppose a country that is currently labor-abundant is in the process of accumulating capital. When it accumulates enough capital, it will have a comparative advantage in capital-intensive industries. However, that does not mean it should try to develop these industries immediately. In the 1980s, for example, South Korea became an exporter of automobiles; it would probably not have been a good idea for South Korea to have tried to develop its auto industry in the 1960s, when capital and skilled labor were still very scarce.

Second, protecting manufacturing does no good unless the protection itself helps make industry competitive. For example, Pakistan and India have protected their manufacturing sectors for decades and have recently begun to develop significant exports of manufactured goods. The goods they export, however, are light manufactures like textiles, not the heavy manufactures that they protected; a good case can be made that they would have developed their manufactured exports even if they had never protected manufacturing. Some economists have warned of the case of the "pseudoinfant industry," in which an industry is initially protected, then becomes competitive for reasons that have nothing to do with the protection. In this case, infant industry protection ends up looking like a success but may actually have been a net cost to the economy.

More generally, the fact that it is costly and time-consuming to build up an industry is not an argument for government intervention unless there is some domestic market failure. If an industry is supposed to be able to earn high enough returns for capital, labor, and other factors of production to be worth developing, then why don't private investors develop the industry without government help? Sometimes, it is argued that private investors take into account only the current returns in an industry and fail to take account of the future prospects, but this argument is not consistent with market behavior. In advanced countries at least, investors often back projects whose returns are uncertain and lie far in the future. (Consider, for example, the U.S. biotechnology industry, which attracted hundreds of millions of dollars of capital years before it made even a single commercial sale.)

Market Failure Justifications for Infant Industry Protection   To justify the infant industry argument, it is necessary to go beyond the plausible but questionable view that industries always need to be sheltered when they are new. Whether infant industry protection is justified depends on an analysis of the kind we discussed in Chapter 10. That is, the argument for protecting an industry in its early growth must be related to some particular set of market failures that prevent private markets from developing the industry as rapidly as they should. Sophisticated proponents of the infant industry argument have identified two market failures as reasons why infant industry protection may be a good idea: **imperfect capital markets** and the problem of **appropriability**.

The *imperfect capital markets justification* for infant industry protection is as follows: If a developing country does not have a set of financial institutions (such as efficient stock markets and banks) that would allow savings from traditional sectors (such as agriculture) to be used to finance investment in new sectors (such as manufacturing), then growth of new industries will be restricted by the ability of firms in these industries to earn current profits. Thus, low initial profits will be an obstacle to investment even if the long-term returns on the investment will be high. The first-best policy is to create a better capital market, but protection of new industries, which would raise profits and thus allow more rapid growth, can be justified as a second-best policy option.

The *appropriability argument* for infant industry protection can take many forms, but all have in common the idea that firms in a new industry generate social benefits for which they are not compensated. For example, the firms that first enter an industry may have to incur "start-up" costs of adapting technology to local circumstances or of opening new markets. If other firms are able to follow their lead without incurring these start-up costs, the pioneers will be prevented from reaping any returns from these outlays. Thus, pioneering firms may, in addition to producing physical output, create intangible benefits (such as knowledge or new markets) in which they are unable to establish property rights. In some cases the social benefits from creation of a new industry will exceed its costs, yet because of the problem of appropriability, no private entrepreneurs will be willing to enter. The first best answer is to compensate firms for their intangible contributions. When this is not possible, however, there is a second-best case for encouraging entry into a new industry by using tariffs or other trade policies.

Both the imperfect capital markets argument and the appropriability case for infant industry protection are clearly special cases of the *market failure* justification for interfering with free trade. The difference is that in this case, the arguments apply specifically to *new* industries rather than to *any* industry. The general problems with the market failure approach remain, however. In practice it is difficult to evaluate which industries really warrant special treatment, and there are risks that a policy intended to promote development will end up being captured by special interests. There are many stories of infant industries that have never grown up and remain dependent on protection.

Promoting Manufacturing Through Protection

Although there are doubts about the infant industry argument, many developing countries have seen this argument as a compelling reason to provide special support for the development of manufacturing industries. In principle, such support could be provided in a variety of ways. For example, countries could provide subsidies to manufacturing production in general, or they could focus their efforts on subsidies for the export of some manufactured goods in which they believe they can develop a comparative advantage. In most developing countries, however, the basic strategy for industrialization has been to develop industries oriented toward the domestic market by using trade restrictions such as tariffs and quotas to encourage the replacement of imported manufactures by domestic products. The strategy of encouraging domestic industry by limiting imports of manufactured goods is known as the strategy of **import-substituting industrialization**.

One might ask why a choice needs to be made. Why not encourage both import substitution and exports? The answer goes back to the general equilibrium analysis of tariffs in Chapter 6: A tariff that reduces imports also necessarily reduces exports. By protecting import-substituting industries, countries draw resources away from actual or potential export sectors. So a country's choice to seek to substitute for imports is also a choice to discourage export growth.

The reasons why import substitution rather than export growth has usually been chosen as an industrialization strategy are a mixture of economics and politics. First, until the 1970s many developing countries were skeptical about the possibility of exporting manufactured goods (although this skepticism also calls into question the infant industry argument for manufacturing protection). They believed that industrialization was necessarily based on a substitution of domestic industry for imports rather than on a growth of manufactured exports. Second, in many cases, import-substituting industrialization policies dovetailed naturally with existing political biases. We have already noted the case of Latin American nations that were compelled to develop substitutes for imports during the 1930s because of the Great Depression and during the first half of the 1940s because of the wartime disruption of trade (Chapter 10). In these countries, import substitution directly benefited powerful, established interest groups, while export promotion had no natural constituency.

It is also worth pointing out that some advocates of a policy of import substitution believed that the world economy was rigged against new entrants—that the advantages of established industrial nations were simply too great to be overcome by newly industrializing economies. Extreme proponents of this view called for a general policy of delinking developing countries from advanced nations; but even among milder advocates of protectionist development strategies, the view that the international economic system systematically works against the interests of developing countries remained common until the 1980s.

The 1950s and 1960s saw the high tide of import-substituting industrialization. Developing countries typically began by protecting final stages of industry, such as food processing and automobile assembly. In the larger developing countries, domestic products almost completely replaced imported consumer goods (although the manufacturing was often carried out by foreign multinational firms). Once the possibilities for replacing consumer goods imports had been exhausted, these countries turned to protection of intermediate goods, such as automobile bodies, steel, and petrochemicals.

In most developing economies, the import-substitution drive stopped short of its logical limit: Sophisticated manufactured goods such as computers, precision machine tools, and so on continued to be imported. Nonetheless, the larger countries pursuing import-substituting industrialization reduced their imports to remarkably low levels. The most extreme case was India: In the early 1970s, India's imports of products other than oil were only about 3 percent of GDP.

As a strategy for encouraging growth of manufacturing, import-substituting industrialization clearly worked. Latin American economies began generating almost as large a share of their output from manufacturing as advanced nations. (India generated less, but only because its poorer population continued to spend a high proportion of its income on food.) For these countries, however, the encouragement of manufacturing was not a goal in itself; rather, it was a means to the end goal of

CASE STUDY   Mexico Abandons Import-Substituting Industrialization

In 1994, Mexico, along with Canada and the United States, signed the North American Free Trade Agreement (NAFTA)—an agreement that, as we explain in Chapter 12, has become highly controversial. But Mexico's turn from import-substituting industrialization to relatively free trade actually began almost a decade before the country joined NAFTA.

Mexico's turn toward free trade reversed a half-century of history. Like many developing countries, Mexico turned protectionist during the Great Depression of the 1930s. After World War II, the policy of industrialization to serve a protected domestic market became explicit. Throughout the 1950s and 1960s, trade barriers were raised higher, as Mexican industry became increasingly self-sufficient. By the 1970s, Mexico had largely restricted imports of manufactured goods to such items as sophisticated machinery that could not be produced domestically except at prohibitive cost.

Mexican industry produced very little for export; the country's foreign earnings came largely from oil and tourism, with the only significant manufacturing exports coming from *maquiladoras*, special factories located near the U.S. border that were exempt from some trade restrictions.

By the late 1970s, however, Mexico was experiencing economic difficulties, including rising inflation and growing foreign debt. The problems came to a head in 1982, when the country found itself unable to make full payments on its foreign debt. This led to a prolonged economic crisis—and to a radical change in policy.

Between 1985 and 1988, Mexico drastically reduced tariffs and removed most of the import quotas that had previously protected its industry. The new policy goal was to make Mexico a major exporter of manufactured goods, closely integrated with the U.S. economy. The coming of NAFTA in the 1990s did little to reduce trade barriers, because Mexico had already done the heavy lifting of trade liberalization in the 1980s. NAFTA did, however, assure investors that the change in policy would not be reversed.

So how did the policy change work? Exports did indeed boom. In 1980, Mexican exports were only 10.7 percent of GDP—and much of that was oil. By 2012, exports were up to 34 percent of GDP, primarily manufactures. Today, Mexican manufacturing, rather than being devoted to serving the small domestic market, is very much part of an integrated North American manufacturing system.

The results for the overall Mexican economy have, however, been somewhat disappointing. Per-capita income has risen over the past 25 years, but the rate of growth has actually been lower than that achieved when Mexico was pursuing a policy of import-substituting industrialization.

Does this mean that trade liberalization was a mistake? Not necessarily. Most (but not all) economists who have looked at Mexican performance blame the relatively low growth on such factors as poor education. But the fact is that Mexico's turn away from import substitution, while highly successful at making Mexico an exporting nation, has not delivered as much as hoped in terms of broader economic progress.

economic development. Did import-substituting industrialization promote economic development? Here serious doubts appeared. Although many economists approved of import-substitution measures in the 1950s and early 1960s, since the 1960s, import-substituting industrialization has come under increasingly harsh criticism. Indeed, much of the focus of economic analysts and of policy makers has shifted from trying to encourage import substitution to trying to correct the damage done by bad import-substitution policies.

Results of Favoring Manufacturing: Problems of Import-Substituting Industrialization

Import-substituting industrialization began to lose favor when it became clear that countries pursuing import substitution were not catching up with advanced countries. In fact, some developing countries lagged further behind advanced countries even as they developed a domestic manufacturing base. India was poorer relative to the United States in 1980 than it had been in 1950, the first year after it achieved independence.

Why didn't import-substituting industrialization work the way it was supposed to? The most important reason seems to be that the infant industry argument is not as universally valid as many people had assumed. A period of protection will not create a competitive manufacturing sector if there are fundamental reasons why a country lacks a comparative advantage in manufacturing. Experience has shown that the reasons for failure to develop often run deeper than a simple lack of experience with manufacturing. Poor countries lack skilled labor, entrepreneurs, and managerial competence and have problems of social organization that make it difficult for these countries to maintain reliable supplies of everything from spare parts to electricity. These problems may not be beyond the reach of economic policy, but they cannot be solved by *trade* policy: An import quota can allow an inefficient manufacturing sector to survive, but it cannot directly make that sector more efficient. The infant industry argument is that, given the temporary shelter of tariffs or quotas, the manufacturing industries of less-developed nations will learn to be efficient. In practice, this is not always, or even usually, true.

With import substitution failing to deliver the promised benefits, attention turned to the costs of the policies used to promote industry. On this issue, a growing body of evidence showed that the protectionist policies of many less-developed countries badly distorted incentives. Part of the problem was that many countries used excessively complex methods to promote their infant industries. That is, they used elaborate and often overlapping import quotas, exchange controls, and domestic content rules instead of simple tariffs. It is often difficult to determine how much protection an administrative regulation is actually providing, and studies show that the degree of protection is often both higher and more variable across industries than the government intended. As Table 11-2 shows, some industries in Latin America and South Asia were protected by regulations that were the equivalent of tariff rates of 200 percent or more. These high rates of effective protection allowed industries to exist even when their cost of production was three or four times the price of the imports they replaced. Even the most enthusiastic advocates of market failure arguments for protection find rates of effective protection that high difficult to defend.

TABLE 11-2	Effective Protection of Manufacturing in Some Developing Countries (percent)
Mexico (1960)	26
Philippines (1965)	61
Brazil (1966)	113
Chile (1961)	182
Pakistan (1963)	271

Source: Bela Balassa, *The Structure of Protection in Developing Countries* (Baltimore: Johns Hopkins Press, 1971), p. 82.

A further cost that has received considerable attention is the tendency of import restrictions to promote production at an inefficiently small scale. The domestic markets of even the largest developing countries are only a small fraction of the size of that of the United States or the European Union. Often, the whole domestic market is not large enough to allow an efficient-scale production facility. Yet, when this small market is protected, say, by an import quota, if only a single firm were to enter the market, it could earn monopoly profits. The competition for these profits typically leads several firms to enter a market that does not really have enough room even for one, and production is carried out at a highly inefficient scale. The answer to the problem of scale for small countries is, as noted in Chapter 8, to specialize in the production and export of a limited range of products and to import other goods. Import-substituting industrialization eliminates this option by focusing industrial production on the domestic market.

Those who criticize import-substituting industrialization also argue that it has aggravated other problems, such as income inequality and unemployment.

By the late 1980s, the critique of import-substituting industrialization had been widely accepted, not only by economists but also by international organizations like the World Bank—and even by policy makers in the developing countries themselves. Statistical evidence appeared to suggest that developing countries that followed relatively free trade policies had, on average, grown more rapidly than those that followed protectionist policies (although this statistical evidence has been challenged by some economists).[2] This intellectual sea change led to a considerable shift in actual policies, as many developing countries removed import quotas and lowered tariff rates.

Trade Liberalization since 1985

Beginning in the mid-1980s, a number of developing countries moved to lower tariff rates and removed import quotas and other restrictions on trade. The shift of developing countries toward freer trade is the big trade policy story of the past two and a half decades.

---

[2]See Francisco Rodriguez and Dani Rodrik, "Trade Policy and Economic Growth: A Skeptic's Guide to the Cross-National Evidence," in Ben Bernanke and Kenneth S. Rogoff, eds., *NBER Macroeconomics Annual 2000*. Cambridge, MA: MIT Press for NBER, 2001.

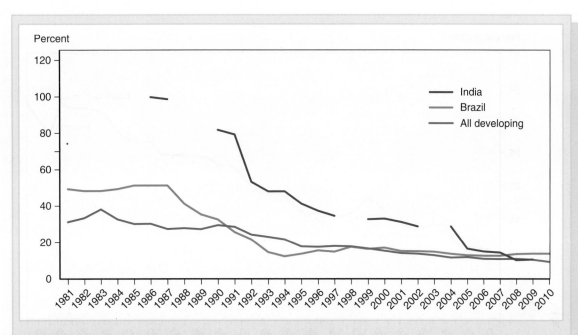

FIGURE 11-1

Tariff Rates in Developing Countries

One measure of the shift away from import-substituting industrialization is the sharp drop in tariff rates in developing countries, which have fallen from an average of more than 30 percent in the early 1980s to only about 10 percent today. Countries that once had especially strong import-substitution policies, like India and Brazil, have also seen the steepest declines in tariff rates.

Source: World Bank.

After 1985, many developing countries reduced tariffs, removed import quotas, and in general opened their economies to import competition. Figure 11-1 shows trends in tariff rates for an average of all developing countries and for two important developing countries, India and Brazil, which once relied heavily on import substitution as a development strategy. As you can see, there has been a dramatic fall in tariff rates in those two countries. Similar if less drastic changes in trade policy took place in many other developing countries.

Trade liberalization in developing countries had two clear effects. One was a dramatic increase in the volume of trade. Figure 11-2 plots exports and imports of developing countries, measured as percentages of GDP, since 1970. As you can see, the share of trade in GDP has tripled over that period, with most of the growth happening after 1985.

The other effect was a change in the nature of trade. Before the change in trade policy, developing countries mainly exported agricultural and mining products. But as we saw in Figure 2-6, that changed after 1980: The share of manufactured goods in developing-country exports surged, coming to dominate the exports of the biggest developing economies.

But trade liberalization, like import substitution, was intended as a means to an end rather than a goal in itself. As we've seen, import substitution fell out of favor as it

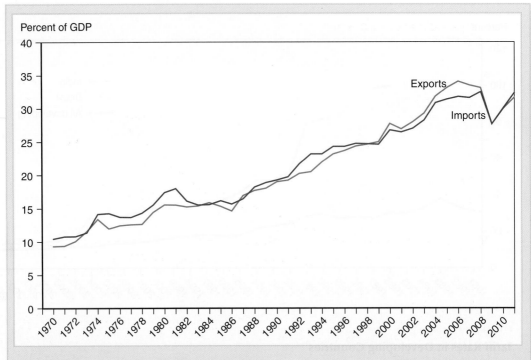

FIGURE 11-2

The Growth of Developing-Country Trade

Beginning in the 1980s, many developing countries began shifting away from import-substitution policies. One result has been a large rise in both exports and imports as a percentage of GDP.

Source: http://data.worldbank.org/indicator/NE.EXP.GNFS.ZS, http://data.worldbank.org/indicator/NE.IMP.GNFS.ZS

became clear that it was not delivering on its promise of rapid economic development. Has the switch to more open trade delivered better results?

The answer is that the picture is mixed. Growth rates in Brazil and other Latin American countries have actually been slower since the trade liberalization of the late 1980s than they were during import-substituting industrialization. India, on the other hand, has experienced an impressive acceleration of growth—but as we'll see in the next section of this chapter, there is intense dispute about how much of that acceleration can be attributed to trade liberalization.

In addition, there is growing concern about rising inequality in developing countries. In Latin America at least, the switch away from import-substituting industrialization seems to have been associated with declining real wages for blue-collar workers, even as earnings of highly skilled workers have risen.

One thing is clear, however: The old view that import substitution is the only path to development has been proved wrong, as a number of developing countries have achieved extraordinary growth while becoming more, not less, open to trade.

Trade and Growth: Takeoff in Asia

As we have seen, by the 1970s there was widespread disillusionment with import-substituting industrialization as a development strategy. But what could take its place?

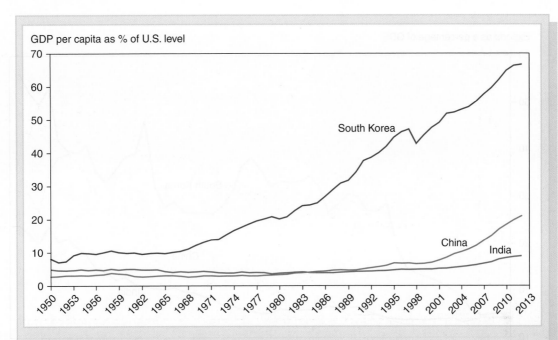

FIGURE 11-3

The Asian Takeoff

Beginning in the 1960s, a series of economies began converging on advanced-country levels of income. Here we show GDP per capita as a percentage of its level in the United States, using a proportional scale to highlight the changes. South Korea began its ascent in the 1960s, China at the end of the 1970s, and India about a decade later.

Source: Total Economy Database.

A possible answer began to emerge as economists and policy makers took note of some surprising success stories in the developing world—cases of economies that experienced a dramatic acceleration in their growth and began to converge on the incomes of advanced nations. At first, these success stories involved a group of relatively small East Asian economies: South Korea, Taiwan, Hong Kong, and Singapore. Over time, however, these successes began to spread; today, the list of countries that have experienced startling economic takeoffs includes the world's two most populous nations, China and India.

Figure 11-3 illustrates the Asian takeoff by showing the experiences of three countries: South Korea, the biggest of the original group of Asian "tigers"; China; and India. In each case, we show per-capita GDP as a percentage of the U.S. level, an indicator that highlights the extent of these nations' economic "catchup." As you can see, South Korea began its economic ascent in the 1960s, China at the end of the 1970s, and India circa 1990.

What caused these economic takeoffs? Each of the countries shown in Figure 11-3 experienced a major change in its economic policy around the time of its takeoff. This new policy involved reduced government regulation in a variety of areas, including a move toward freer trade. The most spectacular change was in China, where Deng Xiaoping, who had taken power in 1978, converted a centrally planned economy into a market economy in which the profit motive had relatively free rein. But as explained in the box on page 319, policy changes in India were dramatic, too.

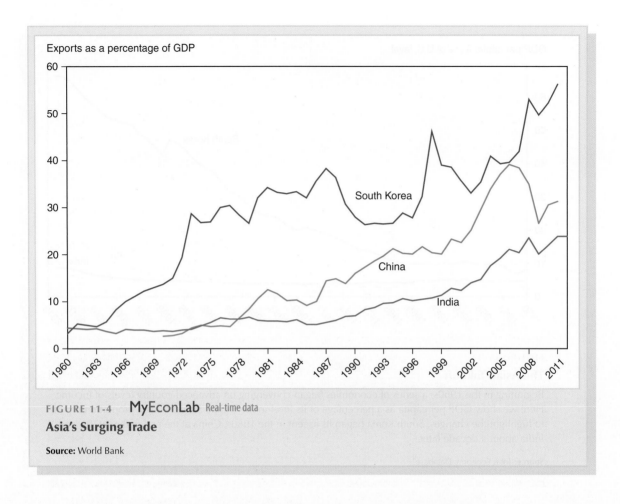

FIGURE 11-4   MyEconLab Real-time data

Asia's Surging Trade

Source: World Bank

In each case, these policy reforms were followed by a large increase in the economy's openness, as measured by the share of exports in GDP (see Figure 11-4). So it seems fair to say that these Asian success stories demonstrated that the proponents of import-substituting industrialization were wrong: It is possible to achieve development through export-oriented growth.

What is less clear is the extent to which trade liberalization explains these success stories. As we have just pointed out, reductions in tariffs and the lifting of other import restrictions were only part of the economic reforms these nations undertook, which makes it difficult to assess the importance of trade liberalization per se. In addition, Latin American nations like Mexico and Brazil, which also sharply liberalized trade and shifted toward exports, did not see comparable economic takeoffs, suggesting at the very least that other factors played a crucial role in the Asian miracle.

So the implications of Asia's economic takeoff remain somewhat controversial. One thing is clear, however: The once widely held view that the world economy is rigged against new entrants and that poor countries cannot become rich have been proved spectacularly wrong. Never before in human history have so many people experienced such a rapid rise in their living standards.

INDIA'S BOOM

India, with a population of more than 1.1 billion people, is the world's second-most-populous country. It's also a growing force in world trade—especially in new forms of trade that involve information rather than physical goods. The Indian city of Bangalore has become famous for its growing role in the global information technology industry.

Yet a generation ago, India was a very minor player in world trade. In part this was because the country's economy performed poorly in general: Until about 1980, India eked out a rate of economic growth—sometimes mocked as the "Hindu rate of growth"—that was only about 1 percentage point higher than population growth.

This slow growth was widely attributed to the stifling effect of bureaucratic restrictions. Observers spoke of a "license Raj": Virtually any kind of business initiative required hard-to-get government permits, which placed a damper on investment and innovation. And India's sluggish economy participated little in world trade. After the country achieved independence in 1948, its leaders adopted a particularly extreme form of import-substituting industrialization as the country's development strategy: India imported almost nothing that it could produce domestically, even if the domestic product was far more expensive and of lower quality than what could be bought abroad. High costs, in turn, crimped exports. So India was a very "closed" economy. In the 1970s, imports and exports averaged only about 5 percent of GDP, close to the lowest levels of any major nation.

Then everything changed. India's growth accelerated dramatically: GDP per capita, which had risen at an annual rate of only 1.3 percent from 1960 to 1980, has grown at close to 4 percent annually since 1980. And India's participation in world trade surged as tariffs were brought down and import quotas were removed. In short, India has become a high-performance economy. It's still a very poor country, but it is rapidly growing richer and has begun to rival China as a focus of world attention.

The big question, of course, is why India's growth rate has increased so dramatically. That question is the subject of heated debate among economists. Some have argued that trade liberalization, which allowed India to participate in the global economy, was crucial.[*] Others point out that India's growth began accelerating around 1980, whereas the big changes in trade policy didn't occur until the beginning of the 1990s.[†]

Whatever caused the change, India's transition has been a welcome development. More than a billion people now have much greater hope for a decent standard of living.

---

[*]See Arvind Panagariya, "The Triumph of India's Market Reforms: The Record of the 1980s and 1990s." Policy Analysis 554, Cato Institute, November 2005.

[†]See Dani Rodrik and Arvind Subramanian, "From 'Hindu Growth' to Productivity Surge: The Mystery of the Indian Growth Transition," *IMF Staff Papers* 55 (2, 2005), pp. 193–228.

SUMMARY

1. Trade policy in less-developed countries can be analyzed using the same analytical tools used to discuss advanced countries. However, the particular issues characteristic of *developing countries* are different from those of advanced countries. In particular, trade policy in developing countries is concerned with two objectives: promoting industrialization and coping with the uneven development of the domestic economy.

2. Government policy to promote industrialization has often been justified by the infant industry argument, which says that new industries need a temporary period of protection against competition from established industries in other countries. However, the infant industry argument is valid only if it can be cast as a market failure argument for intervention. Two usual justifications are the existence of *imperfect capital markets* and the problem of *appropriability* of knowledge generated by pioneering firms.

3. Using the infant industry argument as justification, many less-developed countries pursued policies of *import-substituting industrialization* in which domestic industries are created under the protection of tariffs or import quotas. Although these policies succeeded in promoting manufacturing, by and large they did not deliver the expected gains in economic growth and living standards. Many economists are now harshly critical of the results of import substitution, arguing that it fostered high-cost, inefficient production.

4. Beginning about 1985, many developing countries, dissatisfied with the results of import-substitution policies, greatly reduced rates of protection for manufacturing. As a result, developing-country trade grew rapidly, and the share of manufactured goods in exports rose. The results of this policy change in terms of economic development, however, have been, at best, mixed.

5. The view that economic development must take place via import substitution, and the pessimism about economic development that spread as import-substituting industrialization seemed to fail, have been confounded by the rapid economic growth of a number of Asian economies. These Asian economies have grown not via import substitution but via exports. They are characterized both by very high ratios of trade to national income and by extremely high growth rates. The reasons for the success of these economies are highly disputed, with much controversy over the role played by trade liberalization.

KEY TERMS

appropriability, p. 310
developing countries, p. 307

imperfect capital markets,
p. 310

import-substituting
industrialization, p. 311

PROBLEMS

MyEconLab

1. Two trade theories have been historically prevalent among developing countries, one being import-substituting industrialization and the other is export-led growth. Which one proved to be more effective?

2. "Japan's experience makes the infant industry case for protection better than any theory. In the early 1950s, Japan was a poor nation that survived by exporting textiles and toys. The Japanese government protected what at first were inefficient, high-cost steel and automobile industries, and those industries came to dominate world markets." Discuss critically.

3. A country currently imports automobiles at $8,000 each. Its government believes that, given time, domestic producers could manufacture autos for only $6,000 but that there would be an initial shakedown period during which autos would cost $10,000 to produce domestically.
   a. Suppose each firm that tries to produce autos must go through the shakedown period of high costs on its own. Under what circumstances would the existence of the initial high costs justify infant industry protection?
   b. Now suppose, on the contrary, that once one firm has borne the costs of learning to produce autos at $6,000 each, other firms can imitate it and do the same. Explain how this can prevent development of a domestic industry and how infant industry protection can help.

4. India and Mexico both followed import-substitution policies after World War II. However, India went much further, producing almost everything for itself, while Mexico continued to rely on imports of capital goods. Why do you think this difference may have emerged?

5. What is export-led growth and why is it so popular? Make an example by referring to the Asian miracle.

FURTHER READINGS

W. Arthur Lewis. *The Theory of Economic Development*. Homewood, IL: Irwin, 1955. A good example of the upbeat view taken of trade policies for economic development during the import-substitution high tide of the 1950s and 1960s.

I. M. D. Little, Tibor Scitovsky, and Maurice Scott. *Industry and Trade in Some Developing Countries*. New York: Oxford University Press, 1970. A key work in the emergence of a more downbeat view of import substitution in the 1970s and 1980s.

Barry Naughton. *The Chinese Economy: Transitions and Growth*. Cambridge: MIT Press, 2007. A good overview of the radical changes in Chinese policy over time.

Dani Rodrik. *One Economics, Many Recipes*. Princeton: Princeton University Press, 2007. Views on trade and development from a leading skeptic of prevailing orthodoxies.

T. N. Srinivasan and Suresh D. Tendulkar. *Reintegrating India with the World Economy*. Washington: Institute for International Economics, 2003. How India shifted away from import substitution and what happened as a result.

MyEconLab Can Help You Get a Better Grade

MyEconLab   If your exam were tomorrow, would you be ready? For each chapter, MyEconLab Practice Tests and Study Plans pinpoint which sections you have mastered and those you need to study. That way, you are more efficient with your study time, and you are better prepared for your exams.

To see how it works, turn to page 41 and then go to

www.myeconlab.com

CHAPTER 12

CONTROVERSIES IN TRADE POLICY

As we have seen, the theory of international trade policy, like the theory of international trade itself, has a long, intellectual tradition. Experienced international economists tend to have a cynical attitude toward people who come along with "new" issues in trade—the general feeling tends to be that most supposedly new concerns are simply old fallacies in new bottles.

Every once in a while, however, truly new issues do emerge. This chapter describes three controversies over international trade that have arisen over the past quarter-century, each raising issues that previously had not been seriously analyzed by international economists.

First, in the 1980s, a new set of sophisticated arguments for government intervention in trade emerged in advanced countries. These arguments focused on the "high-technology" industries that came to prominence as a result of the rise of the silicon chip. While some of the arguments were closely related to the market failure analysis in Chapter 10, the new theory of **strategic trade policy** was based on different ideas and created a considerable stir. The dispute over high-technology industries and trade subsided for a while in the 1990s, but it has recently made a comeback as new concerns have emerged about U.S. innovation.

Second, in the 1990s, a heated dispute arose over the effects of growing international trade on workers in developing countries—and whether trade agreements should include standards for wage rates and labor conditions. This dispute often widened into a broader debate about the effects of globalization; it was a debate played out not just in academic journals but also, in some cases, in the streets.

More recently, there has been growing concern about the intersection between environmental issues—which increasingly transcend national boundaries—and trade policy, with a serious economic and legal dispute about whether policies such as "carbon tariffs" are appropriate.

LEARNING GOALS

After reading this chapter, you will be able to:

- Summarize the more sophisticated arguments for interventionist trade policy, especially those related to externalities and economies of scale.
- Evaluate the claims of the anti-globalization movement related to trade effects on workers, labor standards, and the environment in light of the counterarguments.
- Discuss the role of the World Trade Organization (WTO) as a forum for resolving trade disputes and the tension between the rulings of the WTO and individual national interests.
- Discuss key issues in the debate over trade policy and the environment.

Sophisticated Arguments for Activist Trade Policy

Nothing in the analytical framework developed in Chapters 9 and 10 rules out the desirability of government intervention in trade. That framework *does* show that activist government policy needs a specific kind of justification; namely, it must offset some preexisting domestic market failure. The problem with many arguments for activist trade policy is precisely that they do not link the case for government intervention to any particular failure of the assumptions on which the case for laissez-faire rests.

The difficulty with market failure arguments for intervention is being able to recognize a market failure when you see one. Economists studying industrial countries have identified two kinds of market failure that seem to be present and relevant to the trade policies of advanced countries: (1) the inability of firms in high-technology industries to capture the benefits of that part of their contribution to knowledge that spills over to other firms and (2) the presence of monopoly profits in highly concentrated oligopolistic industries.

Technology and Externalities

The discussion of the infant industry argument in Chapter 11 noted that there is a potential market failure arising from difficulties of appropriating knowledge. If firms in an industry generate knowledge that other firms can use without paying for it, the industry is in effect producing some extra output—the marginal social benefit of the knowledge—that is not reflected in the incentives of firms. Where such **externalities** (benefits that accrue to parties other than the firms that produce them) can be shown to be important, there is a good case for subsidizing the industry.

At an abstract level, this argument is the same for the infant industries of less-developed countries as it is for the established industries of the advanced countries. In advanced countries, however, the argument has a special edge because in those countries, there are important high-technology industries in which the generation of knowledge is in many ways the central aspect of the enterprise. In high-technology industries, firms devote a great deal of their resources to improving technology, either by explicitly spending on research and development or by being willing to take initial losses on new products and processes to gain experience. Because such activities take place in nearly all industries, there is no sharp line between high-tech and the rest of the economy. There are clear differences in degree, however, and it makes sense to talk of a high-technology sector in which investment in knowledge is the key part of the business.

The point for activist trade policy is that while firms can appropriate some of the benefits of their own investment in knowledge (otherwise they would not be investing!), they usually cannot appropriate them fully. Some of the benefits accrue to other firms that can imitate the ideas and techniques of the leaders. In electronics, for example, it is not uncommon for firms to "reverse engineer" their rivals' designs, taking their products apart to figure out how they work and how they were made. Because patent laws provide only weak protection for innovators, one can reasonably presume that under laissez-faire, high-technology firms do not receive as strong an incentive to innovate as they should.

The Case for Government Support of High-Technology Industries   Should the U.S. government subsidize high-technology industries? While there is a pretty good case for such a subsidy, we need to exercise some caution. Two questions in particular arise: (1) Can the government target the right industries or activities? and (2) How important, quantitatively, would the gains be from such targeting?

Although high-technology industries probably produce extra social benefits because of the knowledge they generate, much of what goes on even in those industries has nothing to do with generating knowledge. There is no reason to subsidize the employment of capital or nontechnical workers in high-technology industries; on the other hand, innovation and technological spillovers happen to some extent even in industries that are not at all high-tech. A general principle is that trade and industrial policy should be targeted specifically on the activity in which the market failure occurs. Thus, policy should seek to subsidize the generation of knowledge that firms cannot appropriate. The problem, however, is that it is not always easy to identify that knowledge generation; as we'll see shortly, industry practitioners often argue that focusing only on activities specifically labeled "research" is taking far too narrow a view of the problem.

The Rise, Fall, and Rise of High-Tech Worries   Arguments that the United States in particular should have a deliberate policy of promoting high-technology industries and helping them compete against foreign rivals have a curious history. Such arguments gained widespread attention and popularity in the 1980s and early 1990s, then fell from favor, only to experience a strong revival in recent years.

The high-technology discussions of the 1980s and early 1990s were driven in large part by the rise of Japanese firms in some prominent high-tech sectors that had previously been dominated by U.S. producers. Most notably, between 1978 and 1986, the U.S. share of world production of dynamic random access memory chips—a key component of many electronic devices—plunged from about 70 percent to 20 percent, while Japan's share rose from under 30 percent to 75 percent. There was widespread concern that other high-technology products might suffer the same fate. But as described in the box on page 329, the fear that Japan's dominance of the semiconductor memory market would translate into a broader dominance of computers and related technologies proved to be unfounded. Furthermore, Japan's overall growth sputtered in the 1990s, while the United States surged into a renewed period of technological dominance, taking the lead in Internet applications and other information industries.

More recently, however, concerns about the status of U.S. high-technology industries have reemerged. A central factor in these concerns has been the decline in U.S. employment in so-called advanced technology—ATP—products. As Figure 12-1 shows, the United States has moved into a large trade deficit in ICT goods, while as Figure 12-2

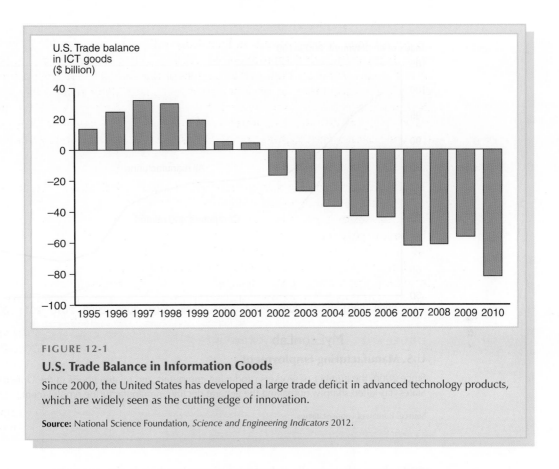

FIGURE 12-1

U.S. Trade Balance in Information Goods

Since 2000, the United States has developed a large trade deficit in advanced technology products, which are widely seen as the cutting edge of innovation.

Source: National Science Foundation, *Science and Engineering Indicators* 2012.

shows U.S. employment in the production of computers and related goods has plunged since 2000, falling substantially faster than overall manufacturing employment.

Does this matter? The United States could, arguably, continue to be at the cutting edge of innovation in information technology while outsourcing much of the actual production of high-technology goods to factories overseas. However, as explained in the box on page 328, some influential voices warn that innovation can't thrive unless the innovators are close, physically and in business terms, to the people who turn those innovations into physical goods.

It's a difficult debate to settle, in large part because it's not at all clear how to put numbers to these concerns. It seems likely, however, that the debate over whether or not high-technology industries need special consideration will grow increasingly intense in the years ahead.

Imperfect Competition and Strategic Trade Policy

During the 1980s, a new argument for industrial targeting received substantial theoretical attention. Originally proposed by economists Barbara Spencer and James Brander of the University of British Columbia, this argument identifies the market failure that justifies government intervention as the lack of perfect competition. In some industries, they point out, there are only a few firms in effective competition. Because of the small number of firms, the assumptions of perfect competition do not apply. In particular, there will typically be **excess returns**; that is, firms will make

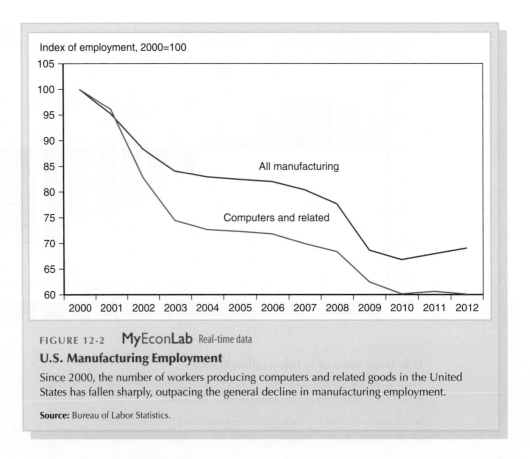

Index of employment, 2000=100

FIGURE 12-2   MyEconLab Real-time data

U.S. Manufacturing Employment

Since 2000, the number of workers producing computers and related goods in the United States has fallen sharply, outpacing the general decline in manufacturing employment.

Source: Bureau of Labor Statistics.

profits above what equally risky investments elsewhere in the economy can earn. There will thus be an international competition over who gets these profits.

Spencer and Brander noticed that, in this case, it is possible in principle for a government to alter the rules of the game to shift these excess returns from foreign to domestic firms. In the simplest case, a subsidy to domestic firms, by deterring investment and production by foreign competitors, can raise the profits of domestic firms by more than the amount of the subsidy. Setting aside the effects on consumers—for example, when firms are selling only in foreign markets—this capture of profits from foreign competitors would mean the subsidy raises national income at other countries' expense.

The Brander-Spencer Analysis: An Example   The **Brander-Spencer analysis** can be illustrated with a simple example in which only two firms compete, each from a different country. Bearing in mind that any resemblance to actual events may be coincidental, let's call the firms Boeing and Airbus and the countries the United States and Europe. Suppose there is a new product, a superjumbo aircraft, that both firms are capable of making. For simplicity, assume each firm can make only a yes/no decision: either to produce superjumbo aircraft or not.

Table 12-1 illustrates how the profits earned by the two firms might depend on their decisions. (The setup is similar to the one we used to examine the interaction of different countries' trade policies in Chapter 10.) Each row corresponds to a particular decision by Boeing; each column corresponds to a decision by Airbus. In each box are two entries: The entry on the lower left represents the profits of Boeing, while that on the upper right represents the profits of Airbus.

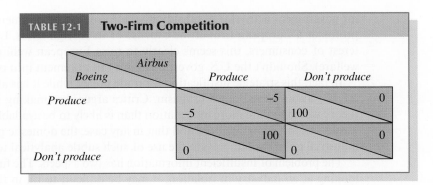

TABLE 12-1	**Two-Firm Competition**				

Boeing / Airbus	Produce		Don't produce	
Produce		−5		0
	−5		100	
Don't produce		100		0
	0		0	

As set up, the table reflects the following assumption: Either firm alone could earn profits making superjumbo aircraft, but if both firms try to produce them, both will incur losses. Which firm will actually get the profits? This depends on who gets there first. Suppose Boeing is able to get a small head start and commits itself to produce superjumbo aircraft before Airbus can get going. Airbus will find that it has no incentive to enter. The outcome will be in the upper right of the table, with Boeing earning profits.

Now comes the Brander-Spencer point: The European government can reverse this situation. Suppose the European government commits itself to pay its firm a subsidy of 25 if it enters. The result will be to change the table of payoffs to that represented in Table 12-2. In this case, it will be profitable for Airbus to produce superjumbo aircraft whatever Boeing does.

Let's work through the implications of this shift. Boeing now knows that whatever it does, it will have to compete with Airbus and will therefore lose money if it chooses to produce. So now it is Boeing that will be deterred from entering. In effect, the government subsidy has removed the advantage of a head start that we assumed was Boeing's and has conferred it on Airbus instead.

The end result is that the equilibrium shifts from the upper right of Table 12-1 to the lower left of Table 12-2. Airbus ends up with profits of 125 instead of 0, profits that arise because of a government subsidy of only 25. That is, the subsidy raises profits by more than the amount of the subsidy itself, because of its deterrent effect on foreign competition. The subsidy has this effect because it creates an advantage for Airbus comparable with the *strategic* advantage Airbus would have had if it, not Boeing, had had a head start in the industry.

Problems with the Brander-Spencer Analysis   This hypothetical example might seem to indicate that this strategic trade policy argument provides a compelling case

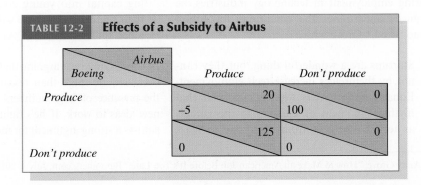

TABLE 12-2	**Effects of a Subsidy to Airbus**				

Boeing / Airbus	Produce		Don't produce	
Produce		20		0
	−5		100	
Don't produce		125		0
	0		0	

for government activism. A subsidy by the European government sharply raises the profits of a European firm at the expense of its foreign rivals. Leaving aside the interest of consumers, this seems clearly to raise European welfare (and reduce U.S. welfare). Shouldn't the U.S. government put this argument into practice?

In fact, this strategic justification for trade policy, while it has attracted much interest, has also received much criticism. Critics argue that making practical use of the theory would require more information than is likely to be available, that such policies would risk foreign retaliation, and that in any case, the domestic politics of trade and industrial policy would prevent the use of such subtle analytical tools.

The problem of insufficient information has two aspects. The first is that even when looking at an industry in isolation, it may be difficult to fill in the entries in a table like Table 12-1 with any confidence. And if the government gets it wrong, a subsidy policy may turn out to be a costly misjudgment. Suppose, for example, that Boeing has some underlying advantage—maybe a better technology—so that even if Airbus enters, Boeing will still find it profitable to produce. Airbus, however, cannot produce profitably if Boeing enters.

In the absence of a subsidy, the outcome will be that Boeing produces and Airbus does not. Now suppose that, as in the previous case, the European government provides a subsidy sufficient to induce Airbus to produce. In this case, however, because of Boeing's underlying advantage, the subsidy won't act as a deterrent to Boeing, and the profits of Airbus will fall short of the subsidy's value—in short, the policy will turn out to have been a costly mistake.

The point is that even though the two cases might look very similar, in one case a subsidy looks like a good idea, while in the other case it looks like a terrible idea. It seems that the desirability of strategic trade policies depends on an exact reading

A WARNING FROM INTEL'S FOUNDER

When Andy Grove speaks about technology, people listen. In 1968, he co-founded Intel, which invented the microprocessor—the chip that drives your computer—and dominated the semiconductor business for decades.

So many people took notice in 2010 when Grove issued a stark warning about the fate of U.S. high technology: The erosion of manufacturing employment in technology industries, he argued, undermines the conditions for future innovation.* Grove wrote:

Startups are a wonderful thing, but they cannot by themselves increase tech employment. Equally important is what comes after that mythical moment of creation in the garage, as technology goes from prototype to mass production. This is the phase where companies scale up. They work out design details, figure out how to make things affordably, build factories, and hire people by the thousands. Scaling is hard work but necessary to make innovation matter.

The scaling process is no longer happening in the U.S. And as long as that's the case, plowing capital into young companies that build their factories elsewhere will continue to yield a bad return in terms of American jobs.

In effect, Grove was arguing that technological spillovers require more than researchers; they require the presence of large numbers of workers putting new ideas to work. If he's right, his assertion constitutes a strong argument for industrial targeting.

*Andy Grove, "How to Make an American Job Before It's Too Late," Bloomberg.com, July 1, 2010.

of the situation. This leads some economists to ask whether we are ever likely to have enough information to use the theory effectively.

The information requirement is complicated because we cannot consider industries in isolation. If one industry is subsidized, it will draw resources from other industries and lead to increases in their costs. Thus, even a policy that succeeds in giving U.S. firms a strategic advantage in one industry will tend to cause strategic disadvantage elsewhere. To ask whether the policy is justified, the U.S. government would need to weigh these offsetting effects. Even if the government has a precise understanding of one industry, this is not enough because it also needs an equally precise understanding of those industries with which that industry competes for resources.

If a proposed strategic trade policy can overcome these criticisms, it still faces the problem of foreign retaliation, essentially the same problem faced when considering the use of a tariff to improve the terms of trade (Chapter 10). Strategic policies are **beggar-thy-neighbor policies** that increase our welfare at other countries' expense. These policies therefore risk a trade war that leaves everyone worse off. Few economists would advocate that the United States be the initiator of such policies. Instead, the furthest that most economists are willing to go is to argue that the United States should be prepared to retaliate when other countries appear to be using strategic policies aggressively.

Finally, can theories like this ever be used in a political context? We discussed this issue in Chapter 10, where the reasons for skepticism were placed in the context of a political skeptic's case for free trade.

CASE STUDY   When the Chips Were Up

During the years when arguments about the effectiveness of strategic trade policy were at their height, advocates of a more interventionist trade policy on the part of the United States often claimed that Japan had prospered by deliberately promoting key industries. By the early 1990s, one example in particular—that of semiconductor chips—had become exhibit A in the case that promoting key industries "works." Indeed, when author James Fallows published a series of articles in 1994 attacking free trade ideology and alleging the superiority of Japanese-style interventionism, he began with a piece titled "The Parable of the Chips." By the end of the 1990s, however, the example of semiconductors had come to seem an object lesson in the pitfalls of activist trade policy.

A semiconductor chip is a small piece of silicon on which complex circuits have been etched. As we saw on page 328, the industry began in the United States when the U.S. firm Intel introduced the first microprocessor, the brains of a computer on a chip. Since then, the industry has experienced rapid yet peculiarly predictable technological change: Roughly every 18 months, the number of circuits that can be etched on a chip doubles, a rule known as Moore's Law. This progress underlies much of the information technology revolution of the last three decades.

Japan broke into the semiconductor market in the late 1970s. The industry was definitely targeted by the Japanese government, which supported a research effort that helped build domestic technological capacity. The sums involved in this subsidy, however, were fairly small. The main component of Japan's activist trade policy, according to U.S. critics, was tacit protectionism. Although Japan had few formal tariffs or other barriers to imports, U.S. firms found that once Japan was able to manufacture a given type of semiconductor chip, few U.S. products were sold in that country. Critics alleged that there was a tacit understanding by Japanese firms in such industries as consumer electronics, in which Japan was already a leading producer, that they should buy domestic semiconductors, even if the price was higher or the quality lower than that for competing U.S. products. Was this assertion true? The facts of the case are in dispute to this day.

Observers also alleged that the protected Japanese market—if that was indeed what it was—indirectly promoted Japan's ability to export semiconductors. The argument went like this: Semiconductor production is characterized by a steep learning curve (recall the discussion of dynamic scale economies in Chapter 7). Guaranteed a large domestic market, Japanese semiconductor producers were certain they would be able to work their way down the learning curve, which meant they were willing to invest in new plants that could also produce for export.

It remains unclear to what extent these policies led to Japan's success in taking a large share of the semiconductor market. Some features of the Japanese industrial system may have given the country a "natural" comparative advantage in semiconductor production, where quality control is a crucial concern. During the 1970s and 1980s, Japanese factories developed a new approach to manufacturing based on, among other things, setting acceptable levels of defects much lower than those that had been standard in the United States.

In any case, by the mid-1980s Japan had surpassed the United States in sales of one type of semiconductor, which was widely regarded as crucial to industry success: random access memories, or RAMs. The argument that RAM production was the key to dominating the whole semiconductor industry rested on the belief that it would yield both strong technological externalities and excess returns. RAMs were the largest-volume form of semiconductors; industry experts asserted that the know-how acquired in RAM production was essential to a nation's ability to keep up with advancing technology in other semiconductors, such as microprocessors. So it was widely predicted that Japan's dominance in RAMs would soon translate into dominance in the production of semiconductors generally—and that this supremacy, in turn, would give Japan an advantage in the production of many other goods that used semiconductors.

It was also widely believed that although the manufacture of RAMs had not been a highly profitable business before 1990, it would eventually become an industry characterized by excess returns. The reason was that the number of firms producing RAMs had steadily fallen: In each successive generation of chips, some producers had exited the sector, with no new entrants. Eventually, many observers thought, there would be only two or three highly profitable RAM producers left.

During the decade of the 1990s, however, both justifications for targeting RAMs—technological externalities and excess returns—apparently failed to materialize. On one side, Japan's lead in RAMs ultimately did not translate into an advantage in other types of semiconductors: For example, American firms retained a secure lead in microprocessors. On the other side, instead of continuing to shrink, the number of RAM producers began to rise again, with the main new entrants from South Korea and other newly industrializing economies. By the end of the 1990s, RAM production was regarded as a "commodity" business: Many people could make RAMs, and there was nothing especially strategic about the sector.

The important lesson seems to be how hard it is to select industries to promote. The semiconductor industry appeared, on its face, to have all the attributes of a sector suitable for activist trade policy. But in the end, it yielded neither strong externalities nor excess returns.

Globalization and Low-Wage Labor

It's a good bet that most of the clothing you are wearing as you read this came from a country far poorer than the United States. The rise of manufactured exports from developing countries has been one of the major shifts in the world economy over the last generation; even a desperately poor nation like Bangladesh, with a per-capita GDP less than 5 percent that of the United States, now relies more on exports of manufactured goods than on exports of traditional agricultural or mineral products. (A government official in a developing country remarked to one of the authors, "We are not a banana republic—we are a pajama republic.")

It should come as no surprise that the workers who produce manufactured goods for export in developing countries are paid very little by advanced-country standards—often less than $1 per hour, sometimes less than $0.50. After all, the workers have few good alternatives in such generally poor economies. Nor should it come as any surprise that the conditions of work are also very bad in many cases—sometimes lethal, as explained in the case study on page 329.

Should low wages and poor working conditions be a cause for concern? Many people think so. In the 1990s, the anti-globalization movement attracted many adherents in advanced countries, especially on college campuses. Outrage over low wages and poor working conditions in developing-country export industries was a large part of the movement's appeal, although other concerns (discussed below) were also part of the story.

It's fair to say that most economists have viewed the anti-globalization movement as, at best, misguided. The standard analysis of comparative advantage suggests that trade is mutually beneficial to the countries that engage in it; it suggests, furthermore, that when labor-abundant countries export labor-intensive manufactured goods like clothing, not only should their national incomes rise but the distribution of income should also shift in favor of labor. But is the anti-globalization movement entirely off base?

The Anti-Globalization Movement

Before 1995, most complaints about international trade made by citizens of advanced countries targeted its effects on people who were also citizens of advanced countries. In the United States, most critics of free trade in the 1980s focused on the alleged threat of competition from Japan; in the early 1990s, there was substantial concern in both the United States and Europe over the effects of imports from low-wage countries on the wages of less-skilled workers at home.

In the second half of the 1990s, however, a rapidly growing movement—drawing considerable support from college students—began stressing the alleged harm that world trade was doing to workers in the developing countries. Activists pointed to the low wages and poor working conditions in third world factories that produced goods for Western markets. A crystallizing event was the discovery in 1996 that clothes sold at Wal-Mart, and endorsed by television personality Kathie Lee Gifford, were produced by very poorly paid workers in Honduras.

The anti-globalization movement grabbed world headlines in November 1999, when a major meeting of the World Trade Organization took place in Seattle. The purpose of the meeting was to start another trade round, following on the Uruguay Round described in Chapter 10. Thousands of activists converged on Seattle, motivated by the belief that the WTO was riding roughshod over national independence and imposing free trade ideas that hurt workers. Despite ample warnings, the police were ill prepared, and the demonstrations brought considerable disruption to the meetings. In any case, negotiations were not going well: Nations had failed to agree on an agenda in advance, and it soon became clear that there was not sufficient agreement on the direction of a new trade round to get one started.

In the end, the meeting was regarded as a failure. Most experts on trade policy believe the meeting would have failed even in the absence of the demonstrations, but the anti-globalization movement had achieved at least the appearance of disrupting an important international conference. Over the next two years, large demonstrations also rocked meetings of the International Monetary Fund and the World Bank in Washington as well as a summit meeting of major economic powers in Genoa; at the latter event, Italian police killed one activist.

In other words, the anti-globalization movement had become a highly visible presence in a relatively short period of time. But what was the movement's goal—and was it right?

Trade and Wages Revisited

One strand of the opposition to globalization is familiar from the analysis in Chapter 3. Activists pointed to the very low wages earned by many workers in developing-country export industries. These critics argued that the low wages (and the associated poor working conditions) showed that, contrary to the claims of free trade advocates, globalization was not helping workers in developing countries.

For example, some activists pointed to the example of Mexico's *maquiladoras*, factories near the U.S. border that had expanded rapidly, roughly doubling in employment, in the five years following the signing of the North American Free Trade Agreement. Wages in those factories were in some cases below $5 per day, and conditions were appalling by U.S. standards. Opponents of the free trade agreement argued that by making it easier for employers to replace high-wage workers in the United States with lower-paid workers in Mexico, the agreement had hurt labor on both sides of the border.

The standard economist's answer to this argument goes back to our analysis in Chapter 3 of the misconceptions about comparative advantage. We saw that it is a common misconception that trade must involve the exploitation of workers if they earn much lower wages than their counterparts in a richer country.

Table 12-3 repeats that analysis briefly. In this case, we assume that there are two countries, the United States and Mexico, and two industries, high-tech and low-tech. We also assume that labor is the only factor of production, and that U.S. labor is more productive than Mexican labor in all industries. Specifically, it takes only one hour of U.S. labor to produce a unit of output in either industry; it takes two hours of Mexican labor to produce a unit of low-tech output and eight hours to produce a unit of high-tech output. The upper part of the table shows the real wages of workers in each country in terms of each good in the absence of trade: The real wage in each case is simply the quantity of each good that a worker could produce in one hour.

Now suppose that trade is opened. In the equilibrium after trade, the relative wage rates of U.S. and Mexican workers would be somewhere between the relative productivity of workers in the two industries—for example, U.S. wages might be four times Mexican wages. Thus, it would be cheaper to produce low-tech goods in Mexico and high-tech goods in the United States.

A critic of globalization might look at this trading equilibrium and conclude that trade works against the interest of workers. First of all, in low-tech industries, highly paid jobs in the United States are replaced with lower-paid jobs in Mexico. Moreover, you could make a plausible case that the Mexican workers are underpaid: Although

TABLE 12-3	Real Wages	
(A) Before Trade		
	High-Tech Goods/Hour	**Low-Tech Goods/Hour**
United States	1	1
Mexico	1/8	1/2
(B) After Trade		
	High-Tech Goods/Hour	**Low-Tech Goods/Hour**
United States	1	2
Mexico	1/4	1/2

they are half as productive in low-tech manufacturing as the U.S. workers they replace, their wage rate is only $\frac{1}{4}$ (not $\frac{1}{2}$) that of U.S. workers.

But as shown in the lower half of Table 12-3, in this example the purchasing power of wages has actually increased in both countries. U.S. workers, all of whom are now employed in high-tech, can purchase more low-tech goods than before: two units per hour of work versus one. Mexican workers, all of whom are now employed in low-tech, find that they can purchase more high-tech goods with an hour's labor than before: $\frac{1}{4}$ instead of $\frac{1}{8}$. Because of trade, the price of each country's imported good in terms of that country's wage rate has fallen.

The point of this example is not to reproduce the real situation in any exact way; it is to show that the evidence usually cited as proof that globalization hurts workers in developing countries is exactly what you would expect to see even if the world were well described by a model that says that trade actually benefits workers in both advanced and developing countries.

One might argue that this model is misleading because it assumes that labor is the only factor of production. It is true that if one turns from the Ricardian model to the factor-proportions model discussed in Chapter 5, it becomes possible that trade hurts workers in the labor-scarce, high-wage country—that is, the United States in this example. But this does not help the claim that trade hurts workers in developing countries. On the contrary, the case for believing that trade is beneficial to workers in the low-wage country actually becomes stronger: Standard economic analysis says that while workers in a capital-abundant nation like the United States might be hurt by trade with a labor-abundant country like Mexico, the workers in the labor-abundant country should benefit from a shift in the distribution of income in their favor.

In the specific case of the *maquiladoras*, economists argue that while wages in the *maquiladoras* are very low compared with wages in the United States, that situation is inevitable because of the lack of other opportunities in Mexico, which has far lower overall productivity. And it follows that while wages and working conditions in the *maquiladoras* may appear terrible, they represent an improvement over the alternatives available in Mexico. Indeed, the rapid rise of employment in those factories indicated that workers preferred the jobs they could find there to the alternatives. (Many of the new workers in the *maquiladoras* are in fact peasants from remote and desperately poor areas of Mexico. One could say that they have moved from intense but invisible poverty to less severe but conspicuous poverty, simultaneously achieving an improvement in their lives and becoming a source of guilt for U.S. residents unaware of their former plight.)

The standard economist's argument, in other words, is that despite the low wages earned by workers in developing countries, those workers are better off than they would have been if globalization had not taken place. Some activists do not accept this argument—they maintain that increased trade makes workers in both advanced and developing countries worse off. It is hard, however, to find a clear statement of the channels through which this is supposed to happen. Perhaps the most popular argument is that capital is mobile internationally, while labor is not; and that this mobility gives capitalists a bargaining advantage. As we saw in Chapter 4, however, international factor mobility is similar in its effects to international trade.

Labor Standards and Trade Negotiations

Free trade proponents and anti-globalization activists may debate the big questions such as, is globalization good for workers or not? Narrower practical policy issues are at stake, however: whether and to what extent international trade agreements should also contain provisions aimed at improving wages and working conditions in poor countries.

The most modest proposals have come from economists who argue for a system that monitors wages and working conditions and makes the results of this monitoring available to consumers. Their argument is a version of the market failure analysis in Chapter 10. Suppose, they suggest, that consumers in advanced countries feel better about buying manufactured goods that they know were produced by decently paid workers. Then a system that allows these consumers to know, without expending large efforts on information gathering, whether the workers were indeed decently paid offers an opportunity for mutual gain. (Kimberly Ann Elliott, cited in the Further Readings list at the end of the chapter, quotes a teenager: "Look, I don't have time to be some kind of major political activist every time I go to the mall. Just tell me what kinds of shoes are okay to buy, okay?") Because consumers can choose to buy only "certified" goods, they are better off because they feel better about their purchases. Meanwhile, workers in the certified factories gain a better standard of living than they otherwise would have had.

Proponents of such a system admit that it would not have a large impact on the standard of living in developing countries, mainly because it would affect only the wages of workers in export factories, who are a small minority of the work force even in highly export-oriented economies. But they argue that it would do some good and little harm.

A stronger step would be to include formal labor standards—that is, conditions that export industries are supposed to meet—as part of trade agreements. Such standards have considerable political support in advanced countries; indeed, President Bill Clinton spoke in favor of such standards at the disastrous Seattle meeting described previously.

The economic argument in favor of labor standards in trade agreements is similar to the argument in favor of a minimum wage rate for domestic workers: While economic theory suggests that the minimum wage reduces the number of low-skill jobs available, some (though by no means all!) reasonable economists argue that such effects are small and are outweighed by the effect of the minimum wage in raising the income of the workers who remain employed.

Labor standards in trade, however, are strongly opposed by most developing countries, which believe that the standards would inevitably be used as a protectionist tool: Politicians in advanced countries would set standards at levels that developing countries could not meet, in effect pricing their goods out of world markets. A particular concern—in fact, it was one of the concerns that led to the collapse of the talks in

Seattle—is that labor standards would be used as the basis for private lawsuits against foreign companies, similar to the way antidumping legislation has been used by private companies to harass foreign competitors.

Environmental and Cultural Issues

Complaints against globalization go beyond labor issues. Many critics argue that globalization is bad for the environment. It is unmistakably true that environmental standards in developing-country export industries are much lower than in advanced-country industries. It is also true that in a number of cases, substantial environmental damage has been and is being done in order to provide goods to advanced-country markets. A notable example is the heavy logging of Southeast Asian forests carried out to produce forest products for sale to Japanese and Western markets.

On the other hand, there are at least as many cases of environmental damage that has occurred in the name of "inward-looking" policies of countries reluctant to integrate with the global economy. A notable example is the destruction of many square miles of rain forest in Brazil, the consequence partly of a domestic policy that subsidizes development in the interior. This policy has nothing to do with exports and in fact began during the years that Brazil was attempting to pursue inward-looking development.

As in the case of labor standards, there is debate over whether trade agreements should include environmental standards. On one side, proponents argue that such agreements can lead to at least modest improvements in the environment, benefiting all concerned. On the other side, opponents insist that attaching environmental standards to trade agreements will in effect shut down potential export industries in poor countries, which cannot afford to maintain anything like Western standards.

An even trickier issue involves the effect of globalization on local and national cultures. It is unmistakably true that the growing integration of markets has led to a homogenization of cultures around the world. People worldwide increasingly tend to wear the same clothing, eat the same food, listen to the same music, and watch the same films and TV shows.

Much but not all of this homogenization is also Americanization. For example, McDonald's is now found almost everywhere, but so is sushi. Hollywood action films dominate the global box office, but stylized fight scenes in Hollywood blockbusters like *The Matrix* are based on the conventions of Hong Kong martial arts films.

It is hard to deny that something is lost as a result of this cultural homogenization. One can therefore make a market failure argument on behalf of policies that attempt to preserve national cultural differences by, for example, limiting the number of American films that can be shown in theaters, or the fraction of TV time that can be taken up with programming from overseas.

As soon as one advances this argument, however, it becomes clear that another principle is involved: the right of individuals in free societies to entertain themselves as they like. How would you feel if someone denied you the right to listen to the Rolling Stones or watch Jackie Chan movies, on the grounds that American cultural independence must be safeguarded?

The WTO and National Independence

One recurrent theme in the anti-globalization movement is that the drive for free trade and free flow of capital has undermined national sovereignty. In the extreme versions of this complaint, the World Trade Organization is characterized as a supranational power able to prevent national governments from pursuing policies in their own interests. How much substance is there to this charge?

The short answer is that the WTO does not look anything like a world government; its authority is basically limited to that of requiring countries to live up to their international trade agreements. However, the small grain of truth in the view of the WTO as a supranational authority is that its mandate allows it to monitor not only the traditional instruments of trade policy—tariffs, export subsidies, and quantitative restrictions—but also domestic policies that are de facto trade policies. And since the line between legitimate domestic policies and de facto protectionism is fuzzy, there have been cases in which the WTO has seemed to some observers to be interfering in domestic policy.

On page 335, we described a well-known example that illustrates the ambiguity of the issue. As we saw, the United States amended its Clean Air Act to require imported gasoline to be no more polluting than the average of gasoline supplied by domestic refineries. The WTO ruled that this requirement was a violation of existing trade agreements. To critics of the WTO, this ruling exemplified how the institution could frustrate an attempt by a democratically elected government to improve the environment.

As defenders of the WTO pointed out, however, the ruling was based on the fact that the United States was applying different standards to imports and to domestic production. After all, some U.S. refineries supply gasoline that is more polluting than the average, yet they are allowed to remain in operation. So the rule in effect prevented the sale of polluting gasoline from Venezuela in U.S. markets but permitted the sale of equally polluting gasoline from a domestic refinery. If the new rule had applied the same standards to domestic and foreign gasoline, it would have been acceptable to the WTO.

CASE STUDY   A Tragedy in Bangladesh

Bangladesh is a very poor country. According to World Bank estimates, in 2010 some 77 percent of Bangladeshis were living on the equivalent of less than $2 a day, and 43 percent were living on less than $1.25 a day. Incredibly, however, these numbers reflected a major improvement from the not-so-distant past: In 1992, 93 percent of the population lived on less than $2 a day in today's dollars, 67 percent on less than $1.25.

This decline in poverty was the byproduct of two decades of impressive economic growth that doubled the nation's GDP per capita. Bangladeshi growth, in turn, relied crucially on rising exports, specifically, exports of apparel. As we noted in Chapter 11, the Bangladeshi clothing industry is a classic case of comparative advantage: It has relatively low productivity, even compared with other developing countries, but Bangladesh has even lower relative productivity in other industries, so it has become a clothing export powerhouse.

Bangladeshi competitiveness in clothing depends, however, on low wages and poor working conditions. How poor? On April 24, 2013, the world was shocked by news that an eight-story building in Bangladesh, containing a number of garment factories, had collapsed, killing more than 1,200 people. Inquiries revealed that cracks had appeared in the building the day before, but garment workers had been ordered back to work anyway. It also appeared that the building was structurally unsuited for manufacturing work and may have had extra stories added without a permit.

And who was buying the clothing made under these unsafe conditions? We were: The factories in the building were supplying clothing to a number of popular Western clothing brands.

Clearly, Bangladesh needs to take steps to protect its workers, starting by enforcing its own building and worker-safety laws. But how should consumers in wealthy nations—that means, among other people, you—respond?

An immediate, instinctive response is that we shouldn't buy goods produced in countries where workers are treated so badly. Yet as we've just seen, Bangladesh desperately needs to keep exporting clothing, and it can only do so if its workers receive very low wages by Western standards. Indeed, it needs to pay less even than China, whose apparel industry has higher productivity. And low wages and poor working conditions tend, whatever we might like, to go together.

Does this mean that nothing can be done to help Bangladeshi workers that won't end up hurting them instead? No. One can imagine trying, either by law or simply through consumer pressure, some basic standards for working conditions that apply not just to Bangladesh but to its competitors. Provided that they're not too ambitious, such standards could make life better for Bangladeshi workers without destroying the exports the country relies on.

But it won't be easy, and one shouldn't expect too much from such measures. For the foreseeable future, two uncomfortable facts will continue to be true when it comes to trade with poor countries: Workers in those countries will suffer from worse wages and working conditions than Westerners can easily imagine, yet refusing to buy what those workers produce would make them much worse off.

Globalization and the Environment

Concerns about human impacts on the environment are growing in much of the world. In turn, these concerns are playing a growing role in domestic politics. For example, in November 2007, the government of Australian Prime Minister John Howard was voted out of office; most political analysts believed the ruling party's decisive defeat had a lot to do with public perceptions that Australia's Liberal Party (which is actually conservative—Labor is on the left) was unwilling to act against environmental threats.

Inevitably, then, environmental issues are playing a growing role in disputes about international trade as well. Some anti-globalization activists claim that growing international trade automatically harms the environment; some also claim that international trade agreements—and the role of the World Trade Organization in particular—have the effect of blocking environmental action. Most international economists view the first claim as simplistic and disagree with the second. That is, they deny that there is a simple relationship between globalization and environmental damage and do not believe that trade agreements prevent countries from having enlightened environmental policies. Nonetheless, the intersection of trade and the environment does raise a number of important issues.

Globalization, Growth, and Pollution

Both production and consumption often lead, as a byproduct, to environmental damage. Factories emit pollution into the air and sometimes dump effluent into rivers; farmers use fertilizer and pesticides that end up in water; consumers drive pollution-emitting cars. As a result—other things equal—economic growth, which increases both production and consumption, leads to greater environmental damage.

However, other things are not equal. For one thing, countries change the mix of their production and consumption as they grow richer, to some extent in ways that tend to reduce the environmental impact. For example, as the U.S. economy becomes increasingly devoted to the production of services rather than goods, it tends to use less energy and raw material per dollar of GDP.

In addition, growing wealth tends to lead to growing political demands for environmental quality. As a result, rich countries generally impose stricter regulations to ensure clean air and water than poorer countries—a difference that is apparent to anyone who has gone back and forth between a major city in the United States or Europe and one in a developing country, and taken a deep breath in both places.

In the early 1990s, Princeton economists Gene Grossman and Alan Krueger, studying the relationship between national income levels and pollutants such as sulfur dioxide, found that these offsetting effects of economic growth lead to a distinctive "inverted U" relationship between per-capita income and environmental damage known as the **environmental Kuznets curve**.[1] This concept, whose relevance has been confirmed by a great deal of further research, is illustrated schematically in Figure 12-3.

The idea is that as a country's income per capita rises due to economic growth, the initial effect is growing damage to the environment. Thus, China, whose economy has surged in recent decades, is in effect moving from point A to point B: As the country burns more coal in its power plants and produces more goods in its factories, it emits more sulfur dioxide into the air and dumps more effluent into its rivers.

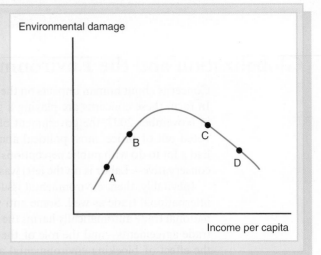

FIGURE 12-3

The Environmental Kuznets Curve

Empirical evidence suggests that as economies grow, they initially do increasing environmental damage—but they become more environmentally friendly once they become sufficiently rich. China, where the environment is deteriorating as the economy expands, is in effect moving from A to B. Richer countries may be moving from C to D, using some of their growth to improve the environment.

[1]Gene Grossman and Alan Krueger, "Environmental Effects of a North American Free Trade Agreement," in Peter Garber, ed., *The U.S. Mexico Free Trade Agreement*. MIT Press, 1994.

But when a country gets sufficiently rich, it can afford to take action to protect the environment. As the United States has grown richer in recent decades, it has also moved to limit pollution. For example, cars are required to have catalytic converters that reduce smog, and a government-licensing scheme limits emissions of sulfur dioxide from power plants. In terms of Figure 12-3, the United States has on some fronts, such as local air pollution, moved from C to D: growing richer and doing less damage to the environment.

What does this have to do with international trade? Trade liberalization is often advocated on the grounds that it will promote economic growth. To the extent that it succeeds in accomplishing this end, it will raise per-capita income. Will this improve or worsen environmental quality? It depends which side of the environmental Kuznets curve an economy is on. In their original paper, which was in part a response to critics of the North American Free Trade Agreement who argued that the agreement would be environmentally harmful, Grossman and Krueger suggested that Mexico might be on the right side of the curve—that is, to the extent that NAFTA raises Mexican income, it might actually lead to a reduction in environmental damage.

However, the environmental Kuznets curve does not, by any means, necessarily imply that globalization is good for the environment. In fact, it's fairly easy to make the argument that at a world level, globalization has indeed harmed the environment—at least so far.

This argument would run as follows: The biggest single beneficiary of globalization has arguably been China, whose export-led economy has experienced incredible growth since 1980. Meanwhile, the single biggest environmental issue is surely climate change: There is broad scientific consensus that emissions of carbon dioxide and other greenhouse gases are leading to a rise in the Earth's average temperature.

China's boom has been associated with a huge increase in its emissions of carbon dioxide. Figure 12-4 shows carbon dioxide emissions of the United States, Europe, and China from 1980 to 2011. In 1980, China was a minor factor in global warming; by 2008, it was, by a substantial margin, the world's leading emitter of greenhouse gases.

It's important to realize, though, that the problem here isn't globalization per se—it's China's economic success, which has to some extent come as a result of globalization. And despite environmental concerns, it's difficult to argue that China's growth, which has raised hundreds of millions of people out of dire poverty, is a bad thing.

The Problem of "Pollution Havens"

When ships get too old to continue operating, they are disassembled to recover their scrap metal and other materials. One way to look at "shipbreaking" is that it is a form of recycling: Instead of leaving a ship to rust, a shipbreaking firm extracts and reuses its components. Ultimately, this salvaging means that less iron ore needs to be mined, less oil extracted, and so on. One might expect shipbreaking to be good for the environment. The task itself, however, can be environmentally hazardous: Everything from the residual oil in a ship's tanks to the plastic in its chairs and interior fittings, if not handled carefully, can be toxic to the local environment.

As a result, shipbreaking in advanced countries is subject to close environmental regulation. When a ship is taken apart in Baltimore or Rotterdam, great care is taken to avoid environmental harm. But these days, shipbreaking rarely takes place in advanced countries. Instead, it's done in places like the Indian shipbreaking center of Alang, where ships are run aground on a beach and then dismantled by men with blowtorches, who leave a lot of pollution in their wake.

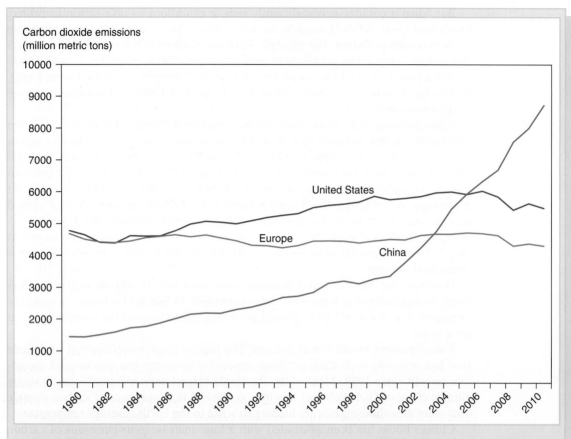

FIGURE 12-4

Carbon Dioxide Emissions

The rapid economic growth of China has turned it from a minor factor in climate change to the world's largest emitter of carbon dioxide.

Source: Energy Information Agency.

In effect, Alang has become a **pollution haven:** Thanks to international trade, an economic activity subject to strong environmental controls in some countries can take place in other countries with less strict regulation. Some activist groups are very concerned about the problem of pollution havens. Indeed, the environmental group Greenpeace made a *cause celebre* out of Alang, demanding that higher environmental standards be imposed. There are really two questions about pollution havens: (1) Are they really an important factor? and (2) Do they deserve to be a subject of international negotiation?

On the first question, most empirical research suggests that the pollution haven effect on international trade is relatively small. That is, there is not much evidence that "dirty" industries move to countries with lax environmental regulation.[2] Even in the case of the

---

[2]See, for example, Josh Ederington, Arik Levinson, and Jenny Minier, "Trade Liberalization and Pollution Havens," Working Paper 10585, National Bureau of Economic Research, June 2004.

shipbreaking industry, India's low wages seem to have been more of a lure than its loose environmental restrictions.

Second, do nations have a legitimate interest in each other's environmental policies? That turns out to depend on the nature of the environmental problem.

Pollution is the classic example of a negative externality—a cost that individuals impose on others but don't pay for. That's why pollution is a valid reason for government intervention. However, different forms of pollution have very different geographical reach—and only those that extend across national boundaries obviously justify international concern.

Thus, to the extent that Indian shipbreaking pollutes the local environment at Alang, this is a problem for India; it's less clear that it is a problem for other countries. Similarly, air pollution in Mexico City is a problem for Mexico; it's not clear why it's a valid U.S. interest. On the other hand, emissions of carbon dioxide affect the future climate for all countries: They're an international externality and deserve to be the subject of international negotiation.

At this point, it's hard to come up with major examples of industries in which the pollution haven phenomenon, to the extent that it occurs, leads to international negative externalities. That situation may change dramatically, however, if some but not all major economies adopt strong policies to limit climate change.

The Carbon Tariff Dispute

In 2009, the U.S. House of Representatives passed a bill that would have created a cap-and-trade system for greenhouse gases—that is, a system under which a limited number of emissions licenses are issued and firms are required to buy enough licenses to cover their actual emissions, in effect putting a price on carbon dioxide and other gases. The Senate failed to pass any comparable bill, so climate-change legislation is on hold for the time being. Nonetheless, there was a key trade provision in the House bill that may represent the shape of things to come: It imposed **carbon tariffs** on imports from countries that fail to enact similar policies.

What was that about? One question that has been raised about climate-change legislation is whether it can be effective if only some countries take action. The United States accounts for only part of the world's emission of greenhouse gases—in fact, as we saw in Figure 12-4, it's not even the largest emitter. So a unilateral reduction in emissions by the United States would have only a limited effect on global emissions, and hence on future climate change. Furthermore, policies that put a high price on carbon might make the pollution haven effect much larger than it has been so far, leading to "carbon leakage" as emissions-intensive industries relocate to countries without strong climate-change policies.

The obvious answer to these concerns is to make the initiative global, to have all major economies adopt similar policies. But there's no guarantee that such an agreement would be forthcoming, especially when some countries like China feel that they deserve the right to have laxer environmental policies than rich countries that have already achieved a high standard of living.

So what's the answer? The idea behind carbon tariffs is to charge importers of goods from countries without climate-change policies an amount proportional to the carbon dioxide emitted in the production of those goods. The charge per ton of emissions would be equal to the price of carbon dioxide emission licenses in the domestic market. This would give overseas producers an incentive to limit their carbon emissions and would remove the incentive to shift production to countries with lax regulation. In addition, it would, possibly, give countries with lax regulations an incentive to adopt climate-change policies of their own.

Critics of carbon tariffs argue that they would be protectionist, and also violate international trade rules, which prohibit discrimination between domestic and foreign products. Supporters argue that they would simply place producers of imported goods and domestic producers on a level playing field when selling to domestic consumers, with both required to pay for their greenhouse gas emissions. And because carbon tariffs create a level playing field, they argue, such tariffs—carefully applied—should also be legal under existing trade rules.

At this point, the issue of carbon tariffs is hypothetical, since no major economy has yet placed a significant price on greenhouse gas emissions. Correspondingly, the WTO hasn't issued any rulings on the legality of such tariffs, and probably won't until or unless a real case emerges. But if climate-change legislation makes a comeback—and it is a good bet that it will sooner or later—it will clearly lead to some major new issues in trade policy.

SUMMARY

1. Some new arguments for government intervention in trade have emerged over the past quarter-century: The theory of *strategic trade policy* offered reasons why countries might gain from promoting particular industries. In the 1990s a new critique of globalization emerged that focused on the effects of globalization on workers in developing countries. And possible action on climate change has raised some major trade issues, including that of the desirability and legality of *carbon tariffs*.

2. Activist trade policy arguments rest on two ideas. One is the argument that governments should promote industries that yield technological *externalities*. The other, which represents a greater departure from standard market failure arguments, is the *Brander-Spencer analysis*, which suggests that strategic intervention can enable nations to capture *excess returns*. These arguments are theoretically persuasive; however, many economists worry that they are too subtle and require too much information to be useful in practice.

3. With the rise of manufactured exports from developing countries, a new movement opposed to globalization has emerged. The central concern of this movement is with the low wages paid to export workers, although there are other themes as well. The response of most economists is that developing-country workers may earn low wages by Western standards, but that trade allows them to earn more than they otherwise would.

4. An examination of cases suggests how difficult the discussion of globalization really is, especially when one tries to view it as a moral issue; it is all too easy for people to do harm when they are trying to do good. The causes most favored by activists, such as labor standards, are feared by developing countries, which believe the standards will be used as protectionist devices.

5. To the extent that globalization promotes economic growth, it has ambiguous effects on the environment. The *environmental Kuznets curve* says that economic growth initially tends to increase environmental damage as a country grows richer but that beyond a certain point, growth is actually good for the environment. Unfortunately, some of the world's fastest-growing economies are still relatively poor and on the "wrong" side of the curve.

6. There is growing concern that globalization may allow highly polluting industries to move to *pollution havens*, where regulation is looser. There is little evidence that

this is a major factor in actual location decisions, at least so far. But that may change if serious climate-change policies are implemented; in that case, there is a strong case for *carbon tariffs*, but also strong criticism of the concept.

KEY TERMS

beggar-thy-neighbor policies, p. 329

Brander-Spencer analysis, p. 326

carbon tariffs, p. 341

environmental Kuznets curve, p. 338

excess returns, p. 325

externalities, p. 323

pollution haven, p. 340

strategic trade policy, p. 322

PROBLEMS

MyEconLab

1. What are the main arguments in favor of an interventionist trade policy? Provide one example of each.
2. Globalization has often attracted a lot of criticism, especially from emerging countries. Taking the analysis made in this chapter into consideration, state your conclusions.
3. If the United States had its way, it would demand that Japan spend more money on basic research in science and less on applied research into industrial applications. Explain why in terms of the analysis of appropriability.
4. Why do strategic trade policies normally attract trade retaliation actions from other countries? Examine a case-study of your choice and analyze its implication.
5. Suppose the European Commission asked you to develop a brief on behalf of subsidizing European development of software for smartphones—bearing in mind that this industry is currently dominated by U.S. firms, notably Apple and Google (whose Android system is used on many phones and tablets). What arguments would you use? What are the weaknesses in those arguments?
6. What is the main critique against the WTO with respect to environmental protection? How does the WTO justify its position on trade disputes that involve environmental issues?
7. France, in addition to its occasional stabs at strategic trade policy, pursues an active nationalist *cultural* policy that promotes French art, music, fashion, cuisine, and so on. This may be primarily a matter of attempting to preserve a national identity in an increasingly homogeneous world, but some French officials also defend this policy on economic grounds. In what sense could some features of such a policy be defended as a kind of strategic trade policy?
8. "The fundamental problem with any attempt to limit climate change is that the countries whose growth poses the greatest threat to the planet are also the countries that can least afford to pay the price of environmental activism." Explain in terms of the environmental Kuznets curve.
9. Many countries have value-added taxes—taxes that are paid by producers, but are intended to fall on consumers. (They're basically just an indirect way of imposing sales taxes.) Such value-added taxes are always accompanied by an equal tax on imports; such import taxes are considered legal because like the value-added tax, they're really an indirect way of taxing all consumer purchases at the same rate. Compare this situation to the argument over carbon tariffs. Why might defenders argue that such tariffs are legal? What objections can you think of?

FURTHER READINGS

James A. Brander and Barbara J. Spencer. "Export Subsidies and International Market Share Rivalry." *Journal of International Economics* 16 (1985), pp. 83–100. A basic reference on the potential role of subsidies as a tool of strategic trade policy.

Kimberly Ann Elliott. *Can Labor Standards Improve Under Globalization?* Washington, D.C.: Institute for International Economics, 2001. A survey of the issues by an economist sympathetic to the cause of the activists.

Edward M. Graham. *Fighting the Wrong Enemy: Antiglobalization Activists and Multinational Corporations.* Washington, D.C.: Institute for International Economics, 2001. A survey of the issues by an economist less sympathetic to the activists.

Elhanan Helpman and Paul Krugman. *Trade Policy and Market Structure.* Cambridge: MIT Press, 1989. A survey and synthesis of the literature on strategic trade policy and related topics.

William Langewiesche. "The Shipbreakers." *The Atlantic Monthly* (August 2000). A fascinating description of the shipbreaking industry of Alang and the dispute it has generated.

Hearing on Trade Aspects of Climate Change Legislation, Before the Subcommittee on Trade, 112th Cong. (March 24 2009) (statement of Joost Pauwelyn). A clear, concise discussion by a trade lawyer of the issues surrounding carbon tariffs, in which he argues that if done carefully, they would be legal under existing agreements.

MyEconLab Can Help You Get a Better Grade

MyEconLab   If your exam were tomorrow, would you be ready? For each chapter, MyEconLab Practice Tests and Study Plans pinpoint sections you have mastered and those you need to study. That way, you are more efficient with your study time, and you are better prepared for your exams.

To see how it works, turn to page 41 and then go to www.myeconlab.com

CHAPTER 13

NATIONAL INCOME ACCOUNTING AND THE BALANCE OF PAYMENTS

B etween 2004 and 2007, the world economy boomed, its total real product growing at an annual average rate of about 5 percent per year. The growth rate of world production slowed to around 3 percent per year in 2008, before dropping to *minus* 0.6 percent in 2009—a reduction in world output unprecedented in the period since World War II. In many countries, including the United States, unemployment soared. While the world's developing and emerging countries quickly returned to an annual growth rate close to 6 per cent per year, advanced economies struggled to grow quickly enough to return to full employment, and the European countries that use the euro again grew at a negative rate in 2012. Can economic analysis help us to understand the behavior of the global economy and the reasons why individual countries' fortunes often differ?

Previous chapters have been concerned primarily with the problem of making the best use of the world's scarce productive resources at a single point in time. The branch of economics called **microeconomics** studies this problem from the perspective of individual firms and consumers. Microeconomics works "from the bottom up" to show how individual economic actors, by pursuing their own interests, collectively determine how resources are used. In our study of international microeconomics, we have learned how individual production and consumption decisions produce patterns of international trade and specialization. We have also seen that while free trade usually encourages efficient resource use, government intervention or market failures can cause waste even when all factors of production are fully employed.

With this chapter, we shift our focus and ask: How can economic policy ensure that factors of production *are* fully employed? And what determines how an economy's capacity to produce goods and services changes over time? To answer these questions, we must understand **macroeconomics**, the branch of economics that studies how economies' overall levels of employment, production, and growth are determined. Like microeconomics, macroeconomics is concerned with the effective use of scarce resources. But while microeconomics focuses on the economic decisions of individuals, macroeconomics analyzes the behavior of an economy as a whole. In our study of international macroeconomics, we will learn how the interactions of national economies influence the worldwide pattern of macroeconomic activity.

Macroeconomic analysis emphasizes four aspects of economic life that, until now, we have usually kept in the background to simplify our discussion of international economics:

1. *Unemployment.* We know that in the real world, workers may be unemployed and factories may be idle. Macroeconomics studies the factors that cause unemployment and the steps governments can take to prevent it. A main concern of international macroeconomics is the problem of ensuring full employment in economies open to international trade.

2. *Saving.* In earlier chapters, we usually assumed that every country consumes an amount exactly equal to its income—no more and no less. In reality, though, households can put aside part of their income to provide for the future, or they can borrow temporarily to spend more than they earn. A country's saving or borrowing behavior affects domestic employment and future levels of national wealth. From the standpoint of the international economy as a whole, the world saving rate determines how quickly the world stock of productive capital can grow.

3. *Trade imbalances.* As we saw in earlier chapters, the value of a country's imports equals the value of its exports when spending equals income. This state of balanced trade is seldom attained by actual economies, however. In the following chapters, trade imbalances play a large role because they redistribute wealth among countries and are a main channel through which one country's macroeconomic policies affect its trading partners. It should be no surprise, therefore, that trade imbalances, particularly when they are large and persistent, quickly can become a source of international discord.

4. *Money and the price level.* The trade theory you have studied so far is a barter theory, one in which goods are exchanged directly for other goods on the basis of their relative prices. In practice, it is more convenient to use money— a widely acceptable medium of exchange—in transactions, and to quote prices in terms of money. Because money changes hands in virtually every transaction that takes place in a modern economy, fluctuations in the supply of money or in the demand for it can affect both output and employment. International macroeconomics takes into account that every country uses a currency and that a monetary change (for example, a change in money supply) in one country can have effects that spill across its borders to other countries. Stability in money price levels is an important goal of international macroeconomic policy.

This chapter takes the first step in our study of international macroeconomics by explaining the accounting concepts economists use to describe a country's level of production and its international transactions. To get a complete picture of the macroeconomic linkages among economies that engage in international trade, we have to master two related and essential tools. The first of these tools, **national income accounting**, records all the expenditures that contribute to a country's income and output. The second tool, **balance of payments accounting**, helps us keep track of both changes in a country's indebtedness to foreigners and the fortunes of its export and import-competing industries. The balance of payments accounts also show the connection between foreign transactions and national money supplies.

LEARNING GOALS

After reading this chapter, you will be able to:

- Discuss the concept of the current account balance.
- Use the current account balance to extend national income accounting to open economies.
- Apply national income accounting to the interaction of saving, investment, and net exports.
- Describe the balance of payments accounts and explain their relationship to the current account balance.
- Relate the current account to changes in a country's net foreign wealth.

The National Income Accounts

Of central concern to macroeconomic analysis is a country's **gross national product (GNP)**, the value of all final goods and services produced by the country's factors of production and sold on the market in a given time period. GNP, which is the basic measure of a country's output studied by macroeconomists, is calculated by adding up the market value of all expenditures on final output. GNP therefore includes the value of goods like bread sold in a supermarket and textbooks sold in a bookstore as well as the value of services provided by stock brokers and plumbers. Because output cannot be produced without the aid of factor inputs, the expenditures that make up GNP are closely linked to the employment of labor, capital, and other factors of production.

To distinguish among the different types of expenditure that make up a country's GNP, government economists and statisticians who compile national income accounts divide GNP among the four possible uses for which a country's final output is purchased: *consumption* (the amount consumed by private domestic residents), *investment* (the amount put aside by private firms to build new plant and equipment for future production), *government purchases* (the amount used by the government), and the *current account balance* (the amount of net exports of goods and services to foreigners). The term *national income accounts*, rather than *national output accounts*, is used to describe this fourfold classification because a country's income in fact equals its output. Thus, the national income accounts can be thought of as classifying each transaction that contributes to national income according to the type of expenditure that gives rise to it. Figure 13-1 shows how U.S. GNP was divided among its four components in the first quarter of 2013.[1]

---

[1]In Figure 13-1 quarterly GNP and its components are measured at an annual rate (that is, they are multiplied by four). Our definition of the current account is not strictly accurate when a country is a net donor or recipient of foreign gifts. This possibility, along with some others, also complicates our identification of GNP with national income. We describe later in this chapter how the definitions of national income and the current account must be changed in such cases.

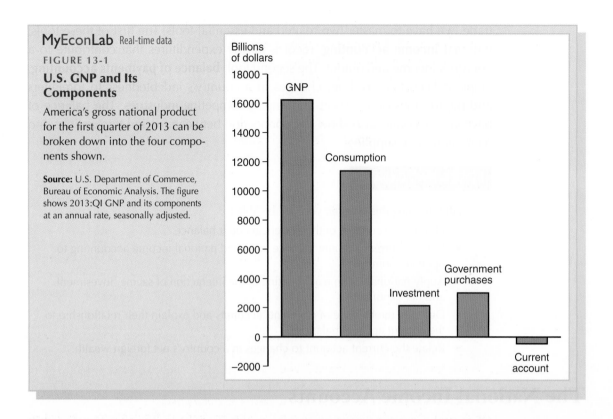

FIGURE 13-1

U.S. GNP and Its Components

America's gross national product for the first quarter of 2013 can be broken down into the four components shown.

Source: U.S. Department of Commerce, Bureau of Economic Analysis. The figure shows 2013:QI GNP and its components at an annual rate, seasonally adjusted.

Why is it useful to divide GNP into consumption, investment, government purchases, and the current account? One major reason is that we cannot hope to understand the cause of a particular recession or boom without knowing how the main categories of spending have changed. And without such an understanding, we cannot recommend a sound policy response. In addition, the national income accounts provide information essential for studying why some countries are rich—that is, have a high level of GNP relative to population size—while some are poor.

National Product and National Income

Our first task in understanding how economists analyze GNP is to explain in greater detail why the GNP a country generates over some time period must equal its **national income**, the income earned in that period by its factors of production.

The reason for this equality is that every dollar used to purchase goods or services automatically ends up in somebody's pocket. A visit to the doctor provides a simple example of how an increase in national output raises national income by the same amount. The $75 you pay the doctor represents the market value of the services he or she provides for you, so your visit raises GNP by $75. But the $75 you pay the doctor also raises his or her income. So national income rises by $75.

The principle that output and income are the same also applies to goods, even goods produced with the help of many factors of production. Consider the example of an economics textbook. When you purchase a new book from the publisher, the value of your purchase enters GNP. But your payment enters the income of the productive factors that cooperated in producing the book because the publisher must pay for their services with the proceeds of sales. First, there are the authors, editors, artists, and compositors who provide the labor inputs necessary for the book's production. Second, there are the publishing company's shareholders, who receive dividends for having financed acquisition of the capital used in production. Finally, there are the suppliers of paper and ink, who provide the intermediate materials used in producing the book.

The paper and ink purchased by the publishing house to produce the book are *not* counted separately in GNP because their contribution to the value of national output is already included in the book's price. It is to avoid such double counting that we allow only the sale of *final* goods and services to enter into the definition of GNP. Sales of intermediate goods, such as paper and ink purchased by a publisher, are not counted. Notice also that the sale of a used textbook does not enter GNP. Our definition counts only final goods and services that are *produced*, and a used textbook does not qualify: It was counted in GNP at the time it was first sold. Equivalently, the sale of a used textbook does not generate income for any factor of production.

Capital Depreciation and International Transfers

Because we have defined GNP and national income so that they are necessarily equal, their equality is really an identity. Two adjustments to the definition of GNP must be made, however, before the identification of GNP and national income is entirely correct in practice.

1. GNP does not take into account the economic loss due to the tendency of machinery and structures to wear out as they are used. This loss, called *depreciation*, reduces the income of capital owners. To calculate national income over a given period, we must therefore subtract from GNP the depreciation of capital over the period. GNP less depreciation is called *net national product* (NNP).
2. A country's income may include gifts from residents of foreign countries, called *unilateral transfers*. Examples of unilateral transfers of income are pension payments to retired citizens living abroad, reparation payments, and foreign aid such as relief funds donated to drought-stricken nations. For the United States in 2012, the balance of such payments amounted to around –$129.7 billion, representing a 0.8 percent of GNP net transfer to foreigners. Net unilateral transfers are part of a country's income but are not part of its product, and they must be added to NNP in calculations of national income.

National income equals GNP *less* depreciation *plus* net unilateral transfers. The difference between GNP and national income is by no means an insignificant amount, but macroeconomics has little to say about it, and it is of little importance for macroeconomic analysis. Therefore, for the purposes of this text, we usually use the terms *GNP* and *national income* interchangeably, emphasizing the distinction between the two only when it is essential.[2]

Gross Domestic Product

Most countries other than the United States have long reported **gross domestic product (GDP)** rather than GNP as their primary measure of national economic activity. In 1991, the United States began to follow this practice as well. GDP is supposed to

---

[2]Strictly speaking, government statisticians refer to what we have called "national income" as *national disposable income*. Their official concept of national income omits foreign net unilateral transfers. Once again, however, the difference between national income and national disposable income is usually unimportant for macroeconomic analysis. Unilateral transfers are alternatively referred to as *secondary income payments* to distinguish them from *primary income payments* consisting of cross-border wage and investment income. We will see this terminology later when we study balance of payments accounting.

measure the volume of production within a country's borders, whereas GNP equals GDP *plus* net receipts of factor income from the rest of the world. For the United States, these net receipts are primarily the income domestic residents earn on wealth they hold in other countries less the payments domestic residents make to foreign owners of wealth that is located in the domestic country.

GDP does not correct, as GNP does, for the portion of countries' production carried out using services provided by foreign-owned capital and labor. Consider an example: The profits of a Spanish factory with British owners are counted in Spain's GDP but are part of Britain's GNP. The services British capital provides in Spain are a service export from Britain, therefore they are added to British GDP in calculating British GNP. At the same time, to figure Spain's GNP, we must subtract from its GDP the corresponding service import from Britain.

As a practical matter, movements in GDP and GNP usually do not differ greatly. We will focus on GNP in this text, however, because GNP tracks national income more closely than GDP does, and national welfare depends more directly on national income than on domestic product.

National Income Accounting for an Open Economy

In this section, we extend to the case of an open economy, the closed-economy national income accounting framework you may have seen in earlier economics courses. We begin with a discussion of the national income accounts because they highlight the key role of international trade in open-economy macroeconomic theory. Since a closed economy's residents cannot purchase foreign output or sell their own to foreigners, all of national income must be allocated to domestic consumption, investment, or government purchases. In an economy open to international trade, however, the closed-economy version of national income accounting must be modified because some domestic output is exported to foreigners while some domestic income is spent on imported foreign products.

The main lesson of this section is the relationship among national saving, investment, and trade imbalances. We will see that in open economies, saving and investment are not necessarily equal, as they are in a closed economy. This occurs because countries can save in the form of foreign wealth by exporting more than they import, and they can *dissave*—that is, reduce their foreign wealth—by exporting less than they import.

Consumption

The portion of GNP purchased by private households to fulfill current wants is called **consumption**. Purchases of movie tickets, food, dental work, and washing machines all fall into this category. Consumption expenditure is the largest component of GNP in most economies. In the United States, for example, the fraction of GNP devoted to consumption has fluctuated in a range from about 62 to 70 percent over the past 60 years.

Investment

The part of output used by private firms to produce future output is called **investment**. Investment spending may be viewed as the portion of GNP used to increase the nation's stock of capital. Steel and bricks used to build a factory are part of investment spending, as are services provided by a technician who helps build business computers. Firms' purchases of inventories are also counted in investment spending because carrying inventories is just another way for firms to transfer output from current use to future use.

Investment is usually more variable than consumption. In the United States, (gross) investment has fluctuated between 11 and 22 percent of GNP in recent years. We often use the word *investment* to describe individual households' purchases of stocks, bonds, or real estate, but you should be careful not to confuse this everyday meaning of the word with the economic definition of investment as a part of GNP. When you buy a share of Microsoft stock, you are buying neither a good nor a service, so your purchase does not show up in GNP.

Government Purchases

Any goods and services purchased by federal, state, or local governments are classified as **government purchases** in the national income accounts. Included in government purchases are federal military spending, government support of cancer research, and government funds spent on highway repair and education. Government purchases include investment as well as consumption purchases. Government transfer payments such as social security and unemployment benefits do not require the recipient to give the government any goods or services in return. Thus, transfer payments are not included in government purchases.

Government purchases currently take up about 20 percent of U.S. GNP, and this share has not changed much since the late 1950s. (The corresponding figure for 1959, for example, was around 20 percent.) In 1929, however, government purchases accounted for only 8.5 percent of U.S. GNP.

The National Income Identity for an Open Economy

In a closed economy, any final good or service not purchased by households or the government must be used by firms to produce new plant, equipment, and inventories. If consumption goods are not sold immediately to consumers or the government, firms (perhaps reluctantly) add them to existing inventories, thereby increasing their investment.

This information leads to a fundamental identity for closed economies. Let Y stand for GNP, C for consumption, I for investment, and G for government purchases. Since all of a closed economy's output must be consumed, invested, or bought by the government, we can write

$$Y = C + I + G.$$

We derived the national income identity for a closed economy by assuming all output is consumed or invested by the country's citizens or purchased by its government. When foreign trade is possible, however, some output is purchased by foreigners while some domestic spending goes to purchase goods and services produced abroad. The GNP identity for open economies shows how the national income a country earns by selling its goods and services is divided between sales to domestic residents and sales to foreign residents.

Since residents of an open economy may spend some of their income on imports, that is, goods and services purchased from abroad, only the portion of their spending not devoted to imports is part of domestic GNP. The value of imports, denoted by IM, must be subtracted from total domestic spending, $C + I + G$, to find the portion of domestic spending that generates domestic national income. Imports from abroad add to foreign countries' GNPs but do not add directly to domestic GNP.

Similarly, the goods and services sold to foreigners make up a country's exports. Exports, denoted by EX, are the amount foreign residents' purchases add to the national income of the domestic economy.

The national income of an open economy is therefore the sum of domestic and foreign expenditures on the goods and services produced by domestic factors of production. Thus, the national income identity for an open economy is

$$Y = C + I + G + EX - IM. \tag{13-1}$$

An Imaginary Open Economy

To make identity (13-1) concrete, let's consider an imaginary closed economy, Agraria, whose only output is wheat. Each citizen of Agraria is a consumer of wheat, but each is also a farmer and therefore can be viewed as a firm. Farmers invest by putting aside a portion of each year's crop as seed for the next year's planting. There is also a government that appropriates part of the crop to feed the Agrarian army. Agraria's total annual crop is 100 bushels of wheat. Agraria can import milk from the rest of the world in exchange for exports of wheat. We cannot draw up the Agrarian national income accounts without knowing the price of milk in terms of wheat because all the components in the GNP identity (13-1) must be measured in the same units. If we assume the price of milk is 0.5 bushel of wheat per gallon, and that at this price, Agrarians want to consume 40 gallons of milk, then Agraria's imports are equal in value to 20 bushels of wheat.

In Table 13-1 we see that Agraria's total output is 100 bushels of wheat. Consumption is divided between wheat and milk, with 55 bushels of wheat and 40 gallons of milk (equal in value to 20 bushels of wheat) consumed over the year. The value of consumption in terms of wheat is $55 + (0.5 \times 40) = 55 + 20 = 75$.

The 100 bushels of wheat produced by Agraria are used as follows: 55 are consumed by domestic residents, 25 are invested, 10 are purchased by the government, and 10 are exported abroad. National income ($Y = 100$) equals domestic spending ($C + I + G = 110$) plus exports ($EX = 10$) less imports ($IM = 20$).

The Current Account and Foreign Indebtedness

In reality, a country's foreign trade is exactly balanced only rarely. The difference between exports of goods and services and imports of goods and services is known as the **current account balance** (or current account). If we denote the current account by CA, we can express this definition in symbols as

$$CA = EX - IM.$$

TABLE 13-1	National Income Accounts for Agraria, an Open Economy (bushels of wheat)				
GNP (total output)	**= Consumption**	**+ Investment**	**+ Government** purchases	**+ Exports**	**− Imports**
100	= 75[a]	+ 25	+ 10	+ 10	− 20[b]

[a] 55 bushels of wheat $+$ (0.5 bushel per gallon) $\times$ (40 gallons of milk).
[b] 0.5 bushel per gallon $\times$ 40 gallons of milk.

When a country's imports exceed its exports, we say the country has a *current account deficit*. A country has a *current account surplus* when its exports exceed its imports.[3]

The GNP identity, equation (13-1), shows one reason why the current account is important in international macroeconomics. Since the right-hand side of (13-1) gives total expenditures on domestic output, changes in the current account can be associated with changes in output and, thus, employment.

The current account is also important because it measures the size and direction of international borrowing. When a country imports more than it exports, it is buying more from foreigners than it sells to them and must somehow finance this current account deficit. How does it pay for additional imports once it has spent its export earnings? Since the country as a whole can import more than it exports only if it can borrow the difference from foreigners, a country with a current account deficit must be increasing its net foreign debts by the amount of the deficit. This is currently the position of the United States, which has a significant current account deficit (and borrowed a sum equal to roughly 3 percent of its GNP in 2012).[4]

Similarly, a country with a current account surplus is earning more from its exports than it spends on imports. This country finances the current account deficit of its trading partners by lending to them. The foreign wealth of a surplus country rises because foreigners pay for any imports not covered by their exports by issuing IOUs that they will eventually have to redeem. The preceding reasoning shows that *a country's current account balance equals the change in its net foreign wealth.*[5]

We have defined the current account as the difference between exports and imports. Equation (13-1) says that the current account is also equal to the difference between national income and domestic residents' total spending $C + I + G$:

$$Y - (C + I + G) = CA.$$

It is only by borrowing abroad that a country can have a current account deficit and use more output than it is currently producing. If it uses less than its output, it has a current account surplus and is lending the surplus to foreigners.[6] International borrowing and lending were identified with *intertemporal trade* in Chapter 6. A country with a current account deficit is importing present consumption and exporting future consumption. A country with a current account surplus is exporting present consumption and importing future consumption.

---

[3]In addition to net exports of goods and services, the current account balance includes net unilateral transfers of income, which we discussed briefly above. Following our earlier assumption, we continue to ignore such transfers for now to simplify the discussion. Later in this chapter, when we analyze the U.S. balance of payments in detail, we will see how transfers of current income enter the current account.

[4]Alternatively, a country could finance a current account deficit by using previously accumulated foreign wealth to pay for imports. This country would be running down its net foreign wealth, which has the same effect on overall wealth as running up its net foreign debts.

Our discussion here is ignoring the possibility that a country receives *gifts* of foreign assets (or gives such gifts), such as when one country agrees to forgive another's debts. As we will discuss below, such asset transfers (unlike transfers of current income) are not part of the current account, but they nonetheless do affect net foreign wealth. They are recorded in the *capital account* of the balance of payments.

[5]Alas, this statement is also not exactly correct, because there are factors that influence net foreign wealth that are not captured in the national income and product accounts. We will abstract from this fact until this chapter's concluding Case Study.

[6]The sum $A = C + I + G$ is often called domestic *absorption* in the literature on international macroeconomics. Using this terminology, we can describe the current account surplus as the difference between income and absorption, $Y - A$.

As an example, consider again the imaginary economy of Agraria described in Table 13-1. The total value of its consumption, investment, and government purchases, at 110 bushels of wheat, is greater than its output of 100 bushels. This inequality would be impossible in a closed economy; it is possible in this open economy because Agraria now imports 40 gallons of milk, worth 20 bushels of wheat, but exports only 10 bushels of wheat. The current account deficit of 10 bushels is the value of Agraria's borrowing from foreigners, which the country will have to repay in the future.

Figure 13-2 gives a vivid illustration of how a string of current account deficits can add up to a large foreign debt. The figure plots the U.S. current account balance since the late 1970s along with a measure of the nation's stock of net foreign wealth, its **net international investment position** (or *IIP*), the difference between its claims on foreigners and its liabilities to them. As you can see, the United States had accumulated substantial foreign wealth by the early 1980s, when a sustained current account deficit of proportions unprecedented in the 20th century opened up. In 1987, the country became

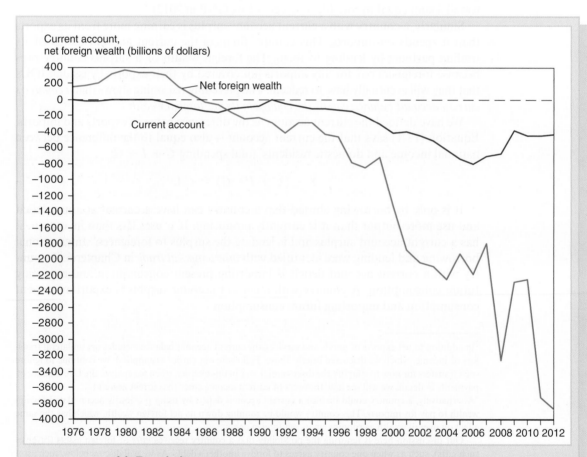

FIGURE 13-2   MyEconLab Real-time data

The U.S. Current Account and Net International Investment Position, 1976–2012

A string of current account deficits starting in the early 1980s reduced America's net foreign wealth until, by the early 21st century, the country had accumulated a substantial net foreign debt.

Source: U.S. Department of Commerce, Bureau of Economic Analysis.

a net debtor to foreigners for the first time since World War I. That foreign debt has continued to grow, and at the start of 2013, it stood at about 25 percent of GNP.

Saving and the Current Account

Simple as it is, the GNP identity has many illuminating implications. To explain the most important of these implications, we define the concept of **national saving**, that is, the portion of output, Y, that is not devoted to household consumption, C, or government purchases, G.[7] *In a closed economy, national saving always equals investment.* This tells us that the closed economy as a whole can increase its wealth only by accumulating new capital.

Let S stand for national saving. Our definition of S tells us that

$$S = Y - C - G.$$

Since the closed-economy GNP identity, $Y = C + I + G$, may also be written as $I = Y - C - G$, then

$$S = I,$$

and national saving must equal investment in a closed economy.

Whereas in a closed economy, saving and investment must always be equal, in an open economy they can differ. Remembering that national saving, S, equals $Y - C - G$ and that $CA = EX - IM$, we can rewrite the GNP identity (13-1) as

$$S = I + CA.$$

The equation highlights an important difference between open and closed economies: An open economy can save either by building up its capital stock or by acquiring foreign wealth, but a closed economy can save only by building up its capital stock.

Unlike a closed economy, an open economy with profitable investment opportunities does not have to increase its saving in order to exploit them. The preceding expression shows that it is possible simultaneously to raise investment and foreign borrowing without changing saving. For example, if New Zealand decides to build a new hydroelectric plant, it can import the materials it needs from the United States and borrow American funds to pay for them. This transaction raises New Zealand's domestic investment because the imported materials contribute to expanding the country's capital stock. The transaction also raises New Zealand's current account deficit by an amount equal to the increase in investment. New Zealand's saving does not have to change, even though investment rises. For this to be possible, however, U.S. residents must be willing to save more so that the resources needed to build the plant are freed for New Zealand's use. The result is another example of intertemporal trade, in which New Zealand imports present output (when it borrows from the United States) and exports future output (when it pays off the loan).

Because one country's savings can be borrowed by a second country in order to increase the second country's stock of capital, a country's current account surplus

---

[7]The U.S. national income accounts assume that government purchases are not used to enlarge the nation's capital stock. We follow this convention here by subtracting *all* government purchases from output to calculate national saving. Most other countries' national accounts distinguish between government consumption and government investment (for example, investment by publicly owned enterprises) and include the latter as part of national saving. Often, however, government investment figures include purchases of military equipment.

is often referred to as its *net foreign investment.* Of course, when one country lends to another to finance investment, part of the income generated by the investment in future years must be used to pay back the lender. Domestic investment and foreign investment are two different ways in which a country can use current savings to increase its future income.

Private and Government Saving

So far our discussion of saving has not stressed the distinction between saving decisions made by the private sector and saving decisions made by the government. Unlike private saving decisions, however, government saving decisions are often made with an eye toward their effect on output and employment. The national income identity can help us to analyze the channels through which government saving decisions influence domestic macroeconomic conditions. To use the national income identity in this way, we first have to divide national saving into its private and government components.

Private saving is defined as the part of disposable income that is saved rather than consumed. Disposable income is national income, Y, less the net taxes collected from households and firms by the government, T.[8] Private saving, denoted S^p, can therefore be expressed as

$$S^p = Y - T - C.$$

Government saving is defined similarly to private saving. The government's "income" is its net tax revenue, T, while its "consumption" is government purchases, G. If we let S^g stand for government saving, then

$$S^g = T - G.$$

The two types of saving we have defined, private and government, add up to national saving. To see why, recall the definition of national saving, S, as $Y - C - G$. Then

$$S = Y - C - G = (Y - T - C) + (T - G) = S^p + S^g.$$

We can use the definitions of private and government saving to rewrite the national income identity in a form that is useful for analyzing the effects of government saving decisions on open economies. Because $S = S^p + S^g = I + CA$,

$$S^p = I + CA - S^g = I + CA - (T - G) = I + CA + (G - T). \quad \text{(13-2)}$$

Equation (13-2) relates private saving to domestic investment, the current account surplus, and government saving. To interpret equation (13-2), we define the **government budget deficit** as $G - T$, that is, as government saving preceded by a minus sign. The government budget deficit measures the extent to which the government is borrowing to finance its expenditures. Equation (13-2) then states that a country's private saving can take three forms: investment in domestic capital (I), purchases of wealth from foreigners (CA), and purchases of the domestic government's newly issued debt ($G - T$).[9]

---

[8]Net taxes are taxes less government transfer payments. The term *government* refers to the federal, state, and local governments considered as a single unit.

[9]In a closed economy, the current account is always zero, so equation (13-2) is simply $S^p = I + (G - T)$.

THE MYSTERY OF THE MISSING DEFICIT

Because each country's exports are other countries' imports, the world's current account balances must add up to zero. But they don't. The accompanying figure shows the pattern in the data. Between 1980 and 2003, the sum of global current accounts was negative, implying either that surpluses were understated or that deficits were overstated. But in 2004, the "mystery of the missing surplus" became a "mystery of the missing deficit." Since that year, the measured global current account has been positive.

Given the inevitable errors in collecting detailed international payments data from many national agencies with differing accuracy and coverage, some discrepancy is unavoidable. What is puzzling is that the global discrepancy should

be *persistently* positive or negative. That pattern suggests that something systematic is going on.

When the global current account balance was negative, it was thought that a big contributing factor was incomplete reporting of international investment income. For example, banks report these to their home governments, but the recipients, some of whom wish to avoid taxes, may not report them at the receiving end.

Not only have tax authorities become better at enforcing compliance, however, the general level of interest rates is now lower than it was in the 1980s and 1990s. Better measurement of international investment income could be responsible for a shrinking negative world current account. But what could have made it turn positive?

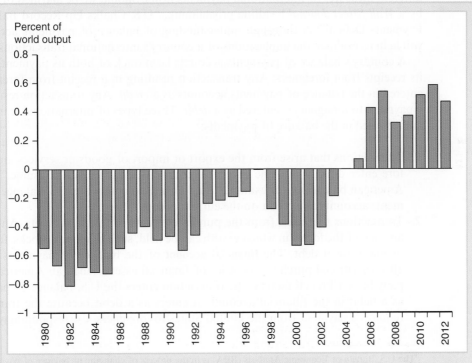

The Global Current Account Discrepancy since 1980

Once big and negative, implying missing current account credits, the global current account balance has become big and positive, implying missing current account debits.

Source: International Monetary Fund, *World Economic Outlook* database, April 2013.

(*Continued*)

One possible culprit is growing international trade in services. For example, a big law firm is likely to report its service exports fairly accurately, but the purchases by many of its smaller customers may escape detection. In a recent detailed review of the question, however, the *Economist* magazine pointed out that errors in measuring merchandise trade have also risen dramatically, and it is less clear that these would create a systematic bias toward an apparent global surplus.* The mystery remains a mystery. In 2012, it was worth $336 billion, or nearly half a percent of world output.

---

*See "Economics Focus: Exports to Mars," *Economist*, November 12, 2011, at http://www.economist.com/node/21538100.

The Balance of Payments Accounts

In addition to national income accounts, government economists and statisticians also keep balance of payments accounts, a detailed record of the composition of the current account balance and of the many transactions that finance it.[10] Balance of payments figures are of great interest to the general public, as indicated by the attention that various news media pay to them. But press reports sometimes confuse different measures of international payments flows. Should we be alarmed or cheered by a *Wall Street Journal* headline proclaiming, "U.S. Chalks Up Record Balance of Payments Deficit"? A thorough understanding of balance of payments accounting will help us evaluate the implications of a country's international transactions.

A country's balance of payments accounts keep track of both its payments to and its receipts from foreigners. Any transaction resulting in a receipt from foreigners is entered in the balance of payments accounts as a *credit*. Any transaction resulting in a payment to foreigners is entered as a *debit*. Three types of international transaction are recorded in the balance of payments:

1. Transactions that arise from the export or import of goods or services and therefore enter directly into the current account. When a French consumer imports American blue jeans, for example, the transaction enters the U.S. balance of payments accounts as a credit on the current account.
2. Transactions that arise from the purchase or sale of financial assets. An **asset** is any one of the forms in which wealth can be held, such as money, stocks, factories, or government debt. The **financial account** of the balance of payments records all international purchases or sales of financial assets. When an American company buys a French factory, the transaction enters the U.S. balance of payments as a debit in the financial account. It enters as a debit because the transaction requires a payment from the United States to foreigners. Correspondingly, a U.S.

---

[10]The U.S. Bureau of Economic Analysis (BEA) is in the process of changing its balance of payments presentation to conform to prevailing international standards, so our discussion in this chapter differs in some respects from that in editions one through eight of this book. We follow the new methodology described by Kristy L. Howell and Robert E. Yuskavage, "Modernizing and Enhancing BEA's International Economic Accounts: Recent Progress and Future Directions," *Survey of Current Business* (May 2010), pp. 6–20. For an update, see Kristy L. Howell and Kyle L. Westmoreland, "Modernizing and Enhancing BEA's International Economic Accounts: A Progress Report and Plans for Implementation," *Survey of Current Business* (May 2013), pp. 44–60. As of this writing, the BEA has not completed a full transition to the new system, but it hopes to do so in June 2014.

sale of assets to foreigners enters the U.S. financial account as a credit. The difference between a country's purchases and sales of foreign assets is called its *financial account balance*, or its *net financial flows*.

3. Certain other activities resulting in transfers of wealth between countries are recorded in the **capital account**. These international asset movements—which are generally very small for the United States—differ from those recorded in the financial account. For the most part they result from nonmarket activities or represent the acquisition or disposal of nonproduced, nonfinancial, and possibly intangible assets (such as copyrights and trademarks). For example, if the U.S. government forgives $1 billion in debt owed to it by the government of Pakistan, U.S. wealth declines by $1 billion and a $1 billion debit is recorded in the U.S. capital account.

You will find the complexities of the balance of payments accounts less confusing if you keep in mind the following simple rule of double-entry bookkeeping: *Every international transaction automatically enters the balance of payments twice, once as a credit and once as a debit.* This principle of balance of payments accounting holds true because every transaction has two sides: If you buy something from a foreigner, you must pay him in some way, and the foreigner must then somehow spend or store your payment.

Examples of Paired Transactions

Some examples will show how the principle of double-entry bookkeeping operates in practice.

1. Imagine you buy an ink-jet fax machine from the Italian company Olivetti and pay for your purchase with a $1,000 check. Your payment to buy a good (the fax machine) from a foreign resident enters the U.S. current account as a debit. But where is the offsetting balance of payments credit? Olivetti's U.S. salesperson must do something with your check—let's say he deposits it in Olivetti's account at Citibank in New York. In this case, Olivetti has purchased, and Citibank has sold, a U.S. asset—a bank deposit worth $1,000—and the transaction shows up as a $1,000 credit in the U.S. financial account. The transaction creates the following two offsetting bookkeeping entries in the U.S. balance of payments:

	Credit	Debit
Fax machine purchase (Current account, U.S. good import)		$1,000
Sale of bank deposit by Citibank (Financial account, U.S. asset sale)	$1,000	

2. As another example, suppose that during your travels in France, you pay $200 for a fine dinner at the Restaurant de l'Escargot d'Or. Lacking cash, you place the charge on your Visa credit card. Your payment, which is a tourist expenditure, will be counted as a service import for the United States, and therefore as a current account debit. Where is the offsetting credit? Your signature on the Visa slip entitles the restaurant to receive $200 (actually, its local currency equivalent) from First Card, the company that issued your Visa card. It is therefore an asset, a claim on a future payment from First Card. So when you pay for your meal abroad with your credit card, you are selling an asset to France and generating

a $200 credit in the U.S. financial account. The pattern of offsetting debits and credits in this case is:

	Credit	Debit
Meal purchase (Current account, U.S. service import)		$200
Sale of claim on First Card		
(Financial account, U.S. asset sale)	$200	

3. Imagine next that your Uncle Sid from Los Angeles buys a newly issued share of stock in the U.K. oil giant British Petroleum (BP). He places his order with his U.S. stockbroker, Go-for-Broke, Inc., paying $95 with funds from his Go-for-Broke money market account. BP, in turn, deposits the $95 Sid has paid into its own U.S. bank account at Second Bank of Chicago. Uncle Sid's acquisition of the stock creates a $95 debit in the U.S. financial account (he has purchased an asset from a foreign resident, BP), while BP's $95 deposit at its Chicago bank is the offsetting financial account credit (BP has expanded its U.S. asset holdings). The mirror-image effects on the U.S. balance of payments therefore both appear in the financial account:

	Credit	Debit
Uncle Sid's purchase of a share of BP		$95
(Financial account, U.S. asset purchase)		
BP's deposit of Uncle Sid's payment at Second Bank of Chicago		
(Financial account, U.S. asset sale)	$95	

4. Finally, let's consider how the U.S. balance of payments accounts are affected when U.S. banks forgive (that is, announce that they will simply forget about) $5,000 in debt owed to them by the government of the imaginary country of Bygonia. In this case, the United States makes a $5,000 capital transfer to Bygonia, which appears as a $5,000 debit entry in the capital account. The associated credit is in the financial account, in the form of a $5,000 reduction in U.S. assets held abroad (a negative "acquisition" of foreign assets, and therefore a balance of payments credit):

	Credit	Debit
U.S. banks' debt forgiveness		$5,000
(Capital account, U.S. transfer payment)		
Reduction in banks' claims on Bygonia		
(Financial account, U.S. asset sale)	$5,000	

These examples show that many circumstances can affect the way a transaction generates its offsetting balance of payments entry. We can never predict with certainty where the flip side of a particular transaction will show up, but we can be sure that it will show up somewhere.

The Fundamental Balance of Payments Identity

Because any international transaction automatically gives rise to offsetting credit and debit entries in the balance of payments, the sum of the current account balance and the capital account balance automatically equals the financial account balance:

$$\text{Current account} + \text{capital account} = \text{Financial account.} \qquad (13\text{-}3)$$

In examples 1, 2, and 4 previously, current or capital account entries have offsetting counterparts in the financial account, while in example 3, two financial account entries offset each other.

You can understand this identity another way. Recall the relationship linking the current account to international lending and borrowing. Because the sum of the current and capital accounts is the total change in a country's net foreign assets (including, through the capital account, nonmarket asset transfers), that sum necessarily equals the difference between a country's purchases of assets from foreigners and its sales of assets to them—that is, the financial account balance (also called net financial flows).

We now turn to a more detailed description of the balance of payments accounts, using as an example the U.S. accounts for 2012.

The Current Account, Once Again

As you have learned, the current account balance measures a country's net exports of goods and services. Table 13-2 shows that U.S. exports (on the credit side) were $2,986.9 billion in 2012, while U.S. imports (on the debit side) were $3,297.7 billion.

The balance of payments accounts divide exports and imports into three finer categories. The first is *goods* trade, that is, exports or imports of merchandise. The second category, *services*, includes items such as payments for legal assistance, tourists' expenditures, and shipping fees. The final category, *income*, is made up mostly of international interest and dividend payments and the earnings of domestically owned firms operating abroad. If you own a share of a German firm's stock and receive a dividend payment of $5, that payment shows up in the accounts as a U.S. investment income receipt of $5. Wages that workers earn abroad can also enter the income account.

We include income on foreign investments in the current account because that income really is compensation for the *services* provided by foreign investments. This idea, as we saw earlier, is behind the distinction between GNP and GDP. When a U.S. corporation builds a plant in Canada, for instance, the productive services the plant generates are viewed as a service export from the United States to Canada equal in value to the profits the plant yields for its American owner. To be consistent, we must be sure to include these profits in American GNP and not in Canadian GNP. Remember, the definition of GNP refers to goods and services generated by a country's factors of production, but it does *not* specify that those factors must work within the borders of the country that owns them.

Before calculating the current account, we must include one additional type of international transaction that we have largely ignored until now. In discussing the relationship between GNP and national income, we defined unilateral transfers between countries as international gifts, that is, payments that do not correspond to the purchase of any good, service, or asset. Net unilateral transfers are considered part of the current account as well as a part of national income, and the identity $Y = C + I + G + CA$ holds exactly if Y is interpreted as GNP *plus* net transfers. In 2012, the U.S. balance of unilateral transfers was −$129.7 billion.

MyEconLab Real-time data

TABLE 13-2	U.S. Balance of Payments Accounts for 2012 (billions of dollars)
Current Account	
(1) Exports	**2,986.9**
Of which:	
Goods	1,561.2
Services	649.3
Income receipts (primary income)	776.3
(2) Imports	**3,297.7**
Of which:	
Goods	2,302.7
Services	442.5
Income payments (primary income)	552.4
(3) Net unilateral transfers (secondary income)	−129.7
Balance on current account	**−440.4**
[(1) − (2) + (3)]	
Capital Account	
(4)	**7.0**
Financial Account	
(5) Net U.S. acquisition of financial assets, excluding financial derivatives	**97.5**
Of which:	
Official reserve assets	4.5
Other assets	93.0
(6) Net U.S. incurrence of liabilities, excluding financial derivatives	**543.9**
Of which:	
Official reserve assets	393.9
Other assets	150.0
(7) Financial derivatives, net	**7.1**
Net financial flows	**−439.4**
[(5) − (6) + (7)]	
Net errors and omissions	−6.0
[Net financial flows less sum of current and capital accounts]	

Source: U.S. Department of Commerce, Bureau of Economic Analysis, June 14, 2013, release. Totals may differ from sums because of rounding.

The table shows a 2012 current account balance of $2,986.9 billion − $3,297.7 − $129.7 billion = −$440.4 billion, a deficit.

The negative sign means that current payments to foreigners exceeded current receipts and that U.S. residents used more output than they produced. Since these current account transactions were paid for in some way, we know that this $440.4 billion net debit entry must be offset by a net $440.4 billion credit elsewhere in the balance of payments.

The Capital Account

The capital account entry in Table 13-2 shows that in 2012, the United States received net capital asset transfers of roughly $7.0 billion. These payments to the United States are a net balance of payments credit. After we add them to the payments deficit implied by the current account, we find that the United States' need to cover its excess payments to foreigners is reduced very slightly, from $440.4 billion to $433.4 billion. Because an excess of national spending over income must be covered by net borrowing from foreigners, this negative current plus capital account balance must be matched by an equal negative balance of net financial flows, representing the net liabilities the United States incurred to foreigners in 2012 in order to fund its deficit.

The Financial Account

While the current account is the difference between sales of goods and services to foreigners and purchases of goods and services from them, the financial account measures the difference between acquisitions of assets from foreigners and the buildup of liabilities to them. When the United States borrows $1 from foreigners, it is selling them an asset—a promise that they will be repaid $1, with interest, in the future. Likewise, when the United States lends abroad, it acquires an asset: the right to claim future repayment from foreigners.

To cover its 2012 current plus capital account deficit of $433.4 billion, the United States needed to borrow from foreigners (or otherwise sell assets to them) in the net amount of $433.4 billion. We can look again at Table 13-2 to see exactly how this net sale of assets to foreigners came about.

The table records separately U.S. acquisitions of foreign financial assets (which are balance of payments debits, because the United States must pay foreigners for those assets) and increases in foreign claims on residents of the United States (which are balance of payments credits, because the United States receives payments when it sells assets overseas).

These data on increases in U.S. asset holdings abroad and foreign holdings of U.S. assets do not include holdings of *financial derivatives*, which are a class of assets that are more complicated than ordinary stocks and bonds, but have values that can depend on stock and bond values. (We will describe some specific derivative securities in the next chapter.) Starting in 2006, the U.S. Department of Commerce was able to assemble data on *net* cross-border derivative flows for the United States (U.S. net purchases of foreign-issued derivatives less foreign net purchases of U.S.-issued derivatives). Derivatives transactions enter the balance of payments accounts in the same way as do other international asset transactions.

According to Table 13-2, U.S.-owned assets abroad (other than derivatives) increased (on a net basis) by $97.5 billion in 2012. The figure is "on a net basis" because some U.S. residents bought foreign assets while others sold foreign assets they already owned, the difference between U.S. gross purchases and sales of foreign assets being $97.5 billion. In the same year (again on a net basis), the United States incurred new liabilities to foreigners equal to $543.9 billion. Some U.S. residents undoubtedly repaid foreign debts, but new borrowing from foreigners exceeded these repayments by $543.9 billion. The balance of U.S. purchases and sales of financial derivatives was $7.1 billion: The United States acquired derivative claims on foreigners greater in value than the derivative claims on the U.S. that foreigners acquired. We calculate the balance on financial account (net financial flows) as $97.5 billion − $543.9 billion + $7.1 billion = −$439.4 billion. The negative value for net financial flows means that in 2012, the United States increased its net liability to foreigners (liabilities minus assets) by $439.4 billion.

Net Errors and Omissions

We come out with net financial flows of −$439.4 billion rather than the −$433.4 billion that we'd expected after adding up the current and capital account balances. According to our data on trade and financial flows, the United States incurred $6.0 billion more in foreign debt than it actually needed to fund its current plus capital account deficit. If every balance of payments credit automatically generates an equal counterpart debit and vice versa, how is this difference possible? The reason is that information about the offsetting debit and credit items associated with a given transaction may be collected from different sources. For example, the import debit that a shipment of DVD players from Japan generates may come from a U.S. customs inspector's report and the corresponding financial account credit from a report by the U.S. bank in which the check paying for the DVD players is deposited. Because data from different sources may differ in coverage, accuracy, and timing, the balance of payments accounts seldom balance in practice as they must in theory. Account keepers force the two sides to balance by adding to the accounts a *net errors and omissions* item. For 2012, unrecorded (or misrecorded) international transactions generated a balancing accounting debit of −$6.0 billion—the difference between the recorded net financial flows and the sum of the recorded current and capital accounts.

We have no way of knowing exactly how to allocate this discrepancy among the current, capital, and financial accounts. (If we did, it wouldn't be a discrepancy!) The financial account is the most likely culprit, since it is notoriously difficult to keep track of the complicated financial trades between residents of different countries. But we cannot conclude that net financial flows were $6 billion higher than recorded because the current account is also highly suspect. Balance of payments accountants consider merchandise trade data relatively reliable, but data on services are not. Service transactions such as sales of financial advice and computer programming assistance may escape detection. Accurate measurement of international interest and dividend receipts is particularly difficult.

Official Reserve Transactions

Although there are many types of financial account transactions, one type is important enough to merit separate discussion. This type of transaction is the purchase or sale of official reserve assets by central banks.

An economy's **central bank** is the institution responsible for managing the supply of money. In the United States, the central bank is the Federal Reserve System. **Official international reserves** are foreign assets held by central banks as a cushion against national economic misfortune. At one time, official reserves consisted largely of gold, but today, central banks' reserves include substantial foreign financial assets, particularly U.S. dollar assets such as Treasury bills. The Federal Reserve itself holds only a small level of official reserve assets other than gold; its own holdings of U.S. dollar assets are not considered international reserves.

Central banks often buy or sell international reserves in private asset markets to affect macroeconomic conditions in their economies. Official transactions of this type are called **official foreign exchange intervention**. One reason why foreign exchange intervention can alter macroeconomic conditions is that it is a way for the central bank to inject money into the economy or withdraw it from circulation. We will have much more to say later about the causes and consequences of foreign exchange intervention.

Government agencies other than central banks may hold foreign reserves and intervene officially in exchange markets. The U.S. Treasury, for example, operates an Exchange Stabilization Fund that at times has played an active role in market trading.

Because the operations of such agencies usually have no noticeable impact on the money supply, however, we will simplify our discussion by speaking (when it is not too misleading) as if the central bank alone holds foreign reserves and intervenes.

When a central bank purchases or sells a foreign asset, the transaction appears in its country's financial account just as if the same transaction had been carried out by a private citizen. A transaction in which the central bank of Japan (the Bank of Japan) acquires dollar assets might occur as follows: A U.S. auto dealer imports a Nissan sedan from Japan and pays the auto company with a check for $20,000. Nissan does not want to invest the money in dollar assets, but it so happens that the Bank of Japan is willing to give Nissan Japanese money in exchange for the $20,000 check. The Bank of Japan's international reserves rise by $20,000 as a result of the deal. Because the Bank of Japan's dollar reserves are part of total Japanese assets held in the United States, the latter rise by $20,000. This transaction therefore results in a $20,000 credit in the U.S. financial account, the other side of the $20,000 debit in the U.S. current account due to the import of the car.[11]

Table 13-2 shows the size and direction of official reserve transactions involving the United States in 2012. U.S. official reserve assets rose by $4.5 billion. Foreign central banks purchased $393.9 billion to add to their reserves. The net increase in U.S. official reserves *less* the increase in foreign official reserve claims on the United States is the level of net central bank financial flows, which stood at $4.5 billion − $393.9 = −$389.4 billion in 2012.

You can think of this −$389.4 billion net central bank financial flow as measuring the degree to which monetary authorities in the United States and abroad joined with other lenders to cover the U.S. current account deficit. In the example above, the Bank of Japan, by acquiring a $20,000 U.S. bank deposit, indirectly finances an American import of a $20,000 Japanese car. The level of net central bank financial flows is called the **official settlements balance** or (in less formal usage) the **balance of payments**. This balance is the sum of the current account and capital account balances, less the nonreserve portion of the financial account balance, and it indicates the payments gap that official reserve transactions need to cover. Thus, the U.S. balance of payments in 2012 was −$389.4 billion.

The balance of payments played an important historical role as a measure of disequilibrium in international payments, and for many countries it still plays this role. A negative balance of payments (a deficit) may signal a crisis, for it means that a country is running down its international reserve assets or incurring debts to foreign monetary authorities. If a country faces the risk of being suddenly cut off from foreign loans, it will want to maintain a "war chest" of international reserves as a precaution. Developing countries, in particular, are in this position (see Chapter 22).

Like any summary measure, however, the balance of payments must be interpreted with caution. To return to our running example, the Bank of Japan's decision to expand its U.S. bank deposit holdings by $20,000 swells the measured U.S. balance of payments deficit by the same amount. Suppose the Bank of Japan instead places its $20,000 with Barclays Bank in London, which in turn deposits the money with Citibank in New York. The United States incurs an extra $20,000 in liabilities to *private* foreigners in this case, and the U.S. balance of payments deficit does not rise. But this "improvement" in the balance of payments is of little economic importance: It makes no real difference to the United States whether it borrows the Bank of Japan's money directly or through a London bank.

---

[11]To test your understanding, see if you can explain why the same sequence of actions causes a $20,000 improvement in Japan's current account and a $20,000 increase in its net financial flows.

CASE STUDY   The Assets and Liabilities of the World's Biggest Debtor

We saw earlier that the current account balance measures the flow of new net claims on foreign wealth that a country acquires by exporting more goods and services than it imports. This flow is not, however, the only important factor that causes a country's net foreign wealth to change. In addition, changes in the market price of wealth previously acquired can alter a country's net foreign wealth. When Japan's stock market lost three-quarters of its value over the 1990s, for example, American and European owners of Japanese shares saw the value of their claims on Japan plummet, and Japan's net *foreign* wealth increased as a result. Exchange rate changes have a similar effect. When the dollar depreciates against foreign currencies, for example, foreigners who hold dollar assets see their wealth fall when measured in their home currencies.

The Bureau of Economic Analysis (BEA) of the U.S. Department of Commerce, which oversees the vast job of data collection behind the U.S. national income and balance of payments statistics, reports annual estimates of the net international investment position of the United States—the country's foreign assets less its foreign liabilities. Because asset price and exchange rate changes alter the dollar values of foreign assets and liabilities alike, the BEA must adjust the values of existing claims to reflect such capital gains and losses in order to estimate U.S. net foreign wealth. These estimates show that at the end of 2012, the United States had a *negative* net foreign wealth position far greater than that of any other country.

Until 1991, foreign direct investments such as foreign factories owned by U.S. corporations were valued at their historical, that is, original, purchase prices. Now the BEA uses two different methods to place current values on foreign direct investments: the *current cost* method, which values direct investments at the cost of buying them today, and the *market value* method, which is meant to measure the price at which the investments could be sold. These methods can lead to different valuations because the cost of replacing a particular direct investment and the price it would command if sold on the market may be hard to measure. (The net foreign wealth data graphed in Figure 13-2 are current cost estimates, which are believed to be more accurate.)

Table 13-3 reproduces the BEA's account of how it made its valuation adjustments to find the U.S. net IIP at the end of 2012. This "headline" estimate values direct investments at current cost. Starting with its estimate of 2011 net foreign wealth (−\$3,730.6 billion), the BEA (column a) added the amount of the 2012 U.S. net financial flow of −\$439.4 billion—recall the figure reported in Table 13-2. Then the BEA adjusted the values of previously held assets and liabilities for various changes in their dollar prices (columns b, c, and d). As a result of these valuation changes, U.S. net foreign wealth fell by an amount smaller than the \$439.4 billion in new net borrowing from foreigners—in fact, U.S. net foreign wealth only declined by \$133.3 billion. The BEA's 2012 estimate of U.S. net foreign wealth, therefore, was −\$3,863.9 billion.

TABLE 13-3 **International Investment Position of the United States at Year End, 2011 and 2012 (millions of dollars)**

Line	Type of investment	Position, 2011 [r]	Changes in position in 2012 — Attributable to: Financial flows (a)	Valuation adjustments — Price changes (b)	Exchange-rate changes [1] (c)	Other changes [2] (d)	Total (a+b+c+d)	Position, 2012 [r]
1	Net international investment position of the United States (lines 2+3)	−3,730,590	−439,351	489,566	5,100	−188,618	−133,302	−3,863,892
2	Financial derivatives, net (line 5 less line 25)[3]	86,039	7,064	(⁴)	(⁴)	⁴−35,327	−28,263	57,776
3	Net international investment position, excluding financial derivatives (line 6 less line 26)	−3,816,629	−446,415	489,566	5,100	−153,291	−105,039	−3,921,668
4	U.S.-owned assets abroad (lines 5+6)	21,636,152	(³)	(³)	(³)	(³)	1,466	21,637,618
5	Financial derivatives (gross positive fair value)	4,716,578	(³)	(³)	(³)	(³)	−1,096,817	3,619,761
6	U.S.-owned assets abroad, excluding financial derivatives (lines 7+12+17)	16,919,574	97,469	990,880	5,909	4,024	1,098,283	18,017,857
7	U.S. official reserve assets	537,037	4,460	33,079	−2,208	0	35,331	572,368
8	Gold	400,355	0	⁵33,079	.....	⁶0	33,079	433,434
9	Special drawing rights	54,956	37	.....	57	0	94	55,050
10	Reserve position in the International Monetary Fund	30,080	4,032	.....	49	0	4,081	34,161
11	Foreign currencies	51,646	391	.....	−2,314	0	−1,923	49,723
12	U.S. government assets, other than official reserve assets	178,901	−85,331	.....	(*)	0	−85,331	93,570
13	U.S. credits and other long-term assets[7]	78,373	5,656	.....	(*)	0	5,656	84,029
14	Repayable in dollars	78,100	5,656	.....	.....	0	5,656	83,756
15	Other[8]	273	0	.....	(*)	.....	0	273
16	U.S. foreign currency holdings and U.S. short-term assets[9]	100,528	−90,987	.....	(*)	.....	−90,987	9,541
17	U.S. private assets	16,203,636	178,341	957,801	8,117	4,024	1,148,283	17,351,919
18	Direct investment at current cost	4,663,142	388,293	25,339	16,234	−15,258	414,608	5,077,750
19	Foreign securities	6,441,350	144,823	932,462	−7,412	20,000	1,089,873	7,531,223
20	Bonds	1,939,912	62,243	139,503	−973	0	200,773	2,140,685
21	Corporate stocks	4,501,438	82,580	792,959	−6,439	20,000	889,100	5,390,538
22	U.S. claims on unaffiliated foreigners reported by U.S. nonbanking concerns	792,953	25,723	.....	3,194	22,882	51,799	844,752
23	U.S. claims reported by U.S. banks and securities brokers, not included elsewhere	4,306,191	−380,498	.....	−3,899	−23,600	−407,997	3,898,194
24	Foreign-owned assets in the United States (lines 25+26)	25,366,742	(³)	(³)	(³)	(³)	134,768	25,501,510
25	Financial derivatives (gross negative fair value)	4,630,539	(³)	(³)	(³)	(³)	−1,068,554	3,561,985
26	Foreign-owned assets in the United States, excluding financial derivatives (lines 27+34)	20,736,203	543,884	501,314	809	157,315	1,203,322	21,939,525
27	Foreign official assets in the United States	5,256,358	393,922	42,110	58	0	436,090	5,692,448
28	U.S. government securities	4,235,886	314,660	−23,650	.....	0	291,010	4,526,896
29	U.S. Treasury securities	3,620,580	433,155	−21,531	.....	0	411,624	4,032,204
30	Other	615,306	−118,495	−2,119	.....	0	−120,614	494,692
31	Other U.S. government liabilities[10]	119,980	8,241	.....	58	0	8,299	128,279
32	U.S. liabilities reported by U.S. banks and securities brokers, not included elsewhere	205,973	−1,572	.....	.....	0	−1,572	204,401
33	Other foreign official assets	694,519	72,593	65,760	.....	0	138,353	832,872
34	Other foreign assets	15,479,845	149,962	459,204	751	157,315	767,232	16,247,077
35	Direct investment at current cost	2,879,531	166,411	20,385	606	−9,607	177,795	3,057,326
36	U.S. Treasury securities	1,386,274	156,385	−1,090	0	0	155,295	1,541,569
37	U.S. securities other than U.S. Treasury securities	6,151,552	196,908	439,909	−897	116,578	752,498	6,904,050
38	Corporate and other bonds	2,894,604	23,584	125,774	−897	18,898	167,359	3,061,963
39	Corporate stocks	3,256,948	173,324	314,135	.....	97,680	585,139	3,842,087
40	U.S. currency	397,086	57,141	.....	.....	0	57,141	454,227
41	U.S. liabilities to unaffiliated foreigners reported by U.S. nonbanking concerns	630,925	−39,505	.....	3,158	61,944	25,597	656,522
42	U.S. liabilities reported by U.S. banks and securities brokers, not included elsewhere	4,034,477	−387,378	.....	−2,116	−11,600	−401,094	3,633,383
	Memoranda:							
43	Direct investment abroad at market value	4,513,863	388,293	301,652	48,194	−2,463	735,676	5,249,539
44	Direct investment in the United States at market value	3,510,395	166,411	260,399	.....	−13,236	413,574	3,923,969

r Revised
* Less than $500,000 (+/−)
..... Not applicable

1. Represents gains or losses on foreign-currency-denominated assets and liabilities due to their revaluation at current exchange rates.
2. Includes changes due to year-to-year shifts in the composition of reporting panels, primarily for bank and nonbank estimates , and to the incorporation of more comprehensive survey results. Also includes capital gains and losses of direct investment affiliates and changes in positions that cannot be allocated to financial flows, price changes, or exchange-rate changes.
3. Financial flows and valuation adjustments for financial derivatives are available only on a net basis, which is shown on line 2; they are not separately available for gross positive fair values and gross negative fair values of financial derivatives. Consequently, columns (a) through (d) on lines 4, 5, 24, and 25 are not available.
4. Data are not separately available for the three types of valuation adjustments; therefore, the sum of all three types is shown in column (d).
5. Reflects changes in the value of the official gold stock due to fluctuations in the market price of gold.
6. Reflects changes in gold stock from U.S. Treasury sales of gold medallions and commemorative and bullion coins; also reflects replenishment through open market purchases. These demonetizations/monetizations are not included in international transactions financial flows.
7. Also includes paid-in capital subscriptions to international financial institutions and outstanding amounts of miscellaneous claims that have been settled through international agreements to be payable to the U.S. government over periods in excess of 1 year. Excludes World War I debts that are not being serviced.
8. Includes indebtedness that the borrower may contractually, or at its option, repay with its currency, or by delivery of materials or transfer of services.
9. Includes foreign-currency-denominated assets obtained through temporary reciprocal currency arrangements between the Federal Reserve System and foreign central banks. These assets are included in the investment position at the dollar value established at the time they were received, reflecting the valuation of these assets in the Federal Reserve System's balance sheet. Changes in exchange rates
10. Includes U.S. government liabilities associated with military sales contracts and U.S. government reserve-related liabilities from allocations of special drawing rights (SDRs).

Source: U.S. Department of Commerce, Bureau of Economic Analysis, June 2013.

This debt is larger than the total foreign debt owed by all the Central and Eastern European countries, which was about $1,240 billion in 2012. To put these figures in perspective, however, it is important to realize that the U.S. net foreign debt amounted to about 25 percent of its GDP, while the foreign liability of Hungary, Poland, Romania, and the other Central and Eastern European debtors was about 67 percent of their collective GDP! Thus, the U.S. external debt represents a much lower domestic income drain.

Changes in exchange rates and securities prices have the potential to change the U.S. net foreign debt sharply, however, because the *gross* foreign assets and liabilities of the United States have become so large in recent years. Figure 13-3 illustrates this dramatic trend. In 1976, U.S. foreign assets stood at only 25 percent of U.S. GDP and liabilities at 16 percent (making the United States a net foreign creditor in the amount of roughly 9 percent of its GDP). In 2012, however, the country's foreign assets amounted to roughly 138 percent of GDP and its liabilities to roughly 163 percent. The tremendous growth in these stocks of wealth reflects the rapid globalization of financial markets in the late 20th century, a phenomenon we will discuss further in Chapter 20.

Think about how wealth positions of this magnitude amplify the effects of exchange rate changes, however. Suppose 70 percent of U.S. foreign assets are denominated in foreign currencies, but all U.S. liabilities to foreigners are denominated in dollars (these are approximately the correct numbers). Because the 2012 U.S. GDP was around $15.7 trillion, a 10 percent depreciation of the dollar would leave U.S. liabilities unchanged but would increase U.S. assets (measured in dollars)

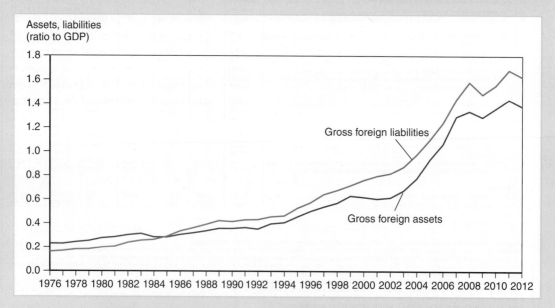

FIGURE 13-3   MyEconLab Real-time data

U.S. Gross Foreign Assets and Liabilities, 1976–2012

Since 1976, both the foreign assets and the liabilities of the United States have increased sharply. But liabilities have risen more quickly, leaving the United States with a substantial net foreign debt.

Source: U.S. Department of Commerce, Bureau of Economic Analysis, June 2013.

by $0.1 \times 0.7 \times 1.38 = 9.7$ percent of GDP, or about $1.5 trillion. This number is approximately 3.4 times the U.S. current account deficit of 2012! Indeed, due to sharp movements in exchange rates and stock prices, the U.S. economy lost about $800 billion in this way between 2007 and 2008 and gained a comparable amount between 2008 and 2009 (see Figure 13-2). The corresponding redistribution of wealth between foreigners and the United States would have been much smaller back in 1976.

Does this possibility mean that policy makers should ignore their countries' current accounts and instead try to manipulate currency values to prevent large buildups of net foreign debt? That would be a perilous strategy because, as we will see in the next chapter, expectations of future exchange rates are central to market participants' behavior. Systematic government attempts to reduce foreign investors' wealth through exchange rate changes would sharply reduce foreigners' demand for domestic currency assets, thus decreasing or eliminating any wealth benefit from depreciating the home currency.

SUMMARY

1. International *macroeconomics* is concerned with the full employment of scarce economic resources and price level stability throughout the world economy. Because they reflect national expenditure patterns and their international repercussions, the *national income accounts* and the *balance of payments accounts* are essential tools for studying the macroeconomics of open, interdependent economies.

2. A country's *gross national product* (GNP) is equal to the income received by its factors of production. The national income accounts divide national income according to the types of spending that generate it: *consumption, investment, government purchases*, and the *current account balance. Gross domestic product* (GDP), equal to GNP less net receipts of factor income from abroad, measures the output produced within a country's territorial borders.

3. In an economy closed to international trade, GNP must be consumed, invested, or purchased by the government. By using current output to build plant, equipment, and inventories, investment transforms present output into future output. For a closed economy, investment is the only way to save in the aggregate, so the sum of the saving carried out by the private and public sectors, *national saving*, must equal investment.

4. In an open economy, GNP equals the sum of consumption, investment, government purchases, and net exports of goods and services. Trade does not have to be balanced if the economy can borrow from and lend to the rest of the world. The difference between the economy's exports and imports, the current account balance, equals the difference between the economy's output and its total use of goods and services.

5. The current account also equals the country's net lending to foreigners. Unlike a closed economy, an open economy can save through domestic *and* foreign investments. National saving therefore equals domestic investment plus the current account balance. The current account is closely related to the change in the *net international investment position*, though usually not equal to that change because of fluctuations in asset values not recorded in the national income and product accounts.

6. Balance of payments accounts provide a detailed picture of the composition and financing of the current account. All transactions between a country and the rest of the world are recorded in the country's balance of payments accounts. The accounts are based on the convention that any transaction resulting in a payment to foreigners is entered as a debit while any transaction resulting in a receipt from foreigners is entered as a credit.

7. Transactions involving goods and services appear in the current account of the balance of payments, while international sales or purchases of *assets* appear in the *financial account*. The *capital account* records mainly nonmarket asset transfers and tends to be small for the United States. The sum of the current and capital account balances must equal the financial account balance (net financial flows). This feature of the accounts reflects the fact that discrepancies between export earnings and import expenditures must be matched by a promise to repay the difference, usually with interest, in the future.

8. International asset transactions carried out by *central banks* are included in the financial account. Any central bank transaction in private markets for foreign currency assets is called *official foreign exchange intervention*. One reason intervention is important is that central banks use it as a way to change the amount of money in circulation. A country has a deficit in its *balance of payments* when it is running down its *official international reserves* or borrowing from foreign central banks; it has a surplus in the opposite case.

KEY TERMS

asset, p. 358
balance of payments
   accounting, p. 347
capital account, p. 359
central bank, p. 364
consumption, p. 350
current account balance, p. 352
financial account, p. 358
government budget deficit,p. 356
government purchases, p. 351

gross domestic product
   (GDP), p. 349
gross national product (GNP),
   p. 347
investment, p. 350
macroeconomics, p. 345
microeconomics, p. 345
national income, p. 348
national income accounting,
   p. 347

national saving, p. 355
net international investment
   position, p. 354
official foreign exchange
   intervention, p. 364
official international reserves,
   p. 364
official settlements balance (or
   balance of payments), p. 365
private saving, p. 356

PROBLEMS

MyEconLab

1. GDP usually includes final goods and services produced in a year. Suppose Honda produced a product in Japan in the year 2013 but sold it in 2014. Would this be included in Japan's GDP calculation for 2014? Explain. Can we include the value of stocks and bonds sold in the same year in GDP? Discuss.

2. Equation (13-2) tells us that to reduce a current account deficit, a country must increase its private saving, reduce domestic investment, or cut its government budget deficit. Nowadays, some people recommend restrictions on imports from China (and other countries) to reduce the American current account deficit. How would higher U.S. barriers to imports affect its private saving, domestic investment, and government deficit? Do you agree that import restrictions would necessarily reduce a U.S. current account deficit?

3. Explain how each of the following transactions generates two entries—a credit and a debit—in the American balance of payments accounts, and describe how each entry would be classified:

   a. An American buys a share of German stock, paying by writing a check on an account with a Swiss bank.

   b. An American buys a share of German stock, paying the seller with a check on an American bank.

   c. The Korean government carries out an official foreign exchange intervention in which it uses dollars held in an American bank to buy Korean currency from its citizens.

   d. A tourist from Detroit buys a meal at an expensive restaurant in Lyons, France, paying with a traveler's check.

   e. A California winemaker contributes a case of cabernet sauvignon for a London wine tasting.

   f. A U.S.-owned factory in Britain uses local earnings to buy additional machinery.

4. A New Yorker travels to New Jersey to buy a $100 telephone answering machine. The New Jersey company that sells the machine then deposits the $100 check in its account at a New York bank. How would these transactions show up in the balance of payments accounts of New York and New Jersey? What if the New Yorker pays cash for the machine?

5. The nation of Pecunia had a current account deficit of $1 billion and a nonreserve financial account surplus of $500 million in 2014.

   a. What was the balance of payments of Pecunia in that year? What happened to the country's net foreign assets?

   b. Assume that foreign central banks neither buy nor sell Pecunian assets. How did the Pecunian central bank's foreign reserves change in 2014? How would this official intervention show up in the balance of payments accounts of Pecunia?

   c. How would your answer to (b) change if you learned that foreign central banks had purchased $600 million of Pecunian assets in 2014? How would these official purchases enter foreign balance of payments accounts?

   d. Draw up the Pecunian balance of payments accounts for 20014 under the assumption that the event described in (c) occurred in that year.

6. Many developing countries have experienced depreciation in their currency during 2013. Do you think the widening current account deficit (CAD) is a reason for such depreciation? If so, explain how the CAD influences the exchange rate?

7. Do data on the U.S. official settlements balance give an accurate picture of the extent to which foreign central banks buy and sell dollars in currency markets?

8. Is it possible for a country to have a current account deficit at the same time it has a surplus in its balance of payments? Explain your answer, using hypothetical figures for the current and nonreserve financial accounts. Be sure to discuss the possible implications for official international reserve flows.

9. Suppose the U.S. net foreign debt is 25 percent of U.S. GDP and foreign assets and liabilities pay an interest rate of 5 percent per year. What would be the drain on U.S. GDP (as a percentage) from paying interest on the net foreign debt? Do you think this is a large number? What if the net foreign debt were 100 percent of GDP? At what point do you think a country's government should become worried about the size of its foreign debt?

10. If you go to the BEA website (http://www.bea.gov) and look at the *Survey of Current Business* for July 2013, the table on "U.S. International Transactions," you will find that in 2012, U.S. income receipts on its foreign assets were $770.1 billion

(line 13), while the country's payments on liabilities to foreigners were $537.8 billion (line 30). Yet we saw in this chapter that the United States is a substantial net debtor to foreigners. How, then, is it possible that the United States received more foreign asset income than it paid out?

11. Assume that China and India's CAD remains unchanged for a prolonged period. If both countries devaluated their currencies against dollar—Chinese Yuan devaluated more compared to Indian Rupee—what will be the likely impact of currency devaluation on the CAD in China and India?

12. We studied that in case of a closed economy, the saving-investment equality holds true. Explain why in case of an open economy the saving investment identity does not hold true? In an open economy, if savings is greater than investments, what will happen to the foreign capital movement and the current account balance of its economy? If the savings were less than investments, is it possible to increase the investments without affecting to the current account of balance of payment?

13. Go to the BEA website at http://www.bea.gov/newsreleases/international/intinv/ intinvnewsrelease.htm and download annual data starting in 1976 on the United States' end-of-year international investment position. For the same time period, download annual data on U.S. nominal GDP from http://www.bea.gov/national/ index.htm#gdp. Then compute the annual ratio of the IIP to nominal GDP starting in 1976, and graph the data. The United States has run current account deficits in almost every year since the mid-1980s. Do the data you have graphed therefore surprise you? (Hint: To answer this question, you will need to compare the current account deficit, as a percent of nominal GDP, with the growth rate of nominal GDP, so you will also need to examine the annual current account data from the BEA website. You may wish to return to this problem after reading Chapter 19.)

FURTHER READINGS

European Commission, International Monetary Fund, Organisation for Economic Co-operation and Development, United Nations, and World Bank. *System of National Accounts 2008.* New York: United Nations, 2009. Definitive guidelines for constructing national income and product accounts.

Christopher A. Gohrband and Kristy L. Howell. "U.S. International Financial Flows and the U.S. Net Investment Position: New Perspectives Arising from New International Standards," in Charles Hulten and Marshall Reinsdorff, eds., *Wealth, Financial Intermediation, and the Real Economy.* Chicago: University of Chicago Press, 2014. Detailed discussion of the IIP statistics for the United States.

William Griever, Gary Lee, and Francis Warnock. "The U.S. System for Measuring Cross-Border Investment in Securities: A Primer with a Discussion of Recent Developments." *Federal Reserve Bulletin* 87 (October 2001), pp. 633–650. Critical description of U.S. procedures for measuring foreign assets and liabilities.

International Monetary Fund. *Balance of Payments and International Investment Position Manual,* 6th edition. Washington, D.C.: International Monetary Fund, 2009. Authoritative treatment of balance of payments accounting.

Philip R. Lane and Gian Maria Milesi-Ferretti. "The External Wealth of Nations Mark II: Revised and Extended Estimates of Foreign Assets and Liabilities, 1970–2004." *Journal of International Economics* 73 (November 2007), pp. 223–250. Applies a common methodology to construct international position data for a large sample of countries.

Catherine L. Mann. "Perspectives on the U.S. Current Account Deficit and Sustainability." *Journal of Economic Perspectives* 16 (Summer 2002), pp. 131–152. Examines the causes and consequences of recent U.S. current account deficits.

James E. Meade. *The Balance of Payments*, Chapters 1–3. London: Oxford University Press, 1952. A classic analytical discussion of balance of payments concepts.

Maurice Obstfeld. "Does the Current Account Still Matter?" *American Economic Review* 102 (May 2012): 1–23. Discusses the significance of the current account in a world of large two-way international asset flows.

Cédric Tille. "The Impact of Exchange Rate Movements on U.S. Foreign Debt." *Current Issues in Economics and Finance* (Federal Reserve Bank of New York) 9 (January 2003), pp. 1–7. Discusses the implications of asset price changes for U.S. foreign assets and liabilities.

CHAPTER 14

EXCHANGE RATES AND THE FOREIGN EXCHANGE MARKET: AN ASSET APPROACH

Around Christmas 2012, Shinzo Abe became prime minister of Japan, immediately pledging to revive its sluggish economy through forceful economic measures including "bold monetary policy." Over the next six months, the prices of Japanese goods measured in the domestic currency, the yen, fell sharply compared to the prices of foreign goods when also measured in yen. One immediate effect was on tourism: A record number of foreign visitors came during Japan's sping 2013 cherry blossom season; at the same time, the number of Japanese travelers to South Korea, a popular tourist destination, dropped sharply. What economic forces made the relative prices of Japanese goods fall so suddenly? One major factor was a 15 percent fall in the dollar price of the yen in the six months after Abe's government came to power.

The price of one currency in terms of another is called an **exchange rate**. At 4 P.M. London time on June 7, 2013, you would have needed 1.3221 dollars to buy one unit of the European currency, the euro, so the dollar's exchange rate against the euro was $1.3221 per euro. Because of their strong influence on the current account and other macroeconomic variables, exchange rates are among the most important prices in an open economy.

Because an exchange rate, the price of one country's money in terms of another's, is also an asset price, the principles governing the behavior of other asset prices also govern the behavior of exchange rates. As you will recall from Chapter 13, the defining characteristic of an asset is that it is a form of wealth, a way of transferring purchasing power from the present into the future. The price an asset commands today is therefore directly related to the purchasing power over goods and services that buyers expect it to yield in the future. Similarly, *today's* dollar/euro exchange rate is closely tied to people's expectations about the *future* level of that rate. Just as the price of Google stock rises immediately upon favorable news about Google's future prospects, so do exchange rates respond immediately to any news concerning future currency values.

Our general goals in this chapter are to understand the role of exchange rates in international trade and to understand how exchange rates are determined. To begin, we first learn how exchange rates allow us to compare the prices of different countries' goods and services. Next, we describe the international asset market in which currencies are traded and show how equilibrium exchange rates are determined in that market. A final section underlines our asset market approach by showing how today's exchange rate responds to changes in the expected future values of exchange rates.

LEARNING GOALS

After reading this chapter, you will be able to:

- Relate exchange rate changes to changes in the relative prices of countries' exports.
- Describe the structure and functions of the foreign exchange market.
- Use exchange rates to calculate and compare returns on assets denominated in different currencies.
- Apply the interest parity condition to find equilibrium exchange rates.
- Find the effects of interest rates and expectation shifts on exchange rates.

Exchange Rates and International Transactions

Exchange rates play a central role in international trade because they allow us to compare the prices of goods and services produced in different countries. A consumer deciding which of two American cars to buy must compare their dollar prices, for example, $44,000 (for a Lincoln Continental) or $27,000 (for a Ford Taurus). But how is the same consumer to compare either of these prices with the 2,500,000 Japanese yen it costs to buy a Nissan Maxima from Japan? To make this comparison, he or she must know the relative price of dollars and yen.

The relative prices of currencies can be viewed in real time on the Internet. Exchange rates are also reported daily in newspapers' financial sections. Table 14-1 shows the dollar exchange rates for currencies traded in London at 4 P.M. on June 7, 2013, as reported in the *Financial Times*. An exchange rate can be quoted in two ways: as the price of the foreign currency in terms of dollars (for example, $0.0102685 per yen) or as its inverse, the price of dollars in terms of the foreign currency (for example, ¥97.3850 per dollar). The first of these exchange rate quotations (dollars per foreign currency unit) is said to be in *direct* (or "American") terms; the second (foreign currency units per dollar) is in *indirect* (or "European") terms.[1]

Households and firms use exchange rates to translate foreign prices into domestic currency terms. Once the money prices of domestic goods and imports have been expressed in terms of the same currency, households and firms can compute the *relative* prices that affect international trade flows.

---

[1]The "mid" rates shown are the average of "bid" and "ask" prices for the U.S. dollar. Generally, a buyer of dollars will pay more (the ask price) than a seller will receive (the bid price) due to costs of intermediating the trade (for example by a bank or broker). The difference—the bid-ask spread—is a measure of transaction costs. In Chapter 19, we will refer to "effective" exchange rate indexes, which are averages of exchange rates against individual trading partner currencies.

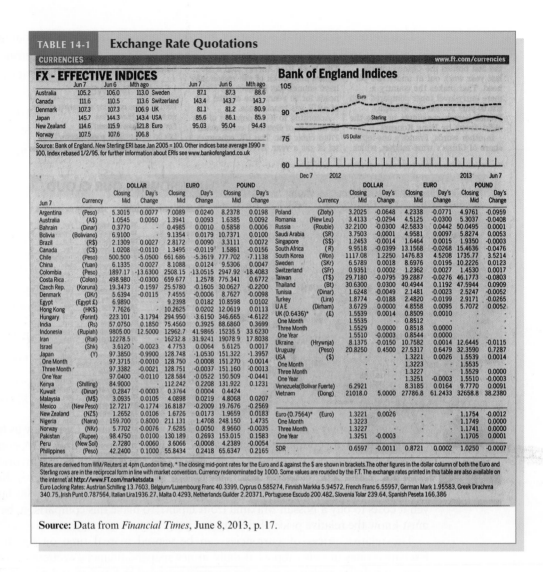

TABLE 14-1   Exchange Rate Quotations

CURRENCIES   www.ft.com/currencies

FX - EFFECTIVE INDICES

	Jun 7	Jun 6	Mth ago		Jun 7	Jun 6	Mth ago
Australia	105.2	106.0	113.0	Sweden	87.1	87.3	88.6
Canada	111.6	110.5	113.6	Switzerland	143.4	143.7	143.7
Denmark	107.3	107.3	106.9	UK	81.1	81.2	80.9
Japan	145.7	144.3	143.4	USA	85.6	86.1	85.9
New Zealand	114.6	115.9	121.8	Euro	95.03	95.04	94.43
Norway	107.5	107.6	106.8				

Source: Bank of England. New Sterling ERI base Jan 2005 = 100. Other indices base average 1990 = 100. Index rebased 1/2/95. for further information about ERIs see www.bankofengland.co.uk

Bank of England Indices

(Graph: Euro, Sterling, US Dollar indices; scale 60–105, Dec 7 2012 to Jun 7 2013)

Jun 7	Currency	DOLLAR Closing Mid	DOLLAR Day's Change	EURO Closing Mid	EURO Day's Change	POUND Closing Mid	POUND Day's Change
Argentina	(Peso)	5.3015	0.0077	7.0089	0.0240	8.2378	0.0198
Australia	(A$)	1.0545	0.0050	1.3941	0.0093	1.6385	0.0092
Bahrain	(Dinar)	0.3770	-	0.4985	0.0010	0.5858	0.0006
Bolivia	(Boliviano)	6.9100	-	9.1354	0.0179	10.7371	0.0100
Brazil	(R$)	2.1309	0.0027	2.8172	0.0090	3.3111	0.0072
Canada	(C$)	1.0208	-0.0110	1.3495	-0.0119	1.5861	-0.0156
Chile	(Peso)	500.500	-5.0500	661.686	-5.3619	777.702	-7.1138
China	(Yuan)	6.1335	-0.0027	8.1088	0.0124	9.5306	0.0047
Colombia	(Peso)	1897.17	-13.6300	2508.15	-13.0515	2947.92	-18.4083
Costa Rica	(Colon)	498.980	-0.0300	659.677	1.2578	775.341	0.6772
Czech Rep.	(Koruna)	19.3473	-0.1597	25.5780	-0.1605	30.0627	-0.2200
Denmark	(DKr)	5.6394	-0.0115	7.4555	-0.0006	8.7627	-0.0098
Egypt	(Egypt £)	6.9890	-	9.2398	0.0182	10.8598	0.0102
Hong Kong	(HK$)	7.7626	-	10.2625	0.0202	12.0619	0.0113
Hungary	(Forint)	223.101	-3.1794	294.950	-3.6150	346.665	-4.6122
India	(Rs)	57.0750	0.1850	75.4560	0.3925	88.6860	0.3699
Indonesia	(Rupiah)	9805.00	12.5000	12962.7	41.9865	15235.5	33.6230
Iran	(Rial)	12278.5	-	16232.8	31.9241	19078.9	17.8038
Israel	(Shk)	3.6120	-0.0023	4.7753	0.0064	5.6125	0.0017
Japan	(Y)	97.3850	-0.9900	128.748	-1.0530	151.322	-1.3957
One Month		97.3715	-0.0010	128.750	-0.0008	151.270	-0.0014
Three Month		97.3382	-0.0021	128.751	-0.0037	151.160	-0.0013
One Year		97.0400	-0.0110	128.584	-0.0522	150.509	-0.0441
Kenya	(Shilling)	84.9000	-	112.242	0.2208	131.922	0.1231
Kuwait	(Dinar)	0.2847	-0.0003	0.3764	0.0004	0.4424	-
Malaysia	(M$)	3.0935	0.0105	4.0898	0.0219	4.8068	0.0207
Mexico	(New Peso)	12.7217	-0.1774	16.8187	-0.2009	19.7676	-0.2569
New Zealand	(NZ$)	1.2652	0.0106	1.6726	0.0173	1.9659	0.0183
Nigeria	(Naira)	159.700	0.8000	211.131	1.4708	248.150	1.4735
Norway	(NKr)	5.7702	-0.0076	7.6285	0.0050	8.9660	-0.0035
Pakistan	(Rupee)	98.4750	0.0100	130.189	0.2693	153.015	0.1583
Peru	(New Sol)	2.7280	-0.0060	3.6066	-0.0008	4.2389	-0.0054
Philippines	(Peso)	42.2400	0.1000	55.8434	0.2418	65.6347	0.2165
Poland	(Zloty)	3.2025	-0.0648	4.2338	-0.0771	4.9761	-0.0959
Romania	(New Leu)	3.4133	-0.0294	4.5125	-0.0300	5.3037	-0.0408
Russia	(Rouble)	32.2100	-0.0300	42.5833	0.0442	50.0495	0.0001
Saudi Arabia	(SR)	3.7503	-0.0001	4.9581	0.0097	5.8274	0.0053
Singapore	(S$)	1.2453	-0.0014	1.6464	0.0015	1.9350	-0.0003
South Africa	(R)	9.9518	-0.0399	13.1568	-0.0268	15.4636	-0.0476
South Korea	(Won)	1117.08	1.2250	1476.83	4.5208	1735.77	3.5214
Sweden	(SKr)	6.5789	0.0018	8.6976	0.0195	10.2226	0.0123
Switzerland	(SFr)	0.9351	0.0002	1.2362	0.0027	1.4530	0.0017
Taiwan	(T$)	29.7180	-0.0795	39.2887	-0.0276	46.1773	-0.0803
Thailand	(Bt)	30.6300	0.0300	40.4944	0.1192	47.5944	0.0909
Tunisia	(Dinar)	1.6248	-0.0049	2.1481	-0.0023	2.5247	-0.0052
Turkey	(Lira)	1.8774	-0.0188	2.4820	-0.0199	2.9171	-0.0265
UAE	(Dirham)	3.6729	0.0000	4.8558	0.0095	5.7072	0.0052
UK (0.6436)*	(£)	1.5539	0.0014	0.8509	0.0010		
One Month		1.5535		0.8512			
Three Month		1.5529	0.0000	0.8518	0.0000		
One Year		1.5510	-0.0003	0.8544	0.0000		
Ukraine	(Hrywnja)	8.1375	-0.0150	10.7582	0.0014	12.6445	-0.0115
Uruguay	(Peso)	20.8250	0.4500	27.5317	0.6479	32.3590	0.7287
USA	($)			1.3221	0.0026	1.5539	0.0014
One Month				1.3223		1.5535	
Three Month				1.3227		1.5529	0.0000
One Year				1.3251	-0.0003	1.5510	-0.0003
Venezuela(Bolivar Fuerte)		6.2921	-	8.3185	0.0164	9.7770	0.0091
Vietnam	(Dong)	21018.0	5.0000	27786.8	61.2433	32658.8	38.2380
Euro (0.7564)*	(Euro)	1.3221	0.0026			1.1754	-0.0012
One Month		1.3223				1.1749	0.0000
Three Month		1.3227				1.1741	0.0000
One Year		1.3251	-0.0003			1.1705	0.0001
SDR		0.6597	-0.0011	0.8721	0.0002	1.0250	-0.0007

Rates are derived from WM/Reuters at 4pm (London time). * The closing mid-point rates for the Euro and £ against the $ are shown in brackets. The other figures in the dollar column of both the Euro and Sterling rows are in the reciprocal form in line with market convention. Currency redenominated by 1000. Some values are rounded by the F.T. The exchange rates printed in this table are also available on the internet at http://www.FT.com/marketsdata

Euro Locking Rates: Austrian Schilling 13.7603, Belgium/Luxembourg Franc 40.3399, Cyprus 0.585274, Finnish Markka 5.94572, French Franc 6.55957, German Mark 1.95583, Greek Drachma 340.75, Irish Punt 0.787564, Italian Lira 1936.27, Malta 0.4293, Netherlands Guilder 2.20371, Portuguese Escudo 200.482, Slovenia Tolar 239.64, Spanish Peseta 166.386

Source: Data from *Financial Times*, June 8, 2013, p. 17.

Domestic and Foreign Prices

If we know the exchange rate between two countries' currencies, we can compute the price of one country's exports in terms of the other country's money. For example, how many dollars would it cost to buy an Edinburgh Woolen Mill sweater costing 50 British pounds (£50)? The answer is found by multiplying the price of the sweater in pounds, 50, by the price of a pound in terms of dollars—the dollar's exchange rate against the pound. At an exchange rate of $1.50 per pound (expressed in American terms), the dollar price of the sweater is

$$(1.50\$/£) \times (£50) = \$75.$$

A change in the dollar/pound exchange rate would alter the sweater's dollar price. At an exchange rate of 1.25 per pound, the sweater would cost only

$$(1.25\$/£) \times (£50) = \$62.50,$$

assuming its price in terms of pounds remained the same. At an exchange rate of $1.75 per pound, the sweater's dollar price would be higher, equal to

$$(1.75\$/\pounds) \times (\pounds 50) = \$87.50.$$

Changes in exchange rates are described as depreciations or appreciations. A **depreciation** of the pound against the dollar is a fall in the dollar price of pounds, for example, a change in the exchange rate from $1.50 per pound to $1.25 per pound. The preceding example shows that *all else equal, a depreciation of a country's currency makes its goods cheaper for foreigners*. A rise in the pound's price in terms of dollars—for example, from $1.50 per pound to $1.75 per pound—is an **appreciation** of the pound against the dollar. *All else equal, an appreciation of a country's currency makes its goods more expensive for foreigners*.

The exchange rate changes discussed in the example simultaneously alter the prices Britons pay for American goods. At an exchange rate of $1.50 per pound, the pound price of a pair of American designer jeans costing $45 is $(\$45)/(1.50\$/\pounds) = \pounds 30$. A change in the exchange rate from $1.50 per pound to $1.25 per pound, while a depreciation of the pound against the dollar, is also a rise in the pound price of dollars, an *appreciation* of the dollar against the pound. This appreciation of the dollar makes the American jeans more expensive for Britons by raising their pound price from £30 to

$$(\$45)/(1.25\$/\pounds) = \pounds 36.$$

The change in the exchange rate from $1.50 per pound to $1.75 per pound—an appreciation of the pound against the dollar but a depreciation of the dollar against the pound—lowers the pound price of the jeans from £30 to

$$(\$45)/(1.75\$/\pounds) = \pounds 25.71.$$

As you can see, descriptions of exchange rate changes as depreciations or appreciations can be bewildering because when one currency depreciates against another, the second currency must simultaneously appreciate against the first. To avoid confusion in discussing exchange rates, we must always keep track of which of the two currencies we are examining has depreciated or appreciated against the other.

If we remember that a depreciation of the dollar against the pound is at the same time an appreciation of the pound against the dollar, we reach the following conclusion: *When a country's currency depreciates, foreigners find that its exports are cheaper and domestic residents find that imports from abroad are more expensive. An appreciation has opposite effects: Foreigners pay more for the country's products and domestic consumers pay less for foreign products.*

Exchange Rates and Relative Prices

Import and export demands, like the demands for all goods and services, are influenced by *relative* prices, such as the price of sweaters in terms of designer jeans. We have just seen how exchange rates allow individuals to compare domestic and foreign money prices by expressing them in a common currency unit. Carrying this analysis one step further, we can see that exchange rates also allow individuals to compute the relative prices of goods and services whose money prices are quoted in different currencies.

An American trying to decide how much to spend on American jeans and how much to spend on British sweaters must translate their prices into a common currency to compute the price of sweaters in terms of jeans. As we have seen, an exchange rate of $1.50 per pound means that an American pays $75 for a sweater priced at £50 in

TABLE 14-2	$/£ Exchange Rates and the Relative Price of American Designer Jeans and British Sweaters		
Exchange rate ($/£)	1.25	1.50	1.75
Relative price (pairs of jeans/sweater)	1.39	1.67	1.94

Note: The above calculations assume unchanged money prices of $45 per pair of jeans and £50 per sweater.

Britain. Because the price of a pair of American jeans is $45, the price of a sweater in terms of a pair of jeans is ($75 per sweater)/($45 per pair of jeans) = 1.67 pairs of jeans per sweater. Naturally, a Briton faces the same relative price of (£50 per sweater)/(£30 per pair of jeans) = 1.67 pairs of jeans per sweater.

Table 14-2 shows the relative prices implied by exchange rates of $1.25 per pound, $1.50 per pound, and $1.75 per pound, on the assumption that the dollar price of jeans and the pound price of sweaters are unaffected by the exchange rate changes. To test your understanding, try to calculate these relative prices for yourself and confirm that the outcome of the calculation is the same for a Briton and for an American.

The table shows that if the goods' money prices do not change, an appreciation of the dollar against the pound makes sweaters cheaper in terms of jeans (each pair of jeans buys more sweaters) while a depreciation of the dollar against the pound makes sweaters more expensive in terms of jeans (each pair of jeans buys fewer sweaters). The computations illustrate a general principle: *All else equal, an appreciation of a country's currency raises the relative price of its exports and lowers the relative price of its imports. Conversely, a depreciation lowers the relative price of a country's exports and raises the relative price of its imports.*

The Foreign Exchange Market

Just as other prices in the economy are determined by the interaction of buyers and sellers, exchange rates are determined by the interaction of the households, firms, and financial institutions that buy and sell foreign currencies to make international payments. The market in which international currency trades take place is called the **foreign exchange market**.

The Actors

The major participants in the foreign exchange market are commercial banks, corporations that engage in international trade, nonbank financial institutions such as asset-management firms and insurance companies, and central banks. Individuals may also participate in the foreign exchange market—for example, the tourist who buys foreign currency at a hotel's front desk—but such cash transactions are an insignificant fraction of total foreign exchange trading.

We now describe the major actors in the market and their roles.

1. *Commercial banks.* Commercial banks are at the center of the foreign exchange market because almost every sizable international transaction involves the debiting and crediting of accounts at commercial banks in various financial centers. Thus, the vast majority of foreign exchange transactions involve the exchange of bank deposits denominated in different currencies.

Let's look at an example. Suppose ExxonMobil Corporation wishes to pay €160,000 to a German supplier. First, ExxonMobil gets an exchange rate quotation

EXCHANGE RATES, AUTO PRICES, AND CURRENCY WARS

Automobiles make up a significant share of international trade, and many advanced economies are significant exporters as well as importers of cars. Competition is fierce—the United States exports Fords, Sweden exports Volvos, Germany exports BMWs, Japan exports Hondas, and Britain exports Land Rovers, to name just a few—and increased auto imports from abroad are likely to mean fewer sales for the domestic producer.

Exchange rates are therefore of critical importance to auto makers. For example, when Korea's currency, the won, appreciates in the foreign exchange market, this hurts Korean producers in two distinct ways. First, the prices of competing imported cars go down because foreign prices look lower when measured in terms of won. Thus, imports flood in and create a more competitive home pricing environment for Korean producers like Hyundai and Kia. Second, foreigners (whose currencies have depreciated against the won) find that the home-currency prices of Korean cars have risen, and they switch their purchases to cheaper suppliers. Korean auto exports suffer as a result. Later in the book (Chapter 16) we will discuss the pricing strategies that producers of specialized products like autos may adopt when trying to defend market shares in the face of exchange rate changes.

These effects of exchange rates on manufacturing producers explain why export industries complain when foreign countries adopt policies that weaken their currencies. In September 2010, as many industrial countries' currencies depreciated because of slow economic growth, Brazil's finance minister accused the richer countries of waging "currency wars" against the poorer emerging market economies. After reading Chapter 17, you will understand why sluggish economic growth and currency depreciation might go together. Chapter 18 discusses how a similar phenomenon of "competitive depreciation" occurred during the Great Depression of the 1930s.

Talk of currency wars emerged once again when Japan's yen depreciated sharply early in 2013 (as described in this chapter's first paragraph). Of course, Japanese auto firms were major beneficiaries, at the expense of their many foreign competitors. According to an Associated Press (AP) report in May 2013, Nissan was able to cut the dollar prices of seven of the 18 models it sells in the United States: at the new dollar exchange rate of the yen, even somewhat lower *dollar* prices produced enough *yen* revenue to cover Japanese production costs as well as higher yen profits. Nissan cut the price of its Altima by $580 and that of its Armada SUV by $4,400. As the AP reported, "Although Nissan denies it, industry analysts say the company can afford to cut prices because of efforts in Japan to weaken the yen against the dollar. That makes cars and parts made in Japan cheaper than goods made in the U.S."*

*"Nissan Cuts Prices on 7 of Its U.S. Models," *USA Today,* May 1, 2013, available at: http://www.usatoday.com/story/money/cars/2013/05/01/nissan-cuts-prices-juke/2127721/

from its own commercial bank, the Third National Bank. Then it instructs Third National to debit ExxonMobil's dollar account and pay €160,000 into the supplier's account at a German bank. If the exchange rate quoted to ExxonMobil by Third National is $1.2 per euro, $192,000 (= $1.2 per euro × €160,000) is debited from ExxonMobil's account. The final result of the transaction is the exchange of a $192,000 deposit at Third National Bank (now owned by the German bank that supplied the euros) for the €160,000 deposit used by Third National to pay ExxonMobil's German supplier.

As the example shows, banks routinely enter the foreign exchange market to meet the needs of their customers—primarily corporations. In addition, a bank will also quote to other banks exchange rates at which it is willing to buy currencies from them and sell currencies to them. Foreign currency trading among banks—called **interbank trading**—accounts for much of the activity in the foreign exchange market. In fact, the exchange rates listed in Table 14-1 are interbank rates, the rates banks charge each other. No amount less than $1 million is traded at those rates. The rates available to corporate customers, called "retail" rates, are usually less favorable than the "wholesale" interbank rates. The difference between the retail and the wholesale rates is the bank's compensation for doing the business.

Because their international operations are so extensive, large commercial banks are well suited to bring buyers and sellers of currencies together. A multinational corporation wishing to convert $100,000 into Swedish kronor might find it difficult and costly to locate other corporations wishing to sell the right amount of kronor. By serving many customers simultaneously through a single large purchase of kronor, a bank can economize on these search costs.

2. *Corporations.* Corporations with operations in several countries frequently make or receive payments in currencies other than that of the country in which they are headquartered. To pay workers at a plant in Mexico, for example, IBM may need Mexican pesos. If IBM has only dollars earned by selling computers in the United States, it can acquire the pesos it needs by buying them with its dollars in the foreign exchange market.

3. *Nonbank financial institutions.* Over the years, deregulation of financial markets in the United States, Japan, and other countries has encouraged nonbank financial institutions such as mutual funds to offer their customers a broader range of services, many of them indistinguishable from those offered by banks. Among these have been services involving foreign exchange transactions. Institutional investors such as pension funds often trade foreign currencies. So do insurance companies. Hedge funds, which cater to very wealthy individuals and are not bound by the government regulations that limit mutual funds' trading strategies, trade actively in the foreign exchange market.

4. *Central banks.* In the last chapter, we learned that central banks sometimes intervene in foreign exchange markets. While the volume of central bank transactions is typically not large, the impact of these transactions may be great. The reason for this impact is that participants in the foreign exchange market watch central bank actions closely for clues about future macroeconomic policies that may affect exchange rates. Government agencies other than central banks may also trade in the foreign exchange market, but central banks are the most regular official participants.

Characteristics of the Market

Foreign exchange trading takes place in many financial centers, with the largest volumes of trade occurring in such major cities as London (the largest market), New York, Tokyo, Frankfurt, and Singapore. The worldwide volume of foreign exchange trading is enormous, and it has ballooned in recent years. In April 1989, the average total value of global foreign exchange trading was close to $600 billion *per day*. A total of $184 billion was traded daily in London, $115 billion in the United States, and $111 billion in Tokyo. Twenty-one years later, in April 2010, the daily global value of foreign exchange trading had jumped to around $4.0 trillion. A total of $1.85 trillion was traded daily in Britain, $904 billion in the United States, and $312 billion in Japan.[2]

---

[2]April 1989 figures come from surveys carried out simultaneously by the Federal Reserve Bank of New York, the Bank of England, the Bank of Japan, the Bank of Canada, and monetary authorities from France, Italy, the Netherlands, Singapore, Hong Kong, and Australia. The April 2010 survey was carried out by 53 central banks. Revised figures are reported in "Triennial Central Bank Survey of Foreign Exchange and Derivatives Market Activity in April 2010: Preliminary Global Results," Bank for International Settlements, Basel, Switzerland, September 2010. Daily U.S. foreign currency trading in 1980 averaged only around $18 billion.

Telephone, fax, and Internet links among the major foreign exchange trading centers make each a part of a single world market on which the sun never sets. Economic news released at any time of the day is immediately transmitted around the world and may set off a flurry of activity by market participants. Even after trading in New York has finished, New York–based banks and corporations with affiliates in other time zones can remain active in the market. Foreign exchange traders may deal from their homes when a late-night communication alerts them to important developments in a financial center on another continent.

The integration of financial centers implies that there can be no significant difference between the dollar/euro exchange rate quoted in New York at 9 A.M. and the dollar/euro exchange rate quoted in London at the same time (which corresponds to 2 P.M. London time). If the euro were selling for $1.1 in New York and $1.2 in London, profits could be made through **arbitrage**, the process of buying a currency cheap and selling it dear. At the prices listed above, a trader could, for instance, purchase €1 million in New York for $1.1 million and immediately sell the euros in London for $1.2 million, making a pure profit of $100,000. If all traders tried to cash in on the opportunity, however, their demand for euros in New York would drive up the dollar price of euros there, and their supply of euros in London would drive down the dollar price of euros there. Very quickly, the difference between the New York and London exchange rates would disappear. Since foreign exchange traders carefully watch their computer screens for arbitrage opportunities, the few that arise are small and very short-lived.

While a foreign exchange transaction can match any two currencies, most transactions (roughly 85 percent in April 2010) are exchanges of foreign currencies for U.S. dollars. This is true even when a bank's goal is to sell one nondollar currency and buy another! A bank wishing to sell Swiss francs and buy Israeli shekels, for example, will usually sell its francs for dollars and then use the dollars to buy shekels. While this procedure may appear roundabout, it is actually cheaper for the bank than the alternative of trying to find a holder of shekels who wishes to buy Swiss francs. The advantage of trading through the dollar is a result of the United States' importance in the world economy. Because the volume of international transactions involving dollars is so great, it is not hard to find parties willing to trade dollars against Swiss francs or shekels. In contrast, relatively few transactions require direct exchanges of Swiss francs for shekels.[3]

Because of its pivotal role in so many foreign exchange deals, the U.S. dollar is sometimes called a **vehicle currency**. A vehicle currency is one that is widely used to denominate international contracts made by parties who do not reside in the country that issues the vehicle currency. It has been suggested that the euro, which was introduced at the start of 1999, will evolve into a vehicle currency on a par with the dollar. By April 2010, about 39 percent of foreign exchange trades were against euros—less than half the share of the dollar, albeit above the figure of 37 percent clocked three years earlier. Japan's yen is the third most important currency, with a market share of 19 percent (out of 200). The pound sterling, once second only to the dollar as a key international currency, has declined greatly in importance.[4]

---

[3]The Swiss franc/shekel exchange rate can be calculated from the dollar/franc and dollar/shekel exchange rates as the dollar/shekel rate divided by the dollar/franc rate. If the dollar/franc rate is $0.80 per franc and the dollar/shekel rate is $0.20 per shekel, then the Swiss franc/shekel rate is (0.20 $/shekel)/(0.80 $/franc) = 0.25 Swiss francs/shekel. Exchange rates between nondollar currencies are called "cross rates" by foreign exchange traders.

[4]For a more detailed discussion of vehicle currencies, see Richard Portes and Hélène Rey, "The Emergence of the Euro as an International Currency," *Economic Policy* 26 (April 1998), pp. 307–343. Data on currency shares come from Bank for International Settlements, *op. cit.*, table 3. For an assessment of the future roles of the dollar and the euro, see the essays in Jean Pisani-Ferry and Adam S. Posen, eds., *The Euro at Ten: The Next Global Currency?* (Washington, D.C.: Peterson Institute for International Economics, 2009). These essays were written before the euro area crisis, to be discussed in Chapter 21.

Spot Rates and Forward Rates

The foreign exchange transactions we have been discussing take place on the spot: Two parties agree to an exchange of bank deposits and execute the deal immediately. Exchange rates governing such "on-the-spot" trading are called **spot exchange rates** and the deal is called a spot transaction.

Foreign exchange deals sometimes specify a *future* transaction date—one that may be 30 days, 90 days, 180 days, or even several years away. The exchange rates quoted in such transactions are called **forward exchange rates**. In a 30-day forward transaction, for example, two parties may commit themselves on April 1 to a spot exchange of £100,000 for $155,000 on May 1. The 30-day forward exchange rate is therefore $1.55 per pound, and it is generally different from the spot rate and from the forward rates applied to different future dates. When you agree to sell pounds for dollars on a future date at a forward rate agreed on today, you have "sold pounds forward" and "bought dollars forward." The future date on which the currencies are actually exchanged is called the *value date*.[5] Table 14-1 shows forward exchange rates for some major currencies.

Forward and spot exchange rates, while not necessarily equal, do move closely together, as illustrated for monthly data on dollar/pound rates in Figure 14-1. The appendix to this chapter, which discusses how forward exchange rates are determined, explains this close relationship between movements in spot and forward rates.

An example shows why parties may wish to engage in forward exchange transactions. Suppose Radio Shack knows that in 30 days it must pay yen to a Japanese supplier for a shipment of radios arriving then. Radio Shack can sell each radio for $100 and must pay its supplier ¥9,000 per radio; its profit depends on the dollar/yen

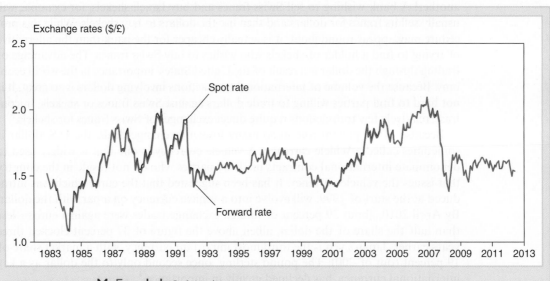

FIGURE 14-1   MyEconLab Real-time data

Dollar/Pound Spot and Forward Exchange Rates, 1983–2013

Spot and forward exchange rates tend to move in a highly correlated fashion.

Source: *Datastream.* Rates shown are 90-day forward exchange rates and spot exchange rates, at end of month.

---

[5]In days past, it would take up to two days to settle even spot foreign exchange transactions. In other words, the value date for a spot transaction was actually two days after the deal was struck. Nowadays, most spot trades of major currencies settle on the same day.

exchange rate. At the current spot exchange rate of $0.0105 per yen, Radio Shack would pay ($0.0105 per yen) × (¥9,000 per radio) = $94.50 per radio and would therefore make $5.50 on each radio imported. But Radio Shack will not have the funds to pay the supplier until the radios arrive and are sold. If over the next 30 days the dollar unexpectedly depreciates to $0.0115 per yen, Radio Shack will have to pay ($0.0115 per yen) × (¥9,000 per radio) = $103.50 per radio and so will take a $3.50 *loss* on each.

To avoid this risk, Radio Shack can make a 30-day forward exchange deal with Bank of America. If Bank of America agrees to sell yen to Radio Shack in 30 days at a rate of $0.0107, Radio Shack is assured of paying exactly ($0.0107 per yen) × (¥9,000 per radio) = $96.30 per radio to the supplier. By buying yen and selling dollars forward, Radio Shack is guaranteed a profit of $3.70 per radio and is insured against the possibility that a sudden exchange rate change will turn a profitable importing deal into a loss. In the jargon of the foreign exchange market, we would say that Radio Shack has *hedged* its foreign currency risk.

From now on, when we mention an exchange rate but don't specify whether it is a spot rate or a forward rate, we will always be referring to the spot rate.

Foreign Exchange Swaps

A foreign exchange *swap* is a spot sale of a currency combined with a forward repurchase of that currency. For example, suppose the Toyota auto company has just received $1 million from American sales and knows it will have to pay those dollars to a California supplier in three months. Toyota's asset-management department would meanwhile like to invest the $1 million in euro bonds. A three-month swap of dollars into euros may result in lower brokers' fees than the two separate transactions of selling dollars for spot euros and selling the euros for dollars on the forward market. Swaps make up a significant proportion of all foreign exchange trading.

Futures and Options

Several other financial instruments traded in the foreign exchange market, like forward contracts, involve future exchanges of currencies. The timing and terms of the exchanges can differ, however, from those specified in forward contracts, giving traders additional flexibility in avoiding foreign exchange risk.

When you buy a *futures contract*, you buy a promise that a specified amount of foreign currency will be delivered on a specified date in the future. A forward contract between you and some other private party is an alternative way to ensure that you receive the same amount of foreign currency on the date in question. But while you have no choice about fulfilling your end of a forward deal, you can sell your futures contract on an organized futures exchange, realizing a profit or loss right away. Such a sale might appear advantageous, for example, if your views about the future spot exchange rate were to change.

A *foreign exchange option* gives its owner the right to buy or sell a specified amount of foreign currency at a specified price at any time up to a specified expiration date. The other party to the deal, the option's seller, is required to sell or buy the foreign currency at the discretion of the option's owner, who is under no obligation to exercise his right.

Imagine you are uncertain about when in the next month a foreign currency payment will arrive. To avoid the risk of a loss, you may wish to buy a *put option* giving you the right to sell the foreign currency at a known exchange rate at any time during the month. If instead you expect to make a payment abroad sometime in the month, a *call option*, which gives you the right to buy foreign currency to make the payment at a known price, might be attractive. Options can be written on many underlying assets (including foreign exchange futures), and, like futures, they are freely bought and sold. Forwards, swaps, futures, and options are all examples of *financial derivatives*, which we encountered in Chapter 13.

The Demand for Foreign Currency Assets

We have now seen how banks, corporations, and other institutions trade foreign currency bank deposits in a worldwide foreign exchange market that operates 24 hours a day. To understand how exchange rates are determined by the foreign exchange market, we first must ask how the major actors' demands for different types of foreign currency deposits are determined.

The demand for a foreign currency bank deposit is influenced by the same considerations that influence the demand for any other asset. Chief among these considerations is our view of what the deposit will be worth in the future. A foreign currency deposit's future value depends in turn on two factors: the interest rate it offers and the expected change in the currency's exchange rate against other currencies.

Assets and Asset Returns

As you will recall, people can hold wealth in many forms—stocks, bonds, cash, real estate, rare wines, diamonds, and so on. The object of acquiring wealth—of saving—is to transfer purchasing power into the future. We may do this to provide for our retirement years, for our heirs, or simply because we earn more than we need to spend in a particular year and prefer to save the balance for a rainy day.

Defining Asset Returns Because the object of saving is to provide for future consumption, we judge the desirability of an asset largely on the basis of its **rate of return**, that is, the percentage increase in value it offers over some time period. For example, suppose that at the beginning of 2015 you pay $100 for a share of stock issued by Financial Soothsayers, Inc. If the stock pays you a dividend of $1 at the beginning of 2016, and if the stock's price rises from $100 to $109 per share over the year, then you have earned a rate of return of 10 percent on the stock over 2015—that is, your initial $100 investment has grown in value to $110, the sum of the $1 dividend and the $109 you could get by selling your share. Had Financial Soothsayers stock still paid out its $1 dividend but dropped in price to $89 per share, your $100 investment would be worth only $90 by year's end, giving a rate of return of *negative* 10 percent.

You often cannot know with certainty the return that an asset will actually pay after you buy it. Both the dividend paid by a share of stock and the share's resale price, for example, may be hard to predict. Your decision therefore must be based on an *expected* rate of return. To calculate an expected rate of return over some time period, you make your best forecast of the asset's total value at the period's end. The percentage difference between that expected future value and the price you pay for the asset today equals the asset's expected rate of return over the time period.

When we measure an asset's rate of return, we compare how an investment in the asset changes in total value between two dates. In the previous example, we compared how the value of an investment in Financial Soothsayers stock changed between 2015 ($100) and 2016 ($110) to conclude that the rate of return on the stock was 10 percent per year.

We call this a *dollar* rate of return because the two values we compare are expressed in terms of dollars. It is also possible, however, to compute different rates of return by expressing the two values in terms of a foreign currency or a commodity such as gold.

The Real Rate of Return   The expected rate of return that savers consider in deciding which assets to hold is the expected **real rate of return**, that is, the rate of return computed by measuring asset values in terms of some broad representative basket

NONDELIVERABLE FORWARD EXCHANGE TRADING IN ASIA

In a standard forward exchange contract, two parties agree to exchange two different currencies at an agreed rate on a future date. The currencies of many developing countries are, however, not fully *convertible*, meaning that they cannot be freely traded on international foreign exchange markets. An important example of an inconvertible currency is China's renminbi, which can be traded within China's borders (by residents) but not freely outside of them (because China's government does not allow nonresidents unrestricted ownership of renminbi deposits in China). Thus, for currencies such as the renminbi, the customary way of trading forward exchange is not possible.

Developing countries with inconvertible currencies such as China's have entered the ranks of the world's largest participants in international trade and investment. Usually, traders use the forward exchange market to hedge their currency risks, but in cases such as China's, as we have seen, a standard forward market cannot exist. Is there no way for foreigners to hedge the currency risk they may take on when they trade with inconvertible-currency countries?

Since the early 1990s, markets in *nondeliverable forward exchange* have sprung up in centers such as Hong Kong and Singapore to facilitate hedging in inconvertible Asian currencies. Among the currencies traded in offshore nondeliverable forward markets are the Chinese renminbi, the Taiwan dollar, and the Indian rupee. By using nondeliverable forward contracts, traders can hedge currency risks without ever actually having to trade inconvertible currencies.

Let's look at a hypothetical example to see how this hedging can be accomplished. General Motors has just sold some car components to China. Its contract with the Chinese importer states that in

three months, GM will receive the dollar equivalent of 10 million yuan in payment for its shipment. (The yuan is the unit in which amounts of renminbi are measured, just as British sterling is measured in pounds.) The People's Bank of China (PBC), the central bank, tightly controls its currency's exchange rate by trading dollars that it holds for renminbi with domestic residents.[*]

Today, the PBC will buy or sell a U.S. dollar for 6.8 yuan. But assume the PBC has been gradually allowing its currency to appreciate against the dollar, and the rate it will quote in three months is uncertain: It could be anywhere between, say, 6.7 and 6.5 yuan per dollar. GM would like to lock in a forward exchange rate of 6.6 yuan per dollar, which the company's chief financial officer might typically do simply by selling the expected 10 million yuan receipts forward for dollars at that rate. Unfortunately, the renminbi's inconvertibility means that GM will actually receive, not renminbi that it can sell forward, but the dollar equivalent of 10 million yuan, dollars that the importer can buy through China's banking system.

Nondeliverable forwards result in a "virtual" forward market, however. They do this by allowing non-Chinese traders to make bets on the renminbi's value that are *payable in dollars*. To lock in a nondeliverable forward exchange rate of 6.6 yuan per dollar, GM can sign a contract requiring it to pay the difference between the number of dollars it actually receives in three months and the amount it would receive if the exchange rate were exactly 6.6 yuan per dollar, equivalent to $1/6.6$ dollars per yuan $= \$0.1515$ per yuan (after rounding). Thus, if the exchange rate turns out to be 6.5 yuan per dollar (which otherwise would be

(Continued)

*China's currency regime is an example of a fixed exchange rate system, which we will study in greater detail in Chapter 18.

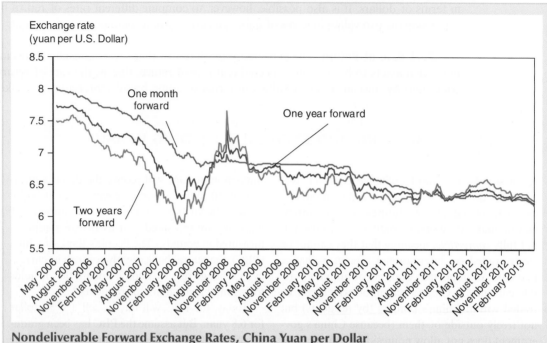

Nondeliverable Forward Exchange Rates, China Yuan per Dollar

Source: *Datastream.*

good luck for GM), GM will have to pay out on its contract $(1/6.5 - 1/6.6$ dollars per yuan$) \times (10,000,000$ yuan$) = (\$0.1538 - \$0.1515$ per yuan$) \times (10,000,000$ yuan$) = \$23,310$.

On the other hand, by giving up the possibility of good luck, GM also avoids the risk of bad luck. If the exchange rate turns out instead to be 6.7 yuan per dollar (which otherwise would be unfavorable for GM), GM will pay the negative amount $(\$0.1493 - \$0.1515$ per yuan$) \times (10,000,000$ yuan$) = -\$22,614$, that is, it will receive \$22,614 from the other contracting party. The nondeliverable forward contract allows GM to immunize itself from exchange risk, even though the parties to the contract need never actually exchange Chinese currency.

The chart above shows daily data on nondeliverable forward rates of yuan for dollars with value dates one month, one year, and two years away. (Far longer maturities are also quoted.) Changes in these rates are more variable at the longer maturities because the rates reflect expectations about China's future exchange rate policy and the far future is relatively more uncertain than the near future.

How have China's exchange rate policies evolved? From July 2005 until July 2008, China followed a widely understood policy of gradually allowing its currency to appreciate against the U.S. dollar. Because of expectations during this period that the yuan/dollar rate would fall over time, the forward rates at which people were willing to trade to cover transactions two years away are below the one-year-ahead forward rates, which in turn are below the one-month-ahead forward rates.

China changed its policy in the summer of 2008, pegging the yuan rigidly to the dollar without any announced end date for that policy. That action altered the relationship among the three forward rates, as you can see in the chart. Two years later, in June 2010, China announced its return to a supposedly more flexible exchange rate for the yuan. Since then, the yuan has continued to appreciate against the dollar—but at a gradual pace.

China's exchange rate system and policies have been a focus of international controversy in recent years, and we will say more about them in later chapters.

of products that savers regularly purchase. It is the expected real return that matters because the ultimate goal of saving is future consumption, and only the *real* return measures the goods and services a saver can buy in the future in return for giving up some consumption (that is, saving) today.

To continue our example, suppose the dollar value of an investment in Financial Soothsayers stock increases by 10 percent between 2015 and 2016 but the dollar prices of all goods and services *also* increase by 10 percent. Then in terms of output—that is, in *real terms*—the investment would be worth no more in 2015 than in 2016. With a real rate of return of zero, Financial Soothsayers stock would not be a very desirable asset.

Although savers care about expected real rates of return, rates of return expressed in terms of a currency can still be used to *compare* real returns on *different* assets. Even if all dollar prices rise by 10 percent between 2015 and 2016, a rare bottle of wine whose dollar price rises by 25 percent is still a better investment than a bond whose dollar value rises by 20 percent. The real rate of return offered by the wine is 15 percent (= 25 percent − 10 percent) while that offered by the bond is only 10 percent (= 20 percent − 10 percent). Notice that the difference between the dollar returns of the two assets (25 percent − 20 percent) must equal the difference between their real returns (15 percent − 10 percent). The reason for this equality is that given the two assets' dollar returns, a change in the rate at which the dollar prices of goods are rising changes both assets' real returns by the same amount.

The distinction between real rates of return and dollar rates of return illustrates an important concept in studying how savers evaluate different assets: The returns on two assets cannot be compared unless they are measured in the *same* units. For example, it makes no sense to compare directly the real return on the bottle of wine (15 percent in our example) with the dollar return on the bond (20 percent) or to compare the dollar return on old paintings with the euro return on gold. Only after the returns are expressed in terms of a common unit of measure—for example, all in terms of dollars—can we tell which asset offers the highest expected real rate of return.

Risk and Liquidity

All else equal, individuals prefer to hold those assets offering the highest expected real rate of return. Our later discussions of particular assets will show, however, that "all else" often is not equal. Some assets may be valued by savers for attributes other than the expected real rate of return they offer. Savers care about two main characteristics of an asset other than its return: its **risk**, the variability it contributes to savers' wealth, and its **liquidity**, the ease with which the asset can be sold or exchanged for goods.

    1. *Risk*. An asset's real return is usually unpredictable and may turn out to be quite different from what savers expected when they purchased the asset. In our last example, savers found the expected real rate of return on an investment in bonds (10 percent) by subtracting from the expected rate of increase in the investment's dollar value (20 percent) the expected rate of increase in dollar prices (10 percent). But if expectations are wrong and the bonds' dollar value stays constant instead of rising by 20 percent, the saver ends up with a real return of negative 10 percent (= 0 percent − 10 percent). Savers dislike uncertainty and are reluctant to

hold assets that make their wealth highly variable. An asset with a high expected rate of return may thus appear undesirable to savers if its realized rate of return fluctuates widely.

2. *Liquidity*. Assets also differ according to the cost and speed at which savers can dispose of them. A house, for example, is not very liquid because its sale usually requires time and the services of brokers and inspectors. To sell a house quickly, one might have to sell at a relatively low price. In contrast, cash is the most liquid of all assets: It is always acceptable at face value as payment for goods or other assets. Savers prefer to hold some liquid assets as a precaution against unexpected pressing expenses that might force them to sell less liquid assets at a loss. They will therefore consider an asset's liquidity as well as its expected return and risk in deciding how much of it to hold.

Interest Rates

As in other asset markets, participants in the foreign exchange market base their demands for deposits of different currencies on a comparison of these assets' expected rates of return. To compare returns on different deposits, market participants need two pieces of information. First, they need to know how the money values of the deposits will change. Second, they need to know how exchange rates will change so that they can translate rates of return measured in different currencies into comparable terms.

The first piece of information needed to compute the rate of return on a deposit of a particular currency is the currency's **interest rate**, the amount of that currency an individual can earn by lending a unit of the currency for a year. At a dollar interest rate of 0.10 (quoted as 10 percent per year), the lender of $1 receives $1.10 at the end of the year, $1 of which is principal and 10 cents of which is interest. Looked at from the other side of the transaction, the interest rate on dollars is also the amount that must be paid to borrow $1 for a year. When you buy a U.S. Treasury bill, you earn the interest rate on dollars because you are lending dollars to the U.S. government.

Interest rates play an important role in the foreign exchange market because the large deposits traded there pay interest, each at a rate reflecting its currency of denomination. For example, when the interest rate on dollars is 10 percent per year, a $100,000 deposit is worth $100,000 after a year; when the interest rate on euros is 5 percent per year, a €100,000 deposit is worth €105,000 after a year. Deposits pay interest because they are really loans from the depositor to the bank. When a corporation or a financial institution deposits a currency in a bank, it is lending that currency to the bank rather than using it for some current expenditure. In other words, the depositor is acquiring an asset denominated in the currency it deposits.

The dollar interest rate is simply the dollar rate of return on dollar deposits. You "buy" the deposit by lending a bank $100,000, and when you are paid back with 10 percent interest at the end of the year, your asset is worth $110,000. This gives a rate of return of $(110,000 - 100,000)/100,000 = 0.10$, or 10 percent per year. Similarly, a foreign currency's interest rate measures the foreign currency return on deposits of that currency. Figure 14-2 shows the monthly behavior of interest rates on the dollar and the Japanese yen from 1978 to 2013. These interest rates are not measured in comparable terms, so there is no reason for them to be close to each other or to move in similar ways over time.

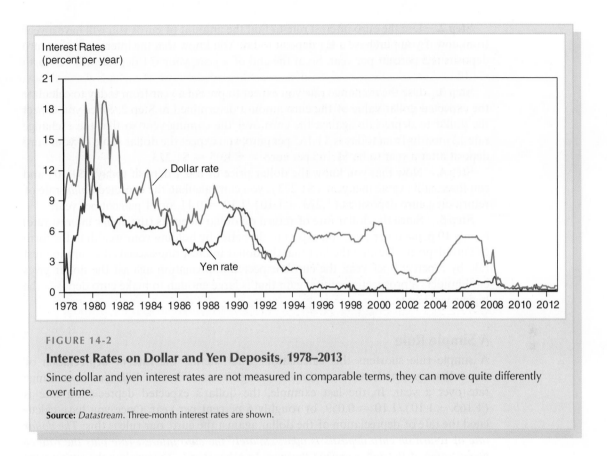

FIGURE 14-2

Interest Rates on Dollar and Yen Deposits, 1978–2013

Since dollar and yen interest rates are not measured in comparable terms, they can move quite differently over time.

Source: *Datastream*. Three-month interest rates are shown.

Exchange Rates and Asset Returns

The interest rates offered by a dollar and a euro deposit tell us how their dollar and euro values will change over a year. The other piece of information we need in order to compare the rates of return offered by dollar and euro deposits is the expected change in the dollar/euro exchange rate over the year. To see which deposit, euro or dollar, offers a higher expected rate of return, you must ask the question: If I use dollars to buy a euro deposit, how many dollars will I get back after a year? When you answer this question, you are calculating the *dollar* rate of return on a euro deposit because you are comparing its *dollar* price today with its *dollar* value a year from today.

To see how to approach this type of calculation, let's look at the following situation: Suppose that today's exchange rate (quoted in American terms) is $1.10 per euro, but that you expect the rate to be $1.165 per euro in a year (perhaps because you expect unfavorable developments in the U.S. economy). Suppose also that the dollar interest rate is 10 percent per year while the euro interest rate is 5 percent per year. This means a deposit of $1.00 pays $1.10 after a year while a deposit of €1 pays €1.05 after a year. Which of these deposits offers the higher return?

The answer can be found in five steps.

Step 1.   Use today's dollar/euro exchange rate to figure out the dollar price of a euro deposit of, say, €1. If the exchange rate today is $1.10 per euro, the dollar price of a €1 deposit is just $1.10.

Step 2.   Use the euro interest rate to find the amount of euros you will have a year from now if you purchase a €1 deposit today. You know that the interest rate on euro deposits is 5 percent per year. So at the end of a year, your €1 deposit will be worth €1.05.

Step 3.   Use the exchange rate you expect to prevail a year from today to calculate the expected dollar value of the euro amount determined in Step 2. Since you expect the dollar to depreciate against the euro over the coming year so that the exchange rate 12 months from today is $1.165 per euro, you expect the dollar value of your euro deposit after a year to be $1.165 per euro × €1.05 = $1.223.

Step 4.   Now that you know the dollar price of a €1 deposit today ($1.10) and can forecast its value in a year ($1.223), you can calculate the expected *dollar* rate of return on a euro deposit as $(1.223 - 1.10)/1.10 = 0.11$, or 11 percent per year.

Step 5.   Since the dollar rate of return on dollar deposits (the dollar interest rate) is only 10 percent per year, you expect to do better by holding your wealth in the form of euro deposits. Despite the fact that the dollar interest rate exceeds the euro interest rate by 5 percent per year, the euro's expected appreciation against the dollar gives euro holders a prospective capital gain that is large enough to make euro deposits the higher-yield asset.

A Simple Rule

A simple rule shortens this calculation. First, define the **rate of depreciation** of the dollar against the euro as the percentage increase in the dollar/euro exchange rate over a year. In the last example, the dollar's expected depreciation rate is $(1.165 - 1.10)/1.10 = 0.059$, or roughly 6 percent per year. Once you have calculated the rate of depreciation of the dollar against the euro, our rule is this: *The dollar rate of return on euro deposits is approximately the euro interest rate plus the rate of depreciation of the dollar against the euro.* In other words, to translate the euro return on euro deposits into dollar terms, you need to add the rate at which the euro's dollar price rises over a year to the euro interest rate.

In our example, the sum of the euro interest rate (5 percent) and the expected depreciation rate of the dollar (roughly 6 percent) is about 11 percent, which is what we found to be the expected dollar return on euro deposits in our first calculation. We summarize our discussion by introducing some notation:

$R_€$ = today's interest rate on one-year euro deposits,

$E_{\$/€}$ = today's dollar/euro exchange rate (number of dollars per euro),

$E^e_{\$/€}$ = dollar/euro exchange rate (number of dollars per euro) expected to prevail a year from today.

(The superscript ^{e} attached to this last exchange rate indicates that it is a forecast of the future exchange rate based on what people know today.)

Using these symbols, we write the expected rate of return on a euro deposit, measured in terms of dollars, as the sum of (1) the euro interest rate and (2) the expected rate of dollar depreciation against the euro:

$$R_€ + (E^e_{\$/€} - E_{\$/€})/E_{\$/€}.$$

This expected return is what must be compared with the interest rate on one-year dollar deposits, $R_\$$, in deciding whether dollar or euro deposits offer the higher expected rate of return.[6] The expected rate of return difference between dollar and euro deposits is therefore equal to $R_\$$ less the previous expression,

$$R_\$ - [R_€ + (E^e_{\$/€} - E_{\$/€})/E_{\$/€}] = R_\$ - R_€ - (E^e_{\$/€} - E_{\$/€})/E_{\$/€}. \quad (14\text{-}1)$$

When the difference above is positive, dollar deposits yield the higher expected rate of return; when it is negative, euro deposits yield the higher expected rate of return.

Table 14-3 carries out some illustrative comparisons. In case 1, the interest difference in favor of dollar deposits is 4 percent per year ($R_\$ - R_€ = 0.10 - 0.06 = 0.04$), and no change in the exchange rate is expected [$(E^e_{\$/€} - E_{\$/€})/E_{\$/€} = 0.00$]. This means that the expected annual real rate of return on dollar deposits is 4 percent higher than that on euro deposits, so that, other things equal, you would prefer to hold your wealth as dollar rather than euro deposits.

In case 2, the interest difference is the same (4 percent), but it is just offset by an expected depreciation rate of the dollar of 4 percent. The two assets therefore have the same expected rate of return.

Case 3 is similar to the one discussed earlier: A 4 percent interest difference in favor of dollar deposits is more than offset by an 8 percent expected depreciation of the dollar, so euro deposits are preferred by market participants.

In case 4, there is a 2 percent interest difference in favor of euro deposits, but the dollar is expected to *appreciate* against the euro by 4 percent over the year. The expected rate of return on dollar deposits is therefore 2 percent per year higher than that on euro deposits.

So far, we have been translating all returns into dollar terms. But the rate of return differentials we calculated would have been the same had we chosen to express

TABLE 14-3	Comparing Dollar Rates of Return on Dollar and Euro Deposits			
	Dollar Interest Rate	Euro Interest Rate	Expected Rate of Dollar Depreciation against Euro	Rate of Return Difference between Dollar and Euro Deposits
Case	$R_\$$	$R_€$	$\dfrac{E^e_{\$/€} - E_{\$/€}}{E_{\$/€}}$	$R_\$ - R_€ - \dfrac{(E^e_{\$/€} - E_{\$/€})}{E_{\$/€}}$
1	0.10	0.06	0.00	0.04
2	0.10	0.06	0.04	0.00
3	0.10	0.06	0.08	−0.04
4	0.10	0.12	−0.04	0.02

---

[6] If you compute the expected dollar return on euro deposits using the exact five-step method we described before introducing the simple rule, you'll find that it actually equals

$$(1 + R_€)(E^e_{\$/€}/E_{\$/€}) - 1.$$

This exact formula can be rewritten, however, as

$$R_€ + (E^e_{\$/€} - E_{\$/€})/E_{\$/€} + R_€ \times (E^e_{\$/€} - E_{\$/€})/E_{\$/€}.$$

The expression above is very close to the formula derived from the simple rule when, as is usually the case, the product $R_€ \times (E^e_{\$/€} - E_{\$/€})/E_{\$/€}$ is a small number.

returns in terms of euros or in terms of some third currency. Suppose, for example, we wanted to measure the return on dollar deposits in terms of euros. Following our simple rule, we would add to the dollar interest rate $R_\$$ the expected rate of depreciation of the euro against the dollar. But the expected rate of depreciation of the euro against the dollar is approximately the expected **rate of appreciation** of the dollar against the euro, that is, the expected rate of depreciation of the dollar against the euro with a minus sign in front of it. This means that in terms of euros, the return on a dollar deposit is

$$R_\$ - (E^e_{\$/\euro} - E_{\$/\euro})/E_{\$/\euro}.$$

The difference between the expression above and $R_\euro$ is identical to expression (14-1). Thus, it makes no difference to our comparison whether we measure returns in terms of dollars or euros, as long as we measure them both in terms of the same currency.

Return, Risk, and Liquidity in the Foreign Exchange Market

We observed earlier that a saver deciding which assets to hold may care about the assets' riskiness and liquidity in addition to their expected real rates of return. Similarly, the demand for foreign currency assets depends not only on returns but also on risk and liquidity. Even if the expected dollar return on euro deposits is higher than that on dollar deposits, for example, people may be reluctant to hold euro deposits if the payoff to holding them varies erratically.

There is no consensus among economists about the importance of risk in the foreign exchange market. Even the definition of "foreign exchange risk" is a topic of debate. For now, we will avoid these complex questions by assuming that the real returns on all deposits have equal riskiness, regardless of the currency of denomination. In other words, we are assuming that risk differences do not influence the demand for foreign currency assets. We discuss the role of foreign exchange risk in greater detail, however, in Chapter 18.[7]

Some market participants may be influenced by liquidity factors in deciding which currencies to hold. Most of these participants are firms and individuals conducting international trade. An American importer of French fashion products or wines, for example, may find it convenient to hold euros for routine payments even if the expected rate of return on euros is lower than that on dollars. Because payments connected with international trade make up a very small fraction of total foreign exchange transactions, we ignore the liquidity motive for holding foreign currencies.

We are therefore assuming for now that participants in the foreign exchange market base their demands for foreign currency assets exclusively on a comparison of those assets' expected rates of return. The main reason for making this assumption is that it simplifies our analysis of how exchange rates are determined in the foreign exchange market. In addition, the risk and liquidity motives for holding foreign currencies

---

[7]In discussing spot and forward foreign exchange transactions, some textbooks make a distinction between foreign exchange "speculators"—market participants who allegedly care only about expected returns—and "hedgers"—market participants whose concern is to avoid risk. We depart from this textbook tradition because it can mislead the unwary: While the speculative and hedging motives are both potentially important in exchange rate determination, the same person can be both a speculator and a hedger if she cares about both return and risk. Our tentative assumption that risk is unimportant in determining the demand for foreign currency assets means, in terms of the traditional language, that the speculative motive for holding foreign currencies is far more important than the hedging motive.

appear to be of secondary importance for many of the international macroeconomic issues discussed in the next few chapters.

Equilibrium in the Foreign Exchange Market

We now use what we have learned about the demand for foreign currency assets to describe how exchange rates are determined. We will show that the exchange rate at which the market settles is the one that makes market participants content to hold existing supplies of deposits of all currencies. When market participants willingly hold the existing supplies of deposits of all currencies, we say that the foreign exchange market is in equilibrium.

The description of exchange rate determination given in this section is only a first step: A full explanation of the exchange rate's current level can be given only after we examine how participants in the foreign exchange market form their expectations about the exchange rates they expect to prevail in the future. The next two chapters look at the factors that influence expectations of future exchange rates. For now, however, we will take expected future exchange rates as given.

Interest Parity: The Basic Equilibrium Condition

The foreign exchange market is in equilibrium when deposits of all currencies offer the same expected rate of return. The condition that the expected returns on deposits of any two currencies are equal when measured in the same currency is called the **interest parity condition**. It implies that potential holders of foreign currency deposits view them all as equally desirable assets, provided their expected rates of return are the same.

Let's see why the foreign exchange market is in equilibrium only when the interest parity condition holds. Suppose the dollar interest rate is 10 percent and the euro interest rate is 6 percent, but that the dollar is expected to depreciate against the euro at an 8 percent rate over a year. (This is case 3 in Table 14-3.) In the circumstances described, the expected rate of return on euro deposits would be 4 percent per year higher than that on dollar deposits. We assumed at the end of the last section that individuals always prefer to hold deposits of currencies offering the highest expected return. This implies that if the expected return on euro deposits is 4 percent greater than that on dollar deposits, no one will be willing to continue holding dollar deposits, and holders of dollar deposits will be trying to sell them for euro deposits. There will therefore be an excess supply of dollar deposits and an excess demand for euro deposits in the foreign exchange market.

As a contrasting example, suppose dollar deposits again offer a 10 percent interest rate but euro deposits offer a 12 percent rate and the dollar is expected to *appreciate* against the euro by 4 percent over the coming year. (This is case 4 in Table 14-3.) Now the return on dollar deposits is 2 percent higher. In this case, no one would demand euro deposits, so they would be in excess supply and dollar deposits would be in excess demand.

When, however, the dollar interest rate is 10 percent, the euro interest rate is 6 percent, and the dollar's expected depreciation rate against the euro is 4 percent, dollar and euro deposits offer the same rate of return and participants in the foreign exchange market are equally willing to hold either. (This is case 2 in Table 14-3.)

Only when all expected rates of return are equal—that is, when the interest parity condition holds—is there no excess supply of some type of deposit and no excess demand for another. The foreign exchange market is in equilibrium when no type of deposit is in excess demand or excess supply. We can therefore say that the foreign exchange market is in equilibrium when, and only when, the interest parity condition holds.

To represent interest parity between dollar and euro deposits symbolically, we use expression (14-1), which shows the difference between the two assets' expected rates of return measured in dollars. The expected rates of return are equal when

$$R_\$ = R_€ + (E_{\$/€}^e - E_{\$/€})/E_{\$/€}. \tag{14-2}$$

You probably suspect that when dollar deposits offer a higher return than euro deposits, the dollar will appreciate against the euro as investors all try to shift their funds into dollars. Conversely, the dollar should depreciate against the euro when it is euro deposits that initially offer the higher return. This intuition is exactly correct. To understand the mechanism at work, however, we must take a careful look at how exchange rate changes like these help to maintain equilibrium in the foreign exchange market.

How Changes in the Current Exchange Rate Affect Expected Returns

As a first step in understanding how the foreign exchange market finds its equilibrium, we examine how changes in today's exchange rate affect the expected return on a foreign currency deposit when interest rates and expectations about the future exchange rate do not change. Our analysis will show that, other things equal, depreciation of a country's currency today *lowers* the expected domestic currency return on foreign currency deposits. Conversely, appreciation of the domestic currency today, all else equal, *raises* the domestic currency return expected of foreign currency deposits.

It is easiest to see why these relationships hold by looking at an example: How does a change in today's dollar/euro exchange rate, all else held constant, change the expected return, measured in terms of dollars, on euro deposits? Suppose today's dollar/euro rate is $1.00 per euro and the exchange rate you expect for this day next year is $1.05 per euro. Then the expected rate of dollar depreciation against the euro is $(1.05 - 1.00)/1.00 = 0.05$, or 5 percent per year. This means that when you buy a euro deposit, you not only earn the interest $R_€$ but also get a 5 percent "bonus" in terms of dollars. Now suppose today's exchange rate suddenly jumps up to $1.03 per euro (a depreciation of the dollar and an appreciation of the euro), but the expected future rate is *still* $1.05 per euro. What happens to the "bonus" you expected to get from the euro's increase in value in terms of dollars? The expected rate of dollar depreciation is now only $(1.05 - 1.03)/1.03 = 0.019$, or 1.9 percent instead of 5 percent. Since $R_€$ has not changed, the dollar return on euro deposits, which is the sum of $R_€$ and the expected rate of dollar depreciation, has *fallen* by 3.1 percentage points per year (5 percent − 1.9 percent).

In Table 14-4, we work out the dollar return on euro deposits for various levels of today's dollar/euro exchange rate $E_{\$/€}$, always assuming that the expected *future* exchange rate remains fixed at $1.05 per euro and the euro interest rate is 5 percent per year. As you can see, a rise in today's dollar/euro exchange rate (a depreciation of the dollar against the euro) always *lowers* the expected dollar return on euro deposits (as in our example), while a fall in today's dollar/euro exchange rate (an appreciation of the dollar against the euro) always *raises* this return.

It may run counter to your intuition that a depreciation of the dollar against the euro makes euro deposits less attractive relative to dollar deposits (by lowering the expected dollar return on euro deposits) while an appreciation of the dollar makes euro deposits more attractive. This result will seem less surprising if you remember we have assumed that the expected future dollar/euro rate and interest rates do

Today's Dollar/Euro Exchange Rate $E_{\$/€}$	Interest Rate on Euro Deposits $R_€$	Expected Dollar Depreciation Rate against Euro $\dfrac{1.05 - E_{\$/€}}{E_{\$/€}}$	Expected Dollar Return on Euro Deposits $R_€ + \dfrac{1.05 - E_{\$/€}}{E_{\$/€}}$
1.07	0.05	−0.019	0.031
1.05	0.05	0.00	0.05
1.03	0.05	0.019	0.069
1.02	0.05	0.029	0.079
1.00	0.05	0.05	0.10

TABLE 14-4 Today's Dollar/Euro Exchange Rate and the Expected Dollar Return on Euro Deposits When $E^e_{\$/€} = \$1.05$ per Euro

not change. A dollar depreciation today, for example, means the dollar now needs to depreciate by a *smaller* amount to reach any given expected future level. If the expected future dollar/euro exchange rate does not change when the dollar depreciates today, the dollar's expected future depreciation against the euro therefore falls, or, alternatively, the dollar's expected future appreciation rises. Since interest rates also are unchanged, today's dollar depreciation thus makes euro deposits less attractive compared with dollar deposits.

Put another way, a current dollar depreciation that affects neither exchange rate expectations nor interest rates leaves the expected future dollar payoff of a euro deposit the same but raises the deposit's current dollar cost. This change naturally makes euro deposits less attractive relative to dollar deposits.

It may also run counter to your intuition that *today's* exchange rate can change while the exchange rate expected for the *future* does not. We will indeed study cases later in this book when both of these rates do change at once. We nonetheless hold the expected future exchange rate constant in the present discussion because that is the clearest way to illustrate the effect of today's exchange rate on expected returns. If it helps, you can imagine we are looking at the impact of a *temporary* change so brief that it has no effect on the exchange rate expected for next year.

Figure 14-3 shows the calculations in Table 14-4 in a graphic form that will be helpful in our analysis of exchange rate determination. The vertical axis in the figure measures today's dollar/euro exchange rate and the horizontal axis measures the expected dollar return on euro deposits. For *fixed* values of the expected future dollar/euro exchange rate and the euro interest rate, the relation between today's dollar/euro exchange rate and the expected dollar return on euro deposits defines a downward-sloping schedule.

The Equilibrium Exchange Rate

Now that we understand why the interest parity condition must hold for the foreign exchange market to be in equilibrium and how today's exchange rate affects the expected return on foreign currency deposits, we can see how equilibrium exchange rates are determined. Our main conclusion will be that exchange rates always adjust to maintain interest parity. We continue to assume the dollar interest rate $R_\$$, the euro interest rate $R_€$, and the expected future dollar/euro exchange rate $E^e_{\$/€}$ are all *given*.

FIGURE 14-3

The Relation between the Current Dollar/Euro Exchange Rate and the Expected Dollar Return on Euro Deposits

Given that $E^e_{\$/€} = 1.05$ and $R_€ = 0.05$, an appreciation of the dollar against the euro raises the expected return on euro deposits, measured in terms of dollars.

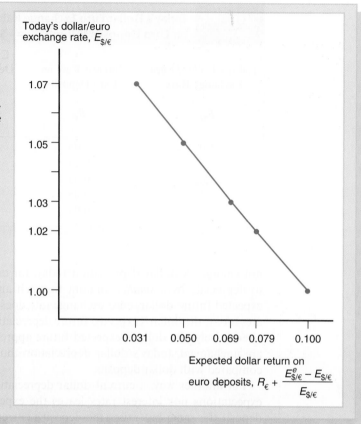

is satisfied.

Figure 14-4 illustrates how the equilibrium dollar/euro exchange rate is determined under these assumptions. The vertical schedule in the graph indicates the given level of $R_\$$, the return on dollar deposits measured in terms of dollars. The downward-sloping schedule shows how the expected return on euro deposits, measured in terms of dollars, depends on the current dollar/euro exchange rate. This second schedule is derived in the same way as the one shown in Figure 14-3.

The equilibrium dollar/euro rate is the one indicated by the intersection of the two schedules at point 1, $E^1_{\$/€}$. At this exchange rate, the returns on dollar and euro deposits are equal, so that the interest parity condition (14-2),

$$R_\$ = R_€ + (E^e_{\$/€} - E^1_{\$/€})/E^1_{\$/€},$$

is satisfied.

Let's see why the exchange rate will tend to settle at point 1 in Figure 14-4 if it is initially at a point such as 2 or 3. Suppose first that we are at point 2, with the exchange rate equal to $E^2_{\$/€}$. The downward-sloping schedule measuring the expected dollar return on euro deposits tells us that at the exchange rate $E^2_{\$/€}$, the rate of return on euro deposits is less than the rate of return on dollar deposits, $R_\$$. In this situation, anyone holding euro deposits wishes to sell them for the more lucrative dollar deposits: The foreign exchange market is out of equilibrium because participants such as banks and multinational corporations are *unwilling* to hold euro deposits.

How does the exchange rate adjust? The unhappy owners of euro deposits attempt to sell them for dollar deposits, but because the return on dollar deposits is higher

FIGURE 14-4

Determination of the Equilibrium Dollar/Euro Exchange Rate

Equilibrium in the foreign exchange market is at point 1, where the expected dollar returns on dollar and euro deposits are equal.

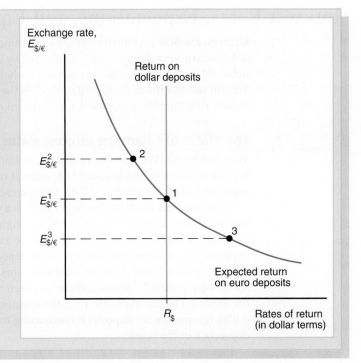

than that on euro deposits at the exchange rate $E^2_{\$/\euro}$, no holder of a dollar deposit is willing to sell it for a euro deposit at that rate. As euro holders try to entice dollar holders to trade by offering them a better price for dollars, the dollar/euro exchange rate falls toward $E^1_{\$/\euro}$; that is, euros become cheaper in terms of dollars. Once the exchange rate reaches $E^1_{\$/\euro}$, euro and dollar deposits offer equal returns, and holders of euro deposits no longer have an incentive to try to sell them for dollars. The foreign exchange market is therefore in equilibrium. In falling from $E^2_{\$/\euro}$ to $E^1_{\$/\euro}$, the exchange rate equalizes the expected returns on the two types of deposit by increasing the rate at which the dollar is expected to depreciate in the future, thereby making euro deposits more attractive.

The same process works in reverse if we are initially at point 3 with an exchange rate of $E^3_{\$/\euro}$, At point 3, the return on euro deposits exceeds that on dollar deposits, so there is now an excess supply of the latter. As unwilling holders of dollar deposits bid for the more attractive euro deposits, the price of euros in terms of dollars tends to rise; that is, the dollar tends to depreciate against the euro. When the exchange rate has moved to $E^1_{\$/\euro}$, rates of return are equalized across currencies and the market is in equilibrium. The depreciation of the dollar from $E^3_{\$/\euro}$ to $E^1_{\$/\euro}$ makes euro deposits less attractive relative to dollar deposits by reducing the rate at which the dollar is expected to depreciate in the future.[8]

---

[8] We could have developed our diagram from the perspective of Europe, with the euro/dollar exchange rate $E_{\euro/\$}$ ($= 1/E_{\$/\euro}$) on the vertical axis, a schedule vertical at $R_\euro$ to indicate the euro return on euro deposits, and a downward-sloping schedule showing how the euro return on dollar deposits varies with $E_{\euro/\$}$. An exercise at the end of the chapter asks you to show that this alternative way of looking at equilibrium in the foreign exchange market gives the same answers as the method used here in the text.

Interest Rates, Expectations, and Equilibrium

Having seen how exchange rates are determined by interest parity, we now take a look at how current exchange rates are affected by changes in interest rates and in expectations about the future, the two factors we held constant in our previous discussions. We will see that the exchange rate (which is the relative price of two assets) responds to factors that alter the expected rates of return on those two assets.

The Effect of Changing Interest Rates on the Current Exchange Rate

We often read in the newspaper that the dollar is strong because U.S. interest rates are high or that it is falling because U.S. interest rates are falling. Can these statements be explained using our analysis of the foreign exchange market?

To answer this question, we again turn to a diagram. Figure 14-5 shows a rise in the interest rate on dollars, from $R_\$^1$ to $R_\$^2$ as a rightward shift of the vertical dollar deposits return schedule. At the initial exchange rate $E_{\$/\euro}^1$, the expected return on dollar deposits is now higher than that on euro deposits by an amount equal to the distance between points 1 and 1′. As we have seen, this difference causes the dollar to appreciate to $E_{\$/\euro}^2$ (point 2). Because there has been no change in the euro interest rate or in the expected future exchange rate, the dollar's appreciation today raises the expected dollar return on euro deposits by increasing the rate at which the dollar is expected to depreciate in the future.

Figure 14-6 shows the effect of a rise in the euro interest rate $R_\euro$. This change causes the downward-sloping schedule (which measures the expected dollar return on euro deposits) to shift rightward. (To see why, ask yourself how a rise in the euro interest rate alters the dollar return on euro deposits, given the current exchange rate and the expected future rate.)

FIGURE 14-5

Effect of a Rise in the Dollar Interest Rate

A rise in the interest rate offered by dollar deposits from $R_\$^1$ to $R_\$^2$ causes the dollar to appreciate from $E_{\$/\euro}^1$ (point 1) to $E_{\$/\euro}^2$ (point 2).

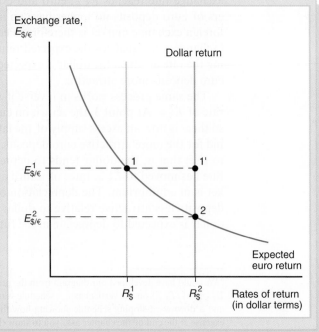

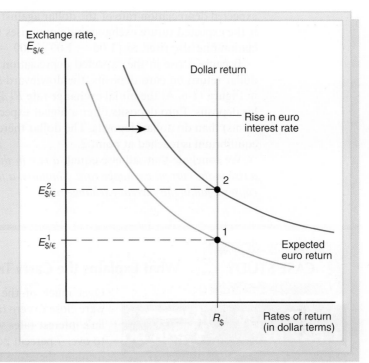

FIGURE 14-6

Effect of a Rise in the Euro Interest Rate

A rise in the interest rate paid by euro deposits causes the dollar to depreciate from $E^1_{\$/€}$ (point 1) to $E^2_{\$/€}$ (point 2). (This figure also describes the effect of a rise in the expected future \$/€ exchange rate.)

At the initial exchange rate $E^1_{\$/€}$, the expected depreciation rate of the dollar is the same as before the rise in $R_€$, so the expected return on euro deposits now exceeds that on dollar deposits. The dollar/euro exchange rate rises (from $E^1_{\$/€}$ to $E^2_{\$/€}$ to eliminate the excess supply of dollar assets at point 1. As before, the dollar's depreciation against the euro eliminates the excess supply of dollar assets by lowering the expected dollar rate of return on euro deposits. A rise in European interest rates therefore leads to a depreciation of the dollar against the euro or, looked at from the European perspective, an appreciation of the euro against the dollar.

Our discussion shows that, all else equal, *an increase in the interest paid on deposits of a currency causes that currency to appreciate against foreign currencies.*

Before we conclude that the newspaper account of the effect of interest rates on exchange rates is correct, we must remember that our assumption of a *constant* expected future exchange rate often is unrealistic. In many cases, a change in interest rates will be accompanied by a change in the expected future exchange rate. This change in the expected future exchange rate will depend, in turn, on the economic causes of the interest rate change. We compare different possible relationships between interest rates and expected future exchange rates in Chapter 16. Keep in mind for now that in the real world, we cannot predict how a given interest rate change will alter exchange rates unless we know *why* the interest rate is changing.

The Effect of Changing Expectations on the Current Exchange Rate

Figure 14-6 may also be used to study the effect on today's exchange rate of a rise in the expected future dollar/euro exchange rate, $E^e_{\$/€}$.

Given today's exchange rate, a rise in the expected future price of euros in terms of dollars raises the dollar's expected depreciation rate. For example, if today's exchange rate is \$1.00 per euro and the rate expected to prevail in a year is \$1.05 per euro, the expected depreciation rate of the dollar against the euro is $(1.05 - 1.00)/1.00 = 0.05$; if the expected future exchange rate now rises to \$1.06 per euro, the expected depreciation rate also rises, to $(1.06 - 1.00)/1.00 = 0.06$.

Because a rise in the expected depreciation rate of the dollar raises the expected dollar return on euro deposits, the downward-sloping schedule shifts to the right, as in Figure 14-6. At the initial exchange rate $E^1_{\$/\in}$, there is now an excess supply of dollar deposits: Euro deposits offer a higher expected rate of return (measured in dollar terms) than do dollar deposits. The dollar therefore depreciates against the euro until equilibrium is reached at point 2.

We conclude that, all else equal, *a rise in the expected future exchange rate causes a rise in the current exchange rate. Similarly, a fall in the expected future exchange rate causes a fall in the current exchange rate.*

CASE STUDY

What Explains the Carry Trade?

Over much of the 2000s, Japanese yen interest rates were close to zero (as Figure 14-2 shows) while Australia's interest rates were comfortably positive, climbing to over 7 percent per year by the spring of 2008. While it might therefore have appeared attractive to borrow yen and invest the proceeds in Australian dollar bonds, the interest parity condition implies that such a strategy should not be *systematically* profitable: On average, shouldn't the interest advantage of Australian dollars be wiped out by relative appreciation of the yen?

Nonetheless, market actors ranging from Japanese housewives to sophisticated hedge funds did in fact pursue this strategy, investing billions in Australian dollars and driving that currency's value up, rather than down, against the yen. More generally, international investors frequently borrow low-interest currencies (called "funding" currencies) and buy high-interest currencies (called "investment" currencies), with results that can be profitable over long periods. This activity is called the *carry trade*, and while it is generally impossible to document the extent of carry trade positions accurately, they can become very large when sizable international interest differentials open up. Is the prevalence of the carry trade evidence that interest parity is wrong?

The honest answer is that while interest parity does not hold exactly in practice—in part because of the risk and liquidity factors mentioned above—economists are still working hard to understand if the carry trade requires additional explanation. Their work is likely to throw further light on the functioning of foreign exchange markets in particular and financial markets in general.

One important hazard of the carry trade is that investment currencies (the high-interest currencies that carry traders target) may experience abrupt crashes. Figure 14-7 illustrates this feature of foreign exchange markets, comparing the cumulative return to investing ¥100 in yen bonds and in Australian dollar bonds over different investment horizons, with the initial investment being made in the final quarter of 2002. As you can see, the yen investment yields next to nothing, whereas Australian dollars pay off handsomely, not only because of a high interest rate but because the yen tended to fall against the Australian dollar through the summer of 2008. But in 2008, the Australian dollar crashed against the yen, falling in price from ¥104 to only ¥61 between July and December. As Figure 14-7 shows, this crash did not wipe out the gains to the carry trade strategy entirely—*if* the strategy had been initiated early enough! Of course, anyone who got into the business late, for example, in 2007, did very poorly indeed. Conversely, anyone savvy enough to unwind the strategy in June 2008 would have doubled his or her money in five and a half years. The carry trade is obviously a very risky business.

We can gain some insight into this pattern by imagining that investors expect a gradual 1 percent annual appreciation of the Australian dollar to occur with high probability (say, 90 percent) and a big 40 percent depreciation to occur with a 10 percent probability. Then the expected appreciation rate of the Australian dollar is:

$$\text{Expected appreciation} = (0.9) \times 1 - (0.1) \times 40 = -3.1 \text{ percent per year.}$$

The negative expected appreciation rate means that the yen is actually expected to appreciate *on average* against the Australian dollar. Moreover, the probability of a crash occurring in the first six years of the investment is only $1 - (0.9)^6 = 1 - 0.53 = 47$ percent, less than fifty-fifty.[9] The resulting pattern of cumulative returns could easily look much like the one shown in Figure 14-7. Calculations like these are suggestive,

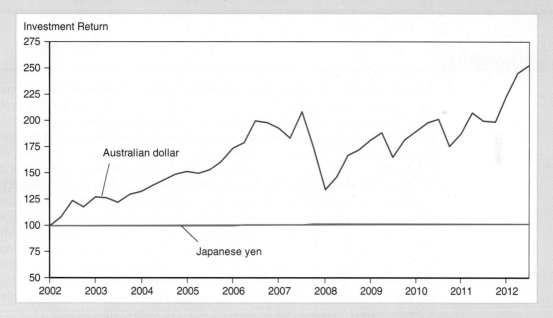

FIGURE 14-7

Cumulative Total Investment Return in Australian Dollar Compared to Japanese Yen, 2003–2013

The Australian dollar-yen carry trade has been profitable on average but is subject to sudden large reversals, as in 2008.

Source: Exchange rates and three-month treasury yields from Global Financial Data.

---

[9]If crashes are independent events over time, the probability that a crash does *not* occur over six years is $(0.9)^6$. Therefore, the probability that a crash does occur in the six-year period is $1 - (0.9)^6$.

and although they are unlikely to explain the full magnitude of carry trade returns, researchers have found that investment currencies are particularly subject to abrupt crashes, and funding currencies to abrupt appreciations.[10]

Complementary explanations based on risk and liquidity considerations have also been advanced. Often, abrupt currency movements occur during financial crises, which are situations in which other wealth is being lost and liquid cash is particularly valuable. In such circumstances, large losses on carry trade positions are extra painful and may force traders to sell other assets they own at a loss.[11] We will say much more about crises in later chapters, but we note for now that the Australian dollar collapse of late 2008 occurred in the midst of a severe global financial crisis.

When big carry trade positions emerge, the government officials responsible for international economic policies often lose sleep. In their early phase, carry trade dynamics will drive investment currencies higher as investors pile in and build up ever-larger exposures to a sudden depreciation of the investment currency. This makes the crash bigger when it occurs, as wrong-footed investors all scramble to repay their funding loans. The result is greater exchange rate volatility in general, as well as the possibility of big trader losses with negative repercussions in stock markets, bond markets, and markets for interbank loans.

SUMMARY

1. An *exchange rate* is the price of one country's currency in terms of another country's currency. Exchange rates play a role in spending decisions because they enable us to translate different countries' prices into comparable terms. All else equal, a *depreciation* of a country's currency against foreign currencies (a rise in the home currency prices of foreign currencies) makes its exports cheaper and its imports more expensive. An *appreciation* of its currency (a fall in the home currency prices of foreign currencies) makes its exports more expensive and its imports cheaper.

2. Exchange rates are determined in the *foreign exchange market*. The major participants in that market are commercial banks, international corporations, nonbank financial institutions, and national central banks. Commercial banks play a pivotal role in the market because they facilitate the exchange of interest-bearing bank deposits, which make up the bulk of foreign exchange trading. Even though foreign exchange trading takes place in many financial centers around the world, modern communication technology links those centers together into a single market that is open 24 hours a day. An important category of foreign

---

[10]See Markus K. Brunnermeier, Stefan Nagel, and Lasse H. Pedersen, "Carry Trades and Currency Crashes," *NBER Macroeconomics Annual* 23 (2008), pp. 313–347. These findings are consistent with the apparently greater empirical success of the interest parity condition over relatively long periods, as documented by Menzie Chinn, "The (Partial) Rehabilitation of Interest Rate Parity in the Floating Rate Era: Longer Horizons, Alternative Expectations, and Emerging Markets," *Journal of International Money and Finance* 25 (February 2006), pp. 7–21.

[11]See Brunnermeier et al., *ibid.*, as well as Craig Burnside, "Carry Trades and Risk," in Jessica James, Ian Marsh, and Lucio Sarno, eds., *Handbook of Exchange Rates* (Hoboken, NJ: John Wiley & Sons, 2012), pp. 283–312.

exchange trading is *forward* trading, in which parties agree to exchange currencies on some future date at a prenegotiated exchange rate. In contrast, *spot* trades are settled immediately.

3. Because the exchange rate is the relative price of two assets, it is most appropriately thought of as being an asset price itself. The basic principle of asset pricing is that an asset's current value depends on its expected future purchasing power. In evaluating an asset, savers look at the expected *rate of return* it offers, that is, the rate at which the value of an investment in the asset is expected to rise over time. It is possible to measure an asset's expected rate of return in different ways, each depending on the units in which the asset's value is measured. Savers care about an asset's expected *real rate of return*, the rate at which its value expressed in terms of a representative output basket is expected to rise.

4. When relative asset returns are relevant, as in the foreign exchange market, it is appropriate to compare expected changes in assets' currency values, provided those values are expressed in the same currency. If *risk* and *liquidity* factors do not strongly influence the demands for foreign currency assets, participants in the foreign exchange market always prefer to hold those assets yielding the highest expected rate of return.

5. The returns on deposits traded in the foreign exchange market depend on *interest rates* and expected exchange rate changes. To compare the expected rates of return offered by dollar and euro deposits, for example, the return on euro deposits must be expressed in dollar terms by adding to the euro interest rate the expected *rate of depreciation* of the dollar against the euro (or *rate of appreciation* of the euro against the dollar) over the deposit's holding period.

6. Equilibrium in the foreign exchange market requires *interest parity*; that is, deposits of all currencies must offer the same expected rate of return when returns are measured in comparable terms.

7. For given interest rates and a given expectation of the future exchange rate, the interest parity condition tells us the current equilibrium exchange rate. When the expected dollar return on euro deposits exceeds that on dollar deposits, for example, the dollar immediately depreciates against the euro. Other things equal, a dollar depreciation today reduces the expected dollar return on euro deposits by reducing the depreciation rate of the dollar against the euro expected for the future. Similarly, when the expected return on euro deposits is below that on dollar deposits, the dollar must immediately appreciate against the euro. Other things equal, a current appreciation of the dollar makes euro deposits more attractive by increasing the dollar's expected future depreciation against the European currency.

8. All else equal, a rise in dollar interest rates causes the dollar to appreciate against the euro while a rise in euro interest rates causes the dollar to depreciate against the euro. Today's exchange rate is also altered by changes in its expected future level. If there is a rise in the expected future level of the dollar/euro rate, for example, then at unchanged interest rates, today's dollar/euro exchange rate will also rise.

KEY TERMS

appreciation, p. 377
arbitrage, p. 381
depreciation, p. 377
exchange rate, p. 374
foreign exchange market, p. 378
forward exchange rate, p. 382

interbank trading, p. 380
interest parity condition, p. 393
interest rate, p. 388
liquidity, p. 387
rate of appreciation, p. 392

rate of depreciation, p. 390
rate of return, p. 384
real rate of return, p. 385
risk, p. 387
spot exchange rate, p. 382
vehicle currency, p. 381

PROBLEMS

1. In Munich, a bratwurst costs 5 euros; a hot dog costs $4 at Boston's Fenway Park. At an exchange rate of $1.05/per euro, what is the price of a bratwurst in terms of a hot dog? All else equal, how does this relative price change if the dollar depreciates to $1.25 per euro? Compared with the initial situation, has a hot dog become more or less expensive relative to a bratwurst?

2. As defined in footnote 3, cross exchange rates are exchange rates quoted against currencies other than the U.S. dollar. If you return to Table 14-1, you will notice that it lists not only exchange rates against the dollar, but also cross rates against the euro and the pound sterling. The fact that we can derive the Swiss franc/Israeli shekel exchange rate, say, from the dollar/franc rate and the dollar/shekel rate follows from ruling out a potentially profitable arbitrage strategy known as *triangular arbitrage*. As an example, suppose the Swiss franc price of a shekel were below the Swiss franc price of a dollar times the dollar price of a shekel. Explain why, rather than buying shekels with dollars, it would be cheaper to buy Swiss francs with dollars and use the francs to buy the shekels. Thus, the hypothesized situation offers a riskless profit opportunity and therefore is not consistent with profit maximization.

3. Table 14-1 reports exchange rates not only against the US dollar, but also against the euro and the pound sterling. (Each row gives the price of the dollar, euro, and pound, respectively, in terms of a different currency.) At the same time, the table gives the spot dollar prices of the euro ($1.3221 per euro) and the pound sterling ($1.5539 per pound). Pick any five currencies from the table and show that the three quoted spot exchange rates (in terms of dollars, euros, and pounds) approximately rule out triangular arbitrage. Why do we need to add the word "approximately"?

4. China faces relatively inelastic demand for oil. Most of China's oil demand is met through imports from oil producing countries. Do you think the depreciation of Chinese yuan against the US dollar will have a favorable impact on its balance of payments in the short run? Explain.

5. Calculate the dollar rates of return on the following assets:
   a. A painting whose price rises from $200,000 to $250,000 in a year.
   b. A bottle of a rare Burgundy, Domaine de la Romanée-Conti 2011, whose price rises from $255 to $275 between 2013 and 2014.
   c. A £10,000 deposit in a London bank in a year when the interest rate on pounds is 10 percent and the $/£ exchange rate moves from $1.50 per pound to $1.38 per pound.

6. What would be the real rates of return on the assets in the preceding question if the price changes described were accompanied by a simultaneous 10 percent increase in all dollar prices?

7. In 2014, Germany's Volkswagen (VW) makes a contract with Malaysia to supply 100 cars in 2015. €700,000 is to be paid on the date of supply. Suppose today's rate is Malaysian ringgit (MYR) 3/€ and the expected exchange rate for next year is MYR 3.15/€. Suppose after the deal, the rate changed to MYR3.10/€. In this case, what will happen to VW's expected gain and loss in bonus in 2015?

8. Traders in asset markets suddenly learn that the interest rate on dollars will decline in the near future. Use the diagrammatic analysis of this chapter to determine the effect on the *current* dollar/euro exchange rate, assuming current interest rates on dollar and euro deposits do not change.

9. We noted that we could have developed our diagrammatic analysis of foreign exchange market equilibrium from the perspective of Europe, with the euro/dollar exchange rate $E_{€/\$}(= 1/E_{\$/€})$ on the vertical axis, a schedule vertical at $R_€$ to indicate the euro return on euro deposits, and a downward-sloping schedule showing how the euro return on dollar deposits varies with $E_{€/\$}$. Derive this alternative picture of equilibrium and use it to examine the effect of changes in interest rates and the expected future exchange rate. Do your answers agree with those we found earlier?

10. The following report appeared in the *New York Times* on August 7, 1989 ("Dollar's Strength a Surprise," p. D1):

    But now the sentiment is that the economy is heading for a "soft landing," with the economy slowing significantly and inflation subsiding, but without a recession.

    This outlook is good for the dollar for two reasons. A soft landing is not as disruptive as a recession, so the foreign investments that support the dollar are more likely to continue.

    Also, a soft landing would not force the Federal Reserve to push interest rates sharply lower to stimulate growth. Falling interest rates can put downward pressure on the dollar because they make investments in dollar-denominated securities less attractive to foreigners, prompting the selling of dollars. In addition, the optimism sparked by the expectation of a soft landing can even offset some of the pressure on the dollar from lower interest rates.

    a. Show how you would interpret the third paragraph of this report using this chapter's model of exchange rate determination.

    b. What additional factors in exchange rate determination might help you explain the second paragraph?

11. If hypothetically, the Japanese yen gives 15 percent interest rate against 10 percent interest rate of Euro deposits—and the expected rate of depreciation of the yen is 10 percent—what will happen to the euro deposits in the foreign exchange market? By how much shall the yen depreciate to bring the foreign exchange market to equilibrium?

12. Does any of the discussion in this chapter lead you to believe that dollar deposits may have liquidity characteristics different from those of other currency deposits? If so, how would the differences affect the interest differential between, say, dollar and Mexican peso deposits? Do you have any guesses about how the liquidity of euro deposits may be changing over time?

13. The current interest rate on one year's Indian rupee deposit is 5 percent and yen (¥) deposit is 12 percent. The current ¥/rupee exchange rate is 2 and after a year, it is expected to exceed 2.4. In this case, which currency would you choose for a higher expected rate of return a year later?

14. Imagine everyone in the world pays a tax of τ percent on interest earnings and on any capital gains due to exchange rate changes. How would such a tax alter the analysis of the interest parity condition? How does your answer change if the tax applies to interest earnings but *not* to capital gains, which are untaxed?

15. Suppose the exchange rate of the Indian rupee depreciated against the dollar. What will be the likely impact of the rupee depreciation on India's exports and imports? How will the GDP and inflation behave when rupee depreciates?

16. Europe's single currency, the euro, was introduced in January 1999, replacing the currencies of 11 European Union members, including France, Germany, Italy,

and Spain (but not Britain; see Chapter 21). Do you think that, immediately after the euro's introduction, the value of foreign exchange trading in euros was greater or less than the euro value of the pre-1999 trade in the 11 original national currencies? Explain your answer.

17. Multinationals generally have production plants in a number of countries. Consequently, they can move production from expensive locations to cheaper ones in response to various economic developments—a phenomenon called *outsourcing* when a domestically based firm moves part of its production abroad. If the dollar depreciates, what would you expect to happen to outsourcing by American companies? Explain and provide an example.

18. The interest rate on U.S. three-month Treasury bills dropped to very low levels at the end of 2008 and remained there for several years. Starting in January 2009 and ending in December 2013, find data on the three-month Treasury bill rate from Federal Reserve Economic Data (FRED) at the Federal Reserve Bank of St. Louis; find data on the exchange rate of the U.S. dollar against the Korean won from the Bank of Korea Economic Statistics System at http://ecos.bok.or.kr/flex/EasySearch_e.jsp; and from the same source, find data on the Korean 91-day Monetary Stabilization Bond interest rate. Imagine that you borrow dollars at the Treasury bill rate to invest in Korean stabilization bonds, thus doing a carry trade that exposes you to the risk of won/dollar exchange rate fluctuations. As in the case study in the text, calculate the total return on your carry trade for every month starting in February 2009 and ending in December 2013.

19. The chapter explained why exporters cheer when their home currency depreciates. At the same time, domestic consumers find that they pay higher prices, so they should be disappointed when the currency becomes weaker. Why do the exporters usually win out, so that governments often seem to welcome depreciations while trying to avoid appreciations? (Hint: Think about the analogy with protective tariffs.)

FURTHER READINGS

Sam Y. Cross. *All about the Foreign Exchange Market in the United States*. New York: Books for Business, 2002. Primer on the United States portion of the market.

Federal Reserve Bank of New York. *The Basics of Foreign Trade and Exchange*, at http://www.ny.frb.org/education/fx/index.html. Broad-ranging but highly accessible account of exchange markets and their role. Also supplies many useful Web links.

Philipp Hartmann. *Currency Competition and Foreign Exchange Markets: The Dollar, the Yen and the Euro*. Cambridge: Cambridge University Press, 1999. Theoretical and empirical micro-oriented study of the role of international currencies in world trade and asset markets.

John Maynard Keynes. *A Tract on Monetary Reform*, Chapter 3. London: MacMillan, 1923. Classic analysis of the forward exchange market and covered interest parity.

Michael R. King, Carol Osler, and Dagfinn Rime. "Foreign Exchange Market Structure, Players, and Evolution," in Jessica James, Ian Marsh, and Lucio Sarno, eds., *Handbook of Exchange Rates*. Hoboken, NJ: John Wiley & Sons, 2012, pp. 3–44. Up-to-date overview of foreign exchange market structure.

Paul R. Krugman. "The International Role of the Dollar: Theory and Prospect," in John F. O. Bilson and Richard C. Marston, eds. *Exchange Rate Theory and Practice*. Chicago: University of Chicago Press, 1984, pp. 261–278. Theoretical and empirical analysis of the dollar's position as an "international money."

Richard M. Levich. *International Financial Markets: Prices and Policies*, 2nd edition. Boston: Irwin McGraw-Hill, 2001. Chapters 3–8 of this comprehensive text focus on the foreign exchange market.

Michael Mussa. "Empirical Regularities in the Behavior of Exchange Rates and Theories of the Foreign Exchange Market," in Karl Brunner and Allan H. Meltzer, eds., *Policies for Employment, Prices and Exchange Rates*, Carnegie-Rochester Conference Series on Public Policy 11. Amsterdam: North-Holland, 1979, pp. 9–57. A classic paper that examines the empirical basis of the asset price approach to exchange rate determination.

David Sawyer. "Continuous Linked Settlement (CLS) and Foreign Exchange Settlement Risk." *Financial Stability Review* 17 (December 2004), pp. 86–92. Describes the functioning of and rationale for the Continuous Linked Settlement system for rapid settlement of foreign exchange transactions.

Julian Walmsley. *The Foreign Exchange and Money Markets Guide*, 2nd edition. New York: John Wiley and Sons, 2000. A basic text on the terminology and institutions of the foreign exchange market.

Tim Weithers. *Foreign Exchange: A Practical Guide to the FX Markets*. Hoboken, NJ: John Wiley & Sons, 2006. A clear introduction to foreign exchange instruments and markets.

MyEconLab Can Help You Get a Better Grade

MyEconLab If your exam were tomorrow, would you be ready? For each chapter, MyEconLab Practice Tests and Study Plans pinpoint sections you have mastered and those you need to study. That way, you are more efficient with your study time, and you are better prepared for your exams.

To see how it works, turn to page 41 and then go to www.myeconlab.com

Forward Exchange Rates and Covered Interest Parity

This appendix explains how forward exchange rates are determined. Under the assumption that the interest parity condition always holds, a forward exchange rate equals the spot exchange rate expected to prevail on the forward contract's value date.

As the first step in the discussion, we point out the close connection among the forward exchange rate between two currencies, their spot exchange rate, and the interest rates on deposits denominated in those currencies. The connection is described by the *covered interest parity* condition, which is similar to the (noncovered) interest parity condition defining foreign exchange market equilibrium but involves the forward exchange rate rather than the expected future spot exchange rate.

To be concrete, we again consider dollar and euro deposits. Suppose you want to buy a euro deposit with dollars but would like to be *certain* about the number of dollars it will be worth at the end of a year. You can avoid exchange rate risk by buying a euro deposit and, at the same time, selling the proceeds of your investment forward. When you buy a euro deposit with dollars and at the same time sell the principal and interest forward for dollars, we say you have "covered" yourself, that is, avoided the possibility of an unexpected depreciation of the euro.

The covered interest parity condition states that the rates of return on dollar deposits and "covered" foreign deposits must be the same. An example will clarify the meaning of the condition and illustrate why it must always hold. Let $F_{\$/€}$ stand for the one-year forward price of euros in terms of dollars, and suppose $F_{\$/€} = \$1.113$ per euro. Assume that at the same time, the spot exchange rate $E_{\$/€} = 1.05$ per euro, $R_\$ = 0.10$, and $R_€ = 0.04$. The (dollar) rate of return on a dollar deposit is clearly 0.10, or 10 percent, per year. What is the rate of return on a covered euro deposit?

We answer this question as we did in the chapter. A €1 deposit costs €1.05 today, and it is worth €1.04 after a year. If you sell €1.04 forward today at the forward exchange rate of $1.113 per euro, the dollar value of your investment at the end of a year is ($1.113 per euro) $\times$ (€1.04) = $1.158. The rate of return on a covered purchase of a euro deposit is therefore $(1.158 - 1.05)/1.05 = 0.103$. This 10.3 percent per year rate of return exceeds the 10 percent offered by dollar deposits, so covered interest parity does not hold. In this situation, no one would be willing to hold dollar deposits; everyone would prefer covered euro deposits.

More formally, we can express the covered return on euro deposits as

$$\frac{F_{\$/€}(1 + R_€) - E_{\$/€}}{E_{\$/€}},$$

which is approximately equal to

$$R_€ + \frac{F_{\$/€} - E_{\$/€}}{E_{\$/€}}$$

when the product $R_€ \times (F_{\$/€} - E_{\$/€})/E_{\$/€}$ is a small number. The covered interest parity condition can therefore be written

$$R_\$ = R_€ + (F_{\$/€} - E_{\$/€})/E_{\$/€}.$$

The quantity

$$(F_{\$/€} - E_{\$/€})/E_{\$/€}$$

is called the *forward premium* on euros against dollars. (It is also called the *forward discount* on dollars against euros.) Using this terminology, we can state the covered interest parity condition as follows: *The interest rate on dollar deposits equals the interest rate on euro deposits plus the forward premium on euros against dollars (the forward discount on dollars against euros).*

There is strong empirical evidence that the covered interest parity condition holds for different foreign currency deposits issued within a single financial center. Indeed, currency traders often set the forward exchange rates they quote by looking at current interest rates and spot exchange rates and using the covered interest parity formula.[12] Deviations from covered interest parity can occur, however, if the deposits being compared are located in different countries. These deviations occur when asset holders fear that governments may impose regulations that will prevent the free movement of foreign funds across national borders. Our derivation of the covered interest parity condition implicitly assumed there was no political risk of this kind. Deviations can occur also because of fears that banks will fail, making them unable to pay off large deposits.[13]

By comparing the (noncovered) interest parity condition,

$$R_{\$} = R_€ + (E_{\$/€}^e - E_{\$/€})/E_{\$/€},$$

with the *covered* interest parity condition, you will find that both conditions can be true at the same time only if the one-year forward rate quoted today equals the spot exchange rate people expect to materialize a year from today:

$$F_{\$/€} = E_{\$/€}^e.$$

This makes intuitive sense. When two parties agree to trade foreign exchange on a date in the future, the exchange rate they agree on is the spot rate they expect to prevail on that date. The important difference between covered and noncovered transactions should be kept in mind, however. Covered transactions do not involve exchange rate risk, whereas noncovered transactions do.

The theory of covered interest parity helps explain the close correlation between the movements in spot and forward exchange rates shown in Table 14-1, a correlation typical of all major currencies. The unexpected economic events that affect expected asset returns often have a relatively small effect on international interest rate differences between deposits with short maturities (for example, three months). To maintain covered

---

[12]Empirical evidence supporting the covered interest parity condition is provided by Frank McCormick in "Covered Interest Arbitrage: Unexploited Profits? Comment," *Journal of Political Economy* 87 (April 1979), pp. 411–417, and by Kevin Clinton in "Transactions Costs and Covered Interest Arbitrage: Theory and Evidence," *Journal of Political Economy* 96 (April 1988), pp. 358–370.

[13]For a more detailed discussion of the role of political risk in the forward exchange market, see Robert Z. Aliber, "The Interest Parity Theorem: A Reinterpretation," *Journal of Political Economy* 81 (November/December 1973), pp. 1451–1459. Of course, actual government restrictions on cross-border money movements can also cause covered interest parity deviations. On the fear of bank failure as a cause for deviations from covered interest parity, see Naohiko Baba and Frank Packer, "Interpreting Deviations from Covered Interest Parity During the Financial Market Turmoil of 2007–2008," Working Paper No. 267, Bank for International Settlements, December 2008. The events underlying this last paper are discussed in Chapter 20.

interest parity, therefore, spot and forward rates for the corresponding maturities must change roughly in proportion to each other.

We conclude this appendix with one further application of the covered interest parity condition. To illustrate the role of forward exchange rates, the chapter used the example of an American importer of Japanese radios anxious about the $/¥ exchange rate it would face in 30 days when the time came to pay the supplier. In the example, Radio Shack solved the problem by selling forward for yen enough dollars to cover the cost of the radios. But Radio Shack could have solved the problem in a different, more complicated way. It could have (1) borrowed dollars from a bank; (2) sold those dollars immediately for yen at the spot exchange rate and placed the yen in a 30-day yen bank deposit; (3) then, after 30 days, used the proceeds of the maturing yen deposit to pay the Japanese supplier; and (4) used the realized proceeds of the U.S. radio sales, less profits, to repay the original dollar loan.

Which course of action—the forward purchase of yen or the sequence of four transactions described in the preceding paragraph—is more profitable for the importer? We leave it to you, as an exercise, to show that the two strategies yield the same profit when the covered interest parity condition holds.

CHAPTER 15

MONEY, INTEREST RATES, AND EXCHANGE RATES

Chapter 14 showed how the exchange rate between currencies depends on two factors—the interest that can be earned on deposits of those currencies and the expected future exchange rate. To understand fully the determination of exchange rates, however, we have to learn how interest rates themselves are determined and how expectations of future exchange rates are formed. In this and the next two chapters, we examine these topics by building an economic model that links exchange rates, interest rates, and other important macroeconomic variables such as the inflation rate and output.

The first step in building the model is to explain the effects of a country's money supply and of the demand for its money on its interest rate and exchange rate. Because exchange rates are the relative prices of national monies, factors that affect a country's money supply or demand are among the most powerful determinants of its currency's exchange rate against foreign currencies. It is therefore natural to begin a deeper study of exchange rate determination with a discussion of money supply and money demand.

Monetary developments influence the exchange rate by changing *both* interest rates *and* people's expectations about future exchange rates. Expectations about future exchange rates are closely connected with expectations about the future money prices of countries' products; these price movements, in turn, depend on changes in money supply and demand. In examining monetary influences on the exchange rate, we therefore look at how monetary factors influence output prices along with interest rates. Expectations of future exchange rates depend on many factors other than money, however, and these nonmonetary factors are taken up in the next chapter.

Once the theories and determinants of money supply and demand are laid out, we use them to examine how equilibrium interest rates are determined by the equality of money supply and money demand. Then we combine our model of interest rate determination with the interest parity condition to study the effects of monetary shifts on the exchange rate, given the prices of goods and services, the level of output, and market expectations about the future. Finally, we take a first look at the long-term effects of monetary changes on output prices and expected future exchange rates.

LEARNING GOALS

After reading this chapter, you will be able to:

- Describe and discuss the national money markets in which interest rates are determined.
- Show how monetary policy and interest rates feed into the foreign exchange market.
- Distinguish between the economy's long-run position and the short run, in which money prices and wages are sticky.
- Explain how price levels and exchange rates respond to monetary factors in the long run.
- Outline the relationship between the short-run and the long-run effects of monetary policy, and explain the concept of short-run exchange rate overshooting.

Money Defined: A Brief Review

We are so accustomed to using money that we seldom notice the roles it plays in almost all of our everyday transactions. As with many other modern conveniences, we take money for granted until something goes wrong with it! In fact, the easiest way to appreciate the importance of money is to imagine what economic life would be like without it.

In this section, we do just that. Our purpose in carrying out this "thought experiment" is to distinguish money from other assets and to describe the characteristics of money that lead people to hold it. These characteristics are central to an analysis of the demand for money.

Money as a Medium of Exchange

The most important function of money is to serve as a *medium of exchange*, a generally accepted means of payment. To see why a medium of exchange is necessary, imagine how time-consuming it would be for people to purchase goods and services in a world where the only type of trade possible is barter trade—the direct trade of goods or services for other goods or services. To have her car repaired, for example, your professor would have to find a mechanic in need of economics lessons!

Money eliminates the enormous search costs connected with a barter system because money is universally acceptable. It eliminates these search costs by enabling an individual to sell the goods and services she produces to people other than the producers of the goods and services she wishes to consume. A complex modern economy would cease functioning without some standardized and convenient means of payment.

Money as a Unit of Account

Money's second important role is as a *unit of account*, that is, as a widely recognized measure of value. It is in this role that we encountered money in Chapter 14: Prices of goods, services, and assets are typically expressed in terms of money. Exchange rates allow us to translate different countries' money prices into comparable terms.

The convention of quoting prices in money terms simplifies economic calculations by making it easy to compare the prices of different commodities. The international price comparisons in Chapter 14, which used exchange rates to compare the prices of different countries' outputs, are similar to the calculations you would have to do many times each day if different commodities' prices were not expressed in terms of a standardized unit of account. If the calculations in Chapter 14 gave you a headache, imagine what it would be like to have to calculate the relative prices of each good and service you consume in terms of several other goods and services—for example, the price of a slice of pizza in terms of bananas. This thought experiment should give you a keener appreciation of using money as a unit of account.

Money as a Store of Value

Because money can be used to transfer purchasing power from the present into the future, it is also an asset, or a *store of value*. This attribute is essential for any medium of exchange because no one would be willing to accept it in payment if its value in terms of goods and services evaporated immediately.

Money's usefulness as a medium of exchange, however, automatically makes it the most *liquid* of all assets. As you will recall from the last chapter, an asset is said to be liquid when it can be transformed into goods and services rapidly and without high transaction costs, such as brokers' fees. Since money is readily acceptable as a means of payment, money sets the standard against which the liquidity of other assets is judged.

What Is Money?

Currency and bank deposits on which checks may be written certainly qualify as money. These are widely accepted means of payment that can be transferred between owners at low cost. Households and firms hold currency and checking deposits as a convenient way of financing routine transactions as they arise. Assets such as real estate do not qualify as money because, unlike currency and checking deposits, they lack the essential property of liquidity.

When we speak in this book of the **money supply**, we are referring to the monetary aggregate the Federal Reserve calls M1, that is, the total amount of currency and checking deposits held by households and firms. In the United States at the end of 2012, the total money supply amounted to $2.5 trillion, equal to roughly 16 percent of that year's GNP.[1]

The large deposits traded by participants in the foreign exchange market are not considered part of the money supply. These deposits are less liquid than money and are not used to finance routine transactions.

How the Money Supply Is Determined

An economy's money supply is controlled by its central bank. The central bank directly regulates the amount of currency in existence and also has indirect control over the amount of checking deposits issued by private banks. The procedures through which the central bank controls the money supply are complex, and we assume for now that the central bank simply sets the size of the money supply at the level it desires. We go into the money supply process in more detail, however, in Chapter 18.

---

[1]A broader Federal Reserve measure of money supply, M2, includes time deposits, but these are less liquid than the assets included in M1 because the funds in them typically cannot be withdrawn early without penalty. An even broader measure, known as M3, is also tracked by the Fed. A decision on where to draw the line between money and near-money must be somewhat arbitrary and therefore controversial. For further discussion of this question, see Chapter 3 of Frederic S. Mishkin, *The Economics of Money, Banking and Financial Markets*, 10th edition (Upper Saddle River, NJ: Prentice Hall, 2013).

The Demand for Money by Individuals

Having discussed the functions of money and the definition of the money supply, we now examine the factors that determine the amount of money an individual desires to hold. The determinants of individual money demand can be derived from the theory of asset demand discussed in the last chapter.

We saw in the last chapter that individuals base their demand for an asset on three characteristics:

1. The expected return the asset offers compared with the returns offered by other assets.
2. The riskiness of the asset's expected return.
3. The asset's liquidity.

While liquidity plays no important role in determining the relative demands for assets traded in the foreign exchange market, households and firms hold money *only* because of its liquidity. To understand how the economy's households and firms decide the amount of money they wish to hold, we must look more closely at how the three considerations listed above influence money demand.

Expected Return

Currency pays no interest. Checking deposits often do pay some interest, but they offer a rate of return that usually fails to keep pace with the higher returns offered by less liquid forms of wealth. When you hold money, you therefore sacrifice the higher interest rate you could earn by holding your wealth in a government bond, a large time deposit, or some other relatively illiquid asset. It is this last rate of interest we have in mind when we refer to "the" interest rate. Since the interest paid on currency is zero while that paid on "checkable" deposits tends to be relatively constant, the difference between the rate of return of money in general and that of less liquid alternative assets is reflected by the market interest rate: The higher the interest rate, the more you sacrifice by holding wealth in the form of money.[2]

Suppose, for example, the interest rate you could earn from a U.S. Treasury bill is 10 percent per year. If you use $10,000 of your wealth to buy a Treasury bill, you will be paid $11,000 by Uncle Sam at the end of a year, but if you choose instead to keep the $10,000 as cash in a safe-deposit box, you give up the $1,000 interest you could have earned by buying the Treasury bill. You thus sacrifice a 10 percent rate of return by holding your $10,000 as money.

The theory of asset demand developed in the last chapter shows how changes in the rate of interest affect the demand for money. The theory states that, other things equal, people prefer assets offering higher expected returns. Because an increase in the interest rate is a rise in the rate of return on less liquid assets relative to the rate of return on money, individuals will want to hold more of their wealth in nonmoney assets that pay the market interest rate and less of their wealth in the form of money

---

[2]Many of the illiquid assets that individuals can choose from do not pay their returns in the form of interest. Stocks, for example, pay returns in the forms of dividends and capital gains. The family summer house on Cape Cod pays a return in the forms of capital gains and the pleasure of vacations at the beach. The assumption behind our analysis of money demand is that once allowance is made for risk, all assets other than money offer an expected rate of return (measured in terms of money) equal to the interest rate. This assumption allows us to use the interest rate to summarize the return an individual forgoes by holding money rather than an illiquid asset.

if the interest rate rises. We conclude that, *all else equal, a rise in the interest rate causes the demand for money to fall*.

We can also describe the influence of the interest rate on money demand in terms of the economic concept of *opportunity cost*—the amount you sacrifice by taking one course of action rather than another. The interest rate measures the opportunity cost of holding money rather than interest-bearing bonds. A rise in the interest rate therefore raises the cost of holding money and causes money demand to fall.

Risk

Risk is not an important factor in money demand. It is risky to hold money because an unexpected increase in the prices of goods and services could reduce the value of your money in terms of the commodities you consume. Since interest-paying assets such as government bonds have face values fixed in terms of money, however, the same unexpected increase in prices would reduce the real value of those assets by the same percentage. Because any change in the riskiness of money causes an equal change in the riskiness of bonds, changes in the risk of holding money need not cause individuals to reduce their demand for money and increase their demand for interest-paying assets.

Liquidity

The main benefit of holding money comes from its liquidity. Households and firms hold money because it is the easiest way of financing their everyday purchases. Some large purchases can be financed through the sale of a substantial illiquid asset. An art collector, for example, could sell one of her Picassos to buy a house. To finance a continuing stream of smaller expenditures at various times and for various amounts, however, households and firms have to hold some money.

An individual's need for liquidity rises when the average daily value of his transactions rises. A student who takes the bus every day, for example, does not need to hold as much cash as a business executive who takes taxis during rush hour. We conclude that *a rise in the average value of transactions carried out by a household or firm causes its demand for money to rise*.

Aggregate Money Demand

Our discussion of how individual households and firms determine their demands for money can now be applied to derive the determinants of **aggregate money demand**, the total demand for money by all households and firms in the economy. Aggregate money demand is just the sum of all the economy's individual money demands.

Three main factors determine aggregate money demand:

1. *The interest rate.* A rise in the interest rate causes each individual in the economy to reduce her demand for money. All else equal, aggregate money demand therefore falls when the interest rate rises.

2. *The price level.* The economy's **price level** is the price of a broad reference basket of goods and services in terms of currency. Generally, the reference basket includes standard, everyday consumption items such as food, clothing, and housing and less routine purchases such as medical care and legal fees. If the price level rises, individual households and firms must spend more money than before to purchase their usual weekly baskets of goods and services. To maintain the same level of liquidity as before the price level increase, they will therefore have to hold more money.

3. *Real national income.* When real national income (GNP) rises, more goods and services are sold in the economy. This increase in the real value of transactions raises the demand for money, given the price level.

If P is the price level, R is the interest rate, and Y is real GNP, the aggregate demand for money, M^d, can be expressed as

$$M^d = P \times L(R, Y), \tag{15-1}$$

where the value of $L(R, Y)$ falls when R rises, and rises when Y rises.[3] To see why we have specified that aggregate money demand is *proportional* to the price level, imagine that all prices doubled but the interest rate and everyone's *real* incomes remained unchanged. The money value of each individual's average daily transactions would then simply double, as would the amount of money each wished to hold.

We usually write the aggregate money demand relation (15-1) in the equivalent form

$$M^d/P = L(R, Y), \tag{15-2}$$

and call $L(R, Y)$ aggregate *real* money demand. This way of expressing money demand shows that the aggregate demand for liquidity, $L(R, Y)$, is not a demand for a certain number of currency units but is instead a demand to hold a certain amount of real purchasing power in liquid form. The ratio M^d/P—that is, desired money holdings measured in terms of a typical reference basket of commodities—equals the amount of real purchasing power people would like to hold in liquid form. For example, if people wished to hold $1,000 in cash at a price level of $100 per commodity basket, their real money holdings would be equivalent to $1,000/($100 per basket) = 10 baskets. If the price level doubled (to $200 per basket), the purchasing power of their $1,000 in cash would be halved, since it would now be worth only 5 baskets.

Figure 15-1 shows how aggregate real money demand is affected by the interest rate for a fixed level of real income, Y. The aggregate real money demand schedule $L(R, Y)$

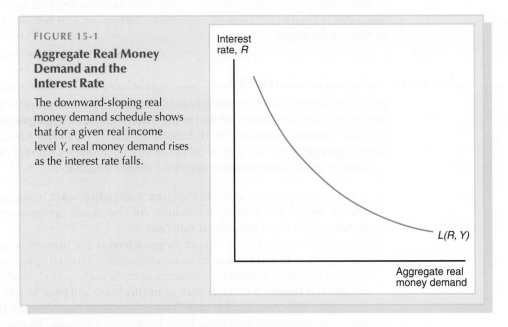

FIGURE 15-1

Aggregate Real Money Demand and the Interest Rate

The downward-sloping real money demand schedule shows that for a given real income level Y, real money demand rises as the interest rate falls.

Interest rate, R

$L(R, Y)$

Aggregate real money demand

---

[3]Naturally, $L(R, Y)$ rises when R falls, and falls when Y falls.

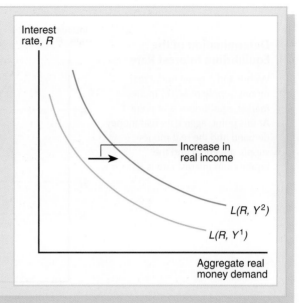

FIGURE 15-2

Effect on the Aggregate Real Money Demand Schedule of a Rise in Real Income

An increase in real income from Y^1 to Y^2 raises the demand for real money balances at every level of the interest rate and causes the whole demand schedule to shift upward.

slopes downward because a fall in the interest rate raises the desired real money holdings of each household and firm in the economy.

For a given level of real GNP, changes in the interest rate cause movements *along* the $L(R,Y)$ schedule. Changes in real GNP, however, cause the schedule itself to shift. Figure 15-2 shows how a rise in real GNP from Y^1 to Y^2 affects the position of the aggregate real money demand schedule. Because a rise in real GNP raises aggregate real money demand for a given interest rate, the schedule $L(R, Y^2)$ lies to the right of $L(R, Y^1)$ when Y^2 is greater than Y^1.

The Equilibrium Interest Rate: The Interaction of Money Supply and Demand

As you might expect from other economics courses you've taken, the money market is in equilibrium when the money supply set by the central bank equals aggregate money demand. In this section, we see how the interest rate is determined by money market equilibrium, given the price level and output, both of which are temporarily assumed to be unaffected by monetary changes.

Equilibrium in the Money Market

If M^s is the money supply, the condition for equilibrium in the money market is

$$M^s = M^d. \tag{15-3}$$

After dividing both sides of this equality by the price level, we can express the money market equilibrium condition in terms of aggregate real money demand as

$$M^s/P = L(R, Y). \tag{15-4}$$

Given the price level, P, and the level of output, Y, the equilibrium interest rate is the one at which aggregate real money demand equals the real money supply.

FIGURE 15-3

Determination of the Equilibrium Interest Rate

With P and Y given and a real money supply of M^S/P, money market equilibrium is at point 1. At this point, aggregate real money demand and the real money supply are equal and the equilibrium interest rate is R^1.

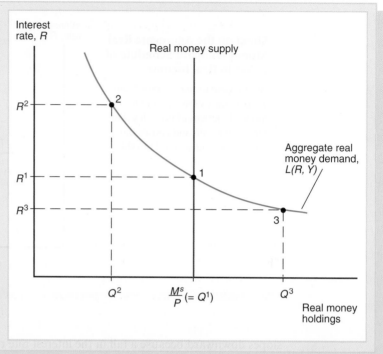

In Figure 15-3, the aggregate real money demand schedule intersects the real money supply schedule at point 1 to give an equilibrium interest rate of R^1. The money supply schedule is vertical at M^s/P because M^s is set by the central bank while P is taken as given.

Let's see why the interest rate tends to settle at its equilibrium level by considering what happens if the market is initially at point 2, with an interest rate, R^2, that is above R^1.

At point 2, the demand for real money holdings falls short of the supply by $Q^1 - Q^2$, so there is an excess supply of money. If individuals are holding more money than they desire given the interest rate of R^2, they will attempt to reduce their liquidity by using some money to purchase interest-bearing assets. In other words, individuals will attempt to get rid of their excess money by lending it to others. Since there is an aggregate excess supply of money at R^2, however, not everyone can succeed in doing this: There are more people who would like to lend money to reduce their liquidity than there are people who would like to borrow money to increase theirs. Those who cannot unload their extra money try to tempt potential borrowers by lowering the interest rate they charge for loans below R^2. The downward pressure on the interest rate continues until the rate reaches R^1. At this interest rate, anyone wishing to lend money can do so because the aggregate excess supply of money has disappeared; that is, supply once again equals demand. Once the market reaches point 1, there is therefore no further tendency for the interest rate to drop.[4]

---

[4]Another way to view this process is as follows: We saw in the last chapter that an asset's rate of return falls when its current price rises relative to its future value. When there is an excess supply of money, the current money prices of illiquid assets that pay interest will be bid up as individuals attempt to reduce their money holdings. This rise in current asset prices lowers the rate of return on nonmoney assets, and since this rate of return is equal to the interest rate (after adjustment for risk), the interest rate also must fall.

Similarly, if the interest rate is initially at a level R^3 below R^1, it will tend to rise. As Figure 15-3 shows, there is excess demand for money equal to $Q^3 - Q^1$ at point 3. Individuals therefore attempt to sell interest-bearing assets such as bonds to increase their money holdings (that is, they sell bonds for cash). At point 3, however, not everyone can succeed in selling enough interest-bearing assets to satisfy his or her demand for money. Thus, people bid for money by offering to borrow at progressively higher interest rates and push the interest rate upward toward R^1. Only when the market has reached point 1 and the excess demand for money has been eliminated does the interest rate stop rising.

We can summarize our findings as follows: *The market always moves toward an interest rate at which the real money supply equals aggregate real money demand. If there is initially an excess supply of money, the interest rate falls, and if there is initially an excess demand, it rises.*

Interest Rates and the Money Supply

The effect of increasing the money supply at a given price level is illustrated in Figure 15-4. Initially, the money market is in equilibrium at point 1, with a money supply M^1 and an interest rate R^1. Since we are holding P constant, a rise in the money supply to M^2 increases the real money supply from M^1/P to M^2/P. With a real money supply of M^2/P, point 2 is the new equilibrium and R^2 is the new, lower interest rate that induces people to hold the increased available real money supply.

The process through which the interest rate falls is by now familiar. After M^s is increased by the central bank, there is initially an excess real supply of money at the old equilibrium interest rate, R^1, which previously balanced the market. Since people are holding more money than they desire, they use their surplus funds to bid for assets that pay interest. The economy as a whole cannot reduce its money holdings,

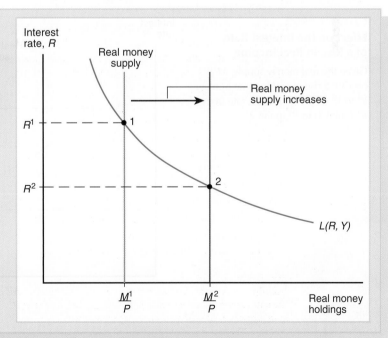

FIGURE 15-4

Effect of an Increase in the Money Supply on the Interest Rate

For a given price level, P, and real income level, Y, an increase in the money supply from M^1 to M^2 reduces the interest rate from R^1 (point 1) to R^2 (point 2).

so interest rates are driven down as unwilling money holders compete to lend their excess cash balances. At point 2 in Figure 15-4, the interest rate has fallen sufficiently to induce an increase in real money demand equal to the increase in the real money supply.

By running the above policy experiment in reverse, we can see how a reduction of the money supply forces interest rates upward. A fall in M^s causes an excess demand for money at the interest rate that previously balanced supply and demand. People attempt to sell interest-bearing assets—that is, to borrow—to rebuild their depleted real money holdings. Since they cannot all be successful when there is excess money demand, the interest rate is pushed upward until everyone is content to hold the smaller real money stock.

We conclude that *an increase in the money supply lowers the interest rate, while a fall in the money supply raises the interest rate, given the price level and output.*

Output and the Interest Rate

Figure 15-5 shows the effect on the interest rate of a rise in the level of output from Y^1 to Y^2, given the money supply and the price level. As we saw earlier, an increase in output causes the entire aggregate real money demand schedule to shift to the right, moving the equilibrium away from point 1. At the old equilibrium interest rate, R^1, there is an excess demand for money equal to $Q^2 - Q^1$ (point 1′). Since the real money supply is given, the interest rate is bid up until it reaches the higher, new equilibrium level R^2 (point 2). A fall in output has opposite effects, causing the aggregate real money demand schedule to shift to the left and therefore causing the equilibrium interest rate to fall.

We conclude that *an increase in real output raises the interest rate, while a fall in real output lowers the interest rate, given the price level and the money supply.*

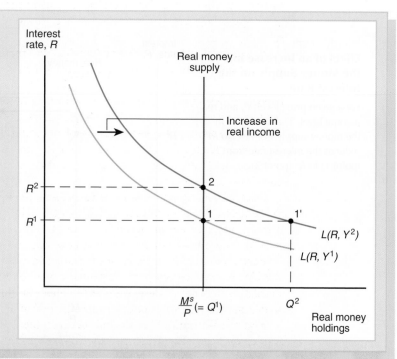

FIGURE 15-5

Effect on the Interest Rate of a Rise in Real Income

Given the real money supply, M^S/P ($= Q^1$), a rise in real income from Y^1 to Y^2 raises the interest rate from R^1 (point 1) to R^2 (point 2).

The Money Supply and the Exchange Rate in the Short Run

In Chapter 14, we learned about the interest parity condition, which predicts how interest rate movements influence the exchange rate, given expectations about the exchange rate's future level. Now that we know how shifts in a country's money supply affect the interest rate on nonmoney assets denominated in its currency, we can see how monetary changes affect the exchange rate. We will discover that *an increase in a country's money supply causes its currency to depreciate in the foreign exchange market, while a reduction in the money supply causes its currency to appreciate.*

In this section, we continue to take the price level (along with real output) as given, and for that reason we label the analysis of this section **short run**. The **long-run** analysis of an economic event allows for the complete adjustment of the price level (which may take a long time) and for full employment of all factors of production. Later in this chapter, we examine the long-run effects of money supply changes on the price level, the exchange rate, and other macroeconomic variables. Our long-run analysis will show how the money supply influences exchange rate expectations, which we also continue to take as given for now.

Linking Money, the Interest Rate, and the Exchange Rate

To analyze the relationship between money and the exchange rate in the short run in Figure 15-6, we combine two diagrams we have already studied separately. Let's assume once again we are looking at the dollar/euro exchange rate, that is, the price of euros in terms of dollars.

The first diagram (introduced as Figure 14-4) shows equilibrium in the foreign exchange market and how it is determined given interest rates and expectations about future exchange rates. This diagram appears as the top part of Figure 15-6. The dollar interest rate, $R_\$^1$, which is determined in the money market, defines the vertical schedule.

As you will remember from Chapter 14, the downward-sloping expected euro return schedule shows the expected return on euro deposits, measured in dollars. The schedule slopes downward because of the effect of current exchange rate changes on expectations of future depreciation: A strengthening of the dollar today (a fall in $E_{\$/€}$) relative to its *given* expected future level makes euro deposits more attractive by leading people to anticipate a sharper dollar depreciation in the future.

At the intersection of the two schedules (point 1'), the expected rates of return on dollar and euro deposits are equal, and therefore interest parity holds. $E_{\$/€}^1$ is the equilibrium exchange rate.

In the second diagram we need to examine the relationship between money and the exchange rate was introduced as Figure 15-3. This figure shows how a country's equilibrium interest rate is determined in its money market, and it appears as the bottom part of Figure 15-6. For convenience, however, the figure has been rotated clockwise by 90 degrees so that dollar interest rates are measured from 0 on the horizontal axis and the U.S. real money supply is measured from 0 on the descending vertical axis. Money market equilibrium is shown at point 1, where the dollar interest rate $R_\$^1$ induces people to demand real balances equal to the U.S. real money supply, M_{US}^s/P_{US}.

Figure 15-6 emphasizes the link between the U.S. money market (bottom) and the foreign exchange market (top)—the U.S. money market determines the dollar interest rate, which in turn affects the exchange rate that maintains interest parity. (Of course,

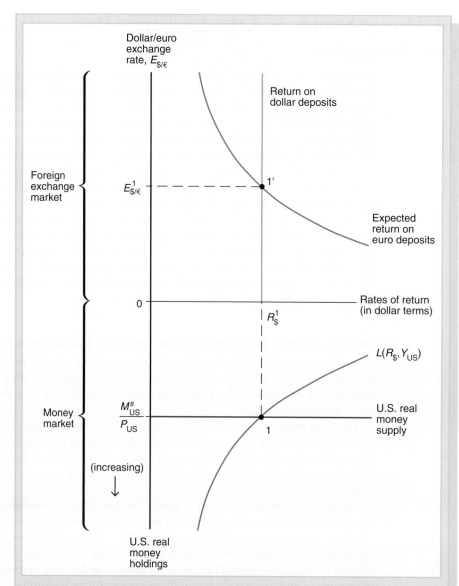

FIGURE 15-6

Simultaneous Equilibrium in the U.S. Money Market and the Foreign Exchange Market

Both asset markets are in equilibrium at the interest rate $R_\$^1$ and exchange rate $E_{\$/\euro}^1$; at these values, money supply equals money demand (point 1) and the interest parity condition holds (point 1').

there is a similar link between the European money market and the foreign exchange market that operates through changes in the euro interest rate.)

Figure 15-7 illustrates these linkages. The U.S. and European central banks, the Federal Reserve System and the European Central Bank (ECB), respectively, determine the U.S. and European money supplies, M_{US}^s and M_E^s. Given the price levels and national incomes of the two countries, equilibrium in national money markets leads to

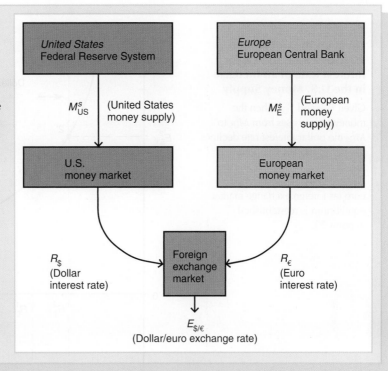

FIGURE 15-7

Money Market/Exchange Rate Linkages

Monetary policy actions by the Fed affect the U.S. interest rate, changing the dollar/euro exchange rate that clears the foreign exchange market. The ECB can affect the exchange rate by changing the European money supply and interest rate.

the dollar and euro interest rates $R_\$$ and $R_€$. These interest rates feed into the foreign exchange market, where, given expectations about the future dollar/euro exchange rate, the current rate $E_{\$/€}$ is determined by the interest parity condition.

U.S. Money Supply and the Dollar/Euro Exchange Rate

We now use our model of asset market linkages (the links between the money and foreign exchange markets) to ask how the dollar/euro exchange rate changes when the Federal Reserve changes the U.S. money supply M_{US}^s. The effects of this change are summarized in Figure 15-8.

At the initial money supply M_{US}^1, the money market is in equilibrium at point 1 with an interest rate $R_\$^1$. Given the euro interest rate and the expected future exchange rate, a dollar interest rate of $R_\$^1$ implies that foreign exchange market equilibrium occurs at point 1′, with an exchange rate equal to $E_{\$/€}^1$.

What happens when the Federal Reserve, perhaps fearing the onset of a recession, raises the U.S. money supply to M_{US}^2? This increase sets in motion the following sequence of events: (1) At the initial interest rate $R_\$^1$, there is an excess supply of money in the U.S. money market, so the dollar interest rate falls to $R_\$^2$ as the money market reaches its new equilibrium position (point 2). (2) Given the initial exchange rate $E_{\$/€}^1$ and the new, lower interest rate on dollars, $R_\$^2$, the expected return on euro deposits is greater than that on dollar deposits. Holders of dollar deposits therefore try to sell them for euro deposits, which are momentarily more attractive. (3) The dollar depreciates to $E_{\$/€}^2$ as holders of dollar deposits bid for euro deposits. The foreign exchange market is once again in equilibrium at point 2′ because the exchange rate's move to $E_{\$/€}^2$ causes a fall in the dollar's expected future depreciation rate sufficient to offset the fall in the dollar interest rate.

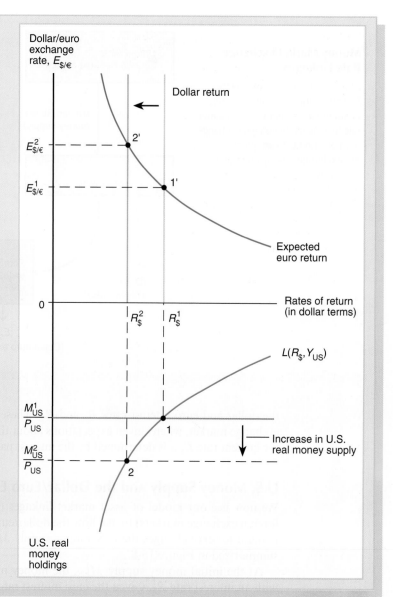

FIGURE 15-8

Effect on the Dollar/Euro Exchange Rate and Dollar Interest Rate of an Increase in the U.S. Money Supply

Given P_{US} and Y_{US} when the money supply rises from M^1_{US} to M^2_{US} the dollar interest rate declines (as money market equilibrium is reestablished at point 2) and the dollar depreciates against the euro (as foreign exchange market equilibrium is reestablished at point 2′).

We conclude that *an increase in a country's money supply causes its currency to depreciate in the foreign exchange market. By running Figure 15-8 in reverse, you can see that a reduction in a country's money supply causes its currency to appreciate in the foreign exchange market.*

Europe's Money Supply and the Dollar/Euro Exchange Rate

The conclusions we have reached also apply when the ECB changes Europe's money supply. Suppose the ECB fears a recession in Europe and hopes to head it off through a looser monetary policy. An increase in M^s_E causes a depreciation of the euro (that is, an appreciation of the dollar, or a fall in $E_{\$/€}$), while a reduction in M^s_E causes an appreciation of the euro (that is, a depreciation of the dollar, or a rise in $E_{\$/€}$).

The mechanism at work, which runs from the European interest rate to the exchange rate, is the same as the one we just analyzed. It is good exercise to verify

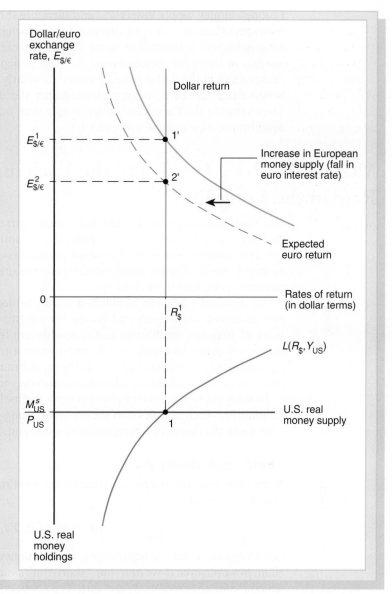

FIGURE 15-9

Effect of an Increase in the European Money Supply on the Dollar/Euro Exchange Rate

By lowering the dollar return on euro deposits (shown as a leftward shift in the expected euro return curve), an increase in Europe's money supply causes the dollar to appreciate against the euro. Equilibrium in the foreign exchange market shifts from point 1' to point 2' but equilibrium in the U.S. money market remains at point 1.

these assertions by drawing figures similar to Figures 15-6 and 15-8 that illustrate the linkage between the European money market and the foreign exchange market.

Here we use a different approach to show how changes in Europe's money supply affect the dollar/euro exchange rate. In Chapter 14, we learned that a fall in the euro interest rate, $R_{\euro}$, shifts the downward-sloping schedule in the upper part of Figure 15-6 to the left. The reason is that for any level of the exchange rate, a fall in $R_{\euro}$ lowers the expected rate of return on euro deposits. Since a rise in the European money supply M_E^s lowers $R_{\euro}$, we can see the effect on the exchange rate by shifting the expected euro return schedule in the top part of Figure 15-6 to the left.

The result of an increase in the European money supply is shown in Figure 15-9. Initially, the U.S. money market is in equilibrium at point 1 and the foreign exchange market is in equilibrium at point 1', with an exchange rate $E_{\$/\euro}^1$. An increase in

Europe's money supply lowers R_ϵ, and therefore shifts to the left the schedule linking the expected return on euro deposits to the exchange rate. Foreign exchange market equilibrium is restored at point 2′, with an exchange rate $E^2_{\$/\epsilon}$. We see that the increase in European money causes the euro to depreciate against the dollar (that is, causes a fall in the dollar price of euros). Similarly, a fall in Europe's money supply would cause the euro to appreciate against the dollar (that is, $E_{\$/\epsilon}$ would rise). The change in the European money supply does not disturb the U.S. money market equilibrium, which remains at point 1.[5]

Money, the Price Level, and the Exchange Rate in the Long Run

Our short-run analysis of the link between countries' money markets and the foreign exchange market rested on the simplifying assumption that price levels and exchange rate expectations were given. To extend our understanding of how money supply and money demand affect exchange rates, we must examine how monetary factors affect a country's price level in the long run.

An economy's **long-run equilibrium** is the position it would eventually reach if no new economic shocks occurred during the adjustment to full employment. You can think of long-run equilibrium as the equilibrium that would be maintained after all wages and prices had had enough time to adjust to their market-clearing levels. An equivalent way of thinking of it is as the equilibrium that would occur if prices were perfectly flexible and always adjusted immediately to preserve full employment.

In studying how monetary changes work themselves out over the long run, we will examine how such changes shift the economy's long-run equilibrium. Our main tool is once again the theory of aggregate money demand.

Money and Money Prices

If the price level and output are fixed in the short run, the condition (15-4) of money market equilibrium,

$$M^s/P = L(R, Y),$$

determines the domestic interest rate, R. The money market always moves to equilibrium, however, even if we drop our "short-run" assumption and think of periods over which P and Y, as well as R, can vary. The above equilibrium condition can therefore be rearranged to give

$$P = M^s/L(R, Y), \tag{15-5}$$

which shows how the price level depends on the interest rate, real output, and the domestic money supply.

The *long-run equilibrium price level* is just the value of P that satisfies condition (15-5) when the interest rate and output are at their long-run levels, that is, at levels consistent with full employment. When the money market is in equilibrium and all factors of production are fully employed, the price level will remain steady if the money

---

[5]The U.S. money market equilibrium remains at point 1 because the price adjustments that equilibrate the European money market and the foreign exchange market after the increase in Europe's money supply do not change either the money supply or money demand in the United States, given Y_{US} and P_{US}.

supply, the aggregate money demand function, and the long-run values of R and Y remain steady.

One of the most important predictions of the previous equation for P concerns the relationship between a country's price level and its money supply, M^s: *All else equal, an increase in a country's money supply causes a proportional increase in its price level.* If, for example, the money supply doubles (to $2M^s$) but output and the interest rate do not change, the price level must also double (to $2P$) to maintain equilibrium in the money market.

The economic reasoning behind this very precise prediction follows from our observation above that the demand for money is a demand for *real* money holdings: Real money demand is not altered by an increase in M^s that leaves R and Y (and thus aggregate real money demand $L(R, Y)$) unchanged. If aggregate real money demand does not change, however, the money market will remain in equilibrium only if the real money supply also stays the same. To keep the real money supply M^s/P constant, P must rise in proportion to M^s.

The Long-Run Effects of Money Supply Changes

Our theory of how the money supply affects the price level *given* the interest rate and output is not yet a theory of how money supply changes affect the price level in the long run. To develop such a theory, we still have to determine the long-run effects of a money supply change on the interest rate and output. This is easier than you might think. As we now argue, *a change in the supply of money has no effect on the long-run values of the interest rate or real output.*[6]

The best way to understand the long-run effects of money supply on the interest rate and output is to think first about a *currency reform*, in which a country's government redefines the national currency unit. For example, the government of Turkey reformed its currency on January 1, 2005, simply by issuing "new" Turkish lira, each equal to 1 million "old" Turkish lira. The effect of this reform was to lower the number of currency units in circulation, and all lira prices, to $\frac{1}{1,000,000}$ of their old lira values. But the redefinition of the monetary unit had no effect on real output, the interest rate, or the relative prices of goods: All that occurred was a one-time change in all values measured in lira. A decision to measure distance in half-miles rather than miles would have as little effect on real economic variables as the Turkish government's decision to chop six zeros off the end of every magnitude measured in terms of money.

An increase in the supply of a country's currency has the same effect in the long run as a currency reform. A doubling of the money supply, for example, has the same long-run effect as a currency reform in which each unit of currency is replaced by two units of "new" currency. If the economy is initially fully employed, every money price in the economy eventually doubles, but real GNP, the interest rate, and all relative prices return to their long-run or full-employment levels.

Why is a money supply change just like a currency reform in its effects on the economy's long-run equilibrium? The full-employment output level is determined by the

---

[6]The preceding statement refers only to changes in the *level* of the nominal money supply and not, for example, to changes in the *rate* at which the money supply is growing over time. The proposition that a one-time change in the level of the money supply has no effects on the long-run values of real economic variables is often called the *long-run neutrality of money*. In contrast, changes in the money supply growth rate need not be neutral in the long run. At the very least, a sustained change in the monetary growth rate will eventually affect equilibrium real money balances by raising the money interest rate (as discussed in the next chapter).

economy's endowments of labor and capital, so in the long run, real output does not depend on the money supply. Similarly, the interest rate is independent of the money supply in the long run. If the money supply and all prices double permanently, there is no reason why people previously willing to exchange $1 today for $1.10 a year from now should not be willing afterward to exchange $2 today for $2.20 a year from now, so the interest rate will remain at 10 percent per annum. Relative prices also remain the same if all money prices double, since relative prices are just ratios of money prices. Thus, money supply changes do not change the long-run allocation of resources. Only the absolute level of money prices changes.[7]

When studying the effect of an increase in the money supply over long time periods, we are therefore justified in assuming that the long-run values of R and Y will not be changed by a change in the supply of money. Thus, we can draw the following conclusion from equation (15-5): *A permanent increase in the money supply causes a proportional increase in the price level's long-run value. In particular, if the economy is initially at full employment, a permanent increase in the money supply eventually will be followed by a proportional increase in the price level.*

Empirical Evidence on Money Supplies and Price Levels

In looking at actual data on money and prices, we should not expect to see an exactly proportional relationship over long periods, partly because output, the interest rate, and the aggregate real money demand function can shift for reasons that have nothing to do with the supply of money. Output changes as a result of capital accumulation and technological advance (for example, more powerful computers), and money demand behavior may change as a result of demographic trends or financial innovations such as electronic cash-transfer facilities. In addition, actual economies are rarely in positions of long-run equilibrium. Nonetheless, we should expect the data to show a clear-cut positive association between money supplies and price levels. If real-world data did not provide strong evidence that money supplies and price levels move together in the long run, the usefulness of the theory of money demand we have developed would be in severe doubt.

The wide swings in Latin American rates of price level increase in recent decades make the region an ideal case study of the relationship between money supplies and price levels. Price level inflation had been high and variable in Latin America for more than a decade, when efforts at macroeconomic reform began to bring inflation lower by the mid-1990s.

On the basis of our theories, we would expect to find such sharp swings in inflation rates accompanied by swings in growth rates of money supplies. This expectation is confirmed by Figure 15-10, which plots annual average growth rates of the money supply against annual inflation rates over the two decades 1987–2007. On average, years with higher money growth also tend to be years with higher inflation. In addition, the data points cluster around the 45-degree line, along which money supplies and price levels increase in proportion.

---

[7]To understand more fully why a one-time change in the money supply does not change the long-run level of the interest rate, it may be useful to think of interest rates measured in terms of money as defining relative prices of currency units available on different dates. If the dollar interest rate is R percent per annum, giving up $1 today buys you $(1 + R)$ next year. Thus, $1/(1 + R)$ is the relative price of future dollars in terms of current dollars, and this relative price would not change if the real value of the monetary units were scaled up or down by the same factor on all dates.

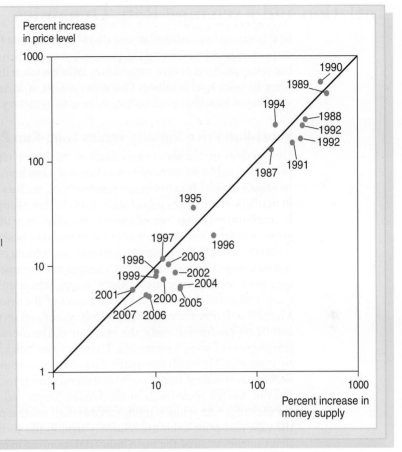

FIGURE 15-10

Average Money Growth and Inflation in Western Hemisphere Developing Countries, by Year, 1987–2007

Even year by year, there is a strong positive relation between average Latin American money supply growth and inflation. (Both axes have logarithmic scales.)

Source: IMF, *World Economic Outlook*, various issues. Regional aggregates are weighted by shares of dollar GDP in total regional dollar GDP.

The main lesson to be drawn from Figure 15-10 is that the data confirm the strong long-run link between national money supplies and national price levels predicted by economic theory.

Money and the Exchange Rate in the Long Run

The domestic currency price of foreign currency is one of the many prices in the economy that rise in the long run after a permanent increase in the money supply. If you think again about the effects of a currency reform, you will see how the exchange rate moves in the long run. Suppose the U.S. government replaced every pair of "old" dollars with one "new" dollar. Then, if the dollar/euro exchange rate had been 1.20 *old* dollars per euro before the reform, it would change to 0.60 *new* dollars per euro immediately after the reform. In much the same way, a halving of the U.S. money supply would eventually lead the dollar to appreciate from an exchange rate of 1.20 dollars/euro to one of 0.60 dollars/euro. Since the dollar prices of all U.S. goods and services would also decrease by half, this 50 percent appreciation of the dollar leaves the *relative* prices of all U.S. and foreign goods and services unchanged.

We conclude that, all else equal, *a permanent increase in a country's money supply causes a proportional long-run depreciation of its currency against foreign currencies. Similarly, a permanent decrease in a country's money supply causes a proportional long-run appreciation of its currency against foreign currencies.*

Inflation and Exchange Rate Dynamics

In this section, we tie together our short- and long-run findings about the effects of monetary changes by examining the process through which the price level adjusts to its long-run position. An economy experiences **inflation** when its price level is rising and **deflation** when its price level is falling. Our examination of inflation will give us a deeper understanding of how the exchange rate adjusts to monetary disturbances in the economy.

Short-Run Price Rigidity versus Long-Run Price Flexibility

Our analysis of the short-run effects of monetary changes assumed that a country's price level, unlike its exchange rate, does not jump immediately. This assumption cannot be exactly correct because many commodities, such as agricultural products, are traded in markets where prices adjust sharply every day as supply or demand conditions shift. In addition, exchange rate changes themselves may affect the prices of some tradable goods and services that enter into the commodity basket defining the price level.

Many prices in the economy, however, are written into long-term contracts and cannot be changed immediately when changes in the money supply occur. The most important prices of this type are workers' wages, which are negotiated only periodically in many industries. Wages do not enter indices of the price level directly, but they make up a large fraction of the cost of producing goods and services. Since output prices depend heavily on production costs, the behavior of the overall price level is influenced by the sluggishness of wage movements. The short-run "stickiness" of price levels is illustrated by Figure 15-11, which compares data on month-to-month percentage changes in the dollar/ yen exchange rate, $E_{\$/¥}$, with data on month-to-month percentage changes in the ratio of money price levels in the United States and Japan, P_{US}/P_J. As you can see, the exchange rate is much more variable than relative price levels, a fact consistent with the view that price levels are relatively rigid in the short run. The pattern shown in the figure applies to all of the main industrial countries in recent decades. In light of this and other evidence, we will therefore continue to assume the price level is given in the short run and does not make significant jumps in response to policy changes.

This assumption would not be reasonable, however, for all countries at all times. In extremely inflationary conditions, such as those seen in the 1980s in some Latin American countries, long-term contracts specifying domestic money payments may go out of use. Automatic price level indexation of wage payments may also be widespread under highly inflationary conditions. Such developments make the price level much less rigid than it would be under moderate inflation, and large price level jumps become possible. Some price rigidity can remain, however, even in the face of inflation rates that would be high by everyday industrial-country standards. For example, Turkey's 30 percent inflation rate for 2002 seems high until it is compared with the 114 percent depreciation of the Turkish lira against the U.S. dollar over the same year.

Our analysis assuming short-run price rigidity is nonetheless most applicable to countries with histories of comparative price level stability, such as the United States. Even in the cases of low-inflation countries, there is a lively academic debate over the possibility that seemingly sticky wages and prices are in reality quite flexible.[8]

---

[8]For a discussion of this debate and empirical evidence that U.S. aggregate prices and wages show significant rigidity, see the book by Hall and Papell listed in Further Readings. Other summaries of U.S. evidence are given by Mark A. Wynne, "Sticky Prices: What Is the Evidence?" *Federal Reserve Bank of Dallas Economic Review* (First Quarter 1995), pp. 1–12; and by Peter J. Klenow and Benjamin A. Malin, "Microeconomic Evidence on Price Setting,"in Benjamin M. Friedman and Michael Woodford, eds., *Handbook of Monetary Economics*, Vol. 3 (Amsterdam: Elsevier, 2010).

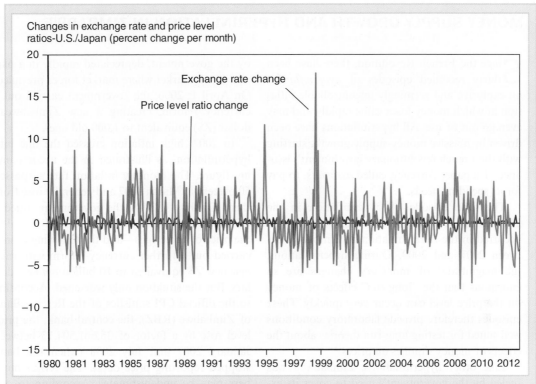

FIGURE 15-11   MyEconLab Real-time data

Month-to-Month Variability of the Dollar/Yen Exchange Rate and of the U.S./Japan Price Level Ratio, 1980–2013

The much greater month-to-month variability of the exchange rate suggests that price levels are relatively sticky in the short run.

Source: Price levels from International Monetary Fund, *International Financial Statistics*. Exchange rate from Global Financial Data.

Although the price level appears to display short-run stickiness in many countries, a change in the money supply creates immediate demand and cost pressures that eventually lead to *future* increases in the price level. These pressures come from three main sources:

1. *Excess demand for output and labor.* An increase in the money supply has an expansionary effect on the economy, raising the total demand for goods and services. To meet this demand, producers of goods and services must employ workers overtime and make new hires. Even if wages are given in the short run, the additional demand for labor allows workers to ask for higher wages in the next round of wage negotiations. Producers are willing to pay these higher wages, for they know that in a booming economy, it will not be hard to pass higher wage costs on to consumers through higher product prices.

2. *Inflationary expectations.* If everyone expects the price level to rise in the future, their expectation will increase the pace of inflation today. Workers bargaining over wage contracts will insist on higher money wages to counteract the effect on their real wages of the anticipated general increase in prices. Producers, once

MONEY SUPPLY GROWTH AND HYPERINFLATION IN ZIMBABWE

Since the French Revolution, there have been thirty recorded episodes of *hyperinflation*: an explosive and seemingly uncontrollable inflation in which money loses value rapidly and may even go out of use. All hyperinflations have been driven by massive money-supply growth, starting with the French revolutionary government's issuance of a paper currency, called *assignats*, to pay for its spending needs.

The lone episode of hyperinflation in the 21st century, but one of the most extreme ever, occurred in the African nation of Zimbabwe between 2007 and 2009. During hyperinflations, the magnitudes of monetary changes are so enormous that the "long-run" effects of money on the price level can occur very quickly. These episodes therefore provide laboratory conditions well suited for testing long-run theories about the effects of money supplies on prices.*

Like other hyperinflations, Zimbabwe's was fueled by the government's need to cover its expenses by printing money. These expenses included a four-year war in the Congo that began in 1998 and large-scale support of agriculture, all at a time when foreigners were withdrawing loans, investment, and aid because of domestic political turbulence. Inflation was the result, and the currency's exchange rate, while officially controlled by the government, depreciated rapidly in a parallel black market where market forces prevailed. On April 1, 2006, the government carried out a currency reform, creating a new Zimbabwean dollar (Z$) equivalent to 1,000 old ones.

In 2007, high inflation crossed the line into hyperinflation, as illustrated in the accompanying figure. The monthly inflation rate surpassed 50 percent in March 2007 and generally rose from there. On July 1, 2008, the government issued a Z$100 billion note—at the time, roughly equal to the price of three eggs—and the following month carried out a further currency reform with each *new* new Z$ equivalent to 10 billion *old* new dollars. But the situation only worsened. According to the official CPI statistics of the Reserve Bank of Zimbabwe (RBZ), the central bank, the price level rose by a factor of 36,661,304.13 between January 2007 and July 2008 (when the bank stopped reporting price data). The RBZ's numbers may be underestimates. According to one report, the rate of inflation for the month of October 2008 alone exceeded 33,000,000 percent![†] Yet another currency reform, on February 3, 2009, created the fourth Z$, equivalent to 1 trillion of the former currency units.

By early 2009, however, the hyperinflation was coming to an end on its own because people

---

*In a classic paper, the late Columbia University economist Phillip Cagan drew the line between inflation and hyperinflation at an inflation rate of 50 percent per month (which, through the power of compounding, comes out to 12,875 percent per year). See "The Monetary Dynamics of Hyperinflation," in Milton Friedman, ed., *Studies in the Quantity Theory of Money* (Chicago: University of Chicago Press, 1956), pp. 25–117. Such eighteenth-century data as are available indicate that the French Revolution episode (1789–1796) reached a peak monthly inflation rate of more than 143 percent.
[†]See Tara McIndoe-Calder, "Hyperinflation in Zimbabwe," unpublished manuscript, Central Bank of Ireland, March 2011.

---

again, will give in to these wage demands if they expect product prices to rise and cover the additional wage costs.

3. *Raw materials prices.* Many raw materials used in the production of final goods, for example, petroleum products and metals, are sold in markets where prices adjust sharply even in the short run. By causing the prices of such materials to jump upward, a money supply increase raises production costs in materials-using industries. Eventually, producers in those industries will raise product prices to cover their higher costs.

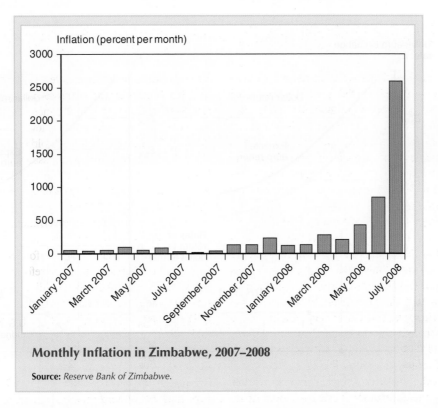

Monthly Inflation in Zimbabwe, 2007–2008

Source: *Reserve Bank of Zimbabwe.*

were avoiding the unstable Z$ and instead relying on foreign currencies such as the U.S. dollar, the South African rand, and the pula of Botswana. A new coalition government legalized foreign currency use, suspended the legal tender status of the Z$, and announced that it would conduct all of its own transactions in U.S. dollars. Importantly, the government (which could no longer print money) adopted a "cash budgeting" rule, allowing itself to spend only the money it brings in through taxes. Because the Z$ quickly went out of use, the RBZ gave up reporting its exchange rate after November 6, 2009. Inflation (now measured in U.S. dollar terms) dropped dramatically in 2009. Although several currencies continue to circulate side by side, the U.S. dollar is by far dominant. In effect, the U.S. Federal Reserve now determines monetary conditions in Zimbabwe.

Zimbabwe still suffers from numerous economic problems, many of them stemming from its years of extreme macroeconomic instability, but inflation is not one of them. Recent inflation has remained low, under 5 percent per year since 2010.**

**For more detailed accounts, see Janet Koech, "Hyperinflation in Zimbabwe," in *Globalization and Monetary Policy Institute 2011 Annual Report,* Federal Reserve Bank of Dallas, pp. 2–12; and Joseph Noko, "Dollarization: The Case of Zimbabwe," *Cato Journal* 31 (Spring/Summer 2011), pp. 339–365.

Permanent Money Supply Changes and the Exchange Rate

We now apply our analysis of inflation to study the adjustment of the dollar/euro exchange rate following a *permanent* increase in the U.S. money supply. Figure 15-12 shows both the short-run (Figure 15-12a) and the long-run (Figure 15-12b) effects of this disturbance. We suppose the economy starts with all variables at

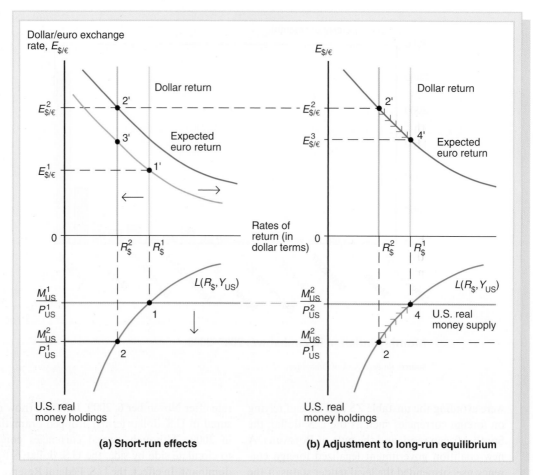

FIGURE 15-12

**Short-Run and Long-Run Effects of an Increase in the U.S. Money Supply
(Given Real Output, Y)**

(a) Short-run adjustment of the asset markets. (b) How the interest rate, price level, and exchange rate move over time as the economy approaches its long-run equilibrium.

their long-run levels and that output remains constant as the economy adjusts to the money supply change.

Figure 15-12a assumes the U.S. price level is initially given at P^1_{US}. An increase in the nominal money supply from M^1_{US} to M^2_{US} therefore raises the real money supply from M^1_{US}/P^1_{US} to M^2_{US}/P^1_{US} in the short run, lowering the interest rate from $R^1_\$$ (point 1) to $R^2_\$$ (point 2). So far, our analysis proceeds exactly as it did earlier in this chapter.

The first change in our analysis comes when we ask how the American money supply change (shown in the bottom part of panel (a)) affects the foreign exchange market (shown in the top part of panel (a)). As before, the fall in the U.S. interest rate is shown as a leftward shift in the vertical schedule giving the dollar return on dollar deposits. This is no longer the whole story, however, for the money supply increase now affects *exchange rate expectations*. Because the U.S. money supply change is permanent, people expect a long-run increase in all dollar prices, including the exchange rate, which is the dollar price of euros. As you know will recall from Chapter 14, a rise in the expected future dollar/euro exchange rate (a future dollar depreciation) raises the expected dollar return on euro deposits; it thus shifts the downward-sloping schedule in the top part of Figure 15-12a to the right. The dollar depreciates against the euro, moving from an exchange rate of $E^1_{\$/€}$ (point 1′) to $E^2_{\$/€}$ (point 2′). Notice that the dollar depreciation is *greater* than it would be if the expected future dollar/euro exchange rate stayed fixed (as it might if the money supply increase were temporary rather than permanent). If the expectation $E^e_{\$/€}$ did not change, the new short-run equilibrium would be at point 3′ rather than at point 3′.

Figure 15-12b shows how the interest rate and exchange rate behave as the price level rises during the economy's adjustment to its long-run equilibrium. The price level begins to rise from the initially given level P^1_{US}, eventually reaching P^2_{US}. Because the long-run increase in the price level must be proportional to the increase in the money supply, the final *real* money supply, M^1_{US}/P^2_{US}, is shown equal to the initial real money supply, M^1_{US}/P^1_{US}. Since output is given and the real money supply has returned to its original level, the equilibrium interest rate must again equal $R^1_\$$ in the long run (point 4). The interest rate therefore rises from $R^2_\$$ (point 2) to $R^1_\$$ (point 4) as the price level rises from P^1_{US} to P^2_{US}.

The rising U.S. interest rate has exchange rate effects that can also be seen in Figure 15-12b: The dollar *appreciates* against the euro in the process of adjustment. If exchange rate expectations do not change further during the adjustment process, the foreign exchange market moves to its long-run position along the downward-sloping schedule defining the dollar return on euro deposits. The market's path is just the path traced out by the vertical dollar interest rate schedule as it moves rightward because of the price level's gradual rise. In the long run (point 4′), the equilibrium exchange rate, $E^3_{\$/€}$, is higher than at the original equilibrium, point 1′. Like the price level, the dollar/euro exchange rate has risen in proportion to the increase in the money supply.

Figure 15-13 shows time paths like the ones just described for the U.S. money supply, the dollar interest rate, the U.S. price level, and the dollar/euro exchange rate. The figure is drawn so that the long-run increases in the price level (Figure 15-13c) and exchange rate (Figure 15-13d) are proportional to the increase in the money supply (Figure 15-13a).

Exchange Rate Overshooting

In its initial depreciation after a money supply rise, the exchange rate jumps from $E^1_{\$/€}$ up to $E^2_{\$/€}$, a depreciation greater than its *long-run* depreciation from $E^1_{\$/€}$ to $E^3_{\$/€}$ (see Figure 15-13d). The exchange rate is said to overshoot when its immediate response to a disturbance is greater than its long-run response. **Exchange rate overshooting** is an important phenomenon because it helps explain why exchange rates move so sharply from day to day.

The economic explanation of overshooting comes from the interest parity condition. The explanation is easiest to grasp if we assume that before the money supply increase first occurs, no change in the dollar/euro exchange rate is expected, so that $R^1_\$$ equals $R_€$, the given interest rate on euro deposits. A permanent increase in the U.S.

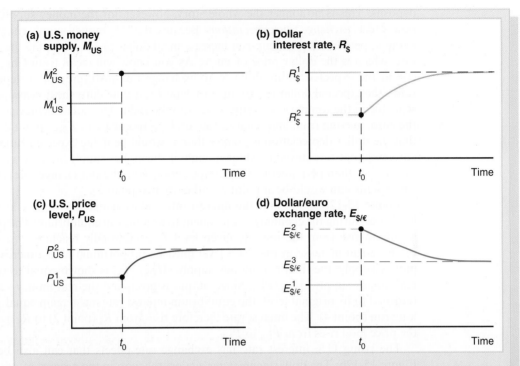

FIGURE 15-13

Time Paths of U.S. Economic Variables after a Permanent Increase in the U.S. Money Supply

After the money supply increases at t_0 in panel (a), the interest rate (in panel (b)), price level (in panel (c)), and exchange rate (in panel (d)) move as shown toward their long-run levels. As indicated in panel (d) by the initial jump from $E^1_{\$/\text{€}}$ to $E^2_{\$/\text{€}}$, the exchange rate overshoots in the short run before settling down to its long-run level, $E^3_{\$/\text{€}}$.

money supply doesn't affect $R_\text{€}$, so it causes $R^1_\$$ to fall below $R_\text{€}$ and remain below that interest rate (Figure 15-13b) until the U.S. price level has completed the long-run adjustment to P^2_US shown in Figure 15-13c. For the foreign exchange market to be in equilibrium during this adjustment process, however, the interest difference in favor of euro deposits must be offset by an expected *appreciation* of the dollar against the euro, that is, by an expected fall in $E_{\$/\text{€}}$. Only if the dollar/euro exchange rate overshoots $E^3_{\$/\text{€}}$ initially will market participants expect a subsequent appreciation of the dollar against the euro.

Overshooting is a direct consequence of the short-run rigidity of the price level. In a hypothetical world where the price level could adjust immediately to its new, long-run level after a money supply increase, the dollar interest rate would not fall because prices *would* adjust immediately and prevent the real money supply from rising. Thus, there would be no need for overshooting to maintain equilibrium in the foreign exchange market. The exchange rate would maintain equilibrium simply by jumping to its new, long-run level right away.

CASE STUDY   **Can Higher Inflation Lead to Currency *Appreciation*? The Implications of Inflation Targeting**

In the overshooting model we have just examined, an increase in the money supply leads to higher inflation and currency depreciation, as shown in Figure 15–13. It may seem puzzling, then, that readers of the financial press often see headlines such as the following one from the *Financial Times* of May 24, 2007: "Inflation Drives Canadian Dollar Higher." In light of the seemingly reasonable model set out in this chapter, can such statements possibly make sense?

A clue comes from reading further in the *Financial Times* news story on Canadian inflation. According to the *FT*:

> [A]nalysts said that the main driver of the recent bout of Canadian dollar appreciation was higher-than-expected April inflation data, which saw the bond market fully price in a 25 basis point rise in Canadian interest rates by the end of the year.

If central banks act to raise interest rates when inflation rises, then because higher interest rates cause currency appreciation, it might be possible to resolve the apparent contradiction to our model. To do so fully, however, we must consider two aspects of the way in which modern central banks actually formulate and implement monetary policy.

> **1.** *The interest rate, not the money supply, is the prime instrument of monetary policy.* Nowadays, most central banks do not actually target the money supply in order to control inflation. They instead target a benchmark short-term rate of interest (such as the overnight "federal funds" rate in the United States). How does our discussion of money market equilibrium help us to understand this process? Consider Figure 15-3, and assume that the central bank wishes to set an interest rate of R^1. It can do so simply by agreeing to provide or take up all of the cash that the market wishes to trade at that rate of interest. If the money supply is initially Q^2, for example, there will be an excess demand for money at the interest rate R^1, so people will sell bonds to the central bank for money (in effect, borrowing) until the money supply has expanded to Q^1 and the excess demand is gone. Central banks tend to set an interest rate, rather than the money supply, because the money demand schedule $L(R, Y)$ shifts around unpredictably in practice. If the central bank were to fix the money supply, the result would be high and possibly damaging interest rate volatility; it is thus more practical to fix the interest rate and let the money supply adjust automatically when necessary.[9]

---

[9]For a nontechnical account of modern central bank policy implementation, see Michael Woodford, "Monetary Policy in a World without Money," *International Finance* 3 (July 2000), pp. 229–260. Woodford's provocative title points to another advantage of the interest rate instrument for central banks: It is possible to conduct monetary policy even if checking deposits pay interest at competitive rates. For many purposes, however, it is reasonable to ignore the variability of the $L(R, Y)$ schedule and simply assume that the central bank directly sets the money supply. In the rest of the book we shall, for the most part, make that simplifying assumption. The major exception will be when we introduce fixed exchange rates in Chapter 18. For a simple reformulation of the theory of monetary policy in terms of an interest rate rather than money supply instrument, see the paper by David Romer in this chapter's Further Readings.

Our preceding discussion of the positive relationship between the money supply and price level will tip you off, however, to one potential problem of an interest rate instrument. If the money supply is free to grow or shrink as markets collectively desire, how can the price level and inflation be kept under control? For example, if market actors doubt the central bank's resolve to control inflation, and suddenly push the price level up because they expect higher prices in the future, they could simply borrow more money from the central bank, thereby bringing about the money supply increase needed to sustain higher prices in the long run. This worrisome possibility brings us to the second pillar of modern monetary policy.

2. *Most central banks adjust their policy interest rates expressly so as to keep inflation in check.* A central bank can keep inflation from getting too high or too low by raising the interest rate when it learns that inflation is running higher than expected, and lowering it when inflation is running lower. As we will see more fully in Chapter 17, a rise in the interest rate, which causes the currency to appreciate, dampens the demand for a country's products by making them more expensive compared to foreign goods. This fall in demand, in turn, promotes lower domestic prices. A fall in the interest rate, symmetrically, supports domestic prices. Indeed, many central banks now follow formal strategies of *inflation targeting*, under which they announce a target (or target range) for the inflation rate and adjust the interest rate to keep inflation on target. Some central banks target so-called *core* inflation, which is inflation in the price level excluding volatile components such as energy prices, rather than *headline* inflation, which is inflation in the total consumer price index. The formal practice of inflation targeting was initiated by New Zealand's central bank in 1990, and the central banks of many other developed and developing areas, including Canada, Chile, Mexico, South Africa, Sweden, Thailand, the United Kingdom, and the euro zone, have followed suit.[10]

We can now understand the "paradox" of higher-than-expected inflation causing currency appreciation rather than depreciation. Suppose market participants unexpectedly push up prices and borrow to enlarge the money supply. Thus, when the Canadian government releases new price data, the data show a price level higher than what market participants had previously predicted. If the Bank of Canada is expected to raise interest rates quickly so as to push the price level and money supply back on course, there is no reason for the future expected exchange rate to change. But with higher Canadian interest rates, interest parity requires an expected future *depreciation* of the Canadian dollar, which is consistent with an unchanged future exchange rate only if the Canadian dollar *appreciates* immediately. The picture of the economy's adjustment after the unexpected increase in money and prices would

---

[10]On inflation-targeting practices and the theory behind them, see the books by Bernanke et al., and by Truman in Further Readings. For a critique of the idea of targeting core rather than headline inflation, see Stephen Cecchetti, "Core Inflation Is an Unreliable Guide," *Financial Times*, September 12, 2006.

look like Figure 15–13 in reverse (that is, constructed to reflect a monetary contraction rather than an expansion)—with the added assumption that the Bank of Canada gradually moves interest rates back to their initial level as the price level returns to its targeted path.[11]

Economists Richard Clarida of Columbia University and Daniel Waldman of Barclays Capital offer striking statistical evidence consistent with this explanation.[12] These writers measure unexpected inflation as the inflation rate estimate initially announced by a government, prior to any data revisions, less the median of inflation forecasts for that period previously published by a set of banking industry analysts. For a sample of ten countries—Australia, Britain, Canada, the euro area, Japan, New Zealand, Norway, Sweden, Switzerland, and the United States—Clarida and Waldman examine the exchange rate changes that occur in the period lasting from five minutes prior to an inflation announcement to five minutes afterward. Their key findings are these:

1. On average for the ten currencies that they study, news that inflation is unexpectedly high does indeed lead a currency to appreciate, not depreciate.
2. The effect is stronger for core than for headline inflation.
3. The effect is much stronger for the inflation-targeting countries than for the United States and Japan, the two countries that did not announce inflation targets. In the case of Canada, for example, the announcement of an annual core inflation rate that is 1 percent per year above the market expectation leads the Canadian dollar to appreciate immediately by about 3 percent against the U.S. dollar. The corresponding effect for the U.S. dollar/euro exchange rate, while in the same direction, is only about one-quarter as big.
4. For countries where sufficiently long data series are available, the strengthening effect of unexpected inflation on the currency is present after the introduction of inflation targeting, but not before.

Scientific theories can be conclusively disproved, of course, but never conclusively proved. So far, however, the theory that strict inflation targeting makes bad news on inflation good news for the currency looks quite persuasive.

---

[11]Strictly speaking, the narrative in the text describes a setting with price level rather than inflation rate targeting. (Can you see the difference?) The reasoning in the case of inflation targeting is nearly identical, however, provided that the central bank's interest rate response to unexpectedly high inflation is sufficiently strong.

[12]See Clarida and Waldman, "Is Bad News About Inflation Good News for the Exchange Rate? And If So, Can That Tell Us Anything about the Conduct of Monetary Policy?" in John Y. Campbell, ed., *Asset Prices and Monetary Policy* (Chicago: University of Chicago Press, 2008). Michael W. Klein of Tufts University and Linda S. Goldberg of the Federal Reserve Bank of New York used a related approach to investigate changing market perceptions of the European Central Bank's inflation aversion after its launch in 1999. See "Evolving Perceptions of Central Bank Credibility: The European Central Bank Experience," *NBER International Seminar on Macroeconomics* 33 (2010), pp. 153–182.

SUMMARY

1. Money is held because of its liquidity. When considered in real terms, *aggregate money demand* is not a demand for a certain number of currency units but is instead a demand for a certain amount of purchasing power. Aggregate real money demand depends negatively on the opportunity cost of holding money (measured by the domestic interest rate) and positively on the volume of transactions in the economy (measured by real GNP).

2. The money market is in equilibrium when the real *money supply* equals aggregate real money demand. With the *price level* and real output given, a rise in the money supply lowers the interest rate and a fall in the money supply raises the interest rate. A rise in real output raises the interest rate, given the price level, while a fall in real output has the opposite effect.

3. By lowering the domestic interest rate, an increase in the money supply causes the domestic currency to depreciate in the foreign exchange market (even when expectations of future exchange rates do not change). Similarly, a fall in the domestic money supply causes the domestic currency to appreciate against foreign currencies.

4. The assumption that the price level is given in the *short run* is a good approximation to reality in countries with moderate *inflation*, but it is a misleading assumption over the *long run*. Permanent changes in the money supply push the *long-run equilibrium* price level proportionally in the same direction but do not influence the long-run values of output, the interest rate, or any relative prices. One important money price whose long-run equilibrium level rises in proportion to a permanent money supply increase is the exchange rate, the domestic currency price of foreign currency.

5. An increase in the money supply can cause the exchange rate to overshoot its long-run level in the short run. If output is given, a permanent money supply increase, for example, causes a more-than-proportional short-run depreciation of the currency, followed by an appreciation of the currency to its long-run exchange rate. *Exchange rate overshooting*, which heightens the volatility of exchange rates, is a direct result of sluggish short-run price level adjustment and the interest parity condition.

KEY TERMS

aggregate money demand, p. 415
deflation, p. 430
exchange rate overshooting,
  p. 435

inflation, p. 430
long run, p. 421
long-run equilibrium,
  p. 426

money supply, p. 413
price level, p. 415
short run, p. 421

PROBLEMS

MyEconLab

1. Suppose there is a reduction in aggregate real money demand, that is, a negative shift in the aggregate real money demand function. Trace the short- and long-run effects on the exchange rate, interest rate, and price level.

2. Do you agree with the view that inflation and interest rate are positively correlated? How would a fall in the interest rate on money demand affect inflation rate in the economy? Would a rise in the country's interest rate adversely affect the economy's GNP? Explain.

3. The velocity of money, V, is defined as the ratio of real GNP to real money holdings, $V = Y/(M/P)$ in this chapter's notation. Use equation (15-4) to derive an

expression for velocity and explain how velocity varies with changes in R and in Y. (Hint: The effect of output changes on V depends on the elasticity of aggregate money demand with respect to real output, which economists believe to be less than unity.) What is the relationship between velocity and the exchange rate?

4. What is the short-run effect on the exchange rate of an increase in domestic real GNP, given expectations about future exchange rates?

5. As an investor you want to choose between two countries—Japan and South Korea. Suppose Japan's nominal interest rate is 12 percent and inflation rate is 7 percent, while South Korea's is 7 percent and 3 percent respectively. Where would you invest and why?

6. During the year 2013, the Indian rupee depreciated sharply against the dollar. To check any further depreciation in the rupee, the central bank of India (Reserve Bank of India or RBI) increased the interest rate in the economy in the short run. How will the increased rate help in controlling the rupee depreciation in the Indian economy? Suppose the RBI increases the money supply instead of the interest rate. Will that check the depreciation of the rupee? Explain using the money supply, interest rate and the exchange rate mechanism.

7. In 1984 and 1985, the small Latin American country of Bolivia experienced hyperinflation. Below are some key macroeconomic data from those years:

Macroeconomic Data for Bolivia, April 1984–October 1985

Month	Money Supply (Billions of Pesos)	Price Level (Relative to 1982 Average = 1	Exchange Rate (Pesos per Dollar)
1984			
April	270	21.1	3,576
May	330	31.1	3,512
June	440	32.3	3,342
July	599	34.0	3,570
August	718	39.1	7,038
September	889	53.7	13,685
October	1,194	85.5	15,205
November	1,495	112.4	18,469
December	3,296	180.9	24,515
1985			
January	4,630	305.3	73,016
February	6,455	863.3	141,101
March	9,089	1,078.6	128,137
April	12,885	1,205.7	167,428
May	21,309	1,635.7	272,375
June	27,778	2,919.1	481,756
July	47,341	4,854.6	885,476
August	74,306	8,081.0	1,182,300
September	103,272	12,647.6	1,087,440
October	132,550	12,411.8	1,120,210

Source: Juan-Antonio Morales, "Inflation Stabilization in Bolivia," in Michael Bruno et al., eds., *Inflation Stabilization: The Experience of Argentina, Brazil, Bolivia, and Mexico*. Cambridge, MA: MIT Press, 1988, table 7A-1. Money supply is M1.

    a. Do the money supply, price level, and exchange rate against the U.S. dollar move broadly as you would expect? Explain.

    b. Calculate the percent changes in the general price level and price of the dollar between April 1984 and July 1985. How do these compare to each other and to the percent increase in the money supply? Can you explain the results? (Hint: Refer back to the discussion of the *velocity* of money in question 3.)

    c. The Bolivian government introduced a dramatic stabilization plan near the end of August 1985. Looking at the price levels and exchange rates for the following two months, do you think it was successful? In light of your answer, explain why the money supply increased by a large amount between September and October 1985.

8. Below is a table of some inflation targeting countries and the years in which they adopted the practice:

Country	Year of adoption
New Zealand	1990
Chile	1991
Canada	1991
Israel	1991
Sweden	1993
Finland	1993
Australia	1994
Brazil	1999
Mexico	1999
South Africa	2000
Indonesia	2005

Go to the International Monetary Fund's most recent *World Economic Outlook* database (accessible directly or through www.imf.org) and collect the annual inflation rate series PCPIEPCH for these countries, starting in 1980. Then graph the data for each country using Excel or some other data analysis package. Just looking at the data, does inflation appear to behave differently after the adoption of inflation targeting?

9. In our discussion of short-run exchange rate overshooting, we assumed real output was given. Assume instead that an increase in the money supply raises real output in the short run (an assumption that will be justified in Chapter 17). How does this affect the extent to which the exchange rate overshoots when the money supply first increases? Is it likely that the exchange rate undershoots? (Hint: In Figure 15-12a, allow the aggregate real money demand schedule to shift in response to the increase in output.)

10. Do you think changes in interest rates affect the total money supply in an economy? Suppose a market is initially at a higher interest rate. Explain, using the demand and supply mechanism, how interest rates tend to settle at the equilibrium.

11. How might a zero interest rate complicate the task of monetary policy? (Hint: At a zero rate of interest, there is no advantage in switching from money to bonds.)

12. As we observed in this chapter, central banks, rather than purposefully setting the level of the money supply, usually set a target level for a short-term interest rate by standing ready to lend or borrow whatever money people wish to trade at that interest rate. (When people need more money for a reason other than a change in the interest rate, the money supply therefore expands, and it contracts when they wish to hold less.)

    a. Describe the problems that might arise if a central bank sets monetary policy by holding the market interest rate constant. (First, consider the flexible-price case, and ask yourself if you can find a unique equilibrium price level when the central bank simply gives people all the money they wish to hold at the pegged interest rate. Then consider the sticky-price case.)

    b. Does the situation change if the central bank raises the interest rate when prices are high, according to a formula such as $R - R_0 = a(P - P_0)$, where a is a positive constant and P_0 a target price level?

    c. Suppose the central bank's policy rule is $R - R_0 = a(P - P_0) + u$, where u is a random movement in the policy interest rate. In the overshooting model shown in Figure 15-13, describe how the economy would adjust to a permanent one-time unexpected fall in the random factor u, and say why. You can interpret the fall in u as an interest rate cut by the central bank, and therefore as an expansionary monetary action. Compare your story with the one depicted in Figure 15-13.

13. Since 1942, the small country of Panama has had no paper currency other than the United States dollar, which circulates freely internally. What would you expect to be true about the inflation rate in Panama compared to that in the United States, and why? Go to the International Monetary Fund's most recent *World Economic Outlook* database (accessible directly or through www.imf.org) and examine comparable consumer-price inflation rates for Panama and the United States? Do the inflation rates you see there conform to your earlier prediction? (After you have read Chapters 16 and 18, you should return to this question as you will then have a deeper understanding of the factors that determine the price level in a country like Panama.)

FURTHER READINGS

Ben S. Bernanke, Thomas Laubach, Frederic S. Mishkin, and Adam S. Posen. *Inflation Targeting: Lessons from the International Experience.* Princeton, NJ: Princeton University Press, 1999. Discusses recent monetary policy experience and the consequences for inflation and other macroeconomic variables.

Rudiger Dornbusch. "Expectations and Exchange Rate Dynamics." *Journal of Political Economy* 84 (December 1976), pp. 1161–1176. A theoretical analysis of exchange rate overshooting.

Jacob A. Frenkel and Michael L. Mussa. "The Efficiency of Foreign Exchange Markets and Measures of Turbulence." *American Economic Review* 70 (May 1980), pp. 374–381. Contrasts the behavior of national price levels with that of exchange rates and other asset prices.

Robert E. Hall and David H. Papell. *Macroeconomics: Economic Growth, Fluctuations, and Policy*, 6th edition. New York: W. W. Norton & Company, 2005. Chapter 15 discusses some theories of nominal price rigidity.

David Romer. "Keynesian Macroeconomics without the *LM* Curve." *Journal of Economic Perspectives* 14 (Spring 2000), pp. 149–169. A macroeconomic model in which the central bank implements monetary policy through the interest rate rather than the money supply.

Edwin M. Truman. *Inflation Targeting in the World Economy*. Washington, D.C.: Institute for International Economics, 2003. Overview of the international aspects of monetary policy frameworks that target low inflation.

MyEconLab Can Help You Get a Better Grade

MyEconLab   If your exam were tomorrow, would you be ready? For each chapter, MyEconLab Practice Tests and Study Plans pinpoint sections you have mastered and those you need to study. That way, you are more efficient with your study time, and you are better prepared for your exams.

To see how it works, turn to page 41 and then go to

www.myeconlab.com

CHAPTER 16

Price Levels and the Exchange Rate in the Long Run

At the end of 1970, you could have bought 358 Japanese yen with a single American dollar; by Christmas 1980, a dollar was worth only 203 yen. Despite a temporary comeback during the 1980s, the dollar's price in yen slumped to 100 by the summer of 2013. Many investors found these price changes difficult to predict, and as a result fortunes were lost—and made—in the foreign exchange market. What economic forces lie behind such dramatic long-term movements in exchange rates?

We have seen that exchange rates are determined by interest rates and expectations about the future, which are, in turn, influenced by conditions in national money markets. To understand fully long-term exchange rate movements, however, we have to extend our model in two directions. First, we must complete our account of the linkages among monetary policies, inflation, interest rates, and exchange rates. Second, we must examine factors other than money supplies and demands—for example, demand shifts in markets for goods and services—that also can have sustained effects on exchange rates.

The model of long-run exchange rate behavior that we develop in this chapter provides the framework that actors in asset markets use to forecast future exchange rates. Because the expectations of these agents influence exchange rates immediately, however, predictions about *long-run* movements in exchange rates are important *even in the short run*. We therefore will draw heavily on this chapter's conclusions when we begin our study in Chapter 17 of *short-run* interactions between exchange rates and output.

In the long run, national price levels play a key role in determining both interest rates and the relative prices at which countries' products are traded. A theory of how national price levels interact with exchange rates is thus central to understanding why exchange rates can change dramatically over periods of several years. We begin our analysis by discussing the theory of **purchasing power parity (PPP)**, which explains movements in the exchange rate between two countries' currencies by changes in the countries' price levels. Next, we examine reasons why PPP may fail to give accurate long-run predictions and show how the theory must sometimes be modified to account for supply or demand shifts in countries' output markets. Finally, we look at what our extended PPP theory predicts about how changes in money and output markets affect exchange and interest rates.

LEARNING GOALS

After reading this chapter, you will be able to:

- Explain the purchasing power parity theory of exchange rates and the theory's relationship to international goods-market integration.
- Describe how monetary factors such as ongoing price level inflation affect exchange rates in the long run.
- Discuss the concept of the real exchange rate.
- Understand factors that affect real exchange rates and relative currency prices in the long run.
- Explain the relationship between international real interest rate differences and expected changes in real exchange rates.

The Law of One Price

To understand the market forces that might give rise to the results predicted by the purchasing power parity theory, we discuss first a related but distinct proposition known as the **law of one price**. The law of one price states that in competitive markets free of transportation costs and official barriers to trade (such as tariffs), identical goods sold in different countries must sell for the same price when their prices are expressed in terms of the same currency. For example, if the dollar/pound exchange rate is $1.50 per pound, a sweater that sells for $45 in New York must sell for £30 in London. The dollar price of the sweater when sold in London is then ($1.50 per pound) × (£30 per sweater) = $45 per sweater, the same as its price in New York.

Let's continue with this example to see why the law of one price must hold when trade is free and there are no transport costs or other trade barriers. If the dollar/pound exchange rate were $1.45 per pound, you could buy a sweater in London by converting $43.50 (= $1.45 per pound × £30) into £30 in the foreign exchange market. Thus, the dollar price of a sweater in London would be only $43.50. If the same sweater were selling for $45 in New York, U.S. importers and British exporters would have an incentive to buy sweaters in London and ship them to New York, pushing the London price up and the New York price down until prices were equal in the two locations. Similarly, at an exchange rate of $1.55 per pound, the dollar price of sweaters in London would be $46.50 (= $1.55 per pound × £30), $1.50 more than in New York. Sweaters would be shipped from west to east until a single price prevailed in the two markets.

The law of one price is a restatement, in terms of currencies, of a principle that was important in the trade theory portion of this book: When trade is open and costless, identical goods must trade at the same relative prices regardless of where they are sold. We remind you of that principle here because it provides one link between the domestic prices of goods and exchange rates. We can state the law of one price formally as follows: Let P^i_{US} be the dollar price of good i when sold in the United States, P^i_E the corresponding euro price in Europe. Then the law of one price implies that the dollar price of good i is the same wherever it is sold.

$$P^i_{US} = (E_{\$/€}) \times (P^i_E).$$

Equivalently, the dollar/euro exchange rate is the ratio of good i's U.S. and European money prices,

$$E_{\$/\euro} = P^i_{US}/P^i_E.$$

Purchasing Power Parity

The theory of purchasing power parity states that the exchange rate between two countries' currencies equals the ratio of the countries' price levels. Recall from Chapter 15 that the domestic purchasing power of a country's currency is reflected in the country's price level, the money price of a reference basket of goods and services. The PPP theory therefore predicts that a fall in a currency's domestic purchasing power (as indicated by an increase in the domestic price level) will be associated with a proportional currency depreciation in the foreign exchange market. Symmetrically, PPP predicts that an increase in the currency's domestic purchasing power will be associated with a proportional currency appreciation.

The basic idea of PPP was put forth in the writings of 19th-century British economists, among them David Ricardo (the originator of the theory of comparative advantage). Gustav Cassel, a Swedish economist writing in the early 20th century, popularized PPP by making it the centerpiece of a theory of exchange rates. While there has been much controversy about the general validity of PPP, the theory does highlight important factors behind exchange rate movements.

To express the PPP theory in symbols, let P_{US} be the dollar price of a reference commodity basket sold in the United States and P_E the euro price of the same basket in Europe. (Assume for now that a single basket accurately measures money's purchasing power in both countries.) Then PPP predicts a dollar/euro exchange rate of

$$E_{\$/\euro} = P_{US}/P_E. \tag{16-1}$$

If, for example, the reference commodity basket costs \$200 in the United States and €160 in Europe, PPP predicts a dollar/euro exchange rate of \$1.25 per euro (\$200 per basket/€160 per basket). If the U.S. price level were to triple (to \$600 per basket), so would the dollar price of a euro: PPP would imply an exchange rate of \$3.75 per euro (= \$600 per basket/€160 per basket).

By rearranging equation (16-1) to read

$$P_{US} = (E_{\$/\euro}) \times (P_E),$$

we get an alternative interpretation of PPP. The left side of this equation is the dollar price of the reference commodity basket in the United States; the right side is the dollar price of the reference basket when purchased in Europe (that is, its euro price multiplied by the dollar price of a euro). These two prices are the same if PPP holds. PPP thus asserts that all countries' price levels are equal when measured in terms of the same currency.

Equivalently, the right side of the last equation measures the purchasing power of a dollar when exchanged for euros and spent in Europe. PPP therefore holds when, at going exchange rates, every currency's domestic purchasing power is always the same as its foreign purchasing power.

The Relationship between PPP and the Law of One Price

Superficially, the statement of PPP given by equation (16-1) looks like the law of one price, which says that $E_{\$/\euro} = P^i_{US}/P^i_E$ for any commodity i. There is a difference between PPP and the law of one price, however: The law of one price applies to individual commodities (such as commodity i), while PPP applies to the general price level, which is a composite of the prices of all the commodities that enter into the reference basket.

If the law of one price holds true for every commodity, of course, PPP must hold automatically as long as the reference baskets used to reckon different countries' price levels are the same. Proponents of the PPP theory argue, however, that its validity (in particular, its validity as a long-run theory) does not require the law of one price to hold exactly.

Even when the law of one price fails to hold for each individual commodity, the argument goes, prices and exchange rates should not stray too far from the relation predicted by PPP. When goods and services become temporarily more expensive in one country than in others, the demands for its currency and its products fall, pushing the exchange rate and domestic prices back in line with PPP. The opposite situation of relatively cheap domestic products leads, analogously, to currency appreciation and price level inflation. PPP thus asserts that even when the law of one price is not literally true, the economic forces behind it will help eventually to equalize a currency's purchasing power in all countries.

Absolute PPP and Relative PPP

The statement that exchange rates equal relative price levels (equation (16-1)) is sometimes referred to as **absolute PPP**. Absolute PPP implies a proposition known as **relative PPP**, which states that the percentage change in the exchange rate between two currencies over any period equals the difference between the percentage changes in national price levels. Relative PPP thus translates absolute PPP from a statement about price and exchange rate *levels* into one about price and exchange rate *changes*. It asserts that prices and exchange rates change in a way that preserves the ratio of each currency's domestic and foreign purchasing powers.

If the U.S. price level rises by 10 percent over a year while Europe's rises by only 5 percent, for example, relative PPP predicts a 5 percent depreciation of the dollar against the euro. The dollar's 5 percent depreciation against the euro just cancels the 5 percent by which U.S. inflation exceeds European inflation, leaving the relative domestic and foreign purchasing powers of both currencies unchanged.

More formally, relative PPP between the United States and Europe would be written as

$$(E_{\$/€, t} - E_{\$/€, t-1})/E_{\$/€, t-1} = \pi_{US, t} - \pi_{E, t} \qquad (16\text{-}2)$$

where π_t denotes an inflation rate (that is, $\pi_t = (P_t - P_{t-1})/P_{t-1}$, the percentage change in a price level between dates t and $t - 1$).[1] Unlike absolute PPP, relative PPP can be defined only with respect to the time interval over which price levels and the exchange rate change.

In practice, national governments do not take pains to compute the price level indexes they publish using an internationally standardized basket of commodities.

---

[1]To be precise, equation (16-1) implies a good approximation to equation (16-2) when rates of change are not too large. The *exact* relationship is

$$E_{\$/€, t}/E_{\$/€, t-1} = (P_{US, t}/P_{US, t-1})/(P_{E, t}/P_{E, t-1}).$$

After subtracting 1 from both sides, we write the preceding exact equation as

$$(E_{\$/€, t} - E_{\$/€, t-1})/E_{\$/€, t-1} = (\pi_{US, t} + 1)(P_{E, t-1}/P_{E, t}) - (P_{E, t}/P_{E, t})$$
$$= (\pi_{US, t} - \pi_{E, t})/(1 + \pi_{E, t})$$
$$= (\pi_{US, t} - \pi_{E, t}) - \pi_{E, t}(\pi_{US, t} - \pi_{E, t})/(1 + \pi_{E, t}).$$

But if $\pi_{US, t}$ and $\pi_{E, t}$ are small, the term $-\pi_{E, t}(\pi_{US, t} - \pi_{E, t})/(1 + \pi_{E, t})$ in the last equality is negligibly small, implying a very good approximation to (16-2).

Absolute PPP makes no sense, however, unless the two baskets whose prices are compared in equation (16-1) are the same. (There is no reason to expect *different* commodity baskets to sell for the same price!) The notion of relative PPP therefore comes in handy when we have to rely on government price level statistics to evaluate PPP. It makes logical sense to compare percentage exchange rate changes to inflation differences, as above, even when countries base their price *level* estimates on product baskets that differ in coverage and composition.

Relative PPP is important also because it may be valid even when absolute PPP is not. Provided the factors causing deviations from absolute PPP are more or less stable over time, percentage *changes* in relative price levels can still approximate percentage *changes* in exchange rates.

A Long-Run Exchange Rate Model Based on PPP

When combined with the framework of money demand and supply that we developed in Chapter 15, the assumption of PPP leads to a useful theory of how exchange rates and monetary factors interact in the long run. Because factors that do not influence money supply or money demand play no explicit role in this theory, it is known as the **monetary approach to the exchange rate**. The monetary approach is this chapter's first step in developing a general long-run theory of exchange rates.

We think of the monetary approach as a *long-run* and not a short-run theory because it does not allow for the price rigidities that seem important in explaining short-run macroeconomic developments, in particular departures from full employment. Instead, the monetary approach proceeds as if prices can adjust right away to maintain full employment as well as PPP. Here, as in the previous chapter, when we refer to a variable's "long-run" value, we mean the variable's equilibrium value in a hypothetical world of perfectly flexible output and factor market prices.

There is actually considerable controversy among macroeconomists about the sources of apparent price level stickiness, with some maintaining that prices and wages only appear rigid and in reality adjust immediately to clear markets. To an economist of the aforementioned school, this chapter's models would describe the short-run behavior of an economy in which the speed of price level adjustment is so great that no significant unemployment ever occurs.

The Fundamental Equation of the Monetary Approach

To develop the monetary approach's predictions for the dollar/euro exchange rate, we will assume that in the long run, the foreign exchange market sets the rate so that PPP holds (see equation (16-1)):

$$E_{\$/€} = P_{US}/P_E.$$

In other words, we assume the above equation would hold in a world where there are no market rigidities to prevent the exchange rate and other prices from adjusting immediately to levels consistent with full employment.

In the previous chapter, equation (15-5) showed how we can explain domestic price levels in terms of domestic money demands and supplies. In the United States,

$$P_{US} = M_{US}^s/L(R_\$, Y_{US}), \tag{16-3}$$

while in Europe,

$$P_E = M_E^s/L(R_€, Y_E). \tag{16-4}$$

As before, we have used the symbol M^s to stand for a country's money supply and $L(R, Y)$ to stand for its aggregate real money demand, which decreases when the interest rate rises and increases when real output rises.[2]

Equations (16-3) and (16-4) show how the monetary approach to the exchange rate comes by its name. According to the statement of PPP in equation (16-1), the dollar price of a euro is simply the dollar price of U.S. output divided by the euro price of European output. These two price levels, in turn, are determined completely by the supply and demand for each currency area's money: The United States' price level is the U.S. money supply divided by U.S. real money demand, as shown in (16-3), and Europe's price level similarly is the European money supply divided by European real money demand, as shown in (16-4). The monetary approach therefore makes the general prediction that *the exchange rate, which is the relative price of American and European money, is fully determined in the long run by the relative supplies of those monies and the relative real demands for them.* Shifts in interest rates and output levels affect the exchange rate only through their influences on money demand.

In addition, the monetary approach makes a number of specific predictions about the long-run effects on the exchange rate of changes in money supplies, interest rates, and output levels:

1. *Money supplies.* Other things equal, a permanent rise in the U.S. money supply M^s_{US} causes a proportional increase in the long-run U.S. price level P_{US}, as equation (16-3) shows. Because under PPP $E_{\$/€} = P_{US}/P_E$, however, $E_{\$/€}$ also rises in the long run in proportion to the increase in the U.S. money supply. (For example, if M^s_{US} rises by 10 percent, P_{US} and $E_{\$/€}$ both eventually rise by 10 percent as well.) Thus, an increase in the U.S. money supply causes a proportional long-run *depreciation* of the dollar against the euro. Conversely, equation (16-4) shows that a permanent increase in the European money supply causes a proportional increase in the long-run European price level. Under PPP, this price level rise implies a proportional long-run *appreciation* of the dollar against the euro (which is the same as a proportional depreciation of the euro against the dollar).

2. *Interest rates.* A rise in the interest rate $R_\$$ on dollar-denominated assets lowers real U.S. money demand $L(R_\$, Y_{US})$. By (16-3), the long-run U.S. price level rises, and under PPP the dollar must depreciate against the euro in proportion to this U.S. price level increase. A rise in the interest rate $R_€$ on euro-denominated assets has the reverse long-run exchange rate effect. Because real European money demand $L(R_€, Y_E)$ falls, Europe's price level rises, by (16-4). Under PPP, the dollar must appreciate against the euro in proportion to Europe's price level increase.

3. *Output levels.* A rise in U.S. output raises real U.S. money demand $L(R_\$, Y_{US})$, leading by (16-3) to a fall in the long-run U.S. price level. According to PPP, there is an appreciation of the dollar against the euro. Symmetrically, a rise in European output raises $L(R_€, Y_E)$ and, by (16-4), causes a fall in Europe's long-run price level. PPP predicts that this development will make the dollar depreciate against the euro.

To understand these predictions, remember that the monetary approach, like any long-run theory, essentially assumes price levels adjust as quickly as exchange rates do—that is, right away. For example, a rise in real U.S. output raises the transactions demand for real U.S. money balances. According to the monetary approach, the U.S.

---

[2]To simplify the notation, we assume identical money demand functions for the United States and Europe.

price level drops *immediately* to bring about a market-clearing increase in the supply of real money balances. PPP implies that this instantaneous American price deflation is accompanied by an instantaneous dollar appreciation on the foreign exchanges.

The monetary approach leads to a result familiar from Chapter 15, that the long-run foreign exchange value of a country's currency moves in proportion to its money supply (prediction 1). The theory also raises what seems to be a paradox (prediction 2). In our previous examples, we always found that a currency *appreciates* when the interest rate it offers rises relative to foreign interest rates. How is it that we have now arrived at precisely the opposite conclusion—that a rise in a country's interest rate *depreciates* its currency by lowering the real demand for its money?

At the end of Chapter 14, we warned that no account of how a change in interest rates affects the exchange rate is complete until we specify *exactly why interest rates have changed*. This point explains the apparent contradiction in our findings about interest and exchange rates. To resolve the puzzle, however, we must first examine more closely how monetary policies and interest rates are connected in the long run.

Ongoing Inflation, Interest Parity, and PPP

In the last chapter, we saw that a permanent increase in the level of a country's money supply ultimately results in a proportional rise in its price level but has no effect on the long-run values of the interest rate or real output. While the conceptual experiment of a one-time, stepwise money supply change is useful for thinking about the long-run effects of money, it is not very realistic as a description of actual monetary policies. More plausibly, the monetary authorities choose a growth rate for the money supply, say, 5, 10, or 50 percent per year and then allow money to grow gradually, through incremental but frequent increases. What are the long-run effects of a policy that allows the money supply to grow smoothly forever at a positive rate?

The reasoning in Chapter 15 suggests that continuing money supply growth will require a continuing rise in the price level—a situation of *ongoing* inflation. As firms and workers catch on to the fact that the money supply is growing steadily at, say, a 10 percent annual rate, they will adjust by raising prices and wages by the same 10 percent every year, thus keeping their real incomes constant. Full-employment output depends on supplies of productive factors, but it is safe to assume that factor supplies, and thus output, are unaffected over the long run by different choices of a constant growth rate for the money supply. *Other things equal, money supply growth at a constant rate eventually results in ongoing price level inflation at the same rate, but changes in this long-run inflation rate do not affect the full-employment output level or the long-run relative prices of goods and services.*

The interest rate, however, is definitely not independent of the money supply growth rate in the long run. While the long-run interest rate does not depend on the absolute *level* of the money supply, continuing *growth* in the money supply eventually will affect the interest rate. The easiest way to see how a permanent increase in inflation affects the long-run interest rate is by combining PPP with the interest rate parity condition on which our previous analysis of exchange rate determination was built.

As in the preceding two chapters, the condition of interest parity between dollar and euro assets is

$$R_\$ = R_\euro + (E^e_{\$/\euro} - E_{\$/\euro})/E_{\$/\euro}$$

(recall equation (14-2), page 394). Now let's ask how this parity condition, which must hold in the long run as well as in the short run, fits with the other parity condition we are assuming in our long-run model, purchasing power parity. According to relative PPP, the percentage change in the dollar/euro exchange rate over the next year, say, will equal the difference between the inflation rates of the United States and Europe over that year (see equation (16-2)). Since people understand this relationship, however, it must also be true that they *expect* the percentage exchange rate change to equal the U.S.–Europe inflation difference. The interest parity condition written on the previous page now tells us the following: *If people expect relative PPP to hold, the difference between the interest rates offered by dollar and euro deposits will equal the difference between the inflation rates expected, over the relevant horizon, in the United States and in Europe.*

Some additional notation is helpful in deriving this result more formally. If P^e is the price level expected in a country for a year from today, the expected inflation rate in that country, π^e, is the expected percentage increase in the price level over the coming year:

$$\pi^e = (P^e - P)/P.$$

If relative PPP holds, however, market participants will also *expect* relative PPP to hold, which means that we can replace the actual depreciation and inflation rates in equation (16-2) with the values the market expects to materialize:

$$(E^e_{\$/\unicode{x20AC}} - E_{\$/\unicode{x20AC}})/E_{\$/\unicode{x20AC}} = \pi^e_{US} - \pi^e_{E}.$$

By combining this "expected" version of relative PPP with the interest parity condition

$$R_\$ = R_\unicode{x20AC} + (E^e_{\$/\unicode{x20AC}} - E_{\$/\unicode{x20AC}})/E_{\$/\unicode{x20AC}}$$

and rearranging, we arrive at a formula that expresses the international interest rate difference as the difference between expected national inflation rates:

$$R_\$ - R_\unicode{x20AC} = \pi^e_{US} - \pi^e_{E}. \tag{16-5}$$

If, as PPP predicts, currency depreciation is expected to offset the international inflation difference (so that the expected dollar depreciation rate is $\pi^e_{US} - \pi^e_{E}$), the interest rate difference must equal the expected inflation difference.

The Fisher Effect

Equation (16-5) gives us the long-run relationship between ongoing inflation and interest rates that we need to explain the monetary approach's predictions about how interest rates affect exchange rates. The equation tells us that *all else equal, a rise in a country's expected inflation rate will eventually cause an equal rise in the interest rate that deposits of its currency offer. Similarly, a fall in the expected inflation rate will eventually cause a fall in the interest rate.*

This long-run relationship between inflation and interest rates is called the **Fisher effect**. The Fisher effect implies, for example, that if U.S. inflation were to rise permanently from a constant level of 5 percent per year to a constant level of 10 percent per year, dollar interest rates would eventually catch up with the higher inflation, rising by 5 percentage points per year from their initial level. These changes would leave the *real rate of return* on dollar assets, measured in terms of U.S. goods and services, unchanged. The Fisher effect is therefore another example of the general idea that in the long run, purely monetary developments should have no effect on an economy's relative prices.[3]

---

[3]The effect is named after Irving Fisher of Yale University, one of the great American economists of the early 20th century. The effect is discussed at length in his book *The Theory of Interest* (New York: Macmillan, 1930). Fisher, incidentally, gave an early account of the interest parity condition on which our theory of foreign exchange market equilibrium is based.

The Fisher effect is behind the seemingly paradoxical monetary approach prediction that a currency depreciates in the foreign exchange market when its interest rate rises relative to foreign currency interest rates. In the long-run equilibrium assumed by the monetary approach, a rise in the difference between home and foreign interest rates occurs only when expected home inflation rises relative to expected foreign inflation. This is certainly not the case in the short run, when the domestic price level is sticky. In the short run, as we saw in Chapter 15, the interest rate can rise when the domestic money supply *falls* because the sticky domestic price level leads to an excess demand for real money balances at the initial interest rate. Under the flexible-price monetary approach, however, the price level would fall right away, leaving the *real* money supply unchanged and thus making the interest rate change unnecessary.

We can better understand how interest rates and exchange rates interact under the monetary approach by thinking through an example. Our example illustrates why the monetary approach associates sustained interest rate hikes with current as well as future currency depreciation, and sustained interest rate declines with appreciation.

Imagine that at time t_0, the Federal Reserve unexpectedly increases the growth rate of the U.S. money supply from π to the higher level $\pi + \Delta\pi$. Figure 16-1 illustrates how this change affects the dollar/euro exchange rate, $E_{\$/€}$, as well as other U.S. variables, under the assumptions of the monetary approach. To simplify the graphs, we assume that in Europe, the inflation rate remains constant at zero.

Figure 16-1a shows the sudden acceleration of U.S. money supply growth at time t_0. (We have scaled the vertical axes of the graphs so that constant slopes represent constant proportional growth rates of variables.) The policy change generates expectations of more rapid currency depreciation in the future: Under PPP the dollar will now depreciate at the rate $\pi + \Delta\pi$ rather than at the lower rate π. Interest parity therefore requires the dollar interest rate to rise, as shown in Figure 16-1b, from its initial level $R_{\$}^1$ to a new level that reflects the extra expected dollar depreciation, $R_{\$}^2 = R_{\$}^1 + \Delta\pi$ (see equation (16-5)). Notice that this adjustment leaves the euro interest rate unchanged; but since Europe's money supply and output haven't changed, the original euro interest rate will still maintain equilibrium in Europe's money market.

You can see from Figure 16-1a that the *level* of the money supply does not actually jump upward at t_0—only the *future growth rate* changes. Since there is no immediate increase in the money supply—but there is an interest rate rise that reduces money demand—there would be an excess supply of real U.S. money balances at the price level prevailing just prior to t_0. In the face of this potential excess supply, the U.S. price level jumps upward at t_0 (see Figure 16-1c), reducing the real money supply so that it again equals real money demand (see equation (16-3)). Consistently with the upward jump in P_{US} at t_0, Figure 16-1d shows the simultaneous proportional upward jump in $E_{\$/€}$ implied by PPP.

How can we visualize the reaction of the foreign exchange market at time t_0? The dollar interest rate rises not because of a change in current levels of money supply or demand, but solely because people expect more rapid future money supply growth and dollar depreciation. As investors respond by moving into foreign deposits, which momentarily offer higher expected returns, the dollar depreciates sharply in the foreign exchange market, moving to a new trend line along which depreciation is more rapid than it was up to time t_0.[4]

Notice how different assumptions about the speed of price level adjustment lead to contrasting predictions about how exchange and interest rates interact. In the example of a fall in the level of the money supply under sticky prices, an interest rate

---

[4]In the general case in which Europe's inflation rate π_E is not zero, the dollar, rather than depreciating against the euro at rate π before t_0 and at rate $\pi + \Delta\pi$ afterward, depreciates at rate $\pi - \pi_E$ until t_0 and at rate $\pi + \Delta\pi - \pi_E$ thereafter.

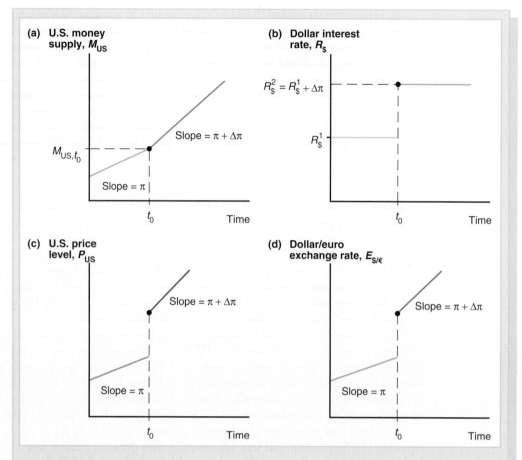

FIGURE 16-1

Long-Run Time Paths of U.S. Economic Variables after a Permanent Increase in the Growth Rate of the U.S. Money Supply

After the money supply growth rate increases at time t_0 in panel (a), the interest rate (in panel (b)), price level (in panel (c)), and exchange rate (in panel (d)) move to new long-run equilibrium paths. (The money supply, price level, and exchange rate are all measured on a *natural logarithmic* scale, which makes variables that change at constant proportional rates appear as straight lines when they are graphed against time. The slope of the line equals the variable's proportional growth rate.)

rise is needed to preserve money market equilibrium, given that the price level cannot do so by dropping immediately in response to the money supply reduction. In that sticky-price case, an interest rate rise is associated with lower expected inflation and a long-run currency appreciation, so the currency appreciates immediately. In our monetary approach example of a rise in money supply growth, however, an interest rate increase is associated with higher expected inflation and a currency that will be weaker on all future dates. An immediate currency *depreciation* is the result.[5]

---

[5]National money supplies typically trend upward over time, as in Figure 16-1a. Such trends lead to corresponding upward trends in price levels; if two countries' price level trends differ, PPP implies a trend in their exchange rate as well. From now on, when we refer to a change in the money supply, price level, or exchange rate, we will mean by this a change in the level of the variable relative to its previously expected trend path— that is, a parallel shift in the trend path. When instead we want to consider changes in the slopes of trend paths themselves, we will say so explicitly.

These contrasting results of interest rate changes underlie our earlier warning that an explanation of exchange rates based on interest rates must carefully account for the factors that cause interest rates to move. These factors can simultaneously affect expected future exchange rates and can therefore have a decisive impact on the foreign exchange market's response to the interest rate change. The appendix to this chapter shows in detail how expectations change in the case we analyzed.

Empirical Evidence on PPP and the Law of One Price

How well does the PPP theory explain actual data on exchange rates and national price levels? A brief answer is that *all versions of the PPP theory do badly* in explaining the facts. In particular, changes in national price levels often tell us relatively little about exchange rate movements.

Do not conclude from this evidence, however, that the effort you've put into learning about PPP has been wasted. As we'll see later in this chapter, PPP is a key building block of exchange rate models that are more realistic than the monetary approach. Indeed, the empirical failures of PPP give us important clues about how more realistic models should be set up.

To test *absolute* PPP, economic researchers compare the international prices of a broad reference basket of commodities, making careful adjustments for intercountry quality differences among supposedly identical goods. These comparisons typically conclude that absolute PPP is way off the mark: The prices of identical commodity baskets, when converted to a single currency, differ substantially across countries. Even the law of one price has not fared well in some recent studies of price data broken down by commodity type. Manufactured goods that seem to be very similar to each other have sold at widely different prices in various markets since the early 1970s. Because the argument leading to absolute PPP builds on the law of one price, it is not surprising that PPP does not stand up well to the data.[6]

Relative PPP is sometimes a reasonable approximation to the data, but it, too, usually performs poorly. Figure 16-2 illustrates relative PPP's weakness by plotting both the yen/dollar exchange rate, $E_{¥/\$}$, and the ratio of the Japanese and U.S. price levels, P_J/P_{US}, through 2012. Price levels are measured by indexes reported by the Japanese and U.S. governments.[7]

Relative PPP predicts that $E_{¥/\$}$ and P_J/P_{US} will move in proportion, but clearly they do not. In the early 1980s, there was a steep appreciation of the dollar against the yen even though, with Japan's price level consistently falling relative to that in the

---

[6]Some of the negative evidence on absolute PPP is discussed in the Case Study to follow. Regarding the law of one price, see, for example, Peter Isard, "How Far Can We Push the Law of One Price?" *American Economic Review* 67 (December 1977), pp. 942–948; Gita Gopinath, Pierre-Olivier Gourinchas, Chang-Tai Hsieh, and Nicholas Li, "International Prices, Costs, and Markup Differences," *American Economic Review* 101 (October 2011), pp. 2450–2486; Mario J. Crucini and Anthony Landry, "Accounting for Real Exchange Rates Using Micro-Data," Working Paper 17812, National Bureau of Economic Research, February 2012; and the paper by Goldberg and Knetter in Further Readings.

[7]The price level measures in Figure 16-2 are index numbers, not dollar amounts. For example, the U.S. consumer price index (CPI) was 100 in the base year 2000 and only about 50 in 1980, so the dollar price of a reference commodity basket of typical U.S. consumption purchases doubled between 1980 and 2000. For Figure 16-2, base years for the U.S. and Japanese price indexes were chosen so that their 1980 ratio would equal the 1980 exchange rate, but this imposed equality does not mean that absolute PPP held in 1980. Although Figure 16-2 uses CPIs, other price indexes lead to similar pictures.

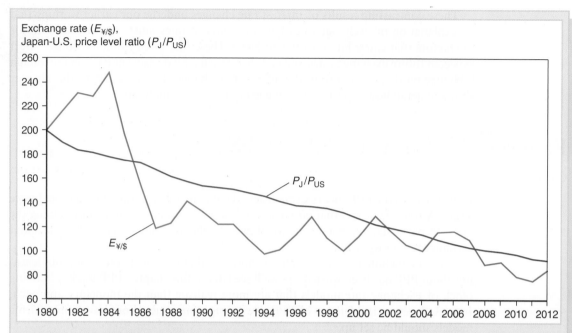

FIGURE 16-2   MyEconLab Real-time data

The Yen/Dollar Exchange Rate and Relative Japan–U.S. Price Levels, 1980–2012

The graph shows that relative PPP does not track the yen/dollar exchange rate during 1980–2012.

Source: IMF, *International Financial Statistics*. Exchange rates and price levels are end-of-year data.

United States, relative PPP suggests that the dollar should have *de*preciated instead. The same inflation trends continued after the mid-1980s, but the yen then appreciated by far more than the amount that PPP would have predicted. Only over fairly long periods is relative PPP approximately satisfied. In view of the lengthy departures from PPP in between, however, that theory appears to be of limited use even as a long-run explanation.

Studies of other currencies largely confirm the results in Figure 16-2. Relative PPP has not held up well.[8] As you will learn later in this book, between the end of World War II in 1945 and the early 1970s, exchange rates were fixed within narrow, internationally agreed-upon margins through the intervention of central banks in the foreign exchange market. During that period of fixed exchange rates, PPP did not do too badly. However, during the first half of the 1920s, when many exchange rates were market-determined as in the 1970s and after, important deviations from relative PPP occurred, just as in recent decades.[9]

---

[8]See, for example, the paper by Taylor and Taylor in this chapter's Further Readings.

[9]See Paul R. Krugman, "Purchasing Power Parity and Exchange Rates: Another Look at the Evidence," *Journal of International Economics* 8 (August 1978), pp. 397–407; Paul De Grauwe, Marc Janssens, and Hilde Leliaert, *Real-Exchange-Rate Variability from 1920 to 1926 and 1973 to 1982*, Princeton Studies in International Finance 56 (International Finance Section, Department of Economics, Princeton University, September 1985); and Hans Genberg, "Purchasing Power Parity under Fixed and Flexible Exchange Rates," *Journal of International Economics* 8 (May 1978), pp. 247–276.

Explaining the Problems with PPP

What explains the negative empirical results described in the previous section? There are several immediate problems with our rationale for the PPP theory of exchange rates, which was based on the law of one price:

1. Contrary to the assumption of the law of one price, transport costs and restrictions on trade certainly do exist. These trade barriers may be high enough to prevent some goods and services from being traded between countries.

2. Monopolistic or oligopolistic practices in goods markets may interact with transport costs and other trade barriers to weaken further the link between the prices of similar goods sold in different countries.

3. Because the inflation data reported in different countries are based on different commodity baskets, there is no reason for exchange rate changes to offset official measures of inflation differences, even when there are no barriers to trade and all products are tradable.

Trade Barriers and Nontradables

Transport costs and governmental trade restrictions make it expensive to move goods between markets located in different countries and therefore weaken the law of one price mechanism underlying PPP. Suppose once again that the same sweater sells for $45 in New York and for £30 in London, but that it costs $2 to ship a sweater between the two cities. At an exchange rate of $1.45 per pound, the dollar price of a London sweater is ($1.45 per pound) × (£30) = $43.50 but an American importer would have to pay $43.50 + $2 = $45.50 to purchase the sweater in London and get it to New York. At an exchange rate of $1.45 per pound, it therefore would not pay to ship sweaters from London to New York even though their dollar price would be higher in the latter location. Similarly, at an exchange rate of $1.55 per pound, an American exporter would lose money by shipping sweaters from New York to London even though the New York price of $45 would then be below the dollar price of the sweater in London, $46.50.

The lesson of this example is that transport costs sever the close link between exchange rates and goods prices implied by the law of one price. The greater the transport costs, the greater the range over which the exchange rate can move, given goods prices in different countries. Official trade restrictions such as tariffs have a similar effect, because a fee paid to the customs inspector affects the importer's profit in the same way as an equivalent shipping fee. Either type of trade impediment weakens the basis of PPP by allowing the purchasing power of a given currency to differ more widely from country to country. For example, in the presence of trade impediments, a dollar need not go as far in London as in Chicago—and it doesn't, as anyone who has ever been to London has found out.

As you will recall from the theory of international trade, transport costs may be so large relative to the cost of producing some goods and services that those items can never be traded internationally at a profit. Such goods and services are called *nontradables*. The time-honored classroom example of a nontradable is the haircut. A Frenchman desiring an American haircut would have to transport himself to the United States or transport an American barber to France; in either case, the cost of transport is so large relative to the price of the service being purchased that (tourists excepted) French haircuts are consumed only by residents of France while American haircuts are consumed only by residents of the United States.

The existence in all countries of nontraded goods and services, whose prices are not linked internationally, allows systematic deviations even from relative PPP. Because the price of a nontradable is determined entirely by its *domestic* supply and demand curves, shifts in those curves may cause the domestic price of a broad commodity basket to change relative to the foreign price of the same basket. Other things equal, a rise in the price of a country's nontradables will raise its price level relative to foreign price levels (measuring all countries' price levels in terms of a single currency). Looked at another way, the purchasing power of any given currency will fall in countries where the prices of nontradables rise.

Each country's price level includes a wide variety of nontradables, including (along with haircuts) routine medical treatment, dance instruction, and housing, among others. Broadly speaking, we can identify traded goods with manufactured products, raw materials, and agricultural products. Nontradables are primarily services and the outputs of the construction industry. There are, naturally, exceptions to this rule. For example, financial services provided by banks and brokerage houses often can be traded internationally. (The rise of the Internet, in particular, has expanded the range of tradable services.) In addition, trade restrictions, if sufficiently severe, can cause goods that would normally be traded to become nontraded. Thus, in most countries, some manufactures are nontraded.

We can get a rough idea of the importance of nontradables in the American economy by looking at the contribution of the service industries to U.S. GNP. In recent years, services have accounted for around 75 percent of the value of U.S. output. While services tend to have smaller shares in poorer economies, nontradables make up an important component of GNP everywhere. Nontradables help explain the wide departures from relative PPP illustrated by Figure 16-2.

Departures from Free Competition

When trade barriers and imperfectly competitive market structures occur together, linkages between national price levels are weakened further. An extreme case occurs when a single firm sells a commodity for different prices in different markets.

When a firm sells the same product for different prices in different markets, we say that it is practicing **pricing to market**. Pricing to market may reflect different demand conditions in different countries. For example, countries where demand is more price-inelastic will tend to be charged higher markups over a monopolistic seller's production cost. Empirical studies of firm-level export data have yielded strong evidence of pervasive pricing to market in manufacturing trade.[10]

In 2011, for example, a Volkswagen Passat cost $4,000 more in Austria than in Ireland despite those countries' shared currency (the euro) and despite the European Union's efforts over many years to remove intra-European trade barriers (see Chapter 21). Such price differentials would be difficult to enforce if it were not costly for consumers to buy autos in Ireland and drive or ship them to Austria or if consumers viewed cheaper cars available in Austria as good substitutes for the Passat. The combination of product differentiation and segmented markets, however, leads to large violations

---

[10]For a detailed review of the evidence, see the paper by Goldberg and Knetter in this chapter's Further Readings. Theoretical contributions on pricing to market include Rudiger Dornbusch, "Exchange Rates and Prices," *American Economic Review* 77 (March 1987), pp. 93–106; Paul R. Krugman, "Pricing to Market When the Exchange Rate Changes," in Sven W. Arndt and J. David Richardson, eds., *Real-Financial Linkages among Open Economies* (Cambridge, MA: MIT Press, 1987); and Andrew Atkeson and Ariel Burstein, "Pricing-to-Market, Trade Costs, and International Relative Prices," *American Economic Review* 98 (December 2008), pp. 1998–2031.

of the law of one price and absolute PPP. Shifts in market structure and demand over time can invalidate relative PPP.

Differences in Consumption Patterns and Price Level Measurement

Government measures of the price level differ from country to country. One reason for these differences is that people living in different countries spend their incomes in different ways. In general, people consume relatively higher proportions of their own country's products—including its tradable products—than of foreign-made products. The average Norwegian consumes more reindeer meat than her American counterpart, the average Japanese more sushi, and the average Indian more chutney. In constructing a reference commodity basket to measure purchasing power, it is therefore likely that the Norwegian government will put a relatively high weight on reindeer, the Japanese government a high weight on sushi, and the Indian government a high weight on chutney.

SOME MEATY EVIDENCE ON THE LAW OF ONE PRICE

In the summer of 1986, the *Economist* magazine conducted an extensive survey on the prices of Big Mac hamburgers at McDonald's restaurants throughout the world. This apparently whimsical undertaking was not the result of an outbreak of editorial giddiness. Rather, the magazine wanted to poke fun at economists who confidently declare exchange rates to be "overvalued" or "undervalued" on the basis of PPP comparisons. Since Big Macs are "sold in 41 countries, with only the most trivial changes of recipe," the magazine argued, a comparison of hamburger prices should serve as a "medium-rare guide to whether currencies are trading at the right exchange rates."* Since 1986, the *Economist* has periodically updated its calculations.

One way of interpreting the *Economist* survey is as a test of the law of one price. Viewed in this way, the results of the initial test were quite startling. The dollar prices of Big Macs turned out to be wildly different in different countries. For example, the price of a Big Mac in New York was 50 percent higher than in Australia and 64 percent higher than in Hong Kong. In contrast, a Parisian Big Mac cost 54 percent more than its New York counterpart, and a Tokyo Big Mac cost 50 percent more. Only in Britain and Ireland were the dollar prices of the burgers close to New York levels.

How can this dramatic violation of the law of one price be explained? As the *Economist* noted, transport costs and government regulations are part of the explanation. Product differentiation is probably an important additional factor. Because relatively few close substitutes for Big Macs are available in some countries, product differentiation may give McDonald's some power to tailor prices to the local market. Finally, remember that the price of a Big Mac must cover not only the cost of ground meat and buns, but also the wages of serving people, rent, electricity, and so on. The prices of these nonfood inputs can differ sharply in different countries. Indeed, the *Economist* has now

*"On the Hamburger Standard," *Economist*, September 6–12, 1986.

(Continued)

introduced a refined version of their index that corrects for the fact that labor costs tend to be lower in poorer countries.**

We have reproduced the results of the *Economist*'s January 2013 survey report. The table shows various countries' prices of Big Macs,

The hamburger standard					
	Big Mac prices		**Implied PPP*** of the dollar	**Actual exchange rate: January 30th**	**Under (−)/over(+) Valuation against the dollar, %**
	in local currency	**in dollars**			
United States	$4.37	4.37	1.00	1.00	0.0
Argentina	Peso 19.00	3.82	4.35	4.98	−12.6
Australia	A$4.70	4.90	1.08	0.96	12.2
Brazil	Real 11.25	5.64	2.58	1.99	29.2
Britain	£2.69	4.25	0.62	0.63	−2.7
Canada	C$5.41	5.39	1.24	1.00	23.5
Chile	Peso 2,050.00	4.35	469.39	471.75	−0.5
China	Yuan 16.00	2.57	3.66	6.22	−41.1
Czech Republic	Koruna 70.33	3.72	16.10	18.89	−14.8
Denmark	DK 28.50	5.18	6.53	5.50	18.7
Egypt	Pound 16.00	2.39	3.66	6.69	−45.2
Euro area	€3.59	4.88	0.82	0.74	11.7
Hong Kong	HK$ 17.00	2.19	3.89	7.76	−49.8
Hungary	Forint 830.00	3.82	190.04	217.47	−12.6
Indonesia	Rupiah 27,939.00	2.86	6,397.18	9,767.50	−34.5
Israel	Shekel 14.90	4.00	3.41	3.72	−8.4
Japan	¥320.00	3.51	73.27	91.07	−19.5
Malaysia	Ringgit 7.95	2.58	1.82	3.08	−41.0
Mexico	Peso 37.00	2.90	8.47	12.74	−33.5
New Zealand	NZ$5.20	4.32	1.19	1.20	−1.0
Norway	Kroner 43.00	7.84	9.84	5.48	79.6
Peru	Sol 10.00	3.91	2.29	2.56	−10.5
Philippines	Peso 118.00	2.91	27.02	40.60	−33.5
Poland	Zloty 9.10	2.94	2.08	3.09	−32.6
Russia	Ruble 72.88	2.43	16.69	30.05	−44.5
Saudi Arabia	Riyal 11.00	2.93	2.52	3.75	−32.8
Singapore	S$4.50	3.64	1.03	1.23	−16.6
South Africa	Rand 18.33	2.03	4.20	9.05	−53.6
South Korea	Won 3,700.00	3.41	847.19	1,085.48	−22.0
Sweden	SKR 48.40	7.62	11.08	6.35	74.5
Switzerland	CHF 6.50	7.12	1.49	0.91	63.1
Taiwan	NT$75.00	2.54	17.17	29.50	−41.8
Thailand	Baht 87.00	2.92	19.92	29.76	−33.1
Turkey	Lire 8.45	4.78	1.93	1.77	9.4

*Purchasing power parity: local price divided by price in United States.

Sources: McDonald's; the *Economist*, January 2013 survey. Exchange rates are local currency per dollar.

**See the Big Mac index website at http://www.economist.com/content/big-mac-index, from which the data below are drawn.

measured in U.S. dollar terms. These range from a high of $7.84 in Norway (79.4 percent above the U.S. price) to only $2.19 in Hong Kong (half the U.S. price).

For each country, we can figure out a "Big Mac PPP," which is the hypothetical level of the exchange rate that would equate the dollar price of a locally sold Big Mac to its $4.37 U.S. price. For example, in January 2013 an American dollar cost only 5.48 kroner in the foreign exchange market, making the dollar price of a Norwegian Big Mac $7.84, quite bit higher than in the U.S. The exchange rate that would have equalized U.S. and Norwegian burger prices, however, was (43 kroner per burger)/(4.37 dollars per burger) = 9.84 kroner per dollar, an exchange rate making the kroner much cheaper in terms of dollars (and therefore making Norwegian burgers cheaper as well).

It is often said that a currency is overvalued when its exchange rate makes domestic goods expensive relative to similar goods sold abroad and undervalued in the opposite case. For the Norwegian krone, for example, the degree of overvaluation on the Big Mac scale is the percentage by which the hypothetical Big Mac PPP kroner price of the dollar exceeds the market rate, or

$$100 \times (9.84 - 5.48)/5.48 = 79.6 \text{ percent.}$$

Of course, apart from rounding error, this is the percentage by which the dollar price of a Norwegian burger exceeds that of a U.S. burger, and therefore the percentage by which the actual dollar price of a kroner exceeds the hypothetical Big Mac price.

Likewise, in January 2013 the dollar price of the Chinese yuan was 41.1 percent *below* the level needed to bring about burger price parity:

That country's currency was *under*valued by 41.1 percent, according to the Big Mac measure. China's currency would have had to appreciate substantially against the dollar to bring the Chinese and U.S. prices of Big Macs into line. Norway's currency, in contrast, would have had to depreciate substantially.

In general, a "PPP exchange rate" is defined as one that equates the international prices of some broad basket of goods and services, not just hamburgers. As we shall see, there are several reasons why we might expect PPP not to hold exactly, even over long periods. Thus, despite the widespread use of terms like *overvaluation*, policy makers have to be very cautious in judging whether any particular level of the exchange rate may signal the need for economic policy changes.

Policy makers would be wise, however, to take into account extremes of over- or undervaluation. Consider the case of Iceland. In January 2006, Iceland had a dollar Big Mac price of $7.44 and a whopping 131 percent currency overvaluation on the Big Mac scale. Then the tiny country was swept up in a global financial crisis that we will discuss in detail in Chapters 19 and 20. From around 68 kronur per dollar in 2006, the currency depreciated all the way to around 120 per dollar by 2010. Unlike many other countries, Iceland imports the burgers' ingredients, the kronur prices of which rose sharply because of the depreciation. The sudden cost increase made the franchise unprofitable without a big rise in prices to customers. But Iceland's economy had suffered severely in the crisis. Rather than boosting prices, the franchise owner closed all three of Iceland's McDonald's restaurants. As a result, the country no longer appears in the *Economist*'s survey.[†]

[†]See Omar R. Valdimarsson, "McDonald's Closes in Iceland after Krona Collapse," Bloomberg News, October 26, 2009. Available at http://www.bloomberg.com/apps/ news?pid=newsarchive&sid=amu4.WTVaqjI

Because relative PPP makes predictions about price *changes* rather than price *levels*, it is a sensible concept regardless of the baskets used to define price levels in the countries being compared. If all U.S. prices increase by 10 percent and the dollar depreciates against foreign currencies by 10 percent, relative PPP will be satisfied (assuming there are no changes abroad) for any domestic and foreign choices of price level indexes.

Change in the relative prices of basket components, however, can cause relative PPP to fail tests that are based on official price indexes. For example, a rise in the relative price of fish would raise the dollar price of a Japanese government reference commodity basket relative to that of a U.S. government basket, simply because fish takes up a larger share of the Japanese basket. Relative price changes could lead to PPP violations like those shown in Figure 16-2 even if trade were free and costless.

PPP in the Short Run and in the Long Run

The factors we have examined so far in explaining the PPP theory's poor empirical performance can cause national price levels to diverge even in the long run, after all prices have had time to adjust to their market-clearing levels. As we discussed in Chapter 15, however, many prices in the economy are sticky and take time to adjust fully. Departures from PPP may therefore be even greater in the short run than in the long run.

An abrupt depreciation of the dollar against foreign currencies, for example, makes farm equipment in the United States cheaper relative to similar equipment produced abroad. As farmers throughout the world shift their demand for tractors and reapers to U.S. producers, the price of American farm equipment tends to rise to reduce the divergence from the law of one price caused by the dollar's depreciation. It takes time for this process of price increase to be complete, however, and prices for U.S. and foreign farm equipment may differ considerably while markets adjust to the exchange rate change.

You might suspect that short-run price stickiness and exchange rate volatility help explain a phenomenon we noted in discussing Figure 16-2—that violations of relative PPP have been much more flagrant over periods when exchange rates have floated. Empirical research supports this interpretation of the data. Figure 15-11, which we used to illustrate the stickiness of goods prices compared with exchange rates, is quite typical of floating-rate episodes. In a careful study covering many countries and historical episodes, economist Michael Mussa compared the extent of short-run deviations from PPP under fixed and floating exchange rates. He found that floating exchange rates systematically lead to much larger and more frequent short-run deviations from relative PPP.[11] The box on pages 467–468 provides an especially vivid illustration of how price stickiness can generate violations of the law of one price even for absolutely identical goods.

Recent research suggests that short-run deviations from PPP such as those due to volatile exchange rates die away over time, with only half the effect of a temporary departure from PPP remaining after four years.[12] Even when these temporary PPP deviations are removed from the data, however, it still appears that the cumulative effect of certain long-run trends causes predictable departures from PPP for many countries. The Case Study entitled "Why Price Levels Are Lower in Poorer Countries" discusses one of the major mechanisms behind such trends.

---

[11]See Mussa, "Nominal Exchange Rate Regimes and the Behavior of Real Exchange Rates: Evidence and Implications," in Karl Brunner and Allan H. Meltzer, eds., *Real Business Cycles, Real Exchange Rates and Actual Policies*, Carnegie-Rochester Conference Series on Public Policy 25 (Amsterdam: North-Holland, 1986), pp. 117–214. Charles Engel of the University of Wisconsin has found that under a floating exchange rate, international price differences for the same good can be more variable than the relative price of different goods within a single country. See Engel, "Real Exchange Rates and Relative Prices: An Empirical Investigation," *Journal of Monetary Economics* 32 (August 1993), pp. 35–50. Also see Gopinath, Gourinchas, Hsieh, and Li, *op. cit.* (footnote 6).

[12]See, for example, Jeffrey A. Frankel and Andrew K. Rose, "A Panel Project on Purchasing Power Parity: Mean Reversion within and between Countries," *Journal of International Economics* 40 (February 1996), pp. 209–224. The statistical validity of these results is challenged by Paul G. J. O'Connell in "The Overvaluation of Purchasing Power Parity," *Journal of International Economics* 44 (February 1998), pp. 1–19.

CASE STUDY

Why Price Levels Are Lower in Poorer Countries

Research on international price level differences has uncovered a striking empirical regularity: When expressed in terms of a single currency, countries' price levels are positively related to the level of real income per capita. In other words, a dollar, when converted to local currency at the market exchange rate, generally goes much further in a poor country than in a rich one. Figure 16-3 illustrates the relation between price levels and income, with each dot representing a different country.

The previous section's discussion of the role of nontraded goods in the determination of national price levels suggests that international variations in the prices of nontradables may contribute to price level discrepancies between rich and poor nations. The available data indeed show that nontradables tend to be more expensive (relative to tradables) in richer countries.

One reason for the lower relative price of nontradables in poor countries was suggested by Bela Balassa and Paul Samuelson.[13] The Balassa-Samuelson theory

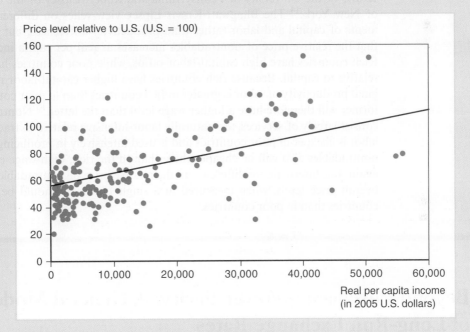

FIGURE 16-3

Price Levels and Real Incomes, 2010

Countries' price levels tend to rise as their real incomes rise. Each dot represents a country. The straight line indicates a statistician's best prediction of a country's price level relative to that of the United States based on knowing its real per capita income.

Source: Penn World Table, version 7.1.

---

[13]See Balassa, "The Purchasing Power Parity Doctrine: A Reappraisal," *Journal of Political Economy* 72 (December 1964), pp. 584–596; and Samuelson, "Theoretical Notes on Trade Problems," *Review of Economics and Statistics* 46 (May 1964), pp. 145–154. The Balassa-Samuelson theory was foreshadowed by some observations of Ricardo. See Jacob Viner, *Studies in the Theory of International Trade* (New York: Harper & Brothers, 1937), p. 315.

assumes the labor forces of poor countries are less productive than those of rich countries in the tradables sector but international productivity differences in nontradables are negligible. If the prices of traded goods are roughly equal in all countries, however, lower labor productivity in the tradables industries of poor countries implies lower wages than abroad, lower production costs in nontradables, and therefore a lower price of nontradables. Rich countries with higher labor productivity in the tradables sector will tend to have higher nontradables prices and higher price levels. Productivity statistics give some empirical support to the Balassa-Samuelson differential productivity postulate. And it is plausible that international productivity differences are sharper in traded than in nontraded goods. Whether a country is rich or poor, a barber can give only so many haircuts in a week, but there may be a significant scope for productivity differences across countries in the manufacture of traded goods like personal computers.

An alternative theory that attempts to explain the lower price levels of poor countries was put forth by Jagdish Bhagwati of Columbia University, and by Irving Kravis of the University of Pennsylvania and Robert Lipsey of the City University of New York.[14] The Bhagwati-Kravis-Lipsey view relies on differences in endowments of capital and labor rather than productivity differences, but it also predicts that the relative price of nontradables increases as real per capita income increases. Rich countries have high capital-labor ratios, while poor countries have more labor relative to capital. Because rich countries have higher capital-labor ratios, the marginal productivity of labor is greater in rich countries than in poor countries, and the former will therefore have a higher wage level than the latter.[15] Nontradables, which consist largely of services, are naturally labor-intensive relative to tradables. Because labor is cheaper in poor countries and is used intensively in producing nontradables, nontradables also will be cheaper there than in the rich, high-wage countries. Once again, this international difference in the relative price of nontradables suggests that overall price levels, when measured in a single currency, should be higher in rich countries than in poor countries.

Beyond Purchasing Power Parity: A General Model of Long-Run Exchange Rates

Why devote so much discussion to the purchasing power parity theory when it is fraught with exceptions and apparently contradicted by the data? We examined the implications of PPP so closely because its basic idea of relating long-run exchange rates to long-run national price levels is a very useful starting point. The monetary approach presented previously, which assumed PPP, is too simple to give accurate

---

[14]See Kravis and Lipsey, *Toward an Explanation of National Price Levels*, Princeton Studies in International Finance 52 (International Finance Section, Department of Economics, Princeton University, November 1983); and Bhagwati, "Why Are Services Cheaper in the Poor Countries?" *Economic Journal* 94 (June 1984), pp. 279–286.

[15]This argument assumes that factor endowment differences between rich and poor countries are sufficiently great that factor-price equalization cannot hold.

predictions about the real world, but we can generalize it by taking account of some of the reasons why PPP predicts badly in practice. In this section, we do just that.

The long-run analysis below continues to ignore short-run complications caused by sticky prices. An understanding of how exchange rates behave in the long run is, as mentioned earlier, a prerequisite for the more complicated short-run analysis that we undertake in the next chapter.

The Real Exchange Rate

As the first step in extending the PPP theory, we define the concept of a **real exchange rate**. The real exchange rate between two countries' currencies is a broad summary measure of the prices of one country's goods and services relative to the other country's. It is natural to introduce the real exchange rate concept at this point because the major prediction of PPP is that real exchange rates never change, at least not permanently. To extend our model so that it describes the world more accurately, we need to examine systematically the forces that can cause dramatic and permanent changes in real exchange rates.

As we will see, real exchange rates are important not only for quantifying deviations from PPP but also for analyzing macroeconomic demand and supply conditions in open economies. When we wish to differentiate a real exchange rate—which is the relative price of two output baskets—from a relative price of two currencies, we will refer to the latter as a **nominal exchange rate**. But when there is no risk of confusion, we will continue to use the shorter term, *exchange rate*, to refer to nominal exchange rates.

Real exchange rates are defined in terms of nominal exchange rates and price levels. Before we can give a more precise definition of real exchange rates, however, we need to clarify the price level measure we will be using. Let P_{US}, as usual, be the price level in the United States, and P_E the price level in Europe. Since we will not be assuming absolute PPP (as we did in our discussion of the monetary approach), we no longer assume the price level can be measured by the same basket of commodities in the United States as in Europe. Because we will soon want to link our analysis to monetary factors, we require instead that each country's price index give a good representation of the purchases that motivate its residents to demand its money supply.

No measure of the price level does this perfectly, but we must settle on some definition before we can formally define the real exchange rate. To be concrete, you can think of P_{US} as the dollar price of an unchanging basket containing the typical weekly purchases of U.S. households and firms; P_E, similarly, is based on an unchanging basket reflecting the typical weekly purchases of European households and firms. The point to remember is that *the U.S. price level will place a relatively heavy weight on commodities produced and consumed in America, and the European price level a relatively heavy weight on commodities produced and consumed in Europe.*[16]

Having described the reference commodity baskets used to measure price levels, we now formally define the *real dollar/euro exchange rate*, denoted $q_{\$/\euro}$, as the dollar price of the European basket relative to that of the American basket. We can express the real exchange rate as the dollar value of Europe's price level divided by the U.S. price level or, in symbols, as

$$q_{\$/\euro} = (E_{\$/\euro} \times P_E)/P_{US}. \tag{16-6}$$

---

[16]Nontradables are one important factor behind the relative preference for home products.

A numerical example will clarify the concept of the real exchange rate. Imagine the European reference commodity basket costs €100 (so that P_E = €100 per European basket), the U.S. basket costs $120 (so that P_{US} = $120 per U.S. basket), and the nominal exchange rate is $E_{\$/€}$ = $1.20 per euro. The real dollar/euro exchange rate would then be

$$q_{\$/€} = \frac{(\$1.20 \text{ per euro}) \times (€100 \text{ per European basket})}{(\$120 \text{ per U.S. basket})}$$

$$= (\$120 \text{ per European basket})/(\$120 \text{ per U.S. basket})$$

$$= 1 \text{ U.S. basket per European basket.}$$

A rise in the real dollar/euro exchange rate $q_{\$/€}$, (which we call a **real depreciation** of the dollar against the euro) can be thought of in several equivalent ways. Most obviously, (16-6) shows this change to be a fall in the purchasing power of a dollar within Europe's borders relative to its purchasing power within the United States. This change in relative purchasing power occurs because the dollar prices of European goods ($E_{\$/€} \times P_E$) rise relative to those of U.S. goods (P_{US}).

In terms of our numerical example, a 10 percent nominal dollar depreciation, to $E_{\$/€}$ = $1.32 per euro, causes $q_{\$/€}$ to rise to 1.1 U.S. baskets per European basket, a *real* dollar depreciation of 10 percent against the euro. (The same change in $q_{\$/€}$ could result from a 10 percent rise in P_E or a 10 percent fall in P_{US}.) The real depreciation means the dollar's purchasing power over European goods and services falls by 10 percent relative to its purchasing power over U.S. goods and services.

Alternatively, even though many of the items entering national price levels are nontraded, it is useful to think of the real exchange rate $q_{\$/€}$ as the relative price of European products in general in terms of American products, that is, the price at which hypothetical trades of American for European commodity baskets would occur if trades at domestic prices were possible. The dollar is considered to *depreciate* in real terms against the euro when $q_{\$/€}$ rises because the hypothetical purchasing power of America's products in general over Europe's declines. America's goods and services thus become cheaper relative to Europe's.

A **real appreciation** of the dollar against the euro is a fall in $q_{\$/€}$. This fall indicates a decrease in the relative price of products purchased in Europe, or a rise in the dollar's European purchasing power compared with that in the United States.[17]

Our convention for describing real depreciations and appreciations of the dollar against the euro is the same one we use for nominal exchange rates (that is, $E_{\$/€}$ up is a dollar depreciation, $E_{\$/€}$ down is an appreciation). Equation (16-6) shows that at *unchanged* output prices, nominal depreciation (appreciation) implies real depreciation (appreciation). Our discussion of real exchange rate changes thus includes, as a special case, an observation we made in Chapter 14: With the domestic money prices of goods held constant, a nominal dollar depreciation makes U.S. goods cheaper compared with foreign goods, while a nominal dollar appreciation makes them more expensive.

Equation (16-6) makes it easy to see why the real exchange rate can never change when relative PPP holds. Under relative PPP, a 10 percent rise in $E_{\$/€}$, for instance, would always be exactly offset by a 10 percent fall in the price level ratio P_E/P_{US}, leaving $q_{\$/€}$ unchanged.

---

[17]This is true because $E_{\$/€} = 1/E_{€/\$}$, implying that a real depreciation of the dollar against the euro is the same as a real appreciation of the euro against the dollar (that is, a rise in the purchasing power of the euro within the United States relative to its purchasing power within Europe, or a fall in the relative price of American products in terms of European products).

Demand, Supply, and the Long-Run Real Exchange Rate

It should come as no surprise that in a world where PPP does not hold, the long-run values of real exchange rates—just like other relative prices that clear markets—depend on demand and supply conditions. Since a real exchange rate tracks changes in the relative price of two countries' expenditure baskets, however, conditions in *both* countries matter. Changes in countries' output markets can be complex, and we do not want to digress into an exhaustive (and exhausting) catalogue of the possibilities. We focus instead on two specific cases that are both easy to grasp and important in practice for explaining why the long-run values of real exchange rates can change.

1. *A change in world relative demand for American products.* Imagine total world spending on American goods and services rises relative to total world spending on European goods and services. Such a change could arise from several sources—for example, a shift in private U.S. demand away from European goods and toward American goods; a similar shift in private foreign demand toward American goods; or an increase in U.S. government demand falling primarily on U.S. output. Any increase in relative world demand for U.S. products causes an excess demand for them at the previous real exchange rate. To restore equilibrium, the relative price of American output in terms of European output will therefore have to rise: The relative prices of U.S. nontradables will rise, and the prices of tradables produced in the United States, and consumed intensively there, will rise relative to the prices of tradables made in Europe. These changes all work to reduce $q_{\$/\unicode{x20AC}}$, the relative price of Europe's reference expenditure basket in terms of the United States'.

STICKY PRICES AND THE LAW OF ONE PRICE: EVIDENCE FROM SCANDINAVIAN DUTY-FREE SHOPS

Sticky nominal prices and wages are central to macroeconomic theories, but just why might it be difficult for money prices to change from day to day as market conditions change? One reason is based on the idea of "menu costs." Menu costs could arise from several factors, such as the actual costs of printing new price lists and catalogs. In addition, firms may perceive a different type of menu cost due to their customers' imperfect information about competitors' prices. When a firm raises its price, some customers will shop around elsewhere and find it convenient to remain with a competing seller even if all sellers have raised their prices. In the presence of these various types of menu costs, sellers will often hold prices constant after a change in market conditions until they are certain the change is permanent enough to make incurring the costs of price changes worthwhile.*

If there were truly no barriers between two markets with goods priced in different currencies, sticky prices would be unable to survive in the face of an exchange rate change. All buyers would simply flock to the market where a good had become cheaper. But when some trade impediments exist, deviations from the law of one price do not induce unlimited arbitrage, so it is feasible for sellers to hold prices constant despite exchange rate changes. In the real world, trade barriers appear to be significant, widespread, and often subtle in nature.

Apparently, arbitrage between two markets may be limited even when the physical distance between them is zero, as a surprising study of pricing behavior in Scandinavian duty-free outlets shows. Swedish economists Marcus Asplund and Richard Friberg studied pricing behavior in the duty-free stores of two Scandinavian ferry

*It is when economic conditions are very volatile that prices seem to become most flexible. For example, restaurant menus will typically price their catch of the day at "market" so that the price charged (and the fish offered) can reflect the high variability in fishing outcomes.

(Continued)

lines whose catalogs quote the prices of each good in several currencies for the convenience of customers from different countries.[†] Since it is costly to print the catalogs, they are reissued with revised prices only from time to time. In the interim, however, fluctuations in exchange rates induce multiple, changing prices for the *same* good. For example, on the Birka Line of ferries between Sweden and Finland, prices were listed in both Finnish markka and Swedish kronor between 1975 and 1998, implying that a relative depreciation of the markka would make it cheaper to buy cigarettes or vodka by paying markka rather than kronor.

Despite such price discrepancies, Birka Line was always able to do business in both currencies—passengers did not rush to buy at the lowest price. Swedish passengers, who held relatively large quantities of their own national currency, tended to buy at the kronor prices, whereas Finnish customers tended to buy at the markka prices.

Often, Birka Line would take advantage of publishing a new catalog to reduce deviations from the law of one price. The average deviation from the law of one price in the month just before such a price adjustment was 7.21 percent, but only 2.22 percent in the month of the price adjustment. One big impediment to taking advantage of the arbitrage opportunities was the cost of changing currencies at the onboard foreign exchange booth—roughly 7.5 percent. That transaction cost, given different passengers' currency preferences at the time of embarkation, acted as an effective trade barrier.[‡]

Surprisingly, Birka Line did not completely eliminate law of one price deviations when it changed catalog prices. Instead, Birka Line practiced a kind of pricing to market on its ferries. Usually, exporters who price to market discriminate among different consumers based on their different locations, but Birka was able to discriminate based on different nationality and currency preferences, even with all potential consumers located on the same ferry boat.

[†]"The Law of One Price in Scandinavian Duty-Free Stores," *American Economic Review* 91 (September 2001), pp. 1072–1083.

[‡]Customers could pay in the currency of their choice not only with cash, but also with credit cards, which involve lower foreign exchange conversion fees but convert at an exchange rate prevailing a few days after the purchase of the goods. Asplund and Friberg suggest that for such small purchases, uncertainty and the costs of calculating relative prices (in addition to the credit-card exchange fees) might have been a sufficient deterrent to transacting in a relatively unfamiliar currency.

We conclude that *an increase in world relative demand for U.S. output causes a long-run real appreciation of the dollar against the euro (a fall in $q_{\$/\euro}$). Similarly, a decrease in world relative demand for U.S. output causes a long-run real depreciation of the dollar against the euro (a rise in $q_{\$/\euro}$).*

2. *A change in relative output supply.* Suppose the productive efficiency of U.S. labor and capital rises. Since Americans spend part of their increased income on foreign goods, the supplies of all types of U.S. goods and services increase relative to the demand for them, the result being an excess relative supply of American output at the previous real exchange rate. A fall in the relative price of American products—both nontradables and tradables—shifts demand toward them and eliminates the excess supply. This price change is a real depreciation of the dollar against the euro, that is, an increase in $q_{\$/\euro}$. *A relative expansion of U.S. output causes a long-run real depreciation of the dollar against the euro ($q_{\$/\euro}$ rises). A relative expansion of European output causes a long-run real appreciation of the dollar against the euro ($q_{\$/\euro}$ falls).*[18]

---

[18]Our discussion of the Balassa-Samuelson effect in the Case Study on pages 463–464 would lead you to expect that a productivity increase concentrated in the U.S. tradables sector might cause the dollar to appreciate, rather than depreciate, in real terms against the euro. In the last paragraph, however, we have in mind a balanced productivity increase that benefits the traded and nontraded sectors in equal proportion, thus resulting in a real dollar depreciation by causing a drop in the prices of nontraded goods and in those of traded goods that are more important in America's consumer price index than in Europe's.

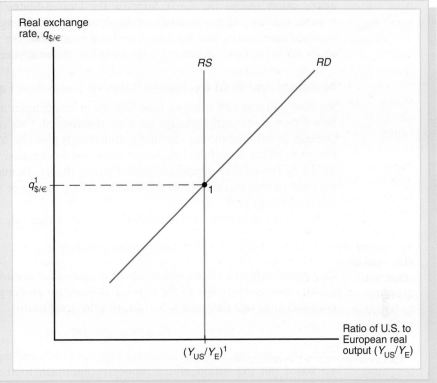

FIGURE 16-4

Determination of the Long-Run Real Exchange Rate

The long-run equilibrium real exchange rate equates world relative demand to the full-employment level of relative supply.

A useful diagram summarizes our discussion of demand, supply, and the long-run real exchange rate. In Figure 16-4, the supply of U.S. output relative to European output, Y_{US}/Y_E, is plotted along the horizontal axis while the real dollar/euro exchange rate, $q_{\$/\in}$, is plotted along the vertical axis.

The equilibrium real exchange rate is determined by the intersection of two schedules. The upward-sloping schedule RD shows that the relative demand for U.S. products in general, relative to the demand for European products, rises as $q_{\$/\in}$ rises, that is, as American products become relatively cheaper. This "demand" curve for U.S. relative to European goods has a positive slope because we are measuring a *fall* in the relative price of U.S. goods by a move *upward* along the vertical axis. What about relative supply? In the long run, relative national output levels are determined by factor supplies and productivity, with little, if any, effect on the real exchange rate. The relative supply curve, RS, therefore is vertical at the long-run (that is, full-employment) relative output ratio, $(Y_{US}/Y_E)^1$. The equilibrium long-run real exchange rate is the one that sets relative demand equal to long-run relative supply (point 1).[19]

The diagram easily illustrates how changes in world markets affect the real exchange rate. Suppose world gasoline prices fall, making American sport-utility vehicles more desirable for people everywhere. This change would be a rise in world relative demand for American goods and would shift RD to the right, causing $q_{\$/\in}$ to fall (a real dollar

---

[19]Notice that these RD and RS schedules differ from the ones used in Chapter 6. The earlier ones referred to relative world demand for and supply of two products that could be produced in either of two countries. In contrast, the RD and RS curves in this chapter refer to the relative world demand for and supply of one country's overall output (its GDP) relative to another's.

appreciation against the euro). Suppose the United States improves its health-care system, reducing illness throughout the American workforce. If workers are able to produce more goods and services in an hour as a result, the rise in U.S. productivity shifts RS to the right, causing $q_{\$/€}$ to rise (a real dollar depreciation against the euro).

Nominal and Real Exchange Rates in Long-Run Equilibrium

We now pull together what we have learned in this chapter and the last one to show how long-run nominal exchange rates are determined. One central conclusion is that changes in national money supplies and demands give rise to the proportional long-run movements in nominal exchange rates and international price level ratios predicted by the relative purchasing power parity theory. Demand and supply shifts in national output markets, however, cause nominal exchange rate movements that do not conform to PPP.

Recall our definition of the real dollar/euro exchange rate as

$$q_{\$/€} = (E_{\$/€} \times P_E)/P_{US}.$$

(See equation (16-6).) If we now solve this equation for the nominal exchange rate, we get an equation that gives us the nominal dollar/euro exchange rate as the real dollar/euro exchange rate times the U.S.–Europe price level ratio:

$$E_{\$/€} = q_{\$/€} \times (P_{US}/P_E). \tag{16-7}$$

Formally speaking, the only difference between (16-7) and equation (16-1), on which we based our exposition of the monetary approach to the exchange rate, is that (16-7) accounts for possible deviations from PPP by adding the *real* exchange rate as an additional determinant of the nominal exchange rate. *The equation implies that for a given real dollar/euro exchange rate, changes in money demand or supply in Europe or the United States affect the long-run nominal dollar/euro exchange rate as in the monetary approach. Changes in the long-run real exchange rate, however, also affect the long-run nominal exchange rate.* The long-run theory of exchange rate determination implied by equation (16-7) thus includes the valid elements of the monetary approach, but in addition it corrects the monetary approach by allowing for nonmonetary factors that can cause sustained deviations from purchasing power parity.

Assuming all variables start out at their long-run levels, we can now understand the most important determinants of long-run swings in nominal exchange rates:

1. *A shift in relative money supply levels.* Suppose the Fed wishes to stimulate the economy and therefore carries out an increase in the level of the U.S. money supply. As you will remember from Chapter 15, a permanent, one-time increase in a country's money supply has no effect on the long-run levels of output, the interest rate, or any relative price (including the real exchange rate). Thus, (16-3) implies once again that P_{US} rises in proportion to M_{US}, while (16-7) shows that the U.S. price level is the sole variable changing in the long run along with the nominal exchange rate $E_{\$/€}$. Because the real exchange rate $q_{\$/€}$ does not change, the nominal exchange rate change is consistent with relative PPP: The only long-run effect of the U.S. money supply increase is to raise all dollar prices, including the dollar price of the euro, in proportion to the increase in the money supply. It should be no surprise that this result is the same as the one we found using the monetary approach, since that approach is designed to account for the long-run effects of monetary changes.

2. *A shift in relative money supply growth rates.* Suppose the Fed concludes, to its dismay, that over the next few years the U.S. price level will fall. (A consistently falling price level is called *deflation.*) A permanent increase in the *growth rate* of the U.S. money supply raises the long-run U.S. inflation rate and, through the Fisher effect, raises the dollar interest rate relative to the euro interest rate. Because relative U.S. real money demand therefore declines, equation (16-3) implies that P_{US} rises (as shown in Figure 16-1). Because the change bringing this outcome about is purely monetary, however, it is neutral in its long-run effects; specifically, it does not alter the long-run *real* dollar/euro exchange rate. According to (16-7), then, $E_{\$/€}$ rises in proportion to the increase in P_{US} (a depreciation of the dollar against the euro). Once again, a purely monetary change brings about a long-run nominal exchange rate shift in line with relative PPP, just as the monetary approach predicted.

3. *A change in relative output demand.* This type of change is *not* covered by the monetary approach, so now the more general perspective we've developed, in which the real exchange rate can change, is essential. Since a change in relative output demand does not affect long-run national price levels—these depend solely on the factors appearing in equations (16-3) and (16-4)—the long-run nominal exchange rate in (16-7) will change only insofar as the real exchange rate changes. Consider an increase in world relative demand for U.S. products. Earlier in this section, we saw that a rise in demand for U.S. products causes a long-run real appreciation of the dollar against the euro (a fall in $q_{\$/€}$); this change is simply a rise in the relative price of U.S. output. Given that long-run national price levels are unchanged, however, (16-7) tells us that a long-run *nominal* appreciation of the dollar against the euro (a fall in $E_{\$/€}$) must also occur. This prediction highlights the important fact that even though exchange rates are nominal prices, they respond to nonmonetary as well as monetary events, even over long horizons.

4. *A change in relative output supply.* As we saw earlier in this section, an increase in relative U.S. output supply causes the dollar to depreciate in real terms against the euro, lowering the relative price of U.S. output. This rise in $q_{\$/€}$ is not, however, the only change in equation (16-7) implied by a relative rise in U.S. output. In addition, the U.S. output increase raises the transaction demand for real U.S. money balances, raising aggregate U.S. real money demand and, by (16-3), pushing the long-run U.S. price level down. Referring back to equation (16-7), you will see that since $q_{\$/€}$ rises while P_{US} falls, the output and money market effects of a change in output supply work in opposite directions, thus making the net effect on $E_{\$/€}$ is *ambiguous.* Our analysis of an output-supply change illustrates that even when a disturbance originates in a single market (in this case, the output market), its influence on exchange rates may depend on repercussion effects that are channeled through other markets.

We conclude that when all disturbances are monetary in nature, exchange rates obey relative PPP in the long run. In the long run, a monetary disturbance affects only the general purchasing power of a currency, and this change in purchasing power changes equally the currency's value in terms of domestic and foreign goods. When disturbances occur in output markets, the exchange rate is unlikely to obey relative PPP, even in the long run. Table 16-1 summarizes these conclusions regarding the effects of monetary and output market changes on long-run nominal exchange rates.

In the chapters that follow, we will appeal to this section's general long-run exchange rate model even when we are discussing *short-run* macroeconomic events. Long-run

TABLE 16-1	Effects of Money Market and Output Market Changes on the Long-Run Nominal Dollar/Euro Exchange Rate, $E_{\$/€}$
Change	**Effect on the Long-Run Nominal Dollar/Euro Exchange Rate, $E_{\$/€}$**
Money market	
1. Increase in U.S. money supply level	Proportional increase (nominal depreciation of $)
2. Increase in European money supply level	Proportional decrease (nominal depreciation of euro)
3. Increase in U.S. money supply growth rate	Increase (nominal depreciation of $)
4. Increase in European money supply growth rate	Decrease (nominal depreciation of euro)
Output market	
1. Increase in demand for U.S. output	Decrease (nominal appreciation of $)
2. Increase in demand for European output	Increase (nominal appreciation of euro)
3. Output supply increase in the United States	Ambiguous
4. Output supply increase in Europe	Ambiguous

factors are important in the short run because of the central role that expectations about the future play in the day-to-day determination of exchange rates. That is why news about the current account, for example, can have a big impact on the exchange rate. The long-run exchange rate model of this section will provide the anchor for market expectations, that is, the framework market participants use to forecast future exchange rates on the basis of information at hand today.

International Interest Rate Differences and the Real Exchange Rate

Earlier in this chapter, we saw that relative PPP, when combined with interest parity, implies that international interest rate differences equal differences in countries' expected inflation rates. Because relative PPP does not hold true in general, however, the relation between international interest rate differences and national inflation rates is likely to be more complex in practice than that simple formula suggests. Despite this complexity, economic policy makers who hope to influence exchange rates, as well as private individuals who wish to forecast them, cannot succeed without understanding the factors that cause countries' interest rates to differ.

In this section, we therefore extend our earlier discussion of the Fisher effect to include real exchange rate movements. We do this by showing that in general, interest rate differences between countries depend not only on differences in expected inflation, as the monetary approach asserts, but also on expected changes in the real exchange rate.

We begin by recalling that the change in $q_{\$/€}$, the real dollar/euro exchange rate, is the *deviation* from relative PPP; that is, the change in $q_{\$/€}$ is the percentage change in the nominal dollar/euro exchange rate less the international difference in inflation rates between the United States and Europe. We thus arrive at the corresponding relationship among the *expected* change in the real exchange rate, the *expected* change in the nominal rate, and *expected* inflation:

$$(q^e_{\$/\euro} - q_{\$/\euro})/q_{\$/\euro} = [(E^e_{\$/\euro} - E_{\$/\euro})/E_{\$/\euro}] - (\pi^e_{US} - \pi^e_E), \qquad \text{(16-8)}$$

where $q^e_{\$/\euro}$ (as per our usual notation) is the real exchange rate expected for a year from today.

Now we return to the interest parity condition between dollar and euro deposits,

$$R_\$ - R_\euro = (E^e_{\$/\euro} - E_{\$/\euro})/E_{\$/\euro}.$$

An easy rearrangement of (16-8) shows the expected rate of change in the *nominal* dollar/euro exchange rate is just the expected rate of change in the *real* dollar/euro exchange rate *plus* the U.S.–Europe expected inflation difference. Combining (16-8) with the above interest parity condition, we thus are led to the following breakdown of the international interest rate gap:

$$R_\$ - R_\euro = [(q^e_{\$/\euro} - q_{\$/\euro})/q_{\$/\euro}] + (\pi^e_{US} - \pi^e_E). \qquad \text{(16-9)}$$

Notice that when the market expects relative PPP to prevail, $q^e_{\$/\euro} = q_{\$/\euro}$ and the first term on the right side of this equation drops out. In this special case, (16-9) reduces to the simpler (16-5), which we derived by assuming relative PPP.

In general, however, the dollar/euro interest difference is the sum of *two* components: (1) the expected rate of real dollar depreciation against the euro and (2) the expected inflation difference between the United States and Europe. For example, if U.S. inflation will be 5 percent per year forever and European inflation will be zero forever, the long-run interest difference between dollar and euro deposits need not be the 5 percent that PPP (when combined with interest parity) would suggest. If, in addition, everyone knows that output demand and supply trends will make the dollar depreciate against the euro in real terms at a rate of 1 percent per year, the international interest spread will actually be 6 percent.

Real Interest Parity

Economics makes an important distinction between **nominal interest rates**, which are rates of return measured in monetary terms, and **real interest rates**, which are rates of return measured in *real* terms, that is, in terms of a country's output. Because real rates of return often are uncertain, we usually will refer to *expected* real interest rates. The interest rates we discussed in connection with the interest parity condition and the determinants of money demand were nominal rates, for example, the dollar return on dollar deposits. But for many other purposes, economists need to analyze behavior in terms of real rates of return. No one who is thinking of investing money, for example, could make a decision knowing only that the nominal interest rate is 15 percent. The investment would be quite attractive at zero inflation, but disastrously unattractive if inflation were bounding along at 100 percent per year![20]

We conclude this chapter by showing that when the nominal interest parity condition equates nominal interest rate differences between currencies to expected changes in *nominal* exchange rates, a *real* interest parity condition equates expected real interest

---

[20]We could get away with examining nominal return differences in the foreign exchange market because (as Chapter 14 showed) nominal return differences equal real return differences for any given investor. In the context of the demand for money, the nominal interest rate is the real rate of return you sacrifice by holding interest-barren currency.

rate differences to expected changes in *real* exchange rates. Only when relative PPP is expected to hold (meaning no real exchange rate change is anticipated) are expected real interest rates in all countries identical.

The expected real interest rate, denoted r^e, is defined as the nominal interest rate, R, less the expected inflation rate, π^e:

$$r^e = R - \pi^e.$$

In other words, the expected real interest rate in a country is just the real rate of return a domestic resident expects to earn on a loan of his or her currency. The definition of the expected real interest rate clarifies the generality of the forces behind the Fisher effect: Any increase in the expected inflation rate that does not alter the expected real interest rate must be reflected, one for one, in the nominal interest rate.

A useful consequence of the preceding definition is a formula for the difference in expected real interest rates between two currency areas such as the United States and Europe:

$$r^e_{US} - r^e_{E} = (R_\$ - \pi^e_{US}) - (R_\euro - \pi^e_{E}).$$

If we rearrange equation (16-9) and combine it with the equation above, we get the desired *real interest parity condition*:

$$r^e_{US} - r^e_{E} = (q^e_{\$/\euro} - q_{\$/\euro})/q_{\$/\euro}. \tag{16-10}$$

Equation (16-10) looks much like the nominal interest parity condition from which it is derived, but it explains differences in expected *real* interest rates between the United States and Europe by expected movements in the dollar/euro *real* exchange rate.

Expected real interest rates are the same in different countries when relative PPP is expected to hold (in which case (16-10) implies that $r^e_{US} = r^e_{E}$). More generally, however, expected real interest rates in different countries need not be equal, even in the long run, if continuing change in output markets is expected.[21] Suppose, for example, that productivity in the South Korean tradables sector is expected to rise during the next two decades, while productivity stagnates in South Korean nontradables and in all U.S. industries. If the Balassa-Samuelson hypothesis is valid, people should expect the U.S. dollar to depreciate in real terms against South Korea's currency, the won, as the prices of South Korea's nontradables trend upward. Equation (16-10) thus implies that the expected real interest rate should be higher in the United States than in South Korea.

Do such real interest differences imply unnoticed profit opportunities for international investors? Not necessarily. A cross-border real interest difference does imply that residents of two countries perceive different real rates of return on wealth. Nominal interest parity tells us, however, that any *given* investor expects the same real return on domestic and foreign currency assets. Two investors residing in different countries need not calculate this single real rate of return in the same way if relative PPP does not link the prices of their consumption baskets, but there is no way either can profit from their disagreement by shifting funds between currencies.

---

[21]In the two-period analysis of international borrowing and lending in Chapter 6, all countries face a single worldwide real interest rate. Relative PPP must hold in that analysis, however, because there is only one consumption good in each period.

SUMMARY

1. The *purchasing power parity* theory, in its absolute form, asserts that the exchange rate between countries' currencies equals the ratio of their price levels, as measured by the money prices of a reference commodity basket. An equivalent statement of PPP is that the purchasing power of any currency is the same in any country. *Absolute PPP* implies a second version of the PPP theory, *relative PPP*, which predicts that percentage changes in exchange rates equal differences in national inflation rates.

2. A building block of the PPP theory is the *law of one price*, which states that under free competition and in the absence of trade impediments, a good must sell for a single price regardless of where in the world it is sold. Proponents of the PPP theory often argue, however, that its validity does not require the law of one price to hold for every commodity.

3. The *monetary approach to the exchange rate* uses PPP to explain long-term exchange rate behavior exclusively in terms of money supply and demand. In that theory, long-run international interest differentials result from different national rates of ongoing inflation, as the *Fisher effect* predicts. Sustained international differences in monetary growth rates are, in turn, behind different long-term rates of continuing inflation. The monetary approach thus finds that a rise in a country's interest rate will be associated with a depreciation of its currency. Relative PPP implies that international interest differences, which equal the expected percentage change in the exchange rate, also equal the international expected inflation gap.

4. The empirical support for PPP and the law of one price is weak in recent data. The failure of these propositions in the real world is related to trade barriers and departures from free competition, factors that can result in *pricing to market* by exporters. In addition, different definitions of price levels in different countries bedevil attempts to test PPP using the price indices governments publish. For some products, including many services, international transport costs are so steep that these products become nontradable.

5. Deviations from relative PPP can be viewed as changes in a country's *real exchange rate*, the price of a typical foreign expenditure basket in terms of the typical domestic expenditure basket. All else equal, a country's currency undergoes a long-run *real appreciation* against foreign currencies when the world relative demand for its output rises. In this case, the country's real exchange rate, as just defined, falls. The home currency undergoes a long-run *real depreciation* against foreign currencies when home output expands relative to foreign output. In this case, the real exchange rate rises.

6. The long-run determination of *nominal exchange rates* can be analyzed by combining two theories: the theory of the long-run *real* exchange rate and the theory of how domestic monetary factors determine long-run price levels. A stepwise increase in a country's money stock ultimately leads to a proportional increase in its price level and a proportional fall in its currency's foreign exchange value, just as relative PPP predicts. Changes in monetary growth rates also have long-run effects consistent with PPP. Supply or demand changes in output markets, however, result in exchange rate movements that do not conform to PPP.

7. The interest parity condition equates international differences in *nominal interest rates* to the expected percentage change in the nominal exchange rate. If interest parity holds in this sense, a real interest parity condition equates international differences in expected *real interest rates* to the expected

change in the real exchange rate. Real interest parity also implies that international differences in nominal interest rates equal the difference in expected inflation *plus* the expected percentage change in the real exchange rate.

KEY TERMS

absolute PPP, p. 448	nominal exchange rate, p. 465	real appreciation, p. 466
Fisher effect, p. 452	nominal interest rate, p. 473	real depreciation, p. 466
law of one price, p. 446	pricing to market, p. 458	real exchange rate, p. 465
monetary approach to	purchasing power parity	real interest rate, p. 473
the exchange rate, p. 449	(PPP), p. 445	relative PPP, p. 448

PROBLEMS   MyEconLab

1. Suppose in the year 2010 (where price level is 100), the Japanese yen and Indian rupee exchange rate (¥/rupee) is 0.54. If the price level in 2013 stands at ¥105 and 110 rupees in Japan and India respectively, what will be the exchange rate in 2013, based on the PPP?

2. Discuss why it is often asserted that exporters suffer when their home currencies appreciate in real terms against foreign currencies and prosper when their home currencies depreciate in real terms.

3. Other things equal, how would you expect the following shifts to affect a currency's real exchange rate against foreign currencies?

   a. The overall level of spending doesn't change, but domestic residents decide to spend more of their income on nontraded products and less on tradables.

   b. Foreign residents shift their demand away from their own goods and toward the home country's exports.

4. Consider the following two cases and explain the validity of the theory of purchasing power parity based on these situations. In the first case, suppose there are trade barriers and an imperfectly competitive market structure in an economy for a product. Explain whether the law of one price holds good here. In the second case, suppose there is no product differentiation, trade barriers, and the market is perfectly competitive for a product. Would the law of one price be applicable in this case? If not, what factor will you attribute to the different prices in different markets for the same product?

5. In the late 1970s, Britain seemed to have struck it rich. Having developed its North Sea oil-producing fields in earlier years, Britain suddenly found its real income higher as a result of a dramatic increase in world oil prices in 1979–1980. In the early 1980s, however, oil prices receded as the world economy slid into a deep recession and world oil demand faltered.

   In the following chart, we show index numbers for the average real exchange rate of the pound against several foreign currencies. (Such average index numbers are called real *effective* exchange rates.) A rise in one of these numbers indicates a real *appreciation* of the pound, that is, an increase in Britain's price level relative to the average price level abroad measured in pounds. A fall is a real depreciation.

Real Effective Exchange Rate of the Pound Sterling, 1976–1984 (1980 = 100)

1976	1977	1978	1979	1980	1981	1982	1983	1984
68.3	66.5	72.2	81.4	100.0	102.8	100.0	92.5	89.8

Source: International Monetary Fund, *International Financial Statistics*. The real exchange rate measures are based on indices of net output prices called value-added deflators.

Use the clues we have given about the British economy to explain the rise and fall of the pound's real effective exchange rate between 1978 and 1984. Pay particular attention to the role of nontradables.

6. With reference to the PPP rationale, explain the relationship between values of currencies in countries with high inflation.

7. At the end of World War I, the Treaty of Versailles imposed an indemnity on Germany, a large annual payment from it to the victorious Allies. (Many historians believe this indemnity played a role in destabilizing financial markets in the interwar period and even in bringing on World War II.) In the 1920s, economists John Maynard Keynes and Bertil Ohlin had a spirited debate in the *Economic Journal* over the possibility that the transfer payment would impose a "secondary burden" on Germany by worsening its terms of trade. Use the theory developed in this chapter to discuss the mechanisms through which a permanent transfer from Poland to the Czech Republic would affect the real zloty/koruna exchange rate in the long run.

8. Given the government price level statistics, would an absolute or relative PPP be more effective while evaluating the PPP between two countries? Explain.

9. A country imposes a tariff on imports from abroad. How does this action change the long-run real exchange rate between the home and foreign currencies? How is the long-run nominal exchange rate affected?

10. Suppose the Samsung smartphone is sold at $100 in the US and 250 real in Brazil. The market exchange rate is 2.4 real/$ and there is a $5 shipping cost from the US to Brazil. Is it profitable for buyers to import from US to Brazil? If the expected exchange rate of the real (real/$) declines by 10 percent, will the buyer then choose to import?

11. Explain how the nominal dollar/euro exchange rate would be affected (all else equal) by permanent changes in the expected rate of real depreciation of the dollar against the euro.

12. Can you suggest an event that would cause a country's nominal interest rate to rise and its currency to appreciate simultaneously, in a world of perfectly flexible prices?

13. Suppose in 2013 the UK pound and Argentine peso interest rate is 7 percent and 5 percent respectively. A year later, if the expected rate of real peso depreciation against pound is 1.2, and the expected inflation rate in UK is 3 percent, calculate Argentina's expected inflation level.

14. In the short run of a model with sticky prices, a reduction in the money supply raises the nominal interest rate and appreciates the currency (see Chapter 15). What happens to the expected real interest rate? Explain why the subsequent path of the real exchange rate satisfies the real interest parity condition.

15. Discuss the following statement: "When a change in a country's nominal interest rate is caused by a rise in the expected real interest rate, the domestic currency appreciates. When the change is caused by a rise in expected inflation, the currency depreciates." (It may help to refer back to Chapter 15.)

16. Nominal interest rates are quoted at a variety of maturities, corresponding to different lengths of loans. For example, in late 2004 the U.S. government could take out ten-year loans at an annual interest rate of slightly over 4 percent, whereas the annual rate it paid on loans of only three months' duration was slightly under 2 percent. (An annualized interest rate of 2 percent on a three-month loan means that if you borrow a dollar, you repay $1.005 = $1 + (3/12) \times 0.02 at the end of three months.) Typically, though not always, long-term interest rates are above short-term rates, as in the preceding example from 2004. In terms of the Fisher effect, what would that pattern say about expected inflation and/or the expected future real interest rate?

17. Continuing with the preceding problem, we can define short- and long-term *real* rates of interest. In all cases, the relevant real interest rate (annualized, that is, expressed in percent per year) is the annualized nominal interest rate at the maturity in question, less the annualized expected inflation rate over the period of the loan. Recall the evidence that relative PPP seems to hold better over long horizons than short ones. In that case, will international real interest differentials be larger at short than at long maturities? Explain your reasoning.

18. Why might it be true that relative PPP holds better in the long run than the short run? (Think about how international trading firms might react to large and persistent cross-border differences in the prices of a tradable good.)

19. Suppose residents of the U.S. consume relatively more of U.S. export goods than residents of foreign countries. In other words, U.S. export goods have a higher weight in the U.S. CPI than they do in other countries. Conversely, foreign exports have a lower weight in the U.S. CPI than they do abroad. What would be the effect on the dollar's real exchange rate of a rise in the U.S. terms of trade (the relative price of U.S. exports in terms of U.S. imports)?

20. The *Economist* magazine has observed that the price of Big Macs is systematically positively related to a country's income level, just as is the general price level (recall the box on pages 459–461). If you go to the *Economist*'s Big Mac standard website, at http://www.economist.com/content/big-mac-index, you will find an Excel spreadsheet containing the data on under/overvaluation for January 2013 (as well as for previous years' surveys). Go to the World Bank's World Development Indicators website, http://data.worldbank.org/indicator/, and find the most recent data on GNI (Gross National Income) per capita, PPP, for all countries. Use these data, together with the *Economist* data on Big Mac dollar prices, to make a graph of income per capita (horizontal axis) versus dollar Big Mac price (vertical axis). What do you find?

FURTHER READINGS

James E. Anderson and Eric van Wincoop. "Trade Costs." *Journal of Economic Literature* 42 (September 2004), pp. 691–751. Comprehensive survey of the nature and effects of costs of international trade.

Gustav Cassel. *Post-War Monetary Stabilization*. New York: Columbia University Press, 1928. Applies the purchasing power parity theory of exchange rates in analyzing the monetary problems that followed World War I.

Robert E. Cumby. "Forecasting Exchange Rates and Relative Prices with the Hamburger Standard: Is What You Want What You Get with McParity?" Working Paper 5675. National Bureau of Economic Research, July 1996. Studies the statistical forecasting power of Big Mac measures of over- and under-valuation.

Angus Deaton and Alan Heston. "Understanding PPPs and PPP-Based National Accounts." *American Economic Journal: Macroeconomics* 2 (October 2010): 1–35. Critical overview of the many obstacles to constructing accurate international price comparisons.

Michael B. Devereux. "Real Exchange Rates and Macroeconomics: Evidence and Theory." *Canadian Journal of Economics* 30 (November 1997), pp. 773–808. Reviews theories of the determinants and effects of real exchange rates.

Rudiger Dornbusch. "The Theory of Flexible Exchange Rate Regimes and Macroeconomic Policy," in Jan Herin, Assar Lindbeck, and Johan Myhrman, eds. *Flexible Exchange Rates and Stabilization Policy*. Boulder, CO: Westview Press, 1977, pp. 123–143. Develops a long-run model of exchange rates incorporating traded and nontraded goods and services.

Pinelopi Koujianou Goldberg and Michael M. Knetter. "Goods Prices and Exchange Rates: What Have We Learned?" *Journal of Economic Literature* 35 (September 1997), pp. 1243–1272. Excellent survey of micro-level evidence on the law of one price, exchange rate pass-through, and pricing to market.

David Hummels. "Transportation Costs and International Trade in the Second Era of Globalization." *Journal of Economic Perspectives* 21 (Summer 2007), pp. 131–154. Surveys the economics of transportation costs in modern international trade.

Jaewoo Lee, Gian Maria Milesi-Ferretti, Jonathan Ostry, Alessandro Prati, and Luca Antonio Ricci. *Exchange Rate Assessments: CGER Methodologies.* Occasional Paper 261, International Monetary Fund, 2008. Describes International Monetary Fund models for evaluating real exchange rates.

Lloyd A. Metzler. "Exchange Rates and the International Monetary Fund," in *International Monetary Policies.* Postwar Economic Studies 7. Washington, D.C.: Board of Governors of the Federal Reserve System, 1947, pp. 1–45. The author applies purchasing power parity with skill and skepticism to evaluate the fixed exchange rates established by the International Monetary Fund after World War II.

Frederic S. Mishkin. *The Economics of Money, Banking and Financial Markets*, 10th edition. Upper Saddle River, NJ: Prentice Hall, 2013. Chapter 5 discusses inflation and the Fisher effect.

Kenneth Rogoff. "The Purchasing Power Parity Puzzle." *Journal of Economic Literature* 34 (June 1996), pp. 647–668. Critical survey of theory and empirical work.

Alan C. Stockman. "The Equilibrium Approach to Exchange Rates." *Federal Reserve Bank of Richmond Economic Review* 73 (March/April 1987), pp. 12–30. Theory and evidence on an equilibrium exchange rate model similar to the long-run model of this chapter.

Alan M. Taylor and Mark P. Taylor. "The Purchasing Power Parity Debate." *Journal of Economic Perspectives* 18 (Fall 2004), pp. 135–158. Surveys recent research on PPP.

MyEconLab Can Help You Get a Better Grade

MyEconLab   If your exam were tomorrow, would you be ready? For each chapter, MyEconLab Practice Tests and Study Plans pinpoint sections you have mastered and those you need to study. That way, you are more efficient with your study time, and you are better prepared for your exams.

To see how it works, turn to page 41 and then go to

www.myeconlab.com

The Fisher Effect, the Interest Rate, and the Exchange Rate under the Flexible-Price Monetary Approach

The monetary approach to exchange rates—which assumes the prices of goods are perfectly flexible—implies that a country's currency depreciates when its nominal interest rates rise because of higher expected future inflation. This appendix supplies a detailed analysis of that important result.

Consider again the dollar/euro exchange rate, and imagine the Federal Reserve raises the future rate of U.S. money supply growth by the amount $\Delta\pi$. Figure 16A-1 provides a diagram that will help us keep track of how various markets respond to that change.

The lower right quadrant in the figure is our usual depiction of equilibrium in the U.S. money market. It shows that before the increase in U.S. money supply growth, the nominal interest rate on dollars equals $R_\$^1$ (point 1). The Fisher effect tells us that a rise $\Delta\pi$ in the future rate of U.S. money supply growth, all else equal, will raise the nominal interest rate on dollars to $R_\$^2 = R_\$^1 + \Delta\pi$ (point 2).

As the diagram shows, the rise in the nominal dollar interest rate reduces money demand and therefore requires an equilibrating fall in the real money supply. But the nominal money stock is unchanged in the short run because it is only the *future* rate of U.S. money supply growth that has risen. What happens? Given the unchanged nominal money supply M_{US}^1, an upward jump in the U.S. price level from P_{US}^1 to P_{US}^2 brings about the needed reduction in American real money holdings. The assumed flexibility of prices allows this jump to occur even in the short run.

To see the exchange rate response, we turn to the lower-left quadrant. The monetary approach assumes purchasing power parity, implying that as P_{US} rises (while the European price level remains constant, which we assume), the dollar/euro exchange rate $E_{\$/€}$ must rise (a depreciation of the dollar). The lower-left quadrant of Figure 16A-1 graphs the implied relationship between U.S. real money holdings, M_{US}/P_{US}, and the nominal exchange rate, $E_{\$/€}$, given an unchanged *nominal* money supply in the United States and an unchanged European price level. Using PPP, we can write the equation graphed there (which is a downward-sloping *hyperbola*) as:

$$E_{\$/€} = P_{US}/P_E = \frac{M_{US}/P_E}{M_{US}/P_{US}}.$$

This equation shows that the fall in the U.S. real money supply, from M_{US}^1/P_{US}^1 to M_{US}^1/P_{US}^2, is associated with a dollar depreciation in which the dollar/euro nominal exchange rate rises from $E_{\$/€}^1$ to $E_{\$/€}^2$ (shown as a movement to the left along the horizontal axis).

The 45-degree line in the upper-left quadrant of Figure 16A-1 allows you to translate the exchange rate change given in the lower-left quadrant to the vertical axis of the upper-right quadrant's diagram. The upper-right quadrant contains our usual portrayal of equilibrium in the foreign exchange market.

There you can see the dollar's depreciation against the euro is associated with a move in the foreign exchange market's equilibrium from point 1′ to point 2′. The picture shows why the dollar depreciates, despite the rise in $R_\$$. The reason is an outward

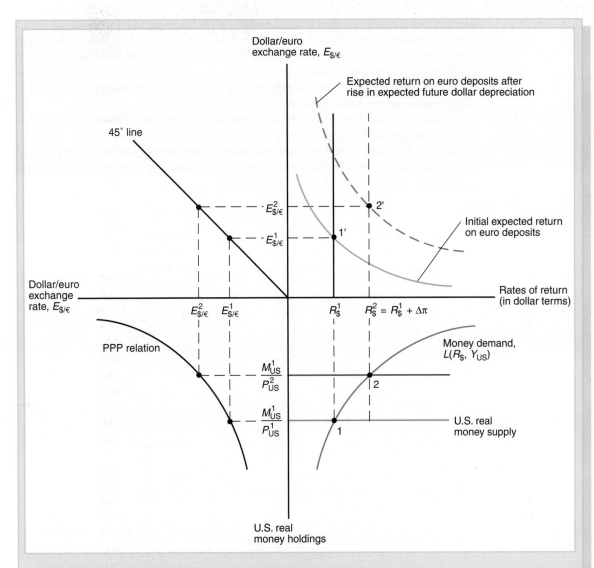

FIGURE 16A-1

How a Rise in U.S. Monetary Growth Affects Dollar Interest Rates and the Dollar/Euro Exchange Rate When Goods Prices Are Flexible

When goods prices are perfectly flexible, the money market equilibrium diagram (southeast quadrant) shows two effects of an increase, $\Delta\pi$, in the future rate of U.S. money supply growth. The change (i) raises the dollar interest rate from $R_\$^1$ to $R_\$^2 = R_\$^2 + \Delta\pi$, in line with the Fisher effect, and (ii) causes the U.S. price level to jump upward, from P_{US}^1 to P_{US}^2. Money market equilibrium therefore moves from point 1 to point 2. (Because M_{US}^1 doesn't change immediately, the real U.S. money supply falls to M_{US}^1/P_{US}^2, bringing the real money supply into line with reduced money demand.) The PPP relationship in the southwest quadrant shows that the price level jump from P_{US}^1 to P_{US}^2 requires a depreciation of the dollar against the euro (the dollar/euro exchange rate moves up, from $E_{\$/€}^1$ to $E_{\$/€}^2$). In the foreign exchange market diagram (northeast quadrant), this dollar depreciation is shown as the move from point 1' to point 2'. The dollar depreciates despite a rise in $R_\$$ because heightened expectations of future dollar depreciation against the euro cause an outward shift of the locus measuring the expected dollar return on euro deposits.

shift in the downward-sloping schedule, which gives the expected dollar rate of return on euro deposits. Why does that schedule shift outward? Higher expected future monetary growth implies faster expected future depreciation of the dollar against the euro and therefore a rise in the attractiveness of euro deposits. It is this change in expectations that leads simultaneously to a rise in the nominal interest rate on dollars and to a depreciation of the dollar in the foreign exchange market.

To summarize, we cannot predict how a rise in the dollar interest rate will affect the dollar's exchange rate without knowing *why* the nominal interest rate has risen. In a flexible-price model in which the home nominal interest rate rises because of higher expected future money supply growth, the home currency will depreciate—not appreciate—thanks to expectations of more rapid future depreciation.

CHAPTER 17

OUTPUT AND THE EXCHANGE RATE IN THE SHORT RUN

The U.S. and Canadian economies registered similar negative rates of output growth during 2009, a year of deep global recession. But while the U.S. dollar depreciated against foreign currencies by about 8 percent over the year, the Canadian dollar *appreciated* by roughly 16 percent. What explains these contrasting experiences? By completing the macroeconomic model built in the last three chapters, this chapter will sort out the complicated factors that cause output, exchange rates, and inflation to change. Chapters 15 and 16 presented the connections among exchange rates, interest rates, and price levels but always assumed that output levels were determined outside of the model. Those chapters gave us only a partial picture of how macroeconomic changes affect an open economy because events that change exchange rates, interest rates, and price levels may also affect output. Now we complete the picture by examining how output and the exchange rate are determined in the short run.

Our discussion combines what we have learned about asset markets and the long-run behavior of exchange rates with a new element, a theory of how the output market adjusts to demand changes when product prices in the economy are themselves slow to adjust. As we learned in Chapter 15, institutional factors like long-term nominal contracts can give rise to "sticky" or slowly adjusting output market prices. By combining a short-run model of the output market with our models of the foreign exchange and money markets (the asset markets), we build a model that explains the short-run behavior of all the important macroeconomic variables in an open economy. The long-run exchange rate model of the preceding chapter provides the framework that participants in the asset markets use to form their expectations about future exchange rates.

Because output changes may push the economy away from full employment, the links among output and other macroeconomic variables, such as the trade balance and the current account, are of great concern to economic policy makers. In the last part of this chapter, we use our short-run model to examine how macroeconomic policy tools affect output and the current account and how those tools can be used to maintain full employment.

After reading this chapter, you will be able to:

- Explain the role of the real exchange rate in determining the aggregate demand for a country's output.
- See how an open economy's short-run equilibrium can be analyzed as the intersection of an asset market equilibrium schedule (*AA*) and an output market equilibrium schedule (*DD*).
- Understand how monetary and fiscal policies affect the exchange rate and national output in the short run.
- Describe and interpret the long-run effects of permanent macroeconomic policy changes.
- Explain the relationship among macroeconomic policies, the current account balance, and the exchange rate.

Determinants of Aggregate Demand in an Open Economy

To analyze how output is determined in the short run when product prices are sticky, we introduce the concept of **aggregate demand** for a country's output. Aggregate demand is the amount of a country's goods and services demanded by households, firms, and governments throughout the world. Just as the output of an individual good or service depends in part on the demand for it, a country's overall short-run output level depends on the aggregate demand for its products. The economy is at full employment in the long run (by definition) because wages and the price level eventually adjust to ensure full employment. In the long run, domestic output therefore depends only on the available domestic supplies of factors of production such as labor and capital. As we will see, however, these productive factors can be over- or underemployed in the short run as a result of shifts in aggregate demand that have not yet had their full long-run effects on prices.

In Chapter 13, we learned an economy's output is the sum of four types of expenditure that generate national income: consumption, investment, government purchases, and the current account. Correspondingly, aggregate demand for an open economy's output is the sum of consumption demand (*C*), investment demand (*I*), government demand (*G*), and net export demand, that is, the current account (*CA*). Each of these components of aggregate demand depends on various factors. In this section we examine the factors that determine consumption demand and the current account. We discuss government demand later in this chapter when we examine the effects of fiscal policy; for now, we assume that *G* is given. To avoid complicating our model, we also assume investment demand is given. The determinants of investment demand are incorporated into the model in the Online Appendix to this chapter.

Determinants of Consumption Demand

In this chapter, we view the amount a country's residents wish to consume as depending on disposable income, Y^d (that is, national income less taxes, $Y - T$).[1] (*C*, *Y*, and *T* are all measured in terms of domestic output units.) With this assumption,

---

[1] A more complete model would allow other factors, such as real wealth, expected future income, and the real interest rate, to affect consumption plans. This chapter's Appendix 1 links the formulation here to the microeconomic theory of the consumer, which was the basis of the discussion in the appendix to Chapter 6.

a country's desired consumption level can be written as a function of disposable income:

$$C = C(Y^d).$$

Because each consumer naturally demands more goods and services as his or her real income rises, we expect consumption to increase as disposable income increases at the aggregate level, too. Thus, consumption demand and disposable income are positively related. However, when disposable income rises, consumption demand generally rises by *less* because part of the income increase is saved.

Determinants of the Current Account

The current account balance, viewed as the demand for a country's exports less that country's own demand for imports, is determined by two main factors: the domestic currency's real exchange rate against foreign currency (that is, the price of a typical foreign expenditure basket in terms of domestic expenditure baskets) and domestic disposable income. (In reality, a country's current account depends on many other factors, such as the level of foreign expenditure, but for now we regard these other factors as being held constant.)[2]

We express a country's current account balance as a function of its currency's real exchange rate, $q = EP^*/P$, and of domestic disposable income, Y^d:

$$CA = CA(EP^*/P, Y^d).$$

As a reminder of the last chapter's discussion, note that the domestic currency prices of representative foreign and domestic expenditure baskets are, respectively, EP^* and P, where E (the nominal exchange rate) is the price of foreign currency in terms of domestic currency, P^* is the foreign price level, and P is the home price level. The *real* exchange rate q, defined as the price of the foreign basket in terms of the domestic one, is therefore EP^*/P. If, for example, the representative basket of European goods and services costs €40 (P^*), the representative U.S. basket costs $50 ($P$), and the dollar/euro exchange rate is $1.10 per euro ($E$), then the price of the European basket in terms of U.S. baskets is

$$EP^*/P = \frac{(1.10\,\$/€) \times (40\,€/\text{European basket})}{(50\,\$/\text{U.S. basket})}$$

$$= 0.88 \text{ U.S. baskets/European basket.}$$

Real exchange rate changes affect the current account because they reflect changes in the prices of domestic goods and services relative to foreign goods and services. Disposable income affects the current account through its effect on total spending by domestic consumers. To understand how these real exchange rate and disposable income effects work, it is helpful to look separately at the demand for a country's exports, EX, and the demand for imports by the country's residents, IM. As we saw in Chapter 13, the current account is related to exports and imports by the identity

$$CA = EX - IM,$$

when CA, EX, and IM all are measured in terms of domestic output.

---

[2]As the previous footnote observed, we are ignoring a number of factors (such as wealth and interest rates) that affect consumption along with disposable income. Since some part of any consumption change goes into imports, these omitted determinants of consumption also help to determine the current account. Following the convention of Chapter 13, we are also ignoring unilateral transfers in analyzing the current account balance.

How Real Exchange Rate Changes Affect the Current Account

You will recall that a representative domestic expenditure basket includes some imported products but places a relatively heavier weight on goods and services produced domestically. At the same time, the representative foreign basket is skewed toward goods and services produced in the foreign country. Thus, a rise in the price of the foreign basket in terms of domestic baskets, say, will be associated with a rise in the relative price of foreign output in general relative to domestic output.[3]

To determine how such a change in the relative price of national outputs affects the current account, other things equal, we must ask how it affects both EX and IM. When EP^*/P rises, for example, foreign products have become more expensive relative to domestic products: Each unit of domestic output now purchases fewer units of foreign output. Foreign consumers will respond to this price shift (a real domestic currency depreciation) by demanding more of our exports. This response by foreigners will therefore raise EX and improve the domestic country's current account.

The effect of the same real exchange rate increase on IM is more complicated. Domestic consumers respond to the price shift by purchasing fewer units of the more expensive foreign products. Their response does not imply, however, that IM must fall, because IM denotes the *value* of imports measured in terms of domestic output, not the *volume* of foreign products imported. Since a rise in EP^*/P (a real depreciation of the domestic currency) tends to raise the value of each unit of imports in terms of domestic output units, imports measured in domestic output units may rise as a result of a rise in EP^*/P even if imports decline when measured in foreign output units. IM can therefore rise or fall when EP^*/P rises, so the effect of a real exchange rate change on the current account CA is ambiguous.

Whether the current account improves or worsens depends on which effect of a real exchange rate change is dominant—the *volume effect* of consumer spending shifts on export and import quantities, or the *value effect*, which changes the domestic output equivalent of a *given* volume of foreign imports. We assume for now that the volume effect of a real exchange rate change always outweighs the value effect, so that, other things equal, a real depreciation of the currency improves the current account and a real appreciation of the currency worsens the current account.[4]

While we have couched our discussion of real exchange rates and the current account in terms of consumers' responses, producers' responses are just as important and work in much the same way. When a country's currency depreciates in real terms, foreign firms will find that the country can supply intermediate production inputs more cheaply. These effects have become stronger as a result of the increasing tendency for multinational firms to locate different stages of their production processes in a variety of countries. For example, the German auto manufacturer BMW can shift production from Germany to its Spartanburg, South Carolina, plant if a dollar depreciation lowers the relative cost of producing in the United States. The production shift represents an increase in world demand for U.S. labor and output.

---

[3]The real exchange rate is being used here essentially as a convenient summary measure of the relative prices of domestic against foreign products. A more exact (but much more complicated) analysis would work explicitly with separate demand and supply functions for each country's nontradables and tradables but would lead to conclusions very much like those we reach below.

[4]This assumption requires that import and export demands be relatively *elastic* with respect to the real exchange rate. Appendix 2 to this chapter describes a precise mathematical condition, called the Marshall-Lerner condition, under which the assumption in the text is valid. The appendix also examines empirical evidence on the time horizon over which the Marshall-Lerner condition holds.

TABLE 17-1	Factors Determining the Current Account
Change	**Effect on Current Account, CA**
Real exchange rate, $EP^*/P\uparrow$	$CA\uparrow$
Real exchange rate, $EP^*/P\downarrow$	$CA\downarrow$
Disposable income, $Y^d\uparrow$	$CA\downarrow$
Disposable income, $Y^d\downarrow$	$CA\uparrow$

How Disposable Income Changes Affect the Current Account

The second factor influencing the current account is domestic disposable income. Since a rise in Y^d causes domestic consumers to increase their spending on *all* goods, including imports from abroad, an increase in disposable income worsens the current account, other things equal. (An increase in Y^d has no effect on export demand because we are holding foreign income constant and not allowing Y^d to affect it.)

Table 17-1 summarizes our discussion of how real exchange rate and disposable income changes influence the domestic current account.

The Equation of Aggregate Demand

We now combine the four components of aggregate demand to get an expression for total aggregate demand, denoted D:

$$D = C(Y - T) + I + G + CA(EP^*/P, Y - T),$$

where we have written disposable income Y^d as output, Y, less taxes, T. This equation shows that aggregate demand for home output can be written as a function of the real exchange rate, disposable income, investment demand, and government spending:

$$D = D(EP^*/P, Y - T, I, G).$$

We now want to see how aggregate demand depends on the real exchange rate and domestic GNP given the level of taxes, T, investment demand, I, and government purchases, G.[5]

The Real Exchange Rate and Aggregate Demand

A rise in EP^*/P makes domestic goods and services cheaper relative to foreign goods and services and shifts both domestic and foreign spending from foreign goods to domestic goods. As a result, CA rises (as assumed in the previous section) and aggregate demand, D, therefore goes up. *A real depreciation of the home currency*

---

[5]As noted above, investment I is taken as given, though we may imagine that it shifts for reasons that are outside the model (in other words, we assume it is an exogenous rather than an endogenous variable). We make the same assumption about G. It would not be hard to make I endogenous, however, as is done in the Online Appendix, where investment is a declining function of the domestic real rate of interest. (That is the assumption made in the standard *IS-LM* model of intermediate macroeconomics courses.) For a given expected future exchange rate and a given full-employment output level, the model of the Online Appendix implies that investment demand can be expressed as $I(E, Y)$, where a rise in E (depreciation of domestic currency) raises investment demand, as does an increase in domestic output Y. Modeling investment in this way within the setup of this chapter would not change our predictions in any important way.

raises aggregate demand for home output, other things equal; a real appreciation lowers aggregate demand for home output.

Real Income and Aggregate Demand

The effect of domestic real income on aggregate demand is slightly more complicated. If taxes are fixed at a given level, a rise in Y represents an equal rise in disposable income Y^d. While this rise in Y^d raises consumption, it worsens the current account by raising home spending on foreign imports. The first of these effects raises aggregate demand, but the second lowers it. Since the increase in consumption is divided between higher spending on home products and higher spending on foreign imports, however, the first effect (the effect of disposable income on total consumption) is greater than the second (the effect of disposable income on import spending alone). Therefore, *a rise in domestic real income raises aggregate demand for home output, other things equal, and a fall in domestic real income lowers aggregate demand for home output.*

Figure 17-1 shows the relation between aggregate demand and real income Y for fixed values of the real exchange rate, taxes, investment demand, and government spending. As Y rises, consumption rises by a fraction of the increase in income. Part of this increase in consumption, moreover, goes into import spending. The effect of an increase in Y on the aggregate demand for home output is therefore smaller than the accompanying rise in consumption demand, which is smaller, in turn, than the increase in Y. We show this in Figure 17-1 by drawing the aggregate demand schedule with a slope less than 1. (The schedule intersects the vertical axis above the origin because investment, government, and foreign demand would make aggregate demand greater than zero, even in the hypothetical case of zero domestic output.)

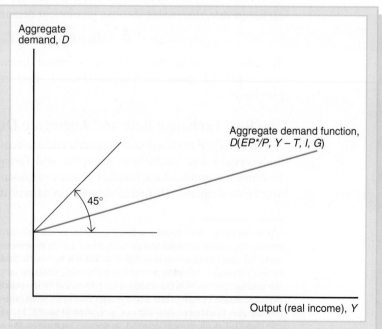

FIGURE 17-1

Aggregate Demand as a Function of Output

Aggregate demand is a function of the real exchange rate (EP^*/P), disposable income ($Y - T$), investment demand (I), and government spending (G). If all other factors remain unchanged, a rise in output (real income), Y, increases aggregate demand. Because the increase in aggregate demand is less than the increase in output, the slope of the aggregate demand function is less than 1 (as indicated by its position within the 45-degree angle).

Aggregate demand, D

Aggregate demand function, $D(EP^*/P, Y - T, I, G)$

45°

Output (real income), Y

How Output Is Determined in the Short Run

Having discussed the factors that influence the demand for an open economy's output, we now study how output is determined in the short run. We show that the output market is in equilibrium when real domestic output, Y, equals the aggregate demand for domestic output:

$$Y = D(EP^*/P, Y - T, I, G). \tag{17-1}$$

The equality of aggregate supply and demand therefore determines the short-run equilibrium output level.[6]

Our analysis of real output determination applies to the short run because we assume that the money prices of goods and services are *temporarily fixed*. As we will see later in the chapter, the short-run real output changes that occur when prices are temporarily fixed eventually cause price level changes that move the economy to its long-run equilibrium. In long-run equilibrium, factors of production are fully employed, the level of real output is completely determined by factor supplies, and the real exchange rate has adjusted to equate long-run real output to aggregate demand.[7]

The determination of national output in the short run is illustrated in Figure 17-2, where we again graph aggregate demand as a function of output for fixed levels of the

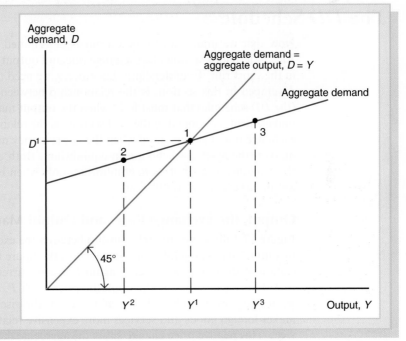

FIGURE 17-2

The Determination of Output in the Short Run

In the short run, output settles at Y^1 (point 1), where aggregate demand, D^1, equals aggregate output, Y^1.

---

[6]Superficially, equation (17-1), which may be written as $Y = C(Y^d) + I + G + CA(EP^*/P, Y^d)$, looks like the GNP identity we discussed in Chapter 13, $Y = C + I + G + CA$. How do the two equations differ? They differ in that (17-1) is an equilibrium condition, not an identity. As you will recall from Chapter 13, the investment quantity I appearing in the GNP identity includes *undesired* or involuntary inventory accumulation by firms, so the GNP identity always holds as a matter of definition. The investment demand appearing in equation (17-1), however, is *desired* or planned investment. Thus, the GNP identity always holds, but equation (17-1) holds only if firms are not unwillingly building up or drawing down inventories of goods.

[7]Thus, equation (17-1) also holds in long-run equilibrium, but the equation determines the long-run real exchange rate when Y is at its long-run value, as in Chapter 16. (We are holding foreign conditions constant.)

real exchange rate, taxes, investment demand, and government spending. The intersection (at point 1) of the aggregate demand schedule and a 45-degree line drawn from the origin (the equation $D = Y$) gives us the unique output level Y^1 at which aggregate demand equals domestic output.

Let's use Figure 17-2 to see why output tends to settle at Y^1 in the short run. At an output level of Y^2, aggregate demand (point 2) is higher than output. Firms therefore increase their production to meet this excess demand. (If they did not, they would have to meet the excess demand out of inventories, reducing investment below the desired level, I.) Thus, output expands until national income reaches Y^1.

At point 3, there is an excess supply of domestic output, and firms find themselves involuntarily accumulating inventories (and involuntarily raising their investment spending above its desired level). As inventories start to build up, firms cut back on production; only when output has fallen to Y^1 will firms be content with their level of production. Once again, output settles at point 1, the point at which output exactly equals aggregate demand. In this short-run equilibrium, consumers, firms, the government, and foreign buyers of domestic products are all able to realize their desired expenditures with no output left over.

Output Market Equilibrium in the Short Run: The *DD* Schedule

Now that we understand how output is determined for a given real exchange rate EP^*/P, let's look at how the exchange rate and output are simultaneously determined in the short run. To understand this process, we need two elements. The first element, developed in this section, is the relationship between output and the exchange rate (the *DD* schedule) that must hold when the output market is in equilibrium. The second element, developed in the next section, is the relationship between output and the exchange rate that must hold when the home money market and the foreign exchange market (the asset markets) are in equilibrium. Both elements are necessary because the economy as a whole is in equilibrium only when both the output market and the asset markets are in equilibrium.

Output, the Exchange Rate, and Output Market Equilibrium

Figure 17-3 illustrates the relationship between the exchange rate and output implied by output market equilibrium. Specifically, the figure illustrates the effect of a depreciation of the domestic currency against foreign currency (that is, a rise in E from E^1 to E^2) for fixed values of the domestic price level, P, and the foreign price level, P^*. With fixed price levels at home and abroad, the rise in the nominal exchange rate makes foreign goods and services more expensive relative to domestic goods and services. This relative price change shifts the aggregate demand schedule upward.

The fall in the relative price of domestic output shifts the aggregate demand schedule upward because at each level of domestic output, the demand for domestic products is higher. For example, foreign and American consumers of autos alike shift their demands toward American models when the dollar depreciates. Output expands from Y^1 to Y^2 as firms find themselves faced with excess demand at initial production levels.

Although we have considered the effect of a change in E with P and P^* held fixed, it is straightforward to analyze the effects of changes in P or P^* on output. *Any rise in the real exchange rate EP^*/P (whether due to a rise in E, a rise in P^*, or a fall in P) will cause an upward shift in the aggregate demand function and an expansion of output, all else equal.* (A rise in P^*, for example, has effects qualitatively identical to those of

FIGURE 17-3

Output Effect of a Currency Depreciation with Fixed Output Prices

A rise in the exchange rate from E^1 to E^2 (a currency depreciation) raises aggregate demand to *Aggregate demand* (E^2) and output to Y^2, all else equal.

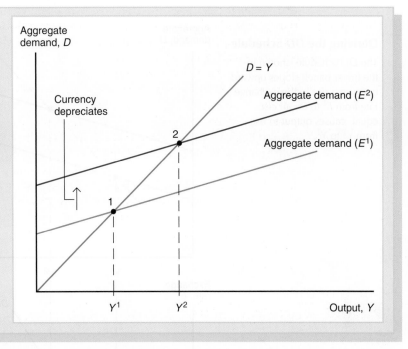

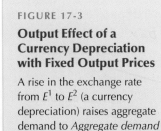

a rise in *E*.) *Similarly, any fall in EP*/P, regardless of its cause (a fall in E, a fall in P*, or a rise in P), will cause output to contract, all else equal.* (A rise in *P*, with *E* and *P** held fixed, for example, makes domestic products more expensive relative to foreign products, reduces aggregate demand for domestic output, and causes output to fall.)

Deriving the *DD* Schedule

If we assume *P* and *P** are fixed in the short run, a depreciation of the domestic currency (a rise in *E*) is associated with a rise in domestic output, *Y*, while an appreciation (a fall in *E*) is associated with a fall in *Y*. This association provides us with one of the two relationships between *E* and *Y* needed to describe the short-run macroeconomic behavior of an open economy. We summarize this relationship by the **DD schedule**, which shows all combinations of output and the exchange rate for which the output market is in short-run equilibrium (aggregate demand = aggregate output).

Figure 17-4 shows how to derive the *DD* schedule, which relates *E* and *Y* when *P* and *P** are fixed. The upper part of the figure reproduces the result of Figure 17-3 (a depreciation of the domestic currency shifts the aggregate demand function upward, causing output to rise). The *DD* schedule in the lower part graphs the resulting relationship between the exchange rate and output (given that *P* and *P** are held constant). Point 1 on the *DD* schedule gives the output level, Y^1, at which aggregate demand equals aggregate supply when the exchange rate is E^1. A depreciation of the currency to E^2 leads to the higher output level Y^2 according to the figure's upper part, and this information allows us to locate point 2 on *DD*.

Factors that Shift the *DD* Schedule

A number of factors affect the position of the *DD* schedule: the levels of government demand, taxes, and investment; the domestic and foreign price levels; variations in domestic consumption behavior; and the foreign demand for home output. To understand the effects of shifts in each of these factors, we must study how the *DD* schedule shifts when it changes. In the following discussions, we assume all other factors remain fixed.

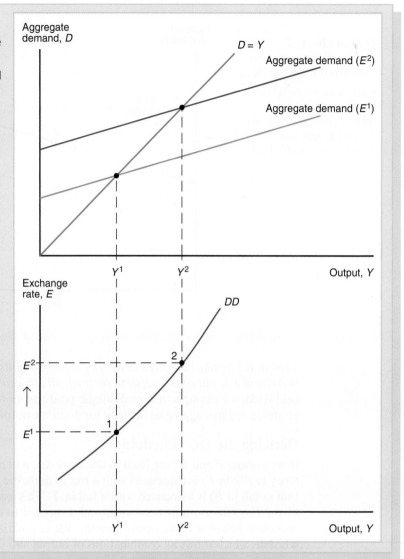

FIGURE 17-4

Deriving the *DD* Schedule

The *DD* schedule (shown in the lower panel) slopes upward because a rise in the exchange rate from E^1 to E^2, all else equal, causes output to rise from Y^1 to Y^2.

1. *A change in G.* Figure 17-5 shows the effect on *DD* of a rise in government purchases from G^1 to G^2, given a constant exchange rate of E^0. An example would be the increase in U.S. military and security expenditures following the September 11, 2001, attacks. As shown in the upper part of the figure, the exchange rate E^0 leads to an equilibrium output level Y^1 at the initial level of government demand; so point 1 is one point on DD^1.

   An increase in *G* causes the aggregate demand schedule in the upper part of the figure to shift upward. Everything else remaining unchanged, output increases from Y^1 to Y^2. Point 2 in the bottom part shows the higher level of output at which aggregate demand and supply are now equal, *given an unchanged exchange rate of E^0.* Point 2 is on a new *DD* curve, DD^2.

   For any given exchange rate, the level of output equating aggregate demand and supply is higher after the increase in *G*. This implies that *an increase in G causes*

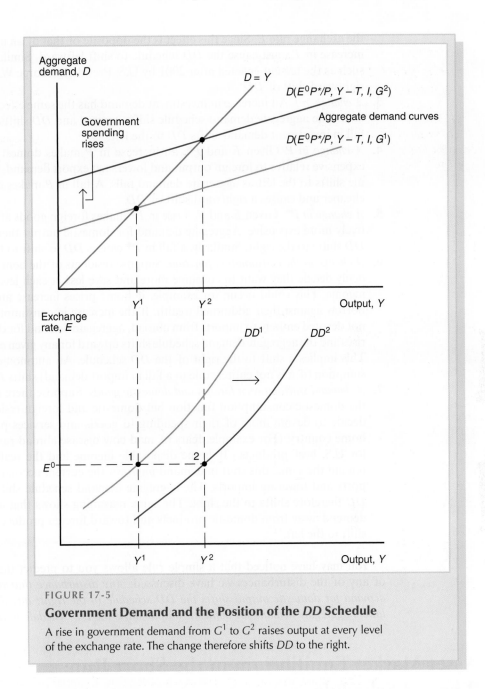

FIGURE 17-5

Government Demand and the Position of the *DD* Schedule

A rise in government demand from G^1 to G^2 raises output at every level of the exchange rate. The change therefore shifts *DD* to the right.

DD to shift to the right, as shown in Figure 17-5. Similarly, a decrease in G causes DD to shift to the left.

The method and reasoning we have just used to study how an increase in *G* shifts the *DD* curve can be applied to all the cases that follow. Here, we summarize the results. To test your understanding, use diagrams similar to Figure 17-5 to illustrate how the economic factors listed below change the curves.

2. *A change in T.* Taxes, *T*, affect aggregate demand by changing disposable income, and thus consumption, for any level of *Y*. It follows that an increase in taxes causes the aggregate demand function of Figure 17-1 to shift *downward* given

the exchange rate E. Since this effect is the opposite of that of an increase in G, an increase in T must cause the DD schedule to shift leftward. Similarly, a fall in T, such as the tax cut enacted after 2001 by U.S. President George W. Bush, causes a rightward shift of DD.

3. *A change in I.* An increase in investment demand has the same effect as an increase in G: The aggregate demand schedule shifts upward and DD shifts to the right. A fall in investment demand shifts DD to the left.

4. *A change in P.* Given E and P^*, an increase in P makes domestic output more expensive relative to foreign output and lowers net export demand. The DD schedule shifts to the left as aggregate demand falls. A fall in P makes domestic goods cheaper and causes a rightward shift of DD.

5. *A change in P^*.* Given E and P, a rise in P^* makes foreign goods and services relatively more expensive. Aggregate demand for domestic output therefore rises and DD shifts to the right. Similarly, a fall in P^* causes DD to shift to the left.

6. *A change in the consumption function.* Suppose residents of the home economy suddenly decide they want to consume more and save less at each level of disposable income. This could occur, for example, if home prices increase and homeowners borrow against their additional wealth. If the increase in consumption spending is not devoted entirely to imports from abroad, aggregate demand for domestic output rises and the aggregate demand schedule shifts upward for any given exchange rate E. This implies a shift to the right of the DD schedule. An autonomous fall in consumption (if it is not entirely due to a fall in import demand) shifts DD to the left.

7. *A demand shift between foreign and domestic goods.* Suppose there is no change in the domestic consumption function but domestic and foreign residents suddenly decide to devote more of their spending to goods and services produced in the home country. (For example, fears of mad cow disease abroad raise the demand for U.S. beef products.) If home disposable income and the real exchange rate remain the same, this shift in demand *improves* the current account by raising exports and lowering imports. The aggregate demand schedule shifts upward and DD therefore shifts to the right. The same reasoning shows that a shift in world demand away from domestic products and toward foreign products causes DD to shift to the left.

You may have noticed that a simple rule allows you to predict the effect on DD of any of the disturbances we have discussed: *Any disturbance that raises aggregate demand for domestic output shifts the DD schedule to the right; any disturbance that lowers aggregate demand for domestic output shifts the DD schedule to the left.*

Asset Market Equilibrium in the Short Run: The *AA* Schedule

We have now derived the first element in our account of short-run exchange rate and income determination, the relation between the exchange rate and output that is consistent with the equality of aggregate demand and supply. That relation is summarized by the DD schedule, which shows all exchange rate and output levels at which the output market is in short-run equilibrium. As we noted at the beginning of the preceding section, however, equilibrium in the economy as a whole requires equilibrium in the asset markets as well as in the output market, and there is no reason in general why points on the DD schedule should lead to asset market equilibrium.

To complete the story of short-run equilibrium, we therefore introduce a second element to ensure that the exchange rate and output level consistent with output market equilibrium are also consistent with asset market equilibrium. The schedule of exchange rate and output combinations that are consistent with equilibrium in the domestic money market and the foreign exchange market is called the *AA* **schedule**.

Output, the Exchange Rate, and Asset Market Equilibrium

In Chapter 14, we studied the interest parity condition, which states that the foreign exchange market is in equilibrium only when the expected rates of return on domestic and foreign currency deposits are equal. In Chapter 15, we learned how the interest rates that enter the interest parity relationship are determined by the equality of real money supply and real money demand in national money markets. Now we combine these asset market equilibrium conditions to see how the exchange rate and output must be related when all asset markets simultaneously clear. Because the focus for now is on the domestic economy, the foreign interest rate is taken as given.

For a given expected future exchange rate, E^e, the interest parity condition describing foreign exchange market equilibrium is equation (14-2),

$$R = R^* + (E^e - E)/E,$$

where R is the interest rate on domestic currency deposits and R^* is the interest rate on foreign currency deposits. In Chapter 15, we saw that the domestic interest rate satisfying the interest parity condition must also equate the real domestic money supply, M^s/P, to aggregate real money demand (see equation (15-4)):

$$M^s/P = L(R, Y).$$

You will recall that aggregate real money demand, $L(R, Y)$, rises when the interest rate falls because a fall in R makes interest-bearing nonmoney assets less attractive to hold. (Conversely, a rise in the interest rate lowers real money demand.) A rise in real output, Y, increases real money demand by raising the volume of monetary transactions people must carry out (and a fall in real output reduces real money demand by reducing people's transactions needs).

We now use the diagrammatic tools developed in Chapter 15 to study the changes in the exchange rate that must accompany output changes so that asset markets remain in equilibrium. Figure 17-6 shows the equilibrium domestic interest rate and exchange rate associated with the output level Y^1 for a given nominal money supply, M^s; a given domestic price level, P; a given foreign interest rate, R^*; and a given value of the expected future exchange rate, E^e. In the lower part of the figure, we see that with real output at Y^1 and the real money supply at M^s/P, the interest rate R^1 clears the home money market (point 1), while the exchange rate E^1 clears the foreign exchange market (point 1′). The exchange rate E^1 clears the foreign exchange market because it equates the expected rate of return on foreign deposits, measured in terms of domestic currency, to R^1.

A rise in output from Y^1 to Y^2 raises aggregate real money demand from $L(R, Y^1)$ to $L(R, Y^2)$, shifting out the entire money demand schedule in the lower part of Figure 17-6. This shift, in turn, raises the equilibrium domestic interest rate to R^2 (point 2). With E^e and R^* fixed, the domestic currency must appreciate from E^1 to E^2 to bring the foreign exchange market back into equilibrium at point 2′. The domestic currency appreciates by just enough that the increase in the rate at which it is expected to *depreciate* in the future offsets the increased interest rate advantage of

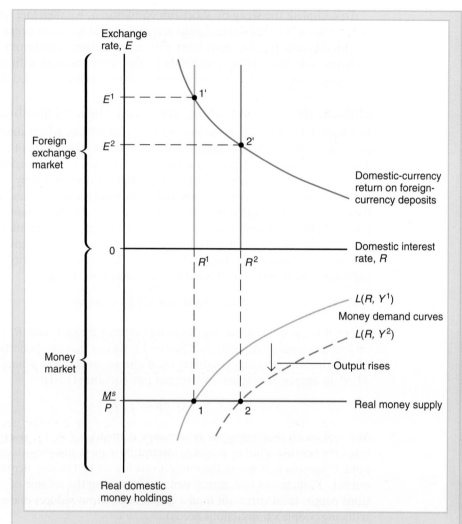

FIGURE 17-6

Output and the Exchange Rate in Asset Market Equilibrium

For the asset (foreign exchange and money) markets to remain in equilibrium, a rise in output must be accompanied by an appreciation of the currency, all else equal.

home currency deposits. *For asset markets to remain in equilibrium, a rise in domestic output must be accompanied by an appreciation of the domestic currency, all else equal, and a fall in domestic output must be accompanied by a depreciation.*

Deriving the *AA* Schedule

While the *DD* schedule plots exchange rates and output levels at which the output market is in equilibrium, the *AA* schedule relates exchange rates and output levels that keep the money and foreign exchange markets in equilibrium. Figure 17-7 shows the *AA* schedule. From Figure 17-6, we see that for any output level Y, there is a unique exchange rate E satisfying the interest parity condition (given the real money supply, the foreign interest rate, and the expected future exchange rate). Our previous

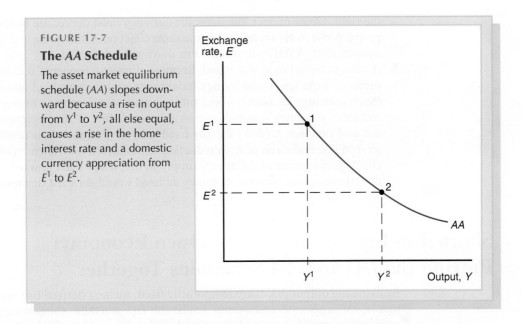

FIGURE 17-7

The AA Schedule

The asset market equilibrium schedule (AA) slopes downward because a rise in output from Y^1 to Y^2, all else equal, causes a rise in the home interest rate and a domestic currency appreciation from E^1 to E^2.

reasoning tells us that other things equal, a rise in Y^1 to Y^2 will produce an appreciation of the domestic currency, that is, a fall in the exchange rate from E^1 to E^2. The AA schedule therefore has a negative slope, as shown in Figure 17-7.

Factors that Shift the AA Schedule

Five factors cause the AA schedule to shift: changes in the domestic money supply, M^s; changes in the domestic price level, P; changes in the expected future exchange rate, E^e; changes in the foreign interest rate, R^*; and shifts in the aggregate real money demand schedule.

1. *A change in M^s.* For a fixed level of output, an increase in M^s causes the domestic currency to depreciate in the foreign exchange market, all else equal (that is, E rises). Since for each level of output the exchange rate, E, is higher after the rise in M^s, the rise in M^s causes AA to shift *upward*. Similarly, a fall in M^s causes AA to shift *downward*.

2. *A change in P.* An increase in P reduces the real money supply and drives the interest rate upward. Other things (including Y) equal, this rise in the interest rate causes E to fall. The effect of a rise in P is therefore a downward shift of AA. A fall in P results in an upward shift of AA.

3. *A change in E^e.* Suppose participants in the foreign exchange market suddenly revise their expectations about the exchange rate's future value so that E^e rises. Such a change shifts the curve in the top part of Figure 17-6 (which measures the expected domestic currency return on foreign currency deposits) to the right. The rise in E^e therefore causes the domestic currency to depreciate, other things equal. Because the exchange rate producing equilibrium in the foreign exchange market is higher after a rise in E^e, given output, AA shifts upward when a rise in the expected future exchange rate occurs. It shifts downward when the expected future exchange rate falls.

4. *A change in R^*.* A rise in R^* raises the expected return on foreign currency deposits and therefore shifts the downward-sloping schedule at the top of Figure 17-6 to

the right. Given output, the domestic currency must depreciate to restore interest parity. A rise in R^* therefore has the same effect on AA as a rise in E^e: It causes an upward shift. A fall in R^* results in a downward shift of AA.

5. *A change in real money demand.* Suppose domestic residents decide they would prefer to hold lower real money balances at each output level and interest rate. (Such a change in asset-holding preferences is a *reduction in money demand.*) A reduction in money demand implies an inward shift of the aggregate real money demand function $L(R,Y)$ for any fixed level of Y, and it thus results in a lower interest rate and a rise in E. A reduction in money demand therefore has the same effect as an increase in the money supply, in that it shifts AA upward. The opposite disturbance of an increase in money demand would shift AA downward.

Short-Run Equilibrium for an Open Economy: Putting the *DD* and *AA* Schedules Together

By assuming output prices are temporarily fixed, we have derived two separate schedules of exchange rate and output levels: the DD schedule, along which the output market is in equilibrium, and the AA schedule, along which the asset markets are in equilibrium. A short-run equilibrium for the economy as a whole must lie on *both* schedules because such a point must bring about equilibrium simultaneously in the output and asset markets. We can therefore find the economy's short-run equilibrium by finding the intersection of the DD and AA schedules. Once again, it is the assumption that domestic output prices are temporarily fixed that makes this intersection a *short-run* equilibrium. The analysis in this section continues to assume the foreign interest rate R^*, the foreign price level P^*, and the expected future exchange rate E^e also are fixed.

Figure 17-8 combines the DD and AA schedules to locate short-run equilibrium. The intersection of DD and AA at point 1 is the only combination of exchange rate

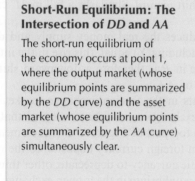

FIGURE 17-8

Short-Run Equilibrium: The Intersection of *DD* and *AA*

The short-run equilibrium of the economy occurs at point 1, where the output market (whose equilibrium points are summarized by the *DD* curve) and the asset market (whose equilibrium points are summarized by the *AA* curve) simultaneously clear.

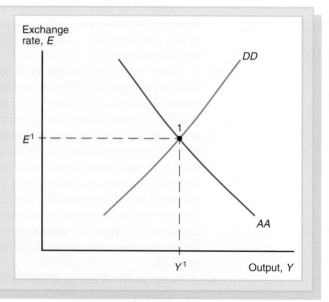

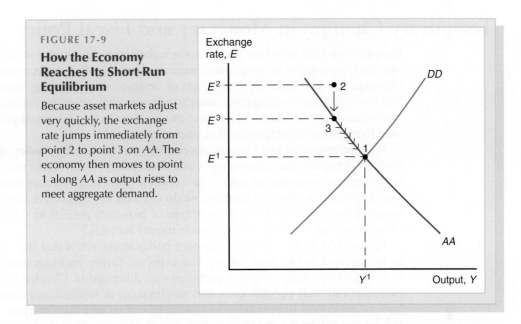

FIGURE 17-9

How the Economy Reaches Its Short-Run Equilibrium

Because asset markets adjust very quickly, the exchange rate jumps immediately from point 2 to point 3 on *AA*. The economy then moves to point 1 along *AA* as output rises to meet aggregate demand.

and output consistent with both the equality of aggregate demand and aggregate supply *and* asset market equilibrium. The short-run equilibrium levels of the exchange rate and output are therefore E^1 and Y^1.

To convince yourself that the economy will indeed settle at point 1, imagine the economy is instead at a position like point 2 in Figure 17-9. At point 2, which lies above *AA* and *DD*, both the output and asset markets are out of equilibrium. Because *E* is so high relative to *AA*, the rate at which *E* is expected to fall in the future is also high relative to the rate that would maintain interest parity. The high expected future appreciation rate of the domestic currency implies that the expected domestic currency return on foreign deposits is below that on domestic deposits, so there is an excess demand for the domestic currency in the foreign exchange market. The high level of *E* at point 2 also makes domestic goods cheap for foreign buyers (given the goods' domestic currency prices), causing an excess demand for output at that point.

The excess demand for domestic currency leads to an immediate fall in the exchange rate from E^2 to E^3. This appreciation equalizes the expected returns on domestic and foreign deposits and places the economy at point 3 on the asset market equilibrium curve *AA*. But since point 3 is above the *DD* schedule, there is still excess demand for domestic output. As firms raise production to avoid depleting their inventories, the economy travels along *AA* to point 1, where aggregate demand and supply are equal. Because asset prices can jump immediately while changes in production plans take some time, the asset markets remain in continual equilibrium even while output is changing.

The exchange rate falls as the economy approaches point 1 along *AA* because rising national output causes money demand to rise, pushing the interest rate steadily upward. (The currency must appreciate steadily to lower the expected rate of future domestic currency appreciation and maintain interest parity.) Once the economy has reached point 1 on *DD*, aggregate demand equals output and producers no longer face involuntary inventory depletion. The economy therefore settles at point 1, the only point at which the output *and* asset markets clear.

Temporary Changes in Monetary and Fiscal Policy

Now that we have seen how the economy's short-run equilibrium is determined, we can study how shifts in government macroeconomic policies affect output and the exchange rate. Our interest in the effects of macroeconomic policies stems from their usefulness in counteracting economic disturbances that cause fluctuations in output, employment, and inflation. In this section, we learn how government policies can be used to maintain full employment in open economies.

We concentrate on two types of government policy, **monetary policy**, which works through changes in the money supply, and **fiscal policy**, which works through changes in government spending or taxes.[8] To avoid the complications that would be introduced by ongoing inflation, however, we do not look at situations in which the money supply grows over time. Thus, the only type of monetary policies we will study explicitly are one-shot increases or decreases in money supplies.[9]

In this section, we examine *temporary* policy shifts, shifts that the public expects to be reversed in the near future. The expected future exchange rate, E^e, is now assumed to equal the long-run exchange rate discussed in Chapter 16, that is, the exchange rate that prevails once full employment is reached and domestic prices have adjusted fully to past disturbances in the output and asset markets. In line with this interpretation, a temporary policy change does *not* affect the long-run expected exchange rate, E^e.

We assume throughout that events in the economy we are studying do not influence the foreign interest rate, R^*, or price level, P^*, and that the domestic price level, P, is fixed in the short run.

Monetary Policy

The short-run effect of a temporary increase in the domestic money supply is shown in Figure 17-10. An increased money supply shifts AA^1 upward to AA^2 but does not affect the position of DD. The upward shift of the asset market equilibrium schedule moves the economy from point 1, with exchange rate E^1 and output Y^1, to point 2, with exchange rate E^2 and output Y^2. An increase in the money supply causes a depreciation of the domestic currency, an expansion of output, and therefore an increase in employment.

We can understand the economic forces causing these results by recalling our earlier discussions of asset market equilibrium and output determination. At the initial output level Y^1 and given the fixed price level, an increase in money supply must push down the home interest rate, R. We have been assuming that the monetary change is temporary and does not affect the expected future exchange rate, E^e, so to preserve interest parity in the face of a decline in R (given that the foreign interest rate, R^*, does not change), the exchange rate must depreciate immediately to create the expectation that the home currency will appreciate in the future at a faster rate than was expected before R fell. The immediate depreciation of the domestic currency, however, makes home products cheaper relative to foreign products. There is therefore an increase in aggregate demand, which must be matched by an increase in output.

---

[8]An example of the latter (as noted earlier) would be the tax cut enacted during the 2001–2005 administration of President George W. Bush. Other policies, such as commercial policies (tariffs, quotas, and so on), have macroeconomic side effects. Such policies, however, are not used routinely for purposes of macroeconomic stabilization, so we do not discuss them in this chapter. (A problem at the end of this chapter does ask you to think about the macroeconomic effects of a tariff.)

[9]You can extend the results below to a setting with ongoing inflation by thinking of the exchange rate and price level changes we describe as departures from time paths along which E and P trend upward at constant rates.

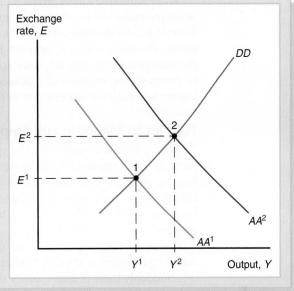

FIGURE 17-10

Effects of a Temporary Increase in the Money Supply

By shifting AA^1 upward, a temporary increase in the money supply causes a currency depreciation and a rise in output.

Fiscal Policy

As we saw earlier, expansionary fiscal policy can take the form of an increase in government spending, a cut in taxes, or some combination of the two that raises aggregate demand. A temporary fiscal expansion (which does not affect the expected future exchange rate) therefore shifts the DD schedule to the right but does not move AA.

Figure 17-11 shows how expansionary fiscal policy affects the economy in the short run. Initially the economy is at point 1, with an exchange rate E^1 and output Y^1. Suppose the government decides to spend \$30 billion to develop a new space shuttle. This one-time increase in government purchases moves the economy to point 2, causing the currency to appreciate to E^2 and output to expand to Y^2. The economy would respond in a similar way to a temporary cut in taxes.

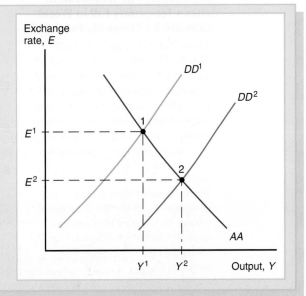

FIGURE 17-11

Effects of a Temporary Fiscal Expansion

By shifting DD^1 to the right, a temporary fiscal expansion causes a currency appreciation and a rise in output.

What economic forces produce the movement from point 1 to point 2? The increase in output caused by the increase in government spending raises the transactions demand for real money holdings. Given the fixed price level, this increase in money demand pushes the interest rate, R, upward. Because the expected future exchange rate, E^e, and the foreign interest rate, R^*, have not changed, the domestic currency must appreciate to create the expectation of a subsequent depreciation just large enough to offset the higher international interest rate difference in favor of domestic currency deposits.

Policies to Maintain Full Employment

The analysis of this section can be applied to the problem of maintaining full employment in open economies. Because temporary monetary expansion and temporary fiscal expansion both raise output and employment, they can be used to counteract the effects of temporary disturbances that lead to recession. Similarly, disturbances that lead to overemployment can be offset through contractionary macroeconomic policies.

Figure 17-12 illustrates this use of macroeconomic policy. Suppose the economy's initial equilibrium is at point 1, where output equals its full-employment level, denoted Y^f. Suddenly there is a temporary shift in consumer tastes away from domestic products. As we saw earlier in this chapter, such a shift is a decrease in aggregate demand for domestic goods, and it causes the curve DD^1 to shift leftward, to DD^2. At point 2, the new short-run equilibrium, the currency has depreciated to E^2 and output, at Y^2, is below its full-employment level: The economy is in a recession. Because the shift in preferences is assumed to be temporary, it does not affect E^e, so there is no change in the position of AA^1.

To restore full employment, the government may use monetary or fiscal policy, or both. A temporary fiscal expansion shifts DD^2 back to its original position, restoring full employment and returning the exchange rate to E^1. A temporary money supply increase shifts the asset market equilibrium curve to AA^2 and places the economy

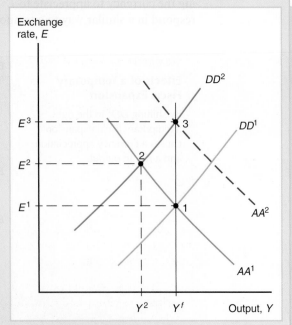

FIGURE 17-12

Maintaining Full Employment after a Temporary Fall in World Demand for Domestic Products

A temporary fall in world demand shifts DD^1 to DD^2, reducing output from Y^f to Y^2 and causing the currency to depreciate from E^1 to E^2 (point 2). Temporary fiscal expansion can restore full employment (point 1) by shifting the DD schedule back to its original position. Temporary monetary expansion can restore full employment (point 3) by shifting AA^1 to AA^2. The two policies differ in their exchange rate effects: The fiscal policy restores the currency to its previous value (E^1), whereas the monetary policy causes the currency to depreciate further, to E^3.

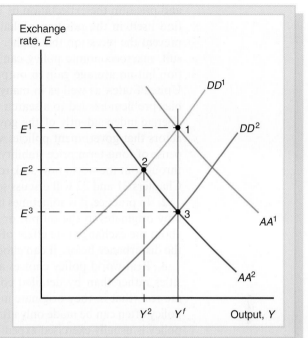

FIGURE 17-13

Policies to Maintain Full Employment after a Money Demand Increase

After a temporary money demand increase (shown by the shift from AA^1 to AA^2), either an increase in the money supply or temporary fiscal expansion can be used to maintain full employment. The two policies have different exchange rate effects: The monetary policy restores the exchange rate back to E^1, whereas the fiscal policy leads to greater appreciation (E^3).

at point 3, a move that restores full employment but causes the home currency to depreciate even further.

Another possible cause of recession is a temporary increase in the demand for money, illustrated in Figure 17-13. An increase in money demand pushes up the domestic interest rate and appreciates the currency, thereby making domestic goods more expensive and causing output to contract. Figure 17-13 shows this asset market disturbance as the downward shift of AA^1 to AA^2, which moves the economy from its initial, full-employment equilibrium at point 1 to point 2.

Expansionary macroeconomic policies can again restore full employment. A temporary money supply increase shifts the AA curve back to AA^1 and returns the economy to its initial position at point 1. This temporary increase in money supply completely offsets the increase in money demand by giving domestic residents the additional money they desire to hold. Temporary fiscal expansion shifts DD^1 to DD^2 and restores full employment at point 3. But the move to point 3 involves an even greater appreciation of the currency.

Inflation Bias and Other Problems of Policy Formulation

The apparent ease with which full employment is maintained in our model is misleading, and you should not come away from our discussion of policy with the idea that it is easy to keep the macroeconomy on a steady course. Here are just a few of the many problems that can arise:

1. Sticky nominal prices not only give a government the power to raise output when it is abnormally low, but also may tempt it to create a politically useful economic boom, say, just before a close election. This temptation causes problems when workers and firms anticipate it in advance, for they will raise wage demands

and prices in the expectation of expansionary policies. The government will then find itself in the position of having to use expansionary policy tools merely to prevent the recession that higher domestic prices otherwise would cause! As a result, macroeconomic policy can display an **inflation bias**, leading to high inflation but no average gain in output. Such an increase in inflation occurred in the United States, as well as in many other countries, during the 1970s. The inflation bias problem has led to a search for institutions—for example, central banks that operate independently of the government in power—that might convince market actors that government policies will not be used in a shortsighted way, at the expense of long-term price stability. As we noted in Chapter 15, many central banks throughout the world now seek to reach announced target levels of (low) inflation. Chapters 21 and 22 will discuss some of these efforts in greater detail.[10]

2. In practice, it is sometimes hard to be sure whether a disturbance to the economy originates in the output or the asset markets. Yet a government concerned about the exchange rate effect of its policy response needs to know the source of the disturbance before it can choose between monetary and fiscal policy.

3. Real-world policy choices are frequently determined by bureaucratic necessities rather than by detailed consideration of whether shocks to the economy are real (that is, they originate in the output market) or monetary. Shifts in fiscal policy often can be made only after lengthy legislative deliberation, while monetary policy is usually exercised expeditiously by the central bank. To avoid procedural delays, governments are likely to respond to disturbances by changing monetary policy even when a shift in fiscal policy would be more appropriate.

4. Another problem with fiscal policy is its impact on the government budget. A tax cut or spending increase may lead to a larger government budget deficit, which must sooner or later be closed by a fiscal reversal, as happened following the multibillion-dollar fiscal stimulus package sponsored by the Obama administration in the United States in 2009. Unfortunately, there is no guarantee the government will have the political will to synchronize these actions with the state of the business cycle. The state of the electoral cycle may be more important, as we have seen.

5. Policies that appear to act swiftly in our simple model operate in reality with lags of varying lengths. At the same time, the difficulty of evaluating the size and persistence of a given shock makes it hard to know precisely how much monetary or fiscal medicine to administer. These uncertainties force policy makers to base their actions on forecasts and hunches that may turn out to be quite wide of the mark.

Permanent Shifts in Monetary and Fiscal Policy

A permanent policy shift affects not only the current value of the government's policy instrument (the money supply, government spending, or taxes) but also the *long-run* exchange rate. This in turn affects expectations about future exchange rates. Because these changes in expectations have a major influence on the exchange rate prevailing

---

[10]For a clear and detailed discussion of the inflation bias problem, see Chapter 14 in Andrew B. Abel, Ben S. Bernanke, and Dean Croushore, *Macroeconomics*, 8th ed. (Upper Saddle River, NJ: Prentice Hall, 2014). The inflation bias problem can arise even when the government's policies are not politically motivated, as Abel, Bernanke, and Croushore explain. The basic idea is that when factors like minimum wage laws keep output inefficiently low by lowering employment, monetary expansion that raises employment may move the economy toward a more efficient use of its total resources. The government might wish to reach a better resource allocation purely on the grounds that such a change potentially benefits everyone in the economy. But the private sector's expectation of such policies still will generate inflation.

in the short run, the effects of permanent policy shifts differ from those of temporary shifts. In this section, we look at the effects of permanent changes in monetary and fiscal policy, in both the short and long runs.[11]

To make it easier to grasp the long-run effects of policies, we assume the economy is initially at a long-run equilibrium position and that the policy changes we examine are the only economic changes that occur (our usual "other things equal" clause). These assumptions mean that the economy starts out at full employment with the exchange rate at its long-run level and with no change in the exchange rate expected. In particular, we know that the domestic interest rate must initially equal the foreign rate, R^*.

A Permanent Increase in the Money Supply

Figure 17-14 shows the short-run effects of a permanent increase in the money supply on an economy initially at its full-employment output level Y^f (point 1). As we saw earlier, even a temporary increase in M^s causes the asset market equilibrium schedule to shift upward from AA^1 to AA^2. Because the increase in M^s is now permanent, however, it also affects the exchange rate expected for the future, E^e. Chapter 15 showed how a permanent increase in the money supply affects the long-run exchange rate: A permanent increase in M^s must ultimately lead to a proportional rise in E. Therefore, the permanent rise in M^s causes E^e, the expected future exchange rate, to rise proportionally.

Because a rise in E^e accompanies a *permanent* increase in the money supply, the upward shift of AA^1 to AA^2 is *greater* than that caused by an equal, but transitory,

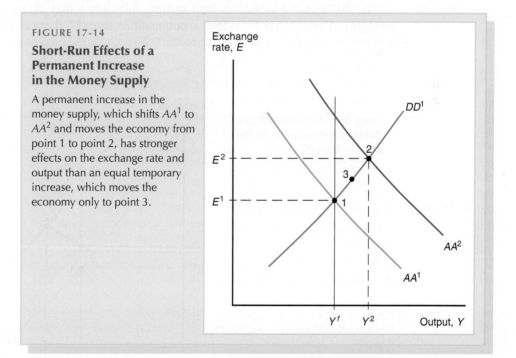

FIGURE 17-14

Short-Run Effects of a Permanent Increase in the Money Supply

A permanent increase in the money supply, which shifts AA^1 to AA^2 and moves the economy from point 1 to point 2, has stronger effects on the exchange rate and output than an equal temporary increase, which moves the economy only to point 3.

---

[11]You may be wondering whether a permanent change in fiscal policy is always possible. For example, if a government starts with a balanced budget, doesn't a fiscal expansion lead to a deficit, and thus require an eventual fiscal contraction? Problem 3 at the end of this chapter suggests an answer.

increase. At point 2, the economy's new short-run equilibrium, Y and E are both higher than they would be were the change in the money supply temporary. (Point 3 shows the equilibrium that might result from a temporary increase in M^s.)

Adjustment to a Permanent Increase in the Money Supply

The increase in the money supply shown in Figure 17-14 is not reversed by the central bank, so it is natural to ask how the economy is affected *over time*. At the short-run equilibrium, shown as point 2 in Figure 17-14, output is above its full-employment level and labor and machines are working overtime. Upward pressure on the price level develops as workers demand higher wages and producers raise prices to cover their increasing production costs. Chapter 15 showed that while an increase in the money supply must eventually cause all money prices to rise in proportion, it has no lasting effect on output, relative prices, or interest rates. Over time, the inflationary pressure that follows a permanent money supply expansion pushes the price level to its new long-run value and returns the economy to full employment.

Figure 17-15 will help you visualize the adjustment back to full employment. Whenever output is greater than its full-employment level, Y^f, and productive factors are working overtime, the price level P is rising to keep up with rising production costs. Although the DD and AA schedules are drawn for a constant price level P, we have seen how increases in P cause the schedules to shift. A rise in P makes domestic goods more expensive relative to foreign goods, discouraging exports and encouraging imports. A rising domestic price level therefore causes DD^1 to shift to the left over time. Because a rising price level steadily reduces the real money supply over time, AA^2 also travels to the left as prices rise.

The DD and AA schedules stop shifting only when they intersect at the full-employment output level Y^f; as long as output differs from Y^f, the price level will change and the two schedules will continue to shift. The schedules' final positions are shown

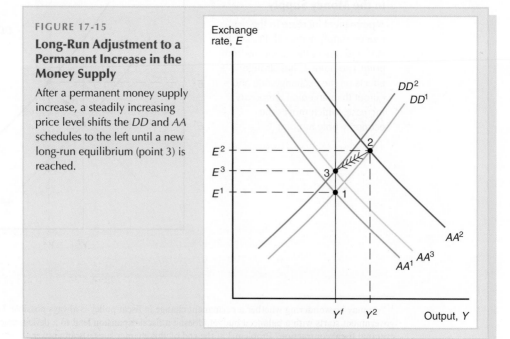

FIGURE 17-15

Long-Run Adjustment to a Permanent Increase in the Money Supply

After a permanent money supply increase, a steadily increasing price level shifts the DD and AA schedules to the left until a new long-run equilibrium (point 3) is reached.

in Figure 17-15 as DD^2 and AA^3. At point 3, their intersection, the exchange rate, E, and the price level, P, have risen in proportion to the increase in the money supply, as required by the long-run neutrality of money. (AA^2 does not shift all the way back to its original position because E^e is permanently higher after a permanent increase in the money supply: It too has risen by the same percentage as M^s.)

Notice that along the adjustment path between the initial short-run equilibrium (point 2) and the long-run equilibrium (point 3), the domestic currency actually appreciates (from E^2 to E^3) following its initial sharp depreciation (from E^1 to E^2). This exchange rate behavior is an example of the *overshooting* phenomenon discussed in Chapter 15, in which the exchange rate's initial response to some change is greater than its long-run response.[12]

We can draw on our conclusions to describe the proper policy response to a permanent monetary disturbance. A permanent increase in money demand, for example, can be offset with a permanent increase of equal magnitude in the money supply. Such a policy maintains full employment, but because the price level would fall in the absence of the policy, the policy will not have inflationary consequences. Instead, monetary expansion can move the economy straight to its long-run, full-employment position. Keep in mind, however, that it is hard in practice to diagnose the origin or persistence of a particular shock to the economy.

A Permanent Fiscal Expansion

A permanent fiscal expansion not only has an immediate impact in the output market but also affects the asset markets through its impact on long-run exchange rate expectations. Figure 17-16 shows the short-run effects of a government decision to spend an

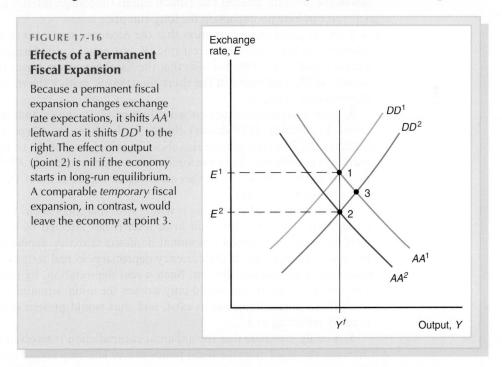

FIGURE 17-16

Effects of a Permanent Fiscal Expansion

Because a permanent fiscal expansion changes exchange rate expectations, it shifts AA^1 leftward as it shifts DD^1 to the right. The effect on output (point 2) is nil if the economy starts in long-run equilibrium. A comparable *temporary* fiscal expansion, in contrast, would leave the economy at point 3.

---

[12]While the exchange rate initially overshoots in the case shown in Figure 17-15, overshooting does not have to occur in all circumstances. Can you explain why, and does the "undershooting" case seem reasonable?

extra $10 billion a year on its space travel program *forever*. As before, the direct effect of this rise in G on aggregate demand causes DD^1 to shift right to DD^2. But because the increase in government demand for domestic goods and services is permanent in this case, it causes a long-run appreciation of the currency, as we saw in Chapter 16. The resulting fall in E^e pushes the asset market equilibrium schedule AA^1 downward to AA^2. Point 2, where the new schedules DD^2 and AA^2 intersect, is the economy's short-run equilibrium, and at that point the currency has appreciated to E^2 from its initial level while output is unchanged at Y^f.

The important result illustrated in Figure 17-16 is that when a fiscal expansion is permanent, the additional currency appreciation caused by the shift in exchange rate expectations reduces the policy's expansionary effect on output. Without this additional expectations effect due to the permanence of the fiscal change, equilibrium would initially be at point 3, with higher output and a smaller appreciation. The greater the downward shift of the asset market equilibrium schedule, the greater the appreciation of the currency. This appreciation "crowds out" aggregate demand for domestic products by making them more expensive relative to foreign products.

Figure 17-16 is drawn to show a case in which fiscal expansion, contrary to what you might have guessed, has *no* net effect on output. This case is not, however, a special one; in fact, it is inevitable under the assumptions we have made. The argument that establishes this point requires five steps; by taking the time to understand them, you will solidify your understanding of the ground we have covered so far:

1. As a first step, convince yourself (perhaps by reviewing Chapter 15) that because the fiscal expansion does not affect the money supply, M^s; the long-run values of the domestic interest rate (which equals the foreign interest rate); or output (Y^f), it can have no impact on the long-run price level.

2. Next, recall our assumption that the economy starts out in long-run equilibrium with the domestic interest rate, R, just equal to the foreign rate, R^*, and output equal to Y^f. Observe also that the fiscal expansion leaves the real money supply, M^s/P, unchanged in the short run (that is, neither the numerator nor the denominator changes).

3. Now imagine, contrary to what Figure 17-16 shows, that output did rise above Y^f. Because M^s/P doesn't change in the short run (Step 2), the domestic interest rate, R, would have to rise above its initial level of R^* to keep the money market in equilibrium. Since the foreign interest rate remains at R^*, however, a rise in Y to any level above Y^f implies an expected depreciation of the domestic currency (by interest parity).

4. Notice next that something is wrong with this conclusion. We already know (from Step 1) that the long-run price level is not affected by the fiscal expansion, so people can expect a nominal domestic currency depreciation just after the policy change only if the currency depreciates in real terms as the economy returns to long-run equilibrium. Such a real depreciation, by making domestic products relatively cheap, would only worsen the initial situation of overemployment that we have imagined to exist, and thus would prevent output from ever actually returning to Y^f.

5. Finally, conclude that the apparent contradiction is resolved only if output does not rise at all after the fiscal policy move. The only logical possibility is that the currency appreciates right away to its new long-run value. This appreciation crowds out just enough net export demand to leave output at the full-employment level despite the higher level of G.

Notice that this exchange rate change, which allows the output market to clear at full employment, leaves the asset markets in equilibrium as well. Since the exchange rate has jumped to its new long-run value, R remains at R^*. With output also at Y^f, however, the long-run money market equilibrium condition $M^s/P = L(R^*, Y^f)$ still holds, as it did before the fiscal action. So our story hangs together: The currency appreciation that a permanent fiscal expansion provokes immediately brings the asset markets as well as the output market to positions of long-run equilibrium.

We conclude that if the economy starts at long-run equilibrium, a permanent change in fiscal policy has no net effect on output. Instead, it causes an immediate and permanent exchange rate jump that offsets exactly the fiscal policy's direct effect on aggregate demand. A fall in net export demand counteracts the rise in government demand.

Macroeconomic Policies and the Current Account

Policy makers are often concerned about the level of the current account. As we will discuss more fully in Chapter 19, an excessive imbalance in the current account—either a surplus or a deficit—may have undesirable long-run effects on national welfare. Large external imbalances may also generate political pressures for governments to impose restrictions on trade. It is therefore important to know how monetary and fiscal policies aimed at domestic objectives affect the current account.

Figure 17-17 shows how the DD-AA model can be extended to illustrate the effects of macroeconomic policies on the current account. In addition to the DD and AA curves, the figure contains a new curve, labeled XX, which shows combinations of the exchange rate and output at which the current account balance would be equal to some desired level, say $CA(EP^*/P, Y - T) = X$. The curve slopes upward because, other things equal, a rise in output encourages spending on imports and thus worsens the current account if it is not accompanied by a currency depreciation. Since the

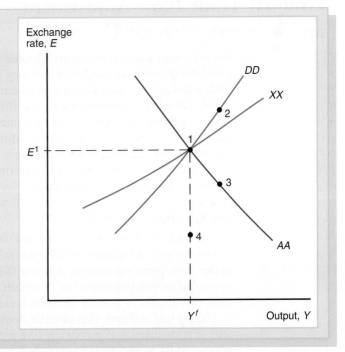

FIGURE 17-17

How Macroeconomic Policies Affect the Current Account

Along the curve XX, the current account is constant at the level $CA = X$. Monetary expansion moves the economy to point 2 and thus raises the current account balance. Temporary fiscal expansion moves the economy to point 3 while permanent fiscal expansion moves it to point 4; in either case, the current account balance falls.

actual level of CA can differ from X, the economy's short-run equilibrium does *not* have to be on the XX curve.

The central feature of Figure 17-17 is that XX is *flatter* than DD. The reason is seen by asking how the current account changes as we move up along the DD curve from point 1, where all three curves intersect (so that, initially, $CA = X$). As we increase Y in moving up along DD, the *domestic* demand for domestic output rises by less than the rise in output itself (since some income is saved and some spending falls on imports). Along DD, however, *total aggregate demand has to equal supply.* To prevent an excess supply of home output, E therefore must rise sharply enough along DD to make export demand rise faster than import demand. In other words, net foreign demand—the current account—must rise sufficiently along DD as output rises to take up the slack left by domestic saving. Thus, to the right of point 1, DD is above the XX curve, where $CA > X$; similar reasoning shows that to the left of point 1, DD lies below the XX curve (where $CA < X$).

The current account effects of macroeconomic policies can now be examined. As shown earlier, an increase in the money supply, for example, shifts the economy to a position like point 2, expanding output and depreciating the currency. Since point 2 lies above XX, the current account has improved as a result of the policy action. *Monetary expansion causes the current account balance to increase in the short run.*

Consider next a temporary fiscal expansion. This action shifts DD to the right and moves the economy to point 3 in the figure. Because the currency appreciates and income rises, there is a deterioration in the current account. A permanent fiscal expansion has the additional effect of shifting AA leftward, producing an equilibrium at point 4. Like point 3, point 4 is below XX, so once again the current account worsens, and by more than in the temporary case. *Expansionary fiscal policy reduces the current account balance.*

Gradual Trade Flow Adjustment and Current Account Dynamics

An important assumption underlying the DD-AA model is that, other things equal, a real depreciation of the home currency immediately improves the current account while a real appreciation causes the current account immediately to worsen. In reality, however, the behavior underlying trade flows may be far more complex than we have so far suggested, involving dynamic elements—on the supply as well as the demand side—that lead the current account to adjust only gradually to exchange rate changes. In this section, we discuss some dynamic factors that seem important in explaining actual patterns of current account adjustment and indicate how their presence might modify the predictions of our model.

The J-Curve

It is sometimes observed that a country's current account *worsens* immediately after a real currency depreciation and begins to improve only some months later, contrary to the assumption we made in deriving the DD curve. If the current account initially worsens after a depreciation, its time path, shown in Figure 17-18, has an initial segment reminiscent of a J and therefore is called the **J-curve**.

The current account, measured in domestic output, can deteriorate sharply right after a real currency depreciation (the move from point 1 to point 2 in the figure) because most import and export orders are placed several months in advance. In the

FIGURE 17-18

The J-Curve

The J-curve describes the time lag with which a real currency depreciation improves the current account.

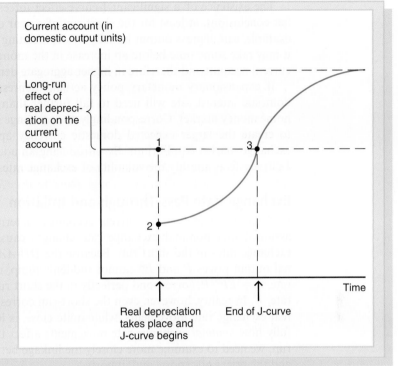

first few months after the depreciation, export and import volumes therefore may reflect buying decisions that were made on the basis of the old real exchange rate: The primary effect of the depreciation is to raise the value of the pre-contracted level of imports in terms of domestic products. Because exports measured in domestic output do not change, while imports measured in domestic output rise, there is an initial fall in the current account, as shown.

Even after the old export and import contracts have been fulfilled, it still takes time for new shipments to adjust fully to the relative price change. On the production side, producers of exports may have to install additional plant and equipment and hire new workers. To the extent that imports consist of intermediate materials used in domestic manufacturing, import adjustment will also occur gradually as importers switch to new production techniques that economize on intermediate inputs. There are lags on the consumption side as well. To expand significantly foreign consumption of domestic exports, for example, it may be necessary to build new retailing outlets abroad, a time-consuming process.

The result of these lags in adjustment is the gradually improving current account shown in Figure 17-18 as the move from point 2 to point 3 and beyond. Eventually, the increase in the current account tapers off as the adjustment to the real depreciation is completed.

Empirical evidence indicates for most industrial countries a J-curve lasting more than six months but less than a year. Thus, point 3 in the figure is typically reached within a year of the real depreciation, and the current account continues to improve afterward.[13]

---

[13]See the discussion of Table 17A2-1 in Appendix 2 of this chapter.

The existence of a significant J-curve effect forces us to modify some of our earlier conclusions, at least for the short run of a year or less. Monetary expansion, for example, can depress output initially by depreciating the home currency. In this case, it may take some time before an increase in the money supply results in an improved current account and therefore in higher aggregate demand.

If expansionary monetary policy actually depresses output in the short run, the domestic interest rate will need to fall further than it normally would to clear the home money market. Correspondingly, the exchange rate will overshoot more sharply to create the larger expected domestic currency appreciation required for foreign exchange market equilibrium. By introducing an additional source of overshooting, J-curve effects amplify the volatility of exchange rates.

Exchange Rate Pass-Through and Inflation

Our discussion of how the current account is determined in the DD-AA model has assumed that nominal exchange rate changes cause proportional changes in real exchange rates in the short run. Because the DD-AA model assumes that the nominal output prices P and P^* cannot suddenly jump, movements in the real exchange rate, $q = EP^*/P$, correspond perfectly in the short run to movements in the nominal rate, E. In reality, however, even the short-run correspondence between nominal and real exchange rate movements, while quite close, is less than perfect. To understand fully how *nominal* exchange rate movements affect the current account in the short run, we need to examine more closely the linkage between the nominal exchange rate and the prices of exports and imports.

The domestic currency price of foreign output is the product of the exchange rate and the foreign currency price, or EP^*. We have assumed until now that when E rises, for example, P^* remains fixed so that the domestic currency price of goods imported from abroad rises in proportion. The percentage by which import prices rise when the home currency depreciates by 1 percent is known as the degree of **pass-through** from the exchange rate to import prices. In the version of the DD-AA model we studied above, the degree of pass-through is 1; any exchange rate change is passed through completely to import prices.

Contrary to this assumption, however, exchange rate pass-through can be incomplete. One possible reason for incomplete pass-through is international market segmentation, which allows imperfectly competitive firms to price to market by charging different prices for the same product in different countries (recall Chapter 16). For example, a large foreign firm supplying automobiles to the United States may be so worried about losing market share that it does not immediately raise its U.S. prices by 10 percent when the dollar depreciates by 10 percent, despite the fact that its revenue from American sales, measured in its own currency, will decline. Similarly, the firm may hesitate to lower its U.S. prices by 10 percent after a dollar appreciation of that size because it can thereby earn higher profits without investing resources immediately in expanding its shipments to the United States. In either case, the firm may wait to find out if the currency movement reflects a definite trend before making price and production commitments that are costly to undo. In practice, many U.S. import prices tend to rise by only around half of a typical dollar depreciation over the following year.

We thus see that while a permanent nominal exchange rate change may be fully reflected in import prices in the long run, the degree of pass-through may be far less than 1 in the short run. Incomplete pass-through will have complicated effects, however, on the timing of current account adjustment. On the one hand, the short-run J-curve effect of a nominal currency change will be dampened by a low responsiveness of import prices to the exchange rate. On the other hand, incomplete pass-through implies that currency movements have less-than-proportional effects on the relative prices determining trade volumes. The failure of relative prices to adjust quickly will in turn be accompanied by a slow adjustment of trade volumes. Notice also how the link between nominal and real exchange rates may be further weakened by *domestic* price responses. In highly inflationary economies, for example, it is difficult to alter the real exchange rate, EP^*/P, simply by changing the nominal rate E, because the resulting increase in aggregate demand quickly sparks domestic inflation, which in turn raises P. To the extent that a country's export prices rise when its currency depreciates, any favorable effect on its competitive position in world markets will be dissipated. Such price increases, however, like partial pass-through, may weaken the J-curve.

The Current Account, Wealth, and Exchange Rate Dynamics

Our theoretical model showed that a permanent fiscal expansion would cause both an appreciation of the currency and a current account deficit. Although our discussion earlier in this chapter focused on the role of price level movements in bringing the economy from its immediate position after a permanent policy change to its long-run position, the definition of the current account should alert you to another underlying dynamic: The net foreign wealth of an economy with a deficit is falling over time.

Although we have not explicitly incorporated wealth effects into our model, we would expect people's consumption to fall as their wealth falls. Because a country with a current account deficit is transferring wealth to foreigners, domestic consumption is falling over time and foreign consumption is rising. What are the exchange rate effects of this international redistribution of consumption demand in favor of foreigners? Foreigners have a relative preference for consuming the goods that they produce, and as a result, the relative world demand for home goods will fall and the home currency will tend to depreciate in real terms.

This longer-run perspective leads to a more complicated picture of the real exchange rate's evolution following a permanent change such as a fiscal expansion. Initially, the home currency will appreciate as the current account balance falls sharply. But then, over time, the currency will begin to depreciate as market participants' expectations focus increasingly on the current account's effect on relative international wealth levels.[14]

The Liquidity Trap

During the lengthy Great Depression of the 1930s, the nominal interest rate hit zero in the United States, and the country found itself caught in what economists call a **liquidity trap**.

Recall from Chapter 15 that money is the most *liquid* of assets, unique in the ease with which it can be exchanged for goods. A liquidity trap is a trap because once an economy's nominal interest rate falls to zero, the central bank cannot reduce it further by increasing the money supply (that is, by increasing the economy's liquidity). Why? At negative nominal interest rates, people would find money strictly preferable to bonds, and bonds therefore would be in excess supply. While a zero interest rate

---

[14]An influential model of exchange rates and the current account is presented by Rudiger Dornbusch and Stanley Fischer, "Exchange Rates and the Current Account," *American Economic Review* 70 (December 1980), pp. 960–971.

may please borrowers who can borrow for free it worries makers of macroeconomic policy, who are trapped in a situation where they may no longer be able to steer the economy through conventional monetary expansion.

Economists thought liquidity traps were a thing of the past until Japan fell into one in the late 1990s. Despite a dramatic lowering of interest rates by the country's central bank, the Bank of Japan (BOJ), the country's economy has stagnated and suffered *de*flation (a falling price level) since at least the mid-1990s. By 1999, the country's short-term interest rates had effectively reached zero. In September 2004, for example, the Bank of Japan reported that the overnight interest rate (the one most immediately affected by monetary policy) was only 0.001 percent per year.

Seeing signs of economic recovery, the BOJ raised interest rates slightly starting in 2006, but retreated back toward zero as a global financial crisis gathered force late in 2008 (see Chapter 19). That crisis also hit the United States hard, and as Figure 14-2 (page 389) suggests, interest rates then plummeted toward zero in the United States as well as in Japan. Simultaneously, other central banks throughout the world slashed their own rates dramatically. The liquidity trap had gone global.

The dilemma a central bank faces when the economy is in a liquidity trap slow-down can be seen by considering the interest parity condition when the domestic interest rate $R = 0$,

$$R = 0 = R^* + (E^e - E)/E.$$

Assume for the moment that the expected future exchange rate, E^e, is fixed. Suppose the central bank raises the domestic money supply so as to depreciate the currency temporarily (that is, to raise E today but return the exchange rate to the level E^e later). The interest parity condition shows that E cannot rise once $R = 0$ because the interest rate would have to become *negative*. Instead, despite the increase in the money supply, the exchange rate remains steady at the level

$$E = E^e/(1 - R^*).$$

The currency cannot depreciate further.

How is this possible? Our usual argument that a temporary increase in the money supply reduces the interest rate (and depreciates the currency) rests on the assumption that people will add money to their portfolios only if bonds become less attractive to hold. At an interest rate of $R = 0$, however, people are indifferent about trades between bonds and money—both yield a nominal rate of return rate equal to zero. An open-market purchase of bonds for money, say, will not disturb the markets: People will be happy to accept the additional money in exchange for their bonds with no change in the interest rate from zero and, thus, no change in the exchange rate. In contrast to the case we examined earlier in this chapter, an increase in the money supply will have no effect on the economy! A central bank that progressively *reduces* the money supply by selling bonds will eventually succeed in pushing the interest rate up— the economy cannot function without some money—but that possibility is not helpful when the economy is in a slump and a *fall* in interest rates is the medicine that it needs.

Figure 17-19 shows how the *DD-AA* diagram can be modified to depict the region of potential equilibrium positions involving a liquidity trap. The *DD* schedule is the same, but the *AA* schedule now has a flat segment at levels of output so low that the money market finds its equilibrium at an interest rate R equal to zero. The flat segment of *AA* shows the currency cannot depreciate beyond the level $E^e/(1 - R^*)$. At the equilibrium point 1 in the diagram, output is trapped at a level Y^1 that is below the full-employment level Y^f.

FIGURE 17-19

A Low-Output Liquidity Trap

At point 1, output is below its full employment level. Because exchange rate expectations E^e are fixed, however, a monetary expansion will merely shift AA to the right, leaving the initial equilibrium point the same. The horizontal stretch of AA gives rise to the liquidity trap.

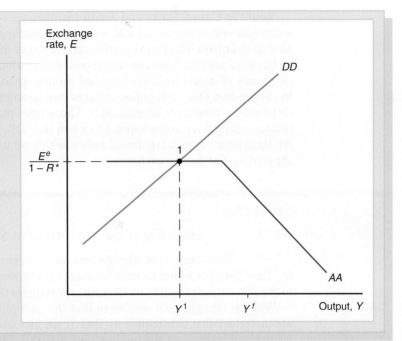

Let's consider next how an open-market expansion of the money supply works in this strange, zero-interest world. Although we do not show it in Figure 17-19, that action would shift *AA to the right*: At an unchanged exchange rate, higher output Y raises money demand, leaving people content to hold the additional money at the unchanged interest rate $R = 0$. The horizontal stretch of AA becomes longer as a result. With more money in circulation, real output and money demand can rise further than before without driving the nominal interest rate to a positive level. (Eventually, as Y rises even further, increased money demand results in progressively higher interest rates R and therefore in progressive currency appreciation along the downward-sloping segment of AA.) The surprising result is that the equilibrium simply remains at point 1. Monetary expansion thus has no effect on output or the exchange rate. This is the sense in which the economy is "trapped."

Our earlier assumption that the expected future exchange rate is fixed is a key ingredient in this liquidity trap story. Suppose the central bank can credibly promise to raise the money supply *permanently*, so that E^e rises at the same time as the current money supply. In that case, the AA schedule will shift up as well as to the right, output will therefore expand, and the currency will depreciate. Observers of Japan's experience have argued, however, that BOJ officials were so fearful of depreciation and inflation (as were many central bankers during the early 1930s) that markets did not believe the officials would be willing to depreciate the currency permanently. Instead, markets suspected an intention to restore an appreciated exchange rate later on, and treated any monetary expansion as temporary. Only in the first half of 2013 did the Japanese government finally announce a credible intention to expand the money supply enough, and keep interest rates at zero long enough, to attain a 2 percent rate of annual inflation. At that point the yen depreciated sharply, as described at the start of Chapter 14.[15]

---

[15]A similar policy was advocated by Paul R. Krugman, "It's Baaack: Japan's Slump and the Return of the Liquidity Trap," *Brookings Papers on Economic Activity* 2 (1998), pp. 137–205

With the United States and Japan maintaining zero interest rates through 2013, some economists feared the Fed would be powerless to stop an American deflation similar to Japan's. The Fed and other central banks responded by adopting what came to be called *unconventional monetary policies*, in which the central bank buys specific categories of assets with newly issued money, greatly increasing the money supply in the process. One such policy involves purchasing long-term government bonds so as to reduce long-term interest rates. Those rates play a big role in determining the interest charged for home loans, and when they fall, housing demand therefore rises. Another possible unconventional policy, which we will discuss in the next chapter, is the purchase of foreign exchange.

CASE STUDY

How Big Is the Government Spending Multiplier?

Many students first encounter the **government spending multiplier** during their initial exposure to macroeconomics. The multiplier measures the size of the increase in output caused by an increase in government spending, or in symbols, $\Delta Y / \Delta G$.

While at first glance it may seem that the multiplier is big, students quickly learn about factors that can reduce its size. If an increase in government spending also leads to an increase in the interest rate, and this, in turn, discourages spending on consumption and investment, then the multiplier is smaller: A part of the potential expansionary impact of the fiscal policy is "crowded out" by the rise in the interest rate.

In the open economy, the multiplier is smaller still. Some private spending leaks out of the economy through imports, and if the exchange rate appreciates, then as we have seen in this chapter, the resulting reduction in net exports is an additional channel for crowding out.

Finally, under conditions of price flexibility and full employment, the multiplier is essentially zero: if the government wishes to consume more, and resources are already fully employed in production, then the private sector must part with the output that the government wants. There is no way to get much more out of the existing, fully employed stocks of productive factors, and so $\Delta Y / \Delta G \approx 0$.

Uncertainty about the multiplier's size raised concerns outside of academia once the world slipped into recession in 2008 as a result of the global financial crisis that we will discuss in later chapters (starting with Chapter 19). The United States, China, and other countries mounted big programs of fiscal expansion, including increased government spending, to prop up their stricken economies. Were these resources wasted, or were they helpful in reducing the severity of the slump? Would it be easy or painful later on to reduce government spending in order to roll back the government deficits the recession caused? The answers depended on the size of the government spending multiplier.

Economists have been studying the question of the multiplier's size for years, but the severity of the 2008–2009 recession inspired a new crop of theoretical and empirical studies. We saw earlier that in the open economy, permanent government spending has no impact on output—the multiplier is zero—but temporary government spending can raise output (recall Figure 17-16). Countercyclical fiscal expansion is most likely to be temporary (because the recession is temporary), and so this is also the case focused upon by recent research.

In an exhaustive survey, Robert E. Hall of Stanford University suggests that most studies find a multiplier between 0.5 and 1.0 (see his paper in Further Readings). That is, when the government raises its consumption by $1, the resulting increase in output will be at most $1—smaller than the big multipliers of the simplest closed-economy models, but still an effect likely to have a substantial positive impact on employment.

We saw earlier, however, that in 2009, many industrial economies lowered their interest rates dramatically, sometimes entering liquidity traps with zero rates of interest. Hall explained that this situation is exceptional because the usual "crowding out" does not occur, and he thought that for economies in liquidity traps the multiplier might be as high as 1.7. Lawrence Christiano, Martin Eichenbaum, and Sergio Rebelo of Northwestern University have suggested a much higher number based on their theoretical modeling: While below 1 normally, their multiplier can be as high as 3.7 in a liquidity trap! Alan Auerbach and Yuriy Gorodnichenko of the University of California, Berkeley, analyze data from the (mostly wealthy) member countries of the Organization for Economic Cooperation and Development and find that for economies in recession (though not necessarily in a liquidity trap), the multiplier is about 2.[16]

Our model of the liquidity trap allow us to see easily that the multiplier is larger when the interest rate is held at zero, and it also yields an interesting additional prediction for the open-economy case. Not only is there no crowding out through the interest rate, there is also no crowding out through the exchange rate.

Figure 17-16 shows the output effect of a temporary increase in G under normal (positive interest rate) conditions. Compare this with the effect on Y of a similar spending increase in Figure 17-19 (assuming R remains at zero). Because (by assumption) the expected future exchange rate E^e does not change when the rise in G is temporary, DD simply slides to the right along the horizontal portion of AA, which itself does not shift. Neither the interest rate nor the expected future exchange rate changes in Figure 17-19, so interest parity implies that the current exchange rate cannot change either. In Figure 17-16, in contrast, the increase in output raises money demand, pushing up R and appreciating the currency. Because the currency appreciation reduces net exports, thereby limiting the net positive effect on output, the multiplier is smaller in Figure 17-16 than in Figure 17-19. In Figure 17-19, in fact, the multiplier is the same as under a *fixed exchange rate*, a case that we will examine in the next chapter.

One region where the multiplier's size became a topic of contentious debate was Europe, where countries simultaneously cut government spending sharply after 2009 in order to reduce public deficits and debts. Our discussion of the multiplier might lead you to believe that the effects were highly contractionary. This is exactly what happened, as we shall see in Chapter 21.

SUMMARY

1. The *aggregate demand* for an open economy's output consists of four components corresponding to the four components of GNP: consumption demand, investment demand, government demand, and the current account (net export demand). An important determinant of the current account is the real exchange rate, the ratio of the foreign price level (measured in domestic currency) to the domestic price level.

---

[16]See Christiano, Eichenbaum, and Rebelo, "When Is the Government Spending Multiplier Large?" *Journal of Political Economy* 119 (February 2011), pp. 78–121; and Auerbach and Gorodnichenko, "Fiscal Multipliers in Recession and Expansion," in Alberto Alesina and Francesco Giavazzi, eds., *Fiscal Policy after the Financial Crisis* (Chicago: University of Chicago Press, 2013), pp. 63–102.

2. Output is determined in the short run by the equality of aggregate demand and aggregate supply. When aggregate demand is greater than output, firms increase production to avoid unintended inventory depletion. When aggregate demand is less than output, firms cut back production to avoid unintended accumulation of inventories.

3. The economy's short-run equilibrium occurs at the exchange rate and output level where—given the price level, the expected future exchange rate, and foreign economic conditions—aggregate demand equals aggregate supply and the asset markets are in equilibrium. In a diagram with the exchange rate and real output on its axes, the short-run equilibrium can be visualized as the intersection of an upward-sloping *DD schedule,* along which the output market clears, and a downward-sloping *AA schedule,* along which the asset markets clear.

4. A temporary increase in the money supply, which does not alter the long-run expected nominal exchange rate, causes a depreciation of the currency and a rise in output. Temporary fiscal expansion also results in a rise in output, but it causes the currency to appreciate. *Monetary policy* and *fiscal policy* can be used by the government to offset the effects of disturbances to output and employment. Temporary monetary expansion is powerless to raise output or move the exchange rate, however, when the economy is in a zero-interest *liquidity trap.*

5. Permanent shifts in the money supply, which do alter the long-run expected nominal exchange rate, cause sharper exchange rate movements and therefore have stronger short-run effects on output than transitory shifts. If the economy is at full employment, a permanent increase in the money supply leads to a rising price level, which ultimately reverses the effect on the real exchange rate of the nominal exchange rate's initial depreciation. In the long run, output returns to its initial level and all money prices rise in proportion to the increase in the money supply.

6. Because permanent fiscal expansion changes the long-run expected exchange rate, it causes a sharper currency appreciation than an equal temporary expansion. If the economy starts out in long-run equilibrium, the additional appreciation makes domestic goods and services so expensive that the resulting "crowding out" of net export demand nullifies the policy's effect on output and employment. In this case, a permanent fiscal expansion has no expansionary effect at all. The *government spending multiplier* is zero for permanent fiscal expansion, unlike for temporary fiscal expansion.

7. A major practical problem is ensuring that the government's ability to stimulate the economy does not tempt it to gear policy to short-term political goals, thus creating an *inflation bias.* Other problems include the difficulty of identifying the sources or durations of economic changes and time lags in implementing policies.

8. If exports and imports adjust gradually to real exchange rate changes, the current account may follow a *J-curve* pattern after a real currency depreciation, first worsening and then improving. If such a J-curve exists, currency depreciation may have an initial contractionary effect on output, and exchange rate overshooting will be amplified. Limited exchange rate *pass-through,* along with domestic price increases, may reduce the effect of a nominal exchange rate change on the real exchange rate.

KEY TERMS

AA schedule, p. 495
aggregate demand, p. 484
DD schedule, p. 491
fiscal policy, p. 500

government spending
  multiplier, p. 516
inflation bias, p. 504
J-curve, p. 510

liquidity trap, p. 513
monetary policy, p. 500
pass-through, p. 512

PROBLEMS

1. If the home currency depreciates in real terms, what will happen to the aggregate demand schedule?

2. Suppose the government imposes a tariff on all imports. Use the *DD-AA* model to analyze the effects this measure would have on the economy. Analyze both temporary and permanent tariffs.

3. Consider the following two independent cases for an economy, which is facing a prolonged recession. In the first case, the government decides to increase its purchases by increasing its expenditure on infrastructure development. How does this increased expenditure affect the economy's aggregate demand and output level? In the second case, if the central bank of the country increases the interest rate (bank rate), how does it affect the economy's aggregate demand schedule and the output?

4. Suppose there is a permanent fall in private aggregate demand for a country's output (a downward shift of the entire aggregate demand schedule). What is the effect on output? What government policy response would you recommend?

5. Why does a temporary increase in government spending cause the current account to fall by a smaller amount than does a permanent increase in government spending?

6. Suppose the Indian rupee depreciated in the international market. What will be the impact of rupee depreciation on the current account balance of India, if the import demand condition is elastic? If personal disposable income rises, along with the rupee depreciation, will the current account balance improve or worsen?

7. You observe that a country's currency depreciates while its current account worsens. What data might you look at to decide if you are witnessing a J-curve effect? What other macroeconomic change might bring about a currency depreciation coupled with a deterioration of the current account, even if there is no J-curve?

8. A new government is elected and announces that once it is inaugurated, it will increase the money supply. Use the *DD-AA* model to study the economy's response to this announcement.

9. Other things being equal, suppose the inflation level in the South African economy increased from 7 percent in 2013 to 12 percent in 2014. What will happen to the asset market schedule for this high inflation level?

10. What does the Marshall-Lerner condition look like if the country whose real exchange rate changes does *not* start out with a current account of zero? (The Marshall-Lerner condition is derived in Appendix 2 under the "standard" assumption of an initially balanced current account.)

11. Our model takes the price level P as given in the short run, but in reality the currency appreciation caused by a permanent fiscal expansion might cause P to fall a bit by lowering some import prices. If P can fall slightly as a result of a permanent fiscal expansion, is it still true that there are no output effects? (As above, assume an initial long-run equilibrium.)

12. Suppose interest parity does not hold exactly, but the true relationship is $R = R* + (E^e - E)/E + \rho$, where ρ is a term measuring the differential riskiness of domestic versus foreign deposits. Suppose a permanent rise in domestic government spending, by creating the prospect of future government deficits, also raises ρ, that is, makes domestic currency deposits more risky. Evaluate the policy's output effects in this situation.

13. If an economy does *not* start out at full employment, is it still true that a permanent change in fiscal policy has no current effect on output?

14. Consider the following linear version of the *AA-DD* model in the text: Consumption is given by $C = (1 - s)Y$ and the current account balance is given by $CA = aE - mY$. (In macroeconomics textbooks, s is sometimes referred to as the *marginal propensity to save* and m is called the *marginal propensity to import*.) Then the condition of equilibrium in the goods market is $Y = C + I + G + CA = (1 - s)Y + I + G + aE - mY$. We will write the condition of money-market equilibrium as $M^s/P = bY - dR$. On the assumption that the central bank can hold both the interest rate R and the exchange rate E constant, and assuming that investment I also is constant, what is the effect of an increase in government spending G on output Y? (This number is often called the *open-economy government spending multiplier,* but as you can see it is relevant only under strict conditions.) Explain your result intuitively.

15. See if you can retrace the steps in the five-step argument on page 508 to show that a permanent fiscal expansion cannot cause output to *fall*.

16. Explain why the expansionary monetary policy becomes ineffective during a liquidity trap? Suppose the government undertakes an expansionary fiscal policy by increasing its expenditure on military equipment. Here, would an expansionary fiscal policy be more effective than expansionary monetary policy to escape a liquidity trap?

17. If you compare low-inflation economies with economies in which inflation is high and very volatile, how might you expect the degree of exchange rate pass-through to differ, and why?

18. In an open economy, imagine there is no change in the monetary policy and the government makes a temporary fiscal expansion through increased government purchases. What will be the immediate impact of fiscal expansion on the domestic currency value and the level of output? Suppose there is a sudden change in the domestic consumers' taste—favoring foreign products—resulting in a decline in domestic demand and employment. How does the monetary policy help the economy to return to its original employment level?

19. Return to problem 14 above and notice that, to complete the model described there, we must add the interest parity conditions. Observe also that if Y^f is the full-employment output level, then the long-run expected exchange rate, E^e, satisfies the equation: $Y^f = (aE^e + I + G)/(s + m)$. (We are again taking investment I as given.) Using these equations, demonstrate algebraically that if the economy starts at full employment with $R = R^*$, an increase in G has no effect on output. What is the effect on the exchange rate? How does the exchange rate change depend on a, and why?

20. We can express a linear approximation to the interest parity condition (accurate for small exchange rate changes) as: $R = R^* + (E^e - E)/E^e$. Adding this to the model of problems 14 and 19, solve for Y as a function of G. What is the government spending multiplier for temporary changes in G (those that do not alter E^e)? How does your answer depend on the parameters a, b, and d, and why?

FURTHER READINGS

Victor Argy and Michael G. Porter. "The Forward Exchange Market and the Effects of Domestic and External Disturbances under Alternative Exchange Rate Systems." *International Monetary Fund Staff Papers* 19 (November 1972), pp. 503–532. Advanced analysis of a macroeconomic model similar to the one in this chapter.

Victor Argy and Joanne K. Salop. "Price and Output Effects of Monetary and Fiscal Policies under Flexible Exchange Rates." *International Monetary Fund Staff Papers* 26 (June 1979), pp. 224–256. Discusses the effects of macroeconomic policies under alternative institutional assumptions about wage indexation and the wage-price adjustment process in general.

Rudiger Dornbusch. "Exchange Rate Expectations and Monetary Policy." *Journal of International Economics* 6 (August 1976), pp. 231–244. A formal examination of monetary policy and the exchange rate in a model with a J-curve.

Rudiger Dornbusch and Paul Krugman. "Flexible Exchange Rates in the Short Run." *Brookings Papers on Economic Activity* 3 (1976), pp. 537–575. Theory and evidence on short-run macroeconomic adjustment under floating exchange rates.

Joseph E. Gagnon. "Productive Capacity, Product Varieties, and the Elasticities Approach to the Trade Balance." *Review of International Economics* 15 (September 2007), pp. 639–659. Looks at the role of new products in determining long-run trade elasticities.

Robert E. Hall. "By How Much Does GDP Rise if the Government Buys More Output?" *Brookings Papers on Economic Activity* 2 (2009), pp. 183–231. Thorough (but advanced) discussion of the government spending multiplier in contemporary macroeconomic models and in practice.

Jaime Marquez. *Estimating Trade Elasticities.* Boston: Kluwer Academic Publishers, 2002. Comprehensive survey on the estimation of trade elasticities.

Subramanian Rangan and Robert Z. Lawrence. *A Prism on Globalization.* Washington, D.C.: Brookings Institution, 1999. An examination of multinational firms' responses to exchange rate movements.

Lars E. O. Svensson. "Escaping from a Liquidity Trap and Deflation: The Foolproof Way and Others." *Journal of Economic Perspectives* 17 (Fall 2003), pp. 145–166. Clear discussion of policy options for economies facing deflation, including unconventional monetary policies.

MyEconLab Can Help You Get a Better Grade

MyEconLab   If your exam were tomorrow, would you be ready? For each chapter, MyEconLab Practice Tests and Study Plans pinpoint sections you have mastered and those you need to study. That way, you are more efficient with your study time, and you are better prepared for your exams.

To see how it works, turn to page 41 and then go to

www.myeconlab.com

Intertemporal Trade and Consumption Demand

We assume in the chapter that private consumption demand is a function of disposable income, $C = C(Y^d)$, with the property that when Y^d rises, consumption rises by less (so that saving, $Y^d - C(Y^d)$, goes up too). This appendix interprets this assumption in the context of the intertemporal model of consumption behavior discussed in the appendix to Chapter 6.

The discussion in Chapter 6 assumed that consumers' welfare depends on present consumption demand D_P and future consumption demand D_F. If present income is Q_P and future income is Q_F, consumers can use borrowing or saving to allocate their consumption over time in any way consistent with the *intertemporal budget constraint*

$$D_P + D_F/(1 + r) = Q_P + Q_F/(1 + r),$$

where r is the real rate of interest.

Figure 17A1-1 reminds you of how consumption and saving were determined in Chapter 6. If present and future output are initially described by the point labeled 1 in the figure, a consumer's wish to pick the highest utility indifference curve consistent with his or her budget constraints leads to consumption at point 1 as well.

We have assumed zero saving at point 1 to show most clearly the effect of a rise in current output, which we turn to next. Suppose present output rises while future output doesn't, moving the income endowment to point 2′, which lies horizontally to the right of point 1. You can see that the consumer will wish to spread the increase in

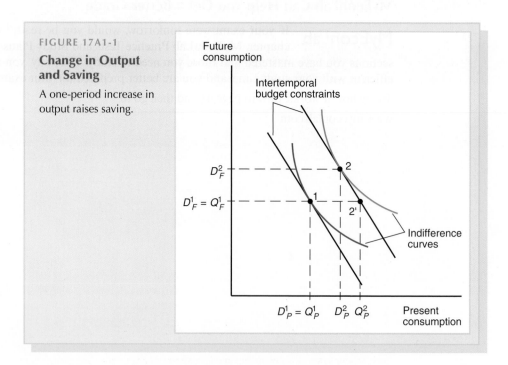

FIGURE 17A1-1

Change in Output and Saving

A one-period increase in output raises saving.

consumption this allows her over her *entire* lifetime. She can do this by saving some of the present income rise, $Q_P^2 - Q_P^1$, and moving up to the left along her budget line from her endowment point 2' to point 2.

If we now reinterpret the notation so that present output, Q_P, corresponds to disposable income, Y^d, and present consumption demand corresponds to $C(Y^d)$, we see that while consumption certainly depends on factors other than current disposable income—notably, future income and the real interest rate—its behavior implies a rise in lifetime income that is concentrated in the present will indeed lead to a rise in current consumption less than the rise in current income. Since the output changes we have been considering in this chapter are all temporary changes that result from the short-run stickiness of domestic money prices, the consumption behavior we simply assumed in the chapter does capture the feature of intertemporal consumption behavior essential for the *DD-AA* model to work.

We could also use 17A1-1 to look at the consumption effects of the real interest rate, which we mentioned in footnote 1. If the economy is initially at point 1, a fall in the real interest rate r causes the budget line to rotate counterclockwise about point 1, causing a rise in present consumption. If initially the economy had been saving a positive amount, however, as at point 2, this effect would be ambiguous, a reflection of the contrary pulls of the income and substitution effects we introduced in the first part of this book on international trade theory. In this second case, the endowment point is point 2', so a fall in the real interest rate causes a counterclockwise rotation of the budget line about point 2'. Empirical evidence indicates that the positive effect of a lower real interest rate on consumption probably is weak.

Use of the preceding framework to analyze the intertemporal aspects of fiscal policy would lead us too far afield, although this is one of the most fascinating topics in macroeconomics. We refer readers instead to any good intermediate macroeconomics text.[17]

---

[17]For example, see Abel, Bernanke, and Croushore, *op. cit.*, Chapter 15.

17

The Marshall-Lerner Condition and Empirical Estimates of Trade Elasticities

The chapter assumed a real depreciation of a country's currency improves its current account. As we noted, however, the validity of this assumption depends on the response of export and import volumes to real exchange rate changes. In this appendix, we derive a condition on those responses for the assumption in the text to be valid. The condition, called the *Marshall-Lerner condition*, states that, all else equal, a real depreciation improves the current account if export and import volumes are sufficiently elastic with respect to the real exchange rate. (The condition is named after two of the economists who discovered it, Alfred Marshall and Abba Lerner.) After deriving the Marshall-Lerner condition, we look at empirical estimates of trade elasticities and analyze their implications for actual current account responses to real exchange rate changes.

To start, write the current account, measured in domestic output units, as the difference between exports and imports of goods and services similarly measured:

$$CA(EP^*/P, Y^d) = EX(EP^*/P) - IM(EP^*/P, Y^d).$$

Above, export demand is written as a function of EP^*/P alone because foreign income is being held constant.

Let q denote the real exchange rate EP^*/P and let EX^* denote domestic imports measured in terms of *foreign*, rather than domestic, output. The notation EX^* is used because domestic imports from abroad, measured in foreign output, equal the volume of foreign exports to the home country. If we identify q with the price of foreign products in terms of domestic products, then IM and EX^* are related by

$$IM = q \times EX^*,$$

that is, imports measured in domestic output = (domestic output units/foreign output unit) $\times$ (imports measured in foreign output units).[18]

The current account can therefore be expressed as

$$CA(q, Y^d) = EX(q) - q \times EX^*(q, Y^d).$$

Now let EX_q stand for the effect of a rise in q (a real depreciation) on export demand, and let EX_q^* stand for the effect of a rise in q on import volume. Thus,

$$EX_q = \Delta EX/\Delta q, EX_q^* = \Delta EX^*/\Delta q.$$

---

[18]As we warned earlier in the chapter, the identification of the real exchange rate with relative output prices is not quite exact since, as we defined it, the real exchange rate is the relative price of expenditure baskets. For most practical purposes, however, the discrepancy is not qualitatively important. A more serious problem with our analysis is that national outputs consist in part of nontradables, and the real exchange rate covers their prices as well as those of tradables. To avoid the additional complexity that would result from a more detailed treatment of the composition of national outputs, we assume in deriving the Marshall-Lerner condition that the real exchange rate can be approximately identified with the relative price of imports in terms of exports.

As we saw in the chapter, EX_q is positive (a real depreciation makes home products relatively cheaper and stimulates exports) while EX_q^* is negative (a relative cheapening of home products reduces domestic import demand). Using these definitions, we can now ask how a rise in q affects the current account, all else equal.

If superscript 1 indicates the initial value of a variable while superscript 2 indicates its value after q has changed by $\Delta q = q^2 - q^1$, then the change in the current account caused by a real exchange rate change Δq is

$$\Delta CA = CA^2 - CA^1 = (EX^2 - q^2 \times EX^{*2}) - (EX^1 - q^1 \times EX^{*1})$$
$$= \Delta EX - (q^2 \times \Delta EX^*) - (\Delta q \times EX^{*1}).$$

Dividing through by Δq gives the current account's response to a change in q,

$$\Delta CA / \Delta q = EX_q - (q^2 \times EX_q^*) - EX^{*1}.$$

This equation summarizes the two current account effects of a real depreciation discussed in the text, the *volume* effect and the *value* effect. The terms involving EX_q and EX_q^* represent the volume effect, the effect of the change in q on the number of output units exported and imported. These terms are always positive because $EX_q > 0$ and $EX_q^* < 0$. The last term above, EX^{*1}, represents the value effect, and it is preceded by a minus sign. This last term tells us that a rise in q worsens the current account to the extent that it raises the domestic output value of the initial volume of imports.

We are interested in knowing when the right-hand side of the equation above is positive, so that a real depreciation causes the current account balance to increase. To answer this question, we first define the *elasticity of export demand* with respect to q,

$$\eta = (q^1 / EX^1) EX_q,$$

and the elasticity of import demand with respect to q,

$$\eta^* = -(q^1 / EX^{*1}) EX_q^*.$$

(The definition of η^* involves a minus sign because $EX_q^* < 0$, and we are defining trade elasticities as positive numbers.) Returning to our equation for $\Delta CA / \Delta q$, we multiply its right-hand side by (q^1 / EX^1) to express it in terms of trade elasticities. Then, if the current account is initially zero (that is, $EX^1 = q^1 \times EX^{*1}$), this last step shows that $\Delta CA / \Delta q$ is positive when

$$\eta + (q^2 / q^1)\eta^* - 1 > 0.$$

If the change in q is assumed to be small, so that $q^2 \approx q^1$, the condition for an increase in q to improve the current account is

$$\eta + \eta^* > 1.$$

This is the Marshall-Lerner condition, which states that if the current account is initially zero, a real currency depreciation causes a current account surplus if the sum of the relative price elasticities of export and import demand exceeds 1. (If the current account is not zero initially, the condition becomes more complex.) In applying the Marshall-Lerner condition, remember that its derivation assumes that disposable income is held constant when q changes.

| | η | | | η* | | |
| TABLE 17A2-1 **Estimated Price Elasticities for International Trade in Manufactured Goods** | | | | | | |
Country	Impact	Short-run	Long-run	Impact	Short-run	Long-run
Austria	0.39	0.71	1.37	0.03	0.36	0.80
Belgium	0.18	0.59	1.55	—	—	0.70
Britain	—	—	0.31	0.60	0.75	0.75
Canada	0.08	0.40	0.71	0.72	0.72	0.72
Denmark	0.82	1.13	1.13	0.55	0.93	1.14
France	0.20	0.48	1.25	—	0.49	0.60
Germany	—	—	1.41	0.57	0.77	0.77
Italy	—	0.56	0.64	0.94	0.94	0.94
Japan	0.59	1.01	1.61	0.16	0.72	0.97
Netherlands	0.24	0.49	0.89	0.71	1.22	1.22
Norway	0.40	0.74	1.49	—	0.01	0.71
Sweden	0.27	0.73	1.59	—	—	0.94
Switzerland	0.28	0.42	0.73	0.25	0.25	0.25
United States	0.18	0.48	1.67	—	1.06	1.06

Source: Estimates are taken from Jacques R. Artus and Malcolm D. Knight, *Issues in the Assessment of the Exchange Rates of Industrial Countries.* Occasional Paper 29. Washington, D.C.: International Monetary Fund, July 1984, table 4. Unavailable estimates are indicated by dashes.

Now that we have the Marshall-Lerner condition, we can ask whether empirical estimates of trade equations imply price elasticities consistent with this chapter's assumption that a real exchange rate depreciation improves the current account. Table 17A2-1 presents International Monetary Fund elasticity estimates for trade in manufactured goods. The table reports export and import price elasticities measured over three successively longer time horizons and thus allows for the possibility that export and import demands adjust gradually to relative price changes, as in our discussion of the J-curve effect. Impact elasticities measure the response of trade flows to relative price changes in the first six months after the change, short-run elasticities apply to a one-year adjustment period, and long-run elasticities measure the response of trade flows to the price changes over a hypothetical infinite adjustment period.

For most countries, the impact elasticities are so small that the sum of the impact export and import elasticities is less than 1. Since the impact elasticities usually fail to satisfy the Marshall-Lerner condition, the estimates support the existence of an initial J-curve effect that causes the current account to deteriorate immediately following a real depreciation.

It is also true, however, that most countries represented in the table satisfy the Marshall-Lerner condition in the short run and that virtually all do so in the long run. The evidence is therefore consistent with the assumption made in the chapter: Except over short time periods, a real depreciation is likely to improve the current account, while a real appreciation is likely to worsen it.

CHAPTER 18

FIXED EXCHANGE RATES AND FOREIGN EXCHANGE INTERVENTION

In the past several chapters, we developed a model that helps us understand how a country's exchange rate and national income are determined by the interaction of asset and output markets. Using that model, we saw how monetary and fiscal policies can be used to maintain full employment and a stable price level.

To keep our discussion simple, we assumed exchange rates are *completely* flexible, that is, that national monetary authorities themselves do not trade in the foreign exchange market to influence exchange rates. In reality, however, the assumption of complete exchange rate flexibility is not always accurate. As we mentioned earlier, the world economy operated under a system of *fixed* dollar exchange rates between the end of World War II and 1973, with central banks routinely trading foreign exchange to hold their exchange rates at internationally agreed levels. Industrialized countries now operate under a hybrid system of **managed floating exchange rates**—a system in which governments may attempt to moderate exchange rate movements without keeping exchange rates rigidly fixed. A number of developing countries have retained some form of government exchange rate fixing, for reasons that we discuss in Chapter 22.

In this chapter, we study how central banks intervene in the foreign exchange market to fix exchange rates and how macroeconomic policies work when exchange rates are fixed. The chapter will help us understand the role of central bank foreign exchange intervention in the determination of exchange rates under a system of managed floating.

After reading this chapter, you will be able to:

▪ Understand how a central bank must manage monetary policy so as to fix its currency's value in the foreign exchange market.

▪ Describe and analyze the relationship among the central bank's foreign exchange reserves, its purchases and sales in the foreign exchange market, and the money supply.

▪ Explain how monetary, fiscal, and sterilized intervention policies affect the economy under a fixed exchange rate.

▪ Discuss causes and effects of balance of payments crises.

▪ Describe how alternative multilateral systems for pegging exchange rates work.

Why Study Fixed Exchange Rates?

A discussion of fixed exchange rates may seem outdated in an era when newspaper headlines regularly highlight sharp changes in the exchange rates of the major industrial-country currencies. There are four reasons why we must understand fixed exchange rates, however, before analyzing contemporary macroeconomic policy problems:

1. *Managed floating.* As previously noted, central banks may intervene in currency markets to influence exchange rates. So while the dollar exchange rates of the industrial countries' currencies are not currently fixed by governments, they are not always left to fluctuate freely, either. The system of floating dollar exchange rates is sometimes referred to as a dirty float, to distinguish it from a clean float in which governments make no direct attempts to influence foreign currency values. (The model of the exchange rate developed in earlier chapters assumed a cleanly floating, or completely flexible, exchange rate.)[1] Because the present monetary system is a hybrid of the "pure" fixed and floating rate systems, an understanding of fixed exchange rates gives us insight into the effects of foreign exchange intervention when it occurs under floating rates.

2. *Regional currency arrangements.* Some countries belong to *exchange rate unions*, organizations whose members agree to fix their mutual exchange rates while allowing their currencies to fluctuate in value against the currencies of nonmember countries. Currently, for example, Denmark pegs its currency's value against the euro within the European Union's *Exchange Rate Mechanism.*

3. *Developing countries.* While industrial countries generally allow their currencies to float against the dollar, these economies account for less than a sixth of the world's countries. Many developing countries try to peg or manage the values of their currencies, often in terms of the dollar, but sometimes in terms of a nondollar currency or some "basket" of currencies chosen by the authorities. Morocco pegs its currency to a basket, for example, while Barbados pegs to the U.S. dollar and Senegal pegs to the euro. No examination of the problems of developing

---

[1]It is questionable whether a truly clean float has ever existed in reality. Most government policies affect the exchange rate, and governments rarely undertake policies without considering the policies' exchange rate implications.

countries would get very far without taking into account the implications of fixed exchange rates.[2]

4. *Lessons of the past for the future.* Fixed exchange rates were the norm in many periods, such as the decades before World War I, between the mid-1920s and 1931, and again between 1945 and 1973. Today, economists and policy makers dissatisfied with floating exchange rates sometimes propose new international agreements that would resurrect a form of fixed-rate system. Would such plans benefit the world economy? Who would gain or lose? To compare the merits of fixed and floating exchange rates, we must understand the functioning of fixed rates.

Central Bank Intervention and the Money Supply

In Chapter 15, we defined an economy's money supply as the total amount of currency and checking deposits held by its households and firms and assumed that the central bank determined the amount of money in circulation. To understand the effects of central bank intervention in the foreign exchange market, we need to look first at how central bank financial transactions affect the money supply.[3]

The Central Bank Balance Sheet and the Money Supply

The main tool we use in studying central bank transactions in asset markets is the **central bank balance sheet**, which records the assets held by the central bank and its liabilities. Like any other balance sheet, the central bank balance sheet is organized according to the principles of double-entry bookkeeping. Any acquisition of an asset by the central bank results in a positive change on the assets side of the balance sheet, while any increase in the bank's liabilities results in a positive change on the balance sheet's liabilities side.

---

[2]The International Monetary Fund (IMF), an international agency that we will discuss in the next chapter, publishes a useful classification of its member countries' exchange rate arrangements. Arrangements as of end-April 2012 can be found on page 4 of its publication, *Annual Report on Exchange Arrangements and Exchange Restrictions 2012*, available at http://www.imf.org/external/pubs/cat/longres.aspx?sk=26012.0. (The IMF calls these "de facto"exchange rate arrangements because they are based on what countries actually do, not what they *say* they do.) As of April 2012, 66 countries, including most major industrial countries and the 17 countries that then used the euro, had "floating" or "freely floating" currencies. (The euro itself floats independently against the dollar and other major currencies, as we discuss in Chapter 21.) Thirteen countries did not have their own currencies (including Ecuador, Panama, and Zimbabwe). Forty-three had "conventional pegs" of the type we will study in this chapter, while 12 more had "currency boards" (a special type of fixed exchange rate scheme to which the analysis of this chapter largely applies). Among the conventional pegs were many mostly poorer countries but also oil-rich Saudi Arabia and European Union member Denmark. Sixteen more countries, including Cambodia, Iraq, Macedonia, and Vietnam, had "stabilized arrangements" in which the authorities fix exchange rates, but without any formal commitment to do so. One country (Tonga) allowed its exchange rate to move within horizontal bands; fifteen others had "crawling pegs," in which the exchange rate is forced to follow a predetermined path, or "crawl-like arrangements." (The latter group includes China.) Finally, 24 countries (including Bangladesh, Nigeria, Russia, and Singapore) had "other managed arrangements." As you can see, there is a bewildering array of different exchange rate systems, and the case of fixed exchange rates remains quite important.

[3]As we pointed out in Chapter 13, government agencies other than central banks may intervene in the foreign exchange market, but their intervention operations, unlike those of central banks, have no significant effect on national money supplies. (In the terminology introduced in the coming pages, interventions by agencies other than central banks are automatically sterilized.) To simplify our discussion, we continue to assume, when the assumption is not misleading, that central banks alone carry out foreign exchange intervention.

A balance sheet for the central bank of the imaginary country of Pecunia is shown below.

Central Bank Balance Sheet

Assets		Liabilities	
Foreign assets	$1,000	Deposits held by private banks	$500
Domestic assets	$1,500	Currency in circulation	$2,000

The assets side of the Bank of Pecunia's balance sheet lists two types of assets, *foreign assets* and *domestic assets*. Foreign assets consist mainly of foreign currency bonds owned by the central bank. These foreign assets make up the central bank's official international reserves, and their level changes when the central bank intervenes in the foreign exchange market by buying or selling foreign exchange. For historical reasons discussed later in this chapter, a central bank's international reserves also include any gold that it owns. The defining characteristic of international reserves is that they be either claims on foreigners or a universally acceptable means of making international payments (for example, gold). In the present example, the central bank holds $1,000 in foreign assets.

Domestic assets are central bank holdings of claims to future payments by its own citizens and domestic institutions. These claims usually take the form of domestic government bonds and loans to domestic private banks. The Bank of Pecunia owns $1,500 in domestic assets. Its total assets therefore equal $2,500, the sum of foreign and domestic asset holdings.

The liabilities side of the balance sheet lists as liabilities the deposits of private banks and currency in circulation, both notes and coin. (Nonbank firms and households generally cannot deposit money at the central bank, while banks are generally required by law to hold central bank deposits as partial backing for their own liabilities.) Private bank deposits are liabilities of the central bank because the money may be withdrawn whenever private banks need it. Currency in circulation is considered a central bank liability mainly for historical reasons: At one time, central banks were obliged to give a certain amount of gold or silver to anyone wishing to exchange domestic currency for one of those precious metals. The balance sheet above shows that Pecunia's private banks have deposited $500 at the central bank. Currency in circulation equals $2,000, so the central bank's total liabilities amount to $2,500.

The central bank's total assets equal its total liabilities plus its net worth, which we have assumed in the present example to be zero. Because changes in central bank net worth are not important to our analysis, we will ignore them.[4]

The additional assumption that net worth is constant means that the changes in central bank assets we will consider *automatically* cause equal changes in central bank liabilities. When the central bank purchases an asset, for example, it can pay for it in one of two ways. A cash payment raises the supply of currency in circulation by the amount of the bank's asset purchase. A payment by check promises the check's owner a central bank deposit equal in value to the asset's price. When the recipient of the check deposits it in her account at a private bank, the private bank's claims on the central bank (and thus the central bank's liabilities to private banks) rise by the same

---

[4]There are several ways in which a central bank's net worth (also called the central bank's *capital*) could change. For example, the government might allow its central bank to keep a fraction of the interest earnings on its assets, and this interest flow would raise the bank's net worth if reinvested. Such changes in net worth tend to be small enough empirically that they can usually be ignored for purposes of macroeconomic analysis. However, see end-of-chapter problem 19.

amount. In either case, the central bank's purchase of assets automatically causes an equal increase in its liabilities. Similarly, asset sales by the central bank involve either the withdrawal of currency from circulation or the reduction of private banks' claims on the central bank, and thus a fall in central bank liabilities to the private sector.

An understanding of the central bank balance sheet is important because changes in the central bank's assets cause changes in the domestic money supply. The preceding paragraph's discussion of the equality between changes in central bank assets and liabilities illustrates the mechanism at work.

When the central bank buys an asset from the public, for example, its payment—whether cash or check—directly enters the money supply. The increase in central bank liabilities associated with the asset purchase thus causes the money supply to expand. The money supply shrinks when the central bank sells an asset to the public because the cash or check the central bank receives in payment goes out of circulation, reducing the central bank's liabilities to the public. Changes in the level of central bank asset holdings cause the money supply to change in the same direction because they require equal changes in the central bank's liabilities.

The process we have described may be familiar to you from studying central bank open-market operations in earlier courses. By definition, open-market operations involve the purchase or sale of domestic assets, but official transactions in foreign assets have the same direct effect on the money supply. You will also recall that when the central bank buys assets, for example, the accompanying increase in the money supply is generally *larger* than the initial asset purchase because of multiple deposit creation within the private banking system. This *money multiplier* effect, which magnifies the impact of central bank transactions on the money supply, reinforces our main conclusion: *Any central bank purchase of assets automatically results in an increase in the domestic money supply, while any central bank sale of assets automatically causes the money supply to decline.*[5]

Foreign Exchange Intervention and the Money Supply

To see in greater detail how foreign exchange intervention affects the money supply, let's look at an example. Suppose the Bank of Pecunia goes to the foreign exchange market and sells $100 worth of foreign bonds for Pecunian money. The sale reduces official holdings of foreign assets from $1,000 to $900, causing the assets side of the central bank balance sheet to shrink from $2,500 to $2,400.

The payment the Bank of Pecunia receives for these foreign assets automatically reduces its liabilities by $100 as well. If the Bank of Pecunia is paid with domestic currency, the currency goes into its vault and out of circulation. Currency in circulation therefore falls by $100. (A problem at the end of the chapter considers the identical money supply effect of payment by check.) As a result of the foreign asset sale, the central bank's balance sheet changes as follows:

Central Bank Balance Sheet after $100 Foreign Asset Sale (Buyer Pays with Currency)

Assets		Liabilities	
Foreign assets	$900	Deposits held by private banks	$500
Domestic assets	$1,500	Currency in circulation	$1,900

---

[5]For a detailed description of multiple deposit creation and the money multiplier, see Frederic S. Mishkin, *The Economics of Money, Banking, and Financial Markets*, 10th ed., Chapter 14 (Upper Saddle River, NJ: Prentice Hall, 2013).

After the sale, assets still equal liabilities, but both have declined by $100, equal to the amount of currency the Bank of Pecunia has taken out of circulation through its intervention in the foreign exchange market. The change in the central bank's balance sheet implies a decline in the Pecunian money supply.

A $100 *purchase* of foreign assets by the Bank of Pecunia would cause its liabilities to increase by $100. If the central bank paid for its purchase in cash, currency in circulation would rise by $100. If it paid by writing a check on itself, private bank deposits at the Bank of Pecunia would ultimately rise by $100. In either case, there would be a rise in the domestic money supply.

Sterilization

Central banks sometimes carry out equal foreign and domestic asset transactions in opposite directions to nullify the impact of their foreign exchange operations on the domestic money supply. This type of policy is called **sterilized foreign exchange intervention**. We can understand how sterilized foreign exchange intervention works by considering the following example.

Suppose once again that the Bank of Pecunia sells $100 of its foreign assets and receives as payment a $100 check on the private bank Pecuniacorp. This transaction causes the central bank's foreign assets and its liabilities to decline simultaneously by $100, and there is therefore a fall in the domestic money supply. If the central bank wishes to negate the effect of its foreign asset sale on the money supply, it can *buy* $100 of domestic assets, such as government bonds. This second action increases the Bank of Pecunia's domestic assets *and* its liabilities by $100 and thus completely cancels the money supply effect of the $100 sale of foreign assets. If the central bank buys the government bonds with a check, for example, the two transactions (a $100 sale of foreign assets and a $100 purchase of domestic assets) have the following net effect on its balance sheet.

Central Bank Balance Sheet before Sterilized $100 Foreign Asset Sale

Assets		Liabilities	
Foreign assets	$1,000	Deposits held by private banks	$500
Domestic assets	$1,500	Currency in circulation	$2,000

Central Bank Balance Sheet after Sterilized $100 Foreign Asset Sale

Assets		Liabilities	
Foreign assets	$900	Deposits held by private banks	$500
Domestic assets	$1,600	Currency in circulation	$2,000

The $100 decrease in the central bank's foreign assets is matched with a $100 increase in domestic assets, and the liabilities side of the balance sheet does not change. The sterilized foreign exchange sale therefore has no effect on the money supply.

Table 18-1 summarizes and compares the effects of sterilized and nonsterilized foreign exchange interventions.

The Balance of Payments and the Money Supply

In our discussion of balance of payments accounting in Chapter 13, we defined a country's balance of payments (or official settlements balance) as net purchases of foreign assets by the home central bank less net purchases of domestic assets by foreign central

TABLE 18-1	Effects of a $100 Foreign Exchange Intervention: Summary		
Domestic Central Bank's Action	**Effect on Domestic Money Supply**	**Effect on Central Bank's Domestic Assets**	**Effect on Central Bank's Foreign Assets**
Nonsterilized foreign exchange purchase	+$100	0	+$100
Sterilized foreign exchange purchase	0	−$100	+$100
Nonsterilized foreign exchange sale	−$100	0	−$100
Sterilized foreign exchange sale	0	+$100	−$100

banks. Looked at differently, the balance of payments equals the current account plus capital account balances *less* the nonreserve component of the financial account balance, that is, the international payments gap that central banks must finance through their reserve transactions. A home balance of payments deficit, for example, means the country's net foreign reserve liabilities are increasing: Some combination of reserve sales by the home central bank and reserve purchases by foreign central banks is covering a home current plus capital account deficit not fully matched by net private sales of assets to foreigners, or a home current account surplus that falls short of net private purchases of financial claims on foreigners.

What we have learned in this section illustrates the important connection between the balance of payments and the growth of money supplies at home and abroad. *If central banks are not sterilizing and the home country has a balance of payments surplus, for example, any associated increase in the home central bank's foreign assets implies an increased home money supply. Similarly, any associated decrease in a foreign central bank's claims on the home country implies a decreased foreign money supply.*

The extent to which a measured balance of payments disparity will affect home and foreign money supplies is, however, quite uncertain in practice. For one thing, we have to know how the burden of balance of payments adjustment is divided among central banks, that is, how much financing of the payments gap is done through home official intervention and how much through foreign. This division depends on various factors, such as the macroeconomic goals of the central banks and the institutional arrangements governing intervention (discussed later in this chapter). Second, central banks may be sterilizing to counter the monetary effects of reserve changes. Finally, as we noted at the end of Chapter 13, some central bank transactions indirectly help to finance a foreign country's balance of payments deficit, but they do not show up in the latter's published balance of payments figures. Such transactions may nonetheless affect the monetary liabilities of the bank that undertakes them.

How the Central Bank Fixes the Exchange Rate

Having seen how central bank foreign exchange transactions affect the money supply, we can now look at how a central bank fixes the domestic currency's exchange rate through foreign exchange intervention.

To hold the exchange rate constant, a central bank must always be willing to trade currencies at the fixed exchange rate with the private actors in the foreign exchange market. For example, to fix the yen/dollar rate at ¥120 per dollar, the Bank of Japan must be willing to buy yen with its dollar reserves, and in any amount the market desires, at a rate of ¥120 per dollar. The bank must also be willing to buy any amount of dollar assets the market wants to sell for yen at that exchange rate. If the Bank of Japan did not remove such excess supplies or demands for yen by intervening in the market, the exchange rate would have to change to restore equilibrium.

The central bank can succeed in holding the exchange rate fixed only if its financial transactions ensure that asset markets remain in equilibrium when the exchange rate is at its fixed level. The process through which asset market equilibrium is maintained is illustrated by the model of simultaneous foreign exchange and money market equilibrium used in previous chapters.

Foreign Exchange Market Equilibrium under a Fixed Exchange Rate

To begin, we consider how equilibrium in the foreign exchange market can be maintained when the central bank fixes the exchange rate permanently at the level E^0. The foreign exchange market is in equilibrium when the interest parity condition holds, that is, when the domestic interest rate, R, equals the foreign interest rate, R^*, plus $(E^e - E)/E$, the expected rate of depreciation of the domestic currency against foreign currency. However, when the exchange rate is fixed at E^0 and market participants expect it to remain fixed, the expected rate of domestic currency depreciation is *zero*. The interest parity condition therefore implies that E^0 is today's equilibrium exchange rate only if

$$R = R^*.$$

Because no exchange rate change is expected by participants in the foreign exchange market, they are content to hold the available supplies of domestic and foreign currency deposits only if these offer the same interest rate.[6]

To ensure equilibrium in the foreign exchange market when the exchange rate is fixed permanently at E^0, the central bank must therefore hold R equal to R^*. Because the domestic interest rate is determined by the interaction of real money demand and the real money supply, we must look at the money market to complete our analysis of exchange rate fixing.

Money Market Equilibrium under a Fixed Exchange Rate

To hold the domestic interest rate at R^*, the central bank's foreign exchange intervention must adjust the money supply so that R^* equates aggregate real domestic money demand and the real money supply:

$$M^s/P = L(R^*, Y).$$

Given P and Y, the above equilibrium condition tells what the money supply must be if a permanently fixed exchange rate is to be consistent with asset market equilibrium at a foreign interest rate of R^*.

When the central bank intervenes to hold the exchange rate fixed, it must *automatically* adjust the domestic money supply so that money market equilibrium is

---

[6]Even when an exchange rate is currently fixed at some level, market participants may expect the central bank to change it. In such situations, the home interest rate must equal the foreign interest rate plus the expected depreciation rate of the domestic currency (as usual) for the foreign exchange market to be in equilibrium. We examine this type of situation later in this chapter, but for now we assume that no one expects the central bank to alter the exchange rate.

maintained with $R = R^*$. Let's look at an example to see how this process works. Suppose the central bank has been fixing E at the level E^0 and asset markets initially are in equilibrium. Suddenly output rises. A necessary condition for holding the exchange rate permanently fixed at E^0 is that the central bank restore current asset market equilibrium at that rate, *given* that people expect E^0 to prevail in the future. So we frame our question as: What monetary measures keep the current exchange rate constant given unchanged expectations about the future exchange rate?

A rise in output raises the demand for domestic money, and this increase in money demand normally would push the domestic interest rate upward. To prevent the appreciation of the home currency that would occur (given that people expect an exchange rate of E^0 in the future), the central bank must intervene in the foreign exchange market by buying foreign assets. This foreign asset purchase eliminates the excess demand for domestic money because the central bank issues money to pay for the foreign assets it buys. The bank automatically increases the money supply in this way until asset markets again clear with $E = E^0$ and $R = R^*$.

If the central bank does not purchase foreign assets when output increases but instead holds the money stock constant, can it still keep the exchange rate fixed at E^0? The answer is no. If the central bank did not satisfy the excess demand for money caused by a rise in output, the domestic interest rate would begin to rise above the foreign rate, R^*, to balance the home money market. Traders in the foreign exchange market, perceiving that domestic currency deposits were offering a higher rate of return (given expectations), would begin to bid up the price of domestic currency in terms of foreign currency. In the absence of central bank intervention, the exchange rate thus would fall below E^0. To prevent this appreciation, the central bank must sell domestic currency and buy foreign assets, thereby increasing the money supply and preventing any excess money demand from pushing the home interest rate above R^*.

A Diagrammatic Analysis

The preceding mechanism of exchange rate fixing can be pictured using a diagrammatic tool developed earlier. Figure 18-1 shows the simultaneous equilibrium of the foreign exchange and domestic money markets when the exchange rate is fixed at E^0 and is expected to remain fixed at E^0 in the future.

Money market equilibrium is initially at point 1 in the lower part of the figure. The diagram shows that for a given price level, P, and a given national income level, Y^1, the money supply must equal M^1 when the domestic interest rate equals the foreign rate, R^*. The upper part of the figure shows the equilibrium of the foreign exchange market at point 1'. If the expected future exchange rate is E^0, the interest parity condition holds when $R = R^*$ only if today's exchange rate also equals E^0.

To see how the central bank must react to macroeconomic changes to hold the exchange rate permanently at E^0, let's look again at the example of an increase in income. A rise in income (from Y^1 to Y^2) raises the demand for real money holdings at every interest rate, thereby shifting the aggregate money demand function in Figure 18-1 downward. As noted above, a necessary condition for maintaining the fixed rate is to restore *current* asset market equilibrium given that E^0 is still the expected future exchange rate. So we can assume that the downward-sloping curve in the figure's top panel doesn't move.

If the central bank were to take no action, the new money market equilibrium would be at point 3. Because the domestic interest rate is above R^* at point 3, the currency would have to appreciate to bring the foreign exchange market to equilibrium at point 3'.

FIGURE 18-1

Asset Market Equilibrium with a Fixed Exchange Rate, E^0

To hold the exchange rate fixed at E^0 when output rises from Y^1 to Y^2, the central bank must purchase foreign assets and thereby raise the money supply from M^1 to M^2.

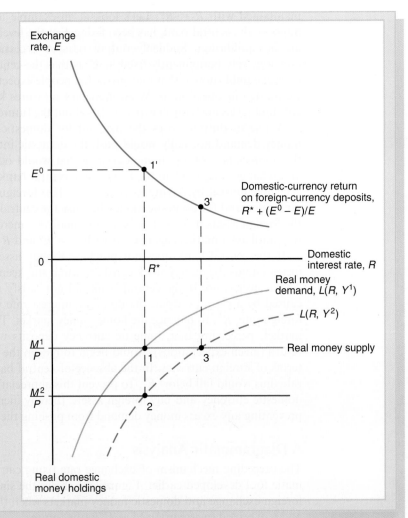

The central bank cannot allow this appreciation of the domestic currency to occur if it is fixing the exchange rate, so it will buy foreign assets. As we have seen, the increase in the central bank's foreign assets is accompanied by an expansion of the domestic money supply. The central bank will continue to purchase foreign assets until the domestic money supply has expanded to M^2. At the resulting money market equilibrium (point 2 in the figure), the domestic interest rate again equals R^*. Given this domestic interest rate, the foreign exchange market equilibrium remains at point $1'$, with the equilibrium exchange rate still equal to E^0.

Stabilization Policies with a Fixed Exchange Rate

Having seen how the central bank uses foreign exchange intervention to fix the exchange rate, we can now analyze the effects of various macroeconomic policies. In this section, we consider three possible policies: monetary policy, fiscal policy, and an abrupt change in the exchange rate's fixed level, E^0.

The stabilization policies we studied in the last chapter have surprisingly different effects when the central bank fixes the exchange rate rather than allowing the foreign exchange market to determine it. By fixing the exchange rate, the central bank gives up its ability to influence the economy through monetary policy. Fiscal policy, however, becomes a more potent tool for affecting output and employment.

As in the last chapter, we use the DD-AA model to describe the economy's short-run equilibrium. You will recall that the DD schedule shows combinations of the exchange rate and output for which the output market is in equilibrium, the AA schedule shows combinations of the exchange rate and output for which the asset markets are in equilibrium, and the short-run equilibrium of the economy as a whole is at the intersection of DD and AA. To apply the model to the case of a permanently fixed exchange rate, we add the assumption that the expected future exchange rate equals the rate at which the central bank is pegging its currency.

Monetary Policy

Figure 18-2 shows the economy's short-run equilibrium as point 1 when the central bank fixes the exchange rate at the level E^0. Output equals Y^1 at point 1, and, as in the last section, the money supply is at the level where a domestic interest rate equal to the foreign rate (R^*) clears the domestic money market. Now suppose that, hoping to increase output, the central bank attempts to increase the money supply through a purchase of domestic assets.

Under a floating exchange rate, the increase in the central bank's domestic assets would push the original asset market equilibrium curve AA^1 rightward to AA^2 and would therefore result in a new equilibrium at point 2 and a currency depreciation. To prevent this depreciation and hold the rate at E^0, the central bank sells foreign assets for domestic money in the foreign exchange market. The money the bank receives goes out of circulation, and the asset market equilibrium curve shifts back toward its initial position as the home money supply falls. Only when the money supply has returned to its original level,

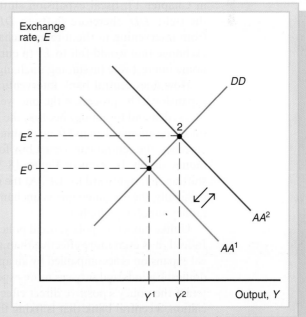

FIGURE 18-2

Monetary Expansion Is Ineffective under a Fixed Exchange Rate

Initial equilibrium is shown at point 1, where the output and asset markets simultaneously clear at a fixed exchange rate of E^0 and an output level of Y^1. Hoping to increase output to Y^2, the central bank decides to increase the money supply by buying domestic assets and shifting AA^1 to AA^2. Because the central bank must maintain E^0, however, it has to sell foreign assets for domestic currency, an action that decreases the money supply immediately and returns AA^2 back to AA^1. The economy's equilibrium therefore remains at point 1, with output unchanged at Y^1

so that the asset market schedule is again AA^1, is the exchange rate no longer under pressure. The attempt to increase the money supply under a fixed exchange rate thus leaves the economy at its initial equilibrium (point 1). *Under a fixed exchange rate, central bank monetary policy tools are powerless to affect the economy's money supply or its output.*

This result is very different from our finding in Chapter 17 that a central bank can use monetary policy to raise the money supply and (apart from liquidity traps) output when the exchange rate floats. So it is instructive to ask why the difference arises. By purchasing domestic assets under a floating rate, the central bank causes an initial excess supply of domestic money that simultaneously pushes the domestic interest rate downward and weakens the currency. Under a fixed exchange rate, however, the central bank will resist any tendency for the currency to depreciate by selling foreign assets for domestic money and thus removing the initial excess supply of money its policy move has caused. Because any increase in the domestic money supply, no matter how small, will cause the domestic currency to depreciate, the central bank must continue selling foreign assets until the money supply has returned to its original level. In the end, the increase in the central bank's domestic assets is exactly offset by an equal *decrease* in the bank's official international reserves. Similarly, an attempt to decrease the money supply through a sale of domestic assets would cause an equal *increase* in foreign reserves that would keep the money supply from changing in the end. Under fixed rates, monetary policy can affect the composition of the central bank's assets but nothing else.

By fixing an exchange rate, then, the central bank loses its ability to use monetary policy for the purpose of macroeconomic stabilization. However, the government's second key stabilization tool, fiscal policy, is more effective under a fixed rate than under a floating rate.

Fiscal Policy

Figure 18-3 illustrates the effects of expansionary fiscal policy, such as a cut in the income tax, when the economy's initial equilibrium is at point 1. As we saw in Chapter 17, fiscal expansion shifts the output market equilibrium schedule to the right. DD^1 therefore shifts to DD^2 in the figure. If the central bank refrained from intervening in the foreign exchange market, output would rise to Y^2 and the exchange rate would fall to E^2 (a currency appreciation) as a result of a rise in the home interest rate (assuming unchanged expectations).

How does central bank intervention hold the exchange rate fixed after the fiscal expansion? The process is the one we illustrated in Figure 18-1. Initially, there is an excess demand for money because the rise in output raises money demand. To prevent the excess money demand from pushing up the home interest rate and appreciating the currency, the central bank must buy foreign assets with money, thereby increasing the money supply. In terms of Figure 18-3, intervention holds the exchange rate at E^0 by shifting AA^1 rightward to AA^2. At the new equilibrium (point 3), output is higher than originally, the exchange rate is unchanged, and official international reserves (and the money supply) are higher.

Unlike monetary policy, fiscal policy can affect output under a fixed exchange rate. Indeed, it is even more effective than under a floating rate! Under a floating rate, fiscal expansion is accompanied by an appreciation of the domestic currency that makes domestic goods and services more expensive in world markets and thus tends to counteract the policy's positive direct effect on aggregate demand. To prevent this appreciation, a central bank that is fixing the exchange rate is forced to expand the money supply through foreign exchange purchases. The additional expansionary effect of

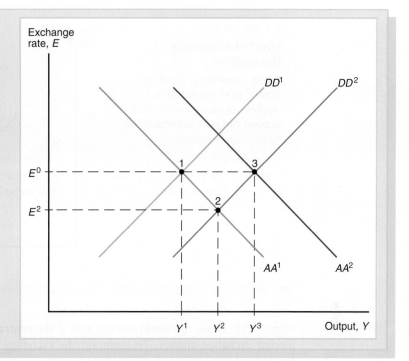

FIGURE 18-3

Fiscal Expansion under a Fixed Exchange Rate

Fiscal expansion (shown by the shift from DD^1 to DD^2) and the intervention that accompanies it (the shift from AA^1 to AA^2) move the economy from point 1 to point 3.

this accompanying increase in the money supply explains why fiscal policy is more potent under a fixed rate than under a floating rate.

Changes in the Exchange Rate

A country that is fixing its exchange rate sometimes decides on a sudden change in the foreign currency value of the domestic currency. This might happen, for example, if the country is quickly losing foreign exchange reserves because of a big current account deficit that far exceeds private financial inflows. A **devaluation** occurs when the central bank raises the domestic currency price of foreign currency, E, and a **revaluation** occurs when the central bank lowers E. All the central bank has to do to devalue or revalue is announce its willingness to trade domestic against foreign currency, in unlimited amounts, at the new exchange rate.[7]

Figure 18-4 shows how a devaluation affects the economy. A rise in the level of the fixed exchange rate, from E^0 to E^1, makes domestic goods and services cheaper relative to foreign goods and services (given that P and P^* are fixed in the short run). Output therefore moves to the higher level Y^2, shown by point 2 on the DD schedule. Point 2, however, does not lie on the initial asset market equilibrium schedule AA^1. At point 2, there is initially an excess demand for money due to the rise in transactions accompanying the output increase. This excess money demand would push the home

---

[7]We usually observe a subtle distinction between the terms *devaluation* and *depreciation* (and between *revaluation* and *appreciation*). Depreciation (appreciation) is a rise in E (a fall in E) when the exchange rate floats, while devaluation (revaluation) is a rise in E (a fall in E) when the exchange rate is fixed. Depreciation (appreciation) thus involves the active voice (as in "the currency appreciated"), while devaluation (revaluation) involves the passive voice (as in "the currency was devalued"). Put another way, devaluation (revaluation) reflects a deliberate government decision, while depreciation (appreciation) is an outcome of government actions and market forces acting together.

FIGURE 18-4

Effect of a Currency Devaluation

When a currency is devalued from E^0 to E^1, the economy's equilibrium moves from point 1 to point 2 as both output and the money supply expand.

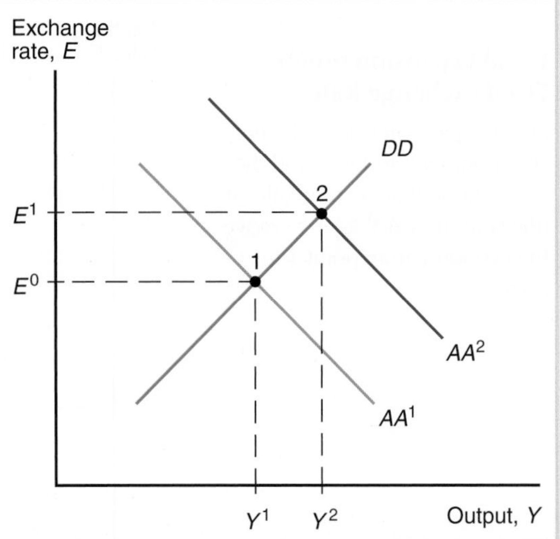

interest rate above the world interest rate if the central bank did not intervene in the foreign exchange market. To maintain the exchange rate at its new fixed level, E^1, the central bank must therefore buy foreign assets and expand the money supply until the asset market curve reaches AA^2 and passes through point 2. Devaluation therefore causes a rise in output, a rise in official reserves, and an expansion of the money supply.[8]

The effects of devaluation illustrate the three main reasons why governments sometimes choose to devalue their currencies. First, devaluation allows the government to fight domestic unemployment despite the lack of effective monetary policy. If government spending and budget deficits are politically unpopular, for example, or if the legislative process is slow, a government may opt for devaluation as the most convenient way of boosting aggregate demand. A second reason for devaluing is the resulting improvement in the current account, a development the government may believe to be desirable. The third motive behind devaluations, one we mentioned at the start of this subsection, is their effect on the central bank's foreign reserves. If the central bank is running low on reserves, a sudden, one-time devaluation (one that nobody expects to be repeated) can be used to draw in more reserves.

Adjustment to Fiscal Policy and Exchange Rate Changes

If fiscal and exchange rate changes occur when there is full employment and the policy changes are maintained indefinitely, they will ultimately cause the domestic price level to move in such a way that full employment is restored. To understand

---

[8]After the home currency is devalued, market participants expect that the new, higher exchange rate, rather than the old rate, will prevail in the future. The change in expectations alone shifts AA^1 the right, but without central bank intervention, this change by itself is insufficient to move AA^1 all the way to AA^2. At point 2, as at point 1, $R = R^*$ if the foreign exchange market clears. Because output is higher at point 2 than at point 1, however, real money demand is also higher at the former point. With P fixed, an expansion of the money supply is therefore necessary to make point 2 a position of money market equilibrium, that is, a point on the new AA schedule. Central bank purchases of foreign assets are therefore a necessary part of the economy's shift to its new fixed exchange rate equilibrium.

this dynamic process, we discuss the economy's adjustment to fiscal expansion and devaluation in turn.

If the economy is initially at full employment, fiscal expansion raises output, and this rise in output above its full-employment level causes the domestic price level, P, to begin rising. As P rises, home output becomes more expensive, so aggregate demand gradually falls, returning output to the initial, full-employment level. Once this point is reached, the upward pressure on the price level comes to an end. There is no real appreciation in the short run, as there is with a floating exchange rate, but regardless of whether the exchange rate is floating or fixed, the real exchange rate appreciates *in the long run* by the same amount.[9] In the present case, real appreciation (a fall in EP^*/P) takes the form of a rise in P rather than a fall in E.

At first glance, the long-run price level increase caused by a fiscal expansion under fixed rates seems inconsistent with Chapter 15's conclusion that for a given output level and interest rate, the price level and the money supply move proportionally in the long run. In fact, there is no inconsistency because fiscal expansion *does* cause a money supply increase by forcing the central bank to intervene in the foreign exchange market. To fix the exchange rate throughout the adjustment process, the central bank ultimately must increase the money supply by intervention purchases in proportion to the long-run increase in P.

The adjustment to a devaluation is similar. In fact, since a devaluation does not change long-run demand or supply conditions in the output market, the increase in the long-run price level caused by a devaluation is proportional to the increase in the exchange rate. A devaluation under a fixed rate has the same long-run effect as a proportional increase in the money supply under a floating rate. Like the latter policy, devaluation is neutral in the long run, in the sense that its only effect on the economy's long-run equilibrium is a proportional rise in all nominal prices and in the domestic money supply.

Balance of Payments Crises and Capital Flight

Until now, we have assumed that participants in the foreign exchange market believe that a fixed exchange rate will be maintained at its current level forever. In many practical situations, however, the central bank may find it undesirable or infeasible to maintain the current fixed exchange rate. The central bank may be running short on foreign reserves, for example, or it may face high domestic unemployment. Because market participants know the central bank may respond to such situations by devaluing the currency, it would be unreasonable for them to expect the current exchange rate to be maintained forever.

The market's belief in an impending change in the exchange rate gives rise to a **balance of payments crisis**, a sharp change in official foreign reserves sparked by a change in expectations about the future exchange rate. In this section, we use our model of asset market equilibrium to examine how balance of payments crises can occur under fixed exchange rates. (In later chapters we will describe a broader range of financial crises.)

Figure 18-5 shows the asset markets in equilibrium at points 1 (the money market) and 1′ (the foreign exchange market) with the exchange rate fixed at E^0 and expected to remain there indefinitely. M^1 is the money supply consistent with this initial equilibrium. Suppose a sudden deterioration in the current account, for example, leads

---

[9]To see this, observe that the long-run equilibrium real exchange rate, EP^*/P, must in either case satisfy the same equation, $Y^f = D(EP^*/P, Y^f - T, I, G)$, where Y^f, as in Chapter 17, is the full-employment output level.

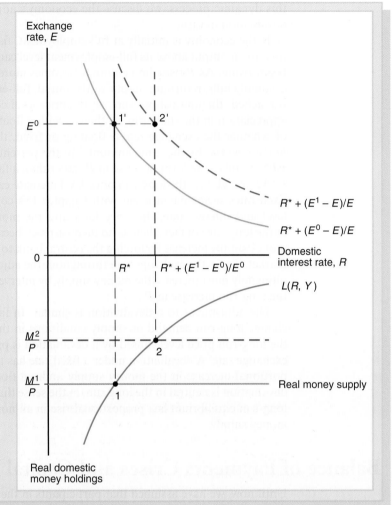

FIGURE 18-5

Capital Flight, the Money Supply, and the Interest Rate

To hold the exchange rate fixed at E^0 after the market decides it will be devalued to E^1, the central bank must use its reserves to finance a private financial outflow that shrinks the money supply and raises the home interest rate.

the foreign exchange market to expect the government to devalue in the future and adopt a new fixed exchange rate, E^1, that is higher than the current rate, E^0. The figure's upper part shows this change in expectations as a rightward shift in the curve that measures the expected domestic currency return on foreign currency deposits. Since the current exchange rate still is E^0, equilibrium in the foreign exchange market (point 2′) requires a rise in the domestic interest rate to $R^* + (E^1 - E^0)/E^0$, which now equals the expected domestic currency return on foreign currency assets.

Initially, however, the domestic interest rate remains at R^*, which is below the new expected return on foreign assets. This differential causes an excess demand for foreign currency assets in the foreign exchange market; to continue holding the exchange rate at E^0, the central bank must sell foreign reserves and thus shrink the domestic money supply. The bank's intervention comes to an end once the money supply has fallen to M^2, so that the money market is in equilibrium at the interest rate $R^* + (E^1 - E^0)/E^0$ that clears the foreign exchange market (point 2). *The expectation of a future devaluation causes a balance of payments crisis marked by a sharp fall in reserves and a rise in the home interest rate above the world interest rate. Similarly, an expected revaluation causes an abrupt rise in foreign reserves together with a fall in the home interest rate below the world rate.*

The reserve loss accompanying a devaluation scare is often labeled **capital flight**. Residents flee the domestic currency by selling it to the central bank for foreign exchange; they then invest the foreign currency abroad. At the same time, foreigners convert holdings of home assets into their own currencies and repatriate the proceeds. When fears of devaluation arise because the central bank's reserves are low to begin with, capital flight is of particular concern to the government. By pushing reserves even lower, capital flight may force the central bank to devalue sooner and by a larger amount than planned.[10]

What causes currency crises? Often, a government is following policies that are not consistent with maintaining a fixed exchange rate over the longer term. Once market expectations take those policies into account, the country's interest rates inevitably are forced up. For example, a country's central bank may be buying bonds from the domestic government to allow the government to run continuing fiscal deficits. Since these central bank purchases of domestic assets cause ongoing losses of central bank foreign exchange reserves, reserves will fall toward a point at which the central bank may find itself without the means to support the exchange rate. As the possibility of a collapse rises over time, so will domestic interest rates, until the central bank indeed runs out of foreign reserves and the fixed exchange rate is abandoned. (Appendix 2 to this chapter presents a detailed model of this type, and shows that the collapse of the currency peg can be caused by a sharp *speculative attack* in which currency traders suddenly acquire all of the central bank's remaining foreign reserves.) The only way for the central bank to avoid this fate is to stop bankrolling the government deficit, hopefully forcing the government to live within its means.

In the last example, exhaustion of foreign reserves and an end of the fixed exchange rate are inevitable, given macroeconomic policies. The financial outflows that accompany a currency crisis only hasten an inevitable collapse, one that would have occurred anyway, albeit in slower motion, even if private financial flows could be banned. Not all crises are of this kind, however. An economy can be vulnerable to currency speculation even without being in such bad shape that a collapse of its fixed exchange rate regime is inevitable. Currency crises that occur in such circumstances often are called **self-fulfilling currency crises**, although it is important to keep in mind that the government may ultimately be responsible for such crises by creating or tolerating domestic economic weaknesses that invite speculators to attack the currency.

As an example, consider an economy in which domestic commercial banks' liabilities are mainly short-term deposits, and in which many of the banks' loans to businesses are likely to go unpaid in the event of a recession. If speculators suspect there will be a devaluation, interest rates will climb, raising banks' borrowing costs sharply while at the same time causing a recession and reducing the value of bank assets. To prevent domestic banks from going out of business, the central bank may well lend money to the banks, in the process losing foreign reserves and possibly its ability to go on pegging the exchange rate. In this case, it is the emergence of devaluation expectations among currency traders that pushes the economy into crisis and forces the exchange rate to be changed.

For the rest of this chapter, we continue to assume that no exchange rate changes are expected by the market when exchange rates are fixed. But we draw on the preceding analysis repeatedly in later chapters when we discuss various countries' unhappy experiences with fixed exchange rates.

---

[10]If aggregate demand depends on the real interest rate (as in the *IS-LM* model of intermediate macroeconomics courses), capital flight reduces output by shrinking the money supply and raising the real interest rate. This possibly contractionary effect of capital flight is another reason why policy makers hope to avoid it.

Managed Floating and Sterilized Intervention

Under managed floating, monetary policy is influenced by exchange rate changes without being completely subordinate to the requirements of a fixed rate. Instead, the central bank faces a trade-off between domestic objectives such as employment or the inflation rate and exchange rate stability. Suppose the central bank tries to expand the money supply to fight domestic unemployment, for example, but at the same time carries out foreign asset sales to restrain the resulting depreciation of the home currency. The foreign exchange intervention will tend to *reduce* the money supply, hindering but not necessarily nullifying the central bank's attempt to reduce unemployment.

Discussions of foreign exchange intervention in policy forums and newspapers often appear to ignore the intimate link between intervention and the money supply that we previously explored in detail. In reality, however, these discussions often assume that foreign exchange intervention is being *sterilized*, so that opposite domestic asset transactions prevent it from affecting the money supply. Empirical studies of central bank behavior confirm this assumption and consistently show central banks to have practiced sterilized intervention under flexible and fixed exchange rate regimes alike.

In spite of widespread sterilized intervention, there is considerable disagreement among economists about its effects. In this section, we study the role of sterilized intervention in exchange rate management.[11]

Perfect Asset Substitutability and the Ineffectiveness of Sterilized Intervention

When a central bank carries out a sterilized foreign exchange intervention, its transactions leave the domestic money supply unchanged. A rationale for such a policy is difficult to find using the model of exchange rate determination previously developed, for the model predicts that without an accompanying change in the money supply, the central bank's intervention will not affect the domestic interest rate and therefore will not affect the exchange rate.

Our model also predicts that sterilization will be fruitless under a fixed exchange rate. The example of a fiscal expansion illustrates why a central bank might wish to sterilize under a fixed rate and why our model says that such a policy will fail. Recall that to hold the exchange rate constant when fiscal policy becomes more expansive, the central bank must buy foreign assets and expand the home money supply. The policy raises output but it eventually also causes inflation, which the central bank may try to avoid by sterilizing the increase in the money supply that its fiscal policy has induced. As quickly as the central bank sells domestic assets to reduce the money supply, however, it will have to *buy* more foreign assets to keep the exchange rate fixed. The ineffectiveness of monetary policy under a fixed exchange rate implies that sterilization is a self-defeating policy.

The key feature of our model that leads to these results is the assumption that the foreign exchange market is in equilibrium only when the expected returns on domestic and foreign currency bonds are the same.[12] This assumption is often called

---

[11]In the United States, the Federal Reserve Bank of New York carries out intervention for the Federal Reserve System, and the interventions are routinely sterilized. See Federal Reserve Bank of New York, "Fedpoint: U.S. Foreign Exchange Intervention," http://www.newyorkfed.org/aboutthefed/fedpoint/fed44.html

[12]We are assuming that all interest-bearing (nonmoney) assets denominated in the same currency, whether illiquid time deposits or government bonds, are perfect substitutes in portfolios. The single term "bonds" will generally be used to refer to all these assets.

perfect asset substitutability. Two assets are perfect substitutes when, as our model assumed, investors don't care how their portfolios are divided between them, provided both yield the same expected rate of return. With perfect asset substitutability in the foreign exchange market, the exchange rate is therefore determined so that the interest parity condition holds. When this is the case, there is nothing a central bank can

CASE STUDY   Can Markets Attack a *Strong* Currency? The Case of Switzerland

The Swiss franc has traditionally been a "safe haven" currency: a currency investors buy when they fear instability in the global economy. When a simmering global financial crisis intensified in September 2008 (as we discuss in later chapters), the usual pattern repeated itself. Investors (many of whom were Swiss and owned substantial assets abroad) rushed to put their money into Switzerland. As you can see in Figure 18-6, the Swiss franc price of euros fell sharply (a Swiss franc appreciation), while the reserves of the central bank, the Swiss National Bank (SNB), rose sharply. (Reserves are measured on the figure's right-hand vertical axis.) Reserves rose because the SNB was intervening in the foreign exchange market, buying euros with francs so as to slow the franc's appreciation.

The SNB cut interest rates quickly, both to stimulate economic activity and to discourage appreciation. By November 2008, Swiss short-term interest rates were essentially at zero (where they remained). The Swiss franc's exchange rate briefly stabilized at levels slightly over CHF 1.5 per euro.

But renewed pressure came when the euro zone entered its own financial crisis late in 2009 (as we discuss in Chapter 21). The Swiss franc appreciated dramatically against the euro and reserves ballooned as a result of further foreign exchange purchases. Switzerland began to suffer from deflation and unemployment as import prices fell and as export industries (such as the watch industry) found themselves priced out of world markets. In August 2011, the currency reached CHF 1.12 per euro.

At that point, the SNB took radical action: in September 2011, it pledged to defend a minimal euro price of CHF 1.2 per euro. It would allow the Swiss franc to depreciate up from that floor, but not to appreciate below it. To accomplish this, the SNB had to buy all the euros the market wished to sell it at a rate of CHF 1.2 per euro.

Figure 18-6 shows that Switzerland's international reserves subsequently rose even more rapidly. As money flooded in from speculators betting that the currency floor would not hold, SNB foreign currency reserves reached a level equal to about three-quarters of a year's national output! When a weak currency is under attack, the defending central bank, which is selling reserves, may run out. But is there any limit to its ability to hold down a *strong* currency by *buying* reserves with its own money, which it has the power to print without limit? The main potential brake is that by buying reserves and allowing the money supply to increase, the central bank sparks excessive inflation. But this did not happen. In part because of the neighboring euro zone's dismal economic growth, Switzerland remained in deflation long after it stepped in to limit the Swiss franc's appreciation.

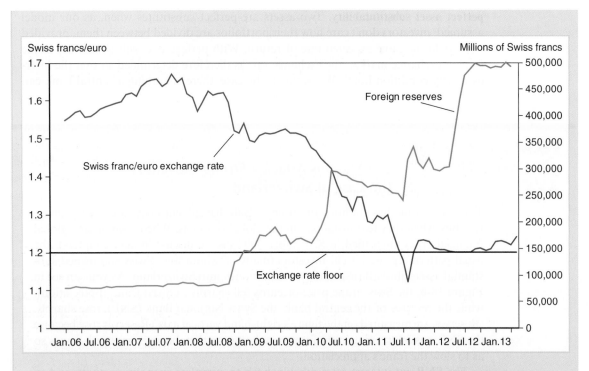

FIGURE 18-6

The Swiss Franc's Exchange Rate against the Euro and Swiss Foreign Exchange Reserves, 2006–2013

The Swiss National Bank intervened heavily to slow the Swiss franc's appreciation against the euro, finally setting a floor under the price of the euro in September 2011.

Source: Swiss National Bank.

do through foreign exchange intervention that it could not do as well through purely domestic open-market operations.

In contrast to perfect asset substitutability, **imperfect asset substitutability** exists when it is possible for assets' expected returns to differ in equilibrium. As we saw in Chapter 14, the main factor that may lead to imperfect asset substitutability in the foreign exchange market is *risk*. If bonds denominated in different currencies have different degrees of risk, investors may be willing to earn lower expected returns on bonds that are less risky. Correspondingly, they will hold a very risky asset only if its expected return is relatively high.

In a world of perfect asset substitutability, participants in the foreign exchange market care only about expected rates of return; since these rates are determined by monetary policy, actions such as sterilized intervention that do not affect the money supply also do not affect the exchange rate. Under imperfect asset substitutability, however, both risk *and* return matter, so central bank actions that alter the riskiness of domestic currency assets can move the exchange rate even when the money supply does not change. To understand how sterilized intervention can alter the riskiness of domestic currency assets, however, we must modify our model of equilibrium in the foreign exchange market.

Foreign Exchange Market Equilibrium under Imperfect Asset Substitutability

When domestic and foreign currency bonds are perfect substitutes, the foreign exchange market is in equilibrium only if the interest parity condition holds:

$$R = R^* + (E^e - E)/E. \tag{18-1}$$

When domestic and foreign currency bonds are *imperfect* substitutes, the condition above does not hold in general. Instead, equilibrium in the foreign exchange market requires that the domestic interest rate equal the expected domestic currency return on foreign bonds *plus* a **risk premium**, ρ, that reflects the difference between the riskiness of domestic and foreign bonds:

$$R = R^* + (E^e - E)/E + \rho. \tag{18-2}$$

Appendix 1 to this chapter develops a detailed model of foreign exchange market equilibrium with imperfect asset substitutability. The main conclusion of that model is that the risk premium on domestic assets rises when the stock of domestic government bonds available to be held by the public rises and falls when the central bank's domestic assets rise. It is not hard to grasp the economic reasoning behind this result. Private investors become more vulnerable to unexpected changes in the home currency's exchange rate as the stock of domestic government bonds they hold rises. Investors will be unwilling to assume the increased risk of holding more domestic government debt, however, unless they are compensated by a higher expected rate of return on domestic currency assets. An increased stock of domestic government debt will therefore raise the difference between the expected returns on domestic and foreign currency bonds. Similarly, when the central bank buys domestic assets, the market need no longer hold them; private vulnerability to home currency exchange rate risk is thus lower, and the risk premium on home currency assets falls.

This alternative model of foreign market equilibrium implies that the risk premium depends positively on the stock of domestic government debt, denoted by B, less the domestic assets of the central bank, denoted by A:

$$\rho = \rho(B - A). \tag{18-3}$$

The risk premium on domestic bonds therefore rises when $B - A$ rises. This relation between the risk premium and the central bank's domestic asset holdings allows the bank to affect the exchange rate through sterilized foreign exchange intervention. It also implies that official operations in domestic and foreign assets may differ in their asset market impacts.[13]

The Effects of Sterilized Intervention with Imperfect Asset Substitutability

Figure 18-7 modifies our earlier picture of asset market equilibrium by adding imperfect asset substitutability to illustrate how sterilized intervention can affect the exchange rate. The lower part of the figure, which shows the money market in equilibrium at point 1, does not change. The upper part of the figure is also much the same

---

[13]The stock of central bank domestic assets is often called central bank *domestic credit*.

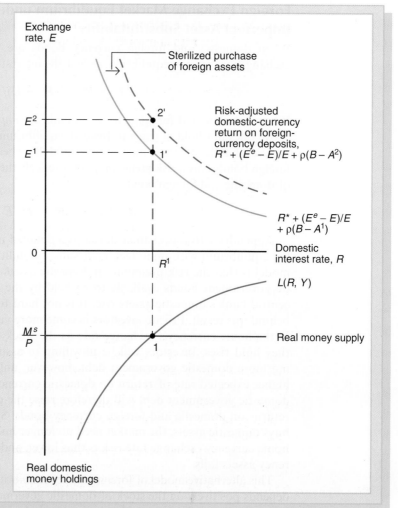

FIGURE 18-7

Effect of a Sterilized Central Bank Purchase of Foreign Assets under Imperfect Asset Substitutability

A sterilized purchase of foreign assets leaves the money supply unchanged but raises the risk-adjusted return that domestic currency deposits must offer in equilibrium. As a result, the return curve in the upper panel shifts up and to the right. Other things equal, this depreciates the domestic currency from E^1 to E^2.

as before, except that the downward-sloping schedule now shows how the *sum* of the expected domestic currency return on foreign assets *and* the risk premium depends on the exchange rate. (The curve continues to slope downward because the risk premium itself is assumed not to depend on the exchange rate.) Equilibrium in the foreign exchange market is at point $1'$, which corresponds to a domestic government debt of B and central bank domestic asset holdings of A^1. At that point, the domestic interest rate equals the risk-adjusted domestic currency return on foreign deposits (as in equation (18-2)).

Let's use the diagram to examine the effects of a sterilized purchase of foreign assets by the central bank. By matching its purchase of foreign assets with a sale of domestic assets, the central bank holds the money supply constant at M^s and avoids any change in the lower part of Figure 18-7. As a result of its domestic asset sale, however, the central bank's domestic assets are lower (they fall to A^2) and the stock of domestic assets that the market must hold, $B - A^2$, is therefore higher than the initial stock $B - A^1$. This increase pushes the risk premium ρ upward and shifts to the right the negatively sloped schedule in the upper part of the figure. The foreign exchange market now settles at point $2'$ and the domestic currency depreciates to E^2.

With imperfect asset substitutability, even sterilized purchases of foreign exchange cause the home currency to depreciate. Similarly, sterilized sales of foreign exchange cause the home currency to appreciate. A slight modification of our analysis shows that the central bank can also use sterilized intervention to hold the exchange rate fixed as it varies the money supply to achieve domestic objectives such as full employment. In effect, the exchange rate and monetary policy can be managed independently of each other in the short run when sterilized intervention is effective.

Evidence on the Effects of Sterilized Intervention

Little evidence has been found to support the idea that sterilized intervention exerts a major influence over exchange rates independent of the stances of monetary and fiscal policies.[14] As we noted in Chapter 14, however, there is also considerable evidence against the view that bonds denominated in different currencies are perfect substitutes.[15] Some economists conclude from these conflicting results that while risk premiums are important, they do not depend on central bank asset transactions in the simple way our model assumes. Others contend that the tests that have been used to detect the effects of sterilized intervention are flawed. Given the meager evidence that sterilized intervention has a reliable effect on exchange rates, however, a skeptical attitude is probably in order.

Our discussion of sterilized intervention has assumed that it does not change the market's exchange rate expectations. If market participants are unsure about the *future* direction of macroeconomic policies, however, sterilized intervention may give an indication of where the central bank expects (or desires) the exchange rate to move. This **signaling effect of foreign exchange intervention**, in turn, can alter the market's view of future monetary or fiscal policies and cause an immediate exchange rate change even when bonds denominated in different currencies are perfect substitutes.

The signaling effect is most important when the government is unhappy with the exchange rate's level and declares in public that it will alter monetary or fiscal policies to bring about a change. By simultaneously intervening on a sterilized basis, the central bank sometimes lends credibility to this announcement. A sterilized purchase of foreign assets, for example, may convince the market that the central bank intends to bring about a home currency depreciation because the bank will lose money if an appreciation occurs instead. Even central banks must watch their budgets!

However, a government may be tempted to exploit the signaling effect for temporary benefits even when it has no intention of changing monetary or fiscal policy to bring about a different long-run exchange rate. The result of crying, "Wolf!" too often is the same in the foreign exchange market as elsewhere. If governments do not follow up on their exchange market signals with concrete policy moves, the signals soon become ineffective. Thus, intervention signaling cannot be viewed as a policy weapon to be wielded independently of monetary and fiscal policy.[16]

---

[14]For evidence on sterilized intervention, see the Further Readings entry by Sarno and Taylor as well as the December 2000 issue of the *Journal of International Financial Markets, Institutions, and Money*.

[15]See the paper by Froot and Thaler in this chapter's Further Readings.

[16]For discussion of the role played by the signaling effect, see Kathryn M. Dominguez and Jeffrey A. Frankel, *Does Foreign Exchange Intervention Work?* (Washington, D.C.: Institute for International Economics, 1993); and Richard T. Baillie, Owen F. Humpage, and William P. Osterberg, "Intervention from an Information Perspective," *Journal of International Financial Markets, Institutions, and Money* 10 (December 2000), pp. 407–421.

Reserve Currencies in the World Monetary System

Until now, we have studied a single country that fixes its exchange rate in terms of a hypothetical single foreign currency by trading domestic for foreign assets when necessary. In the real world there are many currencies, and it is possible for a country to manage the exchange rates of its domestic currency against some foreign currencies while allowing them to float against others.

This section and the next adopt a global perspective and study the macroeconomic behavior of the world economy under two possible systems for fixing the exchange rates of *all* currencies against each other.

The first such fixed-rate system is very much like the one we have been studying. In it, one currency is singled out as a **reserve currency**, the currency central banks hold in their international reserves, and each nation's central bank fixes its currency's exchange rate against the reserve currency by standing ready to trade domestic money for reserve assets at that rate. Between the end of World War II and 1973, the U.S. dollar was the main reserve currency and almost every country pegged the dollar exchange rate of its money.

The second fixed-rate system (studied in the next section) is a **gold standard**. Under a gold standard, central banks peg the prices of their currencies in terms of gold and hold gold as official international reserves. The heyday of the international gold standard was between 1870 and 1914, although many countries attempted unsuccessfully to restore a permanent gold standard after the end of World War I in 1918.

Both reserve currency standards and the gold standard result in fixed exchange rates between *all* pairs of currencies in the world. But the two systems have very different implications about how countries share the burden of balance of payments financing and about the growth and control of national money supplies.

The Mechanics of a Reserve Currency Standard

The workings of a reserve currency system are illustrated by the system based on the U.S. dollar set up at the end of World War II. Under that system, every central bank fixed the dollar exchange rate of its currency through foreign exchange market trades of domestic currency for dollar assets. The frequent need to intervene meant that each central bank had to have on hand sufficient dollar reserves to meet any excess supply of its currency that might arise. Central banks therefore held a large portion of their international reserves in the form of U.S. Treasury bills and short-term dollar deposits, which pay interest and can be turned into cash at relatively low cost.

Because each currency's dollar price was fixed by its central bank, the exchange rate between any two currencies was automatically fixed as well through arbitrage in the foreign exchange market. How did this process work? Consider the following example based on the French franc and the deutsche mark, which were the currencies of France and Germany prior to the introduction of the euro. Let's suppose the French franc price of dollars was fixed at FFr 5 per dollar while the deutsche mark price of dollars was fixed at DM 4 per dollar. The exchange rate between the franc and the DM had to remain constant at DM 0.80 per franc = (DM 4 per dollar) ÷ (FFr 5 per dollar), even though no central bank was directly trading francs for DM to hold the relative price of those two currencies fixed. At a DM/FFr rate of DM 0.85 per franc, for example, you could have made a sure profit of $6.25 by selling $100 to the former French central bank, the Bank of France, for ($100) × (FFr 5 per dollar) = FFr 500, selling your FFr 500 in the foreign exchange market for (FFr 500) × (DM 0.85 per franc) = DM 425, and then selling the DM to the German Bundesbank (Germany's central bank until

1999) for (DM 425) ÷ (DM 4 per dollar) = $106.25. With everyone trying to exploit this profit opportunity by selling francs for DM in the foreign exchange market, however, the DM would have appreciated against the franc until the DM/FFr rate reached DM 0.80 per franc. Similarly, at a rate of DM 0.75 per franc, pressure in the foreign exchange market would have forced the DM to depreciate against the franc until the rate of DM 0.80 per franc was reached.

Even though each central bank tied its currency's exchange rate only to the dollar, market forces automatically held all other exchange rates—called cross rates—constant at the values implied by the dollar rates. Thus, the post–World War II exchange rate system was one in which exchange rates between any two currencies were fixed.[17]

The Asymmetric Position of the Reserve Center

In a reserve currency system, the country whose currency is held as reserves occupies a special position because it never has to intervene in the foreign exchange market. The reason is that if there are N countries with N currencies in the world, there are only $N-1$ exchange rates against the reserve currency. If the $N-1$ nonreserve currency countries fix their exchange rates against the reserve currency, there is no exchange rate left for the reserve center to fix. Thus, the center country need never intervene and bears none of the burden of financing its balance of payments.

This set of arrangements puts the reserve-issuing country in a privileged position because it can use its monetary policy for macroeconomic stabilization even though it has fixed exchange rates. We saw earlier in this chapter that when a country must intervene to hold an exchange rate constant, any attempt to expand its money supply is bound to be frustrated by losses of international reserves. But because the reserve center is the one country in the system that can enjoy fixed exchange rates without the need to intervene, it is still able to use monetary policy for stabilization purposes.

What would be the effect of a purchase of domestic assets by the central bank of the reserve currency country? The resulting expansion in its money supply would momentarily push its interest rate below those prevailing abroad, and thereby cause an excess demand for foreign currencies in the foreign exchange market. To prevent their currencies from appreciating against the reserve currency, all other central banks in the system would be forced to buy reserve assets with their own currencies, expanding their money supplies and pushing their interest rates down to the level established by the reserve center. Output throughout the world, as well as at home, would expand after a purchase of domestic assets by the reserve country.

Our account of monetary policy under a reserve currency system points to a basic asymmetry. The reserve country has the power to affect its own economy, as well as foreign economies, by using monetary policy. Other central banks are forced to relinquish monetary policy as a stabilization tool and instead must passively "import" the monetary policy of the reserve center because of their commitment to peg their currencies to the reserve currency.

This inherent asymmetry of a reserve system places immense economic power in the hands of the reserve country and is therefore likely to lead eventually to policy disputes within the system. Such problems helped cause the breakdown of the postwar "dollar standard" in 1973, a topic we discuss in Chapter 19.

---

[17]The rules of the postwar system actually allowed currencies' dollar values to move as much as 1 percent above or below the "official" values. This meant cross rates could fluctuate by as much as 4 percent.

The Gold Standard

An international gold standard avoids the asymmetry inherent in a reserve currency standard by avoiding the "*N*th currency" problem. Under a gold standard, each country fixes the price of its currency in terms of gold by standing ready to trade domestic currency for gold whenever necessary to defend the official price. Because there are *N* currencies and *N* prices of gold in terms of those currencies, no single country occupies a privileged position within the system: Each is responsible for pegging its currency's price in terms of the official international reserve asset, gold.

The Mechanics of a Gold Standard

Because countries tie their currencies to gold under a gold standard, official international reserves take the form of gold. Gold standard rules also require each country to allow unhindered imports and exports of gold across its borders. Under these arrangements, a gold standard, like a reserve currency system, results in fixed exchange rates between all currencies. For example, if the dollar price of gold is pegged at $35 per ounce by the Federal Reserve while the pound price of gold is pegged at £14.58 per ounce by Britain's central bank, the Bank of England, the dollar/pound exchange rate must be constant at ($35 per ounce) ÷ (£14.58 per ounce) = $2.40 per pound. The same arbitrage process that holds cross exchange rates fixed under a reserve currency system keeps exchange rates fixed under a gold standard as well.[18]

Symmetric Monetary Adjustment under a Gold Standard

Because of the inherent symmetry of a gold standard, no country in the system occupies a privileged position by being relieved of the commitment to intervene. By considering the international effects of a purchase of domestic assets by one central bank, we can see in more detail how monetary policy works under a gold standard.

Suppose the Bank of England decides to increase its money supply through a purchase of domestic assets. The initial increase in Britain's money supply will put downward pressure on British interest rates and make foreign currency assets more attractive than British assets. Holders of pound deposits will attempt to sell them for foreign deposits, but no *private* buyers will come forward. Under floating exchange rates, the pound would depreciate against foreign currencies until interest parity had been reestablished. This depreciation cannot occur when all currencies are tied to gold, however. Why not? Because central banks are obliged to trade their currencies for gold at fixed rates, unhappy holders of pounds can sell these to the Bank of England for gold, sell the gold to other central banks for their currencies, and use these currencies to purchase deposits that offer interest rates higher than the interest rate on pounds. Britain therefore experiences a private financial outflow and foreign countries experience an inflow.

This process reestablishes equilibrium in the foreign exchange market. The Bank of England loses foreign reserves since it is forced to buy pounds and sell gold to keep the pound price of gold fixed. Foreign central banks gain reserves as they *buy* gold with their currencies. Countries share equally in the burden of balance of payments adjustment. Because official foreign reserves are declining in Britain and increasing abroad, the British money supply is falling, pushing the British interest rate back up, and foreign money supplies are rising, pushing foreign interest rates down. Once interest rates

---

[18]In practice, the costs of shipping gold and insuring it in transit determined narrow "gold points" within which currency exchange rates could fluctuate.

have again become equal across countries, asset markets are in equilibrium and there is no further tendency for the Bank of England to lose gold or for foreign central banks to gain it. The total world money supply (not the British money supply) ends up being higher by the amount of the Bank of England's domestic asset purchase. Interest rates are lower throughout the world.

Our example illustrates the symmetric nature of international monetary adjustment under a gold standard. Whenever a country is losing reserves and seeing its money supply shrink as a consequence, foreign countries are gaining reserves and seeing their money supplies expand. In contrast, monetary adjustment under a reserve currency standard is highly asymmetric. Countries can gain or lose reserves without inducing any change in the money supply of the reserve currency country, and only the latter country has the ability to influence domestic and world monetary conditions.[19]

Benefits and Drawbacks of the Gold Standard

Advocates of the gold standard argue that it has another desirable property besides symmetry. Because central banks throughout the world are obliged to fix the money price of gold, they cannot allow their money supplies to grow more rapidly than real money demand, since such rapid monetary growth eventually raises the money prices of all goods and services, including gold. A gold standard therefore places automatic limits on the extent to which central banks can cause increases in national price levels through expansionary monetary policies. These limits can make the real values of national monies more stable and predictable, thereby enhancing the transaction economies arising from the use of money (see Chapter 15). No such limits to money creation exist under a reserve currency system; the reserve currency country faces no automatic barrier to unlimited money creation.

Offsetting this potential benefit of a gold standard are some drawbacks:

1. The gold standard places undesirable constraints on the use of monetary policy to fight unemployment. In a worldwide recession, it might be desirable for all countries to expand their money supplies jointly even if this were to raise the price of gold in terms of national currencies.

2. Tying currency values to gold ensures a stable overall price level only if the relative price of gold and other goods and services is stable. For example, suppose the dollar price of gold is $35 per ounce while the price of gold in terms of a typical output basket is one-third of a basket per ounce. This implies a price level of $105 per output basket. Now suppose that there is a major gold discovery in South America and the relative price of gold in terms of output falls to one-fourth of a basket per ounce. With the dollar price of gold unchanged at $35 per ounce, the price level would have to rise from $105 to $140 per basket. In fact, studies of the gold standard era do reveal surprisingly large price level fluctuations arising from such changes in gold's relative price.[20]

---

[19]Originally, gold coins were a substantial part of the currency supply in gold standard countries. A country's gold losses to foreigners therefore did not have to take the form of a fall in central bank gold holdings: Private citizens could melt gold coins into ingots and ship them abroad, where they were either reminted as foreign gold coins or sold to the foreign central bank for paper currency. In terms of our earlier analysis of the central bank balance sheet, circulating gold coins are considered to make up a component of the monetary base that is not a central bank liability. Either form of gold export would thus result in a fall in the domestic money supply and an increase in foreign money supplies.

[20]See, for example, Richard N. Cooper, "The Gold Standard: Historical Facts and Future Prospects," *Brookings Papers on Economic Activity* 1 (1982), pp. 1–45.

3. An international payments system based on gold is problematic because central banks cannot increase their holdings of international reserves as their economies grow unless there are continual new gold discoveries. Every central bank would need to hold some gold reserves to fix its currency's gold price and serve as a buffer against unforeseen economic mishaps. Central banks might thereby bring about world unemployment as they attempted to compete for reserves by selling domestic assets and thus shrinking their money supplies.

4. The gold standard could give countries with potentially large gold production, such as Russia and South Africa, considerable ability to influence macroeconomic conditions throughout the world through market sales of gold.

Because of these drawbacks, few economists favor a return to the gold standard today. As early as 1923, the British economist John Maynard Keynes characterized gold as a "barbarous relic" of an earlier international monetary system.[21] While most central banks continue to hold some gold as part of their international reserves, the price of gold now plays no special role in influencing countries' monetary policies.

The Bimetallic Standard

Up until the early 1870s, many countries adhered to a **bimetallic standard** in which the currency was based on both silver and gold. The United States was bimetallic from 1837 until the Civil War, although the major bimetallic power of the day was France, which abandoned bimetallism for gold in 1873.

In a bimetallic system, a country's mint will coin specified amounts of gold *or* silver into the national currency unit (typically for a fee). In the United States before the Civil War, for example, 371.25 grains of silver (a grain being 1/480th of an ounce) or 23.22 grains of gold could be turned into, respectively, a silver or a gold dollar. That mint parity made gold worth $371.25/23.22 = 16$ times as much as silver.

The mint parity could differ from the market relative price of the two metals, however, and when it did, one or other might go out of circulation. For example, if the price of gold in terms of silver were to rise to 20:1, a depreciation of silver relative to the mint parity of 16:1, no one would want to turn gold into gold dollar coins at the mint. More dollars could be obtained by instead using the gold to buy silver in the market, and then having the silver coined into dollars. As a result, gold would tend to go out of monetary circulation when its relative market price rose above the mint relative price, and silver coin would tend to disappear in the opposite case.

The advantage of bimetallism was that it might reduce the price level instability resulting from use of one of the metals alone. Were gold to become scarce and expensive, cheaper and relatively abundant silver would become the predominant form of money, thereby mitigating the deflation that a pure gold standard would imply. Notwithstanding this advantage, by the late 19th century most of the world had followed Britain, the leading industrial power of the day, onto a pure gold standard.

The Gold Exchange Standard

Halfway between the gold standard and a pure reserve currency standard is the **gold exchange standard**. Under a gold exchange standard, central banks' reserves consist of gold *and* currencies whose prices in terms of gold are fixed, and each central bank

---

[21]See Keynes, "Alternative Aims in Monetary Policy," reprinted in his *Essays in Persuasion* (New York: W. W. Norton & Company, 1963). For a dissenting view on the gold standard, see Robert A. Mundell, "International Monetary Reform: The Optimal Mix in Big Countries," in James Tobin, ed., *Macroeconomics, Prices and Quantities* (Washington, D.C.: Brookings Institution, 1983), pp. 285–293.

fixes its exchange rate to a currency with a fixed gold price. A gold exchange standard can operate like a gold standard in restraining excessive monetary growth throughout the world, but it allows more flexibility in the growth of international reserves, which can consist of assets besides gold. A gold exchange standard is, however, subject to the other limitations of a gold standard listed previously.

The post–World War II reserve currency system centered on the dollar was, in fact, originally set up as a gold exchange standard. While foreign central banks did the job of pegging exchange rates, the U.S. Federal Reserve was responsible for holding the dollar price of gold at $35 an ounce. By the mid-1960s, the system operated in practice more like a pure reserve currency system than a gold standard. For reasons explained in the next chapter, President Richard M. Nixon unilaterally severed the dollar's link to gold in August 1971, shortly before the system of fixed dollar exchange rates was abandoned.

CASE STUDY   The Demand for International Reserves

The chapter explained that a central bank's assets are divided between domestic currency assets, such as domestic government bonds, and foreign currency assets, the bank's international reserves. Historically and up to the present day, international reserves have been prized by central banks because they can be traded to foreigners for goods and services even in circumstances, such as financial crises and wars, when the value of domestic assets may come into doubt. Gold played the role of international reserve asset *par excellence* under the gold standard—and while the U.S. dollar remains the main reserve asset today, economists debate how long that unique American privilege can last. Because central banks and governments may alter their policies to affect national holdings of international reserves, it is important to understand the factors that influence countries' demands for international reserves.

A good starting point for thinking about international reserves is the model in the chapter in which domestic and foreign bonds are perfect substitutes, the exchange rate is fixed, and confidence in the fixed exchange rate is absolute. In that model, our result that monetary policy is ineffective also implies that individual central banks can painlessly acquire all the international reserves they need! They do so simply by an open-market sale of domestic assets, which immediately causes an equal inflow of foreign assets but no change in the home interest rate or in other domestic economic conditions. In real life, matters may not be so easy, because the circumstances in which countries need reserves are precisely those in which the above conditions of perfect confidence in creditworthiness and in the exchange rate peg are likely to be violated. As a result, central banks manage their reserves in a *precautionary* manner, holding a stock that they believe will be sufficient in future times of crisis.[22]

As usual, there are costs as well as benefits of acquiring and holding reserves, and the level of reserves that a central bank wishes to hold will reflect a balance between those costs and benefits. Some monetary authorities (such as that of Hong Kong) value reserves so highly that the entire money supply is backed by foreign

---

[22]A different problem arises under a system like the gold standard, where the global stock of international reserves may be limited (in contrast to a reserve currency system). The difficulty is that all countries cannot simultaneously increase their reserve holdings, so efforts by many countries to do so at the same time will affect global economic conditions. An end-of-chapter exercise asks you to think about this case.

assets—there are no domestic monetary assets at all. In most cases, however, central banks hold both domestic and foreign assets, with the optimal level of reserves determined by the trade-off between costs and benefits.

Starting in the mid-1960s, economists developed and sought empirical verification of formal theories of the demand for international reserves. In that setting, with international capital markets much more limited than they are today (see Chapter 20), a major threat to reserves was a sudden drop in export earnings, and central banks measured reserve levels in terms of the number of months of import needs those reserves could cover. Accordingly, the variability levels of exports, imports, and international financial flows, all of which could cause reserves to fluctuate too close to zero, were viewed as prime determinants of the demand for international reserves. In this theory, higher variability would raise the demand for reserves. An additional variable raising the average demand for reserves might be the adjustment cost countries would suffer if they suddenly had to raise exports or reduce imports to generate a trade surplus, or raise interest rates to draw in foreign capital. Higher economic openness could make such adjustments easier, thereby reducing the demand for reserves, but might also make an economy more vulnerable to foreign trade shocks, thereby raising desired reserve holdings.[23]

On the other hand, the main cost of holding reserves is their interest cost. A central bank that switches from domestic bonds to foreign reserves loses the interest on the domestic bonds and instead earns the interest on the reserve currency, for example, on dollars. If markets harbor any fears that the domestic currency could be devalued, then domestic bonds will offer a higher interest rate than foreign reserves, implying that it is costly to switch the central bank's portfolio toward reserves. Of course, if the reserve currency does appreciate against domestic currency, the central bank will gain, with a corresponding loss if the reserve currency depreciates.

In addition, reserves may offer lower interest simply because of their higher liquidity. This interest cost of holding relatively liquid reserves is analogous to the interest cost of holding money, which we reviewed in Chapter 15.

It was argued in the 1960s that countries with more flexible exchange rates would find it easier to generate an export surplus if reserves ran low—they could allow their currencies to depreciate, perhaps avoiding the recession that might otherwise be needed to create a trade balance surplus. When industrial countries moved to floating exchange rates in the early 1970s, many economists therefore expected that the demand for international reserves would drop sharply.

Figure 18-8 shows, however, that nothing of the sort happened. For industrial countries, the growth rate of international reserves has not declined since the 1960s. For developing countries, the growth rate of reserves has, if anything, risen on average (though the sharp upsurge in the mid-2000s is to some degree a reflection of huge reserve purchases by China). Accelerating reserve growth has taken place despite the adoption of more flexible exchange rates by many developing countries.

One explanation for this development, which we will discuss further in later chapters, is that the growth of global capital markets has vastly increased the potential variability of financial flows across national borders, especially across the borders

---

[23]An early influential study was by H. Robert Heller, "Optimal International Reserves," *Economic Journal* 76 (June 1966), pp. 296–311.

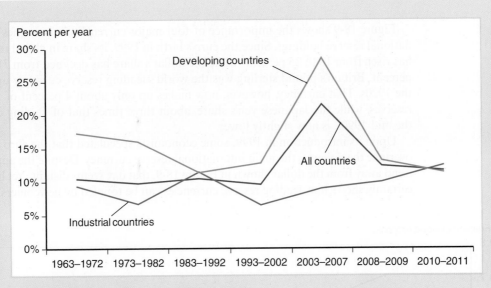

FIGURE 18-8

Growth Rates of International Reserves

Annualized growth rates of international reserves did not decline sharply after the early 1970s. Recently, developing countries have added large sums to their reserve holdings, but their pace of accumulation has slowed starting with the crisis years of 2008–2009. The figure shows averages of annual growth rates.

Source: International Monetary Fund.

of crisis-prone developing countries.[24] The sharp decline in developing-country reserve growth in the 1982–1992 period, shown in the figure, reflects an international debt crisis during the years 1982–1989. In that crisis, foreign lending sources dried up and many developing countries were forced to draw on their reserves. We see another decline in reserve growth during the crisis years of 2008–2009. These episodes illustrate why developing countries have added so eagerly to their reserve holdings. Even a developing country with a floating exchange rate might need to pay off foreign creditors and domestic residents with dollars to avoid a financial crisis and a currency collapse.

Nothing about this explanation contradicts earlier theories. The demand for international reserves still reflects the variability in the balance of payments. The rapid globalization of financial markets in recent years has, however, caused a big increase in potential variability and in the potential risks that variability poses.

Countries can and do choose to hold international reserves in currencies other than the U.S. dollar. They tend to hold only those currencies that are most likely to retain their value over time and to be readily accepted by foreign exporters and creditors. Thanks to the large and generally prosperous geographical region it serves, the euro, introduced in 1999, is the strongest challenger to the dollar's role (although the recent euro area crisis has taken a toll).

---

[24]Recent works on the modern determinants of the demand for international reserves includes those of Robert Flood and Nancy Marion, "Holding International Reserves in an Era of High Capital Mobility," *Brookings Trade Forum* 2001, pp. 1–47; Joshua Aizenman and Jaewoo Lee, "International Reserves: Precautionary versus Mercantilist Views, Theory and Evidence," *Open Economies Review* 18 (April 2007), pp. 191–214; and Maurice Obstfeld, Jay C. Shambaugh, and Alan M. Taylor, "Financial Stability, the Trilemma, and International Reserves," *American Economic Journal: Macroeconomics* 2 (April 2010), pp. 57–94.

Figure 18-9 shows the importance of four major currencies in countries' international reserve holdings. Since the euro's birth in 1999, its share in global reserves has risen from 18 to 25 percent, while the dollar's share has declined from 71 to 62 percent. Britain's pound sterling was the world's leading reserve currency up until the 1920s. That currency, however, now makes up only about 4 percent of global reserves, while the Japanese yen's share, about three times that of sterling during the mid-1990s, is now slightly lower.

Upon its introduction in 1999, some economists speculated that the euro would overtake the dollar as the main international reserve currency. Despite the apparent trend away from the dollar shown in Figure 18-9, that day seems distant. Yet history certainly shows how leading reserve currencies can be toppled by newcomers.[25]

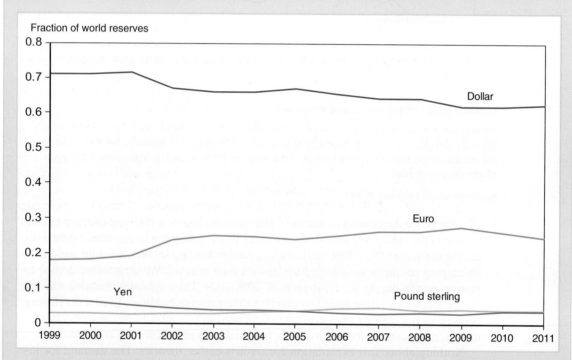

FIGURE 18-9

Currency Composition of Global Reserve Holdings

While the euro's role as a reserve currency has generally increased over time, the dollar remains the overwhelming favorite.

Source: International Monetary Fund, Currency Composition of Foreign Exchange Reserves, at http://www.imf.org/external/np/sta/cofer/eng/index.htm. These data cover only the countries that report reserve composition to the IMF, the major omission being China.

---

[25]A recent assessment of the dollar's reserve status by Eichengreen is listed in Further Readings. Eichengreen presents a comprehensive historical perspective on the dollar's special status in his book *Exorbitant Privilege: The Rise and Fall of the Dollar and the Future of the International Monetary System* (New York: Oxford University Press, 2011). For a formal statistical study, see Menzie Chinn and Jeffrey A. Frankel, "Will the Euro Eventually Surpass the Dollar as Leading International Reserve Currency?" in Richard H. Clarida, ed., *G7 Current Account Imbalances: Sustainability and Adjustment* (Chicago: University of Chicago Press, 2007), pp. 283–322.

SUMMARY

1. There is a direct link between central bank intervention in the foreign exchange market and the domestic money supply. When a country's central bank purchases foreign assets, the country's money supply automatically increases. Similarly, a central bank sale of foreign assets automatically lowers the money supply. The *central bank balance sheet* shows how foreign exchange intervention affects the money supply because the central bank's liabilities, which rise or fall when its assets rise or fall, are the base of the domestic money supply process. The central bank can negate the money supply effect of intervention through *sterilization*. With no sterilization, there is a link between the balance of payments and national money supplies that depends on how central banks share the burden of financing balance of payments gaps.

2. A central bank can fix the exchange rate of its currency against foreign currency if it is willing to trade unlimited amounts of domestic money against foreign assets at that rate. To fix the exchange rate, the central bank must intervene in the foreign exchange market whenever necessary to prevent the emergence of an excess demand or supply of domestic currency assets. In effect, the central bank adjusts its foreign assets—and thus, the domestic money supply—to ensure that asset markets are always in equilibrium under the fixed exchange rate.

3. A commitment to fix an exchange rate forces the central bank to sacrifice its ability to use monetary policy for stabilization. A purchase of domestic assets by the central bank causes an equal fall in its official international reserves, leaving the money supply and output unchanged. Similarly, a sale of domestic assets by the bank causes foreign reserves to rise by the same amount but has no other effects.

4. Fiscal policy, unlike monetary policy, has a more powerful effect on output under fixed exchange rates than under floating rates. Under a fixed exchange rate, fiscal expansion does not, in the short run, cause a real appreciation that "crowds out" aggregate demand. Instead, it forces central bank purchases of foreign assets and an expansion of the money supply. *Devaluation* also raises aggregate demand and the money supply in the short run. (*Revaluation* has opposite effects.) In the long run, fiscal expansion causes a real appreciation, an increase in the money supply, and a rise in the home price level, while devaluation causes the long-run levels of the money supply and prices to rise in proportion to the exchange rate change.

5. *Balance of payments crises* occur when market participants expect the central bank to change the exchange rate from its current level. If the market decides a devaluation is coming, for example, the domestic interest rate rises above the world interest rate and foreign reserves drop sharply as private capital flows abroad. *Self-fulfilling currency crises* can occur when an economy is vulnerable to speculation. In other circumstances an exchange rate collapse may be the inevitable result of inconsistent government policies.

6. A system of *managed floating* allows the central bank to retain some ability to control the domestic money supply, but at the cost of greater exchange rate instability. If domestic and foreign bonds are *imperfect substitutes*, however, the central bank may be able to control both the money supply and the exchange rate through sterilized foreign exchange intervention. Empirical evidence provides little support for the idea that sterilized intervention has a significant direct effect on exchange rates. Even when domestic and foreign bonds are *perfect substitutes*, so that there is no *risk premium*, sterilized intervention may operate indirectly through a *signaling effect* that changes market views of future policies.

7. A world system of fixed exchange rates in which countries peg the prices of their currencies in terms of a *reserve currency* involves a striking asymmetry: The reserve currency country, which does not have to fix any exchange rate, can influence economic activity both at home and abroad through its monetary policy. In contrast, all other countries are unable to influence their output or foreign output through monetary policy. This policy asymmetry reflects the fact that the reserve center bears none of the burden of financing its balance of payments.

8. A *gold standard*, in which all countries fix their currencies' prices in terms of gold, avoids the asymmetry inherent in a reserve currency standard and places constraints on the growth of countries' money supplies. (A related arrangement was the *bimetallic standard* based on both silver and gold.) But the gold standard has serious drawbacks that make it impractical as a way of organizing today's international monetary system. Even the dollar-based *gold exchange standard* set up after World War II ultimately proved unworkable.

KEY TERMS

balance of payments
  crisis, p. 541
bimetallic standard, p. 554
capital flight, p. 543
central bank balance sheet,
  p. 529
devaluation, p. 539
gold exchange standard, p. 554
gold standard, p. 550

imperfect asset substitutability,
  p. 546
managed floating exchange
  rates, p. 527
perfect asset substitutability,
  p. 545
reserve currency, p. 550
revaluation, p. 539
risk premium, p. 547

self-fulfilling currency crises,
  p. 543
signaling effect of foreign
  exchange intervention,
  p. 549
sterilized foreign exchange
  intervention, p. 532

PROBLEMS

MyEconLab

1. Show how an expansion in the central bank's domestic assets ultimately affects its balance sheet under a fixed exchange rate. How are the central bank's transactions in the foreign exchange market reflected in the balance of payments accounts?

2. Do the exercises in the previous problem for an increase in government spending.

3. Describe the effects of an unexpected devaluation on the central bank's balance sheet and on the balance of payments accounts.

4. Explain why a devaluation improves the current account in this chapter's model. (Hint: Consider the *XX* curve developed in the last chapter.)

5. Can you think of reasons why a government might willingly sacrifice some of its ability to use monetary policy so that it can have more stable exchange rates?

6. How does fiscal expansion affect the current account under a fixed exchange rate?

7. Explain why temporary and permanent fiscal expansions do not have different effects under fixed exchange rates, as they do under floating exchange rates.

8. Devaluation is often used by countries to improve their current accounts. Since the current account equals national saving less domestic investment, however (see Chapter 13), this improvement can occur only if investment falls, saving rises, or both. How might devaluation affect national saving and domestic investment?

9. Using the *DD-AA* model, analyze the output and balance of payments effects of an import tariff under fixed exchange rates. What would happen if all countries in the world simultaneously tried to improve employment and the balance of payments by imposing tariffs?

10. When a central bank devalues after a balance of payments crisis, it usually gains foreign reserves. Can this financial inflow be explained using our model? What would happen if the market believed that *another* devaluation would occur in the near future?

11. Suppose that under the postwar "dollar standard" system, foreign central banks had held dollar reserves in the form of green dollar bills hidden in their vaults rather than in the form of U.S. Treasury bills. Would the international monetary adjustment mechanism have been symmetric or asymmetric? (Hint: Think about what happens to the U.S. and Japanese money supplies, for example, when the Bank of Japan sells yen for dollar bills that it then keeps.)

12. "When domestic and foreign bonds are perfect substitutes, a central bank should be indifferent about using domestic or foreign assets to implement monetary policy." Discuss.

13. U.S. foreign exchange intervention is sometimes done by an Exchange Stabilization Fund, or ESF (a branch of the Treasury Department), which manages a portfolio of U.S. government and foreign currency bonds. An ESF intervention to support the yen, for example, would take the form of a portfolio shift out of dollar and into yen assets. Show that ESF interventions are automatically sterilized and thus do not alter money supplies. How do ESF operations affect the foreign exchange risk premium?

14. Use a diagram like Figure 18-7 to explain how a central bank can alter the domestic interest rate, while holding the exchange rate fixed, under imperfect asset substitutability.

15. On page 531 in the text, we analyzed how the sale of $100 worth of its foreign assets affects the central bank's balance sheet. The assumption in that example was that the buyer of the foreign assets paid in the form of domestic currency cash. Suppose instead that the buyer pays with a check drawn on her account at Pecuniacorp, a private domestic bank. Using a balance sheet like the ones presented in the text, show how the transaction affects the central bank's balance sheet and the money supply.

16. We observed in the text that "fixed" exchange-rate systems can result not in absolutely fixed exchange rates but in narrow bands within which the exchange rate can move. For example, the gold points (mentioned in footnote 18) produced such bands under a gold standard. (Typically those bands were on the order of plus or minus 1 percent of the "central" exchange parity.) To what extent would such bands for the exchange rate allow the domestic interest rate to move independently of a foreign rate? Show that the answer depends on the maturity or *term* of the interest rate. To help your intuition, assume plus or minus 1 percent bands for the exchange rate, and consider, alternatively, rates on three-month deposits, on six-month deposits, and on one-year deposits. With such narrow bands, would there be much scope for independence in ten-year loan rates?

17. In a three-country world, a central bank fixes one exchange rate but lets the others float. Can it use monetary policy to affect output? Can it fix both exchange rates?

18. In the Case Study on international reserves (pages 555–558), we asserted that except in the case of a reserve currency system, an attempt by all central banks simultaneously to raise their international reserve holdings through open-market sales of domestic assets could have a contractionary effect on the world economy. Explain by contrasting the cases of a gold standard-type system and a reserve currency system.

19. If a country changes its exchange rate, the value of its foreign reserves, measured in the domestic currency, also changes. This latter change may represent a domestic currency gain or loss for the central bank. What happens when a country devalues its currency against the reserve currency? When it revalues? How might this factor affect the potential cost of holding foreign reserves? Make sure to consider the role of interest parity in formulating your answer.

20. Analyze the result of a permanent devaluation by an economy caught in a liquidity trap of the sort described in Chapter 17.

21. Recall our discussion of the Swiss franc's currency floor in the box on pp. 513–514. Also, recall the last chapter's discussion of the liquidity trap. Because Switzerland has been in a liquidity trap all the time it has defended its currency floor, does our discussion of liquidity trap theory in the last chapter suggest why Swiss inflation has not been raised by the SNB's heavy foreign exchange purchases?

22. Again returning to the case of the Swiss franc currency floor, with Swiss interest rates at zero, what do you think would happen if currency speculators expected the Swiss franc to appreciate by more than the euro rate of interest?

FURTHER READINGS

Graham Bird and Ramkishen Rajan. "Too Much of a Good Thing? The Adequacy of International Reserves in the Aftermath of Crises." *World Economy* 86 (June 2003), pp. 873–891. Accessible review of literature on the demand for international reserves.

William H. Branson. "Causes of Appreciation and Volatility of the Dollar," in *The U.S. Dollar—Recent Developments, Outlook, and Policy Options*. Kansas City: Federal Reserve Bank of Kansas City, 1985, pp. 33–52. Develops and applies a model of exchange rate determination with imperfect asset substitutability.

Barry Eichengreen. "The Dollar Dilemma: The World's Top Currency Faces Competition." *Foreign Affairs* 88 (September/October 2009), pp. 53–68. An assessment of challenges to the dollar's primacy among potential alternative vehicle and reserve currencies.

Milton Friedman. "Bimetallism Revisited." *Journal of Economic Perspectives* 4 (Fall 1990), pp. 85–104. A fascinating reconsideration of economists' assessments of the dual silver-gold standard.

Kenneth A. Froot and Richard H. Thaler. "Anomalies: Foreign Exchange." *Journal of Economic Perspectives* 4 (Summer 1990), pp. 179–192. Clear, nontechnical discussion of the empirical evidence on the interest parity condition.

Karl Habermeier, Annamaria Kokenyne, Romain Veyrune, and Harald Anderson. "Revised System for the Classification of Exchange Rate Arrangements." IMF Working Paper WP/09/211, September 2009. Explains how the International Monetary Fund classifies countries' diverse systems of exchange-rate determination.

Matthew Higgins and Thomas Klitgaard. "Reserve Accumulation: Implications for Global Capital Flows and Financial Markets." *Current Issues in Economics and Finance* 10 (September/October 2004). Analysis of trends in central bank reserve holdings.

Owen F. Humpage. "Institutional Aspects of U.S. Intervention." *Federal Reserve Bank of Cleveland Economic Review* 30 (Quarter 1, 1994), pp. 2–19. How the U.S. Treasury and Federal Reserve coordinate foreign exchange intervention.

Olivier Jeanne. *Currency Crises: A Perspective on Recent Theoretical Developments*. Princeton Special Papers in International Economics 20. International Finance Section, Department of Economics, Princeton University, March 2000. Recent thinking on speculative crises and attacks.

Robert A. Mundell. "Capital Mobility and Stabilization Policy under Fixed and Flexible Exchange Rates." *Canadian Journal of Economics and Political Science* 29 (November 1963), pp. 475–485. Classic account of the effects of monetary and fiscal policies under alternative exchange rate regimes.

Michael Mussa. *The Role of Official Intervention.* Occasional Paper 6. New York: Group of Thirty, 1981. Discusses the theory and practice of central bank foreign exchange intervention under a dirty float.

Christopher J. Neely. "Central Bank Authorities' Beliefs about Foreign Exchange Intervention." Working Paper 2006-045C, Federal Reserve Bank of St. Louis, April 2007. Interesting survey of central bankers' views on the role and limits of intervention.

Maurice Obstfeld. "Models of Currency Crises with Self-Fulfilling Features." *European Economic Review* 40 (April 1996), pp. 1037–1048. More on the nature of balance of payments crises.

Lucio Sarno and Mark P. Taylor. "Official Intervention in the Foreign Exchange Market: Is It Effective and, If So, How Does It Work?" *Journal of Economic Literature* 39 (September 2001), pp. 839–868. An updated survey on foreign exchange intervention.

MyEconLab Can Help You Get a Better Grade

MyEconLab If your exam were tomorrow, would you be ready? For each chapter, MyEconLab Practice Tests and Study Plans pinpoint sections you have mastered and those you need to study. That way, you are more efficient with your study time, and you are better prepared for your exams.

To see how it works, turn to page 41 and then go to

www.myeconlab.com

Equilibrium in the Foreign Exchange Market with Imperfect Asset Substitutability

This appendix develops a model of the foreign exchange market in which risk factors may make domestic currency and foreign currency assets imperfect substitutes. The model gives rise to a risk premium that can separate the expected rates of return on domestic and foreign assets.

Demand

Because individuals dislike risky situations in which their wealth may vary greatly from day to day, they decide how to allocate wealth among different assets by looking at the riskiness of the resulting portfolio as well as at the expected return the portfolio offers. Someone who puts her wealth entirely into British pounds, for example, may expect a high return, but the wealth can be wiped out if the pound unexpectedly depreciates. A more sensible strategy is to invest in several currencies even if some have lower expected returns than the pound, and thus reduce the impact on wealth of bad luck with any one currency. By spreading risk among several currencies, an individual can reduce the variability of her wealth.

Considerations of risk make it reasonable to assume that an individual's demand for interest-bearing domestic currency assets increases when the interest they offer (R) rises relative to the domestic currency return on foreign currency assets $[R^* + (E^e - E)/E]$. Put another way, an individual will be willing to increase the riskiness of her portfolio by investing more heavily in domestic currency assets only if she is compensated by an increase in the relative expected return on those assets.

We summarize this assumption by writing individual i's demand for domestic currency bonds, B_i^d, as an increasing function of the rate-of-return difference between domestic and foreign bonds,

$$B_i^d = B_i^d[R - R^* - (E^e - E)/E].$$

Of course, B_i^d also depends on other factors specific to individual i, such as her wealth and income. The demand for domestic currency bonds can be negative or positive, and in the former case, individual i is a net borrower in the home currency, that is, a *supplier* of domestic currency bonds.

To find the *aggregate* private demand for domestic currency bonds, we need only add up individual demands B_i^d for all individuals i in the world. This summation gives the aggregate demand for domestic currency bonds, B^d, which is also an increasing function of the expected rate-of-return difference in favor of domestic currency assets. Therefore,

$$\text{Demand} = B^d[R - R^* - (E^e - E)/E]$$
$$= \text{sum for all } i \text{ of } B_i^d[R - R^* - (E^e - E)/E].$$

Since some private individuals may be borrowing, and therefore supplying bonds, B^d should be interpreted as the private sector's *net* demand for domestic currency bonds.

Supply

Since we are interpreting B^d as the private sector's *net* demand for domestic currency bonds, the appropriate supply variable to define market equilibrium is the net supply of domestic currency bonds to the private sector, that is, the supply of bonds that are not the liability of any private individual or firm. Net supply therefore equals the value of domestic currency *government* bonds held by the public, B, less the value of domestic currency assets held by the central bank, A:

$$\text{Supply} = B - A.$$

A must be subtracted from B to find the net supply of bonds because purchases of bonds by the central bank reduce the supply available to private investors. (More generally, we would also subtract from B domestic currency assets held by foreign central banks.)

Equilibrium

The risk premium, ρ, is determined by the interaction of supply and demand. The risk premium is defined as

$$\rho = R - R^* - (E^e - E)/E,$$

that is, as the expected return difference between domestic and foreign bonds. We can therefore write the private sector's net demand for domestic currency bonds as an increasing function of ρ. Figure 18A1-1 shows this relationship by drawing the demand curve for domestic currency bonds with a positive slope.

The bond supply curve is vertical at $B - A^1$ because the net supply of bonds to the market is determined by decisions of the government and central bank and is independent of the risk premium. Equilibrium occurs at point 1 (at a risk premium of ρ^1), where the private sector's net demand for domestic currency bonds equals the net supply.

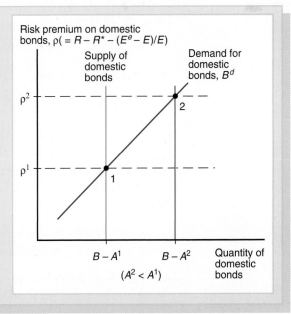

FIGURE 18A1-1

The Domestic Bond Supply and the Foreign Exchange Risk Premium under Imperfect Asset Substitutability

An increase in the supply of domestic currency bonds that the private sector must hold raises the risk premium on domestic currency assets.

Notice that for given values of R, R^*, and E^e, the equilibrium shown in the diagram can also be viewed as determining the exchange rate, since $E = E^e/(1 + R - R^* - \rho)$.

Figure 18A1-1 also shows the effect of a central bank sale of domestic assets that lowers its domestic asset holdings to $A^2 < A^1$. This sale raises the net supply of domestic currency bonds to $B - A^2$ and shifts the supply curve to the right. The new equilibrium occurs at point 2, at a risk premium of $\rho^2 > \rho^1$. Similarly, an increase in the domestic currency government debt, B, would raise the risk premium.

The model therefore establishes that the risk premium is an increasing function of $B - A$, just as we assumed in the discussion of sterilized intervention that led to equation (18-3).

You should recognize that our discussion of risk premium determination is an oversimplification in a number of ways, not least because of the assumption that the home country is small, so that all foreign variables can be taken as given. In general, however, actions taken by foreign governments may also affect the risk premium, which of course can take *negative* as well as positive values. That is, policies or events that make foreign bonds progressively riskier will eventually make investors willing to hold domestic currency bonds at an expected rate of return *below* that on foreign currency bonds.

One way to capture this possibility would be to generalize equation (18-3) in the text and express the risk premium instead as

$$\rho = \rho(B - A, B^* - A^*),$$

where $B^* - A^*$ is the net stock of foreign currency bonds that the public must hold. In this extended formulation, a rise in $B - A$ still raises ρ, but a rise in $B^* - A^*$ causes ρ to fall by making foreign bonds relatively riskier.

18

The Timing of Balance of Payments Crises

In the text, we modeled a balance of payments crisis as a sudden loss of confidence in the central bank's promise to hold the exchange rate fixed in the future. As previously noted, a currency crisis often is not the result of arbitrary shifts in market sentiment, contrary to what exasperated policy makers embroiled in crises often contend. Instead, an exchange rate collapse can be the inevitable result of government policies inconsistent with maintaining a fixed exchange rate permanently. In such cases, simple economic theory may allow us to predict the date of a crisis through a careful analysis of the government policies and the market's rational response to them.[26]

It is easiest to make the main points using the assumptions and notations of the monetary approach to the balance of payments (as developed in Online Appendix A to this chapter) and the monetary approach to the exchange rate (Chapter 16). To simplify, we will assume that output prices are perfectly flexible and that output is constant at its full-employment level. We will also assume that market participants have perfect foresight concerning the future.

The precise timing of a payments crisis cannot be determined independently of government policies. In particular, we have to describe not only how the government is behaving today, but also how it plans to react to future events in the economy. Two assumptions about official behavior are made: (1) The central bank is allowing the stock of central bank domestic credit, A, to expand steadily, and will do so forever. (2) The central bank is currently fixing the exchange rate at the level E^0, but will allow the exchange rate to float freely forever if its foreign reserves, F^*, ever fall to zero. Furthermore, the authorities will defend E^0 to the bitter end by selling foreign reserves at that price as long as they have any to sell.

The problem with the central bank's policies is that they are inconsistent with maintaining a fixed exchange rate indefinitely. The monetary approach suggests that foreign reserves will fall steadily as domestic assets continually rise. Eventually, therefore, reserves will have to run out and the fixed exchange rate E^0 will have to be abandoned. In fact, speculators will force the issue by mounting a speculative attack and buying all of the central bank's reserves while reserves are still at a positive level.

We can describe the timing of this crisis with the help of a definition and a diagram. The *shadow* floating exchange rate at time t, denoted E_t^S, is the exchange rate that would prevail at time t if the central bank held no foreign reserves, allowed the currency to float, but continued to allow domestic credit to grow over time. We know from the monetary approach that the result would be a situation of *ongoing inflation* in which E_t^S trends upward over time in proportion to the domestic credit growth rate. The upper panel of Figure 18A2-1 shows this upward trend in the shadow floating rate, together with the level E^0 at which the exchange rate is initially pegged. The time T indicated on the horizontal axis is defined as the date on which the shadow exchange rate reaches E^0.

---

[26]Alternative models of balance of payments crises are developed in Paul Krugman, "A Model of Balance-of-Payments Crises," *Journal of Money, Credit and Banking* 11 (August 1979), pp. 311–325; Robert P. Flood and Peter M. Garber, "Collapsing Exchange Rate Regimes: Some Linear Examples," *Journal of International Economics* 17 (August 1984), pp. 1–14; and Maurice Obstfeld, "Rational and Self-Fulfilling Balance-of-Payments Crises," *American Economic Review* 76 (March 1986), pp. 72–81. See also the paper by Obstfeld in Further Readings.

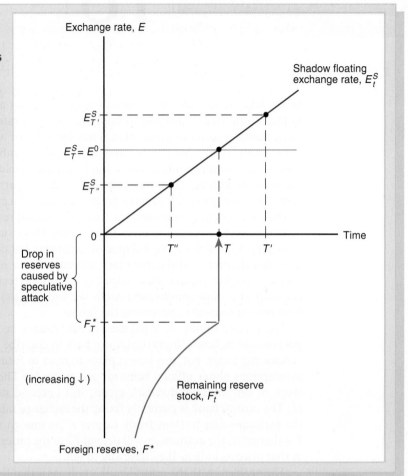

FIGURE 18A2-1

How the Timing of a Balance of Payments Crisis Is Determined

The market stages a speculative attack and buys the remaining foreign reserve stock F_T^* at time T, which is when the shadow floating exchange rate E_t^S just equals the precollapse fixed exchange rate E^0.

The lower panel of the figure shows how reserves behave over time when domestic credit is steadily growing. (An increase in reserves is a move down from the origin along the vertical axis.) We have shown the path of reserves as a kinked curve that falls gradually until time T, at which point reserves drop in a single stroke to zero. This precipitous reserve loss (of size F_T^*) is the speculative attack that forces the end of the fixed exchange rate, and we now argue that such an attack must occur precisely at time T if asset markets are to clear at each moment.

We are assuming that output Y is fixed, so reserves will fall over time at the same rate that domestic credit grows, as long as the domestic interest rate R (and thus the demand for domestic money) doesn't change. What do we know about the behavior of the interest rate? We know that while the exchange rate is convincingly fixed, R will equal the foreign interest rate R^* because no depreciation is expected. Thus, reserves fall gradually over time, as shown in Figure 18A2-1, as long as the exchange rate remains fixed at E^0.

Imagine now that reserves first hit zero at a time such as T', which is *later* than time T. Our shadow exchange rate E^S is defined as the equilibrium floating rate that prevails when foreign reserves are zero, so if reserves first hit zero at time T', the authorities abandon E^0 forever and the exchange rate jumps immediately to the higher level $E_{T'}^S$. There is something wrong with this "equilibrium," however: Each market participant knows that the home currency will depreciate very sharply at time T' and will try to profit by buying foreign reserves from the central bank, at the lower price E^0, just an instant *before* T'. Thus the central bank will lose all of its reserves before T', contrary to our assumption that reserves first hit zero *at* T'. So we have not really been looking at an equilibrium after all.

Do we get to an equilibrium by assuming instead that speculators buy out the official reserve stock at a time like T'' that is *earlier* than time T? Again the answer is no, as you can see by considering the choices facing an individual asset holder. He knows that if central bank reserves reach zero at time T'', the currency will appreciate from E^0 to $E^S_{T''}$ as the central bank leaves the foreign exchange market. It therefore will behoove him not to join any speculative attack that pushes reserves to zero at time T''; in fact, he would prefer to *sell* as much foreign currency as possible to the central bank just before time T'' and then buy it back at the lower market-determined price that would prevail after a crisis. Since every market participant would find it in his or her interest to act in this way, however, a speculative attack simply can't occur before time T. No speculator would want to buy central bank reserves at the price E^0, knowing that an immediate discrete capital loss was at hand.

Only if foreign reserves hit zero precisely at time T are asset markets continually in equilibrium. As noted above, time T is defined by the condition

$$E^S_T = E^0,$$

which states that if reserves suddenly drop to zero at time T, the exchange rate remains initially at its pegged level, and only subsequently floats upward.

The absence of any foreseen initial jump in the exchange rate, either upward or downward, removes the opportunities for arbitrage (described above) that prevent speculative attacks at times like T' or T''. In addition, the money market remains in equilibrium at time T, even though the exchange rate doesn't jump, because two factors offset each other exactly. As reserves drop sharply to zero, the money supply falls. We also know that at the moment the fixed exchange rate is abandoned, people will expect the currency to begin depreciating over time. The domestic interest rate R will therefore move upward to maintain interest parity, reducing real money demand in line with the fall in the real money supply.

We have therefore tied down the exact date on which a balance of payments crisis forces the authorities off the fixed exchange rate. Note once again that in our example, a crisis must occur at *some* point, because profligate monetary policies make one inevitable. The fact that a crisis occurs while the central bank's foreign reserves are still positive might suggest to superficial observers that ill-founded market sentiment is leading to a premature panic. This is not the case here. The speculative attack we have analyzed is the only outcome that does not confront market participants with arbitrage opportunities.[27] However, there are alternative self-fulfilling crisis models in which attacks can occur even when the exchange rate could have been sustained indefinitely in the absence of an attack.

---

[27] Our finding that reserves fall to zero in a single attack comes from our assumptions that the market can foresee the future perfectly and that trading takes place continuously. If we were instead to allow some discrete uncertainty—for example, about the rate of central bank domestic credit growth—the domestic interest rate would rise as a collapse became more probable, causing a series of "speculative" money demand reductions prior to the final depletion of foreign reserves. Each of these preliminary attacks would be similar to the type of crisis described in the chapter.

CHAPTER 19

INTERNATIONAL MONETARY SYSTEMS: AN HISTORICAL OVERVIEW

I n the previous two chapters, we saw how a single country can use monetary, fiscal, and exchange rate policies to change the levels of employment and production within its borders. Although this analysis usually assumes that macroeconomic conditions in the rest of the world are not affected by the actions of the country we are studying, that assumption is not, in general, a valid one: Any change in the home country's real exchange rate automatically implies an opposite change in foreign real exchange rates, and any shift in overall domestic spending is likely to change domestic demand for foreign goods. Unless the home country is insignificantly small, developments within its borders affect macroeconomic conditions abroad and therefore complicate the task of foreign policy makers.

The inherent interdependence of open national economies has sometimes made it more difficult for governments to achieve such policy goals as full employment and price level stability. The channels of interdependence depend, in turn, on the monetary, financial, and exchange rate arrangements that countries adopt—a set of institutions called the *international monetary system*. This chapter examines how the international monetary system influenced macroeconomic policy making and performance during four periods: the gold standard era (1870–1914), the interwar period (1918–1939), the post–World War II years during which exchange rates were fixed under the Bretton Woods agreement (1946–1973), and the recent period of widespread reliance on floating exchange rates (1973–present). As we shall see, alternative international monetary arrangements have posed different trade-offs for macroeconomic policy.

In an open economy, macroeconomic policy has two basic goals, internal balance (full employment with price stability) and external balance (avoiding excessive imbalances in international payments). Because a country cannot alter its international payments position without automatically causing an opposite change of equal magnitude in the payments position of the rest of the world, one country's pursuit of its macroeconomic goals inevitably influences how well other countries attain their goals. The goal of external balance therefore offers a clear illustration of how policy actions taken abroad may change an economy's position relative to the position its government prefers.

Throughout the period since 1870, with its various international currency arrangements, how did countries try to attain internal and external balance, and how successful were they? Why did different international monetary systems prevail at different times? Did policy makers worry about the foreign repercussions of their actions, or did each adopt nationalistic measures that were self-defeating for the world economy as a whole? The answers to these questions depend on the international monetary system in effect at the time.

LEARNING GOALS

After reading this chapter, you will be able to:

- Explain how the goals of internal and external balance motivate economic policy makers in open economies.
- Understand the monetary trilemma that policy makers in open economies inevitably face and how alternative international monetary systems address the trilemma in different ways.
- Describe the structure of the international gold standard that linked countries' exchange rates and policies prior to World War I and the role of the Great Depression of the 1930s in ending efforts to restore the pre-1914 world monetary order.
- Discuss how the post–World War II Bretton Woods system of globally fixed exchange rates was designed to combine exchange rate stability with limited autonomy of national macroeconomic policies.
- Explain how the Bretton Woods system collapsed in 1973 and why many economists at the time favored an international financial system such as the current one based on floating dollar exchange rates.
- Summarize how the monetary and fiscal policies of a large country such as the United States are transmitted abroad under floating exchange rates.
- Discuss how the world economy has performed in recent years and what lessons the post-1973 experience teaches about the need for international policy coordination.

Macroeconomic Policy Goals in an Open Economy

In open economies, policy makers are motivated by the goals of internal and external balance. Simply defined, **internal balance** requires the full employment of a country's resources and domestic price level stability. **External balance** is attained when a country's current account is neither so deeply in deficit that the country may be unable to repay its foreign debts in the future nor so strongly in surplus that foreigners are put in that position.

In practice, neither of these definitions captures the full range of potential policy concerns. Along with full employment and stability of the overall price level, for example, policy makers may have a particular domestic distribution of income as an additional internal target. Depending on exchange rate arrangements or other factors, policy makers may worry about swings in balance of payments accounts other than the current account. To make matters even more complicated, the line between external and internal goals can be fuzzy. How should one classify an employment target for export industries, for example, when export growth influences the economy's ability to repay its foreign debts?

The simple definitions of internal and external balance given previously, however, capture the goals that most policy makers share regardless of the particular economic environment. We therefore organize our analysis around these definitions and discuss possible additional aspects of internal and external balance when they are relevant.

Internal Balance: Full Employment and Price Level Stability

When a country's productive resources are fully employed and its price level is stable, the country is in internal balance. The waste and hardship that occur when resources are underemployed is clear. If a country's economy is "overheated" and resources are *over*employed, however, waste of a different (though probably less harmful) kind occurs. For example, workers on overtime might prefer to work less and enjoy leisure, but their contracts require them to put in longer hours during periods of high demand. Machines worked more intensely than usual will tend to suffer more frequent breakdowns and to depreciate more quickly.

Under- and over-employment also lead to general price level movements that reduce the economy's efficiency by making the real value of the monetary unit less certain and thus a less useful guide for economic decisions. Since domestic wages and prices rise when the demands for labor and output exceed full-employment levels and fall in the opposite case, the government must prevent substantial movements in aggregate demand relative to its full-employment level to maintain a stable, predictable price level.

Inflation or deflation can occur even under conditions of full employment, of course, if the expectations of workers and firms about future monetary policy lead to an upward or downward wage-price spiral. Such a spiral can continue, however, only if the central bank fulfills expectations through continuing injections or withdrawals of money (Chapter 15).

One particularly disruptive result of an unstable price level is its effect on the real value of loan contracts. Because loans tend to be denominated in the monetary unit, unexpected price level changes cause income to be redistributed between creditors and debtors. A sudden increase in the U.S. price level, for example, makes those with dollar debts better off, since the money they owe to lenders is now worth less in terms of goods and services. At the same time, the price level increase makes creditors worse off. Because such accidental income redistribution can cause considerable distress to those who are hurt, governments have another reason to maintain price level stability.[1]

Theoretically, a perfectly predictable trend of rising or falling prices would not be too costly, since everyone would be able to calculate easily the real value of money at any point in the future. But in the real world, there appears to be no such thing as a predictable inflation rate. Indeed, experience shows that the unpredictability of the

---

[1]The situation is somewhat different when the government itself is a major debtor in domestic currency. In such cases, a surprise inflation that reduces the real value of government debt may be a convenient way of taxing the public. This method of taxation was quite common in developing countries in the past (see Chapter 22), but elsewhere it has generally been applied with reluctance and in extreme situations (for example, during or just after wars). A policy of trying to surprise the public with inflation undermines the government's credibility and, through the Fisher effect, worsens the terms on which the government can borrow in the future.

general price level is magnified tremendously in periods of rapid price level change. The costs of inflation have been most apparent in the postwar period in countries such as Argentina, Brazil, Serbia, and Zimbabwe, where astronomical price level increases caused the domestic currencies practically to stop functioning as units of account or stores of value.

To avoid price level instability, therefore, the government must prevent large fluctuations in output, which are also undesirable in themselves. In addition, it must avoid inflation and deflation by ensuring that the money supply does not grow too quickly or too slowly.

External Balance: The Optimal Level of the Current Account

The notion of external balance is more difficult to define than internal balance because there are no unambiguous benchmarks like "full employment" or "stable prices" to apply to an economy's external transactions. Whether an economy's trade with the outside world poses macroeconomic problems depends on several factors, including the economy's particular circumstances, conditions in the outside world, and the institutional arrangements governing its economic relations with foreign countries. A country committed to fixing its exchange rate against a foreign currency, for example, may well adopt a different definition of external balance than a country whose currency floats.

International economics textbooks often identify external balance with balance in a country's current account. While this definition is appropriate in some circumstances, it is not appropriate as a general rule. Recall from Chapter 13 that a country with a current account deficit is borrowing resources from the rest of the world that it will have to repay in the future. This situation is not necessarily undesirable, however. For example, the country's opportunities for investing the borrowed resources may be attractive relative to the opportunities available in the rest of the world. In this case, paying back loans from foreigners poses no problem because a profitable investment will generate a return high enough to cover the interest and principal on those loans. Similarly, a current account surplus may pose no problem if domestic savings are being invested more profitably abroad than they would be at home.

More generally, we may think of current account imbalances as providing another example of how countries gain from trade. The trade involved is what we have called *intertemporal trade*, that is, the trade of consumption over time (see Chapters 6 and 17). Just as countries with differing abilities to produce goods at a single point in time gain from concentrating their production on what they do best and trading, countries can gain from concentrating the world's investment in those economies best able to turn current output into future output. Countries with weak investment opportunities should invest little at home and channel their savings into more productive investment activity abroad. Put another way, countries where investment is relatively unproductive should be net exporters of currently available output (and thus have current account surpluses), while countries where investment is relatively productive should be net importers of current output (and have current account deficits). To pay off their foreign debts when the investments mature, the latter countries export output to the former countries and thereby complete the exchange of present output for future output.

Other considerations may also justify an unbalanced current account. A country where output drops temporarily (for example, because of an unusually bad crop failure) may wish to borrow from foreigners to avoid the sharp temporary fall in its consumption that would otherwise occur. In the absence of this borrowing, the price of present output in terms of future output would be higher in the low-output country than abroad, so the intertemporal trade that eliminates this price difference leads to mutual gains.

Insisting that all countries be in current account equilibrium makes no allowance for these important gains from trade over time. Thus, no realistic policy maker would want to adopt a balanced current account as a policy target appropriate in all circumstances.

At a given point, however, policy makers generally adopt *some* current account target as an objective, and this target defines their external balance goal. While the target level of the current account is generally not zero, governments usually try to avoid extremely large external surpluses or deficits unless they have clear evidence that large imbalances are justified by potential intertemporal trade gains. Governments are cautious because the exact current account balance that maximizes the gains from intertemporal trade is difficult if not impossible to figure out. In addition, this optimal current account balance can change unpredictably over time as conditions in the domestic and global economies change. Current account balances that are very wide of the mark can, however, cause serious problems.

Problems with Excessive Current Account Deficits Why do governments prefer to avoid current account deficits that are too large? As noted, a current account deficit (which means that the economy is borrowing from abroad) may pose no problem if the borrowed funds are channeled into productive domestic investment projects that pay for themselves with the revenue they generate in the future. Sometimes, however, large current account deficits represent temporarily high consumption resulting from misguided government policies or some other malfunction in the economy. At other times, the investment projects that draw on foreign funds may be badly planned and based on overoptimistic expectations about future profitability. In such cases, the government might wish to reduce the current account deficit immediately rather than face problems in repaying debts to foreigners later. In particular, a large current account deficit caused by an expansionary fiscal policy that does not simultaneously make domestic investment opportunities more profitable may signal a need for the government to restore external balance by changing its economic course. Every open economy faces an **intertemporal budget constraint** that limits its spending over time to levels that allow it to pay the interest and principal on its foreign debts. A simple version of that budget constraint was discussed in the appendices to Chapters 6 and 17, and a more realistic version is derived in the following box on New Zealand's foreign borrowing and debt.

At times, the external target is imposed from abroad rather than chosen by the domestic government. When countries begin to have trouble meeting their payments on past foreign loans, foreign creditors become reluctant to lend them new funds and may even demand immediate repayment of the earlier loans. Economists refer to such an event as a **sudden stop** in foreign lending. In such cases, the home government may have to take severe action to reduce the country's desired borrowing from foreigners to feasible levels, as well as to repay maturing loans that foreigners are unwilling to renew. A large current account deficit can undermine foreign investors' confidence and contribute to a sudden stop. In the event of a sudden stop, moreover, the larger the initial deficit, the larger and more painful the fall in domestic spending that is needed to make the economy live strictly within its means.

CAN A COUNTRY BORROW FOREVER? THE CASE OF NEW ZEALAND

The small Pacific country of New Zealand (with a population of about 4.5 million) has run current account deficits every year for many years, as far back as the country's official statistics reach. As a result, its net debt to foreign lenders stands at around 70 percent of its national output. Yet lenders continue to extend credit and seem not to worry about repayment (in contrast to many cases that we will study later on). Is it possible for an indebted country to borrow year after year without going broke? Perhaps surprisingly the answer is yes—if it does not borrow too much.

To understand why, we have to think about a country's budget constraint when it can borrow and lend over a long horizon.[2] (Our analysis will also underline why the *IIP* is so important.) Let's continue to let *IIP* stand for a country's net foreign wealth (claims on foreigners less liabilities), and let *GDP* denote its gross domestic product or production within the country's borders. Let *r* stand for the (constant) interest rate the country both earns on wealth held abroad and pays on its liabilities to foreigners.[3] If we assume for simplicity that gross national product *Y* is the sum of GDP and net foreign investment income, $Y = GDP + rIIP$, then we can express the current account in any year *t* as

$$CA_t = IIP_{t+1} - IIP_t = Y_t - (C_t + I_t + G_t)$$
$$= rIIP_t + GDP_t - (C_t + I_t + G_t).$$

(Think of IIP_{t+1} as net foreign wealth at the *end* of year *t*. We saw in Chapter 13's Case Study that the preceding relationship is not quite accurate because of price gains and losses on net foreign liabilities that are not captured in the national income and product accounts. We say more about this at the end.)

Define net exports, the (possibly negative) difference between what a country produces domestically and what it demands, as $NX_t = GDP_t - (C_t + I_t + G_t)$. (Net exports are sometimes referred to as the "balance of trade.") Then we can rewrite the preceding current account equation as

$$IIP_{t+1} = (1 + r)IIP_t + NX_t.$$

Now we have to resort to some simple, but devious, algebra. Imagine that in the last equation we are starting out in some year labeled $t = 0$ and that there is a year *T* far in the future at which everyone's debts have to be repaid, so that $IIP_T = 0$. We will apply the preceding equation for the *IIP* successively for years 1, 2, 3, and all the way through *T*. To start off, notice that the preceding equation can be manipulated to become

$$IIP_0 = -\frac{1}{1 + r} NX_0 + \frac{1}{1 + r} IIP_1.$$

But a similar relationship to this last one holds true with IIP_1 on the left hand-side and IIP_2 and NX_1 on the right. If we substitute this in for IIP_1 above, we get

$$IIP_0 = -\frac{1}{1 + r} NX_0 - \frac{1}{(1 + r)^2} NX_1$$
$$+ \frac{1}{(1 + r)^2} IIP_2.$$

Of course, we can continue to make these substitutions until we reach $IIP_T = 0$ (the point at

(Continued)

---

[2]Our discussion is closely related to that in the Chapter 6 and 17 appendices, but it is more general because it allows for many time periods (not just two) and for a starting non-zero *IIP*.

[3]A simple interpretation of the model is to imagine that all foreign assets and liabilities are bonds denominated in a single global currency, where *r* is the *nominal* interest rate measured in the global currency. In practice, however, the nominal rates of return on foreign assets and liabilities can differ, and can be somewhat unpredictable, as we discuss further below. In the appendices to Chapters 6 and 17, we interpreted *r* as a global *real* rate of interest, which we could do here too if we measured *GDP*, *Y*, and the *IIP* all in real terms (rather than in terms of the hypothetical global currency).

which all debts have been fully repaid). The resulting equation is the economy's *intertemporal budget constraint*:

$$IIP_0 = -\frac{1}{1 + r} NX_0 - \frac{1}{(1 + r)^2} NX_1$$

$$- \frac{1}{(1 + r)^3} NX_2 - \cdots - \frac{1}{(1 + r)^T} NX_{T-1}.$$

If the country has an initially positive *IIP* (foreign assets in excess of liabilities), this intertemporal constraint states that the country can run a stream of net export deficits in the future ($NX < 0$), provided the *present discounted value* of those deficits is not greater than the economy's initial net claims on foreigners. On the other hand, if initially $IIP < 0$, the economy must have future surpluses of net exports sufficient to repay its net debt to foreigners (with interest, which is why future net exports are discounted by r, and discounted more heavily the farther in the future they occur). So an indebted country such as New Zealand definitely cannot have *net export* or *trade balance* deficits forever. At some point the country must produce more goods and services than it absorbs in order to repay what it owes. Otherwise, it is perpetually borrowing more to repay what it owes—a strategy that must eventually collapse when the country runs out of fresh lenders (and probably long before then).[4]

But what about the current account balance, which equals net exports *plus* the negative flow of net interest payments implied by the country's negative *IIP*? Perhaps surprisingly, it turns out that this sum need *never* be positive for the country to remain creditworthy.

To see why, it is helpful to rewrite the preceding intertemporal budget constraint in terms of *ratios* to nominal output (nominal GDP), $iip = IIP/GDP$ and $nx = NX/GDP$. Assume that nominal GDP grows at a constant annual rate g that is below r – meaning that $GDP_t = (1 + g) GDP_{t-1}$.

Then after dividing the intertemporal budget constraint by GDP in year 0, we can see that

$$iip_0 = \frac{IIP_0}{GDP_0} = -\frac{1}{1 + r} \frac{NX_0}{GDP_0} - \frac{1}{(1 + r)^2} \frac{NX_1}{GDP_1}$$

$$\frac{GDP_1}{GDP_0} - \cdots - \frac{1}{(1 + r)^T} \frac{NX_{T-1}}{GDP_{T-1}} \frac{GDP_{T-1}}{GDP_0}$$

$$= -\frac{1}{1 + r} nx_0 - \frac{1 + g}{(1 + r)^2} nx_1 - \frac{(1 + g)^2}{(1 + r)^3} nx_2$$

$$- \cdots - \frac{(1 + g)^{T-2}}{(1 + r)^T} nx_{T-1}.$$

Let's now apply this version of the country's budget constraint, which we simplify by assuming that the country's time horizon is very long, making the constraint approximately the same as the infinite-summation expression:

$$iip_0 = -\frac{1}{1 + g} \sum_{t=1}^{\infty} \left(\frac{1 + g}{1 + r} \right)^t nx_{t-1}.$$

To illustrate how a country can easily run a perpetual current account deficit, let us ask what *constant* level of net exports $\overline{nx}$ will allow the country to respect this budget constraint. We find this constant net export level by substituting $\overline{nx}$ into the previous equation and simplifying using the summation formula for a geometric series,[5]

$$iip_0 = -\frac{1}{1 + g} \sum_{t=1}^{\infty} \left(\frac{1 + g}{1 + r} \right)^t \overline{nx} = \frac{-\overline{nx}}{r - g}.$$

This solution implies net exports of $\overline{nx} = -(r - g)iip_0$. For example, if iip_0 is negative – the country is a net debtor – then $\overline{nx}$ will need to be positive and by construction, it is just big enough for the country to repay its debt over time.

What level of the current account balance does this imply, though? The country's current account balance in the initial year $t = 0$ (expressed as a fraction of its GDP) is equal to $ca_0 = r(iip_0) + \overline{nx} = r(iip_0) - (r - g)iip_0 =$

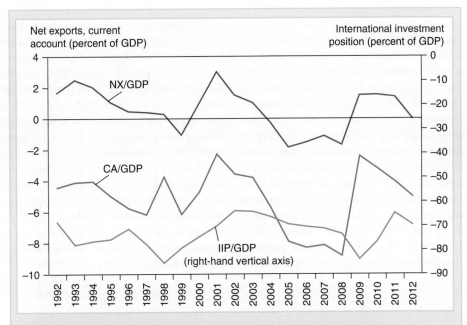

New Zealand's Net Exports, Current Account, and Net International Investment Position, 1992–2012

New Zealand has consistently had a current account deficit for decades, yet its net foreign liabilities have remained near 70 percent of GDP.

Source: Statistics New Zealand.

$g(iip_0)$. For a debtor country such as New Zealand, the initial current account is therefore in deficit. An important further implication of this current account level, however, is that the *IIP* ratio to GDP will remain constant forever at the level $\overline{iip} = iip_0$, so that the current account will also remain constant at $g(\overline{iip})$: this current account level is just enough to keep the ratio of net foreign assets or debt to nominal GDP constant, given that nominal GDP is growing at the rate g.[6] Thus, if the ratio of net exports to GDP is held constant at the right value, a country with an initial net foreign debt will perpetually run deficits in its current account, while still maintaining a constant ratio of net foreign liabilities to national output.

The accompanying figure shows New Zealand data on net exports and the current account (left-hand vertical axis) and the *IIP* (right-hand vertical axis), all expressed as percentages of GDP. In recent

history, as you can see, New Zealand has had a negative current account balance every year, yet its *IIP*-to-GDP ratio has remained roughly constant at −70 percent of GDP. How has this been possible? Because the average growth rate of New Zealand's nominal GDP was 5 percent for 1992–2012, our previous formula suggests that at an interest rate of $r = 6$ percent per year, the *IIP*-to-GDP ratio will remain constant if on average New Zealand has an annual net export surplus equal to

$$\overline{nx} = -(r - g)iip_0 = (.06 - .05) \times (.7)$$
$$= .01 \times .7 = 0.007,$$

or 0.7 percent of GDP. But this is *exactly* the average ratio of New Zealand's net exports to its GDP over the 1992–2012 period shown in the figure![7]

Can we *independently* confirm that the rate of return on New Zealand's *IIP* was around

(Continued)

---

[6]Thus, if nominal GDP grows by 5 percent per year, the current account will raise net foreign assets or debt by 5 percent as well, leaving the ratio constant. Problem 8 at the end of this chapter asks you to verify this algebraically.
[7]The average current account deficit implied by this calculation is rather large: $g(iip_0) = .05 \times .7 = 3.5$ percent of GDP annually.

6 percent per year over this period? Such estimates are not easy to make because we would need detailed data on the country's foreign liabilities and investments and their rates of return (recall our discussion of the U.S. *IIP* at the end of Chapter 13). We can get a partial answer—partial because it ignores capital gains and losses on foreign assets and liabilities—by looking at New Zealand's balance of international investment income, reckoned as a fraction of the *IIP*. Over 1992–2012, New Zealand paid out on average net interest and dividends equal to 8.3 percent of its net foreign debt. This is higher than the 6 percent rate that stabilizes the *IIP* relative to GDP.

What explains the difference? One possibility is that interest inflows to New Zealand are underestimated in the official data, due to the standard under-reporting problem (Chapter 13). In addition, New Zealand's gross foreign liabilities consist largely of bank debt, denominated in New Zealand (or "kiwi") dollars, while its gross foreign assets include substantial stock shares, plus other assets denominated in foreign currencies. Even though the kiwi has appreciated since 1992 (from about 55 to 80 U.S. cents per kiwi dollar), global stock markets have done very well over that period; for example, the Standard and Poor's 500 index of U.S. stock prices has risen roughly fourfold. Evidently, such gains on foreign assets have helped to reduce the average annual *total* cost of New Zealand's negative *IIP* closer to 6 percent.

Problems with Excessive Current Account Surpluses   An excessive current account surplus poses problems that are different from those posed by deficits. A surplus in the current account implies that a country is accumulating assets located abroad. Why are growing domestic claims to foreign wealth ever a problem? One potential reason stems from the fact that, for a given level of national saving, an increased current account surplus implies lower investment in domestic plant and equipment. (This follows from the national income identity, $S = CA + I$, which says that total domestic saving, S, is divided between foreign asset accumulation, CA, and domestic investment, I.) Several factors might lead policy makers to prefer that domestic saving be devoted to higher levels of domestic investment and lower levels of foreign investment. First, the returns on domestic capital may be easier to tax than those on assets located abroad. Second, an addition to the home capital stock may reduce domestic unemployment and therefore lead to higher national income than an equal addition to foreign assets. Finally, domestic investment by one firm may have beneficial technological spillover effects on other domestic producers that the investing firm does not capture.

If a large home current account surplus reflects excessive external borrowing by foreigners, the home country may in the future find itself unable to collect the money it is owed. Put another way, the home country may lose part of its foreign wealth if foreigners find they have borrowed more than they can repay. In contrast, non-repayment of a loan between domestic residents leads to a redistribution of national wealth within the home country but causes no change in the level of national wealth.[8] Excessive current account surpluses may also be inconvenient for political reasons. Countries with large surpluses can become targets for discriminatory import barriers imposed by trading partners with external deficits. Japan has been in this position in the past, and China's surpluses inspire the most visible protectionist threats today. To avoid such damaging restrictions, surplus countries may try to keep their surpluses from becoming too large.

---

[8]This fact was pointed out by John Maynard Keynes in "Foreign Investment and National Advantage," *The Nation and Athenaeum* 35 (1924), pp. 584–587.

Summary   The goal of external balance is a level of the current account that allows the most important gains from trade over time to be realized without risking the problems discussed previously. Because governments do not know this current account level exactly, they may try to avoid large deficits or surpluses unless there is clear evidence of large gains from intertemporal trade.

There is a fundamental asymmetry, however, between the pressures pushing deficit and surplus countries to adjust their external imbalances downward. While big deficits that continue too long may be forcibly eliminated by a sudden stop in lending, there is unlikely to be a sudden stop in borrowing countries' willingness to absorb funds that are supplied by foreigners! Thus, the adjustment pressures that confront deficit countries are generally much stronger than those facing surplus countries.

Classifying Monetary Systems: The Open-Economy Monetary Trilemma

The world economy has evolved through a variety of international monetary systems since the 19th century. A simple insight from the models we studied in the last part of this text will prove very helpful in understanding the key differences between these systems as well as the economic, political, and social factors that lead countries to adopt one system rather than another. The insight we will rely on is that policy makers in an open economy face an inescapable **monetary trilemma** in choosing the currency arrangements that best enable them to attain their internal and external balance goals.

Chapter 18 showed how a country that fixes its currency's exchange rate while allowing free international capital movements gives up control over domestic monetary policy. This sacrifice illustrates the impossibility of a country's having more than two items from the following list:

1. Exchange rate stability.
2. Monetary policy oriented toward domestic goals.
3. Freedom of international capital movements.

Because this list contains properties of an international monetary system that most economists would regard as desirable in themselves, the need to choose only two is a trilemma for policy regimes. It is a *tri*lemma rather than a *di*lemma because the available options are three: 1 and 2, 1 and 3, or 2 and 3.

As we have seen, countries with fixed exchange rates that allow free cross-border capital mobility sacrifice item 2 above, a domestically oriented monetary policy. On the other hand, if a country with a fixed exchange rate restricts international financial flows so that the interest parity condition, $R = R^*$, does not need to hold true (thereby sacrificing item 3 above), it is still able to change the home interest rate so as to influence the domestic economy (thereby preserving item 2). In this way, for example, the country might be able to reduce domestic overheating (getting closer to internal balance by raising the interest rate) without causing a fall in its exports (preventing a potential departure from external balance due to an appreciation of its currency). Finally, as Chapter 17 showed, a country that has a floating exchange rate (and thus gives up item 1 above) can use monetary policy to steer the economy even though financial flows across its borders are free. But the exchange rate might become quite unpredictable as a result, complicating the economic planning of importers and exporters.

Figure 19-1 shows the preceding three desirable properties of an international monetary regime schematically as the vertices of a triangle. Only two can be reached

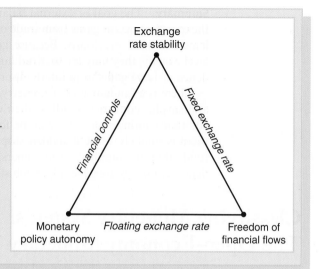

FIGURE 19-1

The Monetary Trilemma for Open Economies

The vertices of the triangle show three features that policy makers in open economies would prefer their monetary system to achieve. Unfortunately, at most two can coexist. Each of the three policy regime labels along the triangle's edges (floating exchange rate, fixed exchange rate, financial controls) is consistent with the two goals that it lies between in the diagram.

simultaneously. Each edge of the triangle represents a policy regime consistent with the two properties shown at the edge's end points.

Of course, the trilemma does not imply that intermediate regimes are impossible, only that they will require the policy maker to trade off between different objectives. For example, more aggressive monetary intervention to manage the exchange rate can reduce exchange rate volatility, but only at the cost of reducing the ability of monetary policy to pursue targets other than the exchange rate. Similarly, a partial opening of the financial account will allow some cross-border borrowing and lending. At the same time, however, fixing the exchange rate in the face of domestic interest rate changes will require larger volumes of intervention, and potentially larger drains on foreign exchange reserves, than would be needed if cross-border financial transactions were entirely prohibited. The central bank's ability to guarantee exchange rate stability (by avoiding devaluations and crises) will therefore decline.

International Macroeconomic Policy under the Gold Standard, 1870–1914

The gold standard period between 1870 and 1914 was based on ideas about international macroeconomic policy very different from those that have formed the basis of international monetary arrangements since World War II. Nevertheless, the period warrants attention because subsequent attempts to reform the international monetary system on the basis of fixed exchange rates can be viewed as attempts to build on the strengths of the gold standard while avoiding its weaknesses. (Some of these strengths and weaknesses were discussed in Chapter 18.) This section looks at how the gold standard functioned in practice before World War I and examines how well it enabled countries to attain goals of internal and external balance.

Origins of the Gold Standard

The gold standard had its origin in the use of gold coins as a medium of exchange, unit of account, and store of value. While gold has played these roles since ancient times, the gold standard as a legal institution dates from 1819, when the British Parliament repealed long-standing restrictions on the export of gold coins and bullion from Britain.

Later in the 19th century, the United States, Germany, Japan, and other countries also adopted the gold standard. At the time, Britain was the world's leading economic power, and other nations hoped to achieve similar economic success by following British precedent. Given Britain's preeminence in international trade and the advanced development of its financial institutions and industry, London naturally became the center of the international monetary system built on the gold standard.

External Balance under the Gold Standard

Under the gold standard, the primary responsibility of a central bank was to fix the exchange rate between its currency and gold. To maintain this official gold price, the central bank needed an adequate stock of gold reserves. Policy makers therefore viewed external balance not in terms of a current account target, but as a situation in which the central bank was neither gaining gold from abroad nor (much more worrisome) losing gold to foreigners at too rapid a rate.

In the modern terminology of Chapter 13, central banks tried to avoid sharp fluctuations in the *balance of payments*, the difference between the current plus capital account balances and the balance of net nonreserve financial flows abroad. Because international reserves took the form of gold during this period, the surplus or deficit in the balance of payments had to be financed by gold shipments between central banks.[9] To avoid large gold movements, central banks adopted policies that pushed the balance of payments toward zero. A country is said to be in **balance of payments equilibrium** when the sum of its current and capital accounts, less the nonreserve component of net financial flows abroad, equals zero, so that the current plus capital account balance is financed entirely by private international lending without official reserve movements.

Many governments took a laissez-faire attitude toward the current account. Britain's current account surplus between 1870 and World War I averaged 5.2 percent of its GNP, a figure that is remarkably high by post-1945 standards. Several borrowing countries, however, did experience difficulty at one time or another in paying their foreign debts. Perhaps because Britain was the world's leading exporter of international economic theory as well as of capital during these years, the economic writing of the gold standard era places little emphasis on problems of current account adjustment.

The Price-Specie-Flow Mechanism

The gold standard contains some powerful automatic mechanisms that contribute to the simultaneous achievement of balance of payments equilibrium by all countries. The most important of these, the **price-specie-flow mechanism,** was recognized by the 18th century (when precious metals were referred to as "specie"). In 1752, David Hume, the Scottish philosopher, described the price-specie-flow mechanism as follows:

> Suppose four-fifths of all the money in Great Britain to be annihilated in one night, and the nation reduced to the same condition, with regard to specie, as in the reigns of the Harrys and the Edwards, what would be the consequence? Must not the

---

[9]In reality, central banks had begun to hold foreign currencies in their reserves even before 1914. (The pound sterling was the leading reserve currency.)

price of all labour and commodities sink in proportion, and everything be sold as cheap as they were in those ages? What nation could then dispute with us in any foreign market, or pretend to navigate or to sell manufactures at the same price, which to us would afford sufficient profit? In how little time, therefore, must this bring back the money which we had lost, and raise us to the level of all the neighbouring nations? Where, after we have arrived, we immediately lose the advantage of the cheapness of labour and commodities; and the farther flowing in of money is stopped by our fulness and repletion.

Again, suppose that all the money in Great Britain were multiplied fivefold in a night, must not the contrary effect follow? Must not all labour and commodities rise to such an exorbitant height, that no neighbouring nations could afford to buy from us; while their commodities, on the other hand, became comparatively so cheap, that, in spite of all the laws which could be formed, they would run in upon us, and our money flow out; till we fall to a level with foreigners, and lose that great superiority of riches which had laid us under such disadvantages?[10]

It is easy to translate Hume's description of the price-specie-flow mechanism into more modern terms. Suppose Britain's current plus capital account surplus is greater than its nonreserve financial account balance. Because foreigners' net imports from Britain are not being financed entirely by British loans, the shortfall must be matched by flows of international reserves—that is, of gold—into Britain. These gold flows automatically reduce foreign money supplies and swell Britain's money supply, pushing foreign prices downward and British prices upward. (Notice that Hume fully understood the lesson of Chapter 15, that price levels and money supplies move proportionally in the long run.)

The simultaneous rise in British prices and fall in foreign prices—a real appreciation of the pound, given the fixed exchange rate—reduces foreign demand for British goods and services and at the same time increases British demand for foreign goods and services. These demand shifts work in the direction of reducing Britain's current account surplus and reducing the foreign current account deficit. Eventually, therefore, reserve movements stop and all countries reach balance of payments equilibrium. The same process also works in reverse, eliminating an initial situation of foreign surplus and British deficit.

The Gold Standard "Rules of the Game": Myth and Reality

In theory, the price-specie-flow mechanism could operate automatically. But the reactions of central banks to gold flows across their borders furnished another potential mechanism to help restore balance of payments equilibrium. Central banks that were persistently losing gold faced the risk of becoming unable to meet their obligations to redeem currency notes. They were therefore motivated to sell domestic assets when gold was being lost, pushing domestic interest rates upward and attracting inflows of funds from abroad. Central banks gaining gold had much weaker incentives to eliminate their own imports of the metal. The main incentive was the greater profitability of interest-bearing domestic assets compared with "barren" gold. A central bank that was accumulating gold might be tempted to purchase domestic assets, thereby lowering home interest rates, increasing financial outflows, and driving gold abroad.

---

[10]Hume, "Of the Balance of Trade," reprinted (in abridged form) in Barry Eichengreen and Marc Flandreau, eds., *The Gold Standard in Theory and History* (London: Routledge, 1997), pp. 33–43.

These domestic credit measures, if undertaken by central banks, reinforced the price-specie-flow mechanism by pushing all countries toward balance of payments equilibrium. After World War I, the practices of selling domestic assets in the face of a deficit and buying domestic assets in the face of a surplus came to be known as the gold standard "rules of the game"—a phrase reportedly coined by Keynes. Because such measures speeded the movement of all countries toward their external balance goals, they increased the efficiency of the automatic adjustment processes inherent in the gold standard.

Later research has shown that the supposed "rules of the game" of the gold standard were frequently violated before 1914. As noted, the incentives to obey the rules applied with greater force to deficit than to surplus countries, so in practice it was the deficit countries that bore the burden of bringing the payments balances of *all* countries into equilibrium. By not always taking action to reduce gold inflows, the surplus countries worsened a problem of international policy coordination inherent in the system: Deficit countries competing for a limited supply of gold reserves might adopt overly contractionary monetary policies that harmed employment while doing little to improve their reserve positions.

In fact, countries often reversed the rules and *sterilized* gold flows, that is, sold domestic assets when foreign reserves were rising and bought domestic assets as foreign reserves fell. Government interference with private gold exports also undermined the system. The picture of smooth and automatic balance of payments adjustment before World War I therefore did not always match reality. Governments sometimes ignored both the "rules of the game" and the effects of their actions on other countries.[11]

Internal Balance under the Gold Standard

By fixing the prices of currencies in terms of gold, the gold standard aimed to limit monetary growth in the world economy and thus to ensure stability in world price levels. While price levels within gold standard countries did not rise as much between 1870 and 1914 as over the period after World War II, national price levels moved unpredictably over shorter horizons as periods of inflation and deflation followed each other. The gold standard's mixed record on price stability reflected a problem discussed in the last chapter: change in the relative prices of gold and other commodities.

In addition, the gold standard does not seem to have done much to ensure full employment. The U.S. unemployment rate, for example, averaged 6.8 percent between 1890 and 1913, whereas it averaged around 5.7 percent between 1948 and 2010.[12]

A fundamental cause of short-term internal instability under the pre-1914 gold standard was the subordination of economic policy to external objectives. Before World War I, governments had not assumed responsibility for maintaining internal balance as fully as they did after World War II. In the United States, the resulting economic distress led to political opposition to the gold standard, as the Case Study that follows explains. In terms of the monetary policy trilemma discussed above, the gold standard allowed high degrees of exchange rate stability and international financial

---

[11]An influential modern study of central bank practices under the gold standard is Arthur I. Bloomfield, *Monetary Policy under the International Gold Standard: 1880–1914* (New York: Federal Reserve Bank of New York, 1959).

[12]Data on price levels are given by Cooper (cited on page 553 in Chapter 18), and data for U.S. unemployment are adapted from the same source. Caution should be used in comparing gold standard and post–World War II unemployment data because the methods used to assemble the earlier data were much cruder. A critical study of pre-1930 U.S. unemployment data is Christina D. Romer, "Spurious Volatility in Historical Unemployment Data," *Journal of Political Economy* 94 (February 1986), pp. 1–37.

capital mobility, but did not allow monetary policy to pursue internal policy goals. These priorities were consistent with the limited political power at the time of those most vulnerable to unemployment.

The importance of internal policy objectives increased after World War II as a result of the worldwide economic instability of the interwar years, 1918–1939. And the unpalatable internal consequences of attempts to restore the gold standard after 1918 helped mold the thinking of the architects of the fixed exchange rate system adopted after 1945. To understand how the post–World War II international monetary system tried to reconcile the goals of internal and external balance, we therefore must examine the economic events of the period between the two world wars.

| CASE STUDY | Gold Smuggling and the Birth of the UAE Dirham |

The Indian rupee was used in what is now the United Arab Emirates (then known as the Trucial States, as they had truce agreements with Britain) and in much of the GCC (Gulf Cooperation Council) countries in the early parts of the 20th century. Originally, the rupee was backed by silver, on which traditional trade was based. However, the discovery of large gold mines in the New World dealt a devastating blow to silver, and thus reduced the purchasing power of the Indian economy compared to that of countries whose currencies were backed by gold. Eventually, India moved away from silver to a pound sterling–based currency system.

Nevertheless, to eliminate the possibility of speculation in gold trading and the likely impact of that speculation on its economy, India banned import and export of gold by private individuals while allowing domestic ownership and trade thereof. In the absence of their own central banking facilities, governments in the Gulf region adopted the Indian rupee as their official currency. The Reserve Bank of India (the Indian central bank) promised convertibility to British pound sterling at the fixed exchange rate once rupees were presented to it. Public confidence in the currency allowed readily accepted status for the rupee even in exchange for gold in the Gulf. The rupee probably was not only used as the medium of exchange,[13] but also served the function of a store of value[14] at the time. This characteristic of the currency provided India with a significant level of seigniorage. **Seigniorage** is the name economists give to the real resources a government earns when it prints money that it spends on goods and services.

Unfortunately, the same feature also contributed to the downfall of the rupee in the region. This is because large quantities of rupees flooded into the region to be exchanged for gold. Afterwards, this gold was smuggled to India. The amount of privately owned gold swelled in the country, and was estimated to be roughly in the neighborhood of 2 trillion U.S. dollars in 1959.[15] This was about two-thirds the value of the currency in circulation. As promised, the Reserve Bank of India exchanged with British pound sterling the rupees presented by the Gulf banks with British pound

---

[13]This is the function of money stating that money is an instrument used in transactions.
[14]This is the function of money stating that money is a vehicle through which today's purchasing power can be transferred to future purchasing power.
[15]http://www.pjsymes.com.au/articles/gulfrupees.htm

sterling. For example, in 1957 India paid out 92.4 million U.S. dollars in sterling to banks in the Gulf. Obviously, some of these rupees were the result of the illegal gold trade. To tackle the problem, on May 1, 1959, the Indian government enacted a law that, in effect, created a special currency, called the Gulf rupee, to be circulated outside the country.[16] The Gulf rupee continued to enjoy the same status as the Indian rupee in most Gulf states, including in today's United Arab Emirates, though some states slowly moved away from it, until June 6, 1966, when India devalued the currency.

Maybe such a move was unavoidable from the perspective of India, which faced an insurmountable array of economic, natural, political, and social problems at the time. As a result, Gulf states stood to incur a large wealth loss because both India and Britain (the patriarch of the original system) refused to assume the consequential financial burden.

This became the beginning of a move to a local currency in the Gulf. Thus, Qatar and Dubai jointly issued a currency called the Qatar-Dubai riyal, which circulated in all emirates of the Trucial States, except Abu Dhabi which adopted the Bahraini dinar in 1966.

Shortly after the emergence of the new currency, all but one of the countries formed the United Arab Emirates on December 2, 1971 (Ras al-Khaimah joined on February 11, 1972), which also saw the introduction of the currency of the new country—i.e., the UAE dirham. Initially, a currency board whose sole responsibility was to issue dirham was established on May 19, 1973. The institutionalization of the system was completed with the launch of the UAE Central Bank in December 1980. After a brief stint with the Special Drawing Rights (SDR), the fictitious currency of the International Monetary Fund (IMF), the dirham has been pegged to the U.S. dollar at the rate of 3.67 dirhams per dollar since November 1997. The dirham has played a significant role in the unification of the nation ever since the currency's inception.

The Interwar Years, 1918–1939

Governments effectively suspended the gold standard during World War I and financed part of their massive military expenditures by printing money. Further, labor forces and productive capacity were reduced sharply through war losses. As a result, price levels were higher everywhere at the war's conclusion in 1918.

Several countries experienced runaway inflation as their governments attempted to aid the reconstruction process through public expenditures. These governments financed their purchases simply by printing the money they needed, as they sometimes had during the war. The result was a sharp rise in money supplies and price levels.

The Fleeting Return to Gold

The United States returned to gold in 1919. In 1922, at a conference in Genoa, Italy, a group of countries including Britain, France, Italy, and Japan agreed on a program calling for a general return to the gold standard and cooperation among central banks

---

[16]France also issues the so-called Central African Franc to be used exclusively in certain African countries, because it has no validity in France.

in attaining external and internal objectives. Realizing that gold supplies might be inadequate to meet central banks' demands for international reserves (a problem of the gold standard noted in Chapter 18), the Genoa Conference sanctioned a partial gold *exchange* standard in which smaller countries could hold as reserves the currencies of several large countries whose own international reserves would consist entirely of gold.

In 1925, Britain returned to the gold standard by pegging the pound to gold at the prewar price. Chancellor of the Exchequer Winston Churchill advocated returning to the old parity on the grounds that any deviation from the prewar price would undermine world confidence in the stability of Britain's financial institutions, which had played the leading role in international finance during the gold standard era. Though Britain's price level had been falling since the war, in 1925 it was still higher than in the days of the prewar gold standard. To return the pound price of gold to its prewar level, the Bank of England was therefore forced to follow contractionary monetary policies that contributed to severe unemployment.

British stagnation in the 1920s accelerated London's decline as the world's leading financial center. Britain's economic weakening proved problematic for the stability of the restored gold standard. In line with the recommendations of the Genoa Conference, many countries held international reserves in the form of deposits in London. Britain's gold reserves were limited, however, and the country's persistent stagnation did little to inspire confidence in its ability to meet its foreign obligations. The onset of the Great Depression in 1929 was shortly followed by bank failures throughout the world. Britain left gold in 1931 when foreign holders of sterling (including several central banks) lost confidence in Britain's promise to maintain its currency's value and began converting their sterling to gold.

International Economic Disintegration

As the depression continued, many countries renounced the gold standard and allowed their currencies to float in the foreign exchange market. In the face of growing unemployment, a resolution of the trilemma in favor of fixed exchange rates became difficult to maintain. The United States left gold in 1933 but returned in 1934, having raised the dollar price of gold from $20.67 to $35 per ounce. Countries that clung to the gold standard without devaluing their currencies suffered most during the Great Depression. Indeed, recent research places much of the blame for the depression's worldwide propagation on the gold standard itself (see the Case Study on page 587).

Major economic harm resulted from restrictions on international trade and payments, which proliferated as countries attempted to discourage imports and keep aggregate demand bottled up at home. The Smoot-Hawley tariff imposed by the United States in 1930 was intended to protect American jobs, but it had a damaging effect on employment abroad. The foreign response involved retaliatory trade restrictions and preferential trading agreements among groups of countries. World trade collapsed dramatically. A measure that raises domestic welfare is called a *beggar-thy-neighbor policy* when it benefits the home country at the cost of worsening economic conditions abroad. However, everyone is hurt when countries *simultaneously* adopt beggar-thy-neighbor policies.

Uncertainty about government policies led to sharp reserve movements for countries with pegged exchange rates and sharp exchange rate movements for those with floating rates. Many countries imposed prohibitions on private financial account transactions to limit these effects of foreign exchange market developments. This was another way of addressing the trilemma. Trade barriers and deflation in the industrial economies of America and Europe led to widespread repudiations of private international debts, particularly by Latin American countries, whose export markets were disappearing. Governments in western Europe repudiated their debts to the United States and Britain incurred because of World War I. In short, the world economy disintegrated into increasingly autarkic (that is, self-sufficient) national units in the early 1930s.

In the face of the Great Depression, most countries resolved the choice between external and internal balance by curtailing their trading links with the rest of the world and eliminating, by government decree, the possibility of any significant external imbalance. By reducing the gains from trade, that approach imposed high costs on the world economy and contributed to the slow recovery from depression, which in many countries was still incomplete in 1939. All countries would have been better off in a world with freer international trade, provided international cooperation had helped each country preserve its external balance and financial stability without sacrificing internal policy goals. It was this realization that inspired the blueprint for the postwar international monetary system, the **Bretton Woods agreement**.

CASE STUDY

The International Gold Standard and the Great Depression

One of the most striking features of the decade-long Great Depression that started in 1929 was its global nature. Rather than being confined to the United States and its main trading partners, the downturn spread rapidly and forcefully to Europe, Latin America, and elsewhere. What explains the Great Depression's nearly universal scope? Recent scholarship shows that the international gold standard played a central role in starting, deepening, and spreading the 20th century's greatest economic crisis.[17]

In 1929, most market economies were once again on the gold standard. At the time, however, the United States, attempting to slow its overheated economy through monetary contraction, and France, having just ended an inflationary period and returned to gold, faced large financial inflows. Through the resulting balance of payments surpluses, both countries were absorbing the world's monetary gold at a startling rate. (By 1932, the two countries alone held more than 70 percent of it!) Other countries on the gold standard had no choice but to engage in domestic asset sales and raise interest rates if they wished to conserve their dwindling

---

[17]Important contributions to this research include Ehsan U. Choudhri and Levis A. Kochin, "The Exchange Rate and the International Transmission of Business Cycle Disturbances: Some Evidence from the Great Depression," *Journal of Money, Credit, and Banking* 12 (1980), pp. 565–574; Peter Temin, *Lessons from the Great Depression* (Cambridge, MA: MIT Press, 1989); and Barry Eichengreen, *Golden Fetters: The Gold Standard and the Great Depression, 1919–1939* (New York: Oxford University Press, 1992). A concise and lucid summary is Ben S. Bernanke, "The World on a Cross of Gold: A Review of 'Golden Fetters: The Gold Standard and the Great Depression, 1919–1939,' " *Journal of Monetary Economics* 31 (April 1993), pp. 251–267.

gold stocks. The resulting worldwide monetary contraction, combined with the shock waves from the October 1929 New York stock market crash, sent the world into deep recession.

A cascade of bank failures around the world only accelerated the global economy's downward spiral. The gold standard again was a key culprit. Many countries desired to safeguard their gold reserves in order to be able to remain on the gold standard. This desire often discouraged their central banks from providing troubled private banks with the loans that might have allowed the banks to stay in business. After all, any cash provided to banks by their home central banks would have increased potential private claims to the government's precious gold holdings.[18]

Perhaps the clearest evidence of the gold standard's role is the contrasting behavior of output and the price level in countries that left the gold standard relatively early, such as Britain, and those that chose a different response to the trilemma and instead stubbornly hung on. Countries that abandoned the gold standard freed themselves to adopt more expansionary monetary policies that limited (or prevented) both domestic deflation and output contraction. The countries with the biggest deflations and output contractions over the years 1929–1935 included France, Switzerland, Belgium, the Netherlands, and Poland, all of which stayed on the gold standard until 1936.

The Bretton Woods System and the International Monetary Fund

In July 1944, representatives of 44 countries meeting in Bretton Woods, New Hampshire, drafted and signed the Articles of Agreement of the **International Monetary Fund (IMF)**. Remembering the disastrous economic events of the interwar period, statesmen in the Allied countries hoped to design an international monetary system that would foster full employment and price stability while allowing individual countries to attain external balance without restrictions on international trade.[19]

The system set up by the Bretton Woods agreement called for fixed exchange rates against the U.S. dollar and an unvarying dollar price of gold—$35 an ounce. Member countries held their official international reserves largely in the form of gold or dollar assets and had the right to sell dollars to the Federal Reserve for gold at the official price. The system was thus a gold exchange standard, with the dollar as its principal reserve currency. In the terminology of Chapter 18, the dollar was the "Nth currency"

---

[18]Chang-Tai Hsieh and Christina D. Romer argue that the fear of being forced off gold cannot explain the U.S. Federal Reserve's unwillingness to expand the money supply in the early 1930s. See "Was the Federal Reserve Constrained by the Gold Standard During the Great Depression? Evidence from the 1932 Open Market Purchase Program," *Journal of Economic History* 66 (March 2006), pp. 140–176.

[19]The same conference set up a second institution, the World Bank, whose goals were to help the belligerents rebuild their shattered economies and to help the former colonial territories develop and modernize theirs. In 1947, the General Agreement on Tariffs and Trade (GATT) was inaugurated as a forum for the multilateral reduction of trade barriers. The GATT was meant as a prelude to the creation of an International Trade Organization (ITO), whose goals in the trade area would parallel those of the IMF in the financial area. Unfortunately, the ITO was doomed by the failures of Congress and Britain's Parliament to ratify its charter. In the 1990s, the GATT became the current World Trade Organization (WTO).

in terms of which the $N - 1$ exchange rates of the system were defined. The United States itself intervened only rarely in the foreign exchange market. Usually, the $N - 1$ foreign central banks intervened when necessary to fix the system's $N - 1$ exchange rates, while the United States was responsible in theory for fixing the dollar price of gold.

Goals and Structure of the IMF

The IMF Articles of Agreement, through a mixture of discipline and flexibility, hoped to avoid a repetition of the turbulent interwar experience.

The major discipline on monetary management was the requirement that exchange rates be fixed to the dollar, which, in turn, was tied to gold. If a central bank other than the Federal Reserve pursued excessive monetary expansion, it would lose international reserves and eventually become unable to maintain the fixed dollar exchange rate of its currency. Since high U.S. monetary growth would lead to dollar accumulation by foreign central banks, the Fed itself was constrained in its monetary policies by its obligation to redeem those dollars for gold. The official gold price of $35 an ounce served as a further brake on American monetary policy, since that price would be pushed upward if too many dollars were created.

Fixed exchange rates were viewed as more than a device for imposing monetary discipline on the system, however. Rightly or wrongly, the interwar experience had convinced the IMF's architects that floating exchange rates were a cause of speculative instability and were harmful to international trade.

The interwar experience had shown also that national governments would not be willing to maintain both free trade and fixed exchange rates at the price of long-term domestic unemployment. After the experience of the Great Depression, governments were widely viewed as responsible for maintaining full employment. The IMF agreement therefore tried to incorporate sufficient flexibility to allow countries to attain external balance in an orderly fashion without sacrificing internal objectives or predictable exchange rates.

Two major features of the IMF Articles of Agreement helped promote this flexibility in external adjustment. First, members of the IMF contributed their currencies and gold to form a pool of financial resources that the IMF could lend to countries in need. Second, although exchange rates against the dollar were fixed, these parities could be adjusted with the agreement of the IMF. Such devaluations and revaluations were supposed to be infrequent and carried out only in cases of an economy in *fundamental disequilibrium*. Although the IMF's Articles did not define "fundamental disequilibrium," the term was intended to cover countries that suffered permanent adverse shifts in the demand for their products, so that without devaluation, the countries would face long periods of unemployment and external deficits. The flexibility of an adjustable exchange rate was not available, however, to the "Nth currency" of the Bretton Woods system, the U.S. dollar.

How did the Bretton Woods system resolve the trilemma? In essence, the system was based on the presumption that movements of private financial capital could be restricted, allowing some degree of independence for domestically oriented monetary policies. The new system thus was diametrically opposed to the gold standard's subordination of monetary policy to external considerations such as freedom of financial flows. After the experience of high interwar unemployment, the architects of the Bretton Woods system hoped to ensure that countries would not be forced to adopt contractionary monetary policies for balance of payments reasons in the face of an economic downturn.

Supporting this emphasis on high employment, restrictions on cross-border financial flows would allow "orderly" exchange rate changes in situations of persistent imbalance. In theory, policy makers would be able to change exchange rates in a deliberate fashion, without the pressure of massive speculative attacks. As we shall see, however, while this approach worked well initially, the very success of the Bretton Woods system in rebuilding international trade made it progressively harder for policy makers to avoid speculative attacks as the years passed.

Convertibility and the Expansion of Private Financial Flows

Just as the general acceptability of national currency eliminates the costs of barter within a single economy, the use of national currencies in international trade makes the world economy function more efficiently. To promote efficient multilateral trade, the IMF Articles of Agreement urged members to make their national currencies convertible as soon as possible. A **convertible currency** is one that may be freely exchanged for foreign currencies. The U.S. and Canadian dollars became convertible in 1945. This meant, for example, that a Canadian resident who acquired U.S. dollars could use them to make purchases in the United States, could sell them in the foreign exchange market for Canadian dollars, or could sell them to the Bank of Canada, which then had the right to sell them to the Federal Reserve (at the fixed dollar/gold exchange rate) in return for gold. General *in*convertibility would make international trade extremely difficult. A French citizen might be unwilling to sell goods to a German in return for inconvertible German marks because these marks would then be usable only subject to restrictions imposed by the German government. With no market in inconvertible French francs, the German would be unable to obtain French currency to pay for the French goods. The only way of trading would therefore be through barter, the direct exchange of goods for goods. Most countries in Europe did not restore convertibility until the end of 1958, with Japan following in 1964.

The early convertibility of the U.S. dollar, together with its special position in the Bretton Woods system and the economic and political dominance of the United States, helped to make the dollar the postwar world's key currency. Because dollars were freely convertible, much international trade tended to be invoiced in dollars, and importers and exporters held dollar balances for transactions. In effect, the dollar became an international money—a universal medium of exchange, unit of account, and store of value. Central banks naturally found it advantageous to hold their international reserves in the form of interest-bearing dollar assets.

The restoration of convertibility in Europe in 1958 gradually began to change the nature of policy makers' external constraints. As foreign exchange trading expanded, financial markets in different countries became more tightly integrated—an important step toward the creation of today's worldwide foreign exchange market. With growing opportunities to move funds across borders, national interest rates became more closely linked, and the speed with which policy changes might cause a country to lose or gain international reserves increased. After 1958, and increasingly over the next 15 years, central banks had to be attentive to foreign financial conditions or take the risk that sudden reserve losses might leave them without the resources needed to peg exchange rates. Faced with a sudden rise in foreign interest rates, for example, a central bank would be forced to sell domestic assets and raise the domestic interest rate to hold its international reserves steady.

The restoration of convertibility did not result in immediate and complete international financial integration, as assumed in the model of fixed exchange rates set out in Chapter 18. On the contrary, most countries continued to maintain restrictions on financial account transactions, a practice that the IMF explicitly allowed. But the opportunities for *disguised* capital flows increased dramatically. For example, importers within a country could effectively purchase foreign assets by accelerating payments to foreign suppliers relative to actual shipments of goods; they could effectively borrow from foreign suppliers by delaying payments. These trade practices— known, respectively, as "leads" and "lags"—provided two of the many ways through which official barriers to private capital movements could be evaded. Even though the condition of international interest rate equality assumed in the last chapter did not hold exactly, the links among countries' interest rates tightened as the Bretton Woods system matured. The Bretton Woods resolution of the trilemma was gradually coming undone.

Speculative Capital Flows and Crises

Current account deficits and surpluses took on added significance under the new conditions of increasingly mobile private financial flows. A country with a large and persistent current account deficit might be suspected of being in "fundamental disequilibrium" under the IMF Articles of Agreement, and thus ripe for a currency devaluation. Suspicion of an impending devaluation could, in turn, spark a balance of payments crisis (see Chapter 18).

Anyone holding pound deposits during a devaluation of the pound, for example, would suffer a loss, since the foreign currency value of pound assets would decrease suddenly by the amount of the exchange rate change. If Britain had a current account deficit, therefore, holders of pounds would become nervous and shift their wealth into other currencies. To hold the pound's exchange rate against the dollar pegged, the Bank of England (Britain's central bank) would have to buy pounds and supply the foreign assets that market participants wished to hold. This loss of foreign reserves, if large enough, might force devaluation by leaving the Bank of England without enough reserves to prop up the exchange rate.

Similarly, countries with large current account surpluses might be viewed by the market as candidates for revaluation. In this case, their central banks would find themselves swamped with official reserves, the result of selling the home currency in the foreign exchange market to keep the currency from appreciating. A country in this position would face the problem of having its money supply grow uncontrollably, a development that could push the price level up and upset internal balance. Governments thus became increasingly reluctant to contemplate exchange rate realignments, fearing the resulting speculative attacks.

Balance of payments crises nonetheless became increasingly frequent and violent throughout the 1960s and early 1970s. A record British trade balance deficit in early 1964 led to a period of intermittent speculation against the pound that complicated British policy making until November 1967, when the pound was finally devalued. France devalued its franc and Germany revalued its mark in 1969 after similar speculative attacks, in which France faced speculative financial outflows and Germany faced speculative financial inflows. (The two countries still had their own currencies at that time.) These crises became so massive by the early 1970s that they eventually brought down the Bretton Woods structure of fixed exchange rates. The possibility of a balance of payments crisis therefore lent increased importance to the external goal of a current account target. Even current account imbalances justified by differing international investment opportunities or caused by purely temporary factors might have fueled market suspicions of an impending parity change. In this environment, policy makers had additional incentives to avoid sharp current account changes.

Analyzing Policy Options for Reaching Internal and External Balance

How were individual countries able to reach internal and external balance under the rules of the Bretton Woods system? A simple diagram will help you to visualize the available policy options. (The problem of the United States under the Bretton Woods system was somewhat different, as we describe later.) In line with the approximate conditions later in the Bretton Woods system, we will assume a high degree of financial capital mobility across borders, so that the domestic interest rate cannot be set independently of the exchange rate.

Our diagrammatic framework actually is applicable whether the exchange rate is fixed, as under the Bretton Woods system, or flexible. The diagram shows how a country's position with respect to its internal and external goals depends on the level of its exchange rate, E, and the level of domestic spending; and that position is not necessarily restricted by the exchange rate regime. Throughout, E is the domestic currency price of the foreign currency (the dollar under Bretton Woods). The analysis applies to the short run because the home and foreign price levels (P and P^*, respectively) are assumed to be fixed.

Maintaining Internal Balance

First consider internal balance, which requires that aggregate demand equal the full-employment level of output, Y^f.[20]

Recall that aggregate demand for domestic output is the sum of consumption, C, investment, I, government purchases, G, and the current account, CA. Of this sum, total domestic spending, also called domestic *absorption*, is denoted by $A = C + I + G$. (Of course, some of this overall domestic spending falls on imports, and therefore does not contribute to the aggregate demand for domestic output, whereas foreign demand for our exports adds to that aggregate demand.) In Chapter 17, we expressed the current account surplus as a decreasing function of disposable income and an increasing function of the real exchange rate, EP^*/P. However, because import spending rises as total domestic spending A rises, we can similarly express the current account as a decreasing function of spending and an increasing function of the real exchange rate, $CA(EP^*/P, A)$. Under this new notation, the condition of internal balance (full-employment output equals aggregate demand) is therefore

$$Y^f = C + I + G + CA(EP^*/P, A) = A + CA(EP^*/P, A). \qquad (19\text{-}1)$$

Equation (19-1) suggests the policy tools that affect aggregate demand and, therefore, output, in the short run. The government can directly influence total spending A through fiscal policy, for example. Fiscal expansion (a rise in G or a fall in T) stimulates aggregate demand and causes output to rise, even though a fraction of the additional spending goes toward import purchases. Similarly, a devaluation of the currency (a rise in E) makes domestic goods and services cheaper relative to those sold abroad and thereby increases demand and output. The policy maker can hold output steady at its full employment level, Y^f, through fiscal policy or exchange rate changes.

---

[20]We will assume the domestic price level is stable at full employment, but if P^* is unstable because of foreign inflation, for example, full employment alone will not guarantee price stability under a fixed exchange rate. This complex problem is considered in the following pages, when we examine worldwide inflation under fixed exchange rates.

Notice that monetary policy is not a policy tool under fixed exchange rates. This is because, as shown in Chapter 18, an attempt by the central bank to alter the money supply by buying or selling domestic assets will cause an offsetting change in foreign reserves, leaving the domestic money supply unchanged. If we were interpreting the diagram to apply to a situation of floating exchange rates, however, we would think of monetary policy as potentially bringing about exchange rate changes consistent with a position of internal and external balance.

The *II* schedule in Figure 19-2 shows combinations of exchange rates and domestic spending that hold output constant at Y^f and thus maintain internal balance. The schedule is downward sloping because currency devaluation (a rise in E) and higher domestic absorption both tend to raise output. To hold output constant, a *revaluation* of the currency (which reduces aggregate demand) must therefore be matched by higher domestic spending (which increases aggregate output demand). Schedule *II* shows precisely how domestic spending must change as E changes to maintain full employment. To the right of *II*, spending is higher than needed for full employment, so the economy's productive factors are overemployed. To the left of *II*, spending is too low, and there is unemployment.

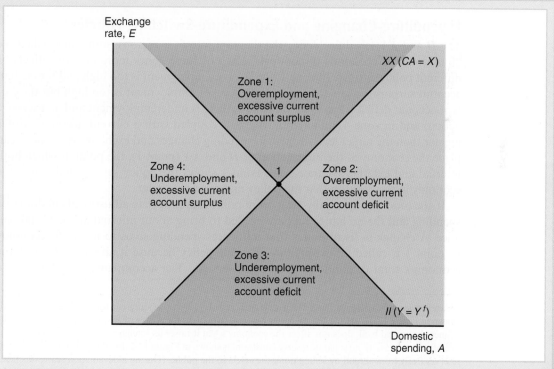

FIGURE 19-2

Internal Balance (*II*), External Balance (*XX*), and the "Four Zones of Economic Discomfort"

The diagram shows what different levels of the exchange rate, E, and overall domestic spending, A, imply for employment and the current account. Along *II*, output is at its full-employment level, Y^f. Along *XX*, the current account is at its target level, X.

Maintaining External Balance

We have seen how domestic spending and exchange rate changes influence output and thus help the government achieve its internal goal of full employment. How do these variables affect the economy's external balance? To answer this question, assume the government has a target value, X, for the current account surplus. The goal of external balance requires the government to manage domestic spending (perhaps through fiscal policy) and the exchange rate so that the equation

$$CA(EP^*/P, A) = X \qquad (19\text{-}2)$$

is satisfied.

Given P and P^*, a rise in E makes domestic goods cheaper and improves the current account. A rise in domestic spending, A, however, has the opposite effect on the current account, because it causes imports to rise. To maintain its current account at X as it devalues the currency (that is, as it raises E), the government must enact policies that raise domestic spending. Figure 19-2 therefore shows that the XX schedule, along which external balance holds, is positively sloped. The XX schedule shows the amount of additional spending that will hold the current account surplus at X as the currency is devalued by a given amount.[21] Since a rise in E raises net exports, the current account is in surplus, relative to its target level X, above XX. Similarly, below XX the current account is in deficit relative to its target level.[22]

Expenditure-Changing and Expenditure-Switching Policies

The II and XX schedules divide the diagram into four regions, sometimes called the "four zones of economic discomfort." Each of these zones represents the effects of different policy settings. In zone 1, the level of employment is too high and the current account surplus too great; in zone 2, the level of employment is too high but the current account deficit is too great; in zone 3, there is underemployment and an excessive deficit; and in zone 4, underemployment is coupled with a current account surplus greater than the target level. Together, spending changes and exchange rate policy can place the economy at the intersection of II and XX (point 1), the point at which both internal and external balance hold. Point 1 shows the policy setting that places the economy in the position that the policy maker would prefer.

If the economy is initially away from point 1, appropriate adjustments in domestic spending and the exchange rate are needed to bring about internal and external balance. A change in fiscal policy that influences spending so as to move the economy to point 1 is called an **expenditure-changing policy** because it alters the *level* of the economy's total demand for goods and services. The accompanying exchange rate

---

[21]Can you see how to derive the XX schedule in Figure 19-2 from the different (but related) XX schedule shown in Figure 17-17? (Hint: Use the latter diagram to analyze the effects of fiscal expansion.)

[22]Since the central bank does not affect the economy when it raises its foreign reserves by an open-market sale of domestic assets, no separate reserve constraint is shown in Figure 19-2. In effect, the bank can borrow reserves freely from abroad by selling domestic assets to the public. (During a devaluation scare, this tactic would not work because no one would want to sell the bank foreign assets for domestic money.) Our analysis, however, assumes perfect asset substitutability between domestic and foreign bonds (see Chapter 18). Under imperfect asset substitutability, central bank domestic asset sales to attract foreign reserves would drive up the domestic interest rate relative to the foreign rate. Thus, while imperfect asset substitutability would give the central bank an additional policy tool (monetary policy), it would also make the bank responsible for an additional policy target (the domestic interest rate). If the government is concerned about the domestic interest rate because it affects investment, for example, the additional policy tool would not necessarily increase the set of attractive policy options. Imperfect substitutability was exploited by central banks under Bretton Woods, but it did not get countries out of the policy dilemmas illustrated in the text.

adjustment is called an **expenditure-switching policy** because it changes the *direction* of demand, shifting it between domestic output and imports. In general, both expenditure changing and expenditure switching are needed to reach internal and external balance. Apart from monetary policy, fiscal policy is the main government lever for pushing total domestic expenditure up or down.

Under the Bretton Woods rules, exchange rate changes (expenditure-switching policy) were supposed to be infrequent. This left fiscal policy as the main policy tool for moving the economy toward internal and external balance. But as Figure 19-2 shows, one instrument, fiscal policy, is generally insufficient to attain the two goals of internal and external balance. Only if the economy had been displaced horizontally from point 1 would fiscal policy be able to do the job alone. In addition, fiscal policy is an unwieldy tool, since it often cannot be implemented without legislative approval. Another drawback is that a fiscal expansion, for example, might have to be reversed after some time if it leads to chronic government budget deficits.

As a result of the exchange rate's inflexibility during the Bretton Woods period, policy makers sometimes found themselves in difficult situations. With the spending level and exchange rate indicated by point 2 in Figure 19-3, there is underemployment and an excessive current account deficit. Only the combination of devaluation and spending expansion indicated in the figure moves the economy to internal and external balance (point 1). Expansionary fiscal policy, acting alone, can eliminate the unemployment by moving the economy to point 3, but the cost of reduced unemployment is a larger external deficit. While contractionary fiscal policy alone can bring about external balance (point 4), output falls as a result and the economy moves further from internal balance. It is no wonder that policy dilemmas such as the one at point 2 gave rise to suspicions that the currency was about to be devalued. Devaluation improves the current account and aggregate demand by raising the real

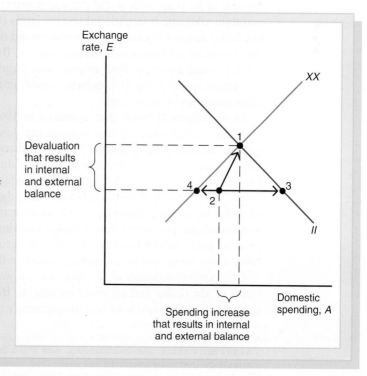

FIGURE 19-3

Policies to Bring about Internal and External Balance

Unless the currency is devalued and the level of domestic spending rises, internal and external balance (point 1) cannot be reached. Acting alone, a change in fiscal policy, for example, enables the economy to attain *either* internal balance (point 3) *or* external balance (point 4), but only at the cost of increasing the economy's distance from the goal that is sacrificed.

exchange rate EP^*/P in one stroke; the alternative is a long and politically unpopular period of unemployment to bring about an equal rise in the real exchange rate through a fall in P.[23]

In practice, countries did sometimes use changes in their exchange rates to move closer to internal and external balance, although the changes were typically accompanied by balance of payments crises. Many countries also tightened controls on financial account transactions to sever the links between domestic and foreign interest rates and make monetary policy more effective (in line with the trilemma). In this they were only partly successful, as the events leading to the breakdown of the system were to prove.

The External Balance Problem of the United States under Bretton Woods

The external balance problem of the United States was different from the one faced by the other countries in the Bretton Woods system. As the issuer of the Nth currency, the United States was not responsible for pegging dollar exchange rates. Its main responsibility was to hold the dollar price of gold at $35 an ounce and, in particular, to guarantee that foreign central banks could convert their dollar holdings into gold at that price. For this purpose, it had to hold sufficient gold reserves.

Because the United States was required to trade gold for dollars with foreign central banks, the possibility that other countries might convert their dollar reserves into gold was a potential external constraint on U.S. macroeconomic policy. In practice, however, foreign central banks were willing to hold on to the dollars they accumulated, since these paid interest and were international money *par excellence*. And the logic of the gold exchange standard dictated that foreign central banks should continue to accumulate dollars. Because world gold supplies were not growing quickly enough to keep up with world economic growth, the only way central banks could maintain adequate international reserve levels (barring deflation) was by accumulating dollar assets. Official gold conversions did occur on occasion, and these depleted the American gold stock and caused concern. But as long as most central banks were willing to add dollars to their reserves and forgo the right of redeeming those dollars for American gold, the U.S. external constraint appeared looser than that faced by other countries in the system.

In an influential book that appeared in 1960, economist Robert Triffin of Yale University called attention to a fundamental long-run problem of the Bretton Woods system, the **confidence problem**.[24] Triffin realized that as central banks' international reserve needs grew over time, their holdings of dollars would necessarily grow until they exceeded the U.S. gold stock. Since the United States had promised to redeem these dollars at $35 an ounce, it would no longer have the ability to meet its obligations should all dollar holders simultaneously try to convert their dollars into gold. This would lead to a confidence problem: Central banks, knowing that their dollars were no longer "as good as gold," might become unwilling to accumulate more dollars and might even bring down the system by attempting to cash in the dollars they already held.

One possible solution at the time was an increase in the official price of gold in terms of the dollar and all other currencies. But such an increase would have been inflationary and would have had the politically unattractive consequence of enriching

---

[23]As an exercise to test your understanding, show that a fall in P, all else equal, lowers both II and XX, moving point 1 vertically downward.

[24]See Triffin, *Gold and the Dollar Crisis* (New Haven: Yale University Press, 1960).

the main gold-supplying countries. Further, an increase in gold's price would have caused central banks to expect further decreases in the gold value of their dollar reserve holdings in the future, thereby possibly worsening the confidence problem rather than solving it!

CASE STUDY

The End of Bretton Woods, Worldwide Inflation, and the Transition to Floating Rates

By the late 1960s, the Bretton Woods system of fixed exchange rates was beginning to show strains that would soon lead to its collapse. These strains were closely related to the special position of the United States, where inflation was gathering strength because of higher monetary growth as well as higher government spending on new social programs such as Medicare and on the unpopular Vietnam War.

The acceleration of American inflation in the late 1960s was a worldwide phenomenon. Table 19-1 shows that by the start of the 1970s, inflation had also broken out in European economies.[25] The worldwide nature of the inflation problem was no accident. The theory in Chapter 18 predicts that when the reserve currency country speeds up its monetary growth, as the United States did in the second half of the 1960s, one effect is an automatic increase in monetary growth rates and inflation abroad as foreign central banks purchase the reserve currency to maintain their exchange rates and expand their money supplies in the process. One interpretation of the Bretton Woods system's collapse is that foreign countries were forced to *import* unwelcome U.S. inflation through the mechanism described in Chapter 18. To stabilize their price levels and regain internal balance, they had to abandon fixed exchange rates and allow their currencies to float. The monetary trilemma implies that these countries could not simultaneously peg their exchange rates and control domestic inflation.

TABLE 19-1	Inflation Rates in Industrial Countries, 1966–1972 (percent per year)						
Country	**1966**	**1967**	**1968**	**1969**	**1970**	**1971**	**1972**
Britain	3.6	2.6	4.6	5.2	6.5	9.7	6.9
France	2.8	2.8	4.4	6.5	5.3	5.5	6.2
Germany	3.4	1.4	2.9	1.9	3.4	5.3	5.5
Italy	2.1	2.1	1.2	2.8	5.1	5.2	5.3
United States	2.9	3.1	4.2	5.5	5.7	4.4	3.2

Source: Organization for Economic Cooperation and Development. *Main Economic Indicators: Historical Statistics, 1964–1983*. Paris: OECD, 1984. Figures are percentage increases in each year's average consumer price index over that of the previous year.

---

[25]The U.S. inflation numbers for 1971 and 1972 are artificially low because of President Nixon's resort to government-administered wage and price controls in August 1971. In principle, the U.S. commitment to peg the market price of gold should have limited U.S. inflation, but in practice, the United States was able to weaken that commitment over time, thus allowing the *market* price of gold to rise while still holding to the promise to redeem dollars from central banks at $35 per ounce. By the late 1960s, the United States was therefore the unique country in the system in that it did not face the full monetary trilemma. It enjoyed fixed exchange rates because *other* countries pegged their currencies to the dollar, yet it could still orient monetary policy toward domestic goals. For recent assessments of the worldwide inflation of the 1970s, see Michael Bordo and Athanasios Orphanides, eds., *The Great Inflation* (Chicago: University of Chicago Press, 2013).

Adding to the tensions, the U.S. economy entered a recession in 1970, and as unemployment rose, markets became increasingly convinced that the dollar would have to be devalued against all the major European currencies. To restore full employment and a balanced current account, the United States somehow had to bring about a real depreciation of the dollar. That real depreciation could be brought about in two ways: The first option was a fall in the U.S. price level in response to domestic unemployment, coupled with a rise in foreign price levels in response to continuing purchases of dollars by foreign central banks. The second option was a fall in the dollar's nominal value in terms of foreign currencies. The first route—unemployment in the United States and inflation abroad—seemed a painful one for policy makers to follow. The markets rightly guessed that a change in the dollar's value was inevitable. This realization led to massive sales of dollars in the foreign exchange market.

After several unsuccessful attempts to stabilize the system (including a unilateral U.S. decision in August 1971 to end completely the dollar's link to gold), the main industrialized countries allowed their dollar exchange rates to float in March 1973.[26] Floating was viewed at the time as a temporary response to unmanageable speculative capital movements. But the interim arrangements adopted in March 1973 turned out to be permanent and marked the end of fixed exchange rates and the beginning of a turbulent new period in international monetary relations.

The Mechanics of Imported Inflation

To understand how inflation can be imported from abroad unless exchange rates are adjusted, look again at the graphical picture of internal and external balance shown in Figure 19-2. Suppose the home country is faced with foreign inflation. Above, the foreign price level, P^*, was assumed to be given; now, however, P^* rises as a result of inflation abroad. Figure 19-4 shows the effect on the home economy.

You can see how the two schedules shift by asking what would happen if the nominal exchange rate were to fall in proportion to the rise in P^*. In this case, the real exchange rate EP^*/P would be unaffected (given P), and the economy would remain in internal balance or in external balance if either of these conditions originally held. Figure 19-4 therefore shows that for a given initial exchange rate, a rise in P^* shifts both II^1 and XX^1 downward by the same distance (approximately equal to the proportional increase in P^* times the initial exchange rate). The intersection of the new schedules II^2 and XX^2 (point 2) lies directly below the original intersection at point 1.

If the economy starts out at point 1, a rise in P^* *given* the fixed exchange rate and the domestic price level therefore strands the economy in zone 1 with overemployment and an undesirably high surplus in its current account. The factor that causes this outcome is a real currency depreciation that shifts world demand toward the home country (EP^*/P rises because P^* rises).

If nothing is done by the government, overemployment puts upward pressure on the domestic price level, and this pressure gradually shifts the two schedules back to their original positions. The schedules stop shifting once P has risen in proportion to

---

[26]Many developing countries continued to peg to the dollar, and a number of European countries were continuing to peg their mutual exchange rates as part of an informal arrangement called the "snake." The snake evolved into the European Monetary System (discussed in Chapter 21) and ultimately led to Europe's single currency, the euro.

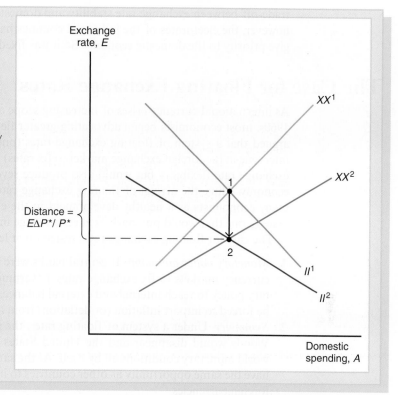

FIGURE 19-4

Effect on Internal and External Balance of a Rise in the Foreign Price Level, P*

After P* rises, point 1 is in zone 1 (overemployment and an excessive surplus). Revaluation (a fall in E) restores balance immediately by moving the policy setting to point 2.

P*. At this stage, the real exchange rate, employment, and the current account are at their initial levels, so point 1 is once again a position of internal and external balance.

The way to avoid the imported inflation is to revalue the currency (that is, lower E) and move to point 2. A revaluation restores internal and external balance immediately, without domestic inflation, by using the nominal exchange rate to offset the effect of the rise in P* on the real exchange rate. Only an expenditure-switching policy is needed to respond to a pure increase in foreign prices.

The rise in domestic prices that occurs when no revaluation takes place requires a rise in the domestic money supply, since prices and the money supply move proportionally in the long run. The mechanism that brings this rise about is foreign exchange intervention by the home central bank. As domestic output and prices rise after the rise in P*, the real money supply shrinks and the demand for real money holdings increases. To prevent the resulting upward pressure on the home interest rate from appreciating the currency, the central bank must purchase international reserves and expand the home money supply. In this way, inflationary policies pursued by the reserve center spill over into foreign countries' money supplies.

Assessment

The collapse of the Bretton Woods system was partly due to the lopsided macroeconomic power of the United States, which allowed it to generate global inflation. But it was also due in large measure to the fact that the key expenditure-switching tool needed for internal and external balance—discrete exchange rate adjustment—inspired speculative attacks that made both internal and external balance progressively more difficult to achieve. The system thus was a victim of the trilemma. As international financial flows became harder to restrain, policy makers faced an increasingly sharp trade-off between exchange rate stability and domestic monetary goals. By the 1970s, however, the electorates of the industrial counties had long expected governments to give priority to the domestic economy. So it was fixed exchange rates that gave way.

The Case for Floating Exchange Rates

As international currency crises of increasing scope and frequency erupted in the late 1960s, most economists began advocating greater flexibility of exchange rates. Many argued that a system of floating exchange rates (one in which central banks do not intervene in the foreign exchange market to fix rates) would not only deliver necessary exchange rate flexibility but would also produce several other benefits for the world economy. Thus, the arrival of floating exchange rates in March 1973 was hailed by many economists as a healthy development in the evolution of the world monetary system, one that would put markets at center stage in determining exchange rates.

The case for floating exchange rates rested on at least four major claims:

1. *Monetary policy autonomy.* If central banks were no longer obliged to intervene in currency markets to fix exchange rates, governments would be able to use monetary policy to reach internal and external balance. Furthermore, no country would be forced to import inflation (or deflation) from abroad.
2. *Symmetry.* Under a system of floating rates, the inherent asymmetries of Bretton Woods would disappear and the United States would no longer be able to set world monetary conditions all by itself. At the same time, the United States would have the same opportunity as other countries to influence its exchange rate against foreign currencies.
3. *Exchange rates as automatic stabilizers.* Even in the absence of an active monetary policy, the swift adjustment of market-determined exchange rates would help countries maintain internal and external balance in the face of changes in aggregate demand. The long and agonizing periods of speculation preceding exchange rate realignments under the Bretton Woods rules would not occur under floating.
4. *Exchange rates and external balance.* Market-determined exchange rates would move automatically so as to prevent the emergence of big current account deficits and surpluses.

Monetary Policy Autonomy

Toward the end of the Bretton Woods fixed-rate system, countries other than the United States had little scope to use monetary policy to attain internal and external balance. Countries could hold their dollar exchange rates fixed only if they kept the domestic interest rate in line with that of the United States. Thus, in the closing years of fixed exchange rates, central banks imposed increasingly stringent restrictions on international payments to keep control over their interest rates and money supplies. However, these restrictions were only partially successful in strengthening monetary policy, and they had the damaging side effect of distorting international trade.

Advocates of floating rates pointed out that removal of the obligation to peg currency values would restore monetary control to central banks. If, for example, the central bank faced unemployment and wished to expand its money supply in response, there would no longer be any legal barrier to the currency depreciation this would cause. Similarly, the central bank of an overheated economy could cool down activity by contracting the money supply without worrying that undesired reserve inflows would undermine its stabilization effort. Enhanced control over monetary policy would allow countries to dismantle their distorting barriers to international payments. In other words, floating rates implied an approach to the monetary trilemma that sacrificed fixed exchange rates in favor of freedom of financial flows and of monetary policy.

Consistent with this view, advocates of floating also argued that floating rates would allow each country to choose its own desired long-run inflation rate rather than having to import passively the inflation rate established abroad. We saw in the last chapter that a country faced with a rise in the foreign price level will be thrown out of balance and ultimately will import the foreign inflation if it holds its exchange rate fixed. By the end of the 1960s, many countries felt that they were importing inflation from the United States. By revaluing its currency—that is, by lowering the domestic currency price of foreign currency—a country can insulate itself completely from an inflationary increase in foreign prices, and so remain in internal and external balance. One of the most telling arguments in favor of floating rates was their ability, in theory, to bring about automatically exchange rate changes that insulate economies from ongoing foreign inflation.

The mechanism behind this insulation is purchasing power parity (see Chapter 16). Recall that when all changes in the world economy are monetary, PPP holds true in the long run: Exchange rates eventually move to offset exactly national differences in inflation. If U.S. monetary growth leads to a long-run doubling of the U.S. price level while Europe's price level remains constant, PPP predicts that the long-run euro price of the dollar will be halved. This nominal exchange rate change leaves the *real* exchange rate between the dollar and the euro unchanged and thus maintains Europe's internal and external balance. In other words, the long-run exchange rate change predicted by PPP is exactly the change that insulates Europe from U.S. inflation.

A money-induced increase in U.S. prices also causes an *immediate* appreciation of foreign currencies against the dollar when the exchange rate floats. In the short run, the size of this appreciation can differ from what PPP predicts, but the foreign exchange speculators who might have mounted an attack on fixed dollar exchange rates speed the adjustment of floating rates. Since they know foreign currencies will appreciate according to PPP in the long run, they act on their expectations and push exchange rates in the direction of their long-run levels.

In contrast, countries operating under the Bretton Woods rules were forced to choose between matching U.S. inflation to hold their dollar exchange rates fixed or deliberately revaluing their currencies in proportion to the rise in U.S. prices. Under floating, however, the foreign exchange market automatically brings about exchange rate changes that shield countries from U.S. inflation. Since this outcome does not require any government policy decisions, the revaluation crises that occurred under fixed exchange rates are avoided.[27]

Symmetry

The second argument put forward by the advocates of floating was that abandonment of the Bretton Woods system would remove the asymmetries that caused so much international disagreement in the 1960s and early 1970s. There were two main asymmetries, both the result of the dollar's central role in the international monetary system. First, because central banks pegged their currencies to the dollar and accumulated dollars as international reserves, the U.S. Federal Reserve played the leading role in determining the world money supply, and central banks abroad had little scope

---

[27]Countries can also avoid importing undesired *deflation* by floating, since the analysis above applies, in reverse, for a fall in the foreign price level.

to determine their own domestic money supplies. Second, any foreign country could devalue its currency against the dollar in conditions of "fundamental disequilibrium," but the system's rules did not give the United States the option to devalue against foreign currencies. Rather, dollar devaluation required a long and economically disruptive period of multilateral negotiation.

A system of floating exchange rates would do away with these asymmetries. Since countries would no longer peg dollar exchange rates, each would be in a position to guide monetary conditions at home. For the same reason, the United States would not face any special obstacle to altering its exchange rate through monetary or fiscal policies. All countries' exchange rates would be determined symmetrically by the foreign exchange market, not by government decisions.[28]

Exchange Rates as Automatic Stabilizers

The third argument in favor of floating rates concerned their ability, theoretically, to promote swift and relatively painless adjustment to certain types of economic changes. One such change, previously discussed, is foreign inflation. Figure 19-5, which uses the DD-AA model presented in Chapter 17, examines another type of change by comparing an economy's response under a fixed and a floating exchange rate to a temporary fall in foreign demand for its exports.

A fall in demand for the home country's exports reduces aggregate demand for every level of the exchange rate, E, and thus shifts the DD schedule leftward from DD^1 to DD^2. (Recall that the DD schedule shows exchange rate and output pairs for which aggregate demand equals aggregate output.) Figure 19-5a shows how this shift affects the economy's equilibrium when the exchange rate floats. Because the demand shift is assumed to be temporary, it does not change the long-run expected exchange rate and so does not move the asset market equilibrium schedule AA^1. (Recall that the AA schedule shows exchange rate and output pairs at which the foreign exchange market and the domestic money market are in equilibrium.) The economy's short-run equilibrium is therefore at point 2; compared with the initial equilibrium at point 1, the currency depreciates (E rises) and output falls. Why does the exchange rate rise from E^1 to E^2? As demand and output fall, reducing the transactions demand for money, the home interest rate must also decline to keep the money market in equilibrium. This fall in the home interest rate causes the domestic currency to depreciate in the foreign exchange market, and the exchange rate therefore rises from E^1 to E^2.

The effect of the same export demand disturbance under a fixed exchange rate is shown in Figure 19-5b. Since the central bank must prevent the currency depreciation that occurs under a floating rate, it buys domestic money with foreign reserves, an action that contracts the money supply and shifts AA^1 left to AA^2. The new short-run equilibrium of the economy under a fixed exchange rate is at point 3, where output equals Y^3.

Figure 19-5 shows that output actually falls more under a fixed rate than under a floating rate, dropping all the way to Y^3 rather than Y^2. In other words, the movement of the floating exchange rate stabilizes the economy by reducing the shock's effect on employment relative to its effect under a fixed rate. Currency depreciation in the floating-rate case makes domestic goods and services cheaper when the demand for them falls, partly offsetting the initial reduction in demand. In addition to reducing

---

[28]The symmetry argument is not an argument against fixed-rate systems in general, but an argument against the specific type of fixed exchange rate system that broke down in the early 1970s. As we saw in Chapter 18, a fixed-rate system based on an international gold standard can be completely symmetric.

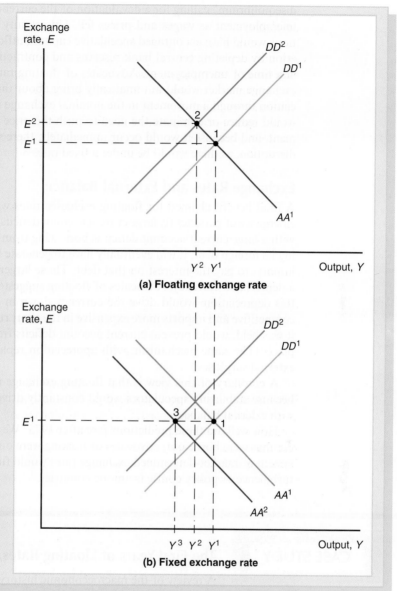

FIGURE 19-5

Effects of a Fall in Export Demand

The response to a fall in export demand (seen in the shift from DD^1 to DD^2) differs under floating and fixed exchange rates. (a) With a floating rate, output falls only to Y^2 as the currency's depreciation (from E^1 to E^2) shifts demand back toward domestic goods. (b) With the exchange rate fixed at E^1, output falls all the way to Y^3 as the central bank reduces the money supply (reflected in the shift from AA^1 to AA^2).

the departure from internal balance caused by the fall in export demand, the depreciation reduces the increased current account deficit that occurs under fixed rates by making domestic products more competitive in international markets.

We have considered the case of a transitory fall in export demand, but even stronger conclusions can be drawn when there is a *permanent* fall in export demand. In this case, the expected exchange rate E^e also rises and AA shifts upward as a result. A permanent shock causes a greater depreciation than does a temporary shock, and the movement of the exchange rate therefore cushions domestic output more when the shock is permanent.

Under the Bretton Woods system, a fall in export demand such as the one shown in Figure 19-5b would, if permanent, have led to a situation of "fundamental disequilibrium" calling for a devaluation of the currency or a long period of domestic unemployment as wages and prices fell. Uncertainty about the government's intentions would have encouraged speculative capital outflows, further worsening the situation by depleting central bank reserves and contracting the domestic money supply at a time of unemployment. Advocates of floating rates pointed out that the foreign exchange market would automatically bring about the required *real* currency depreciation through a movement in the nominal exchange rate. This exchange rate change would reduce or eliminate the need to push the price level down through unemployment, and because it would occur immediately, there would be no risk of speculative disruption, as there would be under a fixed rate.

Exchange Rates and External Balance

A final benefit claimed for floating exchange rates was that they would prevent the emergence of persistently large current account deficits or surpluses. Because a country with a large current account deficit is borrowing from foreigners and thereby increasing its foreign debt, it will eventually have to generate larger surpluses of exports over imports to pay the interest on that debt. Those larger surpluses, in turn, will require a depreciated currency. Advocates of floating suggested that speculators, anticipating this depreciation, would drive the currency down in advance, making exports more competitive and imports more expensive in the short run. Such stabilizing speculation, it was held, would prevent current account deficits from getting too large in the first place. (The same mechanism, with appreciation replacing depreciation, would limit external surpluses.)

A corollary of this view is that floating exchange rates would not be too volatile, because stabilizing speculators would constantly drive them toward levels consistent with external balance.

How well did these predictions fare after 1973? We shall show that while some predictions were borne out, advocates of floating were on the whole too optimistic that a system of market-determined exchange rates would function free of exchange market turbulence or policy conflicts among countries.

CASE STUDY

The First Years of Floating Rates, 1973–1990

A review of the macroeconomic history of the world economy since 1973 offers key data for judging the successes and shortcomings of the modern international monetary system. We begin with a summary of the first turbulent years of floating exchange rates.

INFLATION AND DISINFLATION, 1973–1982

The opening act of the floating exchange rate era was a quadrupling in the world price of petroleum between late 1973 and early 1974, engineered by the newly assertive Organization of Petroleum Exporting Countries (OPEC), an international cartel that includes most large oil producers. Consumption and investment slowed down everywhere and the world economy was thrown into recession. The current account balances of oil-importing countries worsened.

TABLE 19-2	Macroeconomic Data for Key Industrial Regions, 1963–2012					
Period	**1963–1972**	**1973–1982**	**1983–1992**	**1993–2006**	**2007–2009**	**2010–2012**
	Inflation (percent per year)					
United States	3.3	8.7	4.0	2.7	2.1	2.3
Europe	4.4	10.7	5.1	2.4	2.3	2.5
Japan	5.6	8.6	1.8	0.2	0.0	−0.3
	Unemployment (percent of labor force)					
United States	4.7	7.0	6.8	5.3	6.6	8.9
Europe	1.9	5.5	9.4	9.4	7.8	10.0
Japan	1.2	1.9	2.5	4.0	4.3	4.7
	Per Capita Real GDP Growth (percent per year)					
United States	2.8	0.9	2.4	2.1	−0.9	1.4
Europe	3.9	2.0	3.0	2.1	0.6	0.8
Japan	8.5	2.9	3.4	1.0	−3.8	2.1

Source: International Monetary Fund and Eurostat.

The model we developed in Chapters 14 through 18 predicts that inflation tends to rise in boom periods and fall in recessions. As the world went into deep recession in 1974, however, inflation accelerated in most countries. Table 19-2 shows how inflation in the main industrial regions spurted upward in the decade 1973–1982 even though unemployment was rising.

What happened? An important contributing factor was the oil shock itself: By directly raising the prices of petroleum products and the costs of energy-using industries, the increase in the oil price caused price levels to jump upward. Further, the worldwide inflationary pressures that had built up since the end of the 1960s had become entrenched in the wage-setting process and were continuing to contribute to inflation in spite of the deteriorating employment picture. The same inflationary expectations that were driving new wage contracts were also putting additional upward pressure on commodity prices as speculators built up stocks of commodities whose prices they expected to rise. Over the following years, central bankers proved unwilling to combat these inflationary pressures at the cost of yet-higher unemployment.

To describe the unusual macroeconomic conditions of 1974–1975, economists coined a new word that has since become commonplace: **stagflation**, a combination of stagnating output and high inflation. Stagflation was the result of two factors:

1. Increases in commodity prices that directly raised inflation while at the same time depressing aggregate demand and supply
2. Expectations of future inflation that fed into wages and other prices in spite of recession and rising unemployment

Freed of the need to defend a fixed exchange rate, governments responded with expansionary policies that further fueled inflation. Many countries, moving to a different vertex of the trilemma, had even been able to relax the capital controls they had set up before 1974. This relaxation eased the adjustment problem of the developing countries, which were able to borrow more easily from developed-country financial markets to maintain their own spending and economic growth. In turn, the relative strength of the developing world's demand for industrial-country exports helped mitigate the severity of the 1974–1975 recession. But in the industrial countries, unemployment nonetheless jumped upward and remained stubbornly high, as shown in Table 19-2.

In the mid-1970s, the United States attempted to combat this unemployment through expansionary monetary policy, whereas other countries such as Germany and Japan were more worried about inflation. The result of this policy imbalance— vigorous expansion in the United States that was unmatched by expansion abroad— was a steep depreciation of the dollar after 1976. U.S. inflation reached double-digit levels (as did inflation in a number of other countries, including Canada, France, Italy, and the United Kingdom). The depreciation of the dollar in these years is evident in Figure 19-6, which shows both **nominal and real effective exchange rate indexes** of the dollar. These indexes measure, respectively, the price of a dollar in terms of a basket of foreign currencies and the price of U.S. output in terms of a basket of foreign outputs. Thus, a rise in either index is a (nominal or real) dollar appreciation, while a fall is a depreciation.

To restore faith in the dollar, President Jimmy Carter appointed a new Federal Reserve Board chairman with broad experience in international financial affairs, Paul A. Volcker. The dollar began to strengthen in October 1979, when Volcker announced a tightening of U.S. monetary policy and the adoption by the Fed of more stringent procedures for controlling money supply growth.

The fall of the shah of Iran in 1979 sparked a second round of oil price increases by disrupting oil exports from that country. In 1975 macroeconomic policy makers in the industrial countries had responded to the first oil shock with expansionary monetary and fiscal policies. They responded very differently to this second oil shock.

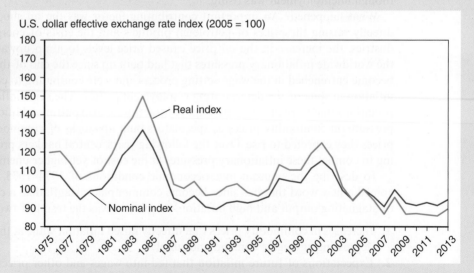

FIGURE 19-6

Nominal and Real Effective Dollar Exchange Rate Indexes, 1975–2013

The indexes are measures of the nominal and real value of the U.S. dollar in terms of a basket of foreign currencies. An increase in the indexes is a dollar appreciation, a decrease a dollar depreciation. For both indexes, the 2005 value is 100.

Source: International Monetary Fund, *International Financial Statistics*.

Over 1979 and 1980, monetary growth was actually *restricted* in most major industrial countries in an attempt to offset the rise in inflation accompanying the oil price increase. This policy approach prevented an upsurge in inflation, but helped cause a worldwide recession.

November 1980 saw the election of President Ronald Reagan, who had campaigned on an anti-inflation platform. In light of the election result and Volcker's monetary slowdown, the dollar's value soared (see Figure 19-6). U.S. interest rates had also risen sharply late in 1979; by 1981, short-term interest rates in the United States were nearly double their 1978 levels.

By pushing up the U.S. interest rate and causing investors to expect a stronger dollar in the future, the U.S. action led to an immediate appreciation of the dollar. This appreciation made U.S. goods more expensive relative to foreign goods, thereby reducing U.S. output.

The dollar's appreciation was not welcomed abroad, however, even though it could, in theory, have lent foreign economies some positive stimulus in a period of slow growth. The reason was that a stronger dollar hindered foreign countries in their own fights against inflation, both by raising the import prices they faced and by encouraging higher wage demands from their workers. A stronger dollar had the opposite effect in the United States, hastening the decline of inflation there. The tight U.S. monetary policy therefore had a beggar-thy-neighbor effect abroad, in that it lowered American inflation in part by exporting inflation to foreign economies.

Foreign central banks responded by intervening in the currency markets to slow the dollar's rise. Through the process of selling dollar reserves and buying their own currencies, some central banks reduced their monetary growth rates for 1980 and 1981, driving interest rates upward. Synchronized monetary contraction in the United States and abroad, following fast on the heels of the second oil shock, threw the world economy into a deep recession, the most severe between the Great Depression of the 1930s and the 2007–2009 crisis a generation later. In 1982 and 1983, unemployment throughout the world rose to levels unprecedented in the post–World War II period. While U.S. unemployment quickly returned to its pre-recession level, unemployment in Japan and especially in Europe remained permanently higher (see Table 19-2). Monetary contraction and the recession it brought quickly led, however, to a dramatic drop in the inflation rates of industrialized countries.

THE STRONG DOLLAR AND THE PLAZA ACCORD

During his election campaign, President Reagan had promised to lower taxes and balance the federal budget. He made good on the first of these promises in 1981. At the same time, the Reagan administration pushed for an acceleration of defense spending. The net result of these and subsequent congressional actions was a ballooning U.S. government budget deficit and a sharp fiscal stimulus to the economy. The U.S. fiscal stance encouraged continuing dollar appreciation (see Figure 19-6). By February 1985, the dollar's cumulative appreciation against the German currency since the end of 1979 was 47.9 percent. The recession reached its low point in the United States in December 1982, and output began to recover both there and abroad as the U.S. fiscal stimulus was transmitted to foreign countries through the dollar's steady appreciation.

While the U.S. fiscal expansion contributed to world recovery, growing federal budget deficits raised serious worries about the future stability of the world economy. Because increasing government deficits were not met with offsetting increases in private saving or decreases in investment, the American current account balance deteriorated sharply. By 1987, the United States had become a net debtor to foreign countries and its current account deficit was at the (then) postwar record level of 3.6 percent of GNP. Some analysts worried that foreign creditors would lose confidence in the future value of the dollar assets they were accumulating and sell them, causing a sudden, precipitous dollar depreciation.

Equally worrisome was the strong dollar's impact on the distribution of income within the United States. The dollar's appreciation had reduced U.S. inflation and allowed consumers to purchase imports more cheaply, but those hurt by the terms of trade change were better organized and more vocal than those who had benefited. Persistently poor economic performance in the 1980s had led to increased pressures on governments to protect industries in import-competing sectors. Protectionist pressures snowballed.

The Reagan administration had, from the start, adopted a policy of "benign neglect" toward the foreign exchange market, refusing to intervene except in unusual circumstances (for example, after a would-be assassin shot President Reagan). By 1985, however, the link between the strong dollar and the gathering protectionist storm became impossible to ignore.

Fearing a disaster for the international trading system, economic officials of the United States, Britain, France, Germany, and Japan announced at New York's Plaza Hotel on September 22, 1985, that they would jointly intervene in the foreign exchange market to bring about dollar depreciation. The dollar dropped sharply the next day and continued to decline through 1986 and early 1987 as the United States maintained a loose monetary policy and pushed dollar interest rates down relative to foreign currency interest rates. (See Figure 19-6.)

Macroeconomic Interdependence under a Floating Rate

Up until now, our modeling of the open economy has focused on the relatively simple case of a small country that cannot affect foreign output, price levels, or interest rates through its own monetary and fiscal policies. That description obviously does not fit the United States, however, with its national output level equal to about a fifth of the world's total product. To discuss macroeconomic interactions between the United States and the rest of the world, we therefore must think about the transmission of policies between countries linked by a floating exchange rate. We will offer a brief and intuitive discussion rather than a formal model, and restrict ourselves to the short run, in which we can assume that nominal output prices are fixed.

Imagine a world economy made up of two large countries, Home and Foreign. Our goal is to evaluate how Home's macroeconomic policies affect Foreign. The main complication is that neither country can be thought of any longer as facing a fixed external interest rate or a fixed level of foreign export demand. To simplify, we consider only the case of *permanent* shifts in monetary and fiscal policy.

Let's look first at a permanent monetary expansion by Home. We know that in the small-country case (Chapter 17), Home's currency would depreciate and its output would rise. The same happens when Home's economy is large, but now, the rest of the world is affected too. Because Home is experiencing real currency depreciation, Foreign must be experiencing real currency *appreciation*, which makes Foreign goods relatively expensive and thus has a depressing effect on Foreign output. The increase in Home output, however, works in the opposite direction, since Home spends some of its extra income on Foreign goods and, on that account, aggregate demand for Foreign output rises. Home's monetary expansion therefore has two opposing effects on Foreign output, with the net result depending on which effect is the stronger. Foreign output may rise or fall.[29]

Next let's think about a permanent expansionary fiscal policy in Home. In the small-country case of Chapter 17, a permanent fiscal expansion caused a real currency appreciation and a current account deterioration that fully nullified any positive effect on aggregate demand. In effect, the expansionary impact of Home's fiscal ease leaked entirely abroad (because the counterpart of Home's lower current account balance must be a higher current account balance abroad). In the large-country case, Foreign output still rises, since Foreign's exports become relatively cheaper when Home's currency appreciates. In addition, now some of Foreign's increased spending increases Home exports, so Home's output actually does increase along with Foreign's.[30]

We summarize our discussion of macroeconomic interdependence between large countries as follows:

1. *Effect of a permanent monetary expansion by Home.* Home output rises, Home's currency depreciates, and Foreign output may rise or fall.
2. *Effect of a permanent fiscal expansion by Home.* Home output rises, Home's currency appreciates, and Foreign output rises.

CASE STUDY

Transformation and Crisis in the World Economy

The fall of the Berlin Wall in 1989 marked the beginning of the end of the Soviet empire. Ultimately, the former Soviet bloc countries would embrace market structures and enter the world economy. At the same time, China was continuing a gradual process of market-oriented reforms begun in 1978, reforms that were starting to lead to rapid economic growth and modernization. These simultaneous changes would greatly increase the size of the global economy and labor force by the turn of the century.

CRISES IN EUROPE AND ASIA, 1990–1999

The reunification of West and East Germany on July 1, 1990, set off inflationary pressures in Germany. At the same time, other European countries were pegging their exchange rates to Germany's former currency, the deutsche mark (DM), within

---

[29]The Foreign money market equilibrium condition is $M^*/P^* = L(R^*, Y^*)$. Because M^* is not changing and P^* is sticky and therefore fixed in the short run, Foreign output can rise only if the Foreign nominal interest rate rises too and can fall only if the Foreign nominal interest rate falls.

[30]By considering the Home money market equilibrium condition (in analogy to the previous footnote), you will see that Home's nominal interest rate must rise. A parallel argument shows that Foreign's interest rate rises at the same time.

the European Union's fixed exchange rate mechanism, the European Monetary System (EMS). Germany's contractionary monetary response to its internal inflation pressures led to slower growth in its EMS partners, many of whom were not afflicted by rising inflation as Germany was. The resulting asymmetric pressures within the EMS led to a massive speculative attack on the EMS fixed parities in 1992.

Japanese inflation rose in 1989, in part the result of a relatively loose monetary policy from 1986 to 1988 designed to avoid further yen appreciation after the sharp post-Plaza Accord rise. Two very visible symptoms of these pressures were skyrocketing prices for Japanese real estate and stocks. The Bank of Japan's strategy of puncturing these asset price bubbles through restrictive monetary policy and high interest rates succeeded well, and Tokyo's Nikkei stock price index lost more than half its value between 1990 and 1992. Unfortunately, the sharp fall in asset prices threw Japan's banking system into crisis and the economy into recession by early 1992.

Recovery never really took hold. By 1998, the Japanese economy seemed to be in free fall, with shrinking GDP, declining prices, and its highest unemployment level in more than four decades. Japan's deflation and stagnation would prove protracted indeed, lasting with little interruption through the following decade and a half.

In 1997–1998, however, the problems of the Japanese economy spilled over to the developing countries in East Asia, with which it trades heavily. As we shall see in Chapter 22, many of these economies had experienced spectacularly rapid rates of GDP growth for many years through 1997. Many of them also held their exchange rates fixed, or in target ranges, against the U.S. dollar. Japan's slowdown in 1997 therefore weakened the East Asian economies.

The eventual result was a cascading series of speculative attacks on East Asian currencies, beginning with Thailand's baht in the spring of 1997 and moving on to Malaysia, Indonesia, and Korea. These economies fell into deep recessions (as we discuss further in Chapter 22), pulled down by Japan but also pulling Japan down in a vicious circle. Russia defaulted on its internal and external debts in 1998, setting off global investor jitters and domestic financial chaos. The fear of a worldwide depression prompted a series of interest rate cuts by the Federal Reserve, as well as an unprecedented coordinated interest rate cut by the 11 European countries preparing to give up their national currencies in 1999 in favor of the euro. These measures helped to avert a global economic meltdown.

THE DOT-COM CRASH AND THE EMERGENCE OF GLOBAL IMBALANCES

The U.S. stock market soared in the late 1990s as money flooded into high-tech, "dot-com" stocks related to new, Internet-based technologies. Investment rose and the U.S. current account deficit swelled. When stock prices began to collapse in 2000, helping to create a recession, the Federal Reserve cut interest rates aggressively. Despite a fall in investment, the U.S. current account deficit was soon on the rise again because of falling saving. One factor reducing U.S. saving was a rapid increase in real estate prices, illustrated in Figure 19-7. Interest rates were low, and as Americans borrowed against their rising home equity values, the net U.S. household saving rate turned negative. As a result, the U.S. current account deficit reached an unprecedented 6 percent of GDP by the middle of the decade (see Figure 13-2), and the dollar began to depreciate (see Figure 19-6). Real estate prices escalated as well in many countries outside the United States, ranging from the United Kingdom to Spain to Estonia, and these countries, like the United States, also tended to run bigger trade deficits.

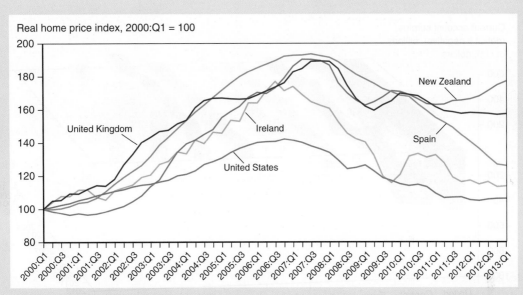

Real home price index, 2000:Q1 = 100

FIGURE 19-7   MyEconLab Real-time data

Real Home Prices in Selected Countries, 2000–2013

Home prices in the United States rose at an accelerating pace through 2006 before collapsing. However, the pace of price increase was even greater in a number of other countries.

Source: Federal Reserve Bank of Dallas, from http://www.dallasfed.org/institute/houseprice/index.cfm. Nominal home price index is divided by a personal consumption price deflator to obtain the real index.

Indeed, during the years after 1999, the pattern of global external imbalances widened sharply. Figure 19-8 gives a picture of this process. It is useful to think of the negative entries in the figure (the deficit entries) as showing net demands for global savings, while the positive entries (the surplus entries) show net supplies of savings (saving in excess of domestic investment needs). In an equilibrium for the global financial markets, the worldwide demand for savings equals the worldwide supply, which is another way of saying that the current account balances of all countries must add up to zero.

On the demand side, the dramatic explosion of the U.S. current account deficit was the dominant development. Because the current account equals saving minus investment, a large U.S. deficit meant that American investment (in effect, a demand for savings) far exceeded the supply of savings generated by American households, firms, and governmental units. Also contributing to the global demand for savings, though on a much smaller scale, was the investment-driven demand coming from the rapidly developing countries of Central and Eastern Europe (see Figure 19-8).

The puzzling feature of the data is that, as the U.S. deficit widened—reflecting an *increase* in American demand for the world's savings—the U.S. real long-term interest rate *fell*, continuing a process that had begun around 2000 when the dot-com crash reduced investment demand and market expectations of future economic growth (see Figure 19-9). Lower real interest rates helped drive American home prices higher, encouraging people to borrow against home equity and spend more out of national income, as noted above. It would seem more natural, instead, for real interest rates to

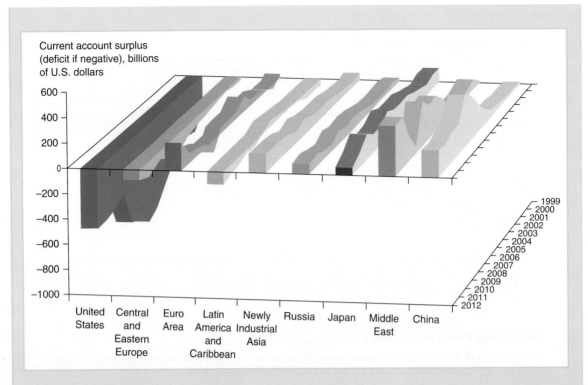

Current account surplus (deficit if negative), billions of U.S. dollars

FIGURE 19-8

Global External Imbalances, 1999–2012

During the 2000s, the large increase in the U.S. current account deficit was financed by increases in the surpluses of Asian countries (notably China), Latin America, and oil exporters. After 2007 the imbalances shrank but remained substantial.

Source: International Monetary Fund, *World Economic Outlook* database.

have *risen*, encouraging U.S. saving and discouraging U.S. investment. How could the opposite, a fall in real interest rates, have happened? Why, moreover, was this phenomenon also seen in other countries, as shown in Figure 19-9? The answer must lie in a change in saving and investment behavior outside of the United States.

Figure 19-8 shows that over the 2000s, current account surpluses rose in Russia, the Middle East, Asia (notably China, but also Japan and newly industrialized countries such as Singapore and Taiwan), and Latin America. The surplus of Africa (not shown in the figure) also increased. Economists still debate the causes of these surpluses, but a number of likely factors stand out. One of these was the emergence of China as a major player in the world economy, especially after it joined the World Trade Organization in December 2001. Growth in the private Chinese economy starting in the late 1970s led to very rapid economic expansion, but also to economic disruption for much of the country's huge population—for example, a reduction in social benefits such as health care, which state-owned firms had earlier supplied. As a precautionary measure, the Chinese saved more than they had in the past. At the same time, China's torrid economic growth (coupled with rather strong growth in the United States) increased the prices of a range of primary commodities, notably petroleum. The revenues from exporting Brazilian soybeans and iron, Malaysian palm oil, and Russian,

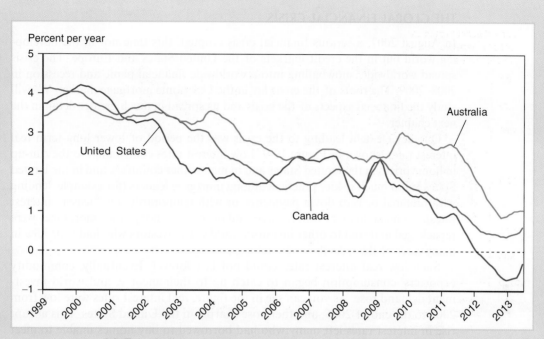

FIGURE 19-9   MyEconLab   Real-time data

Long-Term Real Interest Rates for the United States, Australia, and Canada, 1999–2013

Real interest rates fell to low levels in the 2000s. Many countries followed the same trend.

Source: Global Financial Data. Real interest rates are six-month moving averages of monthly interest rate observations on ten-year inflation-indexed government bonds.

Venezuelan, Congolese, and Saudi petroleum all soared. These economic windfalls, running ahead of the recipients' abilities to spend or invest them, also helped to raise worldwide saving.

A second factor was at work in raising current account surpluses outside the United States. The economic and financial crises of the late 1990s had made poorer countries more cautious in their fiscal policies, and also reduced their willingness to invest. Similarly, economic uncertainty in Japan depressed investment demand there. One result of more conservative economic policies in the developing world was the rapid accumulation of U.S. dollar reserves as mentioned previously, an outcome that provided these poorer countries with a welcome cushion against possible future economic misfortunes.

To summarize, the higher supply of savings from countries outside of the United States, coupled with generally lower investment demand, more than offset the effects on the global financial markets of the higher American current account deficit. The result was a fall in global interest rates, which contributed to global house-price appreciation.[31]

---

[31]Problem 13 at the end of this chapter suggests a simple economic framework that will help you think through the effects of shifts in the world's demand and supply curves for savings. The article by Ben Bernanke in Further Readings offers a detailed analysis of the low real interest rates of the mid-2000s.

THE GLOBAL FINANCIAL CRISIS

In August 2007, a serious financial crisis erupted, this time not in the developing world but in the credit markets of the United States and Europe. The crisis spread worldwide, snowballing into a worldwide financial panic and recession in 2008–2009. The roots of the crisis lay in the U.S. home mortgage market. We will study the financial aspects of the crisis and its spread in much greater detail in the next chapter.

One key element leading to the crisis was the period of lower long-term real interest rates, shown in Figure 19-9. Low interest rates contributed to the run-up in home prices in the United States and in many other countries, and in the United States led to much riskier practices among mortgage lenders (for example, lending with minimal or zero down payments, or with temporarily low "teaser" interest rates). To make matters worse, these "subprime" or "nonprime" mortgages were repackaged and sold to other investors worldwide, investors who had little idea in many cases of the risks they were taking on.

Such low real interest rates could not last forever. Eventually, commodity exporters' consumption began to catch up to their income, and world investment demand rose. As you can see in the figure, real interest rates were low from 2003 to the end of 2005, and then rose sharply in the United States. This abrupt rise in interest rates left many who had borrowed to buy homes unable to meet their monthly mortgage payments. In turn, the homeowners' creditors ran into trouble, and the credit crisis of 2007 erupted. At higher interest rate levels, many of the subprime home loans made earlier in the 2000s by aggressive mortgage lenders started to look as if they would never be repaid. The lenders (including banks around the world) then encountered serious difficulties in borrowing themselves.

Despite interest rate cuts by many central banks and other financial interventions aimed at aiding their economies, the world slipped into recession. The recession deepened dramatically as the financial crisis itself intensified in the autumn of 2008 (for details see Chapter 20). Global trade contracted at a rate initially more rapid than during first stage of the Great Depression.[32] Major countries, including the United States and China, rolled out large fiscal stimulus programs while central banks, in many cases, pushed their target nominal interest rates close to zero. (Figure 14-2 shows the interest rates in the United States and Japan.) While these policies prevented the world economy from going into free fall, unemployment rose sharply the world over (see Table 19-2), and output generally contracted in 2009. By 2010, the world economy had stabilized, but growth remained tepid in the industrial world, unemployment was slow to decline, and the recession left many governments with sharply higher fiscal deficits that could not be sustained indefinitely. Global current account imbalances declined but remained significant. In the years following 2009, much of the developing world recovered more robustly from the crisis than did the industrial world,

---

[32]For a fascinating comparison of 2008 and its aftermath with the Great Depression of the interwar period, see Barry Eichengreen and Kevin Hjortshøj O'Rourke, "What Do the New Data Tell Us?" *Vox: Research-Based Policy Analysis and Commentary from Leading Economists,* March 8, 2010 (at http://www.voxeu.org/article/tale-two-depressions-what-do-new-data-tell-us-february-2010-update#apr609).

but in the United States, Europe, and Japan, recovery from the worst global crisis since the Great Depression remained halting and fragile. Because industrial-country monetary policies remained ultra-loose long after developing countries began to worry again about inflation, developing-country currencies appreciated, causing problems for exporters in those countries. Policymakers in countries such as Brazil accused richer countries of launching "currency wars": easy monetary policies that were forcing poorer countries to choose between less competitive exchange rates and inflation.

In Japan, continuing deflation finally led in 2013, after more than two decades of lethargic economic growth, to an ambitious plan both to revitalize the economy and control a gross government debt that had grown to more than twice the size of GDP. One component of the plan was a Bank of Japan pledge to double the money supply quickly and thereby raise the rate of inflation. The ultimate success of this bold initiative is unknown at the time of writing. In developments that we will take up in Chapter 21, the euro area's recovery stalled and reversed as an existential crisis erupted late in 2009. The euro crisis was driven by the slow growth, unemployment, banking problems, and high public debts bequeathed by the 2007–2009 global crisis, and it also remains unresolved as of this writing.

What Has Been Learned Since 1973?

Earlier in this chapter, we outlined the main elements of the case for floating exchange rates. Having examined the events of the recent floating-rate period, we now briefly compare experience with the predictions made before 1973 by the proponents of floating.

Monetary Policy Autonomy

There is no question that floating gave central banks the ability to control their money supplies and to choose their preferred rates of trend inflation. As a result, floating exchange rates allowed a much larger international divergence in inflation. Did exchange depreciation offset inflation differentials between countries over the floating-rate period? Figure 19-10 compares domestic currency depreciation against the dollar with the difference between domestic and U.S. inflation for the six largest industrial market economies outside the United States. The PPP theory predicts that the points in the figure should lie along the 45-degree line, indicating proportional exchange rate and relative price level changes, but this is not exactly the case. While Figure 19-10 therefore confirms the lesson of Chapter 16 that PPP has not always held closely, even over long periods of time, it does show that on balance, high-inflation countries have tended to have weaker currencies than their low-inflation neighbors. Furthermore, most of the difference in depreciation rates is due to inflation differences, making PPP a major factor behind long-run nominal exchange rate variability.

While the inflation insulation part of the policy autonomy argument is broadly supported as a *long-run* proposition, economic analysis and experience both show that in the short run, the effects of monetary as well as fiscal changes are transmitted across national borders under floating rates. The two-country macroeconomic model

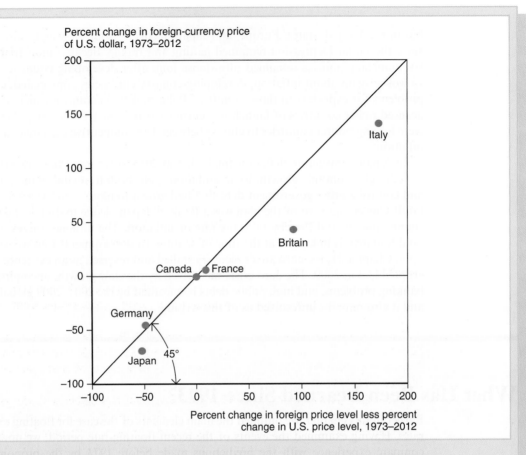

FIGURE 19-10

Exchange Rate Trends and Inflation Differentials, 1973–2012

Over the floating-rate period as a whole, higher inflation has been associated with greater currency depreciation. The exact relationship predicted by relative PPP, however, has not held for most countries. The inflation difference on the horizontal axis is calculated as $(\pi - \pi_{US}) \div (1 + \pi_{US}/100)$ using the exact relative PPP relation given in footnote 1 on page 448.

Source: International Monetary Fund and Global Financial Data.

developed earlier, for example, shows that monetary policy affects output in the short run both at home and abroad as long as it alters the real exchange rate. Skeptics of floating were therefore right in claiming that floating rates would not insulate countries completely from foreign policy shocks.

Symmetry

Because central banks continued to hold dollar reserves and intervene, the international monetary system did not become symmetric after 1973. The euro gained importance as an international reserve currency (and the British pound declined), but the dollar remained the primary component of most central banks' official reserves.

Economist Ronald McKinnon of Stanford University has argued that the current floating-rate system is similar in some ways to the asymmetric reserve currency system underlying the Bretton Woods arrangements.[33] He suggests that changes in the world money supply would have been dampened under a more symmetric monetary adjustment mechanism. In the 2000s, China's policy of limiting its currency's appreciation against the dollar led it to accumulate vast dollar reserves, possibly reinforcing the worldwide economic boom that preceded the 2007–2009 financial crisis. As a result, some economists have characterized the period of the early and mid-2000s as a "revived Bretton Woods system."[34]

The Exchange Rate as an Automatic Stabilizer

The world economy has undergone major structural changes since 1973. Because these shifts changed relative national output prices (Figure 19-6), it is doubtful that any pattern of fixed exchange rates would have been viable without some significant parity changes. The industrial economies certainly wouldn't have weathered the two oil shocks as well as they did while defending fixed exchange rates. In the absence of capital controls, speculative attacks similar to those that brought down the Bretton Woods system would have occurred periodically, as recent experience has shown. Under floating, however, many countries were able to relax the capital controls put in place earlier. The progressive loosening of controls spurred the rapid growth of a global financial industry and allowed countries to realize greater gains from intertemporal trade and from trade in assets.

The effects of the U.S. fiscal expansion after 1981 illustrate the stabilizing properties of a floating exchange rate. As the dollar appreciated, U.S. inflation was slowed, American consumers enjoyed an improvement in their terms of trade, and economic recovery was spread abroad.

The dollar's appreciation after 1981 also illustrates a problem with the view that floating rates can cushion the economy from real disturbances such as shifts in aggregate demand. Even though *overall* output and the price level may be cushioned, some sectors of the economy may be hurt. For example, while the dollar's appreciation helped transmit U.S. fiscal expansion abroad in the 1980s, it worsened the plight of American agriculture, which did not benefit directly from the higher government demand. Real exchange rate changes can do damage by causing excessive adjustment problems in some sectors and by generating calls for increased protection.

Permanent changes in goods market conditions require eventual adjustment in real exchange rates that can be speeded by a floating-rate system. Foreign exchange intervention to peg nominal exchange rates cannot prevent this eventual adjustment because money is neutral in the long run and thus is powerless to alter relative prices permanently. The events of the 1980s show, however, that if it is costly for factors of production to move between sectors of the economy, there is a case for pegging rates in the face of temporary output market shocks. Unfortunately, this lesson leaves policy makers with the difficult task of determining which disturbances are temporary and which are permanent.

External Balance

As Figure 19-8 makes clear, the floating exchange rate system did not prevent large and persistent departures from external balance. True, China's refusal to allow a free

---

[33]Ronald I. McKinnon, *An International Standard for Monetary Stabilization*, Policy Analyses in International Economics 8 (Washington, D.C.: Institute for International Economics, 1984).

[34]See Michael Dooley, David Folkerts-Landau, and Peter Garber, *International Financial Stability: Asia, Interest Rates, and the Dollar*, 2nd edition (New York: Deutsche Bank Securities Inc., 2008).

float of its own currency is part of the story of the large global imbalances of the 2000s. If the Chinese yuan had been free to appreciate in the foreign exchange market, China's surpluses and the corresponding deficits elsewhere in the world might have been smaller.

But even before China's emergence as a world economic power and before the creation of the euro, large current account deficits and surpluses, such as the U.S. deficit of the 1980s and Japan's persistent surpluses, certainly occurred. Financial markets were evidently capable of driving exchange rates far from values consistent with external balance, as suggested by Figure 19-6 for the case of the dollar. Under floating, external imbalances have persisted for years before exchange rates have adjusted. Long swings in real exchange rates that leave countries far from external balance are called *misalignments*, and they frequently inspire political pressures for protection from imports.

The Problem of Policy Coordination

Problems of international policy coordination clearly have not disappeared under floating exchange rates. The problem of resolving global imbalances provides a good example, in the sense that unilateral action by deficit countries to reduce their imbalances would lead to global deflation, while surplus countries have little incentive to avoid that outcome by pumping up their internal demand and appreciating their currencies.

There are other examples that are perhaps even more striking, in the sense that all countries would clearly benefit if they could commit to coordinating their policies rather than going it alone in beggar-thy-neighbor fashion. For example, during the disinflation of the early 1980s, industrial countries as a group could have attained their macroeconomic goals more effectively by negotiating a joint approach to common objectives. The appendix to this chapter presents a formal model, based on that example, to illustrate how all countries can gain through international policy coordination.

Another instance comes from the global fiscal response to the recession that the 2007–2009 crisis caused. We saw earlier in this chapter (and in Chapter 17) that when a country raises government spending, part of the expansionary impact leaks abroad. The country will pay the cost of the policy, however, in the form of a higher government deficit. Since countries do not internalize all the benefits of their own fiscal expansions but pay the cost in full, they will adopt too little of it in a global recession.

If countries could negotiate an agreement *jointly* to expand, however, they might be more effective in fighting the recession (and they might even experience lower fiscal costs). The response to the 2007–2009 crisis was discussed periodically by the Group of Twenty (G20) nations, an informal grouping of leading industrial and developing countries including Argentina, Brazil, China, India, and Russia. In the early stages of the crisis, there was widespread agreement on the fiscal response within the G20. Later on, as countries experienced more divergent rates of recovery, policy coordination became more difficult and G20 meetings yielded fewer concrete results.

Are Fixed Exchange Rates Even an Option for Most Countries?

Is there any practical alternative to floating exchange rates when financial markets are open to international trade? The post-Bretton Woods experience suggests a stark hypothesis: Durable fixed exchange rate arrangements may not even be *possible*. In a financially integrated world in which funds can move instantly between national financial markets, fixed exchange rates cannot be credibly maintained over the long run unless countries are willing to maintain controls over capital movements (as China does), or, at the other extreme, move to a shared single currency with their monetary partners (as in Europe). Short of these measures, the argument goes, attempts to fix exchange rates will necessarily lack credibility and be relatively short-lived. You will recognize that these predictions follow from the trilemma.[35]

This pessimistic view of fixed exchange rates is based on the theory that speculative currency crises can, at least in part, be self-fulfilling events (recall Chapter 18). According to that view, even a country following prudent monetary and fiscal policies is not safe from speculative attacks on its fixed exchange rate. Once the country encounters an economic reversal, as it eventually must, currency speculators will pounce, forcing domestic interest rates sky-high and inflicting enough economic pain that the government will choose to abandon its exchange rate target.

At the turn of the 21st century, speculative attacks on fixed exchange rate arrangements—in Europe, East Asia, and elsewhere—were occurring with seemingly increasing frequency. The number and circumstances of those crises lent increasing plausibility to the argument that it is impossible to peg currency values for long while maintaining open capital markets and national policy sovereignty. Moreover, many countries outside the industrial world have allowed much greater exchange rate flexibility in recent years, and apparently benefited from it, as we shall see in Chapter 22. Some countries appear to be moving toward either greater control over cross-border financial flows or more drastic sacrifices of monetary autonomy (for example, adopting the euro). It seems likely that policy coordination issues will be confronted in the future within a system in which different countries choose different policy regimes, subject to the constraints of the monetary trilemma.

SUMMARY

1. In an open economy, policy makers try to maintain *internal balance* (full employment and a stable price level) and *external balance* (a current account level that is neither so negative that the country may be unable to repay its foreign debts nor so positive that foreigners are put in that position). The definition of external balance depends on a number of factors, including the exchange rate regime and world economic conditions. Because each country's macroeconomic policies have repercussions abroad, a country's ability to reach internal and external balance depends on the policies other countries choose to adopt. A country running large, persistent deficits might appear to be violating its *intertemporal budget constraint*, putting it in danger of facing a *sudden stop* in foreign lending.

2. The limitations of alternative exchange rate regimes can be understood in terms of the open-economy *monetary trilemma*, which states that countries must choose

---

[35]For an early statement of the hypothesis that fixed exchange rates combined with mobile capital can be unstable, see Maurice Obstfeld, "Floating Exchange Rates: Experience and Prospects," *Brookings Papers on Economic Activity* 2 (1985), pp. 369–450. For more recent discussions see Barry Eichengreen, *International Monetary Arrangements for the 21st Century* (Washington, D.C.: Brookings Institution, 1994); Lars E. O. Svensson, "Fixed Exchange Rates as a Means to Price Stability: What Have We Learned?" *European Economic Review* 38 (May 1994), pp. 447–468; Maurice Obstfeld and Kenneth Rogoff, "The Mirage of Fixed Exchange Rates," *Journal of Economic Perspectives* 9 (Fall 1995), pp. 73–96; and the book by Klein and Shambaugh in Further Readings.

two of the following three features of a monetary policy system: exchange rate stability, freedom of cross-border financial flows, and monetary policy autonomy.

3. The gold standard system contained a powerful automatic mechanism for ensuring external balance, the *price-specie-flow mechanism.* The flows of gold accompanying deficits and surpluses caused price changes that reduced current account imbalances and therefore tended to return all countries to external balance. The system's performance in maintaining internal balance was mixed, however. With the eruption of World War I in 1914, the gold standard was suspended.

4. Attempts to return to the prewar gold standard after 1918 were unsuccessful. As the world economy moved into general depression after 1929, the restored gold standard fell apart, and international economic integration weakened. In the turbulent economic conditions of the period, governments made internal balance their main concern and tried to avoid the external balance problem by partially shutting their economies off from the rest of the world. The result was a world economy in which all countries' situations could have been bettered through international cooperation.

5. The architects of the *International Monetary Fund (IMF)* hoped to design a fixed exchange rate system that would encourage growth in international trade while making the demands of external balance sufficiently flexible that they could be met without sacrificing internal balance. To this end, the IMF charter provided financing facilities for deficit countries and allowed exchange rate adjustments under conditions of "fundamental disequilibrium." All countries pegged their currencies to the dollar. The United States pegged to gold and agreed to exchange gold for dollars with foreign central banks at a price of $35 an ounce.

6. After *currency convertibility* was restored in Europe in 1958, countries' financial markets became more closely integrated, monetary policy became less effective (except for the United States), and movements in international reserves became more volatile. These changes revealed a key weakness in the system. To reach internal and external balance at the same time, *expenditure-switching* as well as *expenditure-changing* policies were needed. But the possibility of expenditure-switching policies (exchange rate changes) could give rise to speculative financial flows that would undermine fixed exchange rates. As the main reserve currency country, the United States faced a unique external balance problem: the *confidence problem,* which would arise as foreign official dollar holdings inevitably grew to exceed U.S. gold holdings. A series of international crises led in stages to the abandonment by March 1973 of both the dollar's link to gold and fixed dollar exchange rates for the industrialized countries.

7. Before 1973, the weaknesses of the Bretton Woods system led many economists to advocate floating exchange rates. They made four main arguments in favor of floating. First, they argued that floating rates would give national macroeconomic policy makers greater autonomy in managing their economies. Second, they predicted that floating rates would remove the asymmetries of the Bretton Woods arrangements. Third, they pointed out that floating exchange rates would quickly eliminate the "fundamental disequilibriums" that had led to parity changes and speculative attacks under fixed rates. Fourth, they claimed that these same exchange rate movements would prevent large, persistent departures from external balance.

8. In the early years of floating, floating rates seemed, on the whole, to function well. In particular, it is unlikely that the industrial countries could have maintained fixed exchange rates in the face of the *stagflation* caused by two oil shocks. The

dollar suffered a sharp depreciation after 1976, however, as the United States adopted macroeconomic policies more expansionary than those of other industrial countries.

9. A sharp turn toward slower monetary growth in the United States, coupled with a rising U.S. government budget deficit, contributed to massive dollar appreciation between 1980 and early 1985. Other industrial economies pursued disinflation along with the United States, and the resulting worldwide monetary slowdown, coming soon after the second oil shock, led to a deep global recession. As the recovery from the recession slowed in late 1984 and the U.S. current account began to register record deficits, political pressure for wide-ranging trade restrictions gathered momentum in Washington. At the Plaza Hotel in New York in September 1985, the United States and four other major industrial countries agreed to take concerted action to bring down the dollar.

10. Exchange rate stability was downplayed as a prime policy goal in the 1990s and 2000s. Instead, governments aimed to target low domestic inflation while maintaining economic growth. After 2000, global external imbalances widened dramatically. In the United States and other countries, external deficits were associated with rapidly increasing housing prices. When these collapsed starting in 2006, the global financial system seized up and the world economy went into deep recession.

11. One unambiguous lesson of these experiences seems to be that no exchange rate system functions well when international economic cooperation breaks down. Severe limits on exchange rate flexibility among the major currencies are unlikely to be reinstated in the near future. But increased consultation among international policy makers should improve the performance of the international monetary system.

KEY TERMS

balance of payments equilibrium, p. 581
Bretton Woods agreement, p. 587
confidence problem, p. 596
convertible currency, p. 590
expenditure-changing policy, p. 594

expenditure-switching policy, p. 595
external balance, p. 571
internal balance, p. 571
International Monetary Fund (IMF), p. 588
intertemporal budget constraint, p. 574

monetary trilemma, p. 579
nominal and real effective exchange rate indexes, p. 606
price-specie-flow mechanism, p. 581
stagflation, p. 605
sudden stop, p. 574

PROBLEMS

MyEconLab

1. If you were in charge of macroeconomic policies in a small open economy, what qualitative effect would each of the following events have on your target for external balance?
   a. Large deposits of uranium are discovered in the interior of your country.
   b. The world price of your main export good, copper, rises permanently.
   c. The world price of copper rises temporarily.
   d. There is a temporary rise in the world price of oil.

2. Under a gold standard of the kind analyzed by Hume, describe how balance of payments equilibrium between two countries, A and B, would be restored after a transfer of income from B to A.

3. Is it possible for an indebted country to continue borrowing, if the capital inflow of a country is not sufficient to cover the current account deficit? What impact does this current account deficit put on its domestic currency?

4. Under a gold standard, countries may adopt excessively contractionary monetary policies as all countries scramble in vain for a larger share of the limited supply of world gold reserves. Can the same problem arise under a reserve currency standard when bonds denominated in different currencies are all perfect substitutes?

5. A central bank that adopts a fixed exchange rate may sacrifice its autonomy in setting domestic monetary policy. It is sometimes argued that when this is the case, the central bank also gives up the ability to use monetary policy to combat the wage-price spiral. The argument goes like this: "Suppose workers demand higher wages and employers give in, but the employers then raise output prices to cover their higher costs. Now the price level is higher and real balances are momentarily lower, so to prevent an interest rate rise that would appreciate the currency, the central bank must buy foreign exchange currencies and expand the money supply. This action accommodates the initial wage demands with monetary growth, and the economy moves permanently to a higher level of wages and prices. With a fixed exchange rate, there is thus no way of keeping wages and prices down." What is wrong with this argument?

6. How can one country maintain the balance of output and employment under the flexible exchange rate system? If an economy's currency appreciated in the international market and the domestic spending reduced, what will happen to the employment and the current account balance? What would you suggest (towards the currency and the domestic spending) to maintain full employment level of output?

7. How might restrictions on private financial account transactions alter the problem of attaining internal and external balance with a fixed exchange rate? What costs might such restrictions involve?

8. In the box on New Zealand, we derived an equation showing how the *IIP* changes over time: $IIP_{t+1} = (1 + r)IIP_t + NX_t$. Show that if $g = (GDP_{t+1} - GDP_t)/GDP_t$ is the growth rate of nominal output (GDP), and lower-case variables denote ratios to nominal GDP (as in the chapter), we can express this same equation in the form:

$$iip_{t+1} = \frac{(1 + r)iip_t + nx_t}{1 + g}.$$

   Use this expression to find the ratio of net exports to GDP that holds the *IIP* to GDP ratio *iip* constant over time.

9. You are an economic adviser to the government of China in 2008. The country has a current account surplus and is facing gathering inflationary pressures.

   a. Show the location of the Chinese economy on a diagram like Figure 19-2.

   b. What would be your advice on how the authorities should move the yuan renminbi's exchange rate?

   What would be your advice about fiscal policy? In that regard, you have three pieces of data: First, the current account surplus is big, in excess of 9 percent of GDP. Second, China currently provides a rather low level of government services to its people. Third, China's government would like to attract workers from the rural countryside into manufacturing employment, so Chinese officials would prefer to soften any negative impact of their policy package on urban employment.

10. Use the *DD-AA* model to examine the effects of a one-time rise in the foreign price level, P^*. If the expected future exchange rate E^e falls immediately in proportion to P^* (in line with PPP), show that the exchange rate will also appreciate immediately in proportion to the rise in P^*. If the economy is initially in internal and external balance, will its position be disturbed by such a rise in P^*?

11. Suppose in an open economy, two countries—Brazil and Argentina—have a fixed exchange rate (under Bretton Woods Agreement). If the inflation rate in Brazil is higher than Argentina's, what is the likely impact of the higher inflation on the trade balance between two countries?

12. Imagine that domestic and foreign currency bonds are imperfect substitutes and that investors suddenly shift their demand toward foreign currency bonds, raising the risk premium on domestic assets (Chapter 18). Which exchange rate regime minimizes the effect on output—fixed or floating?

13. The Case Study starting on page 609 discussed the big global imbalances of the 2000s and suggested that one can analyze factors determining world real interest rates in terms of the balance between the world demand for savings (in order to finance investment) and the world supply of savings (just as in a closed economy—which the world is). As a first step in formalizing such an analysis, assume there are no international differences in real interest rates due to expected real exchange rate changes. (For example, you might suppose that yours is a long-run analysis in which real exchange rates are expected to remain at their long-run levels.) As a second step, assume that a higher real interest rate reduces desired investment and raises desired saving throughout the world. Can you then devise a simple supply-demand picture of equilibrium in the world capital market in which quantities (saved or invested) are on the horizontal axis and the real interest rate is on the vertical axis? In such a setting, how would an increase in world saving, defined in the usual way as an outward shift in the entire supply-of-savings schedule, affect equilibrium saving, investment, and the real interest rate? Relate your discussion to the last Case Study in the chapter and to the paper by Ben S. Bernanke in Further Readings. [For a classic exposition of a similar model, see Lloyd A. Metzler, "The Process of International Adjustment under Conditions of Full Employment: A Keynesian View," in Richard E. Caves and Harry G. Johnson, eds., *Readings in International Economics* (Homewood, IL: Richard D. Irwin, Inc. for the American Economic Association, 1968), pp. 465–486.]

14. Assume that Japan and China decide to float their currency in the international market, ceteris paribus. Also, if the People's Bank of China (central bank) declines the interest rate relative to the Japanese rate, what will happen to the exchange rate between the two currencies? What impact does the increase in interest rate have on the current account balance and trade balance of Japan in the short run? (Hint: Explain by using the interest rate and aggregate demand relationship).

15. Under the Bretton Woods Agreement, why is the fiscal policy alone insufficient to maintain internal and external balance? Suppose country 'X'—operating under the agreement—has a lower par exchange rate against the dollar than the market clearing exchange rate. How does the exchange rate impact the price level of country 'X'? To control the price level, list suggestions for the policy maker of country 'X' regarding valuation of its currency in the international market?

16. Like its neighbor New Zealand, Australia has had a long string of current account deficits and is an international debtor. Go to the Australian Bureau of Statistics website at http://www.abs.gov.au/AUSSTATS and find the data you need to carry out an "external sustainability" analysis of the current account such as the one

for New Zealand in the chapter. You will need data starting in 1992 for nominal GDP, the IIP, the current account, and the balance on goods and services *NX* (from "time series spreadsheets"). The goal of the exercise is to find the interest rate *r* on the IIP that stabilizes the ratio *IIP/GDP* at its most recent value given the historical average of *NX* and the historical average of nominal GDP growth (all since 1992). Warning: This is a challenging exercise that requires you to navigate the Australian data system and judge the most appropriate data to use in light of what you learned in Chapter 13.

FURTHER READINGS

Liaquat Ahamed. *Lords of Finance: The Bankers Who Broke the World.* New York: Penguin Press, 2009. Lively historical account of international monetary crises between the world wars of the twentieth century.

Ben S. Bernanke. "The Global Saving Glut and the U.S. Current Account Deficit." Sandridge Lecture, March 10, 2005, at www.federalreserve.gov/boarddocs/speeches/2005/200503102/default.htm. The Federal Reserve chairman's diagnosis of the low real interest rates of the mid-2000s.

Olivier J. Blanchard and Gian Maria Milesi-Ferretti. "(Why) Should Current Account Balances Be Reduced?" *IMF Economic Review* 60 (April 2012), pp. 139–150. The authors offer a concise, up-to-date survey of the hazards of very large current account deficits and surpluses.

Richard H. Clarida. *G-3 Exchange Rate Relationships: A Review of the Record and Proposals for Change.* Princeton Essays in International Economics 219. International Economics Section, Department of Economics, Princeton University, September 2000. Critical review of various target zone proposals for limiting exchange rate movements.

W. Max Corden. "The Geometric Representation of Policies to Attain Internal and External Balance." *Review of Economic Studies* 28 (January 1960): 1–22. A classic diagrammatic analysis of expenditure-switching and expenditure-changing macroeconomic policies.

Barry Eichengreen. *Globalizing Capital: A History of the International Monetary System*, 2nd edition. Princeton: Princeton University Press, 2008. Compact, insightful overview of international monetary history from the gold standard to the present day.

Milton Friedman. "The Case for Flexible Exchange Rates," in *Essays in Positive Economics.* Chicago: University of Chicago Press, 1953, pp. 157–203. A classic exposition of the merits of floating exchange rates.

Joseph E. Gagnon. *Flexible Exchange Rates for a Stable World Economy.* Washington, D.C.: Peterson Institute for International Economics, 2011. The author presents an up-to-date case for exchange rate flexibility.

Charles P. Kindleberger. *The World in Depression 1929–1939*, rev. edition. Berkeley and Los Angeles: University of California Press, 1986. A leading international economist examines the causes and effects of the Great Depression.

Michael W. Klein and Jay C. Shambaugh. *Exchange Rate Regimes in the Modern Era.* Cambridge, MA: MIT Press, 2010. Comprehensive analysis of the causes and consequences of alternative exchange rate regimes.

Maurice Obstfeld. "The International Monetary System: Living with Asymmetry," in Robert C. Feenstra and Alan M. Taylor, eds., *Globalization in an Age of Crisis: Multilateral Cooperation in the Twenty-First Century.* Chicago: University of Chicago Press, 2014, pp. 301–336. Overview of the international monetary system in light of the global financial crisis.

Maurice Obstfeld and Alan M. Taylor. *Global Capital Markets: Integration, Crisis, and Growth.* Cambridge, U.K.: Cambridge University Press, 2004. Overview of the linkages between international financial integration and exchange rate regimes.

Robert Solomon. *The International Monetary System, 1945–1981.* New York: Harper & Row, 1982. Excellent chronicle of the Bretton Woods period and the early years of floating. The author was chief of the Federal Reserve's international finance division during the period leading up to the breakdown of fixed exchange rates.

MyEconLab Can Help You Get a Better Grade

MyEconLab If your exam were tomorrow, would you be ready? For each chapter, MyEconLab Practice Tests and Study Plans pinpoint sections you have mastered and those you need to study. That way, you are more efficient with your study time, and you are better prepared for your exams.

To see how it works, turn to page 41 and then go to

www.myeconlab.com

International Policy Coordination Failures

This appendix illustrates the importance of macroeconomic policy coordination by showing how all countries can suffer as a result of self-centered policy decisions. The phenomenon is another example of the Prisoner's Dilemma of game theory. Governments can achieve macroeconomic outcomes that are better for all if they choose policies cooperatively.

These points are made using an example based on the disinflation of the early 1980s. Recall that contractionary monetary policies in the industrial countries helped throw the world economy into a deep recession in 1981. Countries hoped to reduce inflation by slowing monetary growth, but the situation was complicated by the influence of exchange rates on the price level. A government that adopts a less restrictive monetary policy than its neighbors is likely to face a currency depreciation that partially frustrates its attempts to disinflate.

Many observers feel that in their individual attempts to resist currency depreciation, the industrial countries as a group adopted overly tight monetary policies that deepened the recession. All governments would have been happier if everyone had adopted looser monetary policies, but given the policies that other governments did adopt, it was not in the interest of any individual government to change course.

The argument above can be made more precise with a simple model. There are two countries, Home and Foreign, and each country has two policy options, a very restrictive monetary policy and a somewhat restrictive monetary policy. Figure 19A-1, which is similar to a diagram we used to analyze trade policies, shows the results in Home and Foreign of different policy choices by the two countries. Each row corresponds to a particular monetary policy decision by Home and each column to a decision by Foreign. The boxes contain entries giving changes in Home and Foreign

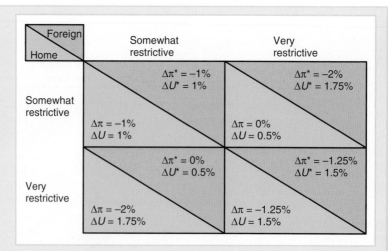

FIGURE 19A-1

Hypothetical Effects of Different Monetary Policy Combinations on Inflation and Unemployment

Monetary policy choices in one country affect the outcomes of monetary policy choices made abroad.

annual inflation rates ($\Delta\pi$ and $\Delta\pi^*$) and unemployment rates (ΔU and ΔU^*). Within each box, lower left entries are Home outcomes and upper right entries are Foreign outcomes.

The hypothetical entries in Figure 19A-1 can be understood in terms of this chapter's two-country model. Under somewhat restrictive policies, for example, inflation rates fall by 1 percent and unemployment rates rise by 1 percent in both countries. If Home suddenly shifts to a very restrictive policy while Foreign stands pat, Home's currency appreciates, its inflation drops further, and its unemployment rises. Home's additional monetary contraction, however, has two effects on Foreign. Foreign's unemployment rate falls, but because Home's currency appreciation is a currency *de*preciation for Foreign, Foreign inflation goes back up to its pre-disinflation level. In Foreign, the deflationary effects of higher unemployment are offset by the inflationary impact of a depreciating currency on import prices and wage demands. Home's sharper monetary crunch therefore has a beggar-thy-neighbor effect on Foreign, which is forced to "import" some inflation from Home.

To translate the outcomes in Figure 19A-1 into policy payoffs, we assume each government wishes to get the biggest reduction in inflation at the lowest cost in terms of unemployment. That is, each government wishes to maximize $-\Delta\pi/\Delta U$, the inflation reduction per point of increased unemployment. The numbers in Figure 19A-1 lead to the payoff matrix shown as Figure 19A-2 .

How do Home and Foreign behave faced with the payoffs in this matrix? Assume each government "goes it alone" and picks the policy that maximizes its own payoff given the other player's policy choice. If Foreign adopts a somewhat restrictive policy, Home does better with a very restrictive policy (payoff $= \frac{8}{7}$) than with a somewhat restrictive one (payoff $= 1$). If Foreign is very restrictive, Home still does better by being very restrictive (payoff $= \frac{5}{6}$) than by being somewhat restrictive (payoff $= 0$). So no matter what Foreign does, Home's government will always choose a very restrictive monetary policy.

Foreign finds itself in a symmetric position. It, too, is better off with a very restrictive policy regardless of what Home does. The result is that both countries will choose very restrictive monetary policies, and each will get a payoff of $\frac{5}{6}$.

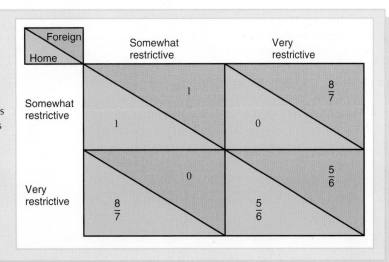

FIGURE 19A-2

Payoff Matrix for Different Monetary Policy Moves

Each entry equals the reduction in inflation per unit rise in the unemployment rate (calculated as $-\Delta\pi/\Delta U$). If each country "goes it alone," they both choose very restrictive policies. Somewhat restrictive policies, if adopted by both countries, lead to an outcome better for both.

Notice, however, that *both* countries are actually better off if they simultaneously adopt the somewhat restrictive policies. The resulting payoff for each is 1, which is greater than $\frac{5}{6}$. Under this last policy configuration, inflation falls less in the two countries, but the rise in unemployment is far less than under very restrictive policies.

Since both countries are better off with somewhat restrictive policies, why aren't these adopted? The answer is at the root of the problem of policy coordination. Our analysis assumed that each country "goes it alone" by maximizing its own payoff. Under this assumption, a situation where both countries were somewhat restrictive would not be stable: Each country would want to reduce its monetary growth further and use its exchange rate to hasten disinflation at its neighbor's expense.

For the superior outcome in the upper left corner of the matrix to occur, Home and Foreign must reach an explicit agreement, that is, they must *coordinate* their policy choices. Both countries must agree to forgo the beggar-thy-neighbor gains offered by very restrictive policies, and each country must abide by this agreement in spite of the incentive to cheat. If Home and Foreign can cooperate, both end up with a preferred mix of inflation and unemployment.

The reality of policy coordination is more complex than in this simple example because the choices and outcomes are more numerous and more uncertain. These added complexities make policy makers less willing to commit themselves to cooperative agreements and less certain that their counterparts abroad will live up to the agreed terms.

CHAPTER 20

FINANCIAL GLOBALIZATION: OPPORTUNITY AND CRISIS

I f a financier named Rip van Winkle had gone to sleep in the 1960s and awakened after 50 years, he would have been shocked by changes in both the nature and the scale of international financial activity. In the early 1960s, for example, most banking business was purely domestic, involving the currency and customers of the bank's home country. Five decades later, many banks were deriving a large share of their profits from international activities. To his surprise, Rip would have found that he could locate branches of Citibank in São Paulo, Brazil, and branches of Britain's Barclays Bank in New York. He would also have discovered that it had long since become routine for a branch of an American bank located in London to accept a deposit denominated in Japanese yen from a Swedish corporation, or to lend Swiss francs to a Dutch manufacturer. Finally, he would have noticed much greater participation by nonbank financial institutions in international markets and a huge expansion in the sheer volume of global transactions.

The market in which residents of different countries trade assets is called the **international capital market**. The international capital market is not really a single market; it is instead a group of closely interconnected markets in which asset exchanges with some international dimension take place. International currency trades take place in the foreign exchange market, which is an important part of the international capital market. The main actors in the international capital market are the same as those in the foreign exchange market (Chapter 14): commercial banks, large corporations, nonbank financial institutions, central banks, and other government agencies. And, like the foreign exchange market, the international capital market's activities take place in a network of world financial centers linked by sophisticated communications systems. The assets traded in the international capital market, however, include different countries' stocks and bonds in addition to bank deposits denominated in their currencies.

This chapter discusses four main questions about the international capital market. First, how can this well-oiled global financial network enhance countries' gains from international trade? Second, what has caused the rapid growth in international financial activity since the early 1960s? Third, what dangers are posed by an integrated world capital market straddling national borders? And fourth, how can policy makers minimize problems raised by the global capital market without sharply reducing the benefits it provides?

After reading this chapter, you will be able to:

▪ Understand the economic function of international portfolio diversification.

▪ Explain factors leading to the explosive recent growth of international financial markets.

▪ Analyze problems in the regulation and supervision of international banks and nonbank financial institutions.

▪ Describe some different methods that have been used to measure the degree of international financial integration.

▪ Understand the factors leading to the worldwide financial crisis that started in 2007.

▪ Evaluate the performance of the international capital market in linking the economies of the industrial countries.

The International Capital Market and the Gains from Trade

In earlier chapters, the discussion of gains from international trade concentrated on exchanges involving goods and services. By providing a worldwide payments system that lowers transaction costs, banks active in the international capital market enlarge the trade gains that result from such exchanges. Furthermore, the international capital market brings borrowers and lenders in different countries together in order to finance the global pattern of current account imbalances. But most deals that take place in the international capital market are exchanges of assets between residents of different countries, for example, the exchange of a share of IBM stock for some British government bonds. Although such asset trades are sometimes derided as unproductive "speculation," they do, in fact, lead to gains from trade that can make consumers everywhere better off.

Three Types of Gain from Trade

All transactions between the residents of different countries fall into one of three categories: trades of goods or services for goods or services, trades of goods or services for assets, and trades of assets for assets. At any moment, a country is generally carrying out trades in each of these categories. Figure 20-1 (which assumes that there are two countries, Home and Foreign) illustrates the three types of international transaction, each of which involves a different set of possible gains from trade.

So far in this book we have discussed two types of trade gain. Chapters 3 through 8 showed that countries can gain by concentrating on the production activities in which they are most efficient and by using some of their output to pay for imports of other products from abroad. This type of trade gain involves the exchange of goods or services for other goods or services. The top horizontal arrow in Figure 20-1 shows exchanges of goods and services between Home and Foreign.

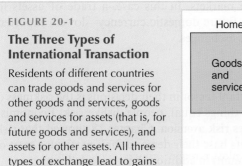

FIGURE 20-1

The Three Types of International Transaction

Residents of different countries can trade goods and services for other goods and services, goods and services for assets (that is, for future goods and services), and assets for other assets. All three types of exchange lead to gains from trade.

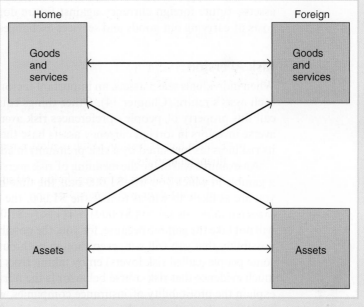

A second set of trade gains results from *intertemporal* trade, which is the exchange of goods and services for claims to future goods and services, that is, for assets (Chapters 6 and 19). When a developing country borrows abroad (that is, sells a bond to foreigners) so that it can import materials for a domestic investment project, it is engaging in intertemporal trade—trade that would not be possible without an international capital market. The diagonal arrows in Figure 20-1 indicate trades of goods and services for assets. If Home has a current account deficit with Foreign, for example, it is a net exporter of assets to Foreign and a net importer of goods and services from Foreign.

The bottom horizontal arrow in Figure 20-1 represents the last category of international transaction, trades of assets for assets, such as the exchange of real estate located in France for U.S. Treasury bonds. In Table 13-2 on page 362, which shows the 2012 U.S. balance of payments accounts, you will see under the financial account both a $97.5 billion purchase of foreign assets by U.S. residents and a $543.9 billion purchase of U.S. assets by foreign residents. (These numbers do not include derivatives; the BEA reports only *net* trade in derivatives.) So while the United States could have financed its current account deficit simply by selling assets to foreigners and not buying any from them, U.S. and foreign residents also engaged in pure asset swapping. Such a large volume of trade in assets between countries occurs in part because international asset trades, like trades involving goods and services, can yield benefits to all the countries involved.

While the preceding distinctions may appear clear-cut in theory, be aware that in the real world, different types of trade may occur together because they are complementary. For example, importers may need to buy foreign goods on the basis of credit from sellers and repay after they have sold the goods to domestic consumers. In this case, the importers' ability to obtain goods today in return for a promise to repay soon after—a form of intertemporal trade—is vital to promoting international exchange of goods and services. As a second example, exporters may need to hedge future foreign exchange receipts in forward exchange markets. In this case, a trade of assets for assets—future foreign currency against future domestic currency—lowers exporters' costs of carrying out goods and services exchanges.

Risk Aversion

When individuals select assets, an important factor in their decisions is the riskiness of each asset's return (Chapter 14). Other things equal, people dislike risk. Economists call this property of people's preferences **risk aversion**. Chapter 18 showed that risk-averse investors in foreign currency assets base their demand for a particular asset on its riskiness (as measured by a risk premium) in addition to its expected return.

An example will make the meaning of risk aversion clearer. Suppose you are offered a gamble in which you win $1,000 half the time but lose $1,000 half the time. Since you are as likely to win as to lose the $1,000, the average payoff on this gamble—its *expected value*—is $\left(\frac{1}{2}\right) \times (\$1,000) + \left(\frac{1}{2}\right) \times (-\$1,000) = 0$. If you are risk averse, you will not take the gamble because, for you, the possibility of losing $1,000 outweighs the possibility that you will win, even though both outcomes are equally likely. Although some people (called risk lovers) enjoy taking risks and would take the gamble, there is much evidence that risk-averse behavior is the norm. For example, risk aversion helps explain the profitability of insurance companies, which sell policies that allow people to protect themselves or their families from the financial risks of theft, illness, and other mishaps.

If people are risk averse, they value a collection (or portfolio) of assets not only on the basis of its expected return but also on the basis of the riskiness of that return. Under risk aversion, for example, people may be willing to hold bonds denominated in several different currencies, even if the interest rates they offer are not linked by the interest parity condition, if the resulting portfolio of assets offers a desirable combination of return and risk. In general, a portfolio whose return fluctuates wildly from year to year is less desirable than one that offers the same average return with only mild year-to-year fluctuations. This observation is basic to understanding why countries exchange assets.

Portfolio Diversification as a Motive for International Asset Trade

International trade in assets can make both parties to the trade better off by allowing them to reduce the riskiness of the return on their wealth. Trade accomplishes this reduction in risk by allowing both parties to diversify their portfolios—to divide their wealth among a wide spectrum of assets and thus reduce the amount of money they have riding on each individual asset. The late economist James Tobin of Yale University, an originator of the theory of portfolio choice with risk aversion, once described the idea of **portfolio diversification** as "Don't put all your eggs in one basket." When an economy is opened to the international capital market, it can reduce the riskiness of its wealth by placing some of its "eggs" in additional foreign "baskets." This reduction in risk is the basic motive for asset trade.

A simple two-country example illustrates how countries are made better off by trade in assets. Imagine there are two countries, Home and Foreign, and residents of each own only one asset, domestic land yielding an annual harvest of kiwi fruit.

The yield of the land is uncertain, however. Half of the time, Home's land yields a harvest of 100 tons of kiwi fruit at the same time as Foreign's land yields a harvest of 50 tons. The other half of the time, the outcomes are reversed: The Foreign harvest is 100 tons, but the Home harvest is only 50. On average, then, each country has a harvest of $\left(\frac{1}{2}\right) \times (100) + \left(\frac{1}{2}\right) \times (50) = 75$ tons of kiwi fruit, but its inhabitants never know whether the next year will bring feast or famine.

Now suppose the two countries can trade shares in the ownership of their respective assets. A Home owner of a 10 percent share in Foreign land, for example, receives 10 percent of the annual Foreign kiwi fruit harvest, and a Foreign owner of a 10 percent share in Home land is similarly entitled to 10 percent of the Home harvest. What happens if international trade in these two assets is allowed? Home residents will buy a 50 percent share of Foreign land, and they will pay for it by giving Foreign residents a 50 percent share in Home land.

To understand why this is the outcome, think about the returns to the Home and Foreign portfolios when both are equally divided between titles to Home and Foreign land. When times are good in Home (and therefore bad in Foreign), each country earns the same return on its portfolio: half of the Home harvest (100 tons of kiwi fruit) plus half of the Foreign harvest (50 tons of kiwi fruit), or 75 tons of fruit. In the opposite case—bad times in Home, good times in Foreign—each country *still* earns 75 tons of fruit. If the countries hold portfolios equally divided between the two assets, therefore, each country earns a *certain* return of 75 tons of fruit—the same as the average or expected harvest each faced before international asset trade was allowed.

Since the two available assets—Home and Foreign land—have the same return on average, any portfolio consisting of those assets yields an expected (or average) return of 75 tons of fruit. People everywhere are risk averse, however, so all prefer to hold the fifty-fifty portfolio described above, which gives a sure return of 75 tons of fruit every year. After trade is opened, therefore, residents of the two counties will swap titles to land until the fifty-fifty outcome is reached. Because this trade eliminates the risk faced by both countries without changing average returns, both countries are clearly better off as a result of asset trade.

The above example is oversimplified because countries can never really eliminate *all* risk through international asset trade. (Unlike the model's world, the real world is a risky place even in the aggregate!) The example does demonstrate that countries can nonetheless *reduce* the riskiness of their wealth by diversifying their asset portfolios internationally. A major function of the international capital market is to make this diversification possible.[1]

The Menu of International Assets: Debt versus Equity

International asset trades can be exchanges of many different types of assets. Among the many assets traded in the international capital market are bonds and deposits denominated in different currencies, shares of stock, and more complicated financial instruments such as stock or currency options. A purchase of foreign real estate and the direct acquisition of a factory in another country are other ways of diversifying abroad.

In thinking about asset trades, it is frequently useful to make a distinction between **debt instruments** and **equity instruments**. Bonds and bank deposits are debt instruments,

---

[1]The Mathematical Postscript to this chapter develops a detailed model of international portfolio diversification. You may have noticed that in our example, countries could reduce risk through transactions other than the asset swap we have described. The high-output country could run a current account surplus and lend to the low-output country, for example, thereby partially evening out the cross-country consumption difference in every state of the world economy. The economic functions of intertemporal trades and of pure asset swaps thus can overlap. To some extent, trade over time can substitute for trade across states of nature, and vice versa, simply because different economic states of the world occur at different points in time. But, in general, the two types of trade are not perfect substitutes for each other.

since they specify that the issuer of the instrument must repay a fixed value (the sum of principal plus interest) regardless of economic circumstances. In contrast, a share of stock is an equity instrument: It is a claim to a firm's profits, rather than to a fixed payment, and its payoff will vary according to circumstances. Similarly, the kiwi fruit shares traded in our example are equity instruments. By choosing how to divide their portfolios between debt and equity instruments, individuals and nations can arrange to stay close to desired consumption and investment levels despite the different eventualities that could occur.

The dividing line between debt and equity is not a neat one in practice. Even if an instrument's money payout is the same in different states of the world, its *real* payout in a particular state will depend on national price levels and exchange rates. In addition, the payments that a given instrument promises to make may not occur in cases of bankruptcy, government seizure of foreign-owned assets, and so on. Assets like low-grade corporate bonds, which superficially appear to be debt, may in reality be like equity in offering payoffs that depend on the doubtful financial fortunes of the issuer. The same has turned out to be true of the debt of many developing countries, as we will see in Chapter 22.

International Banking and the International Capital Market

The Home-Foreign kiwi fruit example above portrayed an imaginary world with only two assets. Since the number of assets available in the real world is enormous, specialized institutions have sprung up to bring together buyers and sellers of assets located in different countries.

The Structure of the International Capital Market

As we noted above, the main actors in the international capital market include commercial banks, corporations, nonbank financial institutions (such as insurance companies, money market funds, hedge funds, and pension funds), central banks, and other government agencies.

1. *Commercial banks.* Commercial banks are at the center of the international capital market, not only because they run the international payments mechanism but also because of the broad range of financial activities they undertake. Bank liabilities consist chiefly of deposits of various maturities, as well as debt and short-term borrowing from other financial institutions, while their assets consist largely of loans (to corporations and governments), deposits at other banks (interbank deposits), and various securities including bonds. Multinational banks are also heavily involved in other types of asset transaction. For example, banks may *underwrite* issues of corporate stocks and bonds by agreeing, for a fee, to find buyers for those securities at a guaranteed price. One of the key facts about international banking is that banks are often free to pursue activities abroad that they would not be allowed to pursue in their home countries. This type of regulatory asymmetry has spurred the growth of international banking over the past 50 years.

2. *Corporations.* Corporations—particularly those with multinational operations such as Coca-Cola, IBM, Toyota, and Nike—routinely finance their investments by drawing on foreign sources of funds. To obtain these funds, corporations may sell shares of stock, which give owners an equity claim to the corporation's assets, or they may use debt finance. Debt finance often takes the form of borrowing from and through international banks or other institutional lenders; firms also sell short-term commercial paper and corporate debt instruments in the international capital market. Corporations frequently denominate their bonds in the currency of the financial center in which the bonds are being offered for sale. Increasingly, however, corporations have been pursuing novel denomination strategies that make their bonds attractive to a wider spectrum of potential buyers.

3. *Nonbank financial institutions.* Nonbank institutions such as insurance companies, pension funds, mutual funds, and hedge funds have become important players in the international capital market as they have moved into foreign assets to diversify their portfolios. Of particular importance are *investment banks*, which are not banks at all but specialize in underwriting sales of stocks and bonds by corporations and (in some cases) governments, providing advice on mergers and acquisitions, and facilitating transactions for clients, among other functions. Investment banks may be free-standing but in most cases belong to large financial conglomerates that also include commercial banks. Prominent examples include Goldman Sachs, Deutsche Bank, Citigroup, and Barclays Capital.

4. *Central banks and other government agencies.* Central banks are routinely involved in the international financial markets through foreign exchange intervention. In addition, other government agencies frequently borrow abroad. Developing-country governments and state-owned enterprises have borrowed substantially from foreign commercial banks, and regularly sell bonds abroad.

On any measure, the scale of transactions in the international capital market has grown much more quickly than world GDP since the early 1970s. One major factor in this development is that, starting with the industrial world, countries have progressively dismantled barriers to private capital flows across their borders.

An important reason for that development is related to exchange rate systems. According to the monetary trilemma of Chapter 19, the widespread adoption of flexible exchange rates since the early 1970s has allowed countries to reconcile open capital markets with domestic monetary autonomy. The individual member countries of the European economic and monetary union (Chapter 21) have followed a different route with respect to their mutual exchange rates. However, the euro floats against foreign currencies and the euro zone as a unit orients its monetary policy toward internal macroeconomic goals while permitting freedom of cross-border payments.

Offshore Banking and Offshore Currency Trading

One of the most pervasive features of today's commercial banking industry is that banking activities have become globalized as banks have branched out from their home countries into foreign financial centers. In 1960, only eight American banks had branches in foreign countries, but now hundreds have such branches. Similarly, the number of foreign bank offices in the United States has risen steadily.

The term **offshore banking** is used to describe the business that banks' foreign offices conduct outside of their home countries. Banks may conduct foreign business through any of three types of institutions:

1. An *agency* office located abroad, which arranges loans and transfers funds but does not accept deposits.

2. A *subsidiary* bank located abroad. A subsidiary of a foreign bank differs from a local bank only in that a foreign bank is the controlling owner. Subsidiaries are subject to the same regulations as local banks but are not subject to the regulations of the parent bank's country.

3. A foreign *branch*, which is simply an office of the home bank in another country. Branches carry out the same business as local banks and are usually subject to local *and* home banking regulations. Often, however, branches can take advantage of cross-border regulatory differences.

The growth of **offshore currency trading** has gone hand in hand with that of offshore banking. An offshore deposit is simply a bank deposit denominated in a currency other than that of the country in which the bank resides—for example, yen deposits in a London bank or dollar deposits in Zurich. Many of the deposits traded in the foreign exchange market are offshore deposits. Offshore currency deposits are usually referred to as **Eurocurrencies**, which is something of a misnomer since much Eurocurrency trading occurs in such non-European centers as Singapore and Hong Kong. Dollar deposits located outside the United States are called **Eurodollars**. Banks that accept deposits denominated in Eurocurrencies (including Eurodollars) are called **Eurobanks**. The advent of the new European currency, the euro, has made this terminology even more confusing!

One motivation for the rapid growth of offshore banking and currency trading has been the growth of international trade and the increasingly multinational nature of corporate activity. American firms engaged in international trade, for example, require overseas financial services, and American banks have naturally expanded their domestic business with these firms into foreign areas. By offering more rapid clearing of payments and the flexibility and trust established in previous dealings, American banks compete with the foreign banks that could also serve American customers. Eurocurrency trading is another natural outgrowth of expanding world trade in goods and services. British importers of American goods frequently need to hold dollar deposits, for example, and it is natural for banks based in London to woo these importers' business.

World trade growth alone, however, cannot explain the growth of international banking since the 1960s. Another factor is the banks' desire to escape domestic government regulations on financial activity (and sometimes taxes) by shifting some of their operations abroad and into foreign currencies. A further factor is in part political: the desire by some depositors to hold currencies outside the jurisdictions of the countries that issue them. In recent years, the tendency for countries to open their financial markets to foreigners has allowed international banks to compete globally for new business.

The major factor behind the continuing profitability of Eurocurrency trading is regulatory: In formulating bank regulations, governments in the main Eurocurrency centers discriminate between deposits denominated in the home currency and those denominated in others and between transactions with domestic customers and those with foreign customers. Domestic currency deposits generally are more heavily regulated as a way of maintaining control over the domestic money supply, while banks are given more freedom in their dealings in foreign currencies.

Regulatory asymmetries explain why those financial centers whose governments historically imposed the fewest restrictions on foreign currency banking became the main Eurocurrency centers. London is the leader in this respect, but it has been followed by Luxembourg, Bahrain, Hong Kong, and other countries that have competed for international banking business by lowering restrictions and taxes on foreign bank operations within their borders.

The Shadow Banking System

In recent decades, a major regulatory asymmetry has arisen between banks and what is often referred to as the **shadow banking system**. Nowadays, numerous financial institutions provide payment and credit services similar to those that banks provide. U.S. money market mutual funds, for example, provide check-writing services to customers and also are major players in providing credit to firms (through commercial paper markets) and in lending dollars to banks outside the United States. Investment banks also have provided credit to other entities while offering payment services. The shadow banking system even has included investment conduits sponsored by banks but supposedly independent of the banks' own balance sheets. However, shadow banks have usually been minimally regulated compared to banks.

Why has this been the case? Historically, monetary policy makers have viewed banks as the prime focus of concern because of their centrality to the payments system, to the flow of credit to firms and household borrowers, and to the implementation of monetary policy. But the shadow banking system has grown dramatically and taken up many of the same functions as traditional banking. Total shadow banking sector assets are difficult to measure precisely, but in the United States today, they are probably comparable to the assets of the traditional banking sector.

Moreover, shadow banks are closely intertwined with banks as both creditors and borrowers. As a result, the stability of the shadow banking network cannot easily be divorced from that of the banks: If a shadow bank gets into trouble, so may the banks that have loaned it money. This became painfully clear during the 2007–2009 global financial crisis, as we shall see later in this chapter. We now turn to a discussion of banking regulation, but readers should be aware that banks are only one category of player in the international financial markets and that banks' fortunes are likely to depend on those of other players. Most of what we say below regarding "banks" also applies to shadow banks.

Banking and Financial Fragility

Many observers believe that the free-wheeling nature of global banking activity up until now left the world financial system vulnerable to bank failure on a massive scale. The financial crisis of 2007–2009, which we will discuss below, supports that belief. To understand what went wrong with financial globalization, we need first to review the inherent fragility of banking activity, even when undertaken in a hypothetical closed economy, and the safeguards national governments have put in place to prevent bank failures.

The Problem of Bank Failure

A bank fails when it is unable to meet its obligations to its depositors and other creditors. Banks use borrowed funds to make loans and to purchase other assets, but some of a bank's borrowers may find themselves unable to repay their loans, or the bank's assets may decline in value for some other reason. When this happens, the bank might be unable to repay its short-term liabilities, including demand deposits, which are largely repayable immediately, without notice.

A peculiar feature of banking is that a bank's financial health depends on depositors' (and other creditors') confidence in the value of its assets. If depositors, for example, come to believe that many of the bank's assets have declined in value, each has an incentive to withdraw his or her funds and place them in a different bank. A bank faced with a large and sudden loss of deposits—a bank run—is likely to close its doors, even if the asset side of its balance sheet is fundamentally sound. The reason is that many bank assets are illiquid and cannot be sold quickly to meet deposit obligations without substantial loss to the bank. If an atmosphere of financial panic develops, therefore, bank failure may not be limited to banks that have mismanaged their assets. It is in the interest of each depositor to withdraw his or her money from a bank if all other depositors are doing the same, even when the bank's assets, if only they could be held until maturity, would suffice to repay fully the bank's liabilities.

Unfortunately, once a single bank gets into trouble, suspicion may fall on other banks that have lent it money: if they lose enough on the loans, they may be unable to meet their own obligations. When banks are highly interconnected through mutual loans and derivative contracts, bank runs therefore can be highly contagious. Unless policymakers can quickly quarantine the panic, the domino effects of a single bank's troubles can result in a generalized, or *systemic*, banking crisis.

It is easiest to understand a bank's vulnerability by looking at its balance sheet. The stylized balance sheet below shows the relationship between the bank's assets, its liabilities, and their difference, the bank's *capital* (its non-borrowed resources, supplied by the bank's owners, who hold the bank's stock):

Bank Balance Sheet			
Assets		**Liabilities**	
Loans	$1,950	Demand deposits	$1,000
Marketable securities	$1,950	Time deposits and long debt	$1,400
Reserves at central bank	$75	Short-term wholesale liabilities	$1,400
Cash on hand	$25	Capital	$200

In this example, the bank's total assets (listed on the Assets side of its balance sheet) are $4,000. They consist of a small amount of cash ($25) and reserves ($75, the latter being deposits at the home central bank), as well as potentially less liquid loans to businesses and households ($1,950) and other securities (such as government or corporate bonds, totaling $1,950). Cash in the bank's vaults obviously can be used any time to meet depositors' withdrawals, as can its central bank deposits, but loans (for example, mortgage loans) cannot be called in at will, and thus are usually highly illiquid. Marketable securities, in contrast, can be sold off, but if market conditions happen to be unfavorable, the bank might have to sell at a loss if forced to do so on short notice. In a financial panic, for example, other banks might simultaneously be trying to unload similar securities, driving down their market prices.

The bank makes its profits by accepting the risk that its assets may fall in value, while at the same time promising depositors and other short-term creditors that they can get their money back whenever they want it. The bank's provision of liquidity to its creditors is reflected on the Liabilities side of its balance sheet. Banks' time deposits and long-term debt ($1,400) are sources of funding that *cannot* flee at the whim of the lenders, and the bank accordingly pays a higher rate of interest on these liabilities than on its two sources of short-term funding, (retail) demand deposits ($1,000) and short-term wholesale liabilities ($1,400). The latter might take various forms, including overnight loans from other banks (including the central bank) or a collateralized *repurchase agreement* (known as "repo"), in which the bank pledges an asset to the lender for cash, promising to buy the asset back later (often the next day) at a slightly higher price. If all wholesale lenders refuse to renew their short-term loans to the bank, however, it will have to scramble for cash by trying to sell off assets, just as in the case of a retail depositor bank run. In general, banks' balance sheets are characterized by *maturity mismatch*—they have more liabilities payable on short notice than they hold of such assets—and this is what makes them vulnerable to runs.

Bank capital (here, $200) is the difference between assets and liabilities, and is the amount the bank could lose on its assets before it becomes *insolvent*, that is, unable to pay off its debts by selling its assets. Without the buffer of bank capital, the bank would have no margin for error and creditors would never believe in the bank's ability always to repay. In that case, the bank could not conduct its business of exploiting the interest difference or "carry" between its liquid liabilities and less liquid assets. Because a bank depends on the confidence of its creditors, even the suspicion that it could be insolvent may lead creditors to demand instant repayment, forcing it to liquidate assets at a loss and making it insolvent in fact. This scenario is most likely in the case of a systemic financial crisis, in which the prices of marketable assets that the bank normally could sell easily are depressed due to distress selling by numerous financial institutions.[2]

The lower a bank's capital, the higher the chance that it becomes insolvent due to losses in asset values, whether these are due to external events in the economy or due to a run by its creditors. It may therefore surprise you that large globally active banks have tended to operate in the past with fairly slim margins of capital. In our example, which is not unrealistic, the ratio of capital to total bank assets is only $200/$4000 = 5 percent, implying that the bank can tolerate at most a 5 percent loss on assets before it fails. Many large global banks have operated with even lower capital levels! Although banks usually avoid big positions in highly risky assets such as stock shares, and they also avoid unhedged or "open" positions in foreign currencies, numerous banks throughout the world still got into trouble during the global financial crisis of 2007–2009. Because of that experience, international policymakers are attempting to ensure that banks throughout the world maintain higher capital levels, as we explain later in this chapter.

Bank failures obviously inflict serious financial harm on individual depositors who lose their money. But beyond these individual losses, bank failure can harm the economy's macroeconomic stability. One bank's problems may easily spread to sounder banks if they are suspected of having lent to the bank that is in trouble. Such a general loss of confidence in banks undermines the credit and payments system on which the economy runs. A rash of bank failures can bring a drastic reduction in the banking system's ability to finance investment, consumer-durable expenditure, and home purchases, thus reducing aggregate demand and throwing the economy into a slump. There is strong evidence that the string of U.S. bank closings in the early 1930s helped start and worsen the Great Depression, and financial panic certainly worsened the severe worldwide recession that began in 2007.[3]

---

[2]Central banks also have capital positions, although we did not emphasize this fact in Chapter 18. Central bank assets normally exceed liabilities and the resulting profits are used to cover the bank's expenses—for example, staff salaries and the operating cost of the central bank's physical plant. Any profits in excess of those expenses are usually turned over to the national treasury. Generally, shares in the central bank's capital are not publicly traded (they are owned by the government), although historically this was not always the case. (To take one notable case, the Bank of England was privately owned from its founding in 1694 until 1946.) If a central bank makes big enough losses—on foreign exchange intervention, for example—this might reduce its capital enough that the central bank is forced to request funding from the government. Central banks prefer not to be in this position because the government might attach conditions that reduce the central bank's independence.

[3]For an evaluation of the 1930s, see Ben S. Bernanke, "Nonmonetary Effects of the Financial Crisis in the Propagation of the Great Depression," Chapter 2 in his *Essays on the Great Depression* (Princeton, NJ: Princeton University Press, 2000). Banking crises may also lead to balance-of-payments crises. The macroeconomic policies needed to counteract the banking system's collapse can make it harder to maintain a fixed exchange rate (as illustrated by the euro area crisis that we discuss later in this book). A classic study is Graciela L. Kaminsky and Carmen M. Reinhart, "The Twin Crises: The Causes of Banking and Balance-of-Payments Problems," *American Economic Review* 89 (June 1999), pp. 473–500.

Government Safeguards against Financial Instability

Because the potential consequences of a banking collapse are so harmful, governments attempt to prevent bank failures through extensive regulation of their domestic banking systems. Well-managed banks themselves take precautions against failure even in the absence of regulation, but the costs of failure extend far beyond the bank's owners. Thus, some banks, taking into account their own self-interest but ignoring the costs of bank failure for society, might be led to shoulder a level of risk greater than what is socially optimal. In addition, even banks with cautious investment strategies may fail if rumors of financial trouble begin circulating. Many of the precautionary bank regulation measures taken by governments today are a direct result of their countries' experiences during the Great Depression.

In most countries, an extensive "safety net" has been set up to reduce the risk of bank failure. The main safeguards are:

1. *Deposit insurance.* One legacy of the Great Depression of the 1930s is deposit insurance. In the United States, the Federal Deposit Insurance Corporation (FDIC) insures bank depositors against losses of up to a current limit of $250,000. Banks are required to make contributions to the FDIC to cover the cost of this insurance. FDIC insurance discourages runs on banks by small depositors who know that their losses will be made good by the government: they no longer have an incentive to withdraw their money just because others are doing so. Since 1989, the FDIC has also provided insurance for deposits with savings and loan (S&L) associations.[4] The absence of government insurance is one reason policymakers sometimes give for the comparatively light regulation of banks' offshore operations as well as of the shadow banking system.

2. *Reserve requirements.* Reserve requirements are one possible tool of monetary policy, influencing the relation between the monetary base and monetary aggregates. At the same time, reserve requirements force the bank to hold a portion of its assets in a liquid form that is easily mobilized to meet sudden deposit outflows. In the United States, banks tend to hold reserves in excess of required reserves, so reserve requirements are not important. In our preceding balance-sheet example, the bank's total liquid reserves (including cash) are $100, only 2.5 percent of its total assets.

3. *Capital requirements and asset restrictions.* U.S. and foreign bank regulators set minimum required levels of bank capital to reduce the system's vulnerability to failure. Other rules prevent banks from holding assets that are "too risky," such as common stocks, whose prices tend to be volatile. Banks must also deal with rules against lending too large a fraction of their assets to a single private customer or to a single foreign government borrower.

4. *Bank examination.* Government supervisors have the right to examine a bank's books to ensure compliance with bank capital standards and other regulations. Banks may be forced to sell assets that the examiner deems too risky or to adjust their balance sheets by writing off loans the examiner thinks will not be repaid. In some countries the central bank is the main bank supervisor, while in others a separate financial supervision authority handles that job.

5. *Lender of last resort facilities.* Banks can borrow from the central bank's discount window or from other facilities the central bank may make available (generally

---

[4]Holders of deposits over $250,000 still have an incentive to run if they suspect trouble, of course, as do uninsured (and uncollateralized) bank creditors other than depositors, including other banks.

after they post assets of comparable or greater value as collateral). While lending to banks is a tool of monetary management, the central bank can also use discounting to prevent or quarantine bank panics. Since a central bank has the ability to create currency, it can lend to banks facing massive deposit outflows as much as they need to satisfy their depositors' claims. When the central bank acts in this way, it is acting as a **lender of last resort (LLR)** to the bank. Indeed, the Federal Reserve was set up in 1913 precisely as a safeguard against financial panic. When depositors know the central bank is standing by as the LLR, they have more confidence in a private bank's ability to withstand a panic and are therefore less likely to run if financial trouble looms. The administration of LLR facilities is complex, however. If banks think the central bank will *always* bail them out, they will take excessive risks. So the central bank must make access to its LLR services conditional on sound management. To decide when banks in trouble have not brought it on themselves through unwise risk taking, the LLR should ideally be closely involved in the bank examination process.

6. *Government-organized restructuring and bailouts.* The central bank's LLR role is intended to tide over banks suffering *temporary* liquidity problems due to jittery creditors. Hopefully the bank will be solvent if the central bank can give it enough time to dispose of assets at favorable prices; and if so, the central bank will not lose money as a result of its intervention. Often, however, creditors are jittery for a good reason and big losses on assets are unavoidable. In this case, the national fiscal authorities, along with taxpayer money, come into the picture. The central bank and fiscal authorities may organize the purchase of a failing bank by healthier institutions, sometimes throwing their own money into the deal as a sweetener. The fiscal authorities may also recapitalize the bank with public monies, in effect making the government a full or part owner of the bank until the bank is back on its feet and the public shares can be sold to private buyers. In these cases, bankruptcy can be avoided thanks to the government's intervention as a crisis manager, but perhaps at public expense. The government may alternatively choose to protect taxpayers by imposing losses—sometimes called *haircuts*—on the claims of unsecured bondholders or uninsured depositors.[5]

How successful have safeguards such as these been? Figure 20-2 shows the frequency of ongoing national banking crises—systemic crises which have affected large portions of countries' banking systems—between 1970 and 2011.[6] Banking crises in the poorer developing and emerging market economies are shown in blue, while crises in industrial economies including the United States are shown in red. Obviously such systemic crises are not rare events! As we will discuss in Chapter 22, through much of recent history poorer countries have regulated their banks much less effectively than richer countries, implying a much greater frequency of financial instability in the developing world. However, that changed in 2007–2009 as many more prosperous economies' banks required extensive government support in order to survive. The 2007–2009 crisis thus revealed serious gaps in the banking safety net, gaps that we will analyze below.

The U.S. commercial bank safety net worked reasonably well until the late 1980s, but as a result of deregulation, the 1990–1991 recession, and a sharp fall in commercial

---

[5]Unsecured bondholders are creditors who have not demanded collateral for their loans. Those who demand collateral receive a lower interest rate because their loans are less risky.

[6]The crisis chronology is taken from Luc Laeven and Fabián Valencia, "Systemic Banking Crises Database," *IMF Economic Review* 61 (June 2013), pp. 225–270.

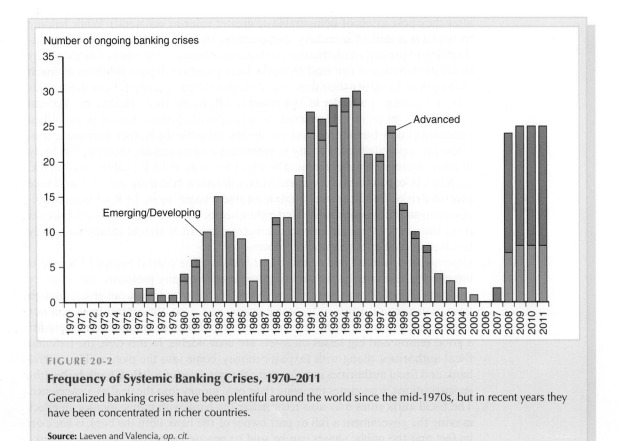

Number of ongoing banking crises

Emerging/Developing

Advanced

FIGURE 20-2

Frequency of Systemic Banking Crises, 1970–2011

Generalized banking crises have been plentiful around the world since the mid-1970s, but in recent years they have been concentrated in richer countries.

Source: Laeven and Valencia, *op. cit.*

property values, bank closings rose dramatically and the FDIC insurance fund was depleted. Like the United States, other countries that deregulated domestic banking in the 1980s—including Japan, the Scandinavian countries, the United Kingdom, and Switzerland—faced serious problems a decade later. Many overhauled their systems of banking safeguards as a result, but as we shall see, those safeguards were not nearly sufficient to prevent the massive financial crisis of 2007–2009.

Moral Hazard and the Problem of "Too Big to Fail"

The banking safeguards listed above fall into two categories: facilities for emergency financial support to banks or their customers and curbs on unwise risk taking by banks.

It is important to realize that these two types of safeguard are complements, not substitutes. An expectation of LLR support or a government-organized bailout package in case of problems may cause banks to extend excessively risky loans and to provision inadequately for investment losses. Deposit insurance will reassure depositors that they need not monitor the bank management's decisions; and without the threat of a bank run to discipline them, bank managers will pursue riskier strategies on the margin, including maintaining an inadequate capital cushion and holding insufficient cash.

The possibility that you will take less care to prevent an accident if you are insured against it is called **moral hazard**. Domestic bank supervision and balance-sheet restrictions are necessary to limit the moral hazard resulting from deposit insurance and access to the lender of last resort, which otherwise would lead banks to make excessively risky loans and inadequate provision for their possible failure.

The FDIC limit of $250,000 on the size of insured deposits is meant to limit moral hazard by encouraging big depositors, and other bank creditors including interbank lenders, to monitor the actions of bank managers. In principle, those big depositors could take their business elsewhere if their bank appears to be taking unwise risks. The problem is that some banks have become so big in global markets, and so interconnected with other banks and shadow banks that their failure might set off a chain reaction that throws the entire financial system into crisis.

When rumors began circulating in May 1984 that the Continental Illinois National Bank had made a large number of bad loans, the bank began rapidly to lose its large, uninsured deposits. At the time the bank was the seventh biggest in the U.S. and many of its deposits were owned by foreign banks, so its failure could have set off a much bigger global banking crisis. As part of its rescue effort, the FDIC extended its insurance coverage to all of Continental Illinois's deposits, regardless of size. This and later episodes have convinced people that the U.S. government is following a "too-big-to-fail" policy of fully protecting all creditors of the largest banks.

When a financial institution is *systemically important*—that is, "too big to fail" or "too interconnected to fail"—its managers and creditors expect that the government will have no choice but to support it in case it gets into trouble. The resulting moral hazard sets off a vicious circle: Because the institution is perceived to be under the umbrella of government support, it can borrow cheaply and engage in risky strategies that (while times are good) yield high returns. The resulting profits allow the institution to become even bigger and more interconnected, leading to more profits, more growth, and more moral hazard. The entire financial system becomes less stable as a result.

THE SIMPLE ALGEBRA OF MORAL HAZARD

The moral hazard that results from a combination of perceived government guarantees and weak regulation of the guaranteed institution has helped fuel excessively speculative investment in many economies. To see how it works, imagine that there is a potential investment—say, a large real estate development—that will cost $70 million up front. If all goes well, the project will yield a return of $100 million; but there is only a one-third chance of this, and a two-thirds chance that the investment will yield only $25 million. The expected payoff, then, is only $(1/3 \times \$100 \text{ million}) + (2/3 \times \$25 \text{ million}) = \$50$ million, which is far below the $70 million up-front cost. Ordinarily, this investment simply would never be made.

Government bailout guarantees change the result, however. Suppose that a real estate developer is able to *borrow* the entire $70 million, because he can convince lenders that the government will protect them if his project fails and he cannot repay. Then from his point of view, he has a one-third chance of making $30 million (= $100 million − $70 million). Otherwise he simply walks away from the project. It's heads he wins, tails the taxpayers lose.

The preceding example may seem extreme, but this kind of logic has led to financial disasters in many countries. The 2007–2009 financial crisis is the most recent example—and the most costly one to date—but it has many precedents. In the 1980s, the U.S. savings and loan industry was granted what amounted to privilege without responsibility: government guarantees on deposits, without close regulation of risk taking. The eventual bill to U.S. taxpayers was $150 billion. Similar mishandling of the financial sector led to much larger bank losses in the 1990s in industrial countries as diverse as Sweden and Japan.

For this reason, economists are increasingly in favor of curbs on the size of financial firms, despite the possible sacrifice of scale efficiencies. As former Federal Reserve chair Alan Greenspan put it, "If they're too big to fail, they're too big." Many economists also favor forcing large complex banks and shadow banks to draw up "living wills" allowing them to be closed and wound down, in case of insolvency, with minimal disruption and minimal cost to taxpayers. The credible threat of bank closure is necessary for limiting moral hazard—bank managers need to know they can be put out of business if they misbehave—but devising concrete procedures is not easy, especially in an international context.

As we shall see, the problem of moral hazard is central to understanding both the 2007–2009 global financial crisis and the measures being proposed to avoid future crises. Another important element in that crisis and its international transmission, however, was the globalized nature of banking.

The Challenge of Regulating International Banking

In this section, we will learn how the internationalization of banking (and financial institutions more generally) weakens purely national safeguards against banking collapse. At the same time, however, global financial interdependence has made the need for effective safeguards more urgent. The result is a second *trilemma* for international policymakers.[7]

The Financial Trilemma

Offshore banking involves a tremendous volume of interbank deposits—roughly 80 percent of all Eurocurrency deposits, for example, are owned by private banks. A high level of interbank depositing implies that problems affecting a single bank can be highly contagious and spread quickly to banks with which it is thought to do business. Through this domino effect, a localized disturbance can set off a banking panic on a global scale, as in the 2007–2009 crisis that we describe below.

Despite these very high stakes, banking regulations of the type used in the United States and other countries become even less effective in an international environment where banks can shift their business among different regulatory jurisdictions. A good way to see why an international banking system is harder to regulate than a national system is to look at how the effectiveness of the U.S. safeguards that we described earlier (pp. 640–641) is reduced as a result of offshore banking activities.

1. **Deposit insurance is essentially absent in international banking.** National deposit insurance systems may protect domestic and foreign depositors alike, but the amount of insurance available is invariably too small to cover the size of the deposits that are usual in international banking. In particular, interbank deposits and other wholesale funding sources are unprotected.

2. **The absence of overseas reserve requirements** was historically a major factor in the growth of Eurocurrency trading. While Eurobanks derived a competitive advantage from escaping the required reserve tax, there was a social cost in terms of the reduced stability of the banking system. No country could solve the problem single-handedly by imposing reserve requirements on its own banks' overseas branches. Concerted international action was blocked, however, by the political and technical difficulty of agreeing on an internationally uniform set of regulations and

---

[7]As you will see, the financial trilemma that we introduce in this section is different from the monetary trilemma that we introduced in Chapter 19 and mentioned again earlier in this chapter. However, both trilemmas concern the connections between international financial integration and other potential policy goals.

by the reluctance of some countries to drive banking business away by tightening regulations. Nowadays, reserve requirements are less important in many countries. In part this is because governments simply realized the requirements' futility in a world of globalized banking.

3. and 4. Bank examination to enforce capital requirements and asset restrictions becomes more difficult in an international setting. National bank regulators usually monitor the balance sheets of domestic banks and their foreign branches on a consolidated basis. But they are less strict in keeping track of banks' foreign subsidiaries and affiliates, which are in theory more tenuously tied to the parent bank but whose financial fortunes may well affect the parent's solvency. Banks have often been able to take advantage of this laxity by shifting risky business that home regulators might question to regulatory jurisdictions where fewer questions are asked. This process is known as **regulatory arbitrage**. Further, it is often unclear which group of regulators would ideally be responsible for monitoring a given bank's assets. Suppose the London subsidiary of an Italian bank deals primarily in Eurodollars. Should the subsidiary's assets be the concern of British, Italian, or American regulators?

5. There is uncertainty over which central bank, if any, is responsible for providing LLR assistance in international banking. The problem is similar to the one that arises in allocating responsibility for bank supervision. Let's return to the example of the London subsidiary of an Italian bank. Should the Fed bear responsibility for saving the subsidiary from a sudden drain of dollar deposits? Should the Bank of England step in? Or should the European Central Bank bear the ultimate responsibility? When central banks provide LLR assistance, they increase their domestic money supplies and may compromise domestic macroeconomic objectives. In an international setting, a central bank may also be providing resources to a bank located abroad whose behavior it is not equipped to monitor. Central banks are therefore reluctant to extend the coverage of their LLR responsibilities.

6. When a bank has assets and liabilities in many countries, several governments may have to share operational and financial responsibility for a rescue or reorganization. The resulting uncertainties can slow down or even impede the operation. Big, complex, highly interconnected global banks know how hard it would be for governments to shut them down and reorganize them rather than simply bailing them out, and this can encourage excessive risk taking.

The preceding difficulties in regulating international financial institutions show that a **financial trilemma** constrains what policymakers in an open economy can achieve. At most two goals from the following list of three are simultaneously feasible:

1. Financial stability.
2. National control over financial safeguard policy.
3. Freedom of international capital movements.

For example, a country that closes itself financially from the outside world can regulate its banks strictly without worrying about regulatory arbitrage across borders, thereby promoting domestic financial stability regardless of what foreign regulators do. On the other hand, if countries were to delegate the design and implementation of financial safeguards to a global regulatory body immune to national political pressures, they could enjoy greater financial stability and financial openness at the same time.[8]

---

[8]For a recent examination of international banking in the context of the financial trilemma, see Dirk Schoenmaker, *Governance of International Banking: The Financial Trilemma* (Oxford: Oxford University Press, 2013).

The utopian goal of an omniscient global financial authority is remote, of course. In its absence, however, national regulators for four decades have been trying to reconcile growing financial integration with financial stability through a process of ever-increasing international cooperation. It is no accident that this process began precisely when the new system of floating exchange rates allowed countries to move to a new edge of the *monetary* trilemma (Chapter 19) by liberalizing international capital movements.

International Regulatory Cooperation through 2007

In the early 1970s, the new regime of floating exchange rates presented a new source of disturbance: a large, unexpected exchange rate change that might wipe out the capital of an exposed bank.

In response to this threat, central bank heads from 11 industrialized countries in 1974 set up a group called the **Basel Committee**, whose job is to achieve "a better coordination of the surveillance exercised by national authorities over the international banking system...." (The group got its name from Basel, Switzerland, the home of the central bankers' meeting place, the Bank for International Settlements, or BIS.) The Basel Committee remains the major forum for cooperation among bank regulators from different countries.

In 1975, the Basel Committee reached an agreement, called the Concordat, which allocates responsibility for supervising multinational banking establishments between parent and host countries. In addition, the Concordat calls for the sharing of information about banks by parent and host regulators and for "the granting of permission for inspections by or on behalf of parent authorities on the territory of the host authority."[9] In 1988, the Basel Committee suggested a minimally prudent level of bank capital (generally speaking, 8 percent of assets) and a system for measuring capital. These guidelines, widely adopted throughout the world, have become known as Basel I. The committee revised the Basel I framework in 2004, issuing a new set of rules for bank capital known as Basel II.

A major change in international financial relations has been the rapidly growing importance of new **emerging markets** as sources and destinations for private capital flows. Emerging markets are the capital markets of industrializing countries that have liberalized their financial systems to allow at least some private asset trade with foreigners. Countries such as Brazil, Mexico, Indonesia, and Thailand were all major recipients of private capital inflows from the industrial world after 1990.

Emerging market financial institutions have, however, proven to be weak in the past. This vulnerability contributed to the emerging markets' severe financial crisis of 1997–1999 (Chapter 22). Among other problems, developing countries tended to lack experience in bank regulation, had looser prudential and accounting standards than developed countries, and had been prone to moral hazard by offering domestic banks implicit guarantees that they will be bailed out if they get into trouble.

Thus, the need to extend internationally accepted "best practice" regulatory standards to emerging market countries became a priority for the Basel Committee. In September 1997, the Committee issued its *Core Principles for Effective Banking Supervision*, worked out in cooperation with representatives from many developing countries (and revised in 2006). That document set out 25 principles deemed to describe the minimum necessary requirements for effective bank supervision, covering

---

[9]The Concordat was summarized in these terms by W. P. Cooke of the Bank of England, then chairman of the Basel Committee, in "Developments in Co-operation among Banking Supervisory Authorities," *Bank of England Quarterly Bulletin* 21 (June 1981), pp. 238–244.

licensing of banks, supervision methods, reporting requirements for banks, and cross-border banking. The Basel Committee and the IMF were monitoring the international implementation of the revised *Core Principles* and Basel II when the global financial crisis erupted in August 2007. The crisis revealed weaknesses in Basel II that led the Basel Committee to agree on a new framework, Basel III, which we will describe further below. The international activities of nonbank financial institutions are another potential trouble spot. The failure of a major actor in the shadow banking system, like the failure of a bank, could seriously disrupt national payments and credit networks. Increasing **securitization** (in which bank assets are repackaged in readily marketable forms and sold off) and trade in options and other derivative securities have made it harder for regulators to get an accurate picture of global financial flows by examining bank balance sheets alone. Indeed, as we shall see, securitization and derivatives were at the heart of the 2007–2009 crisis, which is the subject of the following Case Study.

CASE STUDY

The Global Financial Crisis of 2007–2009

The global financial and economic meltdown of 2007–2009 was the worst since the Great Depression. Banks throughout the world failed or required extensive government support to survive; the global financial system froze; and the entire world economy was thrown into recession. Unlike some recessions, this one originated in a shock to financial markets, and the shock was transmitted from country to country by financial markets, at lightning speed.

The crisis had a seemingly unlikely source: the United States mortgage market.[10] Over the course of the mid-2000s, with U.S. interest rates very low and U.S. home prices bubbling upward (recall Chapter 19), mortgage lenders had extended loans to borrowers with shaky credit. In many cases, the borrowers planned to hold the homes only for brief periods, selling them later for a profit. Many people borrowed at low, temporary "teaser" rates of interest, when in fact they lacked the financial means to meet mortgage payments if interest rates were to rise. And then U.S. interest rates started moving up as the Federal Reserve gradually tightened monetary policy to ward off inflation. U.S. housing prices started to decline in 2006.

The total amount of shaky, "subprime" U.S. mortgage loans was not very big compared to total U.S. financial wealth. However, the subprime loans were securitized quickly and sold off by the original lenders, often bundled with other assets. This factor made it very hard to know exactly which investors were exposed to the risk that subprime mortgage loans would not be repaid. In addition, banks throughout the world, but especially in the United States and Europe, were avid buyers of securitized subprime-related assets, in some cases setting up—outside of the reach of regulators—opaque, off-balance-sheet vehicles for that purpose. A major motivation was regulatory arbitrage. Banks were eager to exploit loopholes in prudential rules, including the Basel II guidelines, in order to minimize the amount of capital

---

[10]For useful accounts of the crisis, see Markus Brunnermeier, "Deciphering the Liquidity and Credit Crunch of 2007–2008," *Journal of Economic Perspectives* 23 (Winter 2009), pp. 77–100; Gary B. Gorton, *Slapped in the Face by the Invisible Hand: The Panic of 2007* (New York: Oxford University Press, 2010); Chapter 9 in Frederic S. Mishkin, *The Economics of Money, Banking, and Financial Markets*, 10th edition (Upper Saddle River, NJ: Prentice Hall, 2013); and the book by Blinder in Further Readings.

they were required to hold against assets and thereby maximize the amount they could borrow to buy securitized credit products. Funding for these banks' securitized asset purchases came from U.S. lenders, including money market mutual funds.[11] Much of the European banks' demand was for U.S. products, but as we noted in Chapter 19, the housing boom of the 2000s was a global phenomenon (recall Figure 19-7), and European banks were also heavily exposed to downturns in highly-priced housing markets outside of the U.S. House prices in those markets would soon follow U.S. prices downward. (In the next chapter, we will see how the problems of Europe's banks led to a crisis in the euro zone.)

As subprime borrowers increasingly missed their payments during 2007, lenders became more aware of the risks they faced, and pulled back from markets. No one could tell who was exposed to subprime risk, or how vulnerable he or she was. Borrowing costs rose, and many participants in financial markets had no choice but to sell assets to get cash. A number of the derivative assets being offered for sale were so poorly understood by the markets that potential buyers could not value them.

During the week of August 9, 2007, central banks provided markets with the most extensive liquidity support since the September 11, 2001, terrorist attacks. On August 9, a major French bank, BNP Paribas, disclosed that three of its investment funds faced potential trouble due to subprime-related investments. Credit markets went into panic, with interbank interest rates rising above central bank target rates around the world. Banks feared that other banks would go under and be unable to repay, and fearing an inability to obtain interbank funding themselves, they all hoarded cash. The European Central Bank stepped in as lender of last resort to the European interbank market, and the Fed followed suit in the United States, announcing that it would accept mortgage-backed securities as collateral for loans to banks. Stock markets fell everywhere. The U.S. economy slipped into recession late in 2007, pushed by the disappearance of credit and a collapsing housing market.

More trouble lay ahead. In March 2008, institutional lenders refused to roll over their short-term credits to the fifth largest investment bank, Bear Stearns, which had extensive subprime-related investments. Even though Bear Stearns was not a bank, it effectively suffered a run by its lenders. In a hastily organized rescue, the Fed bought $30 billion of Bear's "toxic" assets in order to persuade the bank J.P. Morgan Chase to buy Bear at a fire-sale price.

---

[11]For documentation of the two-way financial flows between Europe and the U.S. prior to the crisis, see Ben S. Bernanke, Carol Bertaut, Laurie Pounder DeMarco, and Steven Kamin, "International Capital Flows and the Returns to Safe Assets in the United States, 2003–2007," *Financial Stability Review*, Banque de France 15 (2011), pp. 13–26. Viral V. Acharya and Philipp Schnabl illustrate regulatory arbitrage in "Do Global Banks Spread Global Imbalances? Asset-Backed Commercial Paper during the Financial Crisis of 2007–09," *IMF Economic Review* 58 (August 2010), pp. 37–73. Many securitized U.S. mortgage-backed securities (MBS) were bundled by their issuers so that they would pay off fully except in circumstances where nonpayment of mortgage obligations was extremely widespread—essentially, a severe housing market collapse affecting most regions of the United States. Because rating agencies deemed such an event highly improbable, they gave the MBS their highest ratings. Under the Basel capital guidelines, however, banks were required to hold relatively less capital against such seemingly bullet-proof assets. So European banks piled into MBS and related securities both because of their (slightly) higher returns and because they could thereby borrow and lend on slimmer capital bases.

The Fed was criticized for not wiping out Bear's shareholders (to deter moral hazard) and for putting taxpayer money at risk.

But even after this bailout, financial stability did not return. Foreclosures on delinquent U.S. mortgages were mounting, home prices were still heading downward, and yet banks and shadow banks retained on their books toxic assets that were difficult to value or sell. Against this background the U.S. government took control of the two giant privately owned but government-sponsored mortgage intermediaries, Fannie Mae and Freddie Mac.

The investment bank Lehman Brothers filed for bankruptcy on September 15, 2008, after frantic but unsuccessful efforts by the U.S. Treasury and the Fed to find a buyer. There is still controversy about the legal standing of the U.S. authorities to have prevented the collapse; surely they were still smarting from the criticism over Bear, and hoping that the Lehman fallout could be contained. Instead, the situation quickly spun out of control. A day after Lehman's filing, the giant insurance firm American International Group (AIG, with over $1 trillion in assets) suffered a run. Apparently without the approval of senior management, traders for the firm had issued more than $400 billion in derivatives called *credit default swaps* (CDS), which are insurance policies against nonrepayment of loans (including loans made to Lehman, as well as mortgage-backed securities). With the world financial system in a state of meltdown, those CDS looked increasingly likely to be triggered, yet AIG lacked the funds to cover them. The Fed stepped in immediately with an $85 billion loan, and ultimately the U.S. government loaned AIG billions more.

In the same month, money American market mutual funds (some with claims on Lehman) suffered a run and had their liabilities guaranteed by the U.S. Treasury; Washington Mutual Bank (the sixth largest in the United States) failed; ailing Wachovia (the fourth largest bank) and investment bank Merrill Lynch were bought by Wells Fargo Bank and Bank of America, respectively; the last two independent U.S. investment banks, Goldman Sachs and Morgan Stanley, became bank-holding companies subject to Fed supervision but with access to the Fed's lending facilities; interbank lending spreads over Treasury bill rates reached historic levels; and world stock markets swooned. The U.S. Congress, after much debate, passed a bill allocating $700 billion to buy troubled assets from banks, in hopes that this would allow them to resume normal lending—but the funds were not, in the end, used for that purpose. The post-Lehman turmoil spread to Europe, where a number of financial institutions failed and EU governments issued blanket deposit guarantees to head off bank runs. In addition, a number of countries guaranteed interbank loans. But by this time, the economic downturn had gone global, with devastating effects on output and employment throughout the world.

Limited space prevents a detailed review of the many financial, fiscal, and unconventional monetary policies that central banks and governments undertook to end the global economy's seeming free fall in late 2008 and the first part of 2009.[12] (The box on the next page explores one aspect of the policy response that is especially relevant to international monetary economics.) With housing markets depressed in the industrial countries, however, recovery of financial and household-sector balance sheets was slow, as was the recovery in aggregate demand.

---

[12]A readable account of Fed policies during the crisis is David Wessel, *In Fed We Trust: Ben Bernanke's War on the Great Panic* (New York: Crown Business, 2009). A more comprehensive review of government policy responses is the book by Blinder in Further Readings.

FOREIGN EXCHANGE INSTABILITY AND CENTRAL BANK SWAP LINES

Traditionally, the lender of last resort provides liquidity in its own currency, which it can print freely. The crisis of 2007–2009 made clear, however, that in the modern world of globalized finance, banks may need liquidity in currencies other than that of their home central bank. One area in which central banks innovated during the crisis was in making such support readily available to foreign central banks. In effect, the Federal Reserve, which pioneered this approach, became a *global* LLR for U.S. dollars.

Why was this necessary? The need was a spillover effect of the disruption in U.S. credit markets, particularly interbank markets. As we pointed out above, in the years leading up to the crisis, European banks had invested heavily in U.S. mortgage-backed securities and other similar securitized assets. The European banks did not, however, wish to bear the currency risk of holding these dollar-denominated claims. Lacking an ability to obtain dollars through retail deposits, they borrowed short-term dollars in wholesale markets (from U.S. banks and money market funds) to finance their purchases of U.S. asset-backed securities.

Then the crisis hit and interbank credit markets stopped functioning. European banks did not want to sell their now-toxic U.S. assets at a loss (even if they had been able to), so they needed to borrow dollars to repay their short-term loans and maintain their hedged positions in dollars. Even though the banks' dollar liabilities were on paper balanced with dollar assets, the liquidity mismatch between the assets and liabilities created a currency mismatch once the assets could no longer be sold quickly at face value. Where could these banks get dollars loans quickly now that private dollar credit markets were frozen?

Some, but not all, were able to borrow from the Fed through U.S. affiliates. Other European banks lacked collateral acceptable to the Fed. To make matters worse, the Fed was closed during European morning trading.

The ECB could print euros and lend them to banks, but it could not print U.S. dollars. European banks thus tried to swap the borrowed euros into dollars (selling them in the spot market for dollars and buying them back with forward dollars in the forward market). Under *covered interest parity* (Chapter 14), this complicated operation has the same cost as a straight loan of dollars. But covered interest parity was breaking down because banks did not want to lend dollars to each other. Swaps of euros into dollars thus yielded too few spot dollars and too few forward euros. In particular, this dollar shortage led to a tendency for the dollar to strengthen sharply in the spot market.

The Fed's swap lines, initially extended to the ECB and the Swiss National Bank (SNB) in December 2007, were intended to remedy the shortage and prevent disorderly conditions in foreign exchange markets. The lines allowed the ECB and SNB to borrow dollars directly from the Fed and lend them to domestic banks in need.

But the dollar shortage became much more severe after the Lehman collapse in September 2008. The Fed extended the swaps to a wider set of central banks, including four in emerging countries (Brazil, Mexico, Korea, and Singapore), and made the swap lines unlimited for several industrial-country central banks (including the ECB and SNB), thus fully outsourcing its LLR function. Ultimately the Fed lent hundreds of billions of dollars in this way.*

---

*For further discussion, see Maurice Obstfeld, Jay C. Shambaugh, and Alan M. Taylor, "Financial Instability, Reserves, and Central Bank Swap Lines in the Panic of 2008," *American Economic Review* 99 (May 2009), pp. 480–486; Patrick McGuire and Götz von Peter, "The US Dollar Shortage in Global Banking and the International Policy Response," BIS Working Papers No. 291, October 2009; and Linda S. Goldberg, Craig Kennedy, and Jason Miu, "Central Bank Dollar Swap Lines and Overseas Dollar Funding Costs," *Economic Policy Review*, Federal Reserve Bank of New York (May 2011), pp. 3–20.

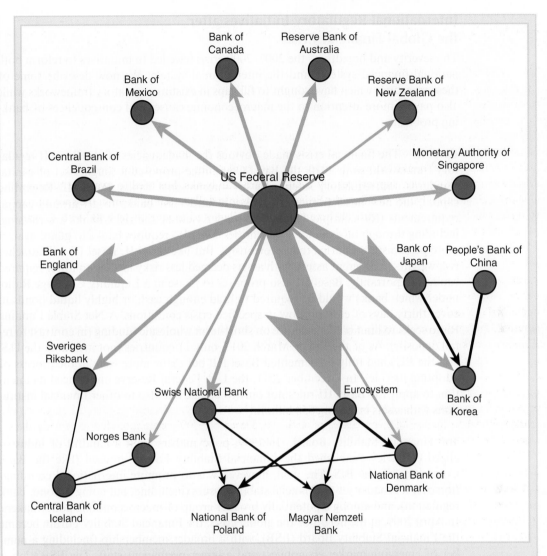

Network of Central Bank Swap Lines during the Crisis of 2007–2009

Light arrows show loans of dollars, dark arrows loans of other currencies. An arrow's direction shows the direction of lending, when known. Arrow thickness is proportional to the size of the swap line or, when the line was unlimited, to the amount lent.

Source: Patrick McGuire and Götz von Peter, "The US Dollar Shortage in Global Banking and the International Policy Response," BIS Working Papers No. 291, October 2009, from http://www.bis.org/publ/work291.pdf © Bank for International Settlements ("BIS")

Central banks other than the Fed likewise extended swap lines in their currencies, though typically these were more limited in scope than the Fed's. The figure above illustrates the remarkable network of swap lines that emerged.

The Fed wound down its swap lines in February 2010 but reactivated some when the European debt crisis erupted shortly afterward and interbank markets again became jittery (Chapter 21). Recent experience clearly shows the need for global lenders of last resort in different currencies, but it is doubtful that national central banks will or can play this role on a permanent basis. One possibility is to assign that function to the IMF, which saw its lending resources triple as world governments responded to the crisis.

International Regulatory Initiatives after the Global Financial Crisis

The severity and breadth of the 2007–2009 crisis have led to initiatives to reform both national financial systems and the international system. We now describe some of these measures, which have sought to fill gaps in existing regulatory frameworks while also paying more attention to the macroeconomic causes and consequences of banking problems.

Basel III   The financial crisis made obvious the inadequacies of the Basel II regulatory framework, so in 2010, the Basel Committee proposed a tougher set of capital standards and regulatory safeguards for international banks, Basel III. Regarding capital, the new Basel framework makes it harder for banks to get around capital requirements (for example, it takes a broader view of the risks banks are running, including through off-balance sheet entities, and also requires banks to guard against more pessimistic scenarios than previously). But like Basel II, Basel III still attaches risk weights to different assets, with assets deemed less risky leading to lower required capital. Importantly, Basel III also proposes to phase in a Liquidity Coverage Ratio, under which banks would be required to hold enough cash or highly liquid bonds to cover thirty days of cash outflow in specified crisis conditions. A Net Stable Funding Ratio seeks to limit banks' reliance on short-term wholesale funding (in contrast to retail deposits). As of the end of March 2013, only 11 countries (not including the U.S. and the EU) had fully implemented Basel III; but many more were in the process of adopting its rules. In December 2011, the U.S. Federal Reserve announced its intention to apply the Basel III rules not only to banks, but also to other financial institutions with assets exceeding $50 billion.[13]

The Financial Stability Board   In 1999, policymakers from a handful of industrialized countries established the Financial Stability Forum, housed (like the Basel Committee) in the BIS. The goal, however, was to promote international coordination over a broader set of financial stability issues (including, but going beyond, bank regulation), and among a potentially broader group of macroeconomic policymakers. In April 2009, at the height of the global crisis, the Financial Stability Forum became the Financial Stability Board (FSB), with a broader membership (including a number of emerging market economies) and a larger permanent staff. The FSB's job is to monitor the global financial system and make recommendations for global policy coordination and reform, sometimes in cooperation with other international agencies such as the IMF.

National Reforms   Individual countries have not limited themselves to implementing the Basel III recommendations. In a number of cases, including the euro zone, the United Kingdom, and the United States, countries have embarked on far-reaching reforms of their domestic financial systems. In 2010, the U.S. Congress passed the Dodd-Frank act, which, among other things, empowers the government to regulate nonbank financial institutions deemed "systemically important" (such as Lehman or AIG) and also allows the government to take over those firms in much the same way that the FDIC takes over and resolves failing banks.[14]

---

[13]You can explore the Basel III framework (and its implementation) on your own at http://www.bis.org/bcbs/basel3.htm?ql=1, on the BIS website.

[14]See Mishkin, *op. cit.*

The Macroprudential Perspective   An important lesson of the global financial crisis is that it is not enough for financial regulators to ensure that each individual financial institution is sound. This in itself will not ensure that the financial system *as a whole* is sound, and in fact, measures that would make an individual institution more resilient, given that the broader financial system is healthy, could put the broader system into jeopardy if implemented simultaneously by all institutions. The **macroprudential perspective** on financial regulation seeks to avoid such fallacies of composition at the aggregate level.[15]

As an example, consider the Basel capital standards, which apply different risk weights to different assets to determine the amount of capital banks need to hold. If there are two assets, A and B, with similar returns, but asset B has the lower Basel risk weight, all banks will wish to hold asset B rather than asset A. But in this case, the system *as a whole* will be more vulnerable to a fall in asset B's price than if banks were more diversified between the two assets. This is exactly what happened in 2007 when U.S. and European banks were all so heavily invested in securities tied to the U.S. housing market, and therefore all vulnerable to the U.S. housing downturn. A major concern about the new Basel rules is that they do not do enough to correct this system-level problem.

However, in other respects the Basel III proposals recognize the macroprudential problem. For example, the Basel Committee has proposed that banks increase their capital ratios during lending booms in order to make the system more resilient during downturns, at which time capital requirements would be loosened. Why is this plan for "countercyclical capital buffers" helpful? If instead all banks simultaneously sell assets to increase their capital buffers in a financial crisis—which is what a *micro* prudential approach might suggest that they do—the result would be an asset "fire sale" that depresses securities prices and therefore endangers the solvency of the system as a whole.

In the United States, the Dodd-Frank act set up a Financial Stability Oversight Council (FSOC), which includes the Fed chair and the Treasury Secretary, to monitor macroeconomic aspects of financial stability, including risks from the shadow banking system. The FSOC has the power to designate individual financial institutions as systemically important and subject them to enhanced supervision. It can also recommend breaking up institutions that are so big or interconnected as to pose a threat to the economy. However, the biggest financial institutions are, if anything, even bigger after the financial crisis, and many observers remain concerned that the U.S. and other countries have done too little to solve the "too big to fail" problem and reduce moral hazard in financial markets. After seeing the effects of the Lehman failure, policymakers still may remain too fearful of contagion to allow a major international bank to fail.

National Sovereignty and the Limits of Globalization   National financial regulators often face fierce lobbying from their home financial institutions, which argue that stricter rules would put them at a disadvantage relative to foreign rivals (while also being ineffective due to the foreign competition). The Basel multilateral process, like multilateral trade liberalization under the GATT and the WTO, plays an essential rule in allowing governments to overcome domestic political pressures against adequate oversight and control of the financial sector. The process partially addresses the financial trilemma by facilitating some limited delegation of national sovereignty over financial policy. The constraints of the trilemma are still important, however.

---

[15]The monograph by Brunnermeier et al., in Further Readings provides an excellent overview.

For example, a country wishing to control a domestic housing boom may forbid its banks from lending too much to prospective home buyers, but may be unable to prevent foreign banks from lending. In this case, there is a tradeoff between financial stability and financial integration; and countries may be tempted to react through capital controls or other measures that segregate domestic financial markets. Unless governments can successfully contain the risks posed by financial markets, it seems unlikely that financial globalization can continue to proceed as it has over recent decades.

How Well Have International Financial Markets Allocated Capital and Risk?

The present structure of the international capital market involves risks of financial instability that can be reduced only through the close cooperation of bank and financial supervisors in many countries. But the same profit motive that leads multinational financial institutions to innovate their way around national regulations can also provide important gains for consumers. As we have seen, the international capital market allows residents of different countries to diversify their portfolios by trading risky assets. Further, by ensuring a rapid international flow of information about investment opportunities around the world, the market can help allocate the world's savings to their most productive uses. How well has the international capital market performed in these respects?

The Extent of International Portfolio Diversification

Since accurate data on the overall portfolio positions of a country's residents are sometimes impossible to assemble, it can be difficult to gauge the extent of international portfolio diversification by direct observation. Nonetheless, some U.S. data can be used to get a rough idea of changes in international diversification in recent years.

In 1970, the foreign assets held by U.S. residents were equal in value to 6.2 percent of the U.S. capital stock (including residential housing). Foreign claims on the United States amounted to 4.0 percent of its capital stock. By 2008, U.S.-owned assets abroad equaled 46.6 percent of U.S. capital, while foreign assets in the United States had risen to about 54.7 percent of U.S. capital.

The recent percentages are much larger than those in 1970 but still seem too small. With full international portfolio diversification, we would expect them to reflect the size of the U.S. economy relative to that of the rest of the world. Thus, in a fully diversified world economy, something like 80 percent of the U.S. capital stock would be owned by foreigners, while U.S. residents' claims on foreigners would equal around 80 percent of the value of the U.S. capital stock. Moreover, the numbers in the previous paragraph describe total foreign assets—stocks, foreign direct investment, and bonds alike—not just stocks and FDI, which alone represent claims on capital. (For the U.S., fewer than half of its foreign assets are stocks and FDI, while less than a third of its foreign liabilities are stocks and FDI.) What makes the apparently incomplete extent of international equity portfolio diversification even more puzzling is the presumption most economists would make that the potential gains from diversification are large. An influential study by the French financial economist Bruno Solnik, for example, estimated that a U.S. investor holding only American stocks could more than halve the riskiness of her portfolio by further diversification into stocks from

European countries.[16] Thus, the observed *home bias* in equity holdings is hard to understand.

The data do show, however, that international asset trade has increased substantially as a result of the growth of the international capital market. Further, international asset holdings are large in absolute terms. At the end of 2012, for example, U.S. claims on foreigners were equal to about 138 percent of the U.S. GNP in that year, while foreign claims on the United States were about 163 percent of U.S. GNP. (Recall Figure 13-3, page 368.) Stock exchanges around the world have established closer communication links, and companies are showing an increasing readiness to sell shares on foreign exchanges. The seemingly incomplete extent of international equity diversification attained so far, however, is not necessarily a strong indictment of the world capital market. The market has certainly contributed to a stunning rise in asset trade in recent decades. Further, the U.S. experience is not necessarily typical. Table 20-1 illustrates the trend over two decades for a sample of industrial countries, showing the countries' gross foreign assets and liabilities as percentages of their GDPs. The United Kingdom, already the world's financial center in the early 1980s,

TABLE 20-1	**Gross Foreign Assets and Liabilities of Selected Industrial Countries, 1983–2011 (percent of GDP)**			
		1983	**1993**	**2011**
Australia				
	Assets	12	34	83
	Liabilities	43	87	140
France				
	Assets	63	80	256
	Liabilities	46	89	289
Germany				
	Assets	38	64	230
	Liabilities	31	54	205
Italy				
	Assets	22	43	106
	Liabilities	26	55	131
Netherlands				
	Assets	93	148	450
	Liabilities	72	133	421
United Kingdom				
	Assets	150	202	694
	Liabilities	134	198	711
United States				
	Assets	31	40	146
	Liabilities	26	46	173

Source: Philip R. Lane and Gian Maria Milesi-Ferretti, "The External Wealth of Nations, Mark II: Revised and Extended Estimates of Foreign Assets and Liabilities, 1970–2004," *Journal of International Economics* 73 (November 2007), pp. 223–250. The table's 2011 figures come from the updated data reported on Philip Lane's home page, http://www.philiplane.org/EWN.html.

[16]See Solnik, "Why Not Diversify Internationally Rather Than Domestically?" *Financial Analysts Journal* (July–August 1974), pp. 48–54.

was deeply engaged in international financial markets then and is even more so now. A small country such as the Netherlands tends to have a high level of foreign assets and liabilities, while all countries in the euro zone (including the Netherlands) have increased their gross foreign investment positions since 1993 as a result of European capital market unification. The same trend is evident, albeit more mildly, for Australia and the United States. Even some emerging markets have begun to engage in significant asset swapping.

The welfare significance of these numbers is far from clear. To the extent that they represent greater diversification of economic risks, as in our analysis at the start of this chapter, they point to a more stable world economy. But most of these external asset and liabilities are debt instruments, including bank debts, in some cases driven by regulatory arbitrage. It is likely that they include systemically risky borrowing, as when a bank in the U.K. borrows short-term funds to invest in less liquid securities abroad. Thus, even though these data show that the volume of international asset transactions has increased enormously over the past decades, they also remind us that there is no foolproof measure of the socially optimal extent of foreign investment.

The Extent of Intertemporal Trade

An alternative way of evaluating the performance of the world capital market was suggested by economists Martin Feldstein and Charles Horioka. Feldstein and Horioka pointed out that a smoothly working international capital market allows countries' domestic investment rates to diverge widely from their saving rates. In such an idealized world, saving seeks out its most productive uses worldwide, regardless of their location; at the same time, domestic investment is not limited by national saving because a global pool of funds is available to finance it.

For many countries, however, differences between national saving and domestic investment rates (that is, current account balances) have not been large since World War II: Countries with high saving rates over long periods also have usually had high investment rates, as Figure 20-3 illustrates. Feldstein and Horioka concluded from this evidence that cross-border capital mobility is low, in the sense that most of any sustained increase in national saving will lead to increased capital accumulation at home. The world capital market, according to this view, does not do a good job of helping countries reap the long-run gains of intertemporal trade.[17]

The main problem with the Feldstein-Horioka argument is that it is impossible to gauge whether the extent of intertemporal trade is deficient without knowing if there are unexploited trade gains, and knowing this requires more knowledge about actual economies than we generally have. For example, a country's saving and investment may usually move together simply because the factors that generate a high saving rate (such as rapid economic growth) also generate a high investment rate. In such cases, the country's gain from intertemporal trade may simply be small. An alternative explanation of high saving-investment correlations is that governments have tried to manage macroeconomic policy to avoid large current account imbalances. In any case, events appear to be overtaking this particular debate. For industrialized countries, the empirical regularity noted by Feldstein and Horioka seems to have weakened recently in the face of the high external imbalances of the United States, Japan, Switzerland, and some of the euro zone countries.

---

[17]See Martin Feldstein and Charles Horioka, "Domestic Savings and International Capital Flows," *Economic Journal* 90 (June 1980), pp. 314–329.

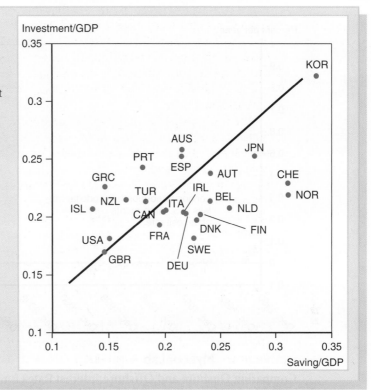

FIGURE 20-3

Saving and Investment Rates for 24 Countries, 1990–2011 Averages

OECD countries' saving and investment ratios to output tend to be positively related. The straight regression line in the graph represents a statistician's best guess of the level of the investment ratio, conditional on the saving ratio, in this country sample.

Source: World Bank, *World Development Indicators*.

Onshore-Offshore Interest Differentials

A quite different barometer of the international capital market's performance is the relationship between onshore and offshore interest rates on similar assets denominated in the same currency. If the world capital market is doing its job of communicating information about global investment opportunities, these interest rates should move closely together and not differ too greatly. Large interest rate differences would be strong evidence of unrealized gains from trade.

Figure 20-4 shows data since the end of 1990 on the interest rate difference between two comparable bank liabilities, three-month dollar deposits in London and three-month certificates of deposit issued in the United States. These data are imperfect because the interest rates compared are not measured at precisely the same moment. Nonetheless, they provide no indication of any large unexploited gains in normal times. The pattern of onshore-offshore interest differences is similar for other industrial countries.

The London-U.S. differential does begin to creep up with the outbreak of global financial turbulence in August 2007, and it reaches a peak in October 2008, the month after the Lehman Brothers collapse. Evidently, investors perceived that the dollar deposits of U.S. banks would be backstopped by the U.S. Treasury and Federal Reserve, but that dollar deposits in London might not receive the same protection.

The Efficiency of the Foreign Exchange Market

The foreign exchange market is a central component of the international capital market, and the exchange rates it sets help determine the profitability of international transactions of all types. Exchange rates therefore communicate important economic

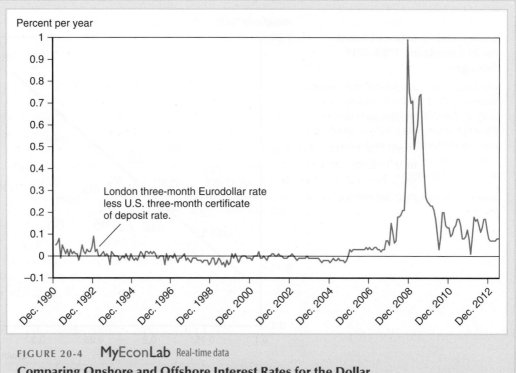

FIGURE 20-4   **MyEconLab** Real-time data

Comparing Onshore and Offshore Interest Rates for the Dollar

The difference between the London and U.S. interest rates on dollar deposits is usually very close to zero, but it spiked up sharply in the fall of 2008 as the investment bank Lehman Brothers collapsed.

Source: Board of Governors of the Federal Reserve System, monthly data.

signals to households and firms engaged in international trade and investment. If these signals do not reflect all available information about market opportunities, a misallocation of resources will result. Studies of the foreign exchange market's use of available information are therefore potentially important in judging whether the international capital market is sending the right signals to markets. We examine three types of tests: tests based on interest parity, tests based on modeling risk premiums, and tests for excessive exchange rate volatility.

Studies Based on Interest Parity   The interest parity condition that was the basis of the discussion of exchange rate determination in Chapter 14 has also been used to study whether market exchange rates incorporate all available information. Recall that interest parity holds when the interest difference between deposits denominated in two different currencies is the market's forecast of the percentage by which the exchange rate between those currencies will change. More formally, if R_t is the date t interest rate on home currency deposits, R_t^* is the interest rate on foreign currency deposits, E_t is the exchange rate (defined as the home currency price of foreign currency), and E_{t+1}^e is the exchange rate that market participants expect when the deposits paying interest R_t and R_t^* mature, the interest parity condition is

$$R_t - R_t^* = (E_{t+1}^e - E_t)/E_t. \tag{20-1}$$

Equation (20-1) implies a simple way to test whether the foreign exchange market is doing a good job of using current information to forecast exchange rates. Since the interest difference, $R_t - R_t^*$, is the market's forecast, a comparison of this *predicted* exchange rate change with the *actual* exchange rate change that subsequently occurs indicates the market's skill in forecasting.[18]

Statistical studies of the relationship between interest rate differences and later depreciation rates show that the interest difference has been a very bad predictor, in the sense that it has failed to catch any of the large swings in exchange rates. We noted this failure in Chapter 14's discussion of the carry trade. Even worse, as we noted there, the interest difference has, on average, failed to predict correctly the *direction* in which the spot exchange rate would change. If the interest rate difference were a poor but unbiased predictor, we could argue that the market is setting the exchange rate according to interest parity and doing the best job possible in a rapidly changing world where prediction is inherently difficult. The finding of bias, however, seems at odds with that interpretation of the data.

The interest parity condition also furnishes a test of a second implication of the hypothesis that the market uses all available information in setting exchange rates. Suppose that E_{t+1} is the actual future exchange rate people are trying to guess; then the forecast error they make in predicting future depreciation, u_{t+1}, can be expressed as actual minus expected depreciation:

$$u_{t+1} = (E_{t+1} - E_t)/E_t - (E_{t+1}^e - E_t)/E_t. \qquad (20\text{-}2)$$

If the market is making use of all available information, its forecast error, u_{t+1}, should be statistically unrelated to data known to the market on date t, when expectations were formed. In other words, there should be no opportunity for the market to exploit known data to reduce its later forecast errors.

Under interest parity, this hypothesis can be tested by writing u_{t+1} as actual currency depreciation less the international interest difference:

$$u_{t+1} = (E_{t+1} - E_t)/E_t - (R_t - R_t^*). \qquad (20\text{-}3)$$

Statistical methods can be used to examine whether u_{t+1} is predictable, on average, on the basis of past information. A number of researchers have found that forecast errors, when defined as above, *can* be predicted. For example, past forecast errors, which are widely known, are useful in predicting future errors.[19]

The Role of Risk Premiums   One explanation of the research results described above is that the foreign exchange market simply ignores easily available information in setting exchange rates. Such a finding would throw doubt on the international capital

---

[18]Most studies of exchange market efficiency study how the forward exchange rate premium does as a predictor of subsequent spot exchange rate changes. That procedure is equivalent to the one we are following if the covered interest parity condition holds, so that the interest difference $R_t - R_t^*$ equals the forward premium (see the appendix to Chapter 14). As noted in Chapter 14, there is strong evidence that covered interest parity holds when the interest rates being compared apply to deposits in the same financial center—for example, London Eurocurrency rates.

[19]For further discussion, see Robert E. Cumby and Maurice Obstfeld, "International Interest Rate and Price Level Linkages Under Flexible Exchange Rates: A Review of Recent Evidence," in John F. O. Bilson and Richard C. Marston, eds., *Exchange Rate Theory and Practice* (Chicago: University of Chicago Press, 1984), pp. 121–151; and Lars Peter Hansen and Robert J. Hodrick, "Forward Exchange Rates as Optimal Predictors of Future Spot Rates: An Econometric Analysis," *Journal of Political Economy* 88 (October 1980), pp. 829–853.

market's ability to communicate appropriate price signals. Before jumping to this conclusion, however, recall that when people are risk averse, the interest parity condition may *not* be a complete account of how exchange rates are determined. If, instead, bonds denominated in different currencies are *imperfect* substitutes for investors, the international interest rate difference equals expected currency depreciation *plus* a risk premium, ρ_t:

$$R_t - R_t^* = (E_{t+1}^e - E_t)/E_t + \rho_t \tag{20-4}$$

(see Chapter 18). In this case, the interest difference is not necessarily the market's forecast of future depreciation. Thus, under imperfect asset substitutability, the empirical results just discussed cannot be used to draw inferences about the foreign exchange market's efficiency in processing information.

Because people's expectations are inherently unobservable, there is no simple way to decide between equation (20-4) and the interest parity condition, which is the special case that occurs when ρ_t is always zero. Several econometric studies have attempted to explain departures from interest parity on the basis of particular theories of the risk premium, but none has been entirely successful.[20]

The mixed empirical record leaves the following two possibilities: Either risk premiums are important in exchange rate determination, or the foreign exchange market has been ignoring the opportunity to profit from easily available information. The second alternative seems unlikely in light of foreign exchange traders' powerful incentives to make profits. The first alternative, however, awaits solid statistical confirmation. It is certainly not supported by the evidence reviewed in Chapter 18, which suggests that sterilized foreign exchange intervention has not been an effective tool for exchange rate management. More sophisticated theories show, however, that sterilized intervention may be powerless even under imperfect asset substitutability. Thus, a finding that sterilized intervention is ineffective does not necessarily imply that risk premiums are absent. Another possibility, raised in Chapter 14's Case Study on the carry trade, is one of expected large but infrequent reversals in currency trends that standard statistical techniques are ill-equipped to detect.

Tests for Excessive Volatility

One of the most worrisome findings is that statistical forecasting models of exchange rates based on standard "fundamental" variables like money supplies, government deficits, and output perform badly—even when *actual* (rather than predicted) values of future fundamentals are used to form exchange rate forecasts! Indeed, in a famous study, Richard A. Meese of Barclays Global Investors and Kenneth Rogoff of Harvard University showed that a naive, "random walk" model, which simply takes today's exchange rate as the best guess of tomorrow's, performs better. Some have viewed this finding as evidence that exchange rates have a life of their own, unrelated to the macroeconomic determinants we have emphasized in our models. More recent research has confirmed, however, that while the random walk outperforms more sophisticated models for forecasts up to a year away, the

---

[20]For useful surveys, see Charles Engel, "The Forward Discount Anomaly and the Risk Premium: A Survey of Recent Evidence," *Journal of Empirical Finance* 3 (1996), pp. 123–192; Karen Lewis, "Puzzles in International Finance," in Gene M. Grossman and Kenneth Rogoff, eds., *Handbook of International Economics*, Vol. 3 (Amsterdam: North-Holland, 1996); and Hanno Lustig and Adrien Verdelhan, "Exchange Rates in a Stochastic Discount Factor Framework," in Jessica James, Ian W. Marsh, and Lucio Sarno, eds., *Handbook of Exchange Rates* (Hoboken, NJ: John Wiley & Sons, 2012), pp. 391–420.

models seem to do better at horizons longer than a year and have explanatory power for long-run exchange rate movements.[21]

An additional line of research on the foreign exchange market examines whether exchange rates have been excessively volatile, perhaps because the foreign exchange market "overreacts" to events. A finding of excessive volatility would prove that the foreign exchange market is sending confusing signals to traders and investors who base their decisions on exchange rates. But how volatile must an exchange rate be before its volatility becomes excessive? As we saw in Chapter 14, exchange rates *should* be volatile, because to send the correct price signals, they must move swiftly in response to economic news. Exchange rates are generally less volatile than stock prices. It is still possible, though, that exchange rates are substantially more volatile than the underlying factors that move them—such as money supplies, national outputs, and fiscal variables. Attempts to compare exchange rates' volatility with those of their underlying determinants have, however, produced inconclusive results. A basic problem underlying tests for excessive volatility is the impossibility of quantifying exactly all the variables that convey relevant news about the economic future. For example, how does one attach a number to a political assassination attempt, a major bank failure, or a terrorist attack?

The Bottom Line The ambiguous evidence on the foreign exchange market's performance warrants an open-minded view. A judgment that the market is doing its job well would support a laissez-faire attitude by governments and a continuation of the present trend toward increased cross-border financial integration in the industrial world. A judgment of market failure, on the other hand, might imply a need for increased foreign exchange intervention by central banks and a reversal of the global trend toward external financial liberalization. The stakes are high, and more research and experience are needed before a firm conclusion can be reached.

SUMMARY

1. When people are *risk averse*, countries can gain through the exchange of risky assets. The gains from trade take the form of a reduction in the riskiness of each country's consumption. International *portfolio diversification* can be carried out through the exchange of *debt instruments* or *equity instruments*.

2. The *international capital market* is the market in which residents of different countries trade assets. One of its important components is the foreign exchange market. Banks are at the center of the international capital market, and many operate offshore, that is, outside the countries where their head offices are based.

3. Regulatory and political factors have encouraged *offshore banking*. The same factors have encouraged *offshore currency trading*, that is, trade in bank deposits

---

[21]The original Meese-Rogoff study is "Empirical Exchange Rate Models of the Seventies: Do They Fit Out of Sample?" *Journal of International Economics* 14 (February 1983), pp. 3–24. On longer-run forecasts, see Menzie D. Chinn and Richard A. Meese, "Banking on Currency Forecasts: How Predictable Is Change in Money?" *Journal of International Economics* 38 (February 1995), pp. 161–178; and Nelson C. Mark, "Exchange Rates and Fundamentals: Evidence on Long-Horizon Predictability," *American Economic Review* 85 (March 1995), pp. 201–218. A recent survey is Pasquale Della Corte and Ilias Tsiakas, "Statistical and Economic Methods for Evaluating Exchange Rate Predictability," in Jessica James, Ian W. Marsh, and Lucio Sarno, eds., *Handbook of Exchange Rates* (Hoboken, NJ: John Wiley & Sons, 2012), pp. 221–263.

denominated in currencies of countries other than the one in which the bank is located. Such *Eurocurrency* trading received a major stimulus from the absence of reserve requirements on deposits in *Eurobanks.*

4. Creation of a Eurocurrency deposit does not occur because that currency leaves its country of origin; rather, all that is required is that a Eurobank accept a deposit liability denominated in the currency. Eurocurrencies therefore pose no threat to central banks' control over their domestic monetary bases, and fears that *Eurodollars*, for example, will some day come "flooding into" the United States are misplaced.

5. Offshore banking is largely unprotected by the safeguards that national governments have imposed to prevent domestic bank failures. In addition, the opportunity that banks have to shift operations offshore, thereby profiting from *regulatory arbitrage*, has undermined the effectiveness of national bank supervision. These problems create a *financial trilemma* that international policymakers have tried to mitigate through increasingly ambitious cross-border collaboration. Since 1974, the *Basel Committee* of industrial-country bank supervisors has worked to enhance global regulatory cooperation, including international standards for *bank capital*. A third generation of proposed prudential regulations (Basel III) was released in 2010 and is in process of implementation by national regulators. There is still uncertainty, however, about a central bank's obligations as an international *lender of last resort*. That uncertainty may reflect an attempt by international authorities to reduce *moral hazard*. The trend toward securitization has increased the need for international cooperation in monitoring and regulating nonbank financial institutions. So has the rise of *emerging markets* and of large *shadow banking systems*. Gaps in the global financial safety net became evident during the global financial crisis of 2007–2009. A key lesson of the crisis is that governments should adopt a *macroprudential perspective* in evaluating financial risks, rather than worrying only about the soundness of individual institutions.

6. The losses caused by financial crises must be evaluated against the gains that international capital markets potentially offer. The international capital market has contributed to an increase in international portfolio diversification since 1970, but the extent of diversification still appears incomplete compared with what economic theory would predict. Similarly, some observers have claimed that the extent of intertemporal trade, as measured by countries' current account balances, has been too small. Such claims are hard to evaluate without more detailed information about the functioning of the world economy than is yet available. Less ambiguous evidence comes from international interest rate comparisons, and this evidence points to a well-functioning market (apart from rare periods of international financial crisis). Rates of return on similar deposits issued in the major financial centers are normally quite close.

7. The foreign exchange market's record in communicating appropriate price signals to international traders and investors is mixed. Tests based on the interest parity condition of Chapter 14 seem to suggest that the market ignores readily available information in setting exchange rates; but because the interest parity theory ignores risk aversion and the resulting risk premiums, the theory may be an oversimplification of reality. Attempts to model risk factors empirically have not, however, been very successful. Tests of excessive exchange rate volatility also yield a mixed verdict on the foreign exchange market's performance. Together with the recent history of financial crises, this is not good news for those who favor a pure laissez-faire approach to financial globalization.

KEY TERMS

PROBLEMS

MyEconLab

1. Which portfolio is better diversified, one that contains stock in a dental supply company and a candy company or one that contains stock in a dental supply company and a dairy product company?

2. Imagine a world of two countries in which the only causes of fluctuations in stock prices are unexpected shifts in monetary policies. Under which exchange rate regime would the gains from international asset trade be greater, fixed or floating?

3. The text points out that covered interest parity holds quite closely for deposits of differing currency denominations issued in a single financial center. Why might covered interest parity fail to hold when deposits issued in *different* financial centers are compared?

4. Consider having a total of $2000 to buy assets from two countries—India and China. Suppose, the annual rate of return from Chinese and Indian assets is 10 percent and 5 percent respectively—this rate may reverse at any time during the year. Where will you invest your money if you are averse to risk? Explain the likely outcome for a risk lover?

5. The Swiss economist Alexander Swoboda has argued that the Eurodollar market's early growth was fueled by the desire of banks outside the United States to appropriate some of the revenue the United States was collecting as issuer of the principal reserve currency. (This argument is made in *The Euro-Dollar Market: An Interpretation*, Princeton Essays in International Finance 64, International Finance Section, Department of Economics, Princeton University, February 1968.) Do you agree with Swoboda's interpretation?

6. After the developing-country debt crisis began in 1982 (see Chapter 22), U.S. bank regulators imposed tighter supervisory restrictions on the lending policies of American banks and their subsidiaries. Over the 1980s, the share of U.S. banks in London banking activity declined. Can you suggest a connection between these two developments?

7. Define moral hazards in a banking system. How would increased moral hazards affect an economy's financial health?

8. Return to the example in the text of the two countries that produce random amounts of kiwi fruit and can trade claims on that fruit. Suppose the two countries also produce raspberries that spoil if shipped between countries and therefore are nontradable. How do you think this would affect the ratio of international asset trade to GNP for Home and Foreign?

9. Sometimes it is claimed that the international equality of *real* interest rates is the most accurate barometer of international financial integration. Do you agree? Why or why not?

10. The Australian Bureau of Statistics shows that between June 1999 and June 2009, Australia's debt to the rest of the world increased sharply. In the meantime the exchange rate of Australian dollar changed in the international market. Do you think that the there is a link between the exchange rate and external debt. If so, how would depreciation in the Australian dollar affect the Australian debt in the future, *ceteris paribus*?

11. In interpreting ratios such as those in Table 20-1, one must be cautious about drawing the conclusion that diversification is rising as rapidly as the reported numbers rise. Suppose a Brazilian buys a U.S. international equity fund, which places its client's money in Brazil's stock market. What happens to Brazilian and U.S. gross foreign assets and liabilities? What happens to Brazilian and U.S. international diversification?

12. Banks are not happy when regulators force them to raise the ratio of capital to total assets: they argue that this reduces their potential profits. When a bank *borrows* more in order to purchase more risky assets, however, the interest rate it must pay on the borrowing should be high enough to compensate the lenders for the risk that the bank cannot repay in full—and the higher interest rate reduces bank profits. In light of this observation, is it obvious to you that it is more profitable for the bank to finance its asset purchase by borrowing, rather than by issuing additional shares of stock (and thereby increasing rather than reducing its ratio of capital to total assets)?

13. Define bank failure. Many countries adopt different measures to safeguard against bank failure. Would increased reserve requirements prevent one? How is a bank's money creation affected if the central bank increases the reserve requirements?

14. If you return to Figure 20-4, you will notice that London Eurodollar interest rates tend to exceed U.S. certificate of deposit rates after the global financial crisis, but not before. Why do you think this is the case? (Be sure to return to this question after you read the next chapter!)

FURTHER READINGS

Viral V. Acharya, Nirupama Kulkarni, and Matthew Richardson. "Capital, Contingent Capital, and Liquidity Requirements," in Viral V. Acharya, Thomas F. Cooley, Matthew P. Richardson, and Ingo Walter, eds., *Regulating Wall Street: The Dodd-Frank Act and the Architecture of Global Finance.* Hoboken, NJ: John Wiley & Sons, 2011, pp. 143–180. Clear discussion of the goals and limitations of the Dodd-Frank act and Basel III.

Anat Admati and Martin Hellwig. *The Bankers' New Clothes: What's Wrong with Banking and What to Do about It.* Princeton, NJ: Princeton University Press, 2013. A lucid account of banks' incentives to propagate financial fragility by financing their asset holdings with debt rather than capital.

Alan S. Blinder. *After the Music Stopped: The Financial Crisis, the Response, and the Work Ahead.* New York: Penguin Press, 2013. An influential economist's account of the origins and repercussions of the global financial crisis of 2007–2009.

Markus K. Brunnermeier, Andrew Crockett, Charles A. E. Goodhart, Avinash Persaud, and Hyun Song Shin. *The Fundamental Principles of Financial Regulation.* Geneva and London: International Center for Monetary and Banking Studies and Centre for Economic Policy Research, 2009. Comprehensive review of regulatory approaches to financial crisis prevention, with emphasis on the macroprudential perspective.

Stijn Claessens, Richard J. Herring, and Dirk Schoenmaker. *A Safer World Financial System: Improving the Resolution of Systemic Institutions.* Geneva and London: International Center for Monetary and Banking Studies and Centre for Economic Policy Research, 2010. Discusses the reorganization of insolvent institutions in a global setting.

Nicolas Coeurdacier and Hélène Rey. "Home Bias in Open Economy Financial Macroeconomics." *Journal of Economic Literature* 51 (March 2012), pp. 63–115. Advanced theoretical and empirical overview of home bias in international asset portfolios.

Barry Eichengreen. "International Financial Regulation after the Crisis." *Daedalus* (Fall 2010), pp. 107–114. Description and critique of the current institutional framework for global cooperation in regulating international finance.

Stanley Fischer. "On the Need for an International Lender of Last Resort." *Journal of Economic Perspectives* 13 (Fall 1999): 85–104. Focuses on the IMF's ability to function as an international LLR.

Charles A. E. Goodhart. "Myths about the Lender of Last Resort." *International Finance* 2 (November 1999), pp. 339–360. Clear discussion of the theory and practice of the LLR function.

Charles P. Kindleberger and Robert Aliber. *Manias, Panics, and Crashes: A History of Financial Crises*, 5th edition. Hoboken, NJ: John Wiley & Sons, 2005. An historical review of international financial crises from the 17th century to the present day.

Richard M. Levich. "Is the Foreign Exchange Market Efficient?" *Oxford Review of Economic Policy* 5 (1989), pp. 40–60. Valuable survey of research on the efficiency of the foreign exchange market.

Haim Levy and Marshall Sarnat. "International Portfolio Diversification," in Richard J. Herring, ed. *Managing Foreign Exchange Risk*. Cambridge, U.K.: Cambridge University Press, 1983, pp. 115–142. A nice exposition of the logic of international asset diversification.

Nelson C. Mark. *International Macroeconomics and Finance*. Oxford: Blackwell Publishers, 2001. Chapter 6 discusses the efficiency of the foreign exchange market.

Maurice Obstfeld. "The Global Capital Market: Benefactor or Menace?" *Journal of Economic Perspectives* 12 (Fall 1998), pp. 9–30. Overview of the functions, operations, and implications for national sovereignty of the international capital market.

Maurice Obstfeld and Kenneth Rogoff. "Global Imbalances and the Financial Crisis: Products of Common Causes," in Reuven Glick and Mark Spiegel, eds. *Asia and the Global Financial Crisis*. San Francisco, CA: Federal Reserve Bank of San Francisco, 2010. An analysis of the links between global financial flows and the financial crisis of 2007–2009.

Carmen M. Reinhart and Kenneth S. Rogoff. *This Time Is Different: Eight Centuries of Financial Folly*. Princeton, NJ: Princeton University Press, 2009. Data-based historical overview of the precedents and effects of financial crises around the world.

Garry J. Schinasi. *Safeguarding Financial Stability: Theory and Practice*. Washington, D.C.: International Monetary Fund, 2006. Thorough overview of financial stability threats in a context of globalized financial markets.

MyEconLab Can Help You Get a Better Grade

MyEconLab If your exam were tomorrow, would you be ready? For each chapter, MyEconLab Practice Tests and Study Plans pinpoint sections you have mastered and those you need to study. That way, you are more efficient with your study time, and you are better prepared for your exams.

To see how it works, turn to page 41 and then go to

www.myeconlab.com

CHAPTER 21

OPTIMUM CURRENCY AREAS AND THE EURO

On January 1, 1999, 11 member countries of the European Union (EU) adopted a common currency, the euro. They have since been joined by seven more EU members. Europe's bold experiment in economic and monetary union (EMU), which many had viewed as a visionary fantasy only a few years earlier, created a currency area with more than 335 million consumers—roughly 7 percent more populous than the United States. If the countries of Eastern Europe all eventually enter the euro zone, it will comprise more than 25 countries and stretch from the Arctic Ocean in the north to the Mediterranean Sea in the south, and from the Atlantic Ocean in the west to the Black Sea in the east. Figure 21-1 shows the extent of the euro zone as of 2014.

The birth of the euro resulted in fixed exchange rates between all EMU member countries. In deciding to form a monetary union, however, EMU countries sacrificed even more sovereignty over their monetary policies than a fixed exchange rate regime normally requires. They agreed to give up national currencies entirely and to hand over control of their monetary policies to a shared European Central Bank (ECB). The euro project thus represents an extreme solution to the monetary policy trilemma of Chapter 19: absolute exchange rate stability, absolute openness to financial trade, but no monetary autonomy whatsoever.

The European experience raises a host of important questions. How and why did Europe set up its single currency? What benefits has the euro delivered for the economies of its members, and why have they found themselves in a protracted crisis? How does the euro affect countries outside of EMU, notably the United States? And what lessons does the European experience carry for other potential currency blocs, such as the Mercosur trading group in South America?

This chapter focuses on Europe's experience of monetary unification to illustrate the economic benefits and costs of fixed exchange rate agreements and more comprehensive currency unification schemes. As we see in Europe's experience, the effects of joining a fixed exchange rate agreement are complex and depend crucially on microeconomic *and* macroeconomic factors. Our discussion

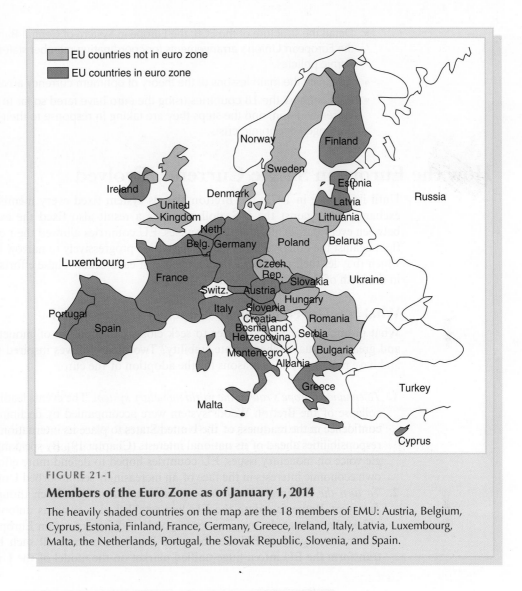

FIGURE 21-1

Members of the Euro Zone as of January 1, 2014

The heavily shaded countries on the map are the 18 members of EMU: Austria, Belgium, Cyprus, Estonia, Finland, France, Germany, Greece, Ireland, Italy, Latvia, Luxembourg, Malta, the Netherlands, Portugal, the Slovak Republic, Slovenia, and Spain.

of Europe will throw light not only on the forces promoting greater unification of national economies but also on the forces that make a country think twice before giving up completely its control over monetary policy.

LEARNING GOALS

After reading this chapter, you will be able to:

- Discuss why Europeans have long sought to stabilize their mutual exchange rates while floating against the U.S. dollar.
- Describe how the European Union, through the Maastricht Treaty of 1991, placed itself on the road to having a single currency, the euro, issued and managed by a European Central Bank (ECB).

- Detail the structure of the ECB, the European System of Central Banks, and the European Union's arrangements for coordinating member states' economic policies.
- Articulate the main lessons of the theory of optimum currency areas.
- Recount how the 18 countries using the euro have fared so far in their currency union, and the steps they are taking in response to their prolonged economic crisis.

How the European Single Currency Evolved

Until its demise in 1973, the Bretton Woods system fixed every member country's exchange rate against the U.S. dollar and as a result also fixed the exchange rate between every pair of nondollar currencies. EU countries allowed their currencies to float against the dollar after 1973, but have tried progressively to narrow the extent to which they let their currencies fluctuate against each other. These efforts culminated in the birth of the euro on January 1, 1999.

What Has Driven European Monetary Cooperation?

What prompted the EU countries to seek closer coordination of monetary policies and greater mutual exchange rate stability? Two main motives inspired these moves and have remained major reasons for the adoption of the euro:

1. *To enhance Europe's role in the world monetary system.* The events leading up to the collapse of the Bretton Woods system were accompanied by declining European confidence in the readiness of the United States to place its international monetary responsibilities ahead of its national interests (Chapter 19). By speaking with a single voice on monetary issues, EU countries hoped to defend more effectively their own economic interests in the face of an increasingly self-absorbed United States.
2. *To turn the European Union into a truly unified market.* Even though the 1957 Treaty of Rome founding the EU had established a customs union, significant official barriers to the movements of goods and factors within Europe remained. A consistent goal of EU members has been to eliminate all such barriers and transform the EU into a huge unified market on the model of the United States.

TABLE 21-1	**A Brief Glossary of Euronyms**
ECB	European Central Bank
EFSF	European Financial Stability Facility
EMS	European Monetary System
EMU	Economic and Monetary Union
ERM	Exchange Rate Mechanism
ESCB	European System of Central Banks
ESM	European Stability Mechanism
EU	European Union
OMT	Outright Monetary Transactions
SGP	Stability and Growth Pact
SRM	Single Resolution Mechanism
SSM	Single Supervisory Mechanism

European officials believed, however, that exchange rate uncertainty, like official trade barriers, was a major factor reducing trade within Europe. They also feared that exchange rate swings causing large changes in intra-European relative prices would strengthen political forces hostile to free trade within Europe.[1]

The key to understanding how Europe has come so far in both market and monetary unification lies in the continent's war-torn history. After the end of World War II in 1945, many European leaders agreed that economic cooperation and integration among the former belligerents would be the best guarantee against a repetition of the 20th century's two devastating wars. The result was a gradual ceding of national economic policy powers to centralized European Union governing bodies, such as the European Commission in Brussels, Belgium (the EU's executive body), and the European Central Bank in Frankfurt, Germany.

The European Monetary System, 1979–1998

The first significant institutional step on the road to European monetary unification was the **European Monetary System (EMS)**. The eight original participants in the EMS's exchange rate mechanism—France, Germany, Italy, Belgium, Denmark, Ireland, Luxembourg, and the Netherlands—began operating a formal network of mutually pegged exchange rates in March 1979. A complex set of EMS intervention arrangements worked to restrict the exchange rates of participating currencies within specified fluctuation margins.[2]

The prospects for a successful fixed-rate area in Europe seemed bleak in early 1979, when recent yearly inflation rates ranged from Germany's 2.7 percent to Italy's 12.1 percent. Through a mixture of policy cooperation and realignment, however, the EMS fixed exchange rate club survived and even grew, adding Spain to its ranks in 1989, Britain in 1990, and Portugal early in 1992. Only in September 1992 did this growth suffer a sudden setback when Britain and Italy left the EMS exchange rate mechanism at the start of a protracted European currency crisis that forced the remaining members to retreat to very wide exchange rate margins.

The EMS's operation was aided by several safety valves that initially helped reduce the frequency of such crises. Most exchange rates "fixed" by the EMS until August 1993 actually could fluctuate up or down by as much as 2.25 percent relative to an assigned par value. A few members were able to negotiate bands of ±6 percent, making a greater sacrifice of exchange rate stability but gaining more room to choose their own monetary policies. In August 1993, EMS countries decided to widen nearly all of the bands to ±15 percent under the pressure of speculative attacks.

As another crucial safety valve, the EMS developed generous provisions for the extension of credit from strong- to weak-currency members. If the French franc (France's former currency) depreciated too far against the deutsche mark (or DM,

---

[1] A very important administrative reason Europeans have sought to avoid big movements in European cross-exchange rates is related to the Common Agricultural Policy (CAP), the EU's system of agricultural price supports. Prior to the euro, agricultural prices were quoted in terms of the European Currency Unit (ECU), a basket of EU currencies. Exchange rate realignments within Europe would abruptly alter the real domestic value of the supported prices, provoking protests from farmers in the revaluing countries. While the annoyance of administering the CAP under exchange rate realignments was undoubtedly crucial in starting Europeans on the road to currency unification, the two motives cited in the text are more important in explaining how Europe ultimately came to embrace a common currency.

[2] As a technical matter, all EU members were members of the EMS, but only those EMS members who enforced the fluctuation margins belonged to the EMS *exchange rate mechanism (ERM)*.

Germany's former currency), Germany's central bank, the Bundesbank, was expected to lend the Bank of France DM to sell for francs in the foreign exchange market.

Finally, during the system's initial years of operation several members (notably France and Italy) reduced the possibility of speculative attack by maintaining capital controls that directly limited domestic residents' sales of home for foreign currencies.

The EMS went through periodic currency realignments. In all, 11 realignments occurred between the start of the EMS in March 1979 and January 1987. Capital controls played the important role of shielding members' reserves from speculators during these adjustments. Starting in 1987, however, a phased removal of capital controls by EMS countries increased the possibility of speculative attacks and thus reduced governments' willingness openly to consider devaluing or revaluing. The removal of controls greatly reduced member countries' monetary independence (a consequence of the monetary policy trilemma), but freedom of payments and capital movements within the EU had always been a key element of EU countries' plan to turn Europe into a unified single market.

For a period of five and a half years after January 1987, no adverse economic event was able to shake the EMS's commitment to its fixed exchange rates. This state of affairs came to an end in 1992, however, as economic shocks caused by the reunification of East and West Germany in 1990 led to asymmetrical macroeconomic pressures in Germany and in its major EMS partners.

The result of reunification was a boom in Germany and higher inflation, which Germany's very inflation-averse central bank, the Bundesbank, resisted through sharply higher interest rates. (Germany's very high inflation after both world wars left permanent scars.) Other EMS countries such as France, Italy, and the United Kingdom, however, were not simultaneously booming. By matching the high German interest rates to hold their currencies fixed against Germany's, they were unwillingly pushing their own economies into deep recession. The policy conflict between Germany and its partners led to a series of fierce speculative attacks on the EMS exchange parities starting in September 1992. By August 1993, as previously noted, the EMS was forced to retreat to very wide (±15 percent) bands, which it kept in force until the introduction of the euro in 1999.

German Monetary Dominance and the Credibility Theory of the EMS

Earlier, we identified two main reasons why the European Union sought to fix internal exchange rates: a desire to defend Europe's economic interests more effectively on the world stage and the ambition to achieve greater internal economic unity.

Europe's experience of high inflation in the 1970s suggests an additional purpose that the EMS grew to fulfill. By fixing their exchange rates against the DM, the other EMS countries in effect imported the German Bundesbank's credibility as an inflation fighter and thus discouraged the development of inflationary pressures at home—pressures they might otherwise have been tempted to accommodate through monetary expansion. This view, the **credibility theory of the EMS**, holds that the political costs of violating an international exchange rate agreement may be useful. They can restrain governments from depreciating their currencies to gain the short-term advantage of an economic boom at the long-term cost of higher inflation.

Policy makers in inflation-prone EMS countries, such as Italy, clearly gained credibility by placing monetary policy decisions in the hands of the inflation-fearing German central bank. Devaluation was still possible, but only subject to EMS restrictions. Because politicians also feared that they would look incompetent to voters

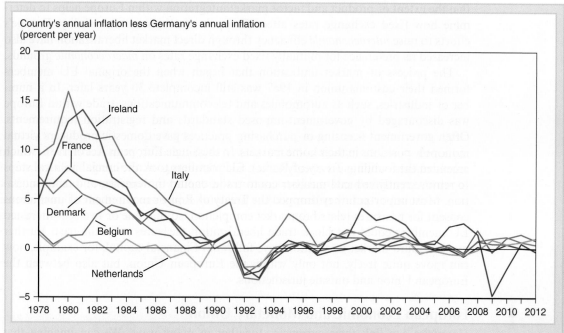

FIGURE 21-2   MyEconLab Real-time data

Inflation Convergence for Six Original EMS Members, 1978–2012

Shown are the differences between domestic inflation and German inflation for six of the original EMS members: Belgium, Denmark, France, Ireland, Italy, and the Netherlands.

Source: CPI inflation rates from International Monetary Fund, *International Financial Statistics.*

if they devalued, a government's decision to peg to the DM reduced both its willingness and its ability to create domestic inflation.[3]

Added support for the credibility theory comes from the behavior of inflation rates relative to Germany's, shown in Figure 21-2 for six of the other original EMS members.[4] As the figure shows, annual inflation rates gradually converged toward the low German levels.[5]

Market Integration Initiatives

The EU countries have tried to achieve greater internal economic unity not only by fixing mutual exchange rates, but also through direct measures to encourage the free flow of goods, services, and factors of production. Later in this chapter you will learn

---

[3]The general theory that an inflation-prone country gains from vesting its monetary policy decisions with a "conservative" central bank is developed in an influential paper by Kenneth Rogoff. See "The Optimal Degree of Commitment to an Intermediate Monetary Target," *Quarterly Journal of Economics* 100 (November 1985), pp. 1169–1189. For application to the EMS, see Francesco Giavazzi and Marco Pagano, "The Advantage of Tying One's Hands: EMS Discipline and Central Bank Credibility," *European Economic Review* 32 (June 1988), pp. 1055–1082.

[4]Figure 21-2 does not include the tiny country of Luxembourg because before 1999, that country had a currency union with Belgium and an inflation rate very close to Belgium's.

[5]Those skeptical of the credibility theory of EMS inflation convergence point out that the United States, Britain, and Japan also reduced inflation to low levels over the 1980s, but did so without fixing their exchange rates. Many other countries have done the same since.

that the extent of product and factor market integration within Europe helps to determine how fixed exchange rates affect Europe's macroeconomic stability. Europe's efforts to raise *microeconomic* efficiency through direct market liberalization have also increased its preference for mutually fixed exchange rates on *macroeconomic* grounds.

The process of market unification that began when the original EU members formed their customs union in 1957 was still incomplete 30 years later. In a number of industries, such as automobiles and telecommunications, trade within Europe was discouraged by government-imposed standards and registration requirements. Often government licensing or purchasing practices gave domestic producers virtual monopoly positions in their home markets. In the Single European Act of 1986 (which amended the founding Treaty of Rome), EU members took the crucial political steps to remove remaining internal barriers to trade, capital movements, and labor migration. Most important, they dropped the Treaty of Rome's requirement of unanimous consent for measures related to market completion, so that one or two self-interested EU members could not block trade liberalization measures as in the past. Further moves toward market integration have followed. Financial capital, for example, now can move quite freely, not only within the European Union, but also between the European Union and outside jurisdictions.

European Economic and Monetary Union

Countries can link their currencies together in many ways. We can imagine that the different modes of linkage form a spectrum, with the arrangements at one end requiring little sacrifice of monetary policy independence and those at the other end requiring independence to be given up entirely.

The early EMS, characterized by frequent currency realignments and widespread government control over capital movements, left some scope for national monetary policies. In 1989, a committee headed by Jacques Delors, president of the European Commission, recommended a three-stage transition to a goal at the extreme end of the policy spectrum just described. That goal was an **economic and monetary union (EMU)**, a European Union in which national currencies would be replaced by a single EU currency managed by a sole central bank operating on behalf of all EU members.

On December 10, 1991, the leaders of the EU countries met at the ancient Dutch city of Maastricht and agreed to propose for national ratification far-reaching amendments to the Treaty of Rome. These amendments were meant to place the EU squarely on the road to EMU. Included in the 250-page **Maastricht Treaty** was a provision calling for the introduction of a single European currency and a European Central Bank no later than January 1, 1999. By 1993, all 12 countries then belonging to the EU had ratified the Maastricht Treaty. The 16 countries that joined the EU afterward accepted the Treaty's provisions upon joining (see Figure 21-1).[6]

Why did the EU countries move away from the EMS and toward the much more ambitious goal of a single shared currency? There were four reasons:

1. They believed a single EU currency would produce a greater degree of European market integration than fixed exchange rates by removing the threat of EMS currency realignments and eliminating the costs to traders of converting one EMS

---

[6]Denmark and the United Kingdom, however, ratified the Maastricht Treaty subject to special exceptions that allow them to "opt out" of the treaty's monetary provisions and retain their national currencies. Sweden has no formal opt out, but it has exploited other technicalities in the Maastricht Treaty to avoid joining the euro zone so far.

currency into another. The single currency was viewed as a necessary complement to plans for melding EU markets into a single, continent-wide market.

2. Some EU leaders thought that Germany's management of EMS monetary policy had placed a one-sided emphasis on German macroeconomic goals at the expense of its EMS partners' interests. The European Central Bank that would replace the German Bundesbank under EMU would have to be more considerate of other countries' problems, and it would automatically give those countries the same opportunity as Germany to participate in system-wide monetary policy decisions.

3. Given the move to complete freedom of capital movements within the EU, there seemed to be little to gain, and much to lose, from keeping national currencies with fixed (but adjustable) parities rather than irrevocably locking parities through a single currency. Any system of fixed exchange rates among distinct national currencies would be subject to ferocious speculative attacks, as in 1992–1993. If Europeans wished to combine permanently fixed exchange rates with freedom of capital movements, a single currency was the best way to accomplish this.

4. As previously noted, all of the EU countries' leaders hoped the Maastricht Treaty's provisions would guarantee the political stability of Europe. Beyond its purely economic functions, the single EU currency was intended as a potent symbol of Europe's desire to place cooperation ahead of the national rivalries that often had led to war in the past. Under this scenario, the new currency would align the economic interests of individual European nations to create an overwhelming political constituency for peace on the continent.

The Maastricht Treaty's critics denied that EMU would have these positive effects and opposed the treaty's provisions for vesting stronger governmental powers with the European Union. To these critics, EMU was symptomatic of a tendency for the European Union's central institutions to ignore local needs, meddle in local affairs, and downgrade prized symbols of national identity (including, of course, national currencies). Germany's citizens in particular, traumatized by memories of severe postwar inflations, feared that the new European Central Bank would not fight inflation as fiercely as their Bundesbank did.

The Euro and Economic Policy in the Euro Zone

How were the initial members of EMU chosen, how are new members admitted, and what is the structure of the complex of financial and political institutions that govern economic policy in the euro zone? This section provides an overview.

The Maastricht Convergence Criteria and the Stability and Growth Pact

The Maastricht Treaty requires EU countries to satisfy several macroeconomic convergence criteria prior to admission to EMU. Among these criteria are:

1. The country's inflation rate in the year before admission must be no more than 1.5 percent above the average rate of the three EU member states with the lowest inflation.

2. The country must have maintained a stable exchange rate within the ERM without devaluing on its own initiative.

3. The country must have a public-sector deficit no higher than 3 percent of its GDP (except in exceptional and temporary circumstances).

4. The country must have a public debt that is below or approaching a reference level of 60 percent of its GDP.

The treaty provides for the ongoing monitoring of criteria 3 and 4 mentioned previously by the European Commission even after admission to EMU, and for the levying of penalties on countries that violate these fiscal rules and do not correct situations of "excessive" deficits and debt. The surveillance and sanctions over high deficits and debts place national governments under constraints in the exercise of their national fiscal powers. For example, a highly indebted EMU country facing a national recession might be unable to use expansionary fiscal policy for fear of breaching the Maastricht limits—a possibly costly loss of policy autonomy, given the absence of a national monetary policy!

In addition, a supplementary **Stability and Growth Pact (SGP)** negotiated by European leaders in 1997 tightened the fiscal straitjacket further. The SGP set out "the medium-term budgetary objective of positions close to balance or in surplus." It also set a timetable for the imposition of financial penalties on countries that fail to correct situations of "excessive" deficits and debt promptly enough. What explains the macroeconomic convergence criteria, the fear of high public debts, and the SGP? Before they would sign the Maastricht Treaty, low-inflation countries such as Germany wanted assurance that their EMU partners had learned to prefer an environment of low inflation and fiscal restraint. They feared that otherwise, the euro might be a weak currency, falling prey to the types of policies that have fueled French, Greek, Italian, Portuguese, Spanish, and United Kingdom inflation at various points since the early 1970s. A highly indebted government that continues to borrow may find that the market demand for its bonds disappears—a nightmare scenario that finally came to pass for several European countries in the euro crisis starting in 2009. Another fear about EMU was that the new European Central Bank would face pressures to purchase government debt directly in such situations, thereby fueling money supply growth and inflation. Voters in traditionally low-inflation countries worried that prudent governments within EMU would be forced to pick up the tab for profligate governments that borrowed more than they could afford to repay. This was especially true in Germany, where taxpayers in the country's western part were bearing the cost of absorbing the formerly Communist east. Consistent with this fear, the Maastricht Treaty also contained a "no bailout clause" prohibiting EU member countries from taking on other members' debts.

As EMU came closer in 1997, German public opinion therefore remained opposed to the euro. The German government demanded the SGP as a way of convincing domestic voters that the new European Central Bank would indeed produce low inflation and avoid bailouts. Ironically, because Germany (along with France) is one of the countries that was subsequently in violation of the Maastricht fiscal rules, the SGP was not enforced in practice during the euro's first decade—even though later experience showed the concerns that motivated it to be valid, as we shall see.

By May 1998, it was clear that 11 EU countries had satisfied the convergence criteria on the basis of 1997 data and would be founding members of EMU: Austria, Belgium, Finland, France, Germany, Ireland, Italy, Luxembourg, the Netherlands, Portugal, and Spain. Greece failed to qualify on any of the criteria in 1998, although it ultimately appeared to pass all of its tests and entered EMU on January 1, 2001. Since then, Slovenia (on January 1, 2007), Cyprus and Malta (both on January 1, 2008), the Slovak Republic (January 1, 2009), Estonia (January 1, 2011), and Latvia (January 1, 2014) also have joined the euro zone.

The European Central Bank and the Eurosystem

The *Eurosystem* conducts monetary policy for the euro zone and consists of the *European Central Bank* (ECB) in Frankfurt plus the 18 national central banks of the euro area, which now play roles analogous to those of the regional Federal Reserve banks in the United States. Decisions of the Eurosystem are made by votes of the governing council of the ECB, consisting of the six-member ECB executive board (including the president of the ECB) and the heads of the national central banks of the euro area. The European System of Central Banks (ESCB) consists of the ECB plus all 28 EU central banks, including those of countries that do not use the euro. Like members of the Eurosystem, non-euro area central banks are committed to pursue domestic price stability as well as various forms of cooperation with the Eurosystem.

The authors of the Maastricht Treaty hoped to create an independent central bank free of the political influences that might lead to inflation.[7] The treaty gives the ECB an overriding mandate to pursue price stability and includes many provisions intended to insulate monetary policy decisions from political influence. In addition, unlike any other central bank in the world, the ECB operates above and beyond the reach of any single national government. In the United States, for example, Congress could easily pass laws reducing the independence of the Federal Reserve. In contrast, while the ECB is required to brief the European Parliament regularly on its activities, the European Parliament has no power to alter the statute of the ECB and ESCB. That would require an amendment to the Maastricht Treaty approved by legislatures or voters in every member country of the EU. However, critics of the treaty argue that it goes too far in shielding the ECB from normal democratic processes.

The Revised Exchange Rate Mechanism

For EU countries that are not yet members of EMU, a revised exchange rate mechanism—referred to as ERM 2—defines broad exchange rate zones against the euro (± 15 percent) and specifies reciprocal intervention arrangements to support these target zones. ERM 2 was viewed as necessary to discourage competitive devaluations against the euro by EU members outside the euro zone and to give would-be EMU entrants a way of satisfying the Maastricht Treaty's exchange rate stability convergence criterion. Under ERM 2 rules, either the ECB or the national central bank of an EU member with its own currency can suspend euro intervention operations if they result in money supply changes that threaten to destabilize the domestic price level. In practice ERM 2 is asymmetric, with peripheral countries pegging to the euro and adjusting passively to ECB decisions on interest rates.

The Theory of Optimum Currency Areas

There is little doubt that the European monetary integration process has helped advance the *political* goals of its founders by giving the European Union a stronger position in international affairs. The survival and future development of the European monetary experiment depend more heavily, however, on its ability to help countries reach their *economic* goals. Here the picture is less clear because a country's decision to fix its exchange rate can in principle lead to economic sacrifices as well as benefits.

We saw in Chapter 19 that by changing its exchange rate, a country may succeed in cushioning the disruptive impact of various economic shocks. On the other hand, exchange rate flexibility can have potentially harmful effects, such as making relative

---

[7]Several studies show that central bank independence appears to be associated with lower inflation. A recent assessment is offered by Christopher Crowe and Ellen E. Meade, "Central Bank Independence and Transparency: Evolution and Effectiveness," *European Journal of Political Economy* 24 (December 2008), pp. 763–777.

prices less predictable or undermining the government's resolve to keep inflation in check. To weigh the economic costs against the advantages of joining a group of countries with mutually fixed exchange rates, we need a framework for thinking systematically about the stabilization powers a country sacrifices and the gains in efficiency and credibility it may reap.

In this section, we show that a country's costs and benefits from joining a fixed exchange rate area such as the euro zone depend on how integrated its economy is with those of its potential partners. The analysis leading to this conclusion, which is known as the theory of **optimum currency areas**, predicts that fixed exchange rates are most appropriate for areas closely integrated through international trade and factor movements.[8]

Economic Integration and the Benefits of a Fixed Exchange Rate Area: The *GG* Schedule

Consider how an individual country, for example, Norway, might approach the decision of whether to join an area of fixed exchange rates, for example, the euro zone. Our goal is to develop a simple diagram that clarifies Norway's choice.

We begin by deriving the first of two elements in the diagram, a schedule called *GG* that shows how the potential gain to Norway from joining the euro zone depends on Norway's trading links with that region. Let us assume that Norway is considering pegging its currency, the krone, to the euro.

A major economic benefit of fixed exchange rates is that they simplify economic calculations and, compared to floating rates, provide a more predictable basis for decisions that involve international transactions. Imagine the time and resources American consumers and businesses would waste every day if each of the 50 United States had its own currency that fluctuated in value against the currencies of all the other states! Norway faces a similar disadvantage in its trade with the euro zone when it allows its krone to float against the euro. The **monetary efficiency gain** from joining the fixed exchange rate system equals the joiner's savings from avoiding the uncertainty, confusion, and calculation and transaction costs that arise when exchange rates float.[9]

In practice, it may be hard to attach a precise number to the total monetary efficiency gain Norway would enjoy as a result of pegging to the euro. We can be sure, however, that this gain will be higher if Norway trades a lot with euro zone countries. For example, if Norway's trade with the euro zone amounts to 50 percent of its GNP while its trade with the United States amounts to only 5 percent of GNP, then, other things equal, a fixed krone/euro exchange rate clearly yields a greater monetary efficiency gain to Norwegian traders than a fixed krone/dollar rate. Similarly, the efficiency gain from a fixed krone/euro rate is greater when trade between Norway and the euro zone is extensive than when it is small.

---

[8]The original reference is Robert A. Mundell's classic article "The Theory of Optimum Currency Areas," *American Economic Review* 51 (September 1961), pp. 717–725. Subsequent contributions are summarized in the book by Tower and Willett listed in Further Readings. Mundell was trying to make the point that the optimum currency area need not coincide with national boundaries. As we shall see, however, recent experience in the euro area suggests that if the currency area does reach beyond national borders, some key governmental functions may need to be delegated to supra-national authorities acting on behalf of the currency union as a whole.

[9]To illustrate just one component of the monetary efficiency gain, potential savings of commissions paid to brokers and banks on foreign exchange transactions, Charles R. Bean of the Bank of England estimated that in 1992, a "round-trip" through all the European Union currencies would result in the loss of fully *half* the original sum. See his paper "Economic and Monetary Union in Europe," *Journal of Economic Perspectives* 6 (Fall 1992), pp. 31–52.

The monetary efficiency gain from pegging the krone to the euro will also be higher if factors of production can migrate freely between Norway and the euro area. Norwegians who invest in euro zone countries benefit when the returns on their investments are more predictable. Similarly, Norwegians who work in euro zone countries may benefit if a fixed exchange rate makes their wages more stable relative to Norway's cost of living.

Our conclusion is that *a high degree of economic integration between a country and a fixed exchange rate area magnifies the monetary efficiency gain the country reaps when it fixes its exchange rate against the area's currencies.* The more extensive are cross-border trade and factor movements, the greater is the gain from a fixed cross-border exchange rate.

The upward-sloping *GG* curve in Figure 21-3 shows the relation between a country's degree of economic integration with a fixed exchange rate area and the monetary efficiency gain to the country from joining the area. The figure's horizontal axis measures the extent to which Norway (the joining country in our example) is economically integrated into euro zone product and factor markets. The vertical axis measures the monetary efficiency gain to Norway from pegging to the euro. *GG*'s positive slope reflects the conclusion that the monetary efficiency gain a country gets by joining a fixed exchange rate area rises as its economic integration with the area increases.

In our example, we have implicitly assumed that the larger exchange rate area, the euro zone, has a stable and predictable price level. If it does not, the greater variability in Norway's price level that would follow a decision to join the exchange rate area would likely offset any monetary efficiency gain a fixed exchange rate might provide. A different problem arises if Norway's commitment to fix the krone's exchange rate is not fully believed by economic actors. In this situation, some exchange rate uncertainty would remain and Norway would therefore enjoy a smaller monetary efficiency gain. If the euro zone's price level is stable and Norway's exchange rate commitment is firm, however, the main conclusion follows: When Norway pegs to the euro, it gains from the stability of its currency against the euro, and this efficiency gain is greater the more closely tied are Norway's markets with euro zone markets.

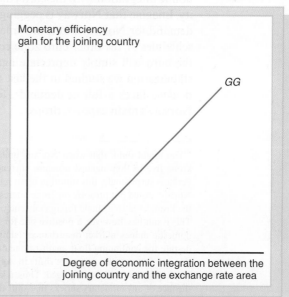

FIGURE 21-3

The *GG* Schedule

The upward-sloping *GG* schedule shows that a country's monetary efficiency gain from joining a fixed exchange rate area rises as the country's economic integration with the area rises.

Earlier in this chapter, we learned that a country may wish to peg its exchange rate to an area of price stability to import the anti-inflationary resolve of the area's monetary authorities. When the economy of the pegging country is well integrated with that of the low-inflation area, however, low domestic inflation is easier to achieve. The reason is that close economic integration leads to international price convergence and therefore lessens the scope for independent variation in the pegging country's price level. This argument provides another reason why high economic integration with a fixed exchange rate area enhances a country's gain from membership.

Economic Integration and the Costs of a Fixed Exchange Rate Area: The *LL* Schedule

Membership in an exchange rate area may involve costs as well as benefits, even when the area has low inflation. These costs arise because a country that joins an exchange rate area gives up its ability to use the exchange rate and monetary policy for the purpose of stabilizing output and employment. This **economic stability loss** from joining, like the country's monetary efficiency gain, is related to the country's economic integration with its exchange rate partners. We can derive a second schedule, the *LL* schedule, that shows the relationship graphically.

In Chapter 19's discussion of the relative merits of fixed and floating exchange rates, we concluded that when the economy is disturbed by a change in the output market (that is, by a shift in the *DD* schedule), a floating exchange rate has an advantage over a fixed rate: It automatically cushions the economy's output and employment by allowing an immediate change in the relative price of domestic and foreign goods. Furthermore, you will recall from Chapter 18 that when the exchange rate is fixed, purposeful stabilization is more difficult to achieve because monetary policy has no power at all to affect domestic output. Given these two conclusions, we would expect changes in the *DD* schedule to have more severe effects on an economy in which the monetary authority is required to fix the exchange rate against a group of foreign currencies. The *extra* instability caused by the fixed exchange rate is the economic stability loss.[10]

To derive the *LL* schedule, we must understand how the extent of Norway's economic integration with the euro zone will affect the size of this loss in economic stability. Imagine that Norway is pegging to the euro and that there is a fall in the aggregate demand for Norway's output—a leftward shift of Norway's *DD* schedule. If the *DD* schedules of the other euro zone countries happen simultaneously to shift to the left, the euro will simply depreciate against outside currencies, providing the automatic stabilization we studied in the last chapter. Norway has a serious problem only when it *alone* faces a fall in demand—for example, if the world demand for oil, one of Norway's main exports, drops.

---

[10]You might think that when Norway unilaterally fixes its exchange rate against the euro but leaves the krone free to float against noneuro currencies, it is able to keep at least some monetary independence. Perhaps surprisingly, this intuition is *wrong*. The reason is that any independent money supply change in Norway would put pressure on krone interest rates and thus on the krone/euro exchange rate. So by pegging the krone even to a single foreign currency, Norway completely surrenders its domestic monetary control. This result has, however, a positive side for Norway. After Norway unilaterally pegs the krone to the euro, domestic money market disturbances (shifts in the *AA* schedule) will no longer affect domestic output, despite the continuing float against noneuro currencies. Why? Because Norway's interest rate must equal the euro interest rate, any pure shifts in *AA* will result in immediate reserve inflows or outflows that leave Norway's interest rate unchanged. Thus, a krone/euro peg alone is enough to provide automatic stability in the face of any monetary shocks that shift the *AA* schedule. This is why the discussion in the text can focus on shifts in the *DD* schedule.

How will Norway adjust to this shock? Since nothing has happened to budge the euro, to which Norway is pegged, its krone will remain stable against *all* foreign currencies. Thus, full employment will be restored only after a period of costly slump during which the prices of Norwegian goods and the wages of Norwegian workers fall.

How does the severity of this slump depend on the level of economic integration between the Norwegian economy and those of the EMU countries? The answer is that greater integration implies a shallower slump, and therefore a less costly adjustment to the adverse shift in *DD*. There are two reasons for this reduction in the cost of adjustment: First, if Norway has close trading links with the euro zone, a small reduction in its prices will lead to an increase in euro zone demand for Norwegian goods that is large relative to Norway's output. Thus, full employment can be restored fairly quickly. Second, if Norway's labor and capital markets are closely meshed with those of its euro zone neighbors, unemployed workers can easily move abroad to find work, and domestic capital can be shifted to more profitable uses in other countries. The ability of factors to migrate abroad thus reduces the severity of unemployment in Norway and the fall in the rate of return available to investors.[11]

Notice that our conclusions also apply to a situation in which Norway experiences an *increase* in demand for its output (a rightward shift of *DD*). If Norway is tightly integrated with euro zone economies, a small increase in Norway's price level, combined with some movement of foreign capital and labor into Norway, quickly eliminates the excess demand for Norwegian products.[12]

Closer trade links between Norway and countries *outside* the euro zone will also aid the country's adjustment to Norwegian *DD* shifts that are not simultaneously experienced by the euro zone. However, greater trade integration with countries outside the euro zone is a double-edged sword, with negative as well as positive implications for macroeconomic stability. The reason is that when Norway pegs the krone to the euro, euro zone disturbances that change the euro's exchange rate will have more powerful effects on Norway's economy when its trading links with noneuro countries are more extensive. The effects would be analogous to an increase in the size of movements in Norway's *DD* curve and would raise Norway's economic stability loss from pegging to the euro. In any case, these arguments do not change our earlier conclusion that Norway's stability loss from fixing the krone/euro exchange rate falls as the extent of its economic integration with the euro zone rises.

An additional consideration that we have not yet discussed strengthens the argument that the economic stability loss to Norway from pegging to the euro is lower

---

[11]Installed plant and equipment typically are costly to transport abroad or to adapt to new uses. Owners of such relatively immobile Norwegian capital therefore will always earn low returns on it after an adverse shift in the demand for Norwegian products. If Norway's capital market is integrated with those of its EMU neighbors, however, Norwegians will invest some of their wealth in other countries, while at the same time part of Norway's capital stock will be owned by foreigners. As a result of this process of international wealth *diversification* (see Chapter 20), unexpected changes in the return to Norway's capital will automatically be shared among investors throughout the fixed exchange rate area. Thus, even owners of capital that cannot be moved can avoid more of the economic stability loss due to fixed exchange rates when Norway's economy is open to capital flows.

When international labor mobility is low or nonexistent, higher international capital mobility may *not* reduce the economic stability loss from fixed exchange rates, as we discuss in evaluating the European experience in the Case Study on pp. 683–686.

[12]The preceding reasoning applies to other economic disturbances that fall unequally on Norway's output market and those of its exchange rate partners. A problem at the end of this chapter asks you to think through the effects of an increase in demand for EMU exports that leaves Norway's export demand schedule unchanged.

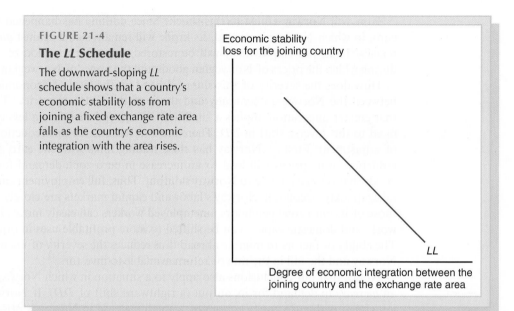

FIGURE 21-4

The *LL* Schedule

The downward-sloping *LL* schedule shows that a country's economic stability loss from joining a fixed exchange rate area falls as the country's economic integration with the area rises.

when Norway and the euro zone engage in a large volume of trade. Since imports from the euro zone make up a large fraction of Norwegian workers' consumption in this case, changes in the krone/euro exchange rate may quickly affect nominal Norwegian wages, reducing any impact on employment. A depreciation of the krone against the euro, for example, causes a sharp fall in Norwegians' living standards when imports from the euro zone are substantial; workers are thus likely to demand higher nominal wages from their employers to compensate for the loss. In this situation the additional macroeconomic stability Norway gets from a floating exchange rate is small, so the country has little to lose by fixing the krone/euro exchange rate.

We conclude that *a high degree of economic integration between a country and the fixed exchange rate area that it joins reduces the resulting economic stability loss due to output market disturbances.*

The *LL* schedule shown in Figure 21-4 summarizes this conclusion. The figure's horizontal axis measures the joining country's economic integration with the fixed exchange rate area, the vertical axis the country's economic stability loss. As we have seen, *LL* has a negative slope because the economic stability loss from pegging to the area's currencies falls as the degree of economic interdependence rises.

The Decision to Join a Currency Area: Putting the *GG* and *LL* Schedules Together

Figure 21-5 combines the *GG* and *LL* schedules to show how Norway should decide whether to fix the krone's exchange rate against the euro. The figure implies that Norway should do so if the degree of economic integration between Norwegian markets and those of the euro zone is at least equal to θ_1, the integration level determined by the intersection of *GG* and *LL* at point 1.

Let's see why Norway should peg to the euro if its degree of economic integration with euro zone markets is at least θ_1. Figure 21-5 shows that for levels of economic integration below θ_1, the *GG* schedule lies below the *LL* schedule. Thus, the loss Norway would suffer from greater output and employment instability after joining exceeds the monetary efficiency gain, and the country would do better to stay out.

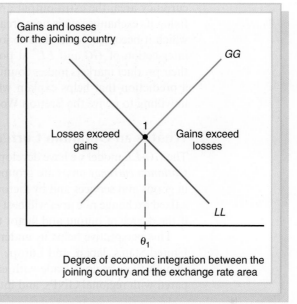

FIGURE 21-5

Deciding When to Peg the Exchange Rate

The intersection of *GG* and *LL* at point 1 determines a critical level of economic integration, θ_1, between a fixed exchange rate area and a country considering whether to join. At any level of integration above θ_1, the decision to join yields positive net economic benefits to the joining country.

Gains and losses for the joining country

GG

1

Losses exceed gains

Gains exceed losses

LL

θ_1

Degree of economic integration between the joining country and the exchange rate area

When the degree of integration is θ_1 or higher, however, the monetary efficiency gain measured by *GG* is greater than the stability sacrifice measured by *LL*, and pegging the krone's exchange rate against the euro results in a net gain for Norway. Thus the intersection of *GG* and *LL* determines the minimum integration level (here, θ_1) at which Norway will desire to peg its currency to the euro.

The *GG-LL* framework has important implications about how changes in a country's economic environment affect its willingness to peg its currency to an outside currency area. Consider, for example, an increase in the size and frequency of sudden shifts in the demand for the country's exports. As shown in Figure 21-6, such a change pushes LL^1 upward to LL^2. At any level of economic integration with the

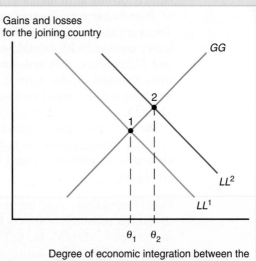

FIGURE 21-6

An Increase in Output Market Variability

A rise in the size and frequency of country-specific disturbances to the joining country's product markets shifts the *LL* schedule upward from LL^1 to LL^2 because for a given level of economic integration with the fixed exchange rate area, the country's economic stability loss from pegging its exchange rate rises. The shift in *LL* raises the critical level of economic integration at which the exchange rate area is joined to θ_2.

Gains and losses for the joining country

GG

2

1

LL^2

LL^1

θ_1 θ_2

Degree of economic integration between the joining country and the exchange rate area

currency area, the extra output and unemployment instability the country suffers by fixing its exchange rate is now greater. As a result, the level of economic integration at which it becomes worthwhile to join the currency area rises to θ_2 (determined by the intersection of GG and LL^2 at point 2). Other things equal, increased variability in their product markets makes countries less willing to enter fixed exchange rate areas— a prediction that helps explain why the oil price shocks after 1973 made countries unwilling to revive the Bretton Woods system of fixed exchange rates (Chapter 19).

What Is an Optimum Currency Area?

The *GG-LL* model we have developed suggests a theory of the optimum currency area. *Optimum currency areas* are groups of regions with economies closely linked by trade in goods and services and by factor mobility. This result follows from our finding that a fixed exchange rate area will best serve the economic interests of each of its members if the degree of output and factor trade among the included economies is high.

This perspective helps us understand, for example, why it may make sense for the United States, Japan, and Europe to allow their mutual exchange rates to float. Even though these regions trade with each other, the extent of that trade is modest compared with regional GNPs, and interregional labor mobility is low.

Other Important Considerations

While the *GG-LL* model is useful for organizing our thinking about optimum currency areas, it is not the whole story. At least three other elements affect our evaluation of the euro currency area's past and prospective performances.

Similarity of Economic Structure The *GG-LL* model tells us that extensive trade with the rest of the currency area makes it easier for a member to adjust to product market disturbances that affect it and its currency partners differently. But it does not tell us what factors will reduce the frequency and size of member-specific product market shocks.

A key element in minimizing such disturbances is similarity in economic structure, especially in the types of products produced. Euro zone countries, for example, are not entirely dissimilar in manufacturing structure, as evidenced by the very high volume of *intra-industry trade*—trade in similar products—within Europe (see Chapter 8). There are also important differences, however. The countries of northern Europe are better endowed with capital and skilled labor than the countries in Europe's south, and EU products that make intensive use of low-skill labor thus are likely to come from Portugal, Spain, Greece, or southern Italy. The different export patterns of northern and southern European countries create more opportunities for asymmetric shocks.

We can view greater structural dissimilarity between a country and its potential currency union partners as shifting the *LL* schedule upward, raising the degree of economic integration required before membership in the currency union becomes a good idea.

Fiscal Federalism Another consideration in evaluating a currency area is its ability to transfer economic resources from members with healthy economies to those suffering economic setbacks. In the United States, for example, states faring poorly relative to the rest of the nation automatically receive support from Washington in the form of welfare benefits and other federal transfer payments that ultimately come out of the taxes other states pay. In addition, the federal tax revenues sent back to Washington automatically decline when the local economy suffers. Such **fiscal federalism** can help offset the economic stability loss due to fixed exchange rates, as it does in the United States. More fiscal federalism shifts the *LL* curve downward.[13]

Banking Union   Suppose that countries in an area of mutually fixed exchange rates maintain national control over banking regulation, supervision, and resolution but at the same time allow freedom of financial transactions across borders, including for banks (and other financial institutions). As we saw in Chapter 20, the *financial trilemma* implies that their financial systems will be less stable than with centralized, supra-national control over financial regulatory policy.

The problem is even worse than usual in an area of fixed exchange rates, however. If member countries print money in large quantities while acting as lenders of last resort, for example, they may run out of international reserves and find themselves in a currency crisis (Chapter 18). Each central bank will therefore be reluctant to act as LLR for its domestic banks, and public perceptions of this reluctance could, in itself, encourage bank runs and thereby raise the risk of financial instability and currency crises. In terms of our *GG-LL* framework, less area-wide unification of banking policy raises the *LL* schedule. As we shall see, this problem has been central to the recent crisis in the euro area, although the preceding example based on the central bank's LLR function works in the EMU context in a more complex fashion.

As the financial trilemma suggests, one way to maintain fixed exchange rates, while retaining national control over financial policy, is to prohibit cross-border capital movements. This is not an option within a currency union such as EMU, with a single shared central bank, because the central bank's interest rate policy could not be transmitted to all the member states if they prevented cross-border borrowing and lending.

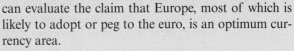

CASE STUDY   Is Europe an Optimum Currency Area?

The critical question for judging the economic success of EMU is whether Europe itself makes up an optimum currency area. A nation's gains and losses from pegging its currency to an exchange rate area are hard to measure numerically, but by combining our theory with information on actual economic performance, we can evaluate the claim that Europe, most of which is likely to adopt or peg to the euro, is an optimum currency area.

THE EXTENT OF INTRA-EUROPEAN TRADE

Our earlier discussion suggested that a country is more likely to benefit from joining a currency area if the area's economy is closely integrated with the country's. The overall degree of economic integration can be judged by looking at the integration of product markets, that is, the extent of trade between the

---

[13]The classic statement of the role of fiscal federalism in the theory of optimum currency areas is by Peter B. Kenen, "The Theory of Optimum Currency Areas: An Eclectic View," in Robert Mundell and Alexander Swoboda, eds., *Monetary Problems of the International Economy* (Chicago: University of Chicago Press, 1969), pp. 41–60. Perhaps surprisingly, the Kenen argument is valid even when people have access to very efficient private markets for sharing risks. See Emmanuel Farhi and Iván Werning, "Fiscal Unions," Working Paper 18280, National Bureau of Economic Research, August 2012.

joining country and the currency area, and at the integration of factor markets, that is, the ease with which labor and capital can migrate between the joining country and the currency area.

In January 1999, at the time of the euro's launch, most EU members exported from 10 to 20 percent of their output to other EU members. That number is far larger than the extent of EU-U.S. trade. While the average volume of intra-EU trade has increased somewhat since the late 1990s, however, it remains below the level of trade between regions of the United States. If we take trade relative to GNP as a measure of goods-market integration, the *GG-LL* model of the last section suggests that a joint float of Europe's currencies against those of the rest of the world is a better strategy for EU members than a fixed dollar/euro exchange rate would be. The extent of intra-European trade, however, is not large enough to convey an overwhelming reason for believing that the European Union itself is an optimum currency area.

When the euro was created, supporters entertained high hopes that it would promote trade substantially within the currency union. These hopes were bolstered by an influential econometric study by Andrew K. Rose, of the University of California—Berkeley, who suggested that on average, members of currency unions trade three times more with each other than with nonmember countries—even after one controls for other determinants of trade flows. A more recent study of EU trade data by Richard Baldwin, of Geneva's Graduate Institute of International and Development Studies, has greatly scaled back the estimates as they apply to the euro zone's experience so far.[14] Baldwin estimated that the euro increased the mutual trade levels of its users only by about 9 percent, with most of the effect taking place in the euro's first year, 1999. But he also concluded that Britain, Denmark, and Sweden, which did not adopt the euro, saw their trade with euro zone countries increase by about 7 percent at the same time. These EU countries therefore would gain little more if they adopted the euro.

EU measures aimed at promoting market integration following the Single European Act of 1986 probably have helped to bolster intra-EU trade. For some goods (such as consumer electronics), there has been considerable price convergence across EU countries, but for others, among them cars, similar items still can sell for widely differing prices in different European locations. One hypothesis about the persistence of price differentials that is favored by euro enthusiasts is that multiple currencies made big price discrepancies possible, but these were bound to disappear under the single currency. Has the euro itself contributed to market integration? In a careful study of European price behavior since 1990, economists Charles Engel of the University of Wisconsin and John Rogers of the Federal Reserve find that intra-European price

---

[14]See Baldwin, *In or Out: Does It Matter? An Evidence-Based Analysis of the Euro's Trade Effects* (London: Centre for Economic Policy Research, 2006). Rose reports his initial analysis and results in "One Money, One Market: The Effects of Common Currencies on Trade," *Economic Policy* 30 (April 2000), pp. 8–45. He based his methods on the "gravity model" of international trade (Chapter 2). Rose scaled down his estimate in Andrew K. Rose and Eric van Wincoop, "National Money as a Barrier to International Trade: The Real Case for Currency Union," *American Economic Review* 91 (May 2001), pp. 386–390. Using a more sophisticated model of international trade patterns, Rose and van Wincoop calculated the trade-creating effect of a currency union to be roughly a 50 percent increase in trade. Even this estimate appears much larger than the increase that followed the euro's introduction.

discrepancies indeed decreased over the 1990s. They find no evidence, however, of further price convergence after the euro's introduction in 1999.[15]

On balance, considering both the price and the quantity evidence to date, it seems unlikely that the combination of Single European Act reforms and the single currency has yet turned the euro zone into an optimum currency area.

HOW MOBILE IS EUROPE'S LABOR FORCE?

The main barriers to labor mobility within Europe are no longer due to border controls. Differences in language and culture discourage labor movements between European countries to a greater extent than is true, for example, between regions of the United States. In a 1990 econometric study comparing unemployment patterns in U.S. regions with those in EU countries, Barry Eichengreen of the University of California–Berkeley found that differences in regional unemployment rates are smaller and less persistent in the United States than are the differences between national unemployment rates in the European Union.[16] Figure 21-7 shows the evolution of selected EU unemployment rates since the early 1990s; the evident divergence after the late 2000s is the result of the recent crisis and will be discussed in the next section.

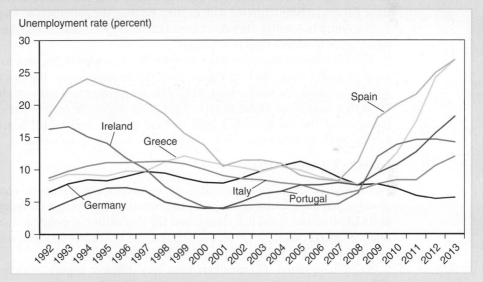

FIGURE 21-7   MyEconLab   Real-time data

Unemployment Rates in Selected EU Countries

Widely divergent unemployment rates moved closer together after the euro's launch in 1999 but since the late 2000s have moved sharply apart.

Source: International Monetary Fund, *World Economic Outlook* database, April 2013. Numbers for 2013 are IMF forecasts.

---

[15]See their paper "European Product Market Integration after the Euro," *Economic Policy* 39 (July 2004), pp. 347–381. For confirmation, see Jesús Crespo Cuaresma, Balázs Égert, and Maria Antoinette Silgoner, "Price Level Convergence in Europe: Did the Introduction of the Euro Matter?" *Monetary Policy and the Economy*, Oesterreichische Nationalbank (Q1 2007), pp. 100–113.

[16]See Eichengreen, "One Money for Europe? Lessons of the U.S. Currency Union," *Economic Policy* 10 (April 1990), pp. 118–166. Further study of the U.S. labor market has shown that regional unemployment is eliminated almost entirely by worker migration rather than by changes in regional real wages. See Olivier Jean Blanchard and Lawrence F. Katz, "Regional Evolutions," *Brookings Papers on Economic Activity* 1 (1992), pp. 1–75.

TABLE 21-2	People Changing Region of Residence in the 1990s (percent of total population)		
Britain	**Germany**	**Italy**	**United States**
1.7	1.1	0.5	3.1

Sources: Peter Huber, "Inter-regional Mobility in Europe: A Note on the Cross-Country Evidence," *Applied Economics Letters* 11 (August 2004), pp. 619–624; and "Geographical Mobility, 2003–2004," U.S. Department of Commerce, March 2004. Table data are for Britain in 1996, Germany in 1990, Italy in 1999, and the United States in 1999.

Even *within* European countries, labor mobility appears limited, partly because of government regulations. For example, the requirement in some countries that workers establish residence before receiving unemployment benefits makes it harder for unemployed workers to seek jobs in regions that are far from their current homes. Table 21-2 presents evidence on the frequency of regional labor movement in three of the largest EU countries, as compared with that in the United States. Although these data must be interpreted with caution because the definition of "region" differs from country to country, they do suggest that in a typical year, Americans are significantly more footloose than Europeans.[17]

There is some evidence that labor mobility has increased in response to the extreme unemployment rates visible in Figure 21-7. But to some degree this is a mixed blessing. The workers that tend to be most mobile are younger and more productive, while those that remain are closer to retirement. This migration pattern can deprive governments of the tax base they need to fund pension and health benefits, thereby worsening fiscal deficits in countries already hit hard by deep recession.

OTHER CONSIDERATIONS

Previously, we identified three additional considerations (alongside economic integration) that are relevant to the costs and benefits of forming a currency area: similarity of structure, fiscal federalism, and the unification of policy toward bank and financial market stability. On all three counts, the EU comes up short, reinforcing the hypothesis that the EU is not an optimum currency area.

As we have noted, EU members have very different export mixes and therefore different vulnerabilities to identical economic disturbances. For example, Portugal competes with China in export markets, whereas China is a big destination market for German machine tools. Thus, higher Chinese growth has very different effects on the Portuguese and German economies.

Regarding fiscal federalism, it is quite limited in the EU, which has no substantial centralized fiscal capacity. Country-specific shocks therefore are not offset by any inflows of budgetary resources from currency-union partners. Finally, regarding financial stability policy, the Maastricht Treaty left virtually all powers at the national level, giving the Eurosystem no explicit authority to oversee financial markets. The story of the euro crisis, to which we turn next, is intimately related to these last two shortcomings in the architecture underlying the single currency.

---

[17]For a more detailed discussion of the evidence, see Maurice Obstfeld and Giovanni Peri, "Regional Non-Adjustment and Fiscal Policy," *Economic Policy* 26 (April 1998), pp. 205–259.

The Euro Crisis and the Future of EMU

Like the rest of the world, the euro area was battered by the global financial crisis of 2007–2009 (described in Chapters 19 and 20). It was only toward the end of the acute phase of the global financial crisis, however—late in 2009—that the euro zone entered a new crisis so severe as to threaten its continuing existence. In this section we help you to understand the nature of the euro crisis, the ways in which it has been managed so far, and the implications for the future of EMU.

Origins of the Crisis

The spark that ignited the crisis came from an unlikely source: Greece, which accounted for only 3 percent of the euro area's output. However, the spark landed on a broad and deep pile of very dry tinder, assembled during the period of low interest rates, real estate speculation, and heightened financial-market growth that preceded the global financial crisis.

The Tinder   The global assets of internationally-active banks grew rapidly in the years leading up to the 2007–2009 crisis, but especially so for European banks, and especially banks in the euro zone. The asset sides of their balance sheets grew through purchases of U.S. credit-backed products, but also through lending to other euro zone countries, including purchases of government debt and lending to finance consumption spending, housing investment, and mortgage lending. This lending helped to fuel, and in turn was fueled by, massive housing booms, especially in Ireland and Spain (recall Figure 19-7). An important factor promoting these developments, as you learned in Chapter 19, was an environment of very low global interest rates, which induced banks to take greater risks in search of profits.

As a result of this credit expansion, bank assets grew to very large levels compared to the GDPs of the banks' home countries. Table 21-3 illustrates the positions of some large euro area banks at the end of 2011; balance sheets were even larger relative to output in 2007. In a number of countries individual banks had become "too big to

TABLE 21-3	Assets of Some Individual Banks as a Ratio to National Output, End-2011	
Bank	**Home country**	**Bank assets**
Erste Group Bank	Austria	0.68
Dexia	Belgium	1.10
BNP Paribas	France	0.97
Deutsche Bank	Germany	0.82
Bank of Ireland	Ireland	0.95
UniCredit	Italy	0.59
ING Group	Netherlands	2.12
Banco Commercial Português	Portugal	0.57
Banco Santander	Spain	1.19

Source: GDP data from International Monetary Fund, *World Economic Outlook* database. Data on bank assets from Viral V. Acharya and Sascha Steffen, "The 'Greatest' Carry Trade Ever? Understanding Eurozone Bank Risks," Discussion Paper 9432, Centre for Economic Policy Research, April 2013.

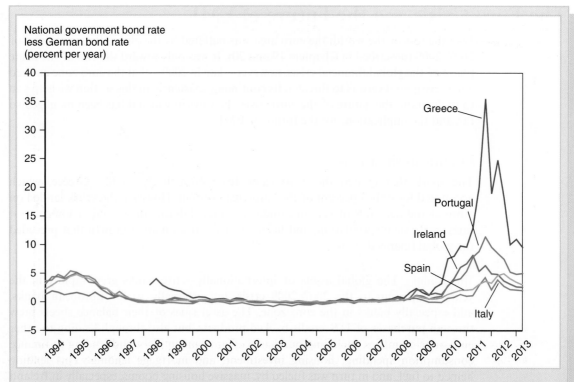

FIGURE 21-8

Nominal Government Borrowing Spreads over Germany

Euro countries' long-term government bond yields converged to Germany's level as they prepared to join the euro. The yields began to diverge again with the global financial crisis of 2007–2009, and moved sharply apart after the euro crisis broke out late in 2009.

Source: European Central Bank. Ten-year government bond interest rates.

save" based on the resources the home government could raise from the home economy alone; and the government's predicament would of course be much worse in a systemic crisis, with several banks in trouble at the same time. For example, if a failed bank's assets are equal to GDP and the government must inject capital equal to 5 percent of assets to restore the bank to solvency, then the government would have to issue debt or raise taxes by 5 percent of GDP—a very big fraction—to keep the bank in operation. And what if several large banks all fail at the same time?

With exchange-rate risk now eliminated between euro area countries, government bond yields moved closer to equality. In addition, markets seemed convinced that no European government would ever **default** on its debts—after all, no advanced country anywhere had done so since the late 1940s. As a result, spreads between the governments judged most creditworthy by ratings agencies such as Moody's (for example, Germany) and the least creditworthy (for example, Greece) became very small—often on the order of 25 basis points or below (see Figure 21-8). This development encouraged more spending and borrowing in countries including Greece, Portugal, and Spain. (A default occurs when a debtor does not make the debt payments it has promised to creditors. The event is called a *sovereign default* when the debtor is a country's government.)

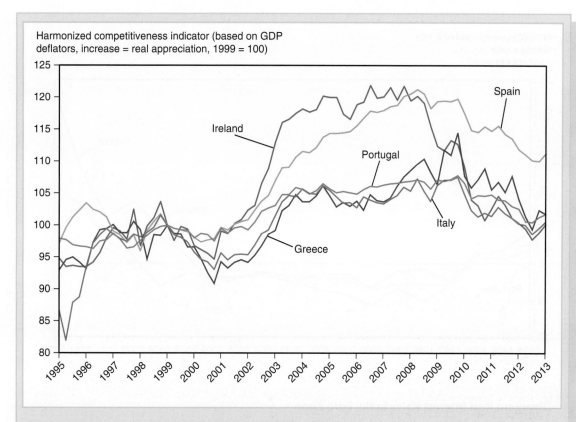

FIGURE 21-9

Real Appreciation in Peripheral Euro Zone Countries

After entry into the euro, real appreciation set in for peripheral euro zone countries, most noticeably the two with massive housing booms, Ireland and Spain.

Source: Eurostat. Harmonized multilateral competitiveness index based on GDP deflators. An increase in the index is a real appreciation (loss in competitiveness).

But with higher spending also came higher inflation relative to the German level. As a result, countries on the euro zone periphery—Ireland, Portugal, Spain, Italy, and Greece—all saw their currencies appreciate in real terms, not only relative to Germany, but relative to all of their trading partners, both within and outside of EMU. Figure 21-9, which reports European Commission indexes of real appreciation with respect to GDP deflators, shows how all of these countries lost competitiveness after the early 2000s, most notably the two countries with the most extreme housing booms, Ireland and Spain. With higher inflation than Germany's, but essentially equal bond rates, these countries had lower *real* interest rates during the mid-2000s, a factor that spurred spending and inflation even further (see Figure 21-10 for real interest rates).[18]

---

[18]This type of monetary instability was predicted by Sir Alan Walters, an economic adviser to Prime Minister Margaret Thatcher of Britain and a prominent opponent of fixed exchange rates within Europe. See his polemical book *Sterling in Danger: Economic Consequences of Fixed Exchange Rates* (London: Fontana, 1990).

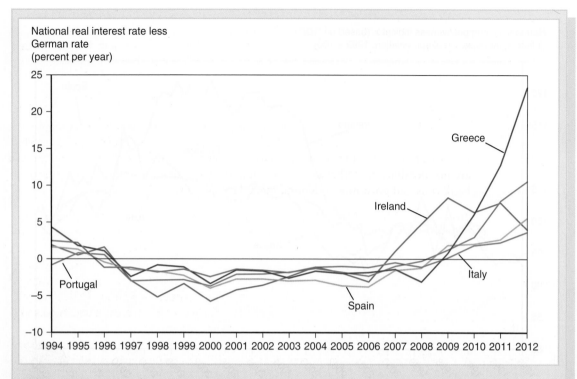

FIGURE 21-10

Divergent Real Interest Rates in the Euro Zone

As the 1999 launch date for the euro approached, nominal long-term bond rates in prospective member countries converged, leading to lower real interest rates in those countries with relatively high inflation. The graph shows each country's long-term real interest rate minus Germany's long-term real interest rate. Real interest rates are average nominal rates on ten-year government bonds minus the same year's inflation rate.

Source: Datastream.

As a result, while Germany had growing current account surpluses, the peripheral countries had growing deficits, in some cases very large ones, as Table 21-4 shows. So external debts built up, raising the question of how these countries would ever generate the net export surpluses necessary to repay foreign creditors. The dilemma

TABLE 21-4	**Current Account Balances of Euro Zone Countries, 2005–2009 (percent of GDP)**					
	Greece	**Ireland**	**Italy**	**Portugal**	**Spain**	**Germany**
2005	−7.5	−3.5	−1.7	−9.4	−7.4	5.1
2006	−11.2	−4.1	−2.6	−9.9	−9.0	6.5
2007	−14.4	−5.3	−2.4	−9.4	−10.0	7.6
2008	−14.6	−5.3	−3.4	−12.0	−9.8	6.7
2009	−11.2	−2.9	−3.1	−10.3	−5.4	5.0

Source: International Monetary Fund.

became more acute once growth slowed as a result of the 2007–2009 global crisis. Because currency devaluation by individual euro area countries was not an option to spur net exports, it became increasingly likely that the adjustment to a more competitive real exchange rate would require a period of low inflation or even deflation, in all likelihood accompanied by significant unemployment due to the rigidity of labor and product markets. Among other negative effects, protracted recession would weaken banks.

In these circumstances, countries with conventional fixed exchange rates might well have fallen victim to speculative currency attacks, forcing the government to devalue. In EMU, however, countries do not have their own currencies, so conventional attacks are not possible. Nonetheless, a different sort of speculation set in, working through bank runs and government debt markets. The effects were devastating.

The Spark   The 2007–2009 crisis certainly caused headaches in the euro zone. Some banks were in trouble due to their exposure to U.S. real estate markets. Also troublesome were exposures to European housing markets, which began to fall following the U.S. example (and with Ireland leading the way; see Figure 19-7). But markets had few fears about the creditworthiness of euro zone governments until Greece's intractable fiscal problems became apparent late in 2008. This was

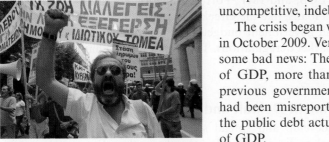

the spark that ignited the tinder of overextended banks and uncompetitive, indebted economies.

The crisis began when a new Greek government was elected in October 2009. Very quickly the new government announced some bad news: The Greek fiscal deficit stood at 12.7 percent of GDP, more than double the numbers announced by the previous government. Apparently the previous government had been misreporting its economic statistics for years, and the public debt actually amounted to more than 100 percent of GDP.

Holders of Greek bonds, including many banks within the euro zone, began to worry about the Greek government's ability to close its yawning deficit and repay its debts. In December 2009, the major rating agencies all downgraded Greek government debt. (As Figure 21-8 shows, the Greek government's borrowing spread over German bonds rose to levels previously seen in late 2008 and early 2009, when global financial markets had been in turmoil over the fallout from the subprime crisis). The Greek government announced harsh budget cuts and raised some taxes in the first months of 2010, but was soon faced with street protests and strikes. Further downgrades followed and Greek borrowing costs soared, making it even harder for the country to repay creditors. Investors began to worry that other deficit countries might face problems similar to those of Greece. The figure shows that borrowing costs for Portugal and Ireland, and even for two larger countries, Spain and Italy, came under pressure. World stock markets plunged as the prospect of a much wider financial crisis in Europe grew.

How did the EU deal with the Greek crisis? A bailout of Greece by richer EU countries would have quelled the market turmoil, but that was exactly the outcome that countries like Germany had wished to avoid when they negotiated the Maastricht Treaty and the SGP. In mid-March 2010, euro zone finance ministers declared their intention to help Greece but provided no details of what they planned to do. With the EU unable to take concrete action, the crisis snowballed, and the value of the euro fell in the foreign exchange markets.

Finally, in mid-April 2010, euro zone countries, working with the IMF, agreed on a €110 billion loan package for Greece. But by this time, the panic over government debt had spread, and the Portuguese, Spanish, and Italian governments (following what Ireland had already undertaken late in 2008) were proposing their own deficit-reduction measures in an effort to keep borrowing spreads from rising to Greek levels. Fearing a continental meltdown, the euro zone's leaders embedded the Greek support within a broader European Financial Stability Facility (EFSF), with funding of €750 billion provided by its own borrowing from markets, the European Commission, and the IMF. (The EFSF was explicitly temporary, but was replaced by a permanent European Stability Mechanism, or ESM, in October 2012.) The ECB then reversed a policy it had earlier announced and began to purchase the bonds of troubled euro zone debtor countries, sparking accusations that it was violating the spirit of the Maastricht Treaty by rewarding fiscal excesses. In fact, the ECB's motivation was to avoid a banking panic by supporting the prices of assets widely held by European banks.

Greek borrowing costs remained high, and soon Ireland's market borrowing rates rose sharply as it became clear that the government's cost of supporting shaky Irish banks would amount to a large fraction of GDP. Late in 2010, Ireland negotiated a €67.5 billion EFSF loan package with the *troika* consisting of the European Commission, ECB, and IMF. Portugal negotiated a €78 billion *troika* loan in May 2011.[19] Both loans, like the Greek loan, came with conditions requiring the recipients to slash government budgets and institute structural economic reforms (such as labor-market deregulation). The *troika* was in charge of monitoring compliance.

Self-Fulfilling Government Default and the "Doom Loop"

Why did market panic develop and spread so quickly? The contentious debate surrounding the initial Greek package made it clear that the northern European countries such as Germany, Finland, and the Netherlands had only a very limited willingness to underwrite the borrowing of countries like Greece facing unfavorable market conditions, either directly or indirectly through support for ECB bond purchases. Some politicians from northern Europe had spoken openly about default by Greece, or even about the possibility that it would exit the euro. Thus, sovereign default on Greek debt, even though EU officials initially denied it as a possibility, appeared eminently possible, as did default by other countries (such as Portugal) with rapidly growing government debts.

The fear of default was a particular problem of the euro area: The government of the United States can always print dollars to pay off its debts, and so is very unlikely to default, but countries using the euro cannot, since the decision to print euros rests with the ECB, not national governments. (This is why Greece, Portugal, and Ireland were in the anomalous position of borrowing euros—their own currency—from the IMF.) The possibility of default gives rise to a self-fulfilling dynamic that is analogous to a bank run (as discussed in Chapter 20) or a self-fulfilling currency crisis (as discussed in Chapter 18): If markets expect a default, they will charge the borrowing government very high interest rates, and if it is unable to raise taxes or cut spending sufficiently,

---

[19]The term *"troika"* came into widespread use during the euro crisis. The word is Russian and refers to a three-horse harness setup for pulling a sleigh.

it will be forced to miss debt repayments and therefore it will default. This is exactly what happened in the euro area.[20]

Because bank balance sheets had become so big, the weakened state of the euro countries' banks strongly reinforced the likelihood of government default. Countries needing to support their banking systems with infusions of public money had to borrow the money, leading to big increases in public debt levels and heightened market fears of default. Figure 21-11 shows the evolution of public debts (as a ratio to GDP) in the euro area. While Greece had by far the largest debt (reaching a staggering 170 percent of GDP by 2011), you can see that other countries' debts were increasing rapidly, fueled in part, in most cases, by the need to bail out banks. Ireland provides the most dramatic example, with debt rising from only 25 percent of GDP in 2007 to more than 90 percent in 2010, driven not only by recession but by a bailout of the banks that had driven the Irish property boom.[21]

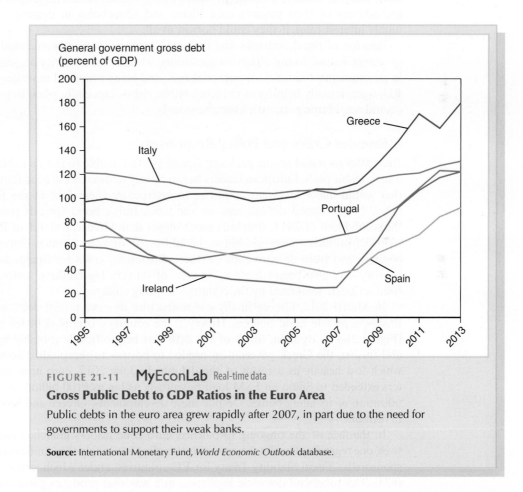

FIGURE 21-11   MyEconLab Real-time data

Gross Public Debt to GDP Ratios in the Euro Area

Public debts in the euro area grew rapidly after 2007, in part due to the need for governments to support their weak banks.

Source: International Monetary Fund, *World Economic Outlook* database.

[20]For a model of this process, see Guillermo A. Calvo, "Servicing the Public Debt: The Role of Expectations," *American Economic Review* 78 (September 1988): 647–661. The model is applied to the euro crisis in the paper by De Grauwe in Further Readings.
[21]Vivid accounts of the Greek and Irish crises are included in Michael Lewis, *Boomerang: Travels in the New Third World* (New York: W.W. Norton & Company, 2011).

To make matters worse, the perilous state of each government's credit, in turn, weakened the solvency of domestic banks. For one thing, banks were heavily invested in their governments' bonds, so when those bonds' prices fell, bank assets and bank capital were reduced. In addition, banks' lenders (including depositors) understood that if the government itself could not obtain cash, it might be unable to make good on promises to support banks, for example, through injections of public capital or deposit insurance.

The two-way feedback from bank distress to government borrowing problems has been labeled a **doom loop** by economists. As a result of the doom loop, private money fled from banks in countries where the government was having trouble borrowing. These countries experienced a *sudden stop* in private lending, and to keep their banks from collapsing, the ECB had to engage in lender of last resort operations on a massive scale. In effect, the euro zone's financial market became segmented along national lines, with the creditworthiness of banks in the weaker countries judged by the creditworthiness of their governments. Firms and households in those countries faced higher interest rates, if they could borrow at all.

Because of fiscal cutbacks and the credit squeeze, output plummeted and unemployment soared. Many observers questioned whether the austerity programs included in governments' financial support packages, and being practiced more generally in the EU, were actually helping in reducing public debts, especially when implemented by several neighboring countries simultaneously.

A Broader Crisis and Policy Responses

Even after its initial rescue package, Greece proved unable to put its public debt onto a sustainable path. European leaders began openly to discuss the need for mechanisms that would allow insolvent countries to restructure their debt in the future. With officially sanctioned default now on the table, Italy's bond spreads rose sharply in the second half of 2011. Italy was much bigger than Greece, Ireland, or Portugal and its fiscal problems were too big to be addressed without a much bigger budgetary commitment from its euro zone partners. Borrowing costs for Spain, another large country, had also been edging up in view of its very big banking sector, which had been seriously weakened by the country's housing collapse.

In March 2012, Greece finally did restructure its government debt, imposing big losses on private bond holders. However, the country's overall debt fell only slightly (Figure 21-11). By then, much of the debt was held officially (notably by the ECB), and further, the Greek government needed to borrow to recapitalize domestic banks, which lost heavily as a result of the default. In June 2012, euro area finance ministers extended to Spain an ESM loan potentially as big as €100 billion to cover recapitalization of its ailing banks. Despite these developments, Greece and Spain remained in turmoil.

In the face of the ongoing turbulence, euro zone leaders launched two key initiatives, one regarding fiscal policy and one regarding banking policy unification. Germany sponsored a Fiscal Stability Treaty for EU countries, under which signatories commit themselves to amend domestic legislation in a way that produces government budgets that are more nearly in balance. The treaty, an updated and more stringent version of the SGP, was motivated by similar concerns and reflected the official German position that the main cause of the crisis was the fiscal misbehavior of national governments. It came into force for the 16 countries that had signed it at the start of 2013.

Critics of the Fiscal Stability Treaty pointed out that countries such as Ireland and Spain had favorable fiscal indicators, with falling levels of debt relative to GDP, prior to the crisis (Figure 21-11). While the German diagnosis described Greece, other countries' debts exploded because their banking systems melted down, and the German strategy did nothing to improve bank supervision, or to break the doom loop between banks and sovereign governments. As in our discussion of optimum currency areas, a closer *banking union* would be needed in order to stabilize the euro zone.

This second direction also was pursued by EU leaders, who met in June 2012 and directed the European Commission to prepare a blueprint for a Single Supervisory Mechanism (SSM) with powers to police banks throughout the euro zone. The leaders also recommended that once the SSM was in place, the ESM should have the power to recapitalize banks *directly*, that is, with any resulting borrowing showing up as a liability of the ESM, that is, as a joint liability of the euro zone and not of any member government, regardless of where the recapitalized banks reside. This important recommendation was intended to reduce the force of the doom loop at the national level, but it made some governments uneasy at the prospect of being forced to bail out banks in other countries.

In response to the summit directive, the Commission in September 2012 recommended a three-pronged approach to banking union, meant to centralize financial supervision, deposit insurance, and the resolution of insolvent banks within the euro area. These measures, as just noted, were meant to deactivate the doom loop at the national level and enhance the quality and credibility of financial oversight for the currency union. Specifically, the Commission recommended the creation of an SSM, of a euro-area wide deposit insurance scheme, and of a Single Resolution Mechanism (SRM), to be operated (like the SSM) at the level of the euro area. In December 2012, the EU leaders endorsed the SSM, housing it in the ECB (although retaining a significant degree of home-country autonomy in the regulation of smaller banks). As of this writing, the SRM remains a work in progress while the idea of centralized euro area deposit insurance is strongly opposed by a group of countries led by Germany. Thus, the doom loop remains substantially in place, and it is hard to see how the ECB will be able to enforce its supervisory edicts if it does not actually have the clout and financial resources to close down and reorganize failing banks in the face of potential opposition from national politicians.

Many observers have recommended that the euro area enhance fiscal federalism through a larger centralized budget, managed by a fiscal authority with the capability to tax, spend, and issue joint eurobonds. This approach is strongly opposed by Germany and other countries and is unlikely to become reality anytime soon.[22]

ECB Outright Monetary Transactions

Despite the preceding reform efforts, markets for peripheral euro zone sovereign debts remained volatile through the summer of 2012, with investors speculating that Greece might even leave EMU. Such an outcome—known colloquially as a "Grexit"—would have destabilized other countries' borrowing rates even more by setting the precedent that a government might abandon the euro and introduce a national currency in its place. On July 26, 2012, ECB President Mario Draghi made the dramatic statement: "Within our mandate, the ECB is ready to do whatever it takes to preserve the euro. And believe me, it will be enough." Six weeks later he unveiled a program called

---

[22]For a survey of eurobond proposals see Stijn Claessens, Ashoka Mody, and Shahin Vallée, "Paths to Eurobonds," Working Paper WP/12/172, International Monetary Fund, July 2012.

Outright Monetary Transactions (OMT) under which the ECB would do exactly that—purchase sovereign bonds, potentially without limit, to prevent their interest rates from rising too far. To qualify for OMT, countries would first have to agree to an ESM stabilization plan.

As of this writing OMT have not been used, but nonetheless, bond yields in the peripheral countries have receded sharply, as Figure 21-11 shows, simply because of the *expectation* of what the ECB could do with its unlimited monetary firepower. However, it is unclear how long this relative calm can last. To start, no one knows what will happen if OMT actually have to be used (and the very idea has been challenged in Germany's constitutional court). In addition, the breathing space given by OMT may have blunted national governments' determination to carry out structural reforms, as well as EU leaders' determination to deliver on necessary institutional innovations. This is just another form of moral hazard, one that encourages governments to postpone tough decisions.

The Future of EMU

Europe's single currency experiment is the boldest attempt ever to reap the efficiency gains from using a single currency over a large and diverse group of sovereign states. If EMU succeeds, it will promote European political as well as economic integration, fostering peace and prosperity in a region that could someday include all of Eastern Europe and even Turkey. If the euro project fails, however, its driving force, the goal of European political unification, will be set back.

EMU must overcome some difficult challenges, however, if it is to survive its current crisis and prosper:

1. Europe is not an optimum currency area. Therefore, asymmetric economic developments within different countries of the euro zone—developments that might well call for different national interest rates under a regime of individual national currencies—will remain hard to handle through monetary policy. The single currency project has taken economic union to a level far beyond what the EU has so far been able (or willing) to do in the area of political union. Nonetheless, in response to the euro crisis, the EU is increasing the centralized control over economic policy beyond the initial ECB blueprint through the Fiscal Stability Treaty, enhanced powers for the Commission, and the euro zone banking union. Many Europeans hoped that economic union would lead to closer political union, but it is possible that continuing quarrels over economic policies will sabotage that aim. Enhanced governmental powers at the center of EMU require enhanced democratic accountability as well, but little has been done to fulfill this need. There is a danger that voters throughout Europe will come to view the euro's superstructure as being under the control of a distant and politically unaccountable group of technocrats who are unresponsive to people's needs.

2. In most EU countries, labor markets remain highly unionized and subject to employment taxes and regulations that impede labor mobility between industries and regions. The result has been persistently high levels of unemployment. Unless labor markets become much more flexible, as in the United States' currency union, individual euro zone countries will have a difficult time adjusting toward full employment and competitive real exchange rates. Other structural problems abound.

It remains to be seen if the euro zone will develop more elaborate institutions for carrying out fiscal transfers from country to country. At the least, some sort of centralized fiscal backstop for the planned banking union is essential to ensure its effectiveness. The euro crisis showed the need for enough of a centralized European fiscal capacity to deal rapidly with inherently contagious member-country financial instability. It also showed the strength of opposition in some countries to such an institutional change. But as we have seen, the economic and political fissures that the crisis revealed have been present from the euro project's start.

Thus, the euro faces significant challenges in the years ahead. The experience of the United States shows that a large monetary union comprising diverse economic regions can work quite well. For the euro zone to achieve comparable economic success, however, it will have to make progress in creating more flexible labor and product markets, in reforming its fiscal and financial regulatory systems, and in deepening its political union. European unification itself will be imperiled unless the euro project and its defining institution, the ECB, succeed in delivering prosperity as well as price stability.

SUMMARY

1. European Union countries have had two main reasons for favoring mutually fixed exchange rates: They believe monetary cooperation will give them a heavier weight in international economic negotiations, and they view fixed exchange rates as a complement to EU initiatives aimed at building a common European market.

2. The *European Monetary System* of fixed intra-EU exchange rates was inaugurated in March 1979 and originally included Belgium, Denmark, France, Germany, Ireland, Italy, Luxembourg, and the Netherlands. Austria, Britain, Portugal, and Spain joined much later. Capital controls and frequent realignments were essential ingredients in maintaining the system until the mid-1980s, but since then, controls have been abolished as part of the European Union's wider program of market unification.

3. In practice, all EMS currencies were pegged to Germany's former currency, the deutsche mark (DM). As a result, Germany was able to set monetary policy for the EMS, just as the United States did in the Bretton Woods system. The *credibility theory of the EMS* holds that participating governments profited from the German Bundesbank's reputation as an inflation fighter. In fact, inflation rates in EMS countries ultimately tended to converge around Germany's generally low inflation rate.

4. On January 1, 1999, 11 EU countries initiated an *economic and monetary union (EMU)* by adopting a common currency, the euro, issued by a European Central Bank (ECB) headquartered in Frankfurt, Germany. (The initial 11 members were joined by several other countries later on.) The Eurosystem consists of euro members' national central banks and the ECB, whose governing council runs monetary policy in EMU. The transition process from the EMS's fixed exchange rate system to EMU was spelled out in the *Maastricht Treaty* signed by European leaders in December 1991.

5. The Maastricht Treaty specified a set of macroeconomic convergence criteria that EU countries would need to satisfy in order to qualify for admission to EMU. A major purpose of the convergence criteria was to reassure voters in low-inflation countries such as Germany that the new, jointly managed European currency would be as resistant to inflation as the DM had been. A *Stability and Growth Pact (SGP)*, devised by EU leaders in 1997 at Germany's insistence, was intended to limit government deficits and debt at the national level.

6. The theory of *optimum currency areas* implies that countries will wish to join fixed exchange rate areas closely linked to their own economies through trade and factor mobility. A country's decision to join an exchange rate area is determined by the difference between the *monetary efficiency gain* from joining and the *economic stability loss* from joining. The *GG-LL* diagram relates both of these factors to the degree of economic integration between the joining country and the larger, fixed exchange rate zone. Only when economic integration passes a critical level is it beneficial to join.

7. The European Union does not appear to satisfy all of the criteria for an optimum currency area. Although many barriers to market integration within the European Union have been removed since the 1980s and the euro appears to have promoted intra-EU trade, the level of trade still is not very extensive. In addition, labor mobility between and even within EU countries appears more limited than that within other large currency areas such as the United States. Finally, the level of *fiscal federalism* in the European Union is too small to cushion member countries from adverse economic events, and policies for banking sector stability are not adequately centralized.

8. The euro crisis was sparked by Greek fiscal problems revealed at the end of 2009, but the crisis spread so widely because euro area banks were overextended and some countries had suffered big real appreciations that they could not unwind through devaluation. The prospect that some governments might *default* on their debts hurt banks, and conversely, bank weakness forced governments into expensive bailouts, in a self-reinforcing *doom loop*. The results were soaring government borrowing rates and capital flight from fiscally stressed countries. The ECB offered massive lender of last resort support to peripheral banks as money fled; at the same time, their governments required loans from other EU members and the IMF, loans that came on condition of fiscal austerity and structural reforms. Austerity combined with tight credit in so many neighboring countries gave rise to deep recessions.

9. Responses to the crisis include revamped fiscal restrictions on euro area governments as well as incomplete progress toward a euro zone banking union. The most effective initiative in pushing government borrowing rates down, however, has been the ECB's promise of Outright Monetary Transactions. But as of this writing, the OMT weapon remains untested.

KEY TERMS

credibility theory of the EMS, p. 670	economic stability loss, p. 678	monetary efficiency gain, p. 676
default, p. 688	European Monetary System (EMS), p. 669	optimum currency areas, p. 676
doom loop, p. 694	fiscal federalism, p. 682	Stability and Growth Pact (SGP), p. 674
economic and monetary union (EMU), p. 672	Maastricht Treaty, p. 672	

PROBLEMS

MyEconLab

1. Define the relationship between bond prices and interest rate. If South Korea issued bonds priced at $2000 with an annual interest of 10 percent, what would happen to the interest rate, if the bond's price falls by $400?

2. In the EMS before September 1992, the Italian lira/DM exchange rate could fluctuate by up to 2.25 percent up *or* down. Assume that the lira/DM central parity

and band were set in this way and could not be changed. What would have been the maximum possible difference between the interest rates on *one-year* lira and DM deposits? What would have been the maximum possible difference between the interest rates on *six-month* lira and DM deposits? On *three-month* deposits? Do the answers surprise you? Give an intuitive explanation.

3. Elaborate the main reason for the EU to allow fixed exchange rate system. The text argues that the prospects of successful fixed exchange rate areas in Europe seemed bleak when the inflation rate between member countries varied widely. Justify the effect of a widening inflation range on the prospects of fixed exchange rate in EU?

4. Do your answers to the last two questions require an assumption that interest rates and expected exchange rate changes are linked by interest parity? Why or why not?

5. Suppose that soon after Norway pegs to the euro, EMU benefits from a favorable shift in the world demand for non-Norwegian EMU exports. What happens to the exchange rate of the Norwegian krone against noneuro currencies? How is Norway affected? How does the size of this effect depend on the volume of trade between Norway and the euro zone economies?

6. Use the *GG-LL* diagram to show how an increase in the size and frequency of unexpected shifts in a country's money demand function affects the level of economic integration with a currency area at which the country will wish to join.

7. During the speculative pressure on the EMS exchange rate mechanism (ERM) shortly before Britain allowed the pound to float in September 1992, the *Economist*, a London weekly news magazine, opined as follows:

> The [British] government's critics want lower interest rates, and think this would be possible if Britain devalued sterling, leaving the ERM if necessary. They are wrong. Quitting the ERM would soon lead to higher, not lower, interest rates, as British economic management lost the degree of credibility already won through ERM membership. Two years ago British government bonds yielded three percentage points more than German ones. Today the gap is half a point, reflecting investors' belief that British inflation is on its way down—permanently. (See "Crisis? What Crisis?" *Economist*, August 29, 1992, p. 51.)

   a. Why might the British government's critics have thought it possible to lower interest rates after taking sterling out of the ERM? (Britain was in a deep recession at the time the article appeared.)

   b. Why did the *Economist* think the opposite would occur soon after Britain exited the ERM?

   c. In what way might ERM membership have gained credibility for British policy makers? (Britain entered the ERM in October 1990.)

   d. Why would a high level of British nominal interest rates relative to German rates have suggested an expectation of high future British inflation? Can you think of other explanations?

   e. Suggest two reasons why British interest rates might have been somewhat higher than German rates at the time of writing, despite the alleged "belief that British inflation is on its way down—permanently."

8. Suppose the ASEAN countries adopt one currency system and fixed exchange rate to achieve greater economic unity and Singapore—part of ASEAN—faced an increased export demand. Will it still be profitable for Singapore to continue with the earlier agreement? Explain using the GG-LL Schedules. Suppose Brunei—also part of ASEAN—is not operating at full employment level. How would its employment be affected by a fall in price level, *ceteris paribus*?

9. Why would the failure to create a unified EU labor market be particularly harmful to the prospects for a smoothly functioning EMU, if at the same time capital is completely free to move among EU countries?

10. Britain belongs to the EU, but it has not yet adopted the euro, and fierce debate rages over the issue.
    a. Find macro data on the British economy's performance since 1998 (inflation, unemployment, real GDP growth) and compare these with euro zone data.
    b. What were nominal interest rates in Britain and the euro zone after 1998? How would Britain have fared if the ECB had been setting Britain's nominal interest rate at the euro zone level and the pound sterling's euro exchange rate had been fixed?

11. Movements in the euro's external exchange rate can be seen as goods-market shocks that have asymmetric effects on different euro zone members. When the euro appreciated against China's currency in 2007, which country suffered the greater fall in aggregate demand, Finland, which does not compete directly with China in its export markets, or Spain, which does? What would have happened had Spain retained its old currency, the peseta?

12. In the United States' currency union, we seem never to worry if a state has a big current account deficit. Have you ever seen such data in the newspaper? Can you even find the data in any U.S. government statistical sources? For example, one would guess that the state of Louisiana ran large current account deficits after it was devastated by Hurricane Katrina in 2005. But Louisiana's possible current account deficit was not deemed worthy of coverage by the financial press. We do know, however, that in 2008, Greece had a current account deficit of 14.6 percent of GDP, Portugal had a deficit of 12 percent of GDP, and Spain had a deficit of 9.8 percent of GDP (Table 21-4). Should the governments of these countries worry about such large deficits? (Hint: Relate your answer to the debate over the need for the SGP.)

13. Go to the IMF website at www.imf.org and find the *World Economic Outlook* database; then download data on the current account balance (as a percent of GDP) for Greece, Spain, Portugal, Italy, and Ireland. What happens to the current accounts of these countries after 2009 during the euro crisis? Can you explain what you see?

14. To curb fiscal deficit, what measures can be taken towards tax rate and government expenditure? What effect does this have on aggregate demand in the economy? Why don't countries operating with EMU increase their exports and current account surpluses through devaluation?

15. In the spring of 2013 Cyprus followed Greece, Ireland, and Portugal in agreeing to an emergency loan from the *troika* of the EU, ECB, and IMF. The cause was big losses in the Cypriot banking system. After imposing losses on some Cypriot bank deposits, the government, with EU approval, imposed capital controls to prevent residents from taking money abroad. Why do you think this step (which violated the EU's single-market philosophy) was taken?

FURTHER READINGS

Alberto Alesina and Francesco Giavazzi, eds. *Europe and the Euro*. Chicago: University of Chicago Press, 2010. Essays on the euro's first decade.

Carlo Bastasin. *Saving Europe: How National Politics Nearly Destroyed the Euro*. Washington, D.C.: Brookings Institution, 2012. Detailed historical account of the political backdrop to the euro crisis and the policy response through 2011.

Lars Calmfors and others. *EMU: A Swedish Perspective.* Berlin: Springer, 1997. This book, which argued against Swedish membership in EMU, is based on a report commissioned by the government of Sweden prior to the launch of the euro.

W. Max Corden. *Monetary Integration.* Princeton Essays in International Finance 32. International Finance Section, Department of Economics, Princeton University, April 1972. Classic analysis of monetary unification.

Paul De Grauwe. "The Governance of a Fragile Eurozone." *Australian Economic Review* 45 (September 2012): 255–268. Interprets the crisis in the euro zone in terms of self-fulfilling speculation in sovereign debt markets.

Barry Eichengreen and Peter Temin. "Fetters of Gold and Paper." *Oxford Review of Economic Policy* 26 (Autumn 2010), pp. 370–384. Explores similarities between the implications of fixed exchange rates in the euro zone, and of the gold standard during the Great Depression.

Martin Feldstein. "The Political Economy of the European Economic and Monetary Union: Political Sources of an Economic Liability." *Journal of Economic Perspectives* 11 (Fall 1997), pp. 23–42. A leading American economist makes the case against EMU.

Harold James. *Making the European Monetary Union.* Cambridge, MA: Harvard University Press, 2012. Detailed historical account of the pre-history of EMU, including negotiations over the design of the ECB.

Peter B. Kenen and Ellen E. Meade. *Regional Monetary Integration.* Cambridge, U.K.: Cambridge University Press, 2008. A comprehensive overview of the euro zone's experience and of the prospects for other large currency areas in East Asia and Latin America.

Philip R. Lane. "The European Sovereign Debt Crisis." *Journal of Economic Perspectives* 26 (Summer 2012), pp. 49–68. Concise overview of the euro area's debt crisis.

Silvia Merler and Jean Pisani-Ferry. "Sudden Stops in the Euro Area." Bruegel Policy Contribution 2012/06, March 2012. An analysis of destabilizing private financial flows within EMU.

Jean Pisani-Ferry, André Sapir, Nicolas Véron, and Guntram B. Wolff. "What Kind of European Banking Union?" Bruegel Policy Contribution 2012/12, June 2012. Compact review of issues in setting up a banking union within the EU.

Jay C. Shambaugh. "The Euro's Three Crises." *Brooking Papers on Economic Activity* 1 (2012), pp. 157–211. A broad look at the euro zone problems leading to the crisis.

Edward Tower and Thomas D. Willett. *The Theory of Optimal Currency Areas and Exchange Rate Flexibility.* Princeton Special Papers in International Economics 11. International Finance Section, Department of Economics, Princeton University, May 1976. Surveys the theory of optimum currency areas.

MyEconLab Can Help You Get a Better Grade

MyEconLab If your exam were tomorrow, would you be ready? For each chapter, MyEconLab Practice Tests and Study Plans pinpoint sections you have mastered and those you need to study. That way, you are more efficient with your study time, and you are better prepared for your exams.

To see how it works, turn to page 41 and then go to

www.myeconlab.com

CHAPTER 22

DEVELOPING COUNTRIES: GROWTH, CRISIS, AND REFORM

U ntil now, we have studied macroeconomic interactions between industrialized market economies like those of the United States and Western Europe. Richly endowed with capital and skilled labor, these politically stable countries generate high levels of income for their residents. And their markets, compared to those of some poorer countries, have long been relatively free of direct government control.

Several times since the 1980s, however, the macroeconomic problems of the world's developing countries have been at the forefront of concerns about the stability of the entire international economy. Over the decades following World War II, trade between developing and industrial nations has expanded, as have developing-country financial transactions with richer lands. In turn, the more extensive links between the two groups of economies have made each group more dependent than before on the economic health of the other. Events in developing countries therefore have a significant impact on welfare and policies in more advanced economies. Since the 1960s, some countries that once were poor have increased their living standards dramatically, while others have fallen even further behind the industrial world. By understanding these contrasting development experiences, we can derive important policy lessons that can spur economic growth in all countries.

This chapter studies the macroeconomic problems of developing countries and the repercussions of those problems on the developed world. Although the insights from international macroeconomics that we gained in previous chapters also apply to developing countries, the distinctive problems those countries have faced in their quest to catch up to the rich economies warrant separate discussion. In addition, the lower income levels of developing areas make macroeconomic slumps there even more painful than in developed economies, with consequences that can threaten political and social cohesion.

After reading this chapter, you will be able to:

- Describe the persistently unequal world distribution of income and the evidence on its causes.
- Summarize the major economic features of developing countries.
- Explain the position of developing countries in the world capital market and the problem of default by developing borrowers.
- Recount the recent history of developing-country financial crises.
- Discuss proposed measures to enhance poorer countries' gains from participation in the world capital market.

Income, Wealth, and Growth in the World Economy

Poverty is the basic problem that developing countries face, and escaping from poverty is their overriding economic and political challenge. Compared with industrialized economies, most developing countries are poor in the factors of production essential to modern industry: capital and skilled labor. The relative scarcity of these factors contributes to low levels of per capita income and often prevents developing countries from realizing the economies of scale from which many richer nations benefit. But factor scarcity is largely a symptom of deeper problems. Political instability, insecure property rights, and misguided economic policies frequently have discouraged investment in capital and skills, while also reducing economic efficiency in other ways.

The Gap between Rich and Poor

The world's economies can be divided into four main categories according to their annual per capita income levels: low-income economies (including Afghanistan, Bangladesh, Nepal, Cambodia, and Haiti, along with parts of sub-Saharan Africa); lower middle-income economies (including China, India, Pakistan, the Philippines, Indonesia, several Middle Eastern countries, many Latin American and Caribbean countries, many former Soviet countries, and most of the remaining African countries); upper middle-income economies (including the remaining Latin American countries, a handful of African countries, a number of Caribbean countries, Turkey, Malaysia, Poland, Latvia, Lithuania, and Russia); and high-income economies (including the rich industrial market economies; the remaining Caribbean countries; a handful of exceptionally fortunate former developing countries such as Israel, Korea, and Singapore; oil-rich Kuwait and Saudi Arabia; and some successfully transitioned Eastern European countries such as the Czech and Slovak Republics, Hungary, and Estonia). The first two categories consist mainly of countries at a backward stage of development relative to industrial economies, while the last two comprise most of the emerging market economies (as well as the industrial economies, of course). Table 22-1 shows 2011 average per capita annual income levels for these country groups, together with another indicator of economic well-being, average life expectancy at birth.

Table 22-1 illustrates the sharp disparities in international income levels in the second decade of the 21st century. Average national income per capita in the richest economies is 69 times that of the average in the poorest developing countries! Even the upper middle-income countries enjoy only about one-sixth of the per capita income

TABLE 22-1	**Indicators of Economic Welfare in Four Groups of Countries, 2011**	
Income Group	**GDP Per Capita (2011 U.S. dollars)**	**Life Expectancy (years)***
Low-income	635	57
Lower middle-income	2,298	66
Upper middle-income	7,239	72
High-income	43,718	80

*Simple average of male and female life expectancies.
Source: World Bank.

of the industrial group. The life expectancy figures generally reflect international differences in income levels. Average life spans fall as relative poverty increases.[1]

Has the World Income Gap Narrowed Over Time?

Explaining the income differences among countries is one of the oldest goals of economics. It is no accident that Adam Smith's classic 1776 book was entitled the *Wealth of Nations*. Since at least a century before Smith's time, economists have sought not only to explain why countries' incomes differ at a given point in time, but also to solve the more challenging puzzle of why some countries become rich while others stagnate. Debate over the best policies for promoting economic growth has been fierce, as we shall see in this chapter.

Both the depth of the economic growth puzzle and the payoff to finding growth-friendly policies are illustrated in Table 22-2, which shows per capita output *growth rates* for several country groups between 1960 and 2010. (These real output data have been corrected to account for departures from purchasing power parity.) Over that period, the United States grew at roughly the 2 to 2.5 percent annual per capita rate that many economists would argue is the long-run maximum for a mature economy. The industrial countries that were most prosperous in 1960 generally grew at mutually comparable rates. As a result, their income gaps compared to the United States changed relatively little. The poorest industrialized countries as of 1960, however, often grew much more quickly than the United States on average, and as a result, their per capita incomes tended to catch up to that of the United States. For example, Ireland, which had been 48 percent poorer than the United States in 1960, was less than 1 percent poorer in 2010—thereby having virtually erased the earlier income gap.

Ireland's catching-up process illustrates the tendency for differences among *industrial* countries' living standards to narrow over the postwar era. The theory behind this observed **convergence** in per capita incomes is deceptively simple. If trade is free, if capital can move to countries offering the highest returns, and if knowledge itself moves across political borders so that countries always have access to cutting-edge production technologies, then there is no reason for international income gaps to persist for long. Some gaps do persist in reality because of policy differences across

---

[1]Chapter 16 showed that an international comparison of *dollar* incomes portrays relative welfare levels inaccurately because countries' price levels measured in a common currency (here, U.S. dollars) generally differ. The World Bank supplies national income numbers that have been adjusted to take account of deviations from purchasing power parity (PPP). Those numbers greatly reduce, but do not eliminate, the disparities in Table 22-1. Table 22-2 reports some PPP-adjusted incomes.

TABLE 22-2	Output Per Capita in Selected Countries, 1960–2010 (in 2005 U.S. dollars)		
	Output Per Capita		
Country	1960	2010	1960–2010 Annual Average Growth Rate (percent per year)
Industrialized in 1960			
Canada	12,946	35,810	2.1
France	9,396	29,145	2.3
Ireland	7,807	41,558	3.4
Italy	7,924	27,227	2.5
Japan	4,404	31,815	4.0
Spain	6,008	25,797	3.0
Sweden	11,710	33,627	2.1
United Kingdom	11,884	32,034	2.0
United States	15,136	41,858	2.1
Africa			
Kenya	978	1,287	0.5
Nigeria	1,442	1,923	0.6
Senegal	1,567	1,480	−0.1
Zimbabwe	3,847	3,959	0.1
Latin America			
Argentina	6,585	12,862	1.3
Brazil	2,354	8,750	2.7
Chile	3,915	12,871	2.4
Colombia	2,814	7,430	2.0
Mexico	5,033	12,189	1.8
Paraguay	1,990	4,666	1.7
Peru	3,939	7,466	1.3
Venezuela	7,307	9,762	0.6
Asia			
China	405	8,727	6.3
Hong Kong	4,518	44,070	4.7
India	734	3,413	3.1
Malaysia	1,624	11,863	4.1
Singapore	3,170	42,360	5.3
South Korea	1,610	28,702	5.9
Taiwan	2,061	32,865	5.7
Thailand	772	8,467	4.9

Note: Data are taken from the Penn World Table, Version 8.0, and use PPP exchange rates to compare national incomes. For a description, see the Penn World Table website at http://www.rug.nl/research/ggdc/data/penn-world-table.

industrial countries; however, the preceding forces of convergence seem to be strong enough to keep industrial-country incomes roughly in the same ballpark. Remember, too, that differences in output *per capita* may overstate differences in output *per employed worker* because most industrial countries have higher unemployment rates and lower labor-force participation rates than the United States.

Despite the appeal of a simple convergence theory, no clear tendency for per capita incomes to converge characterizes the world as a whole, as the rest of Table 22-2 shows. There we see vast discrepancies in long-term growth rates among different regional country groupings, but no general tendency for poorer countries to grow faster. Several countries in sub-Saharan Africa, although at the bottom of the world income scale, have grown (for most of the postwar years) at rates far below those of the main industrial countries.[2] Growth has also been relatively slow in Latin America, where only a few countries (notably Brazil and Chile) have surpassed the average growth rate of the United States, despite lower income levels.

In contrast, East Asian countries *have* tended to grow at rates far above those of the industrialized world, as the convergence theory would predict. South Korea, with an income level close to Senegal's in 1960, has grown nearly 6 percent per year (in per capita terms) since then and in 1997 was classified as a high-income developing country by the World Bank. Singapore's 5.3 percent annual average growth rate likewise propelled it to high-income status. Some of the Eastern European countries that lived under Soviet rule until 1989 have also graduated rapidly to the upper income brackets.

A country that can muster even a 3 percent annual growth rate will see its real per capita income double every generation. But at the growth rates seen in East Asian countries such as Hong Kong, Singapore, South Korea, and Taiwan, per capita real income increases *fivefold* every generation!

What explains the sharply divergent long-run growth patterns in Table 22-2? The answer lies in the economic and political features of developing countries and the ways these have changed over time in response to both world events and internal pressures. The structural features of developing countries have also helped to determine their success in pursuing key macroeconomic goals other than rapid growth, such as low inflation, low unemployment, and financial-sector stability.

Structural Features of Developing Countries

Developing countries differ widely among themselves these days, and no single list of "typical" features would accurately describe all developing countries. In the early 1960s, these countries were much more similar to each other in their approaches to trade policy, macroeconomic policy, and other government interventions in the economy. Then things began to change. East Asian countries abandoned import-substituting industrialization, embracing an export-oriented development strategy instead. This strategy proved very successful. Later on, countries in Latin America also reduced trade barriers while simultaneously attempting to rein in government's role in the economy, reduce chronically high inflation, and, in many cases, open capital accounts to private transactions. These efforts initially met with mixed success but increasingly are bearing fruit.

While many developing countries therefore have reformed their economies to come closer to the structures of the successful industrial economies, the process remains incomplete and many developing countries tend to be characterized by at least some of the following features:

1. There is a history of extensive direct government control of the economy, including restrictions on international trade, government ownership or control of large industrial firms, direct government control of internal financial transactions,

---

[2]On the other hand, other countries in sub-Saharan Africa have now reached upper middle-income status. Botswana in southern Africa did so early. The country enjoyed an average per capita growth rate well above 5 percent per year during the three decades after 1960.

and a high level of government consumption as a share of GNP. Developing countries differ widely among themselves in the extent to which the role of government in the economy has been reduced in these various areas over the past decades.

2. There is a history of high inflation. In many countries, the government was unable to pay for its heavy expenditures and the losses of state-owned enterprises through taxes alone. Tax evasion was rampant, and much economic activity was driven underground, so it proved easiest simply to print money. **Seigniorage** is the name economists give to the real resources a government earns when it prints money that it spends on goods and services. When their governments were expanding money supplies continually to extract high levels of seigniorage, developing countries experienced inflation and even hyperinflation. (See, for example, the discussion of inflation and money supply growth in Latin America in Chapter 15, page 429.)

3. Where domestic financial markets have been liberalized, weak credit institutions often abound. Banks frequently lend funds they have borrowed to finance poor or very risky projects. Loans may be made on the basis of personal connections rather than prospective returns, and government safeguards against financial fragility, such as bank supervision (Chapter 20), tend to be ineffective due to incompetence, inexperience, and outright fraud. While public trade in stock shares has developed in many emerging markets, it is usually harder in developing countries for shareholders to find out how a firm's money is being spent or to control firm managers. The legal framework for resolving asset ownership in cases of bankruptcy typically is also weak. Notwithstanding the recent instability in advanced-country financial markets, it is still true that by comparison, developing countries' financial markets remain less effective in directing savings toward their most efficient investment uses. As a result, developing countries remain even more prone to crisis.

4. Where exchange rates are not pegged outright (as in China), they tend to be managed more heavily by developing-country governments. Government measures to limit exchange rate flexibility reflect both a desire to keep inflation under control and the fear that floating exchange rates would be subject to huge volatility in the relatively thin markets for developing-country currencies. There is a history of allocating foreign exchange through government decree rather than through the market, a practice (called *exchange control*) that some developing countries still maintain. Most developing countries have, in particular, tried to control capital movements by limiting foreign exchange transactions connected with trade in assets. More recently, however, many emerging markets have opened their capital accounts.

5. Natural resources or agricultural commodities make up an important share of exports for many developing countries—for example, Russian petroleum, Malaysian timber, South African gold, and Colombian coffee.

6. Attempts to circumvent government controls, taxes, and regulations have helped to make corrupt practices such as bribery and extortion a way of life in many if not most developing countries. Even though the development of underground economic activity has in some instances aided economic efficiency by restoring a degree of market-based resource allocation, on balance it is clear from the data that corruption and poverty go hand in hand.

For a large sample of developing and industrial countries, Figure 22-1 shows the strong positive relationship between annual real per capita output and an inverse index of corruption—ranging from 1 (most corrupt) to 10 (cleanest)—published by

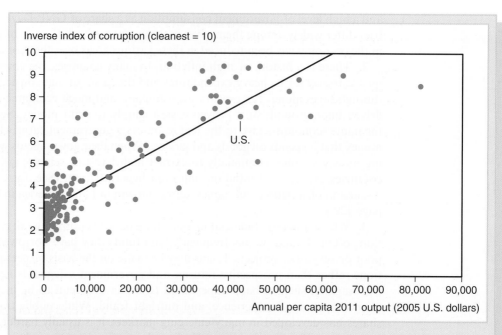

FIGURE 22-1

Corruption and Per Capita Output

Corruption tends to rise as real per capita output falls.

Note: The figure plots 2011 values of an (inverse) index of corruption and 2011 values of PPP-adjusted real per capita output, measured in 2005 U.S. dollars (the amount a dollar could buy in the United States in 2005). The straight line represents a statistician's best guess of a country's corruption level based on its real per capita output.

Source: Transparency International, Corruption Perception Index; World Bank, World Development Indicators.

the organization Transparency International.[3] Several factors underlie this strong positive relationship. Government regulations that promote corruption also harm economic prosperity. Statistical studies have found that corruption itself tends to have net negative effects on economic efficiency and growth.[4] Finally, poorer countries

---

[3]According to Transparency International's 2011 rankings, the cleanest country in the world was New Zealand (scoring a high 9.5), and the most corrupt was Afghanistan (scoring a dismal 1.5). The score for the United States was 7.1. For detailed data and a general overview of the economics of corruption, see Vito Tanzi, "Corruption around the World," *International Monetary Fund Staff Papers* 45 (December 1998), pp. 559–594.

[4]There is, of course, abundant anecdotal evidence on the economic inefficiencies associated with corruption. Consider the following description from 1999 of doing business in Brazil, which had a 2011 Transparency International ranking of 3.8:

> Corruption goes well beyond shaking down street sellers. Almost every conceivable economic activity is subject to some form of official extortion.
>
> Big Brazilian companies generally agree to pay bribes, but multinationals usually refuse and prefer to pay fines. The money—paid at municipal, state and federal levels—is shared out between bureaucrats and their political godfathers. They make sure that it is impossible to comply fully with all of Brazil's tangle of laws, regulations, decrees and directives.
>
> The bribes and fines make up part of the "Brazil Cost," shorthand for the multitude of expenses that inflate the cost of conducting business in Brazil.

See "Death, Decay in São Paulo May Stir Reformist Zeal," *Financial Times*, March 20/21, 1999, p. 4.

lack the resources to police corruption effectively, and poverty itself breeds a greater willingness to go around the rules.

Many of the broad features that still characterize developing countries today took shape in the 1930s and can be traced to the Great Depression (Chapter 19). Most developing countries experimented with direct controls over trade and payments to conserve foreign exchange reserves and safeguard domestic employment. Faced with a massive breakdown of the world market system, industrial and developing countries alike allowed their governments to assume increasingly direct roles in employment and production. Often, governments reorganized labor markets, established stricter control over financial markets, controlled prices, and nationalized key industries. The trend toward government control of the economy proved much more persistent in developing countries, however, where political institutions allowed those with vested financial interests in the status quo to perpetuate it.

Cut off from traditional suppliers of manufactures during World War II, developing countries encouraged new manufacturing industries of their own. Political pressure to protect these industries was one factor behind the popularity of import-substituting industrialization in the first postwar decades. In addition, colonial areas that gained independence after the war believed they could attain the income levels of their former rulers only through rapid, government-directed industrialization and urbanization. Finally, developing-country leaders feared that their efforts to escape poverty would be doomed if they continued to specialize in primary-commodity exports such as coffee, copper, and wheat. In the 1950s, some influential economists argued that developing countries would suffer continually declining terms of trade unless they used commercial policy to move resources out of primary exports and into import substitutes. These forecasts turned out to be wrong, but they did influence developing countries' policies in the first postwar decades.

Developing-Country Borrowing and Debt

One further feature of developing countries is crucial to understanding their macroeconomic problems: Many have relied heavily on financial inflows from abroad to finance domestic investment. Before World War I and in the period up to the Great Depression, developing countries (including the United States for much of the 19th century) received large financial inflows from richer lands. Britain was the biggest international lender, but France, Germany, and other European powers contributed as well to finance industrial development in some then-developing countries (such as Argentina, Australia, Canada, and the United States) and natural resource extraction or plantation agriculture in others (such as Brazil, Peru, Kenya, and Indonesia).

In the decades after World War II, many developing economies again tapped the savings of richer countries and built up a substantial debt to the rest of the world (around $7 trillion in gross terms at the end of 2013). Developing-country debt was at the center of several international lending crises that preoccupied economic policy makers throughout the world starting in the early 1980s.

The Economics of Financial Inflows to Developing Countries

As stated above, many developing countries have received extensive financial inflows from abroad and now carry substantial debts to foreigners. Table 22-3 shows the pattern of borrowing since 1973 by non–oil developing countries (see the second column of data). As you can see, developing countries were consistent borrowers until the very end of the last century (leaving aside the major oil exporters, who run big surpluses

TABLE 22-3	Cumulative Current Account Balances of Major Oil Exporters, Other Developing Countries, and Advanced Countries, 1973–2012 (billions of dollars)		
	Major Oil Exporters	**Other Developing Countries**	**Advanced Countries**
1973–1981	252.9	−246.1	−183.8
1982–1989	−64.6	−143.3	−426.6
1990–1998	−58.2	−522.7	−105.9
1999–2012	3,445.9	1,766.1	−5,576.6

Source: International Monetary Fund, *International Financial Statistics.* Global current accounts generally do not sum to zero because of errors, omissions, and the exclusion of some countries in some periods.

when the world oil price is high). What factors have caused financial inflows to the developing world, and why did the pattern apparently change around the start of the twenty-first century?

Recall the identity (analyzed in Chapter 13) that links national saving, S, domestic investment, I, and the current account balance, $CA : S − I = CA$. If national saving falls short of domestic investment, the difference equals the current account deficit. Because of poverty and poor financial institutions, national saving often is low in developing countries. Because these same countries are relatively poor in capital, however, the opportunities for profitably introducing or expanding plant and equipment can be abundant. Such opportunities justify a high level of investment. By running a deficit in its current account, a country can obtain resources from abroad to invest even if its domestic saving level is low. However, a deficit in the current account implies that the country is borrowing abroad. In return for being able to import more foreign goods today than its current exports can pay for, the country must promise to repay in the future either the interest and principal on loans or the dividends on shares in firms sold to foreigners.

Thus, much developing-country borrowing could potentially be explained by the incentives for *intertemporal trade* examined in Chapter 6. Low-income countries generate too little saving of their own to take advantage of all their profitable investment opportunities, so they must borrow abroad. In capital-rich countries, on the other hand, many productive investment opportunities have been exploited already but saving levels are relatively high. Savers in developed countries can earn higher rates of return, however, by lending to finance investments in the developing world.

Notice that when developing countries borrow to undertake productive investments that they would not otherwise be able to carry out, both they and the lenders reap gains from trade. Borrowers gain because they can build up their capital stocks despite limited national savings. Lenders simultaneously gain because they earn higher returns on their savings than they could earn at home.

While the reasoning above provides a rationale for developing countries' external deficits and debt, it does not imply that all loans from developed to developing countries are justified. Loans that finance unprofitable investments—for example, huge shopping malls that are never occupied—or imports of consumption goods may result in debts that borrowers cannot repay. In addition, faulty government policies that artificially depress national saving rates may lead to excessive foreign borrowing. The 1982–1989 fall in developing-country borrowing evident in Table 22-3 is associated with difficulties that some poorer countries had in keeping up their payments to creditors.

A surprising development starting around 2000 was that developing countries (including many that were not oil exporters) ran surpluses, a counterpart of wealthier countries' deficits (mainly that of the United States). Contrary to what simple economic theory would predict, capital was flowing *uphill*, from poorer to richer countries. We mentioned this pattern of global imbalances in Chapter 19 (pages 611–613), and probe further into the phenomenon later in this chapter. One reason for these surpluses was developing countries' strong desire to accumulate international reserves, as we discuss in the box on page 721.

The Problem of Default

Potential gains from international borrowing and lending will not be realized unless lenders are confident they will be repaid. As we noted in Chapter 21, a loan is said to be in *default* when the borrower, without the agreement of the lender, fails to repay on schedule according to the loan contract. Both social and political instability in developing countries, as well as the frequent weaknesses in their public finances and financial institutions, make it much more risky to lend to developing than to industrial countries. And indeed, the history of financial flows to developing countries is strewn with the wreckage of financial crises and defaulted loan contracts:

1. In the early 19th century, a number of American states defaulted on the European loans they had taken out to finance the building of infrastructure such as canals.
2. Throughout the 19th century, Latin American countries ran into repayment problems. This was particularly true of Argentina, which sparked a global financial crisis in 1890 (the Baring Crisis) when it proved unable to meet its obligations.
3. In 1917, the new communist government of Russia repudiated the foreign debts that had been incurred by previous rulers. The communists closed the Soviet economy to the rest of the world and embarked on a program of centrally planned economic development that was often ruthlessly enforced.
4. During the Great Depression of the 1930s, world economic activity collapsed and developing countries found themselves shut out of industrial-country export markets by a wall of protection (recall Chapter 19). Nearly every developing country defaulted on its external debts as a result, and private financial flows to developing countries dried up for four decades. Several European countries defaulted on their World War I debts to allied governments, mainly the United States.
5. Many developing countries have defaulted (or restructured their foreign debts) in recent decades. For example, in 2005, after lengthy negotiations, most of Argentina's private creditors agreed to settle for only about a third of the contractual values of their claims on the country.

Sharp contractions in a country's output and employment invariably occur after a *sudden stop* in which the country suddenly loses access to all foreign sources of funds (recall Chapter 19). At a very basic level, the necessity for such contractions can be seen from the current account identity, $S - I = CA$. Imagine that a country is running a current account deficit that is 5 percent of its initial GNP, when suddenly foreign lenders become fearful of default and cut off all new loans. Since this action forces the current account balance to be at least zero ($CA \geq 0$), the identity $S - I = CA$ tells us that through some combination of a fall in investment or a rise in saving, $S - I$ must immediately rise by at least 5 percent. The required sharp fall in aggregate demand necessarily depresses the country's output dramatically. Even if the country were not on the verge of default initially—imagine that foreign lenders were originally seized by a sudden irrational panic—the harsh contraction in output that the country would suffer would make default a real possibility.

Indeed, matters are likely to be even worse for the country than the preceding example suggests. Foreign lenders will not only withhold new loans if they fear default, they will naturally also try to get as much money out of the country as possible by demanding the *full* repayment on any loans for which principal can be demanded on short notice (for example, liquid short-term bank deposits). When the developing country repays the principal on debt, it is increasing its *net* foreign wealth. To generate the corresponding positive current account item (see Chapter 13), the country must somehow raise its net exports. Thus, in a sudden stop crisis, the country will not only have to run a current account of zero, it will also actually be called upon to run a *surplus* ($CA > 0$). The bigger the country's *short-term* foreign debt—debt whose principal can be demanded by creditors—the larger the rise in saving or compression of investment that will be needed to avoid a default. You already may have noticed that developing-country sudden stops and default crises can be driven by a self-fulfilling mechanism analogous to the ones behind self-fulfilling balance of payments crises (Chapter 18), bank runs (Chapter 20), and the sovereign debt problems in the euro area (Chapter 21). Indeed, the underlying logic is the same. Furthermore, default crises in developing countries are likely to be accompanied by balance of payments crises (when the exchange rate is pegged) *and* bank runs. A balance of payments crisis results because the country's official foreign exchange reserves may be the only ready means it has to pay off foreign short-term debts. Through running down its official reserves, the government can cushion aggregate demand by reducing the size of the current account surplus needed to meet creditors' demands for repayment.[5] But the loss of its reserves leaves the government unable to peg the exchange rate any longer. At the same time, the banks get into trouble as domestic and foreign depositors, fearing currency depreciation and the consequences of default, withdraw funds and purchase foreign reserves in the hope of repaying foreign-currency debts or sending wealth safely abroad. Since the banks are often weak to begin with, the large-scale withdrawals quickly push them to the brink of failure. Finally, a negative impact on the public finances may complete the doom loop. If the government needs to issue more debt as a result of bailing out the banks, then its own credit standing is weakened, which causes higher borrowing costs and a greater chance of a sovereign default.

Because each of these crisis "triplets" reinforces the others, a developing country's financial crisis is likely to be severe, to have widespread negative effects on the economy, and to snowball very quickly. The immediate origin of such a pervasive economic collapse can be in the financial account (as in a sudden stop), in the foreign exchange market, or in the banking system, depending on the situation of the particular country.

When a government defaults on its obligations, the event is called a *sovereign* default. A conceptually different situation occurs when a large number of *private* domestic borrowers cannot pay their debts to foreigners. In practice in developing countries, however, the two types of default go together. The government might bail out the private sector by taking on its foreign debts, thereby hoping to avoid widespread economic collapse. In addition, a government in trouble may provoke private defaults

---

[5]Make certain you understand why this is so. If necessary, review the open-economy accounting concepts from Chapter 13. For a statistical analysis of the characteristics of default, banking, and currency crises, see Pierre-Oliver Gourinchas and Maurice Obstfeld, "Stories of the Twentieth Century for the Twenty-First," *American Economic Journal: Macroeconomics* 4 (January 2012): 226–265.

by limiting domestic residents' access to its dwindling foreign exchange reserves. That action makes it much harder to pay foreign currency debts. In either case, the government becomes closely involved in the subsequent negotiations with foreign creditors.

Default crises were rare in the first three decades after World War II: Debt issue by developing countries was limited, and the lenders typically were governments or official international agencies such as the International Monetary Fund (IMF) and World Bank. As the free flow of private global capital expanded after the early 1970s, however, major default crises occurred repeatedly (as we shall see), leading many to question the stability of the world capital market.[6]

Alternative Forms of Financial Inflow

When a developing country has a current account deficit, it is selling assets to foreigners to finance the difference between its spending and its income. Although we have lumped these asset sales together under the catchall term *borrowing*, the financial inflows that finance developing countries' deficits (and, indeed, any country's deficit) can take several forms. Different types of financial inflows have predominated in different historical periods. Because different obligations to foreign lenders result, an understanding of the macroeconomic scene in developing countries requires a careful analysis of the five major channels through which these countries have financed their external deficits.

1. *Bond finance.* Developing countries have sometimes sold bonds to private foreign citizens to finance their deficits. Bond finance was dominant in the period up to 1914 and in the interwar years (1918–1939). It regained popularity after 1990 as many developing countries tried to liberalize and modernize their financial markets.

2. *Bank finance.* Between the early 1970s and late 1980s, developing countries borrowed extensively from commercial banks in the advanced economies. In 1970, roughly a quarter of developing-country external finance was provided by banks. In 1981, banks provided an amount of finance roughly equal to the non–oil developing countries' aggregate current account deficit for that year. Banks still lend directly to developing countries, but in the 1990s the importance of bank lending shrank.

3. *Official lending.* Developing countries sometimes borrow from official foreign agencies such as the World Bank or the Inter-American Development Bank. Such loans can be made on a "concessional" basis, that is, at interest rates below market levels, or on a market basis, which allows the lender to earn the market rate of return. Over the post-World War II period, official lending flows to developing nations have shrunk relative to total flows but remain dominant for some countries, for example, many of those in sub-Saharan Africa.

---

[6]On the history of default through the mid-1980s, see Peter H. Lindert and Peter J. Morton, "How Sovereign Debt Has Worked," in Jeffrey D. Sachs, ed., *Developing Country Debt and Economic Performance*, Vol. 1 (Chicago: University of Chicago Press, 1989). A good overview of private capital inflows to developing countries over the same period is given by Eliana A. Cardoso and Rudiger Dornbusch, "Foreign Private Capital Inflows," in Hollis Chenery and T. N. Srinivasan, eds., *Handbook of Development Economics*, Vol. 2 (Amsterdam: Elsevier Science Publishers, 1989). A more recent overview of default crises is in Atish Ghosh et al., *IMF-Supported Programs in Capital Account Crises*, Occasional Paper 210 (Washington, D.C.: International Monetary Fund, 2002). For a comprehensive historical survey, see Carmen Reinhart and Kenneth Rogoff, *This Time Is Different: Eight Centuries of Financial Folly* (Princeton, NJ: Princeton University Press, 2009). Reinhart and Rogoff document that for developing countries, default crises can occur at comparatively low levels of external debt relative to output.

4. *Foreign direct investment.* In foreign direct investment, a firm largely owned by foreign residents acquires or expands a subsidiary firm or factory located in the host developing country (Chapter 8). A loan from IBM to its assembly plant in Mexico, for example, would be a direct investment by the United States in Mexico. The transaction would enter Mexico's balance of payments accounts as a financial asset sale (and the U.S. balance of payments accounts as an equal financial asset acquisition). Since World War II, foreign direct investment has been a consistently important source of developing-country capital.

5. *Portfolio investment in ownership of firms.* Since the early 1990s, investors in developed countries have shown an increased appetite for purchasing shares of stock in developing countries' firms. The trend has been reinforced by many developing countries' efforts at **privatization**—that is, selling to private owners large state-owned enterprises in key areas such as electricity, telecommunications, and petroleum. In the United States, numerous investment companies offer mutual funds specializing in emerging market shares.

The five types of finance just described can be classified into two categories: *debt* finance and *equity* finance (Chapter 20). Bond, bank, and official finance are all forms of debt finance. In this case, the debtor must repay the face value of the loan, plus interest, regardless of its own economic circumstances. Direct investment and portfolio purchases of stock shares are, on the other hand, forms of equity finance. Foreign owners of a direct investment, for example, have a claim to a share of the investment's net return, not a claim to a fixed stream of money payments. Adverse economic events in the host country thus result in an automatic fall in the earnings of direct investments and in the dividends paid to foreigners.

The distinction between debt and equity finance is useful in analyzing how developing-country payments to foreigners adjust to unforeseen events such as recessions or terms of trade changes. When a country's liabilities are in the form of debt, its scheduled payments to creditors do not fall even if its real income falls. It may then become very painful for the country to continue honoring its foreign obligations—painful enough to cause the country to default. Life often is easier, however, with equity finance. In the case of equity, a fall in domestic income automatically reduces the earnings of foreign shareholders without violating any loan agreement. By acquiring equity, foreigners have effectively agreed to share in both the bad and the good times of the economy. Equity rather than debt financing of its investments therefore leaves a developing country much less vulnerable to the risk of a foreign lending crisis.

The Problem of "Original Sin"

When developing countries incur debts to foreigners, those debts are often denominated in terms of a major foreign currency—the U.S. dollar, the euro, or the yen. This practice is not always a matter of choice. In general, lenders from richer countries, fearing the extreme devaluation and inflation that have occurred so often in the past, insist that poorer countries promise to repay them in the lenders' own currencies. If sovereign debts were denominated in domestic rather than foreign currencies—in other words, if the loan contract was a promise to repay foreign lenders with domestic currency—then developing-country governments could simply print their own currencies to repay their creditors. Governments would never need to default, although by creating inflation they would be reducing the *real* value of their obligations.

In contrast to developing countries, richer countries almost always borrow in terms of their own currencies. Thus, the United States borrows dollars from foreigners, Britain borrows pounds sterling, Japan borrows yen, and Switzerland borrows Swiss francs.

For these richer countries, the ability to denominate their foreign debts in their own currencies, while holding foreign assets denominated in foreign currencies, is a considerable advantage—even apart from the leeway it gives to repay in a currency that the home government can print. For example, suppose a fall in world demand for U.S. products leads to a dollar depreciation. We saw in Chapter 19 how such a depreciation can cushion output and employment in the United States. The U.S. portfolio of foreign assets and liabilities, in fact, yields a further cushioning advantage: Because U.S. assets are mostly denominated in foreign currencies, the dollar value of those assets *rises* when the dollar depreciates against foreign currencies. At the same time, because U.S. foreign liabilities are predominantly (about 95 percent) in dollars, their dollar value rises very little. So a fall in world demand for U.S. goods leads to a substantial wealth transfer from foreigners to the United States—a kind of international insurance payment.

For poor countries that must borrow in a major foreign currency, a fall in export demand has the opposite effect. Because poorer countries tend to be net debtors in the major foreign currencies, a depreciation of domestic currency causes a transfer of wealth to foreigners by *raising* the domestic currency value of the net foreign debt. This amounts to negative insurance!

A country that can borrow abroad in its own currency can reduce the real resources it owes to foreigners, without triggering a default, simply by depreciating its currency. A developing country forced to borrow in foreign currency lacks this option, and can reduce what it owes to foreigners only through some form of outright default.[7]

Economists Barry Eichengreen of the University of California–Berkeley and Ricardo Hausmann of Harvard University coined the phrase **original sin** to describe developing countries' inability to borrow in their own currencies.[8] In these economists' view, that inability of poor countries is a structural problem caused primarily by features of the global capital market—such as the limited additional diversification potential that a small country's currency provides to creditors from rich countries, who already hold all the major currencies in their portfolios. Other economists believe that the "sin" of developing countries is not particularly "original" but instead derives from their own histories of ill-advised economic policies. The debate is far from settled, but whatever the truth, it is clear that because of original sin, debt finance in international markets is more problematic for developing than for developed economies.

A related but distinct phenomenon is the large scale of private, *internal* borrowing in dollars or other major foreign currencies in many developing countries. As a result, foreign currency debtors may find themselves in considerable difficulty when the domestic currency depreciates.[9]

---

[7]As we saw in Chapter 21, Greece's government defaulted on its debt in 2012, the first default by a high-income country since the 1940s. Some other euro zone countries could default in the future. Euro zone countries face a unique constraint compared to other high-income countries, however. Because monetary policy is controlled by the ECB, a single euro zone government cannot choose to devalue its debts legally through depreciation of the domestic currency.

[8]See their paper "Exchange Rates and Financial Fragility" in *New Challenges for Monetary Policy* (Kansas City, MO: Federal Reserve Bank of Kansas City, 1999), pp. 329–368.

[9]For insight into the reasons for foreign-currency liability denomination, see the item by Rajan and Tokatlidis in Further Readings. When the currency of denomination is the U.S. dollar, the phenomenon is called **dollarization**. Increasingly, some of the more prosperous emerging market economies' governments have been able to issue domestic-currency bonds in home bond markets, with some demand coming from foreign investors (notably mutual funds). This development has helped to mitigate the original sin problem somewhat.

The Debt Crisis of the 1980s

In 1981–1983, the world economy suffered a steep recession. Just as the Great Depression made it hard for developing countries to make payments on their foreign loans—quickly causing an almost universal default—the great recession of the early 1980s also sparked a crisis over developing-country debt.

Chapter 19 described how the U.S. Federal Reserve in 1979 adopted a tough anti-inflation policy that raised dollar interest rates and helped push the world economy into recession by 1981. The fall in industrial countries' aggregate demand had a direct negative impact on the developing countries, of course, but three other mechanisms were also important. Because the developing world had extensive adjustable-rate dollar-denominated debts (original sin in action), there was an immediate and spectacular rise in the interest burden that debtor countries had to carry. The problem was magnified by the dollar's sharp appreciation in the foreign exchange market, which raised the real value of the dollar debt burden substantially. Finally, primary commodity prices collapsed, depressing the terms of trade of many poor economies.

The crisis began in August 1982 when Mexico announced that its central bank had run out of foreign reserves and that it could no longer meet payments on its foreign debt. Seeing potential similarities between Mexico and other large Latin American debtors such as Argentina, Brazil, and Chile, banks in the industrial countries—the largest private lenders to Latin America at the time—scrambled to reduce their risks by cutting off new credits and demanding repayment on earlier loans.

The results were a widespread inability of developing countries to meet prior debt obligations and a rapid move to the edge of a generalized default. Latin America was perhaps hardest hit, but also hit were Soviet bloc countries like Poland that had borrowed from European banks. African countries, most of whose debts were to official agencies such as the IMF and World Bank, also fell behind on their debts. Most countries in East Asia were able to maintain economic growth and avoid rescheduling their debt (that is, stretching out repayments by promising to pay additional interest in the future). Nonetheless, by the end of 1986 more than 40 countries had encountered severe external financing problems. Growth had slowed sharply (or gone into reverse) in much of the developing world, and developing-country borrowing fell dramatically. Initially, industrial countries, with heavy involvement by the International Monetary Fund, attempted to persuade the large banks to continue lending, arguing that a coordinated lending response was the best assurance that earlier debts would be repaid. Policy makers in the industrialized countries feared that banking giants like Citicorp and Bank of America, which had significant loans in Latin America, would fail in the event of a generalized default, dragging down the world financial system with them.[10] (As you can see, there was more than one near miss on the road to the 2007–2009 financial meltdown!) But the crisis didn't end until 1989 when the United States, fearing political instability to its south, insisted that American banks give some form of debt relief to indebted developing countries. In 1990, banks agreed to reduce Mexico's debt by 12 percent, and within a year, debt-reduction agreements had also been negotiated by the Philippines, Costa Rica, Venezuela, Uruguay, and Niger. When Argentina and Brazil reached preliminary agreements with their creditors in 1992, it looked as if the debt crisis of the 1980s had finally been resolved, but only after years of economic stagnation.

---

[10]By 1981, the developing country loans of the eight largest U.S. banks amounted to 264 percent of their capital, so loan losses of 50 percent would have made them insolvent. See table 5.1a in Federal Deposit Insurance Corporation, *History of the 80s: Lessons for the Future. Volume I: An Examination of the Banking Crises of the 1980s and Early 1990s* (Washington: FDIC, 1997).

Reforms, Capital Inflows, and the Return of Crisis

The early 1990s saw a renewal of private capital flows into developing countries, including some of the highly indebted Latin American countries at the center of the previous decade's debt crisis. As Table 22-3 shows, the foreign borrowing of non–oil-developing countries as a group expanded sharply.

Low interest rates in the United States in the early 1990s certainly provided an initial impetus to these renewed capital flows. Perhaps more important, however, were serious efforts in the recipient economies to stabilize inflation, a move requiring governments to limit their roles in the economy and raise tax revenues. At the same time, governments sought to lower trade barriers, to deregulate labor and product markets, and to improve the efficiency of financial markets. Widespread privatization served both the microeconomic goal of fostering efficiency and competition, and the macroeconomic goal of eliminating the government's need to cover the losses of sheltered and mismanaged state-owned firms.

What finally pushed countries to undertake serious reform despite the vested political interests favoring the status quo? One factor was the 1980s debt crisis itself, which resulted in what many commentators have called a "lost decade" of Latin American growth. Many of the relatively young policy makers who came to power in Latin America as the debt crisis ended were well-trained economists who believed that misguided economic policies and institutions had brought on the crisis and worsened its effects. Another factor was the example of East Asia, which had survived the 1980s debt crisis largely unscathed. Despite having been poorer than Latin America as recently as 1960, East Asia now was richer.

Recent economic reforms have taken different shapes in different Latin American countries, and some have made significant progress. Here we contrast the macroeconomic aspects of the approaches taken in four large countries that have made wide-ranging (though not equally successful) reform attempts.

Argentina Argentina suffered under military rule between 1976 and 1983, but the economy remained a shambles even after the return of democracy. Following years marked by banking crises, fiscal instability, and even hyperinflation, Argentina finally turned to radical institutional reform in the early 1990s. Import tariffs were slashed, government expenditures were cut, major state companies including the national airline were privatized, and tax reforms led to increased government revenues.

The most daring component of Argentina's program, however, was the new Convertibility Law of April 1991 making Argentina's currency fully convertible into U.S. dollars at a *fixed* rate of exactly one peso per dollar. The Convertibility Law also required that the monetary base be backed entirely by gold or foreign currency, so in one stroke it sharply curtailed the central bank's ability to finance government deficits through continuing money creation. Argentina's Convertibility Law represented an extreme version of the exchange rate–based approach to reducing inflation that had been tried many times in the past, but had typically ended in a currency crisis. The 1991 monetary law requiring 100 percent foreign exchange backing for the monetary base made Argentina an example of a **currency board**, in which the monetary base is backed entirely by foreign currency and the central bank therefore holds no domestic assets at all. This time, the approach worked for nearly a decade. Backed as it was by genuine economic and financial reforms, Argentina's plan had a dramatic effect on inflation, which remained low after dropping from 800 percent in 1990 to well under 5 percent by 1995. However, continuing inflation in the first years of the convertibility plan, despite a fixed exchange rate, implied a steep real appreciation of the peso, about

30 percent from 1990 to 1995. The real appreciation led to unemployment and a growing current account deficit.

In the mid-1990s the peso's real appreciation process ended, but unemployment remained high because of rigidities in labor markets. Although by 1997 the economy was growing rapidly, growth subsequently turned negative and the government deficit once again swelled out of control. As the world economy slipped into recession in 2001, Argentina's foreign credit dried up. The country defaulted on its foreign debts in December 2001 and abandoned the peso/dollar peg in January 2002. The peso depreciated sharply and inflation soared once again. Argentine output fell by nearly 11 percent in 2002, although growth returned in 2003 as inflation fell. As of this writing, Argentina is trying to negotiate a settlement with holdout foreign creditors that will allow it to re-enter international capital markets as a borrower.

Brazil   Like Argentina, Brazil suffered runaway inflation in the 1980s as well as multiple failed attempts at stabilization accompanied by currency reforms. The country took longer to get inflation under control, however, and approached its disinflation less systematically than the Argentines did.[11]

In 1994, the Brazilian government introduced a new currency, the real (pronounced ray-AL), pegged to the dollar. At the cost of widespread bank failures, Brazil defended the new exchange rate with high interest rates in 1995, then shifted to a fixed, upwardly crawling peg in the face of substantial real appreciation. Inflation dropped from an annual rate of 2,669 percent (in 1994) to under 10 percent in 1997.

Economic growth remained unimpressive, however. Although Brazil's government undertook a reduction in import barriers, privatization, and fiscal retrenchment, the country's overall progress on economic reform was much slower than in the case of Argentina, and the government's fiscal deficit remained worryingly high. A good part of the problem was the very high interest rate the government had to pay on its debt, a rate that reflected skepticism in markets that the limited upward crawl of the real against the dollar could be maintained.

Finally, in January 1999, Brazil devalued the real by 8 percent and then allowed it to float. Very quickly, the real lost 40 percent of its value against the dollar. Recession followed as the government struggled to prevent the real from going into a free fall. But the recession proved short-lived, inflation did not take off, and (because Brazil's financial institutions had avoided heavy borrowing in dollars), financial-sector collapse was avoided. Brazil elected a populist president, Ignacio Lula da Silva, in October 2002, but the market-friendly policies he ultimately (and rather unexpectedly) adopted have preserved Brazil's access to international credit markets. Economic growth has been healthy and Brazil has become a power in the emerging world. A key factor in Brazil's success has been its strong commodity exports, notably to China.

Chile   Having learned the lessons of deep unemployment and financial collapse at the start of the 1980s, Chile implemented more consistent reforms later in the decade. Very importantly, the country instituted a tough regulatory environment for domestic financial institutions and removed an explicit bailout guarantee that had helped to worsen Chile's earlier debt crisis. A crawling peg type of exchange rate regime was used to bring inflation down gradually, but the system was operated flexibly to avoid extreme real appreciation. The Chilean central bank became independent of the fiscal

[11]For an account, see Rudiger Dornbusch, "Brazil's Incomplete Stabilization and Reform," *Brookings Papers on Economic Activity* 1 (1997), pp. 367–404.

authorities in 1990 (the same year a democratic government replaced the military regime of General Pinochet). That action further solidified the commitment not to finance government deficits by ordering the central bank to print money.[12]

Another new policy required all capital inflows (other than equity purchases) to be accompanied by a one-year, non-interest-bearing deposit equal to as much as 30 percent of the transaction. Because the duration of the deposit requirement was limited, the penalty fell disproportionately on short-term inflows, those most prone to be withdrawn by foreign investors in a crisis. One motivation for the implied capital inflow tax was to limit real currency appreciation; the other was to reduce the risk that a sudden withdrawal of foreign short-term funds would provoke a financial crisis. There is considerable controversy among economists as to whether the Chilean capital inflow barriers succeeded in their aims, although it is doubtful that they did much harm.[13]

Chile's policies have paid off handsomely. Between 1991 and 1997, the country enjoyed GDP growth rates averaging better than 8 percent per year. At the same time, inflation dropped from 26 percent per year in 1990 to only 6 percent by 1997. Chile has been rated not only as being the least corrupt country in Latin America, but also as being less corrupt than several European Union members and the United States.

Mexico   Mexico introduced a broad stabilization and reform program in 1987, combining an aggressive reduction in public-sector deficits and debt with exchange rate targeting and wage-price guidelines negotiated with representatives of industry and labor unions.[14] That same year, the country made a significant commitment to free trade by joining the GATT. (Mexico subsequently joined the Organization for Economic Cooperation and Development and, in 1994, joined the North American Free Trade Agreement.)

Mexico fixed its peso's exchange rate against the U.S. dollar at the end of 1987, moved to a crawling peg at the start of 1989, and moved to a crawling band at the end of 1991. The government kept a level ceiling on the peso's possible appreciation but announced each year after 1991 a gradually rising limit on the currency's allowable extent of depreciation. Thus, the range of possible exchange rate fluctuation was permitted to increase over time.

Despite this potential flexibility, the Mexican authorities held the exchange rate near its appreciation ceiling. The peso therefore appreciated sharply in real terms, and a large current account deficit emerged. During 1994, the country's foreign exchange reserves fell to very low levels. Civil strife, a looming presidential transition, and devaluation fears contributed to this fall. Another important factor behind the

---

[12]For an overview of aspects of the Chilean approach to economic reform, see Barry P. Bosworth, Rudiger Dornbusch, and Raúl Labán, eds., *The Chilean Economy: Policy Lessons and Challenges* (Washington, D.C.: Brookings Institution, 1994). A classic account of Chilean financial problems at the start of the 1980s is Carlos F. Díaz-Alejandro, "Goodbye Financial Repression, Hello Financial Crash," *Journal of Development Economics* 19 (September/October 1985), pp. 1–24. This paper is highly recommended, as the problems discussed by Díaz-Alejandro have proven relevant far beyond the specific context of Chile.

[13]For a discussion, see Chapter 5 of the book by Kenen listed in this chapter's Further Readings. Also see Kevin Cowan and José De Gregorio, "International Borrowing, Capital Controls, and the Exchange Rate: Lessons from Chile," in Sebastian Edwards, ed., *Capital Controls and Capital Flows in Emerging Economies* (Chicago: University of Chicago Press, 2007), pp. 241–296.

[14]The ideas underlying the Mexican approach are explained by one of its architects, Pedro Aspe Armella, an economist trained at the Massachusetts Institute of Technology who was Mexico's finance minister for the period 1988–1994. See his book *Economic Transformation the Mexican Way* (Cambridge, MA: MIT Press, 1993). See also Nora Lustig, *Mexico: The Remaking of an Economy* (Washington, D.C.: Brookings Institution, 1992).

foreign reserve leakage, however, was a continuing extension of government credits to banks experiencing loan losses. Mexico had rapidly privatized its banks without adequate regulatory safeguards, and it had also opened its capital account, thus giving the banks free access to foreign funds. Because banks were confident they would be bailed out by the government if they met trouble, moral hazard was rampant. Hoping to spur growth and reduce a current account deficit that by then was nearly 8 percent of GNP, the new Mexican government that took over in December 1994 devalued the peso 15 percent beyond the depreciation limit promised a year before. The devalued currency peg was immediately attacked by speculators, and the government retreated to a float. Foreign investors panicked, pushing the peso down precipitously, and soon Mexico found itself unable to borrow except at penalty interest rates. As in 1982, default loomed again. The country avoided disaster only with the help of a $50 billion emergency loan orchestrated by the U.S. Treasury and the IMF.

Inflation, which had dropped from 159 percent in 1987 to only 7 percent in 1994, soared as the peso depreciated. Mexico's national output shrank by more than 6 percent in 1995. Unemployment more than doubled amid sharp fiscal cutbacks, sky-high interest rates, and a generalized banking crisis. But the contraction lasted only a year. By 1996, inflation was falling and the economy was recovering as the peso continued to float. Mexico regained access to private capital markets and repaid the U.S. Treasury ahead of schedule. A major achievement of Mexico has been expanding its democratic institutions and moving away from the virtual one-party rule that had characterized much of the country's 20th-century history.

East Asia: Success and Crisis

At the start of 1997, the countries of East Asia were the envy of the developing world. Their rapid growth rates were bringing them far up the development scale, putting several in striking distance of advanced-country status (which several have now reached). Then they were overwhelmed by a disastrous financial crisis. The speed with which East Asia's economic success turned into economic chaos came as a rude shock to most observers. East Asia's setback sparked a broader crisis that engulfed developing countries as distant as Russia and Brazil. In this section, we review the East Asian experience. The lessons, as we will see, reinforce those from Latin America.

The East Asian Economic Miracle

As we saw in Table 22-2, South Korea was a desperately poor nation in the 1960s, with little industry and apparently few economic prospects. In 1963, however, the country launched a series of sweeping economic reforms, shifting from an inward-looking, import-substitution development strategy to one that emphasized exports. And the country began a remarkable economic ascent. Over the next 50 years, South Korea increased its real per capita GDP by a factor of about 16—more than the increase that the United States has achieved over the past century.

Even more remarkable was that South Korea was not alone. Its economic rise was paralleled by that of a number of other East Asian economies. In the first wave were Hong Kong, Taiwan, and Singapore, all of which began growing rapidly in the 1960s. In the course of the 1970s and 1980s, the club of rapidly growing Asian economies expanded to include Malaysia, Thailand, Indonesia, and—awesomely—China, the world's most populous nation. For the first time since the rise of Japan as an industrial power in the late nineteenth century, a substantial part of the world appeared to be making the transition from third world to first.

There remains considerable dispute about the reasons for this economic "miracle." In the early 1990s, it was fashionable among some commentators to ascribe Asia's growth to a common Asian system of industrial policy and business-government cooperation. However, even a cursory look at the economies involved makes the claim of a common system dubious. The high-growth economies did include regimes such as South Korea's, where the government took an active role in the allocation of capital among industries; but it also included regimes such as those of Hong Kong and Taiwan, where this type of industrial policy was largely absent. Some economies, such as those of Taiwan and Singapore, relied heavily on the establishment of local subsidiaries of multinational firms. Others, such as South Korea and Hong Kong, relied mainly on domestic entrepreneurs.

WHY HAVE DEVELOPING COUNTRIES ACCUMULATED SUCH HIGH LEVELS OF INTERNATIONAL RESERVES?

Developing countries facing financial crises typically find that their international reserves have reached very low levels. A country that is fixing its exchange rate may have little choice but to let its currency depreciate once its reserves have run out. A country without liquid foreign exchange reserves may have no means to repay lenders who have previously extended short-term foreign currency loans. Like a run on a bank, market fears about potential default or depreciation can be self-fulfilling. If market confidence fails, reserves will quickly disappear and no new borrowing from foreigners will be possible. The resulting liquidity crunch may make it impossible for a country to meet its remaining foreign obligations.

This type of "bank run" mechanism has been at the heart of many developing-country crises, including the Asian economic crisis of 1997–1998, which we discuss below. Following the Asian crisis, which affected a large number of countries throughout the world, several economists suggested that developing countries take matters into their own hands. Because foreign credit tends to dry up precisely when it is most needed, countries could best protect themselves by accumulating large war chests of ready cash—dollars, euros, and other widely acceptable foreign currencies.

When countries had little involvement with world capital markets (as during the 1950s and early 1960s), reserve adequacy was judged largely by reference to the likelihood that export earnings might temporarily fall short of import needs. But in today's world of globalized finance, the volume of reserves needed to deter an attack might be orders of magnitude greater. As economist Martin Feldstein of Harvard put it, "The most direct way for a country to achieve liquidity is to accumulate substantial amounts of liquid foreign reserves.... [A] government should not judge the adequacy of its reserves in relation to the value of imports. A common reserve goal of, say, six months of imports ignores the fact that currency crises are about capital flows, not trade financing. What matters is the value of reserves relative to the potential selling of assets by speculators even if the country's fundamental economic conditions do not warrant a currency deterioration."*

We touched on the growth of international reserves in Chapter 18. As we observed in that chapter, while reserves have grown for all countries, since the debt crisis of the 1980s they have grown especially quickly for developing countries. For developing countries as a group, however, the pace of reserve accumulation has accelerated most dramatically since the financial crises of the late 1990s. The accompanying figure shows international reserve holdings as a fraction of national output for the group of all developing countries, as well as for Brazil, Russia, India, and China. (These four countries are often referred to as the "BRICs" in view

---

*See Feldstein, "A Self-Help Guide for Emerging Markets," *Foreign Affairs* 78 (March/April 1999), pp. 93–109. For a recent analytical treatment, see Olivier Jeanne, "International Reserves in Emerging Market Countries: Too Much of a Good Thing?" *Brookings Papers on Economic Activity* 1 (2007), pp. 1–79.

(*Continued*)

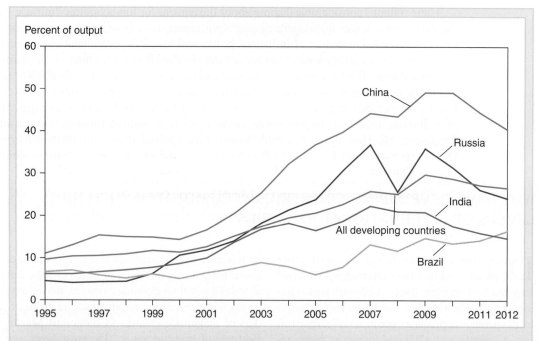

International Reserves Held by Developing Countries

Since the 1990s, developing countries have sharply increased their holdings of foreign currency reserves, mostly U.S dollars.

Source: World Bank, World Development Indicators.

of their recent strong growth performances.) In all the cases shown, reserves better than doubled (as a share of national product) between 1999 and 2009, before falling in three of the four countries. China's reserve ratio rose by a factor of 3.3 over that period and Russia's increased by a factor of 5.7.[†]

For a number of developing countries, the levels of reserves are so high as to exceed their total short-term foreign currency debts to foreigners. These large reserve holdings therefore provide a high degree of protection against a sudden stop of capital inflows. Indeed, they helped the developing countries weather the industrial-country credit crunch of 2007–2009 (recall Chapter 20). As you can see in the figure, developing countries generally spent some reserves to shield themselves during the 2007–2009 crisis.

The self-insurance motive for holding reserves is not the entire story, however. In some cases, reserve growth has been an undesired byproduct of intervention policies to keep the currency from appreciating. China provides a case in point. China's development strategy has relied on increasing export levels of labor-intensive goods to fuel a rapid rise in living standards. In effect, appreciation of the Chinese renminbi makes Chinese labor more expensive relative to foreign labor, so China has tightly limited the currency's appreciation over time by buying up dollars. Despite capital controls limiting inflows of foreign funds, speculative money entered the country in anticipation of future appreciation, and reserves swelled enormously. The government has gradually loosened its capital outflow controls, hoping that reserves will fall as Chinese investors go abroad, but the tactic has had only limited success so far. At the end of 2012, China's reserves still stood at more than 40 percent of national output. We discuss China's policies in greater detail in a Case Study later in this chapter.

[†]Developing countries hold roughly a 60 percent share of their reserves in the form of U.S. dollars. They hold the balance mostly in euros, but also in a few alternative major currencies such as the Japanese yen, British pound, and Swiss franc.

TABLE 22-4	East Asian Current Accounts (annual averages, percent of GDP)		
	1990–1997	**1998–2000**	**2001–2013**
China	1.5	2.1	4.7
Hong Kong	0.5	3.9	8.0
Indonesia	−2.5	4.4	1.2
Malaysia	−5.8	12.7	11.7
South Korea	−1.3	6.7	2.4
Taiwan	3.9	2.2	8.4
Thailand	−6.2	10.2	2.5

Source: International Monetary Fund, World Economic Outlook Database, April 2013.

What the high-growth economies did have in common were high rates of saving and investment; rapidly improving educational levels among the work force; relatively moderate inflation rates; and if not free trade, at least a high degree of openness to and integration with world markets.

Perhaps surprisingly, before 1990 most rapidly growing Asian economies financed the bulk of their high investment rates out of domestic savings. In the 1990s, however, the growing popularity of emerging markets among investors in the advanced world led to substantial lending to developing Asia; as Table 22-4 shows, several of the Asian countries began running, as a counterpart to these loans, large current account deficits as a share of GDP. A few economists worried that these deficits might pose the risk of a crisis similar to the one that had hit Mexico in late 1994, but most observers regarded large capital flows to such rapidly growing and macroeconomically stable economies as justified by the expected profitability of investment opportunities.

Asian Weaknesses

As it turned out, in 1997 Asian economies did indeed experience a severe financial crisis. And with the benefit of hindsight, several weaknesses in their economic structures—some shared by Latin American countries that had gone through crises—became apparent. Three issues in particular stood out:

1. *Productivity.* Although the rapid growth of East Asian economies was not in any sense an illusion, even before the crisis a number of studies had suggested that some limits to expansion were appearing. The most surprising result of several studies was that the bulk of Asian output growth could be explained simply by the rapid growth of production *inputs*—capital and labor—and that there had been relatively little increase in productivity, that is, in output per unit of input. Thus in South Korea, for example, the convergence toward advanced-country output per capita appeared to be mainly due to a rapid shift of workers from agriculture to industry, a rise in educational levels, and a massive increase in the capital-labor ratio within the nonagricultural sector. Evidence for a narrowing of the technological gap with the West was unexpectedly hard to find. The implication of these studies was that continuing high rates of capital accumulation would eventually produce diminishing returns, and, possibly, that the large financial inflows taking place were not justified by future profitability after all.

WHAT DID EAST ASIA DO RIGHT?

The growth of East Asian economies between the 1960s and the 1990s demonstrated that it is possible for a country to move rapidly up the development ladder. But what are the ingredients for such success?

One way to answer this question may be to look at the distinctive attributes of what the World Bank, in its 1993 study entitled *The East Asian Miracle*, dubs the HPAEs, the high-performing Asian economies.

One important ingredient was a high saving rate: In 1990, HPAEs saved 34 percent of GDP, compared with only half that in Latin America, slightly more in South Asia.

Another important ingredient was a strong emphasis on education. Even in 1965, when the HPAEs were still quite poor, they had high enrollment rates in basic education:

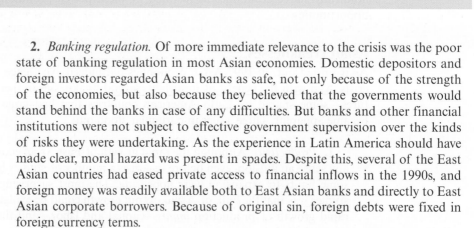

Essentially all children received basic schooling in Hong Kong, Singapore, and South Korea, and even desperately poor Indonesia had a 70 percent enrollment rate. By 1987, rates of enrollment in secondary school in East Asia were well above those in Latin American nations such as Brazil.

Finally, two other characteristics of the HPAEs, as noted earlier, were a relatively stable macroeconomic environment, free from high inflation or major economic slumps, and a high share of trade in GDP. These features made the East Asian economies look quite different from crisis-prone countries in Latin America. These contrasts played an important role in the "conversion" of many leaders in Latin America and elsewhere to the idea of economic reform, in terms of both a commitment to price stability and the opening of markets to the world.

2. *Banking regulation.* Of more immediate relevance to the crisis was the poor state of banking regulation in most Asian economies. Domestic depositors and foreign investors regarded Asian banks as safe, not only because of the strength of the economies, but also because they believed that the governments would stand behind the banks in case of any difficulties. But banks and other financial institutions were not subject to effective government supervision over the kinds of risks they were undertaking. As the experience in Latin America should have made clear, moral hazard was present in spades. Despite this, several of the East Asian countries had eased private access to financial inflows in the 1990s, and foreign money was readily available both to East Asian banks and directly to East Asian corporate borrowers. Because of original sin, foreign debts were fixed in foreign currency terms.

In several Asian countries, close ties between business interests and government officials appear to have helped foster considerable moral hazard in lending. In Thailand, so-called finance companies, often run by relatives of government officials, lent money to highly speculative real estate ventures; in Indonesia, lenders were far too eager to finance ventures by members of the president's family. These factors help to explain how, despite high saving rates, several East Asian countries were led to invest so much that their current accounts were in deficit prior to the crisis.

Some analysts have suggested that excessive lending, driven by moral hazard, helped create an unsustainable boom in Asian economies—especially in real estate—that temporarily concealed the poor quality of many of the investments; and that the inevitable end of this boom caused a downward spiral of declining prices and failing banks. However, while moral hazard was certainly a factor in the run-up to the crisis, its importance remains a subject of considerable dispute.

3. *Legal framework.* One important weakness of Asian economies became apparent only after they'd stumbled: the lack of a good legal framework for dealing with companies in trouble. In the United States, there is a well-established procedure for bankruptcy—that is, for dealing with a company that cannot pay its debts. In such a procedure, the courts take possession of the firm on behalf of its creditors, and then seek to find a way to satisfy their claims as adequately as possible. Often this means keeping the company in existence and converting the debts it cannot pay into ownership shares. In Asian economies, however, bankruptcy law was weak, in part because the astonishing growth of the economies had made corporate failures a rare event. When times did turn bad, a destructive impasse developed. Troubled companies would simply stop paying their debts. They then could not operate effectively because nobody would lend to them until the outstanding debts were repaid. Yet the creditors lacked any way to seize the limping enterprises from their original owners.

Of course, every economy has weaknesses, but the performance of the East Asian economies had been so spectacular that few paid much attention to theirs. Even those who were aware that the "miracle" economies had problems could hardly have anticipated the catastrophe that overtook them in 1997.

The Asian Financial Crisis

The Asian financial crisis is generally considered to have started on July 2, 1997, with the devaluation of the Thai baht. Thailand had been running a huge current account deficit and showing signs of financial strain for more than a year. During 1996, it became apparent that far too many office towers had been built; first the nation's real estate market, then its stock market, went into decline. In the first half of 1997, speculation about a possible devaluation of the baht led to an accelerating loss of foreign exchange reserves, and on July 2 the country attempted a controlled 15 percent devaluation. As in the case of Mexico in 1994, however, the attempted moderate devaluation spun out of control, sparking massive speculation and a far deeper plunge.

Thailand itself is a small economy. However, the sharp drop in the Thai currency was followed by speculation against the currencies first of its immediate neighbor, Malaysia; then of Indonesia; and eventually of the much larger and more developed economy of South Korea. All of these economies seemed to speculators to share with Thailand the weaknesses previously listed; all were feeling the effects in 1997 of renewed economic slowdown in their largest industrial neighbor, Japan. In each case, governments were faced with awkward dilemmas, stemming partly from the dependence of their economies on trade and partly from the fact that domestic banks and companies had large debts denominated in dollars. If the countries had simply allowed their currencies to drop, rising import prices would have threatened to produce dangerous inflation, and the sudden increase in the domestic currency value of debts might have pushed many potentially viable banks and companies into bankruptcy. On the other hand, defending the currencies would have required at least temporary high interest rates to persuade investors to keep their money in the country, and these high interest rates would themselves have produced an economic slump and caused banks to fail.

All of the afflicted countries except Malaysia thus turned to the IMF for assistance and received loans in return for implementation of economic plans that were supposed to contain the damage: higher interest rates to limit the exchange rate depreciation, efforts to avoid large budget deficits, and "structural" reforms that were supposed to deal with the weaknesses that had brought on the crisis in the first place. Despite the IMF's aid, however, the result of the currency crisis was a sharp economic downturn. All of the troubled countries went from growth rates in excess of 6 percent in 1996 to a severe contraction in 1998.

Worst of all was the case of Indonesia, where economic crisis and political instability reinforced each other in a deadly spiral, all made much worse by the collapse of domestic residents' confidence in the nation's banks. By the summer of 1998, the Indonesian rupiah had lost 85 percent of its original value, and few if any major companies were solvent. The Indonesian population was faced with mass unemployment and, in some cases, the inability to afford even basic foodstuffs. Ethnic violence broke out.

As a consequence of the collapse in confidence, the troubled Asian economies were also forced into a dramatic reversal of their current account positions. As Table 22-4 shows, most moved abruptly from sometimes large deficits to huge surpluses. Most of this reversal came not through increased exports but through a huge drop in imports, as the economies contracted.

Currencies eventually stabilized throughout crisis-stricken Asia and interest rates decreased, but the direct spillover from the region's slump caused slowdowns or recessions in several neighboring countries, including Hong Kong, Singapore, and New Zealand. Japan and even parts of Europe and Latin America felt the effects. Most governments continued to take the IMF-prescribed medicine, but in September 1998 Malaysia—which had never accepted an IMF program—broke ranks and imposed extensive controls on capital outflows, hoping that the controls would allow the country to ease monetary and fiscal policies without sending its currency into a tailspin. China and Taiwan, which maintained capital controls and had current account surpluses over the pre-crisis period, were largely unscathed in the crisis.

Fortunately, the downturn in East Asia was "V-shaped": After the sharp output contraction in 1998, growth returned in 1999 as depreciated currencies spurred higher exports. However, not all of the region's economies fared equally well, and controversy remains over the effectiveness of Malaysia's experiment with capital controls. The economies that instead relied on IMF help were generally unhappy with its management of the crisis, which they viewed as clumsy and intrusive. These resentments have proved to be long lived: While governments can turn to the IMF for conditional funding in case of a sudden stop, the Asian crisis countries vowed never to do so again. This determination has been an important motive for "self-insurance" with large stockpiles of international reserves.

Lessons of Developing-Country Crises

The emerging market crisis that started with Thailand's 1997 devaluation produced what might be called an orgy of finger-pointing. Some Westerners blamed the crisis on the policies of the Asians themselves, especially the "crony capitalism" under which businesspeople and politicians had excessively cozy relationships. Some Asian leaders, in turn, blamed the crisis on the machinations of Western financiers; even

Hong Kong, normally a bastion of free market sentiment, began intervening to block what it described as a conspiracy by speculators to drive down its stock market and undermine its currency. And almost everyone criticized the IMF, although some were saying that it was wrong to tell countries to try to limit the depreciation of their currencies, others that it was wrong to allow the currencies to depreciate at all.

Nonetheless, some very clear lessons emerge from a careful study of the Asian crisis and earlier developing-country crises in Latin America and elsewhere.

1. *Choosing the right exchange rate regime.* It is perilous for a developing country to fix its exchange rate unless it has the means and commitment to do so, come what may. East Asian countries found that confidence in official exchange rate targets encouraged borrowing in foreign currencies. When devaluation occurred nonetheless, much of the financial sector and many corporations became insolvent as a result of extensive foreign currency-denominated debts. The developing countries that have successfully stabilized inflation have adopted more flexible exchange rate systems or moved to greater flexibility quickly after an initial period of pegging aimed at reducing inflation expectations. Even in Argentina, where the public's fear of returning to the hyperinflationary past instilled a widely shared determination to prevent inflation, a fixed exchange rate proved untenable over the long term. Mexico's experience since 1995 shows that larger developing countries can manage quite well with a floating exchange rate, and it is hard to believe that, if Mexico had been fixing, it would have survived the Asian crisis repercussions of 1998 without developing a currency crisis of its own.

2. *The central importance of banking.* A large part of what made the Asian crisis so devastating was that it was not purely a currency crisis, but rather a currency crisis inextricably mixed with banking and financial crises. In the most immediate sense, governments were faced with the conflict between restricting the money supply to support the currency and the need to print large quantities of money to deal with bank runs. More broadly, the collapse of many banks disrupted the economy by cutting off channels of credit, which made it difficult for even profitable companies to stay in business. This should not have come as a surprise in Asia. Similar effects of banking fragility played roles in the crises of Argentina, Chile, and Uruguay in the 1980s; of Mexico in 1994–1995; and even in those of industrial countries like Sweden during the 1992 attacks on the EMS (Chapter 21). Unfortunately, Asia's spectacular economic performance prior to its crisis blinded people to its financial vulnerabilities. In the future, wise governments everywhere will devote a great deal of attention to shoring up their banking systems to minimize moral hazard, in the hope of becoming less vulnerable to financial catastrophes.

3. *The proper sequence of reform measures.* Economic reformers in developing countries have learned the hard way that the order in which liberalization measures are taken really does matter. That truth also follows from basic economic theory: The principle of the *second best* tells us that when an economy suffers from multiple distortions, the removal of only a few may make matters worse, not better. Developing countries generally suffer from many, many distortions, so this point is especially important for them. Consider the sequencing of financial account liberalization and financial sector reform, for example. It is clearly a mistake to open up the financial account before sound safeguards and supervision are in place for domestic financial institutions. Otherwise, the ability to borrow abroad will simply encourage reckless lending by domestic banks. When the economy slows down, foreign capital will flee, leaving domestic banks insolvent. Thus, developing countries should delay opening the financial account until the domestic financial system is strong enough to withstand the sometimes violent ebb and flow of world capital. Economists also argue that trade liberalization should precede financial account liberalization. Financial account liberalization may cause real exchange rate volatility and impede the movement of factors of production from nontraded into traded goods industries.

4. *The importance of contagion.* A final lesson of developing-country experience is the vulnerability of even seemingly healthy economies to crises of confidence generated by events elsewhere in the world—a domino effect that has come to be known as **contagion**. Contagion was at work when the crisis in Thailand, a small economy in Southeast Asia, provoked another crisis in South Korea, a much larger economy some 2,000 miles away. An even more spectacular example emerged in August 1998, when a plunge in the Russian ruble sparked massive speculation against Brazil's real. The problem of contagion, and the concern that even the most careful economic management may not offer full immunity, has become central to the discussion of possible reforms of the international financial system, to which we now turn.

Reforming the World's Financial "Architecture"

Economic difficulties lead, inevitably, to proposals for economic reforms. The Asian economic crisis and its repercussions suggested to many people that the international financial and monetary system, or at least the part of it that applies to developing countries, was in need of change. Proposals for such an overhaul have come to be grouped under the impressive if vague title of plans for a new financial "architecture."

Why did the Asian crisis convince nearly everyone of a need for rethinking international monetary relations, when earlier crises of the 1990s did not? One reason was that the Asian countries' problems seemed to stem primarily from their connections with the world capital market. The crisis clearly demonstrated that a country can be vulnerable to a currency crisis even if its own position looks healthy by normal measures. None of the troubled Asian economies had serious budget deficits, excessive rates of monetary expansion, worrisome levels of inflation, or any of the other indicators that have traditionally signaled vulnerability to speculative attack. If there were severe weaknesses in the economies—a proposition that is the subject of dispute, since some economists argue that the economies would have been quite healthy had it not been for the speculative attacks—they involved issues such as the strength of the banking system that might have remained dormant in the absence of sharp currency depreciations.

The second reason for rethinking international finance was the apparent strength of contagion throughout the international capital markets. The speed and force with which market disturbances could be spread between distant economies suggested that preventive measures taken by individual economies might not suffice. Just as a concern about economic interdependence had inspired the Bretton Woods blueprint for the world economy in 1944, world policy makers again put the reform of the international system on their agendas after the Asian crisis.

Developing countries generally recovered quickly from the financial crisis of 2007–2009—this time, unlike after 1982, the rich countries were the ones that suffered protracted recessions (Chapter 19). But it was unclear whether developing-country resilience was due to reforms adopted after the Asian crisis, higher holdings of international reserves, strong commodity prices, greater flexibility of exchange rates, or the historically low interest rates enforced by industrial-country central banks. In view of the breathtaking contagion again displayed as the 2007–2009 crisis spread across the globe, sentiment that international finance needs an overhaul has remained strong. Here we look at some of the main issues involved.

Capital Mobility and the Trilemma of the Exchange Rate Regime

One effect of the Asian crisis was to dispel any illusions we may have had about the availability of easy answers to the problems of international macroeconomics and finance. The crisis and its spread made it all too clear that some well-known policy trade-offs for open economies remain as stark as ever—and perhaps have become even more difficult to manage.

Chapter 19 spelled out the basic *monetary trilemma* for open economies. Of the three goals that most countries share—independence in monetary policy, stability in the exchange rate, and the free movement of capital—only two can be reached simultaneously. Exchange rate stability is more important for the typical developing country than for the typical developed country. Developing countries have less ability to influence their terms of trade than developed countries, and exchange rate stability can be more important for keeping inflation in check and avoiding financial stress in developing countries. In particular, the widespread developing-country practice of borrowing in dollars or other major currencies (both externally and internally) means that currency depreciations can sharply increase the real burden of debts.

The conundrum facing would-be reformers of the world's financial architecture can then be summarized as follows: Because of the threat of the kind of currency crises that hit Mexico in 1994–1995 and Asia in 1997, it seems hard if not impossible to achieve all three objectives at the same time. That is, to achieve one of them, a country must give up one of the other two objectives. Until the late 1970s, most developing countries maintained exchange controls and limited private capital movements in particular, as we have seen. (Some major developing countries, notably China and India, still retain such controls.) While there was considerable evasion of the controls, they did slow up the movement of capital. As a result, countries could peg their exchange rates for extended periods—producing exchange rate stability—yet devalue their currencies on occasion, which offered considerable monetary autonomy. The main problem with controls was that they imposed onerous restrictions on international transactions, thus reducing efficiency and contributing to corruption.

In the last two decades of the 20th century, capital became substantially more mobile, largely because controls were lifted, but also because of improved communications technology. This new capital mobility made adjustable peg regimes extremely vulnerable to speculation, since capital would flee a currency on the slightest hint that it might be devalued. (The same phenomenon occurred among developed countries in the 1960s and early 1970s, as we saw in Chapter 19.) The result has been to drive developing countries toward one or the other sides of the triangle in Figure 19-1: either rigidly fixed exchange rates and a renunciation of monetary autonomy, like dollarization or the currency board system described above, or flexibly managed (and even floating) exchange rates. But despite the lesson of experience that intermediate positions are dangerous, developing countries have been uncomfortable with both extremes. While a major economy like the United States can accept a widely fluctuating exchange rate, a smaller, developing economy often finds the costs of such volatility hard to sustain, in part because it is more open and in part because it suffers from original sin. As a result, even countries claiming to "float" their currencies may display a "fear of floating" and instead limit currency fluctuations over long periods.[15] Meanwhile, a rigid system like a currency board can deprive a country of flexibility, especially when it is dealing with financial crises in which the central bank must act as the lender of last resort.

Several respected economists, including Columbia University's Jagdish Bhagwati and Joseph Stiglitz and Harvard University's Dani Rodrik, have argued that developing countries should keep or reinstate restrictions on capital mobility to be able to exercise monetary autonomy while enjoying stable exchange rates.[16] In the face of the Asian crisis, China and India, for example, put plans to liberalize their capital accounts on hold; some countries that had liberalized capital movements considered the possibility of reimposing restrictions (as Malaysia actually did). Most policy makers, both in the developing world and in the industrial countries, continue to regard capital controls as either difficult to enforce for long or disruptive of normal business relationships (as well as a potent source of corruption). These reservations apply most strongly to controls on capital *outflows*, because restrictions are particularly hard to maintain effectively when wealth owners are fleeing abroad to avoid potentially big losses.

Nonetheless, in recent years a number of emerging market countries, ranging from Brazil to Israel, have become more open to imposing limited controls on financial *inflows*, and even the IMF has become more open to their use. One reason for this change is a *macroprudential* motive: limits on financial inflows could limit excessive bank lending during booms, and thereby temper the resulting contraction in case of a sudden stop or financial-flow reversal later. Equally (if not more) important as a motivation has been the desire to limit real currency appreciation, and the resulting harm to exports, without resorting to inflationary monetary policies.[17]

While there is a renewed openness to capital inflow controls, most discussion of financial architecture has focused instead on meliorative measures—ways to make the remaining choices less painful even when capital controls are not used.

"Prophylactic" Measures

Since the risk of financial crisis is what makes the decisions surrounding the choice of exchange rate regime so difficult, some recent proposals focus on ways to reduce that risk. Typical proposals include calls for the following:

More "transparency." At least part of what went wrong in Asia was that foreign banks and other investors lent money to Asian enterprises without any clear idea of what the risks were, and then pulled their money out equally blindly when it became clear that those risks were larger than they had imagined. There have therefore been many proposals for greater "transparency"—that is, better provision of financial information—in the same way that corporations in the United States are required to provide accurate public reports of their financial positions. The hope is that increased transparency will reduce both the tendency of too much money rushing into

---

[15]See Guillermo A. Calvo and Carmen M. Reinhart, "Fear of Floating," *Quarterly Journal of Economics* 117 (May 2002), pp. 379–408.

[16]See Jagdish N. Bhagwati, "The Capital Myth," *Foreign Affairs* 77 (May–June, 1998), pp. 7–12; Dani Rodrik, "Who Needs Capital-Account Convertibility?" in Stanley Fischer et al., *Should the IMF Pursue Capital-Account Convertibility?* Princeton Essays in International Finance 207 (May 1998); and Joseph E. Stiglitz, *Globalization and Its Discontents* (New York: W. W. Norton & Company, 2003).

[17]As an indication of the IMF's current approach, see, for example, Jonathan D. Ostry, Atish R. Ghosh, Marcos Chamon, and Mahvash S. Qureshi, "Capital Controls: When and Why?" *IMF Economic Review* 59 (2011), pp. 562–580.

a country when things are going well, and the rush for the exits when the truth turns out to be less favorable than the image.

Stronger banking systems. As we have seen, one factor that made the Asian crisis so severe was the way that the currency crisis interacted with bank runs. It is at least possible that these interactions would have been milder if the banks themselves had been stronger. So there have also been many proposals for strengthening banks, through both closer regulation of the risks they take and increased capital requirements, which ensure that substantial amounts of the owners' own money is at risk. Of course, the 2007–2009 crisis demonstrated that industrial-country financial markets were actually less robust than they had seemed. The need for greater transparency and stricter regulation of financial institutions is universal.

Enhanced credit lines. Some reformers also want to establish special credit lines that nations could draw on in the event of a currency crisis, in effect adding to their foreign exchange reserves. The idea would be that the mere existence of these credit lines would usually make them unnecessary: As long as speculators knew that countries had enough credit to meet even a large outflow of funds, they would not hope or fear that their own actions would produce a sudden devaluation. Such credit lines could be provided by private banks, or by public bodies such as the IMF. This reform area, too, can be seen as applicable to richer countries after the events of 2007–2009 (see the box on central bank currency swaps in Chapter 20, pages 650–651).

Increased equity capital inflows relative to debt inflows. If developing countries financed a greater proportion of their private foreign capital inflows through equity portfolio investment or direct foreign investment rather than through debt issuance, the probability of default would be much lower. The countries' payments to foreigners would then be more closely linked to their economic fortunes, and would fall automatically when times were hard. In fact, there has been a trend toward greater emerging-market reliance on foreign equity rather than debt finance, and this development probably enhanced emerging markets' resilience in the face of the 2007–2009 global financial crisis.[18]

The international community recognizes that developing countries play increasingly important roles, as lenders as well as borrowers, in world financial markets. Ongoing discussions, in Basel and elsewhere, of global cooperation in bank regulation increasingly include the main emerging market countries as key participants.

Coping with Crisis

Even with the proposed prophylactic measures, crises would still surely happen. Thus there have also been proposals to modify the way the world responds to such crises.

Many of these proposals relate to the role and policies of the IMF. Here opinion is bitterly divided. Some conservative critics believe that the IMF should simply be abolished, arguing that its very existence encourages irresponsible lending by making borrowers and lenders believe that they will always be saved from the consequences of their actions—a version of the moral hazard argument previously described. Other critics argue that the IMF is necessary, but that it has misconstrued its role—by, for example, trying to insist on structural reform when it should instead restrict itself to

---

[18]This trend is documented by Eswar S. Prasad, "Role Reversal in Global Finance," in *Achieving Maximum Long-Run Growth: A Symposium Sponsored by the Federal Reserve Bank of Kansas City* (Kansas City, MO: Federal Reserve Bank of Kansas City, 2012), pp. 339–390. See also the paper by Forbes listed in Further Readings.

narrow financial issues. A number of Asian countries bitterly resented having to follow IMF advice during their crisis in the late 1990s; for them, as we have seen, one motive for reserve accumulation has been to avoid having to borrow IMF dollars—and accept IMF conditions. Finally, defenders of the IMF—and also some of its critics—argue that the agency has simply been underfunded for its task, that in a world of high capital mobility, it needs to have the ability to provide much larger loans much more quickly than it presently can. IMF resources rose sharply as a result of the 2007–2009 crisis, and moves are afoot to raise the IMF's perceived legitimacy in the developing world by giving poorer countries a greater voting share in the IMF's management. Measures like these should improve the functioning of the international system.

Another set of proposals is based on the idea that sometimes a country simply cannot pay its debts, and that international contracts should therefore be structured so as to speed—and reduce the costs of—renegotiation between creditors and debtors. As we noted in our discussion of the debt crisis of the 1980s, limited debt write-offs did bring that crisis to an end. Even in the euro zone, sovereign bond issues starting in January 2013 contained clauses making it easier for governments to renegotiate their debts with private creditors. Critics argue that such provisions would be either ineffective or counterproductive because they would encourage countries to borrow too much, in the knowledge that they could more easily renegotiate their debts—moral hazard once again.

CASE STUDY   China's Pegged Currency

Over the first decade of the 2000s, China developed a substantial overall current account surplus and a large bilateral trade surplus with the United States. In 2006, the current account surplus reached $239 billion, or 9.1 percent of China's output, and the bilateral surplus with the United States, at $233 billion, was of similar size. A good part of China's exports to the United States consists of reassembled components imported from elsewhere in Asia, a factor that reduces other Asian countries' exports to the United States and increases China's. Nonetheless, trade frictions between the United States and China have escalated, with American critics focusing on China's intervention in currency markets to prevent an abrupt appreciation of its currency, the yuan renminbi, against the U.S. dollar.

Figure 22-2 shows how China fixed the exchange rate at 8.28 yuan per dollar between the Asian crisis period and 2005. Facing the threat of trade sanctions by the U.S. Congress, China carried out a 2.1 percent revaluation of its currency in July 2005, created a narrow currency band for the exchange rate, and allowed the currency to appreciate at a steady, slow rate. By January 2008, the cumulative appreciation from the initial 8.28 yuan-per-dollar rate was about 13 percent—well below the 20 percent or more undervaluation alleged by trade hawks in Congress. Early in the summer of 2008, in the midst of the financial crisis, China pegged its exchange rate once again, this time at roughly 6.83 yuan to the dollar. In response to renewed foreign pressure, China in June 2010 announced it was adopting a "managed float" exchange rate regime, and under this arrangement, the yuan had appreciated to about 6.12 per dollar by the fall of 2013—a further appreciation of about 10 percent.

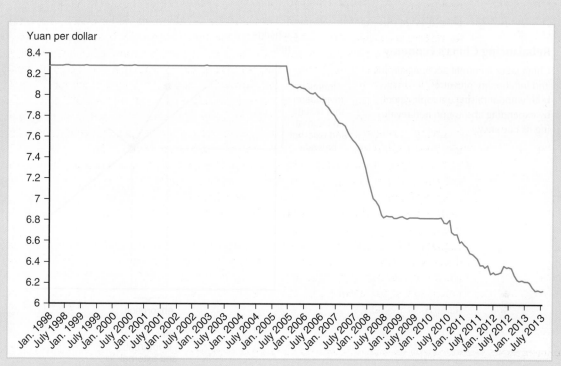

FIGURE 22-2   MyEconLab Real-time data

Yuan/Dollar Exchange Rate, 1998–2013

China's yuan was fixed in value against the U.S. dollar for several years before July 2005. After a 2.1 percent initial revaluation, the currency has appreciated gradually against the dollar.

China's government has moved so slowly because of fears that it would lose export competitiveness and redistribute income domesically by allowing a large exchange rate change. Many economists outside of China believe, however, that a further appreciation of the yuan would be in China's best interest. For one thing, the large reserve increases associated with China's currency peg have caused inflationary pressures in the Chinese economy. Foreign exchange reserves have grown quickly not only because of China's current account surplus, but also because of speculative inflows of money betting on a substantial currency revaluation. To avoid attracting further financial inflows through its porous capital controls, China has hesitated to raise interest rates and choke off inflation. In the past, however, high inflation in China has been associated with significant social unrest.

What policy mix makes sense for China? Figure 22-3 shows the position of China's economy, using the diagram developed earlier in this book as Figure 19-2. In the early 2010s, China was at a point such as 1 in Figure 22-3, with an external surplus and growing inflation pressures—but with a strong reluctance to raise unemployment and thereby slow the movement of labor from the relatively backward countryside into industry. The policy package that moves the economy to both internal and external balance at Figure 22-3's point 2 is a rise in absorption, coupled with currency appreciation. The appreciation works to switch expenditure toward imports and lower inflationary pressures; the absorption increase works

FIGURE 22-3

Rebalancing China's Economy

China faces a current account surplus and inflationary pressures. It can fix both without raising unemployment by expanding absorption and revaluing its currency.

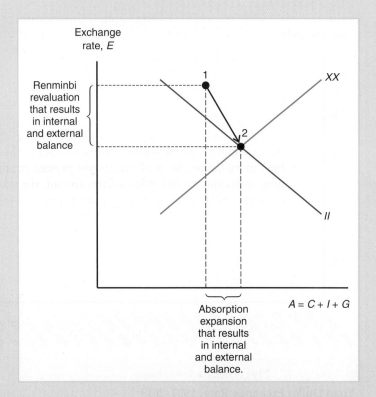

directly to lower the export surplus, at the same time preventing the emergence of unemployment that a stand-alone currency appreciation would bring.

Economists argue further that China should focus on raising both private and government consumption.[19] China's savers put aside more than 45 percent of GNP every year, a staggering number. Saving is so high in part because of a widespread lack of basic services that the government earlier supplied, such as health care. The resulting uncertainty leads people to save in a precautionary manner against the possibility of future misfortunes. By providing a better social safety net, the government would raise private and government consumption at the same time. In addition, there is a strong need for expanded government spending on items such as environmental cleanup, investment in cleaner energy sources, and so on.[20]

While China's leaders have publicly agreed with the needs to raise consumption and appreciate the currency, they have moved very cautiously so far, accelerating their reforms only when external political pressures (such as the threat of trade sanctions) become severe. Whether this pace of change will satisfy external critics, as well as the demands of the majority of Chinese people for higher security and living standards, remains to be seen.

---

[19]For a clear discussion, see Nicholas R. Lardy, "China: Toward a Consumption-Driven Growth Path," *Policy Briefs in International Economics* (Washington, D.C.: Institute for International Economics, October 2006).

[20]Firms also contribute to the very high rate of saving. China's firms pay out relatively little to investors in dividends, retaining their earnings instead and thereby raising corporate saving.

Understanding Global Capital Flows and the Global Distribution of Income: Is Geography Destiny?

As we pointed out at the start of this chapter, today's world is characterized by a vast international dispersion in levels of income and well-being. In contradiction of a simple theory of convergence, however, there is no systematic tendency for poorer countries' income levels to converge, even slowly, to those of richer countries.[21] In conventional macroeconomic models of economic growth, countries' per capita real incomes depend on their stocks of physical and human capital, whose marginal products are highest where stocks are low relative to the stock of unskilled labor. Because high marginal products of investment present strong incentives for capital accumulation, including capital inflows from abroad, the standard models predict that poorer countries will tend to grow more quickly than rich ones. Ultimately, if they have access to the same technologies used in richer countries, poor countries will themselves become rich.

In practice, however, this happy story is the exception rather than the rule. Furthermore, relatively little capital flows to developing countries, despite the prediction of the simple convergence theory that the marginal product of capital, and therefore the returns to foreign investment, should be high there. The scale of capital flows to the developing world is dwarfed by the gross flows between advanced countries. And since the late 1990s (see Table 22-3), net flows to developing countries have reversed as the United States has sucked in most of the world's available current account surpluses.

In fact, the risks of investing in several of the developing countries limit their attractiveness for investors, both foreign and domestic alike; and those risks are closely related to the countries' poor economic growth performances. When governments are unwilling or unable to protect property rights, investors will be unwilling to invest in either physical or human capital, so growth will be nonexistent or low. (The box on the next page probes more deeply into the behavior of capital flows from rich to poor countries.)

What explains the fact that some countries have grown very rich while some attract little or no foreign investment and remain in extreme poverty? Two main schools of thought on the question focus, alternatively, on countries' *geographical features* and on their *institutions of government*.

A leading proponent of the geography theory is UCLA geographer Jared Diamond, whose fascinating and influential book *Guns, Germs, and Steel: The Fates of Human Societies* (New York: W. W. Norton & Company, 1997) won a Pulitzer Prize in 1998. In one version of the geography view, aspects of a country's physical environment such as climate, soil type, diseases, and geographical accessibility determine its long-run economic performance. Thus, for example, unfriendly weather, an absence of easily domesticated large animal species, and the presence of yellow fever and malaria doomed tropical zones to lag behind the more temperate regions of Europe, which could support agricultural innovations such as crop rotation. For these reasons, Diamond argues, it was the Europeans who conquered the inhabitants of the New World and not vice versa.

---

[21]While this statement is true when the unit of study is the country, it is less accurate when the unit of study is the individual. A preponderance of the world's poor in 1960 lived in China and India, two countries that have experienced relatively rapid growth in recent years. A main cause of their growth, however, has been market-friendly economic reforms. For further discussion, see Stanley Fischer, "Globalization and Its Challenges," *American Economic Review* 93 (May 2003), pp. 1–30.

CAPITAL PARADOXES

Although many developing countries have borrowed from developed lenders over the years since World War II, the global pattern of financial flows from rich to poor countries has diverged increasingly from what basic economic theory would seem to predict: a strong flow of lending from high-income countries, rich in capital, to low-income countries, where capital is scarce and where investment opportunities therefore are presumably abundant.

The accompanying figure illustrates the global pattern of current account balances since 1970. Borrowing by non-oil producing developing countries was quite limited, with the partial exception of the decade of the 1990s, when a number of developing borrowers (among them Mexico, Thailand, and the Czech Republic) eventually came to grief. At the same time, current account surpluses by the group of rich countries were small or non-existent. Then, in the 2000s, non-oil developing countries (along with the oil exporters) developed sizable surpluses, while the rich countries borrowed extensively from the poor.

In general, non-oil producing developing countries have not run the big current account deficits predicted by simple development theories. In the early twenty-first century global current account imbalances expanded sharply, but rich countries ran the deficits.

Just before the developing-country borrowing boomlet of the 1990s got under way, economist Robert E. Lucas, Jr., of the University of Chicago, observed that the big income disparities between rich and poor countries, if caused by differences in capital endowments, should imply large opportunities for foreign capital to move profitably into the developing world. Why, then, was investment not far below saving in rich countries, and far higher than saving in poor countries? Lucas suggested that the answer was related to the scarcity in poor countries of *human* capital—in the form of a highly educated work force and managerial know-how. Other scholars put more weight on the

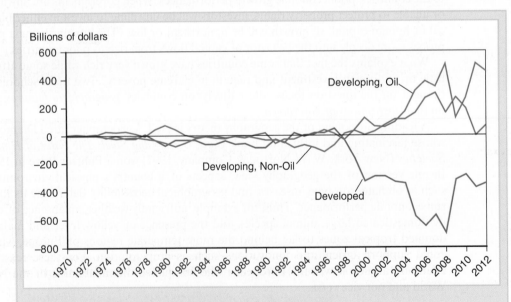

Current Account Balances of Major Country Groups, 1970–2012

Source: International Monetary Fund, *International Financial Statistics*. Note that regional imbalances generally do not sum to zero due to errors and omissions.

greater fragility of property rights and government stability in poorer countries, a position that was partially borne out by the crises of the 1990s.*

Interestingly, the limited postwar flow of capital from rich to poor countries was predicted in the early 1950s by the Columbia University economist Ragnar Nurkse. The nineteenth-century saw a boom in European overseas investment, during which Britain, the leading global lender, invested roughly 4 percent of its income abroad annually for the five decades preceding World War I. Nurkse argued that the conditions of this lending were very special and unlikely to be replicated after World War II. Most of the investment, he noted, flowed to a very few countries of "recent settlement," funding infrastructure (such as railways) needed by the waves of European migrants that accompanied the flow of capital. These migrants transplanted European know-how, as well as governance institutions that made the successful use of investment resources more likely. Not surprisingly, most of the recipient countries—notably Australia, New Zealand, Canada, and the United States—are rich, while most of the poorer "extractive" economies that received a much smaller share of foreign investment before 1914 remain poor today.†

Developments in the twenty-first century made the international pattern of capital flows look even more paradoxical than before. Not only was capital failing to flow from rich to poor countries in appreciable amounts; it was actually flowing *uphill*, from poor to rich, and on a huge scale. Behind this pattern lay a number of specific developments: Asset booms in rich countries spurred consumption and housing investment, for example, causing big current account deficits, while rapid growth in rich countries and especially China boosted commodity prices, allowing many relatively poor exporters of raw materials to run surpluses. As economists looked more carefully at this surprising configuration, however, they discovered new paradoxes even more puzzling than the one Lucas had raised in 1990.

First, experience since 1970 has revealed that on average, foreign capital does not appear to drive economic growth. Instead, the countries that have grown fastest are those that have relied most on domestic savings and run the smallest current account deficits (and often-times, surpluses). For example, the successful economies of East Asia, notably China, generally have had high saving levels. A second, related, paradox, highlighted by Pierre-Olivier Gourinchas of the University of California–Berkeley and Olivier Jeanne of Johns Hopkins University, is called the "allocation puzzle": Countries with lower growth in the productivity of labor and capital actually attract relatively more foreign financial inflows than countries with high productivity growth.

Researchers are still seeking to resolve these new puzzles. Many poor countries have weak financial systems that cannot handle big foreign lending inflows without a high risk of crisis. Thus, countries that generate large volumes of savings themselves may have a growth advantage. Gourinchas and Jeanne suggest their allocation puzzle is related to accumulation of international reserves by some fast-growing economies (such as China's). These economies often do receive substantial inflows of foreign direct investment, but their saving is so high that they still run overall surpluses in their current accounts.‡

---

*These theories are not mutually exclusive; as mentioned above, investment in human capital is discouraged by poor protection of property rights. On the puzzle of low capital flows to poor countries, see Robert E. Lucas, Jr., "Why Doesn't Capital Flow from Rich to Poor Countries?" *American Economic Review* 80 (May 1990), pp. 92–96. A study that ties limited capital flows to poor institutional quality is Laura Alfaro, Sebnem Kalemli-Ozcan, and Vadym Volosovych, "Why Doesn't Capital Flow from Rich to Poor Countries? An Empirical Investigation," *Review of Economics and Statistics* 90 (May 2008), pp. 347–368. Carmen Reinhart and Kenneth Rogoff ascribe the Lucas puzzle to the likelihood of developing-country default. See "Serial Default and the 'Paradox' of Rich-to-Poor Capital Flows," *American Economic Review* 94 (May 2004), pp. 53–58.
†See Nurkse, "International Investment To-Day in the Light of Nineteenth-Century Experience," *Economic Journal* 64 (December 1954), pp. 744–758.
‡See Eswar Prasad, Raghuram Rajan, and Arvind Subramanian, "The Paradox of Capital," *Finance & Development* 44 (March 2007); and Gourinchas and Jeanne, "Capital Flows to Developing Countries: The Allocation Puzzle," *Review of Economic Studies* 80 (October 2013), pp. 1484–1515.

Another factor stressed in some geographical theories is access to international trade. Countries that are landlocked and mountainous trade less with the outside world—and therefore fare worse—than those countries blessed with good ocean harbors, navigable internal waterways, and easily traveled roadways.

In contrast, those favoring the institutions of government as the decisive factor for economic prosperity focus on the success of government in protecting private property rights, thereby encouraging private enterprise, investment, innovation, and ultimately economic growth. According to this view, a country that cannot protect its citizens from arbitrary property confiscation—for example, through extortion by private gangsters or crooked public officials—will be a country in which people do not find it worthwhile to exert effort in the pursuit of wealth.[22] This mechanism is one factor underlying the positive association between lower corruption and higher per capita income shown in Figure 22-1: A low corruption level promotes productive economic activity by ensuring investors that the fruits of their labors will not be arbitrarily seized. As we noted in discussing this evidence, however, the positive slope in the figure is not decisive evidence that national institutions determine national income. It could be, for example, that the slope shown is primarily caused by richer countries' desire to stem corruption and the greater resources they can devote to that task. Even if this is the case, it might still be true that geography determines income levels, and thereby ultimately determines institutions as well. However, if more favorable geography leads to higher income and, through higher income, to a better institutional environment (characterized, among other things, by lower corruption), then the geography school of thought would appear to have it right. For policy makers, the possibility of enhancing economic growth through the reform of institutions would appear bleaker.[23]

How can we hope to distinguish among the various statistical possibilities? One strategy is to find some measurable factor that influences the institutions governing private property but is otherwise unrelated to current per capita income levels. Statisticians call such a variable an *instrumental variable* (or more simply, an *instrument*) for institutions. Because the instrument is not affected by current income, its measured statistical relationship with current income reflects a causal effect of institutions on income rather than the reverse. Unfortunately, because of the complex interrelationships among economic variables, valid instrumental variables are, as a general rule, notoriously hard to find.

Economists Daron Acemoglu and Simon Johnson of the Massachusetts Institute of Technology and James Robinson of Harvard University suggest an imaginative

---

[22]See, for example, Douglass C. North, *Institutions, Institutional Change, and Economic Performance* (Cambridge: Cambridge University Press, 1990).

[23]In countries that formerly were European colonies, current institutions often were implanted by foreign rulers. Geography itself played a role in the types of institutions that colonizers set up. Thus, in the West Indies and the American South, climates and soil were conducive to plantation agriculture based on slave labor and an increasing-returns technology that ensured large farming units and an unequal income distribution. The resulting institutions—even if set up by colonists whose mother countries had limited enlightened rule—were fundamentally hostile to egalitarian political ideals and property protection. Inequality of wealth and power perpetuated itself in many cases, thus hampering long-term growth. For a classic discussion, see Stanley L. Engerman and Kenneth D. Sokoloff, "Factor Endowments, Institutions, and Differential Paths of Growth among New World Economies: A View from Economic Historians of the United States," in Stephen Haber, ed., *How Latin America Fell Behind* (Stanford, CA: Stanford University Press, 1997). The institutions hypothesis allows geography to affect income, but requires that geography affect income only (or mainly) by influencing institutions.

approach to this dilemma. They propose historical mortality rates of early European settlers in former colonies as an instrument for institutional quality.[24] Their case that settler mortality provides a useful instrument rests on two arguments.

First, they argue that the level of settler mortality determined the later institutions governing property rights. (This is another case of geography influencing income *through* its effect on institutions.) In areas with high mortality rates (such as the former Belgian Congo in Africa), Europeans could not settle successfully. Many of these areas were relatively densely populated before Europeans arrived, and the European colonizers' goal was to plunder wealth as effectively as possible, oppressing the native people in the process. The institutions Europeans set up were thus directed to the goal of resource extraction rather than to the protection of property rights, and those exploitative institutions were taken over by new, indigenous ruling elites when the former colonies gained independence. In contrast, Europeans themselves settled in sparsely populated low-mortality regions such as North America and Australia and demanded institutions that would protect political and economic rights, safeguarding private property against arbitrary seizures. (Recall the dispute over taxation without representation that sparked the American Revolution!) Those countries received the biggest inflows of foreign capital in the nineteenth century, and they prospered and are rich today.

A valid instrument must satisfy a second requirement besides having an influence on institutions. It must otherwise not affect today's per capita incomes. Acemoglu, Johnson, and Robinson argue that this requirement is satisfied also. As they put it,

> The great majority of European deaths in the colonies were caused by malaria and yellow fever. Although these diseases were fatal to Europeans who had no immunity, they had limited effect on indigenous adults who had developed various types of immunities. These diseases are therefore unlikely to be the reason why many countries in Africa and Asia are very poor today.... This notion is supported by the [lower] mortality rates of local people in these areas.[25]

Acemoglu, Johnson, and Robinson show that the effect of early European settler mortality rates on current per capita income, operating through the influence of mortality on later institutions, is large. They further argue that once the latter effect is taken into account, geographical variables such as distance from the equator and malarial infection rates have no independent influence on current income levels. Provided that one accepts the premises of the statistical analysis, the institutions theory would seem to emerge victorious over the geography theory. But the debate has not ended there.

Some critics have suggested that Acemoglu, Johnson, and Robinson's measures of institutional quality are inadequate; others argue that their mortality data are faulty or even that historical mortality rates could be related directly to productivity today. In one recent paper, a group of economists argues that the main influence on institutions is human capital, that is, the accumulated skills and education of the population. Even an authoritarian dictatorship may establish democracy and property rights as its citizens become more educated. These writers point out that South Korea did just this, and suggest that perhaps European settlers' human capital, not their transplantation

---

[24]The data cover soldiers, sailors, and bishops and are drawn from the seventeenth through the nineteenth centuries. See Daron Acemoglu, Simon Johnson, and James Robinson, "The Colonial Origins of Comparative Development: An Empirical Investigation," *American Economic Review* 91 (December 2001), pp. 1369–1401.

[25]Acemoglu, Johnson, and Robinson, *ibid.*, p. 1371.

of institutions, is what spurred subsequent growth.[26] As we pointed out earlier, one cause of East Asia's high subsequent growth was a high level of investment in education, often decreed by nondemocratic governments.

A number of Asian former colonies arguably offer counterexamples to the theory of Acemoglu, Johnson, and Robinson. India, Indonesia, and Malaysia, for example, all were European colonies with overwhelmingly indigenous populations, yet their economic growth rates generally have exceeded those of the advanced economies.

SUMMARY

1. There are vast differences in per capita income and in well-being among countries at different stages of economic development. Furthermore, developing countries have not shown a uniform tendency of *convergence* to the income levels of industrial countries. However, some developing countries, notably several in East Asia, have seen dramatic increases in living standards since the 1960s. Explaining why some countries remain poor and which policies can promote economic growth remains one of the most important challenges in economics.

2. Developing countries form a heterogeneous group, especially since many have embarked on wide-ranging economic reform in recent years. Many have at least some of the following features: heavy government involvement in the economy, including a large share of public spending in GNP; a track record of high inflation, usually reflecting government attempts to extract *seigniorage* from the economy in the face of ineffective tax collection; weak credit institutions and undeveloped capital markets; pegged exchange rates and exchange or capital controls, including crawling peg exchange rate regimes aimed at either controlling inflation or preventing real appreciation; a heavy reliance on primary commodity exports. Corruption seems to increase as a country's relative poverty rises. Many of the preceding developing-country features date from the Great Depression of the 1930s, when industrialized countries turned inward and world markets collapsed.

3. Because many developing economies offer potentially rich opportunities for investment, it is natural for them to have current account deficits and to borrow from richer countries. In principle, developing-country borrowing can cause gains from trade that make both borrowers and lenders better off. In practice, however, borrowing by developing countries has sometimes led to default crises that generally cause currency and banking crises. Like currency and banking crises, default crises can contain a self-fulfilling element even though their occurrence depends on fundamental weaknesses in the borrowing country. Often default crises begin with a sudden stop of financial inflows.

4. In the 1970s, as the Bretton Woods system collapsed, countries in Latin America entered an era of distinctly inferior macroeconomic performance with respect to

---

[26]See Edward L. Glaeser, Rafael La Porta, Florencio Lopez-de-Silanes, and Andrei Shleifer, "Do Institutions Cause Growth?" *Journal of Economic Growth* 9 (September 2004), pp. 271–303. In support of institutional over geographical explanations, see Dani Rodrik, Arvind Subramanian, and Francesco Trebbi, "Institutions Rule: The Primacy of Institutions over Geography and Integration in Economic Development," *Journal of Economic Growth* 9 (June 2004), pp. 131–165. For a contrary view, see Jeffrey D. Sachs, "Institutions Don't Rule: Direct Effects of Geography on Per Capita Income," Working Paper 9490, National Bureau of Economic Research, February 2003. The role of international trade in growth is another focus of current research. Rodrik and his co-authors argue that openness to international trade is not a prime direct determinant of per capita income, but rather that openness leads to better institutions, and, through that indirect channel, to higher income.

growth and inflation. Uncontrolled external borrowing led, in the 1980s, to a generalized developing-country debt crisis, its greatest impact being in Latin America and Africa. Starting with Chile in the mid-1980s, some large Latin American countries started to undertake more thorough economic reform, including not just disinflation but also control of the government budget, vigorous *privatization*, deregulation, and trade policy reform. Argentina adopted a *currency board* in 1991. Not all the Latin American reformers succeeded equally in strengthening their banks, and failures were evident in a number of countries. For example, Argentina's currency board collapsed after ten years.

5. Despite their astoundingly good records of high output growth and low inflation and budget deficits, several key developing countries in East Asia were hit by severe panics and devastating currency depreciation in 1997. In retrospect, the affected countries had several vulnerabilities, most of them related to widespread moral hazard in domestic banking and finance and linked to the *original sin* of foreign currency denominated debts. The effects of the crisis spilled over to countries as distant as Russia and Brazil, illustrating the element of *contagion* in modern-day international financial crises. This factor, plus the fact that the East Asian countries had few apparent problems before their crises struck, has given rise to demands for rethinking the international financial "architecture." These demands were reinforced by the global nature of the 2007–2009 financial crisis.

6. Proposals to reform the international architecture can be grouped as preventive measures or as ex post (that is, after the fact) measures, with the latter applied once safeguards have failed to stop a crisis. Among preventive measures are greater transparency concerning countries' policies and financial positions; enhanced regulation of domestic banking; and more extensive credit lines, either from private sources or from the IMF. Ex post measures that have been suggested include more extensive and flexible lending by the IMF. Some observers suggest more extensive use of capital controls, both to prevent and manage crises, but in general not too many countries have taken this route. In the years to come, developing countries will no doubt experiment with capital controls, *dollarization*, floating exchange rates, and other regimes. The architecture that will ultimately emerge is not at all clear.

7. Recent research on the ultimate determinants of economic growth in developing countries has focused on geographical issues such as the disease environment, institutional features such as government protection of property rights, and human capital endowments. The flow of capital from rich to poor countries also depends on these factors. While economists agree that all of these determinants are important, it is less clear where policy should focus first in its attempts to lift poor countries out of their poverty. For example, institutional reform might be an appropriate first step if human capital accumulation depends on the protection of property rights and personal security. On the other hand, it makes little sense to create an institutional framework for government if there is insufficient human capital to run government effectively. In that case, education should come first. Because the statistical obstacles to reaching unambiguous answers are formidable, a balanced effort on all fronts is warranted.

KEY TERMS

contagion, p. 728	dollarization, p. 715	privatization, p. 714
convergence, p. 704	original sin, p. 715	seigniorage, p. 707
currency board, p. 717		

PROBLEMS

1. Can a government always collect more seigniorage simply by letting the money supply grow faster? Explain your answer.

2. Assume that a country's inflation rate was 100 percent per year in both 1990 and 2000 but that inflation was falling in the first year and rising in the second. Other things equal, in which year was seigniorage revenue greater? (Assume that asset holders correctly anticipated the path of inflation.)

3. In the early 1980s, Brazil's government, through an average inflation rate of 147 percent per year, got only 1.0 percent of output as seigniorage, while Sierra Leone's government got 2.4 percent through an inflation rate less than a third as high as Brazil's. Can you think of differences in financial structure that might partially explain this contrast? (Hint: In Sierra Leone, the ratio of currency to nominal output averaged 7.7 percent; in Brazil, it averaged only 1.4 percent.)

4. Suppose the average current account deficit (CAD) of a country is 4 percent. The gap is filled through foreign borrowing. The social and political instability stopped borrowing from foreign sources. How should the government adjust its savings and investments to keep the CAD at zero? What would happen to the aggregate demand and output of the economy?

5. The external debt buildup of some developing countries (such as Argentina) in the 1970s was due, in part, to (legal or illegal) capital flight in the face of expected currency devaluation. (Governments and central banks borrowed foreign currencies to prop up their exchange rates, and these funds found their way into private hands and into bank accounts in New York and elsewhere.) Since capital flight leaves a government with a large debt but creates an offsetting foreign asset for citizens who take money abroad, the consolidated net debt of the country as a whole does not change. Does this mean that countries whose external government debt is largely the result of capital flight face no debt problem?

6. Suppose all foreign debts of Argentina are fixed at a nominal interest rate and loans repayments are in Peso. What affect would increased domestic inflation have on the real burden of debt payment in Argentina? Does the real burden change if the repayments to the external loans were in US dollars instead of Peso?

7. Can a country with high international currency reserves protect its currency from depreciation in the international market? Justify.

8. Given output, a country can improve its current account by cutting either investment or consumption (private or government). After the debt crisis of the 1980s began, many developing countries achieved improvements in their current accounts by cutting investment. Was this a sensible strategy?

9. Why would Argentina have to give the United States seigniorage if it gave up its peso and completely dollarized its economy? How would you measure the size of Argentina's sacrifice of seigniorage? (To complete this exercise, think through the actual steps Argentina would have to take to dollarize its economy. You may assume that the Argentine central bank's assets consist of 100 percent of interest-bearing U.S. Treasury bonds.)

10. Early studies of the economic convergence hypothesis, which looked at data for a group of currently industrialized countries, found that those that were relatively poor a century ago subsequently grew more quickly. Is it valid to infer from this finding that the convergence hypothesis is true?

11. Some critics of the adoption of fixed exchange rates by emerging market economies argue that these exchange rates create a kind of moral hazard. Do you agree?

(Hint: Might borrowers behave differently if they knew exchange rates were changeable from day to day?)

12. Collect the per capita GDP data from the World Bank Database of 7 ASEAN countries—Indonesia, Malaysia, Philippines, Singapore, Thailand, Brunei, and Vietnam. Take the data for the year 1990 and 2012. Find out whether the convergence principle is satisfied in these countries (Hint: by comparing the per capita GDP of low income countries with the high income countries.)

13. Suppose the production function for aggregate output in the United States is the same as in India, $Y = AK^\alpha L^{1-\alpha}$, where A is a total productivity factor, K is the capital stock, and L is the supply of labor. From Table 22-2, calculate the ratio of per capita incomes Y/L in India and the United States in 2010. Use this information to figure out the ratio of capital's marginal product in India and the U.S. (The marginal product of capital is given by $\alpha AK^{\alpha-1} L^{1-\alpha}$.) Relate the answer to the Lucas puzzle of capital flows from rich to poor. How much would A have to differ between India and the U.S. to make the marginal product of capital the same in the two countries?

FURTHER READINGS

Jahangir Aziz, Steven V. Dunaway, and Eswar Prasad, eds. *China and India: Learning from Each Other*. Washington, D.C.: International Monetary Fund, 2006. Essays on Chinese and Indian strategies for promoting economic stability and growth.

Guillermo A. Calvo and Frederic S. Mishkin. "The Mirage of Exchange Rate Regimes for Emerging Market Countries." *Journal of Economic Perspectives* 17 (Winter 2003), pp. 99–118. Argues that institutions are more important than exchange rate regimes for understanding developing-country macroeconomic performance.

Barry Eichengreen and Ricardo Hausmann, eds. *Other People's Money: Debt Denomination and Financial Instability in Emerging Market Economies*. Chicago: University of Chicago Press, 2005. Essays on original sin.

Albert Fishlow. "Lessons from the Past: Capital Markets During the 19th Century and the Interwar Period." *International Organization* 39 (Summer 1985), pp. 383–439. Historical review of the international borrowing experience, including comparisons with the post-1982 debt crisis.

Kristin Forbes. "The 'Big C': Identifying and Mitigating Contagion." In *The Changing Policy Landscape: A Symposium Sponsored by the Federal Reserve Bank of Kansas City*. Kansas City, MO: Federal Reserve Bank of Kansas City, 2013, pp. 23–87. A comprehensive survey of contagious shock transmission through international markets.

Morris Goldstein. *Managed Floating Plus*. Washington, D.C.: Institute for International Economics, 2002. A proposal for managing exchange rate flexibility by emerging market economies.

Morris Goldstein and Nicholas R. Lardy. *The Future of China's Exchange Rate Policy*. Washington, D.C.: Peterson Institute for International Economics, 2009. Compact but thorough analysis of China's macroeconomic challenges.

Peter B. Kenen. *The International Financial Architecture: What's New? What's Missing?* Washington, D.C.: Institute for International Economics, 2001. Reviews emerging market crises and the consequent proposals to reform the global financial system.

M. Ayhan Kose and Eswar S. Prasad. *Emerging Markets: Resilience and Growth amid Global Turmoil*. Washington, D.C.: Brookings Institution, 2010. A wide-ranging study of the relative resilience of emerging economies in the face of the 2007–2009 global financial crisis.

David S. Landes. *The Wealth and Poverty of Nations*. New York: W. W. Norton & Company, 1999. Broad-ranging overview of the global development experience.

Ronald I. McKinnon. *The Order of Economic Liberalization: Financial Control in the Transition to a Market Economy*, 2nd edition. Baltimore: Johns Hopkins University Press, 1993. Essays on the proper sequencing of economic reforms.

Edward Miguel. *Africa's Turn?* Cambridge, MA: MIT Press, 2009. A presentation of perspectives on Africa's economic performance and prospects.

Peter J. Montiel. *Macroeconomics in Emerging Markets.* Cambridge: Cambridge University Press, 2003. Comprehensive analytical overview of macroeconomic policy issues for developing economies.

Raghuram G. Rajan and Ioannis Tokatlidis. "Dollar Shortages and Crises." *International Journal of Central Banking* 1 (September 2005), pp. 177–220. Excellent overview of the institutional weaknesses in developing economies that give rise to liability dollarization.

Dani Rodrik. *One Economics, Many Recipes: Globalization, Institutions, and Economic Growth.* Princeton: Princeton University Press, 2007. Essays on the interplay of institutions and globalization in the process of economic growth.

Nouriel Roubini and Brad Setser. *Bailouts or Bail-ins? Responding to Financial Crises in Emerging Economies.* Washington, D.C.: Institute for International Economics, 2004. Analysis and proposals on the international financial "architecture."

Joseph E. Stiglitz and others. *The Stiglitz Report: Reforming the International Monetary and Financial Systems in the Wake of the Global Crisis.* New York: The New Press, 2010. Report of a United Nations commission of financial experts, with a focus on implications for developing economies.

The Factor-Proportions Model

In this postscript we set out a formal mathematical treatment for the factor-proportions model of production explained in Chapter 5. The mathematical treatment is useful in deepening your understanding of the model.

Factor Prices and Costs

Consider the production of some good that requires capital and labor as factors of production. Provided the good is produced with constant returns to scale, the technology of production may be summarized in terms of the *unit isoquant* (*II* in Figure 5P-1), a curve showing all the combinations of capital and labor that can be used to produce one unit of the good. Curve *II* shows that there is a trade-off between the quantity of capital used per unit of output, a_K, and the quantity of labor per unit of output, a_L. The curvature of the unit isoquant reflects the assumption that it becomes increasingly difficult to substitute capital for labor as the capital-labor ratio increases, and vice-versa.

In a competitive market economy, producers will choose the capital-labor ratio in production that minimizes their cost. Such a cost-minimizing production choice is shown in Figure 5P-1 as point E, the point at which the unit isoquant *II* is tangent to a line whose slope is equal to minus the ratio of the price of labor, w, to the price of capital, r.

The actual cost of production is equal to the sum of the cost of capital and labor inputs,

$$c = a_K r + a_L w, \tag{5P-1}$$

where the input coefficients, a_K and a_L, have been chosen to minimize c.

Because the capital-labor ratio has been chosen to minimize costs, it follows that a change in that ratio cannot reduce costs. Costs cannot be reduced by increasing a_K while reducing a_L, nor conversely. It follows that an infinitesimal change in the capital-labor ratio from the cost-minimizing choice must have no effect on cost. Let da_K, da_L be small changes from the optimal input choices. Then

$$r da_K + w da_L = 0 \tag{5P-2}$$

for any movement along the unit isoquant.

Consider next what happens if the factor prices r and w change. This will have two effects: It will change the choice of a_K and a_L, and it will change the cost of production.

First, consider the effect on the relative quantities of capital and labor used to produce one unit of output. The cost-minimizing labor-capital ratio depends on the ratio of the price of labor to that of capital:

$$\frac{a_K}{a_L} = \Phi\left(\frac{w}{r}\right). \tag{5P-3}$$

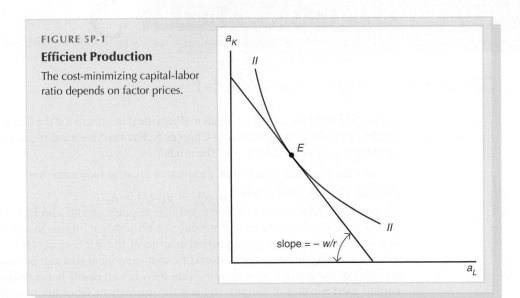

FIGURE 5P-1

Efficient Production

The cost-minimizing capital-labor ratio depends on factor prices.

The cost of production will also change. For small changes in factor prices dr and dw, the change in production cost is

$$dc = a_K dr + a_L dw + r da_K + w da_L. \tag{5P-4}$$

From equation (5P-2), however, we already know that the last two terms of equation (5P-4) sum to zero. Hence the effect of factor prices on cost may be written

$$dc = a_K dr + a_L dw. \tag{5P-4'}$$

It turns out to be very convenient to derive a somewhat different equation from equation (5P-4'). Dividing and multiplying some of the elements of the equation leads to the following new equation:

$$\frac{dc}{c} = \left(\frac{a_K r}{c}\right)\left(\frac{dr}{r}\right) + \left(\frac{a_L w}{c}\right)\left(\frac{dw}{w}\right). \tag{5P-5}$$

The term dc/c may be interpreted as the *percentage change* in c, and may conveniently be designated as $\hat{c}$; similarly, let $dr/r = \hat{r}$ and $dw/w = \hat{w}$. The term $a_K r/c$ may be interpreted as the *share of capital in total production costs*; it may be conveniently designated θ_K. Thus equation (5P-5) can be compactly written

$$\hat{c} = \theta_K \hat{r} + \theta_L \hat{w}, \tag{5P-5'}$$

where

$$\theta_K + \theta_L = 1.$$

This is an example of "hat algebra," an extremely useful way to express mathematical relationships in international economics.

The Basic Equations in the Factor-Proportions Model

Suppose a country produces two goods, cloth C and food F, using two factors of production, capital and labor. Assume that food production is capital-intensive. The price of each good must equal its production cost:

$$P_F = a_{KF}r + a_{LF}w, \tag{5P-6}$$

$$P_C = a_{KC}r + a_{LC}w, \tag{5P-7}$$

where $a_{KF}, a_{LF}, a_{KC}, a_{LC}$ are the cost-minimizing input choices given the price of capital, r and labor, w.

Also, the economy's factors of production must be fully employed:

$$a_{KF}Q_F + a_{KC}Q_C = K, \tag{5P-8}$$

$$a_{LF}Q_F + a_{LC}Q_C = L, \tag{5P-9}$$

where K, L are the total supplies of capital and labor.

The factor-price equations (5P-6) and (5P-7) imply equations for the rate of change for factor prices.

$$\hat{P}_F = \theta_{KF}\hat{r} + \theta_{LF}\hat{w}, \tag{5P-10}$$

$$\hat{P}_C = \theta_{KC}\hat{r} + \theta_{LC}\hat{w}, \tag{5P-11}$$

where θ_{KF} is the share of capital in production cost of F, etc., $\theta_{KF} > \theta_{KC}$ and $\theta_{LF} < \theta_{LC}$ because F is more capital-intensive than C.

The quantity equations (5P-8) and (5P-9) must be treated more carefully. The unit inputs a_{KF}, etc., can change if factor prices change. If goods prices are held constant, however, then factor prices will not change. Thus for *given* prices of F and C, it is also possible to write hat equations in terms of factor supplies and outputs:

$$\alpha_{KF}\hat{Q}_F + \alpha_{KC}\hat{Q}_C = \hat{K}, \tag{5P-12}$$

$$\alpha_{LF}\hat{Q}_F + \alpha_{LC}\hat{Q}_C = \hat{L}, \tag{5P-13}$$

where α_{KF} is the share of the economy's capital supply that is used in production of F, etc. $\alpha_{KF} > \alpha_{LF}$ and $\alpha_{KC} < \alpha_{LC}$ because of the greater capital intensity of F production.

Goods Prices and Factor Prices

The factor-price equations (5P-10) and (5P-11) may be solved together to express factor prices as the outcome of goods prices (these solutions make use of the fact that $\theta_{LF} = 1 - \theta_{KF}$ and $\theta_{LC} = 1 - \theta_{KC}$):

$$\hat{r} = \left(\frac{1}{D}\right)[(1 - \theta_{KC})\hat{P}_F - \theta_{LF}\hat{P}_C], \tag{5P-14}$$

$$\hat{w} = \left(\frac{1}{D}\right)[\theta_{KF}\hat{P}_C - \theta_{KC}\hat{P}_F], \tag{5P-15}$$

where $D = \theta_{KF} - \theta_{KC}$ (implying that $D > 0$). These may be arranged in the form

$$\hat{r} = \hat{P}_F + \left(\frac{\theta_{LF}}{D}\right)(\hat{P}_F - \hat{P}_C), \tag{5P-14'}$$

$$\hat{w} = \hat{P}_C + \left(\frac{\theta_{KC}}{D}\right)(\hat{P}_F - \hat{P}_C). \tag{5P-15'}$$

Suppose that the price of F rises relative to the price of C, so that $\hat{P}_F > \hat{P}_C$. Then it follows that

$$\hat{r} > \hat{P}_F > \hat{P}_C > \hat{w}. \tag{5P-16}$$

That is, the real price of capital rises in terms of both goods, while the real price of labor falls in terms of both goods. In particular, if the price of F were to rise with no change in the price of C, the wage rate would actually fall.

Factor Supplies and Outputs

As long as goods prices may be taken as given, equations (5P-12) and (5P-13) can be solved, using the fact that $\alpha_{KC} = 1 - \alpha_{KF}$ and $\alpha_{LC} = 1 - \alpha_{LF}$, to express the change in output of each good as the outcome of changes in factor supplies:

$$\hat{Q}_F = \left(\frac{1}{\Delta}\right)[\alpha_{LC}\hat{K} - \alpha_{KC}\hat{L}], \tag{5P-17}$$

$$\hat{Q}_C = \left(\frac{1}{\Delta}\right)[-\alpha_{LF}\hat{K} + \alpha_{KF}\hat{L}], \tag{5P-18}$$

where $\Delta = \alpha_{KF} - \alpha_{LF}$, $\Delta > 0$.

These equations may be rewritten

$$\hat{Q}_F = \hat{K} + \left(\frac{\alpha_{KC}}{\Delta}\right)(\hat{K} - \hat{L}), \tag{5P-17'}$$

$$\hat{Q}_F = \hat{L} - \left(\frac{\alpha_{LF}}{\Delta}\right)(\hat{K} - \hat{L}). \tag{5P-18'}$$

Suppose that P_F and P_C remain constant, while the supply of capital rises relative to the supply of labor—$\hat{K} > \hat{L}$. Then it is immediately apparent that

$$\hat{Q}_F > \hat{K} > \hat{L} > \hat{Q}_C. \tag{5P-19}$$

In particular, if K rises with L remaining constant, output of F will rise more than in proportion while output of C will actually fall.

The Trading World Economy

Supply, Demand, and Equilibrium

World Equilibrium

Although for graphical purposes it is easiest to express world equilibrium as an equality between relative supply and relative demand, for a mathematical treatment, it is preferable to use an alternative formulation. This approach focuses on the conditions of equality between supply and demand of either one of the two goods, cloth and food. It does not matter which good is chosen because equilibrium in the cloth market implies equilibrium in the food market and vice versa.

To see this condition, let Q_C, Q_C^* be the output of cloth in Home and Foreign, respectively; D_C, D_C^* the quantity demanded in each country; and corresponding variables with an F subscript the food market. Also, let p be the price of cloth relative to that of food.

In all cases, world expenditure will be equal to world income. World income is the sum of income earned from sales of cloth and sales of food; world expenditure is the sum of purchases of cloth and purchases of food. Thus the equality of income and expenditure may be written

$$p(Q_C + Q_C^*) + Q_F + Q_F^* = p(D_C + D_C^*) + D_F + D_F^*. \tag{6P-1}$$

Now suppose that the world market for cloth is in equilibrium; that is,

$$Q_C + Q_C^* = D_C + D_C^*. \tag{6P-2}$$

Then from equation (6P-1), it follows that

$$Q_F + Q_F^* = D_F + D_F^*. \tag{6P-3}$$

That is, the market for food must be in equilibrium as well. Clearly the converse is also true: If the market for food is in equilibrium, so too is the market for cloth.

It is therefore sufficient to focus on the market for cloth to determine the equilibrium relative price.

Production and Income

Each country has a production possibility frontier along which it can trade off between producing cloth and producing food. The economy chooses the point on the frontier that maximizes the value of output at the given relative price of cloth. This value may be written

$$V = pQ_C + Q_F. \tag{6P-4}$$

As in the cost-minimization cases described in the earlier postscript, the fact that the output mix chosen maximizes value implies that a small shift in production along the production possibility frontier away from the optimal mix has no effect on the value of output:

$$pdQ_C + dQ_F = 0. \tag{6P-5}$$

A change in the relative price of cloth will lead to both a change in the output mix and a change in the value of output. The change in the value of output is

$$dV = Q_C dp + p dQ_C + dQ_F. \tag{6P-6}$$

However, because the last two terms are, by equation (6P-5), equal to zero, this expression reduces to

$$dV = Q_C dp. \tag{6P-6$'$}$$

Similarly, in Foreign,

$$dV^* = Q_C^* dp. \tag{6P-7}$$

Income, Prices, and Utility

Each country is treated as if it were one individual. The tastes of the country can be represented by a utility function depending on consumption of cloth and food:

$$U = U(D_C, D_F). \tag{6P-8}$$

Suppose a country has an income I in terms of food. Its total expenditure must be equal to this income, so that

$$p D_C + D_F = I. \tag{6P-9}$$

Consumers will maximize utility given their income and the prices they face. Let MU_C, MU_F be the marginal utility that consumers derive from cloth and food; then the change in utility that results from any change in consumption is

$$dU = MU_C dD_C + MU_F dD_F. \tag{6P-10}$$

Because consumers are maximizing utility given income and prices, there cannot be any affordable change in consumption that makes them better off. This condition implies that at the optimum,

$$\frac{MU_C}{MU_F} = p. \tag{6P-11}$$

Now consider the effect on utility of changing income and prices. Differentiating equation (6P-9) yields

$$p dD_C + dD_F = dI - D_C dp. \tag{6P-12}$$

But from equations (6P-10) and (6P-11),

$$dU = MU_F[p dD_C + dD_F]. \tag{6P-13}$$

Thus,

$$dU = MU_F[dI - D_C dp]. \tag{6P-14}$$

It is convenient to introduce now a new definition: The change in utility divided by the marginal utility of food, which is the commodity in which income is measured, may be defined as the change in *real income*, and indicated by the symbol dy:

$$dy = \frac{dU}{MU_F} = dI - D_C dp. \tag{6P-15}$$

For the economy as a whole, income equals the value of output: $I = V$. Thus the effect of a change in the relative price of cloth on the economy's real income is

$$dy = [Q_C - D_C]dp. \tag{6P-16}$$

The quantity $Q_C - D_C$ is the economy's exports of cloth. A rise in the relative price of cloth, then, will benefit an economy that exports cloth; it is thus an improvement in that economy's terms of trade. It is instructive to restate this idea in a slightly different way:

$$dy = [p(Q_C - D_C)]\left(\frac{dp}{p}\right). \tag{6P-17}$$

The term in brackets is the value of exports; the term in parentheses is the percentage change in the terms of trade. The expression therefore says that the real income gain from a given percentage in terms of trade change is equal to the percentage change in the terms of trade multiplied by the initial value of exports. If a country is initially exporting \$100 billion and its terms of trade improve by 10 percent, the gain is equivalent to a gain in national income of \$10 billion.

Supply, Demand, and the Stability of Equilibrium

In the market for cloth, a change in the relative price will induce changes in both supply and demand.

On the supply side, a rise in p will lead both Home and Foreign to produce more cloth. We will denote this supply response as in Home and Foreign, respectively, so that

$$dQ_C = s\, dp, \tag{6P-18}$$

$$dQ_C^* = s^*dp. \tag{6P-19}$$

The demand side is more complex. A change in p will lead to both *income* and *substitution* effects. These effects are illustrated in Figure 6P-1. The figure shows an economy that initially faces a relative price indicated by the slope of the line VV^0.

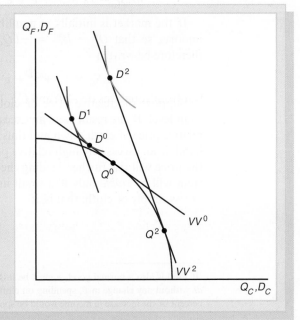

FIGURE 6P-1

Consumption Effects of a Price Change

A change in relative prices produces both income and substitution effects.

Given this relative price, the economy produces at point Q^0 and consumes at point D^0. Now suppose the relative price of cloth rises to the level indicated by the slope of VV^2. If there were no increase in utility, consumption would shift to D^1, which would involve an unambiguous fall in consumption of cloth. There is also, however, a change in the economy's real income; in this case, because the economy is initially a net exporter of cloth, real income rises. This change leads to consumption at D^2 rather than D^1, and this income effect tends to raise consumption of cloth. Analyzing the effect of change in p on demand requires taking account of both the substitution effect, which is the change in consumption that would take place if real income were held constant, and the income effect, which is the additional change in consumption that is the consequence of the fact that real income changes.

Let the substitution effect be denoted by $-e\,dp$; it is always negative. Also, let the income effect be denoted by $n\,dy$; as long as cloth is a normal good for which demand rises with real income, it is positive if the country is a net exporter of cloth, negative if it is a net importer.[1] Then the total effect of a change in p on Home's demand for cloth is

$$dD_C = -e\,dp + n\,dy$$

$$= [-e + n(Q_C - D_C)]dp. \qquad \text{(6P-20)}$$

The effect on Foreign's demand similarly is

$$dD_C^* = [-e^* + n^*(Q_C^* - D_C^*)]dp. \qquad \text{(6P-21)}$$

Because $Q_C^* - D_C^*$ is negative, the income effect in Foreign is negative.

The demand and supply effect can now be put together to get the overall effect of a change in p on the market for cloth. The *excess supply* of cloth is the difference between desired world production and consumption:

$$ES_C = Q_C + Q_C^* - D_C - D_C^* . \qquad \text{(6P-22)}$$

The effect of a change in p on world excess supply is

$$dES_C = [s + s^* + e + e^* - n(Q_C - D_C) - n^*(Q_C^* - D_C^*)]dp. \qquad \text{(6P-23)}$$

If the market is initially in equilibrium, however, Home's exports equal Foreign's imports, so that $Q_C^* - D_C^* = -(Q_C - D_C)$; the effect of p on excess supply may therefore be written

$$dES_C = [s + s^* + e + e^* - (n - n^*)(Q_C - D_C)]dp. \qquad \text{(6P-23')}$$

Suppose the relative price of cloth were initially a little higher than its equilibrium level. If the result were an excess supply of cloth, market forces would push the relative price of cloth down and thus lead to restoration of equilibrium. On the other hand, if an excessively high relative price of cloth leads to an excess *demand* for cloth, the price will rise further, leading the economy away from equilibrium. Thus equilibrium will be *stable* only if a small increase in the relative price of cloth leads to an excess supply of cloth; that is, if

$$\frac{dES_C}{dp} > 0. \qquad \text{(6P-24)}$$

---

[1]If food is also a normal good, n must be less than $1/p$. To see this effect, notice that if I were to rise by dI without any change in p, spending on cloth would rise by $np\,dI$. Unless $n < 1/p$, then, more than 100 percent of the increase in income would be spent on cloth.

Inspection of equation (6P-23′) reveals the factors determining whether or not equilibrium is stable. Both supply effects and substitution effects in demand work toward stability. The only possible source of instability lies in income effects. The net income effect is of ambiguous sign: It depends on whether $n > n^*$; that is, on whether Home has a higher marginal propensity to consume cloth when its real income increases than Foreign does. If $n > n^*$, the income effect works against stability, while if $n < n^*$, it reinforces the other reasons for stability. The income effects can lead to equilibrium instability because they can generate a relative demand curve for the world that is upward sloping.

In what follows, it will be assumed that equation (6P-24) holds, so that the equilibrium of the world economy is in fact stable.

Effects of Changes in Supply and Demand

The Method of Comparative Statics

To evaluate the effects of changes in the world economy, a method known as *comparative statics* is applied. In each of the cases considered in the text, the world economy is subjected to some change that will lead to a change in the world relative price of cloth. The first step in the method of comparative statics is to calculate the effect of the change in the world economy on the excess supply of cloth *at the original p*. This change is denoted by $dES|_p$. Then the change in the relative price needed to restore equilibrium is calculated by

$$dp = \frac{-dES|_p}{(dES/dp)},\qquad(6P\text{-}25)$$

where dES/dp reflects the supply, income, and substitution effects described earlier.

The effects of a given change on national welfare can be calculated in two stages. First there is whatever direct effect the change has on real income, which we can denote by $dy|_p$; then there is the indirect effect of the resulting change in the terms of trade, which can be calculated using equation (6P-16). Thus the total effect on welfare is

$$dy = dy|_p + (Q_C - D_C)dp.\qquad(6P\text{-}26)$$

Economic Growth

Consider the effect of growth in the Home economy. As pointed out in the text, by growth we mean an outward shift in the production possibility frontier. This change will lead to changes in both cloth and food output at the initial relative price p; let dQ_C, dQ_F be these changes in output. If growth is strongly biased, one or the other of these changes may be negative, but because production possibilities have expanded, the value of output at the initial p must rise:

$$dV = p\,dQ_C + dQ_F = dy|_p > 0.\qquad(6P\text{-}27)$$

At the initial p, the supply of cloth will rise by the amount dQ_C. The demand for cloth will also rise, by an amount $n\,dy|_p$. The net effect on world excess supply of cloth will therefore be

$$dES|_p = dQ_C - n(p\,dQ_C + dQ_F).\qquad(6P\text{-}28)$$

This expression can have either sign. Suppose first that growth is biased toward cloth, so that while $dQ_C > 0$, $dQ_F \leq 0$. Then demand for cloth will rise by

$$dD_C = n(p\,dQ_C + dQ_F) \leq np\,dQ_C > dQ_C.$$

(See footnote 1.)

Thus the overall effect on excess supply will be

$$dES|_p = dQ_C - dD_C > 0.$$

As a result, $dp = -dES|_p/(dES/dp) < 0$: Home's terms of trade worsen.

On the other hand, suppose that growth is strongly biased toward food, so that $dQ_C \leq 0, dQ_F > 0$. Then the effect on the supply of cloth at the initial p is negative, but the effect on the demand for cloth remains positive. It follows that

$$dES|_p = dQ_C - dD_C < 0,$$

so that $dp > 0$. Home's terms of trade improve.

Growth that is less strongly biased can move p either way, depending on the strength of the bias compared with the way Home divides its income at the margin.

Turning next to the welfare effects, the effect on Foreign depends only on the terms of trade. The effect on Home, however, depends on the combination of the initial income change and the subsequent change in the terms of trade, as shown in equation (6P-26). If growth turns the terms of trade against Home, this condition will oppose the immediate favorable effect of growth.

But can growth worsen the terms of trade sufficiently to make the growing country actually worse off? To see that it can, consider first the case of a country that experiences a biased shift in its production possibilities that raises Q_C and lowers Q_F while leaving the value of its output unchanged at initial relative prices. (This change would not necessarily be considered growth, because it violates the assumption of equation (6P-27), but it is a useful reference point.) Then there would be no change in demand at the initial p, whereas the supply of cloth rises; hence p must fall. The change in real income is $dy|_p - (Q_C - D_C)dp$; by construction, however, this is a case in which $dy|_p = 0$, so dy is certainly negative.

Now, this country did not grow, in the usual sense, because the value of output at initial prices did not rise. By allowing the output of either good to rise slightly more, however, we would have a case in which the definition of growth is satisfied. If the extra growth is sufficiently small, however, it will not outweigh the welfare loss from the fall in p. Therefore, sufficiently biased growth can leave the growing country worse off.

A Transfer of Income

We now describe how a transfer of income (say as foreign aid) affects the terms of trade.[2] Suppose Home makes a transfer of some of its income to Foreign. Let the amount of the transfer, measured in terms of food, be da. What effect does this aid have on the terms of trade?

At unchanged relative prices, there is no effect on supply. The only effect is on demand. Home's income is reduced by da, while Foreign's is raised by the same amount. This adjustment leads to a decline in D_C by $-n\,da$, while D_C^* rises by n^*da. Thus,

$$dES|_p = (n - n^*)da \tag{6P-29}$$

and the change in the terms of trade is

$$dp = -da\frac{(n - n^*)}{(dES/dp)}. \tag{6P-30}$$

---

[2]In the online appendix to Chapter 6, we discuss an important historical example of a large income transfer and its implications for the terms of trade of the donor and recipient countries.

Home's terms of trade will worsen if $n > n^*$, which is widely regarded as the normal case; they will, however, improve if $n^* > n$.

The effect on Home's real income combines a direct negative effect from the transfer and an indirect terms of trade effect that can go either way. Is it possible for a favorable terms of trade effect to outweigh the income loss? In this model it is not.

To see the reason, notice that

$$
\begin{aligned}
dy &= dy|_n + (Q_C - D_C)dp \\
&= -da + (Q_C - D_C)dp \\
&= -da\left\{1 + \frac{(n - n^*)(Q_C - D_C)}{s + s^* + e + e^* - (n - n^*)(Q_C - D_C)}\right\} \\
&= -da\frac{(s + s^* + e + e^*)}{[s + s^* + e + e^* - (n - n^*)(Q_C - D_C)]} < 0.
\end{aligned}
\tag{6P-31}
$$

Similar algebra will reveal correspondingly that a transfer cannot make the recipient worse off.

An intuitive explanation of this result is the following. Suppose p were to rise sufficiently to leave Home as well off as it would be if it made no transfer and to leave Foreign no better off as a result of the transfer. Then there would be no income effects on demand in the world economy. But the rise in price would produce both increased output of cloth and substitution in demand away from cloth, leading to an excess supply that would drive down the price. This result demonstrates that a p sufficiently high to reverse the direct welfare effects of a transfer is above the equilibrium p.

A Tariff

Suppose Home places a tariff on imports, imposing a tax equal to the fraction t of the price. Then for a given world relative price of cloth p, Home consumers and producers will face an internal relative price $\bar{p} = p/(1 + t)$. If the tariff is sufficiently small, the internal relative price will be approximately equal to

$$
\bar{p} = p - p.
\tag{6P-32}
$$

In addition to affecting p, a tariff will raise revenue, which will be assumed to be redistributed to the rest of the economy.

At the initial terms of trade, a tariff will influence the excess supply of cloth in two ways. First, the fall in relative price of cloth inside Home will lower production of cloth and induce consumers to substitute away from food toward cloth. Second, the tariff may affect Home's real income, with resulting income effects on demand. If Home starts with no tariff and imposes a small tariff, however, the problem may be simplified, because the tariff will have a negligible effect on real income. To see this relation, recall that

$$
dy = p\,dD_C + dD_F.
$$

The value of output and the value of consumption must always be equal at world prices, so that

$$
p\,dD_C + dD_F = p\,dQ_C + dQ_F
$$

at the initial terms of trade. But because the economy was maximizing the value of output before the tariff was imposed,

$$
p\,dQ_C + dQ_F = 0.
$$

Because there is no income effect, only the substitution effect is left. The fall in the internal relative price $\bar{p}$ induces a decline in production and a rise in consumption:

$$dQ_C = -sp\, dt, \tag{6P-33}$$

$$dD_C = ep\, dt, \tag{6P-34}$$

where dt is the tariff increase. Hence,

$$dES|_p = -(s + e)p\, dt < 0, \tag{6P-35}$$

implying

$$dp = \frac{-dES|_p}{(dES/dp)}$$

$$= \frac{p\, dt(s + e)}{[s + s^* + e + e^* - (n - n^*)(Q_C - D_C)]} > 0. \tag{6P-36}$$

This expression shows that a tariff unambiguously improves the terms of trade of the country that imposes it.

The Monopolistic Competition Model

We want to consider the effects of changes in the size of the market on equilibrium in a monopolistically competitive industry. Each firm has the total cost relationship

$$C = F + cX, \tag{8P-1}$$

where c is marginal cost, F a fixed cost, and X the firm's output. This implies an average cost curve of the form

$$AC = C/X = F/X + c. \tag{8P-2}$$

Also, each firm faces a demand curve of the form

$$X = S[1/n - b(P - \overline{P})], \tag{8P-3}$$

where S is total industry sales (taken as given), n is the number of firms, and $\overline{P}$ is the average price charged by other firms (which each firm is assumed to take as given).

Each firm chooses its price to maximize profits. Profits of a typical firm are

$$\pi = PX - C = PS[1/n - b(P - \overline{P})] - F - cS[1/n - b(P - \overline{P})]. \tag{8P-4}$$

To maximize profits, a firm sets the derivative $d\pi/dP = 0$. This implies

$$X - SbP + Sbc = 0. \tag{8P-5}$$

Since all firms are symmetric, however, in equilibrium, $P = \overline{P}$ and $X = S/n$. Thus (8P-5) implies

$$P = 1/bn + c, \tag{8P-6}$$

which is the relationship derived in the text.

Since $X = S/n$, average cost is a function of S and n,

$$AC = Fn/S + c. \tag{8P-7}$$

In zero-profit equilibrium, however, the price charged by a typical firm must also equal its average cost. So we must have

$$1/bn + c = Fn/S + c, \tag{8P-8}$$

which in turn implies

$$n = \sqrt{S/bF}. \tag{8P-9}$$

This shows that an increase in the size of the market, S, will lead to an increase in the number of firms, n, but not in proportion—for example, a doubling of the size of the market will increase the number of firms by a factor of approximately 1.4.

The price charged by the representative firm is

$$P = 1/bn + c = c + \sqrt{F/Sb},$$ (8P-10)

which shows that an increase in the size of the market leads to lower prices.

Finally, notice that the sales per firm, X, equal

$$X = S/n = \sqrt{SbF}.$$ (8P-11)

This shows that the scale of each individual firm also increases with the size of the market.

Risk Aversion and International Portfolio Diversification

This postscript develops a model of international portfolio diversification by risk-averse investors. The model shows that investors generally care about the risk as well as the return of their portfolios. In particular, people may hold assets whose expected returns are lower than those of other assets if this strategy reduces the overall riskiness of their wealth.

A representative investor can divide her real wealth, W, between a Home asset and a Foreign asset. Two possible states of nature can occur in the future, and it is impossible to predict in advance which one it will be. In state 1, which occurs with probability q, a unit of wealth invested in the Home asset pays out H_1 units of output and a unit of wealth invested in the Foreign asset pays out F_1 units of output. In state 2, which occurs with probability $1 - q$, the payoffs to unit investments in the Home and Foreign assets are H_2 and F_2, respectively.

Let α be the share of wealth invested in the Home asset and $1 - \alpha$ the share invested in the Foreign asset. Then if state 1 occurs, the investor will be able to consume the weighted average of her two assets' values,

$$C_1 = [\alpha H_1 + (1 - \alpha)F_1] \times W. \tag{20P-1}$$

Similarly, consumption in state 2 is

$$C_2 = [\alpha H_2 + (1 - \alpha)F_2] \times W. \tag{20P-2}$$

In either state, the investor derives utility $U(C)$ from a consumption level of C. Since the investor does not know beforehand which state will occur, she makes the portfolio decision to maximize the average or *expected* utility from future consumption,

$$qU(C_1) + (1 - q)U(C_2).$$

An Analytical Derivation of the Optimal Portfolio

After the state 1 and state 2 consumption levels given by (20P-1) and (20P-2) are substituted into the expected utility function above, the investor's decision problem can be expressed as follows: Choose the portfolio share α to maximize expected utility,

$$qU\{[\alpha H_1 + (1 - \alpha)F_1] \times W\} + (1 - q)U\{[\alpha H_2 + (1 - \alpha)F_2] \times W\}.$$

This problem is solved (as usual) by differentiating the expected utility above with respect to α and setting the resulting derivative equal to 0.

Let $U'(C)$ be the derivative of the utility function $U(C)$ with respect to C; that is, $U'(C)$ is the *marginal utility* of consumption. Then α maximizes expected utility if

$$\frac{H_1 - F_1}{H_2 - F_2} = -\frac{(1 - q)U'\{[\alpha H_2 + (1 - \alpha)F_2] \times W\}}{qU'\{[\alpha H_1 + (1 - \alpha)F_1] \times W\}}. \tag{20P-3}$$

This equation can be solved for α, the optimal portfolio share.

759

For a risk-averse investor, the marginal utility of consumption, $U'(C)$, falls as consumption rises. Declining marginal utility explains why someone who is risk averse will not take a gamble with an expected payoff of zero: The extra consumption made possible by a win yields less utility than the utility sacrificed if the gamble is lost. If the marginal utility of consumption does not change as consumption changes, we say the investor is *risk neutral* rather than risk averse. A risk-neutral investor is willing to take gambles with a zero expected payoff.

If the investor is risk neutral, however, so that $U'(C)$ is constant for all C, equation (20P-3) becomes

$$qH_1 + (1 - q)H_2 = qF_1 + (1 - q)F_2,$$

which states that *the expected rates of return on Home and Foreign assets are equal*. This result is the basis for the assertion in Chapter 14 that all assets must yield the same expected return in equilibrium when considerations of risk (and liquidity) are ignored. Thus, the interest parity condition of Chapter 14 is valid under risk-neutral behavior, but not, in general, under risk aversion.

For the analysis above to make sense, neither of the assets can yield a higher return than the other in *both* states of nature. If one asset did dominate the other in this way, the left-hand side of equation (20P-3) would be positive while its right-hand side would be negative (because the marginal utility of consumption is usually assumed to be positive). Thus, (20P-3) would have no solution. Intuitively, no one would want to hold a particular asset if another asset that *always* did better were available. Indeed, if anyone did wish to do so, other investors would be able to make riskless arbitrage profits by issuing the low-return asset and using the proceeds to purchase the high-return asset.

To be definite, we therefore assume that $H_1 > F_1$ and $H_2 < F_2$, so that the Home asset does better in state 1 but does worse in state 2. This assumption is now used to develop a diagrammatic analysis that helps illustrate additional implications of the model.

A Diagrammatic Derivation of the Optimal Portfolio

Figure 20P-1 shows indifference curves for the expected utility function described by $qU(C_1) + (1 - q)U(C_2)$. The points in the diagram should be thought of as contingency plans showing the level of consumption that will occur in each state of nature. The preferences represented apply to these contingent consumption plans rather than to consumption of different goods in a single state of nature. As with standard indifference curves, however, each curve in the figure represents a set of contingency plans for consumption with which the investor is equally satisfied.

To compensate the investor for a reduction of consumption in state 1 (C_1), consumption in state 2 (C_2) must rise. The indifference curves therefore slope downward. Each curve becomes flatter, however, as C_1 falls and C_2 rises. This property of the curves reflects the property of $U(C)$ that the marginal utility of consumption declines when C rises. As C_1 falls, the investor can be kept on her original indifference curve only by successively greater increments in C_2: Additions to C_2 are becoming less beneficial at the same time as subtractions from C_1 are becoming more painful.

Equations (20P-1) and (20P-2) imply that by choosing the portfolio division given by α, the investor also chooses her consumption levels in the two states of nature. Thus, the problem of choosing an optimal portfolio is equivalent to the problem of optimally choosing the contingent consumption levels C_1 and C_2. Accordingly, the indifference

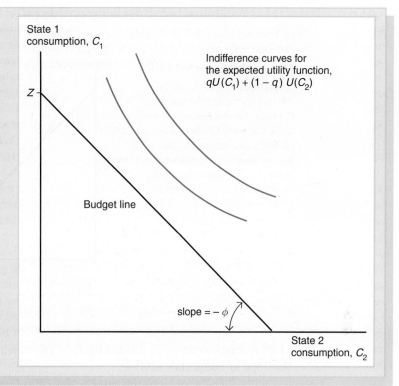

FIGURE 20P-1

Indifference Curves for Uncertain Consumption Levels

The indifference curves are sets of state-contingent consumption plans with which the individual is equally happy. The budget line describes the trade-off between state 1 and state 2 consumption that results from portfolio shifts between Home and Foreign assets.

State 1 consumption, C_1

Indifference curves for the expected utility function, $qU(C_1) + (1-q) U(C_2)$

Z

Budget line

slope $= -\phi$

State 2 consumption, C_2

curves in Figure 20P-1 can be used to determine the optimal portfolio for the investor. All that is needed to complete the analysis is a budget line showing the trade-off between state 1 consumption and state 2 consumption that the market makes available.

This trade-off is given by equations (20P-1) and (20P-2). If equation (20P-2) is solved for α, the result is

$$\alpha = \frac{F_2 W - C_2}{F_2 W - H_2 W}.$$

After substitution of this expression for α in (20P-1), the latter equation becomes

$$C_1 + \phi C_2 = Z, \tag{20P-4}$$

where $\phi = (H_1 - F_1)/(F_2 - H_2)$ and $Z = W \times (H_1 F_2 - H_2 F_1)/(F_2 - H_2)$. Notice that because $H_1 > F_1$ and $H_2 < F_2$, both ϕ and Z are positive. Thus, equation (20P-4) looks like the budget line that appears in the usual analysis of consumer choice, with ϕ playing the role of a relative price and Z the role of income measured in terms of state 1 consumption. This budget line is graphed in Figure 20P-1 as a straight line with slope $-\phi$ intersecting the vertical axis at Z.

To interpret ϕ as the market trade-off between state 2 and state 1 consumption (that is, as the price of state 2 consumption in terms of state 1 consumption), suppose the investor shifts one unit of her wealth from the Home to the Foreign asset. Since the Home asset has the higher payoff in state 1, her net loss of state 1 consumption is H_1 *less* the Foreign asset's state 1 payoff, F_1. Similarly, her net gain in state 2 consumption is $F_2 - H_2$. To obtain additional state 2 consumption of $F_2 - H_2$, the investor therefore must sacrifice $H_1 - F_1$ in state 1. The price of a single unit of C_2 in terms

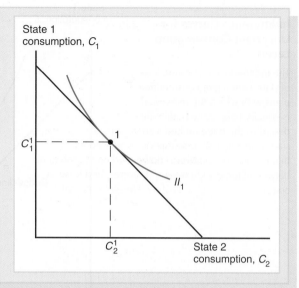

Maximizing Expected Utility

To maximize expected utility, the investor makes the state-contingent consumption choices shown at point 1, where the budget line is tangent to the highest attainable indifference curve, II_1. The optimal portfolio share, α, can be calculated as $(F_2W - C_2^1) \div (F_2W - H_2W)$.

of C_1 is therefore $H_1 - F_1$ divided by $F_2 - H_2$, which equals ϕ, the absolute value of the slope of budget line (20P-4).

Figure 20P-2 shows how the choices of C_1 and C_2—and, by implication, the choice of the portfolio share α—are determined. As usual, the investor picks the consumption levels given by point 1, where the budget line just touches the highest attainable indifference curve, II_1. Given the optimal choices of C_1 and C_2, α can be calculated using equation (20P-1) or (20P-2). As we move downward and to the right along the budget constraint, the Home asset's portfolio share, α, falls. (Why?)

For some values of C_1 and C_2, α may be negative or greater than 1. These possibilities raise no conceptual problems. A negative α, for example, means that the investor has "gone short" in the Home asset, that is, issued some positive quantity of state-contingent claims that promise to pay their holders H_1 units of output in state 1 and H_2 units in state 2. The proceeds of this borrowing are used to increase the Foreign asset's portfolio share, $1 - \alpha$, above 1.

Figure 20P-3 shows the points on the investor's budget constraint at which $\alpha = 1$ (so that $C_1 = H_1W$, $C_2 = H_2W$) and $\alpha = 0$ (so that $C_1 = F_1W$, $C_2 = F_2W$). Starting from $\alpha = 1$, the investor can move upward and to the left along the constraint by going short in the Foreign asset (thereby making α greater than 1 and $1 - \alpha$ negative). She can move downward and to the right from $\alpha = 0$ by going short in the Home asset.

The Effects of Changing Rates of Return

The diagram we have developed can be used to illustrate the effect of changes in rates of return under risk aversion. Suppose, for example, the Home asset's state 1 payoff rises while all other payoffs and the investor's wealth, W, stay the same. The rise in H_1 raises ϕ, the relative price of state 2 consumption, and therefore steepens the budget line shown in Figure 20P-3.

We need more information, however, to describe completely how the position of the budget line in Figure 20P-3 changes when H_1 rises. The following reasoning fills the gap. Consider the portfolio allocation $\alpha = 0$ in Figure 20P-3, under which all

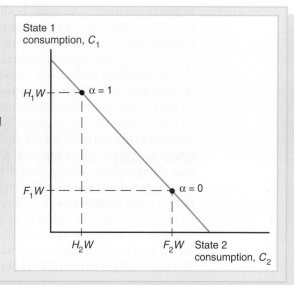

FIGURE 20P-3

Nondiversified Portfolios

When $\alpha = 1$, the investor holds all her wealth in the Home asset. When $\alpha = 0$, she holds all her wealth in the Foreign asset. Moves along the budget constraint upward and to the left from $\alpha = 1$ correspond to short sales of the Foreign asset, which raise α above 1. Moves downward and to the right from $\alpha = 0$ correspond to short sales of the Home asset, which push α below 0.

wealth is invested in the Foreign asset. The contingent consumption levels that result from this investment strategy, $C_1 = F_1 W$, $C_2 = F_2 W$, do not change as a result of a rise in H_1, because the portfolio we are considering does not involve the Home asset. Since the consumption pair associated with $\alpha = 0$ does not change when H_1 rises, we see that $C_1 = F_1 W$, $C_2 = F_2 W$ is a point on the new budget constraint: After a rise in H_1, it is still feasible for the investor to put all of her wealth into the Foreign asset. It follows that the effect of a rise in H_1 is to make the budget constraint in Figure 20P-3 pivot clockwise around the point $\alpha = 0$.

The effect on the investor of a rise in H_1 is shown in Figure 20P-4, which assumes that initially, $\alpha > 0$ (that is, the investor initially owns a positive amount

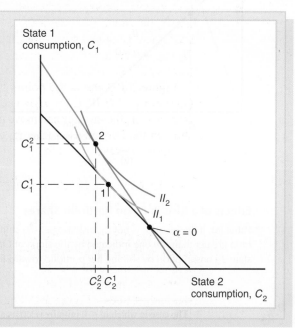

FIGURE 20P-4

Effects of a Rise in H_1 on Consumption

A rise in H_1 causes the budget line to pivot clockwise around $\alpha = 0$, and the investor's optimum shifts to point 2. State 1 consumption always rises; in the case shown, state 2 consumption falls.

of the Home asset).[1] As usual, both a "substitution" and an "income" effect influence the shift of the investor's contingent consumption plan from point 1 to point 2. The substitution effect is a tendency to demand more C_1, whose relative price has fallen, and less C_2, whose relative price has risen. The income effect of the rise in H_1, however, pushes the entire budget line outward and tends to raise consumption in *both* states (as long as $\alpha > 0$ initially). Because the investor will be richer in state 1, she can afford to shift some of her wealth toward the Foreign asset (which has the higher payoff in state 2) and thereby even out her consumption in the two states of nature. Risk aversion explains the investor's desire to avoid large consumption fluctuations across states. As Figure 20P-4 suggests, C_1 definitely rises while C_2 may rise or fall. (In the case illustrated, the substitution effect is stronger than the income effect, and C_2 falls.)

Corresponding to this ambiguity is an ambiguity concerning the effect of the rise in H_1 on the portfolio share, α. Figure 20P-5 illustrates the two possibilities. The key to understanding this figure is to observe that if the investor does *not* change α in response to the rise in H_1, her consumption choices are given by point 1', which lies on the new budget constraint vertically above the initial consumption point 1. Why is this the case? Equation (20P-2) implies that $C_2^1 = [\alpha H_2 + (1 - \alpha)F_2] \times W$ doesn't

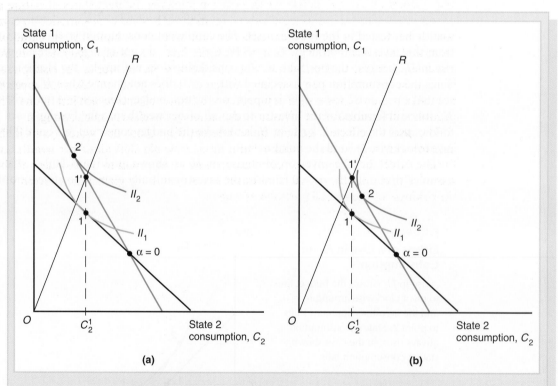

FIGURE 20P-5

Effects of a Rise in H_1 on Portfolio Shares

Panel (a): If the investor is not too risk averse, she shifts her portfolio toward the Home asset, picking a C_1/C_2 ratio greater than the one indicated by the slope of OR. Panel (b): A very risk-averse investor might increase state 2 consumption by shifting her portfolio toward the Foreign asset.

---

[1]The case in which $\alpha < 0$ initially is left as an exercise.

change if α doesn't change; the new, higher value of state 1 consumption corresponding to the original portfolio choice is then given by the point on the new budget constraint directly above C_2^1. In both panels of Figure 20P-5, the slope of the ray OR connecting the origin and point 1′ shows the ratio C_1/C_2 implied by the initial portfolio composition after the rise in H_1.

It is now clear, however, that to shift to a lower value of C_2, the investor must raise α above its initial value, that is, shift the portfolio toward the Home asset. To raise C_2, she must lower α, that is, shift toward the Foreign asset. Figure 20P-5a shows again the case in which the substitution effect outweighs the income effect. In that case, C_2 falls as the investor shifts her portfolio toward the Home asset, whose expected rate of return has risen relative to that on the Foreign asset. This case corresponds to those we studied in the text, in which the portfolio share of an asset rises as its relative expected rate of return rises.

Figure 20P-5b shows the opposite case, in which C_2 rises and α falls, implying a portfolio shift toward the Foreign asset. You can see that the factor giving rise to this possibility is the sharper curvature of the indifference curves II in Figure 20P-5b. This curvature is precisely what economists mean by the term *risk aversion*. An investor who becomes more risk averse regards consumptions in different states of nature as poorer substitutes, and thus requires a larger increase in state 1 consumption to compensate her for a fall in state 2 consumption (and vice versa). Note that the paradoxical case shown in Figure 20P-5b, in which a rise in an asset's expected rate of return can cause investors to demand *less* of it, is unlikely in the real world. For example, an increase in the interest rate a currency offers, other things equal, raises the expected rate of return on deposits of that currency in all states of nature, not just in one. The portfolio substitution effect in favor of the currency therefore is much stronger.

The results we have found are quite different from those that would occur if the investor were risk neutral. A risk-neutral investor would shift all of her wealth into the asset with the higher expected return, paying no attention to the riskiness of this move.[2] The greater the degree of risk aversion, however, the greater the concern with the riskiness of the overall portfolio of assets.

---

[2]In fact, a risk-neutral investor would always like to take the maximum possible short position in the low-return asset and, correspondingly, the maximum possible long position in the high-return asset. It is this behavior that gives rise to the interest parity condition.

Chapter 3   p. 65: AP Images; p. 68: North Wind/North Wind Picture Archives

Chapter 4   p. 104: Library of Congress Prints and Photographs Division [LC-D4-12683]

Chapter 8   p. 221: Si Wei/Color China Photo/AP Images; p. 229: © 2004 Drew Dernavich/The New Yorker Collection/www.cartoonbank.com

Chapter 9   p. 248: Courtesy of Subaru of America, Inc.; p. 251: Jockel Finck/AP Images; p. 255: Rachel Youdelman/Pearson Education, Inc.; p. 258: McClatchy-Tribune Information Services/Alamy

Chapter 14   p. 376: Ahn Young-Joon/AP Images

Chapter 16   p. 430: Imagebroker.net/SuperStock

Chapter 19   p. 587: Franklin D. Roosevelt Library and Museum; p. 604: AP Images

Chapter 20   p. 648: Richard Drew/AP Images

Chapter 21   p. 683: Domenico Stinellis/AP Images; p. 691: Dimitri Messinis/AP Images

Chapter 22   p. 724: Peter Turnley/Corbis

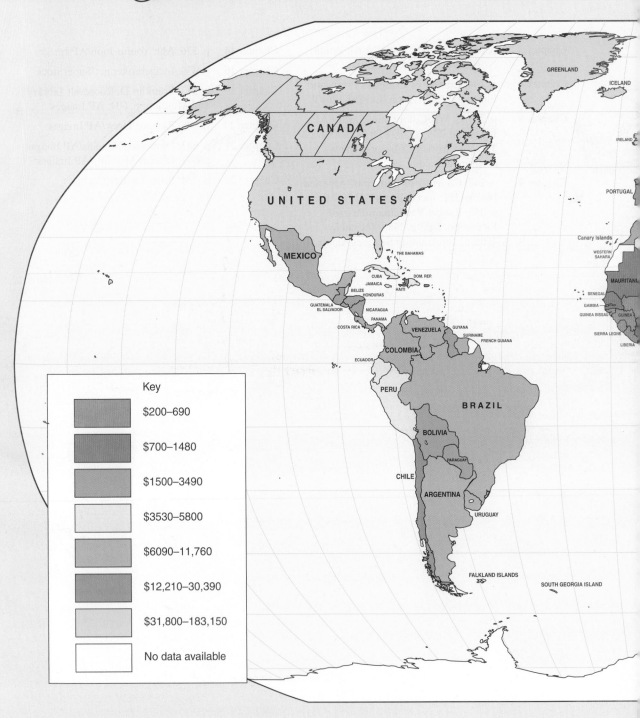

Gross National Product per Capita (in 2011 d

Key

- $200–690
- $700–1480
- $1500–3490
- $3530–5800
- $6090–11,760
- $12,210–30,390
- $31,800–183,150
- No data available

rs)

Source: World Bank, *World Development Indicators,* 2013. Data are measured in 2011 United States dollars.